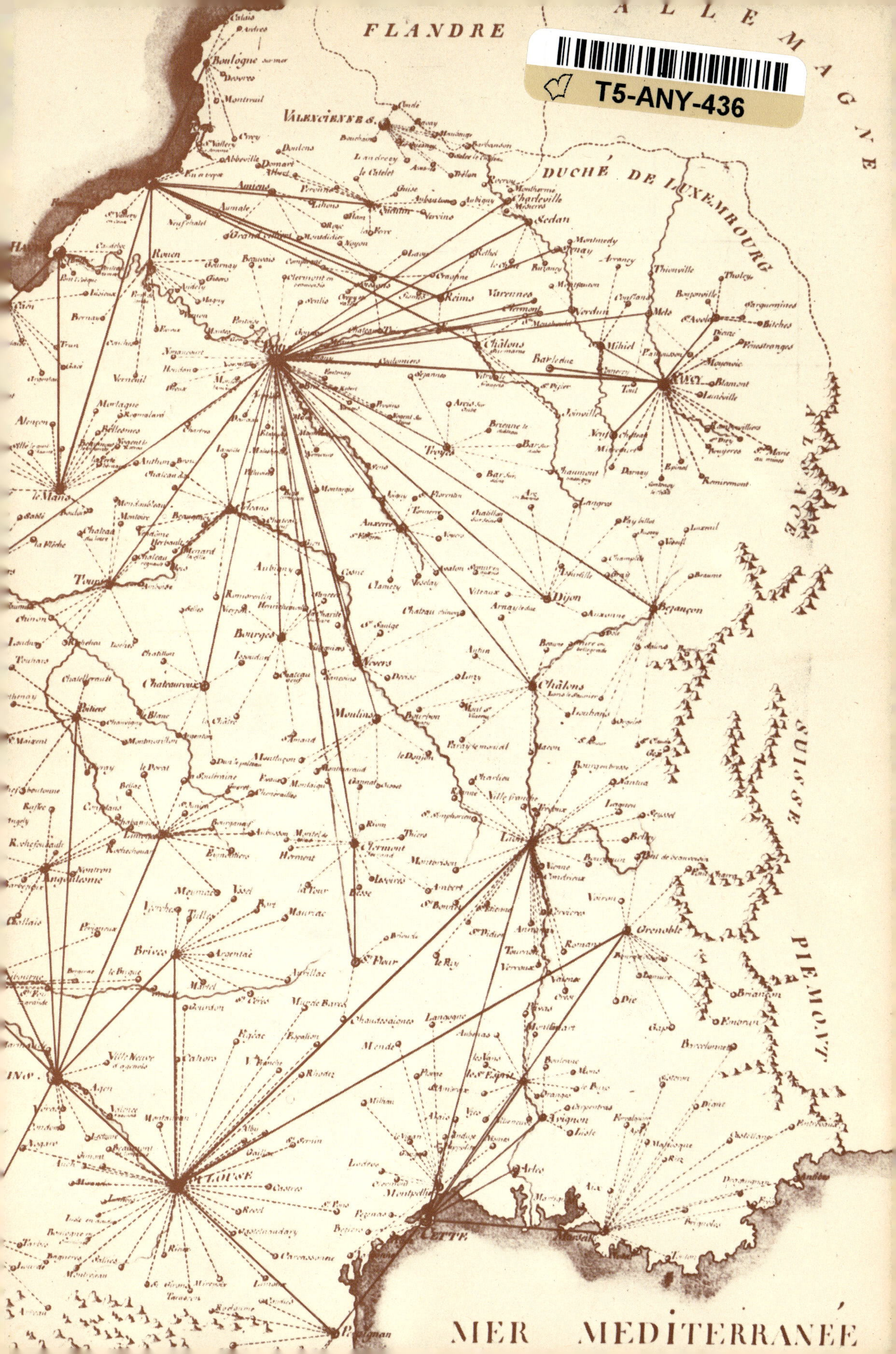
FLANDRE
ALLEMAGNE
DUCHÉ DE LUXEMBOURG
ALSACE
SUISSE
PIEMONT
MER MEDITERRANEÉ
Boulogne
Valenciennes
Amiens
Rouen
Reims
Sedan
Châlons
Verdun
Nancy
Troyes
Dijon
Besançon
Orléans
Tours
le Mans
Bourges
Chateauroux
Nevers
Moulins
Limoges
Angoulême
Poitiers
Clermont
Brives
Lyon
Grenoble
Avignon
Montpellier
Cette
Marseille
Perpignan
Briançon

FRANCE AND THE CHESAPEAKE

Samuel Bernard in 1727
By P. I. Drevet after H. Rigaud, courtesy of B. N. Estampes.

France
and the
Chesapeake

*A History of the French Tobacco Monopoly,
1674–1791, and of Its Relationship to the
British and American Tobacco Trades*

Volume 1

JACOB M. PRICE

Ann Arbor
THE UNIVERSITY OF MICHIGAN PRESS

Copyright © by The University of Michigan 1973
All rights reserved
ISBN 0-472-08738-X
Library of Congress Catalog Card No. 74-124438
Published in the United States of America by
The University of Michigan Press and simultaneously
in Don Mills, Canada, by Longman Canada Limited
Manufactured in the United States of America

Published with the assistance of a grant
from the Horace H. Rackham School of Graduate Studies
of the University of Michigan

To the memory of my cousin
Lieutenant Harvey Blacher, U.S.A.A.F.
*an American pilot, based in England,
killed while returning from a mission
over Europe, October 1944*

IN THE COMMON CAUSE

Contents

Volume 1

Preface — xi
Introduction: An Argument on Three Levels — xvii

PART I. France: Institutions and Interests, 1674–1791

Period A. The Foundations of the Monopoly, 1674–1718

1. The Prehistory of Tobacco in Seventeenth-Century France — 3
   The Beginnings of Consumption, Cultivation, and Commerce — 3
   The Beginnings of Tobacco Taxation: The Age of Import Duties, 1621–74 — 11

2. The Creation of the Monopoly: The Age of de Lagny and Hénault, 1674–97 — 17
   The Origins of the First Monopoly and the First Monopolists — 17
   The Brief, Inglorious History of the Jean Breton Company, 1674–80 — 25
   The First Union with the United Farms, 1680–97 — 37

3. The Creation of the Monopoly: The Age of Samuel Bernard, 1697–1718 — 52

4. Colonial Supplies and the Crisis of St. Domingue, 1674–1709 — 73
   The Windward Islands as a Source of Supply, 1600–1674 — 73
   Colbert in Search of a Policy, 1661–74 — 78
   The Fate of St. Domingue, 1674–1709 — 83
   West Indian Tobacco under Louis XV, 1715–74: A Postscript — 110
   Appendix to Chapter 4: A Note on Spanish Tobacco — 114

5. Some Administrative Problems of the Tobacco Monopoly, 1674–1718 — 116
   The Administrative Framework — 116
   Administrative Problems and Legal Redress — 120
   The Varieties and Geography of Tobacco Contraband — 127

6. The Domestic Cultivation of Tobacco during the Early Farms, 1674–1718 — 143
   The Restrictive Policy and Its Critics — 143
   The General Enforcement of Restriction, 1674–1718 — 147
   Tobacco Cultivation in the Southwest, 1674–1718 — 153

7. Merchants and Manufacturers: The Business Activities of the Monopoly, 1674–1718	173
The Buying Policy of the Monopoly, 1674–1718	173
The Manufacturing Activity of the Monopoly, 1674–1718	189

Period B. The Law Interlude and Its Antecedents, 1715–21

8. Tobacco in the Genesis of Law's Company, 1716–18	196
9. The Struggle for the Tobacco Farm, 1711–18	221
10. Tobacco under "The System," 1718–21	247

Period C. The Monopoly Triumphant, 1721–91

11. After the Fall, 1721–23	268
The Restoration of the Monopoly, 1721–23	268
The Return of the Indies Company, 1723–30	276
The Suppression of Planting, 1720–26	294
12. Louisiana Tobacco under the Company, 1717–31	302
13. Louisiana Tobacco under "Free Trade," 1731–63	329
The Age of Maurepas, 1731–49	329
The Last Years of French Louisiana, 1748–63	348
After the Loss of Louisiana, 1763–75	358
14. The Tobacco Monopoly under the United Farms: The Leases of 1730–86	361
15. Purchasing Policy and Its Critics, 1721–75	376
The Purchasing Policy of the Monopoly, 1721–75	376
Russia, the Seven Years' War, and Purchasing Policy	392
The Monopoly's Purchasing Policy and the Critics of 1758–63	406
16. The Internal Structure and Operation of the Tobacco Monopoly, 1721–91	411
The Manufacturing Establishments	411
The Organization of the Monopoly, 1730–91	427
17. Administrative Problems of the Tobacco Monopoly, 1721–91	440
Laws and Authorities	440
Smuggling by Sea, 1718–91	446
Smuggling by Land, 1721–91	454
The Struggle against Illicit Trade within the Frontiers of the Monopoly, 1721–91	463

18. French Territories outside the Monopoly
and the 1749 Import Duty ... 477
Bayonne and the Pays de Labourd ... 478
The Alsatian Tobacco Trade and the Monopoly ... 485
The Northern Provinces and Dunkirk ... 493

PART II. Britain and the Chesapeake: Monopsonistic Elements in an Open Market

19. Britain and the French Market up to the Treaty of Utrecht ... 509
The Beginnings (to 1711) ... 509
The Commercial Treaty of Utrecht, 1709–14 ... 522

20. The French Agency in London: The Early Agents, 1697–1739 ... 531

21. The French Agency in London: The Rise of the Abbé Huber and the FitzGeralds ... 544
The MacKercher-Huber Mission of 1737–38 ... 544
Who Were the FitzGeralds? ... 557

22. The Purchasing Commission during the War Years, 1739–63 ... 563
Postscript to Chapter 22 ... 585

23. The French Agency in the English Outports and in Scotland, 1725–65 ... 588
The General Situation ... 588
French Buying at Whitehaven, 1742–75 ... 594
The French Agents in Scotland ... 604

24. The Last Great Struggle for the French Agency in Great Britain, 1766–75 ... 618

25. The French Monopoly as a Monopsonistic Buyer in the British Tobacco Market, 1700–1775; Some Economic Implications ... 649
Appendix to Chapter 25: The French in the British Tobacco Market, 1748–75: A Price Chronicle ... 671

Volume 2

PART III. Postscript, 1775–91

26. The War Years, 1775–83 ... 681
Sir Robert Herries' War, 1776–78 ... 681
Walpole v. Alexander ... 691
The Affairs of Benjamin Franklin, 1776–78 ... 700
French Tobacco Supplies during the War, 1778–82 ... 717

27. The Tobacco Trade during the Last Years
    of the Monopoly, 1783–91 . . . 728
    The General Lines of Development . . . 728
    The Alexander and Morris Contracts . . . 738
    The Aftermath of Berni, 1786–89 . . . 769

28. An Interrupted History . . . 788
    The Withering Away, 1789–91 . . . 788
    Some Implications of Monopoly . . . 839

Appendix: Statistics . . . 843

Abbreviations . . . 853

Notes . . . 855

Bibliography . . . 1123

Index . . . 1141

Illustrations . . . *following* 40

Map of the Tobacco-Growing Area in Guienne, ca. 1710 . . . 145

Map of Generalities and Intendancies, 1789 . . . 428

Lavoisier's Map of Distribution Network of
French Tobacco Monopoly, ca. 1780 . . . *end papers*

Preface

In 1949, the present writer began to work on the British-Chesapeake tobacco trade in the seventeenth and eighteenth centuries. He found that although much had been written on the institutional side of the plantation system and the trade, existing work was weak in several respects. Among other things, there was a noticeable lack of quantification, which in turn made it impossible to describe either the growth or the vicissitudes of cultivation or trade over time. There was an equally troublesome lack of material on the markets to which the tobacco of Virginia and Maryland was sent. A few things had been written about the tobacco merchants of London, but virtually nothing about what they did with the tobacco they bought. From the first, therefore, the present writer developed a sharp curiosity about the destinations of the tobacco exported from the Chesapeake. Out of this came his tangential study on the efforts to reexport Chesapeake tobacco to Russia.[1]

With the passage of time, it became evident that attention could be concentrated upon four major markets: that in Britain itself, and the reexport markets to Germany, the Low Countries and France. With the compilation of statistical data on reexports, particularly from Scotland, it became evident that the French market, hitherto little remarked, was actually the first or second most important market in the half-century preceding the American Revolution. Surviving mercantile correspondence was filled with cryptic references to the "French agents" and the "French price." The present writer became convinced that an understanding of the dynamics behind the Chesapeake economy required a fuller understanding of French demand. He soon discovered that a considerable amount had been published in France on the history of the French tobacco monopoly of 1674–1791, much of it as theses for law degrees.[2] He at first imagined that these works would say all that could be said about the history of the monopoly, and envisaged his own task as simply that of attempting a few articles on the French agents in Britain and the effect of their activities upon the British-American tobacco trade. (The first and only one of the articles envisaged appeared in 1957.)[3] By 1960–61, however, further reading had shown that the existing works dealt almost exclusively with the legal and administrative history of the monopoly and had relatively little to say about its financial and political history and even less about its commercial activities. Therefore, by 1961, he had resolved to write a full-scale history of both the French tobacco monopoly and of its activities in world markets. This was written in 1963–66.

The work was planned from the start as a history of the French tobacco monopoly and not as a history of tobacco in France. Only the brief first chapter is devoted to the premonopoly period of tobacco in France, while the history of tobacco cultivation and trade in the frontier provinces outside the jurisdiction of the tobacco monopoly is given only a brief survey in Chapter 18. (A substantial monograph could be written on the history of tobacco in Alsace alone.) Similarly, taking into account previous work on the subject, it was decided from the start to be relatively brief about those topics discussed by previous writers (legal and administrative history, planting in France before 1720) but to explore more fully those previously neglected. The emphasis therefore has been on the political, financial and commercial history of the monopoly: who were the tobacco monopolists? how did they get their farm? at what rent? how did they run their business? and, particularly, where did they buy their tobacco? Covering these varied topics over a period of more than a century involved difficult choices of emphasis. More effort and space were consistently devoted to investigating the economic implications of the monopoly's marketing decisions upon St. Domingue, Louisiana, Glasgow, and the Chesapeake, and relatively less attention to topics of more local interest, such as planting in Guienne before 1720.

The problem of emphasis has naturally been influenced by the availability of materials. Revenue farms are by necessity secretive. It is likely that most destroyed all their records shortly after the books of a particular lease were closed. The farmers-general had a deliberate policy of concentrating all their archives in Paris where they were destroyed after some years.[4] Few of their internal records have therefore survived in French departmental archives. It is generally believed that the central archives of the company in existence in Paris at the time of its suppression in 1791 (none of it antedating 1750) were officially destroyed, about 1810–11, as part of the Napoleonic definitive settlement of the company's accounts.[5] This gap can be made up only to a very limited extent from the records of the office of the Controller-General of Finance. Unlike the records of the contemporary ministries of foreign affairs and the navy, these have been most erratically preserved, victims both of dispersal after 1791 and perhaps of destruction. Thus, research has had to be based in large part upon the assembly of fragments from the Archives Nationales, Archives des Affaires Etrangères, Bibliothèque Nationale, notarial archives, printed works, and other sources. Only in the chapters touching foreign and colonial affairs was it possible to use full archives systematically preserved. For the British and American sections, the problem has been even more difficult. The British government was only rarely concerned officially with the activities of the French agents in Britain. The archives of public offices in Britain therefore contain relatively little information on the British-French tobacco trade. It is, for example, hardly ever mentioned in the dispatches of the British envoys in Paris, though we know that several of them were much concerned about it privately. The strength of the British materials has been largely on the statistical side, compensating usefully for weaknesses in corresponding French data. Although virtually nothing is known about some of the French tobacco buying agents in Britain, relatively rich data have come to light on others, particularly Sir Robert Herries. American data are also very thin, though they become much richer after 1775.

The work has been divided into three parts, each of which could, with some alterations, stand as a separate monograph. The longest, Part I, is a history of the French tobacco monopoly, with considerable emphasis upon its tobacco purchasing policies and their implication for French colonies and French foreign trade. It is in turn divided into three sections: Chapters 2–7 discuss the early history of the tobacco monopoly, 1674–1718; Chapters 8–10, the Law interruption; and Chapters 11–18 the main period of the farm's history, 1721–91. Perhaps a disproportionate attention has been given to the Law years and their sequel, 1721–30. The author hopes, however, that after reading the relevant chapters the reader will agree that the tobacco monopoly played a most significant role financially in the inception of the Law scheme and in the subsequent history of the Indies Company. (Needless to say, the author would have been delighted if he could have used Professor Earl J. Hamilton's long-awaited magnum opus on Law. He also regrets that volume III of Professor Marcel Giraud's masterly history of Louisiana, covering 1717–20, appeared too late to be used properly.)

Part II is a monographic study of the French tobacco agents in Britain and of the effects of their purchases upon the structure, geographic distribution, and rate of growth of the British-American tobacco trade. The implications for the Chesapeake have been largely confined to a general essay in Chapter 25, inasmuch as it is hoped to explore some of these topics further in a future book on the Chesapeake economy. Part III is a "Postscript" on the years 1775–91, investigating the fate of the monopoly and of its commercial policies in the turbulent years preceding its abolition. This is a postscript both in circumstance and in subject. At first, it was planned to end the book in 1775, with the close of the classic period of the American-British-French tobacco trade (1723–75). Further investigation and reflection suggested that this might both disappoint and deceive the reader. A very large part of the old order survived into the 1780's. It was therefore decided to bring the story down to its proper legal terminus in 1791. The author pretends to no expertise in the history of either the American or the French Revolution, nor does he argue that the tobacco trade was too important in either. In subject matter, these chapters are very much a postscript, discussing what had happened to the debris of the old system after it lost control of its own destiny.

Some methodologically minded readers will notice that in this book we are dealing simultaneously with three quite distinct conceptual "systems": (1) the classic system of the *market;* (2) the less frequently analyzed system of *administrative logic* or *convenience;* and (3) the much looser quasi system or "human comedy" of interpersonal connections or relationships (including kinship, marriage, dependency, reciprocal obligation, and partnership) which had a dynamism of its own and at the same time channeled the dynamism of the other more self-evident systems.[6] A basic decision of state being made and adhered to (in this case, to maximize the fiscal yield of tobacco through a royal monopoly), all kinds of subsidiary administrative decisions sooner or later logically, almost inevitably, followed (bureaucratic arrangements, penal codes, regulations affecting agriculture, foreign trade, navigation and the colonies); these in turn had each greater or lesser impact upon the world market; all created opportunities for patronage in decisions over farms, contracts, and appointments. Such patronage, once granted, created new interests which in turn exerted influence backward upon state and administrative "decision-making."

Some readers might well feel that the operation of these three systems might have been depicted more clearly if each were disentangled from the whole and separately presented. Such a criticism would have great validity were this a work in econometric history or in political science. For the historian *tout court,* such a disentanglement and reconstruction, however convenient, have one serious drawback, indeed fatal flaw: they destroy the historicity of the problem. The wheels of market, administration and patronage did not turn in isolation; each was tightly enmeshed with the other two; pressure anywhere was felt throughout the whole. To understand the "decision-making process" historically, one must understand the interconnectedness of the three sets of pressures upon the "decision makers." (We have nevertheless attempted a partial disentanglement in Part I by presenting separate chapters on the political, administrative, and commercial history of the monopoly.)

Readers might also feel that the scale of the work is unjustified, that the whole story, the three monographs, could have condensed into a volume one-half or one-third as long. The writer has given this problem much thought. He is not concerned simply with formal state policy whose essential outlines can be succinctly described, nor with the mere description of institutions whose lack of complexity makes possible a treatment almost as brief. He is concerned rather with *process:* the process by which state, administrative and market decisions are made, and the process by which the implications of decisions are felt through the multitudinous layers of the administration and the market in the lives of people insignificant, colonies unfamiliar and indeed foreign places unknown to the decision makers. To describe these infinitely complex and interlinked chains of happening, the historian is very much in a position analogous to that of the microbiologist: only at a sufficiently high level of magnification does matter become process.

A generation ago, it was fashionable to dub every particular or microcosmic investigation a "case study." For some, perhaps for most readers, the value or interest of this work will be that of a *representative* or "case" study in the interrelatedness of statecraft, finance, commerce, and society in the *ancien régime*. Its "representative" quality should not, however, be exaggerated: the very size of the tobacco farm made it unlike most other monopolies held by companies or corporate bodies. Only its sometime connection, the Indies Company, could compare with it in magnitude, yet the fate of the Indies Company was for the most part governed by decisions as "national" and antifiscal, as those governing the tobacco monopoly were fiscal and antinational. For other readers, the interest of this study may well be not representative but particular: i.e., for historians of finance, colonies, and international trade. There is yet a third way of conceiving of the problem, a way often in the mind of the author when writing, a way which combines both representative and particular significance: if the seine of experience is one, then to know the fate of one central strand is to know something of the fate of the whole.

The author would like to thank the archivists and librarians of the various institutions cited in the Bibliography for their much appreciated help and courtesy. (Mr. William J. Van Schreeven, State Archivist of Virginia, was particularly helpful.) He would also like to express his indebtedness to Mrs. Eaves Walton, Mme E. Hubert, Mme R. A. Aussedat, Mlle M. Rochette, and Miss Judith Reynolds for assistance in research. To Professors Lionel Rothkrug, John Hemphill, and Julian P. Boyd, he is most grateful for the loan of valuable microfilms; to Professors M. Braure, Lawrence A. Harper, and Donald Wiedner, he is deeply indebted for important statistical data. J. S. Bromley has listened patiently and commented shrewdly over the many years this work was in gestation. For permission to consult and quote from their records, he is highly indebted to the appropriate officers of the Bank of England, the Bank of Scotland, the Royal Bank of Scotland, Martin's Bank Ltd., and Messrs. Coutts & Co. To Professor C. Colleer Abbott, he is most grateful for access to the papers of Sir William Forbes and to the late Professor Edward Hughes for access to the Lutwidge letter-books. For their kind hospitality and permission to consult their muniments, he should particularly like to thank Lady Bosanquet, Sir James Hunter Blair, bart., Lt. Col. W. H. Olivier, Major R. A. Oswald, and the Hon. Andrew Vanneck. For the privilege of examining their family papers, he is also indebted to the duke of Norfolk, the earl of Dartmouth, the earl of Lonsdale, and David Holland, Esq.

Last but not least, he must acknowledge the extremely important financial assistance he has received from the John Simon Guggenheim Memorial Foundation, the Social Science Research Council, and the Faculty Research Fund of the Horace H. Rackham School of Graduate Studies of the University of Michigan.

Introduction

An Argument on Three Levels

Philosophers may argue about the ultimate function of the state, be it carrier/realizer of an idea, a national mission or spirit, or a class interest. To the historian dealing with short- and middle-range phenomena, however, the state, particularly the state of the *ancien régime,* more often than not appears to act as if it were its own justification, an end in itself. That is, the preponderant bulk of governmental decisions of the early modern state, whether examined under the microscope of the decision-making process or analyzed from a distance for their longer-run significance, seem best understandable as state-building efforts and little more. This narrow view of state policy seems particularly suitable when seeking to explain state fiscal decision making. Whether states spent their revenues on armies, navies, foreign subsidies, royal extravagance or economic development, or on anything else, revenues were the ultimate measure of the grandeur and power of the state; thus, their enhancement was a primary state objective. Though one can point out examples here and there where fiscal interests were subordinated to considerations of economic development or of the need for autarkical supplies of strategic commodities, the general primacy of fiscal interests seems unchallengeable.

Historians, of course, like to chop up the life of state and society into pieces labeled court, administration, church, law, army, navy, fisc, and so on. None of these categories, it goes without saying, exists in isolation. Decisions and developments in one sphere affect other spheres. At the highest level, influences from many spheres frequently affect single decisions. Things would be easier for the historian and his reader if everything stayed in its own box and if each box could be examined by itself. Life, however, is not neat; just as realistic history must allow for the irrational as well as the rational, for the accidental as well as the deliberate, for the incoherent as well as the coherent, so it must allow for the confusing interrelatedness of seemingly disparate spheres of activity which it would be "so much easier" to study separately.

This work centers upon the study of a fiscal institution of the French *ancien régime,* the tobacco monopoly, an entity whose annals are not only interesting in themselves to the historian but are significant for what they reveal of the interplay of fiscal, administrative, and political-court considerations which governed the fate of all fiscal institutions of the *ancien régime*. This particular institution differed from others in that it involved the monopolization of a commodity which (unlike salt) came to be purchased normally in open world markets where heavy French buying exerted pressures approaching monopsonistic. Thus, once the historian understands the state decision to raise revenue by a tobacco monopoly, he must follow the implications of this decision through three distinct "systems": (1) administrative convenience; (2) the market; and (3) the vast network of interpersonal relationships (familial, patron-client, and other) that governed the vast official and commercial patronage created by the monopoly and which, to varying degrees, exerted pressure laterally on decisions in the other systems and indeed even backward upon the basic state decision-making process.

Tobacco was hardly introduced into common consumption in Europe before seventeenth-century governments discovered that they could extract a significant state revenue from it by taxing it at rates exceeding 100 percent of cost. Only in England and a few other places were these very high duties obtained by import duties and/or excises alone. In Spain, Portugal, most German and Italian states, and elsewhere it was soon found that the highest yields could be obtained only by a state monopoly. It was probably inevitable that France follow this latter example, for, without fiscal unity, its administrative apparatus and legal powers for collecting import duties and uniform excises were quite imperfect. In fact, the French state had collected only very modest amounts from tobacco before the monopoly was established in 1674. Yields under the new arrangements were at first disappointing but grew significantly from 1697 with the gradual social and geographical diffusion of the practice of tobacco and snuff taking. (Compared to other west European states, France was relatively backward in picking up this habit.) By 1730, however, yields to the state were about twenty times those of the 1670's and were to increase fourfold more by 1789. This impressive increase in yields rendered unassailable the original decision to establish the monopoly. (The brief suspension of the monopoly in the chaotic last months of Law's ascendancy only made the monopoly seem more incontrovertibly orthodox thereafter.)

The decision to establish a monopoly implied a triumph of fiscal considerations over the interests of agriculture and commerce. Only time was to show how absolute was this victory. From the 1670's, the districts within the monopoly's jurisdiction in which tobacco cultivation was permitted were severely limited. Under the protection of the intendants, cultivation continued and even prospered in these constricted regions for two generations, until suppressed by John Law in his hour of ruthless experimentation. Similarly, government at first hoped that, despite the monopoly, tobacco would continue to be shipped to France from the French colonies in America. At the test, however, it appeared that West Indian tobacco production needed a price about double that of Chesapeake tobacco to be economic. As the monopolists were not prepared to pay such a price, the once great St. Domingue tobacco cultivation had become more or less extinct by 1700; for essentially the same reasons, the Louisiana tobacco cultivation, though much talked about and favored in the next century, never produced more than one or two percent of France's needs. Thus, the victory of fiscal over agricultural and commercial-colonial considerations, though qualified initially, was to be absolute in the long run. With neither domestic nor colonial supplies available, the French monopolists became entirely dependent upon foreign sources from the 1720's onward.

To this general picture of the triumph of fiscality, there were however some local exceptions—the frontier provinces outside the jurisdiction of the monopoly: the "Belgic provinces" (Flanders, Artois, Hainault, Cambrésis), Alsace, Franche Comté and, at the other end of France, the *pays de Labourd* about Bayonne. Because of treaty and other contractual obligations (in some cases) and because of a persistent state policy of indulging the militarily exposed frontier provinces, these areas were never subject to the monopoly and in some of them there was much planting (Lower Alsace, Flanders, Artois) and manufacturing (Strasbourg, St. Omer, Dunkirk). The monopoly fought against and limited these privileges but, in the end, they survived to 1791 to triumph over the monopoly.

The center of the picture is thus clear: the financial needs of the state determined the decision to establish the tobacco monopoly. The swelling yields of the monopoly strengthened the original resolution and led to the sacrifice of both French domestic cultivation and colonial trade to the advancement of those ever mounting yields. The consequences and implications of these basic state decisions we can follow through the three "systems" previously mentioned: (1) the seine of kinship, friendship, partnership, and clientage that ties person to person to person; (2) the inherent logic of administrative convenience that makes a thousand little decisions follow from a few big ones; and (3) the market.

1. "Who Whom?" Once the basic decision was made to establish a monopoly, the first question became who would obtain that monopoly on farm, since all French indirect taxation was then farmed. Three things at least were required of a successful revenue farming company: usable connections in court and administration; financial resources; and some administrative ability. The initial monopoly company had more of the first than of the latter two. Their lack of operating success led to the transfer of the monopoly in 1680 to the United General Farms who were possessed of all three. The government was, however, still dissatisfied with yields and so in 1697 (contrary to the normal policy) took the monopoly away from the powerful united farms and confided it to an equally powerful company headed by Samuel Bernard, Antoine Crozat, and Vincent Maynon. This group had influence, resources, and administrative ability but also offered a considerably higher price to the state and demonstrated the ability to get foreign tobacco even in the most difficult war years. With consumption rising, this new group gave every appearance of making a very good thing out of the monopoly. Their prosperity stirred great jealousy and numerous rival companies came forward, but not till the rise of John Law did an influence emerge powerful enough to conquer that of Bernard & Co. Even so, Law had to offer a price almost double that of the old group to break their grip on the farm in 1718.

After Law's collapse, the dominant influence in matters of public finance was that of the brothers Paris. It was they who restored the Colbertian monopoly in 1721 and had it transferred to the reformed Indies Company in 1723, before they were themselves undone in the disgrace of the duke of Bourbon in 1726. The ensuing new regime of the young king and the old Cardinal Fleury was characterized by extreme fiscal conservatism. Under such a policy, it was not surprising that the United General Farms should be fully restored in 1726 or that the tobacco monopoly should be transferred to them (from the Indies Company) in 1730. That powerful society retained its hold on the monopoly until both went down in 1791. Throughout, the "who whom?" of the tobacco monopoly was to be intimately associated with the "who whom?" of the highest levels of court, administration, and Paris financial circles.

Kinship and connection not only influenced what company got the tobacco farm and who were its partners, but also influenced the internal staffing policies of the monopoly. The tobacco privilege alone by the 1780's had about 10,000 employees, exclusive of its 40,000 licensed retailers. The intercession of courtiers, high government officials, farmers-general, their relations and mistresses was extremely helpful in obtaining the higher positions in the monopoly or the farms generally. At lower levels within the monopoly, the higher officials had their own networks of clientage among the lower. Even outside the company proper, the merchants who held the lucrative contracts for buying the monopoly's tobacco in London, Amsterdam, and elsewhere owed their commissions in part to their personal connections not only in the company but in Paris court and administrative circles generally. The triumph of Madame du Barry, for example, was to determine who got the French commission to buy tobacco at Glasgow.

These influences were not operative only in the procuring of positions and contracts. Collectively, they formed a vast social weight working against innovations that might disturb so many happy family arrangements.

2. *Administrative Convenience.* To create a productive state monopoly, it was not enough for the king simply to sign a *déclaration* setting up such a monopoly and a *résultat du conseil* awarding it on lease to some company or other. The successful operation of such a monopoly required vast administrative and legal elaboration. The monopolists were from the start given most of the powers needed to set up their own manufacturing, distribution, and account-keeping systems and to make the regulations neces-

sary for the direction of their employees and licensed retailers. However, to deal with merchants, sailors, the inhabitants of frontier zones, and the public generally, inevitably the monopoly required the continuing use of the legislative powers of the state. Year after year, administrative necessity or convenience sent the monopolists back to the controller-general for more *arrêts* and *ordonnances,* spelling out in ever greater detail and exactitude the legal rights of the monopoly vis-à-vis all and sundry. Just as administrative convenience at first restricted and then abolished the right to grow tobacco within the jurisdiction of the monopoly, so it came to limit the ports at which the importation of tobacco was allowed, the ships in which it could be carried, their routes, the warehouses in which it could be stored, the conditions for its export, the areas in the frontier provinces outside the monopoly in which it was permitted to be grown or traded, and so on. Increasingly elaborate and severe penal codes were developed to cover every conceivable variety of fraud.

The France of the *ancien régime* was a complex corporative society in which groups great and small jealously guarded their particular privileges, liberties, exemptions. The administrative logic of the tobacco monopoly inevitably brought it into conflict with this regime of privilege. Municipalities did not like the exemptions from tolls given to the property of the monopoly or the exemptions from services given to its employees. Religious bodies, seigneurs, foreign ambassadors, officers of royal residences all complained about the search powers of the guards of the monopoly. Law courts high and low *(cours des aides* and *élections* in particular) did not like the exemptions given to the monopoly which cut down on their jurisdictions and fees. Wherever possible the monopoly preferred to use extraordinary tribunals established for fiscal offenses, much to the annoyance of the regular courts. Although the victory of the monopoly over the courts seemed clear by the 1720's, throughout the century the regional *parlements* and *cours des aides* sustained against it an intermittent guerilla war which burgeoned into a full-scale conflict in the 1780's.

3. *The Market.* Despite its public character and legal privileges, the tobacco monopoly was also a manufacturing and distributing company which had to buy and sell as much as others did. Even monopoly selling was complicated, for leases fixed maximum retail prices. Sometimes, those maxima were charged; at other times the monopoly deliberately sold for less either to develop a wider market for its more highly manufactured snuff or to discourage smuggling in areas near the frontiers. Buying the raw material was even more difficult as most of it had to be obtained in the open commodity markets of Holland, Germany, and Britain. As tobacco of the desired quantities, qualities, and prices could most readily be obtained in Britain, about 90 percent of French purchases came to be made there between the 1720's and 1770's. A great single buyer could not, however, enter even a classically perfect market (many buyers, many sellers) and attempt to buy up to 25 percent or more of imports without seriously disturbing that

market. The French came ultimately to depend upon a few large sellers in London, Whitehaven, and Scotland. The French presence helps to explain many of the structural changes in the British tobacco trade in the eighteenth century: the emergence of the larger firms trading on their own, the chains of stores in the Chesapeake, the shift of the trade to Whitehaven and Glasgow.

In the end, this peculiar marriage of a French monopoly with the British acts of trade was dissolved by the American Revolution. But the melody lingered on for another generation. Because tobacco could be purchased in Britain so expeditiously, and, relatively speaking, so inexpensively, the farmers-general would have preferred continuing their purchases there even after the American Revolution but were prevented from doing so by French state policy which called for the encouragement of direct trade with the new United States. Dissatisfied as ever with the workings of the open market, the monopoly found itself forced to buy through a series of exclusive agents in America. Whether they bought in French ports or through Robert Morris and other agents in the United States, most of the tobacco sold to the French after 1783 came ultimately from the Chesapeake agents of the same Scottish firms which had supplied them before the war. The old regime really ended only when the National Assembly in 1791 abolished the monopoly and permitted tobacco cultivation throughout France. When the monopoly was reestablished by Napoleon, it was to be on more autarkical lines utilizing French home tobaccos. In that form, it survives to the present.

The old Virginia tobacco trade was at its secular height in 1791 when the French monopoly was abolished. Before that decade was over, it had gone into the decline from which it has never recovered. The old tobacco trade (as distinct from the modern) was built upon the purchase sight unseen (by warehouse notes) of ungraded tobacco. The buyers did their own sorting later, knowing in advance of purchase that the poorest grades passing the public inspectors could always be sold to the French, while the better qualities could be put aside for sale to more exacting markets. With the disappearance of the bulk purchases of the French monopoly, most speculative bulk purchases in America became too risky. In the changed market conditions, much of the production of Tidewater Virginia proved submarginal and disappeared.

The systems here sketched can be readily enough followed in outline. In the text, however, we have not been able to keep the history of each distinct. Abstractly, we can conceive of a set of state interests and decisions from which three separate chains of consequences follow. In the historical situation, the various chains or systems are not isolated but interact with each other and upon the original state decision-making process. Some readers may find this intermingling of ill-sorted elements a rather unfelicitous design; but the architecture of life is untidy.

Part I

France: Institutions and Interests, 1674–1791

CHAPTER 1

The Prehistory of Tobacco in Seventeenth-Century France

The Beginnings of Consumption, Cultivation, and Commerce

MOST LITERATE PEOPLE are vaguely aware that the introduction of tobacco into northwestern Europe had something to do with someone named Nicot whom we remember in the words *nicotinus,* the botanical name for the plant, and *nicotine,* its most characteristic ingredient. Jean Nicot (1530–1600) was in fact French ambassador in Lisbon in 1560, a time when tobacco was already relatively well known in the Iberian peninsula, but almost unknown to Europeans outside it. From a Flemish merchant in Lisbon, he obtained some tobacco seed reputedly from Florida which he sent in 1560 as a curiosity to the queen mother, Catherine de Medici. At her command, it was cultivated in the royal botanical gardens, and thence spread to other gardens of the unusual. From the persons associated with its introduction, tobacco was known in sixteenth-century France both as *nicotiane* and as *herbe à la reine.* The reputation of both Nicot and his queen as the introducers of tobacco may, however, be somewhat ill deserved, for the French Franciscan and geographer, André Thevet, who had been on the French expedition to Brazil in 1555, claimed in 1576 that he had grown tobacco from the superior Brazil seed in France as early as 1556.[1]

Whether Thevet or the queen's gardener first planted tobacco in France is actually of little concern to us here. In the second half of the sixteenth century, tobacco was cultivated in France either for ornamental purposes or for experiments by the more adventurous among herbalists and apothecaries. Though Frenchmen might be given it as a medicine or salve, it was not until well into the seventeenth century that any number of them voluntarily took it for pleasure. Thus the true popular history of tobacco in France begins not in the age of Catherine de Medici but in that of Louis XIII (1610–43). The French have a reputation for relative conservatism in habits of consumption. One cannot be exact, but our little evidence suggests that the French were among the slowest in western Europe to adopt the tobacco habit. In France, the general chronology of the spread of tobacco taking seems to follow about a generation behind that in England.

Some would have Louis XIII introducing the use of the pipe into France.[2] True or not, it was during the first two decades of his reign that we find the significant beginnings of the public history of tobacco in France: commerce, agriculture, and, above all, taxation. As early as 1599, on the re-

3

turn of the *Marguerite* to Le Havre from a voyage as much of exploration as of trade to the West Indies and Brazil, we find in its cargo an unspecified quantity of "petun," the Indian word by which tobacco was known in France in the sixteenth and seventeenth centuries.[3] We have to wait a generation, however, to find evidence of the importation of tobacco in any volume and with any regularity. By 1613–15, we do find it imported in commercially significant quantities at Marseilles from Lisbon, Cadiz, and Seville. This was a most predictable trading pattern. From the Iberian ports whither tobacco from the Spanish colonies in America had compulsorily to be brought, tobacco was carried first to those ports in France, like Marseilles, closest to Iberia in taste and in trade. When the Franco-Spanish War of 1635–59 interrupted normal traffic, the expanding network of the tobacco trade provided other sources of supply. By 1636, Marseilles was importing Spanish tobacco indirectly from Genoa and other types of tobacco from Bristol and Holland.[4] The revolt of Portugal against Hapsburg suzerainty in 1640 enabled its merchants to resume trade with states at war with Spain and may have helped Portuguese (Brazilian) tobacco supplant Spanish (then Venezuelan) tobacco in French taste. Of 20,550 lb. of tobacco sent from Bordeaux to Toulouse in 1646, 18,950 lb. or 92 percent were Brazilian.[5] Major imports from Spain and Portugal were supplemented from the mid-1620's by importations from the new French settlements on St. Christopher and later elsewhere in the West Indies. As shall be explained in Chapter 4, the French colonies founded in the West Indies in the 1620's and 1630's were in their first years essentially tobacco colonies.[6] Though we lack data on which to be explicit, it seems likely that by 1650, the half dozen principal French ports (Marseilles, Bordeaux, La Rochelle, Nantes, St. Malo, and Le Havre-Rouen and perhaps Dieppe) each had significant commercial imports of tobacco, most probably in the five figure range (10,000–99,999 lb. p.a.) —commercially significant but economically not very important yet.[7]

But tobacco in France was not simply a matter of ports and foreign traders. The same early years of Louis XIII which saw the beginnings of significant imports saw also the beginnings of the cultivation of tobacco on French soils. Too much should probably not be made of Thevet's claims to have introduced the culture in the southwest.[8] A curiosity is not a commercial crop. From the 1620's, however, significant amounts were being grown at Mondragon on the Rhone, in the Angoumois, and particularly in the Agenais in the middle Garonne valley. In the not yet French east, we hear of the introduction of tobacco planting in Alsace—at Bischwiller (1618)[9] and Strasbourg (1620–21)[10]—in Artois (1620), and in Lorraine.[11] In Normandy in 1626, one René de Montesson obtained permission under royal letters-patent to plant tobacco.[12] A great stimulus to the domestic plantation may have come from the adoption of the first import duties on tobacco in 1621 and 1629. The latter high duty of 30 *sols* per lb. on foreign tobaccos (equal to 300 percent and more on common grades) was designed to encourage the new French colonies in the West Indies whose product was exempt.[13] In fact, the principal immediate benefit was realized by growers in France, particularly those in the southwest. By the 1640's, tobacco cultivation had become relatively common along the middle Garonne, particularly in the Agenais and Condomois, and by the 1660's was also established in the upper Garonne valley toward Montauban and in the upper Dordogne. The growing production appears to have reached something between 1.5 and 2.0 million lb. in 1679 and about three million lb. in 1696.[14] Though these figures are not overwhelming, it should be kept in mind that the famous Brazilian tobacco industry sent only 3.5 million lb. to Portugal in 1689.[15]

Thus, though we find references in the late seventeenth century to small importations into France of tobacco from Spain, England, and the United Provinces and larger importations from Portugal,[16] France had colonial and domestic supplies sufficient to meet all its consumption needs, if it so chose. In fact, from the 1630's onward, the development of this great domestic culture and the somewhat smaller production in the French West Indies made possible French tobacco exports. From the 1630's, a prosperous trade developed at Marseilles, exporting Guienne tobacco to the Mediterranean world, particularly Italy, and even to Hamburg and England. This trade was hurt when in 1660 a special tobacco sales tax of 20s. per lb. was established in Provence for the benefit of the hospitals of Aix, Marseilles, and Toulon. Even though this tax was reduced in 1664 to 10s. per lb. on Brazil tobacco and 5s. per lb. on domestic tobacco, it remained a burden of over 100 percent of wholesale prices. Even though tobacco in transit for export was not taxed, it was subject to the controls of the *fermier* of this duty. Exports of domestic tobacco at Marseilles, which had been much larger, fell to only 403,500 lb. in Nov. 1661–Nov. 1662 and to only 285,750 lb. p.a. in the next two years. To avoid the special situation in Provence, tobacco was shipped from Guienne via Montauban to the Languedoc ports of Narbonne and Agde for export.[17]

The Atlantic ports of France also had a significant though less extensive export trade in tobacco, particularly in the 1660's and 1670's, though for them, French West Indian tobacco was more important than the domestic leaf. Most of it was bought by the Dutch for shipment to Holland and reexport thence to the Baltic where a steady demand was created. We learn from mercantile correspondence that in 1668, "Martinique tobacco always sells well at Danzig and at Königsberg, going for 12 to 15 groschen per lb." Königsberg alone imported 100,000 lb. of French leaf about 1670.[18] At Danzig, we find St. Christopher's tobacco mentioned in the printed price-currents as late as 1699.[19] We also hear of English ships in 1673 carrying French tobacco to Sweden,[20] where legislation of the 1660's recognized

French tobacco as one of the types in common use there.[21] Colbert at one time had high hopes of developing these northern markets for French and French colonial tobacco into something of national importance.[22]

One of the reasons the French had so much tobacco to export in the mid-seventeenth century was that compared to other nations they consumed relatively modest amounts themselves. From what has been written above about the growth of French domestic and colonial production and trade, one might get the impression that by Colbert's time, France was a nation of tobacco users. This was only partly true; all through the seventeenth century, we find traces of a suspicion of and hostility to tobacco in France and its neighbors that effectively disappeared from England with the death of James I.

When in 1626 René de Montesson presented to the *parlement* of Rouen letters-patent from the king authorizing him to introduce and propagandize the cultivation of tobacco in Normandy for twenty years, the judges decided (29 April) that they would consent to the registration of the letters-patent only on condition that none of the said *petun* be sold for human consumption until inspected by the physicians of Rouen who were to report to the *parlement* on its "usefulness or harmfulness."[23] Others were prepared to go farther. By an *ordonnance* of 12 February 1628, Charles IV, duke of Lorraine, forbad the cultivation of tobacco in his territories. (Throughout western and central Europe, many feared that growing tobacco would take land away from the cultivation of foodstuffs.) This led the Lothringian tobacco "undertakers" to transfer their activities in 1628–29 to lands under the authority of the king of France, starting with the baron de Rorthey's *seigneurie* of Malpierre in the canton of Vaucouleurs within the jurisdiction of Metz; the tobacco so grown was sold to merchants in Metz.[24] The results must have been financially attractive both to landlord and undertakers, for within a very few years, with permission from the governors, the dukes of La Valette and Epernon, the cultivation spread within the Messin. This innovation was viewed with extreme hostility by the local peasantry, probably because of the danger to the food supply, and a widespread series of riots ensued in 1634 in which mobs attacked fields growing tobacco and pulled up the plants. At least eight localities were affected, some forty *journaux* destroyed. The properietors of the tobacco brought suit in the *parlement* of Metz, claiming 50,000 *l.t.* damages, and were awarded 11,500.[25]

This hostile attitude was by no means confined to the rude peasants of the *vaux de Metz*. At about the same time, the *procureur-général* informed the *parlement* of Paris that the physicians and surgeons of the Conciergerie had reported to him that many prisoners there took tobacco "which was dangerous both for them and others who might inhale the smoke, for it could cause serious illness." The *parlement* so warned on 24 May 1631 forbad, under penalty of flogging, the bringing in or using of tobacco in any of the prisons of Paris.[26] By the late 1620's, "tobacco-seller" had become a recognized but not an accepted occupation.[27] The general police *ordonnance* for Paris of 30 March 1635, citing an *arrêt* of the *conseil d'état* of 11 February 1634, forbad anyone to sell tobacco except apothecaries, and they only on the prescription of a physician. Publicans were specifically enjoined against keeping tobacco on hand for the use of their customers.[28] This and related *ordonnances* were specifically confirmed as late as the 1660's by a *déclaration* of the king of 18 December 1660, and by an edict of December 1666.[29]

If Paris was suspicious, one might well expect to find the provinces paranoid about tobacco. The use of the new herb spread inland from the ports only slowly. As late as 1661, the Senate of Berne in Switzerland established a special "Tobacco Court" to act against those using the leaf.[30] Burgundy is perhaps the most inland province of France: the public use of tobacco was supposed to have been introduced there only during the wars by the army of Galas in 1636.[31] The local authorities were markedly hostile to this unwelcome innovation and Dijon, like a number of other inland towns, had a local ordinance against taking tobacco. In fact, the police tolerated a number of illicit, secret *cabarets, académies,* or *stecqs* where the public could get pipes and tobacco and smoke sociably. If this suggests an analogy with more modern experience with prohibition and "speak-easies," the ensuing will suggest an even more current analogy. In 1662, a young man smoking in one such establishment, suddenly fell dead. His father, a surgeon, accused the *cabaretier* of murder by tobacco poisoning and had him arrested. In the event, two other surgeons who made the autopsy, though sympathetic to their colleague, the bereaved father, could find no evidence that would support such a serious accusation in court. The local municipal council was however sufficiently incensed to renew its longstanding prohibitions against *cabaretiers, hosteliers,* and *académistes* keeping places of resort where the public might obtain pipes and tobacco—on pain of corporal punishment and 150 *l.t.* fine for a first offense. In 1665, that same body made it an offense for the public to attend such *stecqs* or even to take tobacco.[32] As late as 1679, the *parlement* of Burgundy, on the recommendation of its *procureur-général,* confirmed for the whole province the prohibitions on either keeping or attending such places of ill resort, with penalties of corporal punishment and 500 *l.t.* fine, and ordered public officials to search out such establishments and arrest their keepers and the vagabonds and debauched persons frequenting them.[33]

Burgundy may have been even more isolated and conservative in its consumption tastes than the rest of provincial France, but when we view together the local regulations on tobacco in Paris and Dijon down through the 1660's and 1670's, we sense that the history of tobacco in seventeenth-century France is somewhat more complicated than the frequent mention of the product in commercial accounts would suggest. We are told that literary references to tobacco in the 1630's are commonly hostile, that the pipe was never accepted at court and had been banished from the better bourgeois cafés by the end of the reign of Louis XIV.[34] According to an Englishman, writing some years later, "from the year 1684 to 1691 during my stay in France, smoking of Tobacco was so scandalous, & offensive, that none but Mariners & people in the Sea Port Towns used it, except in urgent cases for preservation of health, & that was done in secret, & with bashfullness."[35] All in all, we gain the impression that however fashionable and popular tobacco may have become in the eighteenth century—the age of snuff—in the seventeenth century, the age of the hot, reeking clay pipe,[36] both polite and mass acceptance of the new product were decidedly restrained.

Thus far, our suggestion of the relative slowness with which the French took to tobacco has been based on the texts of laws and curious anecdotes. This kind of evidence can be misleading, for laws are not necessarily enforced and the bizarre is often more readily remembered than the commonplace. We can, however, attempt a more "scientific" demonstration of this slow acceptance. After the tobacco monopoly was established in 1674, we can find more precise records of tobacco consumption in France.

The levels of tobacco consumption accepted as "normal" today are unlike anything known in the seventeenth or eighteenth centuries. In 1956, tobacco consumption per adult per annum in advanced nations ranged from 3.1 lb. in Italy to 8.3 lb. in the Netherlands (the highest in Europe) and 9.8 lb. in the United States. If we assume that one-third of the population in 1956 consisted of children, then consumption per head of population would have been about 2.1 for Italy, 5.5 for the Netherlands and 6.6 for the United States. For the United Kingdom and France, the figures were 6.3 and 3.7 respectively per adult or 4.2 and 2.5 per head of population. France had the lowest consumption of any country in Europe except for Italy. The situation was substantially the same in 1935.[37] For a seventeenth or eighteenth-century tobacco merchant, these modern levels of consumption would have seemed extraordinarily high. The only familiar element would have been the relatively low ranking of France.

In the late seventeenth and eighteenth centuries, England and Wales with one of the most fully developed tobacco trades in Europe had a consumption of only one to two pounds per head of population per annum.[38] As we shall see in a subsequent chapter, it was not to be until the middle of the eighteenth century that France should even approach a consumption of even one pound per head of population per annum.[39] When the tobacco monopoly was first established in 1674, it found consumption levels scarcely one-tenth those suggested for contemporary England.

In the early years of the monopoly, figures were compiled of sales in each *généralité* for the years 1675–79. These figures do not include the eastern provinces outside the monopoly (Artois, Hainault, Flanders, Alsace, and the Franche Comté) nor the new *généralité* (1694) of La Rochelle nor Béarn or Roussillon. For the late seventeenth century, we have population estimates by Vauban, adjusted by Alfred des Cilleuls. Since these were also compiled by *généralités,* it is relatively easy to compute an estimate of the population living within those areas of the monopoly's jurisdiction for which we have sales data. Out of a total population for France of about 19.3 millions, some 17.34 millions lived within the relevant provinces of the monopoly.[40] Table I summarizes the results.

TABLE I

Sales of Tobacco within the Territories of the Monopoly
1676–79, 1690[41]

Year	Total	Per Head of Population
1676	1,471,116	.085 lb.
1677	1,458,140	.084 lb.
1678	1,314,042	.076 lb.
1679	1,144,360	.066 lb.
1690	1,490,626 (+ ?)	—

These figures seem to suggest that at a time when England had a tobacco consumption of over one pound per head of population per annum, France had a consumption of only about eight one-hundredths of a pound per annum, or roughly one-twelfth as much. Even if we were to double or treble the French figures to allow for smuggling and the consumption of untaxed tobacco in the growing regions, we should have an *overall* rate of consumption for France strikingly below current rates for England. To understand this phenomenon, we must look at the geographical breakdown of French consumption in Table II.

Even though this table has been derived from the crudest of data, certain remarkable patterns emerge. (Even if the population data were pushed up or down by 25 percent and the consumption data by 50 percent, the basic pattern would persist.) We may ignore the *généralités* of Bordeaux and Montauban where tobacco was grown in great quantities and where the possibilities for fraudulent or legitimate consumption outside of regular channels make our data too suspect. Looking at the rest, we see a clear enough pattern. Brittany alone accounted for over one-third the consumption within the monopoly, though it had less than one-tenth the population of the area. The contiguous *généralités* of Brittany, Normandy, Amiens, and Paris account for almost 74 percent of the whole consumption though they account for only 30 percent of the population covered. Looking at the rates of consumption only, we see the highest rates in Brittany, Amiens, Normandy and northern Champagne (Soissons) followed by the nearby but further inland *généralités* of Paris, southern Champagne (Châlons) and Metz, together with Provence on the southern coast and Poitiers on the

10   FRANCE AND THE CHESAPEAKE

Table II

Consumption of Tobacco in France, 1676, by *Généralités*[42]

Généralité	Consumption in Pounds	Population	Rate per Head in Pounds
Brittany	534,177	1,700,000	.314
Amiens	136,353 (143,561) *	497,351	.274 (.289) †
Normandy (3 gen.)	262,565	1,540,000	.170
Soissons	48,410 (82,056)	322,500	.150 (.254)
Paris	152,375	1,576,938	.097
Provence	99,543 (137,892)	1,044,350	.095 (.132)
Châlons	51,827	693,244	.075
3 Bishoprics (gen. Metz)	24,196	362,063	.067
Poitiers[43]	20,552	363,729	.057
Languedoc (Toulouse & Montpellier)	56,222 (64,551)	1,441,896	.039 (.045)
Orléans	22,448 (29,072)	607,165	.037 (.048)
Lyons	11,729 (26,344)	363,000	.032 (.073)
Bourges	2,966	201,232	.015
Tours	11,425 (15,524)	1,069,616	.011
Moulins	2,862	324,332	.009
Burgundy	11,431 (11,745)	1,266,359	.009
Grenoble (Dauphiné)	3,892	543,585	.007
Montauban	4,627 (21,594)	798,600	.006 (.027)
Riom	3,344	557,068	.006
Bordeaux[43]	8,988 (149,257)	1,482,304	.006 (.101)
Limoges[43]	1,182 (8,252)	585,000	.002 (.014)
Total	1,471,114	17,340,332	

*The highest annual consumption of tobacco in pounds during 1676–79 is indicated in parentheses.

†The highest annual rate per head of consumption of tobacco during 1676–79 is indicated in parentheses.

western coast. Next comes coastal Languedoc, commercial Lyons, and Orléans lying immediately to the south of Paris. Far, far behind are the inland *généralités* of the south and center. Despite the shakiness of our data, the general pattern is unassailable. Coastal smuggling cannot be too important for the coastal areas have higher rates of consumption than their inland neighbors. Overland smuggling might possibly account for the low consumption in Dauphiné, but the frontier *généralités* of Picardy (Amiens) and

Champagne (Soissons and Châlons) had relatively high rates of consumption.

We may therefore, with some degree of assurance, conclude that our data for the 1670's suggest that tobacco consumption then was still in the process of establishing itself in much of France. The habit had been brought to France by sailors, merchants, and travelers and established itself first in the coastal districts, particularly in the north. Only gradually did it work its way inland. Thus, Brittany and Normandy had a higher rate of consumption than did the *généralité* of Paris. Those inland areas closest to the coast in trade and culture followed next. The more isolated inland areas were least affected. Thus, the legislation of the *parlement* of Dijon in 1679 was not just oldfogeyism. Tobacco consumption had not yet established itself broadly in Burgundy.

The limited geographic and social penetration of tobacco in seventeenth-century France will help explain an ambiguity in public policy. While a controller-general and a minister of the navy might be trying to stimulate the tobacco revenue and trade, secretaries of state charged with internal administration, lieutenants general of police, and parliamentary and local magistrates might simultaneously be striving to check the consumption of a pernicious weed. Such an ambiguity in policy could go unresolved only so long as the question itself remained in the obscurity of comparative unimportance.

The Beginnings of Tobacco Taxation: The Age of Import Duties, 1621–74

Several dozen books published between the late eighteenth century and today tell us that the taxation of tobacco in France was first conceived by Cardinal Richelieu about 1625 and introduced formally by the king's *déclaration* of 17 November 1629. Eighteenth-century manuscript accounts tell the same story. Yet, as long ago as 1738, Du Fresne de Francheville pointed out that tobacco had actually been taxed by its then common name *petun* some years earlier, before Richelieu's ascendancy. In the midst of the campaign against the Huguenots in the south, when the court was in the field, a *déclaration* was issued at Cognac on 30 June 1621 for the levying of import and export duties on goods passing between the territories of the *cinq grosses fermes* (northern France except for Brittany) and the outlying provinces (Brittany and the south). The "Five Great Farms" of the import and export duties embraced roughly the northern half of the kingdom, containing about two-thirds of its population and most of its wealth (though excluding the important commercial centers of Bordeaux, Marseilles and Lyons). Though there were numerous toll (*péage, octroi*) barriers within it, this zone was something of a customs union, in relation to which the outlying provinces were considered fiscally foreign. By the *déclaration* of 1621, an import duty of two *l.t.* or forty *sols* per quintal (100 lb.) and an export duty ranging upward from 66*s.* 8*d.* per quintal were established on tobacco entering or leaving the territories of the *cinq grosses fermes*.[44] There was nothing exceptional about such a tax at such a time; other countries were doing as much or more: in England, for example, tobacco had been subject to much heavier taxation from the last years of Elizabeth and received constant fiscal attention from 1604 onward.[45] The duties levied at Cognac were in fact exceptionally light by any standard.

In the succeeding trouble-filled years, when the royal finances were so inadequate for the ambitious work Richelieu (1624–42) had in hand, it is not surprising that someone should suggest that tobacco could make a heavier contribution to the king's support. Among the papers of Richelieu there is in fact a *mémoire* tentatively dated 1625 in which it is proposed that the costs of an ambitious anti-Spanish naval and commercial policy in the Mediterranean might be met by additional taxes on sugar and tobacco. The *mémoire* estimated French consumption at about two million pounds a year (a high estimate) of which a great part was fraudulent. A tax paying consumption of 800,000–900,000 lb. p.a. under a duty of 10 *sols* per lb. would produce about 400,000 *l.t.* p.a. gross. Once the revenue was well established, the rate could be raised to 20*s.* per lb., or fifty times the existing import duty under the tariff of 1621.[46] The *mémoire* implies that this would be a revenue raising excise, on domestic as well as foreign tobaccos. Nothing came of this proposal at the time, though we are told that the scheme was presented to the Assembly of Notables in December 1626.[47] The impost ultimately adopted in 1629, though, bears interesting resemblances to and contrasts with the proposal of 1625.

By 1629, France, as we shall see, had acquired a tentative colonial supply of tobacco at St. Christopher which she had not possessed in 1625. This changed circumstance was to be reflected in the actual terms of the *déclaration* of 17 November 1629 which provided for an additional entry duty of not ten or twenty but thirty *sols* per lb. on all tobacco imported except that coming from St. Christopher or other islands belonging to the new French West India Company. (This was 75 times the existing duty under the tariff of 1621.) Quite recently, the *déclaration* stated, tobacco had been imported into France without paying any duty on the pretext that it was not listed on any of the old or current tariffs or *pancartes*. (This was stretching the truth a bit.) This de facto exemption from duty had so cheapened the product that Frenchmen had begun taking it "at all hours" to the prejudice of their health. Even so, French colonial tobacco was to be exempted from the new health-protecting duty for the announced purpose of encouraging the new West India Company.[48] In other words, if people wanted to use an unhealthful plant, they could at least support the state's colonial ambitions. Little was said of the king's fiscal interest so explicit in the 1625 *mémoire*. In the long run, though, the needs of the treasury were to prove a stronger influence on tobacco policy than either public health or colonial ambitions.

It is difficult to imagine the new impost yielding as much as 100,000 *l.t.* p.a., for both French domestic and French colonial tobaccos were exempt. Our limited evidence suggests, however, that the *déclaration* of 1629, though registered, was in fact never put into effect. We hear nothing of its being repealed, nor of its being enforced; it is not mentioned in the texts of other legislation. In every practical way, the relevant precedent for the next half century was to be not the *déclaration* of 1629, but that of 1621.[49]

By a *déclaration* of 14 August and an *arrêt du conseil* of 27 October 1632, the king of France established a new *Tariffe général* for the territories within the *cinq grosses fermes* replacing that of 1621. The new tariff revised both the rates of import and export duties and the evaluation of goods paying ad valorem duties by class. Tobacco was listed under drugs and spices for which the general rate was 4 percent (compared to 2 percent on other merchandise). The specific duty of 40 *sols* per quintal under the 1621 tariff (equivalent to 4 percent on an evaluation of 50 *l.t.* per quintal) was replaced with a new specific duty of 7 *l.t.* per quintal.[50] In subsequent decades, on top of this 1632 duty there were piled various surcharges which were not uniform along all the frontiers of the *cinq grosses fermes*. Thus, by the early 1660's, the effective import duty on tobacco had become 23 *l.t.* 1s. 5d. per quintal on entering Normandy, 20 *l.t.* 3s. 7d. for Picardy, Burgundy, Champagne, Poitou, Berry, and the Bourbonnais, and only 11 *l.t.* 15s. 5d. in most of Anjou.[51] Even the highest of these was, however, less than a sixth of the 30s. per lb. mentioned in the *déclaration* of 1629. On the other hand, while the 1629 duty would have exempted and thus protected both the production of the French colonies and that of France itself, the 1632 duty and supplements applied to both. In the colonies, there does not seem to have been any immediately discouraging effect, for production was increasing till the late 1630's, but, in the long run, these duties would have speeded the redirection of colonial efforts to other commodities.

For French domestic tobacco, the 1632 duty and supplements may have had more profound effects. Guienne lay outside the territories of the *cinq grosses fermes* and its tobacco was thus liable to duty when going north; the tobacco of Guienne was cheap and depended for a good part of its market on underselling the better tobaccos of the Americas. In 1655, it sold at Tonneins for as little as 36–40s. per quintal.[52] Even when it sold for three, four, or five times as much, it could not easily bear a duty of from seven to 23 *l.t.* per quintal on shipment northward into the jurisdiction of the *cinq grosses fermes*. In the previous section, we noted a trading pattern developing as early as the mid-1630's in which the tobacco of Guienne was shipped overland to Marseilles, Narbonne, and Agde for export to Italy and elsewhere in the Mediterranean. Around the turn of the century, the then tobacco monopolists were censured because Guienne tobacco, when not exported, was sold only in the south of France. Far from being innovations of the then *fermiers,* both appear to be persistent consumption patterns having their probable origins in the same tariff of 1632.

The new tariff also altered the export duties on tobacco. Tobacco, hitherto valued at 50 *l.t.* per quintal was now listed at 60 *l.t.* On exportation from Normandy, Picardy, Poitou, Aunis, La Rochelle, and Berry, where the rate was 16 *deniers* per *l.t.* of value, this meant a rise in duty from 3 *l.t.* 6*s.* 8*d.* to 4 *l.t.* per *quintal;* in Burgundy where the rate was 20*d.* per *l.t.* of value, the rates should have gone up from 4 *l.t.* 3*s.* 4*d.* to 5 *l.t.* per quintal; and in Champagne where the rate was 23*d.* per *l.t.*, from 4 *l.t.* 15*s.* 10*d.* to 5 *l.t.* 5*s.*[53] These could be very high tolls on the less expensive grades of tobacco, but the practical effects were probably less than that of the import duty. Virtually no tobacco was grown in the territory of the *cinq grosses fermes* except around Léry in Normandy and that was all consumed locally. The export toll, if collected, would have been more onerous for French colonial tobaccos reexported. It would have had the effect of redirecting the entrepôt in French colonial tobacco away from the ports of the *cinq grosses fermes* to the cheaper ports of Brittany and Guienne. This was partly mitigated by later legislation.

In addition to the relatively heavy import and export duties of 1629 and 1632, tobacco was subject to a number of lesser special tolls. As a measure of war finance, an edict was issued at St. Germain in November 1640 providing for a general turnover tax of 5 percent on all commercial transactions; on the plea of merchants and traders that such a tax would be very irksome to them and very hard to collect, the tax was changed by the *déclaration* of 8 January 1641 into a toll on the entry of all goods (except basic foodstuffs) into walled cities and towns. Foreign goods paying import duties were exempted on entry into the town of their importation. For purposes of this duty, tobacco was assessed at five *l.t.* per quintal, or one *sol* per pound.[54] This assessment was much closer to actual market values particularly for French domestic tobacco, than the sixty *l.t.* per quintal in the external tariff of 1632. On such an assessment, the actual duty at 5 percent came to only three-fifths of a *denier* per pound. However, a pound of tobacco might have to pay this duty many times over as it passed through many a town gate on its road from producer to consumer. In addition, several towns had their own special tolls on tobacco. Of these, the highest and most complained about was the sales tax on tobacco established in the chief Provençal towns in 1660 for the benefit of the hospitals of Aix, Marseilles, and Toulon. Originally 20*s.*, per lb., it was reduced in 1664 to 10*s.* per lb. on Brazil tobacco and 5*s.* per lb. on domestic tobacco. Even these reduced rates were in excess of 100 percent, for Brazil tobacco delivered at Marseilles sold for only eight *sols* per lb. and domestic for three *sols,* six *deniers.*[55]

With the arrival of Colbert in power, there was a return to the colonial protectionist policy embodied in the abortive impost of 1629, but not in the tariffs of 1621 and 1632. While the 1629 measure would have exempted both French domestic and colonial tobacco, the tariffs taxed both on entry into or shipment from the territories of the *cinq grosses fermes*. This meant, as Colbert was reminded in 1662, that Antilles tobacco worth hardly more than 20 *l.t.* per quintal had to pay at least eleven *l.t.* in duties passing through France.[56] This burden was provisionally lightened by an *arrêt* of 30 May 1664, by which all products imported from the Antilles or exported thither by the new French West India Company (*Compagnie d'Occident*) were to be exempt from one-half the normal duties.[57] A few months later, the core of the French customs system was reformed by Colbert's famous new *tarif général* of 18 September 1664. This reforming measure unified into a single tariff the varying charges hitherto collected on goods passing into and out of the jurisdiction of the *cinq grosses fermes*. (The outlying provinces were still not included.) By this measure, all export duties on tobacco were now removed, to the considerable advantage of colonial planters. (Those in Guienne and Languedoc, already outside, would not have been affected.) While import duties were made uniform on all frontiers of the *cinq grosses fermes,* a differential was reestablished between tobaccos of French and foreign origin. For tobacco coming directly from the French West Indies, the duty was only four *l.t.* per quintal, but Verinas (Venezuela), Virginia, Brazil, and all other foreign tobaccos were to pay 13 *l.t.* per quintal.[58] The exemption from half the duties on goods imported, granted to the West India Company in May, was now withdrawn, but, after some complaints, a further *arrêt* of 7 May 1666 reduced the duty on both tobacco and sugar from the French islands from 4 *l.t.* to 2 *l.t.* per quintal.[59]

The tariff of 1664 as a whole was considered by later generations to represent a very moderate level of duties. This was definitely true for tobacco. Though French duties now ranged from about 10 percent for French colonial tobacco (after 1666) to something over 50 percent ad valorem for most foreign tobaccos, they were decidedly moderate by the standards of the age. A duty of two *l.t.* per quintal on French West Indies tobacco was equivalent to only 4.8 *deniers* per lb. By contrast the English act of tonnage and poundage of 1660 provided a nominal duty of 2*d.* per lb. and an effective duty of 1*d.*3/4 on English colonial tobacco. With the metallic ratio of English money to French at 13.3:1 after 1666, the English duty was the equivalent of 23.275 French *deniers* per lb., or almost five times the post-1666 French rate on colonial tobacco. The discrepancy on foreign tobacco imported into England was as great.[60] This difference can best be explained by the fact that tobacco had already established itself as an item of mass consumption in England with a demand relatively inelastic over a wide price range. This was not yet the case in France.

The next few years saw a continuation of the moderate taxation policy for tobacco embodied in the tariff of 1664. The charter of the French West India Company in 1664 had granted it freedom from all import and export duties on goods in entrepôt in all French ports (inside and outside the *cinq grosses fermes*), that is, goods in transit from French America intended for reexport. This was challenged in practice by farmers of various import and export duties, but specifically confirmed by an *arrêt du conseil* of 26 August 1665.[61] This free entrepôt actually gave French tobacco exporters an advantage over those in England where about one-quarter of the import duties was not returned at exportation.[62] The free entrepôt policy was specifically confirmed for the whole kingdom by the *arrêt* of 10 September 1668 (which reestablished the French colonial laws in full vigor after the laxness of the war just concluded)[63] and by those of 12 August 1671[64] and 15 July 1673. The 1666 reduction in the duty from four *l.t.* to two *l.t.* per quintal had also to be confirmed by *arrêts* of 10 December 1670[65] and 15 July 1673.[66]

This was to be the end of Colbert's low duty liberalism toward the tobacco trade. The coming of the long Dutch war of 1672–78 placed severe strains on French royal finances. For the rest of the reign of Louis XIV, and long thereafter, the history of the tobacco revenue was to be dependent upon the exigencies of French war finance.

One important question must be raised about French experimentation with import duties on tobacco. Prior to the establishment of the monopoly in 1674, France never really attempted systematically to derive a significant income from tobacco through heavy import duties (100 percent and above) on colonial and foreign tobacco, comparable to those levied in England. Why not? It may well have been that the absence of a unified customs system in France precluded the collection of duties of such magnitude on tobacco. France, with treble the population, never in the eighteenth century obtained from *traites* the revenue which Great Britain obtained from customs. Thus, there may never have been a real choice in France between obtaining a major revenue from tobacco via an import duty and obtaining one through a monopoly. In the absence of a unified and effective customs system, monopoly may well have seemed and even have been the only way.

CHAPTER 2

The Creation of the Monopoly: The Age of de Lagny and Hénault, 1674–97

The Origins of the First Monopoly and the First Monopolists

There is nothing remarkable about France adopting a tobacco monopoly in 1674. The war demanded additional state revenues. England had experimented with a nominal tobacco monopoly in the 1630's.[1] Monopolies, farms or "stanks" were introduced into Castile and Léon in 1636, into Venice in 1657, into the Papal States and Portugal in 1664, and into the Archduchy of Austria in 1670.[2] It was an idea very much in the air. Colbert himself had just (1672) granted two Protestant Zeelanders a twelve-year monopoly of the manufacture of *tabac matiné,* a blended tobacco pressed in *briques* or plugs, hitherto unknown in France, provided that within three years they established a working manufacture at La Rochelle.[3]

Yet it does not appear that the idea of a tobacco monopoly was originally that of Colbert. It came rather from a rising circle of *financiers* around Madame de Maintenon. Several later memoirs refer to these events. The best account seems to be that of about 1715 by an anonymous farmer-general:

> In the year 1674 Madame de Montespan on the solicitation of M. de Lagny who was protected by Madame de Maintenon requested of the king the exclusive privilege for selling tobacco throughout the realm for a fixed time. This privilege was granted to her [him?] but M. Colbert having pointed out to the king that it would be much better to make the tobacco monopoly a *ferme* to the profit of His Majesty, compensating Madame de Montespan for it, the council so decided [and] the lease was granted in the name of Jean Breton to Messrs. de Lagny, Dodun, Caze and Tronchain [Tronchin] with the hallmark and stamping privilege on pewter throughout the realm for 500,000 livres per year.[4]

Everything about the above account accords perfectly with what we otherwise know of these events. The one doubtful point is the suggestion that the financial benefit of the original scheme was to be primarily that of Madame de Montespan. It is possible that she was to get something out of the transaction, but it would seem that the pressing financial need at the moment was that of the future Madame de Maintenon. In the so-called

"Memoirs of the count of Maurepas" we are told, without reference to dates or details, about the rise in the favors of Louis XIV of the last named lady, then only the widow Scarron:

> This prince offered to make her a duchess [by marriage to the duke of Villars]: she refused that dignity; but she added that simply by buying an estate, she would bear the title that went with it; she thanked him very much and said to him that, in order that it should cost him nothing, he could establish some exclusive privilege to be held by a company and that she would use the money which those interested in the company would give to buy the marquisate of Maintenon which was then for sale and for which they were asking 400,000 livres, and by this means she would cost the state nothing.
> The king told the minister of finance to provide 400,000 livres for the widow Scarron to buy the marquisate of Maintenon.[5]

The events referred to here can be dated 1674 because we know when the widow Scarron refused Villars and acquired the chatellany of Maintenon, though the figure 400,000 is much too high. Otherwise the account fits well with what else we know of the affairs of the *marquise* and her share in the promotion of the first tobacco farm.

In 1674, Françoise d'Aubigné, widow of the poet and playwright Scarron, former Huguenot turned ultra-Catholic, was not yet favorite of Louis XIV in name or fact. She had since 1669 been governess to the numerous offspring of that monarch by Madame de Montespan. The legitimization of those children in 1674 brought the governess more fully into court life and more frequent meetings with her king, but did not make her position any more to her liking. Aside from the frequent tumultuous breaks and reconciliations between the king and Montespan, her own relations to that lady were not easy. She had long been promised a pension or other compensation for her services as royal governess. She now decided to ask for her reward (suggesting herself the figure 100,000 *livres*), buy some real estate for her own security and retire from court. In wartime, finding an uncommitted 100,000 *livres* was not easy. Hence her preference for a privilege which she could sell without ostensibly costing the government anything. In the event, the king would not hear of her leaving and promised her 200,000 *livres* if she would stay at court and continue as governess to his children. She agreed and embarked on that course which ultimately made her the king's morganatic wife.[6]

It was not too strange that the widow Scarron should have sought her 100,000 *livres* in the byways of public finance. She appears to have known her way well in those mazes: brought up in poverty, married to a bankrupt, plagued throughout her life by the claims of ever necessitous kindred, she had a very matter-of-fact attitude toward money. Earlier that same crucial year, 1674, we find her intervening with M. and Mme Colbert to get the farmer-general Arnaud continued in office at the renewal of his company's lease. For her good offices, her brother received some substantial consideration from the grateful Arnould.[7] We do not know when she first became acquainted with de Lagny, but from 1675 onward, as both their stars were in the ascendant, we find her in frequent correspondence with him about the affairs of the *fermes,* about getting a job for a Huguenot cousin, marrying, and otherwise arranging the affairs of her brother. From her correspondence with de Lagny, we learn that for her good offices at the lease of the united farms in 1681, she earned for her brother a consideration of 108,000 *l.t.* from the *fermiers-généraux.*[8]

Putting our scraps of evidence together, we obtain the following tentative "court interpretation" of what happened in the summer and fall of 1674. The widow Scarron, anxious to get her promised 100,000 *l.t.* and retire from court, was willing to listen to proposals that might get her that sum without depending on an uncertain wartime treasury. When her acquaintance de Lagny suggested the tobacco monopoly scheme (with or without the attached farm for hallmarking pewter), she was interested and introduced him to Madame de Montespan. It was probably understood that the widow Scarron would sell any monopoly granted her for 100,000 *l.t.* (or more) to de Lagny and friends or that she would at least receive 100,000 *l.t.* clear over and above any sums which the *fermiers*-to-be would have to pay to the crown. Madame de Montespan was agreeable, perhaps because she was not loth to see Mme Scarron go, perhaps because she too was to receive a consideration. (As she was quite adequately provided for by the king, this last consideration can probably be ignored.) Montespan thus presented the de Lagny proposals to the king. By the time Colbert got wind of what was afoot, the plan had been agreed to. The finance minister had then to remonstrate with his master that a tobacco monopoly was potentially too lucrative to be thus estranged. The king thereupon reversed himself and decided to provide otherwise to retain the widow Scarron at court and to farm the tobacco monopoly directly from his treasury. On 30 September 1674, the king granted to Françoise d'Aubigné, *veuve* Scarron, the exclusive privilege of constructing hearths for the ovens and stoves of pastrycooks, bakers, and dyers throughout the kingdom (A few months later she acquired the chatellany of Maintenon.)[9] Three days before, on 27 September 1674, the king issued the *déclaration* establishing a state tobacco monopoly in France.[10]

The only thing questionable about this "court interpretation" of the origins of the tobacco monopoly of 1674 is that it ascribes too little a role to Colbert. Can we really believe that he knew nothing of the scheme until after the king had agreed to it in principle? Some further insights into the political character of the origins of the tobacco farm can be obtained from documents arising out of the attack on the Colbert party after his death by his inveterate enemies, the chancellor Le Tellier and his son, the secretary of state for war, Louvois. Shortly after the death in September 1683 of their enemy, the great Colbert, the Le Tellier family and their creature, the new controller-general Claude Le Peletier, obtained the disgrace of the ablest member of Colbert's family, his nephew, Nicolas Desmaretz, *intendant des finances* and chief threat to Le Peletier. This disgrace had been obtained through the *affaire des pièces de quatre sols*.[11] In 1674, as a measure of war finance, and to relieve the shortage of small change, Colbert had farmed to a Lyons syndicate for three years the right to coin moderately debased silver pieces with fiat values of two, three, and four *sols*. The contract was not renewed when it expired in 1677, and in 1679, after the return of peace, Colbert on the advice of Desmaretz restored the coinage by a series of moves including the devaluation of the *pièces de quatre sols* to three and one half *sols* and the two *sol* pieces in proportion. (No three *sol* pieces were coined.) After Colbert's death and long after the coining company had wound up its affairs and destroyed its records, the matter was reopened by the Le Telliers and a ruinous fine or *restitution* of 1,529,040 *l.t.* inflicted on the company. In the course of the investigations, Colbert's other right hand man, the *directeur général du commerce,* the Italian François Bellinzani, was arrested. To save himself, Bellinzani talked freely, though he was able to reveal little incriminating about the *quatre sols* affair. He did reveal, however, that he and Desmaretz had shared large *gratifications* from the united farms and many particular farms, including the *quatre sols* and tobacco! From the tobacco farm they had received 40,000 *l.t.* p.a., of which 25,000 allegedly went to Desmaretz, 3,000 to de Breteuil, confidential clerk to Colbert, and 10,000–12,000 to Bellinzani.[12] It was understood by the king and everyone else that the controller-general received a significant gratuity on the granting or renewal of each major *ferme*. From Colbert's time onward, though, it was considered improper for lesser officials to be so interested. Hence, the ruinous fines on Bellinzani and his heirs and the exclusion of Desmaretz from public office for the next twenty years. For our present purposes, however, it is by no means certain that the payment of these alleged *gratifications* to Desmaretz and Bellinzani proved that these officials had anything to do with the inception of the tobacco monopoly. Bellinzani insisted that the *gratifications* were routine courtesies and implied no *quid pro quo*.

Shortly afterward, however, in 1685, some merchants of Paris prepared a memoir on French trade which has survived among the papers of La Reynie, *lieutenant général de la police de Paris,* an adherent of the Le Telliers. In it the merchants attempted to attack the tobacco farm by questioning its origins:

> As for the tobacco farm, one has only to remember the person [Desmaretz] who inspired its recommendation and creation to presume at once that it would be useful to examine with what views, in what

time and by what persons it was inspired, what have been its unfortunate results and what remedy ought to be applied.

The view of the person who effected this innovation was, as everyone knew, to obtain the pensions which he got thereon. The instigators, who were also the first farmers, were at that time living in his house and he had a share in their undertakings; shortly thereafter, they were also the instigators and partners in the *affaire des pièces de quatre sols*—two affairs (among many which were born in his house) which have caused such prejudice to the state and to trade.[13]

The merchants of Paris seem to be ascribing full credit for the inception of the tobacco monopoly to Desmaretz's greed. But such charges must be taken with more than a grain of salt. In the aftermath of the *quatre sols,* it was very shrewd of the enemies of the tobacco monopoly to link the two. The document in question has survived in the papers of La Reynie and was most likely intended for his patrons, the Le Telliers. One could not more surely compromise the tobacco farm in the eyes of those grandees than by associating it with Desmaretz. (No one dared allude in ink to Madame de Maintenon in this connection until after the death of Louis XIV.) Under the circumstances, the Paris memoir of 1685 must be regarded as a tract for the times and not as a statement of historical record. Whatever Desmaretz received from the farmers, he was too young and relatively unimportant in 1674 to have played a decisive part in the creation of the tobacco monopoly.

In short, the promoters of the tobacco monopoly of 1674 would seem to have cultivated an interest around Colbert as well as one with the widow Scarron. For reasons now unknown—perhaps Colbert's colonial concerns—their interest with the minister was insufficient for their purposes. Thus the intervention of the future Madame de Maintenon was necessary.

For the public, the preamble to the *déclaration du roi* of 27 September 1674 explained that the use of tobacco had become so widespread that most neighboring princes were able to derive a substantial revenue from it. The king believed that, in order to help meet the costs of the current war, he might appropriately derive an important income from its retail sale, particularly as it was not a commodity necessary for life. Its importation and exportation would remain unrestricted and a revenue could be extracted from an internal monopoly without raising the retail price. Henceforth, no tobacco of the growth of France, the French West Indies, Brazil, or elsewhere was to be sold anywhere in the kingdom, either wholesale or retail, except by those named by the king and at prices fixed by the king, to wit, 20 *sols* per lb. for French domestic tobacco; 40 *sols* per lb. for Brazilian (and presumably other foreign and colonial) tobacco. All inland traders and dealers were to report their stocks within three days and to have them purchased by the new farmers of the monopoly within three months. Merchants in ports had the option of exporting their stocks. They could continue to import and export tobacco but could sell it within France only to the monopolists. All previous special arrangements were revoked, including the special sales tax in Marseilles of 5 *sols* per lb. for the benefit of the hospitals of Marseilles, Aix, and Toulon.[14] As the French West India Company was itself to be suppressed in 1674, its privileges no longer mattered.[15]

One very important point should be emphasized about this new monopoly: its authority transcended the older and current distinctions between provinces in France, applying both to the jurisdiction of the *cinq grosses fermes* and to most of the provinces traditionally *réputées étrangères* (Brittany and the south) but not to the major new territories acquired in 1648 or later: Alsace, Dunkirk, Artois, Hainault, the Cambrésis, French Flanders, and later the Franche Comté and Lorraine.

The *déclaration* of 27 September 1674 established the legal authority for the monopoly; it did not grant the monopoly itself. Colbert had snatched the tobacco monopoly from the grasping hands of Madame de Maintenon's protégé de Lagny and friends, but he could not long keep it from them. He now joined the internal tobacco monopoly to the concession for the compulsory hallmarking of pewter ("*contrôle et marque d'étain*") and offered them up to the highest bidder. Notices were according to form posted on the gates of the palace of Versailles announcing that the lease for six years of the tobacco and pewter privileges would be auctioned to the highest bidder at proceedings to start at the council on 13 October; the bidding would start at 400,000 *l.t.,* already offered by the *avocat au conseil,* Jean Frizon. (Lawyers entitled to act before council regularly appeared in such matters for the real principals.) On the appointed day, no higher bid was received, nor was any heard at the next opportunity on 20 October. At the third bidding at St. Germain en Laye on 27 October, two *avocats au conseil,* Maîtres Chassebras and Chanu, bid the price up to 450,000 whereupon Chanu offered 500,000 for the first two years and 600,000 for the last four (with the first three months free). This bid was not surpassed when the candle (which measured the allotted bidding time) burned out, nor were any further bids received at the final opportunity on 13 November. The lease was thereupon adjudged to Chanu for his principals and signed on 30 November.[16]

The lease thus concluded on 30 November was in the name of "Maistre Jean Breton Bourgeois de Paris." To the end of the *ancien régime* all leases of major *fermes* were in the name of straw men who had nothing to to do but lend their names and sign everything put in front of them. They were generally persons of modest means who had little to lose and were pretty well paid for their trouble. In the eighteenth century, the system became something of a joke, the right to be the straw man for the united general farms becoming for a time a perquisite of the senior porter of the then controller-general of finance.[17] Of John Breton we know only that he was chief bookkeeper in the Levant Company; of his successors we know nothing; but we need not trouble ourselves enquiring. The important question for each farm lease is not who was the *adjudicataire* (nominal lessee) but who were the *interessés* in his *ferme*, the men who signed his lease as sureties or bondsmen (*cautions*) but were really the principals, the men who put up the risk capital, who bore the losses or realized the profits from the gamble that revenue farming was.

The actual men behind the name "Jean Breton," the real lessees of the tobacco monopoly during 1674–80, were six: Jean-Baptiste de Lagny, Gaspard Dodun, Jean Tronchin, César Caze, Gaspard Hindret, and Gabriel Bronot.[18] Of these, Hindret and Bronot were the least important. We at present know nothing of Bronot (Bronod) except that he came from Lyons and was involved at this very time in the *affaire des pièces de quatre sols*.[19] In the 1680's, he appears in notarial documents as *receveur des restes de la cour des comptes aydes et finances de Provence*.[20] Gaspard Hindret, sieur de Beaulieu, son of a judge at the Châtelet (the Paris court of general jurisdiction), was himself a sometime silver refiner at Lyons and one of the principal proprietors of the *quatre sols* minting company. He also appears, about 1678–84, as one of the proprietors of the new woolen manufacture at Clermont in Languedoc, sponsored by Colbert and subsidized by the estates of Languedoc. He fled to England in December 1683 at the beginnings of the *quatre sols* investigations but was permitted to return safely in 1684, presumably paid his fine, and was soon being consulted again on minting matters by Le Peletier.[21] He subsequently appears dabbling in revenue farms in the 1690's, as *inspecteur général des monnaies de France* in 1702 and as a participant in the several minting contracts, 1702–12, involving the great Hogguer brothers of St. Gall.[22]

Caze and Tronchin also had Lyons connections, but came from rather better-known families—Huguenot families, however, whose position in society was about to be destroyed. The Cazes from Lyons had occupied prominent offices in public finance from the sixteenth century. Jean Caze, the father of César, had been provided in 1648 with the office of *conseiller et maître d'hôtel ordinaire du roi;* he was also an elder and benefactor of the reformed church in Lyons. He married Marie Huguetan, of a well-known Huguenot family of booksellers in Lyons who were to become even better known as booksellers and bankers in Amsterdam in the next century. The young César (born 1641) married in 1677 Catherine, daughter of the Huguenot farmer-general, Etienne Monginot, sieur du Plessis-la-Salle. In 1683, both father and son fled to Holland, whence the father proceeded to Geneva, where the family were honored with free citizenship by the republic; they managed to extract from France a fair amount of their wealth.[23] The tobacco farm of 1674–80 was young César Caze's only known venture into finance. The increasing difficulties facing Protestants trying to acquire traditional offices may have forced him into this more speculative course. He was the richest member of the company and its financial bulwark.

Jean Tronchin (later styled du Breuil) was born in Geneva in 1641 of a prominent Huguenot family; his father, Jacques, and brother, Jacques *fils,* later became active merchants at Lyons. Young Jean was educated at Saumur, where he was something of a prodigy, but eventually found study too much of a strain upon his eyes. Proceeding to Paris while still quite young, he entered "les affaires," becoming a great favorite of Colbert who unsuccessfully tried to persuade him to change his religion. He reportedly lost heavily in the unsuccessful scheme of the 1660's to connect the Saône and the Loire by the *canal de Longpendu* (later built as the *canal du Centre*). Both he and Caze were Paris directors of Colbert's experimental Levant Companies of 1670 and 1678, in which Bellinzani represented the king and Jean Breton was bookkeeper.[24] His closeness to Colbert would make him as important a person in the farm as de Lagny's relationship to Madame de Maintenon made him.

If Caze and Tronchin represented the declining star of Huguenot finance, de Lagny and Dodun represented well the rising star of the newer court finance that was to enrich so many families, enabling them ultimately to move into the securer world of purchased offices and purchased titles of nobility. Gaspard Dodun (1621–1701) is remembered, if at all, as the grandfather of the Charles-Gaspard Dodun, marquis d'Herbault (1679–1736), controller-general during 1722–26. The grandfather with whom we are here concerned, the son of an *avocat* of Troyes, acquired nobility through the purchase of the office of *secrétaire du roi* which he held for the necessary twenty years (1655 to 1675). He sold this office about the time we first observe him entering *finance* as then understood, i.e., revenue farming and other speculative ventures in the "affaires du roi." The tobacco farm of 1674–80 is his earliest known venture of this kind. In the 1680's, he became a farmer-general of the united farms, but dropped out after 1687. Between 1689 and 1699, he was interested in at least fifteen contracts in the *affaires extraordinaires de finances,* most of them concerned with the sale of offices. His son later resigned the post of *conseiller* in the *parlement* of Paris in 1702 to become *receveur général des finances* at La Rochelle and Bordeaux.[25]

The last and most important of the tobacco farmers of 1674 was Jean-Baptiste de Lagny, the protégé of Madame de Maintenon. His origins are most obscure; his first known post was that of a *commis* in the powder and saltpetre monopoly at La Rochelle. He subsequently held the slightly more important position of *contrôleur* in the *ferme des traites* (customs duties) at Dunkirk. In 1669 (the year Madame Scarron became *gouvernante* to the first of the king's children by Madame de Montespan), de Lagny emerges from obscurity as one of the directors of the *Compagnie du Nord* at La Rochelle. He traveled extensively in the North for the company and was very much in Colbert's eye. As with Dodun, the tobacco *ferme* of 1674 seems to have been his first important venture into public finance on his own account. Like Dodun, he became a farmer-general in 1680 and was still interested in the

United General Farms at the time of his death in December 1700. (Unlike Dodun, he took little interest in the lesser *affaires extraordinaires* of royal finance after 1689.) As a channel of communication between the farms and Madame de Maintenon, his influence must have been very great among his colleagues. Following her acknowledgment by and supposed marriage to the king in 1684, de Lagny acquired the title of *secrétaire du roi* in 1685, and in 1686 was appointed to Bellinzani's old post of *directeur-général du commerce* by the minister of the navy, Colbert's son Seignelay; in that capacity he served as the principal deputy to the minister for matters concerning foreign trade and taxation. About this same time, he was also appointed government representative on the boards of directors of the new Guinea Company, the Mediterranean Company, and the East India Company.[26]

Although at least two of the tobacco farmers of 1674 were to become very important in the court finance of the middle years of the reign of Louis XIV, it would be wrong to assume that they were either terribly influential or terribly successful in this earlier venture. The farm of the tobacco monopoly in 1674 was a most risky undertaking. Unlike almost all other farms, it was not a matter of taking over an existing body of taxation, or even levying a new tax through an existing tax-collecting establishment. For the new tobacco farmers of 1674, everything had to be created out of nothing: warehouses and buying offices, manufacturing establishments, distributing centers in every province, all to be leased and set up, retailers to be licensed by the thousand and guards, inspectors, and auditors to be appointed to put some check on fraud. For all of this, there was no preexisting administrative or legal framework. Putting down the foundations was to be an extremely difficult task. In a subsequent chapter, we shall discuss the administrative history of the monopoly. In this chapter, we shall confine ourselves to its political and financial history.

The Brief, Inglorious History of the Jean Breton Company, 1674–80

The *bail général de la ferme du tabac et marque de l'étain*[27] provides us, as it did contemporaries, with only the roughest idea of how the *ferme* of the Jean Breton Company was to operate. The lease was to run for six years from 1 December 1674 to 30 November 1680. Six years was then becoming the normal duration for the leases of the United General Farms and its major components when separated. The tobacco and pewter farm would thus be running over roughly the same period as the major components of the united farms which had been split up at the end of the Le Gendre lease (1668–74).[28] As the Breton lease was not signed till 30 November, though decided on several weeks before, there must have been considerable confusion involved in starting its operation on 1 December. An emergency *arrêt* had to be issued for interim legal authority for the farm until the lease itself was formally registered in the various *parlements* (regional supreme courts) and *cours des aides* (regional high fiscal courts).[29]

The price of the lease was 500,000 *l.t.* for the first two years and 600,000 *l.t.* for the last four. We are told on reasonably good authority that it was understood that three-fifths of this was for tobacco and two-fifths for pewter.[30]

Although the *déclaration* of 27 September had left the external trade in tobacco free, the lease limited the ports at which tobacco could be generally imported to four, Marseilles, Bordeaux, La Rochelle, and Rouen. In addition, tobacco could be imported at Dieppe for sale in Normandy only, and at Morlaix, St. Malo, and Nantes for sale in Brittany only. These exceptions undoubtedly recognized the substantial manufacturing trade that had already developed at Dieppe and Morlaix and the intrenched trading interests of St. Malo and Nantes. The farmers themselves later recognized these vested interests by establishing their own manufactures at Dieppe and Morlaix.[31] The short list of ports was obviously motivated by the desire of the new farmers to simplify their purchasing and particularly their defenses against smuggling. Nevertheless, such a list was bound to offend excluded ports. An *arrêt* of 25 January 1676 limiting the ports at which the *export* of tobacco was permitted included not only the above but also les Sables d'Olonne, St. Valéry, Narbonne, Cette, Agde, and Toulon.[32] Honfleur was added in 1680.[33]

The September *déclaration* had limited the monopolists' wholesale prices to not more than 20 *sols* per lb. for French domestic and colonial tobacco and 40*s.* per lb. for foreign tobaccos. The lease now added that licensed retailers could not resell the same for more than 25 and 50*s.* per lb. respectively. Snuff too was to be sold only by licensed snuffmakers and retailers at prices not to exceed 10*s.* per ounce for ordinary, 20*s.* per ounce for perfumed, and 25*s.* per ounce for "Malta," "Pontgibon" (both made primarily from a Virginia base) and other exotic snuffs. At the end of the lease, all tobacco in the hands of the monopolists was to be purchased by their successors.

The immediate problem was the abrupt transition from a system of open trade to one of strict controls. Both the September *déclaration* and the November lease provided that all merchants and dealers were to stop selling, report all their stocks, and have them marked pending purchase by the new farmers. But Colbert did not get around to sending out the *déclaration* of 27 September 1674 for registration in the various *parlements* until 31 October.[34] This and the delay in signing the lease put everything behind. An *arrêt du conseil* had to be issued on 22 November 1674 for "Jean Breton" to enter into the enjoyment of "his" farm on 1 December even though the lease had not yet been signed, registered, or despatched. The *arrêt* again specifically ordered all grocers, perfumers, etc. to declare their stocks on hand immediately to the agents of Breton who were to mark, inventory, and purchase the same within three months.³⁵ All this was easier said than done. No established wholesaler or retailer found it in his interest to rush his declaration to Breton's men, and the latter were not prompt in getting started. An *arrêt* of 26 January 1675 extended to 28 February the time within which established dealers could continue selling tobacco, though such activity was supposed to have ceased three days after the publication of the *déclaration* of the previous 27 September.³⁶ Under the circumstances we are not surprised to find that the intendant of Auvergne waited until 26 August 1675 to issue an *ordonnance* for the enforcement of the *déclaration* of 27 September 1674 and the *arrêt* of 22 November 1674. Only then did he order all dealers in tobacco to declare their stocks within eight days at the *bureaux* of the *ferme* by then established in eight electoral seats (towns where there were fiscal courts called *élections*).³⁷ We gain an inkling of the growing network of administrative apparatus which the new *ferme* was building up. We also gain the impression that with such delays the first year must have been a grievous disappointment for Jean Breton and his sureties.

We get a clearer picture of the administrative and financial difficulties involved from events in Normandy where Pellot, president of the *parlement* of Rouen, the intendant Creil, and the marquis of Beuvron, lieutenant-general of the province, took an active role in smoothing over the introduction of the new *ferme*. Meetings were held in their presence early in June 1675 between representatives of the monopoly and the aggrieved tradesmen of Rouen and Dieppe. The aforenamed officials were able to satisfy the retailers by getting the agents of the farm to agree to buy all their tobacco at prices fixed by disinterested experts. With the wholesalers and manufacturers the problem was more difficult. The wholesalers were angry because the September 1674 *déclaration* which gave them three months to sell their stocks (as they interpreted it) was only published in Rouen on 28 February, the last day for selling any tobacco under the *arrêt* of 26 January 1675. Thus, they alleged, they lost through ignorance all chance of selling their stock. Their tobacco, locked up since 28 February, was slowly going bad. The *fermier* refused to buy their tobacco as he did that of the retailers, but gave them the option only of exporting it (by which they would lose duties and expenses) or of buying from him a special license to sell at home for a premium of 10s. per lb. for Brazil tobacco and 5s. for domestic. The wholesalers insisted that at current prices they would lose heavily paying such fines. Pellot wondered why the monopolists didn't buy up all the tobacco in Normandy (which they could do for 80,000–100,000 *l.t.*) and then be in the much stronger position of being able to set their own prices. It is apparent, however, that the new *fermiers* were short of capital and were trying to avoid laying out large sums to buy up stocks before the product of their own sales came in.

The manufacturers at Dieppe were the least happy of all. The industry had been established there eight or ten years before and they had by then laid out considerable sums on stocks and tools. They employed some

300–400 persons in the town plus 400–500 peasant families in the vicinity who grew tobacco for them. They could not afford to pay the monopolist 5s. per lb. for a license to sell when their normal selling price was only 5–6s. per lb. They too wanted the *fermier* to buy all their manufactured and unmanufactured stocks quickly. In addition, the good president Pellot felt that the new monopoly would ruin the import trade from the colonies too, for no one would bring tobacco in if he had to deal with such people, "but His Majesty has undoubtedly considered that the profit and advantage he gets out of this business in a time when he has need of money must be held above all these considerations."[38]

The situation of the new tobacco monopoly in the spring of 1675 was not easy: the monopolists were ruining the businesses of hundreds of importers, wholesalers, and manufacturers and thousands of retailers without themselves having the funds at hand to buy up the perishing stocks which their own monopoly made unsaleable. The discontent of these numerous groups must be kept in mind as an important cause contributing to the major riots which struck western France in 1675. Mixed in, of course, were the complaints against the new duties on salt, pewter, and stamped paper for legal documents (1673). Underlying all was the widespread distress in the maritime regions caused by the Dutch war of 1672–78 and the mass discontent with the whole fiscal apparatus of the state. The riots began in Bordeaux in March 1675: four days of serious disturbances (26–29) persuaded the governor (the marshal d'Albret) to have the *parlement* suspend the tobacco monopoly and the new pewter, transfer, and stamp duties; both *parlement* and the municipal council (jurats) petitioned the king for a general amnesty, which was granted in April. From the beginning, however, some of this appeared less than fully spontaneous. As early as 6 March, the jurats, advised by the leading traders, had warned the intendant that there was likely to be trouble over tobacco and recommended that the introduction of the new monopoly be suspended, at least during the spring fair.[39] On 24 April, the intendant himself wrote to Colbert explaining that the tobacco merchants and wholesalers were very much annoyed at the loss of their trade and at the refusal of the new monopolists to take their existing stocks of tobacco off their hands. Under the circumstances, they were very well pleased with the riots, thanks to which they and the retailers continued to sell tobacco. The other merchants sat back, letting themselves be persuaded that, after tobacco, other commodities were in line for monopolization.[40] However, an Englishman shrewdly observed at the time "that if Toulouse ... do not oppose this tax as well as Bordeaux, that city will receive much damage."[41] In the end, further disorders in August were put down by troops, after which the monopoly was restored (November-December) and the city corporatively punished by military occupation (November-March) and the removal of its *parlement* and *cour des aides*.

Much more serious and more complex were the disturbances in Brittany which have been much more fully studied.[42] They are generally known as the "Stamped Paper Revolt" or the "Red Cap Revolt" after the *bonnets rouges* worn by peasant insurgents. However, in its earliest phases the upheaval was largely directed against the offices of the new tobacco and pewter monopoly and against Huguenot *temples* and homes. One of the special features of the riots in Brittany was the stirring of the anti-Protestant feelings of the ultra-Catholic masses through the identification as Huguenots of several of the tobacco farmers and many of their employees.[43]

The trouble began when news arrived at Rennes on 3 April 1675 of the disturbances in Bordeaux. The initial disorders were immediately repressed by the authorities at Rennes and elsewhere in Brittany under the leadership of d'Argouges, *premier président* of the *parlement* of Brittany. Privately, d'Argouges asked the agents of the farm to keep their offices open, but to take no action against offenders for a fortnight. The uneasy "truce" broke down on 18 April when the grocers of Rennes, claiming that the mob threatened to wreck their shops if they did not concur, asked permission to resume selling tobacco in the old premonopoly way. Receiving only an ambiguous answer from the *premier président,* the grocers took the initiative and, to protect their shops, directed the wrath of the commonalty against the *ferme;* the mob thus diverted sacked the regional distribution center (*bureau général*) of the tobacco monopoly. With the duke of Chaulnes, governor of Brittany, and de Coëtlogon, governor of Rennes, both absent, the son of the latter assumed responsibility, assembled twenty to thirty gentlemen and attacked and dispersed the mob, killing more than a dozen and wounding over fifty. The tobacco monopoly had drawn its first blood in Brittany.

On the next day, 19 April, word of the goings-on at Rennes reached St. Malo, which was filled with more than two thousand sailors on the eve of the sailing of the Newfoundland fleet. There was talk of a mob attack on the offices of the tobacco monopoly, but the local officials and leading citizens, having no taste for sailor riots, took the precautions necessary to avert trouble; at the same time, they ordered the officials of the farm to stay indoors and to take no measures against retailers selling tobacco until after the fleet had sailed. The monopoly was less lucky at Nantes; murmurings started there on 20 April with the arrival of the news from Rennes, but the real riots didn't start till the twenty-second and twenty-third when the local headquarters of the tobacco and pewter monopoly were sacked, with the cry, "Vive le roy sans maltôte." On that occasion, the governor of the château with twenty to thirty gentlemen and substantial citizens was able to disperse the mob before they reached the stamped paper office. Those premises were, however, destroyed a few days later in a much more serious riot on 3 May, involving almost the whole population except the very "top people" (and in which, at one time, the bishop was taken prisoner by the mob).

This was to be the peak of the urban disturbances in Brittany. On 2 May, the duke of Chaulnes returned to Rennes with troops which he chose to use as little as possible. He moved on to Nantes a few days later.

By tact, persuasion, and his very presence, he restored order as he went, punishing little but conceding nothing. At Nantes, one person was executed and a number banished or otherwise punished lest the governor's moderation should be misunderstood. By 28 May, the duke could report back to Paris that all tax offices were reopened and back in business.[44]

The tobacco monopoly had had a lot to do with the start of the disturbances in Brittany, but not with their later history. There were further disturbances in mid-June calmed by the duke of Chaulnes without bloodshed, but these had nothing to do with tobacco. At this point, the disturbances moved from the town to the country and from Upper Brittany to Lower Brittany (the peninsula) where in the latter part of June and in July a full-scale peasant revolt broke out against seigneurs, complete with murders and the burning of châteaux. This *jacquerie* eventually spread back into Upper Brittany where the peasants vented their spleen on gentry, priests, and bourgeois—and a few tax collectors as well. The movement had either burned itself out or been repressed everywhere by September. These rural disturbances of the summer had little in common with the urban disturbances of the spring except timing. Their roots were far more profound than petty bourgeois annoyance at a few new taxes.[45]

The duke of Chaulnes, in classic fashion, suspected that sinister forces were behind the riots, that those in his own Brittany were not just accidentally connected with those at Bordeaux. He noted that, in the end, more noise had been made in Brittany about the stamped paper duties, which affected only a few, than about the tobacco duties which touched the many.[46] In the case of tobacco, wholesalers and retailers had some interest in the riots, but the actual consumers who did most of the rioting were simply venting their annoyance at higher prices and the disruption of normal supplies during the "changeover" period.

Even though somewhat superficial in their social character, the tobacco riots were widespread. (If there was any coordination or even correspondence between the riot centers, we shall never know now.) The *Gazette de Bruxelles* reported riots everywhere, with agents of the monopoly manhandled by the mob at Moulins, and troops sent into Normandy to restore order.[47] Nevertheless by 15 November the situation seemed well enough in hand for the king to issue a *déclaration* superseding any local concessions made during the riots and ordering the rigorous collection of all duties in the manner prescribed by law.[48]

Midst all this disorder, the tobacco monopoly could only have gotten off to a disappointing start, but would not be shaken. Its farmers refused to make concessions to mollify public opinion, pushing ahead wherever the inexorable logic of their monopoly led them. As we shall see, the yields of the first few years were disappointing. The company apparently decided that their principal trouble was not nonconsumption but fraudulent consumption, fed not so much by foreign tobacco smuggled in as by domestic tobacco which evaded their reach. Since they were only a small *ferme,* they could not afford the vast armies of guards and inspectors employed for example by the *gabelles* (salt monopoly). Without such an army, they could not afford to watch every back garden in France in which a few *perches* of tobacco might be grown. The logical solution was to restrict the area of cultivation to that convenient for guarding. There was nothing particularly revolutionary in this decision. The growth of tobacco was forbidden in several European states: the pre-Civil War, Interregnum, and Restoration governments in England alike outlawed it throughout that whole realm. At this very time, the English government, after a twenty-year administrative effort involving the use of cavalry, finally suppressed planting by about 1681.[49]

Thus, a few months after the suppression of the tobacco riots, the government issued an *arrêt du conseil* on 14 March 1676 limiting the areas in which the cultivation of tobacco was permitted to the *généralités* of Bordeaux and Montauban and the environs of Mondragon, "Saint Maixent," Léry, and Metz.[50] Of the latter, only Léry in Normandy and St. Maixent or Mexant in Limousin created any administrative difficulties: Metz was frontier territory, an enclave in the alien duchy of Lorraine, cut off then from other French territory, and Mondragon was a French enclave in the papal Comtat Venaissin on the Rhône. To simplify the policing problems of the monopoly and to prevent the spread of cultivation to new, as yet unpoliced villages, a further *arrêt* of 6 February 1677 restricted the cultivation of tobacco within the *généralités* of Bordeaux and Montauban to those 22 communities therein named where the crop had been grown before 1674.[51]

In a subsequent chapter, we shall discuss relations between the tobacco monopoly and the few localities where cultivation was still permitted. Suffice it to say here that the limiting of tobacco planting in France to a little over two dozen localities was the most fundamental administrative accomplishment of the first tobacco *ferme* of 1674–80, ranking in policy making second only to the decision to create the monopoly itself. There can be no doubt that this was a basic policy decision, the implications of which Colbert fully understood. When Henri d'Aguesseau, intendant at Toulouse, wrote him in 1679 about ways in which the operation of the privilege in Languedoc might be mitigated, Colbert replied:

> In regard to the memoir concerning the changes which could be made in that farm, the king does not wish to effect any change; nor does His Majesty wish to ease the conditions under which tobacco is raised in the realm; on the contrary, H.M. wishes to ruin this cultivation if possible, because it ruins the colonies in the American islands.[52]

This had in fact been Colbert's "line" since 1677.[53] Local cultivation, of course, also ruined the revenue potentialities of the monopoly, but that was not part of the official rhetoric. It is quite clear that the basic policy decision to sacrifice French domestic cultivation to the interests of the state had been made as early as the time of Colbert, but two generations of French growers and French local officials refused to see this and continued to blame all their difficulties on the tricks and misrepresentations of the monopolists.

TABLE I

Gross Receipts of the Tobacco Farm, 1675–79 (in *l.t.*) [54]

Généralités	1675	1676	1677	1678	1679 (1st half)
Paris	101,670	219,483	216,049	194,689	110,991
Rouen	70,941	231,055	216,978	218,402	89,353
Caen	11,202	28,746	45,199	34,473	21,110
Alençon	920	2,982	—	—	—
Bretagne	21,617	388,143	339,243	285,143	109,820
Poitiers	6,376	22,048	26,026	19,110	7,331
Limoges	1,258	1,686	—	4,044	6,879
Bordeaux	97	12,975	51,930	39,223	44,427
Montauban	453	3,775	9,156	9,670	2,054
Toulouse & Montpellier	2,983	77,449	88,347	74,567	43,306
Provence	27,774	91,694	96,747	111,859	52,895
Bourgogne & Bresse	6,662	15,844	14,940	16,548	4,999
Orléans	10,480	43,107	55,040	45,576	18,529
Tours	5,699	20,023	17,912	15,709	12,239
Soissons	16,508	29,785	39,954	27,359	13,807
Amiens	32,984	137,273	149,312	111,553	34,495
Metz	16,500	21,637	18,842	14,839	6,317
Châlons	24,782	56,659	56,839	53,592	17,864
Bourges	1,938	4,420	—	—	—
Moulins	2,984	5,379	—	—	—
Riom	1,613	7,207	5,130	3,344	2,575
Lyon	14,240	19,458	45,060	44,403	23,379
Grenoble	7,015	9,153	—	—	—
"Plus-Value"	69,253	50,908	—	—	—
Total	455,950	1,500,888	1,492,205	1,324,102	622,371

Despite this achievement, the financial history of the Jean Breton lease was not very happy. In the previous chapter, we reported the quantities sold in each province during 1675–79 in order to point out how limited tobacco consumption then was outside of the maritime districts. In Table I, we now summarize the gross receipts (*produit général*) of the monopoly during these same years.

From these figures, we can see at a glance how devastating the results of the disturbances of 1675 were, particularly in Brittany where receipts were kept down to 21,617 *l.t.* in 1675, against their average of over 350,000 *l.t.* p.a. in the next three years (1676–78). Again we notice how dependent the farm was on the consumption of Paris and the maritime provinces, Picardy (Amiens), Normandy (particularly the *généralité* of Rouen where all the important Norman ports were located), Brittany, and Provence. The inland regions contributed disappointingly little. In most cases, this was probably the result of as yet low consumption, though in frontier districts like Soissons, Châlons, and Grenoble, sales were possibly already depressed by smuggling. Receipts were also noticeably low in the *généralités* where tobacco growing was permitted: Bordeaux, Montauban, and Metz. Receipts in Bordeaux and Montauban recovered noticeably after the repression of the disorders of 1675 and the restriction of planting in 1676–77, but, particularly in Bordeaux, were probably still regarded as disappointingly low by the monopoly.

These figures are only gross receipts. What the net yield to the farm was in these years, we do not know. At an estimated price of 25 *l.t.* per *quintal* for imported tobacco, the cost of the tobacco sold was probably about 20 percent of gross receipts, or rather less, depending on the proportion of cheap domestic tobacco used.[55] Administrative expenditures, though, were probably very large in the early years, when the proprietors were starting a new organization and had to acquire leaseholds and equip offices. Costs of inspection and law suits should have been particularly onerous in these years. In addition there were the more routine outlays for manufacture and transport.

Did the farm make enough to pay its contractual dues to the government and still have something left over for its own profit? We have no precise accounts, but on several sides we are told that it did not. One well-informed memoir writer in fact insisted that the farmers offered to surrender their lease at the end of the first year and forfeit their advance to the government.[56] They were persuaded to stay on, but the government must have made some concession, for it does not seem that they paid the full price of their lease after their first year. Mallet, *premier commis des finances* under Desmaretz (1708–15), in a book written about 1720 gives some interesting data on government receipts at this time, summarized in Table II. Since Mallet labels his equivalent of our third column, "prix de baux," we can only assume that the original price provided in the lease of 1674 was adjusted downward when the farmers found their farm a losing proposition. The 12,000 *l.t.* charge was undoubtedly the annual compensation paid to the hospitals of Provence when they lost their income from the older sales tax on tobacco in Marseilles. (One can only guess why it was not paid in 1678; it was probably only delayed.) The remainder of the charges are prob-

TABLE II

Government Receipts from the Tobacco and Pewter Monopoly, 1675–80[57]

Original Price in the Contract l.t.	Year	Adjusted Contract Price Received l.t.	Charges l.t.	Net Receipts l.t.
500,000	1675	500,000	12,000	488,000
500,000	1676	366,000	65,730	300,270
600,000	1677	570,000	12,000	558,000
600,000	1678	552,000	—	552,000
600,000	1679	570,000	168,000	402,000
600,000	1680	322,000	60,000	262,000

ably payments of various obligations of the government assigned against the receipts from the tobacco farm.

However we look at our data, the financial record of the new farm was not good. Its payments to the government, one way or another, had had to be scaled down. More sinister was the declining pattern of tobacco receipts after 1676. If we can estimate the receipts for 1679 by doubling those of the first six months, we get the following from Table I:

gross receipts	1676	1,500,888 l.t.
" "	1677	1,492,205 l.t.
" "	1678	1,324,102 l.t.
" "	1679	1,244,742 l.t.

Either consumption was declining (as was alleged at the time) or the smugglers were perfecting their organization faster than the farm its own. The return of peace in 1678 would have made maritime smuggling distinctly easier and may have deprived the farm of part of its sales to the army. There is other evidence that some sort of a crisis was reached in 1679. Bellinzani later testified that the affairs of the farm were in such straits during the fifth year (1679) that he and Desmaretz volunteered to give up their *gratification* of 40,000 *l.t.* for that year—but the offer was declined.[58] Under the circumstances, we can well believe the later memoir writers who tell us that at the end of the lease the farmers of the Jean Breton company asked to be relieved of their responsibility.[59] Their offer was accepted.

The inglorious end of the first lease of the tobacco monopoly coincided with a basic change in French religious policy. Hitherto, Huguenots, though excluded from judicial and an increasing number of financial offices, had been able to play an important part in the royal farms, which were technically private companies. Now, by the *règlement des fermes* of 11 June

1680 and an *arrêt du conseil* of 17 June 1680, the farms were closed to Protestants.[60] Thus, when the head of the new united farms, Nicolas de Frémont (grandfather of St. Simon's duchess), brought de Lagny and Dodun into the amalgamated company in 1680,[61] Caze and Tronchin could not follow, regardless of qualifications. This forcible split helps explain the bitterness and protracted disputes between the former partners.

From the interminable litigation over the accounts of the defunct tobacco monopoly, we learn something of its internal affairs. The family of César Caze, for example, insisted in one document that he had been responsible for setting up the original organization of the company and, as its richest member, had alone kept it going after the financial disappointments of the first year. Because of outside (i.e., court) pressures, the company had been obliged to appoint as their receiver-general or chief cashier, one Claude Du Fresnoy, *dit la Mare*, a person without experience or capacity; to watch him they had named Jean Tronchin's brother Pierre as their *contrôleur général* (auditor). When Dodun and de Lagny went into the general farms, they took la Mare with them, leaving the accounts and day-to-day transactions of the former tobacco farm in the hands of Pierre Tronchin. About the same time, the dragonades started against the Huguenots and Caze and Tronchin, deciding to emigrate, began a series of complex bill of exchange operations to extract their funds from France. (These involved in particular the Lyons house of Jacques Tronchin, *père et fils*.) In this, perhaps not entirely from ignorance or incompetence, Pierre Tronchin frequently confused the private affairs of his brother Jean and Caze with those of the company. When Dodun and de Lagny sensed that their interests might be in jeopardy and began legal action, Caze returned to Paris and obtained an *arrêt du conseil* on 22 November 1681, giving him and Tronchin two years' grace to settle accounts. (Colbert and Bellinzani were still helpful behind the scenes.) On 23 January 1682, de Lagny, Hindret, Bronot and Dodun gave a complete discharge to César Caze who thereupon withdrew to the United Provinces where he settled in the refugee colony at Balk in Friesland and dabbled in scientific writing. The company also settled with Jacques Tronchin *fils* of Lyons in 1682.

These discharges may have been based on the premise of (technical) insolvency for two years later (January 1684) Bellinzani testified that after the "failure" of Caze and Tronchin, he and Desmaretz offered to return to the remaining partners the entire *gratification* they had received over six years (240,000 *l.t.*). This offer was declined for the former company just then received over 300,000 *l.t.* from the sale of the tobacco on hand at the end of their lease to their successors. Bellinzani did, however, lend them then 50,000 *écus* (150,000 *l.t.*) to tide them over. Late in 1683, when de Lagny and Dodun found the company's bills of exchange with Hindret's signature protested because of the latter's involvement in the then breaking *quatre sols* affair, Bellinzani (before his own arrest) and Desmaretz lent them another 30,000 and 40,000 *l.t.* respectively.

Meanwhile, in 1679, the Tronchins and Caze had sent to Amsterdam for a commercial speculation one Pierre du Mou[s]tier de Montforton, a Huguenot clerk in the tobacco farm; with the expulsion of the Huguenots from the farms in 1680, Montforton was instructed to remain in Holland where on 14 November 1681 he was admitted as a merchant to the citizenship of Amsterdam. In the next few months large sums were remitted to him from such places as Paris, Lyons, Geneva, and Frankfort on the account of Caze and Jean Tronchin. (Quittance for these transactions was included in the general settlement made in 1682 between Caze and Tronchin and their former partners.) In November 1683, shortly after the death of their protector Colbert, Jean and Pierre Tronchin left for Holland with the Cazes, sending ahead to Montforton several trunk loads of papers of the old tobacco farm. The émigrés could not have felt too secure for on arrival in Holland all altered their names: Montforton styling himself Le Noir, C. Caze adding d'Harmonville, Pierre Tronchin du May and Jean Tronchin du Breuil (the name under which he became famous as the publisher of the Amsterdam *Gazette Française*).

Accounts appeared settled and the matter closed until one Daniel Bousanquet, another Huguenot émigré and former employee of the monopoly, for whom no provision could be made in Holland, returned to France with stories of an alleged fortune surreptitiously extracted from France by Caze and Tronchin. Immediately following the revocation of the Edict of Nantes, Dodun and de Lagny took advantage of the current mood in France to reopen the case. In 1686, they obtained from chancery a decree voiding their 1682 settlement with Caze and Tronchin, while the Châtelet in 1686–87 recognized their claims against their erstwhile partners for 172,900 *l.t.* plus interest and declared Caze, Jean and Pierre Tronchin, Montforton, and others fraudulent bankrupts and absconders and sentenced them to death in absentia. With their French condemnation papers, Dodun and de Lagny began suit in 1686 against the émigres in the United Provinces, and on court order had Montforton arrested in Amsterdam and Tronchin in Friesland and their effects detained, including funds of Caze and the Tronchins and the papers of the old tobacco farm. However, on the morrow of the revocation of the Edict of Nantes, Protestant refugees were objects of sympathy in the United Provinces and the courts ordered both Montforton and Tronchin released. (Caze was more successfully pursued by Bousanquet for a private debt but chose to remain in debtor's prison in Friesland from 1688 to ca. 1700 rather than let his rich father pay an unjust claim.) Unable to obtain justice in Holland, de Lagny and Dodun initiated action in 1687 in the Council of State in Paris against the city of Amsterdam. On 10 November 1688 (after the war had started) the king granted them letters of reprisal against the goods of citizens of Amsterdam wherever found, up to a maximum of 279,746 *l.t.* By this authority, considerable property of Amsterdam citizens at Bordeaux and Rouen was in fact seized in 1689. Not satisfied, de Lagny and Dodun also initiated action against the property of the family in France of César Caze's wife, Catherine née Monginot. This tactic does not seem to have been very successful, but was still under litigation in 1698.[62]

The First Union with the United Farms, 1680–97

While the "Jean Breton" company was being thus leisurely wound up, Colbert was faced with the immediate problem of what to do about the tobacco monopoly. As we shall see in Chapter 4 on the colonies, he had been under pressure since 1677 from colonial officials to abolish or alter the monopoly in favor of the tobacco producers of St. Domingue. The only practical results of this pressure would seem to have been the laws restricting the permitted zones of tobacco cultivation in France. Succeeding students of Colbert have, however, made much of the contention that Colbert really wanted to abolish the tobacco farm with the return of peace in 1678.[63] This thesis would seem to be based upon a single document of about 1680, a "Memoir to report to the king on the state of his finances" which concludes with "Items which ought to receive the reductions in taxes and other improvements if the king decides to reduce his expenses." One item in this list is "to abolish the tobacco farm and that of stamped paper which are prejudicial to the trade of the kingdom."[64] There does not in fact seem to be very much evidence to suggest that Colbert ever seriously thought the king would retrench expenses to the point where he would be able to reduce and remove taxes wholesale.

The evidence we have suggests rather that all Colbert's thought on the tobacco monopoly in the two years following the end of the war was moving in exactly the opposite direction: how, in fact, could he get a higher yield out of this disappointing farm? As early as 9 January 1679, he sent a circular letter to all intendants announcing that the king planned to continue the tobacco farm and expected to increase its yield. On the basis of the revenues produced by tobacco in neighboring states, the farm which because of fraud now realized only 500,000 *l.t.* or so should produce 400,000–500,000 *écus* (i.e., 1.2–1.5 million *l.t.*). This monopoly, he explained, was an ideal source of revenue because the tax itself was burdenless: every individual was free to choose whether to use tobacco or not. The intendants were to give this farm their personal attention.[65] Two months later, Colbert wrote again repeating the message and asking all intendants to submit reports on what the farm then produced in their *généralités* and what it might produce.[66] He attacked complacency and satisfaction with current yields in letters to the intendants of Languedoc[67] and Montauban. "You should keep it for a maxim," he reminded the latter, "that there is no farm in the kingdom that cannot easily be made to yield more."[68] From that sensitive tobacco growing region, he wanted a report every six months on the current and future product of the monopoly.[69]

Clamageran estimates the annual average gross income of the French government during 1662–83 at about 104,304,000 *l.t.* of which 56,961,000 came from the *fermes* (indirect taxes), the rest (38,693,000) from the *taille* and related land taxes. Perhaps 20 percent should be deducted for various charges.[70] However we calculate, it is quite clear that the 500,000 *l.t.* or so which Colbert was getting from the tobacco and pewter farm was hardly one-half of one percent of the total revenues of the French state and indeed, less than 1 percent of the contractual yield from all indirect taxes. This is remarkably little by any standard. We need not credit Colbert with the prophetic vision of foreseeing the immense revenues modern states would get from tobacco, or even the forty-fold increase in yield that would be achieved in France by the mid-eighteenth century. With the limited information at his disposal, he felt that something more, perhaps two or three times as much, might be realized from this branch of the revenue. The decision to continue the monopoly and increase its value had been made before January 1679 and was actively implemented in the next eighteen or so months. At some point in those months, it must have become apparent to Colbert that the increased yield he desired could only be achieved by reducing fraud and that this in turn would require a more elaborate police force than that which a small *ferme* could maintain. Other considerations also suggested a policy of amalgamation. With Caze, the only wealthy member of the existing company, a Protestant and thus ineligible to continue in the farm by the new policy of 1680, some radical change would have been necessary even if the financial results of the farm hadn't been as disappointing as they were to all concerned. With all avowed Protestants withdrawing from the farms at once, there must have been a general shortage of affluent and experienced persons to participate as principals. This helps in some part explain the policy of amalgamation of the farms that re-created the United General Farms in 1680–81.[71] Thus, Colbert's decision in 1680 to attach the tobacco farm to the united farms was both necessary in itself and part of a similar broader necessity.

Of the conditions under which the tobacco monopoly was transferred in 1680 to the united farms, we know relatively little. The outgoing Breton company, we have just seen, received 300,000 *l.t.* for their stock and tools. Their facilities and personnel were taken over by their successors. In computing the annual contractual price paid by the united farms to the government, it is likely that the tobacco monopoly was valued at something between 500,000 and 700,000 *l.t.* (since we know it to have been valued at 700,000 *l.t.* a year later).[72]

The transfer of the monopoly demanded the development for the first time of a procedure, later to become standard, for an ordered transition between the two *régimes*. By a lease or leases of 27 June 1680, the separate sections of the general farms (leased since 1674 to three separate companies under the names of Saulnier, Dufrénoy, and La Planch) were, together with the tobacco monopoly, granted to one company under the name of Claude Boutet.[73] The lease was to commence on 1 October 1680. (The original lease to Jean Breton of 1674 was to run till 30 November 1680. The last two months of the Breton bail were presumably voluntarily surrendered by the old company or taken away by an *arrêt du conseil*.) Two days later, on 29 June 1680, two special *arrêts* were issued for the tobacco farm. One merely confirmed the lease and permitted Boutet (i.e., the company of the United General Farms) to take over the monopoly on schedule on 1 October whether or not the lease were registered in all the proper courts by then.[74] The second warned all retailers that they could sell tobacco bought or to be bought from the Breton company only through 30 September. They could sell no tobacco from 1 October without the express permission of Claude Boutet.[75] This *arrêt* hindered the old "Jean Breton" company from disposing of their tobacco and was amended by a further *arrêt* of 17 August which specifically permitted and encouraged retailers to continue buying from Breton and ordered the incoming Boutet company to supply *gratis* their new marks or stamps needed to sell such tobacco after 1 October. Records were, however, to be kept of all tobacco purchased from Breton by the retailers in the last weeks of the old lease.[76] For this purpose, the Boutet company was permitted to place its own employees in the Breton company's warehouses to record all sales after 1 July. This was designed to discourage retailers buying smuggled tobacco during the confusion of the changeover.[77] After the new lease came into effect, the retailers had to be further instructed by an *arrêt* of 19 October to declare all their old "Breton" tobacco within fifteen days to the agents of Boutet and have the same remarked for sale with the Boutet seal. No tobacco without the Boutet mark or seal could be sold at the expiry of the fifteen days.[78]

In the event, the Claude Boutet lease which was supposed to run for six years only lasted twelve months. Colbert was striving to create a truly monolithic revenue farming company. The Boutet lease included all the important indirect taxes plus the salt and tobacco monopolies, but did not include the *domaines* (the remnants of the king's feudal income, but in the eighteenth century to include many stamp and transfer taxes). With the farm of the *domaines* ending in 1681, he decided to reconstitute the united general farms that year to include *domaines* as well: hence the new lease to Jean Fauconnet. This should *not* be thought of as taking the farms away from Boutet and giving them to Fauconnet, for behind both names were substantially the same interests.[79]

Thus, on 26 July 1681, the same day as the other branches of the revenue were so granted, a lease of the tobacco monopoly was awarded to the company of the United General Farms under the name of Jean Fauconnet for six years starting 1 October 1681.[80] The same day, the usual confirmatory *arrêt* was issued authorizing him to take over the tobacco monopoly on 1 October whether or not his lease had been registered by that day.[81] (The French administrative system met in advance the normal delays of the law as well as the possible noncooperation of the law courts.)

The great achievement of the United General Farms in taking over the tobacco monopoly in 1680 was to systematize its internal organization and the legal basis of its activities. The old Jean Breton company of 1674–80 had gotten along with minimal recourse to the king's council. In July 1681, almost simultaneously with the complete unification of the farms in the Fauconnet lease, the government at the behest of the new company issued a series of extremely detailed *ordonnances* codifying and amplifying the public law relating to the revenue farms. One of these July *ordonnances* referred exclusively to the tobacco monopoly and shall be discussed in Chapter 5 on the administrative history of the farm.

Aside from legal and administrative history, we know relatively little about the internal history of the Boutet and Fauconnet leases. Nicolas de Frémont, head of the united farms, was apparently dissatisfied with the de Lagny-Dodun management and about 1685 asked Jean Rémy Hénault (1648–1737, father of the president Hénault) to become director-general of the tobacco monopoly, promising him that he would be made a farmer-general of the united farms at the first opportunity. We do not know what administrative experience Hénault had had, but he remained in charge of the tobacco monopoly until 1697 and became a farmer-general during 1689–1718. Hénault (writing in 1714) boasted that he had doubled the profit *(produit)* of the farm in his first three years and had been awarded 30,000 *l.t.* by Frémont in the name of the company.[82] This seems possible for the farm was not very prosperous during the years preceding his appointment. We have, by chance, a rather complete financial statement of the income and outgo of the united farms for the pre-Hénault period, the first three years of the Fauconnet lease, 1 October 1681–30 September 1684. The section relating to the tobacco monopoly is summarized in Table III.

These figures at first say very little, but can be made to tell a bit of a story with some manipulation. Total "receipts" for the three years average 1,846,295 *l.t.* p.a. This would seem to mark a considerable advance on the receipts of the old Jean Breton farm which had averaged 1,439,065 for the three years 1676–78. However, this difference is almost entirely made up of the strange item in the "receipts" of stock on hand at the end of year. Though an asset, this is not normally considered a receipt and was not counted as such in the Breton data. If we eliminate this line which averages 371,557 *l.t.* above, the average receipts for 1681–84 fall to 1,474,624, just a hair's breadth above the old company's receipts for 1676–78. The rising value of stock on hand at the end of the year, while sales remain relatively stagnant, suggests disappointments in sales.

Joseph Paris Duverney
By Avelines after Vanloo, courtesy of B. N. Estampes.

Jean Paris de Montmartel
*By L. J. Cathelin after
M. Q. de la Tour, courtesy of
B. N. Estampes.*

John Law
*By Belle, courtesy of National
Portrait Gallery.*

Antoine Crozat
By Largilière, courtesy of B. N. Estampes.

OPERATIONS OF A ROYAL TOBACCO FACTORY
From the Recueil de planches, *I (1762),
accompanying Diderot's* Encyclopédie.

Opening hogsheads and sorting.

Preparing wrappers and moistening.

OPERATIONS OF A ROYAL TOBACCO FACTORY *(Cont.)*

Boys stemming leaves.

Spinning, both manually *(right) à la françoise,* and mechanically *(left) à la hollandoise.*

OPERATIONS OF A ROYAL TOBACCO FACTORY *(Cont.)*

Rolling *(right)* and pressing rolls *(left)*.

Unrolling spun tobacco and cutting into pieces.

OPERATIONS OF A ROYAL TOBACCO FACTORY *(Cont.)*

Pressing pieces into *carottes*.

OPERATIONS OF A ROYAL TOBACCO FACTORY *(Cont.)*

Winding string around *carottes (ficellage)*.

Trimming bound *carottes*.

Daniel MacKercher
*By J. Brooke after T. Stevens,
courtesy of the British Museum.*

Abbé Huber
By M. Q. de la Tour, courtesy of
Musée de l'Art et de l'Histoire,
Geneva.

Gerard Van Neck
By MacArdell after Vanloo, courtesy of the British Museum.

Sir Joshua Van Neck *(left)* and His Family at
Putney, 1752 (with Thomas Walpole, *center left*)
By A. Devis, from the Collection of Miss Helen Frick.

J. J. de la Borde
By Lalive de Jully after Roslin, courtesy of B. N. Estampes.

Vray Citoyen, vertueux Pere,
Sensible Epoux fidel amy,
Son plus grand bonheur sur la terre
Est de faire celuy d'autruy.

Abbé Terray
By L. J. Cathelin after Roslin, courtesy of B. N. Estampes.

Sir James Hunter Blair, 1st Bart.
By Raeburn, courtesy of Sir James Hunter Blair of Blairquhan and Scottish National Portrait Gallery.

Sir William Forbes, Bart.
By Reynolds, courtesy of Scottish National Portrait Gallery.

William Short
By J. Neagle, courtesy of Historical Society of Pennsylvania.

Robert Morris
By C. W. Peale, National Park Service Photo.

Pierre Louis Roederer
By Courbe after Labadye, courtesy of B. N. Estampes.

A. L. Lavoisier and His Wife (*née* Paulze)
By David, courtesy of Rockefeller University.

TABLE III

Income and Expenditure of the Tobacco Section of the
United General Farms, 1 October 1681–30 September 1684[83]

	1st Year	2d Year	3rd Year
"Income"	*(in livres tournois)*		
From sale of tobacco	1,172,059	1,204,115	1,265,200
Tobacco on hand at end of year	322,056	339,416	453,199
Extra value of retail stocks	55,832	58,584	82,101
From fines and confiscations	10,167	9,097	10,859
Subfarm of Brittany	180,000	180,000	180,000
Subfarm of Metz district	4,275	5,925	6,000
Total	1,744,388	1,797,136	1,997,360
"Expenditure"			
Tobacco bought from Boutet company	487,307		
Other purchases of tobacco	339,918	no information	
Salaries of employees	76,685		
Other expenses	92,336		
Total	996,246		

It is not exactly clear what is meant by item "extra value of retail stocks" (*"plus-values des tabacs ès main des marchands"*). We find a similar item in the old farm's accounts for 1675–76. It most probably means nothing more than the book profit on tobacco delivered to retailers but not yet paid for. (Alternatively, it may imply some sort of special payment on tobacco supplied to retailers by licensed manufacturers or wholesalers without passing through the company's hands. Such arrangements were permitted in the tobacco growing regions of the south and occasionally elsewhere. It may also include the income from certain local monopolies granted by the company.) [84]

One of the most interesting items in the accounts is the indication that Brittany and the *pays Messin* (territory around Metz) were let out as subfarms. The *Messin* was a frontier area cut off from easy communication with France proper by the intervening jurisdictions of Lorraine; on all sides it was surrounded by territories in which the planting of tobacco was legal. To have attempted to administer it as part of the farm in the rest of France would probably have cost more than it was worth. Under such circumstances, the 4,275–6,000 *l.t.* which the sublease (to one Jean Le-Mot) brought in may have been all that could have been hoped for. The subfarm of Brittany (to a company in the name of Louis Bouget) was another matter. The disturbances there in 1675 may have encouraged the general farms to rid themselves of this political difficulty. Then too, since Brittany was a *pays d'état* (a province with its own estates) and outside the *cinq grosses fermes,* the united farms were accustomed to dealing with it as a special case.[85] The general practice of subfarming introduced at this time was to remain one of the marked features of the history of the tobacco monopoly for the next forty years.

The figures on the expenditure side seem very modest. The 76,685 *l.t.* for the salaries of *commis* could have provided only the most rudimentary distribution system. Since there is no specific mention of costs of manufacture, we must assume that the monopoly still bought most of its tobacco in a semimanufactured state (both Brazilian and French West Indian tobaccos were imported in rolls of spun tobacco and Guienne tobacco was generally sold in that condition too) and left most additional processing to subcontractors or retailers. The snuff works were an exception, but their employment was small.) The 92,336 *l.t.* for miscellaneous expenses would have covered such things as transport, headquarters and auditing expenses, costs of prosecutions, and the tobacco farm's contribution to the general expenses of the united farms for guards.

Was the tobacco monopoly profitable for the United General Farms during the first three years of the Fauconnet lease? The price at which the tobacco monopoly was estimated in calculating the total price of the Fauconnet lease of the united farms (over 56 millions) was a well-kept secret, but a contemporary memorandum by the minister of the navy Seignelay indicates that the figure was actually 700,000 *l.t.*[86] Using the figures given in Table III, which treat stock on hand at the end of the year as income, the difference between "receipts" and "expenditures" in the first year of the Fauconnet lease was 748,142 *l.t.* With the price of the lease at 700,000 *l.t.*, this would have been just getting by. Even then, it was getting by only on paper and not in cash receipts, for two of the items in its balance represented as yet unrealized assets: the 322,056 *l.t.* for stock on hand and the 55,813 for excess value of stock in retailers' hands. In succeeding years, the position should have been easier for the company would have been spared the heavy initial real outlay on stock. Yet, for an undertaking more financial than commercial, such accounts could not have been very attractive.

After Hénault took over the management of the tobacco monopoly, ca. 1685, a more vigorous policy was pursued. In subsequent chapters, we shall notice the steps taken to check planting at this time, including the buying up of tobacco privileges in enclaves along the frontiers and in the interior.[87] Hénault also seems to have attempted to cut costs in Paris by closing the monopoly's own snuff manufacture there and contracting out the snuff grinding work.[88] (This policy was continued in the next two leases.) [89] In thinly populated and unprofitable areas, the snuff monopoly was sublet separately on condition that the subfarmers buy all their snuff from the company at Paris or Mondragon: for such a privilege, the subfarmers for Haute Auvergne in 1685 paid only 3,000 *l.t.* annually.[90] Even the rights to sell ordinary tobacco were sublet in difficult districts: the *élection* of Chartres, where great numbers of soldiers and workmen were employed in improving the river Eure, was sublet during 1685–87 to one Pierre Dupré, *marchand de tabac à Paris,* on condition that he purchase at least 23,500 lb. of roll or spun tobacco *(en corde)* each year.[91]

This increased "efficiency" in the tobacco monopoly came at a politically delicate time. With the death of Colbert in 1683, the driving passion disappeared behind the union of all revenue farms into the one great company. His successor, Claude Le Peletier (1683–89), a nonentity advanced by the Le Telliers, was an administrator rather than a policy innovator. His years in office were peace years and he was able to keep the revenues from the farms at or near the highest levels reached under Colbert. When the more difficult conditions of wartime threatened, he resigned. He was hardly the person to resist the centripetal forces in the farms provided the government suffered no obvious losses of revenue. Nor was he one to resist very effectively encroachment on his departmental preserves by his more forceful fellow ministers. The latter challenge developed first.

At the death of Colbert, his authority was divided between his successors as minister of the navy (his son Seignelay), controller-general (Le Peletier), superintendent of royal buildings (the war minister Louvois), and others. In the echoing void of departed greatness, a spirit was soon manifest of general but undirected criticism both of the policies of the late minister and of the current social state of France. Rather than let this new spirit be turned against himself and his family, Seignelay chose to give it leadership and direction. His department became the center of a most extensive investigation into the state of France, economic and social.[92] This investigation was begun in 1685–86 by his deputy, Marius Basile Morel de Boistiroux, successor to Bellinzani as *directeur général du commerce* and *commissaire des fermes.* When Morel died early in 1686, he was succeeded as *directeur* for foreign trade, companies and farms by the former tobacco farmer and current farmer-general, Jean Baptiste de Lagny.[93] The investigations continued through 1687–89, but with, for our purposes, one great difference. While Morel was alive, considerable attention was devoted to the tobacco monopoly and its effects upon trade and the colonies; many were encouraged to send in memorials on this subject; after he was succeeded by de Lagny, the investigations concentrated on other subjects, memorials ceased to come in on tobacco, the subject was "forgotten."

Early in 1685, Morel, on the instructions of Seignelay, entered into correspondence with merchants all over the country soliciting information on and analyses of the current state of the economy. One result of this correspondence was the 1685 memoir from some merchants of Paris, already mentioned, so highly critical of the tobacco monopoly for ruining the West Indian tobacco trade and driving the *habitants* to filibustering or emigration. The monopolists had also ruined the hopeful new French manufacture of *tabac mâtiné* (established at La Rochelle, ca. 1672) which had seemed likely to supplant the Dutch in northern markets. They recommended the return to free trade with a customs duty slightly above the rates (2 *l.t.* per *quintal*) prevailing before 1674. With the inevitable increased consumption, the king should realize a larger revenue than under the monopoly.[94]

Another memoir from Rouen developed much the same ideas. The monopoly had ruined the St. Domingue trade, driven the settlers to piracy, spoiled the great and growing export trade in French manufactured tobacco to the Baltic, and, in addition, hurt the French trade with Portugal by reducing purchases of Brazil and Marignan (Maranhão) tobacco. This last had, in turn, ruined more than 1,000 persons in the Rouen area manufacturing textiles for export to Portugal. Tobacco consumption in France was alleged to have decreased by nine-tenths since the introduction of the monopoly but would recover this loss if the privilege were abolished.[95] A version exists of extracts from this Rouen memoir (together with contemporary memoirs from Bordeaux, Nantes, St. Malo, La Rochelle, Dieppe, Le Havre, and Dunkirk) with marginal notes by Seignelay. This extremely interesting document can by internal evidence be dated as late 1685 or early 1686, before the death of Morel.[96]

From these marginal notes ("Apostil de Monseigneur"),[97] we learn that Seignelay was very much interested in the question of the tobacco farm, even though it did not technically concern his department: "This concerns finance, but it will be useful to investigate this matter and consider whether the suppression [of the monopoly] would bring about a great diminution in the king's revenues." He was particularly intrigued by the allegation in the Rouen memorial that *consumption* there (probably imports at all Norman ports) had declined from 60,000 rolls p.a. (at least three million lb.) before the farm to only 6,000–7,000 rolls p.a. then. He had letters written to the various ports asking for more information on this point. The answers were almost as extravagant. From Nantes, he was informed that imports there and in the nearby south Breton ports had declined from 20,000 rolls in 1674 to 2,600 rolls in 1684 and that many peasants had turned to chewing liquorice because they could no longer afford tobacco. From Saint Malo, he was told that imports there had declined from 15,000 rolls p.a. before the monopoly to scarcely one-sixth as much. At Bordeaux, near the tobacco growing regions, they estimated imports before the monopoly at only 2,000 rolls per year but could not say what they had since become. The Saint Malo merchants thought the production of St. Domingue had declined from 200,000 rolls before 1674 to 20,000 then; those at Rouen suggested a decline from 260,000 to 20,000: i.e., from 10–13 million lb. to one million lb. p.a.

Seignelay calculated that if one could count on an importation from the colonies of only 200,000 rolls p.a. (which at 50 lb. per roll would equal 10 million lb. or 100,000 quintals), then a duty of eight *l.t.* per quintal would produce 800,000 *l.t.* (or 100,000 *l.t.* more than the monopoly was then producing in the united farms) without counting anything that might come in from the importation of Spanish or Portuguese tobaccos. (The pre-1674 duties were two *l.t.* for French colonial and 13 *l.t.* per quintal for foreign tobacco.) Since the price of ordinary St. Domingue tobacco purchased by the monopoly in France was then around 25 *l.t.* per quintal, eight *l.t.* per quintal would have been equivalent to a duty of about 32 percent.

It wasn't to be all that simple, however, as Seignelay soon found out. He added in his own hand:

> The farmers do not agree with these facts. It is difficult to achieve the suppression [of the monopoly]. There would be only one way to do it: let the merchants form among themselves a company to collect the duty which they want placed anew on tobacco, and undertake to compensate the [united] farms. But I regard that as hardly practicable.

The proposition was however made to the merchant complainers—and not simply in private. On 19 January 1686, an *arrêt du conseil* was issued calling for the advertisement for bids for the monopoly of the sale of tobacco for seven years starting 1 October 1686. The privilege would not be held directly from the crown but would be a subfarm held of the united farms for the last year of Fauconnet and for the whole of the next six year lease.[98] There was no satisfactory response. As another hand added after Seignelay's note (above), "The merchants do not wish to enter into this proposition."[99]

With the failure of the January 1686 scheme to subfarm the tobacco monopoly in France, Seignelay's attention turned to an even more bizarre proposition. As we shall observe in our discussion of the colonies at this time (Chapter 4), there had been a steady stream of complaint from the West Indies against the tobacco monopoly almost from its inception. Its discouraging effects on prices were reported to have greatly diminished the cultivation of tobacco, particularly in St. Domingue. To such complaints and pleas for the abolition of the monopoly, the government of Colbert had paid little heed. There were people in the colonial administration, however, who realized that the changed tone of government after 1683 might provide an opportunity for such complaints to be heard. One such was Michel Begon. Formerly *intendant de la marine* at Le Havre, Begon had been sent out to the West Indies in 1682 as *intendant général;* he was recalled in 1685 to become *intendant des galères* at Marseilles. Before leaving for France, he and the governor-general of the islands, the count of Blénac, drew up a joint report on the commodities grown in the French West Indies (dated Martinique, 18 March 1685). In it, the two officials alluded cautiously to tobacco, pointing out the desirability of encouraging its cultivation in St. Domingue to supply the other French islands and Canada, as well as the mother country.[100] Begon, however, realized even then that nothing could be done to increase tobacco production in St. Domingue as long as prices remained so unattractive. On 25 January 1685, he and Saint Laurent, another official in the West Indies, had written to Seignelay, suggesting that tobacco production would be greatly encouraged if the king would abolish the monopoly and accept in its place a payment of one-quarter of all the tobacco from St. Domingue landed in France, all expenses paid.[101] (We shall discuss the economics of this proposition below in Chapter 4.) This letter only alluded to the farm as a cause of low prices. After their return to France later that same year, the two officials submitted or were asked to submit the same proposals to Seignelay in a memoir much more strongly critical of the monopoly.[102] Seignelay became actively interested when his negotiations of January-February 1686 with the metropolitan merchants for a new farm broke down. On 28 February 1686, he wrote to de Cussy, governor of St. Domingue, sending along a copy of the memoir of Begon and Saint Laurent and asking for more information.[103] De Cussy instructed his district officers to call meetings of the settlers in their respective districts and read to them the proposals of Begon and Saint Laurent. The results were disappointing. In every case of which we have record, the settlers pleaded that extreme poverty made them incapable of paying even one quarter of their crops to the crown, particularly after freight and local taxes had been paid.[104] That was the end of the scheme in Saint Domingue.

With the failure of these double negotiations in 1685–86 to find an alternative to the tobacco monopoly, Seignelay seems to have lost interest in the subject. His last measure of initiative was the letter of 28 February 1686 to de Cussy in St. Domingue. Within the ensuing few weeks, his principal deputy Morel had died and was replaced by de Lagny, farmer-general and apologist for the status quo.[105] Not for another forty years was the navy ministry to take again any initiative in the matter of the tobacco monopoly, a subject belonging more properly to the office of the controller general.

When the leases of the United General Farms came to be renewed in normal course in 1687, there was in fact a division, though not a very serious one. Tobacco was not affected. *Aides* (internal excise taxes, particularly on wine) and *domaines,* about three-sevenths of the old united company's revenue, were by lease of 18 March 1687 farmed to a company under the name of Christophe Charrière for 27 millions, while the remaining four-sevenths—*gabelles* (salt monopoly and taxes), *traites* (customs on imports and exports), *domaine d'Occident* (customs on colonial commerce and certain taxes in America) and the tobacco monopoly—went to another company under the name of Pierre Domergue for 36 millions. The total was more than a million under what Colbert had obtained in the Fauconnet lease of 1681, but that was as good as the less adept Le Peletier could do.[106] The Domergue lease, though a step backwards in the rationalization of French revenue farming, was an important document in the history of the tobacco farm. It contained many clauses which filled in gaps in the legal support for the farm provided by the *ordonnance* of 1681. As such, it was regularly cited in subsequent leases for at least two generations.[107]

We know little more about the internal history of the tobacco monopoly during the Pierre Domergue lease than we do of its history during the preceding Fauconnet farm. The new company procured from the government a special *arrêt* giving them maximum liberty in every kind of subfarming and other reorganization.[108] They used this quite purposefully, their general policy being to sublease the snuff monopoly wherever possible but to bring the more important distribution of roll tobacco (for smoking and chewing) under their more immediate supervision and control. They abandoned the policy of allowing private wholesale merchants to supply roll tobacco to retailers in areas where there were no *entrepôts* of the monopoly. All stocks in the hands of wholesalers were bought up and orders given for opening new distribution facilities in poorly served areas.[109] *Arrêts du conseil* of 10 June and 19 August 1687 also provided for winding up the subfarms to Louis Bouget in Brittany and Jean le Mot in Metz. The Domergue company obtained the now usual right to send *contrôleurs* into the offices of Bouget and le Mot during their last three months (July-September) to note all sales made to retailers.[110]

This general policy was violated only in the case of remote and exposed Provence (and three attached *bailliages* in Dauphiné). There a subfarm of *tabac en corde* was made to a Parisian group, using the name Estienne Veron, for 87,000 *l.t.* p.a. Almost immediately, the subfarm ran into trouble and some of the partners had to be replaced early in 1688.[111] By the end of the first year in October 1688, Veron's principals realized that they were losing money and could not continue. The Domergue company then agreed retroactively to convert the subfarm of the first year into a *régie* or administration at their own risk, run for them by the partners in the Veron company. For the second and succeeding years, the central Domergue company and the Veron subfarmers in Provence would go partners, half and half. Even so, the losses continued and an order was needed from the Council of State to get the Veron partners to pay their share.[112] Finally, the tobacco subfarm was taken away from that concern and with the snuff subfarm in Provence given for the last four years of its lease at the reduced price of 72,000 *l.t.* p.a. to a company of persons domiciled in Provence using the name of Louis Codoneau.[113] Almost immediately, the partners in this new firm were quarreling among themselves, and carrying their differences to the intendant and the Council of State.[114] However, they must have found their combined subfarm profitable, for three of the six, under the name of Jean Reaux, reconstracted for the same sublease for 1691-97 at the enhanced price of 80,000 *l.t.* p.a.[115]

In the rest of the country, the Domergue company subfarmed only snuff. This made some sense for snuff then was a much more exotic and expensive product than it was to become in the eighteenth century. It might sell for ten times or more the price of roll tobacco. It was more highly manufactured into a greater number of products varying from each other in scents as well as in types of leaf tobacco used. It posed exceptionally difficult administrative problems which the Domergue company thought best to pass off onto others. Administrators trained in distributing a monopolized commodity like salt were hardly the best equipped to get the most out of a fashion-tossed luxury whose hundreds of varieties were sold at prices from 10 *sols* per ounce up.

In the early months of 1688, the snuff monopoly in the entire country (with the apparent exception of valuable Brittany and valueless Burgundy) was leased by the Domergue general farms to four regional syndicates: (1) a group resident at St. Flour in Auvergne, under the name of Jean Roux, took Auvergne, Bourbonnais, Berry, and La Marche for 13,500 *l.t.* annually;[116] (2) a Paris company under the name of Jacques Vallois leased the northeastern *généralités* of the Three Bishoprics, Soissons, Amiens, and Châlons plus the Boulonnais, the Rethelais, and the town of Cateau-Cambrésis for 12,400 *l.t.* annually;[117] (3) another Paris syndicate under the name of Antoine Cornel leased the southwestern *généralités* of Poitiers, Limoges, Toulouse, Montauban, and Bordeaux, plus Béarn, Roussillon, and the viscounty of Turenne for 24,000 *l.t.* annually;[118] (4) another unknown group under the name of Pierre Mabile for an unknown price leased most of the rest of the country, the *généralités* of Paris, Orléans, and Tours, the three Norman *généralités,* plus the Lyonnais, Dauphiné, Provence, and Languedoc (minus Toulouse). In each case, the subfarmers agreed to buy all their snuff from Domergue according to a fairly uniform table of prices. If they exceeded a quota, which varied with the price of their leases, they would have to pay a higher price per pound for any further deliveries.

Below these subfarmers were sub-subfarmers. In January 1689, the Mabile firm sublet its northern area (Normandy and the *généralités* of Paris, Orléans, and Tours) for 55,000 *l.t.* annually to another Paris group, under the name of Marin Poupart; after the failure of Mabile, this company subleased its concession directly from Domergue and subsequently took over Burgundy and the northeastern *généralités* (from the Vallois firm).[119] This Poupart group in turn appears to have sublet Paris and vicinity to another company.[120] There were also much smaller sub-subfarms. The Cornel syndicate in the southwest sublet Roussillon for 7,000 *l.t.* p.a. to a company headed by Etienne Richer, sieur des Hayes, though using the name of François Gaudé, sieur des Roziers. The Mabile firm or their successors sublet the *généralité* of Montpellier in Languedoc in two pieces in 1690: the dioceses of Montpellier, Agde, Béziers, St. Pons, Lodève, and Narbonne for 12,750 *l.t.* p.a. to two merchants of Béziers; and the dioceses of Nîmes, Alais, Uzès, Viviers, Mende, and Lepuy for 19,000 *l.t.* p.a. to two merchants of St. Esprit.[121] And so on. There was nothing unusual about this. The system of subfarms and sub-subfarms was fully characteristic of public finance in the last years of Louis XIV. It does seem, though, that snuff was only a minor branch of the tobacco business in France at this date, though relatively more popular in the south (closer to its Spanish origin) than in the north.

For the four years of the lease of Pierre Domergue starting 1 October 1687, we are fortunate to have rather fuller accounts than we had for the preceding Fauconnet lease. (They are the last such accounts we have till the 1750's.) They are in the same style and are summarized in Table IV.

Everything about this account suggests at the very least increased activity in the tobacco farm. Receipts from sales which had averaged 1.44

TABLE IV

Income and Expenditure of the Tobacco Section of the Domergue General Farms, 1 October 1687–30 September 1691 [122]

"Income"	1687–88	1688–89	1689–90	1690–91
	\multicolumn{4}{c}{(*in* livres tournois)}
From sale of tobacco & snuff	1,985,988	2,030,727	2,426,792	2,308,920
Duty on excess-value of tobacco in hands of dealers	93,220	58,550	60,842	58,200
Duty on pewter in Brittany	5,104	4,536	4,599	4,768
From subfarms and contracts	160,434	253,595	196,143	196,350
Realized from seizures	10,091	6,588	7,094	9,701
From monetary changes	0	75	2,018	0
Value of tobacco and tools on hand in bureaux at end of yr.	630,079	738,977	779,728	1,727,005
Total	2,884,916	3,093,048	3,477,217	4,304,944
"Expenditures"				
Tobacco on hand at beginning of year and purchases	1,146,686	1,216,732	1,610,705	2,012,264
Salaries of employees	188,528	235,828	219,535	208,999
Carriage and other expenses	245,204	226,240	344,476	380,721
Purchases of tools	36,660	36,347	43,578	38,046
Rents of offices, warehouses	45,786	14,234	17,437	18,658
Leases of frontier jurisdictions, etc.	5,717	12,972	10,372	10,372
Excess value of tobacco in hands of dealers at beginning of year	56,303	86,303	56,303	60,695
Indemnity to subfarmer Mabille	0	0	15,800	0
Losses on merchandise returned	991	1,198	7,470	25,014
Extraordinary expenses in Paris	0	0	0	3,948
Total	1,695,883	1,799,854	2,325,675	2,758,718
Trading balance	1,189,033	1,293,193	1,151,542	1,546,227

millions in 1681–84 now average 2,188,107 *l.t.* p.a. in 1687–91. Most of this increase, over the earlier 1680's can be accounted for by the addition of Brittany to the regular revenues of the farm, after having been subfarmed in 1681–87. (This province alone had brought 337,500 *l.t.* p.a. during 1676-78 before being subfarmed.) The 200,000 *l.t.* plus, which the company now received from the subfarms of snuff and Provence, represented a slight advance, for Provence alone had produced something under 100,000 p.a. gross in the 1670's, and snuff then was unimportant. A comfortable contribution still came from the duties on the mysterious "excess-value."

The trading balances which we now for the first time have over an extended period suggest that the farm could have born a price of 700,000–1,000,000 *l.t.* but not much more. The seeming leap in profits the last year is deceptive. It is primarily the result of a jump of almost one million *l.t.* in the value of stock in hand. This rise takes some explaining. It is based upon an increase in purchases of only 360,808 *l.t.* and a decrease of sales of only 117,872, together only 478,670 *l.t.* or less than half the rise in stock on hand.[123] (Adding in the 38,046 spent on tools should raise the total to 516,616 *l.t.* but would not affect the argument.) This can only mean that the company was valuing its tobacco on hand at year's end at something above cost. This may have been reasonable when we consider transport and warehousing charges and the special circumstances of the war. As we shall see in Chapter 7, with the start of the war, many of the company's usual overseas sources of supply were cut off, but it did have a new and relatively abundant cheap supply in prize tobacco. It was wise to buy all of this one could in wartime and not unreasonable to raise its value somewhat in inventorying. Thus the swollen figure for stock on hand for 1690–91 was in part a logical result of the war; it was also the logical result of revaluing upwards one's stock in the last year of a farm prior to transferring that stock to one's successors.

War finance is ever one of the most difficult of state problems, and not the least so in the France of Louis XIV. The times demanded a tougher man and in 1689, the man of routine, the administrator Claude Le Peletier gave way at the *contrôle-général* to the man of many resources, Louis Phélypeaux de Pontchartrain (usually styled the elder), another old enemy of Colbert. Pontchartrain's forte was finding money or seeming to find money at any cost. As much as any man, he must be considered the father of that great morass of *affaires extraordinaires* that characterized French public finance in the last twenty-five years of Louis XIV.

War normally meant a decline in French revenues from indirect taxes (due to the decline in foreign trade and increased smuggling by soldiers, in particular). Pontchartrain attempted to avert this by permitting the two separate companies between whom the general farms were split—Pierre Domergue and Christophe Charrière—to surrender their leases at the end of their fourth year on 30 September 1691. By *bail* and *résultat* of 11 September 1691, the general farms were reunited and granted for six years from 1 October 1691 to a company under the name of Pierre Pointeau, in fact the merged companies of Domergue and Charrière. This united company of forty farmers-general in its administrative and financial arrangements was to be the model of the United General Farms for the next two generations and more. (The United General Farms, except for tobacco, were never again split till the time of Necker, 1777–81.) Even though the rent under the united Pointeau lease was slightly under the combined totals of the Domergue and Charrière leases, both sides realized almost from the beginning that it would not be earned in wartime, and had agreed privately that the government should compensate the united farms for any losses. By the end of the lease in 1697, these losses had run up to fifty millions, almost one year's yield, all of which the farmers were forgiven.[124]

There is nothing to suggest that the tobacco monopoly contributed to the distress of the United General Farms during the Pointeau lease, 1691–97. In all probability, it was one of the few branches of the revenue that held its own, though we do not have any detailed accounts of this period.[125] Nevertheless, the farm was hurt rather seriously by the financial stratagems of Pontchartrain. The most important and most characteristic damage came through the sale of offices. Creating new offices, usually unneeded, to be sold for a capital sum had for the past two hundred years been a familiar French device for public borrowing in wartime. As the income realized from such offices was hardly more than the current interest earnable by the capital, such sales were at bottom but an elaborately dressed up way of borrowing money on perpetual but terminable annuities. Selling all the offices that could be invented or multiplied in the French state did not, however, raise sufficient funds for the demands of the war. Therefore, someone conceived the idea of creating offices for sale in the various branches of the United General Farms, including customs, excise, *domaines,* and the salt and tobacco monopolies. Such offices, commonly styled *receveurs,* were in fact created and offered for sale by an edict of December 1694.[126] They carried with them many privileges, including exemption from *taille* and from billetting. To make the posts more attractive, those who purchased them needed not execute them but could engage deputies of their own choosing for whom they remained responsible.[127]

Although the united farms received a credit toward the annual price of their lease for the sums paid in salaries to these unwanted officials, the company was not so easily quit of the implications of this new system. A significant part of their local administration passed into the hands of people completely outside their power to dismiss or discipline. These alienated posts remained a thorn in the side of the farms until abolished by the Regency in 1716–17.[128]

CHAPTER 3

The Creation of the Monopoly: The Age of Samuel Bernard, 1697–1718

"On use aujourd'hui du Tabac autant à la Cour qu'à la Ville; on voit les Princes & les grands Seigneurs s'en servir comme le peuple; il a part aux inclin[a]tions des Dames les plus illustres, & les Bourgeoises qui tâchent de les imiter en tout, ne s'oublient point en cette occasion. Il est la passion des Prélats, des Abés & des Religieux même. . . . Les artisans & les gens du commun ont mis en usage le tabac en corde pour le mâcher ou pour le mettre en poudre, & le prendre par le nez, & c'est une espece de divertissement & de plaisir pour eux que de joüer de la rape. On sait que le Tabac en fumée est familier aux soldats, aux gens de mer; & ceux qui sont exposés à de mauvaises exhalaisons, ne peuvent plus se passer de la pipe."

[J. Brunet ?], *Le bon usage du tabac en poudre* . . . (Paris, 1700) 3–4.

In the generation 1680–97, the history of the tobacco farm was confusingly and obscurely intertwined with that of the general farms of which it formed a part. By contrast, between 1697 and 1730 it was once again a separate farm, with its own history. This was not simply a matter of the legal separation of tobacco from the united farms; the financial experience of tobacco was also different. The rest of the farming system collapsed in the last years of the reign of Louis XIV. From 1703 to the end of the reign, first one, then gradually all sections of the united farms became unfarmable and were in fact simply managed by the united farms company for the account and risk of the government.[1] The great exception to this rule was the tobacco farm: through every crisis of these crisis-filled years it remained solvent, paying in full its obligations to the government. In more than one way, therefore, 1697 stands out as a turning point: behind the emergence of the tobacco monopoly as an important branch of the public revenue in France, we can detect the gradual but now sensible diffusion of tobacco consumption in France.

As the Pointeau lease of 1691–97 drew to its close, negotiations ensued in the normal course between the company of the United General Farms and the government for the renewal of the lease. It would appear that in these discussions it was taken for granted that tobacco would continue as part of the united farms. The *résultat du conseil* of 30 April 1697,[2] confirmed and made operative by the *arrêt du conseil* of 14 May,[3] granted the lease of the United General Farms and tobacco to substantially the same company, now under the name of Thomas Templier, for six further years to start 1 October 1697. The company proceeded, in the now established way, to organize itself into three major committees to administer the farms. By its resolution (*délibération*) of 6 May 1697, the customs duties (*traites*) and tobacco were entrusted to a division of fourteen farmers-general including Jean-Baptiste de Lagny, the father of the farm of 1674, and François Le Gendre, son of the farmer-general of the same name who had earlier in his career been the straw man for the first united farms of 1668.[4] These arrangements were approved by an *arrêt du conseil* of 21 May 1697.[5]

Since the death of Colbert, each succeeding lease of the general farms had produced a slightly smaller yield than the preceding, the highest for the reign of Louis XIV being Colbert's Fauconnet lease of 1681. The Templier lease had been negotiated under conditions of extreme fiscal confusion with the war still dragging on and the financial community particularly demoralized by the glaring failure of the Pointeau lease of 1691–97. In the course of the summer, as peace became more certain, Controller-General Pontchartrain began to have second thoughts about the relatively disadvantageous Templier lease which he had just made but which had not yet gone into operation. Out of these second thoughts came an effective rethinking of the place of tobacco in the general scheme of public revenues.

The tobacco monopoly had been valued at 700,000 *l.t.* in calculating the Fauconnet lease of 1681–87,[6] at something near that in the Pointeau lease of 1691–97, and at 800,000 *l.t.* for the new Templier lease to start 1 October 1697.[7] This last sum (at 16:1) was the equivalent of about £50,000 sterling. This was a very modest yield for tobacco in a great country like France after almost twenty-three years of monopoly. At this very time, England, with only one-third the population of France and no monopoly, was deriving a public revenue of about £200,000 stg. p.a. from tobacco.[8] And the consumer paid less for his tobacco in England than in France. Yet consumption was increasing in France. Pontchartrain knew most of this and decided that the time had come to get something more for the state out of the tobacco monopoly. The wretched condition of the public finances at the end of the Nine Years' War made hardheadedness necessary; the approach of peace made it probable that ruthlessness would be profitable.

The fullest account we have of what ensued in the summer of 1697 comes from the same well-informed memoir of about 1715 which gave us the account of Madame de Maintenon's part in the founding of the monopoly in 1674. Pontchartrain, we are told, decided that the tobacco monopoly was not producing what it should for the state because it was mixed in with the other revenues in the united farms and no one in that great company was giving it the attention it deserved. He decided that it should be made a distinct subfarm entrusted to a company that would be responsible for nothing else. Bids were invited by the usual public advertisement. Various companies came forward with bids and counter bids. It was finally granted to the highest bidder, a sieur Accault and company, for 1,345,000 *l.t.* (as against the 800,000 *l.t.* calculated in the new Templier lease of the united farms). Pontchartrain was, however, dissatisfied with the standing of the bondsmen, i.e., the principals in the Accault company. He felt that, instead of the usual petty farmers and concession-speculators, men were needed with an experience of international trade, for tobacco, unlike salt, had to be bought in the world market.

> Judging moreover that men of commerce were needed with credit in foreign lands, he turned towards M. Bernard, who was very much attached to him, to whom he said that he wanted [the tobacco monopoly to yield] 1500 thousand livres excluding the entry duties; and he charged him [Bernard] to put together a company for him [that would farm the monopoly on these terms]. M. Bernard spoke about it to M. Crozat with whom he was then working closely and the two of them together approached M. Maynon to whom the price appeared excessive because of the knowledge which he had of the yields.

Maynon, who alone of the key three was in the united farms, explained his reservations to Pontchartrain and also reminded the minister that he could not go into a subfarm because the farmers-general of the united farms in the deed of partnership for the new Templier lease, signed in May, had stipulated that no member of their company could be interested in any subfarm on penalty of 50,000 *l.t.* forfeit. Pontchartrain therefore decided not to make the tobacco monopoly a subfarm of the united farms but instead to detach it and set it up as a separate *ferme générale*.[9]

By *résultat du conseil* and *arrêt* of 17 September 1697, the lease of the tobacco monopoly was taken away from Thomas Templier (i.e., the United General Farms) and given instead to Nicolas du Plantier (i.e., the new Bernard-Crozat-Maynon company) for 1.5 million *l.t.* under the usual transfer conditions. The new company was to have complete freedom to subfarm.[10] As understood in advance, "Nicolas du Plantier," by a notarial act of 28 November 1697, agreed to pay "Thomas Templier" 100,000 *l.t.* p.a. over and above the regular price of his lease to the crown, as composition for all import, export and transit duties to which the united farms might lay claim.[11] (This was to be standard in all subsequent leases down to 1730.) This made the effective price paid by the new farmers 1.6 millions. In the *résultat* of 17 September 1697, as amplified by an *arrêt du conseil* of 11 March 1698, the new company was given power to buy back compulsorily any office of receiver of tobacco which had been sold to a private person under the edicts of December 1694 and May 1696. Such offices would then be their property, to be purchased from them by any successor company.[12] This was a necessary step in establishing the authority of the du Plantier company in their own farm and apparently important in their own eyes if they were to pay the larger sum for which they had contracted.

The company which took over the tobacco monopoly as of 1 October 1697 under the name of Nicolas du Plantier was to retain that farm without interruption but with a few changes in personnel for twenty-one years (1697–1718). During those twenty-one years, the tobacco farm was to develop those buying and other business policies which were to cling to it through storm and calm down to the end of the *ancien régime*. This is a company worth close examination. It was formed by deed of partnership on 22 September 1697 with an initial capital of 500,000 *l.t.;* and consisted of nine partners usually listed in this order: Vincent Maynon, Antoine Crozat, Samuel Bernard, Pierre Thomé, François Le Gendre, Charles Ponthon, Charles Le Jongleur, Pierre Pellard, and Charles de la Condamine.[13] Of the nine, three were also interested in the current United General Farms (Templier lease);[14] most of the remainder belonged more conspicuously to the world of *finance* than to those of trade or revenue farming.

They were not, however, a chance grouping. Of the nine, four represented a single interest: Crozat *le riche,* his brother-in-law, Le Gendre, and his two protégés, Ponthon and Le Jongleur;[15] Pellard, on the other hand, was a creature of Bernard.[16] Of much greater significance were the ties that bound Crozat and Bernard: these were far from casual. The memoir quoted above referred to the fact that these two great financiers were then working closely together. During 1697–1701, we find them acting together in at least four contracts for the sale of government offices.[17] That very year, 1697, they had become for a time directors of the derelict French East India company and had tried to take over the company till bought off by the other directors.[18] The next year, when the new *compagnie royale de Saint-Domingue* was chartered, we find among its seven nonofficial members four of our tobacco farmers, Samuel Bernard, Antoine Crozat, Pierre Thomé, and Vincent Maynon, as well as Nicolas Magon de la Chipaudière of St. Malo, a close collaborator of Bernard and Crozat.[19] When de Lagny's unsuccessful Guinea company was reorganized on 9 July 1701 and entrusted to seven directors, we find four of them to be from our tobacco farm group: Maynon, Thomé, Bernard, and Crozat; two of the remaining three were from the same world: Joseph Le Gendre, sieur d'Arminy, brother of the tobacco farmer, François Le Gendre, and Etienne Landais, from the St. Domingue company. When the company was expanded later in the year to take over the Asiento (technically the French Asiento Company was a separate company in which the new Guinea Company shared halves with the kings of France and Spain but provided virtually all the capital), the principals added included the two tobacco farmers, Charles Le Jongleur and Charles Ponthon, as well as Louis Doublet, brother-in-law of Crozat and the Le Gendre, Claude-César Rasle, brought in by Bernard, plus further important figures from the St. Domingue company, Jacques de Vanolles and Jean Ducasse, governor of St. Domingue.[20] For all practical purposes, the tobacco farm of 1697, the St. Domingue company of 1698, and the Guinea-Asiento company of 1701 were one and the same interest.

Rather more peripheral was the further interest of these same persons in the "new company" formed in 1698 for illicit trade to the coasts of South America, variously styled the *compagnie royale de la mer pacifique* or the *compagnie de la mer du sud*. Although created by the adventurer Jean Jourdan de Grouée, its directors included both Samuel Bernard and Antoine Crozat plus François Le Gendre and several familiar names from the simultaneously launched St. Domingue company: Michel Begon, *commissaire général de la marine,* Jacque de Vanolles, *trésorier général de la marine,* and the close ally of Bernard and Crozat, the St. Malo magnate, Nicholas Magon de la Chipaudière.[21] The same cluster pattern of investment/speculation—"hunting in packs"—can thus be discerned here too.

The tobacco farmers of 1697, the *cautions* of Nicolas du Plantier, were significant not just as a group but also as individuals. The most important of them was Samuel Bernard (1651–1739), the son of a Huguenot court painter of the same name, ultimately the greatest international trader and financier of his generation. Bernard was already an important merchant and banker before 1685. Through a nominal "conversion" he escaped the punitive effects of the revocation of the edict of Nantes in that year, though a country house of his suffered 10,000 *l.t.* damages through an "accidental" dragonading. He prospered greatly in the succeeding years, rumor had it through handling millions which Huguenot *émigrés* left in his hands for expatriation, more obviously through the great part he played in privateering and in the *affaires du roi* during the long wars which started in 1688. His specialty was remitting money abroad for the French army and procuring foreign bullion: In the famine years 1693–94, he was employed to buy grain abroad. During 1693–1702, he was also very active in the syndicates which bought blocks of offices from the government for resale, occasionally in collaboration with Maynon, Thomé, Crozat, and the Le Gendre, father and sons. In 1697, he was at the height of his repute: "Samuel Bernard," wrote the marquis of Dangeau, "is at present the most famous banker in Europe." It seemed he had only to snap his fingers and vast sums could be conjured up for the king's service anywhere in Europe. In the ensuing war years he became the linchpin of the entire structure of French governmental credit and financial operations. His collapse in the service of the state in 1709 was interpreted by everyone as the collapse of French royal credit. Out of this débâcle, he was yet able to extract the bulk of his vast estate and his strong standing at court. So pervasive was his influence, so unique his position that the generation between 1697 and the rise of Law can, in the history of French public finance, without exaggeration be called the age of Samuel Bernard.[22] This was also the life span of "his" tobacco farming company.

Almost as wealthy as the "new Catholic" Samuel Bernard, as influential as he perhaps within France but lacking his Europe-wide connections in (particularly Protestant) banking circles was his old Catholic collaborator, Antoine Crozat (1655–1738). More provincial and obscure in his origins,

Antoine Crozat was the son of a self-made banker and *capitoul* (magistrate) of Toulouse of the same name. Young Antoine and his brother Pierre started out in life as clerks in the office of Pierre Louis de Reich de Pennautier, treasurer of the estates of Languedoc and receiver-general of the clergy of France; under his patronage and that of Bâville, intendant of Languedoc, Pierre soon became cashier (really deputy) and *caution* or bondsman for his employer (i.e., acquired an interest in his office). Both also purchased offices of their own. It was Reich de Pennautier, who signed at Paris as representative of the elder Crozat (then dying in Toulouse) when in 1690 Antoine Crozat the son married the daughter of the minor financier, François Le Gendre (also a *capitoul* of Toulouse). By that time, the younger Crozat was already *receveur-général des finances* for the *généralité* of Bordeaux and had moved into the greater financial world of Paris where he was building two splendid houses. He prospered greatly in the next generation and became, perhaps after Bernard, the richest financier in France. He was much more a courtier than Bernard and was particularly notorious in his own time for the monstrous social ambition that forced his children into the most pretentious if unhappy marriages and bought for him for a time the right to wear the *cordon bleu* of the *Ordre du Saint-Esprit*.[23] (Bernard and other great financiers were content with the *Ordre de Saint-Michel*.) If Bernard can be thought of as a conventional merchant-banker who moved into public finance under the extraordinary conditions of the wars of 1688–1713, Antoine Crozat should be thought of as someone who rose within the safe, traditional world of public finance and purchased offices, and then, in his affluence, came to speculate in the most venturesome and farflung of commercial undertakings. (During 1694–1701, he too was active with Maynon, Thomé and Bernard in the *traités* for the sale of government offices.) From 1697 onward, we find him mixed up in virtually every risky commercial venture from South America to China culminating in 1712 in his assumption singlehandedly of responsibility for the entire colony of Louisiana. If Louisiana was a disappointment, his other commercial speculations were remarkably successful. The *Chambre de Justice* of 1716 recognized his preeminence by assessing him 6.6 million *l.t.*, the largest *taxe* levied on anyone in France (roughly £330,000 sterling). (Samuel Bernard had exempted himself from the jurisdiction of the *chambre* by paying a composition of six millions.) [24]

Closely allied with Antoine Crozat were his brothers-in-law the Le Gendre. This common family name has given historians great trouble. Some have confused Crozat's relations with the family of Thomas Le Gendre, great former Huguenot merchant of Rouen and correspondent of Samuel Bernard.[25] Others have confused them with the family originally from Lyons, the Le Gendre de Villemorien, which produced several farmers-general in the eighteenth century; or with the old Parisian family, the Le Gendre de Lormoy et St. Aubin, one of whose members was intendant of Montauban, etc. at this time.[26] Our Le Gendre, like the Crozat, may have been originally from Toulouse, though a Paris origin is as likely. François Le Gendre came out of nowhere to lend his name to the first company of the United General Farms in 1668–74. Some modern writers have assumed that he was actually "interested" in that company; in fact, he was only the usual straw man.[27] In the 1680's, he appears in documents only as "bourgeois de Paris," though obviously a person of means and wide interests, acting for example as financial agent for Prince Philippe, chevalier de Lorraine.[28] A great upward turn in his family's fortunes came in 1690 when his daughter married the rising young Antoine Crozat. Earlier that year, we find him a *capitoul* of Toulouse and acquiring a share in the Orléans canal. Shortly thereafter he moved from the rue de Richelieu to the Place des Victoires, the residence of the greatest financiers, and acquired the style of *écuyer* and the ennobling rank of *secrétaire du roi*.[29] In 1695, one year before his death, he paid 450,000 *l.t.* to acquire the post of farmer-general from the creditors of the bankrupt Jean Arnaud: he was the only "straw man" in the history of the united farms ever to become "the real thing."[30]

The rise of the Le Gendre family continued after François' death in 1696. In 1690, the marriage contract of his daughter Marie Marguerite and Antoine Crozat had been witnessed by the duke of Orléans.[31] Fourteen years later, that of a younger daughter Françoise to Jean-Baptiste Bosc, *procureur général* in the *cour des aides,* was to be witnessed by the king, the Dauphin, the royal dukes of Burgundy, Berry and Orléans, all the principal officers of state, the leading members of the rival Phélypeaux and Colbert families and all the senior officers of finance.[32] (In between, another daughter, the noted Marie Anne, had in 1698 married Louis Doublet, *secrétaire des commandements* to the duke of Orléans and an investor in the Asiento company;[33] while her sister Louise in 1701 married Jean-Baptiste Durey de Vieuxcourt, *trésorier général de l'extraordinaire des guerres* and connected with two important financial families.) [34]

François Le Gendre also had two sons: the elder, François, succeeded his father as farmer-general[35] and was one of the new tobacco monopolists of 1697; the younger, Joseph Le Gendre, sieur d'Armi(g)ny, was one of the founders of the Asiento Company and went out to America to establish its organization there during 1702–4; after his return to Paris he served successively as director of its trade (ca. 1704–6) and as director-general of the St. Domingue Company (ca.1710–14); he also succeeded his brother François in the tobacco monopoly in 1703, and followed his brother-in-law Doublet in the service of the younger duke of Orléans.[36] Aside from their family connection with Crozat, the brothers Le Gendre were very much of our group. One or another of them was active in all the great trading companies of 1697–1701 in which the Bernard-Crozat element was so conspicuous. Their father, the farmer-general, had been active in many of the *affaires extraordinaires* (including jobbing of offices and new revenues) between 1689 and his death in 1696, usually in collaboration with his fellow farmer-general Charles Le Normant (1634–1712), but sometimes too in collaboration with his other fellow farmers-general, Maynon and Thomé, and on one occasion with Samuel Bernard. Shortly after his death, we find his son François venturing into a *traité de la distribution du papier et parchemin timbré* (April 1697). The brothers in general were not as active in this sort of thing as their father had been, but on one occasion in 1699, we find both brothers taking a flyer in a small *traité* along with Samuel Bernard.[37]

If history has hitherto left a veil of obscurity about the Le Gendre brothers, the same cannot be said of their collaborator in the tobacco farm, Vincent Maynon (1645–1728), *ecuyer, seigneur de* Châtillon, Boissy-le-Brouart, Chambon, Bouville, *secrétaire du roi,* one of the leading farmers-general of his time. The son of a Paris draper, his own son became a *conseiller* in the *parlement* of Paris, his grandson (like the grandson of Dodun) a controller-general (Etienne Maynon d'Invault, 1768–69).[38] Maynon was a leading member of the United General Farms from 1691 down to the Law upheaval in 1718. He was also interested in a considerable number of lesser farms and syndicates for the jobbing of offices during 1689–98 (usually with Thomé, the Le Gendre, or Crozat), but dropped such activities thereafter, perhaps because of the new stricter rules of the united farms, perhaps because he was increasingly absorbed in other work. He seems to have been an exceptional administrator.[39] About 1714, we find him business manager[40] to the king's grandson, the duke of Berry (as Crozat had earlier been to the duke of Vendôme, great-grandson of Henry IV). In 1692–93, he had served on the farmers-generals' tobacco committee, and in the plan for the United General Farms of 1697–1703, he was head of one of the three great committees, that in charge of *aides* and *domaines* (mostly internal excise duties).[41] Though he had only a limited background in tobacco, we have already seen how he was brought into the new tobacco farm by Bernard because of his administrative ability. In fact, he was the administrative head of the tobacco farm for the next twenty-one years, in charge of personnel and operations, the farm itself to its employees, the person too who conducted all correspondence with the government and drafted the innumerable *arrêts du conseil* solicited by the company. He performed similar functions in other farms,[42] as well as in the Guinea-Asiento company, where he acted as *orateur* (spokesman) of the assembly of directors.[43] In 1716, his estate was valued at 4.2 million *net* (ca. £205,000 stg.), making him not a Bernard or Crozat but richer than the Le Gendre brothers or the Paris brothers and far above any of his other colleagues in the tobacco farm.[44]

Very close to Maynon and quite similar in background, though slightly less important for the tobacco farm, was his frequent colleague, Pierre Thomé (1649–1711), seigneur de Montmagny et de Ferrières. Thomé belonged rather to the older generation, that of de Lagny and Dodun. In fact, about 1678–84 we find him partners with the old tobacco farmer, Gaspard Hindret de Beaulieu, in the proprietorship of the new cloth manufacture at Clermont in Languedoc.[45] He was also a colleague of de Lagny in the Mediterranean Company (1686) as well as in the farms.[46] We first meet him as *trésorier général des écuries* (stables) *du roi* (ca. 1674–1702), and subsequently as *trésorier général des galères de France,* about 1692–1711. When he died, the latter office was sold by his estate for 350,000 *l.t.* He was a farmer-general from 1687 until his death in 1711, when he was succeeded by his son André Romain (for the remainder of that lease only).[47] Pierre Thomé was active in the *affaires extraordinaires* during 1689–98, almost always in collaboration with Maynon.[48] He was, as noted above, a regular investor in all the trading companies which attracted our group in 1697–1701, and later speculated in Crozat's East Indian ventures.[49] Though an important person, his interest in the tobacco farm from 1697 to 1711 would seem to have been that simply of an investor or speculator, not an active participant.

Ostensibly of similar background to that of Thomé and Maynon was their collaborator in the tobacco farm, Pierre Pellard, *écuyer, conseiller du roy, interessé dan les fermes,* partner in the leather manufacture at Sens, army supplier, farmer-general of the United General Farms from 1703 until at least 1721.[50] Yet, Pellard is suspect. In 1716, his entire estate was valued at only 151,660 *l.t.*[51] In 1718, he had to borrow 300,000 *l.t.* from Samuel Bernard for his share in the capital of the new Aymard Lambert lease of the United General Farms.[52] He had been active on a very small scale in some of *affaires extraordinaires* during 1696–97, e.g., a syndicate which paid the crown 360,000 *l.t.* for the right to confirm letters of naturalization and certificates for the legitimization of bastards. It was not until the Spanish War (particularly 1702–5), however, that he became impressively active in a great number of the most substantial contracts for the sale of offices, etc.—precisely at the time when Bernard and Crozat withdrew from such undertakings.[53] Considering Pellard's dependence upon Bernard in 1718, it seems highly likely that his participation in the United General Farms from 1703 and in the *affaires extraordinaires* after 1702 was not primarily on his own account but as a "front man" for Bernard or others. This would explain the modest proportions of his estate in 1716. This would also explain why he entered the *affaires extraordinaires* on a large scale in 1702 just as Bernard withdrew, why he left the same after 1705 at a time when Bernard was assuming other great obligations in the king's financial affairs, and why his return in 1710–13 (after Bernard's "failure" in 1709) was so modest. It might also help to explain why it was Pellard who of all his company was accused in 1707 of trafficking in offices in the united farms.[54]

The remaining three members of the new tobacco farming company of 1697 were relatively less important: Charles Ponthon, Charles Le Jongleur, Charles de la Condamine. Except for one occasion, the three had nothing to do with other national revenue farming or the *affaires extraordinaires*. In

1703 and 1706, we find all three of them acting as principals in the sublease of the *domaines* and *gabelles* for three and then nine years in the frontier provinces of the Three Bishoprics, Alsace, and the Franche Comté.[55] Charles de la Condamine (1649–1711), *conseiller* subsequently *secrétaire du roy, receveur général des finances* for the *généralité* of Moulins, sprung from a *cévenolle* Protestant family, father of a famous scientist, would appear to have been an affluent person whose presence in the tobacco farm was purely that of an investor. In 1705, we find him also taking a 10,000 *l.t.* share (the largest) in the *Compagnie royale de la Chine*;[56] he later speculated in Crozat's East Indian ventures.[57] In 1706, he appears as a member of a syndicate of seven (with a 3/20th share) which took over the *manufacture royale* of tinware and tinplate at Beaumont-la-Ferrière in the Nivernais (established in 1695 with a twenty years' privilege).[58] Both Ponthon and Le Jongleur, by contrast, were administrators long in the service of the monopoly. Charles Ponthon, *avocat en parlement,* was the grandson of a mayor of Calais and brother-in-law of the farmer-general Jean Rémy Hénault. He prospered greatly from shares in Crozat's overseas ventures and was able to buy the ennobling position of *secrétaire du roi,* to lend money to the duke of Antin (legitimate son of Madame de Montespan) and to become *secrétaire des commandements* to the duke of Berry, grandson of the king (whom Maynon also served). Earlier in life when his brother-in-law Hénault had charge of the tobacco monopoly under the united farms, Ponthon served as his deputy for eight years. Because of his technical skill, he was continued in that capacity under Maynon in the new company. Considering his legal background, he must have helped Maynon draft the great mass of *arrêts* which the monopoly obtained from the Council between 1689 and his own death in 1713.[59] Far more obscure was Charles Le Jongleur of whom little more is known than his previously mentioned involvement with Ponthon and others in the Guinea-Asiento company of 1701 and in the frontier subfarms of 1703–15. He appears to have resided for a time in Brittany and to have been interested in local tax farming and other business at St. Malo. He can only have been an administrator brought into the company because of his technical skills, for we know him to have had charge at one time of the company's great tobacco manufactory at Morlaix in Brittany which he was accused of burning to defraud the king.[60]

In retrospect the tobacco company of 1697 reveals a good representation from the united farms (Maynon, Thomé, François Le Gendre, Pellard), from the official financial world of *receveurs-généraux* and *trésoriers-généraux* (Crozat, Thomé again, La Condamine) and from the shadow world of office-jobbing and petty farms (all nine), but only one person from the orthodox world of international trade and private banking, i.e., Samuel Bernard. In practice, we are told, the company was run by its three chief members: Maynon, the old tax farmer, taking charge of its internal administration; Crozat, who had grown up in various receivers' offices, taking charge of financial matters; and Bernard, the only one with mercantile connections abroad, taking charge of procuring supplies. In this task, so difficult after the start of the war in 1702, Bernard had no ready assistance. This may explain why in 1703 François Le Gendre, the farmer-general, yielded his place in the company to his merchant brother, Joseph Le Gendre d'Arminy, to be assumed on the latter's return from the West Indies in 1704.[61]

The formal history of the new tobacco company during their first or du Plantier lease of 1697–1703 is rather sparse. Perhaps because the united farms were not too happy about losing the tobacco monopoly, perhaps because they knew the new company consisted of some of the wealthiest men in France, the Templier company (united farms) created considerable trouble over the prices to be charged for the tobacco, furniture, and tools transferred to the new company; the matter had ultimately to be referred to the government, an *arrêt du conseil* of 27 July 1700 fixing the compensation at 821,675 *l.t.*[62] Much more important was an immediate shift in policy made by the new group. It had been the apparent policy of the united farms while they held the tobacco monopoly during 1680–97 to subfarm the snuff privilege while keeping most of the distribution of roll tobacco under their immediate management. Major exceptions to the latter rule were made only for Brittany and Metz during 1681–87, for Guienne ca. 1696–97, and for Provence during 1687–97.[63] The new du Plantier company (which contained few or none with any specific tobacco experience) must have decided that this policy was too risky, considering the enhanced price they had agreed to pay for the monopoly; for insurance, they embarked upon a policy of more general subfarming in the south and along the eastern frontier, i.e., in areas marginal in profit or difficult to administer. The *généralités* of Toulouse, Montpellier, Montauban, and the county of Roussillon were sublet to a syndicate under the name of Etienne Brisbault, while Provence went to another group behind Nicolas Dieul. Companies under various names but all managed by René Lemoyne (previously interested in a Guienne subfarm, ca. 1696) took subleases on the *généralités* of Limoges (Duplessis), Poitiers and La Rochelle (Pierre Cochart) and Bordeaux (Jacques Picot);[64] while in the southeast the *généralités* of Grenoble, Lyons, Riom, Moulins, and Bourges all went for 120,000 *l.t.* p.a. to another group using the name of Pierre Mauret.[65] The national (du Plantier) company had the greatest difficulty trying to sublet the eastern frontier provinces of Burgundy, Champagne, and the Three Bishoprics. These were let in 1698 to a syndicate of nine persons in the name of Jean Gadel for 146,000 *l.t.* p.a., but the sublessees ran into serious trouble with smugglers; first they obtained a reduction in their price to 110,000 *l.t.*, then they threw up their lease completely. New bids were called for and a new group in the name of François Robillard picked up the sublease at the old price of 110,000 *l.t.*[66]

At least one subfarming company (the Duplessis group in Limoges) in turn sublet the snuff monopoly in individual *élections;* parallel companies probably did the same. In an apparent effort to preserve established consumption patterns, contracts for the lease of 1697–1703 specified that subfarmers and sub-subfarmers must buy their snuff from the workshops of the monopoly at Paris and Mondragon—or (in the Limoges case) from a specified private manufacturer at Tonneins. By contrast, a subfarming company was free to import its roll tobacco or buy it from the private manufacturers in the growing areas of the south; if it chose to buy such *tabacs en corde* from the central company, it was guaranteed a certain quantity of each variety at stated prices. In later wartime leases, the national company could promise no such supplies to the regional sublessees.[67]

Despite setbacks and difficulties, the policy of extensive subfarming introduced in 1697 persisted through the successive leases of the Bernard-Maynon-Crozat company down to 1718. This practice of course made it increasingly difficult for either the contemporary government or the farmers-general of tobacco themselves (not to mention subsequent historians) to know exactly what was the turnover of the tobacco monopoly and its net earnings.

This problem lay in the future. Of far more immediate import was the public ferment and crisis of policy-making that filled the peace years, 1697–1702, culminating in the creation of the new Council of Commerce in 1700. In the deliberations of the council and the preceding discussion, every aspect of governmental economic policy came up for review and criticism. It is hardly to be expected that the tobacco monopoly should escape its share of hostile attention. It was attacked on several counts: (1) its purchasing policies and prices were alleged to have ruined the production of tobacco in the French West Indies; (2) the resulting decline of the West Indian tobacco cultivation had deprived France of a valuable reexport to the Baltic and North, leaving that trade firmly in the hands of the Dutch (both points will be discussed more fully in the next chapter); (3) the same purchasing policies and prices allegedly discouraged the production of tobacco in France (to be discussed in Chapter 6); (4) the market for French manufactures in Portugal had been ruined when the monopoly ceased buying Portuguese tobacco; (5) with the drying up of the colonial, Portuguese, and domestic supplies, France had become dependent on its enemies Holland and England for its supplies (these two points to be discussed in Chapter 7); and (6) high monopoly prices at home had inhibited the growth of consumption in France, thus ultimately depriving the king of the much higher revenue which he might have received from an open trade moderately taxed.

As in 1685–86, very little attempt was made by the monopoly to answer these criticisms. The only comprehensive answer found came in a long memoir written quite early in the controversy by Jean-Baptiste de Lagny, the founder of the tobacco monopoly of 1674, a farmer-general of the united farms (since 1680) and director-general for foreign trade and taxation in the navy ministry (since 1686). Sensing the impending onslaught, de Lagny in January 1697 prepared a memoir defending *in toto* French economic policy since 1659. At the time he wrote, the tobacco monopoly was still part of the united farms; hence both pride and interest moved him to justify it fully. Conceding nothing, he flatly denied all charges against the monopoly: the French colonies, he claimed, sent so much tobacco to France that there was a surplus for export to the Baltic at good prices; the French plantations on the Garonne also produced a considerable surplus available for export to Italy and elsewhere; the monopoly had established thriving manufactures so that France had no longer to import processed tobacco; the king had his revenue, the landlords their rent, all was well with the world.[68]

No one but de Lagny attempted such a bold-faced denial of all the charges against the monopoly. Far more representative of the spirit of the times was the much longer memoir written by the official, Jean Pottier de la Hestroy the next year (1698). In general, de la Hestroy was conservative, defending from the inside the French administrative tradition as it had come down from Colbert. When he came to tobacco, however, he became quite critical, sketching out in 1698 most of the criticisms of the monopoly elaborated by the Council of Commerce in 1701: the buying practices of the monopoly had ruined the West Indian tobacco trade, thus forcing France to buy its tobacco abroad; by not buying from Portugal, the monopoly had destroyed the export trade of French textiles thither; the king should abolish the monopoly; import duties reestablished at or slightly above the levels prevailing before 1674 would, thanks to increased consumption, bring the crown as much revenue as the monopoly did; the domestic plantations should pay so much per *arpent* for permission to grow tobacco.[69] Whether de la Hestroy's memoir was widely circulated or not, the ideas and suggestions presented in it were common property, as the deliberations at the council were to show.

The Council of Commerce was established by an *arrêt du conseil* of 29 June 1700. The council was to consist of the controller-general, the secretary of state for the navy, other high officials, plus merchant deputies from the principal ports and a few important inland towns (Paris, Lyons). Its composition was thus heavily weighted in favor of "liberal" commercial interests as opposed to "protectionist" manufacturing interests. One of the two deputies named by the king for Paris (the others were elected by local merchants and worthies) was Samuel Bernard, international banker, royal man of business, and, incidentally, a principal *interessé* in the tobacco monopoly.[70] Bernard was the only deputy who never submitted a formal memoir to the council; yet, in the end, his interests survived its scrutiny quite comfortably.

In the memoirs[71] submitted to the council by its own members and by outsiders, though criticism of the tobacco monopoly was widespread, there were significant differences of opinion on remedies for it. One body of opinion, following the arguments sketched out by Pottier de la Hestroy in 1698, felt that the most important thing was to abolish the monopoly and return to an open trade under a moderate duty. In a printed memorial submitted by a local magistrate, Jean Le Pelletier, in behalf of the magistrates of Rouen, the tobacco and beaver farms were held up as the two worst examples of the ways in which trades were ruined by monopoly; domestic employment, the colonies and the trade to the North had all been hurt; only open trade could remedy the situation.[72] The memoir submitted by Antoine Le Pelletier, Bernard's co-deputy from Paris, called for the abolition of the monopoly without giving any explanation; he devoted his space to an exposition of the general tightening of legal penalties needed to make a simple duty effective.[73] The fullest statement of this position came from Noé Piécourt (Piedcourt), deputy from Dunkirk, the very port at which Pottier had long been a senior admiralty official. (Dunkirk was outside the jurisdiction of the monopoly, but had a growing tobacco manufacturing industry which was denied a market in France proper.) Piécourt repeated all of Pottier's arguments about ruining the colonial and Portuguese trades and called for the reestablishment of open trade with a duty of 5–6 percent on French colonial tobacco and 12–15 percent on foreign tobacco.[74] Only the merchants of St. Malo were hard-headed enough to suggest that duties in the vicinity of 60–80 percent on French colonial tobacco would be necessary to compensate the crown for the abolition of the monopoly—but no attention was paid to their opinion. By contrast, in England, where the desired "free trade" actually prevailed, duties at that time were about 100 percent on English colonial tobacco and three times as heavy on foreign.[75]

Other opinion on the council was much less severe on the monopoly. Many deputies failed to mention it at all. Nicolas Mesnager, deputy from Rouen, one of the most influential, if the most conservative, members of the council, merely asked for the encouragement of both domestic and colonial production and the moderation of the fiscal burden on the trade.[76] Others, less restrained, attacked the monopoly, but with a difference. Such was the tack taken by Joachim Descazeaux du Hallay, deputy from the great port of Nantes, rising center of the West Indian trade. (Descazeaux subsequently had business with Bernard, but it is not known whether he had had any before this time.)[77] As a spokesman for the West India trade, he concentrated his attack upon the harm done by the monopoly to colonial tobacco production. He also would prefer to have the monopoly replaced by open trade, though he admitted it would be necessary to have a stiff import duty to recompense the king. He hoped that increased consumption from lower prices would provide part of this increase. If open trade were impracticable, he would want the tobacco farmers obliged to purchase St. Domingue tobacco only. Unlike the Dunkirk spokesmen, he thought buying from Portugal as bad as buying from Holland. Unlike the conservative Pottier, he saw no point in encouraging French domestic production; he would in fact extend an older policy of Colbert and *prohibit* domestic production in the interest of the colonies.[78]

The council does not appear to have been absolutely certain what procedure it should follow. For example, on 12 February 1701, it received a memorial from the merchants of Honfleur, which, among other things, attacked the tobacco monopoly for ruining the St. Domingue plantations and called for its abolition. These complaints were referred to the United General Farms who replied for the tobacco monopoly that "this proposition has been rejected as often as it has been proposed; the farm cost a lot to establish and now brings in an assured revenue to the king": who knows what it would yield if converted to an import duty? The Honfleur merchants came back (28 March 1701) with further complaints against the monopoly and its purchasing policies. Meanwhile, however, the deputies had agreed that they would attempt no specific statement on the Honfleur grievances concerning the West Indian trade, but would wait until they could prepare a general report on the subject.[79]

By 10 June 1701, the deputies were ready to draw up a "Memoir on the Company of Guinea, on the Trade of the French Colonies in America, . . . and on privileged ports and monopolies, particularly on the monopolies of tobacco and sugar."[80] One version or draft of this memoir has survived, prepared it would seem by one of the most zealous opponents of monopoly on the council.[81] The section of this draft memoir concerning tobacco[82] is quite strong in tone and recapitulates the most extreme arguments raised in the council against the monopoly. The farmers were accused of conspiring not only to minimize the production of tobacco in France, but in the West Indies as well. Instead they preferred to buy from Portugal, Holland, and England, to the ruin of the French colonies, navigation and export trade to the North and the Levant. (In synthesizing all the arguments made before the council, the author of the draft was inconsistent for he at the same time censured the farmers for buying from Portugal, as in Descazeaux's argument, while blaming them for ruining the textile export trade to Portugal by ceasing to buy Portuguese tobacco, as in the Dunkirk arguments.) The draft concludes with a recommendation that the monopoly be abolished and a simple and moderate import duty established in its place. Hopefully, with the expected increase in consumption, such a duty would produce as much revenue as the monopoly did.

The tobacco section of the draft ended with a peculiar salute to Samuel Bernard. One of the members of this council, it announced, was also interested in the monopoly and was one of the most experienced merchants in France: even he agreed that this farm and all other monopolies granted to companies or ports were the true cause of the ruin of trade. If Bernard was correctly reported, he was in effect saying that if his monopoly ought to be abolished, so also should the monopolies of the East India Company, of

Marseilles in the Levant trade, of Lyons in the silk trade, and so on. It was a shrewd defense to seem to concur with one's accusers.

The draft report on the Guinea and West Indies trades and on the monopolies, prepared at the session of 10 June 1701, was read and discussed at the meeting of the Council of Commerce on 1 July. This was an intensely topical subject at that moment, for within the month the Guinea trade was to be taken away from the old (de Lagny) company and regranted to the new (Bernard-Crozat-Maynon-Thomé) company and negotiations opened for the acquisition of the Asiento. In reading the draft, various clauses were questioned by one or another of the members present. When the recommendations were read for abolishing the tobacco monopoly and throwing the trade open under a moderate duty, objection was made that the assumption was highly speculative that the king's revenue would automatically be compensated for the loss of the monopoly by an equivalent revenue from a moderate duty and a higher rate of consumption; the king might well lose by such an experiment. The council ordered that the deputies (the merchant members) enlarge the memoir to include answers to such objections. For the present, further consideration of the memoir was deferred.[83]

On 13 January 1702, the deputies again memorialized the council, going over the same ground: the monopoly had ruined colonial production, necessitating heavy purchases from foreign countries; if a free trade were reestablished, the settlers on St. Domingue would resume growing tobacco and thus save France millions in foreign exchange and encourage navigation; *even if there were no radical increase in consumption,* the king would not lose, for the costs and profits of the monopoly would be saved, there would be higher duties on foreign tobaccos and prosperity on St. Domingue would mean increased revenues to the king from export duties on other goods sent thither. The deputies were ordered to draw up a memoir on the abolition of the farm and on ways of reimbursing the king.[84] Nothing ever came of this. As of 27 February 1704, the minutes of the council show that the matter was still pending and that no decision had been reached.[85]

We should not let our attention be distracted by the brightly painted pictures of the settlers of St. Domingue driven from tobacco planting to buccaneering, or of the "Jews of Lisbon" accepting vast quantities of outmoded French fabrics, ribbons, and millinery in exchange for Brazilian tobacco. From its inception, the tobacco monopoly was a fiscal device; to get rid of it, one had first to produce an equivalent revenue from another source. All that the merchant opponents of the monopoly in 1701–2 could promise was that *in the long run* increased consumption would produce an equivalent revenue from a moderate import duty. But there could be no *long run* for the fiscally pressed government of Louis XIV (or of his successors). In such a situation, the businessmen-deputies seem like "babes in the woods" when confronting the hard-headed objectivity of the bureaucrats.

Thus, the tobacco monopoly and the Bernard-Crozat-Maynon company escaped the many-sided onslaught of the Council of Commerce of 1700–1702. Their contract was due to expire on 30 September 1703 and from the spring of 1702 other groups came forward suggesting to Controller-General Chamillart that they might bid more for the monopoly. With the onset of maritime hostilities (war was declared by England and Holland on 4–15 May 1702) no one in France could really have viewed the tobacco farm as anything but a very risky business. The most interesting proposal came from a "M. Paris," probably Antoine, eldest of the famous Paris brothers: he proposed to give 100,000 *l.t.* more than the current farmers, to reestablish a free tobacco trade within the kingdom, with importation allowed from anywhere and to permit planting *everywhere* in the kingdom.[86] Internal planting and unrestricted importation would, of course, compensate for the cutting off by war of imports from the colonies and from England and Holland. Nothing came of his proposal. It is nevertheless interesting because of its sponsorship. A generation later, the Paris brothers, by then war-rich government contractors turned mighty financiers, shall return to our story as partisans of a somewhat more orthodox fiscality.

In the event, in those uncertain times, no one came forward with a firm, better offer; the current farmers themselves seemed reluctant to continue since the war made procurement so difficult. One of their number, the author of the 1715 memoir, later reported that they agreed to continue only as a favor to the government and to show their loyalty.[87] The matter was not settled until almost the last minute: by lease, *résultat* and *arrêt du conseil* of 18 September 1703, the tobacco monopoly was farmed for six further years starting 1 October to the same company, this time under the name of Germain Gaultier. The preamble to the *résultat* stated that because of the war the usual legal procedure of advertising for bids had been dispensed with; the existing lessees, though wishing to withdraw and feeling a lower price justified, had, at the behest of the controller-general and for patriotic motives, agreed to continue at the old price (1.5 million plus 100,000 *l.t.* in lieu of all duties and tolls). They were to have the right to subfarm any and all sections of this farm without even the usual restrictions of having to advertise for bids.[88] A special *arrêt* of the same date gave Gaultier & Co. the continuing right to repurchase from the holders any offices in the tobacco administration sold under the scheme of 1694.[89]

The nine "sureties" of Gaultier were the same as those of du Plantier with one exception: Joseph Le Gendre d'Arminy, the merchant, replaced his brother François Le Gendre, the farmer-general of the united farms.[90] He must have assumed his responsibilities upon his return from America in 1704. This bringing in of an experienced merchant may have been thought necessary because of the special difficulties of procurement in wartime. In the course of the lease, in 1707, one of the company died: Charles Le Jongleur, minor inside figure and sometime supervisor of the manufactory at Morlaix.

He was replaced for the duration of the lease by Philibert-Antoine Chevalier de Montigny, a minor venturer in the *affaires extraordinaires* and second son of Louis Chevalier of the united farms.[91] Like his predecessor, Chevalier de Montigny was also actively engaged in the administration of the company.[92]

The nominal capital of the company, which had been 500,000 *l.t.* in 1697, was raised to one million *l.t.* for the Gaultier lease of 1703–9. However, at least one managerially active member of the company, Le Jongleur, was permitted to pay in only half his share and to give a personal note for the remainder. In general, there seems to have been an effort to encourage those members of the company who were doing the work as distinct from those who were merely investors. At the beginning of the lease in 1703, Samuel Bernard's share in the company had been 20 percent; shortly thereafter he sold a quarter of this to the two active members of the company, Ponthon and Le Jongleur (2.5 percent each), raising both their shares from 10 to 12.5 percent.[93]

Among the papers of the controller-general is an invaluable account of the individual shares of the partners in the company toward the end of the Gaultier lease, after the death of Le Jongleur in 1707.[94] For purposes of this calculation the company (as was usual in contemporary French accounting) was, like a *livre tournois* or a pound, divisible into fractions of one-twentieth (*sols*) and one two hundred and fortieth (*deniers*).

Maynon	2s.10d.	(14.2%)
Bernard	3s.	(15 %)
Crozat	2s. 7d.	(12.9%)
Thomé	2s. 7d.	(12.9%)
Ponthon	2s. 6d.	(12.5%)
d'Arminy	2s.	(10 %)
Chevalier de Montigny	2s.	(10 %)
Le Jongleur heirs	6d.	(2.5%)
Pellard	1s.	(5 %)
La Condamine	1s.	(5 %)

This information confirms the preeminence of the four great names (Maynon, Bernard, Crozat, and Thomé) and the relative unimportance of Pellard and La Condamine suggested above.

During the Gaultier lease, the practice of subletting the southern provinces continued on an extensive scale: Provence, the easternmost *bailliages* of Dauphiné, Languedoc, Roussillon and the *généralité* of Montauban (to a company under the name of Pierre Mauret for 295,000 *l.t.* p.a.); the rest of Dauphiné and the *généralités* of Lyons, Bourges, Bourbonnais (Moulins) and Auvergne (Riom) (co. Pierre Fraisse for 135,000 *l.t.* p.a.); the *généralités* of Poitiers, La Rochelle and Limoges (co. Jean Trezon for 68,000 *l.t.* p.a.). Farms of Burgundy and Champagne were also attempted but failed because of smuggling across the complex eastern frontiers; at the end of the Gaultier lease, these last provinces were under the direct administration (*régie*) of the central company, except for Bresse and Bugey in southern Burgundy which had been attached to the Fraisse sublease of the Lyonnais group. The principal areas retained under the direct administration of the company were the northern provinces of Brittany, Normandy, Picardy, Anjou, Maine, Touraine, the Orléanais, and the Ile-de-France. There is evidence that would suggest that this compact area between the Loire and the Somme produced better than three-fourths of the company's revenue, at least enough to meet the price of the lease.[95]

Except where the surety bonds (*cautionnements*) can be found in the notarial archives, we do not normally have information on the real investors behind the straw men who took the subleases. Such information as we do have suggests that these subleases which in the time of Domergue (1687–91) had been largely in the hands of Parisians had by this time (i.e., the Gaultier lease of 1703–9) passed in good part into the hands of local people with local knowledge. For example, the five sureties or principals in the Fraisse sublease of the Lyonnais group included two Parisians and three provincials, residents of Lyons, Moulins and Clermont-en-Auvergne. The last, one Antoine Chappus, was involved in every subfarm for snuff or tobacco in Auvergne between 1680 and 1715. Of the five, three described themselves professionally as *interessés aux fermes*.[96] In the case of the Trezon company which subfarmed the *généralités* of Poitiers, La Rochelle, and Limoges at this same time, the principals included, besides three investor-types from Paris and Bordeaux, the receiver of customs for La Rochelle and the receiver-general, controller, and *banquier* (probably cashier) of the tobacco office at La Rochelle. Though the office of a "receiver" might be purchased, the others were probably career positions. Such men had the specialized knowledge to make revenue farming much less of a risk.[97] (In the next lease of 1709–15, by contrast, there appears to have been a reintroduction of more Parisians, including some senior employees of the monopoly, as well as clients of court patronage.)[98]

The years of the Germain Gaultier lease (1703–9) were trying times for French state finances. In 1705, a surcharge of 10 percent had to be imposed on most branches of the united farms: the tobacco monopoly, however, escaped.[99] When all river tolls were doubled in 1708, tobacco was again exempted.[100] Nevertheless, these were years of great difficulty for the Bernard-Crozat-Maynon company. As we shall see in succeeding chapters, smuggling did not decrease because of the war, but obtaining supplies became more difficult. The united farms and many special farms collapsed in these years and were administered to the end of the war by their former farmers for the account of the government (a *régie* rather than a *ferme*). The tobacco monopoly was one of the very few branches of the revenue which remained in farm during all the financial disasters of the War of the Spanish Succession. Like the others, it was forced to lend financial support to the government through the issue of bearer notes (*billets au porteur*) which it advanced to the government in anticipation of the regular payments due from the farm. According to a memoir of December 1704, the company then had 1,575,000 *l.t.* in such bearer notes outstanding and the government was pressing it for another million.[101]

In spite of all these difficulties, the fact that the tobacco farm kept going when most everything else financial was collapsing impressed contemporaries. Some time early in 1708, another group came forward to bid for the farm, including the farmers-general of the united farms Des Espoisses, Lallement, and Chevalier and his son, Chevalier de Montigny (in the existing tobacco farm), the future farmer-general de Vitry, Pierre Dodun (probably a son of the tobacco farmer of 1674), André Auvray, army contractor (*munitionnaire*), Antoine Neyret, *interessé dans les affaires,* and others. Both Dodun and Neyret had been interested in the subfarm of Provence during 1691–97. There are various estimates in the papers of Controller-General Chamillart and his successor Desmaretz about the possible yield of the farm, but little came of these negotiations or calculations. The existing company sent in their offer to continue the farm at the same price and upon virtually the same terms for another six years (1709–15). Considering the chaos of the times, the enormous financial services which Bernard was then performing for the government and the considerable financial advances of the existing company to the treasury, it would have been very difficult for the controller-general to have changed horses at that moment. The memoir from the old company was marked "bon" and a copy of the *résultat* of 1703 defining the terms of the existing lease was brought to the king who wrote in the margin: "The present Resultat and all its clauses is my will [for the next lease]."[102]

On 24 July 1708, more than fourteen months before the expiry of the existing lease, and without any public advertisement for bids, a *résultat du conseil* was issued granting a new lease under the name of Charles Michault to the existing company for a further six years through 30 September 1715. The price at which they could sell St. Domingue tobacco was raised in their favor to that for foreign tobaccos. Otherwise, the provisions were the same as those of the 1703–9 (Germain Gaultier) farm. (The new lease was confirmed or expedited by *arrêts du conseil* of 24 July 1708 and 24 July 1709, royal letters-patent of 9 July 1709, and an *arrêt de la cour des aides* of 5 September 1709.)[103]

The membership of the Charles Michault company for 1709–15 was the same and in the same proportions as that of the Germain Gaultier company for 1703–9 with minimal changes. The 12.5 percent share held by the late Charles Le Jongleur during 1703–7, most of which had been acquired by Louis Chevalier de Montigny, son of the farmer-general, now passed from both de Montigny and the Le Jongleur heirs and was divided equally (6.25

percent each) between the new figures de Vitry and de la Roche Céry.[104] Of Pierre Philippe Jacques, sieur de Vitry, we know only that he was *receveur des tailles* (land tax) for the city of Limoges, had ventured in the gunpowder monopoly of 1706, and was to enter the United General Farms at this same time (1709).[105] He had been one of the unsuccessful Des Espoisses group trying to take over the monopoly in 1708, but had been taken care of nonetheless. Louis Claude de la Roche, sieur de Céry, son of the governor and captain of the town and castle of La Haye-en-Touraine, had in 1696 married the stepdaughter of Le Jongleur. He seems to have succeeded his stepfather-in-law first as director general of the tobacco monopoly in Brittany and eventually in 1709 as farmer-general of tobacco.[106] If de Vitry appears a true *financier,* La Roche Céry was, like Le Jongleur before him, more a technician.

The history of the Maynon-Crozat-Bernard tobacco monopoly company during the Charles Michault lease (1709–15) was very much of a piece with what it had been during the two preceding leases. It continued to sublet the southern provinces;[107] it continued to make very substantial advances to the government in bearer notes (a million at a time);[108] midst the collapse of the credit of the French state in 1709–10, the national wave of bankruptcies, the failure of so many other branches of the revenue, it continued to meet the price of its farm and inferentially to make profits. In a subsequent chapter we shall see that when the time came for its lease to be renewed in 1714–15, though several rival groups came forward in the improved conditions of the peace, the same "old gang," with a bit of new blood, obtained from the controller-general Desmaretz one further renewal of their lease (for 1715–21). It took the rise of John Law to break their grip on the tobacco monopoly in 1718.

When we view the whole history of the tobacco monopoly from 1674 to 1715 or 1718, three principal points should emerge clearly: (1) the Maynon-Crozat-Bernard company could never have kept the monopoly going during the disasters of the Spanish War if their revenues had not been supported by a significantly even if slowly rising consumption of tobacco in France; (2) assuming the monopoly to have been profitable after 1697, the Maynon-Crozat-Bernard company could never have held on to the farm if they were not such important people in their own right; and (3) all state decisions on the monopoly were ultimately fiscal decisions. However much politicians and memoir writers might scribble about the interests of commerce, the colonies, and domestic agriculture, at the test fiscal considerations always weighed most. If this was true of the *ancien régime* generally, it was particularly true in wartime. We must keep this hard truth always in mind when in the next few chapters we examine the impact of the monopoly upon the French colonies, French administrative practices, and French agriculture.

CHAPTER 4

Colonial Supplies and the Crisis of St. Domingue, 1674–1709

The Windward Islands as a Source of Supply, 1600–1674

From the earliest days of the French presence in the West Indies, tobacco had been a significant item of commercial pursuit. French as well as English and Dutch interloping vessels were attracted to Spanish Trinidad about 1600 to exchange forbidden European manufactures for the native tobacco (and probably that of Venezuela as well). Sir Thomas Roe reported in 1611 that he had seen in Trinidad at one time "Fifteen sayle of ships . . . English, French and Dutch" freighting tobacco.[1] When the French began their own settlements in the next generation in what they called the Windward Islands (*Iles du Vent*),[2] tobacco was to play a major part in the economics of the first few decades of settlement.

When the first French company was organized at Le Havre about 1623–24 to trade to the West Indies, it was understood from the beginning that tobacco would be one of the principal items of their attention. The first expedition of 1625–26 from Le Havre was led by Pierre d'Esnambuc who had previously served on French royal filibustering expeditions to the West Indies and was thus quite cognizant of the commodities that might advantageously be obtained there. When he arrived at St. Christopher in October 1625, he found that an English expedition under Thomas Warner and Thomas Painton had been settled there since 1622 growing tobacco. (Warner had taken 9,500 lb. of tobacco back to England with him in 1625.) The English had been joined there by some eighty Frenchmen, the remnants of an unsuccessful Guiana expedition of 1624. As the English and French were both weak and had common enemies in the Spaniards and the Caribs, they found it relatively easy at first to live and work together. This was the beginning of the joint English and French occupation of St. Christopher that lasted—with subsequent increasing difficulty—until 1713. From these French settlers, d'Esnambuc purchased some tobacco and other goods and returned to France. He arrived at Le Havre in September 1626 where he sold his cargo to advantage.

With money in his pocket, d'Esnambuc and his associate Urbain de Roissey, seigneur de Chardonville, were able to persuade Cardinal Richelieu to charter a *Compagnie des Iles* in October 1626 for trade, settlement, and missionary work. D'Esnambuc returned to St. Christopher in 1627 where he formally divided the island with the English. While he was absent on a trip back to France in 1628, a Dutch vessel visited the island trading food to the needy settlers for their tobacco. This early, the French settlers had neglected growing food to concentrate on their staple tobacco. From that time onward, the tobacco grown by the French settlers was as likely to end up in the hands of Dutch or English merchants as French. The settlers abandoned the island temporarily in 1629 when attacked by a Spanish fleet but soon returned and resumed their tobacco planting. As the company obtained successive orders from the French government prohibiting French private traders from visiting the island without the company's permission, the settlers were confirmed in their preference for trading with Dutch and English merchants. The weak (capital only 45,000 *l.t.*) and understandably unsuccessful first company had to be wound up and replaced by a stronger in 1635.[3]

In that very year, the French under d'Esnambuc (d.1636) and his nephew Jacques Diel du Parquet began the settlement of Martinique. There too tobacco was the first commercial product grown; its superior quality made it a magnet for merchant shipping.[4] The Jesuit Bouton in his description of Martinique (published 1640) could write, "Tobacco has been up to now the only merchandise imported into France from that island and from the other islands which the French have settled."[5] The same pattern was repeated on Guadeloupe.[6] The missionary Breton wrote of that island, about 1646, "This is the true country for *petun* or tobacco and it is our greatest trade."[7] In a pamphlet published about 1651 for a projected company to settle the mainland of equatorial America, it was taken for granted that tobacco would be one of the staples of the proposed colony.[8]

All the early descriptions stress the point that tobacco was well suited to be a crop of initial settlement because it required little capital equipment or skill, relatively little land to be cleared at first and could, if need be, be grown by a single man working alone. An optimistic projector ventured that a single man could grow 2,000 lb. of tobacco a year if someone else were available to grow his food;[9] the more sober du Tertre estimated that a man could grow from 1,000 to 1,500 lb. of tobacco plus his own food.[10] (This was more nearly consistent with later Virginia experience.) At the high prices prevailing in the 1620's and early 1630's, this could be an attractive crop. But when the production of St. Christopher came to be supplemented after 1635 by that of Martinique and Guadeloupe, signs of glut and lower prices were soon evident. In fact, something like an international crisis of oversupply seems to have developed in 1638. We do not have specific data on the French side, but the figures for tobacco imports at London make the dimensions of this crisis very clear (Table I).

From these figures (London accounted for at least two-thirds of English imports) we get a fairly clear idea of the proportions of the glut of 1638–39 and the discouraging effects it had on subsequent West Indian production. The French felt the ill effects of this surplus as much as the English, perhaps more so because tobacco consumption was probably not as wide-

Table I

Tobacco Imported into London (by Pounds) Lady Day 1637–Lady Day 1642[11]

Type	1637–38	1638–39	1639–40	1641–42
Virginia	1,080,827	2,361,999	1,102,773	1,044,554
Barbados	125,318	204,956	28,010	66,895
St. Christopher	270,629	473,833	108,212	139,451
Spanish	60,597	93,306	115,773	6,379
Total	1,537,371	3,134,094	1,354,768	1,257,279

spread in France as in England. From about 1635, when the French West India Company was refounded and the settlement of Martinique and Guadeloupe begun, instructions had been sent out for the settlers to alternate tobacco one year with cotton the next, with no one permitted to grow more than 900 lb. of tobacco in any one year. These well-intentioned rules were not observed, probably because tobacco cultivation was easier than cotton and prices were still attractive. Some merchants of Dieppe had agreed to take all the tobacco grown on Guadeloupe at ten *sols* per lb. (50 *l.t.* per quintal), a very attractive price by the standards of all that was to follow. When prices collapsed after the glut imports into Europe in 1638, the now alarmed tobacco growers recognized that something drastic had to be done. On 26 May 1639, Sir Thomas Warner, governor of the English half of St. Christopher, and Philippe Longvilliers de Poincy, governor-general of the French West Indies, signed an agreement by which all tobacco growing in either half of the island on 31 October/10 November 1639 was to be pulled up and no more planted for eighteen months. It was hoped that this agreement would be observed on the other islands as well, but the Dutch do not seem to have cooperated and the French officials on Guadeloupe considered their island exempt because of their agreement with the merchants of Dieppe.[12]

The disastrous prices of 1638–39 drove the settlers first to other known commodities such as cotton, indigo, and roucou. It was, however, precisely at this time—1639—that Trezel, a Dutch merchant at Rouen, was engaged by the West Indies company to introduce the planting and processing of sugar into Martinique. In the course of the 1640's, sugar cultivation was also introduced into Guadeloupe and St. Christopher. Its progress was at first very slow because, while tobacco could be and was grown by the poorest free white settlers, sugar then needed both capital equipment and slaves. At first, the only slaves most French settlers could get were those they could buy from Dutch or English traders.[13] Nevertheless, the decades 1640–70 saw a silent revolution throughout most of the French Windward Islands: the gradual retreat from tobacco, experiments with cotton and indigo, and, most striking, the inexorable advance of sugar, slowed only by the limits of the available supplies of capital and slave labor. These changes were not a matter of policy but of market economics. Tobacco exhausted its soil quickly and required an abundance of cheap land available on St. Domingue or in Virginia but not on the smaller islands of the Lesser Antilles. Then too the price of tobacco moved generally downward in the century from the 1630's to the 1730's. The abandonment of tobacco was an experience common to the English, French, and Dutch islands. Even vast Brazil suffered.[14] Only in Virginia and Maryland where land was cheap and where there were no feasible alternative crops did tobacco production continue to grow throughout the seventeenth century, even in the face of falling prices.[15]

The precise chronology by which tobacco yielded place to sugar in the Lesser Antilles between 1640 and 1670 is, however, difficult to establish. As early as 1640, the Jesuit Bouton foretold the end of the preeminence of tobacco because of its low price and perishability and the new sugar fad.[16] Profits of doom are often aforetimes. Sugar required too much capital for most small planters; people who couldn't do any better soon adjusted their horizons to the new lower prices of tobacco, even while complaining; the problem of spoilage was met by soaking the tobacco in various preservative fluids, spinning or twisting the leaves into a long cord which was then rolled onto a stick much as thread is wound about a spool. This method seems to have come into the French West Indies from Brazil. We soon find in the French islands a class of skilled workers known as "torqueurs" or spinners who were entitled to one-tenth the weight of their output for their troubles.[17] The resulting product was well liked for chewing, less so for smoking, and was to be at a serious disadvantage vis-à-vis the dried leaf of Virginia when taste in Europe at the end of the century went over to snuff.

Thus, when Maurile de St. Michel visited Guadeloupe in 1647, he reported that the governor made sugar, but that the average planter was still raising tobacco.[18] He was amazed at the number of English, French, and Dutch vessels that came for this tobacco.[19] The same theme was repeated in the first (1658) edition of Rochefort's *History of the Antilles,* with particular reference to St. Christopher.[20] Yet signs that sugar was gaining were not missing. Up to 1661, taxes and public salaries in the islands were payable in tobacco. In that year, the law was altered to provide for optional payment in tobacco or sugar. Thereafter the rate of change seems to have accelerated. (By 1679–80, tobacco payments had virtually disappeared except on St. Domingue.)[21] In 1669–74, on the eve of the tobacco monopoly, Guadeloupe produced 80,000–100,000 lb. of tobacco a year, equivalent in weight to its production of cotton or ginger, but negligible compared to the millions of pounds of sugar produced by its 113 *sucreries*.[22] (By contrast, a single ship had carried 250,000 lb. of tobacco from St. Christopher to La Rochelle in 1646.)[23] At Martinique, in 1671, some 107,000 square yards of arable were devoted to victuals, 76,700 to sugar and only 36,400 to tobacco. Only in the neighborhoods of Marigot, Le Prêcheur, and the famous Macouba did the acreage devoted to tobacco exceed that given over to sugar.[24] At La Rochelle, during 1670–75, sugar accounted for nine-tenths of imports from the West

Indies by weight, followed by indigo (68 entries), ginger (58), cotton (46), and tobacco (36) in fifth place.[25]

Thus by 1674, on the eve of the adoption of the tobacco monopoly in France, throughout the *Isles du Vent* (particularly St. Christopher, Martinique, and Guadeloupe) tobacco had everywhere yielded pride of place to sugar but was still a significant if minor local production. The *coup de grâce* was rendered by the new monopoly. By 1680, tobacco production had virtually ceased on Martinique and Guadeloupe and the intendant-general of the Isles, Jean-Baptiste Patoulet, could report that 4,000–5,000 small planters had been deprived of their livelihood.[26] The governor-general de Blénac and the intendant-general, Michel Begon (Patoulet's successor), reported in 1685 that all the *Isles du Vent* had given up tobacco so completely that they were obliged to import what they needed for their own consumption from St. Domingue. They wished the islanders would resume making spun tobacco and *tabac en andouilles* (small rolls for chewing and smoking) in the Brazilian fashion if only to sell to Acadia and Canada (where the Indians preferred Brazil tobacco); they also wished that the small French islands would try making dried leaf tobacco in imitation of the sort the English made at Antigua—and in the Chesapeake—so that France would not have to go to England for the leaf needed for snuff, then a rather new fashion.[27] In fact, there seems to have been something of a revival of tobacco planting in the lesser French islands by the end of the century, but chiefly for local consumption. (Labat, writing ca. 1700, reports some planting almost everywhere.)[28] Only St. Christopher tobacco continued to be known in world markets, at least till almost the end of the century; but the tobacco still grown on the French part of that island was probably marketed surreptitiously through the English part.[29]

Patoulet's complaint in 1680 that the decline of tobacco cultivation left thousands of small men without a livelihood may have been exaggerated but it did reflect the profound social reconstruction that was changing the smaller French islands from settlements of a numerous white peasantry to lands of large plantations with a predominantly slave population. This was the social meaning of the transition from tobacco to sugar. For a time it seemed that the great exception was St. Domingue. With its much more extensive territories, its ill-disciplined population—part settlers, part buccaneers, in considerable part both—the French end of Hispaniola was for most of the seventeenth century too disordered a place to attract investment in slaves or sugar refining plants. Thus it remained peculiarly the land of the small white settler and of the crops favored by such. Its free population was considerably augmented after 1660 by migration from the Windward Islands where free land was now gone and small men found it difficult to compete with the encroaching sugar plantations, but easy to sell out and move. In retrospect, we can see that the social evolution of St. Domingue was merely one or two generations behind that of the smaller islands. This very lag meant that about 1660–74 tobacco production, declining elsewhere, was still rising on St. Domingue.[30] Thus, the real story—or tragedy—of the impact of the monopoly of 1674 on the West Indies is the tale of St. Domingue.

Colbert in Search of a Policy, 1661–74

There is no particular reason why Colbert on his arrival in power in 1661 should have had any policy toward tobacco. Considering the many great problems facing him concerning subsistence, rural poverty, taxation, industries to be developed, and shipping and commercial activity to be wrenched from the Dutch, tobacco was a minor issue indeed. Nevertheless, like countless other minor issues, it eventually received considerable attention from the great minister. Yet, these assembled bits of attention did not necessarily add up to a policy; in fact, as we shall see, they were not to any degree mutually consistent.

Colbert, as every textbook reader knows, attached enormous, probably excessive importance to colonial trade and navigation. This can be shown to be part of a broader policy of economy building; yet it was also a matter of national prestige. When he came to power, a considerable part of the trade and carrying business of the French West Indies was in the hands of the Dutch. Dutch traders sold manufactured goods and food to the colonists more cheaply than did their French competitors, they offered higher prices for West Indian goods, and quoted cheaper freight rates to planters who wished to ship their produce back to Europe on their own account. In the case of tobacco, the freight rates offered by the Dutch in the 1650's were only one-ninth the cargo by weight—a very modest freight—with free passage thrown in for anyone shipping 3,000 lb. For many French planters, taking advantage of such economies meant shipping one's tobacco and other goods to Flushing or Middleburg rather than to La Rochelle or Nantes.[31] In 1664, Colbert estimated that the Dutch drew from the French West Indies two million *l.t.* worth of sugar and one million *l.t.* worth of tobacco and other goods each year.[32] His answer to this problem is well known: by numerous pieces of royal legislation, from 1664 the Dutch and other foreigners were progressively excluded from the French islands and the French settlers obliged to sell their produce to French merchants or to send them to France for sale.[33] At the same time, the free movement of French merchants to and among the islands was hindered by the special privileges granted to the new West India Company, that of 1664–74.[34] Such policies restricted competition and had the effect of lowering the prices offered the planters for their tobacco and other goods and of raising freight charges and the costs of imported supplies. Intrinsically, there is no reason why the growers of tobacco should have suffered any more during the years of Colbert's company than the growers of other products. In fact, tobacco was yielding place to other crops in all the islands except St. Domingue during these years. In retrospect, we may explain this by reference to such factors as soil exhaustion, overproduction, declining prices of tobacco on world markets, and the greater profitability of other crops as labor and capital became available. To contemporaries, however, it often seemed that tobacco suffered more than other crops from the new state policies applied after 1664.

One state reaction to this distress, we shall see, was for the government to intervene and fix freight rates.[35] Another was to revive an older policy that attempted to improve the quality of the tobacco raised in the French islands. As was the case in regulating many industries in France, official opinion felt that the sequence of overproduction, glut, declining prices, and declining production was caused fundamentally by market resistance to products of poor quality. If the quality of the tobacco could be raised to the minimum demanded by most consumers, then world markets could and would take at attractive prices all that the islands produced. Quality control, however, was rather difficult for French West Indian tobacco which was usually grown by many small settlers and which was not marketed in the leaf (an easily inspected condition) but was spun and rolled before sale. This processing allegedly preserved it better for its long ocean voyage and long wait before use; in fact, by concealing the inner leaf, spinning and rolling made numerous frauds possible.

By the 1660's, there was a well-established policy in the islands, probably going back to the 1640's, requiring all tobacco before being sold and shipped to be weighed at public scales and viewed by public inspectors who had power to seize and destroy any inferior or fraudulently packed tobacco.[36] It was realized that the practice of using tobacco as money encouraged planters and traders to push into circulation the worst tobacco they had on hand in payment of debts expressed only as so many pounds of tobacco. To prevent this, Bertrand d'Ogeron, governor of St. Domingue and Tortuga, issued an *ordonnance* in September 1669, ending the use of tobacco as money and requiring all debts to be settled either in cash or in drafts on France against the produce of tobacco consigned there for sale. The *ordonnance* was not enforced, however, and the customary use of tobacco as money continued.[37]

A much more comprehensive attack on the problem was attempted by Jean-Charles de Baas, governor-general of the French West Indies, in his *ordonnance* of 5 February 1671. Lest poor quality be caused by inadequate attention in cultivation, de Baas limited production to 500 plants per laborer, slave or free—a limitation comparable to some later adopted in the Chesapeake, but equally ineffective. Standards were prescribed, including those for cultivating the growing plants, for gathering the leaf, for drying, and for spinning. The leaf was not to be submerged but salt water could be sprinkled on the rolls; the sticks in the center might not be more than two pounds in weight, the entire roll not more than sixty pounds; old leaf might not be spun in with new.[38] These were to remain the ideal standards of manufacture as long as roll tobacco remained in demand in Europe.

The government in Paris seems to have been aware of and approved these efforts to limit production and control quality. Hearing about attempts to grow tobacco in Canada, Colbert instructed the new intendant departing for Quebec in 1672 that the government did not want such planting; it would only hurt the West Indian colonies. The settlers in Canada had much better things to do with their time.[39]

Another way of solving the problem of glut, of course, would be to find greater markets in Europe. Before Colbert's time, the transit trade through France to other markets was difficult because French import duties were relatively high (compared to the Dutch) and French law gave few free entrepôt facilities or drawbacks, but frequently charged export as well as import duties on goods in transit.[40] Exemptions, such as those made for the Company of the American Islands in 1642, were neither permanent nor general.[41] Colbert, however, understood this problem. When the new West India Company was formed in 1664, its charter (confirmed by an *arrêt du conseil* of 26 August 1665) gave it the privilege of absolute free entrepôt for goods in transit through France between the West Indies and foreign countries.[42] An *arrêt du conseil* of 10 September 1668 extended this privilege to the goods of private merchants licensed by the company to trade in the West Indies.[43]

This freedom of entrepôt was very much to the point, for there seems to have been something of a market for French West Indian tobacco in the Baltic. (French domestic tobacco was exported to Italy and the Mediterranean littoral.) When Queen Hedwig Eleanora of Sweden issued a proclamation in 1665 regulating the prices at which tobacco might be sold by the local monopoly, French tobacco was one of the three specified imported grades—and the cheapest:

Fine twisted Virginia tobacco—8 copper marks per lb.
Medium heavy tobacco twisted from Dutch leaves—7 c/mks. per lb.
Heavy tobacco twisted from French leaves—4 c/mks. per lb.

As late as 1673 we find reference to an English ship carrying sixty rolls of French tobacco to Sweden.[44] This marketability seems to have been general throughout the Baltic. The merchant brothers Formont, surveying Baltic trade in 1668, reported that Martinique tobacco always sold well at Danzig and Königsberg. A few small shipments of French domestic had also been sent there experimentally. About 1670, Königsberg alone imported 100,000 lb. weight of French tobacco.[45]

Colbert naturally viewed these developments with favor. In his report to the king on public finance in 1670, he specifically boasted of the growing reexport trades in sugar and tobacco.[46] He was on the lookout for new markets. In 1670, he wrote to Mouslier, the French resident at Geneva, asking him to find out the prices of sugar and tobacco in Switzerland and whether they were generally imported from Holland or elsewhere; he wanted such information to see whether new markets could be developed for the returns from the French East and West Indian trades.[47]

Markets in the Baltic and dream-markets in Switzerland were all very well, but ultimately the prosperity of the tobacco trade in the French West Indies had to depend upon the size of the market in France itself. With consumption developing only slowly, much would depend upon French fiscal policy. All the other objectives of Colbert's policy were to be peripheral; the fisc alone was to be central.

As explained in Chapter 1, both foreign and French colonial tobacco had from 1632 been subject to duties rising from 7 to 23 *l.t.* per quintal on entering the territories of the *cinq grosses fermes*. These were by 1660 equal perhaps to ad valorem rates of 33 1/3–100 percent on the West Indian price or perhaps 25–75 percent on the price in French ports. This was a high duty by French or Dutch standards though comparable to contemporary English practice. When the new French West India Company (*Compagnie d'Occident*) was established in 1664, however, it was granted a reduction of one-half the duties on the goods it imported from or exported to its colonies.[48] A more significant concession was obtained from Colbert's tariff of 18 September 1664; by it, import duties on tobacco from the French colonies were set at only four *l.t.* per quintal while foreign tobaccos paid thirteen *l.t.* per quintal.[49]

When word reached the West Indies of the establishment in May 1664 of the new *Compagnie d'Occident* with monopoly privileges, and of the concession to it of a rebate of one-half the duties normally collected on imports of sugar, tobacco, and other goods, the governor-general of the islands, Alexandre de Prouville, seigneur des deux Tracys (generally called simply "de Tracy"), issued a set of *règlements* on 17 March 1665, governing trade under the new monopoly conditions. Under the misapprehension that the company was still exempt from one-half the import duties, he fixed a uniform and quite high freight of seven *l.t.* per quintal for the carriage by the company of all sugar, indigo, and tobacco from the islands to France. Out of this, the company itself was to pay all import duties in France.[50] The company complained to the government on the grounds that they had lost the concession of half duties by the new tariff of September 1664: this argument was a bit forced since the tariff lowered the effective duty to 4 *l.t.* Nevertheless, to avoid controversy and encourage the colonial trade, an *arrêt du conseil* of 7 May 1666 reduced the duties on all sugar and tobacco imported from the French West Indies by half to only 40 *sols* per quintal.[51] Thus, the import duty on tobacco during 1666–74 was reduced to the original levels of 1621, the lowest ever.

These same years, 1666–74, which saw the highest tobacco production in the French West Indies, were years of the greatest official leniency in the regulation of colonial trade. An *arrêt* of 1 July 1671 abolished all export duties on goods shipped from France to the French West Indies and reduced from five to three percent the toll which French private merchants had to pay to the company on the sugar, indigo, and tobacco which they brought back from the islands.[52] An edict of February 1669 had established a general right of free entrepôt for French subjects and foreigners in all French ports.[53] Thus, even the tobacco brought back by a private merchant could avoid all duty if intended for reexport.

This then was the relatively favorable economic and legal position of the French West Indian tobacco trade when in the fall of 1674, the old monopoly, the West India Company of 1664–74, was abolished, and the new monopoly, the tobacco farm, was established. For the moment, there were some appearances that these changes did not constitute a basic reversal of the government policy which had hitherto encouraged the West Indian tobacco trade. By the terms of the lease of the new monopoly, French colonial tobacco was to be sold wholesale and retail for only one-half the price of other imported tobaccos.[54] There were gestures at lesser concessions, too. On 1 December 1674, the same day on which the edict[55] was issued dissolving the West India Company and opening the trade freely to all French subjects, an *arrêt du conseil*,[56] was issued confirming to private merchants all the privileges previously granted to the company. In addition, the farmers of the *domaine d'Occident*, who took over the tax revenues of the defunct company, were only to pay one-half or 20 *sols* per quintal on the sugar and tobacco which they brought back from the islands. That very same day, the tobacco monopoly granted to the Jean Breton company went into effect.

Whatever the government intended or pretended, the new monopoly, necessitated as it was by the exigencies of war finance, constituted a basic reversal in the existing policy toward the West Indian tobacco trade. The West India company of 1664 had never had even a nominal, not to mention an effective, monopsony (right of exclusive purchase). Yet monopsony was inherent in the new tobacco farm from its inception. In an era of declining world tobacco prices, this could have only the direst portent for the incomes of French tobacco growers. The protectionist policy embodied in the tariff of 1664 would have tended to give French domestic and West Indian tobacco growers a price somewhat above world market prices for equivalent qualities. There was no reason why a monopsony should pay anything above the world price. Where quality was unsatisfactory, it could refuse to buy at all. If merchants wanted to reexport their tobacco (as they were entitled to do without restriction by the *déclaration* of 27 September 1674), the agents of the monopoly-monopsony could discover a thousand stratagems of delay in order to bring pressure on the merchant to sell at the proffered price. The import of all this was made quite clear in the experience of St. Domingue after 1674.

The Fate of St. Domingue, 1674–1709

Most accounts suggest that the St. Domingue tobacco trade was at least expanding if not fully prosperous in the years immediately preceding the establishment of the monopoly in 1674. Land was still easily obtainable and the very factors which were driving the smaller settlers from the Lesser Antilles were drawing them to "the coasts" of the greater island. For men with relatively few slaves or servants, meager capital but abundant land, tobacco was still the most suitable crop. It is difficult, though, to say precisely how much tobacco might have been grown on St. Domingue at this time. In the 1680's, polemicists attacking the monopoly suggested that as much as thirteen million pounds of tobacco were grown yearly on St. Domingue before 1674.[57] No contemporary evidence would support such a figure. Bertrand d'Ogeron, the governor of Tortuga and St. Domingue who first established order and the reality of French authority over much of those lawless coasts, reported in 1669 that local production had reached 1.2 million lb.[58] A very well informed memoir writer of 1692 suggested a production of about three million pounds for St. Domingue in 1674.[59] Putting this evidence together with that above on the lesser islands, one might well hazard that during 1661–74 tobacco production was rising on St. Domingue, while declining on the other islands; as of 1674, at most it could have equaled three million pounds for the whole French West Indies; of this, perhaps 2.5 million should be assigned to St. Domingue and not more than 0.5 million to all the lesser islands. Though three million pounds seems like a modest production compared to that of the Chesapeake (16 million French lb. in 1672), it was probably as much as the total exportation of Brazil in this generation.[60]

The rapid growth of tobacco production on St. Domingue from about 1.2 million lb. in 1669 to about 2.5 million lb. in 1674 was felt in the markets and led to frequent complaints of overproduction. In 1670–71, the settlers on St. Domingue rose against their governor, Bertrand d'Ogeron, when he tried in the name of the West India Company to stop their trading with the Dutch.[61] During the winter of 1670–71, Gabaret, the naval commander responsible for driving off the Dutch and putting down the rebellion, submitted a plan for suppressing the insurrection without bloodshed. He pointed out that the rebels about Cul-de-Sac were all tobacco growers who traded their tobacco to foreign vessels for supplies and arms. He suggested placing a naval vessel of thirty to thirty-six guns on this coast from February when the tobacco was cut till mid-July when it began to spoil if not shipped off. This would prevent the planters from trading with the Dutch and would bring effective pressure on them to come to terms before their tobacco spoiled. To use military force, by contrast, would only drive the rebels in fury to Jamaica.[62] Tactics very much like this were successful, for the settlers had returned to "obedience" by mid-1671. There was a general pardon.

When Gabaret returned to France in June 1671, he sent to Colbert a memoir on the condition of St. Domingue. He doubted that very much of a colony could be built up in the south around Cul-de-Sac because the area was not suited for sugar or indigo and "the quantity of tobacco which could be made there alone . . . would bring the price so low that the merchant finding it profitless would cease to be interested in trading thither."[63] Ogeron too was quite aware of the overproduction problem for when one of his officers, Renou, returned to France that summer, he included in the list of things about which he should speak to Colbert, "Ways of facilitating the sale of tobacco which is made in such quantity."[64] He explained that since St. Domingue raised three or four times as much tobacco as could be sold in France, ways had to be found to sell the surplus elsewhere.[65] By the next year, Ogeron was blaming the tobacco surplus and low prices for the wretchedness of the settlers.[66]

There were also serious questions about the quality of St. Domingue tobacco, even in its supposed hour of greatest prosperity. There was no market for it at all in important sections of northern France from 1668 to 1674.[67] A memoir of 1672 by someone familiar with local conditions explained that much of this may have been due to quality. Because tobacco continued to be used as money on St. Domingue and tended to circulate at one price, there was little incentive to improve quality but great incentive to expand the quantity produced. It was in any event very difficult to tell about the quality of roll tobacco without undoing the roll. The *ordonnance* of 1671 was likely to be of only limited effectiveness. The memorialist saw no way of inducing the planters to grow less and better tobacco short of demonetizing the crop so that tobacco could be sold on the market at varying prices according to its quality.[68] (Ogeron's demonetization *ordonnance* of 1669 had not been enforced.)

Plagued with such problems of overproduction, low prices, and poor quality, St. Domingue was hardly in a strong position to meet the new troubles brought on by the tobacco monopoly of 1674. In the other islands, where tobacco cultivation was long in decline and a relatively minor part of the economy, existing trends were merely accelerated. We hear few complaints. On Tortuga and St. Domingue, however, tobacco was still the staple; for most planters changing to another commodity was not a practical alternative. The real alternatives were emigrating or buccaneering. With a war on, the last was a very easy and even legitimate choice. Whichever the course, the colony suffered. When de Pouançay, the new governor, arrived at his post in 1676, he was distressed to find many of the small planters on Tortuga talking of giving up tobacco and moving to the mainland of St. Domingue—where at least the hunting was better. If only the tobacco trade were free, he wrote, St. Domingue could load thirty tobacco ships a year.[69] The next year, he sent in a much fuller report attacking the monopoly and making it clear that the evil effects were felt not just on Tortuga, but all through St. Domingue.

Because of the monopoly, settlers everywhere were giving up tobacco and abandoning their homesteads. More than a hundred *habitations* had been given up at Cul-de-Sac alone. If only the government would go back to the old open trade, even with a high duty of ten *l.t.* per quintal (compared to the two *l.t.* per quintal last levied, 1666–74), then the settlers would all go back to work again and the high duties would oblige them to raise only the best quality. The colony would produce enough for thirty ships. He did not see how France could ever again begin new colonies, since on all the islands settlement had begun with tobacco.[70]

With the return of peace in 1678, the situation became worse. Buccaneering or filibustering was no longer privateering but piracy; the French had to suppress it to keep open their own surreptitious but desirable trade with the Spaniards. Yet, for men reduced in many cases to subsistence agriculture, piracy had its attractions. There was no chance of getting any relief from the Jean Breton tobacco monopoly company, whose own affairs were in an embarrassed condition during its last years (1678–80). De Pouançay tried to keep the smaller planters from emigrating to Dutch Curaçao or to English Jamaica by releasing letters from Bellinzani, director-general of commerce in the navy ministry, "in which he gives great hopes that the tobacco farm will be suppressed at the end of the lease [in 1680], or converted into an entry duty." By such stratagems, he wrote Colbert early in 1680, he had kept the settlers on the island for the time being, but he feared "that the colony will perish entirely within three years if that monopoly persists." He warned the minister that the information and excuses furnished by the tobacco farmers were not to be believed, that "there were no rigors or hardships which they had not exercised against the poor settlers in this land in order to get their goods almost for nothing, without considering their expenses for manufacture and transport to France." On the other hand, the excessively high prices they charged at resale in France had diminished consumption there by one-half. Once more, the governor asked for the restoration of open trade, with an entry duty and a tax on the domestic growth in France—or, better still, a prohibition after the English fashion of all tobacco growing at home.[71] All that the government would concede was a relatively meaningless confirmation of the right of free entrepôt in France for colonial tobacco.[72]

By January 1681, de Pouançay had given up all hope for tobacco on St. Domingue, in view of the overproduction and depressed prices.[73] A few months later, however, he and the settlers tried another tack. On orders from de Blénac, governor-general of the islands, in May 1681 he called a meeting of the officeholders and principal inhabitants of St. Domingue. The assembled worthies drew up a memorial to Colbert blaming all their distress on the low price which the monopolists in France paid for their tobacco, forcing the merchants trading to the island to charge more for the supplies they brought and forcing many of the inhabitants to give up agriculture for filibustering. They asked for the abolition of the monopoly, or alternatively for the prohibition both of tobacco growing in France and of the importation of foreign tobaccos. (They wished to meet the power of monopsony with a monopoly of their own.) On their part, they would agree to regulate the quantity and quality of their production: no settler would be allowed to have more than four slaves (unless he had one white indentured servant for each surplus slave to keep up the white population), the amount of tobacco sold would be strictly limited by legal quotas and only large leaf could be marketed.[74]

In a covering letter, de Pouançay stressed the importance of restricting tobacco production in St. Domingue, forcing the settlers to turn from their monoculture to such products as sugar, cotton, cacao, and indigo. He suggested a limitation of 4,000 plants for each field hand, free or slave. (The *ordonnance* of governor-general de Baas in 1671—of which little more was ever heard—had called for a limit of 5,000.) He also wanted a royal *ordonnance* prohibiting the marketing of *rejettons* or leaves of second and third growth from the same roots. This would limit quantity as well as raise quality.[75] These seconds were in all countries considered inferior to first growth and when mixed in with the latter gave the resulting product a bad reputation. The marketing of seconds had been prohibited in Virginia as early as 1632 and in Maryland in 1657,[76] but remained characteristic of French colonial production throughout the *ancien régime*. When Labat visited the French West Indies, about 1700, the matter was still subject to much local debate. In his view:

> The settlers won't stop mixing them [the seconds] with the first leaves, their economy persuading them that they can get from a plant all that it can produce, and that anything is all right, when one knows how to get it by.... It is this poorly understood economy and this mixture of second and third growths which have ruined the reputation of the tobacco of the islands, which had always been equal to the best tobaccos of Brazil in the days when they made them with care and honesty.[77]

At the time—1681—de Pouançay was unable to persuade the home government to intervene, nor could he persuade the settlers voluntarily to adopt any form of effective *quality* control. Some sort of *quantity* control was adopted, however, for the next year de Pouançay reported that the total refusal of many merchants to buy tobacco had forced the settlers to agree to limit production to twelve rolls per field hand. At the normal 50 lb. each, this should have meant a quota of about 600 lb. per laborer but it would have been relatively easy for "cheaters" to make their rolls larger. More significantly, he reported that many disgusted settlers were turning finally to indigo and cotton, a few only to sugar, some to cacao, though many were also imitating their Spanish neighbors by taking up the large-scale raising of cattle, sheep, and goats.[78]

The inability of de Pouançay to influence the formation of central policy on tobacco set the pattern for the efforts of his successors as governors of Tortuga and St. Domingue. He himself—and Colbert—died in 1683. His successor de Cussy (1683-91) upon his arrival in April 1684 was at first absorbed primarily in his struggle to restore order and suppress filibustering. The initiative in economic matters passed to the intendant Michel Begon and to St. Laurent, governor of St. Christopher since about 1666. They had submitted a number of joint memoirs on economic subjects since Begon's arrival in 1683. On the eve of their joint return to France in 1685, they prepared for Seignelay a special report on St. Domingue, pointing out the importance of tobacco in establishing a population of settled agriculturalists on that island. Ever since the establishment of the monopoly, though, it had been impossible to earn a living from tobacco. They suggested as a remedy that the planters of St. Domingue would be prepared to pay to the king one-quarter of their tobacco landed in France if the monopoly and all other duties were removed.[79]

On their return to France in the spring of 1685, Begon and St. Laurent found that the situation seemed suddenly to have become propitious for changes in the tobacco monopoly. Seignelay and his deputy Morel were conducting their inquiries, and memorials were coming in from important mercantile groups highly critical of the tobacco monopoly. One from some merchants of Paris blamed the whole piracy problem in St. Domingue on the ill effects of the tobacco monopoly which left the poor *habitants* with nothing to do but turn filibuster or emigrate.[80] Much the same arguments were made in the memorial from Rouen, with the startling "statistic" added that before the monopoly, France (changed by another hand to read "Rouen alone") had consumed 60,000 rolls (three million lb.) of St. Domingue tobacco, but then only 6,000-7,000 rolls (300,000-350,000 lb.). Seignelay was curious about this and wrote around to other ports for comparable information. From Nantes, he was told that imports in the south Breton ports had fallen from 20,000 rolls (one million lb.) before the monopoly to only 2,600 rolls (130,000 lb.); from St. Malo, that imports had dropped from 15,000 rolls to less than 2,500 and that the general production of St. Domingue had declined from 200,000 rolls (ten million lb.) to only 20,000 rolls (one million lb.). Rouen suggested 260,000 rolls (13 million lb.) for the 1674 production of all the French West Indies. The figures given for current activity are eminently reasonable; those for pre-1674 conditions as suggested above belong to the world of airy speculation. (The merchants wanted to show that the trade had declined to a tenth its former state in order to suggest that if the monopoly were abolished and the trade made open under a modest duty, the volume of activity would increase tenfold and the king's revenue be no loser.) Only Bordeaux, which hadn't perhaps received "the message," admitted to an importation of all colonial and foreign tobaccos before 1674 of as little as 2,000 rolls or 100,000 lb. Seignelay and Morel were nevertheless sufficiently impressed to undertake during the winter of 1685-86 their unsuccessful negotiations to find a syndicate of merchants prepared to take over the tobacco farm on an open trade basis.[81]

By February 1686 it had become apparent that nothing was going to come of the negotiations with the metropolitan merchants, and Seignelay turned to the St. Domingue proposals. Begon and St. Laurent had submitted, most probably after their return to France, a further memoir repeating with greater detail their picture of the woes of St. Domingue under the monopoly and their proposal for abolishing the monopoly and establishing in its place a toll of one-quarter of the tobacco imported, paid in kind.[82] On 28 February 1686, Seignelay wrote about this scheme to de Cussy, governor of St. Domingue, enclosing a copy of the Begon-St. Laurent memoir. The minister, skeptical no doubt of the merchants' figures, asked for more precise information on production and alleged quality deterioration.[83]

De Cussy, it would seem, did not welcome Seignelay's interest in the Begon-St. Laurent proposals. De Cussy, it should be noted, was the only governor of St. Domingue in the two generations following 1665 who never once made formal representations to the home government about the distressed condition of the tobacco planters in his government. At this juncture he simply gave instructions for the local officers in the principal divisions of his command to assemble the settlers in their districts and read to them the letter from Seignelay and the Begon-St.Laurent proposals. The surviving replies from Tortuga and the Cape, though obsequiously loyal, both paint in pathetic colors the wretchedness of the settlers and plead an utter incapacity to pay the suggested duty of one-quarter of their tobacco. That from Tortuga was quite vague, that from the Cape interestingly specific: a typical household of ten or twelve persons would include only three or four slaves or *engagés* capable of working in the fields, who at most could make 100 rolls of tobacco (ca. 5,000 lb.). From this, one-tenth would have to be paid to the artisan who spun the tobacco and one-twentieth to the artisan who rolled it, making fifteen rolls together. Then, one roll per head in the household would have to be paid to the local surgeon and another roll per head for the support of the *curé* and the church: between them, another twenty to twenty-four rolls. Freight at one *sol* per lb. would be the equivalent of one-fifth the value of the tobacco shipped. Then, there was the pilferage and damage on shipboard. Thus, with a quarter going to the king, almost two-thirds would be gone before the consigning planter received any returns:

Tobacco Rolls

15	for spinning and rolling
12	to surgeon
12	for church
12	for freight
1	for pilferage
12	to king
36	left to consigning planter
100	total for typical household

The example is a bit forced. Many of the smaller *habitants,* whose households surely were not that large, could spin and roll their own. Most planters too would seem to have sold, when they could, to merchants in the colony and not to have consigned on their own account. The hostility of the planters to the scheme, though based partly on ignorance, probably represents the advice given by the merchants, in a time of higher prices, to the more substantial planters. They were afraid, as the Cape memorial specifically said, that the one-quarter paid to the king would suffice for the consumption of the kingdom and that the importers would be forced to reexport the rest, thus getting no real benefit from their tax.[84] A more general reply to the same effect was made in the name of all the settlers on St. Domingue by the *conseil souverain*.[85]

During the remainder of the governorship of de Cussy, there was hardly another murmur out of the island, though there is evidence that all was not well.[86] In November 1686, the meat dealers had to be constrained by an order of the council at Petit Goave to accept tobacco in payment for meat as hitherto.[87] In 1688, the weather was bad and so little tobacco made that the clergy had to be paid in indigo, cotton, and other goods.[88] In 1689, de Cussy could report that the more substantial planters were going over to indigo, reputedly almost as good as that of Guatemala. If prices kept up, they would be on a very solid footing indeed, but he feared for the smaller settlers who knew only tobacco. In a rare note of alarm, he reported that these small men could scarce earn enough from tobacco to clothe themselves and he feared a revolt if things weren't put right.[89]

The extremely short crop of 1687–88 had repercussions at home. The planters would seem to have attempted to recoup some of this loss and to take advantage of the higher prices by recourse to those old frauds and irregularities designed to increase the weight of tobacco sold. The metropolitan merchants, despairing perhaps of the pro-*colon* mentality of Seignelay, complained to the controller-general Le Peletier who took the unusual initiative of writing directly to the *intendant-général des îles,* Dumaitz de Goimpy: the minister reported the complaints of poor quality and suggested that perhaps a new *ordonnance* was needed. De Goimpy replied rather brashly and stupidly that there was nothing wrong with St. Domingue tobacco that higher prices wouldn't mend. The low prices offered by the monopoly not only discouraged the planters but induced the merchants in France to hold their tobacco back from the market to try to raise the price; it was in their French warehouses or in their ships that the spoilage took place. With an adequate price, fixed in advance, he would guarantee the quantity and quality desired without any new legislation.[90] It was not the sort of answer Le Peletier could have expected or desired, but in any event he was to leave office shortly thereafter.

We have a rare insight into the precise character of the market for St. Domingue tobacco in France at this time in a unique account prepared for Seignelay's office by the United General Farms. It specifies the quantities of all tobacco imported from St. Domingue into France during 1683–88, the amount purchased by the united farms and the prices paid.

TABLE II

Tobacco Imported into France from St. Domingue and Purchased by the Farm, 1683–88[91]

Year	Imported	Purchased (Total)	Purchased (Prices Specified)	Price (Average) (per quintal)	Price (Median) (per quintal)
	rolls	rolls	rolls	l.t.	l.t.
1683	47,822	8,913	8,913	26.2	25
1684	17,213	11,211	11,211	27.8	25
1685	25,153	6,300	4,112	33.0	25
1686	35,590	14,126	11,426	30.0	30
1687	45,500	6,781	6,772	31.1	31
1688	12,767	7,955	6,781	22.0	22
Total	184,045	55,286	49,215		
Average, yearly	30,674	9,214	8,202	28.1	27

The first thing that may be observed from this table is the extreme sensitivity of prices to supply even under conditions of monopsony. We must of course see the effects of the importation of any one year (the greater part coming in the second half of the year) as influencing not the prices of that year but rather of the following year. The heavy importations of 1683 are reflected in low prices that year and the next. The exceptionally small importation of 1684 and the less than normal import of 1685 led to a substantial rise in prices in 1685 sustained through 1686 and 1687. This ultimately brought forth from St. Domingue the very heavy shipments of 1687 which sent prices tumbling in 1688. These prices were all low compared to prices earlier in the century, but not inexplicably so. The median price for 1683 was 25 *l.t.* per quintal or five sols per lb. At 13.3:1, this would be equivalent to 4*d*.1/2 sterling per lb. In February 1683, the London price currents show Antigua leaf (the only West Indian variety cited) as 4*d*. 3/4 per lb. ashore. As duty was roughly 1*d*. 3/4 per lb. net, this was equivalent to 3*d*. per lb. before duty. Thus, St. Domingue roll sold to the monopoly in France in 1683 realized a considerably better price than Antigua leaf sold that same year on the London free market. (The French pound, of course, was 9 percent heavier than the English pound.) Another London price-current for December 1684 shows about the same price for St. Christopher roll tobacco as that cited the previous year for Antigua leaf. There was however no rise in the London price (excluding duty) in 1685 to correspond to the rise in French prices in 1685.[92] Thus, it would seem that when supplies were abundant, the world price acted as something of a floor for French prices; but when shortage developed in France, the prices paid by the monopoly could rise considerably above the world price. This is what we would expect since the French merchants who imported the tobacco from St. Domingue (either on their own account or on consignment) had the right to reexport to foreign countries; merchants in London or Amsterdam would not however be likely to venture shipments to a monopsonized market unless specifically so ordered. Thus, however much the planters of St. Domingue might complain of falling prices, they could not with justice then claim that the monopoly forced upon them prices below open market levels.

As significant as the price data are the quantity data. In an average year during 1683–88, there was shipped from St. Domingue to France over 30,000 rolls or roughly 1.5 million lb. of which the farm bought less than 10,000 rolls or 500,000 lb. If we remember that production at St. Domingue had before the establishment of the monopoly been rising from about 1.2 million lb. p.a. in 1669 to 2.5 or at most three million pounds by 1674, we can see that production there had in fact dropped 40–50 percent from its peak but was still a considerable quantity even by premonopoly standards. What is most revealing of all is the fact that the monopoly purchased less than one-third of the tobacco landed in France from St. Domingue. Here we see most concretely the importance of the northern markets developed in the 1660's; here we also see the importance of the various legal concessions of free *entrepôt* and a good explanation of the fury of many merchants and other complainants against the dilatory tactics of the agents of the monopoly in giving permits for reexport, tactics which sellers could only interpret as devices to force down local prices, particularly when, as in 1685–87, prices were abnormally high.

The stratagems of the monopoly delaying reexports were in fact the subject of a formal complaint from the consuls of La Rochelle in 1686 and an investigation by the intendant there,[93] and to them were devoted extensive sections of two similar memoirs of about 1687–89, one by Chauvel, a merchant of Dieppe, the other by Blondel, an official. As soon as a vessel arrived in a French port with tobacco from the West Indies, it was boarded by agents of the farm who supervised the unloading of the tobacco into special warehouses under the farmer's key. The monopoly, it was alleged, was slow to buy and even slower to release for reexport. The merchant frequently lost his foreign market through such delays. Appeals to Paris and lawsuits were at times needed to get the tobacco released. Frequently, the merchants gave in and sold the tobacco to the monopoly on its own terms.

Chauvel admitted that there had been a boom in imports in the mid-1680's. The pacification policy of de Cussy had induced many of the *flibustiers* to return to St. Domingue, a settled life and tobacco cultivation. News of this induced some French merchants to send out additional ships to the coast in 1685 and 1686. Even so, the trade was regarded as so little profitable that in most cases the merchants gave instructions to their supercargoes not to buy the tobacco but to take it back only on freight and consignment at the planter's risk. After local tolls, freight, and handling charges had been deducted, there was often little or nothing left of the sale price for the consigning planter. In certain cases, the tobacco had to be abandoned on arrival in France, for sale would not even meet freight charges. The consigners were understandably deeply disappointed. Many would be forced to return to their former evil ways of buccaneering on the Guinea coast and against the Spaniards, both so prejudicial to legitimate French trade. Chauvel could see no way of preventing a reversion to filibustering unless the legitimate tobacco (and sugar) trades were made more attractive.[94]

Whether a consigning planter had his tobacco sold for a good price or abandoned for the freight was not just a matter of luck. It might also depend upon the quality of the tobacco and the care with which it had been prepared and packed. That some had to be abandoned was not just an allegation of Chauvel and Blondel. Apoil, a merchant who received many consignments from St. Domingue (and was also de Cussy's personal agent), submitted to the secretary of state for the navy in 1687 a list of 235 rolls consigned to him from St. Domingue which had to be abandoned in French ports or which were sold in Amsterdam for less than the freight and charges.[95]

The government's response was nothing but a few paper concessions. When an *arrêt du conseil* of 9 March 1688 repealing the general right of free entrepôt established by an *arrêt* of 6 April 1680 was interpreted by the farmers-general as applying also to tobacco (despite its special rights of transit confirmed by an *arrêt* of 8 April 1687[96] and articles xi and xii of the general tobacco *ordonnance* of July 1681), the government hastened to issue an *arrêt* on 13 July 1688 specifically confirming the right of entrepôt for tobacco under the arduous rules of 1681.[97] A further *arrêt* of 16 December 1690 gave particular privileges of unrestricted free *entrepôt* for tobacco and other goods to the Senegal Company (which sold its slaves in the West Indies for these goods).[98] None of these orders touched the crucial problem of delay. When, however, the new Senegal Company was chartered, its letters-patent of March 1696 were more explicit. The officers of the monopoly had thenceforth to declare within fifteen days of the arrival in France of the company's tobacco whether they intended to buy or not. At the end of this time, the Senegal Company was to have an unrestricted right of immediate reexport. Procedures were also established for fixing the prices of sale quickly.[99] For ordinary merchants, there were no such shortcuts. An anonymous memoir by a well-informed official, written about 1692 but describing conditions at the beginning of the war, saw easier reexport as the only possible and effective reform, but was still bleakly pessimistic about the future of the tobacco trade on St. Domingue.[100]

Such were the conditions at the start of the war with England in 1689. In 1688–89, the St. Domingue trade seems to have shrunk to a level (12,000–

15,000 rolls) less than half the average for 1683–88 (30,000 rolls) and perhaps only one-quarter the level of 1674. Yet, even at that level (600,000–750,000 lb), it could make a major contribution to the still modest French consumption. But the trade entered the war years in feeble condition and the war was to kill it off. Once dead, nothing that the government was prepared to do could revive it. This final blow was indubitably the result of the war itself. Hostilities of course meant that many of the small, poor, marginal settlers, the characteristic planters of tobacco, would give up agriculture for the duration and turn once more to the sea and their more interesting career of privateering.[101] Hostilities too meant the disruption of normal sea communications between St. Domingue and France. There was little point in paying the higher freight rates and risking the dangers of the sea with a commodity whose price in France might artificially be prevented from rising to reflect the new higher costs and risks. With shipping scarce and irregular, long waits for space were inevitable. It was too risky holding a perishable commodity like St. Domingue roll tobacco when other less perishable commodities could be grown instead. For shipowners who charged freight by weight, tobacco was not as attractive a cargo as the much denser sugar or indigo.

In France, the start of the war meant turning loose the privateers of St. Malo and Dunkirk on the lumbering English tobacco vessels from the Chesapeake. In Chapter 7 we shall try to calculate exactly how much English tobacco the French might have obtained by this device. Suffice it to observe here that an ordinary English tobacco ship contained more tobacco than the French imported from England in an average year before 1689. If the French captured one Chesapeake tobacco ship in ten (twenty out of 200) they obtained more tobacco than France was accustomed to import from the whole world before 1689, and at least four times the retained importation from St. Domingue in the 1680's. The worst of it all for St. Domingue was that the French consumer discovered that he liked Virginia tobacco. The dried Virginia leaf (easily preserved) was highly adaptable. It could be made into any variety of roll or twist tobacco for smoking or chewing; it was also eminently suitable for conversion into the newly fashionable snuff. The development of a mass demand for tobacco in France dates only from the introduction of Virginia tobacco in the 1690's. Once the French consumer came to know, to like and to expect Virginia tobacco in those years, he would not readily return to St. Domingue. Since the monopolists could make as much profit selling Virginia as they ever did selling St. Domingue (and control smuggling better), they would find no reason to deny the consumer what he wanted. In changed consumer tastes, the war of the 1690's was to strike the unexpected but fatal blow that extinguished forever any place for St. Domingue tobacco in the French market.

On 21 January 1691, de Cussy, governor of St. Domingue since 1684, was killed fighting the Spaniards. In June 1691, there arrived as his successor, Jean Ducasse, the future admiral, without doubt the most celebrated governor of that colony. Of the petty nobility of southwest France, he went to sea first in the service of the Senegal Company, then entered the royal navy, about 1680. His most famous achievement as governor was shaping the ill-disciplined *flibustiers* of St. Domingue into the effective force that captured and sacked Cartagena. This was the making of his own fortune and that of many of his lieutenants. (This substantial injection of capital must be seen as an important factor facilitating the extensive introduction of the more heavily capitalized sugar industry into St. Domingue in the ensuing generation.) His was a personality of remarkable force. This passionate energy bellows forth from the pages of his correspondence. Unlike the reticent de Cussy, he was to speak out vigorously on economic and social as well as on military matters.[102]

In an early letter of 1691 on economic conditions, Ducasse made it clear that the agrarian economy of St. Domingue was still quite different from that of the lesser islands. Sugar was not mentioned. The main hope was indigo which needed better customs protection in France. Cotton and hides were also staples, but the planters were still prepared to grow more than enough tobacco for French needs if unspecified but well understood conditions were met.[103] Circumstances forced Paris to ponder this offer almost immediately. In 1692, there was a five months drought on St. Domingue and most crops were severely reduced; many ships had to return to France without cargoes. The monopoly thus received almost no tobacco from St. Domingue at a stage in the war when captures by the French privateers of Virginiamen were not yet sufficiently numerous to meet all their needs. The United General Farms were thus forced in the latter part of 1692 to make representations to Pontchartrain (both controller-general and navy secretary) requesting, ironically enough, that Ducasse be instructed to use all his endeavors to encourage the settlers on St. Domingue to make more tobacco. The governor replied that he would do what he could but wished the united farms would treat the tobacco growers more encouragingly.[104] A year later he described his command as singularly cursed among French colonies because of the tobacco monopoly and the failure of the African companies to bring slaves.[105] In 1693, the monopoly for its part was so distressed by the continued failure of any tobacco to arrive from St. Domingue through the usual mercantile channels that they obtained special permission to send out a vessel on their own account to see if they could find any tobacco there. They had earlier sent out to St. Domingue an employee charged with buying what tobacco he could.[106]

Despite the virtually complete cessation of imports from St. Domingue, the monopoly seems to have gotten by during the next few years, probably from prizes, licensed imports from Holland, and greater use of inferior domestic tobacco. However, their position became very difficult in the last two years of the war—1696 and 1697—when tobacco became scarce throughout Europe and Amsterdam prices rose to their highest level in a generation, almost double that of 1688.¹⁰⁷ This inevitably sharpened the interest of the united farms in West Indian tobacco and we are not surprised to find them complaining to the government again, early in 1696, about the failure of supplies from St. Domingue. On 11 January, Pontchartrain wrote to the *munitionnaire* (military contractor) and farmer-general Jean Germain at La Rochelle, asking him to consult the merchants there about ways of getting more tobacco from St. Domingue. The merchants replied that nothing short of the abolition of the monopoly would induce the settlers on St. Domingue to return to tobacco.¹⁰⁸ A few months later, Pontchartrain's son, Jérôme Phélypeaux, held similar discussions at the same port. Realizing that there could be no thought of abolishing the monopoly midst the financial crises of the war, young Pontchartrain recommended only that the monopoly be obliged to declare within thirty days whether it wanted to buy imported tobacco; if not, export permission should be given automatically. This long-demanded entrepôt reform (conceded a few months before to the Senegal Company) would, Jérôme thought, revive merchant interest in tobacco and in turn rekindle that of the planters.¹⁰⁹ However, the same high external prices that made such a reform attractive to the merchants made it impossible for the monopoly.

Pontchartrain did nothing about his son's suggestion, but he was moved to action by distressing information sent by Ducasse from St. Domingue. Raids by the English and Spanish upon the north coast of the island had caused the settlers to abandon several *quartiers*. Ducasse was trying to resettle these areas, but found it extremely difficult to get the old *habitants* to return or new ones to take their place unless there was some crop to make their efforts worthwhile. Tobacco in these areas was traditionally the only crop for men without capital. Ducasse felt that the settlers would return to their *habitations* and to tobacco if guaranteed a price of six *écus* (eighteen *l.t.*) per quintal in the islands for tobacco of minimum acceptable quality. On 9 May 1696, Pontchartrain instructed the United General Farms to confer with de Lagny, also a farmer-general but acting here as *directeur-général du commerce* in the navy ministry, and make a joint report on the amount of tobacco the farm could take from St. Domingue, the rules which must be followed in its preparation, and related points.¹¹⁰

The united farms replied with a long and valuable account of the St. Domingue tobacco trade as it existed during the war. Since 1690, no tobacco had arrived from that island that was fit to be sold for chewing, its traditional use and that for which it fetched the best price. The small amount of tobacco that had arrived, all defective, could only be ground up for snuff, for which it was less suited and for which a lower price had to be paid. Only the carelessness of the St. Domingue planters could account for the condition in which the tobacco had arrived—"dry, odorless, rusty, stuck together, worm-eaten, sandy and almost entirely rotten." However, since the monopoly could not obtain enough Virginia prize tobacco and since there was still some demand for St. Domingue for chewing, the farmers, to encourage the return to cultivation on the island, offered to take up to 12,000 rolls (600,000 lb.) of good quality chewing tobacco at a price in France considerably above the 18 *l.t.* per quintal previously offered. Recognizing that some of the delicate St. Domingue tobacco would always spoil in the ocean crossing, they agreed to take at a lower price another thousand rolls of defective tobacco for manufacture into snuff—for a total of 13,000 rolls or 650,000 lb. Their terms were familiar. (1) An end was to be made to the fraud of putting wooden rods of up to nine or ten pounds in the center of the rolls, when only three pounds was customarily allowed for tare. The rods thenceforth were to be made according to the official standard of the island, were not to exceed three pounds in weight, were not to be made of green wood and were to bear the mark of the planter. (2) The rolls themselves were not to exceed fifty pounds in weight. (3) Only sea water was to be used in moistening the leaves during manufacture and the water was to be used for only one dipping. The reuse of the water (to which planters far from the seacoast were prone) left sand in the second batch of tobacco and ruined its taste for chewing. Sea water, they insisted, preserved the tobacco while fresh water hastened its decay. (4) The planters were to cease mixing together leaves of first, second, and third growth and were never to use the poor, dirty bottom leaves, or grafted leaves. For the first crop (and largest) leaves, which must be packed separately, the company offered to give at least 25 *l.t.* per quintal in France; for the seconds, 20–22 *l.t.*; for the thirds or *rejettons* (sprouts) only 16–18 *l.t.*; for the thousand rolls damaged in transit to be used for snuff they would give 12–15 *l.t.* In addition, to encourage the planters not to try to slip in any worm-eaten or spotted leaves with the good ones, they offered to take up to 30,000 lb. of such leaf separately for 8–10 *l.t.* per quintal. If the planters would resume making the *tabacs exquis* of old, the farmers would pay 30 *l.t.* for the first quality; 25 *l.t.* for the second or good; 20 *l.t.* for the third or middling; 15 *l.t.* for the ship-damaged suitable for snuff; and 10 *l.t.* for the defective leaves.[111]

It is quite obvious from all this that, despite the regulations on the books, there were no controls in operation on St. Domingue (analogous to those long known in Virginia and Maryland) which placed any restriction on the quality of the tobacco shipped. The only way the monopoly could induce the planters not to mix inferior with superior leaf was to offer to take even the worst leaf at a price. The prices offered, however, were lower than those paid in peacetime in the 1680's. Despite high prices in Europe, the monopolists obviously had grave doubts about the quality of anything coming from St. Domingue.

On 23 May 1696, Pontchartrain wrote Ducasse that the government fully appreciated the importance of tobacco to the small settlers and was prepared to take any action not prejudicial to the farm.[112] On 18 July, he sent the governor two memoirs from the united farms specifying the terms outlined above. He agreed that a single price of eighteen *l.t.* per quintal in France was inadequate and suggested that Ducasse issue an order fixing prices for every grade to avoid quarrels. He warned him not to be lulled by plausible arguments from the planters but to exert himself to make sure that the farm was not cheated by those frauds in manufacture and packing which had ruined the St. Domingue tobacco trade in the past.[113] (In a subsequent letter, he promised that the government would also do all it could to see that St. Domingue received a greater supply of slaves for indigo, tobacco still being thought of as the cultivation of the man with few or no slaves.)[114] In correspondence with others, the minister was rather skeptical about the analysis of de Lagny and the monopoly, but equally optimistic that the measures then taken would solve the problem.[115]

When the offer and terms of the united farms reached Ducasse, the governor replied bluntly that all the promises of the monopoly would never persuade the settlers to return to tobacco, for they knew from personal experience the hard bargaining of that company in days when tobacco was abundant. In any event, he saw no point in all the proposed regulations to guarantee quality and prevent fraud. The tobacco then grown on St. Domingue just wasn't very good and spoiled too easily as he and some friends had discovered from recent experience. He wondered whether this deterioration in their tobacco was due to the degeneration of the seed they used or whether clearing so much of the country of trees had created too much dust. (This was Ducasse's first hint of the problem of soil exhaustion.)

In *Le Quartier* (Léogane), the planters had done well switching to indigo and Ducasse saw no reason for them to return to tobacco. The Cape, he admitted, was not suited to indigo nor did the poor settlers there have the slaves for that crop. They might grow a little more tobacco if—as he had suggested before—they were guaranteed by the king eighteen *l.t.* per quintal *in St. Domingue.* (The monopoly's prices were for deliveries in France.) During the preceding three years, the merchants had refused to take any tobacco, except to settle old debts. He doubted that 100 lb. had been made that year! He saw the St. Domingue tobacco trade going the way of that of the Windward Islands and could imagine no way of resurrecting it short of abolishing the monopoly and following the successful English example.

The annotations in the ministry on Ducasse's letter, most probably by de Lagny, are revealing: they emphasize all that the governor had written about the poor quality of the tobacco and the hopelessness of improving it. The suggested price of eighteen *l.t.* in St. Domingue, though, was "hardly practicable." St. Domingue tobacco wasn't as good as Jamaica tobacco or any of the other English varieties; it couldn't even compete with that of Clairac. Thus, all analogies with English experience were inapplicable because of different qualities. Because of this, the annotator noted, St. Domingue tobacco had always been a disappointment, even before the monopoly. Half of that sent to France spoiled on the way. Small men had planted it only because they didn't know what else to grow. Now that they had changed to other commodities, it was not in the interest of the state to draw them back to tobacco, and the scheme of the previous summer should be abandoned; France could supply itself adequately from other sources.[116]

Such was the state of affairs and official opinion early in 1697. Ducasse appears to have done nothing to put the monopolists' scheme into operation on St. Domingue. In Paris, Pontchartrain let the matter drop for the time being, as he busied himself with the renewal of the lease of the united farms. In the course of 1697, it will be remembered, Pontchartrain was to change his mind about the tobacco monopoly, take it away from the united farms and give it to the Bernard-Crozat-Maynon company. He did not do this because of St. Domingue, but his experiences with St. Domingue made him more fully informed than he might otherwise have been of the details of the tobacco trade and its revenue possibilities.

The months which saw the transfer of the tobacco monopoly from the united farms to the Bernard-Crozat-Maynon company (August-September) and the conclusion of the peace of Ryswick (September-October 1697) also saw a basic shift of power within the navy ministry. Although de Lagny apparently was not formally dismissed from his position as *directeur-général du commerce,* his name ceases to appear in the records from this time until his death in 1700. He was bypassed or ignored. His functions seem to have been divided among three officials of that ministry now each styled alike as "premier commis de M. de Pontchartrain": Joseph de la Touche, Charles de Salabéry, and Michel Begon. This meant that there no longer sat at the policy-making center of the navy ministry a person like Jean-Baptiste de Lagny who was not only a farmer-general but also one peculiarly associated with the tobacco monopoly from its inception in 1674 and peculiarly defensive of its reputation and interests.[117]

With the return of peace, the government had the leisure to reconsider the whole question of reviving the St. Domingue tobacco trade. (Private projectors came forward with their own schemes.)[118] On 17 December 1697, Ducasse reopened the question by sending to Pontchartrain a general attack on the tobacco monopoly and calling for its abolition.[119] This outburst, seemingly uncalled for, was probably written when Ducasse received his first inklings from home of the transfer of the monopoly in August-September 1697. Not knowing any of the details, Ducasse yet may have thought it worth while to call attention again to the plight of the settlers and to attack the idea of monopoly, lest St. Domingue be entirely forgotten in these changes.

What first drew Pontchartrain's attention back to St. Domingue was apparently not tobacco but sugar. Up to this time, little cane had been grown there. In February 1698, however, a ship arrived from St. Domingue loaded entirely with sugar, and the minister learned that the islanders (aided perhaps by their Cartagena loot) were planning to go more into that commodity. On 26 February 1698, he wrote in some dudgeon about this both to Ducasse[120] and to the *intendant de la marine,* Michel Begon.[121] There was no point in St. Domingue changing to sugar; enough was already grown in the Windward Islands; it would be difficult to find a market for any more. It was much more in St. Domingue's interest to concentrate on indigo, cotton, cocoa, *and tobacco.*

When these ministerial predilections reached Ducasse, the governor replied with characteristic vigor. For the first time, he developed fully the theme of soil exhaustion. The great quantities of tobacco and indigo grown on St. Domingue over so many years had ruined the soil, as had earlier happened on the Windward Islands. Just as the smaller islands had a generation or two ago been forced for this reason to turn to sugar, so must St. Domingue now change. If forbidden to make sugar, great stretches of cleared land would have to be abandoned. The whole area about Léogane had already reached the point where it must turn to sugar. The price of indigo had already fallen by 40 percent and the reestablishment of the settlements at the Cape and about Port-de-Paix would further increase the supply. Many small settlers were in fact talking of going back to tobacco, but he could not envisage as many as 500 of them taking it up without feeling the ill effects of overproduction and falling prices. The monopolists didn't want more than 20,000–25,000 rolls and the Dutch market couldn't take more than 30,000 rolls. This 50,000–55,000 roll total (2.5–2.75 million lb.) could be made by 200 small settlers (inferring now that even a small settler had about ten field hands). What was to happen to the production of the 300?[122]

Others were more sanguine. De Galiffet, Ducasse's subordinate as governor of the Cape, the locus classicus of the small tobacco planter, submitted a memoir while home in France in 1698 calling for a large scale return to tobacco cultivation on St. Domingue, where every desired quality could be grown. He frankly suggested that, to help its balance of payments, France should ban tobacco imports from foreigners and willingly pay more than the world price for those from St. Domingue. He even recommended prohibiting tobacco cultivation in France, ostensibly to release land for food. If St. Domingue thus encouraged grew more tobacco than France could consume, permission should be given to ship the surplus directly from that island to foreign countries (a very attractive notion when prices were as high as they were in Europe that year).[123]

Pontchartrain's much more sober answer to the sugar threat of 1698 was to pull out and dust off the pigeon-holed proposals of 1696 for reviving the St. Domingue tobacco trade. With the high prices of 1696–97 continuing surprisingly into the peace,[124] the new Bernard-Crozat-Maynon monopoly company seems to have been rather more willing than their predecessors to push the scheme. On 20 June 1698, an *arrêt* or technically *résultat du conseil* was issued "for the planting of tobacco in St. Domingue." It was phrased in the form of the king's acceptance of offers made by the new tobacco farmers. In content, it was essentially the proposal of the old tobacco monopolists (the united farms) in 1696 with the change, suggested by Ducasse, that delivery be taken not in France, but in St. Domingue—though at prices considerably under the 18 *l.t.* recommended by the governor. All planters were to register in advance the amount of ground they intended to plant with tobacco. The monopoly would buy 700,000 lb. per annum (starting in 1699) plus up to 100,000 lb. surplus if the planters grew more. If anything over 800,000 lb. were grown, it was to be destroyed by the public officials in St. Domingue, pro rata among the various planters according to their declared acreage. No tobacco was to be sold to anyone except the agents of the monopoly, under penalty of confiscation. The company would take 500,000 lb. of first growth leaf (450,000 in roll and 50,000 in dried leaf) at 16 *l.t.* per quintal; 200,000 lb. of second growth in roll at 13 *l.t.* and up to 100,000 of the "excess" in roll at 10 *l.t.* per quintal. The monopoly could at any time give three months notice that they wanted more than the 700,000 lb. specified. No rods were to be used in the rolls except those supplied by the company with its mark and weighing exactly the four pounds to be deducted for tare. The agents of the company would pay for the tobacco on delivery either in cash or in bills of exchange on France at four months sight, at the company's choice. The monopoly would be obliged to use only 100,000 lb. of their purchases for consumption within France and could reship the rest abroad with free *entrepôt* (except for 3 percent duty to the *domaine d'Occident*). There were various quality controls including a ban on the use of anything but sea water in manufacture. The new rules were to be read aloud in all settlements and the settlers were to sign their names as evidence of having heard the same.[125]

This *arrêt* of June 1698 was part of a more general policy pursued that year to encourage the development of the colony, including in particular the chartering in August of the *Compagnie Royale de St. Domingue* to develop the Ile des Vaches (Ile à Vache) and the southerly parts of the colony. That same month, Pontchartrain wrote to Ducasse about the new arrangements, instructing him to reserve 200,000 lb. out of the 800,000 lb. quota for the intended plantations of the new company.[126] In this new *compagnie royale,* Jean-Baptiste Ducasse was strangely conjoined as partner with the four principal members of the new tobacco monopoly company: Samuel Bernard, Antoine Crozat, Pierre Thomé, and Vincent Maynon.[127] Since Ducasse was not in France when these arrangements were being made, his participation probably represented the king's will rather any preference of his own. Only after his return to France late in 1700, did Ducasse begin to work closely with his new partners (in the negotiations for the Asiento, in particular). During his last two years on St. Domingue (1698–1700), he continued to fight them in the name of the *petits habitants* of his colony.

As soon as Ducasse heard of the *arrêt* of June 1698, he wrote back attacking it violently. He was particularly opposed to the exclusive purchasing privilege in St. Domingue, to the limitation of the crop to only 700,000–800,000 lb., and to the permission granted to the monopoly to use as little as 100,000 lb. of the tobacco in France. Against these arguments, he paraded all kinds of grossly inflated historical data about past production and sales; e.g., during the first lease of 1674–80, the monopolists had sold two million pounds of St. Domingue tobacco a year in France (actually ca. 410,000 lb.); and now their successors doubted they could sell one-twentieth as much. The whole thing to him was a plot to enable the monopolists to take advantage of the high European prices prevailing and to resell St. Domingue tobacco in Holland at great profit for 50 *l.t.* per quintal. He had no objections to the quality controls though he thought they would be impossible to enforce, as the small settlers used every stratagem to cheat the hated monopolists. The amount now ordered (800,000 lb.) was so trivial that fifty small planters could make it all (implying now that even small settlers had 12–16 field hands). The scheme could be made to work only if the farm would agree to take 1.2–2.0 million lb. at 20 *l.t.* per quintal and if the colony were given permission to send any excess it might grow directly to Holland. "It is impossible," Ducasse felt, "to reconcile the interests of the colony with those of the monopolist, the settlers dream only of increasing their worldly goods by their labor and the farmers only of drawing a profit out of their lease in whatever manner they can without consideration for the good of the state or that of private individuals."[128]

Ducasse was to keep up a steady stream of complaints against the new arrangements until his return home in late 1700. Although in September 1698, he insisted that the 800,000 lb. quota was grossly inadequate, in January 1699, he announced that less than that had actually been planted the previous fall. The agents of the farm had arrived without adequate funds and he had had to lend them money to keep them from starving. He was incensed at the monopolists for writing him letters of instruction as if he were their clerk.[129] In February, he was pointing out that the small tobacco planters were not persons who could use the bills of exchange on France which the agents of the monopoly offered them for their tobacco.[130] In March, he was explaining that the ruin of the tobacco trade would make very difficult the establishment of the new colonies in the southern part of St. Domingue (which he otherwise favored). Without this low-capital first crop, it would be necessary for the settlers to proceed immediately to crops like indigo and sugar requiring for a start a minimum of ten slaves per establishment. All this would require great credit advances by the new company.[131] In April, he expatiated on the plight of the independent merchants whose ships, thanks to the new rules, could find no tobacco cargoes in St. Domingue.[132]

Pontchartrain coldly assured Ducasse on 11 March and 8 April 1699 that he knew exactly what he was doing when he obtained the *arrêt* of the previous June. It would take many years to reestablish in France the by then forgotten taste for St. Domingue tobacco. In the meanwhile, if the monopolists, to help the small planters, guaranteed to buy as large a quantity as 800,000 lb., they had to be free to export to Holland what they couldn't sell in France. If Ducasse (who had received permission to return to France) wanted to help the cause, he would do better to complain less and cease writing rude letters to Crozat and instead bestir himself to induce the planters to improve the quality of their tobacco.[133] Ducasse quickly apologized for the affront to the monopolist, Antoine Crozat; he didn't agree with the policy of giving the company a monopoly of the reexport trade to Holland as well as that of the internal French trade, but would follow instructions precisely; he was glad that the tobacco farmers were now sending their agents some cash to pay the small planters who would not take bills of exchange; he only wished they had sent more and earlier. He could not refrain from adding that the farmers had made no arrangements for shipping so that tobacco which should have been in Holland in June was still sitting rotting in St. Domingue in August.[134]

A month later, Ducasse wrote with heavy formality that he understood the minister's policy exactly and would never trouble him again about tobacco.[135] This promise he was able to fulfill because that same month Pontchartrain gave up his joint tenure of the controller-generalship and the navy department to become chancellor. This implied no change of policy because his successor as secretary of state for the navy was his son Jérôme, who since 1693 had been active in the department as successor-designate and had in that capacity corresponded with Ducasse and other colonial officials. Early in 1700, Ducasse, at the Cape on his way back to France, flattered the new secretary by an optimistic report of the rôle tobacco was playing in reestablishing the devastated colonies of Port-de-Paix and the Cape.[136] After a few more months waiting and another harvest, his normal pessimism returned, as we shall see.

The government did not intend the visit home of Ducasse to make any difference in policy. When the *inspecteur-général de la marine,* de la Boulaye, was sent out on a tour of inspection to the West Indies, he was given detailed instructions (26 August 1699) calling his attention to the arrangements made with the monopoly the previous year for encouraging the St. Domingue tobacco trade and to Ducasse's reports of the indifference of the settlers to the new terms offered them. He was to explain to the planters their interest in accepting the new terms and the importance of raising tobacco that would meet the monopoly's standards. He was, however, to report if he found the settlers' arguments against the new terms reasonable.[137]

Far more important were to be the efforts in this same direction of the chevalier de Galiffet, *lieutenant de roi* or subgovernor at the Cape (the principal tobacco growing region in the North) and acting governor of all St. Domingue in Ducasse's absence. He arrived in St. Domingue (from a visit to France) early in March 1699, just after the gathering in of the first crop grown under the "encouragement" of the *arrêt* of June 1698.[138] In July he submitted a long report to the minister on the workings of the new system. The small planters, ignorant and suspicious of everything that emanated from the monopoly, had taken a violent dislike to the terms of the new *arrêt-résultat* from the moment of its publication. In fact, had he been on the island the previous fall, he would not have permitted its publication in the form in which it had come from France. He had done his best to mollify the hostility of the small settlers and answer their doubts, but had for his troubles been branded by rumor-mongers as secretly interested in the monopoly. Using an authorization from the monopolists to change details of the new rules, he had, in consultation with their agents, in fact altered virtually every clause to get the plan going on some feasible basis.

The most immediate problem was the means of payment. The smallest planters had no use for bills of exchange and the larger ones were suspicious of the bills drawn by the agents of the farm. De Galiffet had allayed the latter fears by countersigning the bills, but the problem itself was only solved when the cash sent out by the company belatedly arrived. Of more fundamental importance were the questions of prices and of compulsory sale to the farm. With peace restored (and world tobacco prices high) the merchants felt that the Dutch market alone could absorb 40,000 rolls (two million lb.), while the entire crop called for by the *arrêt* was only 800,000 lb., which three of the largest planters allegedly could raise alone. Hampered by all these restrictions, suddenly so vexatious in the light of attractive European prices, the private merchants were stirring up the planters against the farm by offering 20 *l.t.* per quintal when the maximum price provided by the *arrêt* was only 16 *l.t.* It would appear that de Galiffet closed his eyes to this now prohibited private trade. The distinction between the price of 16 *l.t.* for the first growth and 13 *l.t.* for the second growth, he also reported, only caused trouble, since there was no way generally accepted in the colony to distinguish first growth from second. Had there been, he insisted, the planters would long ago have stopped raising a second growth from the same roots, something they attempted only because they thought they could pass it off as first.

To make the new scheme a bit more palatable, de Galiffet had ordered the agents of the farm to give up the deduction of 4 percent for "good weight" in buying tobacco and not to insist on the prescribed proportion of English-style dried leaf along with the usual St. Domingue roll tobacco. Since the dried leaf weighed considerably less than the equivalent leaf in roll, the planters had refused to make it at the price offered. He simplified the arrangements obliging the planters to use only the company's rods in their rolls and waived most of the rules for registering and inspecting the acreage planted and for burning anything grown above the allotted quota.

He suggested that the *arrêt* itself be changed to accord with his alterations and that the planters be given an unrestricted right to raise all the tobacco they desired and to sell to private merchants any the farm didn't want.

To demonstrate the sincerity and dispassionateness of their criticism of the new arrangements—and encouraged no doubt by the high prices still reported from Europe—de Galiffet and Ducasse (who had not yet left the colony) offered themselves at this juncture (July 1699) to form a company to buy 1.6 million lb. of tobacco from the St. Domingue planters (twice the monopolists' quota) at a flat price of 15 *l.t.* per quintal without regard to first or second growth, without deductions of 4 percent for "good weight" or of the four pounds for the center rods, with full liberty to planters to grow more than that amount and sell their surplus wherever they pleased if the new company would not buy it at the same price.[139]

The rules as altered by de Galiffet and his assurances that the monopoly would buy in 1700 as they had in 1699 seem to have allayed the worst fears of the planters, for that winter he was able to report that enough tobacco had been planted in the fall to promise a crop in February 1700 of some 1.5 million lb.[140] He was shortly advised that both the minister and the tobacco monopoly approved of the changes he had made in the 1698 rules and that the monopoly would buy the full 1.5 million lb. of the expected crop. With such agreeable news from home, de Galiffet undertook to persuade the appeased planters to convert a substantial proportion of their crops into English-style dried leaf instead of spinning it. In the early months of 1700, de Galiffet supervised a number of experiments to establish a fair price ratio between spun and leaf tobacco.[141] One hundred pounds of dried leaf would make 190 lb. in roll tobacco, but if one started with leaf not fully dried, as was normal in the colony, the increase in weight was only 30–40 percent. De Galiffet's solution both to the weight problem and to the problem of the quality of manufacture by the numerous small planters was for the monopoly to buy the leaf green and have it processed in its own workshops on the island.[142] In the end, nothing came of all his experiments and suggestions.

In the latter part of 1699, European tobacco prices began to recede from their high levels of the preceding three or four years. Thus, when word arrived in Paris late in 1699 of the various changes in the rules which de Galiffet had made that spring, the whole question had to be reviewed in a colder light. Although both young Pontchartrain and the tobacco farmers recognized the need for de Galiffet's alterations as a means to calm the fears of the planters, both sought a more secure basis of operation for the future. The new secretary of state wrote de Galiffet that three solutions seemed possible: (1) the new company proposed by himself and Ducasse; (2) a return to conditions prevailing before the new rules of June 1698, but with an undertaking by the colony to supply to the monopoly 400,000 lb. of dried leaf tobacco at the prices offered in 1698 for roll; or (3) continuation under the unamended *résultat* of 1698. In answer to the first, with prices now dropping in Europe, both de Galiffet and Ducasse hastened to write separately in March 1700 that they were no longer interested in their proposed company, an idea which each ascribed to the other, advanced only as an emergency measure to protect the small planters. In any event, there was no time to put it into effect that year. The second proposition seemed impractical to de Galiffet because the planters would not sell dried leaf for the same price as roll; to Ducasse because the highly perishable roll tobacco could never be disposed of through the old French entrepôt system before it spoiled. Both agreed that the third proposal was equally impractical if the farmers insisted on the letter of the *résultat*. The various temporary changes made by de Galiffet, particularly paying in cash rather than bills of exchange, would, they insisted, have to be continued. In particular, a price differential would have to be worked out between leaf and roll tobacco. Ducasse added that he thought it ridiculous to expect St. Domingue tobacco (a special product designed for chewing) to be processed like Virginia, grown in such a different climate and designed for smoking. Let the monopolists buy the tobacco from the planters for 25 *l.t.* per quintal green and process it themselves any way they liked; they would get all they wanted; alternatively, let the planters send their tobacco in French vessels to foreign markets. Nothing in between would work.[143]

The early months of 1700 brought one disaster after another to the briefly revived tobacco industry of St. Domingue. There had been four months of very dry winter weather and much of the tobacco was lost in the fields. Just as the planters started to bring in the crop in February and March, the effects of the lower prices in Europe began to be felt: the agents of the farm announced that they had received new instructions from Paris forbidding them to take the enlarged crop on the new easier terms, and enjoining them strictly to take only so much and on such conditions (including payment in bills of exchange) as were specified in the *résultat* of 1698. To make matters worse, in April the agents at Port-de-Paix received word that all bills drawn by them the previous fall had been returned from France protested. Private traders, alert to the price changes, refused to touch the leaf, and no one would touch the agents' bills. In fury, many planters ripped out and destroyed any tobacco they still had growing. More swore never to plant the crop again. De Galiffet continued to write brave, optimistic letters suggesting ways in which all difficulties could be resolved and cultivation continued. Yet, to save the planters from complete ruin, he and Ducasse had to buy up the unsaleable tobacco at 15 *l.t.* per quintal and charter two vessels to take it directly to Hamburg with special licenses on their own authority. By the time he left the colony at the end of July 1700, Ducasse at least perceived that his worst fears had been realized, that the revival had been a failure and that the tobacco industry on St. Domingue was again and truly dead.[144]

It is quite evident that the best explanation of the abortive revival of the St. Domingue tobacco trade in 1698–1700 lies in the history of prices. With the upward movement of prices in 1696 was born the monopolists' first interest in reviving cultivation there. The Amsterdam prices best explain the terms inserted by the new Bernard-Crozat-Maynon company into the *résultat* of June 1698 enabling them to limit production (to keep prices up), to preempt the entire crop (to control the market), and to reexport virtually their entire purchase to the Dutch and nearby markets. But word of these same high prices of course reached others in France and St. Domingue. In the first months of the peace, St. Domingue tobacco sold in French ports for 45–46 *l.t.* per quintal and even higher prices were realized in Holland. This caused a considerable flurry of interest in tobacco among private merchants which rendered the farm's privilege of exclusive purchase (monopsony) illusory. But news of these same high prices rendered the planters all the more furious at the *arrêt-résultat* of 1698 and its wretched 13–16 *l.t.* prices. The sudden change in the market in the latter part of 1699 explains in turn why Ducasse and de Galiffet, who had been so ready early that year to form a company to buy up virtually the whole production of St. Domingue, were so prompt to withdraw their offer by early 1700. The fall of prices also helps explain why the monopoly at first seemed to approve the alterations in the *arrêt-résultat* of 1698 and then during the winter of 1699–1700 sent word to their agents to purchase only as provided by the letter of that document.[145]

In retrospect, then, the abortive revival of tobacco planting in St. Domingue during 1698–1700 did not represent a serious effort by the government, tobacco monopoly, and planters to reach new realistic terms based upon the long-range prospects of the market. Rather did it represent only a flurry of speculative activity on all sides caused by the persistence of exceptionally high prices in Europe during the first year or two of the peace. When these disappeared, so too did the tobacco revival. The planters of St. Domingue had more remunerative ways in which to employ their resources than in growing tobacco for the world market as it existed then or in the coming century. And, no tobacco monopoly company in France would long agree to pay a price substantially above the world price, even if (as was not the case) French consumers had retained any liking for the tobaccos of St. Domingue.

The ups and downs of world tobacco prices during 1696–1700 and the aborted hopes of reviving the St. Domingue tobacco industry must also be kept in mind as part of the immediate background of the discussion of the tobacco question in the new Council of Commerce established in 1700. The merchants of the western and northern ports had seen the new tobacco monopoly company try to grab from them the profits of reexporting to Holland in the good years around 1698; the new council gave them the opportunity to vent their grievances. In the discussion of the tobacco trade in the various memoirs of 1700–1701, we find arguments not self-evidently consistent. On the one hand, most of the complainants (as noted in the previous chapter) called for the abolition of the monopoly and the reestablishment of an open trade under a moderate duty for the alleged purpose of supplying France in the future from a revived St. Domingue tobacco industry, so selfishly destroyed by the monopoly. But when the memorialists came to recite the misdeeds of the tobacco company, they devoted the greatest vehemence and detail to the ways in which the company impeded the reexport trade. A free entrepôt and a prosperous reexport trade might be all very well for some French merchants and even for St. Domingue, but this has nothing to do with supplying French internal demand. On reflection we might surmise that for most French merchants in 1700–1701, supplying the home market was a distant chimera, but reexporting to Holland and the North was a quite immediate business activity in which great profits were to be made as recently as 1697–99 by those who could circumvent the delays of the monopolists.

Statements developing the St. Domingue and reexport arguments came from Jean Le Pelletier, a former official of Rouen,[146] from the merchants of Honfleur[147] and particularly from Joachim Descazeaux du Hallay, the deputy of Nantes,[148] and from Jean Pottier de la Hestroy, an old official in the navy ministry in the time of Seignelay, subsequently an admiralty judge at Dunkirk.[149] The last two were particularly well informed on recent developments in St. Domingue. By contrast, the deputy Mesnager from Rouen merely thought the St. Domingue trade should be encouraged[150] while Piedcourt, the deputy from Dunkirk (with little colonial trade), seemed more interested in encouraging imports from Portugal than from the French colonies.[151] The draft report to the crown drawn up for consideration by the council developed in full in its tobacco section the grievances both of St. Domingue and of the reexport trade and reflected in its detail the marked influence of both Descazeaux and Pottier.[152]

But all of this, as we have seen before, was to very little purpose. The St. Domingue tobacco industry was not to be revived by memoirs or debates in council. In St. Domingue itself, tobacco was all but forgotten as sugar profits soared and the new sugar excitement spread.[153] With Ducasse gone to France and soon (July-August 1701) to join his erstwhile enemies the tobacco farmers in the new Asiento Company, de Galiffet, his deputy in the colony, became very circumspect in his references to the tobacco question. He assured the government once more that it was impossible to make dried leaf tobacco in the colony, for labor there, for unspecified reasons, was six times as expensive as in Virginia. As before, he suggested higher prices from the monopoly or permission to export directly to Holland, and, when these were not forthcoming, assured the secretary of state that not one roll would be made during the 1700–1701 season. The sieur de St. Martin, the expert sent out by the monopoly to improve processing methods in St. Domingue, died and was not replaced.[154] The little tobacco that was raised continued to be plagued with excessive spoilage.[155]

With the return of Ducasse to St. Domingue in the summer of 1702, the silence about tobacco becomes more ominous, considering his former volubility and his new partners. The start of the war that same year meant the end of the first sugar boom on St. Domingue. Both slaves and shipping became painfully scarcer. The small men suffered more than their great neighbors. Yet, as a class, they refused to return to tobacco; any pretense of carrying out the contract implied in the *résultat* of 1698 was abandoned.[156] Yet, some tobacco was obviously raised, for in 1703 we hear of 10 bales and 56 rolls of St. Domingue tobacco being shipped from Nantes to Ostend.[157] (As late as 1711, St. Domingue tobacco can be found in the printed prices-current at Hamburg, though with the price left blank, mute evidence to an imminent demise.)

The last governmental effort to revive tobacco cultivation in St. Domingue came in 1706–7 when Amsterdam prices were even higher than in the 1690's and when France was once more having wartime difficulties obtaining overseas supplies. In 1706, the secretary of state, Jérôme de Pontchartrain, sent out instructions to the governor (Auger) and intendant to urge the settlers to resume planting tobacco. The sieur Deslandes, *commissaire-ordonnateur de la marine et des colonies,* acting as intendant for St. Domingue, issued a *règlement* on 6 January 1707 for the better ordering and encouraging of the cultivation and manufacture of tobacco. On its regulative side, it was a very mild document. (For example, it contained nothing to prevent the use of leaves of second or third growth.) Following precedents going back to the 1660's, it established certain standards for the manufacture of roll tobacco, including: only whole, unblemished leaves were to be used; and only sea water was to be used for moistening. The planters were urged to make dried leaf in imitation of that of Virginia, but (unlike 1698) were not required to do so. Those who made tobacco were to have an absolute liberty to sell to private French merchants; in case the latter did not buy all that was available, public agents would be named at the Cape and at Léogane to buy the remainder. A fair price was promised but left unspecified. Young men could have free land near Léogane to grow tobacco. Small *habitants* who agreed to grow tobacco would be sold slaves by the government on credit, to be paid for out of the proceeds of the tobacco they raised.[158] We wonder whether the government of St. Domingue was ever in a position to carry out this last clause, so tempting to the small man without slaves, for this *règlement* seems to have been forgotten as soon as it was issued. (Its author died a few months later.) [159]

The true measure of government policy can be taken not in the issue of unheeded *règlements* in St. Domingue, but in certain financial negotiations in Paris. In the mixed bag of odd bits and scraps of legislation and rulings and government contracts passing as policy which the succeeding generations had inherited from Colbert, one item remained which seemed to suggest sincere commitment to the encouragement of the West Indian tobacco trade. The original lease of 1674 and the *ordonnance* of 1681 which established the general legislative framework for the entire tobacco monopoly had provided that the monopoly should sell St. Domingue tobacco at wholesale and retail in France for one-half the price charged for foreign tobacco. This meant that if the French consumer became indifferent to St. Domingue chewing tobacco, it was not the price which drove him away. It meant also that St. Domingue tobacco was the least profitable imported product carried by the monopoly, the one least in their interest to "push." Yet these arrangements persisted until 1708. In that year of general financial crisis for the French state, the contract with the tobacco farm came up rather early for its sexennial renewal (from 1 October 1709). Due to the war and the general embarrassment of state finances, there was no serious likelihood of advertising for bids in the legally "normal" way. On 21 July 1708, the bondsmen or principals in the current (Germain Gaultier) lease offered to renew the lease for six further years at the same price but "begged" the controller-general (now Nicolas Desmaretz) to permit them to sell St. Domingue tobacco at the same price as other imported tobaccos (40 *sols* per lb. wholesale and 50 retail). They explained that although they now had to sell St. Domingue tobacco at one-half price, it actually cost them more than any other imported tobacco. If this favor were granted, they would be in a position to reestablish the long abandoned tobacco trade of St. Domingue. The treasury was obviously under great pressure, for these terms were immediately accepted and the *résultat* regranting the lease (under the name of Charles Michault) for six more years from 1 October 1709 was signed three days later, 24 July 1708.[160] Thus passed the last vestige of state encouragement for the St. Domingue tobacco industry.

When the count of Choiseul Beaupré, the new governor of St. Domingue, arrived at his post early in 1708, he sent home some pious platitudes about encouraging some larger planters to grow tobacco once more as a good example for the smaller settlers.[161] Nothing of course changed. An account of all the produce of St. Domingue in the year 1 May 1709–1 May 1710 shows the now heavy preponderance of indigo followed by sugar—with *no* tobacco.[162] From time to time thereafter, particularly during the exciting years 1715–20, various persons were to come forward with schemes to revive large scale tobacco production on St. Domingue, with equal lack of success. Just before the death of Louis XIV, the new directors of the St. Domingue company (who had replaced the tobacco farmers in that company) proposed that an *ordonnance* be issued requiring each settler to plant a specified proportion of tobacco.[163] The next year, the same proposition came from the company, but in a new reign and new atmosphere more sympathetic to change. It was now specifically suggested that each settler be obliged to employ one-third of his land and slaves in this culture. To make it pay, however, the monopoly, if not abolished, should be obliged to buy the tobacco for 50 *l.t.* per quintal for dried leaf (and 50*s.* per lb. for any snuff obtained from trade with the Spaniards).[164] (It is interesting that even this ambitious project could find no place for the traditional St. Domingue roll tobacco for chewing.) All such schemes, of course, were to be lost sight of in the next few years as all eyes turned toward the Mississippi.

West Indian Tobacco under Louis XV, 1715–74: A Postscript

Well before the accession of Louis XV in 1715, large-scale commercial tobacco growing had, we have seen, disappeared from the French Antilles. Yet, from time to time in the long reign of *le bien aimé*, statesmen in Paris and officials in the field were to question this decision-by-default; some even attempted to see if it could not be reversed. This sporadic questioning and experimentation was most noticeable during the long sojourn (1723–49) at the navy ministry of the count of Maurepas, grandson of the chancellor and son of the secretary Pontchartrain.

In the early 1730's, Maurepas undertook a concerted program to encourage tobacco production in the French colonies, as we shall remark below in Chapter 13 on Louisiana. This activity also reached St. Domingue. In 1727, he had been informed that some settlers there in quarters unsuited for indigo or sugar were prepared to resume tobacco production if the then monopoly offered them a high enough price.[165] Nothing was done about this at the time but four years later, Maurepas wrote to the governor of St. Domingue, the marquis of Vienne, of his hopes of reviving tobacco there, both as a stimulus to seaborn trade and as a support for a larger population of small white settlers which the colony needed. He recognized realistically that the sort of prepared tobacco now made on the island by the settlers for their own use would not be suitable for the manufactures of the farm and that price was likely to be a serious stumbling block. To proceed systematically and convince the monopoly objectively of the usefulness of St. Domingue tobacco, the minister instructed Vienne to ask the intendant Jean-Baptiste Duclos to have prepared in each *quartier* of the colony where tobacco grew well a sample of 500–600 lb. of dried leaf tobacco in hands or bunches (*tabac en manoque*) to be shipped suitably labeled to La Rochelle for delivery to the monopoly. The samples would be paid for by the government. The secretary warned the governor, however, that the settlers must not expect to get for any future staple production of tobacco the prices they then received for the small quantities raised for local consumption and specialized export. Looking backward, Maurepas admitted that tobacco would probably travel better from St. Domingue if spun and made into rolls; but that tobacco had such a bad reputation for fraud from times past that the farmers general could never be induced to take it unless, after sending experts out to examine the actual processing, they could be persuaded that St. Domingue roll was by then manufactured more carefully.[166]

These instructions would appear to have been taken fairly seriously on the island. The new governor, the marquis of Fayet (1732–35), discussed them with leading inhabitants in his travels through the colony. The *commissaire-ordonnateur*, Pierre de Sartre, wrote about, asking individuals in different *quartiers* to undertake the necessary experiments. At La Petite Anse in the *canton du Bonnet à L'Evêque*, Asselin, a member of the *conseil supérieur* at The Cape was quite enthusiastic. He thought tobacco was just the crop to repeople the waste sections of the colony with free white settlers. He consulted the oldest inhabitants about the proper methods and had some tobacco grown experimentally. He preferred *andouilles* (small pressed rolls) to dried leaf for he feared too much weight was lost the latter way. There was no chance of bringing back spun tobacco for there was no one left who remembered how to spin (*torquer*) and what workers were available lived too far from the seawater needed for spinning. In the end, there is no evidence to suggest that anything came of all this experimentation and correspondence.[167]

Thus, although there ceased to be any significant tobacco industry on St. Domingue after 1700, some tobacco understandably continued to be made there for local consumption, and for shipment in modest quantities to other colonies. Charlevoix, writing ca. 1724, reported that none of the French merchants at St. Domingue would touch tobacco, except those from Dunkirk, a free port outside the jurisdiction of the monopoly.[168] As early as 1685, the intendant Michel Begon had pointed out that there might be a big market for French West Indian tobacco in Acadia and Canada.[169] In 1736, there was actually imported at Quebec in *carottes* (strands of spun tobacco pressed together):

from St. Domingue	2,002 lb.
from St. Vincent	75 lb.
from Louisiana	944 lb.
plus Spanish snuff	780 lb.[170]

This little trade, for any potential it might have had, disappeared of course with the loss of Canada. Official statistics on exports from St. Domingue during 1764–76 once more show *no tobacco*.[171]

Not just on St. Vincent,[172] but on all the smaller islands generally, some cultivation and preparation of tobacco probably persisted throughout the century following the advent of the monopoly in 1674—if only for domestic consumption. That on Guadeloupe could not have been very significant. Statistical reports of cultivation in 1730 and 1739 show no tobacco.[173] There was rather more activity on Martinique. For some years in the 1730's, from 100 to 1,000 quintals (10,000 to 100,000 lb.) of tobacco were sent to France annually. Thereafter the trade was less active, except in unusual years, though it was to revive to an annual level of ca. 2,000 quintals during 1783–87.[174] Part of this was the famous rose or violet scented snuff grown and made in the Macouba district of Martinique, "le plus recherché de tous les tabacs de l'Amérique,"[175] an exotic and expensive product, but not one on which a staple branch of agriculture could be built. Good but less *recherchés* tobaccos grown in the Basse Pointe, Grand'ance and Marigot *quartiers* of Martinique were frequently also passed off as "Macouba." They were manufactured into long *carottes* of three to four pounds which were aged for a year and then ground up into snuff. The normal markets were in the French, British, and Dutch islands of the West Indies.[176]

During 1739–41, some thought was given to the possibility of reviving tobacco in the French Windward Islands. Partly because of the British-Spanish war, tobacco prices rose temporarily in Europe.[177] In 1739, de la Croix, the intendant of the isles at Martinique, sent in a report on the subject. The next year, de Clieu, governor of Guadeloupe, sent home a sample of Guadeloupe tobacco for inspection by the farmers-general. On the basis of a favorable report from that company, the minister Maurepas wrote to the marquis of Champigny, governor of the *Iles du Vent,* and to de la Croix in February 1741. The Guadeloupe tobacco was quite good, he reported, but he had doubts whether a price could be worked out that would be mutually satisfactory considering the high freights from the West Indies. He asked for a continuation of the Guadeloupe experiment and for information on the other islands.[178] Champigny and de la Croix replied that they had instructed de Clieu to continue his experiments on Guadeloupe and were ordering the governors of the other islands to encourage tobacco where possible, but that they doubted that much would come of all this in the *Iles du Vent:* everything there—land, labor and especially transport—was too expensive to permit raising tobacco that could compete in Europe with the Virginia product.[179] They were of course good prophets.

Meanwhile, the farmers-general had had second thoughts. In February they had reported that Guadeloupe tobacco was "de tres bonne qualité" and mixed with Virginia "à Merveille." When asked by the minister about prices, they replied in March that the price of their farm was based upon an estimated and actually relatively stable English price of 22–23 *l.t.* per quintal; that they were able to pay 25 *l.t.* for that from Louisiana only because not too much came thence; that they would pay as much to Guadeloupe if the minister so requested them, but didn't think it wise to encourage the Antilles to compete with the mainland.[180] As Maurepas had suspected from the very beginning, this price did not prove attractive—Macouba snuff sold in the islands for 50–60 *s.* per lb.—and the entire matter was forgotten.

Why then did all efforts to encourage tobacco planting on St. Domingue and the lesser islands fail? The most popular, indeed almost the only, explanation during the years of travail, 1674–1700, and afterward throughout the eighteenth century[181] was monopsonistic. That is, the establishment of the tobacco monopoly in 1674 had created a single buyer in France for colonial tobacco; it was in the interest of this exclusive buyer to keep the price of the tobacco he bought as low as possible. "He" drove down the price until he killed the colonial industry. No other explanation was thought necessary—even though the practice of subfarming whole provinces meant there couldn't be a pure monopsony in France. Yet, there were other explanations.

In the late seventeenth century, tobacco production did not simply decline in the French West Indian islands where there were monopsonistic pressures, but in the West Indies generally, including the English West Indies where there was not the slightest trace of a privileged buyer. There obviously were factors at work which transcended the institutional arrangements of any one country. One such factor was simply a matter of taste. St. Domingue roll tobacco, like Brazilian tobacco on which it was patterned, was preferred as a chewing tobacco; but chewing was going out of fashion (not that it had ever really been "in fashion") in the France of Louis XIV. As the lower classes imitated their betters, first smoking then snuff became more acceptable. For these latter uses, fully dried leaf tobacco was more suitable. As early as 1685, the intendant Michel Begon noted that France had to import dried leaf from Antigua and other English colonies. He suggested that there might be a greater future for French colonial tobacco prepared in the English fashion.[182] But the planters of St. Domingue were reluctant to invest either the time or the trouble in preparing their tobacco in a way which would produce from a given quantity of green leaf only one-half as much by weight as did their traditional well-watered roll. This of course calls our attention to a second factor, that of prices, or more specifically the secular downward trend of world market prices for tobacco in the latter part of the seventeenth century. No one ever seriously accused the tobacco monopolists in France of offering less than the world price for any protracted time. It was painful enough for the growers and traders that the farm used its monopsonist powers to force down the French price to something approaching the world price. At that level, however, *no* West Indian production could compete with the cheap and plentiful production of the Chesapeake and of Holland and Germany.

Contributing to the unsatisfactory prices received by St. Domingue tobacco in Europe were considerations of quality, our third factor. In March 1717, the tobacco farmer François Le Gendre submitted to the government a detailed report from Thomas, head of the great tobacco manufacturing establishment of the monopoly at Dieppe, with more than thirty years' experience in this work. Dieppe was already an important tobacco manufacturing center when the monopoly was established in 1674, but never to his knowledge, either before or since that date, had French West Indian leaf tobacco been used in the manufacture there. It was, he reported, characteristically picked before it was fully mature and was never properly and fully dried. Some French colonial tobacco came to Dieppe already manufactured (in roll) for chewing, but because of its inadequate preparation, a high proportion of it spoiled in transit and had to be thrown away by the importing merchants. In 1701–2, the works at Dieppe had as an experiment manufactured several thousand pounds of St. Domingue tobacco. The leaf arrived in poor shape and did not improve in manufacture. The results were so unattractive that they could only be disposed of by mixing them into the cheap grade of tobacco sold to soldiers, to the evident unhappiness of the troops. In Thomas' opinion, "the tobaccos of French America because of their defectiveness are not suitable in any way for manufacture in France."[183]

To Thomas, who had no direct experience of St. Domingue, the root of the trouble was moral, the ignorance and laziness of the tobacco planters. Both Labat and Ducasse who were infinitely more knowledgeable hinted at similar qualities, particularly, as we have seen, when they discussed such matters as the settlers' persistent efforts to pass off leaf of second and third growth as first crop. But all three of them also wondered whether there might not be physical reasons why good tobacco could not be made in the French colonies. We have already seen that by 1698–1700, Ducasse had become convinced that it was no longer possible to make traditional roll tobacco there which would endure the ocean crossing, nor was it possible at the prices offered to make dried leaf. He wondered whether the seed had degenerated or whether the extensive clearances of the forest had dried up or otherwise impoverished the soil.[184] Thomas did not know why, but it was clear to him in 1716–17 that "the soil is not suitable for making tobacco of good quality."[185] Labat, whose chapter on tobacco is dated 1700, was fully aware of the problem of tropical soil exhaustion. He recommended that trees be left standing to protect the soil from wind, rain, and sun. He was particularly vehement about the folly of raising seconds and thirds from the same roots which only hastened the process of soil exhaustion in old settled areas like the French Windward Islands. Labat was an enthusiastic promoter both of the French colonies and of tobacco cultivation. Thus, his awareness of soil exhaustion is all the more suggestive.[186]

Whether because of soil exhaustion, degeneration of seed, ignorance, sloth, high labor and related costs, or simply the relatively greater attractiveness of other crops, the planters of St. Domingue were not prepared after 1700 to grow marketable tobacco at the world price. The understandable sin of the tobacco monopolists was that they would not pay more than the world price for their tobacco. The state could have required them to do so in their lease, but in the end the state negotiated revenue leases to obtain the greatest possible revenue.

Appendix to Chapter 4: A Note on Spanish Tobacco

In addition to the normal trade on St. Domingue in the native tobacco of that colony, there was also a more shadowy trade in tobacco from the Spanish colonies, both the manufactured Verinas tobacco from Venezuela, the most expensive luxury tobacco of the seventeenth century, and Havana tobacco, in great demand for snuff in the eighteenth century. About 1705, the French Asiento Company acquired a substantial amount of Havana tobacco from its trade in Cuba which it tried unsuccessfully to sell to the Spanish monopoly.[187] De Charrite, a great planter and sugar pioneer in northern St. Domingue and governor at the Cape after 1706, enticed some skilled workers from Havana to establish at the Cape a snuff manufacture in the Cuban style. The manufacture, however, had to use Havana and not St. Domingue leaf and received little encouragement in the colony.[188] After the war, though, before the Spanish administration was effectively tightened up, we find among the exports of St. Domingue quantities both of Verinas tobacco and of snuff from de Charrite's experiment:

1715: Verinas tobacco	468 quintals	@ 95 *l.t.*	44,470 *l.t.*
snuff	44,600 lb.	@ 13 *sols*	28,990 *l.t.*
1716: Verinas tobacco	283 quintals	@ 90 *l.t.*	25,470 *l.t.*
snuff	4,710 lb.	@ 12 *sols*	2,826 *l.t.*

The tobacco was shipped from Léogane, better situated for communication with the Spanish Main, while the snuff went from the Cape, easier of access to Cuba.[189] This is all very interesting, but does nothing to alter the general picture of a St. Domingue tobacco industry dormant after 1700.

CHAPTER 5

Some Administrative Problems of the Tobacco Monopoly, 1674–1718

The Administrative Framework

In this volume, our primary concern is with the political and commercial history of the tobacco monopoly, rather than with its administrative and legal evolution. Nevertheless, one cannot understand much of the business activity or policies of the farm without knowing something of the internal problems it faced. Administrative convenience and fiscal security, we shall see, were often the considerations governing decisions as to which tobaccos it was most or least in the interest of the monopoly to use in France.

We know relatively little about the internal administration of the tobacco farm during its first thirteen years, 1674–87. It seems to have maintained a headquarters at Paris, snuff worshops at Paris and Mondragon (Provence), and a tobacco factory at Dieppe. Around the country it had in 1687 about fifty warehouses or offices (*bureaux*) from which licensed retailers obtained their tobacco. These warehouses were not evenly distributed over the country, but were clustered in the coastal and northern areas where we have already seen consumption was concentrated. Of fifty offices listed outside Paris in an inventory of 1687, no fewer than twenty-one were in Normandy, Picardy, Ile-de-France, and Champagne, while thirteen were in the extreme south (Guienne, Béarn, Foix, Roussillon, Languedoc, and Provence). With six in external sovereignties or appanages leased from their princes, this left only ten warehouses to serve the rest of the country (Le Mans, Angers, Tours, Orléans, Clermont-en-Auvergne, Bourges, Limoges, La Rochelle, Dijon, and Chalon-sur-Saône). Brittany and the Three Bishoprics were subfarmed during the lease of 1681–87, as the Lyonnais and Dauphiné seem to have been by 1687.[1] Those inland provinces where the monopoly maintained no distribution centers were supplied by licensed private trade. In the remote Bourbonnais, for example, certain wholesale traders received special permissions to buy *tabac en corde* from the warehouses of the farm at Bordeaux, La Rochelle, Bourges, Orléans, Limoges, or Clermont and bring it into their province, reporting on arrival to the local agents of the monopoly who checked to see if the seals and papers were in order; these same agents would restamp or remark the tobacco if the traders wished to break up large parcels into small. The tobacco so brought in was sold retail by the importing traders or more commonly resold to retailers for petty sales.[2]

At the start of the Domergue lease in 1687, all this was changed. The tobacco division of the united farms, under the management of Jean-Rémy Hénault, was thoroughly reorganized. Farmers-general and senior employees (*commis-généraux à l'inspection*) were sent out with sweeping powers to open new warehouses wherever needed, to terminate the licensed private wholesale trade and to buy up the tobacco remaining in the hands of the former private wholesalers.[3] Out of this reorganization came the basic organizational structure of the tobacco farm which persisted through many vicissitudes down to the end of the *ancien régime*. Order and hierarchy replaced improvisation.

Under the new arrangements, from one to four *généralités* (the basic geographic divisions of France for fiscal purposes) constituted a *direction* or *département* of the farm, divided in turn into a few rather large districts whose head offices were styled *bureaux-généraux*. These districts were subdivided into lesser ones, each containing a local distributing office called a *bureau d'entrepôt*, one of which would in time be found in every market town. The *bureaux-généraux* were intermediate distribution centers, receiving their tobacco directly from the ports, from the company's own manufacturing establishments or from special regional warehouses on main navigable rivers. The *entrepôts* were local distributing centers which received their supplies from their appropriate *bureaux-généraux* (never too far away) and which did not have to carry very large stocks. The *entrepôts* sold some tobacco retail but their primary function was to supply the retailers (*débitants*) both in their own town and in the villages of the surrounding countryside for about seven leagues around. The retailers were usually small shopkeepers, but sometimes innkeepers or *cabaretiers* as well, though the latter were discouraged by the farm. Sales by hawkers, peddlers, street-vendors, and the like were prohibited. While the staff of the *bureaux* and *entrepôts* were employees of the farms on salaries or commissions, the retailers were private traders licensed by the monopoly. Their earnings came from the controlled mark-up (ca. 25 percent) between the price they paid at the *entrepôts* and the price at which they were permitted to sell retail. Nothing except constant vigilance by the inspectors of the monopoly could keep the retailers from mixing in cheap smuggled tobacco with the more expensive product they bought from their official suppliers.

The entire system was given precision by Hénault at the beginning of the Domergue lease (1 October 1687). Formal printed instructions issued in the first year of that lease defined the functions of each *bureau-général*, *entrepôt* and retailer. At the head of the system was the *directeur général de la ferme* in Paris who supervised the day-to-day operations of the monopoly for the United General Farms. Under him in each direction were one or two travelling *directeurs* who supervised the local *bureaux-généraux* and reported directly to Paris. In each *bureau-général* there were a receiver-general and a controller-general (who acted as a check on each other) as well as lesser officials; each *entrepôt* had its own receiver or *entreposeur* and controller too as well as its distinctive mark which appeared on all the tobacco it sold. The regulations provided for six different types of daybooks, journals and ledgers which were to be kept in each *bureau-général*. Other ledgers, etc., were prescribed for the *entrepôts*, for the buying offices in the tobacco growing regions and for the manufactories. In the last named, for example, there were to be separate ledgers of shipments in, shipments out, day-by-day expenses, labor expenses and receipts and inventories of all miscellaneous products used in manufacture. The receiver of an *entrepôt* was to be advanced a limited stock on credit on taking up his office; thereafter, he was to pay in cash for additional stock needed. Retailers were not to buy less than three pounds at a time and must pay in cash. Their numbers were to be limited, but there was to be at least one in each parish. The duties of inspectors and guards were all carefully prescribed, including their regular visits to the retailers' shops.[4]

The full system, although clear on paper by 1687-88, did not reach all sections of the country at once. Paris might need 1200 licensed retailers in 1708, each selling an estimated three pounds per day.[5] The provinces of the interior, with thin populations and low levels of consumption per capita, had more modest needs. When a distributive system was finally brought to the Bourbonnais in 1688, it provided only for a *bureau-général* or *entrepôt* in each *ville d'élection* (seat of a fiscal court): this was not the same as the ultimate office in every market town. In Burgundy, where tobacco seems to have arrived last of all, there were still only two *bureaux* in 1689 (Dijon, Chalon) and, because of the absence of *entrepôts*, merchants had to be given permission to sell the tobacco they bought at these *bureaux* anywhere in the province. Under a *bureau-général* at Lyons, there were only four *entrepôts* to serve the Lyonnais proper plus Le Forest (Forez), Bresse, Bugey, and Valromey. In Dauphiné, there were three *bureaux-généraux* (one at Grenoble for the city and *élection,* another at Gap, and a third at Valence) but seemingly few *entrepôts*.[6]

In other provinces, both north and south, where consumption was higher, we find a fuller development of the *entrepôt* system. In Picardy in 1698, there were three *bureaux-généraux* and fourteen *entrepôts*.[7] While a single *bureau-général* at Perpignan could supply the tiny territory of Roussillon, the *bureau-général* at Montpellier to supply the *généralité* of that name required no fewer than thirteen *entrepôts*. In its own administration, the farm generally followed the existing boundaries of *généralités* and *élections* or dioceses except where there were good economic reasons not to do so. Thus, the *entrepôts* at Privas and Annonay in the *généralité* of Montpellier were instructed to get their tobacco from the *bureau-général* at Valence (in Dauphiné) only ten leagues away, rather than cart it the eighteen and thirty-eight leagues from Montpellier itself. Transportation costs were important. At the *entrepôts* near Montpellier (Pézénas, Béziers, Narbonne, Clermont de Lodève, and Sumène) the staff were allowed three *sols* per pound sold to cover carriage, wastage and an allowance in lieu of salaries. At the *entrepôts* further away from Montpellier (Florac, Marvejols, Le Puy, Annonay, Privas, and St. Esprit), four *sols* had to be allowed. Comparable arrangements prevailed in the *direction* of Toulouse, covering nine dioceses in the *généralité* of Toulouse and nine dioceses in the *géneralité* of Montauban. Under the *bureau-général* at Toulouse were 24 *entrepôts* covering a territory whose legitimate consumption must have been considerably impaired by local growth in Montauban.[8]

A 1689 report from the farmer-general Le Juge on the *département* of Orléans shows an even more comprehensive distribution network (approaching Paris levels). The *bureau-général* at Orléans served directly 38 retailers in that city plus 42 in the remainder of the *élection* and 13 in the *élection* of Beaugency. From this same *bureau-général* were also supplied a number of *entrepôts* including: (1) Montargis serving 53 retailers in that town and 21 parishes of the *élection* of Nemours; (2) Pithiviers serving 47 retailers in 12 parishes of the *élection* of Orléans and 15 parishes in the *élection* of Montargis; (3) Gien serving 46 retailers in the *élections* of Orléans, Montargis, and Bourges; (4) St. Fargeau serving 19 retailers in the *élections* of Gien, Clamecy and Joigny; (5) Clamecy serving 28 retailers in the *élections* of Vezelay, Nemours, and Auxerre; (6) Vendôme serving 26 retailers in the *élections* of Vendôme and Chateaudun; (7) Blois serving 39 retailers in the *élections* of Blois and Chateaudun; (8) Romorantin serving 36 retailers in its own *élection;* and (9) Chateaudun serving 60 retailers in its own *élection*. This last figure was thought excessive and a separate *entrepôt* was recommended for Brou, only four leagues away. In this part of France, unlike the south, or Burgundy, retailers had to buy from their own *entrepôt* and permission was denied them to obtain supplies elsewhere, even from the *bureau-général* at Orléans. (Consumers, however, found ways to shop around between districts both for quality and price until the farm could eliminate such differentials.)[9]

The network of *entrepôts* in Picardy and the Orléannais and to a lesser extent those based on Toulouse and Montpellier represent the fully developed system which was to be characteristic of the whole country in the next century. A province such as Burgundy with only two outlets for the farm in 1689 was "retarded" but would in time catch up. The varying degrees of administrative elaboration in different parts of France at this time are thus a measurement of the degree to which the tobacco habit had taken hold in those several areas.

In most parts of France, retailers were left free to buy as much as they pleased. In Provence, however, a different system had been employed analagous to that for snuff. During the Fauconnet lease (1681–87), the United General Farms distributed tobacco and snuff from three *bureaux-généraux* in Marseilles, Aix, and Toulon to subcontractors or *consommateurs* for each town; the latter agreed, by *traités de consommation,* to purchase a fixed quantity each year. These they sold in their respective towns through retail agents or *distributeurs.* During the ensuing Domergue lease (1687–91), however, the united farms decided to sublet the tobacco and snuff monopolies separately in Provence. Both the new subfarming companies eventually eliminated both the existing *consommateurs* and *distributeurs* as either inefficient or corrupt and established for roll tobacco the conventional *entrepôt* system selling to ordinary retailers as elsewhere in France.[10]

Administrative Problems and Legal Redress

Since so few administrative papers of the tobacco farm of 1674–1718 have survived, we are dependent for our knowledge of much of its workings and of the problems it faced on the record of its appeals to the state for general and specific aid. Such state aid could take the form of general laws for the governance of the farm, of specific orders to cover individual and general problems and of appeals to the *conseil d'état* in its judicial capacity against decisions of lower courts disadvantageous to the monopoly.

The *déclaration* of 27 September[11] creating the monopoly and the lease of 30 November 1674[12] granting the farm to the Jean Breton company contained only the barest outline of the rights and regulations under which the new monopoly was to operate. As we noted in Chapter 2, de Lagny and colleagues had to return frequently to the council for *arrêts* explaining and expanding their powers. When the United General Farms took over the tobacco monopoly in 1680, they obtained in their lease (Boutet) a much fuller definition of their legal position.[13] This new legal formulation was repeated and amplified in the important tobacco *ordonnance* of 22 July 1681, one of a series of *ordonnances* issued that month covering all branches of the revenue farms.[14] This *ordonnance* was to be the basic legal code for the tobacco farm for the next two generations, cited in every lease and every lawsuit. It summarized existing law on the ports permitted for the import and export of tobacco, the procedures for importing, warehousing and exporting, the proper sealing and marking of the tobacco of the monopoly, the character of its various exclusive privileges, control of the cultivation, manufacture and internal transport of tobacco, the prices to be charged by the company, and the various punishments for infraction of the tobacco laws. About the same time, the United General Farms issued printed instructions for their own inspectors, guards and other employees establishing procedures under the new laws for inspecting shops, hawkers and peddlers, for searching out illicitly planted tobacco and for making seizures.[15]

With the passage of time, the legislative edifice of 1680–81 proved inadequate. Various loopholes appeared in the law and had to be plugged. In negotiating the Pierre Domergue lease in 1687, the general farms insisted on a whole catalogue of further provisions buttressing their existing legal rights. In future years, this lease of 18 March 1687 was also cited along with the *ordonnances* of 1681 to define the terms on which subsequent leases were granted.[16] The new tobacco farmers who took over the monopoly in 1697 found still other loopholes and weaknesses in procedure. After some years of enlightening experience, their administrative head, Vincent Maynon, obtained royal approval for the *déclaration* of 6 December 1707 which further codified and strengthened the rules against various forms of fraud in the tobacco revenue.[17] In addition to these three great codifications of 1681, 1687, and 1707, there were hundreds of individual orders (*arrêts*) and other acts of authority which the monopoly obtained from the king and council at various times between 1674 and 1718.

The lesser courts, by contrast, were not always as helpful as they might be. Often they appear in the record more as obstacles than as aids to the enforcement of the rights of the monopoly. French magistrates, who purchased their offices and had roots deep in local society, had no reason to view with anything except deep suspicion the intrusion into their jurisdictions of a new monopoly threatening alike their own privileges and the ease of their neighbors.

It took months to get a new lease registered in the *cour des aides* at Paris (high fiscal court from which appeal went only to the king in council) and the provincial courts of parallel jurisdiction. Until their lease was registered, revenue farmers could pursue no suits in those courts. Thus, in the earliest months of the farm in 1675 and again at the change in 1680, it was necessary to give the intendants temporary commissions to hear all cases arising out of the new monopoly[18] and to name a master of requests in Paris to hear all appeals to the council.[19] A subsequent *arrêt* of 18 December 1677 transferred complete jurisdiction in tobacco away from the local fiscal courts (*élections*) to the courts of the intendants and their *subdélégués*;[20] the *ordonnance* of July 1681, however, restored jurisdiction to the *élections* and other usual local fiscal courts, with appeal to the regional *cours des aides*.[21]

The local fiscal courts (*élections*, etc.) were usually far more troublesome than the great *cours des aides* for all their delays.[22] Every employee of the farm who might make or prosecute a seizure had to register his commission in the clerk's office of the local *élection* and take his oath of office there. In addition, the *ordonnance* of 1681 provided for the registration in these same courts of the seals and marks used to identify the tobacco of the farm. Every time the lease of the monopoly changed, there were new marks and seals to be registered and local magistrates to claim that all employees of the monopoly should take their oaths over again, at the usual fee. In addition there were fee-hungry magistrates to claim that those employees of the monopoly whose duties took them into several *élections* should register in each. Considering the hundreds of such jurisdictions in France, the monopoly might well have been at the mercy of this rapacious magistracy had not the state intervened. Starting in 1680, we find *arrêts* appearing regularly fixing the fees which great courts could charge for registering leases and which lesser courts could charge for registering commissions and for tendering oaths.[23] An *arrêt* of 25 October 1681 fixed at 30 *sols* the fee which all the officers of an *élection* together could charge for registering marks and seals or for tendering an oath of office to an employee of the tobacco farm.[24] The figure for the latter service remained standard thereafter, but those for registering marks and seals were raised to 3 *l.t.* in 1697.[25]

Nevertheless, the war continued between the tobacco monopoly and the petty courts. The *procureur* (crown attorney) in the *élection* of Mantes tried to get all retailers to register their licenses in his court, until stopped in 1688 by an order of council.[26] Further *arrêts* were necessary to establish the point that employees of the farm having registered their commissions and taken their oaths in a high court could thereafter exercise their office within any *élection* of that court without repeating the oath or paying any further fees,[27] and that sworn employees of other branches of the united farms could make tobacco seizures without swearing an additional oath for that service.[28] About 1709–10, a series of orders were required to check the efforts of some local magistrates to oblige the monopoly to register the royal order (*résultat*) granting its lease in their *élections* with quite high fees; hitherto it had always been understood that *résultats* were registered only in the *cours des aides*.[29]

In general, the tobacco monopoly, like all the farms, was successful in gaining for its employees (if not its retailers) exemptions from onerous local burdens such as billeting, militia duty, and certain local taxes.[30] On more important taxes, it was as frequently defeated, particularly on the *taille*.[31]

These same employees were by their very number both a strength and a weakness for the company. They could make enemies for the farm by sloth or malfeasance. They did not have the best reputation.[32] At the same time, their numbers and salaries gave the company the social weight of a valuable body of patronage. In the next century, this was to become a major concern of the monopoly; from the earliest days, it was important. In Chapter 2, we observed outside influence at work in the appointment of the first chief clerks of the company.[33] In 1705, we can find Nicolas Desmaretz, then *directeur des finances* under Chamillart, requesting from the farm the post of head of the *entrepôt* at Versailles for his concièrge. In 1708, as controller-general, he wanted another post for a protégé of the duke of Lauzun.[34] At a more disreputable level, some of the farmers-general themselves, particularly in the early Bernard-Crozat-Maynon years after 1697, were accused of trafficking in offices in the farm and in lining their own pockets with parts of the salaries of their "clients." (The exemption from billeting made many willing to pay handsomely for minor positions in the tobacco monopoly during the wars of 1688–1715.)[35]

During these same years, of course, many higher posts in the farm had by state action been placed completely outside the control of the farmers-general of tobacco. Exigencies of war finance had led the government of Pontchartrain to create a considerable number of posts in the farms for sale, including many *receveurs du tabac* (edicts of December 1694 and May 1696).[36] The farm did not lose any money from these creations, for it received credit in its accounts for all "salaries" paid to these receivers. The farm did, however, lose effective control over nominal subordinates who handled much of its money. The leases of 1697 and later contained clauses empowering the company, when they saw fit, to buy compulsorily at face value from the owners any such alienated office. A repurchased office became the property of the then farming company, to be purchased from it by its successor. Evidence suggests that many such compulsory purchases were in fact made.[37] The problem itself was only eliminated by the suppression and reimbursement of the alienated offices in all the farms by the edicts of August 1716 and June 1717, particularly the latter.[38]

A further element of privilege which created considerable difficulty for the tobacco monopoly was the fiscal independence of many municipalities. In addition to the royal taxation on tobacco, many local authorities, by royal grant or otherwise, taxed the tobacco consumed within their jurisdictions, either by excises collected from vendors or more commonly by tolls (*octrois*) collected on tobacco and other goods passing through the town gates. The revenues so collected might be retained locally, or all or part might have been alienated to the crown. We hear, for example, of a duty in the 1650's on sugar, wine, and tobacco consumed in Rouen which was united to the *cinq grosses fermes* in 1660.[39] That same year, a much heavier impost was levied on all the tobacco sold in the towns of Provence for the benefit of the hospitals of Aix, Marseilles, and Toulon.[40] When the freedom of the port of Marseilles was reestablished by the edict and letters patent of March 1669, an exception was made for the local and royal duties on tobacco.[41] In the event, this anomaly was removed when the monopoly was established in 1674: by article XIV of the lease the impost was abolished in Provence, but an annuity of 12,000 *l.t.* p.a. was granted by the crown to the three hospitals, assigned upon the monopoly's rent.[42] The lesser, more localized *octrois* throughout the country continued. We find, for example, an *octroi* at Amiens in 1689 which included a toll of 6 *l.t.* per quintal on tobacco.[43]

We hear little of this problem during the years when the tobacco monopoly was administered by the united farms (1680–97) —in all probability because the united farms shared in many *octrois* on behalf of the king and had long experience in working together with the towns in their collection.[44] When, however, the Bernard-Crozat-Maynon company took over the farm in 1697 at double the old price, they were anxious to define all their contractual obligations in the most specific terms. Thus, over and above the 1.5 million due the crown annually for their farm, they agreed to pay 100,000 *l.t.* annually to the United General Farms in return for an exemption from all import, export, and transit duties or tolls.[45] When this exemption was challenged by various subfarmers of the united farms in Paris, Brittany, and elsewhere, a confirmatory *arrêt* was obtained from the council on 6 September 1701 giving to the 1697 contract the status of public law.[46]

Thereafter, the issue moved to a much pettier plane. In 1703, the farmer of the *aides* of Normandy within the *élection* of Caudebec (one half of which went to the king) entered into litigation with the keeper of the tobacco *entrepôt* at Caudebec about a local toll which he insisted the tobacco monopoly owed him. The case was appealed twice to the royal council: in both instances, the council ruled that the contract of 1697 exempted the monopoly from all local *octrois* and that precedents before 1674 were irrelevent.[47] Similar decisions were rendered against Orléans in 1710,[48] Avranches[49] and Nantes[50] in 1711, and Pont-Audemer (Normandy)[51] and Mézières[52] in 1712. In the Avranches case, the local collectors of the *octrois* had attempted without success to proceed not against the farm but against its licensed retailers. In both the Avranches and Nantes cases (by far the most important for the amounts involved), the council again disallowed arguments based on precedents before 1674. This flurry of cases would seem to have settled the issue.

Thus far we have been considering problems created by the mere existence of the tobacco monopoly as a body claiming privileges. When we move from status to operation, we shall of course come across a range of much more serious problems. As a revenue farm, the tobacco monopoly had to employ guards and inspectors who occasionally arrested persons smuggling or otherwise in possession of contraband tobacco. To punish the malefactors so detected, it was necessary to bring suit in the local electoral and other fiscal courts—institutions, we have already observed, proud of their prerogatives and procedures, deeply embedded in local society, and rather unsympathetic to the "alien" monopolists. But the monopoly was also a business. As such, it could not view with equanimity long and expensive lawsuits, particularly suits against poor men from whom little could be recovered. As such, it became a prime interest of the farm (as of all the farms) to obtain for itself the quickest and least expensive legal procedures possible. In this, of course, its interest ran counter to that of the vast body of entrenched magistrates, crown attorneys, clerks of courts, and the legal profession generally.

The *déclaration* of 27 September 1674 creating the tobacco monopoly established a fine of 1,000 *l.t.* for anyone selling tobacco illegally.[53] By the lease of 30 November 1674, this would seem to have been reduced to 500 *l.t.* for a first offense (art. ii).[54] Yet almost immediately, judges began levying fines of as little as 10–30 *l.t.* on the grounds that the levels provided in the *déclaration* were impossibly high. Complaints were made to the crown that such leniency encouraged repeated offenses. A new *déclaration* was issued on 20 February 1677 for tobacco and stamped paper reducing the fines to 100 *l.t.* for a first offense and 300 *l.t.* for a second. Judges were permitted to levy higher fines when justified by the damage to the revenue, but they were forbidden to go below the minima here established.[55] The judges, it soon transpired, generally assessed only the minimum penalties prescribed regardless of the enormity of the offense. A further *déclaration* had to be issued on 27 September 1678 establishing a sliding scale for offenses against the tobacco monopoly: in cases involving up to 500 lb. of tobacco or 10 lb. of snuff, the fine was to continue 100 *l.t.* for the first offense and 300 *l.t.* for the second; in cases of from 500 to 1,000 lb. of tobacco, the penalty would be 500 *l.t.* for the first offense and 1,000 *l.t.* for the subsequent; anything over 1,000 lb. would bring a fine of 1,000 *l.t.* Judges would be personally responsible should they mitigate any penalties.[56]

For a complete system of fines and punishment, however, French law had to wait for the tobacco *ordonnance* of July 1681. The existing sliding scale was considerably stiffened: a first offense in tobacco could now bring a forfeit of 500 *l.t.* for only 10–50 lb. while anything over 50 lb. meant a 1,000 *l.t.* fine, a second offense brought a 2,000 *l.t.* fine and three years' banishment while a third offense meant the pillory and perpetual banishment. Comparable scales were established for snuff, reflecting the higher values per pound (art. xxix). The same *ordonnance* now for the first time established a separate scale of punishments for the propertyless wretches involved in smuggling bands for whom fines might be meaningless. Anyone convicted of counterfeiting the seal or marks of the monopoly (art. xxiv) or transporting contraband tobacco in armed bands (art. xxv) was to be condemned to the galleys for five years for the first offense and life for the second. Vagabonds and other poor persons arrested with illegal tobacco in their possession and unable to pay the fines were to be sentenced to the pillory for a first offense, public whipping for a second, and five years in the galleys for a third offense (art. xxvi). Anyone harboring tobacco smugglers or storing contraband tobacco was to be guilty of complicity (art. xvii).[57]

These punishments would still seem to have been inadequate for the purposes intended. The Domergue lease of 1687, art. 338, provided that the minimum punishment for selling, transporting, or concealing contraband tobacco would be confiscation and a 500 *l.t.* fine, even in cases involving less than 10 lb.[58] By a *déclaration* of 18 September 1703[59] and art. i of the *déclaration* of 6 December 1707, the minimum fine for every variety of offense against the tobacco monopoly was raised to 1,000 *l.t.* plus confiscation of all horses, carts, wagons, and gear; by art. ii, these heavy punishments were extended to those who merely bought illegal tobacco.[60]

These punishments established specially for tobacco were not exceptionally severe by the standards of the age. Even critics of the monopoly, such as the intendant Le Bret and Antoine Le Pelletier, deputy to the Council of Commerce in 1701, could only suggest harsher penalties to suppress fraud.[61] To fight the revival of all kinds of large scale smuggling in the peace interlude, 1697–1702, the government pursued general measures as rigorous as anything attempted exclusively for tobacco. A *déclaration* of 1699 raised to nine years in the galleys the punishment for smuggling prohibited goods in armed bands.[62] Another *déclaration* of 1701 tried to suppress the corruption of revenue officials by traders: merchants or tradesmen convicted of corrupting fiscal officials were for the rest of their lives to be prohibited from engaging in wholesale or retail trade; employees or agents implicated were to be pilloried for three days; the guilty officials, however, were to be sent to the galleys for nine years and lose any property they might have had in their offices.[63]

Insofar as vagabonds and other propertyless persons were concerned, the law admitted that merely monetary punishments were intended as much for terror as for compensation. Thus, the farm insisted on keeping an unrestricted right to make compositions for lesser sums without any intervention from the courts or official collectors of fines.[64] When fines could not be paid and were not compounded, it was the normal practice in French fiscal courts to convert the sentences to a time in the pillory. The *parlement* of Brittany ordered in 1689 that vagabonds and common laborers convicted of tobacco frauds who had not paid their fines or appealed within three months should *automatically* have their sentences converted to the pillory.[65] Of course, for persons not overly concerned with honor, the stocks might appear far preferable to a fine; some thus requested and obtained from the courts the immediate conversion of their fines into the pillory. A special *déclaration* had to be issued in 1705 forbidding such conversions without permission of the monopoly.[66] To block such loopholes, the *déclaration* of 1707 provided, in cases involving such persons as vagabonds, sailors, and common workmen, that if at least 300 *l.t.* of the fine had not been paid within one month of sentencing, the sentence would, on the simple request of the farm, without any hearing or legal expense, be converted into the galleys![67] Such galley service was later fixed at three years.[68] All this seemed excessively severe to some courts. There are records of a number of cases in the next few years where local courts ignored the letter of the law and let culprits off with trifling fines. In those cases printed, the monopoly appealed successfully.[69] There were undoubtedly other cases where they did not choose to appeal.

Regardless of what penalty a smuggler received, the case could be very expensive for the monopoly. Thus, a constant stream of special orders had to be solicited from the government to reduce the costs of litigation. The officers and guards of the monopoly making an arrest or seizure of goods were excused from having to go to a fiscal judge, but could make their depositions before the nearest royal judge or his lieutenant or—after 1712—before the nearest royal notary. Seized goods, other than tobacco, could be sold in the nearest market.[70] The seized tobacco did not have to be carried to the offices of the local *élection* but could be kept in the warehouses of the farm.[71] After the *déclaration* of 1707, seizures anywhere could be made by just one sworn officer, accompanied by any local official, even though the officer sworn was not an employee of the tobacco farm.[72] The fate of such seizures would in due time be decided by a single fiscal judge solely upon the evidence of the seizing officers' depositions and normally without a hearing unless the accused within a limited time (three days after 1707) filed depositions of his own (*inscriptions des faux*) challenging the facts presented in the officers' statement. (In an extreme case, the *parlement* of Brittany, in order to check perjury, ruled that *inscriptions des faux* would be received only if filed within 24 hours of the officers' original deposition.) These quite summary procedures used in petty smuggling or planting cases were termed *voies ordinaires* and were normal for cases involving only civil penalties. The courts were forbidden to use the more time-consuming, complicated, and expensive procedures (*voies extraordinaires*) involving the interrogation of the accused and of witnesses, which were reserved for "criminal" offenses, e.g., smuggling in armed bands. The difference was often artificial for "civil" fines were, if not promptly paid, automatically converted into "criminal" punishments ranging from the pillory to the galleys.[73]

Great delays and expenses for the farm were also caused by appeals by petty offenders who hoped by legal chicanery to fatigue the farm into dropping their charges. To defend themselves against such tactics—and on the apparent assumption that accused contrabanders were to be presumed guilty unless proved innocent—the monopoly obtained a provision in the Domergue lease of 1687,[74] confirmed by a *déclaration* of 25 January 1689,[75] providing that no person convicted of an offense against the tobacco farm could appeal unless he first deposited in the court within thirty days of sentencing the full amount of his fine up to 300 *l.t.*

The Varieties and Geography of Tobacco Contraband

All this litigation suggests that a considerable amount of contraband tobacco was getting into France. Some of it of course was grown there. In the next chapter, we shall discuss the domestic cultivation of tobacco as an administrative problem and as a leak in the revenue. In the remainder of this chapter, we shall confine our attention to those other sources of contraband commonly called "smuggling."

When some writers mention the "smuggling" of the seventeenth or eighteenth centuries they seem to be thinking of dishonest masters running part of the cargo of merchant ships ashore in small boats on a dark night. Some of this did of course occur, but it was generally the least important sort of fraud with which customs officials had to contend. Ships had to carry too many papers. More important, there were relatively few masters or owners who would risk the forfeiture of a large ship and its entire cargo to run a few things ashore. Where such frauds occurred, they were most often the result of the complicity of customs officers. The small private ventures that sailors might carry ashore on their persons were rarely of aggregate importance.

Serious smuggling was thus not usually a side-line to legitimate commerce, but rather the work of "specialists" using small boats devoted primarily to this service. Most trade goods were shipped in packages too large for convenient handling in smuggling. Brazil tobacco came in rolls of 250 lb.; Virginia tobacco in hogsheads rising in weight from 300 lb. in the late seventeenth century to 1,000 lb. in the mid-eighteenth. Tea, brandy, and particularly wine were commonly shipped in containers too large for any smuggler to handle. Repacking could take place on shipboard, but could more conveniently be done in friendly foreign harbors; hence, the extreme importance in the geography of seventeenth- and eighteenth-century smuggling of free ports and cheap ports (like those of Holland) and of islands outside normal customs jurisdiction.

At Marseilles in the 1680's there were reports of almost every form of smuggling by sea, facilitated and complicated by the privileges of the port. One report estimated that one-half the tobacco consumed in Provence was smuggled. Merchants could use an ostensible open and legal transit trade in Guienne and Brazil tobacco as cover for large-scale frauds. Brazil tobacco in transit was normally stored in the united farms' warehouse, though the merchants complained of the cost. Guienne tobacco passing through the port was stored in the merchants' own warehouses, under double lock, though the farm suspected the merchants of having secret doors by which they could remove legitimate tobacco for sale and substitute smuggled. In 1688, the intendant calmed both sides by inducing the *échevins* of the city to provide a free warehouse in which all transit tobacco might be securely kept. The monopoly accused some local merchants of employing small, fast boats to run tobacco ashore from incoming vessels. To prevent this, the monopoly employed an armed *chaloupe* to visit vessels approaching the harbor and post guards on board if the cargo included tobacco. The Bureau of Health, however, whose duty it was to prevent the introduction of plague from other Mediterranean ports, argued that it was unsafe for the tobacco guards to board such vessels before they had been visited by the inspectors of health. The intendant Le Bret, in April 1688, ordered the monopoly to cease such practices, even though the company complained bitterly that this restriction gave the smugglers those valuable extra hours to run their tobacco on shore in small boats near the city. For this work, armed bands were employed on shore, stronger than the forces of the farm. Once ashore and safely hid, the tobacco could be brought into the city quietly in smaller parcels as needed.

The most serious problem was not however the smuggling in of Brazilian and other foreign tobaccos which were quite expensive and hard to come by in large quantities in that part of the world, but rather the *relanding* of the cheap, plentiful Guienne tobaccos exported in great quantities from the ports of Languedoc and Provence. A merchant of Marseilles or Agde might take out papers to export some Clairac tobacco to Nice, Villefranche, Genoa, or any other port in Italy or Spain; the ship's master would however be instructed once out of the harbor to transfer the tobacco to a small boat for relanding secretly on the French Mediterranean coast. When the master eventually came back from Genoa or another port, he would bring with him forged certificates pretending that the tobacco had been landed at its foreign destination. (The return of such certificates to clear bonds given at export was compulsory under art. xx of the tobacco *ordonnance* of July 1681.) To prevent such practices, prevalent particularly in the Mediterranean, the united farms obtained a provision in the Domergue lease of 1687 (art. 336) obliging vessels exporting tobacco to take on board a guard of the monopoly who would accompany the tobacco to its foreign destination and certify its lawful export. At first, the merchants of Marseilles agreed to take such agents on board their ships, but then refused on the grounds that they would be in a position to spy into and reveal all their trade secrets. They also refused to have their outbound tobacco ships stop at Antibes so that the agents of the farm could check that none of their cargo had been relanded along the Provençal coast. The *échevins* of Marseilles supported the merchants despite allegations by the subfarmer of Provence that 120,000 lb. of Clairac tobacco had been relanded on the coasts of that province in nine months of 1688–89. To appease him, the united farms and the intendant Le Bret obtained an order from the council establishing heavy penalties for relanding or returning any Guienne tobacco exported from Marseilles.[76]

On the west coast of France there seems to have been relatively less smuggling activity in the early decades of the monopoly. The great rolls imported from Portugal were too heavy for ideal smuggling and there was no significant export trade here in native tobacco that could be used as a cover for relanding. Yet there was obviously some irregular activity along this coast. The Domergue lease of 1687 specifically provided that the tobacco monopoly was to include the islands of Ré, Noirmoutier, and Belle-Ile.[77] Nothing was done at first to establish offices of the monopoly on those islands, in all probability because it was suspected that the income from sales would not meet the costs incurred. In 1689, Jean Germain, a government contractor and farmer-general at La Rochelle, reported to the new controller-general, Pontchartrain, that there was an open trade in tobacco going on at the Ile de Ré and that the island was becoming a depot for smuggling tobacco onto the mainland. He recommended that the farm license retailers on the island who would be permitted to sell tobacco at a lower price than on the mainland—as was already done on nearby Oléron.[78] Similar measures were in all likelihood attempted there in the next few years and on Noirmoutier to the north, where, however, the residents violently resisted establishment of a *bureau de tabac* and the royal council had to intervene.[79] (Only when the crown purchased Noirmoutier from the prince of Condé in the last years of Louis XV was this question conclusively settled.) [80]

Compared to Marseilles there were relatively few complaints of smuggling in the principal ports of the west coast. Quite the contrary, after the sterner regime was established under Maynon in 1697, the complaints that survive are chiefly of the excessive zeal of the officers of the monopoly, particularly of Jean de Montigny, director at Bordeaux. Ships visiting that port were rigorously searched by his agents and every ounce of tobacco in ship's stores was locked up while the vessel was in port, forcing the poor sailor to buy from the farm to fill his pipe. Montigny was universally detested in Bordeaux, but after more than thirty years in the farm obviously had the confidence of his superiors in Paris.[81]

The situation was far more serious in these same years on the northern coast of France, close to the main centers of population and the chief seats of tobacco consumption, close too to the abundant supplies of England and Holland. England proper was not too convenient a base for tobacco smuggling into France because duties were high there, particularly after 1685, and the English government, to prevent relanding on its own coasts, was, in these very years, adopting ever more stringent regulations forbidding the export of tobacco in small parcels or on board small vessels suitable for running.[82] A more serious threat to the French monopoly than England itself were the English Channel Islands, outside English customs jurisdiction, virtually free ports and only too close to the north Breton coast.[83] From them every variety of tobacco, even that of St. Domingue, could be smuggled into France.[84]

On 13 August 1688, Controller-General Claude Le Peletier sent a circular letter to the intendants of the three Norman *généralités* announcing a new rigorous policy of administration for the tobacco farm in Normandy, an innovation provoked by the large quantities of English tobacco recently seized and by the disturbances ("especes de rébellions") associated with the smuggling.[85] The same problem also existed in germ in Brittany in the 1680's. Smugglers from thence were already finding their way to the Channel Islands and back with tobacco.[86] As early as 1685, the *parlement* of Brittany had had to issue special orders for tobacco searches on all vessels entering Breton waters.[87]

The situation in the 1680's was as nothing, however, compared to the flood of tobacco smuggling that swept over Brittany with the return of peace in 1697. The proportions of this problem are made quite clear by the official English figures for exports of tobacco to the Channel Islands (Table I).

The reader will notice immediately the differences in the volume of these shipments in peace and war. If we assume that the Channel Islands might have needed about 50,000 lb. of tobacco p.a. for their own consumption and legitimate sales to visiting ships, then shipments thither in wartime would have left only a small surplus for smuggling to England or France. Yet even in wartime, more was probably going to France than to England. On 1 March 1694/5 o.s., the English customs board reported to the Treasury that "it seems more propable [sic], That the storing of tobacco in those Islands beyond what is necessary for the Consumption thereof is rather to gaine Opportunity of stealing it into France then to returne it Backe into England."[88] If such was the case in wartime, we shall not be surprised at the much greater activity in peacetime when the seas were safer and much greater quantities were being shipped to the islands.

Yet there is something more involved than just an alternation of war and peace. The peaceful years of the 1680's saw nothing like the tempest of smuggling activity that struck after 1697. In the 1680's, there was only a limited demand for English tobacco in France. Most Frenchmen had yet to

TABLE I

English Exports of Tobacco to the Channel Islands, 1696–1714[89]

Year	Guernsey lb.	Jersey lb.	Total lb.
Mich. 1696–Mich. 1697	62,546	0	62,546
Mich. 1697–Xmas 1698	486,479	31,219	517,698
Xmas 1698–Xmas 1699	184,469	88,097	272,566
1700	151,809	108,086	259,895
1701	124,930	200,627	325,557
1702	4,172	0	4,172
1703	0	25,390	25,390
1704	37,846	3,756	41,602
1705	7,338	73,232	80,570
1706	11,009	0	11,009
1707	64,671	14,755	79,426
1708	96,686	17,528	114,214
1709	0	0	0
1710	94,179	47,648	141,827
1711	78,663	0	78,663
1712	221,915	66,761	288,676
1713	419,877	74,000	493,877
1714	249,003	256,021	505,024

be introduced to it. But, as we shall see, during the war of 1689–97, millions of pounds of Virginia tobacco were taken prize by Breton privateers and manufactured for French consumption in the workshops of the farm. A greatly increased demand had by the accidents of war been created in France for Virginia tobacco which the smugglers as well as the farm were prepared to help satisfy in peacetime.

On 20 April 1698, Béchameil de Nointel, intendant in Brittany, reported to Controller-General Pontchartrain that a great number of cadets of noble families on the North Breton coast between Tréguier and Saint-Brieuc had formed an association to go in *chaloupes* to Jersey and Guernsey to load tobacco. Since the beginning of the year, they had run 50,000 lb. into the province. The *parlement* of Brittany had been informed but the judges did not think they had the necessary means to "prosecute the guilty who have as accomplices all the inhabitants of the coast and who carry on their trade openly." The intendant felt that reliance on normal judicial procedures would only embolden "ces gentilshommes-là"; he recommended arresting two or three of them arbitrarily and holding them in prison a few months to intimidate the others. In a case later that year when a judge did sentence two gentlemen to the galleys for tobacco smuggling, the *parlement* of Brittany reduced the sentences to 1,000 *l.t.* fines on grounds that proceeding in armed bands had not been proven. The intendant of Brittany was afraid that if strong steps were not taken the evil would spread to Normandy.[90] In the event, the following year, the intendant at Caen was also to send several reports to the controller-general on tobacco smuggling from Jersey and Guernsey into his *généralité*.[91]

The government obviously regarded the situation as of some seriousness, and acted on several fronts during 1698–99. On 15 May and 15 July 1698 *arrêts* were issued by the *parlement* of Brittany citing the rebellious activity of the armed gangs that went to Jersey and Guernsey for tobacco. The populace were forbidden to give shelter, food, or drink to such smugglers; all were summoned to pursue and arrest them dead or alive; judges were enjoined to inflict the full penalties of the law on the sole evidence of the depositions of the employees of the farm without other witnesses.[92] The next year, priests and sacristans were warned not to let their churches be used to hide tobacco on pain of being held accomplices.[93] These orders had little effect in the milieu of north Brittany where the entire population identified themselves with the smugglers: even preachers attacked the monopoly from the pulpit and bishops harrassed its agents in their courts.[94] Whenever a tobacco smuggler was arrested, any number of local people were prepared to come forward and perjure themselves to defend the accused and gainsay the depositions of the officers of the farm. To limit the opportunities for such forswearing, the *parlement* of Brittany on 4 July 1701, following a precedent already established for the *gabelles,* ordered that *inscriptions en faux* against the depositions of seizing officers of the tobacco farm must be made within twenty-four hours.[95]

Royal officials were also active. On 16 July 1698, the *commissaire général de la marine* for Brittany issued a general prohibition against small boats going to Jersey and Guernsey, under threat of having their crews condemned to the galleys.[96] In 1700, the magistrates of St. Malo became alarmed at a report that this ban on trade with the islands would be extended to all vessels. They argued that such traffic was necessary to procure English wool for French manufacturers.[97] The entire matter was ultimately referred to the new Council of Commerce which reported in 1702 that France gained more from this trade than it lost in that the Channel Islands were an important base for the smuggling of French textiles and spirits into England; they recommended, however, that normal precautions be intensified against tobacco smuggling and currency export on the coasts near the Channel Islands.[98]

With the resumption of war in 1702, complaints of smuggling activity on the north Breton coast died down for a time. This may have been partly a result of security measures in the islands which made illicit traffic more difficult. (When the St. Malo merchant, Paul Causserouge de St. Paul, went to Guernsey in January 1703, to buy £6,000 sterling worth of tobacco, he was arrested, despite protestations of being a secret Huguenot and a would-be English agent.)[99] However, in the latter years of the war, the insular authorities relented and French boats flocked back to the islands.[100] This was reflected in more frequent reports of tobacco smuggling into France after 1709[101] and in a revived repressive effort. On 7 December 1710 the *parlement* at Rennes had to renew its standing prohibitions against giving succor to tobacco smugglers.[102]

With the return of "peace," the situation deteriorated remarkably. The controller-general's papers for 1713 are filled with reports from north Brittany of riots and violent resistance to the officers of the tobacco farm.[103] Despite an *arrêt du conseil* of 24 June 1713 calling for the enforcement of all laws relating to the tobacco farm, rumors were abroad in the province that the tobacco monopoly was about to be abolished. The *parlement* of Rennes had to deny them publicly and repeat its long standing injunctions on 11 August 1713[104] and 7 December 1717.[105] Even the commercial treaty of Utrecht seems to have encouraged the illicit trade. When vessels smuggling tobacco were seized, inhabitants of Jersey and Guernsey came forward as the ostensible owners, claiming the protection of the treaty. Sometimes English diplomats intervened.[106] The situation seemed to be getting out of hand. The revenues of the tobacco farm's *bureaux* at Morlaix and St. Brieuc did not cover expenses. An emergency *arrêt* was needed conferring extraordinary jurisdiction upon the intendant of Brittany from September 1713 to September 1714, to the prejudice and displeasure of the *parlement* at Rennes.[107] Yet, reports of violent resistance continued to come from those shores during the last unquiet years of Louis XIV.[108]

If smuggling by sea was a serious local problem in Provence and above all in Brittany, a far greater national problem was smuggling by land. On France's ocean frontier, only a few isolated spots like Jersey and Guernsey were well situated as bases for tobacco smuggling. The territories bordering France on the east all the way from Switzerland to the North Sea were, however, one continuous base from which tobacco could be smuggled into France. The jurisdiction of the tobacco monopoly extended by and large only over those territories (less Alsace) which had belonged to France before 1659. By the 1680's, therefore, there existed along France's eastern frontier a string of newly acquired territories outside the jurisdiction of the monopoly, including Franche-Comté, Alsace, Lorraine (in French occupation, 1670–97), Artois, Hainault, and Flanders. In two of these, Alsace and Flanders, there were significant tobacco growing industries. In all of them, tobacco planting was permitted. It was hopeless to challenge the local privileges and exemptions so recently confirmed by treaties and royal charters and grants. Of all the eastern provinces, only in the Three Bishoprics (the *généralité* of Metz) were the powers of the farm officially operative.[109] France's own eastern territories were therefore the base whence came the greater part of the contraband "foreign" tobacco which so plagued the farm.

The first land frontier to become an active center of tobacco smuggling was that between Picardy within the monopoly and Artois without. Here an artificial line across open country separated the great consuming areas of Paris and Normandy from the not too distant growers of Lille and the manufacturers of St. Omer. Shortly after the peace of Nijmegen, de Ris, acting for the intendant of Picardy, issued an *ordonnance* warning the inhabitants of that province to have nothing to do with the tobacco smugglers and to let no tobacco be found on their premises, in transit or otherwise.[110] The real solution, however, lay not on the Picard but on the Artesian side of the frontier. At the behest of the king, the estates of Artois, anxious to preserve their privileges, had on 29 July 1678 ordered the inhabitants of the parishes lying within three leagues of the frontier of Picardy to cease planting tobacco (under threat of a 1,000 *l.t.* fine). The inhabitants appeared to obey, but continued to smuggle nonetheless. Instead of dealing in their own "home grown" tobacco, the more enterprising inhabitants of the three league zone imported tobacco from elsewhere in Artois or from Flanders and sold it to smugglers or sent it into Picardy on their own account. To check these new practices, Le Tonnelier de Breteuil, intendant of Picardy and Artois, issued an *ordonnance* on 16 September 1681, codifying various separate measures adopted since 1678 by, or with the assent of, the estates of Artois. Henceforth persons living within the three league frontier zone were prohibited not just from planting tobacco but also from manufacturing, selling, or storing leaf or roll tobacco. No one was to have in his possession more than one month's personal supply, calculated at the rate of two pounds per month per household. Punishments, however, were rather moderate: confiscation plus fines of 25 *l.t.* for a first offense, 50 *l.t.* for a second, and 100 *l.t.* for a third offense, with corporal punishment threatened if necessary.[111]

When the inhabitants of the three league zone subsequently resumed planting and trading on the pretext that the *ordonnance* applied only to the Boutet lease of 1680 and not to the Fauconnet lease of 1681, the terms of the intendant's arrangement were confirmed and made permanent by an order of the Council of State in 1685.[112] In 1687, by article 340 of the Domergue lease, the zone was once more confirmed and the penalty for infraction raised to 1,500 *l.t.*[113] A slight complication arose from the town of Bapaume in Artois, within three leagues of Picardy, which had a local monopoly of tobacco farmed to a small syndicate. The rights of the farmers of tobacco at Bapaume had been specifically confirmed by an *ordonnance* of the intendant de Breteuil in 1681[114] and by the royal *arrêt* of 1685. To prevent such a small local farm from becoming a cover for smuggling, the general farms took over its concession from the lessee Bertrand in 1688.[115]

It need not be surprising that diseases and remedies suitable to the frontier between Picardy and Artois should appear in time along other sections of the frontier of the monopoly further inland. About this very time, a certain Fiévé obtained for 750 *l.t.* p.a. the right to sell tobacco in the town of Cateau in Cambrésis. The Cambrésis, like adjacent Hainault and Artois, was outside the monopoly's authority. Tobacco planting was permitted, though relatively little was grown. Fiévé immediately started buying large quantities of tobacco in Lille, St. Omer, Valenciennes, and elsewhere, allegedly for his new contract. In one eight-month period, he sent over 58,000 lb. to Cateau, although it was alleged that the town and its environs could consume only 2,000–3,000 lb. p.a. The surplus soon found its way into the territories of the monopoly. Other quantities he bought and shipped toward Picardy and Champagne without even bothering going through Cateau. When the matter was brought to the attention of the government in 1686, Controller-General Le Peletier instructed Bagnols, intendant in Flanders, that the king did not want to disturb the freedom of planting or trade in the Cambrésis, but that the united farms should take over Fiévé's contract. A somewhat more rigorous solution was effected a few months later. The farmers-general took over the Fiévé lease for six years, paying the magistrates of Cateau-Cambrésis twice the old rent, or 1,500 *l.t.* At the same time, the ban on keeping stores of tobacco, already in force in those parts of Artois within three leagues of Picardy, was now extended to the town of Cateau and to those sections of the Cambrésis and Hainault lying within three leagues of the frontier of Picardy. No household was to keep more than a month's supply—two pounds—on hand. The penalties were to be 100 *l.t.* for the first offense and 500 *l.t.* for the second.[116]

The enforcement of the three league ban was not easy or uniform. In 1687, Chauvelin, intendant for Picardy and Artois, reported that a recent enforcement of the prohibition against planting in the three league zone had provoked armed riots. He recommended taking legal proceedings against the disobedient parishes as well as sending cavalry into the disaffected districts.[117] Part of the difficulty lay in defining exactly which parishes were included within the three league zone. In his *ordonnance* of 1681, Breteuil, the then intendant, had taken an existing list of parishes already in use for the security of the *gabelles*. This, however, omitted the boundary between Artois and the Boulonnais (which was subject to the tobacco monopoly but not the *gabelles*) even though that territory was intended to be included. To avoid such difficulties, a new list of the affected parishes was drawn up by a committee of the estates of Artois and confirmed by the Council of State in 1690.[118] Yet, a new measurement of the three league zone had to be ordered again in 1705.[119]

All these steps along the northern frontier were only partially successful. In 1707, the tobacco farm reported to the controller-general that the law was disregarded in several sections of the zone and that two villages openly grew tobacco. The armed bands that carried this tobacco into Picardy and all the way to Paris were so strong that they frightened off the guards of the farm. Instructions were sent to the intendant to use the *maréchaussée* (mounted rural police) where necessary.[120] From Normandy too, reports were received of armed bands operating up to the gates of Rouen.[121] In 1711, with the approach of peace, instructions had to be given to the intendants in Normandy, Picardy, and neighboring provinces to take the most strenuous measures to break up and arrest these armed bands smuggling tobacco; all police elements were to be regularly used; communities giving any assistance to these vagabonds were to be collectively fined.[122]

Inside the area of the tobacco monopoly, once the frontier had been passed, the chief problem was of course to prevent by patrols and inspections at bridges and town gates the easy movement of contraband tobacco. Successive measures provided for the searching of public coaches and wagons and the punishment (including confiscation of horses and carriages) of coach and wagon proprietors who let their equipment be used to convey contraband tobacco.[123] There were also long standing arrangements for revenue officers to search private premises, accompanied by a local magistrate. Such procedures had most recently been codified in the *ordonnance* of 1681 for all the farms, but proved inadequate as far as privileged places, ecclesiastical and seigneurial, were concerned.[124] Another *arrêt* of 14 August 1688 established a special procedure for officers of the tobacco farm, accompanied by an officer of the local *élection,* to search such places as privileged châteaux, royal residences, and convents.[125] This proved a delicate regulation to enforce as officers of the royal households were sometimes involved.[126] There are on the other hand records of very severe sentences against members of religious orders implicated.[127]

An even more difficult problem of security was created by the large French army stationed near the frontier in peace and war, constantly on the march across the line which separated the territories within the tobacco monopoly from the frontier provinces where tobacco could be obtained so much more cheaply. To appease the troops and make it less worth their while to smuggle, a policy had been instituted by the early 1680's of selling tobacco to them at reduced prices. In the Domergue lease of 1687, it was specified that common domestic tobacco should be sold to the ranks for 12 *sols* per lb. (and 9 *deniers* per ounce), less than one-half the price (25 *sols* per lb.) charged by licensed retailers.[128] This immediately made it necessary to take steps (usually rationing) to prevent soldiers from reselling their tobacco to civilians in garrison towns.[129] Despite these favors, there were repeated reports of large scale smuggling by the troops, particularly in the distressed years around 1709 when pay was long in arrears.[130]

For many years, going back at least to the 1640's, it had been the practice of the French government to issue frequent general orders to the troops forbidding them to smuggle salt and other goods or defraud the collectors of the *aides* on wines. Punishments ranging up to the death penalty were specified.[131] No special mention was made of tobacco. The tobacco *ordonnance* of July 1681 for the first time provided that soldiers or sailors selling contraband tobacco were to receive corporal punishment and a 300 *l.t.* fine.[132] This was quite mild compared to other punishments then in force. The situation would seem to have deteriorated in the later 1680's, for Controller-General Le Peletier sent out numerous instructions to intendants in 1687 calling upon them to exert themselves to check tobacco smuggling by the troops.[133]

With the start of the war in 1688, the situation became more acute, for hundreds of thousand of troops would thenceforth regularly be passing back and forth across the limits of the tobacco monopoly. Many of them would have had some experience with tobacco smuggling, particularly during the Spanish Succession War when many petty convicted tobacco and salt smugglers who could not pay their fines were drafted into the army instead of being sent to the galleys. The first *ordonnance* devoted particularly to tobacco smuggling among the troops was issued on 16 October 1688. Soldiers were forbidden to have in their possession more than one ounce of tobacco at a time, under penalty of prison and public beating ("d'être passez par les Baguettes"). Those who smuggled tobacco in armed bands or who were repeated offenders in lesser trafficking in contraband tobacco were to be sent to the galleys. The guards of the farm could search the gear of officers and men. Officers who were negligent in enforcing these regulations would be fined.[134] The next autumn, 1689, another *ordonnance* was issued warning troops returning to winter quarters after the campaigns not to attempt to bring any tobacco back with them under threat of the galleys. An *ordonnance* of similar content was thereafter issued regularly every fall during that war and the next.[135] In the process, the penalties gradually became harsher. All horses or carts used for tobacco contraband were to be confiscated, regardless of whether they belonged to the soldiers involved, to officers, or to others. The 1707 *ordonnance* specified life sentences on the galleys. The most severe change came in 1709, when French government finances were most desperate, and the temptation to smuggling greatest among the soldiers whose pay was so long in arrears. Efforts were made to tighten army controls, and a new *ordonnance* was issued, parallel to the old one, governing smuggling by troops in garrison. The death penalty for smuggling by soldiers in armed bands, which had applied to salt since 1682, was now extended to tobacco. On complaint of an agent of the farm, soldiers accused were to be tried immediately by courts martial and sentences as promptly carried out. Even unarmed smuggling was to be punished by the galleys for life. Soldiers in garrison were forbidden to appear out of uniform nor were they to leave their garrison towns without written passes. Soldiers arresting smugglers could keep the horses and gear seized and were to receive cash rewards in proportion to the amount of salt or tobacco seized and the number of smugglers captured.[136] This garrison *ordonnance* was also issued annually thereafter.[137] A royal *déclaration* of 30 January 1717 codified the law governing all kinds of smuggling by troops. Thereafter, soldiers offering any kind of violent resistance or obstruction to the employees of any revenue farm were to be punished by death.[138] It is doubtful if the death sentence for tobacco smuggling was carried out very frequently, if at all, in this generation; however, life sentences on the galleys were given.[139] Nevertheless, a further death penalty was established in 1718 for soldiers on guard against tobacco contraband in Picardy, Champagne, and the Soissonnais who took bribes from the smugglers.[140]

Officials of the tobacco farm could thus by the turn of the century search châteaux, convents, royal palaces, travelers' baggage, and soldiers' packs. They could not, however, search odd corners of the kingdom whose lords had either by the vagaries of history or by rather recent royal grants retained or obtained rights of "sovereignty." Such appanages or sovereignties could be very embarrassing to the monopoly, for they were too often enclaves surrounded by French territory, but outside their own authority. As such they made excellent bases for smuggling tobacco into France. Since there was no immediate hope of terminating their privileges, the farm could only end the vexations from these jurisdictions by buying them out. For a price, the several princes would usually agree to lease to the united farms or tobacco farm of France the tobacco monopoly or revenues in their several territories. This gave the French monopoly the right to send in agents who were usually able to put an end to smuggling.

This new policy was put into effect by the united farms about the year 1686, just after Hénault took over the management of tobacco. On the northeastern frontier (in the modern department of the Ardennes) was the sovereignty of Arches and Charleville, belonging to the Gonzagas, dukes of Mantua (reunited to the French crown in 1708 by the death of the last duke, but regranted to the prince of Condé). By a contract of 7 May 1686 with the duke and the local magistrates, the united farms of France acquired the tobacco monopoly in Arches and Charleville, agreeing to buy up most of the tobacco then on hand. No tobacco was to be planted thereafter during the duration of the lease.[141] At Charleville, the tobacco farmers were later in 1703 to establish an important tobacco manufactory.[142] Nearby (also in the modern Ardennes) was the county of Rethel, sold by the duke of Mantua to the duke of Mazarin in 1663. By a contract of 18 May 1686, the united farms also obtained the tobacco farm in that jurisdiction for 3,300 *l.t.* p.a.[143] Slightly further to the east (in the modern department of the Meuse) were the jurisdictions of Clermont, Stenay, Dun, and Jamets (belonging to the prince of Condé) whose tobacco monopoly was leased about the same time— 1686—for a mere 800 *l.t.* p.a.[144] Again in 1686, though at the other end of France, the united farms acquired from the duke of Bouillon the lease of the tobacco monopoly in the viscounty of Turenne (in the modern department of Corrèze).¹⁴⁵ This lease was primarily an attempt to check an important tobacco growing industry, as we shall see in the next chapter.

Other territories of varying importance escaped the farm's control in the two generations between 1674 and 1718. These included the substantial principality of Dombes, north of Lyons, which in 1681 passed into the possession of the duke of Maine (son of Louis XIV and Madame de Montespan) and was not reunited to France till 1762.¹⁴⁶ Equally exempt were such lesser jurisdictions as the *pays de Labourd* (about Bayonne) and the minute *pays de Soule* on the Spanish border which imported its tobacco from Bayonne. On the other hand, while Nice was occupied by French troops in the War of the Spanish Succession, the subfarmer of tobacco in Provence leased the tobacco monopoly from the Senate there (ca. 1711) to prevent that city from being used as a base for smuggling operations into his jurisdiction.¹⁴⁷

More important than all these jurisdictions together, however, was the great frontier duchy of Lorraine.¹⁴⁸ Tobacco had been known there from the beginning of the seventeenth century; in fact, its cultivation had been prohibited in 1628 as a danger to the food supply. During the time when Lorraine was occupied by French troops between 1670 and 1697, a tobacco monopoly was established along the general lines prevailing in France after 1674.¹⁴⁹ When the duchies of Lorraine and Bar were restored to duke Leopold by the treaty of Ryswick in 1697, a brief period of confusion ensued for tobacco. Cultivation was permitted and the manufacture and trade were left uncontrolled. Very soon, however, the fiscal interest of the restored duke asserted itself and by a lease of 21 January 1700, the re-established tobacco monopoly in Lorraine was leased for eight years to a company headed by the Genoese, Marc Antoine Boncony or Boccony, baron of St. Lazarre. Although the price of the lease was the ridiculously low figure of 12,000 *l.l.* annually, the new monopoly company was soon in trouble, for its lease fixed at absurdly low levels its sale prices on Lorraine-grown tobaccos. At the same time, it had no real protection against the smuggling in of choicer, more expensive foreign tobaccos which many in the duchies preferred. To rescue the monopoly, the duke on 7 December 1703 issued a *règlement* covering all aspects of the tobacco trade in Lorraine. Planters had to obtain a license from the monopoly and deliver all their growth to it. In the French fashion, all manufactured tobacco had to be appropriately sealed or marked. Finally, sales prices were raised significantly, as is suggested by Table II.

Although prices were raised in Lorraine in 1703, they were still extremely low by the standards of France, where very little manufactured tobacco (except that for the troops) sold for less than 25 *sols* per lb. and most for much more. Lorraine understandably became a great depot for the smuggling of cheap tobaccos into France. In the most affected of French frontier provinces, the enclaved Three Bishoprics, all serious efforts were abandoned to enforce the monopoly in the countryside.¹⁵⁰ A memoir prepared for the French monopoly in 1707 or 1708 estimated that of some

TABLE II

Authorized Prices of Manufactured Tobacco
in Lorraine, 1700 and 1703[151]
(in local money)

Manufactured Tobacco	1700 per lb.	1703 per lb.
Rouge commun filé	5 s.	7 s.
Rouge fin à fumer	6 s.	9 s.
Tabac noir	3 s.	6 s.
Twists for snuffmaking	22 s.	22 s.

700,000 lb. of tobacco grown annually in Lorraine, only 200,000 lb. were consumed in the duchy, the rest being smuggled into France. By that time, the yield to the duke's treasury had risen to 27,000 l.l. annually from the monopoly. The French farmers (then the Bernard-Crozat-Maynon company) did the only logical thing: in February 1708, for 40,000 l.l. annually to the duke, they leased the tobacco monopoly in Lorraine and Bar for six years in the name of their then straw-man, Germain Gaultier. In 1714, the lease was renewed for six years at 55,000 l.l. in the name of Nicolas Bogelot or Beaujelot.[152] Though a generation later, the acquisition of the Lorraine farm in 1708 by the Bernard-Crozat-Maynon company marks an obvious continuation of the policy of leasing troublesome tobacco monopolies beyond their own frontiers started by the united farms under Hénault's management in 1686.

In the end, though, when we add up all the elaborate precautions taken by the tobacco farm to check smuggling by land and sea—leasing the tobacco farms in sovereignties, establishing frontier zones, searching everywhere, threatening with ever more dire punishments, striving for ever more summary justice—we realize that one great flaw still persisted throughout the whole system, the thousands and tens of thousands of small retailers all over the country, including keepers of public houses of every description, who sold the consumer his tobacco by the quarter pound, the ounce, or even the pipeful. These small men possessed unique opportunities to mix contraband leaf with legal, and thus were as much the principal vendors of contraband as they were of legal tobacco. Without their collusion, it would have been impossible for smuggled tobacco to reach the consumer in any quantity.

Among these retailers, we may distinguish two general classes: regular dealers in tobacco licensed by the monopoly; and public house keepers, *cabaretiers, académistes,* and the like who kept a little tobacco on hand for the convenience of their guests. In the latter category, we may also include petty shopkeepers who handled a little tobacco as a convenience for their neighbors in villages with no licensed tobacco dealer. Even though the original lease of 1674 (art. ii) and the tobacco *ordonnance* of July 1681 (art. i) provided that no one was to sell tobacco without the license of the monopoly, such petty transactions had been tolerated for a time as a convenience to the public. The opportunities for fraud were obvious. The letter of the law was finally put into effect by an order of the *cour des aides* in 1686 which prohibited *cabaretiers, académistes,* and the like from supplying pipes and tobacco to their guests (or letting anyone do so on their premises) without first registering with the officers of the farm.[153] These new controls were formalized by an order of the Council of State of 23 December 1688 which established penalties of 500 and 1,000 *l.t.* for violators; and granted the agents of the farm a general right of search.[154] There is some evidence that these rules were enforced.[155] In those inland provinces, too, so poorly supplied with *entrepôts* by the first monopolists, where some private, unlicensed trade had at first had to be tolerated, the law against unlicensed vending was gradually brought into operation in the course of the 1680's.[156]

Even with all retailers licensed and all innkeepers registered, the problem was not solved. As long as tobacco was sold in very small quantities, it would be possible to mix in contraband with legal leaf. To check this, the tobacco *ordonnance* of July 1681 had provided that all the tobacco of the farm should bear distinctive marks or seals, with heavy fines provided by art. ix for anyone selling unmarked or unsealed tobacco. Most commonly, before delivery to retailers, the spun tobacco was cut from the rolls and pressed into pieces (*bouts*) to which, at one end, wax seals were applied. The customer normally either chewed the tobacco or grated it himself for smoking. Since any further processing prior to sale would involve the removal of the seals, licensed retailers and all others were forbidden by the *ordonnance* of 1681 to manufacture French or foreign tobacco into snuff—or even to possess cutting or grinding mills.[157] (Licensed tobacco retailers were, however, permitted to carry rasps for sale to consumers to grate their own tobacco.) [158] In the special case of snuff, the monopoly in its first dozen or so years tried to minimize fraud by forcing retailers large and small (*marchands* and *débitants*) to sign contracts (*traités de consommation*) by which they agreed to buy from the farm a specific quantity of *poudre* each year, ranging from 45 lb. p.a. in Cahors to 500 lb. p.a. in a Paris case. After 1687, we have seen, this policy was abandoned in favor of subfarming the snuff privilege in groups of provinces.[159]

Roll tobacco, however, remained the heart of the fraud problem. There being no automatic reason why a licensed retailer should necessarily obey the letter of the law, Maynon had recourse to terror after 1697. The fines of 1681 proving inadequate, a royal *déclaration* was obtained in 1703 prohibiting the sale of unsealed tobacco under penalty of a 1,000 *l.t.* fine for the first offense and corporal punishment for the second.[160] The draconian *déclaration* of 1707 made the galleys the punishment for even a first offense by shopkeepers, prohibiting any judicial moderation or commutation of sentences.[161]

The monopoly would continue to struggle with the problem of retailers and contraband down to 1789. The solutions of the reign of Louis XIV were of only limited success. In these insoluble problems we must see the peculiar logic of the position of the farm. Because contraband could not be eliminated, the entire trade, including customers' taste, had to be organized in such a way as to minimize its impact. Since, with all due allowances for Brittany and Provence, smuggling by sea was generally much less serious than smuggling by land, it was in the interest of the farm to import tobacco by sea rather than by land—and to create in France a taste for those types of tobacco which came by sea and not for those which came by land. As early as 1681, the importation of tobacco by land was prohibited.[162] Never in the first century of the monopoly would the company buy significant quantities of tobacco from the eastern provinces immediately outside its jurisdiction. The less French consumers knew about the tobaccos of Alsace and Flanders, the better.

Herein lies the ultimate commercial importance of the administrative problems of the farm: the better Frenchmen liked overseas tobaccos, the easier the monopoly would be to enforce. We cannot therefore understand the buying policy of the farm without appreciating its enforcement problems. With such an appreciation, we shall also be better able to understand the monopoly's policy toward the domestic cultivation of tobacco in France.

CHAPTER 6

The Domestic Cultivation of Tobacco During the Early Farms, 1674–1718

The Restrictive Policy and Its Critics

Every first-year university student knows that a most basic principle of "mercantilist" state economic policy in the seventeenth and eighteenth centuries was never to import what could be readily produced at home. Yet, French state action, even in the lifetime of the great Colbert, discouraged the production of tobacco at home and willfully stimulated greater imports from abroad. Fiscal necessity, the missing chapter in so many accounts of mercantilism, does of course and must indeed explain a lot.

There was nothing in the *déclaration* of 27 September 1674 setting up the tobacco monopoly, nor in the first lease of 30 November 1674 to the Jean Breton company, which suggested that the government was thinking of prohibiting or restricting the plantation of tobacco in France. Quite the contrary, the lease specifically protected the minimal interests of the growers and exporters of French domestic tobacco. Such tobacco was either to be sold to the monopoly or exported. Foreigners were specifically given liberty to come into France to buy and ship out French tobacco giving bond for its due exportation. The officers of the farm were to give all exporters passes specifying the route by which they could send their tobacco across French territory to the ports of exportation.[1] An *arrêt* of 25 January 1676 limited the ports at which tobacco could be exported, but this was self-evidently to simplify administration and guard against relanding.[2] The list of ports was quite generous, nine ports on the Atlantic and five in the Mediterranean.[3] Of these, those on the Mediterranean were the most important since, for reasons which are not entirely clear, Italy rather than France itself, even before the establishment of the monopoly in 1674, had become the principal market for French domestic tobacco.

A basic innovation in policy came only a few months later, though it was not presented as such. By an *arrêt* of 14 March 1676, the royal council forbade the planting of tobacco anywhere in the kingdom except in the *généralités* of Bordeaux and Montauban and the vicinity of Mondragon, Saint Mexant (near Tulle in Limousin), Léry (Normandy), and Metz. Mondragon was a French enclave in the papal Comtat-Venaissin on the Rhone. Metz was as yet a French enclave in Lorraine; tobacco had been planted there since the 1620's. All these were allegedly the only areas in which tobacco had been planted before the creation of the monopoly in

1674. The declared intention of the *arrêt,* for the sake of administrative convenience, was merely to prevent the spread of cultivation into new regions.[4] The same explanation was used a year later when a new *arrêt* of 6 February 1677 further limited the areas of cultivation permitted within the *généralités* of Bordeaux and Montauban. Its preamble explained that, as soon as the agents of the farm had opened their offices in the districts where tobacco had commonly been cultivated, evil-minded men began planting in other, entirely new neighborhoods with the sole and obvious intention of escaping the vigilance of the farm. To check such evasion, the cultivation of tobacco was thereafter limited to those places in the two *généralités* where it had reportedly been grown before 1674:

Bordeaux (*all in modern department of Lot-et-Garonne*)	Montauban* (*all in modern department of Tarn-et-Garonne*)
Deux Tonneins	Meauzac
Clairac	Villeneuve-la-Garde
Aiguillon	Villemade
Damazan	Saint Porquier
Monheurt	Escatalens
Puch-de-Gontaut	Montech
Villeton	Castelsarrasin
Le Mas d'Agenais	
La Gruère	
Gontaud	
Fauillet	
Grateloup	
La Parade	
La Fitte	
Caumont	
Verteuil	

*All (except Villemade) in Bas-Montauban, later transferred to *généralité* of Toulouse

Each of these was a *communauté* or township, embracing several parishes. Illegal planting elsewhere was to be punished by confiscation of the crop and a 1,000 *l.t.* fine.[5]

The tobacco *ordonnance* of July 1681 repeated all these provisions: in the *généralité* of Bordeaux, it added a place given as "Bouseau" (perhaps Boussès in Lot-et-Garonne); in Normandy, it amplified the "vicinity of Léry" to include Léry, Les Damps, and Vaudreuil (all in the modern department of Eure). It also established more elaborate procedures in the growing regions. Before planting, the would-be cultivator was obliged to report to the appropriate officials of his municipality exactly where and how much he intended to grow; within one month of planting, he had to report the same to the officers of the farm. If, at the harvest, the tobacco were not immediately

The Tobacco-Growing Area in Guienne, ca. 1710
(Tobacco jurisdictions indicated by "T")
*From J.-B. Nolin's map of Direction of Bordeaux,
courtesy of the British Museum.*

exported, the grower or buyer would have to store the same at his own expense in an approved warehouse under the key of the farm. Buyers for export had to report their purchases immediately and obtain the necessary papers. Any infractions brought confiscation and a 500 *l.t.* fine.[6]

The restrictive innovations of 1676–81 seem to have attracted relatively little attention at the time. In the entire first generation of the monopoly, 1674–97, virtually no documents have come to light questioning the principle on which the new legislation was proceeding, except a few from officials in areas immediately concerned. In 1680, de Pouançay, governor of St. Domingue, wrote to Colbert suggesting that in the interests of that colony, tobacco planting be *prohibited* entirely in France, "just as they do in England" (where tobacco planting had been outlawed since 1619, primarily in the interest of Virginia) .[7] On the other side, Henri d'Aguesseau, intendant in Languedoc, had written Colbert the previous year suggesting various ways in which the cultivation of tobacco might be encouraged in France. Colbert replied rather testily, "His Majesty does not wish to encourage tobacco growing in the kingdom; on the contrary, he wishes to ruin it if possible, because that cultivation ruins the colonies on the American islands."[8] Yet Colbert never quite dared follow the recommendations of de Pouançay and abolish the cultivation in France entirely. His compromise of 1676–77, restricting cultivation to a few specified places, was to persist for two generations until challenged by a more daring innovator.

Only in the years of debate between the wars, 1697–1702, was the nature of this whole "compromise" examined and then only cursorily. For de Lagny, writing in 1697, everything was all right. Three million pounds of tobacco were raised in the *généralités* of Bordeaux and Montauban, most of which was usefully exported to Italy and Spain.[9] He did not think it necessary to discuss why this leaf wasn't consumed at home, or why more wasn't grown in France. Others were less complacent. Writing in 1698, Jean Pottier, sieur de la Hestroy, a retired official in the navy ministry and sometime admiralty judge at Dunkirk, saw no reason why domestic production might not be increased. He suggested that the monopoly be abolished and domestic growers required to pay a license fee of so much per arpent which, on the basis of average yields, could be calculated to come to the same as the import duties levied on French colonial tobaccos. A resident of the north of France, he seemed hardly aware that any tobacco was then being grown in France.[10] In a subsequent version of his memoir, written ca. 1711, Pottier appeared as a much more ardent advocate of the tobaccos of Guienne and Artois. He would give those provinces preference even over the French colonies in supplying France with tobacco (an attitude reflecting the difficulties which France was having in obtaining tobacco during the long War of the Spanish Succession) .[11]

When the Council of Commerce met in 1701, the question of domestic production received very little attention, principally because the deputies represented commerce and not agriculture. Only the conservative deputy from Rouen, Mesnager, like the conservative Pottier, thought that more tobacco might be grown in France.[12] Most of the rest ignored the question. The only other deputy who discussed it, Joachim Descazeaux du Hallay, representative of Nantes and of the West India trade, believed that all cultivation in France should be prohibited to help the colonies.[13] This suggestion was not, however, incorporated in the draft recommendations from the council to the king.

With publicists and public men uninterested, the plaints of the cultivators had to be addressed to the local authorities, particularly the intendants. It was thus at the level of local administration that the real debate took place over the policy of restricting tobacco production.

The General Enforcement of Restriction, 1674–1718

For convenience, we can divide the general administrative problem of the government and the monopoly in restricting tobacco cultivation into local problems defined by geography: (a) the greater part of the kingdom where a total prohibition of planting had to be enforced; (b) the isolated areas, such as the parishes in Normandy, where a little tobacco cultivation was permitted; and (c) the principal growing areas in the southwest where millions of pounds of tobacco were produced.

Hardly had the first prohibitions on planting been issued in 1676 when the farm found itself in litigation with the widowed countess of Verton who claimed an exemption based on ancient grants. Her three villages of Verton, Berq, and Merlimont (near Montreuil) had obtained exemptions from *aides* and *gabelles* at a time when they were French enclaves in alien Artois. The royal council ruled now, however, that as they were undeniably part of France and not Artois, they were subject to the ban on planting.[14]

The *dame seigneur de Verton* was obviously not the only person in France who chose to ignore the initial ban on tobacco planting. On 4 June 1680, Colbert sent a circular letter to all the intendants calling their attention to the problem. Although the letter was sent out in the very month in which the tobacco monopoly was transferred from the old Breton company to the United General Farms, the minister chose to stress not the fiscal but the colonial and subsistence aspects of the problem: much better, healthier tobacco could be grown in the colonies than in France; tobacco used land which could be better employed in wheat. He asked each intendant to report precisely how much tobacco was grown in his *généralité*, exactly where, what was its quality, and how much more did the cultivators make from the tobacco than from other crops which might be grown on the same land.[15] The only reply located was that from the intendant of Bordeaux, in whose jurisdiction most of the tobacco growing regions lay. He characteristically called for an extension of the permitted acreage, particularly in the *élections* of

Agen and Condom.[16] Neither his report nor those of any of the other intendants could have influenced Colbert very much—we already know his general attitude toward domestic cultivation—for the tobacco *ordonnance* of the next year, as already noted, continued the existing restrictive code substantially unchanged.

In the subsequent enforcement of these restrictions, physicians and apothecaries seem to have been particularly troublesome, pretending that what all others were prohibited to grow they could raise for medicinal purposes. Thus, the Domergue lease of 1687 had specifically to declare that the prohibition of planting by the *ordonnance* of 1681 applied to physicians and apothecaries (art. 337). It also declared that proprietors allowing their land to be used illegally for tobacco planting would have such land confiscated (art. 338). Nevertheless, after the war started in 1688 and tobacco became scarcer and more expensive, even for smugglers, apothecaries and others attempted once more to circumvent the laws, only insisting now that what they were growing was legally not really tobacco. When officers of the farm detected an apothecary at Clermont in Auvergne growing tobacco, he insisted that it was really the *herbe Nicotianne* and thus not covered by the language of the *ordonnance* of 1681. His argument was supported by the gild (*corps*) of apothecaries of Clermont and was allowed by the fiscal judges (*élus*) there and, on appeal, by the *cour des aides* of Clermont. The Council of State, however, reversed the decision on higher appeal and ruled that art. xiv of the tobacco *ordonnance* of July 1681 prohibited the planting of tobacco under any name.[17] A year and a half later, the *parlement* of Paris also had to prohibit the growing of certain degenerate forms of tobacco under the pretense that such was really henbane (*jusquiame*) or anything else.[18] After the new company took over the monopoly in 1697, they found it still necessary to obtain a further *déclaration* from the king prohibiting the planting of tobacco under the names of *nicotiane, herbe à la Reine, herbe Sainte-Catherine* or whatever.[19]

Nevertheless, in 1710 (when everything fiscal seemed to be going wrong) a mason in Paris was fined only 6 *l.t.* instead of 1,000 *l.t.* on the grounds that what he had been caught growing was not *tabac* but *nicotiane*. On appeal, the distinction was upheld by the *cour des aides*, ignoring the Clermont case of 1689 and greatly annoying Controller-General Desmaretz.[20] On higher appeal, the Council of State reversed the decision, fined the mason 1,000 *l.t.* plus expenses, specifically confirmed the Clermont decision, and prohibited again the planting of tobacco under the names of *nicotiane, herbe à la Reine, herbe au Grand Prieur,* or any other.[21]

By the *arrêt* of 1676[22] and the *ordonnance* of 1681, the fine for growing tobacco in unauthorized places became confiscation plus a 1,000 *l.t.* fine. In addition, the *ordonnance* provided a 500 *l.t.* fine for growers in permitted localities who failed to report their planting plans to the municipal officers and the agents of the farm within the times prescribed.[23] These rules were considerably tightened by the *déclaration* of 18 September 1703 which forbade any person of any quality to plant tobacco without getting written permission in advance from the officers of the farm, subject to a 1,000 *l.t.* fine, double that of 1681 for the permitted areas. In addition, the guards of the monopoly could in the English fashion destroy on the spot any tobacco growing illegally without judicial process.[24] This last provision seems to have led to considerable violence in rural districts in the next few years, with peasants banding together to drive off officers of the farm who came to pull up their tobacco. In 1707, we have reports of several such disturbances in the *généralités* of Tours and Rouen.[25] There were also several reports from different parts of the country about 1708–14 of plantations within monastic grounds allegedly for the ease of the poor monks, who also knew how to use violence to drive off the agents of the farm.[26] In 1710, troops had to be sent to support the farm at Thuillières in Champagne.[27] (Cavalry had had to be regularly used in England until the domestic plantations were finally suppressed in the 1680's.)

Questions of jurisdiction were also raised similar to that posed in the first months of the prohibition by the *dame seigneur de Verton*. In 1694, the council had to tell the inhabitants of the *isle de Bouin* (off the Poitevin coast) that they could not plant tobacco, whatever they might think of their privileges.[28] A much more serious jurisdictional problem was posed by the rather vague language of the early legislation restricting tobacco plantations. Just what did the *arrêts* of 1676–77 and the *ordonnance* of 1681 mean by the "environs" of such and such a place? This became a problem in Normandy in the very first days of the prohibitions. The *arrêts* of 1676–77 had said only that tobacco could be planted in the vicinity of Léry. Did *environs* embrace neighboring villages as well? The area affected was quite small, a few parishes between Pont-de-l'Arche and Louviers, a few miles south of Rouen on the left bank of the Seine, in the modern department of the Eure.

Tobacco cultivation had been introduced into Léry about 1620. From there it had spread to the neighboring communities of Vaudreuil, Les Damps, Romilly, and Pitres, utilizing the alluvial sediment left by river flooding at the confluence of the Seine, the Eure, and the Andelle.[29] By 1674, Norman production was still a small affair, though important for those in the five parishes concerned who had perhaps no equally remunerative use to which they could put their exposed river lands. When the monopoly was established in 1674, the manufacturers of Dieppe alleged that they employed 300–400 workers in the town and 400–500 families growing tobacco thereabouts (presumably about Léry).[30] When the new policy of restricting production was announced in March 1676, tolerating in all Normandy only that at Léry, the intendant Le Blanc wrote at once to Colbert, inquiring about the other neighboring parishes. Colbert answered on 8 May:

> In regard to the parishes round about Louviers which raise tobacco, it is no great evil that they should cease to cultivate it, since their tobaccos are not as good as those which come from the islands of Amer-

ica, and since in time, they might decrease the commerce carried on in those islands.

Nevertheless, on 14 May, the minister relented and wrote that he would instruct the farmers of tobacco to let the peasants harvest the tobacco then growing in the five parishes in the *élection* of Pont-de-l'Arche, but he warned the intendant that "measures must be taken to stop the cultivation of the herb in all Normandy," not just for the colonies but for the security of the grain supply as well.[31]

The next year—1677—the comedy was repeated all over again. When informed by the intendant that the parishes in the *élection* of Pont-de-l'Arche were once again planting tobacco, Colbert replied in June that the monopoly was quite right in wanting to stop this, for it would ruin the colonial trade. "Thus, all that can be done for these parishes is to indulge them for this year, without however, giving them any inkling of such." On the contrary, the agents of the farm should make themselves sufficiently difficult to convince the peasants that the government was in earnest. In 1678, at the very latest, it would be necessary to pull up the tobacco completely. The intendant, however, did not appreciate the minister's deviousness. To the farm's great annoyance, he issued an *ordonnance* on 2 July calling for a census of all the lands then planted with tobacco in the five parishes and forbidding the agents of the monopoly to destroy any so growing until further orders. Colbert reprimanded him on 30 July, "You ought not have issued that *ordonnance,* because it can embolden the people to continue and expand that planting; on the contrary, it is necessary to make some demonstration of wanting to pull up the tobacco . . . so that they will be clearly warned." Once proper warning was given, it would be easier the next year to pull up the tobacco, if cultivation continued.[32]

Yet, despite all the official rhetoric about encouraging colonies, in the end, peasant stubbornness won. When the *ordonnance* of 1681 was issued, the list of permitted places in Normandy was expanded from just Léry to include Les Damps and Vaudreuil as well.[33] This "compromise" could not last very long, for the Norman villages were located so close to the principal centers of consumption that any cultivation must have seemed an incitement to fraud to the United General Farms. When the new Domergue lease was being negotiated in 1687, that company offered to pay the owners of the tobacco lands in the three parishes of Léry, Les Damps, and Vaudreuil an annual compensation of eighteen *l.t.* per acre on up to sixty acres provided that no tobacco were planted in any of the three parishes. The proposal was referred by the council's *arrêt* of 16 August 1687 to the intendant at Rouen, Feydeau de Brou, who, like his predecessors, was most sympathetic to the interests and arguments of the poor peasants. The growers, he reported on 15 December, felt that their cultivation was useful to the nation, particularly when supplies did not arrive from the West Indies. Yet, the farm only paid them 10 *l.t.* per quintal then, although previously they had sold their tobacco for up to 50 *l.t.* per quintal. The land used for tobacco could not be used for wheat. The compensation offered by the monopoly would indemnify the owners of the land but not the day-laborers (*journaliers*) who could find employment only in growing or processing tobacco. The monopoly's own figures showed that out of the 200 *l.t* received from the product of an acre of tobacco, 192 *l.t.* went in expenses, primarily wages to day-laborers. Only such income enabled small men to pay their *taille*. The inhabitants wanted their rights of cultivation confirmed and the price paid by the monopoly raised from 10 to 20 *l.t.* per quintal. The farm, however, would not consider higher prices, since Norman tobacco was of poor quality and was difficult to sell to consumers even when mixed with imported leaf.

On the recommendation of the intendant Feydeau (10 January 1688), the Council of State ordered—13 January 1688—that cultivation in the three Norman parishes be limited to 100 acres; that the growers be allowed until 20 March after each harvest to export what they wanted; that all not exported must then be sold to the monopoly for 10 *l.t.* per quintal. (The monopoly would have preferred total abolition or a limit of no more than 80 acres.) [34] There was considerable overplanting the first year, but the scheme seems to have been reasonably well enforced thereafter.[35]

When the new Bernard-Crozat-Maynon company took·over the monopoly in 1697, they tried to tighten up the administration, with only limited success. The new group felt that the key to the fraud in Normandy lay in the fact that the cultivators dried and prepared the tobacco themselves, thus giving them a product much better suited to fraud than were freshly gathered leaves. To check this, the company agreed with the planters in 1704 to buy their tobacco green, making allowance in the price for normal dehydration. (To their surprise, they found that an acre produced 3,800 lb. green, even in a bad year, while formerly they had never received more than 2,000 lb. dry leaf from an acre. This last figure, which was considerably higher than the Virginia figure, must have included bottom leaves and anything else the cultivators could pick.) Some of the inhabitants, at the harvest, refused to sell green as agreed and were taken into court. When the *cour des aides* of Normandy ruled that it lacked jurisdiction, the monopoly in 1705 tried unsuccessfully to get the necessary powers from the royal council, but the government was unwilling to stop the cultivation, particularly in wartime. When Desmaretz, then *directeur des finances,* and Maynon from the farm, could not work out a settlement fair to the cultivators, the matter was referred for settlement to the more sympathetic intendant (May 1706) and not heard of again.[36]

By an *ordonnance* of 10 May 1688, the then intendant, Feydeau de Brou, had divided the 100 acres among the various parishes:[37]

Léry   55 acres (reduced from 60)
Vaudreuil   27 acres (originally 22)
Les Damps   5 acres (reduced from 13)
St. Cyr-du-Vaudreuil   13 acres (originally 5)

Actually, rather less than this seems to have been cultivated most years, particularly at Léry. We have the exact data for 1705:[38]

	Planters	Acres	Tobacco Delivered (dry)	Productivity (lb. per acre)
Léry	152	42.1	69,618 lb.	1,660
Vaudreuil	86	21.8	30,372 lb.	1,400
Les Damps	37	4.9	9,689 lb.	1,970
St. Cyr	84	10.8	20,245 lb.	1,868
Total	359	79.6	129,924 lb.	1,633

The men of St. Cyr thought their quota much too small particularly since Léry did not use its in full. They persuaded the intendant Lamoignon de Courson to issue an *ordonnance* on 23 March 1709 raising their quota from 13 to 20 and reducing that of Léry, then only 52, to 45. The monopoly immediately protested on the grounds that the tobacco of St. Cyr was the worst of the lot and a complete loss to the farm.[39] The royal council ordered St. Cyr's quota returned to thirteen acres.[40]

A comparable small-scale history can be found at Mondragon on the Rhône at the other end of France. In this small French enclave in the Comtat Venaissin, tobacco had been grown from rather early in the seventeenth century. Before the establishment of the monopoly in 1674, the local leaf, allegedly good for smoking, chewing, and snuff, was for the most part sold at the fair of Beaucaire. The Jean Breton or first monopoly company established a manufacture there which used all the local production it could acquire. This arrangement continued under the succeeding farming companies and, after 1687, under the subfarmers for Provence. Mondragon was one of the places where cultivation was permitted to continue after the restrictions of 1676–77. During the Nine Years War, when tobacco was generally scarce in France, the monopolists encouraged the local peasantry to expand their production, guaranteeing them in 1694 fourteen *l.t.* per quintal for all their superior leaf and ten *l.t.* for all the ordinary. About 1700, the subfarmers for Provence under the new Bernard-Crozat-Maynon company decided that Mondragon tobacco no longer suited either them or their customers and tried to drop the 1694 agreement on the grounds that they had not been parties to it. The cultivators appealed to the intendant who obtained an order of council (8 October 1701) obliging the subfarmers to continue on condition that: (1) production at Mondragon be limited to 200 *saunées* (something less than 200 acres) and (2) the company be obliged to purchase only three-fourths of a production of perhaps 170,000 lb., the rest presumably to be exported. In subsequent years, the subfarmers of Provence tried to evade this obligation to purchase leaf which they found vile and unsaleable; they were kept to the mark only through active intervention on behalf of the cultivators by Le Bret, intendant of Provence.[41]

The production of neither Normandy nor Mondragon was very large, yet each could conceivably have supplied something around 10 percent of the consumption of France in the 1670's or 1680's. Yet the monopolists were reluctant to encourage either production: in Normandy, from the very beginning, owing to poor quality and the facility for fraud; in remoter Provence, more slowly, as quality seemingly deteriorated, or perhaps as popular taste changed. (They dared not offer Mondragon tobacco for sale in Paris, the monopoly claimed in 1703.) In both cases, the local cultivators were saved only by the intervention of a series of intendants, solicitous all for the poor peasant. In so doing, the intendants could safely ignore official policy in favor of the colonies. Up to a point, they could even ignore policy protective of the interests of the revenue. No less solicitous were the intendants in Guienne. There, where production was ten times as vast as that in Normandy or Provence, the early monopoly companies were to meet their most redoubtable foes.

Tobacco Cultivation in the Southwest, 1674–1718

Thus far, we have been discussing tobacco planting in areas where it posed serious administrative problems or where it was of some local importance. Only when we come to the southwest, do we encounter an area where tobacco planting was of national significance. In the valleys of the tributaries of the Gironde was grown nine-tenths or more of the tobacco raised within the jurisdiction of the monopoly.

The vast *gouvernement* of Guienne and Gascony was—roughly speaking—divided first into two and then into three *généralités:* Bordeaux in the west, Montauban in the east and Auch in the south, created in 1716 out of parts of Montauban and Bordeaux plus Pau. The *généralité* of Bordeaux included the Bordelais, the tobacco growing *pays* of the Agenais and Condomois, as well as Périgord to the north; Montauban consisted essentially of Haute Guienne (Rouergue and Quercy) and a small piece of Languedoc— within the diocese of Bas Montauban—wherein tobacco was also planted. To the northward, on the border of Guienne (Quercy) and Limousin, stretching from above the Isle to below the Dordogne, was the viscounty of Turenne, a privileged fief belonging to the dukes of Bouillon until sold to the crown in 1738. Because of its special status, it was the third area in or contiguous to the *gouvernement* of Guienne in which tobacco was planted after 1677. (Saint Mexant, where tobacco cultivation was permitted in Limousin, was very close to the territories of Turenne.)

We have already noticed in Normandy that the land used for tobacco growing was located at the confluence of the Seine, the Eure, and the

Andelle, where river flooding left an alluvial sediment on which tobacco thrived. In the southwest too, we shall find tobacco growing commonly situated in river valleys, frequently at the confluence of two streams, in many cases in areas then or shortly before subject to flooding. In an account of 1720, we are told:

> Sandy and gravelly soils are the best for planting tobacco, because they are the mildest [plus doux]. Such are the soils along the left bank of the Lot from Aiguillon to Granges, where they harvest the best tobacco in Guienne. The rich [grasses] soils produce the fullest [plus rondes] thickest [plus nourries] leaves, but they are more watery and less pithy.[42]

Tobacco could thus be planted in odd bits of land near the rivers not suited for other crops, because of the character of the soils, the awkward shape of the fields, or the danger of spring floods. This last danger could be avoided in the case of tobacco, since it was the practice in Guienne to plant the tobacco seeds in manured beds between 1 February and 15 March and not to transplant them in open fields till late May or June, after the danger of flooding was past.[43]

Tobacco growing was first introduced into Guienne some time in the 1620's or 1630's, the later the account the earlier the starting date given. The members of the *Société d'Agriculture, Sciences et Arts* of Agen reported in 1804 a local tradition that tobacco was first raised commercially in France on the Lot at Clairac in the Agenais, by one Labat in 1620.[44] However, the *chevalier* de Vivens, reporting a similar story in 1756, placed the beginning of cultivation at Clairac at ca. 1630, though he and others had some years before put the start at ca. 1637.[45] Even earlier, in a memorial presented by the inhabitants of Clairac to the intendant of Bordeaux in 1699, it was reported that the seed had first been brought thither about sixty years before by a local man who had traveled abroad.[46] This would place the introduction in or about 1639. Several recent scholars favor 1637,[47] or 1635.[48] By 1640, we are told by another modern author, the cultivation had spread over much of the Agenais and Condomois.[49] The center of planting was the triangle Clairac-Tonneins-Aiguillon at the confluence of the Lot and Garonne; from there the cultivation spread up the Lot toward Villeneuve-sur-Lot and down the Garonne toward Marmande. The *arrêts* of 1676–77 were to recognize in this area seventeen *communautés* (jurisdictions or townships) containing over seventy parishes[50] as already having established tobacco cultures. Of these *communautés*, Clairac was the best known as the original seat of cultivation and as the home of the preferred leaf: it ultimately gave its name to the entire product of the Agenais and Condomois. Nearby Tonneins, however, was ultimately to replace Clairac as the marketing and manufacturing center of the trade.

Clairac, Aiguillon, and particularly Tonneins had been important fortified Huguenot centers early in the seventeenth century. After they lost their military privileges, they remained important Protestant seats throughout the *ancien régime*. The spread of cultivation outside the original area about the confluence of the Lot and Garonne took place along lines of trade and Protestant family connection. The second major area of cultivation at the confluence of the Tarn and Garonne lay within the marketing area of the very Protestant city of Montauban. A recent scholar suggests that the earliest cultivation here was in the village of Meauzac on the left bank of the Tarn below Montauban on land owned by a Protestant *seigneur* whose wife came from Clairac and who had himself resided there for some time. From Meauzac, cultivation spread upriver to Villeneuve-La Garde and Villemade toward the marketing center at Montauban. Only later, after demand grew, did it spread into the nearby Garonne valley to Saint Porquier, Escatalens, Montech, and even Castelsarrasin-la-catholique. Soil conditions were comparable to those about Clairac. Much of the land in all the villages affected was owned by citizens of Montauban. At first, though, marketing was controlled from Clairac. Only after cultivation spread to the Garonne about Castelsarrasin did the merchants of Montauban intervene.[51]

A third area of cultivation of much less importance lay to the northward along the borders of Guienne (Périgord and Quercy) and Limousin. In the middle of the seventeenth century, tobacco was grown to a limited degree at various spots along the Dordogne, the Isle, and the Vézère.[52] The most important cultivations in this region were those along the Dordogne within the privileged viscounty of Turenne at Montvalent, Martel, and, from about 1660, at Souillac (all in the northern part of the present department of Lot).[53] Although unmentioned in the *arrêts* of 1676–77 and the *ordonnance* of 1681, these places at first escaped the attention of the law because of their protected position in the viscounty.[54] By an *arrêt* of 14 August 1685, the Council of State at last tried to prohibit the planting, manufacture, and trade of tobacco in Turenne and ordered a mill there for grinding snuff destroyed.[55] This may have been intended only to frighten the duke of Bouillon, the lord of the viscounty. Seventeen months later, as part of the new policy of leasing awkward liberties, the United General Farms of France took over from a private person (Louis Brean) the tobacco farm in Turenne and farmed it thereafter directly from the duke for about 800 *l.t.* p.a.[56] They were enabled by this lease to control but not suppress tobacco cultivation in the viscounty.

There were thus in the southwest three distinct areas of cultivation commonly styled "of Guienne": the original and most important about the confluence of the Lot and Garonne in the Agenais and Condomois; the second about the confluence of the Aveyron, Tarn, and Garonne near Montauban; and the third on the northern limits of Quercy in that part of the valley of the Dordogne that flowed through the viscounty of Turenne. How much tobacco was grown in all these areas? We are embarassed here by perhaps too many estimates and reports, some of them undated, not all of them consistent. Putting this mixed bag of evidence together, we can nevertheless draw a fairly consistent picture.

During the last year of the first tobacco farm, 1679–80, Colbert received various reports on tobacco under the new regime. A report from de Ris, intendant of Bordeaux, in 1680 painted a glowing picture of tobacco cultivation in his *généralité,* tobacco markedly superior to that of Montauban, much of it being exported to Italy and Spain. He reported that in 1679 in the *élections* of Agen and Condom, 1,368 1/2 *journaux* had been planted in tobacco. (A *journal* was slightly more than an English acre.) At his estimated yield of twelve quintals per *journal*, this would suggest a production of about 1,642,000 lb.[57] Using a more conservative contemporary estimate of nine quintals per *journal*,[58] we would get a production of only 1,231,650 lb. The intendant de Ris added that he had heard that nearly twice as much was planted the next year. This addendum need not be taken too literally, for de Ris was arguing in this report that the areas in which tobacco cultivation was permitted should be expanded to embrace all of the Agenais and Condomois. His argument would be better supported the higher he could show current planting to be. There is no reason to believe, however, that the detailed figures he gave for 1679 were significantly defective.

The de Ris data for 1679 include only the eighteen jurisdictions in the Agenais and Condomois. We must add something for production near Montauban and in the viscounty of Turenne. One modern writer has suggested that production near Montauban was 80 percent of that about Clairac, without giving any source of his calculation.[59] The only precise figures we have—for ca. 1719—suggest that then production in the Montauban-St. Porquier region was only 13 percent of that about Clairac.[60] Using this as our solid point of departure, it would seem that if we allowed 20 percent extra for both the Montauban-St. Porquier and Turenne productions, we would be erring if at all on the side of generosity. Adding this 20 percent to the figures given in the previous paragraph for the production of the Agenais and Condomois in 1679, we get a total production for the southwest in that year of from 1,478,000 to 1,971,000 lb. A production of this magnitude, though trivial by Chesapeake standards (around 20 million French pounds in 1681), was still more than France legitimately consumed at this time.

De Ris suggested that production in 1680 might be twice that of 1679. Though he was probably exaggerating at the time, his remark suggests that the general tendency of production was upward. This fits in with what else we know. Early in 1689, an anonymous official in the growing regions, hostile to the monopoly, estimated production in the Clairac area alone at three million pounds annually while an official of the monopoly placed it rather higher for "Clairac" and Bas Montauban and wanted it reduced to three millions. In 1697, the father of the tobacco monopoly, the farmer-general and *directeur-général de commerce,* Jean-Baptiste de Lagny, also estimated production at that time (i.e., ca. 1696) in the *généralités* of Bordeaux and Montauban at three million pounds.[61] (Food shortages in the 1690's may have diverted efforts away from tobacco.) From this data, we may assume that tobacco production in the southwest had grown from about 1.5–2.0 million lb. in 1679 to over 3.0 million in 1688, near or below which level it stagnated through the war.

Low tobacco prices (Table II), as well as food shortage, half explain the failure of Guienne leaf production to increase during the war years when French colonial supplies failed and importation from anywhere was difficult. (We have already noted how the farm tried to get more from Mondragon in the 1690's.) The higher prices characteristic of the Spanish Succession War acted as a more effective stimulant. In the viscounty of Turenne, where planting seems to have been relatively minor before the wars, production reached only 200,000 lb. p.a. during 1693–1700 but 800,000 lb. p.a. during 1700–1715.[62] This marked expansion of production during the Spanish war seems to have been general. La Bourdonnaye, intendant at Bordeaux, in a memoir of 18 June 1708, estimated production in the eighteen jurisdictions in his *généralité* (i.e., in the Agenais and Condomois) as 5,000,000–6,000,000 lb.[63] If we add 13 percent more, as before, for the production of the Montauban-St. Porquier area and 800,000 lb. for the viscounty of Turenne, we obtain a total production for the southwest of 6.45–7.45 million lb. or at least twice the 3.0 million suggested by de Lagny for 1696. Growth of this magnitude is not unlikely, considering the shortage of tobacco and high prices all through Europe during the war years after 1702. (Dutch production also doubled in these years.)[64] About 1712, two antimonopoly memoirs estimated production in the Agenais and Condomois at about five million pounds, or at La Bourdonnaye's lower limit, but this perhaps only reflects the poor crops of 1710–12.[65]

The high levels of production reached during the Spanish war seem to have continued into the peace. Two memoirs of these years have survived, both dating from about 1719–22. One breaks down tobacco production about 1716–19 by administrative districts:[66]

Dist. Tonneins (north of Garonne)	50,000 quintals
Dist. Layrac (to east, south of Garonne)	3,000–4,000 quintals
Dist. St. Porquier (near Montauban)	7,000 quintals
Total	60,000–61,000 quintals

If we add 800,000 lb. for the production of the viscounty of Turenne, we get a total production for the southwest about 1719 of about 6,800,000 lb., fully consistent with the range 6.45–7.45 million lb. suggested for 1708. The other memoir of this same time fits in less easily: it suggests that in the eighteen jurisdictions about Clairac (corresponding to the Tonneins and Layrac districts above) 8,375 *journaux* were planted with tobacco, about 1719. At the rate of nine quintals per *journal* offered in the same memoir, we obtain an estimated production of 75,375 quintals—almost 50 percent more than that just reported for the same districts at the same time.[67] The difference can probably be accounted for by the fact that the latter account was in all probability compiled from the acreage which peasants registered for planting at the beginning of each season—as required in the *ordonnance* of July 1681. Since one might be punished for underdeclaring, but not for overdeclaring, there would be a natural tendency for the cultivators to overregister when in doubt.[68]

In summary, then, the available evidence, though spotty, suggests a consistent picture of production in the southwest rising from ca. 1.5–2.0 million lb. in 1679 to ca. 3.0 million lb. in 1688 and 1696 to ca. 6.4–7.5 million lb. in 1708, which level was more or less maintained down to 1720.

Though not a major branch of agriculture in the southwest, tobacco cultivation was important in the areas in which it was permitted, as is clearly suggested by Table I.

TABLE I

Lands Registered for Tobacco Cultivation in the
Agenais and the Condomois, ca. 1719

Election	Jurisdiction	Area Reg'd. for Tob'o[69]	Share of Arable[70]
		journaux	percentage
Agenais	Clairac	1,660	23
	Tonneins-Dessus	650	33
	Tonneins-Dessous	700	27
	Aiguillon	300	22
	La Parade	55	7
	La Fitte	400	50
	Grateloup	350	22
	Verteuil	20	8
	Gontaud	300	33
	Caumont	200	10
	Fauillet	800	50
Condomois	Le Mas d'Agenais	450	25
	La Gruère	400	31
	Calonges	450	29
	Puch-de-Gontaut	400	17
	Damazan	500	16
	Monheurt	400	33
	Villeton	400	33
Total		8,375	

The last two columns (Table I) are *not* derived from the same source. They both suggest, nevertheless, that a substantial, proportion of the arable in the eighteen jurisdictions (embracing 85 villages) was registered for tobacco.

The market price for Clairac tobacco seems in normal times to have hovered around 10 *l.t.* per quintal, though it went much higher in wartime, as is shown in Table II.

TABLE II
Prices per Quintal of Guienne Tobacco[71]
(All prices are for "Clairac" leaf unless otherwise specified.)

Year	l.t.		Year	l.t.
1647	18–20	Montauban	1690	10
			1691	12
1665	8–10	Tarn Valley	1692	8–10
	7	St. Porquier	1693	8
			1694	12–13
1679	5–20		1695	11
	8–9	average		
			1708	28
1684	17½–18½	superior	1709–10	18–19
	7½	common	1710–11	[25–30 manufactured]
1685	16–18		1712	25–26
1686	11–14			[30–35 manufactured to export]
1687	9–10			
1688	7–8		1713	22–23
1689	6–7		ca.1715	12–13
				[26–27 manufactured]
			1719	10–11

On the one hand, these prices were quite cheap compared to what the farm had to pay for St. Domingue or any other imported tobacco. Yet they do not seem to have been inconsistent with the prosperity of the cultivators. A small man with two or three *journaux* might perhaps expect to receive 70–80 *l.t.* per *journal* gross, a very respectable cash income which, as many frequently observed, alone enabled him to pay his *taille*.[72] In fact, lands within the *crus* (the jurisdictions where cultivation was permitted) reportedly sold for double the price of equivalent lands outside.[73] They also were supposed to be more heavily taxed than lands elsewhere in Guienne.[74] So prosperous did the privileged areas appear that de Dregny, a nephew of Colbert, and former inspector-general of the united farms about 1680–91, wrote in 1704 to his cousin Desmaretz, *directeur des finances,* that a substantial amount could be extracted from occupiers in those districts in the form of loans to the crown (*finance*) for the planting privilege.[75]

Within the jurisdictions, the legal tobacco trade was only very loosely regulated by the monopoly. Private merchants and manufacturers controlled much of the trade, advancing sums to the peasants, and contracting in advance for their tobacco. The merchants of Montauban obtained theirs by making advances to small country traders who bought from the cultivators. Big merchants of Marseilles as well as the monopoly made large advances to the principal dealers of Tonneins who advanced to the manufacturers who ultimately made their own advances to the growers. During the two months of the year following the harvest, about 15,000 persons (including women, children, and the elderly) were employed preparing the tobacco in the growing areas. The reputation of Clairac tobacco was aided by the fact that it was not the local custom to grow "seconds" from the same roots after the first leaves had been gathered—in part because the growing season was too short before the time for fall plowing for grain. The top or best leaves of the plant were "stemmed," i.e., had their midribs removed, and were made into the superior grades of spun tobacco known as *sans-côtes* or pressed into *prin* or *briquet*. (The stalks, stems, midribs and other waste parts of the plant were used as fertilizer.) The midribs were left in the lower, less desirable leaves which were made up into the cheaper sorts of spun tobacco known as *exprès* (from leaf of middling quality) and *commun* (from refuse leaf).[76]

The domestic market for "Clairac" tobacco lay almost exclusively in the south of France from Aunis to Provence. As explained in Chapter 2, this geographical restriction probably had its origin in the decades before the introduction of the monopoly in 1674, when the movement of Guienne tobaccos northward would have been impeded by the customs duties of the *cinq grosses fermes*. After the monopoly was established, sales data for 1675–78 show significant (if declining) sales for Clairac manufactured tobaccos in the north only in Paris and Brittany, the latter also being outside the *cinq grosses fermes*.[77] It was not in the interest of the monopoly to introduce this product into the interior, lest familiarity encourage smuggling from the south. During the Fauconnet lease (1681–87), when Brittany was subfarmed, the united farms appear to have ceased shipping Clairac tobacco northward in a manufactured form. Surviving purchase contracts for 1684–87 specify that the various forms of roll and pressed tobaccos were for the southern market and that only dried leaf was to be shipped northward to the monopoly's manufactures at Dieppe and Paris.[78] In this form, the Clairac tobacco could be mixed with other domestic and foreign tobaccos and manufactured in styles distinct from those of the south.

Clairac tobacco was noted principally for its strength (*sève*), which made it particularly suited for use in snuff, but not in smoking tobacco. In the 1670's and 1680's, snuff taking was still exotic outside of Paris; it was, though, relatively more common in the south than in the north, reinforcing the market limitations for Clairac tobacco. Even when the taste for snuff taking did begin to develop more widely in the north (from the 1690's), it was to be for snuff not from a Clairac but from a Virginia base. (Snuffs termed "de Malthe," "de Pontgibon," or "de Gênes" were in fact two-thirds Virginia.) During the War of the Spanish Succession, when Virginia supplies became very difficult, the monopoly had to use more Clairac in their northern snuff and tobacco works, but they mixed it with Virginia to make it palatable to northern taste. Thus, even in time of shortage, they bought only dried leaf in Guienne, which they had sent in hogsheads from Tonneins via Bordeaux by sea to their works at Morlaix, Dieppe, and Paris for blending.[79]

With the markets within France for the tobacco of Clairac thus severely restricted, it is readily understandable that France as a whole took only a minor proportion of the production of Guienne. Data for 1679 suggest that less than one-fifth of southwestern production could have been distributed in France through the monopoly.[80] In 1689[81] and again in 1712, the growers of Clairac, in representations to authority, claimed that only one-sixth of their production was purchased by the monopolies.[82] Thus the prosperity of tobacco cultivation in the southwest obviously depended not on the home but on the export market, lying almost exclusively in the Mediterranean, primarily in Italy.

As early as the 1640's, we find a fully developed trade exporting Clairac tobacco to Italy. The trade throughout was dominated primarily by the merchants of Tonneins and Clairac, to the exclusion of their great neighbors in Bordeaux. From the Clairac area, the tobacco was shipped up the Garonne to Toulouse and thence overland to the ports of Agde and Narbonne from which at this time it was usually carried by coastal craft to the great market at Marseilles. From there it was commonly exported in larger ships to Genoa usually on the account of Genoese purchasers or occasionally on that of Marseilles merchants (acting for themselves or for principals in Tonneins and elsewhere). At first the merchants of Montauban also sent their tobacco to the same big merchants in Toulouse who acted as factors and forwarders for the Tonneins merchants. The older pattern was disturbed about 1653 by the Fronde and by the plague during which Toulouse was for a time quarantined. Both the tobacco from the Montauban area as well as much from Clairac-Tonneins had for a time to be shipped up the Tarn to Montauban and thence overland via l'Isle-sur-Tarn, Puylaurens, and Revel to Castelnaudary where it rejoined the main road to Narbonne.[83] The disturbances of 1653 also affected Marseilles. By about 1647-51, the town had developed a considerable trade reexporting the tobacco of Guienne to Genoa, Leghorn, Catalonia, North Africa, and the Levant. When the plague and other disturbances cut off supplies in 1653, both French and foreign merchants resident at Marseilles went into Guienne to buy tobacco at the source. By 1670, domestic and foreign tobacco worth 300,000 *l.t.* annually was being shipped into Marseilles for local consumption and reexport.[84] If we can assume that this tobacco had an average value of 20 *l.t.* per quintal (probably high), it would represent at least 1.5 million lb., equivalent to almost the whole production of Guienne at this time.

The basic pattern of trade established before 1674, drawing the greater part of the production of Guienne to Italian and other foreign markets, was not seriously affected by the establishment of the monopoly in that year. In his report of 1680, de Ris, intendant of Bordeaux, reported that the superior tobaccos of Clairac (rather more so that the less acceptable ones of Montauban) were exported in considerable quantity to Italy and Spain.[85] (The Spanish was largely a smuggling market supplied from the *bureaux* early established by the monopoly not just in Perpignan and Pau, but also in Tarascon, St. Girons, and St. Béat in the central Pyrenees—though the Spanish monopoly did occasionally buy in France when in need.)[86] In his complacent memoir of January 1697, de Lagny too admitted that the greater part of the three million pounds of tobacco raised in the southwest was exported, either by land to Spain or by sea to Italy, both directly from the ports of Languedoc and indirectly via the entrepôt at Marseilles. He stressed the liberty which the rules of the farm gave to foreign merchants to buy and export this tobacco.[87] In 1699, a French merchant reported a great trade in Guienne tobacco at Genoa.[88] The Italians, according to de la Bourdonnaye, intendant of Bordeaux, in 1708, preferred Clairac tobacco above all others.[89] His successor, Lamoignon de Courson, reported in 1715 that close to four million pounds of domestic tobacco was by then being shipped to Languedoc and Marseilles, from whence most of it was exported to Genoa and elsewhere in Italy. Of Clairac, so "contaminated by protestant heresy," he wrote, "All the tobacco is sent to Genoa." He stressed that this was a trade which brought back silver from Spain and Italy.[90]

The heavy orientation of Guienne production toward export and its inability to satisfy more than a small proportion of French domestic taste, were, we have seen, based in the first instance on the physical characteristics of Guienne tobacco: its suitability for snuff at a time when little snuff was consumed in the north of France; its ill suitability for the chewing and smoking tobacco still most widely used through most parts of France. To at least one person, it appeared that this poor fit need not be permanent. Why not change the manner of making tobacco in Guienne so that it would more closely resemble the Brazilian so preferred in many parts of France for smoking and particularly for chewing. Out of this self-evident opportunity came an "enterprise" characteristic of the last years of Louis XIV.

Roland Duclos, a native of Bayonne, had resided in Portugal for many years and dealt extensively in tobacco there. He had made several trips to Brazil as a ship's captain and claimed to have been interested for many years in the tobacco monopoly in Portugal. He turned up in Paris, at the end of 1697, just at the time when the new Bernard-Crozat-Maynon company had taken over the tobacco monopoly from the United General Farms. He got the new company slightly interested in his claims that he could manufacture the tobacco of Clairac and Tonneins to resemble that of Brazil. They encouraged him to go to the Agenais in 1698 and experiment with his new methods, but they refused to sign a formal contract with him or to use their influence to get him the grant of a crown monopoly. He then acquired some more venturesome partners: Antoine Dieure (counsellor in the *parlement* of Metz) and Antoine Adelé Desliberdières. On their advice, and through their connections, the matter was "put into the hands of" the president de Mesmes (Jean Antoine de Mesmes, comte d'Avaux, *président à mortier* in the *parlement* of Paris from 1689, subsequently *premier président*). Through the influence of that worthy, royal letters-patent were obtained on 31 August 1700 granting Duclos a twenty-year monopoly of manufacturing Clairac tobacco in the Brazilian style, provided only that all was exported. (This last proviso reflects the influence and skepticism of the monopoly.) A company was then formed in which the president de Mesmes received a 25 percent interest for his "help." Dieure and Desliberdières each received 10 percent for their help and 4,000 *l.t.* advanced for Duclos' trip to the Agenais. Further partners were brought in to raise capital: Jean Baptiste Louis Berrier de la Ferrière and the inveterate speculator, Paul Poisson de Bourvalais. Dieure went out with Duclos to Tonneins in 1701 and supervised the establishment of the workshop. By the end of the first year, 1701—during which Duclos had manufactured all of three *barriques* and 25 *demi-barriques* of "Brazil" tobacco— the partners were at each others' throats in litigation. The company had gotten off to a rather poor start.[91]

In May 1705, Duclos, his affairs by then in considerable disorder, submitted to Romain Dalon, *premier président* of the *parlement* of Bordeaux, a lengthy memorial with elaborate calculations alleging to show how his manufactures could save the nation millions. By this time, Duclos was manufacturing not only "Brazilian" but also "Dutch" mixed *briquet*. The scheme, forwarded by Dalon to Controller-General Chamillart on 9 May 1705 with his personal good word, purported to show how Dutch and Brazilian manufactured tobaccos then imported could be made in France for one-half the price paid abroad to the obvious benefit of the consumer and of the balance of trade. From a trade so reorganized, the king could obtain a revenue of five million *l.t.* annually compared to the 1.5 million then paid by the existing monopolists. The matter was referred to Desmaretz, principal deputy to Chamillart, who inquired about quality, quantity, and price. What Desmaretz found out was obviously not in Duclos' favor, for, on 27 May, Chamillart wrote Dalon that there was nothing new in Duclos' proposal, that he had in his existing "privilege" all the legal powers he needed but had so far failed to produce tobacco as good as the Brazilian or Dutch models: "you can see for yourself by the evidence what one can expect of him."[92]

With this, Duclos passed from the scene. In a report of 1708, the intendant of Bordeaux referred to Duclos' manufacture at Tonneins as something which had failed some time before.[93] His company seems to have staggered on for a number of years trying to sell the thousands of pounds of tobacco which Duclos had made up before 1706. As of 1713, they still had 500 rolls of this "Brazil" tobacco on hand at Tonneins for which they could not find a foreign market though obliged by their "privilege" to export all they made. In 1712, they applied to de Montigny, director of the monopoly in the *généralité* of Bordeaux, asking permission to sell the tobacco for fertilizer. Suspecting that they really wanted to sell it to contrabanders, he refused. Desmaretz finally ordered in 1713 that the tobacco be burned and the ash only sold for fertilizer. With that, there passed from the scene the splendid scheme of Roland Duclos, so much more adept at writing memoirs than at making tobacco.[94]

In 1708, in the months preceding the renewal of the sexennial lease of the tobacco farm, and at a time when overseas tobacco supplies were particularly difficult and prices in Europe very high, other groups offered to start similar new manufactures of their own in the Agenais, not for export, but to supply France. One group promised to import skilled workers from Portugal or other countries. Once the lease was renewed (24 July 1708), nothing more was heard of these schemes. However, the next year, the great *traitant* Paul Poisson de Bourvalais, who had been interested in Duclos' company, obtained letters-patent (28 December 1709, 2 December 1710) transferring the Duclos privilege for a new period of thirty years to one Jean Henriques, a native of Portugal then settled at Bayonne. Henriques had resided in Brazil for twelve years and allegedly knew more about tobacco making than Duclos. He entered into a new partnership with Bourvalais and moved to Tonneins, but soon had to give up the manufacture: he could not sell his product. However, Jean Venant, who had been a foreman or manager under both Duclos and Henriques, continued some sort of "Brazilian" manufacture at Tonneins until 1720 when all private manufacture was abolished.[95]

The Duclos affair suggests in general terms the very cautious attitude of the monopoly toward the domestic cultivation in the southwest. We have seen repeatedly how solicitous were the intendants of Bordeaux, Montauban, and Languedoc, like the intendants of Rouen and Provence, for the domestic plantations and planters. In an age when a favorable balance of trade was still an omen of grand portent, the monopoly could not be so indiscreet as to *seem to prefer* imported tobacco to native. After the death of Colbert, who conspicuously preferred to encourage colonial tobacco rather than domestic, the monopoly understandably followed a discreet policy toward cultivation in the southwest. After the codifying *ordonnance* of July 1681, the United General Farms made no further effort to restrict the areas of production. They left the pre-1674 organization of the trade and manufacture more or less alone; rather than preempting supplies, they contracted for their limited needs with a few large merchants at Tonneins and Clairac.[96] For the rest, they confined their administrative activity to patrolling the growing areas and the transport routes from Tonneins to the Mediterranean.

Even such technical activity could, however, lead to serious disputes. To facilitate the work of their patrols, the administration of the monopoly, under the reinvigorating leadership of Hénault, tried to make a detailed written survey determining exactly which pieces of ground were entitled to grow tobacco. The task was complicated because the jurisdictions permitted to grow tobacco by the *ordonnance* of 1681 each consisted of several parishes and fragments of parishes. *Communautés* not listed in the *ordonnance* might depend for some governmental purpose upon one of the privileged jurisdictions and thus could advance a tenuous claim to planting rights. A detailed survey of April 1689 revealed some parishes planting without legal justification and others growing an inferior leaf unsaleable except to smugglers. The united farms wanted to prohibit the former practice and discourage the latter by strict quotas for each jurisdiction and parish.[97] This was prevented at the time (1689–90) by the hostility of the intendant and by protests to the controller-general, but a few years later, the monopoly obtained an order from the *élus* (fiscal magistrates) of Agen (20 December 1692) calling for a new survey of the planting area and prescribing elaborate new registration and permit procedures for the planters.[98] The latter were, however, revoked and replaced by much simpler procedures by an *ordonnance* of 8 November 1693 issued by the intendant Bazin de Bezons, classically sympathetic to the small planters and taxpayers.[99] This hostile sympathy sustained during his long intendancy (1686–1700) made it impossible for the monopoly despite legal efforts, ca. 1694, to take planting rights away from parishes which had long enjoyed them.[100]

Neither Bazin de Bezons nor anyone else in Guienne was, however, notified when the united farms procured the *arrêt du conseil* of 12 April 1689. Ostensibly an order confirming arrangements made between the united farms and the estates of Languedoc fixing the values at which Guienne tobacco would pay transit tolls (*droit forain*) on its way through that province to the Mediterranean ports, the *arrêt* further provided that leaf and the superior grades of manufactured tobacco in transit must be bound in bales (*emballés et emboutés*) and that the manufactured rolls (*rouleaux*) must be of a standard size: two feet long (in place of the customary one) and five strands (*cordes*) of spun tobacco deep (in place of the usual four).[101] This uniformity would make it easy for the guards to check the contents of shipments and would also result in an awkward, heavy product (weighing over ten pounds) difficult for a smuggler or anyone else to conceal or even carry. The manufacturers of Tonneins protested bitterly that there was no market for such bulky *rouleaux* at Genoa or elsewhere and that the whole thing was just a plot by the monopoly to make the output of Guienne unmarketable so that they could buy up cheaply in wartime what they hardly looked at in peace.[102] After many protests, Bazin de Bezons got the monopoly to relent on manufacturing details, provided that the tobacco was shipped in bales.[103]

Far more serious was the question of prices. During the early 1680's, tobacco prices generally were quite high, but started slipping after 1686 and were universally low by 1688. (Cf. Table II above and Table II in Chapter 4 for St. Domingue prices.)[104] With prices in Guienne at the exceptionally low level of 7 and 8 *l.t.* per quintal in 1688, the monopoly took the precaution at the start of the war to preempt the entire crop of 1688. In April 1689, discussions were held at Bordeaux, in the presence of the intendant Bezons, between representatives of the monopoly and the planters. The delegates from the *cru* objected not only to preemption but also to the normal practice of the monopoly engaging in advance for their needs with a few big dealers to whom they made large cash advances. These advances enabled the contractors to make forward contracts with manufacturers who did the same with growers. All this "forestalling" naturally depressed the market.[105] Nothing came of the discussions and in the fall of 1689 the monopoly, allegedly by delaying export licenses, further depressed leaf prices to a mere 6 or 7 *l.t.* (the lowest level reached between the establishment of the monopoly in 1674 and the abolition of cultivation in 1720).[106] War and market pressures forced prices back up to 10 in 1690 and for the next few years they fluctuated between 8 and 12 (Table II).

With prices moderately higher and with the monopoly in Guienne subfarmed during the lease of 1691–97, there was less controversy concerning the buying policies of the monopoly during the middle years of the War of the League of Augsburg. However, all the old disputes came very quickly to the surface again when tobacco prices all over Europe soared during 1696–97. With other supplies so dear, René Lemoine, manager of the subfarm in the *généralité* of Bordeaux, decided in 1696 that he would need 400,000 lb. instead of 20,000 the year before. The national farmers-general also decided that they needed increased leaf supplies for Brittany; they asked the intendant Bezons to help them get what they needed. The Tonneins houses acting as buying agents for the farmers-general and the Bordeaux subfarmers offered 12 *l.t.* per quintal in 1696 for top quality, as high a price as had been known since 1686, but the growers and manufacturers demanded at least 14 *l.t.* A local cartel was formed by which those needing cash agreed to sell not to the monopolies but to a local merchant (Sageran Cavalier, who probably had financial backing from Marseilles) for 12 *l.t.* for mixed qualities ('*cap et queue*'). The monopolists retaliated by refusing export permits. A visit by the farmer-general, Le Courtois d'Averly, and the intervention of the intendant led to some sort of settlement: in all probability, the monopolists agreed to pay a good bit extra during 1696–97.[107]

The advent of the peace in 1697 brought the transfer of the monopoly from the united farms to the Bernard-Crozat-Maynon company, but the *généralité* of Bordeaux continued under the subfarming company managed by Lemoine. The exceptionally high tobacco prices prevalent throughout Europe during the last year of the war also continued into 1698 and 1699, exacerbated in the case of Guienne by a very bad crop in the last year. This disaster gave the association of planters and dealers, which had continued from 1696, the most grandiose ideas of the prices they could get for the 1699 crop, while general market conditions made not only the subfarmers but even the national company interested in Guienne's output. The Bernard-Crozat-Maynon company sent down one of their partners, François Le Gendre, who met at Clairac with delegates from the different communities of the *cru*. The private merchants, who bought for the national monopoly and the subfarmers, had suggested prices of 25–30 *l.t* for that year. The delegates of the growers talked of 40 but retreated to 34. Le Gendre bluffed about 10 but offered 25, then left town before anything could be settled.[108] The local *fournisseurs*, who normally bought for the monopoly, may subsequently have reached a compromise price with the delegates of the growers. However, the decline in the European price at the very end of 1699 would have made the national company much less interested in Clairac tobaccos. For our purposes, the most interesting thing about these fragmentary reports on the d'Averly visit of 1696 and the Le Gendre visit of 1699 is their revelation of the way monopsonist pressures in the market created countervailing organization and market discipline on the part of sellers.

Although the Bernard-Crozat-Maynon company greatly expanded subfarming in the south, they do not appear to have sublet the *généralité* of Bordeaux after 1703. This might have been an obvious precaution to facilitate procurement in wartime. Despite the war and generally high prices in Europe, the relations between the monopolists and the merchants and growers of the *cru* remained quiet during the lease of 1703–9—in part because of good crops and relatively low prices most years in Guienne, in part because the then *directeur* of the monopoly in those parts, one Peyron, was a Huguenot who had his own understandings with the Huguenot manufacturers and merchants of Tonneins and who preferred to avoid controversy for fear of being *recherché sur sa religion*.[109] Quite different was Peyron's successor as *directeur* after 1709, one Jean de Montigny, an old hand active in the farm since about 1676, who proved a tactless and too literal executor of the toughening policies of the monopoly.[110] His personal honesty was also suspect as was that of the equally unpopular Jacques Jacob de St. Elie, principal figure in the company which under various names subfarmed Languedoc and the *généralité* of Montauban for a generation.[111]

Relations between the monopolists and merchants of the *cru de Guienne* grew much more strained during the first four years of the lease of 1709–15, opening with the semibankruptcy of the French state in 1709 and coinciding with the disastrous famine-filled last years of the War of the Spanish Succession. While Jacob and other subfarmers preferred to buy their tobacco year by year, the national company, for greater security contracted for its full requirements for the six year lease with two merchants of Tonneins, Larrard (their customary supplier), and Degals. Normally, these supply contracts were easy to fulfill because the national company and the combined subfarmers only took from 400,000 to 500,000 pounds each out of a Guienne production of over six million pounds. However, conditions comparable to those in 1696–99 returned with the three successive poor crops of 1710, 1711, and 1712. For their limited customary supplies the national company was at first covered by their contract price of 18 *l.t.*, 10 *s.* per quintal even though prices soared to 25–30 in 1711 and 30–35 the next year. The southern subfarmers who bought year by year, however, were terribly squeezed.[112] About the beginning of December 1711, a joint complaint about supply conditions was made by the various subfarmers in the southern provinces, i.e., the companies in the names of René Mortier (Languedoc, Roussillon and the *généralité* of Montauban), Jean Petre (*généralités* of La Rochelle, Poitiers, and Limoges), Nicolas David (Provence), Jean Molon (Lyonnais and Dauphiné), and Jean Lucot (*généralités* of Bourges, Riom and Moulins). They complained that the merchants at Tonneins-Clairac and St. Porquier had conspired to force up the price of tobacco to the point where the solvency of their subfarms was threatened. The matter had both that year and the previous year been referred to Lamoignon de Bâville, intendant of Languedoc (for St. Porquier), and to Lamoignon de Courson, intendant of Bordeaux (for Clairac-Tonneins). (These two famous intendants were father and son.) The complainants had so far received no satisfaction. Their representations, with a supporting memoir from the national tobacco farming company of 8 December 1711, were presented to the controller-general.[113] Desmaretz wrote once more to the two intendants on 20 December 1711, enclosing an order of council of 12 December assigning the matter to their adjudication.

On 2 February 1712, Courson replied from Bordeaux that he had assembled the principal manufacturers and landowners of the Clairac district together with de Montigny, the *directeur* of the monopoly in his *généralité*, and Jacob, managing partner in the René Mortier company that subfarmed Montauban and Languedoc. The manufacturers insisted that they preferred selling to the monopoly and the subfarming companies (whose prices and credit were generally good), but that lately they had had so much trouble with Jacob that none wanted to deal with him any more. They claimed that he would, for example, agree in advance to take a certain quantity of their tobacco at 24 *l.t.* per quintal, only to refuse all that was offered to him on one pretext or another—but then two weeks later come back and offer them 18 *l.t.* for the same. With the selling season almost gone, they often had to agree to his terms. They did not accuse the *directeur* de Montigny of such stratagems, though they also found him a difficult person with whom to deal. Despite the reluctance of the manufacturers to have any further dealings with Jacob, Courson induced them to sell all their remaining tobacco in stock to the monopoly and the various subfarming companies. His father, Bâville, subsequently made equivalent agreements for the production about St. Porquier in Languedoc. It is significant that Courson reported that he could have made a longer agreement to run through 1715, but that de Montigny and Jacob felt sure that one good crop would bring down the price.[114]

Bâville and Courson had procured for the various farming companies the tobacco they then so badly needed, but they had not settled the matter to the satisfaction of the national monopoly. With leaf supplies difficult, the company decided they needed leaf from the south (for their Breton manufactory) as well as the usual quantities of manufactured for sale in Guienne. Working very quietly, without any outside publicity, the Bernard-Crozat-Maynon company in the spring of 1712 set about strengthening their legal position so that they could get that leaf.

The *ordonnance* of July 1681 (art. xvii) forbade anyone to mix tobaccos or grind them into snuff (to disguise the smuggled) but permitted growers (and by inference others) to spin tobacco into roll; article xix permitted growers to sell for immediate export only; and article xxi gave the monopoly the right to preempt all the domestic tobacco they needed either at the market price or at a price to be determined by bargaining. In spite of these regulations, which said nothing about middlemen, a more complex organization soon came to characterize the industry in the southwest. Instead of spinning themselves, the growers came increasingly to sell their dried leaf to master manufacturers, who, after processing, sold it to merchants who arranged for its export. The greater merchants also bought leaf directly which they "put out" for manufacture. It was these latter greater merchants who commonly dealt with the farm, forcing it to pay for two levels of middlemen.

Of the varying qualities of tobacco manufactured in the southwest, the commoner grades were made primarily for export to Italy: *exprès* (from the whole leaf) and *demi-côte* (half-stemmed) at 7–8 *l.t.* per quintal in most years, and *commun* (made from scrap and the worst whole leaf) at 4–5 *l.t.* Only for the best *sans côte pressé,* made only from the stemmed, higher leaves and selling usually for 18–20 *l.t.* (but costing the farm 28–30 in 1711) was there a demand in France by 1712. Contrabanders carried this as far as Paris. If the monopoly could buy all of the best leaf available, they could check the supply of the contrabanders at the source. When they tried to do this, they either found the merchants reluctant to sell unless they would also take some of the inferior, or they found that the tobacco sold to them as best had lesser grades mixed in. To circumvent the stratagems of the merchants and manufacturers, the farm tried to buy the best leaf directly from the cultivators. In this, they were rebuffed, being told that the growers had contracted several years in advance to deliver all the tobacco they raised to the merchants and manufacturers who had advanced them money. The monopoly suspected that some of these alleged contracts were fictitious, but had no means of proving it.

To remedy this situation, the Bernard-Crozat-Maynon company obtained an *arrêt du conseil* of 3 May 1712 which ordered that henceforth: (1) the monopoly should by art. xxi of the *ordonnance* of 1681 have the same right to preempt dried leaf at market price from the growers as they enjoyed in procuring both leaf and manufactured tobacco from the merchants; and (2) that tobacco cultivators in Guienne and Languedoc could contract for the sale of their tobacco only one year in advance and only by a written contract before a notary, the agents of the farm being duly notified.[115]

The monopoly does not appear to have made public the *arrêt* of 3 May 1712 until 21 September when the current crop was ready for market. Protests erupted from every side. A general *remonstrance* to the king and council was prepared in the name of the inhabitants, cultivators, merchants and manufacturers of the *crû du tabac de Guienne*. (Besides attacking the *arrêt,* they charged de Montigny and Jacob with private schemes to monopolize the short crop of that year for their personal gain.) Another memoir claimed that the farm didn't really want the leaf tobacco but was trying to help some merchants it favored. The *curés* of Tonneins and twenty-eight other nearby parishes submitted statements charging the merchants with mistreating the cultivators (who did not necessarily receive prices in proportion to the prices obtained by the merchants). The master manufacturers (*marchands fabriquans*) of Guienne protested to the intendant of Bordeaux both against the new *arrêt* and against the allegations of the parish priests. The consuls of Clairac wrote directly to Controller-General Desmaretz. Most of these papers were in October referred to the monopoly which in due course prepared an elaborate response to which there were replies and counterreplies. On 26–29 November, the entire matter was not uncharacteristically referred back to Lamoignon de Courson, intendant of Bordeaux.[116]

The following April Courson reported most sympathetically on the complaints of the local people against the *arrêt* of 3 May 1712. The cultivators had greatly expanded production in the preceding years only because their advance agreements with the master manufacturers assured them of a ready market for all they produced. This trade and the advances they received enabled them to pay their taxes without trouble. Without the assurance of long term advance contracts, the master manufacturers would never advance substantial sums and the cultivators would be less likely to plant as much as they then did. If the monopoly were given the same preemptive rights over leaf which they then had over manufactured tobacco, others would be reluctant to buy leaf till the company had made its purchases in the market, thus depressing prices. The manufacturers felt they needed all four varieties to make up the assortment (*assortiment*) best for the export trade. If there was any chance that the monopoly would preempt all of the best grades of tobacco, then the manufacturers could not make advance contracts involving those grades with the merchant-exporters who in turn would be unable to make advance commitments to their correspondents abroad. Thus a trade would be compromised which earned two million *l.t.* annually from exports. (The monopoly thought the figure was closer to 500,000 *l.t.*)

In the opinion of de Courson, registration of all contracts before a notary was totally impractical since the quantities involved were so small and so many of the peasants poor and illiterate. A petty cultivator who sold tobacco worth only twenty *l.t.* annually could not afford the fees and taxes for a notarial document. Though some of the subfarmers in the south might want this leaf, Courson doubted seriously whether the monopoly itself sincerely wanted any. In their manufactories, they usually used foreign leaf, which, with peace imminent, they could import very cheaply. He thought the farm wanted the superior qualities only out of malice; he ignored their avowed motive of seeking to preempt the superior leaf in order to keep it out of contraband channels within France.

All things considered, Courson felt that the interests of the 30,000 families that allegedly grew the tobacco and the 10,000 laborers allegedly employed in the manufacture as well as the state's interest in their ability to pay taxes, demanded that the *arrêt* of 3 May 1712 not be executed.[117] In all likelihood, the *arrêt* was never actually enforced. (The monopoly was unable to get deliveries under the *arrêt* on their 1709 contract and had to pay much higher prices for the crops of 1712–14.)[118] In a report of 1715, de Courson still refers to the preemption of leaf as something to which the monopoly has no right and which should never be conceded to them.[119] With the return of peace, the supply problem of the monopoly disappeared; the fiscal advantages of preempting the best leaf was not a pressing enough motive for them to challenge the two formidable intendants particularly at a time when, as we shall see, their own position was anything but secure.

In summary, then, by the last years of the Bernard-Crozat-Maynon company, 1713 to 1718, the relations between the monopoly and the domestic cultivators and manufacturers had reached something of an impasse. From the introduction of the monopoly in 1674 to Colbert's death in 1683, the government had consistently if not always firmly supported a policy of restricting domestic cultivation in the interests of the colonies. After Colbert's death and particularly after the collapse of colonial production in the 1690's, the company found it more difficult to evoke government sympathy for a policy of further restrictions, particularly when the domestic cultivators were so eloquently defended by their respective intendants. During the years of war and shortages, 1689–1713, difficulties of procurement forced the monopoly to try to buy or preempt a larger proportion of the better tobacco grown in the southwest. (Such purchases would also have kept the superior grades out of the hands of the contrabanders.) These enlarged purchases were partially effected by deliberate delays in issuing permits for exports. When the company tried to obtain royal sanction for a policy of total preemption of superior leaf, however, they drew forth the resistance of the intendants. With overseas supplies easily available after 1713, they abandoned such efforts and matters seemed to revert to a condition of impasse once more.

There is reason to believe, however, that in the minds of the partners in the monopoly, this impasse was far from acceptable. On 13 October 1711, the Dauphin forwarded to Controller-General Desmaretz a scheme which had come to him from some unknown group proposing to take over the tobacco farm for two million *l.t.* annually instead of the 1.5 million then paid by the monopolists, with the understanding that they would encourage the plantations in the southwest to the point where they would be able to supply all the needs of France. Nothing came of this scheme, of course. What is most interesting about it, though, is the answer to it from the then monopolists. Extending the legal cultivation area, they insisted, was one sure way *not* to increase the yield of the farm. Tobacco was "une Marchandise de Fantaisie" and any successful monopolists would have to govern themselves by public taste. Outside of the south, they insisted, no one wanted Guienne tobacco. Not even the soldiers would take it at canteen prices from three-fifths to four-fifths below normal retail prices. Even the Duclos company had eventually discovered this at very great cost. No monopoly could be run in France without importing Brazil and Virginia tobacco demanded by public taste. The lands in the southwest could much better be employed under wheat. The only thing that made tobacco economically more attractive than wheat was the opportunity of selling part of the crop fraudulently. At Léry in Normandy, though cultivation was permitted on only 100 acres, the monopoly claimed they had had to spend 50,000 *l.t.* annually on a staff of 60 guards and clerks, and still half the production went to the contrabanders. In Guienne, the permitted production zone was so extensive that the monopoly had had to abandon its first attempts at detailed supervision. To limit the fraudulent trade there, the company had had to offer its own tobacco for sale retail in that neighborhood at one-half the usual price or less. If the government really wanted to increase the yield of the farm, the wise thing would be to abolish the domestic plantation entirely! They would pay well for this. If, on the other hand, a general extension of the cultivation zone was being contemplated, they averred that they would not be interested in continuing the farm at any price.[120]

Disregarding the rhetoric on either side, what is significant about this exchange is that, as of 1711, the company which had been exploiting the monopoly since 1697 felt that the interests of the revenue required the total abolition of the domestic cultivation and were not abashed to say so. If those disturbed and distressed times were unpropitious for such a drastic change, other times and other men would come.

CHAPTER 7

Merchants and Manufacturers: The Business Activities of the Monopoly, 1674–1718

Thus far, we have been largely concerned with the activities of the succeeding tobacco monopolies in France, 1674–1718, as they reflected or influenced public policy. We cannot leave this period without attempting to sum up what little we know of the purely business activities of the monopoly, particularly buying and manufacturing. (In the administrative chapter, we have already discussed their distributive network.)

The Buying Policy of the Monopoly, 1674–1718

No activity of the monopoly was felt more keenly at the time, or is more significant for our study, than its buying. By purchasing decisions, the monopoly could, as we have seen, decide the prosperity or despair of tobacco growers in the French colonies and in the growing jurisdictions within France; such choices could affect the French balance of trade and France's relations with friend and foe. Yet ultimately the monopoly as a revenue farm was under even stronger pressures to maximize profits by giving the consumer the tobacco he wanted (which otherwise he would try to get from contrabanders), by cultivating consumer taste for varieties least accessible to contrabanders, and by buying in the cheapest market supplies acceptable within these criteria.

We have already several times noted that long before the monopoly was established in 1674, there was an active tobacco market at Marseilles in Portuguese (Brazilian), Spanish and Guienne tobaccos. In the ports of northern France, an even greater variety could be found offered on the market. A printed price-current from Rouen of 25 January 1669 gives the following prices for the day.[1]

Verinas tobacco	per lb.	—
Verinas, 2nd sort	"	—
Brazil tobacco	"	17–18s.
Marignan [Maranhão]	"	16–17s.
Virginia tobacco	per quintal	66 l.t.
St. Christopher, good	"	55 l.t.
Holland, pressé	"	64 l.t.

Verinas was the exotic and very expensive Spanish tobacco from Venezuela carried out by the Dutch as often as by the Spanish. "Marignan" [Maranhão]

173

described those tobaccos from the more northerly parts of Brazil. We have here then virtually all of the varieties of tobacco well known in maritime trade. The conspicuous exceptions are surprisingly the tobacco of St. Domingue (which, however, appears in a later Rouen price-current)[2] and of Guienne. It would thus appear that five years before the monopoly was established, northern France had an established market for the principal international varieties of tobacco, but had no place for that of France's own southwest or of St. Domingue. Much that was later blamed on the monopoly can be found presaged in this price-current.

For the varieties given above, the price range is from 55 *l.t.* per quintal for St. Christopher's to 80–90 *l.t.* per quintal for Marignan and Brazil. St. Domingue could probably be had then for no more than St. Christopher, while the tobacco of the southwest could probably be bought in the growing areas for about 10 *l.t.* per quintal and need only pay a duty of 2–4 *l.t.* on entering Normandy. The principal imported varieties were closely enough priced so that price itself was unlikely to be the determining factor governing consumer choice. The marked cheapness of the tobaccos of the southwest did not seem to make them any more welcome in the north of France.

In the early days of the monopoly, the consumer was supplied with all the varieties of tobacco he had known before, as is shown in Table I.

TABLE I
Sales of Tobacco (in Pounds) in the Offices of the Monopoly, 1675–79[3]

	1675	1676	1677	1678	1679 (6 mo.)
Brazil & Marignan	56,496	240,243	267,028	224,622	127,397
St. Domingue	168,435	634,423	564,859	433,727	124,092
Léry, Other French & German	79,957	271,085	276,547	413,691	223,311
Clairac *pressé*	35,136	251,580	223,462	98,849	7,107
English	6,642	14,314	51,320	58,453	26,097
Dutch	7,533	30,916	17,999	30,115	36,983
Verinas	42	147	511	178	51
Snuff	5,256	16,107	39,865	46,967	27,142
Total	359,497	1,458,816	1,441,590	1,306,602	572,180

This information is most interesting. It reveals right off that, despite all complaints, the early monopoly followed a rather "patriotic" purchasing and selling policy (or at least responded to consumer demand in a "patriotic" way). Except for the last year (incomplete), at least three-quarters of sales were accounted for by French and French colonial tobaccos. The only major imported supply was that of Brazil and Marignan tobacco from Portugal. This was in response to a well-established consumer demand and from a "friendly" power. Nevertheless, the figures show some interesting trends. (We can disregard 1675 when the monopoly was in the process of being established, and should double in our minds the figures in the last column to make a complete year.) While the sales of Brazil tobacco were relatively constant from 1676 to 1679, those of St. Domingue, the leading type in 1675–76, weakened steadily from 1676 to 1679. The turn of consumer taste away from this type, which we observed in the colonial chapter, was obviously already in operation in the 1670's. The demand for the relatively expensive "Clairac pressé" declined abruptly from 1676 to 1679 (due to contraband) while the market for the cheaper Léry and other French and frontier tobaccos rose. Of little immediate importance, though significant for the future, was the modest rise in the demand for English and Dutch tobaccos. Equally modest

TABLE II

Inventory of Stock (in Pounds) in Hands of Monopoly, 30 September 1687 (excluding Brittany and the Three Bishoprics)[4]

Foreign	Leaf	Manufactured	Total
Brazil	0	109,437	109,437
Marignan	0	2,690	2,690
Holland	0	14,912	14,912
Germany & Alsace	0	434	434
Virginia	4,021	134	4,155
Verinas	0	153	153
Snuffs:			
Malta	—	303	303
Pontgibon	—	736	736
Spain	—	3,134	3,134
Rome	—	94	94
National			
St. Domingue	0	366,802	366,802
Dieppe	0	100,335	100,335
Léry	97,157	9,315	106,472
Charleville	59,451	Tobacco: 3,749 Snuff: 7,168	70,368
Artois	974	2,467	3,441
St. Mexant	0	355	355
Clairac	37,607	146,974	184,581
Mondragon	25,768	Snuff: 28,971	54,739
Other snuff	—	207,762	207,762
Total, foreign	4,021	132,027	136,148
Total, national	220,957	873,898	1,094,855
Grand total	224,978	1,005,925	1,230,903

but significant was the steady rise in sales of snuff, portending the great revolution in taste that took place in the next century.

Quite similar is the picture presented by the inventory of the monopoly's stock on hand at the end of the Fauconnet lease, 30 September 1687, covering all of France except the sublet provinces of Brittany and the Three Bishoprics. Snuff had grown somewhat in relative importance by 1687, but supply was still based solidly on "national" sources. The proportion of imported tobaccos would perhaps be a little higher if we had data on Brittany, and if we knew what proportion of Virginia tobacco (the only foreign leaf imported) was disguised in the mixed "Dieppe" rolls, and perhaps in the national snuff as well (Table II).

There is, of course, one big difficulty in using an inventory as evidence of purchasing policy. Not everything purchased by the company was passed on to consumers equally quickly. We know, for example, from the colonial chapter that the company's purchases of St. Domingue tobacco during 1683–88 averaged 9,214 rolls annually or 460,700 lb. at 50 lb. each—rather below the level of sales of 1676–77.[5] Assuming that the company was behaving intelligently, this suggests a declining consumer interest in St. Domingue roll tobacco. In fact, the detailed inventory shows that of the 366,802 lb. of St. Domingue roll shown in Table II, fully 52,448 lb. had sat so long in storage as to be too dry for chewing and would have to be ground up into a cheap snuff, while another 54,085 lb. were unfit for any use.

Similarly, it is possible that consumer demand for foreign tobaccos was brisker than average so that warehouse stocks were disproportionately low. That this was in fact so is suggested by an unofficial document about 1700–1705 describing consumption as of 1690:[6]

Brazil tobacco	312,600 lb.
Briquet imported from Holland	449,680 lb.
Briquet from Morlaix manufacture	330,300 lb.
Briquet from Dieppe manufacture	398,046 lb.
Total	1,490,626 lb.

Although the account seems to suggest a consumption static since the 1670's it should be noted that it does not include snuff or the tobacco manufactured in private workshops in the Clairac-Tonneins area for use in the south. What is most striking about this account is the growing importance of imported tobacco, even when compared to the mid-1680's. If the consumption of Brazil had risen only modestly since the 1670's, that of Dutch had soared. St. Domingue had disappeared completely, while even the Morlaix and Dieppe products contained some Virginia leaf mixed in with the Léry and Clairac for quality. This evidence suggesting growing foreign purchases in the late 1680's is reinforced by a later memoir by Jean-Rémy Hénault, head of the tobacco monopoly, 1685–97. The monopoly, he insisted, had had to buy

Dutch and Portuguese tobacco to meet specific consumer tastes which they could not otherwise satisfy. (They maintained regular correspondents in Amsterdam and Lisbon to buy this tobacco for them but eventually became dissatisfied with the Brazil they were receiving and sent one of their own employees to Lisbon to make the selection.) [7]

The year 1690 was still early enough in the war for a significant proportion of the tobacco sold then to have been imported into France before the formal declarations of belligerency. The Nine Years' War was to witness a crucial transition in French tobacco consumption habits. As we have seen, it ended any place for St. Domingue tobacco in the French market. With all overseas supplies difficult to obtain, the domestic plantations in the southwest and south could be and were expanded—but French consumer taste could not be supplied entirely from that source. Every sort of tobacco could, of course, be obtained even in wartime from Amsterdam, the greatest tobacco market in Europe. The States-General made significant efforts to prevent imports from enemy France but tolerated most exports except gunpowder and other obvious contraband of war. Such authorized trade could easily be carried on in neutral or licensed vessels.[8] An even greater source of imports was created by the war itself through the capture by French privateers of English tobacco vessels from Virginia and Maryland. This was to reach proportions substantial enough to satisfy French demand in some years and to alter French taste.

Long before 1689, English tobacco was known in France (as was evident from the Rouen price-current of 1669) but was slow in becoming important. English data show that in 1660, 33,084 lb. of tobacco worth £827 were exported from London to France.[9] This would suggest total exports for all England of about 50,000 lb. By the year Michaelmas 1668–69, this would seem to have risen to 160,818 lb. exported to France from London, or about 240,000 lb. from all England.[10] In the two years following the establishment of the tobacco monopoly in France in 1674, sales of English tobacco were insignificant, but they recovered thereafter. During 1677–79, we have seen, sales of English tobacco by the farm averaged 54,348 French lb. annually—or almost 60,000 English lb.[11] (If the English tobacco were sent to France in leaf and manufactured there, as was later the case, we must allow for waste in manufacture: it would have taken at least 80,000 lb. of English exports to produce this 60,000 lb. for sale.)

In the 1680's, as supplies arriving in France from St. Domingue declined, imports from England would seem to have risen significantly as is suggested by these English figures on exports to France:

	London	English Outports	Total
Mich. 1685–86	131,783 lb.	59,769	191,552 lb.[12]
Mich. 1686–87	169,778 lb.	325,903	496,281 lb.[13]

The figures for 1686–87 were probably exceptional, but even those for the prior year represent more than a doubling of the probable shipments in 1677–79. The seeming erratic quality of these figures was probably just a logical reaction by the united farms to market conditions after the English ban on imports from France lapsed in 1685. We have already noted in Chapter 4 that tobacco imports into France from St. Domingue were exceptionally low in 1684 and below normal in 1685, leading to a sharp rise in price in 1685 that was sustained through 1686 and 1687. We also noted in that chapter that even in 1683 and 1684, prices for Virginia tobacco in London were almost a third below prices for St. Domingue tobacco in France, and did not rise significantly when French prices rose in 1685.[14] It would seem that there had been a tendency for the prices of tobacco in England to rise early in 1685 but that a new heavy impost of $3d.$ per lb. on tobacco consumed domestically (effective 24 June 1685), while it enhanced the price of old tobacco already entered, tended to depress the price of new tobacco arriving after the effective date, making the latter particularly cheap for export. The drop in export prices seems to have been more marked in the outports than in London, explaining in all probability the upsurge in French buying at the outports noted in 1686. At a time when the prices paid by the united farms for St. Domingue in France ranged between $4d.\frac{1}{2}$ and $5d.$ sterling, prices at Bristol for ordinary export tobacco on board were:[15]

1684	$2d.\frac{1}{4}$
1685	$2d.\frac{3}{4}$
1686	$2d.\frac{1}{4}$
1687	$2d.\frac{1}{4}-\frac{3}{8}$

There were thus the amplest of market motives for an expansion of French purchases in England, and in the English outports in particular, in the middle 1680's.

Thus, when we juxtapose our French and English data, we seem to see English shipments to France declining with the establishment of the monopoly from about 240,000 lb. in 1668–69 to about 80,000 p.a. during 1677–79 and then recovering to about 200,000 lb. in 1685–86 and about 500,000 lb. in 1686–87. Nevertheless, these figures are not overly impressive, considering that total English exports in the 1680's were in all probability well over ten million pounds annually. France in the 1680's can be considered only a tertiary market for English tobacco exports, while England was little more than a secondary source for French tobacco supplies.

The Nine Years' War, we repeat, changed everything. As we shall see below, after that war, both France and Flanders (Dunkirk) became major vents for English tobacco, taking many times any quantity they were known to have taken before the war. By the turn of the century, we know, the St. Domingue tobacco trade was virtually extinct. By that time, too, a real demand was manifest in France for English tobacco. That demand, as English merchants at the time realized, had in fact been created by the familiarity and acceptability of English tobacco among French consumers established during the war years when millions of pounds of Chesapeake leaf were captured by French privateers and dumped onto the French market.[16] Through these "losses," the English planter and merchant were to capture a permanent place in French consumer taste.

Just how much English tobacco might French privateers have captured in the course of the war? This is a very difficult question because modern scholarship has yet to establish any generally agreed upon quantitative data for privateering activity during this war. In 1783, the baron of Sainte-Croix published a study of English naval power in which he stated, without giving any source, that in the Nine Years' War, the English had lost 4,200 merchant vessels worth thirty million sterling.[17] We are concerned with the number of ships rather than the estimate of value, which seems rather high—over £7,000 per vessel. The most distinguished modern scholar on this subject has suggested that the number of prizes given by Sainte-Croix is much too high.[18] There is, nevertheless, other evidence that would suggest that this estimate is not too far off the mark. In 1708, when British losses during the Spanish Succession War were under discussion, the Lord High Admiral officially conveyed to the House of Lords his department's estimate that in the previous war, "the Trading Part of the Nation had the Misfortune to lose near 4,000 Ships."[19] Figures of this magnitude for the 1689–97 war are also fully consistent with the losses which impeccable modern scholarship has established for the 1702–12 war.[20] If we concede that "near 4,000" may have meant as little as 3,600, we must still think in terms of English losses to the French of at least 400 vessels a year during the Nine Years' War.

Of these 400 or so ships a year lost to the French, what proportion might have been in the Chesapeake trade? A recent scholar has suggested that about 6 percent of English tonnage entering English ports in the peaceful year 1686 was from the tobacco colonies.[21] Six percent of even 400 English vessels captured by the French annually from 1689 to 1697 would have been 24 vessels per year. As convoys were rather better outward bound than coming home, it may be safe to assume that of the 24, two-thirds or 16 were inbound with tobacco and the remaining one-third or eight outward bound. The best available evidence would suggest that the average vessel in the tobacco trade then carried about 120,000 or 130,000 lb. of tobacco.[22] Sixteen vessels brought into French ports with 120,000 lb. of tobacco on board each would have given the French 1,920,000 lb. of tobacco yearly, or more than enough to supply the entire needs of the monopoly for imported tobacco. This is also almost four times as much tobacco as was exported from England to France in the best prewar year known (1686–87).

Though the figure 1,920,000 lb. per annum for English tobacco taken prize by the French may seem large, it most likely errs on the modest side.

For one thing, it probably underestimates the cargo of the average vessel taken by the French. Privateers were on the lookout for the larger and richer prizes and were less likely to ransom them. English merchant protests in the 1690's are filled with references to great tobacco ships taken by the French which would have paid from £8,000 to £14,000 sterling in customs had they arrived safely at London or Bristol.[23] It would have taken 480,000 lb. of tobacco paying the full nominal duty of 5d. per lb. to produce £10,000 to the crown—on paper. (If the duty were calculated net after all possible discounts for prompt payment, it would have taken 640,000 lb. to yield £10,000.) [24] Yet it is safest to ignore such data as merely picturesque.

Much more important is the question of whether the Chesapeake trade accounted for only six percent of English tonnage entered inward during 1689–97. In wartime, English shipping activity declined as much of the carriage between England and northern Europe in particular passed into neutral bottoms. This meant that the undiminished trade with the tobacco colonies would have occupied a relatively larger place in total English traffic. One surviving account of arrivals in the port of London in the year ending Michaelmas 1692 shows 19 percent of the English ships entered and 23.4 percent of the inward tonnage coming from Virginia, Maryland, and Carolina.[25] This would suggest that instead of just 24 vessels a year, the French may well have captured (after deducting 10 percent for the Carolinas) somewhere between 70 and 90 vessels a year to and from the tobacco colonies, or perhaps 46 to 60 homeward bound.

Thus far we have been attempting to calculate various proportions of the macro-figure of 400 French prizes a year which might have carried tobacco. It is possible to calculate also from the microcosm upward. From detailed lists, we know that Bristol lost to the French an average of four ships from Virginia yearly in the five years from late 1690 to early 1695.[26] Since Bristol accounted for 10–15 percent of the English tobacco trade,[27] this would suggest total losses to the French during those five years of 24–40 ships yearly inbound from the Chesapeake. This falls between the modest 16 and the rash 46–60 suggested as extremes. In one group of Bristol Virginia ships lost, the average cargo was 412 hogsheads.[28] This would produce an average cargo by weight of 154,500 lb. instead of the 120,000 lb. used above, indicating again the conservatism of those calculations.

In short, by the most conservative of calculations from the English data, the French would appear to have taken as prize 1.92 million lb. of English tobacco annually during the Nine Years' War. It is quite possible that the actual figures were substantially higher.

On the French side, our data are more fragmentary. At the start of the war, there was a real shortage of tobacco in northern France and steps were taken to facilitate the shipment of unexpectedly large quantities of southern tobacco northward via Bordeaux.[29] (Government help was also received to facilitate the overland shipment of Brazil tobacco from Marseilles to Paris without paying Lyons tolls.) Special dispensations were obtained to import Dutch manufactured tobacco overland via Ghent.[30] From the first day of the war, however, substantial Virginia ships were captured by French privateers.[31] By June 1690, warehouses at Nantes were filling up with captured tobacco.[32] Government intervention facilitated purchases by the monopoly from the privateers on convenient terms.[33] By 1696, the united farms themselves could admit the good fortune which had enabled them to replace the disappeared St. Domingue tobacco with the Virginia leaf from prizes "at a rather reasonable price."[34] So abundant were supplies that they had never had to pay more than 20 *l.t.* per quintal for such tobacco during the entire war.[35] (This was markedly cheaper than prices for tobacco in London, Dunkirk, or Amsterdam in the latter years of the war.)

When peace returned in the fall of 1697, Frenchmen had been consuming relatively cheap Virginia tobacco for eight and one half years. With the complete disappearance of St. Domingue production and the limited acceptability of Guienne tobacco in northern France, it was self-evident that the future prosperity of the tobacco farm was to depend upon imported tobaccos, primarily from England and Holland. Samuel Bernard was brought into the new tobacco monopoly company by the elder Pontchartrain in 1697 because he alone of French merchants had the correspondence throughout Europe that could guarantee imported supplies in peace and in war.[36] What actually happened to English tobacco exports to France and Flanders is told in Table III.

TABLE III
English Tobacco Exports (in Pounds) to France and Flanders
1696–1703[37]

	Flanders (Dunkirk & Ostend)	*France*	*Both*
Mich. 1696–Mich. 1697	626,633	0	626,633
Mich. 1697–Xmas 1698	1,152,703	110,926	1,263,629
Xmas 1698–Xmas 1699	1,202,087	296,990	1,499,077
Xmas 1699–Xmas 1700	716,035	1,756,244	2,472,279
Xmas 1700–Xmas 1701	921,009	2,241,041	3,162,050
Xmas 1701–Xmas 1702	312,699	191,550	504,249
Xmas 1702–Xmas 1703	0	0	0

The most obvious fact to be derived from Table III is that in 1700 and 1701, for the first time, England became a major supplier of tobacco to France through the open market. That this did not happen immediately in 1698 and 1699 was probably due to the carry-over of wartime captures and the extremely high prices prevailing in London in the first two years of peace. Rather than pay these high prices, the monopoly ran down its old stocks and may have had recourse to such devices as purchasing Dutch spun tobacco in which a small amount of Virginia leaf was mixed with native Dutch leaf. When prices dropped in 1700–1701, the monopoly responded to the logic of the marketplace and bought directly and substantially in England. When prices rose again in London at the end of 1701, the monopoly again trimmed its purchases even before the war started.[38]

It was not, of course, entirely necessary for France to buy at this time from her erstwhile enemies, England and Holland. Supplies of superior tobacco could also be obtained from Spain and Portugal. We need not concern ourselves much with Spain. Its tobacco—whether from Venezuela (Verinas) or from Cuba—was several times more expensive than any other on the European market and was only used by the French for mixing in luxury snuffs,[39] except along the Pyrennean frontier where there was a special local demand for it.[40] When Ducasse's expedition to Cartagena in 1697 captured a large quantity of Verinas tobacco, he realized immediately that it was too expensive to be sold well in France and could best be sold only in Amsterdam.[41] Similarly, when the Asiento Company sent home a shipment of Spanish snuff in 1705–6, its sale was very difficult since the monopoly found it too dear for their purchases—even though many members of the monopoly were also directors of the Asiento.[42]

Brazil tobacco, by contrast, sold at much more competitive prices and all through the seventeenth century played a significant part in the French tobacco market. We have already noted that one estimate placed French consumption of Brazil tobacco in 1690 at over 300,000 lb. annually. Perhaps five times as much was reportedly purchased in Lisbon about 1699 when tobacco prices were very high in London and Amsterdam.[43] That purchases were seldom as high and never rose higher may have been partly a matter of taste. (Brazil tobacco then was used in France primarily as a chewing tobacco; it was unacceptable in snuff unless mixed with two-thirds Virginia.) The French failure to buy more from Portugal was also a matter of restricted supply: the quantity of Brazilian tobacco reaching Europe was always quite limited compared to supplies available from other sources.

In 1666, the Brazil fleet brought to Portugal only two million pounds of tobacco (less than usual)[44] compared to about fifteen million imported into England from its colonies about that time. In 1689, the same fleets brought 22,000 rolls or about 3.5 million lb. of tobacco from Brazil to Portugal,[45] while English imports had risen to about 28 million lb. By 1698–1708, official accounts at Lisbon show tobacco shipments from Brazil to Portugal of about seven million Portuguese (or English) pounds annually, about nine-tenths coming from Bahia, the remainder being "Maranhão" tobacco shipped from Recife. By comparison, in the decade ending Christmas 1708, English imports (almost entirely from the Chesapeake) averaged 28.6 million lb. annually.[46] In other words, total imports into Portugal were too modest in the seventeenth century (compared to supplies available in England or even Holland) to permit major expansion of exports to France without seriously disturbing prices. (There were firmly established markets for Portuguese tobacco all through Europe, in the African slave trade and even in the Hudson's Bay trade.)

Despite the actual limitations of the market, there were many in France all too willing to criticize the succeeding monopolists for not buying more Brazilian tobacco. An anonymous memoir writer (probably an official), writing in 1691 but describing conditions at the beginning of the war, condemned the monopoly not only for discouraging tobacco cultivation in France and St. Domingue, but also for ruining France's trade with Portugal. The returns from French trade with Portugal had formerly been made almost entirely in Brazil and Marignan tobacco, he alleged; with the monopoly now refusing to buy these returns, the whole Portuguese trade was ruined.[47] This was to be an ever more frequent charge in the next ten years. In January 1696, when Pontchartrain sought the views of the merchants of La Rochelle on reviving the St. Domingue trade, they used the occasion to inform the minister that the trade to Portugal—the most important neutral market still available as an entrepôt for the export of French manufactures—was also in ruins. They blamed this in great part on the hostility of the united farms toward Brazilian tobacco.[48] Six months later, when Pontchartrain's son, Jérôme Phélypeaux, visited La Rochelle, the merchants complained to him too about the importance of tobacco as a return from Portugal, the low prices offered for Brazilian tobacco by the monopoly, and the obstructions placed in the way of merchants who wanted to reexport any.[49] In his memoirs of 1698 and 1711,[50] the former admiralty and naval official Jean Pottier de la Hestroy repeated the same arguments about Portuguese tobacco in greater detail, adding that Portugal had been a particularly valuable market for French manufactures, inasmuch as out-of-fashion silks which could be sold nowhere else could be sold in Lisbon for reexport to Brazil where no one knew the difference.

In his aforesaid memoirs, Pottier de la Hestroy began the general attack on the monopoly for wasting foreign exchange by buying tobacco for cash from foreign states (England and Holland) instead of from national sources or from a foreign state like Portugal with whom France had a favorable balance of trade. In his second memoir, he admitted that buying tobacco from such countries as England and Holland was cheaper for the monopolists, but thought this an insufficient reason to waste three million *l.t.*[51] These themes were to be reiterated during the sittings of the Council of Commerce in 1701–2. The merchants of Honfleur protested against a policy that encouraged importation from Holland rather than the French colonies just because it was profitable for the monopolist.[52] Piedcourt, the deputy from Dunkirk, who on this as on other points, was very close to la Hestroy in his arguments, stressed the harmful effects of the monopoly's policies upon the Portugal trade as much as upon the West India trade.[53] By contrast, Descazeaux du Hallay, deputy from the great West India trading center of Nantes, thought buying from Portugal as bad as buying from Holland. To buy from anywhere but the West Indies was to waste more than two million *l.t.* annually.[54] All these criticisms were to be found in the draft report from the Council to the king: on the one hand, it condemned the monopoly for wasting millions in specie buying tobacco from England, Holland, *and* Portugal; on the other hand, it blamed the monopoly for ruining the Portuguese trade, the favored mart for outmoded and unsaleable goods, by refusing to buy enough Brazilian tobacco.[55]

It is clear, then, that by 1698–1701, informed opinion was quite aware that the tobacco monopoly had become dependent for a substantial proportion of its supplies upon imports from England, Holland, and Portugal. Those who discussed it all thought it an egregious waste of foreign exchange. Some, but not all, would make an exception for Portugal with whom France had a favorable balance of trade. Nothing came of these complaints at the time, but the criticism thus early sounded was never to be silenced till the monopoly itself disappeared a century later.

In the War of the Spanish Succession, the monopoly was to have a much more difficult time obtaining supplies than it had had in the previous war. Although more than 4,000 British vessels were taken prize by the French in this war too,[56] a sufficient number of tobacco ships do not seem to have been captured to satisfy the needs of the monopoly. Consumption was rising and the place of imported leaf had become even more fixed in French taste in the interwar years. Part of the trouble may also have been due to the fact that in the early years of the war, the number of English ships sailing from the Chesapeake was sharply reduced—there were thus fewer ships available for capture. The reduced shipping was reflected in peak prices for English tobacco at Amsterdam in 1703 and 1706. After 1707, the English convoy system seems to have markedly improved.[57] On the French side, a member of the company thought the paucity of prize tobacco was caused by the fact that the Malouins, great specialists in privateering, had redirected part of their effort during the Spanish War to the South Seas trade.[58] By January 1704, Maynon, the administrative head of the monopoly, begged Controller-General Chamillart to be very secretive about the company's affairs lest the merchants and privateer-owners discover how desperately short of tobacco the monopoly then actually was. In the previous war, he reported, they had never paid more than 20 *l.t.* per quintal for captured Virginia leaf; now they were offering 25, but the captors were holding out for 45: "the needs of the farm are so great that it must absolutely have them [the prize tobaccos] at whatever price is necessary." None of the prize tobacco could be spared for France's ally Spain.[59] By 1708, the monopoly was offering 66 *l.t.* for Brazil prize tobacco and 28 *l.t.* for Virginia and still had to appeal to the controller-general to force privateer owners at Calais and La Rochelle to sell at these prices.[60]

The war years then were years of continuous supply crisis for the monopoly. Part of the shortage was met, as we observed in the last chapter, by trying to preempt a larger percentage of the rising production of the southwest. (In the viscounty of Turenne, for example, production which had averaged 200,000 lb. during 1693–1700 rose to 800,000 lb. annually during 1700–1715.) [61] But the monopoly also needed imported supplies. It was in the end saved only by the extensive foreign connections of that wonder-worker, Samuel Bernard. An apologist later explained:

> ... the exchange having become very unfavorable and the Malouins ... having given up privateering the monopoly having no more prize tobacco found itself without any supply because of the total prohibition of commerce which developed in 1704 between England, Holland and France and fell into a penury that put it on the very brink of ruin. Any other [company] with less credit and which did not have the industry to procure its supplies by indirect routes (nothing less was at stake than the lives of its correspondents in England who nevertheless willingly risked them) —any other [company], I say, would undoubtedly have succumbed to these misfortunes . . .[62]

But not Samuel Bernard. We do not know all the *voyes obliques* through which he got English or Dutch tobacco to France. During 1703 and 1704, when there was a serious effort by the English and Dutch governments to stop trading with the enemy, he had to use very indirect routes indeed. English export statistics suggest that these probably were via Baltic and Scandinavian ports.[63] That such a roundabout route was in fact used is substantiated by a document from the farm listing four neutral vessels which carried 667 hogsheads of Virginia leaf tobacco from Gothenburg in Sweden to Dieppe and Morlaix in 1703 or 1704, "for the account of M. Bernard."[64] Another Swedish vessel carried tobacco from London to Dieppe twice in 1704, while ostensibly bound for Leghorn.[65]

From 1705 onward, when the Dutch government became much more permissive about trading with the enemy, the French could easily procure both English and Dutch tobaccos in Holland. Such trade, of course, required a great mass of special papers, permits, and passes, at the collecting of which Samuel Bernard was also most expert. About 1706, we find the monopoly protesting against the seizure by French privateers of Portuguese and Dutch vessels carrying the farm's tobacco to France.[66] In and about 1708, we find them writing frequently to the government for special passes for vessels bringing tobacco from Holland, sometimes for passes for two or three named vessels at a time, at others for blank passes for twelve vessels at once. In 1707, they even obtained for some tobacco ships a waiver of the usual rule that licensed vessels importing goods from enemy states must carry away the equivalent value in French produce. On other occasions, the company applied for passes to bring overland from Holland across Spanish Flanders 500 rolls of Brazil tobacco or 1,500 hogsheads of Virginia leaf.[67] Irish ship captains domiciled in France regularly received permits from the French king to trade to their homeland in wartime in ships manned by Irish crews primarily to get provisions needed in France. In 1711, we learn, such ships received special passes to visit Ostend and Holland to bring Dutch tobacco back for the monopoly—despite a general prohibition on trading with the United Provinces then in force in France.[68] Early in 1713, on the eve of the peace, when Franco-Dutch relations were at their nadir and commerce between them once again prohibited on both sides, the monopoly still needing tobacco in the Dutch style, bought it at Hamburg and had it shipped to Liège and thence sent via Namur into France.[69]

The purchasing agents of the French tobacco monopoly in Holland were the great banking house of André Pels & Son, the Amsterdam correspondents of Samuel Bernard.[70] In London, his and their correspondents were the Huguenot firm of Tourton & Guiguer, an offshoot of the more important Paris house of the same name, though with different partners. The story of this firm will be discussed in greater detail in Chapter 20. Suffice it to say here that their great triumph came in 1708 when working through more influential houses in the London banking community, they were able to obtain special passes from the British government permitting direct export of tobacco to France.[71] With obvious satisfaction, Maynon could write to Controller-General Desmaretz in January 1709, "The tobacco farmers desiring to profit from the arrival of the Virginia fleet in England by having purchased the tobacco necessary for their manufactures which are in danger of falling into ruin, Monseigneur is very humbly begged to be so kind as to grant them six blank passports. . . ."[72] Although no tobacco had been cleared out from England directly to France in 1703–8, no fewer than 1,212,382 lb. were so dispatched in 1709.[73] The trade was interrupted in 1710, but resumed the next year, facilitated by an act of Parliament permitting the return of French wines.

For the middle years of the war, we have a most detailed estimate of the direct operations of the monopoly dated May 1708. It was probably prepared for the controller-general preparatory to the renewal of the lease of the farm in 1709. It is an estimate of current operations rather than the record of any particular year. Coming from the farm, it is probably accurate in its proportions—though there were of course reasons for the monopoly to inflate prices or to under-report its total operations. It does not include purchases by the subfarmers in southern France. The account (Table IV on page 187) shows that the monopoly then required for its operations in northern France 2,956,000 lb. of tobacco annually. Of this a shade over 60 percent (1,836,000 lb.) was purchased in leaf, a shade under 40 percent (1,120,000 lb.) in a manufactured or semimanufactured state. The account is interesting in that it suggests that in 1708, one of the most disastrous years of the war, with French state finances in a shambles and the exchanges heavy against France, Samuel Bernard was able to procure about 1,000,000 lb. of enemy (British and Dutch) tobacco. Another 540,000 lb. were obtained from hostile Portugal. The 165,000 lb. of Havana and Verinas were more

TABLE IV

Tobacco Purchases of the Monopoly, ca. 1708 (with Prices per Quintal)[74]

Snuff		120,000 lb.
Havana	45,000 at 150 *l.t.*	
Clairac, etc.	75,000 at 50	
Spun, Roll, Corde, etc.		1,000,000 lb.
Strasbourg	350,000 at 30–75	
Brazil	500,000 at 100	
Holland	150,000 at 110	
Leaf		1,836,000 lb.
Virginia	700,000 at 37:10	
Amersfort (Dutch)	150,000 at 42:10	
Havana	80,000 at 40	
Verinas	40,000 at 40	
Marignan	40,000 at 40	
Artois	100,000 at 19	
Clairac	600,000 at 28	
Léry	126,000 at 18	
Total		2,956,000 lb.

likely obtained in Holland or brought back directly from the West Indies by the Asiento Company rather than imported from Spain. Only 801,000 lb. were obtained from Guienne (Clairac) and Normandy (Léry) within the territories of the monopoly. Another 450,000 lb. were obtained from France's eastern frontier provinces (Artois and Alsace) outside the jurisdiction of the farm. (These purchases on the frontier were a wartime lapse from policy and were not repeated till the American Revolution.) The total obtained from French territories was less than half total needs. (By contrast, the 1687 inventory—Table II—had shown about five-sixths from "national" sources.)

Prices were rather distorted by the war. Léry and Artois were understandably cheap, but probably twice their peacetime levels. The even higher price for Clairac tobacco reflects the real difficulty the monopoly had buying in Guienne against foreign competitors. Although Virginia tobacco sold in Holland for twice the price of Dutch native (Amersfort) tobacco, here Amersfort is shown costing slightly more than Virginia. This undoubtedly reflects the fact that a goodly proportion of the Virginia came from prizes which the monopoly could obtain cheaply, while the Amersfort had to be bought in enemy territories and shipped at considerable expense under wartime conditions. That Havana and Verinas leaf were as cheap as they were probably meant that they were obtained from the Asiento Company on specially favorable terms.

These figures for 1708 should not be taken for a description of the supply position of the farm in a normal year. They rather show how, at one of the worst times in the war, the farm could get by. With the return of peace, we should expect to get a much fairer representation of the supply problems of the farm, governed not by wartime exigencies, but by consumer taste and the play of the open market. In fact, we find in Table V that some radical changes had taken place by 1715–16.

TABLE V
French Tobacco Imports (in Pounds), 1715–16[75]

From:	1715 Leaf	1715 Snuff	1716 Leaf	1716 Snuff
England	2,392,487	—	2,344,291	—
Un. Provs.	1,003,844	4,857	950,660	9,334
Aus. Flanders	149,614	7,370	95,086	3,372
Spain	57,571	410,038	50,030	127,968
Portugal	97,500	15,800	88,200	—
Fr. W. I.	—	—	2,028	15,368
Total	3,701,016	438,065	3,530,295	156,042

These figures date from about the time of the establishment of the French statistical office for foreign trade, the *Bureau de la Balance du Commerce,* and may well have originated there. Such an origin, as well as the title on the unsigned document, suggests that it refers to all France (except Dunkirk), not just to the territories of the monopoly. This would probably explain the imports from Austrian Flanders where the farm is never known to have bought. Though these must have gone to the exempt eastern provinces, virtually all the remaining imports probably went to the territories of the monopoly. When the figures here given for imports from England are compared with English figures for exports to France and due allowance is made for differences in the pound weight and the fiscal years used, they come to within one percent of each other for the two years—remarkably closer than most skeptics about eighteenth century commercial statistics would have thought likely.[76]

Comparing these 1715–16 figures with those for 1708 or earlier, the most striking change is the complete elimination of the importation of manufactured roll tobacco. This would reflect both changing consumer tastes in France and the preference of the monopoly to buy only raw materials and do its manufacturing in France when it could. The most serious sufferer from this change was Brazil roll tobacco, used for chewing. As late as 1708, its consumption in northern France alone was estimated at 500,000 lb. p.a. With the return of peace, we rarely hear of it again. The other side of this taste change is the growing popularity of snuff, reflected here in the imports from Spain and the French West Indies (St. Domingue), both made from Havana leaf.[77] Ultimately, however, the growing French taste for snuff was to be met in the eighteenth century not by imports of the manufactured product but by manufacture within France from imported leaf, particularly the versatile Virginia leaf. Thus, the aspect of the postwar data most significant for the long run is the much enhanced place occupied by imports of Virginia tobacco. Imports from England now account for 65 percent of all leaf imports and 60 percent of all imports.

The growing importance of French tobacco imports from England after the peace is confirmed by the English data in Table VI.

TABLE VI
English Tobacco Exports (in Pounds) to France and Flanders, 1703–18[78]

Year Ending Christmas	Flanders (Dunkirk & Ostend)	France	Both
1703–1708 (av.)	51,407	0	51,407
1709	107,407	1,121,382	1,228,789
1710	97,832	0	97,832
1711	240,694	3,505,807	3,746,501
1712	219,635	864,376	1,084,011
1713	3,008,814	790,800	3,799,614
1714	1,709,608	2,491,814	4,201,422
1715	489,100	2,332,898	2,821,998
1716	866,577	2,910,799	3,777,376
1717	460,723	3,153,513	3,614,236
1718	894,255	2,580,760	3,475,015

In the years 1711, 1716, and 1717, France for the first time passed Germany to become the second most important export market after Holland for English tobacco.

One important point of reference should be kept in mind when we consider all these figures. French tobacco consumption was rising very slowly. Our data for 1676–78 show sales by the monopoly of about 1.4 million lb.[79] The estimates for 1708 show purchases of 2,956,000 lb., which after losses in manufacture produce 2,432,633 lb. of saleable tobacco. To this should be added perhaps 20 or 25 percent for sales within the provinces subfarmed.[80] Consumption in the immediate postwar years could have been only slightly above this. In other words, consumption had only slightly more than doubled in the forty years between 1676–78 and 1716–18. At both times, per capita consumption in France—only a small fraction of a pound of tobacco per head per year—was well below that in England, Holland, and other north and west European countries. Frenchmen would appear never to have really cared very much for seventeenth-century smoking or chewing tobacco. Only after the widespread introduction of snuff in the next generation was French tobacco consumption to catch up with that of the rest of Europe.

The Manufacturing Activity of the Monopoly, 1674–1718

There were literally dozens of varieties of prepared tobacco known to the trade about 1700.[81] How were all these manufactured for the consumer after the establishment of the monopoly in 1674? In his apologia of 1697, de Lagny boasted that (but did not say when) the monopoly had established manufactories which made native leaf into both twist (roll) and *tabac mâtiné* (a mixture of tobaccos pressed into a *brique* or plug) comparable to the varieties imported from Holland and England.[82] Such *tabac en corde* for smoking and snuffing and *mâtiné* for chewing would have satisfied most needs but not the demand for more exotic varieties. Hence, we are faced with two problems: (1) how soon did the monopoly establish its own workshops; and (2) how did it satisfy the demand for varieties it did not manufacture or import itself?

There is very little evidence concerning manufacturing activity by the original monopoly company of 1674–80. During the first year or two of its existence, it most probably did no manufacturing at all. Most of the varieties needed it would have purchased already manufactured, including the roll tobacco of Brazil and St. Domingue, the *pressés and andouilles* (small rolls or plugs) from England and Holland, and the Clairac *pressé*. In the main growing areas of Guienne, it and its successors permitted the existing manufacturers to continue under its close fiscal inspection. It may have permitted private manufacturers elsewhere to continue for a while, but it soon closed them down. A hostile memoir from some merchants of Paris in 1685 accused the first monopoly of having suppressed the new and successful manufacture of *tabac mâtiné* at La Rochelle which surpassed the famous product of the Dutch.[83] (The special privileges granted in 1672 to the Zeeland merchants who introduced the new process there were revoked when the monopoly was established in 1674.) [84] In 1676, the monopoly took the momentous step of establishing its own manufactory at Dieppe. Though this was ultimately to become a great industrial undertaking, it would appear at first to have been a rather small operation.[85]

When the monopoly was transferred to the United General Farms in 1680, manufacturing activity continued at first along established, rather modest lines. Snuff, in which sales were limited but profit per pound highest and fraud easiest, was ground in the company's own workshops at Paris, Mondragon and Perpignan; spun tobacco, by contrast, was made only at the company's big works at Dieppe. (Brittany which had its own spinning works at Morlaix was subfarmed during 1681–87.) In 1686, when the French monopoly took over the tobacco farm in the eastern frontier sovereignty of Charleville, it acquired a further small spinning and snuff works there. Still, of the million pounds of manufactured tobacco and snuff in the monopoly's inventory as of 30 September 1687 (Table II), only about a third had been made in the company's own establishments—and most of that was snuff.[86]

After 1687, the company increased its tobacco spinning activity, but reduced its snuffmaking as part of its general policy of subletting the snuff privilege. In 1687, the snuff works at Perpignan were transferred to the company which sublet the snuff monopoly in Languedoc and Roussillon; when they sub-sublet Roussillon, they transferred the manufacture to new works at Toulouse[87] and later established another snuff manufactory at (Pont) St. Esprit on the Rhône (near Mondragon on the opposite side).[88] The other groups which subfarmed the snuff privilege, 1687–97, were, however, still obliged to buy their snuff from the national monopoly's works and warehouses at Paris and Mondragon.[89] In 1697, however, the new Bernard-Crozat-Maynon company, as part of its new policy of subfarming both tobacco and snuff in the south, transferred the Mondragon snuff works to the company subleasing Provence and eastern Dauphiné.[90] (It was probably also about this time that the company subfarming Auvergne, Bourbonnais, Berry, and La Marche established its own snuff works at Clermont.)[91] This left the monopoly only with the Paris snuff works and, during 1687–97 at least, they contracted out the actual snuff grinding work there.[92] In the new century, it became for a time very fashionable for even polite snuff takers (following a practice introduced by soldiers and workmen) to carry about elegantly decorated rasps and to grate their own snuff from twists as needed. This made it less necessary for the monopoly to grind snuff for them.[93]

While reducing its snuff-making activity, the monopoly would appear to have expanded its tobacco spinning. After 1687, it had two large manufactories at Dieppe and Morlaix and a smaller one on the frontier at Charleville. Although no new spinning works were added down to 1718, these were expanded. In the company's accounts for 1687–91, we find substantial and rising expenditures for tools and equipment for these works.[94] Morlaix supplied Brittany, Anjou, and Touraine, while Dieppe provisioned Normandy, the Ile-de-France, Champagne, Burgundy, and most of Picardy.[95] Charleville made cheaper tobaccos for sale at reduced prices to the troops and in the exposed frontier territories where the farm had to compete in price with smugglers.[96]

The great expansion in manufacture at Dieppe and Morlaix would appear to have occurred in the 1690's as a result of the altered supply situation caused by the war. The war ended importations of manufactured tobacco from St. Domingue and hindered such importations from Holland and Portugal. At the same time, the privateers of St. Malo, Dunkirk, and elsewhere made available to the monopoly millions of pounds of captured Virginia leaf tobacco. This all had to be manufactured at Dieppe and Morlaix. Their preeminence thus dates primarily from the 1690's.[97]

Dieppe and Morlaix were undoubtedly chosen for the sites of works because they had a previous history of manufacturing and an available supply of skilled labor. In the case of Morlaix, this is only inference. It was a major center of the north Breton linen industry and as such had close trading connections with Cadiz. This liaison would have made for an early familiarity with both the use and preparation of Spanish tobacco. It also had close trading connections with England and was particularly well situated to obtain tobacco cheaply from the English southwestern ports which were very important in the seventeenth-century tobacco trade. A recorded shipment of

7,524 lb. of leaf tobacco from Bristol to Morlaix in 1677 suggests that there was some sort of manufacture there, either of or licensed by the monopoly.[98] There clearly was a manufactory there during the Breton subfarm of 1681–87, for an employee of the United Farms was sent there in 1687 to supervise the transfer at the end of the lease.[99] By 1690, the Morlaix works were making at least 330,000 lb. of spun tobacco yearly.[100] During the 1690's, the first small establishment at Morlaix was damaged by a fire ascribed to enemy bombardment.[101] With the return of peace, it was replaced by a much larger works on the outskirts of the town at the manor of Penanrue en Ploujean.[102]

On Dieppe, we are better informed. The first substantial *petunerie* was established there in 1664 by a company of local merchants, employing workers from Poland and Brazil, probably imported via Holland. Other firms followed with further workers imported from Holland—though eventually native workers were trained.[103] The town was well situated for both imported and Norman tobaccos, and easily accessible to the Paris market. The establishment of the monopoly in 1674 led to two years of bitter disputes between the new monopolists and the nineteen or so *marchands bourgeois de Dieppe* engaged in the tobacco trade as dealers or manufacturers. This transitional period ended with the establishment of the monopoly's own manufactory there in 1676. Thereafter, local merchants continued to import tobacco but only for sale to the farm. In 1694, the old workshops were also destroyed during an enemy bombardment of the town and the resultant fire. They were reconstructed on a more ample scale thereafter.[104]

By 1715, the tobacco manufactory at Dieppe was big enough to have a major labor disturbance. The works, which were entirely devoted to the manufacture of spun tobacco, then employed about 1,000–1,100 workers. Of these, about 200 were skilled adults employed in the spinning operation. The bulk of the remainder were children between nine and sixteen employed in preparing the tobacco for spinning. The company became disturbed at the amount of tobacco which the adult spinners were stealing from the workshops in their clothes. They gave orders for the guards to search the workers as they left the premises and take away from them any tobacco found on their persons. As compensation, they announced that the company would give each adult worker one pound of tobacco monthly for his own use. The workers formed a *cabale* and threatened strikes, so the company took the precaution of training some of the older and stronger boys to act as spinners. On 1 July 1715, the adult workers struck and attacked the manufactory to prevent the boys from replacing them as spinners. This aroused the townspeople, the relations and friends of the child laborers, who formed another mob to drive off the strikers, accusing them of maltreating the children and of trying to deprive them of their livelihood. Troops were called out and restored order. The strikers eventually trickled back to work individually.[105] The whole story is as suggestive of the problems of early (perhaps premature) industrialization as that of the contemporary strikes at the van Robais woolen works at Abbeville.

For the year 1708 we have rather detailed estimates of all the manufacturing operations of the monopoly.[106] The company's purchases given in Table IV can be summarized as:

Snuff	120,000 lb.	97,500 l.t.
Spun or *corde*	1,000,000 lb.	828,000 l.t.
Leaf	1,836,000 lb.	600,930 l.t.
Total	2,956,000 lb.	1,526,430 l.t.

The 120,000 lb. of snuff consisted of 45,000 lb. of Havana snuff and 75,000 lb. of Clairac and other cheaper materials. They were mixed and flavored at the workshops at Paris to produce 60,000 lb. of the expensive (7 *l.t.* per lb.) "Spanish" snuff and 60,000 of the much cheaper *tabac grené* (moist snuff in balls or pellets).

The million pounds of spun or *corde* tobacco consisted of 500,000 lb. of Brazil, 150,000 of Dutch, and 350,000 lb. of Alsatian. The Brazil and Dutch were apparently sold as purchased, the former for chewing, the latter for smoking or snuffmaking. The 350,000 lb. of Alsatian were further prepared by subcontractors at Strasbourg into the following types:

baton à raper (for consumer-prepared snuff)	40,000 lb.
canasse et brique (expensive smoking, chewing)	100,000 lb.
ordinary twist (medium price smoking, snuffmaking)	200,000 lb.
inferior (cheap smoking, snuffmaking)	60,000 lb.

The 1,836,000 lb. of leaf tobacco from Clairac, Virginia, etc. (broken down in Table IV), were sent to the manufactories at Dieppe and Morlaix. With a normal loss in manufacture of about 30 percent, they yielded the following chewing (*mâtiné*), smoking and snuffmaking tobaccos:

At Dieppe: grosses andouilles	506,632 lb. at 2 *l.t.* per lb.[107]
rouge (*demi-andouille*)	145,900 lb. at 1 *l.t.*
pressé mâtiné	6,321 lb. at 1 *l.t.*
cantine (for troops)	143,780 lb. at 12s.
Total	802,633 lb.
At Morlaix: andouillettes	60,000 lb. at 2 *l.t.* per lb.
Morlaix pressé	300,000 lb. at 1:10s.
"English"	130,000 lb. at 1 *l.t.*
cantine (for troops)	20,000 lb. at 10s.
Total	510,000 lb.
Combined total	1,312,633 lb.

Total sales therefore were:

Product of Dieppe and Morlaix factories	1,312,633 lb.	1,912,935 *l.t.*[108]
Snuff from Paris workshops	120,000 lb.	570,000 *l.t.*
Strasbourg manufactures (private)	350,000 lb.	321,750 *l.t.*
Imported Brazil and Dutch	650,000 lb.	1,267,500 *l.t.*
Total	2,432,633 lb.	4,072,185 *l.t.*

In addition to the 4,072,185 *l.t.* shown here from its sales, the monopoly realized 14,000 *l.t.* from the export sales of 350,000 lb. of the stems and midribs of the tobacco leaf not used in the manufacture (at 4 *l.t.* per quintal). In addition, of course, there was 500,000 *l.t.* annually from the subfarms of the southern provinces, making a total receipt of 4,586,185 *l.t.*

Against this income, there were in the first instance the primary expenses of 1,526,430 *l.t.* for tobacco purchases and 827,000 *l.t.* for operating expenses. (Tobacco purchasing costs were relatively high in wartime.) The operating expenses are broken down into:

	l.t.
Operation of factories at Morlaix and Dieppe	90,000
Operation of workshops at Paris	35,000
Transportation	150,000
River and quay tolls	15,000
Wastage at sea	12,000
Central office at Paris	40,000
Provincial administration and guards	250,000
Pensions to officers of *cinq grosses fermes*	30,000
"Gratifications" to *juges des fermes* and other useful persons	20,000
Legal and other expenses	150,000
Rent of buildings	35,000
Total	827,000

It will be seen at a glance that the costs of manufacture and transportation were relatively minor compared to administrative and legal expenses.

Finally, there were the direct costs of the monopoly. Although the price to the government was supposed to be only 1.5 million *l.t.* annually, this line in fact appears on the accounts as 1.7 million. Presumably there were 200,000 *l.t.* annually in pensions or ministerial gratifications charged to the farm. In addition, there was the quite proper payment of 100,000 *l.t.* to the United General Farms in lieu of all import duties. Then there was also an item of 120,000 for 10 percent interest on the 1,200,000 *l.t.* which the monopoly had borrowed from its partners or others, and part of which was advanced to the government.[109] The final statement showed therefore:

Gross Receipts: (in *l.t.*)			4,586,185
Charges:	Tobacco purchases	1,526,430	
	Operating expenses	827,000	
	Price of farm	1,700,000	
	Composition to U.G.F.	100,000	
	Interest on advance	120,000	
		4,273,430	
	Net Profit	312,755	
			4,586,185

These figures could, of course, be interpreted as implying that the final profits of the monopoly (less than 7 percent of gross receipts) were too modest to support any rise in the price of the farm. That was undoubtedly the purpose to which they were put in 1708–9. The same figures could also be interpreted to suggest that if in 1708, one of the worst years of the war, the monopoly could still clear over 300,000 *l.t.* then it might very well have had much greater profits in less disturbed years.

With the return of peace and "better times," all kinds of men began to wonder how much further those profits might well be made to go.

CHAPTER 8

Tobacco in the Genesis of Law's Company, 1716–18

To write about the history of the tobacco monopoly during the hectic years of John Law and the Mississippi Bubble is both a very difficult and a somewhat foolhardy project at the present time. Although much has been written on the "System" during the past century and more, the existing literature on the subject does not devote much attention to the place of the tobacco monopoly in the scheme. Three great scholars, Professors Harsin, Giraud, and Hamilton, have since the 1920's undertaken the most extensive researches into the life and times of Law, but we still await the final results of their labors. Had I the pleasure of seeing their completed work, these chapters probably need only have been in great part a synthesis.[1] Without those greatly needed guides, however, this section has had to be based on the author's own gropings among the primary sources. The reader should keep in mind one charitable distinction: the general treatment of Law's scheme is intended only as an interpretive sketch; only the sections on the tobacco monopoly proper in this and the next two chapters attempt anything more.

It will occur to many who have read this far that one of the most striking features of John Law's scheme was that it proposed to take over all the principal activities, individual and collective, of the Bernard-Crozat-Maynon group with which we have been concerned: the trading monopoly to Louisiana which Crozat had had since 1712,[2] the Guinea trade, the St. Domingue company, the Pacific and Asian trades in which Crozat and others of them were active, and, not least, the tobacco monopoly which the group had enjoyed to their apparent profit since 1697. Law himself from the very beginning seemed to recognize and avow his enemies.[3]

We know very little about the formation of the mind of John Law. His perceptive ideas on banking seem based upon a real familiarity with and understanding of contemporary advanced English, Scottish, and Dutch practice. Less certain is where he got his knowledge of and ideas about overseas trade. A single copy of a long manuscript has survived, signed by John Law and dated 4 October 1715, shortly after his arrival in Paris, when he was struggling to get his banking proposals considered. A little over a quarter of the manuscript is about banking and is clearly by Law. The remaining three-fourths contain an ambitious description of French commerce and recommendations for its restoration. Its most striking feature is a proposal to form a *compagnie générale du commerce maritime* which would absorb all existing French companies trading abroad and would monopolize the trade to the East and West Indies, Africa, Canada, Louisiana, the Baltic, the whale fisheries, and much more. This would seem to suggest that Law had the whole plan for the "System" at hand from his arrival in Paris.[4] Yet, there is no known external evidence of such a memoir being in existence at the time. Moreover, close textual examination reveals that about 40 percent of the memoir, and about 60 percent of its commercial sections, were lifted almost verbatim from a 1698 memoir by the official Jean Pottier de la Hestroy, which we have already discussed in Chapter 3. So careless was this borrowing that passages referring to Pottier personally were left in the text.[5] Most of the historical and descriptive material in the memoir comes from Pottier, but not the more sweeping recommendations, such as that for a single great trading company.

An interesting exception to this last generalization is the long section on the tobacco monopoly:[6] although this section contains the "sweeping recommendation" for the abolition of the monopoly, it was in fact copied almost verbatim from Pottier's 1698 memoir.[7] In other words, if we accept the authenticity of this 1715 memoir, then we have the innovator John Law taking over intact the criticism of the tobacco monopoly compiled in 1698 by a conservative, elderly official who looked back to the golden days of Colbert and Seignelay, under the latter of whom he had served. Law thus accepted Pottier's criticism of the monopoly for buying tobacco from England and Holland instead of from the French colonies, the French domestic planters and Portugal, as well as his recommendations for abolishing the monopoly and establishing in its place a simple import duty of 5–10 percent. In the event, Law was ultimately to carry out Pottier's proposal, though with a duty raised far above the judge's suggestion to a level approaching the 100 percent import duty then prevailing in Britain.

In summary, then, textual evidence suggests that only the banking section can be accepted unquestionably as belonging to Law and September-October 1715. The remainder was probably put together for him from various papers that had come into his possession, perhaps by 1715, perhaps later. However concocted, the historical importance of the memoir lies in its suggestion that, from his first arrival in France, Law had a "grand design" for the economic reconstruction of that war-harried land. This thesis cannot, however, be automatically accepted, for other documents emanating from Law or his circle make no such claim,[8] nor is there any external evidence of the memoir being circulated. In the fall of 1715, John Law was principally engaged in pushing his temporarily unsuccessful scheme for a great state bank. (The Regent was sympathetic but the scheme was blocked at the time by the opposition of the duke of Noailles, president of the Council of Finance.) It is possible that, as ammunition in this struggle, Law commissioned someone to put together the long memoir from papers in his possession, but, in the end, decided not to circulate it.

Whatever the true history of the long memoir of 1715, it tells us nothing about the actual origins of the Mississippi Bubble. By necessity or by nature, Law was to act his hour upon the stage not as a systematic innovator but as an improvisor, changing his tactics with circumstances. The contingencies from which he created his great Indies Company had their origin not with him, but with those whom he supplanted. To understand the beginnings of the Mississippi, we must look therefore not to the rising but to the setting suns.

Despite the death of the king and the reorganization of the government in 1715, the position of the old group of financiers seemed for the moment as strong as ever. They were after all able to stop Law in October of that year. If Maynon was passing into retirement, Samuel Bernard was as active as ever. The world continued to be amazed at the vast sums he could procure and shuffle about for the government.[9] Crozat, though he withdrew from the tobacco farm in 1715, was at the height of his influence, shortly to achieve the highest honor of his career in the treasurership of the king's orders, including the ultra-aristocratic *ordre du Saint-Esprit*.[10] Yet the "old gang" had their difficulties: they had had fallings-out since the difficult times of 1708–9 and no longer can be thought of as a group acting together as in 1697–1701. Many of the companies in which they invested, particularly the Guinea and St. Domingue companies, were now in shambles. Even Crozat's not unprofitable Louisiana trading monopoly needed a vast infusion of additional capital.[11] Out of their understandable efforts to restore order to this confusion came the first proposals which grew ultimately into Law's Occident Company.

One possible way of salvaging something was to join the pieces together, one fragment supporting another. A good place to start would be the Guinea and St. Domingue companies, both controlled by substantially the same interests.[12] The Guinea Company, it will be remembered, had been originally chartered in 1685 for twenty years. In 1701, its administration was transferred to the group including Bernard, Crozat, and Maynon which shortly thereafter set up the Asiento Company as a joint undertaking between the existing Guinea Company and the French and Spanish crowns. The formal monopoly of the Guinea Company expired in 1705; this was of much less import to it than the peace of Utrecht by which France lost the Asiento to England. With the expiration of the Asiento (formally renounced as of 24 June 1714), the question became what to do about the rump of the Guinea Company.[13]

On 19 September 1713, the directors of the St. Domingue company wrote to Pontchartrain suggesting that the expired monopoly of the Guinea Company (which they also controlled) be transferred to them. The secretary of state for the navy replied on 8 October that the king had decided to throw open the Guinea trade to all his subjects. Special passports would be required and would be given out in sufficient number. The St. Domingue company was to cease giving out such passports on its own authority.[14] The new policy (effective November 1713) was specifically confirmed by letters-patent of January 1716 which removed the need for passports but restricted the French ports which could take part in the slave trade.[15] In this new "liberal" policy, both the governments of Louis XIV and the Regency chose to respect the preferences of the West Indian planters rather than those of the metropolitan financier-investors.

From the moment its bid to take over the Guinea trade monopoly was rejected, the affairs of the St. Domingue company began to turn very sour indeed for its directors. From its early days, Crozat had been one of the two most active directors of this company (the other being de la Boulaye).[16] In 1712, he disappeared from its active leadership, probably to devote himself to his Louisiana venture, the managing director by then being his brother-in-law, Joseph Le Gendre d'Arminy.[17]

At first it seemed that the affluent directors of the St. Domingue company would be prepared to invest more of their own money for the postwar reconstruction of their colony. On 29 December 1712, Le Gendre d'Arminy had written to Pontchartrain of the directors' resolution to raise another 187,000 *l.t.* The secretary replied on 1 February 1713, urging them to try to raise a much larger sum to clear the debts of the company and reestablish the colony.[18] He wrote to Maynon privately the same day to the same effect.[19] In May 1713, an *arrêt du conseil* was issued ordering the directors to put in another 800,000 *l.t.*, but the directors chose to ignore it.[20] By October, the minister was reduced to cajolery, writing to Bernard and Crozat individually to contribute and to use their good offices to get the other directors to advance the sums ordered. As an inducement, Pontchartrain obtained another *arrêt* granting the company exemption from one-half the duties it normally would have paid on its returns to France.[21] Crozat seemed agreeable as of 18 October, but after the company's request for the Guinea monopoly was turned down in November, the directors became reluctant once more. On 7 December, Le Gendre d'Arminy wrote to Pontchartrain that a group of recalcitrant directors refused to invest the further sums in the company called for by the *arrêt*. With the exception of de la Boulaye, an old navy official, they had decided to come to some sort of financial agreement with the directors who preferred to remain and to leave the company.[22]

Matters came to a head in 1714. In January, Pontchartrain persuaded Bernard and other disgruntled directors to stay in the company for the time being and keep it alive until another group could be formed to take it over.[23] Meanwhile, de la Boulaye conducted negotiations with a new monied group headed by Pierre Galabin who were prepared to put up something like one million *l.t.* Details were worked out by July when the new contract of partnership was signed. In the end, Le Gendre d'Arminy and the original directors Bernard, Crozat, Thomé, Maynon, Landais, and the official Charles de Salabery all decided to withdraw.[24] Only de la Boulaye, de Vanolles, and Magon de la Chipaudière remained, to join the incoming directors. The new managing directors were Galabin and Gayot, already active in the Canadian beaver monopoly.[25] On 19 February, the new administrators of the St. Domingue company went in turn to Pontchartrain with a request of their own that they be granted the Guinea monopoly. They too were refused in the name of the free trade so much desired by the planters of the West Indies and the merchants of France.[26]

Thus, it should be rather clear that even before the death of Louis XIV, well before the return of John Law to France, there were forces within the French financial (as opposed to commercial) community who were trying to unite in one company remnants of the old trading monopolies to Guinea, St. Domingue, and even Canada. Under the changed conditions of the Regency, these same forces were to come out into the open with more such plans, without waiting for John Law to take any lead.

The first concrete proposal toward a great trading company came in mid-1716 from one of the former directors of the St. Domingue company who can almost certainly be identified as Joseph Le Gendre d'Arminy. This may seem a rather undocumented identification, but it is rather likely: (1) a few months later, in the early months of 1717, we find other memoirs by or about d'Arminy by name which are consistent with his authorship of the 1716 memoir; (2) by explicit statement, the 1716 memoir is by a former director of the St. Domingue company who referred to himself in the first person: he cannot be Crozat, Thomé, Maynon, or Bernard who were referred to in the text by name in the third person; this leaves only Etienne Landais, Charles de Salabery, and Joseph Le Gendre d'Arminy. Neither Landais (*trésorier-général de l'artillerie de France*) nor de Salabery (president in the *chambre des comptes,* Paris) had the practical experience of St. Domingue and the slave trade shown by the author. There remains therefore only Le Gendre d'Arminy: he had lived in the colony, about 1702-4, and had the widest relevant experience. Brother-in-law to Crozat, he was an original Asientist of 1701 and had gone to the West Indies in 1702-4 to manage the affairs of that company there. On his return to France, he continued as *directeur du commerce royal de l'Asiento* and acquired a share in the tobacco monopoly. In 1709, he bought into the St. Domingue company and was its *directeur-général* during 1710-14, selling out finally in 1715.[27] The long connection of his family with that of the Regent (to whom he was now *secrétaire des finances* and business agent) might also help to explain why he was emboldened to speak out at this juncture.[28]

The mysterious memoir itself[29] was presented to the Navy Council (*Conseil de la Marine*) in "July 1716," at the very time when the government was confirming the new regulations which the Company of St. Domingue had issued for its colony (sometimes called the colony of Saint Louis to distinguish it from the French settlements in the northern part of St. Domingue which were not within the jurisdiction of the company). According to the author, Le Gendre d'Arminy, the transfer to new directors had been something of a fiasco. The new act of partnership had never been dated or formally deposited with notaries. Des Ruaux (one of the Galabin group), to whom Crozat and Maynon had sold their shares, had not yet been able to be formally admitted to the company and was now under arrest at Rochefort, presumably for debts. It was difficult for the new directors to get a quorum for a meeting. The wretched colonists were left to their own devices, subsisting by trade, most of it illegal. Yet the colony could not be abandoned; it was an important military bulwark against the English in Jamaica. Only a big company could fulfill such strategic obligations. Yet d'Arminy admitted that big trading companies had expenses that small firms avoided. They could not sustain such outlays and compete unless they were given some sort of monopoly. Hence, he was recommending the formation of a new big monopoly trading company.

The company recommended by Le Gendre d'Arminy would not simply be another *compagnie de Saint-Domingue*. The future of that island, he saw, lay not in white settlement, which by the charter of 1698 the company was to promote, but in its slave supply; ten Negroes would be necessary for every white settler. Therefore, d'Arminy recommended (as he and his colleagues had done in 1713) that the monopoly of the Guinea trade also be granted to the new company. Furthermore, he suggested that his brother-in-law Antoine Crozat's Mississippi trading monopoly be taken away and given to the new company. He envisaged Louisiana supplying St. Domingue with the forest and other products of the temperate zone which the British colonies in North America furnished to the British West Indies. He also concocted a wild scheme to use a combination of force and kindness to induce Indians from the Mississippi Valley to settle on St. Domingue as free laborers. (It is obvious that his travels had never taken him to that great valley.) Finally, he would add to his great company the farm of the *domaine d'Occident* (the king's tax revenues from trade in and with the American colonies). The rent due the crown from this farm could be used in the first few years to pay the king's subscription to the capital of the new company. The numerous employees of the farm in the ports of France and the colonies would provide the perfect skeletal administration for the new company. (The *domaine d'Occident* was then losing so much money that its farmers would probably willingly give it up.) [30]

Here then we have from an old member of the Bernard-Crozat-Maynon connection a suggestion for a great trading company embracing St. Domingue, Louisiana, the slave trade and the *domaine d'Occident*—a full year before Law became actively interested in the idea at all. It differed from the scheme ultimately worked out chiefly in that it included no British

"South Sea" gimmick for absorbing part of the national debt into the capital of the company. It was a purely commercial scheme. Its occasion was the distress of the colony of St. Louis and the weakness of the reformed St. Domingue company.

There was reason for the government to be concerned with the condition of the settlement in southern St. Domingue: it was not only from the disgruntled former directors that they received advice. A few months later, the current directors of the company also submitted a memoir to the Navy Council. It was no ambitious project for a greatly expanded trading company, but simply a request for routine financial and material assistance. The memoir did, however, have one clause concerning tobacco which showed clearly that the new directors of the *compagnie royale de Saint-Domingue* were Paris financiers without any real knowledge of the economic geography of their colony.

On 30 July 1715, the new directors of the St. Domingue company, as noted in Chapter 4, had requested from the government an *ordonnance* obliging all the settlers on St. Domingue to plant a certain quantity of tobacco each year[31]—despite the very solid reasons underlying the decline and disappearance of the tobacco trade there. In their memoir of late 1716, the same directors repeated the suggestion in more specific form. Each planter was to be required to use one-third of his land [sic!] and one-third of his slaves in producing tobacco! To make this worth while, they would like to see the monopoly abolished and a simple entry duty of 15–20 *l.t.* per quintal established (harking back to Pottier's suggestion of 1698 picked up by Law in 1715, though here at a much higher rate, approaching 100 percent). If this were not practical, they would like to see the tobacco monopoly make a contract with the St. Domingue company by which the farm agreed to take all their tobacco at 50 *l.t.* per quintal for dried leaf (more than double any previously discussed price for St. Domingue tobacco) and 50 *sols* per lb. for any Spanish snuff they might obtain through commerce.[32] All this was taken seriously enough at the time for the tobacco farmer, François Le Gendre (brother of Le Gendre d'Arminy) with the aid of the officer in charge of the Dieppe manufactory to prepare technical reports on the inadequacies of St. Domingue tobacco which were presented to the count of Toulouse, head of the Navy Council, in March 1717.[33]

Though they may have been concerned about St. Domingue in 1716, the government in fact did nothing about that colony, for the Regent and his ministers had much more pressing matters in hand then. The principal concern of course was the 750 million floating debt inherited by the Regency from the wars of Louis XIV, reduced by the *Visa* of 1715–16 into 250 millions of *billets d'état,* which the inadequate revenues of the day showed no signs of being able to diminish further.[34] Le Gendre d'Arminy himself recognized in his July 1716 memoir that the general financial tightness made that an unpropitious time to float a great new company:

... it will be objected that the now prevailing lack of confidence (*discredit*) makes any such project chimerical. Without doubt, it would not be easy to collect such capital funds, but one must also admit that the present situation (*conjoncture*) is favorable for forcing compliances. Monsieur the duke of Noailles, in his administration of finance, can render the state a great service in this matter.[35]

When Le Gendre d'Arminy wrote that the "present situation is favorable for forcing compliances," he referred to what was on everyone's mind in Paris financial circles in 1716—the *Chambre de Justice*. After the Visa, the Regency had, following a historic French practice, set up an emergency tribunal in 1716 to look into the estates and accounts of all those who had enriched themselves at the state's expense during the past war—revenue farmers and subfarmers, office jobbers, government suppliers, and miscellaneous contractors. It was, in effect, a retrospective profits tax averaging 25 percent of the estates assessed.[36] Of the 220 million *l.t.* in fines ultimately assessed, the first list approved in the Council of Finance on 27 November 1716 brought in ca. 26 million, of which almost half came from two men—Bernard and Crozat. To preserve his foreign credit for the benefit of the state, Samuel Bernard was permitted to exempt himself entirely from the scrutiny of the chamber by a composition of six millions; Antoine Crozat was assessed 6.6 millions. (The two Le Gendre brothers were taxed 300,000 *l.t.* each in January.) [37]

We shall examine these assessments in detail in the next chapter. What is important here is to appreciate the psychological impact in Paris financial circles when the news of these great sums burst upon the city at the end of November 1716. The effects were almost entirely psychological, for most of the great assessments seem to have been settled by balancing off depreciated debts owed by the crown to the financiers. Even so, these assessments seem to have had a particularly demoralizing effect upon the old Bernard-Crozat-Maynon connection. On the one hand, their preeminent assessments impaired at least for the time being their ability to undertake extensive new commitments such as the great new trading company envisaged by Le Gendre d'Arminy. On the other hand, these same assessments mortified them publicly and rendered them reluctant out of pique or calculation to do any more "favors" for the state in the immediate future. Samuel Bernard and Antoine Crozat were both probably worth at least twenty million after settling their accounts—and as such richer each of them than any contemporary financier in England.[38] Both lived long thereafter, yet for both of them 1716 marked the end of their most active, public careers and the beginnings of their semi-retirement.

Perhaps the angriest man in France at the moment was Antoine Crozat, even though in the end he paid less than a fifth of his *taxe*.[39] He felt that the greater part of his fortune had been made honestly and at great risk in wartime ventures to the East Indies, and that it was rank injustice to confound him in the proceedings of the Chamber of Justice with "all the rascals" in France who had made their fortunes during the war at jobbing offices or profiteering on contracts.[40] Though Crozat had been holding back for some time on enlarging his capital commitments in Louisiana, he realized clearly enough the vast sums needed to develop that colony.[41] Toward the end of December 1716, i.e., within a few weeks of the announcement of his assessment and while he was in the process of settling his accounts with the Chamber of Justice,[42] Crozat decided that he could not continue with his monopoly of the Louisiana trade. This decision was embodied in a series of memoirs which he presented to the government late in December and early in January 1717.

Toward the end of December 1716, Crozat wrote to the count of Toulouse, head of the Navy Council, protesting that he had been prepared to devote to the development of Louisiana the fortune which it had taken him 45 years to accumulate, that he had great hopes in particular for the mines and tobacco cultivation to be developed there—but that the assessment of the Chamber of Justice had rendered him incapable of continuing. He asked that there be applied toward his *taxe* various sums arising from his surrender of the Louisiana trade: two million *l.t.* compensation for the loss of his monopoly, 960,000 *l.t.* for his trading goods in Louisiana, and 300,000 *l.t.* for sums advanced in the king's service.[43] In the next few weeks, he poured memoirs upon the government. A trade which up to then had been a desperate proposition[44] was suddenly endowed with incredible profits and prospects for which he demanded compensation. In one of these memoirs, he discussed the general importance and promise of Louisiana and the need to maintain it in a strong condition as a bulwark against British expansion. For this purpose, it was necessary for the king to spend 120,000–150,000 *l.t.* annually and to form a company with a capital of 1.5 million *l.t.*[45] In a second memoir addressed to "Monseigneur" (probably the marshal duke of Estrées, president of the Navy Council), he explained his ideas about the company: "It appears necessary to form a company promptly, strong enough not merely to sustain that affair [Louisiana] but actually to begin operations on a large scale." A really big company could so strengthen Louisiana in two years that it would thereafter have nothing to fear from the British. Such a company should not only take over his Louisiana trading and mining monopoly, but should also be given the North American beaver trading monopoly (which he never had) since the Gayot and Neret grant was about to expire at the end of 1717. For this company he recommended a capital of 1.5 million for Louisiana alone or two million with the beaver monopoly, divided into shares of 3,000 *l.t.* each. Crozat recognized that it would be difficult to raise new capital under existing conditions and so suggested that subscribers be permitted to pay in *billets d'état* (depreciated state obligations) provided that the government agreed that these particular notes would be paid off in installments over the coming three years. He urged speed so that two additional vessels could be despatched to Louisiana by 1 April.[46]

A third memoir, addressed to the duke of Noailles, president of the Council of Finance, repeated the plans for a company of 1.5 million capital with shares subscribed in *billets d'état*. (It did not mention the beaver alternative and may thus be slightly earlier than the second memoir discussed above.) As was appropriate to its addressee, this version repeated the appeal that Noailles permit Crozat to count toward his *taxe* the value of his surrendered monopoly and the sums which he had advanced for government expenses in Louisiana.[47]

Crozat's scheme, therefore, was for a company limited to Louisiana and the beaver trade in contrast to the earlier more ambitious scheme of his brother-in-law, Le Gendre d'Arminy, which called for a monopoly embracing Louisiana, St. Domingue, the Guinea trade and the *domaine d'Occident*. The somewhat novel feature about Crozat's scheme was the suggestion that the subscription be made in *billets d'état;* in his hands, however, this became a very timid suggestion. In the flotation of the British South Sea Company of 1711 or of Law's *banque générale* in 1716, the government paper subscribed was incorporated into the capital of the company. All that Crozat was suggesting in January 1717 was that the *billets d'état* subscribed should be held by the new company until preferentially repaid in specie by the government within three years. This was in the old tradition of French royal finance under which insiders got paid off early, while ordinary creditors waited.

On 11 January 1717, the marshal duke of Estrées presented to the Regency Council in the name of the Navy Council the memoirs presented to the latter body by Crozat. It was decided that the government would work toward forming a company to take over Louisiana as suggested by Crozat.[48] On the thirteenth, the matter was further considered by the Navy Council which decided that a rather strong company would be needed, but referred to the Council of Finance all questions of compensation to Crozat.[49]

Crozat's surrender of January 1717 completely changed the prospects of floating a new company. For six months, the Navy Council had had before it Le Gendre d'Arminy's scheme for a great new trading company, but there was no pressing reason to do anything about this. Crozat's surrender meant that something would have to be decided soon about Louisiana and that decision-making would have to be shared by the Navy Council with the Council of Finance under the presidency of Noailles. The latter appears at this stage to have been particularly anxious to do something about Louisiana quickly only lest it involve the hard-pressed Treasury in new expense.

One of the first persons to act upon the new situation was Le Gendre d'Arminy. On 3 March 1717, he wrote to Noailles enclosing a copy of the scheme for a great company which he had submitted to the Navy Council in July 1716. In the accompanying letter, he admitted, though, that the scheme as presented was hardly acceptable because of "the view which you [Noailles] have on the Mississippi, which you make a principal objective, while the establishment or rather the support of the colony of St. Louis [on St. Domingue] . . . is the capital point of my proposition." Even if the government decided to go ahead with a separate company for Louisiana, there would also be room, he insisted, for his sort of company to take over (in addition to the *domaine d'Occident*) the Guinea trade and the St. Domingue company, for those two trades were mutually dependent while Louisiana was a matter by itself. As the issues were rather technical, d'Arminy suggested that Noailles refer the whole matter to two *commissaires,* Louis Charles de Machault, then a member of the Council of Commerce, and Antoine François Ferrand, a member of both the Council of Commerce and the Navy Council. As an afterthought, he suggested that some of the capital might be subscribed in the form of *billets d'état* which could be used to pay the annual rent to the crown for the *domaine d'Occident* and thus retired.[50]

Two weeks later, Le Gendre d'Arminy was back with a different and more novel scheme. In the interval the decision had been reached to abolish the Chamber of Justice, and risk-takers were once more venturing out of their shells. The duke of Noailles was not interested in his great African-St. Domingue company but was interested in Louisiana and in reducing the great load of *billets d'état* that so weighed down public credit: d'Arminy proceeded accordingly. In a new memoir of 17 March 1717,[51] he proposed a *compagnie du Mississippi* for Louisiana and the beaver monopoly only. He had heard it said that three millions in working capital would be needed to start the trade to Louisiana. That was ten times too much for a start and even four times too much when the trade was in full swing. He proposed a company with a nominal capital of four million *l.t.* Of this, the king would subscribe one million, payable in ten annual installments of 100,000 *l.t.,* assignable against the king's revenues from the tobacco or postal farms. Ten directors would subscribe another million in *billets d'état;* the public would subscribe the remaining two millions also in *billets d'état*. The three million capital in *billets d'état* would not be redeemed by the state (as in the Crozat scheme) but would be held by the company as an indefinite loan to the government at 4 percent. In addition, during the first ten years, the government would give the *compagnie du Mississipi* an annual subsidy of 200,000 *l.t.,* assignable on the tobacco monopoly! (Le Gendre d'Arminy had left the tobacco company in 1715.) In order that this should cost the government nothing, he suggested that the price of foreign tobacco to the consumer be raised and the rent of the farm to the crown increased proportionately. In order to do this, it might be necessary to break the current lease of that farm, "which had caused so much jealousy"—but he did not suggest transferring the lease to any other group. In summary, then, for its actual working capital during its first ten years, d'Arminy's Mississippi Company would have an annual cash in-flow, all from the government, of:

4% interest on 3m. *l.t.* loan to state	120,000 *l.t.*
Subsidy (assigned on tobacco farm)	200,000 *l.t.*
King's annual payment of subscription	100,000 *l.t.*

or 420,000 *l.t.*, out of which it would have to provide its own working capital and perhaps pay some dividends.[52]

The most significant financial arrangements subsequently embodied in Law's *Compagnie d'Occident* were present in miniature in d'Arminy's scheme of 17 March: (1) the entire capital subscribed by the public was to be received in the form of *billets d'état* and held by the company as a permanent loan to the state; (2) for working capital, the company would depend upon the interest from that loan and other payments from the state; and (3) for the security of the company, payments including those due from the crown were to be assigned upon specific branches of the revenue.

The various company proposals of January-March were at an unknown date (probably ca. 1 April) referred to a special commission headed by Jean-Baptiste Duché, a merchant and naval supplier of La Rochelle interested in the Louisiana trade before 1712 and much consulted by the Navy Council. Its other members were Le Gendre d'Arminy, Jean-Baptiste Fénelon, deputy from Bordeaux in the Council of Commerce, René Moreau, deputy from St. Malo, and Gérard Heusch de Janvry, a Paris lawyer of Protestant banking background, then serving as deputy from Bayonne. In 1715, Fénelon had supported and Heusch opposed Law's banking scheme before the Regency Council. Although Fénelon had since become *inspecteur* of Law's *Banque Générale* and Duché and Moreau were to become directors of Law's *Compagnie d'Occident*, at first the prevailing tone of the committee was very conservative. They worked out a draft for a *Compagnie Royalle de la Louisianne* that was much closer to Crozat's scheme of January than to d'Arminy's scheme of March. The company was to have the monopoly of trade to Louisiana (including the exclusive right to import slaves into that colony from Africa) and the Canadian beaver trade monopoly. The capital was to be 2.4 million (instead of Crozat's two million) in 800 shares of 3,000 *l.t.* each, discouraging to small investors. The king was not to take a share. Though the capital was to be subscribed in *billets d'état*, there was to be no permanent loan to the crown, for the king was to undertake to redeem these *billets* (as in the Crozat scheme) in regular payments over five years.[53]

It was probably at this juncture (ca. April 1717), while the commissioners were working out their very conservative plan that they consulted François Le Bart(s), a Paris financier of Breton origin, treasurer to her serene highness the Princess of Conti, tobacco subfarmer and partner for one-tenth in Crozat's old Louisiana company.[54] With his special knowledge, the views he expressed in several memoirs and conferences were of some influence. He thought that the Canadian beaver monopoly ought not be joined to a Mississippi company lest the beaver trade of Louisiana be sacrificed to that of the St. Lawrence.[55] He for the first time seriously and concretely introduced tobacco into the discussion. Crozat's interest in Louisiana had been primarily in mines and in trade and very little attention had been paid to agriculture. Only when Crozat was about to surrender his monopoly did he submit memoirs suggesting that Louisiana might produce tobacco as good as that of Virginia and in quantity sufficient to supply all France.[56] Le Bart repeated these predictions, placing tobacco second only to silk in the agricultural potential of the colony. To realize this potential, though, it would be necessary to oblige the tobacco monopoly to take all the tobacco delivered to it from Louisiana at 75 *l.t.* per quintal—about three times their highest usual buying price. Few in France knew very much about tobacco prices; the prospect of self-sufficiency was, however, attractive. Finally, Le Bart did not think much of d'Arminy's scheme for a *Compagnie du Mississippi*. It was much too ambitious. Who needed a great company with ten directors when all the trade to Louisiana then envisionable could be handled by three or four ships a year with cargoes of 40,000–50,000 *l.t.* each? "A single man with a book-keeper and a junior clerk would not be overburdened fitting out four vessels of this character every year; and if I were master of 300,000 *l.t.* I would undertake alone to take care of all the trade of Louisiana about which, however, so much noise is being made." He warned emphatically against letting such a company fall into the hands of the sort of person inexperienced in foreign trade who had been the ruin of so many Paris-based companies.[57]

Paris in the spring and summer of 1717 heard from the sieur Le Bart and his like exactly what it wanted to hear: glowing prospects for silk, tobacco, and mines; it ignored his awkward remarks about one merchant and two clerks being able to handle all of Louisiana's immediately likely trade. (Similarly, Le Bart's partner, the former governor of Louisiana, La Mothe Cadillac, was in September imprisoned by Law for casting doubts upon the officially brilliant prospects of Louisiana.) Thus, while Le Bart criticized d'Arminy's March scheme as being too ambitious, in the end it, like so many other schemes, proved too modest. At some point, the cautious but desperate duke of Noailles, president of the Council of Finance, became seriously interested in the various plans for a Louisiana company as a means of getting rid of or funding the greatest possible amount of *billets d'etat*, the state's foundering floating debt. The change in official attitude came abruptly in May.

Early in May 1717, the five commissioners were still working on Duché's picayune scheme for a company with a capital of 2.4 million. Things went rather slowly with Duché lecturing them on the history of the colony from its first discovery, for none of the others knew anything about Louisiana except d'Arminy and he, according to Duché, had some rather wild ideas. The commissioners had just about agreed on the final draft of letters-patent for Duché's 2.4 million company when d'Arminy broke ranks and submitted a radically new scheme for a twelve million *l.t.* company. Duché was furious, but the three provincial deputies (Moreau, Fénelon, and Heusch de Janvry) hesitated; both sides appealed to authority.[58] D'Arminy worked through his brother-in-law Crozat whom he apparently persuaded to come forward at this juncture as cosponsor of his scheme. Crozat now had a very good reason for dropping his modest January proposal and coming out for something much grander, for the bigger the new company, the better able it would be to reimburse him handsomely for his rights and the property he was abandoning in Louisiana. Such compensation was stressed in several of his memoirs at this time[59] as well as in that of his partner Le Bart previously mentioned, but was inadequately provided for in the draft for Duché's 2.4 million company.

The d'Arminy-Crozat proposal of 14 May 1717[60] for a twelve million *l.t.* company is essentially the d'Arminy 17 March proposal for a four million company multiplied by three. The king would still subscribe one quarter, now three millions, to be paid 200,000 annually over fifteen years. The nine millions subscribed by the public (including two millions by twenty directors at 100,000 *l.t.* each) would still be paid entirely in *billets d'état*. The interest from these *billets* at 4 percent would bring the company 360,000 *l.t.* annually which, with the king's annual payment of 200,000 *l.t.* toward his subscription, would give the company an annual cash flow of 560,000 *l.t.* during its first fifteen years to devote to its trade. By accepting only *billets* with interest due since 1 January 1717, the new company would have as of 1 July 1717 one-half year's interest or 180,000 *l.t.* cash with which to start trading. Some significant features of the March scheme were altered to give the new plan greater political attractiveness: the state subsidy of 200,000 *l.t.* annually was dropped, and, following Le Bart's advice, the projectors gave up their claim to the Canadian beaver trade. For tighter control there would be, above the twenty directors, seven *commissaires,* five chosen by the directors, two named by the crown.

The May scheme differed from that of March in another important respect. The earlier scheme had called for assuring some of the payments due the company from the state by assigning to the company certain crown revenues, including part of the rent due from the tobacco monopoly—even if this meant breaking the current lease of the tobacco farm and raising prices to the consumer—but it did not call for taking the tobacco lease away from its existing lessors. The May scheme also called for appropriating from the tobacco rent the entire 560,000 *l.t.* due annually from the crown to the company, but with this difference—to secure this revenue, the new scheme called for the Mississippi company to take over the tobacco farm. Though this was necessary purely for financial reasons, it was justified secondarily on the grounds that Louisiana could grow excellent tobacco which would free France from dependence on that of Virginia. Of the twenty directors, ten (exactly the number interested in the existing tobacco company) would be in charge of the tobacco monopoly.

Although both Crozat and d'Arminy had left the tobacco farming company in 1715, this last proposal need not be interpreted as an effort by them to use their new Mississippi company to take over the tobacco farm. They both retained close relations with their former colleagues in the tobacco company: d'Arminy's brother and Crozat's brother-in-law, François Le Gendre, was a prominent and active member of that company. Since the affluent directors of the tobacco monopoly could easily buy directors' places (at 100,000 *l.t.* in *billets d'état* each) in the proposed company, the plan may equally well be interpreted as an effort by the current tobacco farmers (who, as we shall see, were under attack) to transfer their interests to a new trading company and thereby secure their monopoly indefinitely. Some suspected this at the time. Turned inside out, the d'Arminy-Crozat plan of 14 May 1717 is a blueprint of the financial details of what Law's company achieved in 1718.

With the d'Arminy-Crozat scheme of 14 May and Duché's protest of 19 May before it, the government had at last to make up its mind. It is most likely at this point that Noailles became actively interested in the possibility of using the subscription to a Mississippi Company to absorb a substantial proportion of the state's floating debt. The majority of the five commissioners sensed the new atmosphere and hurried to do what was expected of them. In their report (submitted sometime after 19 May) they informed Estrées and the Navy Council that they had considered two proposals: one (Duché's) calling for a company with a 2.4 million capital subscribed in *billets* which the crown would redeem over five years; a second (that of Le Gendre d'Arminy and Crozat) calling for a capital of 12 million and the absorption of the tobacco monopoly "which was strong enough to meet anything." However, after considering all that had to be done in trade, fortifications, and Indian relations, they had become convinced that a capital would be needed of at least 25 million in *billets d'état,* producing an annual assured revenue of one million!

Though this sudden jump to 25 million may seem radical, the rest of the commissioners' recommendations were a compromise between the frank experimentalism of d'Arminy and the caution of Duché. As suggested by d'Arminy, the full 25 million was to be held as capital, with the company operating on the interest—yet any revenues that might accrue to the king from his mineral rights in Louisiana should be reserved for paying off the *billets d'état* that made up the 25 million. The company would have enough to do without getting involved in the Canadian beaver trade. The king should not subscribe anything: private investors would prefer a purely private undertaking (whereas d'Arminy had argued that official patronage encouraged private investment). Although there was to be no public subsidy, the crown was to buy all of Crozat's property and rights and present them to the company which would then be obliged to expend the equivalent value on transporting settlers to Louisiana—all as Duché had suggested. Funds which the company advanced for the expenses of government and defense in Louisiana should be reimbursed out of a specially pledged branch of the revenue in France, so that the company would not be kept waiting for payment as Crozat had been.

Finally, when they came to the key proposal of the company's taking over the tobacco farm so as to guarantee the 4 percent interest on the 25 million, the commissioners in their report straddled the issue exactly if awkwardly: on the one hand, they thought it a nefarious stratagem to preserve the monopoly; on the other hand, they admitted it was probably necessary.

> This [Louisiana] company needs no other support than that which it can expect from the protection of His Majesty. We totally reject the proferred support of the wealth which the duties of the tobacco farm bring to those who are its farmers. The monopolization of this merchandise is monstrous. One would not know how to measure the infinite prejudice which the state, our colonies and our navigation have suffered from it. This assistance is only offered [N. B.] to prevent the abolition of a farm which everyone has attacked for so long a time.
>
> But if in the end, by a chance which ought not to be expected, the propositions and offers which are made on the monopoly's behalf are listened to, we feel that it will at least be necessary to unite the tobacco farm to the Louisiana Company in order to procure for the company the total benefit of that farm which it will employ for the good of the state in supporting a project which should be very advantageous to the trade of the realm. Ministers are frequently obliged to tolerate an evil to obtain a good which exceeds the harm, but in this case the company should be required to distribute throughout the kingdom only the tobacco grown at home or in our colonies.

Subject to all these provisos, the commissioners thought there would be no trouble in inducing private investors to subscribe in depreciated *billets d'état* since they had so little to lose and so much to gain.[61]

Only at this point does John Law enter the scene. In the months between the flotation of his *Banque Générale* in May-June 1716 and their ultimate quarrel in September 1717, he was on very good terms with the duke of Noailles, president of the Council of Finance. In a subsequent retrospective memoir of about 1724, Law tells us that the council became interested in the plans for the Mississippi Company solely as a device to fund some of the floating debt. They lacked confidence in the persons who were proposing such a company, however, and sent two government officials to him asking if he would lend his name to a two million *l.t.* scheme as encouragement to private persons to invest. (The shares of Law's bank were then selling above par.) He suspected that some were also interested in drawing him into an unsound scheme in order to ruin his reputation. Law studied the various suggestions and claimed to see in them not just a chance to get a few million in *billets d'état* off the money market but opportunities for the commercial expansion of France all over the world. In place of the two million capital suggested, he offered to undertake the flotation of a company with a 50 million capital to be subscribed in *billets d'état*. When some seemed shocked at this figure, Law, "piqued" at such narrowness, retorted he would make it 100 million and thereby raise *billets d'état* from 70 percent discount to par.[62]

That was the way Law (or whoever wrote for him) remembered things about 1724. The outlines of the story are highly plausible and in all probability true. The author, however, forgot certain inconvenient details. The jump in the bidding wasn't simply from two million to fifty million. In between, there had been serious schemes for capitalization at four, twelve, and twenty-five millions. What Law did essentially was to extract from "all the papers" Le Gendre d'Arminy's scheme of July 1716 for a general commercial company monopolizing many trades and the same person's 1717 scheme for a company with a subscribed capital entirely in government debt, the interest on which would supply its trading funds. This last was no more original with d'Arminy than with Law, for it was the organizing principle of the British South Sea Company in 1711–12. The difference was that, while Britons could trust their government to pay the interest on its debt fairly regularly, Frenchmen could not. Therefore, d'Arminy had added a revenue farm to all his schemes so that his company could from the sums it collected as *fermier* pay itself the interest owed to it as government creditor —without going through the Treasury. As Law himself was later to show, this assured revenue was the *sine qua non* in France for the establishment of subscriber confidence.

The basic plan of John Law was expressed in a memoir of ca. June or July 1717. For the first time, we meet the title *Compagnie d'Occident* which he preferred to d'Arminy's *Compagnie du Mississippi* because it was less precise and would not give the British or the Spanish any advance warning that great projects were to be started in Louisiana. Characteristically, he did not explain how such secrecy was consistent with the publicity attendant on the flotation of a great public company. A petty trading company, according to the memoir, could not create the customers and suppliers it would need in Louisiana; only a big company could manage and develop such a large territory. His company should be vested with Louisiana plus the Canadian beaver monopoly (expiring at the end of 1717) and the Guinea slave trade (open since 1716), whose expansion was so necessary both for Louisiana and all the French colonies. The capital of his company would be fifty million "and perhaps more" subscribed in *billets d'état*. Shares would be fully transferable. The *billets d'état* would be converted into permanent government annuities *(rentes)* at 4 percent. (The surrendered *billets* should be publicly burned to create public confidence by visibly reducing the quantity known to be in circulation.) As in the d'Arminy May scheme, the income from the *billets* or *rentes* for the first year, 1717, would be used for the working capital of the company. (This would be two million, i.e., 4 percent of fifty million.) From the second year, 1718, the *rentes* received from the government would all be reserved for the payment of a minimum 4 percent dividend by the company. Subscribers would of course be attracted by the prospect of higher dividends in the long run arising out of the trading profits of the company. The *rentes* due the company from the government would be made a charge on the stamp tax farm (the farm for the stamping of the acts of notaries and others), but that farm itself would not be taken over by the new company.[63] In that sense, the revenues of the new company were far less well secured than under the d'Arminy-Crozat scheme of 14 May which had suggested that the new company take over the tobacco farm to secure its obligations from the state.

Law then shied away at this point from an effort to take over the tobacco monopoly. There are many plausible explanations for this: (1) he avoided a direct confrontation with the powerful figures led by Samuel Bernard in the tobacco monopoly and with those influential persons in the administration of finance who were primarily concerned with the security of the revenue; (2) several of the special commissioners considering his plan, particularly Duché, appear to have been hostile to any connection with the tobacco monopoly: there was widespread sentiment in the mercantile community, which they represented, that the monopoly should be abolished; (3) Law himself may have privately hoped to abolish the tobacco monopoly when the proper occasion offered: he had incorporated Pottier's recommendations to that effect in his memoir of 1715 already mentioned, and in 1720 he was to carry out just such an experiment on the English model. That something similar may have been in his mind in June-July 1717 is suggested by a further memoir of this period (written by him or Duché) comparing his scheme with that of the British South Sea Company. The author stressed (in a way not heard before this year) the central importance of tobacco in the agricultural development of Louisiana. With an adequate supply of slaves, an extensive production of tobacco was promised by 1719 and enough to supply all France by 1721.[64] This implies, if it does not state in so many words, some change in at least the buying practices of the tobacco monopoly.

Between 19 and 26 June 1717, at a succession of regular and special meetings of the Regency Council, the duke of Noailles, president of the Council of Finance, presented an extended survey of the various measures taken to alleviate the economic and fiscal distress of France since the death of Louis XIV. After his conclusion on the twenty-sixth, the Regent appointed a special committee of grandees, members of the Regency Council and of the lesser councils, to consider Noailles' report and recommend further specific measures of amelioration.[65] No minutes of this special committee have survived, but it would appear that from the moment of its creation, all further consideration of the proposals for a Louisiana company came within its jurisdiction. On 19, 21, and 23 August, the duke of Noailles reported to the Regency Council the recommendations of the special commissioners in the form of four draft edicts and one draft *déclaration*. They were approved by the Regency Council and presented to the *parlement* for registration on 28 August; after considerable difficulty they were registered on 5 and 10 September. The measures so adopted were all designed to reduce the volume of outstanding *billets d'état* and included a lottery, sale of part of the *domaines*, creation of life annuities and the "establishment of a company of commerce under the name of the *Compagnie d'Occident*," the whole being intended, as an officer of the *parlement* noted, "to achieve the extinction of the *billets d'état*."[66] Of the 750 million in floating debt at the beginning of the reign, there was still some 300 million clogging the market in *billets d'état* and *billets* of the receivers-general, the former depreciated by 60–70 percent.[67] It was thus as part of a fiscal package to reduce this burden that Crozat's modest proposal of January for a stopgap for Louisiana came to be adopted in August in such a grandiose form.

Although we do not have any record of the proceedings of the extraordinary committee of June-August 1717, we do have draft letters-patent representing the several stages through which the project went during its sittings. The successive changes did not necessarily take place at these sittings, but may have been handled in private, preparatory conferences involving Noailles, Law, and others. Though the ultimate terms were those of Law, much of the drafting work may have been done by Duché, for Law was not, as he himself admitted, a man for fine detail.[68] The earliest detailed draft is still for a *Compagnie du Mississippi* (d'Arminy's title) and is self-avowedly based upon earlier drafts by Duché. It bears the mark of his extreme fiscal conservatism: instead of 4 percent, the king was to pay the company 6 percent for his debt to them, in return for which the debt would be considered liquidated after twenty years. Such an arrangement which would also have appealed to many in the government, was inconsistent with the assuredness of dividends necessary for a successful flotation at this stage. Many of the other clauses reflect Law more clearly, including his preference for keeping accounts in the "hard" *écu de banque* and thus avoiding fluctuations in the *livre*. One of the clauses appearing in the first and surviving to the final draft was that making the government's obligations to the company a charge upon the revenue from the stamp tax farm.[69] In the next version, the company has become the *Compagnie des Indes Occidentales*, the 50 million ceiling omitted, the shares dropped to a cheap 500 *l.t.*, and all pretense of paying off the crown's debt to the company abandoned and the interest accordingly dropped to 4 percent.[70] When we come to the project bearing the name *Compagnie d'Occident,* we have arrived at the final draft.[71] There was only one important change between this draft and the edict ultimately enacted: at the last moment the monopoly of the Guinea trade was dropped from the scheme. The government was not yet ready to abandon this experiment in "free" trade so pleasing to the West Indian colonists.

"Letters-patent in form of an edict establishing a trading company under the name of the *Compagnie d'Occident"* were passed in August 1717 and registered at the *parlement* of Paris on 10 September.[72] They provided for a company with 25-year monopolies of the Louisiana and Canadian beaver trades. The entire capital of the company, divisible into shares of 500 *l.t.* each, was to be subscribed by the public and payable in *billets d'état:* these were to be surrendered by the company to the government in return for perpetual annuities *(rentes)* at 4 percent charged against government receipts from the stamp farm. The first year's interest on these *billets* (from 1 January 1717) was to be used by the company for its trading fund; all interest accruing after 1 January 1718 was reserved for paying dividends on the shares. Virtually all of these provisions could be found in the earlier schemes presented in March and May by Le Gendre d'Arminy and Crozat. Only one detail was entirely original with Law: whereas everyone else's schemes had provided for a definite capital sum to be subscribed, the letters-patent of August 1717 left that detail to be settled later. Perhaps Law was dreaming of swallowing up the entire 250 millions in *billets d'état* then in circulation. (After all, the British South Sea subscription of 1711 had absorbed almost as much: £9.1 million sterling at 20:1 being 182 million *l.t.*) Perhaps he merely wished to try the market before setting his limit.

Thanks to the recent work of Professor Giraud, we are well informed about the first year of Law's company. The subscriptions went rather well during its first ten days and then slowed down markedly: 28.5 millions were subscribed between 14 and 24 September, but this had risen to only 29.8 million by 6 October. It is doubtful if as much as 40 millions were subscribed by the end of the year. Nor were all subscriptions paid promptly or in full. When the first conversion of *billets d'état* into perpetual annuities *(rentes)* was made in February 1718, only 24 million had been received. The company had got off to a bad start.[73] The duke of Saint-Simon, who was in a position to know, reported that this failure was due to the hostility of Noailles. Professor Giraud is unwilling to accept this explanation at its face value because he can find no evidence of Noailles' overt resistance.[74] Yet Law himself later reported that his and the Regent's break with Noailles came in September, though Noailles did not resign from the presidency of the Council of Finance till January.[75] It is likely that something happened at the highest levels in September and that this was not unconnected with the willingness or unwillingness of many monied men to participate. At first, for example, there were rumors that Crozat would go into the new company. He acted for it at La Rochelle in September in chartering ships to be sent to Louisiana.[76] A plan of organization for the company drawn up early in September bracketed his name with Law at the head of the strategic financial department of the company.[77] Yet when the *arrêt* was issued on 12 September naming the seven directors of the company, Crozat's name was omitted.[78]

Considering the enormous credits toward his *taxe* which Crozat hoped to obtain from the government in return for the surrender of his Louisiana interests, that financier had every reason to appear to support the government's darling new company. The omission of his name from the directorate is thus particularly significant and strikingly revelatory of the elements supporting or failing to support Law's company. Subscriptions among Paris money-men who held so much government paper were unlikely to have been encouraged by the fact that the first seven directors named included no well-known Paris financier or banker. Representation of the western trading ports was, by contrast, generous: Jean-Baptiste Duché, the veteran merchant and contractor of La Rochelle, his brother-in-law, François Mouchard, deputy for that port in the Council of Commerce, as well as René Moreau and Jean Piou, deputies for St. Malo and Nantes. (Duché and Moreau, of course, were among the five commissioners who first considered the various proposals for a company and were thus in a sense in on the scheme from the beginning; Piou more strikingly, had been a supporter of Law's banking scheme before the Regency Council in 1715.) [79]

In analyzing both the directors and the first subscribers, Professor Lüthy has suggested that certain patterns can be vaguely discerned: was not Law drawing to his support merchants in those ports which traded primarily to North Europe (so hurt by state policy since 1672) in contradistinction to those merchants who traded to Spain and who knew how to use government need for Spanish silver to extract concessions?[80] Professor Giraud objects to this dichotomy, citing the presence on the directorate of René Moreau from St. Malo, a great center of the Spanish trade.[81] But where were the Magon and the rest of St. Malo? It does seem that Law's appeal was rather more marked toward those who were "outsiders" (including Huguenots and foreigners) rather than "insiders" in the financial power structure of the previous reign.

Professor Lüthy also suggests that we may see a distinction between those who supported and those who opposed Law's company in the old rivalry between the Senegal Company and the Guinea Company for control of the African trade. Many directors of the Senegal Company subsequently joined his board, but none from the Guinea Company.[82] This is a more useful distinction for our purposes, though we cannot view the Guinea Company alone. We must remember that the tobacco farm of 1697–1718, the St. Domingue company of 1698–1714, and the Guinea-Asiento company of 1701–16 were controlled by substantially overlapping groups centering around Bernard, Crozat, Maynon, and Thomé. (The Le Gendre brothers were active in all three.) We may well regard this connection as one interest in 1717, for we do not find a single pre-1715 member of any of its three parts subscribing to Law's company.[83] Nevertheless, we should avoid rigid dichotomies in classifying our data. As we shall see in the next chapter, there were numerous contending factions among those who failed to support John Law.

With the subscription to the *Compagnie d'Occident* languishing in the fall of 1717 and the *billets d'état* even slower in coming in, John Law had to rethink his plans for the company.[84] He could hardly inspire confidence unless he made some effort to start the company's trade—yet he could hardly trade without funds. By the letters-patent, the sums owed by the government to the company were a charge upon the income from the stamp tax farm. This particular revenue seems to have been heavily overcommitted and funds from it difficult to extract. Law later complained that Noailles cheated the company out of the four million *l.t.* interest on its *billets d'état* retroactive to 1 January 1717; by this he meant 4 percent of 100 millions. Yet no such sum could have been due *in* 1717 for by the end of that year, the company had not received more than 24 millions in *billets d'état*.[85] Even so, it would have been entitled to close to one million in back interest in 1717 from the stamp tax revenues—but there is no evidence that it received this at the time. Professor Giraud has searched the surviving accounts and cannot find evidence of the company having received more than 250,000 *l.t.* from the stamp tax farm in 1717.[86] This could hardly have been a secret in Paris financial circles.

To allay some of these not unreasonable doubts, John Law persuaded the government to issue an edict in December 1717 amending that of August. The capital of the company was now fixed at 100 millions, which, when and if fully subscribed, would require annual interest payments from the government to the company of four millions. Recognizing that the overpledged stamp tax farm could not supply this, the December edict provided that of the four millions, two million only should be charged to the stamp tax farm, one million to the post office farm and one million to the tobacco farm.[87] Thus did tobacco reenter the financial history of Law's great company.

In practice, the tobacco monopoly seems to have provided all the revenues of the company in the ensuing months. Since the company had taken in only 24 millions in *billets d'état* as of February, it was of course not yet entitled to payment of four million, but only 960,000 *l.t.* annually, or just within the million pledged from the tobacco farm. One million was in fact all that the government then had available from that monopoly. The contracted rent of the farm was two million per annum up to 1 October 1717 and 2.2 million thereafter. Of this, 12,000–18,000 was pledged, primarily to the support of orphanages and hospitals in Marseilles, Aix, and Toulon.[88] One million annually was paid in cash into the royal treasury. The remainder was assigned for the maintenance of the household of the dowager duchess of Berry, disreputable daughter of the Regent and widow of the grandson of Louis XIV. This allocation was not accidental, for Vincent Maynon, managing partner of the tobacco monopoly, had also been chief financial officer *(surintendant des maisons et finances)* to the late duke of Berry, and continued to perform such functions for the dowager.

Thus, the one million *l.t.* allocated from the tobacco farm price to pay the 1718 *rentes* due Law's company was the government's entire disposable income from that farm that year. In addition, however, the government by *arrêt* of 8 January 1718 borrowed one million *l.t.* from the tobacco monopoly at 7 1/2 percent (credited against the rent of the farm for the year July 1719–June 1720) to be paid to the *Compagnie d'Occident* for its arrears of 1717 in twelve monthly installments of 83,333: 6s. 8d. each. Although we only have record of payment of the first month's allocation from the tobacco monopoly to the company, it is highly probable that the farm paid what was due from it.[89] Although the tobacco monopoly under the management of Bernard and Maynon had been accused of virtually every offense conceivable to the mercantilist imagination, it was never accused of not paying its debts with reasonable promptness. By contrast, there is no record of the *Compagnie d'Occident* receiving anything from the stamp tax or postal farms in 1718.

This then was Law's situation at the beginning of May 1718. The only assured income for his company was that assigned against the tobacco farm—and that was limited to one million *l.t.* annually, while he would need four millions p.a. if the full 100 millions were ever subscribed. Subscriptions meanwhile were almost stagnant and payments on old subscriptions embarrassingly slow. The 24 millions in *billets d'état* converted into government annuities in February had only been raised to 30 million by 11 June.[90] The twentieth of June, the crisis day in Law's fight with the *parlement* of Paris, appears to have been the turning point in his fortunes. By July, everything had changed. The investing public suddenly became interested once more in the *Compagnie d'Occident;* shares were re-offered on very favorable terms by an *arrêt* of 12 June,[91] not made public until the twenty-fifth,[92] and by 15 July, the remainder of the 100 million had been snapped up.[93] The *billets d'état* were a little slower in being paid but 45 millions more came in by September, the rest by the end of the year.[94] The "System" had finally gotten started. How do we account for this sudden change of mood?

The crisis came in May and June 1718. In those months, the government fought and won its battle with the *parlement* of Paris over the recoinage. Whether or not Law was responsible for the recoinage, the government's victory seemed to have restored public confidence and thus strengthened his position.[95] Only after the defeat of the *parlement* did he release the *arrêt* of 12 June reopening the sale of his company's shares. At the same time, by his victory, Law introduced an inflationary element in the investing psychology of Paris. He had depreciated the metallic content of the *livre tournois* (a money of account) by one-third.[96] This would tend to make businessmen and investors, particularly foreigners, reluctant, for fear of further devaluation, to keep assets in *livres*—particularly in such a suspect form of the *livre* as the *billet d'état*. The flight from the *billet d'état* was marked. An option to convert them as part of the recoinage brought in 110 million worth, while Law's company absorbed 70 million more, all in a few months.[97] The terms on which the company's shares were reoffered in June as amended by an *arrêt* of 28 June[98] were particularly attractive to speculators, especially foreigners: only one-fifth down (the rest by October), with both shares and receipts for subscriptions issued to "the bearer," with no register of names of subscribers to be kept. This seemed to promise to speculators an exemption from the scrutiny of any future Chamber of Justice, and to foreigners a way of hiding part of their wealth from the *aubaine* or forfeiture of the estates of deceased foreigners.

The mood had then changed. The question is whether this change of mood itself could have drawn 70 millions into the *Compagnie d'Occident* if there had not been some improvement in the earning prospects of that company. To be sure, the company started paying dividends as of 1 July 1718, but what assurance did the investor have that it would be able to continue paying those dividends regularly and in full. The payment of the company's basic 4 percent dividend was contingent upon its receipt of the annuities due it from the government, an uncertain resource for the past several decades. The assurance investors needed came in fact in August and September when, as we shall see in the next chapter, the tobacco farm was taken away from the Bernard-Maynon syndicate and given to Law's company at a rent of 4,020,000 *l.t.* per annum. At the same time, the full four million due annually to the company from the government was made a charge upon that same tobacco farm.[99] That meant that the company would as tobacco farmer pay itself each year the four million in annuities which the government owed it—without going through the royal treasury. For the cautious investor, so rightly suspicious of the state's credit, this meant that the company would be paid its *rentes* on time when it itself was paymaster. For the speculator, there was also the possibility that the tobacco farm might produce considerably more than the contracted price of 4.02 million, to the enticing advantage of the company. The past solvency of this farm, the presence at its head up to then of people like Bernard and Maynon suggested that this was not a farm on which one could go wrong.

All this had not been formally achieved until *after* the company's full 100 million in capital had been subscribed in early July. It was only on 18 July that a meeting of the company's directors decided to ask the king to make the full four million *rentes* now due the company a charge upon the tobacco farm;[100] this was not legally effected until August and September, all ostensibly too late to affect the subscriptions of early July. Yet the preliminary steps had been taken months earlier. By an *arrêt* of 10 May, the existing lease to the Bernard-Maynon company had been abrogated;[101] the same day, instructions were given for the printing of public notices inviting bids.[102] By the twenty-first, it was common knowledge that great new bids were being made.[103] While no one could be sure that the *Compagnie d'Occident* would get the tobacco farm, the victory of Law over the chancellor Daguesseau and Noailles in January and over the *parlement* of Paris in June made such an award probable enough by the end of June to be worth gambling on. (It is obvious that Law himself knew for a certainty that he was going to get the tobacco farm at a price of at least four million sometime before 18 July or else his company could not have decided that day to have four million from that source mortgaged to them.) [104]

Thus, in the end, John Law was forced to adopt the one major clause in the previous plans of Joseph Le Gendre d'Arminy for a Mississippi company which he had not at first chosen to borrow—establishing the fiscal security of the Louisiana or Mississippi or West India company upon the assured revenues and profits of the tobacco farm. Law had tried other resources but had been forced back on d'Arminy's suggestion because in the France of 1717–18 there was no other revenue farm which intelligent investing opinion thought securer, more undercommitted, or more underpriced.

The ultimate importance of tobacco then in the genesis of Law's company was financial rather than commercial. Crozat and Le Bart and d'Arminy and Duché and Law all mentioned the great potentiality of Louisiana as a producer of tobacco that would free France from dependence on the British Chesapeake. But they also wrote and talked of the future of Louisiana as a great producer of silk and as the inevitable home of silver mines rivaling those of Mexico of which they were supposed to be a geological continuation. This was promotional talk to which investors and government officials were congenitally resistant. The tobacco farm was quite another matter. This was a French institution which everyone knew and which most thought was a very good thing for its proprietors. A company which got its hands on that would offer attractive possibilities to both investors and speculators. Thus the struggle for the tobacco farm was the struggle for the life of the newborn *Compagnie d'Occident*.

To understand why so many informed persons in the Paris money market of 1718 thought that the tobacco farm was underpriced, we must investigate the history of that institution during the preceding seven fat but troubled years.

CHAPTER 9

The Struggle for the Tobacco Farm, 1711–18

In his scheme of 17 March 1717, Joseph Le Gendre d'Arminy suggested for the support of his proposed Mississippi Company a rise in both the retail price of imported tobacco and the rent of the tobacco farm, the proceeds to be used for the payment of the government's obligations toward the company. To do this, he admitted, "it would doubtlessly be necessary to begin by breaking the current lease of that farm which has caused so much jealousy and so much activity disagreeable (I dare say) to the company which is vested with it."[1] What were these jealousies and disagreeable activities which so plagued the company about 1717–18 and about which everyone seemed only too well informed? They did not arise from the absolute importance of the tobacco farm in the state revenues. About 1706, for example, the tobacco farm at 1.5 million *l.t.* p.a. accounted for only about 2½ percent of state revenues from all farms (59.5m.) and 1 percent of total state revenues (148m.).[2] The absolute importance of this monopoly was still in the future. At the time, the difficulties rose rather from the observation that this was one of the few farms which had got through the War of the Spanish Succession without apparent financial difficulty and from the suspicion, based on the secrecy with which its leases were renewed, that it was a very lucrative business indeed for its proprietors.[3]

On 24 July 1708, at one of the most financially difficult times during the War of the Spanish Succession, the lease of the tobacco monopoly, without any public invitation for bids, was renewed by the new controller-general Desmaretz for six years (1 October 1709–30 September 1715) at the same price (1.5 million) and to substantially the same group which had held it since 1697: Maynon, Bernard, Crozat, Thomé, Ponthon, Le Gendre d'Arminy, Pellard, La Condamine. Only two new persons were brought into the company at this time, Pierre Philippe Jacques, sieur de Vitry, who also entered the united farms at the same time, and Louis Claude de la Roche, sieur de Céry, an experienced employee of the monopoly, formerly its director in Brittany.[4]

In the chaotic conditions of 1708–9, there was relatively little difficulty about this renewal. However, when the prospects of peace became more definite in 1711, sundry people began to calculate that the tobacco farm might be worth having and that possibly it might be pried away from its current lessees by outsiders offering the government better terms. On 13 October 1711, the Dauphin forwarded to the controller-general a proposal presented to him by a company which offered to take over the tobacco monopoly from 1 October 1712 at a rent 500,000 *l.t.* p.a. higher than that currently in force. They also promised to save 1.8 million in foreign exchange annually by expanding the cultivation in Guienne and ultimately to reduce the price to the consumer. The incumbent farmers replied that if one wanted to increase the price of the farm, the best way would be to abolish, not to expand, the domestic cultivation which caused them such heavy administrative expense for supervision and patrols.[5] Substantially the same proposals were made in December 1712, in neither case with any practical results.[6] The office of the controller-general was, however, accumulating some information: one angry memoir of this time in defense of Guienne insisted that the farm could produce over three million to the crown which would be evident if the existing farmers weren't so successfully secretive about their foreign purchases and other practices.[7]

With the return of peace, the existing monopolists began to have their own troubles. Vincent Maynon, the managing director of the company, was also *surintendant des batiments et finances* to the king's grandson, the duke of Berry, who wanted him to give up outside activities. Maynon informed Controller-General Desmaretz of this command and of his intention of withdrawing, offering "to put together for him a good, solvent company composed of intelligent men knowledgeable in the administration of that farm who would give 500,000 livres more." The duke of Berry conveniently died in May 1714, so Maynon did not have to make this personal sacrifice—but considerable changes were nevertheless to be made in the company.[8] Even before May 1714, Maynon realized that the existing company would have to give one-third more for their monopoly.

According to a subsequent memoir by a member of the company, Desmaretz demanded that Maynon and associates continue for another six years.[9] We know only that on 12 July 1714, more than a year before the expiry of their lease, the incumbent tobacco farmers submitted a formal proposal to Desmaretz offering to take the farm for another six years from 1 October 1715, for two million per year (plus the usual 100,000 *l.t.* annually to the united farms in lieu of all import and transit duties) provided that certain conditions were met. Most of these were technical continuations of concessions previously made, such as preemptive purchase of prize tobacco, exemptions for their employees from municipal taxes, and the right to maintain offices on the islands of Ré, Noirmoutier, Bouin, and Belle-Ile. Others were new efforts to solve old problems, such as a request for still another survey of the three league line beyond the frontiers of Picardy. Other conditions involved new concessions: (a) the monopoly should be extended into the recently acquired Principality of Orange and into the territories acquired at the Treaty of Utrecht from the duke of Savoy in compensation for the French territories exchanged; (b) the farm should be extended into the city of Bayonne and surrounding *pays de Labourd,* from which it had hitherto been excluded by local privileges of challengeable legality; and (c) the prices of foreign tobacco should be raised from 40s. wholesale and 50s. per lb. in retailers' shops to 50s. wholesale and 64s. retail; while domestic tobacco should go up from 20 to 24s. wholesale and from 25 to 32s. retail.[10]

Desmaretz' own experience of the tobacco farm went back to the days when he had served in the office of the controller-general under his uncle Colbert and had been accused of taking substantial "tips" at the granting of the first tobacco monopoly in 1674. Well might he ponder the offer of the incumbent tobacco farmers: five months passed before a decision was made. All of the memoirs of the time contain rumors of great bids expected. Among the people with whom he was in correspondence was one of the farmers-general on the Council of Commerce, Jean Rémy Hénault, who had been in charge of the tobacco monopoly under the united farms, during 1685–97. Desmaretz seems to have asked him whether, if the monopoly were transferred to the united farms or to another company, the problem of assigning a value to the tobacco and tools to be transferred would be insuperable. Hénault replied that in 1697 both sides had haggled for six months but had finally agreed to refer the matter to him as expert arbitrator, and that he had settled the matter in eight days at 1.5 millions.' The evaluation at transfer could be handled as easily in the future.

A more serious problem was the size of the tobacco reserves transferred. Desmaretz seemed afraid that the existing monopolists would let their stocks run down and that the incoming farmers would face a shortage that would create trouble and consumer dissatisfaction. Hénault assured him that this could easily be avoided by requiring from the farm an account of their stocks on hand as of 1 January 1714, so that the incoming farmers could order their supplies well in advance of their entering into their lease. Far more serious, he thought, was the danger that the existing farmers would overbuy if they had a chance to buy tobacco cheaply, thus putting an impossible financial strain on their successors. He reported that during the last war, such overstocking (defended on grounds of difficulty in obtaining supplies in wartime) had frightened off rivals who thought of bidding for the farm.

Hénault was very angry with the tobacco company because, when his brother-in-law, the tobacco farmer Ponthon, had died in 1713, the company had given his place to an outsider and had refused to recognize that his son, the *président* Charles Jean François Hénault, as residuary legatee to Ponthon, had any claim on the farm except for the reimbursement of his uncle's share in the farm's loan to the crown. His memoir was long and rambling, showing signs of the eccentricity of age if not of senility, but filled with information, some of it out of date. He wrote as if it were still the 1680's and Brazil tobacco was still the chief foreign variety imported. Virginia tobacco for him was something that Bernard had been clever enough to get when the war made imports from Portugal difficult. For all its anachronisms, though, his memoir conveys graphically the mood of expected change. He strongly preferred reattaching tobacco to the united farms. For this reason, he had abruptly rejected overtures from persons unknown to him (probably Maynon) asking him to head a new company to bid for the tobacco farm under the protection of the late duke of Berry.[11]

Desmaretz was also in communication with persons who could give him more up-to-date information. One of these was Jean Dussol or du Sault, *intendant* to her serene highness the dowager duchess of Vendôme (widow of the famous general), and one of the prime movers against the existing tobacco company. He had either been given (perhaps as successor to the deceased Ponthon) or been promised a place in that farm, but preferred to conspire in behalf of a new company. On 30 September 1714, he wrote to Desmaretz that he had seen Antoine Paris, eldest of the four brothers (who had in 1702 himself made an unsuccessful offer for the tobacco farm) but had found him disheartened about taking the initiative with Desmaretz for a new tobacco company. Paris in fact advised du Sault to make his peace with the existing company in order to save his place. Du Sault, however, who was actively sponsored by the duchess of Vendôme, was determined to persevere and submitted to Desmaretz as promised some accounts and calculations about the tobacco farm. He also presented proposals for a new company.[12]

The accounts[13] which du Sault submitted are most interesting. The subfarms produced only 510,000 *l.t.* p.a. (only 10,000 more than in 1708):

	l.t.
Languedoc, Montauban, Roussillon, etc.	180,000
Provence, upper Dauphiné	120,000
Auvergne, Berry, Bourbonnais	83,000
Lyonnais, Forêt, Beaujolais, lower Dauphiné	52,000
Gens. of Poitiers, Limoges & La Rochelle	75,000

Because of smuggling in the eastern provinces and local planting in the southwest, the exposed provinces under the direct administration of the monopoly produced very little in sales revenue:

	l.t.
Orléans and Beauce	40,000
Picardy	30,000
Champagne	25,000
Burgundy	20,000
Guienne, Béarn, Navarre, Périgord, Angoumois	25,000
3 Bishoprics (Metz, Toul, Verdun)	20,000
Total	160,000

The basic revenues of the monopoly thus came primarily from Paris, Normandy, and Brittany as is shown by du Sault's recapitulation:

	l.t.
Subfarms	510,000
Exposed provinces	160,000
Paris (city & *généralité*)	2,129,200
Normandy	1,800,000
Brittany	1,800,000
Gross Receipts	6,399,200
Deduct for cost of raw materials, transport, manufacture and administration	2,399,200
Possible gross profit	4,000,000
Deduct for possibility of overestimate	1,000,000
Fair Price of Farm	3,000,000

Du Sault had detailed figures for Paris only. Even so, his estimate of the overwhelming importance of the three northern provinces is most impressive. He blamed the low sales in the interior provinces entirely on smuggling. Even so, we see the persisting pattern of tobacco consumption greatest in the maritime provinces and gradually spreading inland. (Tobacco consumption in France at this time was still far from the peaks it was to reach in a generation or two.) The only disappointing maritime districts were Bordeaux and La Rochelle, close to the planting districts in southwestern France.

His account was apparently very influential, for much of the talk in the next four years about what the farm should yield (down to Law's successful bid of four millions in 1718) was within the range suggested by du Sault. He omitted only two cost items: the 100,000 *l.t.* annually to the united farms and interest on sums borrowed for advances to the crown or for working capital. His figure of 2,399,200 *l.t.* for all costs left very little margin. In 1708, the same items had come to 2,353,430 *l.t.*[14] Although unit costs had undoubtedly gone down since then with the return of peace, sales (hence purchases) had gone up. Of course, the margin of one million suggested by du Sault would cover all this.

As a result of his exchanges with Desmaretz, du Sault must have come to the conclusion that the controller-general was unsympathetic. The group which he had helped form or simply joined thereupon decided that they would need more powerful political support. Sometime in October 1714, they presented their offer (nominally addressed to Desmaretz) to the duke of Maine, son of Louis XIV and Madame de Montespan, then of great political importance. This proved to be a tactical error, for the duke did nothing about it for several months. This plan called for an offer of 2.5 million compared to the 1.5 million at which the farm had been priced since 1697 and the two million which the existing farmers had offered in July for its continuation. In addition, they offered to pay six months' rent as a loan or advance to the crown in place of the three months' rent usually paid.[15]

This group was sometimes styled in the records "du Tertre & Co.," after its first spokesman, Adrien Caniou du Tertre, a discharged employee of the tobacco farm, subsequently employed as *inspecteur* in the general farms. Though the tobacco farmers referred to him as a "600 *livre* junior clerk," he insisted that he had been employed in that farm from the age of nineteen and was in fact an expert. On the basis of this expertise, he induced men of capital to give him a share in their projects.[16] In his memoir to the duke of Maine, he maintained that his proposed company, unlike the existing company, consisted primarily of merchants and bankers, rather than old fiscal speculators. Actually, its members were drawn primarily from the conventional world of public finance: they included five receivers-general of the land taxes (*finances*),[17] three bankers,[18] a big government victualling contractor (François Raffy), three holders of lesser purchased offices,[19] four persons "interested in the farms of the king," including *two avocats au conseil*,[20] plus du Sault, intendant to the duchess of Vendôme, and du Tertre himself.

What happened next is a bit mysterious though it appears from accusations made later that an element of secrecy and perhaps deception was involved. Desmaretz and the existing tobacco company, undoubtedly well informed about what was going on about the duke of Maine, apparently decided to settle the matter of the new tobacco contract before higher political pressures could be brought to bear. Acting in secrecy, without any public invitation for bids, a lease was signed in the name of Guillaume Filtz and a *résultat* passed at the council on 18 December 1714 accepting the lease. The preamble stated that other offers had been received, but that the king desired the existing bondsmen of the Michault lease (1709–15) to continue. The matter was being taken care of very early because it was necessary for the farmers to construct new buildings and make purchases well in advance of the start of the new lease. In all likelihood, there had been some bargaining by Desmaretz because the terms were not those advanced by the old or Michault company in July. Instead of the two million offered, the price was set at two million for the first two years (1 October 1715–30 September 1717) and 2.2 million for the last four (1717–21). The routine technical clauses asked for by the old company in July were all granted, including that for a new survey of the three league limit beyond the frontiers of Picardy, and the inclusion of the Principality of Orange and the territories ceded by Savoy. Desmaretz, however, rejected their request for higher consumer prices and for the inclusion of Bayonne and the district of Labourd. In addition to the usual advance of the last quarter's rent at the beginning of the lease, the company agreed to a further immediate advance of one-half year's rent (one million *l.t.*) at 5 percent, 500,000 *l.t.* against the first quarter's rent, the other 500,000 against the third quarter of 1716.[21]

The group around du Tertre refused to accept the rather irregular *résultat* of 18 December 1714. Early in January, one of their number, the *avocat au conseil* Girardin (such bids were always made technically through *avocats au conseil*), wrote formally to the controller-general offering in behalf of a named company to lease the tobacco monopoly for nine years at 2.5 million annually (plus the usual 100,000 *l.t.* to the united farms). Seven of the seventeen names in the original October company were missing from his January list,[22] though other names had taken their place. The new names were heavy with prestigious bankers,[23] receivers-general,[24] lesser *traitants*[25] with a few unknowns.[26] With the duke of Maine's protection, this was indeed a company deserving consideration. It may be that these impressive names were challenged, for between 18 January and 2 February, Girardin was busy handing in powers of attorney from his backers, authorizing him to bid for them.[27] In the end, the offer of the rival company was rejected, reportedly by the king himself, in an *arrêt du conseil*.[28] There is evidence, though, that their patron, the duke of Maine, was appeased by an anonymous pension of 15,000 *l.t.* annually for six years guaranteed by Maynon but assigned on the subfarm of Languedoc, which seems to have been for the benefit of Girardin and Henry Daugère, *valet de chambre* and subsequently controller-general of the household of the duke.[29]

Although everyone considered the new Guillaume Filtz company just a continuation of that of Charles Michault (1709–15) there was in fact more turnover at this than at any other renewal in the history of the ongoing company. Bernard, Maynon, and Pellard of the original partners continued with de Vitry and La Roche Céry who had come in in 1709 and young Thomé who had succeeded his father in 1711. La Condamine also died in 1711, as had Ponthon in 1713. Joseph Le Gendre d'Arminy now yielded his place to his brother, François Le Gendre, while their brother-in-law Crozat also chose this moment to withdraw. We can only guess at the motives which induced these retreats. There may well have been differences of opinion: this is suggested not so much by Crozat's interests in Louisiana (he did nothing for tobacco planting there) or by d'Arminy's in St. Domingue (Bernard, Maynon, Thomé, and others also were or had been interested in the St. Domingue Company) as by the fact that in their memoirs of 1716–17 both Crozat and d'Arminy were moderately critical of the company they had recently left.

Their places were taken by the sieurs Barré, Darras, Gallet, and Duverney, the first two of whom had since 1709 been interested in the tobacco subfarms for the *généralités* of La Rochelle, Poitiers, Limoges, Montpellier, Montauban, Toulouse, and the *pays* de Roussillon.[30]

Of Charles-Nicolas Barré, we know little except that he was born in 1666 at Corbeil, the son of Nicolas Barré and Marie de Court, and died in 1737. He may have been a protégé of Crozat, for in 1719 he procured enoblement by acquiring the latter's place of *secrétaire du roi*.[31] Jean Darras would appear to have started as a career employee of the tobacco farm and risen to become *caissier* and *sous-fermier*. Through this and other interests in the *affaires du roi,* he accumulated enough to be fined 550,000 *l.t.* by the Chamber of Justice in 1716. He subsequently became a wealthy merchant and government supplier.[32]

Gallet was probably the Vincent-Robert Gallet (born at Ancone in Dauphiné in 1675), who held various financial offices. His father, Jacques Gallet, sieur de Coulanges, receiver of the farms at St. Malo, had been active in the farms for forty years, had been ejected from seven contracts in 1708 but was still trying that year to get into the united farms. An older brother, Jean-Jacques Gallet (b.1672), subsequently controller-general of the king's household, was styled seigneur de Coulanges et de Mondragon! Whether this implied any long family connection with Mondragon in Provence, where tobacco was grown, is not apparent.[33]

The most important of the new members was, however, Joseph Paris Duverney, third of the almost legendary Paris brothers whose family history is virtually the history of French public finance from 1689 to 1770.[34] They were the sons of a prosperous innkeeper in Dauphiné with pretensions to nobility. The two elder brothers, Antoine (1668–1733) and Claude (1670–1745), styled de la Montagne, had early prospered in army victualling contracts in the 1690's. The two younger brothers Joseph (1684–1770), styled Duverney, and Jean (1690–1766), sieur de Montmartel, joined their elder brothers in this work as soon as they were old enough. By the end of the war in 1713, all four brothers were rich and powerful. They were employed by the duke of Noailles, one of their great patrons, in managing the Visa in 1715–16 and were to be employed in similar work after the collapse of Law's scheme.

Their connection with the tobacco farm had some history. In 1702, we have already noted, a "M. Paris," undoubtedly Antoine the eldest (who alone went by that style), had attempted to bid for the tobacco farm.[35] In 1714, presumably the same "M. Paris" had been approached by du Sault when the latter was trying to put together a rival tobacco company, but had refused to become involved.[36] The second brother, de la Montagne, had in 1708 married one Elisabeth de la Roche and was thus possibly connected to the tobacco farmer, Louis Claude de la Roche, sieur de Céry.[37] The third and fourth brothers, Duverney and Montmartel, were to have long and complex, if somewhat peripheral relations with the tobacco trade and Louisiana during the next half century. At this stage in their careers, the brothers are believed to have been on very good terms with Samuel Bernard who helped them in their rise.[38] Antoine's rejection of du Sault's approach in 1714 and Duverney's entry into the tobacco farm the same year are precisely consistent with such an alliance.

The defeat by the entrenched monopolists of the rival offer of 300,000–500,000 *l.t.* more from the imposing company protected by the duke of Maine caused a scandal which echoed through the memoirs of the next three years. The death of Louis XIV on 1 September 1715 meant the dismissal of Controller-General Nicolas Desmaretz, last relic of Colbertian finance. With Bernard and the Paris brothers on good relations with Noailles, the new conciliar or polysynodical regime of the Regency did not seem immediately likely to upset the tobacco monopoly company. The tide began to turn against them, however, in 1716 with the establishment of the Chamber of Justice. As individuals, they were heavily assessed:

	l.t.
Antoine Crozat	6,600,000[39]
Samuel Bernard (composition)	6,000,000
Vincent Maynon	2,742,000[40]
Family of late Pierre Thomé	
Widow Thomé	621,000
son, Pierre	139,000
son, Louis	200,000
son, André Romain	55,000
son, Philippe	150,000[41]
François Le Gendre	300,000[42]
Joseph Le Gendre d'Arminy	300,000
Widow Le Gendre, their mother	183,000
Louis Claude de la Roche Céry	243,000[43]
Pierre Philippe Jacques de Vitry	143,000[41]
Nicolas Du Plantier	125,000[44]
Jean Darras	550,000
Nicolas Charles Barré	40,000[45]
Le Jongleur heiress	40,000[46]
Charles Michault	20,000[40]
Charles La Condamine (heir)	10,000
Pierre Pellard	10,000
Robert Vincent Gallet	6,800[46]

These assessments would not in themselves have hurt the standing of the tobacco farmers very much. As pointed out in the preceding chapter, most of them were government creditors who would pay off their *taxes* in depreciated state paper. Nor was it simply a matter of loss of face. What was most important was the mood of the hour. By establishing the Chamber of Justice, the Regency gave official recognition to all the resentments and hostile stories that had been circulating about the *financiers* and *traitants* during the previous generation. The latter were now officially labelled as robbers of the state. The public were invited to submit *placets* or petitions of grievances. Midst such an orgy of incrimination, how could the obviously profitable Bernard-Maynon tobacco company go unchallenged?

In May 1716, shortly after the establishment of the Chamber of Justice, the company which had made the offer for the farm in January

1715 stirred itself once more. It no longer looked for protection to the fallen duke of Maine, but rather to the duke of Albret, *grand prieur de France* (heir of the duke of Bouillon), the marshal duke of Estrées, president of the Navy Council, and the duke of Aumont, peer and great courtier. On 21 May, the whole rival group or that fraction of it which included du Tertre presented to the Regent a petition (*placet*) offering to bid for the tobacco farm, with annexed memoirs. In one supporting document, they pointed out that the king of France with 18–19 million subjects received until very recently only 1.5 million from tobacco, while the king of Portugal with only 1.2–1.3 million inhabitants had an income of 3.1 million *l.t.* and the king of Spain with 5–6 million subjects, an income of 4.5 million *l.t.* from tobacco. (This was probably taken from an old memoir by Roland Duclos.) They offered to present a company of unexceptionable sureties who would offer to take the tobacco farm for nine years at 2.5 million *l.t.* annual rent during the first six years and 2.8 million *l.t.* during the last three (plus the usual 100,000 *l.t.* to the united farms). They would sell French domestic tobacco throughout the kingdom, not just in the southern parts as then practiced, and would encourage colonial production. They would reduce the wholesale price of *corde* tobacco (the basic type consumed) from 40s. to 30s. per pound. Finally, they would submit detailed accounts of their operations to the crown. The *placet* and supporting memoirs were referred by the Regent, insofar as they related to the tobacco revenue, to Hilaire Rouillé du Coudray, *conseiller d'état, directeur général des finances* and the member of the Council of Finance specifically responsible for the tobacco monopoly, and, insofar as they related to commerce, to Estrées, president of the Navy Council. Rouillé, whom du Tertre accused of being close to Maynon, allegedly chose to do nothing. The supporters of the rival company persuaded the duke of Bourbon to write personally in remonstrance to the Regent (the letter being carried by du Tertre).[47] Eventually, Rouillé, who had in routine fashion been consulting the existing farmers, made some sort of a report.

While the May papers were being shuffled about, the sieur du Sault, *intendant* to the duchess of Vendôme and one of the original counterbidders of 1714, entered with a variant scheme. He would form a company which would offer 2.5 million based upon a sale of 5.5 million lb. or less; if sales went above that, they would pay the crown 10 *sols* per lb. for every extra pound sold. He too would cut the price 25 percent to the consumer, would endeavor to encourage French and colonial production, and would sell Guienne tobacco throughout the kingdom. His company would do all its manufacturing in France. He accused the existing company of such cheats as mixing domestic tobacco with foreign and selling the whole as imported. If tobacco, alone of the major branches of revenue, had never gone out of farm, it was because it alone was so profitable to its farmers. The du Sault plan of August is a cautious improvement upon the du Tertre plan of May: it provided a possibility of still higher revenues for the crown without binding the company.[48] It is not clear whether du Sault was simply offering a substitute proposal from the same group or a new proposal from a different group.

By August, the Council of Finance had received answering memoirs from the existing farmers, but Rouillé refused to show them to the rival group—even though they threatened to denounce him to the Chamber of Justice! On 29 August and 17 September, the duke of Albret wrote again to Noailles enclosing new copies of all the memoirs submitted since May and further memoirs answering what they thought to be the company's defense of its anti-Guienne and anti-St. Domingue policies. Just as Hénault had predicted in 1714, the existing or Filtz company advanced in its defense that it had on hand six million *l.t.* worth of tobacco and tools which any incoming company must be prepared to purchase for cash. A memoir of 10 September denounced this as a trick and urged Noailles to strip the tobacco company of the secrecy which alone protected it.[49]

One of the memoirs forwarded by Albret reminded Noailles that the Regent had taken the matter away from Rouillé and had referred it to the count of Toulouse (head of the Navy Council) to report on the colonial implications and to Amelot, president of the Council of Commerce, to report on the foreign trade implications. Their several reports were now ready, if only Noailles would ask for them.[50] The matter seems to have been decided by Noailles without outside advice. On 6 October 1716, a memorandum was drawn up within his office (perhaps by his secretary Tradet) summarizing all the memoirs received.[51] The next day, an alternative scheme was presented by the *avocat au conseil* Millain on behalf of what appears to be a different faction of the company bidding since 1714 acting under the protection of the duke of Bourbon. (Millain himself was *secrétaire des commandements* to Bourbon.) Their offer differed from du Tertre's May offer by including the sliding scale suggested by du Sault in August.[52] At this point, negotiations ceased. Noailles had apparently decided to take no action.

In the ensuing months, all was far from quiet. As we observed in the last chapter, the new St. Domingue company chose this time to repeat their earlier request that the tobacco farm encourage the reestablishment of tobacco in their colony by offering for its tobacco a price far above the world market. While the farm was busy drawing up memoirs to answer this request, the greater world was shaken by the announcement of the assessments of the Chamber of Justice, leading among other things to Crozat's decision to abandon his Louisiana monopoly. Du Tertre, the most desperate member of the bidding company, decided to take advantage of the moment and appeal to the Chamber of Justice.

On 14 October 1716 (hardly a week after Noailles apparently decided to take no action on his associates' applications), du Tertre filed a denunciation at the Chamber of Justice against the Bernard-Maynon tobacco farming company. He had little specific information against them: they permitted retailers to sell above the legal prices; they had destroyed colonial production; they discouraged French production by refusing to sell Guienne tobacco in the northern two-thirds of France; they had misapplied some of the funds arising from the king's sale of offices in their farm; they must have made great individual fortunes for the late Charles Ponthon, who had started as a clerk and had only a one-twentieth share in the company, left an estate of 900,000 l.t. There were few facts and figures, nor did du Tertre name individuals who might be called by the court to give such information. Something simply had to be wrong when the king of France got so very much less for his tobacco farm than did the kings of Spain and Portugal.[53] (Very few Parisians could conceive that French provincials did not take as much tobacco as did most foreigners.)

Du Tertre's "denunciation" ran into immediate trouble. On 24 October 1716, he presented a "request" to the Chamber of Justice, protesting against a family plot against him. The *procureur-général* of the chamber was Charles Michel Bouvard de Fourqueux, former *procureur-général* of the *chambre des comptes*. Fourqueux himself was married to the sister of Rouillé du Coudray whom du Tertre had already denounced as an ally of Maynon; Fourqueux' daughter was married to young Vincent Maynon, son of the terrible tobacco farmer. Du Tertre asked that the case be placed in other hands. In addition, he asked that the chamber disallow the argument that the *arrêt du conseil* issued in the last year of Louis XIV, clearing the tobacco company of all charges against it, could restrict the jurisdiction of the court.[54] On the twenty-sixth, he wrote to the same effect to Noailles, adding that he alone had been responsible for the extra 500,000–700,000 l.t. annually which the crown obtained from the tobacco farm in the renewal of 1714.[55] All this should not be taken too seriously, for we know that his personal finances were in desperate straits at this time, and du Tertre had to magnify his claims upon the government for special consideration.[56]

Affairs not proceeding as well as they might in the Chamber of Justice, du Tertre on 31 October extended his charges to include the subfarms. This was a rather sensitive area, for, as a contemporary memoir pointed out, it was well known that the subfarms were a haven for the friends, relatives and dependents of the greater farmers.[57] The controversial subfarm of the tobacco monopoly in Languedoc at this very time included among its principals Joseph Nantiat, brother-in-law of the tobacco farmer Darras, and François Le Bart, partner of Crozat in the Louisiana company, who was also interested in the subfarm for Provence.[58] Du Tertre told stories of the millions reportedly made by the sieurs Jacob (de St. Elie) and Montanier, principals in the subfarm of Languedoc since ca. 1690–97, both of whom had started with nothing. He ascribed this affluence to such frauds as the mixing in of olive leaves which he had observed in 1699 on a visit on the farm's account to the subfarmers' headquarters at St. Esprit in Languedoc. These frauds were in great part the responsibility of the national tobacco company: it was their decision to subfarm all the southern provinces; although the lease of 1697 obliged them to maintain the manufactories at Paris, Morlaix, Dieppe, and Mondragon, they chose in 1699 to lease the last (from which they had formerly compulsorily supplied all the southern subfarmers) to the subfarm of Languedoc, leaving to the other subfarms the option of buying from Languedoc or of importing on their own account via the Mediterranean (previously forbidden). Du Tertre ignored supply difficulties in wartime and insisted that the entire policy was designed to confuse the accounts and make it more difficult for the government or anyone to know how much the monopoly or any of the subfarms was making.[59]

Though his affluent colleagues remained scrupulously silent after October, the desperate du Tertre kept up a steady stream of letters and memoirs to Noailles all during the winter of 1716–17, the winter of the Chamber of Justice. He promised letters from the marshal duke of Estrées, president of the Navy Council, and Amelot, president of the Council of Commerce, that would prove him the only true begetter of the rise in the tobacco farm's rent in 1714–15. If the government would just give him a special commission to inspect the activities of the monopoly throughout the land, he felt sure he could, on return from such a mission, present a company that would farm the tobacco privilege for four million![60] Unfortunately, while the various memoirs and proposals which were submitted in behalf of the new company by the duke of Albret between May and October 1716 were formally considered by the government, it is not apparent that any of the many communications sent in by du Tertre alone between October 1716 and March 1717 were read by anyone other than the clerks in Noailles' office. Insofar as most of them were highly repetitious, it would not appear that much information was thereby lost.

At this point, Adrien de Caniou, sieur du Tertre, leaves the center of the stage and the principal actors begin to return. The entire mood of public affairs changed suddenly in mid-March 1717. On the ninth, the marquis of Dangeau reported in his *Journal* in routine fashion that François Raffy, the great victualling contractor (and one of the original supporters of du Tertre's new company in 1714), had been taxed 2.3 million at the Regency Council that day. Two days later, on the eleventh, he suddenly recorded that the Regency Council would decide very soon "the day when the Chamber of Justice will end, and it was not doubted that it would be before Easter." On Tuesday the sixteenth he could report that it was set for next Monday, the twenty-second, when in fact the court was closed. At that time he noted, "Some changes in public finance are spoken of; but they are such uncertain rumors that one does not know what to believe."[61]

We can see in retrospect that the sudden termination of the Chamber of Justice in March 1717 marked a basic turning point in the financial history of the Regency. For the first eighteen months, all was retrenchment and revenge. Government expenditure was significantly cut; government indebtedness and interest payments were radically reduced by the operation of the Visa; finally, in the Chamber of Justice, a highly publicized effort was made to make war-profiteers disgorge and help the Treasury. But the duke of St. Simon was not the only person to realize that much of this, and particularly the chamber, was not good for business and that four years after the war, France was still suffering from trade depression, inadequate state revenues, and a general lack of public confidence.[62] With the suppression of the chamber, government policy turned abruptly in effect from retrenchment toward measures for stimulating the economy, increasing state revenues and redeeming the state floating debt in ways attractive to the holders of *billets d'état*. Noailles' report to the Regency Council in June, the secret "committee" of council during the summer, the various edicts of August, including the chartering of the *Compagnie d'Occident,* were successive steps in this redefinition of policy, but the basic reorientation had come abruptly in March. (It will be remembered from the last chapter that Le Gendre d'Arminy had written rather dispiritedly to Noailles on 3 March, but two weeks later had come back with the germinal idea for a Mississippi Company financed with *billets d'état*.)

Much of this was months in the future in March 1717. The immediate question at hand following the suppression of the Chamber of Justice was Noailles' effort to reform the revenue farms and get more money out of them. At their meeting of 17 March, when the Regency Council authorized the edict suppressing the Chamber of Justice, they also approved a series of *déclarations* defining the relations to that tribunal of farmers-general, receivers-general, and treasurers-general, among others. In return for a total exemption of their official concerns from the cognizance of this or any future chamber of justice, these functionaries were thenceforth prohibited from participating in government contracts or in the *affaires extraordinaires de finances*. The last category was commonly understood to include subfarms and special farms such as the tobacco monopoly.[63] These new rules precipitated an immediate upheaval in the farms. On 20, 24, and 27 April, Dangeau correctly reported rumors that the united farms were to be thoroughly reorganized, that fourteen farmers-general were to be removed and only four new ones appointed, thus reducing the company from forty to thirty; in particular, he had heard that among the senior farmers-general, Vincent Maynon and Paul-Etienne Brunet, seigneur de Rancy, had asked to be relieved and wished only to get their capital back without any compensation for their lost places.[64] The new legislation immediately affected the tobacco farm, for there were four individuals who were in both it and the united farms: Maynon, François Le Gendre, Pellard, and de Vitry. Of these, Maynon and Pellard resigned from the united farms to stay in the tobacco farm, while de Vitry and François Le Gendre stayed in the united farms and presumably resigned from the tobacco farm. The latter had only to transfer his share back to his brother d'Arminy who might have retained a concealed interest in it all along. (Le Gendre was now a very important farmer-general, representing his company at the Council of Commerce.) [65]

For those who were trying to replace the intrenched tobacco company, these changes of March-May 1717 meant new opportunities but also new difficulties. Since their last offer had been shelved in October 1716, they had been quiet while the Chamber of Justice went through the financial community with its scythe: only the desperate du Tertre had kept up his stream of futile memoirs. Now, with the threat of the chamber gone, the bidding company was ready to come out again, but would first have to reform itself, for its old membership had been heavy with receivers-general. The reconstituted company, operating for the moment through the duke of St. Simon as patron, included five members of the original company of November 1714 (the banker Cadet, the office-owners de l'Auvergne and Goubert, the lawyer Thierry and du Tertre); plus six of the next contingent who had joined in January 1715 (the Paris bankers the Bertrand brothers and Pierre DuMolin; the *traitant* Nicolas Le Vasseur, Berlan and Colomyer); plus eight new members. Of these last, the most interesting were: the important Paris Huguenot banker, Etienne Demeuves, related to Pierre DuMolin; the pre-1715 farmer-general of the united farms, Jacques de Mons; Crozat's estranged (?) partner, the tobacco subfarmer of Provence and Languedoc, François Le Bart; and Etienne Bourgeois, treasurer of Law's *Banque Generale* and subsequently of the *Compagnie d'Occident*.[66] It is conceivable that Bourgeois was standing in for Law and even that Le Bart was standing in for Crozat.

In the latter part of March 1717, the St. Simon bidding company presented to the Regent and the duke of Noailles a new "submission," essentially that of May 1716 offering 2.5 million annually while undertaking to sell tobacco to the consumer at one fourth under the prices then prevailing and promising to do all possible to reestablish tobacco cultivation in the French colonies. The new company suggested that their plan be referred to anyone except Maynon's connection Rouillé du Coudray, preferably to Amelot, president of the Council of Commerce, to whom in fact it was sent.[67]

Consideration of such offers was necessarily suspended by the appointment in June 1717 of the special "committee" of grandees to consider Noailles' long report. We do not know what went on during the sittings of that body between June and August; though its labors eventually brought forth the *Compagnie d'Occident*, they did not bring forth any suggestions touching the revenue farms of the kingdom. It may very well be that the *éminence grise* in this decision was the former controller-general Desmaretz. One of the few documents traceable dating from the weeks of the committee's sittings is a memoir by Desmaretz of 9 July 1717 on "the augmentation of the revenues." Here was his judgment on the charges made against the tobacco farm:

> The price of the last lease now in force is two million, two hundred thousand livres.
>
> Memoirs have been submitted in which it is claimed to prove that the tobacco farm produces for its shareholders more than five millions, and even near six millions. When examined in depth, crude errors have been found in them and it has been necessary to reject them.
>
> M. Mainon who has administered this farm for several years and who by his effort has enlarged it and raised it to its current price, gave grounds for hope that without waiting for the expiration of the lease, he would increase it before the end of the fourth year and would raise it to three millions.
>
> The tobacco farm is very different from the others. It consists of an exclusive sale, that is a trade which requires much skill and intelligence and, moreover, correspondents in Holland, England and Portugal.
>
> I cannot refrain from saying what I know of that farm: it will decline and perhaps even fail if the farmers and the manner of administering it are changed.[68]

It is very clear from this important document that all the papers had been referred to Desmaretz and that he had interviewed Maynon before giving his advice to alter nothing. Maynon felt sufficiently insecure to offer three million for the last two years of the lease (1719–21) instead of the 2.2 million contracted for. At the very least, we may assume that tobacco consumption had grown since the peace at a faster rate than the farmers had guessed likely in 1714. We may also assume that the figure three millions given out by the weary Maynon was soon known to well-placed people who made their plans accordingly.

Thus, in the summer of 1717, the Maynon-Bernard tobacco monopoly company beat off the attacks of those who would break its lease, just as in the last chapter we saw it beat off the simultaneous attacks of those who would attach it in some way to a new Mississippi company. Both victories gave it only six months of peace. In December 1717, we observed in the last chapter, one million *l.t.* of the crown's revenues from the tobacco farm were assigned to the new *Compagnie d'Occident*. That same month, in a reorganization of responsibilities within the Council of Finance, the tobacco monopoly was taken away from Rouillé du Coudray, the friend of Maynon.[69] In January 1718, Noailles, president of the Council of Finance, was replaced by the seemingly more flexible Argenson. The reaction in certain circles was immediate. At once, offers and counteroffers for the tobacco farm were dusted off and rushed to the new president of the Council of Finance in the hope that he would see in them virtues his predecessor had overlooked.

Du Tertre was quickly in with his personal claims,[70] but was as quickly pushed aside by stouter contestants, now that the contest had become worth fighting. In the first week of skirmishing (14–20 February 1718), two companies alone were engaged, both continuators of the Millain company of 7 October 1716 protected by the duke of Bourbon and both still protected by that duke. (The related company of March 1717 protected by the duke of St. Simon had disappeared, those of its members who were still interested presumably joining or rejoining one or another of the Bourbon companies.) One of the new companies protected by *Monseigneur le duc,* styled the "company of Colomyer," submitted a scheme on 20 February essentially the same as that submitted by Millain on 7 October 1716: 2.5 million *l.t.* p.a. with 10s. per lb. for all tobacco sold over a quota of 5.5 million lb., and a reduction of 25 percent in the price to the consumer.[71] (A slightly more attractive variant of this was submitted by du Tertre a month or so later in the name of Eloy Le Febvre, raising the price for the last three years to 2.8 million and reducing the quota to 5 million lb.[72] The second group protected by Bourbon, styled the "company of Boignard" had on 15 February submitted through Millain a variant plan without any reduction in retail price but offering a higher annual rent of three million *l.t.* and 20s. per lb. on all sales over 5.5 million lb.[73] The first or Colomyer group in their memoirs had stressed the importance of reducing the retail price, not simply as an act of social justice, but to encourage consumption and discourage smuggling. These and the memoirs which followed were like those of the preceding year referred to Amelot, now a member of the Finance Council, acting with the abbé Jean Paul Bignon, *conseiller d'état.*

The two old bidding companies were not long to have the stage to themselves. Schemes now poured in, though few got very much attention from Argenson.[74] The report late in April by his *premier commis,* Gilbert Clautrier, on some memoirs submitted by the Colomyer group in February seems to suggest that that company had made very little impression with their price reduction ideas: Clautrier only wondered why they should be offering 2.5 million when others were offering three.[75] One proposal, however, which attracted immediate attention, came from an entirely new or third company of merchants of Paris, St. Malo and Lyons describing themselves as very rich. It seems to have been put together by Pierre du Molin, an early (1715) member of the original bidding company and a Paris banker, and César Pierre Landais de Soiselle, chevalier, *secrétaire du roi,* of St. Malo. They employed as their soliciting agent the *avocat* Jacques Thierry, a member of one or another of the bidding companies since 1714. A 25 percent share (5 sols) had been taken by Antoine and Etienne Bertrand, the Paris bankers, who had also been involved in the bidding companies since 1715. Little is known of the Lyons or other St. Malo members.[76]

The new and old members (du Molin, Bertrand, Thierry) realized that in the changed atmosphere after the advent of the *Compagnie d'Occident* one had to do more than offer a slightly higher price if one hoped to induce the government to break the lease of the entrenched tobacco company. This was unlikely to be done for just 300,000–400,000 *l.t.* more annually. In an unsigned memoir on 13 March 1718 the third company thus proposed to give everything the other companies were bidding, plus some extras: (1) they offered to take the farm for twelve years at three million p.a. plus 100,000 *l.t.* to the united farms (the price promised by Maynon and offered by the Boignard company); (2) they offered to reduce retail prices within two years by one-quarter (a key provision in the offer of the Colomyer company but annotated in Argenson's office, "Useless to put in the advertisements for bids and likely to discourage . . . bidders"); (3) after two years, they would buy only French and French colonial tobacco (annotated "useless to stipulate . . . but very good to carry out"); (4) they would use only French ships and sailors for the importation of their tobacco and other ventures (annotated "good to carry out"); (5) they would use the tobacco monopoly as a means to develop the African slave trade, sending out French and other tobacco to Guinea to buy slaves to be sold in the French West Indies for tobacco to be returned to France (annotated "strange for a farm"); and finally (6) they proposed to pay for the assets of the existing tobacco company in four installments at six month intervals. This last was annotated, "must be paid for in a single payment."[77] This last was a very difficult point for, although the existing tobacco company now estimated its stock and tools as worth only four rather than six million, this was an enormous sum of money to have to pay out at one time before one had started making any profits. It was a subject of continuing correspondence with all the rival bidding companies.[78] Perhaps no group smaller than the *Compagnie d'Occident* could ever get over this hurdle. When this third company came to sign its proposals on 16 March, they retained the four installments clause but deleted the Guinea trade proposal which the minister found "strange" as well as the promise to use only French ships.[79] This last omission implied that in fact they were thinking of continuing imports from Britain and Holland for some time and provoked a quite negative response from Argenson's office.[80]

The new "colonial" approach of the St. Malo-Paris group was very attractive to the government. The official who reported on the scheme to Argenson (most probably Clautrier) was generally sympathetic to the new company, though he thought even more might be done for the colonies. He had absorbed the argument of the St. Domingue company that the monopoly would have to guarantee a high price to the planters if tobacco planting was to be reestablished in St. Domingue. (Nothing was said of Mr. Law's Louisiana.) The reporting official also thought that an even higher price than three millions might be obtained for the monopoly and perhaps a large loan to the government.[81]

The Paris members of the new Paris-St. Malo company were all drawn from the group bidding in March 1717 protected by the duke of St. Simon. Another member of that same group was one Nicolas Le Vasseur (a member too of the original 1714 bidding company), who now in 1718 also decided to form a syndicate of his own and make a bid very much like that of the Boignard company. His troubles show the difficulty of forming solid concerns under the more stringent rules adopted in 1717. He had got together a company of sorts on paper on 21 March 1718, but hesitated to submit the document till 5 May—so obscure were his names: minor financial officials, the son of a *commis* to Colbert and the nephew of the former preceptor to the duke of Albret.[82] Later in May, he submitted a memoir[83] in which he explained that he had been precluded from approaching most established financial names because of the *déclaration* of 17 March 1717 forbidding receivers-general and others from having shares in special farms. There were receivers-general who would sign only if they were sure he could get a waiver from Argenson. He had approached the important former farmers-general, Jean-Baptiste Langlois and Charles Louis Lallemant, who in 1717 had withdrawn from the united farms in favor of their sons, but found them uninterested in new engagements. Others preferred to stay for the time being where they were in the stamp tax farm,[84] the Breton revenues, or wherever.[85] It seems likely that as more powerful interests moved into the competition for the tobacco farm and bid the price up, the more knowledgeable sort of speculator shied away from that affair.

Others viewed this bidding and counterbidding with profound hostility. There were elements in the French business community who were distressed that breaking the old lease should simply be the occasion for delivering the monopoly into new hands. As early as 24 February, de la Boulaye had written Argenson against the whole idea of monopoly. An *inspecteur général de la marine*, he had been one of the original directors of the St. Domingue company in 1698, and had remained in it when the Bernard-Crozat-Maynon-d'Arminy element had been replaced by the new Gayot-Galabin directorate in 1714. The reformed St. Domingue company had been attacking the tobacco monopoly vigorously since at least 1716 when it proposed that the monopoly be abolished or that the existing monopolists be forced to take St. Domingue tobacco at double the world price to encourage the reintroduction of cultivation there. This had evoked elaborate countermemorials from the monopoly about the technical inadequacies of St. Domingue tobacco.[86] His letter and memoir to Argenson of 24 February suggest that de la Boulaye may have been one of the sources of the preposterous stories about the profits of the tobacco monopoly referred to by Desmaretz. By estimating the farm's sales at six million pounds, he computed their profits to be 5,640,000 *l.t.* p.a. He thought the king should get five million from the tobacco farm, but hoped that the monopoly would be abolished and a free trade established for the good of the French colonies. The proposal was referred by Argenson to his senior clerk (*premier commis*)

Gilbert Clautrier who reported a month or so later that it was not so much a proposition as a series of charges about which it would be interesting to have more evidence.[87]

In March or April, de la Boulaye or someone like-minded seems to have procured from the merchants of the western ports remonstrances addressed to the council attacking the whole idea of monopoly and calling for a free trade.[88] In answer to these exaggerated attacks, someone in the monopoly submitted a defense of the farm some time before 10 May. The author was probably Joseph Le Gendre d'Arminy (who had apparently rejoined the farm when his brother left the previous year), the author of many memoirs critical of the St. Domingue company since he left its direction in 1714. His basic argument was that the French public did not like and would not accept St. Domingue tobacco as the monopoly had found out many times to their cost. The monopoly had never bought more than three million pounds of Virginia tobacco p.a. Dreams of the St. Domingue trade employing 300 vessels were therefore grossly exaggerated, for 19 vessels carrying only 80 tons each could bring 3,040,000 lb. from St. Domingue. Similarly, stories of the monopoly wasting 3–4 million *l.t.* annually in foreign exchange were as exaggerated, for three million lb. at 30 *l.t.* per quintal cost only 900,000 *l.t.* He warned finally that, were the guards of the monopoly once removed, untaxable tobacco cultivation would spread all over France and the king's revenue from this source be utterly destroyed, while St. Domingue gained nothing.[89]

In the event, the advocates of open trade in the spring of 1718 were voices crying in the wilderness. There were no politically powerful forces whose interest at that juncture lay in the abolition of the monopoly. When John Law had concocted his memoir on commerce in 1715, he had copied verbatim from Pottier de la Hestroy's memoir of 1698 those paragraphs calling for an open trade in tobacco.[90] Even though Law eventually carried out that experiment in 1720, it was not in his interest at this juncture to back the representations of de la Boulaye and the merchants of the western ports. To stimulate a revival of subscriptions to his languishing company, he needed prospects of an assured income for it. In May, his attention was to be drawn to the tobacco farm as a promising source for that income, but he could not then afford to suggest any risky changes in the way that revenue would be obtained. Whatever Law may have said or done after he obtained the tobacco monopoly (in August), there is no evidence of any sort to suggest that in the crucial months before that happy event, he even so much as hinted at a change in the basic scheme of the monopoly.

From the dates of various internal reports from Gilbert Clautrier, his *premier commis,* and from marginal annotations, it would seem that Argenson only began to become seriously interested in the question of a new tobacco farm at the end of April and beginning of May 1718. Argenson's own outlook in this was somewhat ambiguous. Law later wrote of the

Keeper of the Seals' attitude on taking office: "He formed intrigues against him [Law], he recalled the proscribed tax-leeches (*maltôtiers*), fawned upon them, had pity on them, made them great promises, he sought out bankers hostile to Mr. Law and his enemies."[91] According to Law, he himself "proposed to the Regent to have the tobacco farm put up for public bidding so that the [Occident] company could put in its bid." The company "immediately carried it [the bidding] to three million, and after much time, contradiction and trouble, it was awarded to the company for four millions."[92] Law's meager account has the appearance of truth in all details that can be verified, even though we know with certainty only that the *arrêt* breaking the existing Guillaume Filtz lease was issued on 10 May and that the farm was awarded to Law's company on 1 August.

On 10 May, the same day as the *arrêt* for breaking the existing lease, Argenson sent to Paul du Jardin, clerk (*greffier*) and secretary to the Council of State for finance, a draft for the public notice inviting bids. Even before either of these documents had been made public, an office memorandum of the twelfth notes that bids had been received in the unrevealing names of various *avocats au conseil*. On 14 May 1718, "Mgr the Keeper of the Seals [Argenson] sent to M. du Jardin the original of a submission from M. l'Enfant *avocat au conseil* for three millions for the farm of tobacco with an *arrêt* for breaking the lease to Guillaume Filtz and a [further] draft of the invitation for bids to be published."[93] This would seem to confirm Law's account of the bidding starting at three millions.

What happened between 10 May when the old lease was broken and 1 August when the lease was awarded to Law's company is a complete mystery. Although there is nothing to suggest that Law or his company had been among the bidders for the farm before this time, his own account suggests that he or his company or someone acting for them put in a bid immediately on the old lease's being broken. The only picture we have of what the bidding may have been like is a final memoir from the indefatigable du Tertre probably written in early July.[94] In it, he discussed the principal offers then being considered and related suggestions. He had seen a scheme from someone proposing to abolish the monopoly entirely and substitute a simply duty:

French domestic tobacco	6*s.* per lb.
French colonial tobacco	12*s.* per lb.
Foreign tobacco	20*s.* per lb.
Spanish snuff	30*s.* per lb.

The author of the scheme estimated French consumption then at about 13–14 million lb. per year, about double that suggested by any other memorialist. Du Tertre was not hostile to the plan, but pointed out that the crown could not judge it because it did not have adequate statistics. Only his own company would give the crown the data on which to judge such plans for the future.

Du Tertre described his proposal as a consolidated one encompassing all the previous schemes submitted under the protection of the duke of Bourbon. (It was essentially the same as his "Eloy Le Febvre" draft of the previous March or April.) It had the quota and sliding scale common to plans of both the Colomyer and Boignard companies of February, but, where those schemes differed, du Tertre leaned toward the Colomyer position: lower consumer prices and lower contract price. He thought his plan would ultimately produce six million to the crown through increased consumption and a reduction in fraud. Its novel features were the abolition of the subfarms and permission to the crown to establish auditors in all the principal offices of the farm: these two provisions between them would permit the government to know exactly what the monopoly was producing and thus guarantee maximum yields to the state in the future. His company as before would encourage the production of tobacco in France and the French colonies. Although his offer had many attractive features for the long run, there is no evidence that it received very much attention after higher bids had been received by the government.

Du Tertre had also heard of another company bidding, which was offering 3.5 million and was suggesting that it might go to four; he considered this company nothing more than a "front" for Maynon who did not want to make an offer in his own name. Even more noteworthy is another offer of which du Tertre had even less good to say: "The sieurs Paris were the first to want to take advantage of the council in proposing to take in discharge of the state's debt one hundred and ten million of the state's own *billets* provided that they were granted the lease of the tobacco farm for twenty years, the yield of which during that said time would certainly have been more than one hundred sixty million on the basis of expected growth."[95] The profit to the Paris brothers would be at least one hundred millions over the twenty years, implying a real price of only sixty millions equivalent to three million per annum.

The passage just quoted, if not too lucid or coherent, is nevertheless a remarkable piece of evidence. It is important that du Tertre writing about 1 July did not mention any offer coming from Law or his company, though Law later wrote that he had been responsible for a bid on the tobacco farm immediately on bidding being opened in May. We must therefore assume that the Paris brothers were bidding for Law. To understand what the passage in question means, we must look a bit closer at the relations between Law and the brothers Paris in 1718.

In any standard account of these years, one will read that in August 1718, the united farms were taken away from the old company which had farmed or administered them since 1681 and granted to the brothers Paris. The brothers Paris then in September reorganized the farms as a public company and offered 100 millions in shares to the public in exchange for *billets d'état:* these shares were snapped up by the public and were soon selling for higher prices than the similar shares of Law's *Compagnie d'Occident.* Law came to regard this new company as a challenge to his own influence and power and the next year (1719) had the lease to the Paris company (under the name of Aymard Lambert) broken and the united farms transferred to his own company (under the name of Armand Pillavoine). Because of the retrospective threat to Law's preeminence, the rival company of the Paris brothers is usually called the "Anti-System" or the "Contra-System."

However, the fact that Law came to break with the Paris brothers in 1719 does not mean that he was always hostile to them. They invested in his bank in 1716[96] and the youngest of them, Paris de Montmartel, was an early subscriber to the *Compagnie d'Occident.*[97] Law himself later wrote that he had sponsored the reorganization of the united farms as a joint stock company in August 1718 with the intention of eventually attaching those farms to his company. He had not done so at the time only because all the experienced administrators of the farms insisted strenuously that the farms be kept separate to preserve their skilled management.[98] This is consistent with the fuller account recorded subsequently by Paris de la Montagne: the government having decided to terminate the 1715 lease of the united farms at the end of the third year on 30 September 1718, wanted at least 45 millions annually from that source, but the old company would offer only 43. Without the brothers' knowledge, Law and the duke of La Force, vice-president of the Finance Council, suggested them to the Regent as the right persons to take over the united farms at a rent attractive to the state. Paris de la Montagne insisted that the brothers were reluctant to assume this responsibility because of their inexperience in the farms, and because "a large part of our wealth and that of our creditors was still in the hands of the king," i.e., was owing to them from the government. Only after Law and La Force got the Regent to promise that the brothers would be paid all that was owing to them before the end of the year, and under pressure from the Regent, did they bid up the price to 48.5 million (or 5.5 million above the original bid of the old company, which dropped out only because they saw that the Regent was determined to give the lease to the Paris.) In September, after the lease had been awarded them, Law proposed merging the united farms with his company. They resisted and got 29 out of the 30 directors of the united farms to agree with them against the Scot. This, according to Paris de la Montagne, was the beginning of the brothers' split with Law.[99]

The accounts of Law and Paris de la Montagne about the origin of the 1718 or Aymard Lambert lease of the united farms are in essential agreement. The brothers acted on Law's initiative, and subject to his influence with the Regent. Both accounts are vague about dates; it is likely, however, that the initial events described took place as early as April and May of 1718, for by 21 May, the marquis of Dangeau had heard that bidding had raised the price of the united farms by 5.5 millions.[100] Against the background of this close cooperation between Law and the Paris brothers in the bidding for the united farms, it is easy enough to conceive that from the beginning of May the Paris brothers may also have been bidding at John Law's initiative for the tobacco farm—even though one of the brothers, Paris Duverney, was a shareholder in the existing tobacco monopoly company.

Although the intervention of the Paris brothers in Law's behalf is therefore easily understood, the rest of du Tertre's statement is less easy to explicate: (1) the Paris brothers bid 110 millions in *billets* for a twenty-year lease of the tobacco farm; (2) with consumption increasing, the farm would probably realize 160 millions over the twenty years, making the monopolists' profit at least 100 millions, implying a real cost to them of only 60 millions.[101] Assuming du Tertre knew the facts, he may have meant one of two different things. At the more obvious level, he seems to be suggesting that the Paris brothers bid a lump sum payment of 110 million in *billets d'état* for a twenty year concession during which the tobacco monopoly was likely to net 160 millions. At existing rates of depreciation,[102] 110 millions in *billets* were worth less than 60 millions cash, creating a real profit of over 100 million. Less obviously, du Tertre might have meant that a company promoted by the Paris brothers would fund 110 million of *billets d'état* held by the public into a permanent loan to the crown if granted the tobacco monopoly for twenty years at 60 million or three million per annum. The latter arrangement would have been similar to the company the Paris were organizing to take over the united farms and fund 100 million in *billets d'état*. Understood either way, the Paris scheme reported by du Tertre would have involved a public subscription of 110 millions. It is not indicated whether this subscription would have been taken by a new or an existing company. (By July 1718, Law's Occident Company would have been in a position to contemplate further subscriptions.)

Putting together all our fragmentary evidence, what happened to the tobacco farm up to early July 1718 may be *tentatively* reconstructed as follows (others may prefer other reconstructions):

(1) Through Law's influence with the Regent, the decision to break the lease of the tobacco farm to the Bernard-Maynon company was finally taken on 10 May 1718.

(2) At Law's suggestion, the Paris brothers put in an initial bid for three millions (compared to the old price of 2.2 million.) Either at once or at some time prior to early July, this may have

been changed into a scheme involving either the payment or funding of 110 millions in *billets d'état* for a twenty-year lease.

(3) The Colomyer (or du Tertre) company protected by the duke of Bourbon also put in a bid for 2.5 million and a sliding scale based on sales, but was never a serious contender. There may also have been an ineffective bid from western port elements desiring a simple import duty. The only other serious bidder was a company representing the old Maynon interests which by early July had bid 3.5 million and had announced its intention to bid four if necessary. All the other companies of the spring of 1718 had dropped out by then.

Suddenly in mid-July 1718, Law apparently decided to drop the device of bidding through the Paris brothers and put in a bid directly on behalf of the *Compagnie d'Occident*, ostensibly because of his great hopes of developing tobacco cultivation in Louisiana. His decision may have been influenced by the unwillingness of the Paris brothers on their own to bid higher than the four million which the company representing the old Maynon interests was prepared to offer. What was probably crucial in deciding him to act directly was the wave of confidence in the first two weeks of July which filled the full one hundred million subscription to the *Compagnie d'Occident*. With his full 100 millions subscribed, Law needed quickly a revenue source to guarantee the four millions required for annual dividends. He had since January been getting one million yearly in monthly payments from the tobacco farm with some regularity; why not get the full four million from that source and the profits of the farm to boot, if he could?

On 15 July, the marquis of Dangeau reported that the 100 million subscription to the *Compagnie d'Occident* had been filled.[103] Three days later, on 18 July, the directors of that company voted to petition the king to make the full four million due them yearly in interest a charge upon the tobacco farm.[104] It is clear then that by 18 July, Law was certain that the price at which the tobacco farm would be awarded would be at least four millions; he was also by that date reasonably confident of getting the tobacco monopoly for the company, for he would not have been likely to have risked the entire financial security of his company upon a single revenue source which he could not control or guarantee. In the next week or so, word got out that the *Compagnie d'Occident* had put in a bid for the tobacco farm on pretense of helping to develop Louisiana. The Colomyer (du Tertre) company thereupon rushed in a memoir in opposition which Argenson referred to Gilbert Clautrier, his *premier commis*, on 29 July. Clautrier reported with studied neutrality that the *Compagnie d'Occident*'s proposals to use the tobacco monopoly to develop Louisiana were not more implausible or riskier in time of war than the earlier proposals of the protesting (Colomyer) company to develop tobacco cultivation on St. Domingue.[105]

Final bids were received at the Council of State on 1 August. The successful bid of 4,020,000 *l.t.* came from the *avocat aux conseils*, Jean-Baptiste Mignot. The next day, he appeared at the clerk's office of the Council of State to declare that his successful bid was in behalf of the straw man Jean Ladmiral, bourgeois of Paris, who would have as sureties the *Compagnie d'Occident*.[106] That same day, 2 August 1718, an *arrêt de conseil* added to the directorship of the *Compagnie d'Occident* three members of the outgoing tobacco monopoly company (Joseph Paris Duverney, Louis Claude de la Roche, sieur de Céry and Charles-Nicolas Barré) plus the outgoing *sous-fermier* of tobacco in Provence, François Berger.[107] On 4 August 1718, a further statement was deposited at the clerk's office of the Council of State[108] to the effect that the twelve sureties for the new Jean Ladmiral lease of the tobacco farm would be eight existing directors[109] and the four new directors of the *Compagnie d'Occident*, all acting *ex-officio*.

From 1711 to the early months of 1718, a succession of companies had fought to break the grip of the old Bernard-Crozat-Maynon company on the tobacco farm. They had offered higher prices and promises of freeing France from dependence on imported supplies of tobacco. None of them had been able to match the influence of the old company and the preference of French fiscal administration for proven sources of revenue. In the end, it took the combined influence of John Law and the Paris brothers to do the work. For John Law, obtaining the tobacco farm was crucial for the well-being of his *Compagnie d'Occident:* not so much because there were bright if uncertain hopes of developing tobacco cultivation in Louisiana, as because the financial structure of that company required an assured income from the state of four million a year. Once the company itself was farmer of the tobacco monopoly, that income was assured without going through the Treasury, provided only that the monopoly produced at least four millions a year. The final terms on which he obtained the monopoly, including the price and the vesting in the *Compagnie d'Occident,* were thus preeminently Law's handiwork about which the Paris brothers and the experts brought over from the outgoing company (La Roche Céry, Barré, Berger) had marked doubts. From the hour of its birth, there was ample matter for misunderstanding within John Law's new tobacco monopoly administration.

CHAPTER 10

Tobacco under "The System," 1718–21

We do not propose to give any sort of account, detailed or otherwise, of Law's "System" during its heyday, 1718–20. For that, the reader must turn to the old accounts or await the definitive work of Professor Hamilton. In order to understand the history of the tobacco revenue during these years, of course, the reader should keep in mind the following chronology, remembering that the speculative mania in the shares of Law's company really got under way only in the last four months of 1719 and was at its height in January 1720:[1]

1718, Dec.: *Compagnie d'Occident* absorbs *Compagnie du Sénégal*.
    Dec.: *Banque Générale* becomes *Banque Royale*.
1719, May: *Compagnie d'Occident* absorbs the old East Indies and China cos. and becomes the *Compagnie des Indes*.
    July: New *Compagnie des Indes* absorbs *Compagnie d'Afrique* (for North African trade). Shares reach 1,000 (200%).
    July: *Compagnie des Indes* receives minting privilege for nine years.
    Aug.: United Farms taken away from Paris brothers (Aymard Lambert lease) and granted to *Compagnie des Indes* (Pillavoine lease) effective 1 October 1719.
    Aug.-Oct.: *Compagnie des Indes* lends government 1.5 billion *l.t.* to repay capital to owners of suppressed offices; massive new issue of company shares at increasing premiums.
    Oct.-Dec.: Period of most pronounced speculative rise: shares pass 10,000 *l.t.*
1720, Jan.: Law becomes controller-general; difficulties begin.
    Feb.: Royal Bank absorbed by *Compagnie des Indes*.
    Mar.: Crisis of system; efforts to sustain market value of shares by having company buy them back at 9,000. Creates great inflation.
    May: Redemption price of company shares and value of bank notes reduced. System discredited. Law dismissed as controller-general.
    June: Shares down to 6,000. Law restored to favor; Argenson disgraced and Paris brothers exiled.
    July: Bank unable to redeem its notes.
    Sept.: *Compagnie des Indes* absorbs St. Domingue company and Guinea trade monopoly.
    Oct.: Company shares depressed by forced payment of arrears of subscriptions.

Nov.: Company shares further depressed by compulsory loan from shareholders to company. End of Law's influence.

Dec.: Law leaves France; return of the Paris brothers.

Against this hectic background, the tobacco farm worked out its quieter, less conspicuous but equally turbulent fate. On 1 August 1718, the farm had been awarded by *adjudication* of council to Jean Ladmiral, straw man for the Occident Company, for six years starting 1 October 1718 at the price of 4,020,000 *l.t.* per annum.[2] Law was not satisfied with these terms and by a subsequent *arrêt* of 4 September 1718,[3] confirmed by an *arrêt/résultat* of 16 September,[4] the period of the lease was extended from six to nine years at the same price. These *arrêts* and *résultats* had most of the usual clauses with one or two striking exceptions: after a three year transition period, the company promised that, from 1 October 1721, it would import no more foreign tobacco and would supply all the imported tobacco needed in France from the French colonies, particularly Louisiana. (Any persons or company taking over the tobacco farm at the end of the nine years would also be limited to French colonial tobacco and would have to buy half of all tobacco needed from Louisiana through the Occident Company at the open market price.) Thus did Law overbid all the other contenders who had promised to "encourage" tobacco cultivation in the French colonies. As we shall see subsequently in Chapter 12 on Louisiana, this was a very rash commitment to undertake. In the event and fortunately for the company, it never became operative.

The lease and *résultat* of 16 September of course spelled out in detail the terms on which the tobacco farm was to operate during the next nine years. Most of the articles were quite familiar provisions borrowed from the Guillaume Filtz lease of December 1714. The conventional payment to the united farm of 100,000 *l.t.* per annum in lieu of all internal and external tolls was retained, as were other terms. One further important innovation was, however, made: all tobacco, regardless of its provenance, was to be sold for 40s. per lb. wholesale and 50s. retail, thus ending the old Colbertian policy of giving a price preference to French tobaccos. This preference had been withdrawn from the disappearing French colonial tobaccos in 1709; now it was also taken away from French domestic tobaccos. Clearly, from the very beginning, Law was prepared to sacrifice metropolitan plantations to the interests of Louisiana and his company.

At the same time, the financial relations of the tobacco farm, the Occident Company, and the government were redefined. By the edict of December 1717, it will be remembered, the four million *l.t.* per annum due the Occident Company (when its full 100 million capital had been subscribed) was assigned upon the crown's revenues from the stamp tax farm (two millions), the postal farm (one million), and the tobacco farm (one million). As requested by the Occident Company in July, a new edict was issued in September[5] replacing that of the previous December and providing that the full four million in perpetual annuities (*rentes*) due the company from the government should be a charge upon the crown's income from the tobacco farm. In effect, this meant that of the 4.02 million which the company owed the government annually for the tobacco farm, it would actually pay itself four millions for the annuities due it and pay into the Treasury only the 20,000 *l.t.* balance. Anyone else taking over the tobacco farm at the expiration of the company's nine year lease would automatically assume the obligation of paying the company its four million p.a.

The most serious problem arising out of the transfer of the tobacco monopoly from the outgoing Bernard-Maynon company (the Guillaume Filtz lessees) to the incoming Occident Company (the Jean Ladmiral lessees) was the question of evaluating existing stocks on the transfer date. An *arrêt du conseil* of 8 January 1719 set up a special procedure of joint evaluation, with difficulties referred to experts appointed by the *intendants* of the several *généralités*.[6] An even more complicated problem was created by tobacco in the hands of retailers but not yet paid for, hence belonging to the outgoing farmers. An unprecedented clause inserted in the Guillaume Filtz lease of 12 December 1714 provided that on termination of that lease, such tobacco should be sold for the account of the outgoing farmer who was to pay his successor only a flat composition of 30,000 *l.t.* in compensation. This would of course provide a cover for retailers to sell the tobacco which they had not obtained from the new monopoly for months and years after the new company had started its lease. To avoid this, the lease of 16 September 1718 to Jean Ladmiral (the Occident Company) provided that the *tabacs de retrouve*, as they were called, should instead be sold for the account of the incoming company which should compensate the outgoing company for their value up to a maximum of 30,000 *l.t.* This immediately caused trouble because the outgoing company insisted that the clause in their 1714 lease was still operative and that the *tabacs de retrouve* were worth far more than 30,000 *l.t.* A special *arrêt* of 28 November 1718 formally annulled the relevant clause in the December 1714 lease (on grounds of the irregularities in the granting of that lease) and provided that the *tabacs de retrouve* should be inventoried and evaluated by experts and that the incoming tobacco company should compensate the outgoing for their actual cost (as was done with the tobacco in the company's warehouses and manufactories).[7]

These difficulties over the transition from the old lease to the new were in the end only technicalities. Much more serious were Law's relations with his new collaborators, the Paris brothers, and with the four expert directors he had added to the Occident Company from the old monopoly to manage the tobacco business, Paris Duverney, Barré, La Roche Céry, and Berger. Law's difficulties with them seem to have started immediately, even before his new tobacco lease went into effect on 1 October 1718. It was in September, it will be remembered, that Law had proposed to the Paris brothers that they merge their new company for the united farms with his Occident Company. The had refused and twenty-nine of the thirty new directors or farmers-general of the united farms agreed with them. Some weeks later, according to a later memoir by Paris de la Montagne, Law had come to Paris Duverney with a scheme to convert the company's six or nine year lease of the tobacco farm into a lease in perpetuity in return for which the 100 millions owing from the state to the company would in some manner be extinguished. We do not know the details of this scheme, but La Montagne tells us that his brother Duverney made a calculation which showed that at the end of 25 years, the king would have gained only 25 millions and the company only sixteen millions. Law was dissatisfied with this calculation and made one of his own showing a profit to the company of 216 millions.

> My brother expressed some surprise at these figures and showed him the error in his calculation, [de la Montagne writes]. Law merely answered him that he was a bad politician, and that one must never tell princes the truth.[8]

Law dropped this scheme for the moment as he dropped for the moment his proposal to merge the Occident Company and the united farms. Nevertheless, quarrels continued.

According to Paris de la Montagne, at a meeting of the directors of the Occident Company in September 1718, Law proposed that, when they took over the tobacco farm on 1 October, they abolish the monopoly and in its place establish a simple import duty on the model of Great Britain. (In his project of 1715, Law had copied just such a proposal from Pottier's 1698 memoir, but in the spring of 1718 he had given no support to similar suggestions from La Boulaye and the merchants of the western ports. Strengthened since then by his victories of the summer of 1718, Law could now indulge his fancies.) When these fancies were sprung upon the directors, La Montagne tells us that his brother Duverney and La Roche Céry, an expert director brought over from the old tobacco monopoly, strongly opposed the suggestion, insisting it would ruin the farm. Law was extremely irritated by this resistance and tried both cajolery and threats to win them over, to no avail. At a subsequent meeting on 30 September, all four "expert" directors, charged with managing the tobacco farm, presented written statements opposing the proposed change from a sales monopoly to a simple import duty.

Paris de la Montagne, in the "discourse" of 1729, justified his brother's opposition by pointing to the allegedly disastrous results which ensued when Law actually abolished the monopoly and when, Paris claimed, the net yield of the farm disappeared completely.[9] It must be remembered, however, that Paris de la Montagne was writing in 1729, a time when the brothers were in disgrace and when it was widely believed that they had taken advantage of the chaos which followed the collapse of Law's "System" to help themselves by advising the reestablishment of the tobacco monopoly at an unnecessarily low price. There may thus very well be another side to the story of their quarrel with Law.

According to Dutot, an official of the Indies Company under Law who later wrote in his defense, the role of the four directors from the old tobacco monopoly was far more ambiguous. At the crucial meeting (which he places on 1 October rather than 30 September), they warned the other directors of the Occident Company that they had contracted for the tobacco farm at a very high price and would probably lose money on it initially since it was unlikely to produce much above three millions in the first year. They advised against subfarming the whole monopoly and against continuing the old policy of subfarming individual provinces; on these points, their advice was taken. Dutot insists, however, that when the idea of substituting an import duty for the monopoly was raised, far from opposing it, the tobacco "experts" (Paris Duverney, Barré, La Roche Céry, and Berger) told the other directors that this would be an excellent idea provided that they could persuade the Regent to forbid tobacco planting in France as it was in Britain. This would remove the principal source of untaxed tobacco within France. They did not think external smuggling would be as serious under a simple duty as it had been under the monopoly.[10] If this is in fact what Paris Duverney and the other "expert" directors recommended in 1718, they would understandably have found it convenient to forget much in subsequent years. Of course, any such advice may only have been a delaying tactic in that Paris Duverney and his comrades anticipated that government approval for such sweeping changes would be difficult to procure, particularly when local *intendants* could be counted upon to oppose ending the domestic plantation as detrimental to agricultural interests.

There is among Argenson's office papers a twenty-one page memoir dated October 1718 strongly opposing the proposed change to a simple import duty. The author had an expert knowledge of the tobacco farm and would appear to have been an old man who remembered Seignelay's efforts in 1686 to get merchants to farm the tobacco revenue as a simple import duty rather than as a monopoly; either Maynon or Hénault would have remembered those days well. The author insisted that the argument that the British king received five millions a year from a simple import duty in a country with a smaller population than France was not valid. The current exchange rates, so unfavorable to France, exaggerated the British figures. More important, tobacco taking, particularly smoking, was much more widespread in Britain than in France. Finally, Britain had to contend only with smuggling by sea; France not only had sea coasts open to smuggling both from Britain and the Levant, but also had a great land frontier exposed to tobacco smuggling from Spain, Savoy, Switzerland, Germany and the Low Countries and the exempted enclaves. Then, too, by giving up the monopoly, the Occident Company would lose its most effective tool for giving preferential treatment to Louisiana. More immediately, there was the question of yields: the author thought experienced farmers could pay a rent of three million *l.t.* on a consumption of 4.5 million lb. That same quantity paying an import duty of 10s. per lb. net would produce a revenue of only 2.25 million, from which a million would have to be deducted for expenses, leaving only 1.25 million to the crown. More could of course be obtained by abolishing the domestic plantations. Finally, he doubted whether there were merchants in France rich enough to finance the importation and aging (one year for Virginia; three years for Havana) of the tobacco needed for the consumption of all France.[11]

This memoir of October 1718 is one of the most expert expressions of the administrative problems of the tobacco monopoly. It may well have made Argenson cautious; it does not seem to have influenced either Law or the duke of Orléans. At this juncture, the Scot seems to have been able to persuade the Regent and the majority of the directors of the company that they should persevere with his plan for the conversion of the tobacco monopoly into an import duty, but postpone its execution until the company had a chance to take over the southern subfarming companies and their stocks. (Overly precipitous action might have let these stocks pass into private hands with the loss of perhaps a million to the farm.) This decision was conveyed in early October in confidential letters from the Regent and the directors of the company to intendant de Bernage of Languedoc, and presumably to the intendants of other *généralités* subfarmed. In asking for their assistance in the speedy liquidation of the subfarms, the decision to convert the monopoly into an entry duty was announced as accepted in principle, though nothing was said of the date of its implementation or of the fate of the domestic plantations. It may be politically significant that the Regent rather than Argenson sent the first letter; it is indubitably significant that the directors' letter was signed by none of their number from the old tobacco monopoly: Paris Duverney, Barré, La Roche Céry, or Berger.[12]

Paris de la Montagne insisted that at the climactic meeting which he placed on 30 September, the exchange between Law and the four directors from the old tobacco monopoly was so bitter that those four gentlemen then volunteered to resign their positions in the Occident Company. Law, according to de la Montagne, refused to permit their withdrawal, but they insisted both verbally and in writing until an *arrêt du conseil* was obtained permitting their departure.[13] In fact, that *arrêt* permitting them to withdraw as directors and as sureties for the tobacco farm was not issued until 27 January 1719.[14]

This withdrawal exposed to the entire world the growing tension between John Law and the brothers Paris. His great victory over them came of course with the *arrêt* of 27 August 1719,[15] which abrogated the Aymard Lambert lease of the united farms to the Paris brothers' company and granted it instead under the name of Armand Pillavoine to Law's company, now styled the Indies Company (*Compagnie des Indes*). Midst all these changes continuity and discontinuity were strangely mixed. The four Paris brothers and their allies, La Roche Céry, Barré and Pierre Pellard of course ceased being farmers-general when the Aymard Lambert lease was broken. However, at the same time, Law added seventeen former farmers-general to the directorate of the Indies Company, including François Le Gendre! A very few of these had been in the original Manis lease of 1715, had been kept on by the Paris brothers in the Lambert lease of 1718 and were again kept on by Law in the Pillavoine lease. At least eight, however, who had been dropped by the Paris in the Lambert lease now came back into the management of the farms under Law, while five who first became farmers-general under the Paris were yet retained by Law. Midst the greatest upheavals of the next few years, we shall observe comparable continuity in the highest ranks of the old and new finance.[16]

With so many preoccupations in 1719, John Law gave little attention to the tobacco farm during the eleven months or so following the withdrawal in January of Paris Duverney and the other old tobacco farmers. The tobacco monopoly was then presumably supervised by the directors of the company acting as a whole. After the merger of the enlarged and renamed *Compagnie des Indes* with the united farms in August-September 1719, it was necessary to set up committees of the directors to handle individual departments. By a *délibération* of 18 September 1719, the tobacco monopoly was entrusted from 1 October 1719 to MM. Raudot, Mouchard, Gilly, Corneau, and Berthelot.[17] Antoine Denis Raudot, *intendant des classes de la marine* (naval reserves), had been a director of the Occident Company since February 1718; François Mouchard, deputy for La Rochelle in the Council of Commerce, was one of the original 1717 directors; Elizée Gilly de Montaud,[18] a Paris merchant interested in the West Indies with a Languedoc Protestant background and good connections in Geneva, had been a director since February 1718; all three had been among the directors who stood surety for the lease of the tobacco farm when it was adjudged to the Occident Company in August 1718. If Jean Corneau was an obscure *avocat au conseil* who became a director only at this time, Louis Henri Berthelot, seigneur de St. Laurent, came from a great family of financiers. He had, following his father, been a farmer-general from 1703, with a seat on the Council of Commerce from 1716, until dropped by the Paris brothers in 1718. (As important, his niece was the marchioness of Prie, mistress to the duke of Bourbon and later mistress of France during the years of the duke's ascendency, 1723-26.) [19]

These arrangements lasted only a few weeks. By a subsequent *délibération* of 2 October 1719, the administration of the tobacco monopoly was merged with that of the united farms and entrusted to a committee consisting of Law, Berthelot, Mouchard, Raudot, Gilly-de-Montaud (the last four just described) plus Piou, Desvieux, de Lalive, and Le Gendre.[20] Jean Piou, deputy from Nantes in the Council of Commerce, was one of the original directors of August 1717. Louis Philippe Desvieux (1677–1735) [21] and Louis Denis de Lalive de Bellegarde[22] (1679–1755) had both first become farmers-general of the united farms in 1715 and were to continue in such functions until their deaths (although the latter had been dropped for one year by the Paris brothers). Le Gendre is of course François Le Gendre, farmer-general since 1696 and brother-in-law of Crozat, the only one of the old tobacco company to go along with Law. (Le Gendre, Berthelot, Piou and Desvieux also represented the Indies Company on the Council of Commerce where the first two had previously sat for the united farms.) This merger of committees in October 1719 suggests that Law was then already planning the early merger of the administration of the tobacco farm with that of the united farms. He was in fact to do just that before the end of the year.

At the same time as the directors were being divided into committees, the company itself was being divided into *bureaux,* each under a staff *directeur.* Above these, six secretaries of the company were named, four for commerce, one for the united farms, and one for tobacco. The director of the tobacco bureau and the secretary for the tobacco farm were the same person, François Dupleix, father of the famous governor of Pondichéry.[23] François Dupleix (1664–1735), himself the son of a shopkeeper at Chatellerault, was one of several functionaries (others being Le Jongleur, La Roche Céry, La Gombaude) who rose to head the tobacco farm after service in the administration of the farm in Brittany. During the du Plantier lease (1697–1703) he was receiver for the tobacco farm at Brest; from about 1706 to 1718 he was also head of the great tobacco manufactory at Morlaix.[24] He was representative of a significant body of "technicians" who broke through into the highest posts in finance during the time of Law.

Aside from organizational shifts, we hear very little of the tobacco farm between January and December 1719. There were even remarkably few *arrêts du conseil* concerning its administration in that year.[25] Following Law's success in reducing the general rate of interest on government indebtedness to 3 percent, an *arrêt du conseil* of 19 September 1719 lowered that due the company on its original 100 million loan to the state from 4 percent to 3 percent (through the circumlocution of permitting the company to lend the government 100 million at 3 percent to repay to itself the 100 million principal of the 4 percent annuities it had received the previous year.) The assignment against the tobacco farm was thus reduced from four to three millions annually.[26]

At the end of December, Law suddenly became interested in the tobacco farm once more. The timing is most important. This is precisely the period when the speculative fever on the Rue Quincampoix seemed to have reached and temporarily declined from its peak, and thus when Law would have had to begin to worry about how he was going to keep prices up.[27] He was therefore under considerable pressure to disclose new wonders every day. The greatest of these wonders was the soaring dividend of the Indies Company.

On 30 December 1719, to help sustain the high price of shares, Law announced to a general meeting of the shareholders, attended by the Regent, the company's intention of paying a regular 40 percent dividend. This of course would mean an income of only 2 percent on the current value of old shares now risen twenty-fold. Nevertheless, it was tremendously buoyant news. After his fall, Law was criticized for announcing such a dividend with allegedly no real basis in current earnings. To justify himself, in later years he compiled some rather vague figures which claimed to show that the company was in fact earning enough to pay such a dividend. He reported enormous profits on the united farms in 1720 which were probably due primarily to speculative hoarding of taxed commodities by people afraid to hold paper money. In addition, Law put the tobacco farm down for the impressive figure of six millions in profits, including the 4.02 million price of that farm (which the company of course also retained).[28] In December 1719, Law did not reveal specific figures to prove that his company could pay 40 percent, but that figure would seem more credible to the public if any sources of increased income could be suggested. A change in the method of collecting the tobacco revenue would of course suggest to many that "improvements" were being made which would be reflected in the company's balance sheet.

There is a further reason, which cannot be proved but only suggested, why it would have been convenient to change the tobacco farm at that moment. The apogee of the Law system was connected with large scale emission of paper money reflected in the deterioration in the bill market of the rates of exchange between the French *livre* and foreign currencies. For example, exchange on Paris at London had declined from around 45 at the beginning of March 1718 to 32 on 29 May o.s. (9 June n.s.) following the reminting decreed in May 1718. The rate thereafter held steady for a year at about 29–30, but in the latter part of 1719, as Law's "System" went into full operation, declined to about 24–25 at the end of December 1719 (o.s.).[29] This last deterioration of the exchanges must have proven especially embarrassing to the tobacco farm which even before Law's time had spent a million *l.t.* yearly on foreign tobaccos; with increased importation and unfavorable exchanges, this may easily have exceeded three millions in 1719. The sum itself may not have bothered Law too much except that retail prices of tobacco were fixed and could not be raised to reflect rising costs. What would have been even more embarrassing to his position would be having the trading activities of his own company help turn the exchanges against France. This could be avoided by having the company get out of the tobacco importing business entirely. Such a change would also extricate Law from the rash promise to supply from the French colonies all the imported tobacco needed in France after 1 October 1721.

Whatever his motives, Law may have met some resistance on high. Although the Regent had agreed to the change in principle in October 1718, he appears to have retained some doubts about the fiscal as opposed to the commercial desirability of the change. The duke is reported to have expressed these doubts publicly at the shareholders' meeting on 30 December when announcement was made of the impending change in the tobacco farm.[30] Nevertheless, the basic decision had been taken.

The previous day—29 December 1719—Law had obtained an *arrêt du conseil*[31] overturning the entire legislative structure of the tobacco farm built up since 1674. Its basic provisions were: (1) the monopoly was abolished; (2) anyone might import tobacco into France on payment of a simple import duty; (3) anyone might engage in the wholesale or retail trade in tobacco or in its manufacture; and (4) the planting of tobacco was prohibited (for the security of the revenue) in all France except the eastern frontier provinces, traditionally exempt from the tobacco and many other fiscal arrangements. (The first three points but not the last had been foretold by the Regent's letter of 3 October 1718.)

Although the new import duty rates gave a marked preference to the tobacco of the French colonies and the French eastern provinces, they were on all categories of tobacco *very high,* reflecting Law's desperate need for revenues. Under normal conditions, they would have been the equivalent of from 100–400 percent; under the inflationary conditions of 1720, they may have amounted to much less. They were on tobacco from:

Louisiana during the company's privilege	25 *l.t.* per quintal
Louisiana after expiry of company's privilege	50 *l.t.* per quintal
Artois, Alsace, Flanders, Lorraine, Franche-Comté, etc.	30 *l.t.* per quintal
St. Domingue and all French colonies except Louisiana	60 *l.t.* per quintal
Virginia (i.e., all British colonies)	75 *l.t.* per quintal
Brazil	150 *l.t.* per quintal
Spanish snuff	200 *l.t.* per quintal

By a subsequent *arrêt* of 3 March 1720, the list was extended to include Havana leaf tobacco (200 *l.t.* per quintal) and Levant tobacco (75 *l.t.* per quintal).[32] Both were relatively new types destined to become much more important in the eighteenth century.

The remaining provisions of the *arrêt* of 29 December 1719 were technical but interesting: the ports and frontier points through which tobacco could be imported were specified;[33] on the British model, minimum weights were established for the package in which tobacco was imported, e.g., 500 lb. for leaf tobacco; tobacco imported by sea must come in vessels of at least fifty tons; that imported by land must move in wagons along specified roads. Tobacco planting was prohibited in France proper including Metz, Mondragon, and all the specified places in Normandy and the southwest where it had up to then been permitted. An unprecedentedly heavy fine of 10,000 *l.t.* was established for planting, assessable against both tenants and proprietors. All stocks of domestic tobacco on hand were to be exported within six months or a duty for domestic use of fifteen *l.t.* per quintal for whole leaf and thirty *l.t.* per quintal for stemmed tobacco had to be paid. Finally, as presaged in the reorganization of October, the tobacco revenue was merged with the united farms.

In Chapter 11, we shall discuss the seven years of administrative headaches arising from the suppression of tobacco planting. The more immediate problem facing the administrators of the dissolved monopoly was selling off their buildings, tools, and accumulated stocks. These would have come to considerable sums, easily several million *l.t.*, since it was the normal practice of the tobacco farm to have about a year's tobacco supply on hand. In February 1720, everything was put up for auction on 1 March: manufactured tobacco was to be sold in moderate sized lots, but leaf tobacco at each manufactory was to be sold in a single lot (together with all the tools and equipment at the works) to a single bidder who had also to agree to buy or to take over the leases of the buildings in which the manufactory was located.[34] Apparently there was a shortage of acceptable bidders, for in April, new announcements were made repeating the same terms for new bidding to be held on 1 June. Until the workshops were actually sold on 1 June, the Indies Company continued their operation to supply retail demand.[35] The prices obtained should have been very high inasmuch as the wealthy were by then trying to get rid of paper money. Nevertheless, in the case of the works at Montpellier (an old manufactory of the subfarm for Languedoc), *arrêts du conseil* of 23 July and 12 October 1720 cancelled the June auction and ordered new bids to be received.[36] It is not clear whether *all* the workshops and equipment were finally sold or not.

The Montpellier case at least was atypical. The manufactories at Paris, Dieppe, and many other unspecified places in the realm were bought by a single company nominally headed by Jean-Maurice de Montigny. (This might conceivably be the same Jean de Montigny who was for many years *directeur* of the tobacco farm in the *généralité* of Bordeaux.) The principal shareholders in this *Société pour le commerce général du tabac* were the partners Jean Salaville and Jean-Robert de la Prade (6*s*.3*d*. or 31.25 percent), a sieur Petit de St. Lienne holding 2*s*. or 10 percent, while the remaining 59.75 percent was held by the sieurs de Montigny, de Maugin, Dorlyé, Philippe, de Breton du Prat, de Nesle, Dupré de Plaisance, and Pingault, all quite obscure and drawn apparently from outside the circles of Paris finance. (Pingault was a senior employee of the Indies Company itself.) They seem to have devoted themselves primarily to manufacture and to have farmed out the distribution of their tobacco to lesser firms in different parts of the country. They also appear to have been a very large and ambitious company, formed at a time when money was easily come by—but in the end disastrously unsuccessful.[37]

A special problem was created by the needs of the army and the navy for large quantities of cheap tobacco for sale to the lower ranks. The monopoly throughout its existence had traditionally supplied such *tabac de cantine* at a price far below that normally charged in its *entrepôts* or by its licensed retailers, i.e., about 12s. per lb. instead of 40–60s. When the Indies Company sold the tobacco manufactories of the old tobacco farm, the supply of *tabac de cantine* was suddenly cut off. De Montigny & Co., who had acquired most of the tobacco manufacturing facilities, announced that they could not undertake to supply the troops at the old low price (because they had to pay import duty on all the tobacco they manufactured and could no longer buy the cheap tobaccos of the southwest) . An arrangement was finally reached, confirmed by the *résultat du conseil* of 16 July 1720, whereby de Montigny & Co. agreed to supply *tabac de cantine* at the old prices from 1 August 1720 to 1 October 1721 in return for a state subsidy of 8s. per lb. At the same time, de Montigny & Co. were permitted to import manufactured tobaccos (prohibited by the new rules) suitable for *tabac de cantine,* paying for all its imported tobacco, whether in leaf or manufactured, only the low import duty of 30 *l.t.* per quintal established for the leaf of France's eastern provinces. The Indies Company also agreed to transfer to de Montigny & Co. its lease of the tobacco monopoly in the frontier territory of Charleville from the princess and duchess of Brunswick (at 4,500 *l.t.* p.a.) . The tobacco manufactory at Charleville had for many years been used not only to supply that minuscule territory but also to make *tabac de cantine* for the large numbers of French troops stationed along the eastern frontier.[38] These new arrangements were explained to the army in a royal *règlement* of 30 July 1720 which limited sales to the troops to one pound per head per month.[39]

When word got out early in January 1720 that the tobacco monopoly was to be abolished,[40] considerable speculative activity was engendered in Paris, the French ports, London, Bristol, and elsewhere. French merchants rushed to order tobacco from abroad; foreign merchants hurried not only to fill their French correspondents' orders, but to send tobacco on their own account. Those who got their tobacco to France in the earliest months probably did quite well. The deteriorating exchange, of course, ate up much of their book profits as the year progressed. By the end of the year, there appears to have been so much tobacco in France that it became unsaleable. We do not hear much of the success stories; the disasters, however, are most informative.

Sir Abraham Elton, Bart., a well-known tobacco merchant and mayor of Bristol, in July and August 1720 sent on his own account 273 hogsheads of tobacco to his correspondent, Sir Edward Rigby, merchant at Port Louis and L'Orient. Rigby (presumably an Irish émigré) had become a director of Law's company in February 1719 and was in charge of the company's affairs at L'Orient. When the tobacco trade was opened, Rigby established a manufactory at L'Orient as a private venture. After Law's fall, all of Rigby's effects (including Elton's tobacco) were seized as security for Rigby's accounts with the Indies Company. It took the personal intervention of the British ambassador in Paris in 1721 to get Elton's tobacco released from seizure and sold for his account. He could not have got very much for it by that time.[41] Joseph Read and William Marsland, merchants of London, sent 70 hogsheads of tobacco on their own account to George Arbuthnot and Charles Irvine, merchants at Rouen. So great was the glut that the tobacco could not be sold at all, nor reexported under French law. It was not until December 1723 that the tobacco was finally sold to the re-established French monopoly (then the Indies Company again). A considerable loss was suffered on the transaction.[42]

The most interesting speculator was William Law, brother of the controller-general. Daniel Pulteney, a British special commissioner in Paris, thought that the publication of the *arrêt* of 29 December was delayed until early February to give the Indies Company a chance to reduce its large stocks of tobacco.[43] This was undoubtedly *not* the reason, for the Indies Company itself continued to buy tobacco in London until March or April 1720. When still a merchant in London, William Law had been employed by the Indies Company to buy tobacco there between February and August 1719.[44] He then went over to Paris leaving the company's London purchases to one Claude Bettifort.[45] Despite the abrogation of the monopoly, Bettifort continued to buy for the company until at least March 1720; as late as April we can find traces in the books of George Middleton, the London banker of the Indies Company, of payments to Bettifort for tobacco bought on the company's account. Quite apart from these were to be the purchases made for William Law personally. On 11/22 January 1719/20, more than ten days before the *arrêt* ending the monopoly was published in Paris, a Mr. Harrold walked into Middleton's counting house with word that he was to buy 700 hogsheads of tobacco for William Law in Paris (about 400,000 lb.) and be paid by Middleton. During the next two months, Middleton's correspondence with William Law is filled with references to such purchases by Harrold and by James Douglas, another London merchant. William Law paid for these by getting special permission to export gold from France to Pels in Amsterdam on whom Middleton drew.[46]

Even so, William Law and his brother were heavily indebted to Middleton at the time of John Law's banishment in December 1720. To cover part of this debt, William Law transferred some of his hoarded copper and tobacco at Rouen and Chaillot to Thomas Pitt, lord Londonderry, to hold for Middleton. Londonderry was in Paris during the Bubble to sell his father's "great diamond" and lesser baubles and speculated deeply on his own. (The diamonds sold well in that inflationary frenzy.) However, after the fall of Law, the merchant companies (guilds) of Paris, supported by the *parlement,* searched zealously for wholesale quantities of commodities in store in Paris and environs which belonged to persons not authorized to trade there. Large caches belonging to the dukes of La Force and Estrées, peers of France, were found and confiscated. Under the circumstances, Londonderry could not take delivery of the goods at Chaillot, which were found and seized as the property of John and William Law. The 325 hogsheads of tobacco at Rouen, however, in the hands of Robert Arbuthnot, William Law's agent there, were safe, though it took two years of applications to the Regent and successive controllers-general by Sir Robert Sutton and Sir Luke Schaub, British ambassadors in Paris, and Thomas Crawfurd, British resident there, to get the restored monopoly to buy them eventually in May 1723.[47]

Even William Law, the insider, who imported his tobacco ahead of the pack in March and April 1720, could not dispose of it all to advantage in the monetary chaos of that year. Others less knowing, like Elton, Read, and Marsland, who continued sending tobacco to France in July, August, and September 1720, were even more likely to have got their fingers burned, for France was grossly overstocked with tobacco by then. The Indies Company in any event obviously had large receipts between February and July 1720 from the very high import duty on British and other foreign tobaccos. Once the glut developed, however, importations and import duties must both have dried up. It was inevitable under such circumstances for someone to suggest a further change in the status of the tobacco revenue to get money flowing in again to the Indies Company and/or the state.

A period of extreme uncertainty began with the dismissal of Law from the controller-generalship on 29 May 1720. For a moment, it seemed as if Argenson, the inveterate foe of Law and protector of the brothers Paris, had triumphed, but on 2 June Law was recalled to favor and resumed direction of the bank and company. He was now given the title of *intendant général du commerce,* but not the controller-generalship which on 7 June was entrusted to "triumvirs" headed by Le Peletier Des Forts as *commissaire général des finances*. With the resumption of office by the exiled chancellor Daguesseau, Argenson (also Keeper of the Seals) was totally disgraced; the financial officials associated with him (Le Pelletier de la Houssaye, Fagon, Dodun) either resigned or were discharged.[48] The appointment of Des Forts, nephew of Claude Le Peletier, controller-general in the 1680's, suggests an apparent wish to return to the conventional financial administration of Louis XIV's time, with its vices as well as its virtues. On the day of Law's dismissal, the *livre tournois* had been further devalued in its metallic equivalent.[49] The exchange rate on Paris at London (quoted in pence sterling per nominal *écu* of three livres) after hovering between 28 and 32 between the devaluation of May 1718 and April 1719, dropped steadily from near 25 at the beginning of 1720 to 17–18 in April and May and then abruptly to 12½ in early June, following the latest devaluation. By September, it was down to six, even four and, on some days, "no exchange."[50] Law's seeming return to favor and office only added to the uncertainty. When his foes, the Paris brothers, were exiled on 1 July, Pulteney, British special commissioner in

Paris, reported that while the Regent was determined to appear to support the "System," in reality he no longer supported Law.[51] Leaders of the old finance, headed by Samuel Bernard, were consulted by the Regency Council. To counteract their influence, Law tried to persuade the Regent to bring pressure upon Bernard and Crozat to bring back to France in specie the many millions they were supposed to have abroad.[52] Rumors begat rumors.

To check this uncertainty, it was felt necessary to issue an *arrêt du conseil* on 22 July 1720, specifically denying reports that the crown intended to divorce the farms from the Indies Company. Article I confirmed the grant of the tobacco revenue to the company.[53] The day before, an *arrêt* had been issued granting the company its commercial privileges in perpetuity.[54] A month later, on 29 August, a further *arrêt* was issued reorganizing the Indies Company. The duke of Orléans was declared Protector and Perpetual Governor of the company; the directors were reduced in number to 24 and purged. Instead of being headed by a committee, each department of the company was now entrusted to just two directors. The *cinq grosses fermes* (primarily import duties) and tobacco were entrusted to François Le Gendre and François Dupleix (who became a director at this time).[55] Dupleix, it will be remembered, had been an employee of the tobacco farm from about 1697 until it was absorbed into the Occident Company in 1718 and he summoned to Paris. If his expertise were now required, it could only be to reestablish the monopoly; he had no other expertise to offer. The old bureaucrats were coming back as well as the old financiers.

It is very likely that when the contract was made on 16 July 1720 for de Montigny & Co. to supply *tabac de cantine* for the remarkably short period of August 1720–September 1721, it was understood in some quarters that before those fourteen months were up, the monopoly would in fact be reestablished. The actual restoration came slowly, in two stages, reflecting the gradual decline of Law and the reemergence of the old finance. The first stage came with the *déclaration* of 17 October 1720.[56] Its preamble stated that the benefits expected from the open trade established by the *arrêt* of 29 December 1719 had not been realized: prices had gone up (this was hardly to be ascribed primarily to the open trade) and much tobacco had been smuggled in. The *déclaration* preserved the internal free trade in the manufacture, wholesale, and retail selling of tobacco. At the same time, it reestablished the exclusive privilege of importing tobacco which it vested in the Indies Company for the remainder of the nine-year lease of 1718 at that lease's price of 4.02 million *l.t.* per annum. All the old regulations about the importation of tobacco going back to the *ordonnance* of 1681 were reestablished. The prohibition of domestic planting was specifically confirmed. Any private merchants importing tobacco must sell the same to the importing monopoly or reexport it. The ports of importation were limited to Marseilles, Bordeaux, La Rochelle, Nantes, Morlaix, St. Malo, Rouen, and Dieppe. At each of these, the import monopoly was to have an auction at least once every three months at which manufacturers could supply themselves. The resale of unmanufactured tobacco was prohibited. No manufacture or storage facility for tobacco could be established within three leagues of the coast or of the land frontiers, except in the ports of legal entry. Each manufacturer was to have a distinctive mark to appear on all his tobacco. No tobacco was to be shipped by coast or by road without a pass from the monopoly. A subsequent *arrêt* of 17 November 1720 added L'Orient to the list of permitted ports of importation, thus permitting Rigby's manufacture there to continue.[57]

On the face of it, the *déclaration* of 17 October 1720 was a very good thing for the Indies Company. Without having to undertake the expenses of reestablishing workshops and the vast network of *entrepôts* and *bureaux* necessary to supply all parts of the country, with the large running stocks they entailed, the company would nevertheless derive the monopoly profits of exclusive importation. This assumed, of course, that there would be an active market in France for imported tobacco offered at auction and made no allowance for the utterly demoralized condition of the company and the French business community in the months following. Even more urgent, the new policy made no allowance for the enormous quantities of tobacco imported into France during the months of free trade in 1720 and hoarded both by speculators (afraid of paper money and forbidden to hold specie) and by the new manufacturers. One memoir of mid-1721 claimed that there was then, from licit and illicit importation, a five or six years' supply of tobacco in France: thus, the great "profits" earned for the company by the tobacco monopoly during the first two years (October 1718–September 1720), had, it asserted, turned in the third year to a loss approaching two millions; that is, the tobacco import duties were bringing the company two million p.a. less than the 4.02 million for which it was farming that revenue.[58] In addition, the company couldn't collect the large sums owing them from de Montigny & Co., the largest of the manufacturers.[59] In the long run, of course, the monopoly might again have been a very good thing for the Indies Company—but 1721 was to be a year of short views.

The last drops of influence retained by Law evaporated during November 1720—though, when his fall came, it came suddenly and even unexpectedly. On 11 December, there were rumors of strong court intrigues against Law. On the twelfth, Le Peletier Des Forts was dismissed as *commissaire général des finances* and the post of controller-general was revived for Le Pelletier de la Houssaye, chancellor to the duke of Orléans and inveterate enemy of the company. La Houssaye had given up all his financial posts on 7 June with the return of Law and the disgrace of Argenson. He now refused to accept the controller-generalship unless Law left Paris. The Scot surrendered his posts and left provisionally on the thirteenth and finally on the nineteenth,[60] reaching Brussels destitute on the twenty-second.[61] Immediately, all eyes turned to Bernard and Crozat, but those aged worthies, though generous with advice, preferred not to take an interest or an active role in the company. (La Houssaye also consulted the dying Desmaretz.) Younger hands were needed: on the fourteenth, the Paris brothers, whom everyone had hitherto considered creatures of Argenson, were invited back, reportedly to take over the united farms. By Christmas, when they had all arrived in Paris, it was apparent to some that they would have charge not just of the farms but of financial affairs generally.[62] In fact, the brothers were to be responsible for the most important financial measures of the next six years. Paris Duverney was the most active of them, personally supervising the dismemberment and reorganization of the Indies Company.[63]

On 29 December, a general meeting of the demoralized shareholders of the Indies Company, at the threatening suggestion of the Regent, voted to surrender all their noncommercial privileges except the tobacco monopoly.[64] An *arrêt* of 5 January 1721 actually took away from the company, effective 1 January, the collection of the land taxes (*recettes générales des finances*) and the privilege and profits of minting and abrogated the Armand Pillavoine lease of the united farms which still had about seven years to run. It excepted only the tobacco farm.[65]

The last was not long to remain a consolation. The company was rendered insolvent by an *arrêt* of 26 January 1721 making it responsible for all the debts of the bank.[66] On 7 April 1721, two *arrêts* were issued in effect placing the Indies Company in receivership: the rights and powers of shareholders, directors, and syndics were suspended and four councillors of state (Trudaine, Fagon, Ferrand, and de Machault) named to settle the accounts of the company and the bank with the state.[67] A subsequent *arrêt* of 15 April created five lesser commissioners (Baillon de Blancpignon, Begon, Duché, Dumoulin, and Moreau) who were to be in charge of the day-to-day operations of the company and report to the commissioners of council.[68] Of these five, Jean-Baptiste Duché and René Moreau de Maupertuis, of course, had been original directors of the *Compagnie d'Occident* in 1717 but had dropped out when it became the *Compagnie des Indes* in May 1719. The other three had no official connection with the company before, although Michel Begon (the younger), financier sport of an administrative family, and connected to Mme de Prie, had been an original subscriber to the company in 1717. François Baillon de Blancpignon, like Moreau, was from St. Malo; Pierre Dumoulin (DuMolin) was a substantial Paris banker related to Étienne Demeuves, one of the syndics chosen by the shareholders just before the suspension.[69] As none of the five, or their general manager (*directeur-général*) Le Cordier, had any background in the tobacco farm, it was fairly evident that that revenue was considered as good as lost to the company.

That the blow did not come until another three months had passed was probably due to the confusion of the moment and the time needed to prepare all the documents and make the necessary arrangements. Finally, on

29 July 1721, an *arrêt du conseil* abrogated as of 1 September the lease of the tobacco monopoly to the Indies Company (which was to have run through September 1727). The preamble declared that the company was not in a condition to carry out the monopoly granted to it by the *déclaration* of 17 October 1720. It had sold all its tobacco at public auction on 1 June 1720 and could not supply the trade as it was supposed to do. From legitimate and fraudulent imports during the preceding eighteen months, enough tobacco had accumulated in France to supply the country for several years, causing the company to lose money on its tobacco farm. It was therefore in its interest that the lease at the high rent of 4.02 million yearly be broken.[70]

Three days later, on 1 August 1721, a very important *déclaration* was issued reestablishing the full tobacco monopoly as it had existed before Law's time.[71] This long document (which must have been weeks in preparation) replaced the *ordonnance* of 1681 as the legal foundation and principal legal code under which the monopoly operated down to its abolition in 1791. The giddy days of experiment were over.

How can one sum up the thirty-five months of the "age of Law" in the history of the tobacco farm? A critical memoir of the summer of 1721 reported that the tobacco monopoly had earned over twelve million *l.t.* p.a. for the company during the first two years (October 1718–September 1720) or eight million over the contract price of 4.02 million p.a. (These figures are preposterous for 1718–19, but quite credible for inflationary and experimental 1719–20.) By the third year, however, the memoirist reported that receipts dropped by five-sixths, threatening the company with a two million loss on the lease price.[72] Paris Duverney also later claimed that, in the end, the lease of the tobacco farm had become "very onerous" to the Indies Company and that it was well rid of it.[73] He was, however, writing many years later to justify his part in taking the monopoly away from that company in 1721 and giving it to others at a much lower price. In answer to Duverney, Dutot, an old official of the company, prepared some figures to show that over the whole thirty-five months (1 October 1718–31 August 1721) during which the company had farmed the tobacco revenue in one form or another, it had netted 2.4 million annually over and above the 4.02 million price of the farm.[74]

Gross receipts (35 months)	21,026,654 *l.t.* 2*s*.
All expenses (price of lease, raw materials, manufacturing, administrations, etc.)	−13,974,470 *l.t.*19*s*.
Clear Net	7,052,093 *l.t.* 3*s*.
(or per annum)	2,417,860 *l.t.*

These figures seem to show that the gross yield of the farm was 4,020,000 plus 2,417,860 or 6,437,860 *l.t.* annually, very close to the six million estimated by Law (in his later memoirs) as available for dividends. Dutot's figures, however, merit some scrutiny. On 1 June 1720 and afterward, the company sold off at auction all its accumulated stocks and tools. These must have been worth quite a few million because the monopoly normally had a year's supply of tobacco on hand and had continued foreign purchases (presumably as a speculation) through at least April 1720. A few days before the June sale, the country had been subject to a further round of monetary devaluation: the *livre* was now worth one-fourth its "normal" value in exchange with sterling. Everyone in France who could was trying to convert his paper money into real estate or goods, the only things safe and legal to hoard. The prices realized for the tobacco sold under under such circumstances must have been several times those realizable in "normal" times. We must use the comparison with "normal" times because the price of four million was bid by Law in 1718 during something approaching settled conditions. Similarly, in those months in the spring and summer of 1720 when the importation of tobacco was open to all at rather high duties, the desire of French businessmen to get rid of their paper money persuaded many to invest in tobacco, quite apart from the more understandable purchases by those starting up as manufacturers.[75] For a few months, the company should have had exceptionally large receipts from its import duties, quite apart from its profits on what it may have imported speculatively. Dutot's "gross receipts," assuming them to be correct to the last *sou,* are therefore still unknown quantities to us.

Similarly, it is very difficult to say what Dutot did or did not include in his figure of near fourteen million for expenses. If, from his total expenses of 13,974,470 *l.t.* we deduct the price of the farm (@ 4.02 million p.a.) or 11,725,000 *l.t.* for thirty-five months, we find that he has allowed only 2,249,470 *l.t.* for all other expenses during the thirty-five months, or 771,247 *l.t.* annually. This is a ridiculously low figure, even allowing for the fact that the farm had no manufacturing plant or sales distribution apparatus in operation during its last fifteen months. In Chapter 7, we discussed some accounts of the farm presented in 1708.[76] At a time when tobacco consumption was much lower than in Law's time, these showed:

Tobacco purchases	1,526,430 *l.t.* p.a.
Manufacturing, transport and administration	827,000 *l.t.* p.a.
Total direct costs	2,353,430 *l.t.* p.a.

In Chapter 9, we discussed the well-informed estimates which du Sault gave Desmaretz about the accounts of the tobacco farm in 1714.[77] Du Sault estimated direct costs at 2,399,200 *l.t.,* remarkably close to the 1708 estimate and about three times as much as Dutot assigned to the same items for 1718–21. Moreover, both the 1708 estimator and du Sault were concerned only with the expenses in the provinces administered directly by the monopoly and not subfarmed; we should perhaps add a third to their figures to allow for costs in the southern subfarmed provinces. Thus, Dutot's "cost" data are even less meaningful than his income data. Since Dutot did not choose to give a breakdown of his figures, he presumably knew what he was about.

Dutot, writing in the 1740's,[78] and Professor Harsin in the 1920's[79] have argued that the farm may well have netted in 1719 the sum claimed for it by Law because subsequently it produced about seven million yearly during 1723–30 and was leased for eight million in the later 1730's. This is a much stronger argument than that based on Dutot's figures and avoids the thorny problem of what happened to the company's yields during the free trade interlude of 1720–21. It is, however, subject to three important qualifications. In 1723–30 and later, there was no domestic plantation of tobacco in France, though of course there had been before 1720. This cultivation was the principal source of contraband tobacco in southern France and involved the farm in police expenditures of several hundred thousand *l.t.* annually, quite apart from the sales revenue lost to the contrabanders. The elimination of domestic planting was easily worth from 500,000 to a million *l.t.* annually to the farm. Second, the years after 1723 were years of relatively low commodity prices throughout Europe when (except for 1725) tobacco could be purchased for one-third less than during Maynon's postwar leases or Law's monopoly farm (1713–19).[80] (British tobacco export prices were also lowered by an act of Parliament[81] in 1723 which refunded the last retained duty at exportation, saving the foreign buyer three-eighths of a penny per pound in sterling or 3 *l.t.* 15*s*. per quintal in French money.) Savings from these lower prices were worth more than a million a year to the farm by the 1730's. Third, and perhaps most important of all, we have at this point come to the generation when tobacco consumption in France began to grow very rapidly. This was something about which the farm was very conscious and which all its critics tended to forget. Until about 1713, tobacco consumption in France was markedly below that in other European countries. Smoking had never really taken on in France, and chewing tobacco was acceptable only in limited circles. Only when we come to the age of snuff, which is the age of Louis XV, do Frenchmen begin to take tobacco widely and in quantity. Whether the new reign gave new opportunities for new tastes to be introduced in the world of fashion and then spread downward, or whether the habits were introduced directly among the common people by returning soldiers and others, we do not know. Perhaps this phenomenon is simply the culmination and acceleration of changes in consumption habits that had been going on for a century. That the change took place, there can be no doubt. In 1737–43, when Paris Duverney and Dutot were writing, England alone (exclusive of Scotland) exported to France about five times as much tobacco annually as it had in 1711–18; as early as 1724–29 it sent two and one half times as much. (Yet even in 1711–18, England was France's primary supplier.)[82] Therefore, one cannot use any yield figures for the later 1720's or 1730's for fair comparisons with Maynon's time or Law's.

In retrospect, it seems likely that the 4.02 million which Law contracted to pay in 1718 was a very safe price to bid in that it was based on the Maynon group's counterbid of four million. The earnings of the farm probably covered that price easily down to the end of the monopoly and the sale of the manufacturing plant on 1 June 1720. The danger in Law's bid lay not in the price, but in the promise to import nothing but Louisiana tobacco after 1 October 1721. We shall see in Chapter 12 that he must soon have discovered that he could not live up to that promise. (The Regent's letter of October 1718 suggests he knew it from the beginning.) Then too, his own inflation made the price-controlled monopoly of diminishing attraction in late 1719. His general position in December of that year made bold steps necessary. Who knew what a combination of an open trade, a high entry duty and the abolition of domestic planting might not produce? Why not try and find out? Above all, Law was a plunger. At the very least, he would get himself out of those traps of his own making: Louisiana and deteriorating exchanges. With so many other things to worry about, the decision to discard the monopoly could not have seemed more than a trivial risk to Law.

We shall never know the final balance sheet of the open trade experiment of 1720–21. Any big book profits the company might have made would have come not from import duties paid but from the once only windfall gains made in June 1720 by the sale at inflated prices of their accumulated stocks. (The ca. six million [Fr.] pounds[83] imported from England in 1720, perhaps 90 percent of total French imports, had they all been imported in the free trade months, would have paid in duty only 4.5 million *l.t.* gross, while the previous year the old monopoly allegedly netted six million for the company.)

The Maynon-Bernard company had had a very good thing in the tobacco monopoly, but they cannot be accused of fraud for not knowing, when they signed their December 1714 contract, how much tobacco would be consumed in France in 1739 or 1729 or even 1719. Law perceived, he did not create, the pattern of increased consumption. His good guess about consumption was balanced out by his poor judgment about Louisiana production and by his blind plunge into open trade. In retrospect, his most lasting mark on the French tobacco monopoly was the decision to abolish the domestic cultivation.

CHAPTER 11

After the Fall, 1721–30

The Restoration of the Monopoly, 1721–23

The *arrêt du conseil* of 29 July 1721 broke the lease of the tobacco monopoly to the Indies Company as of 1 September;[1] the *déclaration* of 1 August 1721 reestablished the monopoly under a new legal code, yet much as it had been before Law's time—except for one or two important additions that would add to the value of the monopoly in the future. Instead of the old maximum prices of 40s. per lb. wholesale and 50s. per lb. retail established by the *ordonnance* of 1681, it was now provided (art. vii) that *tabacs supérieurs en corde* were to sell for 50s. per lb. wholesale and 60s. per lb. retail, while Brazil was to sell for up to 70s. per lb. wholesale and 80s. per lb. retail. Article xxii confirmed the prohibition of tobacco planting in France proper.[2] The tobacco monopoly would henceforth be an even more attractive property than in the past. The only question was, who would get it.

In the demoralized but hectic atmosphere of 1721, there appears to have been little question of putting the reestablished tobacco monopoly up for the proper competitive bids. Instead, a "company of Dupleix" was put together with the blessings of the brothers Paris to lease the monopoly for nine years without giving anyone else a chance to bid. François Dupleix, of course, was the veteran employee of the old Bernard-Maynon company who had been put in charge of the tobacco monopoly by Law in 1718 and became a director of the Indies Company in 1720, just before the fall. Because of the expenses involved in reestablishing the monopoly (particularly acquiring premises and staff and buying up private stocks), this company proposed paying only 1.3 million *l.t.* for the first 13 months (September 1721–September 1722), 1.8 million for the second year, 2.5 million for the third year and 3 million each for the last six years.

The only opposition to these arrangements came from an anonymous projector who claimed to be *au fait* with the tobacco farm but whose writings in fact reveal no inside knowledge of the workings of the monopoly. He sent a long memoir to the *intendant des finances* de Gaumont, with a précis for the controller-general, attacking the management of the farm by Dupleix under the company, and calling for a three-year *régie* (contractual administration on crown account) so that the ministers could find out how much the monopoly was really worth.[3] As it was obvious that the government was determined to farm, a rival offer was evoked from a "company of Ruminet" in which the anonymous projector appears to have been interested. This group at first offered only a slightly higher price for the first three years: 2.1 million for the first and second years, and three million for the third. In addition, they offered to pay all net earnings to the crown, reserving for themselves only a commission of 15 percent on the profits. This was really another *régie,* though for a longer period and in a slightly riskier form.[4] When it became apparent that this scheme too had no chance, essentially the same group came forward with a proposition for an ordinary farm at a still higher price: 2.1 million each for the first and second years, 2.8 for the third, and 3.5 for the last six, with a bonus of 3.5 million if guaranteed the contract for the full nine years. This came to 28 million for the nine years, or 31.5 with the bonus, compared to only 23.6 for the proposal of the Dupleix company.[5] There is no indication, however, that these offers were ever seriously considered. In fact, many of the projector's associates refused to let their names be given to the council because they felt sure the offer had no chance.[6]

The projector complained in his memoirs that he lacked the support at court which the Dupleix company enjoyed. He also seemed to lack much support in the Paris financial community. This apparently meant a lack of capital, for in his various schemes he called for selling receivers' and controllers' places in the monopoly to raise working capital. His "company of Ruminet" described itself as consisting of "good merchants of La Rochelle, Bordeaux, St. Malo, Nantes and Lille, and other hard workers who know the management of that farm in depth." This string of cities suggests the directors of the Indies Company in Law's time, as well as the syndics elected by the shareholders in January 1721 and the commissioners appointed to administer the company in April. It also suggests in particular the "company of Paris and St. Malo" (whose Paris members were the bankers the Bertrand brothers and Pierre DuMolin) which had tried to bid for the monopoly in the spring of 1718. Common members of these overlapping groups were to remain interested in bidding for the farm for some time.

In the end, after relatively brief negotiations and without any public invitation for bids, the monopoly was by the lease and *résultat du conseil* of 19 August 1721 granted on the recommendation of the all powerful Paris brothers to the Dupleix company under the name of Edouard du Verdier for nine years and one month at the price offered.[7] This lease at a low price rising only to three million in the fourth year caused more scandal than any other lease in the history of the tobacco farm, not excepting the unhappy Filtz lease of 1714. It was not simply that Law had bid four millions in 1718: nothing that Law had done could be cited as a precedent in 1721. It was rather that well-informed persons knew that others, even the old Maynon-Bernard company, had been prepared to go to four million in 1718 and that the Indies Company had not lost on its four million price in 1718–19. Even those less well informed could guess what was up. There were rumors that the Paris brothers had taken a *croupe* or "cut," i.e., a secret share.[8] Dutot, rather better informed, reported that they had not taken a share but had reserved for themselves the exclusive contract to buy all the foreign tobacco for the monopoly in England at a commission of 3 percent.[9] Others had it that Madame de Prie had received a pension on this farm and had wisely insisted that it be paid to her seven years in advance.[10]

Paris Duverney later defended himself against the attacks of Dutot and others by insisting that the lease of 1721 was only intended to last until the monopoly was firmly and soundly reestablished.[11] That claim makes a certain amount of sense, though it is hard to make it gibe with the exceptionally long, nine-year contract. It was realized at the time that the secret granting of the du Verdier lease without public invitations for bids would cause a scandal and the preamble devoted several pages to explaining the reasons for this procedure. The public was informed that the combination of free internal trade and monopoly of importation established in October 1720 had been a failure. The Indies Company had not imported tobacco on its own account or established warehouses in the principal ports as it was supposed to do, but had simply sold licenses to private merchants to import. So much tobacco had either been smuggled in after the tobacco monopoly was separated from the united farms in January 1721 and left defenseless, or had been legally imported in the open trade and license periods that it would be years before the monopoly could be made effective again. The new company would also have to pay treble prices buying tobacco abroad due to the existing unfavorable exchanges. The annual rents were described as very favorable compared to those of the Filtz lease of 1714; they could not be compared to the Ladmiral (Occident Company) lease of 1718 because the latter was made on commercial rather than fiscal principles; that is, Law's company bid for the lease at a losing price in order to develop the trade of Louisiana! The lease was being made secretly, even before the terms of the *déclaration* of 1 August had been made public, in order that private traders and manufacturers would not be forewarned and conceal their tobacco.[12]

The reasons given in the preamble were all factual and plausible, except that most persons then and subsequently did not believe that the Indies Company had actually lost money on its 4.02 million monopoly lease during 1718–19. Even strong critics of the Dupleix-du Verdier lease did not deny, though, that the originally profitable tobacco monopoly had become a loss for the Indies Company by 1720–21. Granted that the shaken company did not have the hard cash to buy tobacco abroad and to reestablish the manufacturing and distribution network in France, there still remained the question of whether the crown could have gotten better terms than those in the du Verdier lease. Some at least thought that the government should have tried a *régie* either for nine years (the Ruminet scheme) or for at least three years in order to find out empirically what tobacco could yield.[13] The award to the Dupleix company was, however, made so quickly and quietly that memoir writers never really got a chance to discuss the alternatives.

Who were the company set up by the Paris brothers under the name of Edouard du Verdier? In the days of the Bernard-Crozat-Maynon company, the identity of the partners had been something of a secret. There was no secret about the new company; their names and addresses, following the new custom of publicity introduced for the united farms in 1704 and for most everything else in Law's time, were published on *arrêts*[14] and in the *Almanach Royal*:[15] they were the *sieurs* Bonnevie, Ralet de Challet, de la Gombaude, de Vitry, Dupleix, Du Vau de Rosnay, Gallet, Girard de Bussou, Lallemant de Betz, Moufle de la Tuillerie, Le Franc de Brunpré, and Pingault. All these names do not convey very much, for they were, taken as a whole, a rather obscure lot. There were no Samuel Bernards or Antoine Crozats in this company, although Lallemant de Betz and Bonnevie were as well known as Thomé or the Le Gendre.

The company was to a certain degree an assembly of technicians, giving some semblance to the claims of Paris Duverney that its task was primarily organizational. Of these technicians, we have already mentioned François Dupleix, a man who was to devote virtually his entire professional life to the tobacco monopoly. A person who was probably a protégé of Dupleix was Jean Pingault. In 1719–20, he was head of the *bureau* of the Indies Company for the *domaine d'Occident*, at a time when Dupleix was head of the equivalent *bureau* for the tobacco monopoly. In 1720–21, in the last months before the suspension of the company, when Dupleix was promoted to director in charge of both *tabac* and *domaine d'Occident*, Pingault became *chef du bureau* for both those revenues. In 1720 he also became a partner in de Montigny & Co. which bought the large tobacco manufactories at Paris, Dieppe, and elsewhere from the Indies Company.[16] (He may also be the same Pingault who approached the government in 1712 with an offer for the tobacco monopoly.) [17] An equally obvious technician was Antoine de la Gombaude. Like Dupleix and others before him who had risen to important positions in the monopoly, he began in the company's service in Brittany. A native of Rennes, allegedly the son of a laundress, he started out as a boy in some lowly employment in the tobacco farm there, rose to become controller of the *bureau-général* at Rennes, then director of the monopoly in Brittany, finally director-general of the farm's main office in Paris. This was his first entry into high finance, though he was ultimately to become a farmer-general.[18] He was very close to the former tobacco farmer, Charles-Nicolas Barré,[19] who was in turn close to Paris Duverney, which may also help explain his elevation at this time. A possible further member of this Breton clique was Ralet de Chalet; he is probably the Antoine Ralet (subsequently de Chalet), farmer of the local taxes at Saint Brieuc in 1709;[20] either he or a son must be the Ralet de Chalet, merchant and slave-trader of Nantes, who was active with Paris de Montmartel and Dupleix's son, Dupleix de Bacquencourt, in the consolidation of two large slave-trading companies in 1750.[21] Another possible technician was DuVau de Rosnay of Moulins, the only member of the company not resident at Paris. Of him we know nothing.[22]

Others were more conventional figures in the world of royal finance. Barthélémy Moufle da la Tuillerie had been a most active office-jobber of the last years of the reign of Louis XIV, taxed 60,000 *l.t.* by the Chamber of Justice in 1717. His other interests extended to the Hungarian copper manufacture at St. Denis.[23] De Vitry and Gallet had been minor members of the old Bernard-Maynon tobacco company, de Vitry from 1709, Gallet from 1715. De Vitry had also been a farmer-general of the united farms from 1709 until 1718.[24] Lallemant de Betz and Bonnevie were farmers-general of the newly reestablished united farms' *régie* (Cordier lease). Lallemant de Betz had become a farmer-general when his father resigned in the purge of the receivers-general in 1717. He had been temporarily out under the Paris brothers and Law, but was to live to see them all dead or exiled and himself the senior farmer-general and one of those responsible for ultimately returning the tobacco monopoly to the united farms. As no friend of the Paris brothers, his presence in the company is probably ascribable to his family connection with the controller-general Le Pelletier de la Houssaye.[25] Jean Bonnevie (1662–1733), the son of a Paris jeweller, had been sufficiently active in a great variety of farms, subfarms, and *traites* to have been taxed 100,000 *l.t.* by the Chamber of Justice in 1716.[26] He first became a farmer-general under the Paris brothers in 1718–19; he returned to that company on its reestablishment in 1721 and remained in it until his death.[27]

And finally there were the hangers-on. Jean-Gerard Le Franc de Brunpré, the son of a director of the mint at Reims, had had an obscure career as a government official and minor *traitant:* he was assessed only 22,500 *l.t.* by the Chamber of Justice in 1717. He could only owe his inclusion to his place as *secrétaire des comptes et deniers* to the duke of Bourbon.[28] An even more striking case was that of Martin Girard de Bussou. Through the influence of his brother, who was *secrétaire des commandements* to the same duke, he obtained places in the tobacco farm and subsequently in the united farms; he was dismissed from the latter by Cardinal Fleury at the renewal of the united farms' lease in 1726 when clients of the exiled duke of Bourbon were proscribed. He was not active in management, but signed everything that was put in front of him.[29] There is, of course, also the possibility that some of the more obscure members of the du Verdier company may in whole or in part have been standing in for more prominent figures like the Paris brothers or Bernard. (Just as earlier the capital for Pellard's share in the united farms had been supplied by Bernard.)

On 1 September 1721, when the new tobacco monopoly company doing business under the name of Edouard du Verdier started operations, it faced a most difficult task. It had to buy tobacco, acquire and equip manufacturing establishments, set up an administrative and policing apparatus,[30] and end the activities of all the merchants and dealers who had sprung into activity during the fifteen months of effective open trade (1 June 1720–31 August 1721). The task of the new company was made simpler by article xvii in the *déclaration* of 1 August 1721[31] and article iv in their lease of 19

August[32] which gave them preemptive rights on all buildings used as manufactories, storehouses, or offices by the previous monopoly. Many of these buildings, including the manufactories at Paris and Dieppe, had been acquired by Jean Maurice de Montigny & Co. (in which firm one of the new company—Pingault—had been interested); that firm now had no option but to sell out to the new du Verdier monopoly on du Verdier's terms.[33] (The new company by article xii of the lease also assumed the obligation to supply the troops with *tabac de cantine* at the old low price of 12s. per lb. and without the subsidy which the government had granted to de Montigny & Co. in 1720.)[34] These transactions gave the reestablished company a skeleton structure at once, including workshops and offices.

Much more serious were the host of small manufacturers and unlicensed dealers that had sprung up during the open months. (Private manufacture had of course also been tolerated in the southwestern growing regions since the establishment of the monopoly in 1674.) All private manufacture was now to cease on 1 September 1721 when all such establishments were to be inventoried and their tobacco and tools transferred to sealed warehouses. Henceforth any form of private manufacture, even the possession of tools by retailers or anyone else, was prohibited. The old manufacturers could sell their equipment to the new monopoly or export it; they and anyone else possessing unmanufactured tobacco could also sell it to the same monopoly or export it. The new du Verdier company did not, however, have the resources or the inclination to buy up all the manufactured tobacco in the country (which they would only have to resell again in any event). Thus the *déclaration* and the lease permitted wholesale traders and retailers to retain and continue trading in their manufactured tobacco subject to the payment of a *droit de marque*. On 1 September 1721, all manufactured tobacco in the hands of private traders was to be reported and inventoried and taxed and stamped or marked with the seal of the new company indicating that the tax had been paid. Tobacco so marked could be traded freely; any sold not so marked was to be confiscated and its vendors fined 1,000 *l.t.* If the trader was not in a position to pay the *droit de marque* on all his tobacco at once, or if some of it was in bulk and not in a condition to be marked, it could be placed in sealed warehouses until the duty was paid and the marks affixed. The tariff of the *droit de marque* was to be: 7s.6d. per lb. on ordinary manufactured tobacco; 10s. per lb. on most snuffs; and 20s. per lb. on Spanish snuff of first quality. Once this duty had been paid and the tobacco marked, unrestricted right of sale, wholesale and retail, was promised.[35]

We are told that the *droit de marque* proved very profitable for the du Verdier company and its members.[36] It is obvious that it would have provided them with a large cash income in the opening months of their lease without their first having had to spend any funds of their own on tobacco, tools, etc. Nevertheless, in the longer run it proved rather complicated to administer. Implicit in it were obvious facilities for fraud. The former manufacturers and wholesalers interpreted the *déclaration* of 1 August 1721 as giving an indefinite right of sale and resale. The farm maintained that the right of sale was a special exemption from the general monopoly, accorded only to those who had paid the *droit de marque*. Litigation ensued till compromised by an *arrêt du conseil* of 10 March 1722: the right of sale was in general confined to those who had paid the *droit de marque;* however, a manufacturer or wholesaler paying it could obtain up to six *permissions* (depending on how much tobacco he had declared) transferring this right of sale to retailers who bought tobacco from him. The *permissions* could be renewed by the wholesaler but could not be transferred to a third person by the retailer.[37] In this way, the monopoly kept track of every pound of tobacco which had paid the *droit de marque* until it passed into the consumer's pocket, or was exported. These and later analagous rules were particularly hard on the larger dealers of Tonneins in the old growing region of Guienne, four of whom held 600,000 lb. of superior roll tobacco. The new monopoly was probably being consciously difficult with them (even though they were protected by the intendant Boucher) in order to force them to export their great stocks. For the same reasons, the monopoly insisted on keeping their buying and selling prices of Guienne tobacco artificially low.[38]

Difficulties thus continued between the monopoly and the private traders winding up. An *arrêt* of 15 September 1722,[39] similarly motivated, provided that dealers must take their tobacco out of the sealed warehouses and pay duty in not more than six installments; freedom of transit for private tobacco was confirmed subject to the usual passes, but private dealers were prohibited from charging more than the maximum prices for tobacco established in the *déclaration* of 1 August 1721. All these rules were of course designed to bring more pressure to export upon the merchants with the big stocks of Guienne tobacco who were keeping its price above the 25s. per lb. retail limit. The efforts of the intendant on behalf of the big Tonneins merchants were of no avail.[40] Ultimately, on grounds that the tobacco was spoiling in storage, an *arrêt* of 4 September 1723 suppressed the *droit de marque* on all tobacco still in the sealed warehouses and gave its proprietors four months to export it.[41]

Article xv of the lease of 19 August 1721 gave to the company under the name of Edouard du Verdier the right to subfarm any portion of their monopoly.[42] This was to be the last time in the history of the French tobacco monopoly that subletting was practiced. Only one subfarm was made, but it was a large one: Provence, Dauphiné, Lyonnais, Languedoc, and Roussillon were sublet for the nine years of the parent lease to a company under the name of Jean-Baptiste Tournelles. Of its seven known shareholders, four (de Nesle, Dupré de Plaisance, de Maugin, and Dorlyé) had been partners in the interregnum firm, de Montigny & Co. One of the remaining three, Berger de Fontigny is probably the François Berger who had been interested in the subfarm for Provence before 1718 and had for a few months in 1718–19 been an expert director of Law's company, along with Paris Duverney.[43]

The Tournelles subfarm seems to have met more resistance in reestablishing the monopoly than did the du Verdier national company. Despite the fact that article vi of the lease of 19 August 1721 provided that, in return for the 100,000 *l.t.* paid the united farms as before, the tobacco monopoly would be exempt from all duties and tolls on the transit of its goods, various local authorities tried to collect tolls (*octrois*) from the Tournelles company. An *arrêt* of 2 January 1722 ordered the magistrates of troublesome Toulouse to desist from such demands;[44] a more general *arrêt* of 20 February 1722 extended this prohibition to all other authorities.[45] The most serious problems came in Provence, in no mood to be cooperative after its traumatic experience of the plague of 1720–21. Merchants in Marseilles and elsewhere had in Law's time gotten rid of their *billets de banque* by buying up large quantities of tobacco from the Indies Company and the growers of the southwest. Tournelles estimated that they had stock on hand in late 1721 equivalent to five years' consumption in the province. To enable them to sell this tobacco, the Provençal merchants did everything in their power to delay the return of the monopoly. According to the Tournelles company, a conspiracy was formed in pursuance of which two persons brought some defective tobacco into the *cour des aides* at Aix, alleging that it had been purchased from the monopoly. On the basis of this questionable evidence, the court on 3 February 1722 appointed commissioners to inspect all the tobacco on the premises of the Tournelles company within its jurisdiction, although such an inspection was clearly illegal under the precedents of the old monopoly. The commissioners found all the tobacco satisfactory except for one parcel of 350 lb. of cheap snuff (called *briailles*). This allegedly had foreign matter in it, although the Tournelles company claimed that it had been purchased as made from "pure Virginia stems" only. It was part of 47,000 lb. of the same obtained from a Marseilles merchant named Fiquet at the start of their lease to tide them over till their own manufactories came into operation. By an *arrêt* of 3 June 1722, the case was transferred to the Council of State where nothing more was heard of it. In the meantime, however, the reputation of the new company had been damaged by wild stories about impurities.[46]

In a more flagrant case, a Marseilles merchant named François Ricfaux got a series of orders in the spring of 1722 from the *procureur* of the maritime court of Marseilles, in the absence of the judge, ordering the Tournelles company to let him, Ricfaux, take his tobacco out of the sealed warehouse when and as he pleased and permitting him to sell it with the court's mark if Tournelles would not mark it for him. Another *arrêt* from the Council of State was needed to make the king's attorney at Marseilles obey the law.[47]

After a year or so of such travail, the monopoly was effectively reestablished, to the evident satisfaction and profit of its farmers and subfarmers. Their good fortune was not, however, to go unobserved.

The Return of the Indies Company, 1723-30

The circumstances under which the Édouard du Verdier company had received its lease of the tobacco monopoly in 1721 were exceptional: the political and financial worlds were reeling from the fall of Law and the collapse of the "System"; the Indies Company was in receivership and thus was incapable of the investment and administrative exertion necessary to reestablish the tobacco monopoly. From the first, however, the du Verdier company obviously realized that these extraordinary conditions would not last indefinitely and that it was extremely likely that efforts would be made to break its nine-year lease before very many of those years had run. To protect itself against alterations in the terms of its farm, the company had inserted into the lease itself various special protective clauses. We have already mentioned the proviso that if tobacco cultivation was restored, the price of their lease was to be reduced 500,000 l.t. annually.[48] They were also protected against war, plague, famine or alterations in the metallic equivalent of the *livre* of account.[49] The sureties of du Verdier, their subfarmers, agents, and employees were all "never to be subject to any investigation by a Chamber of Justice or to be assessed" for their earnings under that lease or its subleases.[50] Finally, the lease was not to be broken before its termination—but, if it should be, the du Verdier company was to be compensated by their successors 200,000 l.t. annually for as many years as their lease still had to run.[51] These unprecedented clauses all suggest the extreme skepticism with which those doing business with the government regarded royal promises in 1721. Such skepticism was to be well justified in the case of the du Verdier company.

The political situation began to change almost at once. In April 1722, the controller-general, Le Pelletier de la Houssaye, resigned because of ill health and died the next year. His behavior and attitude in 1721 gave him the reputation of an implacable foe of the Indies Company. His post was offered to but declined by Louis Fagon, another member of that group of high financial officials around Argenson who had resigned or were dismissed when Law returned temporarily in June 1720. The position thus went to Charles Gaspard Dodun (subsequently marquis of Herbault), grandson of the 1674 tobacco farmer, Gaspard Dodun. Dodun d'Herbault was one of the weaker figures to hold that high office, seeming to contemporaries to list as court winds blew.[52] The office itself seemed comtemptible by having changed hands four times in two years. The political situation was further complicated in February 1723 when Louis XV turned thirteen and officially came of age. The Regency was over, but the duke of Orléans continued as first minister.

Orléans himself was regarded by contemporaries as one who in his heart of hearts remained secretly a friend to Law and his "System." Perhaps Law thought so, for he never attacked or exposed the Regent, even after the latter's death. After the Regent, the most important friend the Indies Company had in the next few years was Paris Duverney. Though an implacable foe of Law and anything that smacked of the "System," he seemed genuinely to have had the interests of the company at heart. The shareholders recognized both his concern and his influence by electing him in 1724 *syndic général* or their chief spokesman. He and his brother Montmartel had acquired large concessions in Louisiana and were to show themselves actively interested in the affairs of the company and colony during 1723-26.

The commissioners of council who had been appointed in April 1721 to investigate the affairs of the Indies Company and settle its accounts with the government completed their work in March 1723. It was decided at the highest levels of state to let the company continue not merely in a solvent condition but with some regular assured income, other than its trading prospects, that would give the much squeezed shareholders some assurance of dividends. Therefore all that the company owed the state on account of the bank was allowed to be canceled out by all that the state owed the company for debts assumed. This left the state owing the company only the original 100 million capital of the Occident Company subscribed in *billets d'état* and converted in 1718-19 into formal contracts of perpetual state annuities (*rentes*) at 4 percent. By the *arrêt* of 19 September 1719, these *rentes* were supposed to have been surrendered and new ones constituted at 3 percent. Law apparently never carried out the letter of that *arrêt* and simply reduced the interest payments to the company to 3 percent without surrendering the old contracts assignable on the tobacco farm. Therefore, the company alone of the mass of state creditors was still in possession of pre-"System" (i.e., pre-August 1719) contracts of state *rentes* which the ministry now proposed to honor as a means towards reestablishing the company and its credit.[53]

The reestablishment and reorganization of the Indies Company were effected by a series of *arrêts du conseil* on 22-24 March 1723. One *arrêt* of 22 March reorganized the capital structure of the company at 56,000 shares (of 2,000 *l.t.* par).[54] Another of the same date announced that since the Indies Company was now in a position to settle its accounts with the state, the king saw fit to restore to it its property including the three million *l.t.* per annum which had been alienated to it by the contracts of 1718-19 as interest on the 100 millions which it had lent the state and for the payment of which the revenue from the tobacco farm had been pledged. Since the tobacco monopoly itself had originally been granted in 1718 as security for those payments, the king could think, the *arrêt* stated, of no better way to assure these payments for the future than by regranting to the Indies Company the tobacco monopoly itself. The king therefore transferred the tobacco monopoly to the Indies Company from 1 October 1723 on the same terms as that under which the du Verdier company then leased it. The king would, however, deem the monopoly as the equivalent of only 2.5 million *l.t.* p.a. (its price during the third year of the du Verdier lease starting the next 1 October) and would make other arrangements to pay the Indies Company the remaining 500,000 *l.t.* p.a. which was once more owing to it.[55] The next day (23 March 1723) an *arrêt* was issued granting to the Indies Company the revenues of the *domaine d'Occident* to make up the remaining 500,000 *l.t.* of the full three million p.a.[56]

Paris Duverney is generally thought to have been the guiding spirit behind these new arrangements. The evaluation of the tobacco monopoly at the low figure of 2.5 million p.a. was fully consistent with his arguments since 1718 that the revenue possibilities of the farm were quite limited. Should it produce more, his error would of course be the greatest of favors to the Indies Company.

On 24 March, the important *arrêt*[57] was issued reorganizing the Indies Company and fixing its dividends at nil for 1721, 100 *l.t.* per share for 1722 and 150 *l.t.* per share for 1723. If the financial details discussed above reflect the influence of Paris Duverney, the new organization on the Spanish model was thought to mirror the statist proclivities of Cardinal Dubois, whose influence, since Law's departure, had emanated outward from foreign affairs to embrace the general operation of the government. He now gave the company a Council of the Indies with himself as head (*chef*) and the controller-general Dodun as president; of the twenty councillors, ten only would be businessmen, the other ten officials: two councillors of state (Fagon and de Fortas), four masters of requests and four naval officials. This council suggested only a very limited continuity of management: one of the masters of requests (Peirenc de Moras), alone of the twenty, had been elected a syndic by the shareholders at the only previous election in January 1721; two of the merchant members (Baillon de Blancpignon and J. B. Duché) had been among the special commissioners charged with the management of the company during the receivership; only three of the merchant members had been in the last regular board of September 1720. For some purposes, the official members of the council were to meet separately as the First Bureau and the merchant members as the Second Bureau; for other they were to meet together.

Although it was hoped and expected that the favorable dispositions of the government towards the company announced in March would silence critics and lead to a rise in the value of the company's shares, this did not in fact take place. Investors were suspicious of and shareholders antagonistic to the heavy official representation in the management of the company. Nothing was done to implement the transfer of the tobacco monopoly from the du Verdier company to the Indies Company. In the event, the death of Cardinal Dubois was to render the March settlement stillborn, with all details to be worked out afresh.

Cardinal Dubois died on 10 August 1723, making the former Regent, the duke of Orléans, first minister in fact as well as in name. Five days later, on 15 August, Paris Duverney submitted a memorandum suggesting major alterations in the organization of the company adopted in March, alterations in the direction both of greater centralization and greater shareholder participation. In a somewhat watered down version, Paris Duverney's suggestions were adopted by an *arrêt* of 30 August 1723. The duke of Orléans became titular governor and the duke of Bourbon titular vice-governor of the company, the controller-general remaining president. At the effective level, the ten official councillors were replaced by four official *inspecteurs* who, precisely because they were given no departmental duties within the company, became its policy-makers and coordinators. (In 1730, one *commissaire-général* was substituted for the four inspectors, as originally suggested by Paris Duverney.) The shareholders were to elect five or six syndics, also with general supervisory powers, but less effective than the royal inspectors. In addition, there were to be twelve directors charged with the administration of the twelve commercial departments of the company and eight separate directors who were to be responsible for the tobacco monopoly. These were to be initially named by the king, but thereafter elected by the shareholders.[58] The next day, 31 August, the coffee monopoly was given to the company in place of the *domaine d'Occident* promised in March but never conveyed.[59] This was to make up the 500,000 *l.t.* between the 2.5 million at which the tobacco monopoly was evaluated and the three million annually which the king now owed the company.

The next few days were to be equally busy ones for Paris Duverney and the tobacco monopoly. The former now saw his opportunity to put the affairs of both the monopoly and the company on so secure a footing that the normal upheavals of the court could not shake them. The simple arrangement promised in March by which the Indies Company was to have the tobacco monopoly for 2.5 million annually was now abandoned. By an *arrêt* of 1 September 1723, it was ordered that commissioners of council be named (as they were by letters-patent of the same day) to transfer the tobacco monopoly forever from the crown to the Indies Company. In return the crown was to be quit of ninety millions of its hundred million debt to the company. Ninety of the hundred annuity contracts (of one million capital value each) made in 1718–19 were to be canceled, but ten were to remain in force. In practice this meant that the crown was letting the company have the tobacco monopoly indefinitely for 2.7 million yearly (the interest on 90 millions at 3 percent.[60] It was later assumed that this contract meant that if the king wanted to break this "perpetual" grant, he would have to pay back the ninety millions in one lump sum.[61] In French court finance, nothing was quite that clear.

This was followed on 6 September by an *arrêt* which finally broke the lease to the du Verdier company, threatened since March.[62] No mention was made of the 200,000 *l.t.* p.a. compensation which the du Verdier company could have claimed under its 1721 lease. The next day, 7 September, a further *arrêt* was issued which named the eight special directors of the Indies Company charged with the administration of the tobacco monopoly: Bonnevie, de la Gombaude, Begon, Berlan, Nicolas, Luillier, Girard, and Laugeois.[63] Three of these—Bonnevie, de la Gombaude, and Girard (de Bussou)—had been partners in the outgoing du Verdier company and were thus taken care of by Paris Duverney or their other protectors. Nicolas is probably Jean Nicolas, a former partner of Samuel Bernard, who was also being taken care of.[64] Michel Begon the younger, from an important administrative family related to Colbert, had been a great *traitant* and army contractor during the War of the Spanish Succession.[65] He subsequently lost heavily in the North African trade and was in reduced circumstances by 1716. An early subscriber to the Occident Company, he took no part in its management in Law's time. In April 1721, he had nonetheless been named one of the five merchant commissioners to run the company during its receivership. He belonged to the clientèle of the Paris and of Mme de Prie, whose brother had married his daughter.[66] Claude Luillier had also been a big *traitant* and army victualling contractor during the same war, usually in partnership with Berthelot Duchy, the uncle of Mme de Prie.[67] Both he and Berlan were members of the original bidding company of 1714-15 that tried unsuccessfully to get the tobacco monopoly away from the Bernard-Maynon company. Berlan, of whom nothing else is known, was still in the bidding company in 1717.[68] Jean-Baptiste Laugeois had been a petty *traitant* taxed 10,000 *l.t.* by the Chamber of Justice in 1716. In 1717, he suddenly sprang to inexplicable importance when he became a farmer-general at a time when many of the old farmers-general were forced out because they were also receivers-general or interested in other farms. He was continued by the Paris brothers (1718-19) and by Law (1719-21).[69] He may well have been a technician advanced for his administrative abilities.

As of 11 September, letters-patent had yet to be registered, sealed or even drawn on either the original *arrêt* of 22 March 1723 granting the tobacco monopoly to the Indies Company or the new *arrêt* of 1 September alienating it forever for a capital sum of ninety millions. Nevertheless, on that day, an interim *arrêt* was issued for the Indies Company to take possession of the monopoly on 1 October under the name of Pierre Le Sueur. Sales prices and other technical terms were specified similar to those prevailing in the revoked du Verdier lease.[70] This is the only occasion in the history of the tobacco monopoly in which the farm was transferred without mention of a formal lease (*bail*) or a confirmatory *résultat du conseil*.

Only at this point in time does what was happening to the tobacco farm seem to have become general knowledge. During the next week, there was an intense effort to upset these arrangements. It would seem that Dodun the controller-general suddenly realized that under the terms of the *arrêt* of 1 September, the Indies Company was likely to make millions annually above the 2.7 million (90 million capital at 3 percent) at which the farm was officially valued at its alienation. On the twelfth, he brought forward a company that offered to bid six million p.a. for the monopoly; as one contemporary understood it, three million of this would go to the Indies Company and three million to the crown.[71] Dutot later suggested that the very people who had been interested in the underpriced du Verdier lease of 1721 may have also been behind this six million offer.[72] This could hardly have been true of Bonnevie, de la Gombaude, and Girard, who went from the du Verdier company to the Indies Company on 7 September to run the tobacco monopoly. It may very well have been true, though, of other important figures in the du Verdier company, particularly the farmer-general Lallemant de Betz and the expert manager Dupleix, who were left out of Paris Duverney's new arrangements.

One contemporary heard that the six million offer came from "le sieur de Meuve et le sieur Bertrand, banquiers de Languedoc."[73] He was obviously not familiar with the Paris financial community, for the individuals named were well-known Paris bankers only one of whom, Bertrand, had a Languedoc background. More important for our purposes, these names evoke the whole history of the leading element in the succession of bidding companies that had been trying to get the monopoly since the last days of Louis XIV. In the formal submission of an offer made by the *avocat* Girardin in January 1715, the first three names on his list were: Bertrand *frères*, DuMolin, and Demeuves *fils*, though the name of Demeuves *fils* was crossed out without explanation.[74] In the submission made in March 1717 for the derivative company sponsored by the duke of St. Simon, the first five names were: Rouillé de Péray, Bertrand *frères*, DuMolin, Cadet, and Demeuves.[75] In the Paris-St. Malo-Lyons company that bid in April 1718, the Paris members were Bertrand & Co. and Pierre DuMolin.[76] (DuMolin was related to Demeuves.) We have already stated our suspicions that the same elements may have been behind the unsuccessful Ruminet company of 1721.[77]

Both the Bertrand and Demeuves families were originally Huguenots. The Bertrand brothers and their father, all originally from Montpellier, protected their protestantism by moving temporarily to Geneva and acquiring citizenship there in 1704;[78] the Demeuves of Paris became nominally conforming "new Catholics."[79] Both were outsiders in another way, perhaps more important in 1723. They were not part of the Paris or Bernard clientèle that seemed to be so helpful at this time.[80] The Demeuves would seem to have been on bad terms with Samuel Bernard ever since the failure of the elder Demeuves, a great Paris banker, in 1705. The younger Demeuves had also been an early subscriber to Law's company[81] who had never withdrawn. The Bertrand brothers were part of the circle about François-Marie Fargès, the great victualling contractor of the last years of the war and implacable foe of the Paris brothers.[82] Fargès had also been in Law's company from the beginning.[83] When, after Law's flight, the shareholders of the Indies Company were for the first time permitted to elect spokesmen, they chose on 2 January 1721 eight syndics who included Fargès, his son-in-law Abraham Peirenc de Moras, his former business associates Antoine Bertrand and

Pierre Cavalier, plus Demeuves.[84] When the Paris brothers organized the receivership of the Indies Company in April 1721, these syndics had been ignored, but the managing commissioners then selected by the government, if they included none of the Fargès circle, did include Demeuves' kinsman Pierre DuMolin.

The Demeuves-Bertrand-Fargès group, though excluded from power in the Indies Company and the tobacco farm, kept up their pressure on the Paris brothers' settlement. In 1722, Demeuves presented the new controller-general Dodun with a proposal for a bank![85] In 1723, one of them (probably Demeuves) wrote to Fleuriau d'Arménonville (Keeper of the Seals since the death of Argenson in 1722) about the lack of recognition he had received from the state. He had helped restore French trade to China but had been squeezed out by Law; he had formed a company in Louis XIV's time to bid for the tobacco monopoly; the company was well on its way to success until also squeezed out by Law. He solicited the support of the Keeper in this latest struggle.[86] Nevertheless, the struggle was once more in vain. The generally understood support of the duke of Orléans for the Indies Company as well as the specific support of the duke of Bourbon for Paris Duverney could not be overcome. After a hidden struggle of a few days, the decision was rendered public on 17 September when the duke of Orléans and the duke of Bourbon attended the general meeting of the shareholders called to elect five syndics. The prime minister announced that the king would confirm the monopolies of tobacco and coffee which he had granted to the Indies Company.[87] Nevertheless, the opposition had its consolation, four out of five of the syndics chosen at the election that same day had been among those elected in the Fargès sweep of January 1721: Demeuves, Bertrand, Cavalier, and Saintard.[88] That Demeuves and Bertrand were elected suggests that a majority of the shareholders felt that it would have been better for the Indies Company to subfarm the tobacco monopoly for a high rent rather than try to manage it itself. The election of this hostile board of syndics was partly balanced in the spring, after the death of the duke of Orléans, when Paris Duverney was elected *syndic-général* (15 March 1724).

Although a consciousness of the six million offer hung in the air for the next few years,[89] the matter seemed settled for the moment by the duke of Orléans' announcement of 17 September. The directors of the Indies Company charged with the administration of the tobacco monopoly felt relieved enough to boast that they would eventually get their monopoly to yield fourteen or fifteen million a year to the company, whose shares rose from 900 *l.t* in the summer to 1,400 *l.t.* by 30 September. Only that perpetual Cassandra, the defeated and excluded Jean-Baptiste Duché, warned, against the huzzas of profit, that the dividends fixed in March were too high and would embarrass the company.[90]

At the technical level, the *cour des aides* by an order of 23 September 1723 permitted Pierre Le Sueur (i.e., the Indies Company) to assume the monopoly on 1 October while granting "him" till 1 December to have the necessary letters-patent on the *arrêts* of March and September registered.[91] (For reasons unknown but suggesting hidden opposition, these letters-patent were not actually registered in the *cour des aides* until 1726 and were never registered in the *chambre des comptes*.) On 25 October, the company named nine of its directors[92] as special deputies to contract with the commissioners of council[93] named on 1 September for the alienation of the monopoly. The contract transferring the tobacco monopoly to the Indies Company "forever" was passed before notaries on 19 November 1723.[94]

The restoration of the Indies Company to some degree of prosperity through the regranting of the tobacco monopoly in September 1723 provided the solid fact that gave verisimilitude to all sorts of rumors in the next few months of new schemes afoot, including banks, paper money, and even the recall of Law.[95] There was some truth to the stories of a new bank[96] and perhaps even some basis to that about Law. However substantial the rumors, they were all rendered empty by the sudden death of the duke of Orléans in December 1723. This unexpected event dashed forever the hopes of Arménonville and any other defenders of the "System" in the government of returning to an adventurous financial policy. It meant the absolute triumph of Paris Duverney, for he had since 1721 attached himself firmly to the duke of Bourbon, who now became first minister, and to Mme de Prie, the duke's mistress, now mistress of France.

The duke and Mme de Prie were of such unconstant disposition that it was not at first evident that Paris Duverney would be able to preserve the new status of the tobacco monopoly and the Indies Company. During the financially difficult years 1724 and 1725, numerous memoirs were prepared attacking the company and the arrangements of September 1723.[97] To counter this attack, a number of carefully thought out measures were taken to strengthen the company in fact and in the public's eye. On 8 February 1724, an *arrêt* was issued permitting the company to send employees of the tobacco farm into the customs offices of the united farms to guard more effectively against tobacco smuggling.[98] On 25 April, an even more impressive *arrêt* was issued ordering the royal treasury to pay to the company 3.25 million *l.t.* for arrears on sums due the company on its old annuities contracts assigned against the royal income from the tobacco farm.[99]

In the early months of 1725, a number of expert memoirs were also prepared defending the company.[100] One of them pointed out that the company had raised the yield of the tobacco farm from 2.2 million to 4.02 million in 1718; it was now producing six millions for the company! Private farmers had ruined tobacco planting on St. Domingue and would be incapable of developing Louisiana. They might offer six millions but would find excuses not to fulfill their contracts because of alleged low consumption or high prices of raw materials or shipwrecks or whatnot.[101] Another memoir of the same months ably defended the principle of monopoly companies for overseas trade as in the best French tradition: when combined into one general company, the profitable trades like that to the East Indies could compensate for unprofitable ones like that of Louisiana. This memoir defended the retention of the tobacco monopoly by the Indies Company as an act of justice. Most of the shareholders in the company had not become so voluntarily, but had been forced into it by the various operations of the "System." Anything the company was making on the tobacco monopoly then would be only minor compensation for the vast sums which those shareholders had lost. Private merchants were not interested in sending their ships to Louisiana, but there was a good chance that within three or four years, the company would be able to supply all of France's tobacco needs from there, saving the country two millions yearly in foreign exchange.[102]

All these memoirs were conscious propaganda to procure from the government of the duke of Bourbon a formal statement confirming the privileges granted the company by the late duke of Orléans. The last memoir unambiguously stated that such a confirmation and good administration could raise to and maintain the price of shares in the company at between 2,000 and 3,000 *l.t.* The "perpetual and irrevocable" edict of confirmation was in the event issued in June 1725. Article v confirmed the concession of the Louisiana trade monopoly. Article vii reviewed the history of the company's first 100 million of capital and its relationship to the tobacco monopoly and confirmed the permanent grant of the monopoly. The king, it said, "recognized more and more that if the same capital of ninety millions, which is the patrimony of the shareholders, had remained in the commercial stock of the company, it would have produced much greater profits than can the monopoly of tobacco." Article viii stated that the tobacco monopoly belonged to the company "en pleine propriété" subject only to the limitation on prices to be charged. The enjoyment of that property required no *arrêt de prise de possession* such as was normally issued at the beginning of a revenue lease.[103]

This particular edict was one of a series of eight edicts and one *déclaration* issued simultaneously at the beginning of June 1725. Several of the other edicts affected the Indies Company, but the most unpopular items were those levying new taxes. The registration of the whole batch was refused by the *parlement* and required a *lit de justice*. That ceremony on 8 June may be held to mark the high point of the "post-System" of Paris Duverney, the duke of Bourbon and Mme de Prie.[104] A year later, on 28 May 1726, the letters patent were finally issued ordering the carrying out of the *arrêts* of 22 March and 1 September 1723 granting the tobacco monopoly to the Indies Company.[105] This three-year delay suggests that the arrangements of Paris Duverney were never quite as solidly founded as appearances would suggest.

The next day, 29 May 1726, the annual general meeting of the shareholders of the company was held: the official tone was optimistic. The company considered its assets to be 139 millions including 100 millions for the capital value of the king's engagements toward it. During the first year of the tobacco monopoly (October 1723–30 September 1724) the monopoly had produced 8.4 million for the company! This had dropped to 7,788,431 in the second year, 1724–25, but this was to be expected since in the first year they had extraordinary profits of 510,000 *l.t.* on the *tabacs de retrouve* in the hands of retailers and acquired by them from the outgoing farmers. Gross receipts for the first six months of the third year were above those of the preceding year. By contrast, the coffee monopoly had netted them only 182,993 *l.t.* The combined profits of the tobacco and coffee monopolies had not sufficed to pay the high dividend to which they were pledged (a dividend of 150 *l.t.* on 56,000 shares would require 8.4 million) but they had been able to use 1.2 million from their trading funds for this.[106]

Less than two weeks after this promising picture was painted, the whole political world was once more overturned. The king was now sixteen years old and beginning to have ideas of his own. He liked his cousin Bourbon as little as did the rest of France. On 11 June, the duke of Bourbon was dismissed as first minister and exiled from Paris. Within two days, Mme de Prie and the four Paris brothers were also to be exiled. (Mme de Prie committed suicide the next year midst the boredom of Normandy, but the brothers, particularly the two younger—Duverney and Montmartel—lived to fight another day.) Cardinal Fleury, the septuagenarian tutor of the king was now first minister in fact if not in name. The unpopular Dodun was dismissed as controller-general and replaced by Le Peletier Des Forts, nephew of the controller-general of the 1680's. At least one observer thought that the good old days had returned.[107]

In fact, the year 1726 marks a major turning point in French financial history, the end of a generation of chaos that had started during the War of the Spanish Succession. One of the last "achievements" of Paris Duverney had been an edict of January 1726 for a deflationary reminting which increased the metallic content of the *livre* of account. The long period of monetary fluctuations was over. From May 1726 until the French Revolution, the *livre tournois* was stable at between 24 and 25 to the pound sterling. State revenues were also put on a more stable basis that year. One of the first actions of the new Fleury-Des Forts financial administration was to restore the traditional operation of the united farms. For the greater part of the time since 1709, what were called the "united farms" had not in fact been farmed at all; the company of the United General Farms merely administered them for the government for a fee or commission. This was called a *régie* as opposed to a *ferme* in which the farmers took the risks and the profits. There was some opinion in France that that country had outgrown revenue farming and that a *régie* was intrinsically better than a *ferme*. However, to fiscal conservatives like Fleury and Des Forts, a *régie* was a confession of failure, a public admission that the finances of the country were so disordered that no responsible financiers were prepared to contract for their farming at a reasonable price. This general distaste for a *régie* was reinforced by the chaos and rumors of corruption and peculation that accompanied the actual administration of the *régie* during the Cordier lease (1721–26), particularly during the three year reign of Madame de Prie. A month after the fall of the duke of Bourbon, the Cordier lease was broken (9 July 1726); a month later (19 August), the company of the United General Farms signed the Carlier lease (1726–32) in which they agreed to take the united farms as a pure *ferme* at the unprecedentedly high but still safe price of 80 million *l.t.* annually. The orthodox regime thus restored to the united farms in 1726 remained essentially unchanged down to 1780.[108]

It was not at first apparent just what the banishment of the Paris brothers and the advent of the new conservative Fleury-Des Forts financial policy would mean for the Indies Company or the tobacco monopoly. The cautious nature of the new ministers as well as the close relations of many of them with Samuel Bernard[109] made it unlikely that there would be any sudden radical moves. On 26 August, the *cour des aides* decided to permit the registration on its records of the letters patent of 28 May which ordered the carrying out of the *arrêts* of 22 March and 1 September 1723 granting the tobacco monopoly to the Indies Company—but with the proviso that the letters patent should be observed only so long as the king judged it necessary because of his debt to the Indies Company; thereafter they hoped the king would farm the monopoly for his own advantage, since the profits which the Indies Company were then drawing from tobacco far exceeded any interest owing them by the king.[110] The ministry ignored for the time being the door thus left temptingly ajar by the *cour des aides*.

In 1725, there had been some minor changes in the structure of the Indies Company in which the number of directors in charge of the tobacco monopoly had been reduced from eight to five: Bonnevie, de la Gombaude, Begon, Luillier, Laugeois.[111] Those dropped (Berlan, Nicolas, and Girard de Bussou) were by all appearances "extra baggage," persons of no administrative or financial importance who had been originally included only as court favors. On 17 July 1726, following the political upheavals of June, the company was more seriously changed. The directors for commerce were reduced in number from twelve to eight, six of whom still went back to Law's time. The directors for the tobacco and coffee monopolies were reduced from five to four by dropping Bonnevie, *the last tie between the company and the united farms!* In place of the imprisoned Paris Duverney, the former director Le Cordier became a syndic (the other syndics being unchanged since 1723).[112] There were no further changes until 1728 when Begon (clearly also "extra weight") died and was replaced in the direction of the tobacco monopoly by Dupleix and Morel.[113] Morel is an unknown, entirely new to the higher administration of the tobacco monopoly and the Indies Company. Dupleix by contrast had been the administrative head of the monopoly under both Law and the du Verdier company until dropped by Paris Duverney in 1723. He now returned to his familiar work after the fall of the Paris. In the meantime, de la Gombaude had since 1723 become the administrative head of the monopoly.[114]

The only significant measure of legislation affecting the farm in the early years of Fleury's administration was an *arrêt* of 9 December 1727 which declared that the continued presence in retail shops of tobacco imported before 1721 and legitimized by the payment of the *droit de marque* could only be a cover for fraud. The *arrêt* ordered all such tobacco vended in from three to twelve months, or sold to the company or exported—thus ending the last traces of John Law's open trade experiment.[115]

Having survived the fall of the duke of Bourbon and the Paris brothers, the Indies Company can after 1726 be thought of as gradually becoming part of the accepted financial establishment of France. As such, it could be readily attacked but not easily vanquished except by a more powerful part of that establishment. The only such entity in France was now the United General Farms. The inherent hostility between the Indies Company and the farms was manifest in the complete absence, after Bonnevie's departure in 1726, of a single person who was both a farmer-general and a director or syndic of the company.

That the Indies Company stood off the imperialism of the united farms for four years is usually ascribed to the influence of Le Peletier Des Forts, the controller-general, both a conservative spirit and a consistent friend of the company. Cardinal Fleury was not obviously unfriendly to the company, but we are told that, after Des Forts, he was most influenced in financial matters by de la Porte, the head of the united farms.[116] Jean François de la Porte had succeeded his deceased father as farmer-general in 1695.[117] As such his own memory and personal experience went back to the days before 1697 when the tobacco monopoly had been part of the united farms. He and his brother, de la Porte de Feraucourt, also a farmer-general, had been dropped from the united farms in 1718–19 by the Paris brothers but were among the farmers-general whom Law brought into the directorship of the Indies Company in 1719–20. As such, he had further first hand knowledge of the tobacco monopoly at that critical time. Perhaps the next most important man in the united farms, actually the one who later succeeded de la Porte as head, was Lallemant de Betz. (Both represented the farms on the Council of Commerce.) He had succeeded his father, Charles Louis Lallemant, as farmer-general in 1717, had also been dropped by the Paris brothers in 1718 and been brought back by Law in 1719. As has already been discussed, he had obtained a share (probably through the influence of La Houssaye) in the du Verdier company of 1721–23 but was not continued by Paris Duverney in the tobacco monopoly management after the Indies Company took over in 1723.[118]

There were thus at the head of the united farms persons with a good knowledge of the tobacco monopoly. Other farmers-general were as well or better informed. Bonnevie had been in the du Verdier tobacco company, 1721–23 and had been a director of the Indies Company for tobacco from 1723 to 1726. Desvieux (also in the Council of Commerce) and Lalive de Bellegarde had been among the directors of the Indies Company responsible for the tobacco monopoly between October 1719 and its abolition in June 1720. P.-A. Chevalier had himself been briefly interested in the Bernard-Maynon tobacco monopoly company during 1703–9. Lalive, de July and Masson had been among the bidders for the tobacco farm during 1714–18. When the "forty thieves" met in conclave, there can be little wonder that their conversation turned to tobacco.

Nevertheless, the farmers-general, however anxious they might have been to take over tobacco, prudently held their fire until they could see victory. What ultimately seems to have given them their opportunity was the unsatisfactory financial condition of the Indies Company due to its overly generous dividends policy (the heritage of Paris Duverney's victory over J. B. Duché) and its failure to show any progress in the tobacco monopoly after the amazing first year. This last is quite evident in Table I.

TABLE I

Gross and Net Profits of the Indies Company from the Tobacco Monopoly
1 October 1723–30 September 1730

Year	Gross Profits[119]	Net Profits[120] (after losses from monetary deflation)
	l.t.	l.t.
1723–1724	8,400,000	7,914,735
1724–1725	7,788,431	7,358,313
1725–1726	7,898,505	6,914,171
1726–1727	7,014,648	6,905,227
1727–1728	7,338,239	7,125,672
1728–1729	7,502,979	6,832,704
1729–1730	7,079,862	7,033,145
Total	53,022,664	50,083,968
Average	7,574,666	7,154,853

It will be seen at a glance that the profits of the first year in both columns were never again realized during the succeeding six. Even if it is admitted in the company's defense that during the first year they had made a windfall profit on the *tabac de retrouve* (the tobacco in retailers' hands acquired at a low price from the outgoing farmers), this item came to only 510,000 *l.t.* in the accounts of the first year. Deducting it, the first year still stands above the succeeding. There are no signs of profit growth; assuming that consumption and sales were rising, a larger proportion of receipts was probably being absorbed by increasing expenditures on administration, guards and the like.

(Much of this of course duplicated the facilities of the united farms.) We also know that, thanks in part to very high leaf prices in 1725, the capital employed in the Indies Company's tobacco division (mostly stock on hand) was constantly rising:

31 January	1725	1,355,033[121]
22 April	1727	2,306,719[122]
30 April	1728	2,562,734[123]

None of this would have been too serious if the company had not been pledged to a high dividend policy. To pay 150 *l.t.* a year on 56,000 shares required 8.4 million in profits. In reestablishing the company in 1723, it had been hoped that the income from the tobacco and coffee monopolies (the latter quite small) [124] would be sufficient to pay the dividends, permitting the company to reinvest the profits from its trading activities in further expansion. Trading profits were not large because the gains in the East Indies trade were partly offset by losses in most of the other branches of trade, particularly that to Louisiana. With the receipts from the tobacco and coffee monopolies unable to meet the pledged dividends, the company had to dig into its trading funds. In the report to the general meeting of the shareholders on 29 May 1726, the officers reported that they had had to use 1.2 million from the trading funds to pay the last year's dividends.[125] At the next year's meeting on 11 June 1727, they announced that they had had to use 1,614,986 *l.t.* to supplement the yield of the tobacco monopoly in paying dividends *and annuities* on sums borrowed, and foresaw the necessity of so using 1.5 million annually in the future.[126] In fact, interest payments (*rentes*) on sums borrowed by the company rose from nil in 1725–26 to 1,281,254 *l.t.* in 1729–30.[127] Since the sums borrowed were to a considerable extent dissipated in dividends and interest payments, these policies had a tendency to inhibit the accumulation of capital and even to contribute to its wastage.

TABLE II

Assets of the Indies Company Exclusive of the 100 Million Royal Debt

31 January 1725	37,326,689 *l.t.*[128]
February 1725	39,385,941 *l.t.*
April 1726	38,974,653 *l.t.*[129]
22 April 1727	38,814,396 *l.t.*[130]
30 April 1728	29,310,285 *l.t.*[131]

The crisis stage appears to have been reached in the latter part of 1729: "something had to be done" and all sorts of schemes were forthcoming about what should be done. Most of the proposals that have survived recommended taking some or all of its monopolies away from the company. A memoir to the controller-general Des Forts dated 8 September 1729 from the farmer-general Desvieux (representative of the united farms on the Council of Commerce) recommended abolishing the company and transferring all its trading activities to a new company composed of the merchants of the greatest wealth and credit in the country. He was particularly critical of the sloppy way in which the Indies Company had been managing the tobacco farm. They had lost great sums because of the ignorance and dishonesty of their provincial employees: one egregious case involved a nephew of one of the directors who had stolen 300,000 l.t. Desvieux did not think that anything better could be expected from the company whose personnel policy was governed by the patronage of directors or of "seigneurs de la cour." By contrast, the farmers-general were having excellent results managing the *cinq grosses fermes;* if the tobacco monopoly were transferred to them, the merger would make it possible to eliminate half of the administrative and policing expenditures of the tobacco farm. Hence, the united farms could and would offer a good price for tobacco. A rent of 7.5 million annually would enable the king to pay an annuity of 150 l.t. p.a. on 50,000 shares in the dissolved company, converting the erstwhile shareholders into the safest of state rentiers.[132] Though, in the event, the company was not to be abolished, enough of the Desvieux proposal was carried out to classify it as most influential.

In the annual report made to the shareholders on 11 June 1727, the officers admitted that from a commercial standpoint the company might better employ all its capital in the profitable East Indies trade; however, they added, there were important state objectives to be pursued in the other trades, such as the development of tobacco production in Louisiana.[133] The qualification of the report reflects a basic division within the company between the shareholders' interest (properly represented by the syndics) and the government interest (maintained alike by inspectors and directors). The shareholder viewpoint was very ably represented in another memoir submitted to the government late in 1729. The author ably argued that the company had undertaken too many responsibilities for its resources. He recommended that henceforth it confine its trade to the East Indies and China only. It should give up the Senegal and Barbary trades to new companies and even give up the Canadian beaver monopoly, though profitable. In particular, it should give up its unprofitable Louisiana concession. (If the government wanted more tobacco from there, they could forbid the settlers to plant anything else.) Finally, he wanted the company to farm out the tobacco monopoly. He thought they could get eight million a year net by subfarming and could thereby withdraw the near three millions in capital they had tied up in it. Those three millions plus a two million advance they could easily get from whoever farmed the monopoly would give them five million more in working capital for their East India and China trades.[134] It should be remembered that in September 1723 Bertrand and Demeuves had wanted the company to subfarm the monopoly for six millions rather than to try to administer it themselves. They had been defeated then but ever since had served as elected syndics of the company. Either of them might have been the author of this memoir so sharply attuned to the shareholders' best commercial interest.

This businessman's memoir was answered by someone named Plissay, a self-avowed expert of conservative orientation, probably a naval official. He objected to the abandonment of Louisiana which he defended strongly. At the same time, he was not at all averse to having the company farm out the tobacco monopoly if they could find someone who would give them as much for it as they were then earning. They could well use the three million working capital elsewhere.[135]

Several rather different memoirs were submitted in 1730 recommending that the Indies Company confine its attention to the East India and China trades. One thought the company could get eight million rent for the tobacco monopoly, or 1.5 million more than it was then making.[136] One rather friendly to the company thought that as quid pro quo, the company should be ready to give up the tobacco monopoly if it could get rid of its unprofitable trades to Louisiana and elsewhere.[137] Another, more hostile, did not see why the shareholders of the Indies Company should be entitled to 7½ percent (150 *l.t.* on 2,000 *l.t.*, the nominal values of their reformed shares) when all the other victims of the Visa of 1721–22 had had to be content with 2½ percent. He thought that tobacco should be taken away from the company as an act of justice, the company being compensated only by a guaranteed payment of 2½ percent on its old 100 million loan to the crown.[138]

What is interesting in these projects of 1729–30 is that friend and foe alike of the company, amateurs and professionals, members of the united farms and spokesmen for the company's own shareholders all agreed that the company should get rid of the tobacco farm, though they differed radically on the terms. The best informed projects saw it was a way of alleviating the company's shortage of working capital. It is not surprising therefore that when the company came to give up the tobacco monopoly in 1730, the transaction was in form at least its own idea. Before that could take place, however, the company had to be shaken by two terrible and unexpected blows.

On or shortly before 14 March 1730,[139] word reached Paris of the bloody uprising of the Indians at Natchez on the Mississippi in 1729 during which hundreds of Frenchmen were killed and the principal center of tobacco cultivation in Louisiana destroyed. (The details will be discussed in the next chapter.) Ever since the company was restored in 1723, its leaders had been saying that in three or four years' time they would be getting enough tobacco from Louisiana to supply the monopoly and free France from dependence on British supplies. With the destruction of Natchez, it became impossible to sustain this illusion any more and Louisiana was cruelly exposed for what it was, a drain on the human and material resources of the company. A few days later, a greater scandal broke upon the city. Thousands of unissued or deposited shares of the Indies Company, worth it was rumored five or six millions, were discovered to be missing from its vaults. The official responsible implicated the wife of the controller-general Le Peletier Des Forts and her brother, the *conseiller d'état* Lamoignon de Courson (member of the Councils of Commerce and Finance); the trail led ultimately to the controller-general himself, the man who restored probity to French public finance after the Regency and the reign of Madame de Prie. On 19 March, he was dismissed. His successor, Philibert Orry, count of Vignory, was a relative nonentity advanced by Fleury.[140] Nevertheless, until toppled by the Paris brothers in 1745, he gave France the longest period of stable fiscal administration in the eighteenth century.

On the heels of their March disasters, the directors of the Indies Company came forward with various schemes to improve the administration of the company for the future,[141] but patching was not to be enough. The disorders of their company (particularly when compared to the regularity and prosperity of the United General Farms since 1726) made it evident that surgery would be necessary. Subsequent memoir writers recognized that at this hour the influence of the united farms was at its peak and invincible.[142] We do not know exactly what happened between March and June, though as early as 14 April the agent of Bayonne in Paris had reported the rumor that the tobacco monopoly would be transferred to the united farms.[143] In all probability, the directors and syndics of the Indies Company early perceived that, at the existing juncture of business and politics, they would have to lease the tobacco monopoly to the United General Farms as a step toward restoring their finances; the four months were probably spent in negotiation to obtain the best possible terms for their company. One technical memoir has been found representing the last stages in the negotiation: in it, it is assumed as settled that the Indies Company will farm out the tobacco monopoly for eight years. The only question is whether the Indies Company has a clear legal title to the tobacco monopoly since the concessionary *arrêts* of March and September 1723 were never registered in the *chambre des comptes*. Various ways of getting around this are discussed.[144]

By early July, the details had been worked out. By a *délibération* of its council (inspectors, syndics, directors) of 12 July 1730, the Indies Company formally accepted the idea of an alienation of the tobacco monopoly through a lease to the United General Farms. The *délibération* stated that in the six years 1 October 1723–30 September 1729, the company had earned 43,136,173 *l.t.* net from the tobacco monopoly, or 7,189,362 p.a. (very close to the final figures given in Table I, page 288). During those six years, they had advanced to the tobacco department for working capital an average of 3,042,964 *l.t.* annually for which they had charged that department at the rate of 10 percent p.a. If they were to continue to manage the tobacco monopoly, they would have to expect increasing expenditures on administration and police:

> ... that in truth, no private company could in all probability have raised the yield higher during the years of the administration of the Indies Company; and that MM. the farmers general were the only ones in the kingdom capable of increasing its yield significantly by eliminating [separate] clerks and guards for tobacco, those of the [united] farms being sufficient for both purposes ...

Therefore, the *délibération* concluded, if the united farms were to see fit to make an offer to lease the tobacco monopoly from the company for eight years for an annual rent of 7.5 million for the first four years and eight million *l.t.* for the last four, "the company would find a very great advantage in accepting the aforesaid offers," both because of the greater net receipts it would realize from the tobacco monopoly and because such a farm would release substantial sums of the company's own capital for employment in the East India and China trades.[145]

The lease between the Indies Company and the United General Farms embodying these terms was passed before notaries on 5 September 1730[146] and authorized by a *résultat* of the Council of State the same day.[147] The whole was duly confirmed by the *arrêt pour la prise de possession* of 12 September[148] and by the usual *arrêt* of the *cour des aides* of 22 September 1730.[149] The United General Farms entered into the management and profits of the tobacco monopoly on 1 October 1730. Although the initial lease was only for eight years, in fact, as we shall see in later chapters, the united farms were to retain control of the tobacco monopoly until both disappeared in 1791.

The taking over of the tobacco monopoly by the united farms in 1730 should not be thought of as a sharp break with the past. The key managerial staff headed by the *caissier général* Sonnois were all continued. The technician de la Gombaude was made a farmer-general for two years (1730–32) to help in the transition;[150] he served on all the committees[151] of the company connected with that revenue. The important purchasing and manufacturing committee was headed by de la Porte, the senior farmer-general; the *régie* (distribution and police) committee was headed by Lallemant de Betz, the auditing committee by Bonnevie. All three, as pointed out earlier in this chapter, had had extensive previous experience with the tobacco farm, as had many of their fellow farmers-general. In recapitulation, of the thirteen members of the important new tobacco manufacturing and purchasing committee of the united farms, all but two (Mazade and Darlus) had had some previous connection with the tobacco monopoly: three had been actively involved in the farm during 1721–30 (de la Gombaude, Bonnevie and Lallemant de Betz), eight had been directors of Law's Indies Company during 1719–20 (de la Porte, Le Normand, Chevalier, Desvieux, de Lalive, Lallemant de Betz, de Villemur, and Savalette), two had been bidders for the company during 1714–18 (de Lalive and Masson), one (de la Gombaude) had been a professional employee of the old Bernard-Maynon company, another (Chevalier) had been a partner in that company during 1707–9, while one (de la Porte) had been a member of the tobacco committee of the old united farms in 1697 where he had sat beside Jean-Baptiste de Lagny, the founder of the monopoly.[152]

The Suppression of Planting, 1720–26

While the tobacco monopoly was thus passing through the turbulent court revolutions of the 1720's, the peasants of the planting districts in the southwest were trying to get for themselves some compensation for the loss of their right to cultivate tobacco. As has been explained before, the plan of this book does not include an investigation of the local history of the various planting regions. All that can be indicated here is an outline of the problem in the 1720's.

At the height of Law's "System," as part of his plan to establish, on the British model, an open trade in tobacco subject only to a high import duty, the *arrêt* of 29 December 1719 prohibited tobacco planting in France proper—excepting only the eastern frontier provinces of French Flanders, Artois, Hainault, Cambrésis, Alsace, and Franche Comté which had always been outside the jurisdiction of the monopoly. The *arrêt* specifically included within the ban thirty-four localities, mostly along the Garonne, where such cultivation had hitherto been tolerated. An unprecedentedly heavy fine of 10,000 *l.t.* was established for violations of the ban, a penalty to which both proprietors and tenants were liable.[153] The ban was specifically confirmed by the *déclaration* of 17 October 1720,[154] and, after Law's fall, by both the *déclaration* of 1 August 1721[155] reestablishing the full monopoly and the du Verdier lease of 19 August 1721. The last named in fact contained the previously mentioned clause providing that, should planting be permitted again, the farmers were to be entitled to a deduction of 500,000 *l.t.* annually in the price of their lease.[156] In letters of 22 October 1720, 10 January and 3 March 1721, the new intendant of Bordeaux, Boucher, had informed Le Peletier Des Forts and his successor, the new controller-general Le Pelletier de la Houssaye, that Law's ban was costing his *généralité* eight million *l.t.* a year and that both he and his predecessor Lamoignon de Courson thought that cultivation should be permitted again. La Houssaye, however, wrote back on 3 September 1721 that *all* the companies which had recently bid for the tobacco lease had insisted on compensation of 500,000 *l.t.* p.a. should cultivation be restored. Since the government was not prepared to make this sacrifice, the ban was to be kept.[157]

The decision to ban tobacco cultivation, made in December 1719, was only communicated to the southwest by a letter from the new controller-general Law of 27 January 1720, and made public in the *généralité* of Bordeaux by the intendant's *ordonnance* of 17 February 1720. This caused great excitement and protests among the affected peasantry but the government was able to enforce the new ban without violent resistance. This was undoubtedly made easier by the limited geographical areas in which tobacco cultivation had up to then been permitted. More complex was the problem of profiteering and compensation. On news of the planting ban, the prices of tobacco in the southwest immediately rose from about 10 *l.t.* to 50–60 *l.t.* per quintal—to the immense profit of seven local merchants (including the former buying agents of the Indies Company) who had got advance word of the impending ban and had bought up most of the local tobacco on contracts for later delivery. (Peasants normally made such contracts with the merchant-manufacturers who in turn made such contracts with the exporting merchants.) About March 1720, Lamoignon de Courson reported the intensity of local feeling against these contracts, which so cruelly defrauded the peasants who would in any event be the chief sufferers from the ban.[158]

On receipt of this information, Law obtained an *arrêt* from the Council of State on 16 March 1720 which voided all contracts for the sale of tobacco in Guienne made since 1 November 1719. The proprietors of the tobacco (i.e., the merchant-manufacturers) could now sell their tobacco at the going market price, but were to pay to the peasant-cultivators a compensation according to a scale to be devised by the intendant, Lamoignon de Courson.[159] These arrangements for the *généralité* of Bordeaux were by a subsequent *arrêt* of 27 July 1720 extended to the growing region of Bas Montauban in the *généralité* of Toulouse and to the *pays de Layrac* in the *généralité* of Auch;[160] by the *arrêt* of 1 October 1720, they were further extended to the parish of Villemade in the *généralité* of Montauban.[161] In each case, the responsibility for establishing the compensation to be paid to the peasants was ascribed to the respective intendant.

Lamoignon de Courson, intendant of Bordeaux, sympathetic to the big merchants as he had never been to the monopoly, investigated promptly and sent Law, as controller-general, a draft *arrêt* letting the buyers keep their tobacco while granting the cultivators additional compensation of only 8 *l.t.* per quintal for all leaf sold. Law, however, left office before anything was done. With prices rising and disputes between merchant-buyers and manufacturers growing more acrimonious, Courson assembled the principal businessmen involved and got them to agree to a *convention* on 8 July 1720 (subsequently confirmed by a conciliar *arrêt* of 27 July 1720). With prices ever higher, manufacturers were now to pay to the cultivators a bonus of 25 *l.t.* per quintal over and above the price originally contracted (around 10 *l.t.* per quintal). The merchants were to pay to the manufacturers for worked up tobacco delivered between 1 November 1719 and the receipt of the *arrêt* of 16 March 1720 the said 25 *l.t.* per quintal to cover the compensation to the growers and were to raise their purchase price to 45 *l.t.* for rolls made from stemmed leaves and 30 *l.t.* for ordinary roll tobacco. Private contracts at higher prices were allowed to stand.[162] On the advice of the subdelegate for Bas Montauban and the intendant of Languedoc, these arrangements were extended to the growing region of Bas Montauban (the St. Porquier district) by the Council of State's order of 26 October 1720. (The indemnity to the planters in Languedoc was actually only 20 *l.t.* 15*s.* instead of 25 *l.t.*, making allowance for differences in weights used and preparation.) However, the intendant of Auch, Le Clerc de Lesseville, made a separate arrangement (*ordonnance* of 23 October 1720) for the district of Layrac by which cultivators there received an indemnity of 38 *l.t.* per quintal, instead of 25.[163]

These generous terms were granted at the height of the Law inflation when merchants and financiers had more *billets de banque* than they knew what to do with and credit was very easy. (The seven great merchants of Tonneins easily borrowed over 600,000 *l.t.* toward the supplementary payments on the tobacco they had purchased.) Sellers, of course, would be much less willing to accept this ever more dubious paper money. The progressive demonetization of the *billets* by the *arrêts* of 15 August, 15 September and 10 October 1720,[164] all denominations ceasing to be legal tender after 1 November, made the merchants ever more anxious to pay them out (permitted for old debts during the transition) and the manufacturers and planters ever more reluctant to receive them. Trouble started in September 1720 when the cultivators in Guienne refused to accept their indemnities in the larger bills which were to be "hors de cours" after 1 October, forcing the merchants to deposit them with public trustees. The intendant of Bordeaux tried in vain to get a supply of smaller bills or permission to cut up the larger ones, but his efforts were rendered futile by the *arrêt* of 10 October demonetizing even the smaller notes after 1 November.[165] At this absolute impasse, and with a storm of litigation threatening, on the petition of the big tobacco dealers of Tonneins, an *arrêt* of 4 April 1721 referred the entire compensation question to the intendants of Languedoc, Montauban, Auch, and Bordeaux.[166]

In Languedoc, the intendant de Bernage acted quickly and obtained an *arrêt du conseil* of 15 July 1721, reducing the scale of compensation to cultivators (and manufacturers) by one-half.[167] The *déclaration* of 1 August 1721 reestablishing the full monopoly made things even more difficult for the merchants by establishing maximum prices for manufactured tobacco made from French domestic leaf of only 25*s.* per lb. wholesale and 32*s.* retail —or one-half the prices fixed for imported tobacco.[168] At first the wholesalers and retailers (who were permitted to continue private trading after paying the *droit de marque*) ignored these price restrictions and charged up to 80–96*s.* per lb. for the now rare Guienne tobacco. The new monopolists (or rather their subfarmers in the south) decided to stop this and obtained an *arrêt* from the *cour des aides* of Montpellier on 15 January 1722 obliging the private traders to keep within the prices fixed.[169] While the national monopoly desired such price limitation to force private traders to export, the southern subfarmers sought the same to induce private traders to sell out to them at the legal prices. When this hint did not prove sufficient, the same subfarmers obtained a further *arrêt* from the same court at Montpellier giving them a right of preemptive purchase of manufactured tobacco still in private traders' hands at the legal wholesale price of 25s. per lb.[170] Under such circumstances, it was no longer possible for private traders to pay the generous compensation to the peasants ordered. The three great wholesale merchants of Tonneins, de Gals, Larrard, and Seilhade, petitioned the king for relief; an *arrêt* of the Council of State of 22 September 1722 admitted their inability to pay the bonuses even at the reduced scale established for Languedoc in 1721 and cut those payments further to a mere 35s. per quintal to cultivators and in proportion to manufacturers.[171]

In Guienne, the problem of the indemnity to the planters was much greater than in Languedoc because of the greater quantities involved: in the *généralité* of Bordeaux, the total nominal "indemnity" came to 2,626,599 *l.t.*, payable to about 6,000 cultivators. The leading merchants, de Gals, Seilhade and Larrard, refused to pay the cash indemnity in Guienne which they had paid in Languedoc, even at the reduced rate of 1722, on the sound legal grounds that, pursuant to the *convention* of 8 July 1720, they had in September 1720 deposited the full "indemnity" in *billets de banque* with the trustees named by the intendant. If the government had demonetized the *billets,* that was not the fault of the merchants. Nothing came of an exchange of memoirs in 1722–23 between the intendant, the controller-general, the new tobacco monopoly and the merchants. Finally, the crown in 1730 compulsorily converted these deposited *billets* into annuities to the cultivators payable from the receipts of the *taille* in the Agenais. In 1742, the government agreed to refund the principal of the annuities. In some parishes, these funds were eventually distributed to the individual claimants; in others they were used for public improvements: at Tonneins, a clock tower was built with the money.[172]

Here and there in the 1720's, recalcitrant peasants in obscure villages throughout the country chose to defy the monopoly and its bans on planting. An *arrêt* of the Council of State of 1 December 1722 ordered the inhabitants of Rarecourt in the bishopric of Verdun to appear before the intendant of Champagne with the documentary evidence supporting their pretended privilege of planting tobacco.[173] The *parlement* of Britanny sternly punished someone near Brest who tried the old ruse of claiming that the tobacco found growing on his property was really something else.[174] If the guards of the monopoly had only a little trouble pulling up the tobacco of the Brothers of Charity at Condom, a more serious case of armed resistance by the inhabitants of Lartigues near Auch to protect their illegally cultivated tobacco had to be referred by the Council of State to the intendant of Auch.[175]

The only area of protracted difficulty, however, was the viscounty of Turenne and its attached county of Montfort, belonging to the dukes of Bouillon. As already mentioned in Chapter 6, the precise fiscal privileges of this feudal jurisdiction were ill defined. The French government had never officially recognized the right of the inhabitants of the viscounty to raise tobacco and, in fact, by an *arrêt* of 1685 had ordered them to cease. However, rather than become involved in protracted litigation with political complications, the united farms in 1686 had leased the tobacco monopoly in Turenne from the duke of Bouillon, thus obtaining control of the tobacco trade within the territory. This lease was apparently continued without any trouble until Law's time. Just after his fall, during the 1721 vacuum of no tobacco policy, the then duke of Bouillon died and was succeeded by his arrogant son whom we met in a previous chapter as the duke of Albret, protector of the bidding company of 1716. The family had the right to the title "Serene Highness" and the rank of foreign princes at the French court from the Bouillon territories in modern Belgium, though their most important possessions were in France. The new duke of Bouillon amused contemporaries by having himself proclaimed "by the grace of God." Such a grandee had the spirit, the position, and the knowledge to make trouble for the tobacco monopoly in France.

The viscounty of Turenne was a scattered jurisdiction that stretched out along the borders of Guienne (Périgord and Quercy) and Limousin. Administratively, parts of it lay within the cognizance of the intendants of Bordeaux, Montauban, Limoges, and Riom (Auvergne). Whether for administrative or political or other reasons, the farmers of the restored tobacco monopoly during the du Verdier lease (1721–23) appear to have ignored the viscounty. When the more powerful Indies Company took over the tobacco monopoly on 1 October 1723, a confrontation was inevitable. The company obtained from the Council of State an *arrêt* on 16 February 1724 prohibiting the growing, manufacture, or sale of tobacco within the viscounty of Turenne. In no way did the document even allude to any pretended exemptions of that jurisdiction. The preamble merely recited that, in violation of the *déclaration* of 17 October 1720, the inhabitants of the viscounty were growing and manufacturing tobacco and carrying the same into neighboring territories, sometimes in armed bands. It ordered them to cease and desist and to report within one month all the tobacco they possessed, for sale to the company or exportation.[176] The controller-general made it clear to the intendants that he wanted this strictly enforced and made troops available as needed.[177] An *arrêt* of 29 June 1724 gave a delay for the reports until mid-July, but permitted the Indies Company to make searches and ordered the four intendants concerned to enforce the law rigorously.[178] Further *arrêts* of 14 and 22 July gave the four intendants extraordinary jurisdiction to hear all civil and criminal questions arising from the enforcement of the tobacco ban in the viscounty, to the exclusion of all ordinary courts.[179]

The intendants introduced the new policy firmly but discreetly.[180] In the course of 1724, the inhabitants of the viscounty of Turenne and county of Montfort made the following declarations:

1,819	declarations at Souillac	(*gén.* Montauban)	764,687 lb.
1,482	declarations at Brives	(*gén.* Limoges)	353,296 lb.
320	declarations at Sarlat	(*gén.* Bordeaux)	70,967 lb.
	Total		1,188,950 lb.

On 8 October and again on 20 November 1724, the Indies Company made the owners formal offers to pay 30 *l.t.* per quintal for their tobacco of the crops of 1721, 1722, and 1723 of the first quality stemmed; and in proportion for inferior qualities. The inhabitants, in writing on 25 November 1724, refused the price as inadequate. Lest this tobacco stored all over the viscounty become an object of smuggling, an *arrêt* of 19 December 1724 gave the inhabitants one month to accept the company's last offer or to export their tobacco; if they had not done either by the end of that month, they must at their own expense within eight days transport their tobacco to one of the company's storehouses at Brives, Souillac, or Sarlat to be stored there at their own expense under double key until exported. At the end of the thirty and eight days, the company was given power to search for and seize any tobacco found in the viscounty not so stored.[181]

There is evidence that the employees of the company, backed by troops, proceeded to go over the viscounty with a fine tooth comb. Their rigor provoked the bitter resentment of the inhabitants, but only the pulling up of illicit plantations led to the few cases of armed resistance. That there were not more was due to the discretion of the company, the controller-general Dodun and the intendants.[182] At the annual meeting of the shareholders of the Indies Company on 29 May 1726, it was reported that "the plantations of tobacco have been entirely destroyed in the viscounty of Turenne; what remains of that sort of tobacco in the four contiguous provinces is almost consumed; and in the sales offices in these four provinces, sales are noticeably increasing day by day."[183]

There is evidence that during the latter part of 1726, following the political changes of June, there was some discussion about restoring tobacco cultivation in France. Memoirs were written for and against the idea.[184] In the event, nothing came of such proposals: influential opinion was too delighted at having the Indies Company back on its feet to think much about the poor peasants of the Garonne. The project was not heard of again until the 1740's when France was at war with Great Britain and imported supplies were precarious and expensive. About 1744–46, the intendant of Bordeaux, Tourny, proposed reviving planting in the Agenais, with the cultivators obliged to sell only to the united farms and with the zones of cultivation carefully delimited. Cardinal Fleury had allegedly been most sympathetic when the idea had earlier been broached to him by others. (The government had since 1739 been sympathetically investigating plans to stimulate production in Louisiana and to revive that in the Antilles.) The farmers-general also appeared to be interested, but attached such onerous conditions (including special courts to handle all disputes arising from the planting) that Tourny dropped the project.[185]

Others, however, kept the idea alive. The *chevalier* de Vivens, a resident of the former planting district in the Agenais who had advised both Boucher and Tourny on local conditions, published a book on Guienne agriculture in 1756, in which he devoted several chapters to demonstrating the desirability of reviving cultivation. If this could not be done with the cooperation of the united farms, he recommended abolishing the tobacco monopoly and substituting a simple import duty.[186] Though his work received little national recognition at the time, his ideas kept cropping up. On 21 July 1764, after the disasters of the Seven Years' War, the *parlement* of Bordeaux sent a memoir to the king (in support of similar memoirs from Normandy and Brittany) recommending free-trade policies to speed the postwar reconstruction of French trade. One paragraph called attention to the former splendid tobacco plantations along the Garonne destroyed by the *soi-disant Génie tutélaire* (Law); the glorious days of Louis XIV were invoked. The more than 200 million *l.t.* which had been spent by France on British tobacco since 1720 helped account for Great Britain's naval superiority over France. The prosperity and public order created in the southwest by a revived cultivation would more than compensate the king for any revenues lost.[187] When serious debate was resumed by the intendant Dupré de St. Maur in the 1780's, the arguments used were essentially those of his predecessor Tourny and de Vivens.[188] Though nothing was done about any of the proposals of midcentury when made, we cannot say that at any time between 1720 and the 1780's was the memory of the old tobacco cultivation along the Garonne ever totally erased.[189]

The principal growing areas along the Garonne, Lot, and Tarn were too exposed to have harbored any significant illegal cultivation of tobacco during the seventy years of the ban. The peasants turned instead to hemp and later to coleseed.[190] We are told, though, that in tiny patches on craggy slopes high above the Dordogne and Cére (i.e., in the viscounty of Turenne), where the guards of the *ferme* never climbed, tobacco cultivation continued throughout the *ancien régime*.[191] Elsewhere in the country only rare isolated cases of planting have left any trace on the record.[192] The government did not even find it necessary to reissue the prohibitions against the planting until 1777 when the American Revolution for a time made tobacco scarce and expensive in Europe.[193]

In retrospect, the twelve years 1718–30 marked the coming of age of the tobacco monopoly in France. In those years, tobacco consumption clearly emerged as a mass phenomenon offering great fiscal possibilities. After the dust had cleared from the chaos of Law's downfall, that potential was effectively realized during 1721–30. In those years, the monopoly was firmly reestablished along legal, institutional, and commercial lines that were to persist to the end of the *ancien régime*. Both tobacco consumption and revenue yields were to increase vastly in the decades after 1730, but the tobacco monopoly handed over by the Indies Company to the united farms in 1730 was a "going concern" not significantly different from that abolished by the Constituent Assembly in 1791. The eight millions annual revenue which the Indies Company received from the united farms for the tobacco monopoly in the 1730's and 1740's secured its dividends and thus provided the company that secure financial-political position necessary for the great work attempted in India during those same years. Ironically, though, in the end the monopoly reestablished and refashioned by Dupleix *père* in 1721–23 proved more lasting than the conquests of Dupleix *fils* which it made possible.

CHAPTER 12

Louisiana Tobacco under the Company, 1717–31

John Law obtained the farm of the tobacco monopoly for his Occident Company in 1718 on condition that the company undertake to develop tobacco production in Louisiana and thus free France from dependence on Great Britain for that product. By the lease of 1 August and the *arrêt* of 4 September 1718, Law bound his company to import no tobacco except that from Louisiana and other French colonies after 1 October 1721; if the monopoly were transferred thereafter to any other company, such company would similarly be bound both to import only French colonial tobacco and to buy half its needs from Louisiana.[1] Law squirmed out of this obligation by abandoning the tobacco monopoly itself for an open trade in December 1719. When the monopoly was reestablished in 1720–21, nothing further was said about the obligation to buy only from Louisiana. The lease of 19 August 1721 merely stated that the monopoly was obliged to purchase any tobacco imported from Louisiana or any other French colony at the same price it paid for tobacco from Virginia or Alsace to which it could most nearly be compared in quality. (In practice, this would mean a rather low price.) However, the monopoly was not obliged to purchase more French colonial tobacco than it could sell "competitively with an assorted stock of French-grown [Alsatian and Flemish] and foreign tobaccos."[2] This minimal obligation was automatically assumed by the Indies Company when it resumed control of the tobacco monopoly in 1723. The irony is that the Indies Company exerted itself as strenuously as it did to develop tobacco cultivation in Louisiana.

Louisiana had not originally been thought of by the French as an agricultural colony, least of all as a colony producing tropical and semitropical products in competition with those of the French Antilles. Rather was it envisioned as a great strategic position to limit the expansion of the English colonies westward and southward, as a base for trade with both the Spaniards around the Gulf of Mexico and the Indians of the Mississippi Valley, as a source for timber and other forest products for the West Indian colonies and finally as a new El Dorado in which all kinds of mineral wealth might be discovered.[3]

Nevertheless, it was bound to occur to many that a territory of hundreds of thousands of square miles did have interesting agricultural potentialities. In January 1704, at a time when the English-Dutch commercial blockade of France was most effective and French imports of tobacco most difficult, the secretary of state for the navy, Jérôme Phélypeaux de Pontchartrain, wrote to Jean-Baptiste Le Moyne de Bienville, governor of Louisiana:

> It is very important that you apply yourself carefully to the cultivation of the land in order that the colony may be able to subsist by itself in difficult times when assistance from Europe may fail you. I think that you ought to begin with the tobacco plantations which will serve to render the lands capable of producing other things after the first clearing, in addition to the fact that tobacco will probably grow very well there and will be of the quality of that of Virginia, the reputation of which in commerce you know. On these plantations, follow as far as you can the method of the English colonies about which you can obtain information.[4]

Nothing very much was done at the time about this excellent advice. Capital, labor, and technical skill were all lacking. When the ever-cautious Jean Baptiste Duché (whom we have met in previous chapters as a subsequent director, 1717–19, and *régisseur*, 1721–23, of Law's company, but at this time a merchant of La Rochelle) was negotiating with Pontchartrain in 1708 to take over the trade to Louisiana, he treated tobacco cultivation as a very remote prospect for that colony:

> Tobacco can no longer be a great consideration since we see that the settlers on St. Domingue abandoned its cultivation. It is, however, still certain that quite good tobacco can be made there: that is easy to understand considering the proximity of that country to Havana and Virginia whence come the best tobaccos. The tobacco which would come from Louisiana might perhaps prove to be of a different quality but as esteemed as the others—and it is always something to employ the small settlers.[5]

In other words, by 1708–9, reasonably well informed merchants and ministers regarded tobacco cultivation as something which might conceivably be developed in the infant colony of Louisiana, but not as something of immediate importance.

Meanwhile, back in Louisiana, the garrison, settlers, and traders were left to their own resources without pay or supplies from home. Desperate but small-scale efforts were made to raise food and tobacco for their own consumption. In a letter of 1709 on the desperate state of the colony, the *commissaire de la marine,* Jean Martin d'Artaguiette d'Iron (subsequently a director of the Indies Company) added a hopeful note on the wheat grown near Biloxi and on tobacco: "The tobacco which grows here is excellent according to those who use it; much has been planted this year."[6] Out of this desperate necessity to grow one's own if one was to smoke or chew at all came the beginnings of the Louisiana tobacco industry. In 1711, Governor Bienville wrote that the experiments with wheat had been a failure, so that "the inhabitants of this place [Ile Dauphine] are devoting themselves for the most part to the planting of tobacco which everybody gives assurance is superior to that of Virginia."[7] When d'Artaguiette returned to France on leave in 1712, the ship which brought him home carried tobacco as its principal freight,[8] yet when he arrived in France, he did not bother mentioning that commodity in his report to the government.[9] It is thus likely that most of the tobacco sent home came from Cuba.[10]

Though Crozat later claimed that tobacco cultivation had been introduced into Louisiana during his administration,[11] it is apparent that some cultivation had begun well before his time. In actuality, tobacco supply played almost no part in the grant of the Louisiana trading and mining monopoly to Crozat in 1712. That commodity was not mentioned in Crozat's proposals to the government for that monopoly, though a great number of other commodities including silk were discussed;[12] nor was it mentioned in the royal letters patent of 14 September 1712 granting him the concession.[13] This is perfectly understandable, for Crozat was then a member of the tobacco monopoly company and had no desire to embarrass that lucrative interest; his concern with Louisiana was always understood to be primarily in its mines and trading prospects.

Nevertheless, Jérôme Pontchartrain maintained a slight but consistent interest in developing a national source of tobacco in this new colony. In a letter to Crozat in November 1712, the secretary of state urged him to "take your measures for the establishment of a tobacco manufacture in Louisiana which will not differ . . . in any way from that of Havana and in which you could find a considerable profit."[14] The next month, in the king's formal instructions to the new governor, de la Mothe Cadillac, Pontchartrain recommended tobacco as a temporary crop peculiarly suited to the small settler without the resources to attempt anything more capital-intensive.[15] In the simultaneous instructions to the naval official, Jean-Baptiste du Bois du Clos, sent out as the first *commissaire-ordonnateur* in Louisiana, the secretary recommended the cultivation of both indigo and tobacco. Crozat would have to introduce indigo cultivation from St. Domingue; tobacco, however, was already established: the secretary had heard from the former governor Bienville that "the settlers in Louisiana engage in that cultivation which is as good as that of Virginia [and] it will sell well if it is made faithfully and without deception."[16] When du Clos got out to Mobile Bay, he found however that such instructions were easier urged than executed. Tobacco of a good quality could in fact be grown there but it was a very discouraging crop: it was hardly above ground before it was attacked by worms (*vers*). The settlers had despaired of it as a commercial crop. Du Clos hoped that this condition was engendered only by the heavy forests in which the worms bred and that as the country was cleared, they would disappear.[17] (Forests had also been blamed for most natural afflictions in seventeenth-century Virginia.)

Du Clos' discouraging reports about insects consuming all the tobacco were repeated by the governor de la Mothe Cadillac. The settlers hadn't even been able to grow enough to supply their own needs and had to import tobacco from St. Domingue and Cuba. Since little else would grow in the black and white sands about Mobile Bay, he concluded that those sands were good for nothing but hourglasses.[18] This pessimistic analysis was passed on by Crozat in his own reports to Pontchartrain. Only up the Mississippi would they find lands with a real agricultural potential.[19] In Crozat's time, however, French efforts in the Mississippi valley proper remained feeble. About January 1716, the governor de la Mothe Cadillac was only able to send a sample of two pounds of tobacco grown *chez les Yassous,* about forty leagues north of the Natchez post. He thought, though, that something might conceivably come of it if skilled persons were sent out from France to demonstrate its proper cultivation and preparation.[20]

Despite discouragements, the new government of the Regency was from the first as interested in the tobacco possibilities of Louisiana as Jérôme Pontchartrain had been before them. The official instructions given in October 1716 to Jean Michiele de Lépinay, successor to de la Mothe Cadillac as governor, and to Marc-Antoine Hubert, successor to du Clos as *commissaire-ordonnateur,* both stated that tobacco would grow well in Louisiana and that the settlers there should be encouraged to grow it.[21]

Crozat's attitude was more ambivalent. As long as he planned to keep the Louisiana monopoly, his reports to the government were very pessimistic, stressing among other things his losses, the sums owing him, and the poor agricultural and trading prospects. Thus between 1712 and mid-1716, he never once wrote optimistically about the prospects for tobacco in Louisiana. As soon as he decided to surrender his monopoly, however, his tone changed at once: Louisiana became a colony of the solidest profits and of the most dazzling prospects; for the surrender of such a property, he was understandably entitled to millions in compensation. In one of the earliest of such memoirs, written in the latter part of 1716, shortly before he announced his abandonment of the concession, Crozat spoke glowingly of Louisiana's prospects of some day supplying France with all its needs in copper, lead, and tobacco, the last as good as that of Virginia.[22] A month or two later, after his great *taxe* by the Chamber of Justice, Crozat, in his memoir surrendering the Louisiana privilege, could claim that the establishment of tobacco cultivation there to compete with that of Virginia had always been one of his principal goals. Since Louisiana was at the same latitude as Virginia and "contiguous" to it, he saw no reason why tobaccos as good as those of the Chesapeake could not be grown on the Mississippi.[23] All through 1717, while the question was pending of compensation to Crozat for his surrendered privilege, memoirs flowed into the government from him[24] and his partner Le Bart,[25] stressing the dazzling prospects of Louisiana, not the least as a great producer of tobacco.

Though much of this was only self-interested rhetoric, it did evoke a positive response in the government. Though perhaps not originally intended, the development of Louisiana as a major supplier of tobacco became an important element in the discussions and projects that led to the creation of the Occident Company in 1717. This association had all been worked out in some detail by the time of the Crozat-d'Arminy company scheme of 14 May 1717. In this important document, discussed in Chapter 8, the two former tobacco farmers used the importance of developing tobacco cultivation in Louisiana as justification for taking the tobacco farm away from their former partners and granting it instead to the new company they were proposing.[26] The same point was rather differently made in the subsequent report from the commissioners (including d'Arminy) to whom had been referred the plans for chartering a new company to take over the Louisiana trade. The report was most probably written by the conservative Duché, who had himself, about 1708–9, been interested in taking over the Louisiana trade. His report emphasized the mines in Louisiana much more than tobacco or any branch of agriculture. It also deplored the idea of continuing the tobacco monopoly. Yet it came to the reluctant conclusion that the tobacco monopoly in France might well be granted to the proposed company to provide it with the income needed to develop Louisiana—provided that the new company-cum-monopoly be obliged by law to sell in France only the tobaccos of France and the French colonies.[27] Even the cautious Duché thus assumed that Crozat was correct in prophesying that Louisiana could easily supply France's tobacco needs. His report is also of considerable importance in that it first suggested that contractual obligation to supply France with tobacco from the French colonies that Law later assumed.

Law did not walk into that trap unaware. In a memoir of the summer of 1717 on his proposed Occident Company, he sketched out his plans:

> By the measures which the company proposes to take, it is as certain as human prudence can foresee, that the cultivation of tobacco will begin to produce significantly in 1719; that in 1720 it will increase; and that in 1721 there will be enough settlers and slaves, negroes or savages, in the colony to be able to furnish the kingdom with the same quality of tobacco which we get yearly from Virginia. The same vessels which bring it back will be ballasted with lead and it is almost certain that in 1721, the company will furnish the kingdom with all the lead and all the tobacco which we now get from the English.[28]

In other words, the rather vague suggestion by the commissioners in May 1717 that any Mississippi company granted the tobacco monopoly for its financial support also be obliged to sell only French and French colonial tobacco was metamorphosed a few months later into the boast from Law's projected company that it would by 1721 be supplying all of France's imported tobacco from Louisiana! This promise was not taken up at the time because the new Occident Company did not get the tobacco monopoly in 1717. However, when the tobacco monopoly was transferred to it in August-September 1718, it was done with the proviso that from 1 October 1721 the company import tobacco only from the French colonies.[29] Thus, although no one had as yet demonstrated that tobacco could be grown economically in commercial quantities in Louisiana, the propaganda war about that colony, first started by Crozat in December 1716, had ended by convincing the government and everyone else that the claim was self-evidently true. (In the end, France was to lose Louisiana before it could realize that blithe assumption.)

Law, having assumed for his company the commitment to supply all French tobacco needs from Louisiana, proceeded energetically with the steps necessary to carry out that obligation. One of the announced reasons for absorbing the Senegal Company in December 1718 was the need to procure slaves to grow tobacco in Louisiana. For the needed skills, some German peasants from the Rhineland, a tobacco growing area, were sent out in 1719.[30] In the fall of 1718, immediately after taking over the tobacco monopoly, the company despatched laborers from the Clairac district on the Garonne, skilled in tobacco growing. To supervise them, the company also hired from that same region the sieur de Montplaisir de la Guchay, at a salary of 1,500 *l.t.* annually plus all expenses, and the sieur Richer at 1,000 *l.t.*: each was to supervise a tobacco plantation to be established on the company's account.[31] In addition, owners of private concessions also sent out experienced tobacco hands, including some from Mondragon, as well as from Clairac. To encourage private settlers to grow tobacco, the company on 25 April 1719 instructed its factors in Louisiana to accept all tobacco offered them at 25 *l.t.* per quintal for the best quality, and in proportion for lesser qualities.[32] This was further defined the next year as 25 *l.t.* for the first quality, 20 *l.t.* for the second and 15 *l.t.* for the third.[33]

Despite these careful plans, tobacco cultivation in Louisiana got off to a rather poor start. Although the new governor Bienville had at first been rather optimistic about the prospects for tobacco,[34] letters sent home in 1719 reported that most of the private settlers as well as the Indians were too lazy to grow tobacco; the settlers could make money more easily in trade. The prices offered for tobacco were unattractive.[35] Of three vessels sent out to Louisiana in the spring of 1718 and returned to France early in 1719, two arrived back in ballast, the third with 75,000 lb. of Havana tobacco purchased in trade with the Spaniards.[36] At least one of the subsequent vessels which returned at the end of 1720 also came back in ballast.[37]

The tobacco workers from Clairac sent out at the end of 1718 arrived at Dauphine Island at the mouth of Mobile Bay too late in the spring of 1719 to start planting that year. A council of commerce (including the governor Bienville and the *commissaire-ordonnateur* Hubert) decided on 10 April 1719:

> Since the season is too far advanced to clear the land and plant tobacco in it this year and it has not appeared to us that there was any cleared place either around Mobile or around New Orleans suitable for establishing a plantation for tobacco because there was nobody to clear land and because the Indians will not work at it at all after they obtain what they need, the Council has decided to send the tobacco workers who have come on the *Comte de Toulouse* [to a place] just below English Turn on the west side four leagues from New Orleans where there is a tract of land [that is] very spacious and almost cleared.[38]

At the same time, the company in France was informed that neither Mobile Bay with its insects nor the lower reaches of the Mississippi subject to flooding were suitable for tobacco cultivation. That activity would have to be located on higher land farther up the river.[39] In October 1719, the council of commerce in the colony finally decided to locate the company's tobacco growing activity not at English Turn but higher up at Natchez, "the most suitable place to gather the best tobacco," and to send thither the company's tobacco workers from Clairac under Montplaisir.[40] Thus began the fateful association of Louisiana tobacco growing with the settlement among the Natchez Indians.

After sitting idle on Dauphine Island for almost a year, the "Clairacs" finally arrived at Natchez early in 1720 only to find that no arrangements had been made to feed them. With the greater part of their efforts necessarily diverted to growing food, only a small start could be made that year on tobacco.[41] Thus, Montplaisir's first proud shipment to the company in 1721 was only 500 lb.[42] Yet, the company was supposed to have been in a position by 1 October 1721 to supply from the French colonies all of France's tobacco needs—between four million and six million pounds annually!

Such was the state of affairs early in 1721, following Law's fall. The disappointments in tobacco were matched by equivalent disappointments in the other branches of trade to Louisiana. By early 1722, these losses had been calculated at over 3.25 million *l.t.*, exclusive of any losses from monetary revaluations.[43] Nevertheless, there remained a continuing pressure in high government circles to push on with the Louisiana and tobacco experiments. Despite the meteoric rise and fall of Law, there remained a considerable continuity in influential persons in important places concerned with Louisiana. The first directors of the Occident Company in 1717 included Jean-Baptiste Duché of La Rochelle, who had traded to Louisiana for many years before Crozat's time, and Jean Martin d'Artaguiette d'Iron, the naval official, who had served in Louisiana, also before Crozat's time. Though Duché dropped out of Law's Company in 1719, d'Artaguiette became during 1719–21 the director particularly charged with the affairs of that colony. When the Indies Company went into official receivership in 1721–23, one of the five commissioners charged with the interim administration of its commercial affairs was of course Jean-Baptiste Duché. When the Company was restored in March 1723, Duché was named to its directorate. Though he was dropped, as too conservative on dividend policy, in the reorganization of 30 August 1723, his former colleague d'Artaguiette d'Iron reemerged in September as an elected syndic of the company, in which capacity he remained till the further reorganization of 1731. Other directors appointed on 30 August 1723 included men who had served as directors in Law's company since 1717 (Castanier, Mouchard) or early 1718 (Boyvin d'Hardancourt) and who thus were familiar with the Louisiana tobacco experiment from its start.[44]

Then too during the full flood of the "System," extensive territories along the Mississippi had been granted to influential people in France: to Law himself, to the secretary of state Le Blanc (the great enemy of the Paris), to Paris Duverney himself and his brother Montmartel, to the future controller-general Dodun, to the general and courtier, the count of Belle-Isle, to the mysterious Oglethorpe sisters (siblings of the founder of Georgia), their husbands, the marquis of Mézières and the marquis des Marches, and their partners, the army contractor Fargès (another great enemy of the Paris) and his son-in-law, Abraham Peirenc de Moras, and many others.[45] All these people were interested in preserving the value of their concessions after the fall of Law. But this of course meant continuing with the encouragement of the colony, for their concessions could not be developed in isolation. Paris Duverney, in particular, used his great influence during 1721–26 in behalf of the colony and company. In return, the Indies Company instructed its agents to reserve a certain number of slaves in consignments to Louisiana for the concession of M. Duverney.[46] When Le Blanc returned to power in 1726, similar consideration was extended to his properties.[47]

In the history of tobacco, the most important concession was that at Natchez belonging originally to Marc-Antoine Hubert. As *commissaire-or-donnateur* in Louisiana at the start of Law's scheme, Hubert was in a position to obtain for himself some of the best soil. He chose land at Natchez near to where the colony's council of commerce decided to establish the company's own principal tobacco plantation.[48] On the eve of his return to France in 1721, Hubert sold his Natchez property for 50,000 *l.t.* to Jean-Baptiste Faucon Dumanoir for the account of the latter's employers, the Paris syndicate of Coetlogon & Deucher, also styled the "St. Catherine's company." This society, formed in September 1719 to exploit concessions made separately to the abbé Charles-Elisabeth Coetlogon, nephew of the vice-admiral Alain Emmanuel, marquis de Coetlogon, subsequently marshal of France, and to a more bourgeois group centered about Jean Deucher, who had other business dealings at this time with the abbé. The Deucher brothers, citizens of Steckborn in Switzerland, were merchants at Strasbourg and Basel and interested in a bank at Paris. They had close business relations with Fargès and belonged to that circle of businessmen about Fargès and his protector Le Blanc who entered fully into Law's scheme and profited greatly from it, Jean Deucher being taxed 1.5 million in the Visa of 1721–22. The other investors in Coetlogon & Deucher included Jean-Baptiste Fénelon, former deputy from Bordeaux in the Council of Commerce and now inspector of Law's *Banque Royale,* Etienne Bourgeois, Paris banker and now cashier or "treasurer" of that same great bank, as well as Law himself. The management was left to Deucher and another shareholder, Jean Daniel Kolly, a Swiss banker in the service of the elector of Bavaria and original investor in the Occident Company who made enough in the "System" to be taxed 2.1 million by the Visa. (In Louisiana, this company was referred to as "the Malouins," presumably because many of its senior local employees came from St. Malo and elsewhere in Brittany.) [49]

Quite apart from the continuity of personnel and of interests, there were objective reasons why the Louisiana and tobacco experiments should be continued after the fall of Law. Although very little had been extracted from Louisiana, millions had been invested in it. The white population there had risen from an estimated 400 at the beginning of 1717 to about 5,400 at the beginning of 1721 (after allowing for some two thousand who had died, deserted or returned to France). To the 600 Negro slaves in the colony at the beginning of 1720, the company added close to 1,900 more in 1720 and early 1721. All of this represented an investment which need not be abandoned, from which indeed much might be expected if adequately supported. An optimistic memoir of 1721, while admitting that 1722 would probably have to be written off for reorganization, suggested that by 1723, there might be 4,000 field hands in Louisiana (2,500 Negro and 1,500 white) who theoretically could produce eight million pounds of tobacco; even allowing for distractions and disorganization, they should conservatively be able to produce at least four million pounds, or half the consumption of the monopoly. If the Indies Company would only continue sending 500–600 slaves a year to Louisiana, that colony should in a very few years be able to supply all France's needs.[50] In the event, these calculations proved wildly optimistic. Nevertheless, they are important for showing an awareness in 1721 that the very real investment and settlement made in Louisiana since 1717 ought not be thoughtlessly abandoned.[51]

Despite all the political turmoil of 1720 and succeeding years, we find in practice a remarkable continuity in attitude toward the tobacco experiment in Louisiana. The French national interest in obtaining an autarkic source of tobacco was so self-evident that when all else in Law's work seemed threatened, no one seriously suggested abandoning the efforts to encourage that crop along the Mississippi. When du Vergier was sent out to Louisiana as *directeur ordonnateur,* his instructions of 15 September 1720 reminded him that tobacco ought to become one of the principal products of that colony and ordered him to let the new settlers grow that crop anywhere they liked.[52] When the commissioners in receivership took over the management of the Indies Company in 1721, one of the first things they did was to send encouragement to the sieur de Montplaisir, in charge of the company's plantation at Natchez (who had just sent home his first 500 lb. of tobacco), and to order the company's officials at Biloxi to send him 100 slaves as well as the agricultural implements and skilled workmen he needed.[53]

In September 1721, an *ordonnance* or *règlement* for the encouragement of Louisiana was issued in the name of the *commissaires du conseil* responsible for the company. Slaves were to be sold to the settlers at reasonable prices. Tobacco was to be bought at the company's offices at Biloxi, Mobile or New Orleans in good condition in dried leaf, either loose or in hands (*manoques*) at a flat price of 25 *l.t.* per quintal. The growers could pack it in the preferred hogsheads (*futailles*) or in chests (*caisses*) of at least 200 lb.[54] Officials were reminded that tobacco was the most important branch of agriculture in the colony and to be encouraged accordingly.[55]

The basic trouble afflicting tobacco cultivation from the very beginning was geographical. As the earliest memoirs noted, the soil at Natchez was excellent for its growth.[56] By 1723, officials in the colony were writing home that all tobacco growing efforts should be concentrated there, for the lands lower down the river were thought to be too wet for the leaf. Since the little cleared land about Natchez was in the hands of the Indians, it was necessary, in order to expand production there, to clear the forests, for which considerable manpower was needed.[57] But most of the population of Louisiana was concentrated around Mobile, Biloxi, and New Orleans, with relatively few venturing as far upriver as Natchez. When Charles Legac, a director for the company in Louisiana during 1718-21, returned to France, he estimated that the population of the colony when he left on 5 March 1721 was 6,000 whites and 600 Negroes. As of that same date, however, he reported that the total staff of the company's plantation at Natchez under Montplaisir was only forty, white and black. The nearby plantation of Marc-Antoine Hubert (shortly to be sold to the St. Catherine's company) had only 25 slaves, both Indian and Negro. With a few smaller establishments nearby, this wretched settlement then was expected to supply all of France's tobacco needs.[58] When Father P. F. X. de Charlevoix visited Natchez at the end of 1721, he was very favorably impressed by the size (four leagues square each) and fertility of the tobacco plantations of both the Indies Company and "the Malouins" but had to report that most of the skilled tobacco workmen from Clairac whom Law had sent to staff the company's plantation had quit Natchez and gone back to France.[59]

With their principal tobacco plantation thus abandoned before it could be developed, it is not surprising that the administrators and commissioners of council in charge of the company's affairs should decide that the company should leave tobacco growing to private enterprise. At some time between late 1721 and early 1723, they sold the company's "Terre Blanche" plantation at Natchez to a group known at first as "Le Blanc and Associates."[60] The last we hear of the efforts of Montplaisir and his men of Clairac is a report of 1724 that the tobacco they had raised at Natchez, presumably in 1721, was all rotting in the warehouse at New Orleans.[61]

The new owners of the company's Natchez plantation were a powerful group who had earlier received other individual and collective concessions including one further north on the Yazoo. They included the secretary of state for war, Claude Le Blanc, and his close coadjutor, Gérard Michel de la Jonchère, *trésorier de l'extraordinaire des guerres*,[62] and the prominent soldiers, the count of Belle-Isle and the marquis of Asfeld, with La Jonchère acting as manager.[63] The fraud filled bankruptcy of La Jonchère and the resulting dismissal and exile of his patron Le Blanc during 1723–26 slowed the development of this concession. On the death of Le Blanc in 1728, control was assumed by the count (subsequently marshal duke) of Belle-Isle but he was unable to do much to develop "Terre Blanche."[64]

In the end, therefore, the years of receivership, 1721–23, were years of stagnation or retrogression. According to the *ordonnateur* Hubert and many other officials in Louisiana, much of the failure of the years after 1717 could be ascribed to Bienville, governor from 1717 to 1726. He was, however, protected by Jean-Baptiste Duché, one of the *régisseurs* during 1721–23, and thus could not be corrected from home.[65] Nevertheless, at the end of their *régie* in early 1723, the *régisseurs* made a report that was at once complacent and optimistic. After the East India trade, Louisiana should be the principal activity of the restored Indies Company. Louisiana, after such vast investments, was now on the verge of producing something. Since the tobacco monopoly was to be regranted to the Indies Company, all efforts in Louisiana should be devoted to producing tobacco. For this, all that was needed was slave labor: there were then 5,000–6,000 white settlers in the colony and over 1,000 slaves, but at least 4,000 of the latter were needed. White labor could not be counted on to produce tobacco or indigo. Several vessels were then at sea bringing slaves to Louisiana; several more should be sent out immediately. With adequate labor, success was guaranteed.[66]

In March 1723, the Indies Company was restored to its directors; in September, its first elected syndics were chosen; on 1 October it resumed the farm of the tobacco monopoly. In these months, the new management had to consider seriously its unending expenses in Louisiana and its obligations to develop that colony as a source of supply for its tobacco monopoly. On 23 August 1723, three of the directors (Le Cordier, Fromaget, and Deshayes) wrote to the council at New Orleans for detailed information on the private plantations in the colony, how much tobacco each was then raising, how much more it might raise if supplied with all the slaves it could pay for.

They had heard from persons recently returned from Louisiana that the Le Blanc ("Terre Blanche") and Kolly (St. Catherine's) concessions at Natchez alone had enough land cleared and enough labor to fill a *flute* or fly-boat with tobacco. The company wanted the council at New Orleans to give all possible aid to those two concessions, while persuading them to concentrate on tobacco. This was both the intention of their owners and the interest of the company as it resumed control of the tobacco monopoly.

The council at New Orleans sent this letter to Jean Baptiste Faucon Dumanoir, director-general of the "colony of St. Catherine." He replied indignantly that the Indies Company had no right to tell him what to raise. It was more remunerative for him to use his slaves growing food and indigo, rather than to devote them entirely to tobacco and have to buy high-priced victuals. Thirty-six slaves could produce indigo worth 15,000–18,000 *l.t.*, while they could at most produce tobacco worth 6,000–7,000 *l.t.* He would therefore grow tobacco only if the company paid him the difference. It was not true, he insisted, that a slave could produce 1,000 lb. of tobacco annually. In that climate, continuous cultivation was necessary and, with the losses from insects, a slave might produce as little as 600 lb. yearly, worth only 150 *l.t.* at the company's price of 25 *l.t.* per quintal. The planters could not dry and pack their leaf in hands (*manoques*) in hogsheads to be delivered to France exactly as tobacco came from Virginia: they lacked hogsheads and the coopers to make them. If the company wanted more tobacco, it should take delivery in the leaf at Natchez and pack and transport the crop at its own expense.

The council at New Orleans sent home a sycophantic letter on 4 January 1724 expressing horror at Dumanoir's truculence: small planters might have to be left to their own choices, but Dumanoir ought to have loftier views. They felt sure that de Kolly could expect only tobacco from a plantation that had cost almost 100,000 *l.t.* to develop.

The council had also sent the company's letter to Desfontaines, director of the Le Blanc concession. Even before its receipt, Desfontaines had decided that tobacco was a very dubious proposition under the conditions then prevailing. On 24 October 1723, before he had heard of the disgrace of La Jonchère and Le Blanc, he wrote to the former recommending the temporary abandonment of the "Terre Blanche" concession at Natchez until more slaves were available, and the transfer of the slaves then there to indigo planting at the company's other establishment at Chaouachas; indigo was of course more profitable. Le Blanc & Co. had, to be sure, acquired "Terre Blanche" to grow tobacco, but he also doubted that that crop was profitable at the monopoly's price of 25 *l.t.* per quintal, considering packing and transportation costs. The largest available river boat would carry only 4,000 lb. of tobacco which would yield 1,000 *l.t.* at the Indies Company's stores at New Orleans. But (presumably for security) Desfontaines estimated that such a boat required twelve men and a supervisor. With the boat two months going to New Orleans and back, he estimated total costs for transport alone at 1,115 *l.t.* or more than the tobacco produced. Larger boats would be more economical, but he saw no real solution until the company paid much higher prices for tobacco.

Such being the private opinions of Desfontaines, it is not surprising that his reply to the Indies Company's queries of 26 August 1723 was quite negative. Small planters everywhere started with tobacco but changed to indigo as soon as they had acquired sufficient capital and changed again to sugar when they had accumulated still more. The only thing that kept some small planters on tobacco near Natchez was the opportunity to sell it in small quantities for consumption in the colony at prices equivalent to 200 *l.t.* per quintal and above. If they had to sell it all to the company at the offered price of 25 *l.t.* per quintal, none would continue with it. He saw no way of persuading anyone to plant tobacco unless the company sold them slaves for tobacco at an attractive rate. He too was sure that it was against the interest of his proprietors for him to grow tobacco and rejected the idea that the company had any right to make him do so.[67]

The company pondered these reports carefully. They could buy tobacco in England delivered in France in good condition for under 30 *l.t.* per quintal. By the rules of September 1721, the company took delivery of tobacco at Mobile, Biloxi, or New Orleans at 25 *l.t.* per quintal in hogshead or chest; with overhead costs in Louisiana and transport costs back to France, such tobacco must have cost them well over 40 *l.t.* per quintal by the time it arrived in France. Yet this price was inadequate to draw forth from Louisiana any significant quantities of tobacco. In October 1724, someone well informed drew up a "Memoir on the difficulties of encouraging tobacco production at the Natchez," which summarized the data in the answers of the directors of the Kolly (Coëtlogon & Deucher) and Le Blanc concessions: although the land at Natchez was well suited for tobacco, production was difficult there because (a) the settlers were unable to get hogsheads for packing; (b) there was a shortage of boats there to transport the tobacco down to New Orleans; (c) the company could send boats up to Natchez for the tobacco only at excessive expense; and (d) the company sent too few vessels a year to Louisiana to carry any significant quantity of tobacco back to France. The last circumstance implied that much of the tobacco would stay at New Orleans long enough to spoil, as much of the tobacco grown by Montplaisir had in fact done.

To meet these difficulties, the author of the memoir (who might conceivably have been the syndic d'Artaguiette d'Iron) recommended going back to the practices of Law's time and establishing a company-owned cultivation at Natchez. This would be a model plantation demonstrating to the smaller settlers how tobacco should be grown and prepared; it could be discontinued once the private settlers started bringing in enough dried leaf tobacco. He also recommended establishing a workshop there to make hogsheads and a shop to spin the tobacco and make it into *carotte* or *brique*. The last seemingly backward step was frankly an experiment to see if ways could be found to put the tobacco in a condition in which it could be preserved over longer periods of time more surely than it could in dried leaf. The author estimated that such an establishment would cost 25,770 *l.t.* during its first year (10,370 *l.t.* for the wages and living allowances of the French staff; 5,400 *l.t.* for 34 Negro slaves amortized at 130 *l.t.* annually; and 10,000 *l.t.* for tools, materials and transport). It might cost less in succeeding years as slaves were trained to perform some of the tasks of the skilled French workers.[68]

These suggestions were very seriously considered by the "committee of Louisiana," that is, the syndics and directors of the Indies Company responsible for that colony. The committee accepted in full the recommendations of the author of the October memoir: in their report to the council of directors and syndics, they recommended the establishment at Natchez both of a plantation and a manufacturing workshop where the tobacco would be spun into roll and pressed into *brique*. They estimated that by manufacturing only stemmed tobacco, they would reduce the bulk of the tobacco by five-sixths and thus solve the transport problem from Natchez to New Orleans and from the Mississippi to France. When, however, the committee's report came before the full council on 8 November, skeptical voices prevailed. Some must have queried whether the savings to be made would be worth the added investment of sending thirty more slaves to Natchez and the high costs of hiring skilled French workmen to go there. In the end, the council approved the establishment of a plantation or *habitation* at Natchez that would actually be little more than a trading and shipping station. Only 15–20 Negro field hands were to be sent for the demonstration plantation. But, to encourage tobacco cultivation, the company would accept tobacco "in hands" packed in loose bundles at both New Orleans and Natchez at a price of 6s. per lb. or 30 *l.t.* per quintal.[69] From the standpoint of the Natchez planters, these terms would be a considerable improvement over those of 1721 under which the company paid 25 *l.t.* per quintal for tobacco only if it were packed in hogsheads or chests and delivered to New Orleans, Biloxi, or Mobile.

That same month, the company appointed as their principal agent at Natchez Marc-Antoine de la Loire des Ursins who was already in the country and had previously served as a factor under Crozat. He was to be assisted by the sieur de La Broc (La Bros?) who had previously served as principal assistant to Montplaisir, manager of the company's earlier tobacco plantation at Natchez during 1720–1722. The instructions of 29 November 1724 to de la Loire des Ursins indicate clearly that his operation was to be primarily commercial and only secondarily agricultural. He was to use his French carpenters and woodcutters and his fifteen to twenty slaves first of all to clear the land and build buildings; the primary agricultural assignment of the slaves was to be to grow food for the whole trading station; they were then to be used to raise tobacco only if the local planters did not bring in enough. Two of the French workmen were to be constantly employed in making barrel staves for hogsheads of from four hundred to five hundred pounds capacity. To reduce bulk, experiments were to be made with larger hogsheads and with a small amount of stemmed tobacco. It was economically impossible to send boats up from New Orleans to bring the tobacco down from Natchez. Therefore, several of the workmen would have to be employed constantly making flatboats which would be sold on arrival at New Orleans; these were likened to the barges (*chalans*) which were sold for breaking up after unloading in Paris. All payments at Natchez would be made in cash or in notes on New Orleans whence the local planters would have to order their goods. The company did not intend to maintain a retail establishment at Natchez.[70]

These new arrangements had hardly been announced when they were liberalized. Prices of Virginia tobacco were exceptionally high in Europe in 1725, higher in fact than they were to be again until the American Revolution.[71] Pinched by these prices, the Indies Company reconsidered its buying policy in Louisiana: most of the planters there were heavily in debt to the company and very slow in paying their debts. Newly received information stressed the unattractiveness of existing prices to Natchez planters. By a new *ordonnance* of 27 June 1725, the company's agents in Louisiana were instructed to accept in payment of debts contracted before August 1724 tobacco in hands unpacked at the rate of 40 *l.t* per quintal, instead of the 30 ordered in November. Planters who owed nothing could take advantage of the temporarily higher rates to buy drafts on Paris. Debtors in difficulties need only apply half the proceeds of their tobacco to clearing old debts; the other half could be used to buy goods from the company or drafts on Paris.[72]

The impact of all this encouragement on Louisiana was only slowly perceived. On 25 May 1725, five of the councillors in Louisiana wrote privately to the company that the settlers were delighted by the new rules of November 1724. All they still needed was an adequate supply of slave labor. For three years, they had been promised slaves but none had come, the company preferring to ship only to the islands. If none came this year, many honest and industrious settlers would return to France.[73] The council sent the same message in August: the failure of the company to send Negro slaves had demoralized the settlers, most of whom now wanted to return to France. At Natchez, nothing could be done without slaves. Since de la Loire des Ursins didn't want to reside there, they had placed a half-pay captain named Ignace Broutin in charge and had engaged a man from Clairac named Ricart or Ricard to start the cultivation there. (This was Pierre Ricard, one of the "Clairacs" sent out in 1718; he is to be distinguished from François Ricard who had gone out in 1720 as *inspecteur en tabac* for the concession of the marquis of Ancenis and had by 1722 become an *"officier"* of the St. Catherine's concession at Natchez.) The company's only reaction to this message was an annotation that the new governor Périer should take out some tobacco growers with him.[74]

When the old governor, Bienville, returned to France in 1725, he gave substantially the same advice. Excellent tobacco could be grown at the Natchez and Yazoo settlements. It could also be grown farther down the river, but the settlers there preferred indigo. The key problem was slaves. There were only 900 working slaves in the whole colony, including 100 retained by the company to work on fortifications. There were only fifteen planters in the whole colony who owned more than twenty working slaves. Three-fourths owned none. At Natchez, there were slaves only on the Le Blanc and Kolly concessions; there were few on the Illinois or at Mobile Bay. Only around New Orleans were slaves and slave plantations numerous.[75]

The Indies Company was slow to acknowledge that its new arrangements adopted in November 1724 were insufficient to stimulate tobacco production in Louisiana. The annual report to the shareholders in the spring of 1725 admitted that the settlers had yet to turn to tobacco, but blamed this on the du Verdier tobacco monopoly of 1721–23 which had offered them such wretched terms. These had now been corrected, and the company looked forward to a speedy increase in tobacco deliveries.[76] In their report the next year (29 May 1726), however, the syndics and directors were much franker. Both vessels bringing returns from Louisiana had been lost in 1725, one at the Ile Dauphine where harbor conditions were notoriously dangerous, the other off the coast of Cuba. The shortage of slaves retarded the economic development of Louisiana: only 180 Negro slaves had been imported there in the previous four years. The company had recognized this and sent two vessels to Senegal in 1725 to carry 500 slaves to Louisiana. However, both vessels had stopped at St. Domingue and been persuaded by the local people to sell their slaves there, leaving Louisiana totally deprived of the expected reinforcements. The company had attempted to remedy this by making arrangements to send 600 more slaves to Louisiana who should have arrived there early that spring, 1726. They were planning to send 500 more slaves in the spring of the next year, 1727.[77] Meanwhile, nothing more than samples of tobacco had arrived from Louisiana.[78]

In the instructions to Périer, who went out as governor in the fall of 1726, tobacco and Natchez were stressed. He was to encourage the settlers around Mobile Bay to switch to tobacco and indigo since pitch and tar would not pay their own freight. He was to recognize the importance of the tobacco efforts at Natchez by visiting it soon after his arrival. The *commissaire* de la Chaise had been instructed to treat the settlers there equally with those around New Orleans in selling slaves. Périer could, however, give a preference to Natchez if he deemed it advisable; the concessions of Kolly and *monseigneur* Le Blanc were specifically mentioned. Broutin was confirmed in charge at Natchez under the supervisory authority of the councillor de la Loire, but the latter was to be required to reside at Natchez once the *habitation* there was a going concern.[79]

In 1726, at about the time that Périer was setting out, the company also embarked upon new serious efforts to improve the quality of Louisiana tobaccos. That year, they received some leaf from thence, the first fruits of the new policy of encouragement adopted in November 1724. They had some of this leaf manufactured into roll tobacco at their manufactories at Morlaix and Dieppe; they hoped to give Cardinal Fleury a roll from each manufactory as a gift on New Year's Day 1727 to show what they were doing to develop Louisiana. However, before making the present, they sampled the tobacco at a full meeting of the directors of the company. They found to their consternation that the tobacco so manufactured had retained the taste of Guienne or Alsace, the two areas from which Law had sent workers and seed to Louisiana almost ten years before. They recognized at once that the French consumer had developed such a marked preference for Virginia tobaccos (plus certain Dutch manufactured tobaccos made primarily from Virginia leaf) that he would never accept a product that smelled of Guienne or Alsace. They therefore decided to abandon their projected gift to the cardinal and keep the entire matter a secret.

For the future, the directors resolved that they must obtain seed from Virginia to introduce into Louisiana so that the tobacco grown along the Mississippi would more closely resemble that from the Chesapeake. They asked Pierre Cavalier, a syndic of the company who was also their buying agent in London, to engage "an intelligent person" to go to Virginia and bring back some seed, particularly the seed of the varieties used by the Dutch manufacturer Scholt whose output was so much to the French taste. Six thousand *l.t.* were promised for the successful completion of the mission. Cavalier engaged a young Swiss Protestant named Lunel who successfully completed his mission. On his return to France, he was engaged by the company in 1728 to go out to Louisiana and teach the settlers at Natchez to cultivate and prepare tobacco as he had seen it done in Virginia.[80]

Meanwhile, the company had also written to the chief officials of its colony in St. Domingue asking them to try to get tobacco seed from Virginia vessels that might trade their way.[81] When the new governor Périer, outward bound to Louisiana, stopped at Cap François on the north coast of St. Domingue, he found there three Englishmen allegedly familiar with tobacco, including one from Carolina who styled himself a "master manufacturer"; he engaged all three to go with him to Louisiana to teach the Louisianans how to grow tobacco in the best English manner.[82] The heritage of "the Clairacs" was being diluted.

Périer and Bienville, his predecessor and successor, between them administered Louisiana from 1717 to 1743. Both preferred to tell Paris what Paris wanted to hear, but neither could invent deliveries. Hence, the pattern of correspondence so common under both those gentlemen: optimistic letters in the spring and early summer about great crops of tobacco then in the fields; sorrowful explanations in the fall that rain or drought or insects or hurricane had resulted in much smaller crops than expected. Périer arrived at New Orleans on 15 March 1727. By the end of April he was sending the expected glowing optimistic letters to the controller-general,[83] to the count of Maurepas, the young secretary of state for the navy,[84] and the abbé Raguet, a director of the Indies Company.[85] The fullest and frankest letter, however, was that from Périer and de la Chaise, the *commissaire-ordonnateur*, to the company; in it we can see that all was not too well. The previous year, 1726, the planters in all Louisiana had raised only 20,000 lb. of tobacco, the product of a single medium-sized plantation in Virginia. Allegedly not knowing that the company wanted dried leaf in hands, the settlers about Natchez had, in the bad, old tradition of St. Domingue, manufactured their tobacco into small rolls; de la Chaise had allowed them 50 *l.t.* per quintal (10*s.* per lb.) for this—instead of the authorized price of 30—to compensate them for the costs of manufacture, but they all claimed to have lost on the transaction. In the coming year, the planters not only at Natchez but at Choupetoulas ("Chapitoulas") would grow much more tobacco: 200,000 lb. were promised, 100,000 lb. from Choupetoulas alone, though some doubts were expressed. Much more tobacco could be grown farther down the river were it not for the very heavy expense of clearing the forests and the unfortunate proclivity of the settlers to plant tobacco on the richest soils where it seemed peculiarly susceptible to insects.

Many planters were, they reported, reluctant to undertake the costs of clearing forests and building drying sheds for tobacco for fear that the company would not adhere to its terms announced in 1724-25: 30 *l.t.* per quintal nominal price, but 40 *l.t.* when credited against old debts. The growers suspected that the company would lower terms once tobacco was produced in any quantity in the colony. What they wanted were prices guaranteed for ten years: 50 *l.t.* in credit against debts; 40 *l.t.* in cash; or 35 *l.t.*, without discount, in bills of exchange on France. Périer and de la Chaise couldn't alter the prices set by the company, but they did waive the 10 percent discount (premium) on bills of exchange. The settlers did not remit these to France themselves because few of them had correspondents there, but rather used them to buy European goods which ships' officers had brought along as private ventures (*pacotilles*). In addition, the officials reported, many of the planters claimed that their tobacco was not suitable for drying and packing in hands (*en manoque*); they asked permission to continue manufacturing it for its better preservation. Périer and de la Chaise thought that the planters should be indulged in this (after all, the monopoly could always sell the roll tobacco to the troops), as well as in the requested ten-year guarantee of price.[86] In short, since the company had agreed to accept delivery at Natchez, the transportation problem had disappeared. Enough slaves had arrived in the past year to take the edge off complaints about the labor supply.[87] Conditions of delivery—dried leaf versus manufactured rolls—were still a problem, particularly in a climate in which many of the planters found it difficult to preserve their tobacco while waiting for the rare company ship. But the crucial problem to Périer and de la Chaise was fixing the price of tobacco high enough to make it more attractive to the planters than other commodities. This might well mean valuing it at two or three times the world price.

When the autumn of 1727 arrived, things were not quite as Périer had predicted in the spring. He was as optimistic as ever in his letter to the count of Maurepas—Louisiana was some day going to make better silk than China[88]—but he had to discuss facts with the company. Not as much tobacco had been grown as expected: he could only send 25,000 lb. on the *Prince de Conti,* which had just brought 266 slaves, but he hoped to send more on a subsequent vessel, perhaps 100,000 lb. more, once the tobacco from Natchez came down. At the same time he and de la Chaise had to admit that the tobacco was not all that it might be. Despite warnings, many planters had insisted on spinning their tobacco and pressing it into *carottes.* They alleged that they did not have the laborers to build sheds for drying or curing their tobacco in the Virginia style; therefore, they had processed it to preserve it. The council had decided that since they had not followed instructions, the planters should only get 40 *l.t.* per quintal for these *carottes* instead of the 50 *l.t.* paid the previous year. The planters had, however, complained that they would be ruined, and—so as not to discourage them—the council had raised the price to 50 *l.t.* again. One sieur de Beaulieu of Choupetoulas had been deceived by an incompetent employee who prepared thoroughly bad *carottes* and only mediocre dried tobacco. They had however also taken his output lest the poor fellow be ruined. Their Carolina "experts" had obviously proven inadequate for they beseeched the company to send them from France someone skilled in harvesting the leaf at maturity and in drying it. They were not discouraged, though, for "everybody is going to begin to cultivate this plant and . . . next year certainly the returns in it will be considerable."[89]

The company was not at all amused by these going on during Périer's first year in Louisiana. As soon as they received his first letters asking for more generous price terms, they wrote him in the fall of 1727 firmly expounding their policy. They could, they informed him, buy Virginia tobacco delivered in France for less than one-half what Louisiana tobacco cost them, including the freight home. Nevertheless, they were prepared to pay this premium for the time being as an encouragement to the colony and as an experiment. They could not however guarantee to go on paying those prices for the next ten years—let alone pay more—for many reasons: to do so would be binding on them without any equivalent obligations of quantity or quality on the part of the planters; and, since they had yet to receive any accurate information on how much tobacco an average slave could produce in a normal year, they had no way of ascertaining the real costs of tobacco to the planter.

The governor and *ordonnateur* were instructed that, until such time as ships could be built cheaply in Louisiana, they were not to encourage tobacco production beyond the capacity of the shipping then planned for that colony. Under existing trading conditions, it would not pay the company to send extra ships thither just to bring back tobacco. Furthermore, the company did not want noneconomic arguments used to persuade planters to grow tobacco rather than indigo or any other crop. Each planter should be left to follow his own best interest, for the prosperity of the company lay in the total prosperity of the colony!

The company's ardor for Louisiana tobacco was obviously cooling by 1727. This is partly understandable in terms of the decline in European prices for Virginia tobacco since 1725; it may also be explained by the quality of what they had received from Louisiana. The crop of 1726 sent home in 1727 was a great disappointment: both the *carottes* (three-fourths spoiled) and the dried leaf sent in chests were bad. The directors wanted only hogsheads used in the future. Although the leaf grown by Coustilhas at Choupetoulas was very good, that from Natchez was small, ill-scented, and worm-eaten. It appeared to be mostly second growth. (The inference was that the Natchez planters had disposed of their first growth elsewhere.) The company would make experiments to see if they could use second and third growth but such leaf should not be passed off as first.[90]

When the crop of 1727 came home in 1728, the company was even less happy. It was not simply the obviously rotten tobacco of the sieur de Beaulieu, about which Périer and de la Chaise continued to apologize for several years.[91] Even presents of supposedly choice tobacco could be disasters. Father de Beaubois, a priest in the colony, sent a chest of tobacco as a gift to Cardinal Fleury. The abbé Raguet, a director of the company, wrote him never, never to do that again, for when the chest was opened, the cardinal's apartment was "infected" by the stench; the whole chest had to be thrown out, and Raguet forced into an ex tempore "harangue" to "lessen the inconvenient consequences of that gift."[92]

The company's more positive reaction to this disappointing quality was, as noted above, to send out to Louisiana in 1728 the sieur Lunel, their Swiss spy just returned from the Chesapeake. Before setting out for the Mississippi, Lunel had a manual printed on the proper Chesapeake way to raise and cure tobacco. He was instructed to teach English methods and distribute English seed (and Havana, if he could get any), starting with the company's plantation near New Orleans and then visiting all the principal planting areas. At the harvest, he was to inspect all receipts and records, making sure that the various qualities correctly declared were not mixed in a single hogshead. He was also to build a press for the proper packing of the hogsheads, as was done in the Chesapeake.[93] Lunel arrived in Louisiana in December 1728. He, his "Instructions" from the company, and his manual for the planters were all well received by the officers and settlers—though the governor did not always accept his strict judgments on inspections. His own reports were critical of Clairac methods but optimistic about the country and its soils. In the fall of 1729, he made his headquarters temporarily at Natchez.[94]

Although Périer and de la Chaise were still trying to get the company to guarantee for a few years ahead the 30 and 40 l.t. per quintal prices established in 1724–25,[95] the directors moved in the opposite direction. They apparently decided that the poor quality of receipts in 1727 and 1728 did not merit those prices and that uniform prices discouraged effort. By article ix of his instructions, Lunel was directed to announce that starting in 1729, the company would pay 30 l.t. per quintal only for perfect dried leaf in hands of the quality called "the first sort" (and made only from the first growth of the plant). For the "second sort" they would pay only 20 l.t. per quintal. The "third sort" they would not accept at all.[96]

In Louisiana, meanwhile, disasters and apologies followed fast on each other's heels. In 1728, forty days of summer rain, though admirable for the rice, destroyed the greater part of the tobacco crop in the lower reaches of the colony—yet Périer still hoped to send 200,000 lb. home from Natchez.[97] It is unlikely that that figure was actually reached for the second ship carrying home the crop of that year left early in 1729 with only 66,983 lb., all that was available.[98] In the following summer of 1729, there were again weeks of heavy rain which destroyed much of the tobacco growing in the lower reaches of the colony—but again Périer and de la Chaise hoped to send 300,000 lb. home.[99] It is certain that that figure was not reached either.

Internal transport remained a problem. Early in 1729, Périer experimented by sending the ocean-going vessel which had come for tobacco up the river to see if it could reach Natchez. It had to stop at Trois Chenaux (Three Channels), eight leagues below the fort and have the tobacco brought down to it in boats. The next year, the governor intended to send demigalleys up from New Orleans.[100] No one wanted to assume responsibility for transporting anyone else's tobacco by water—so great was the fear of spoilage.[101]

Quality, though, remained the insuperable problem. In the spring of 1728, Périer and de la Chaise assured the company that the poor quality of the tobacco sent the previous years on the *Baleine* arose not from the dishonesty or laziness of the planters, but from their ignorance. More expert instructors were requested, before and after the arrival of Lunel. In the meantime, the officers were taking stringent steps to guard against the repetition of such unfortunate shipments: rigorous inspection would assure the receipt of nothing but perfectly made tobacco, carefully dried, packed in hogsheads. They had given permission to manufacture some tobacco experimentally at Natchez, but each roll was to be marked indicating whether it was made from leaf of the first, second, or third qualities. They were sure that the tobacco they were then sending home on the *Duc de Noailles* would give complete satisfaction.[102] (One year later, they were writing apologetically about the poor quality of the tobacco on the *Duc de Noailles*.)[103] In the fall of 1728, those same officials assured the company that they had announced publicly and firmly that they would accept no tobacco except that properly made, dried, and packed in hands. To make sure that none else was received, they had appointed inspectors: at New Orleans Antoine Descairac, a Clairac emigrant of 1718, who had made the good tobacco for Coustilhas at Choupetoulas, and at Natchez one of the Ricards (Ricart), an "expert" long in the colony. (They only wished again that the company had sent them out more experienced men from Clairac as demonstrators.) [104]

Yet that same winter Périer and de la Chaise were to overrule Lunel on some rejections and some of the tobacco thus sent home in the *Diane* was found by the company to be worthless: "It would be better to burn this poor stuff in Louisiana than to send it to France. Nothing discredits the colony more."[105] Again in the spring of 1729, when cargo was hard to find because of the poor crop the previous year, 6,000 lb. of roll tobacco similar to that sent on the *Diane* were sent on the *Flore* and also found to be worthless on arrival in France. The company was so indignant that they threatened to make de la Chaise pay damages if he tried such a trick again.[106] The directors were also indignant because Périer and de la Chaise, to get around the shortage of hogsheads, had had tobacco packed in the empty water casks of slave ships returning to France, ruining them as water casks. The company reversed itself once more and ordered the planters to supply their own hogsheads, even if it was necessary to allow them something for costs.[107] Périer and de la Chaise in turn pleaded for more coopers (and carpenters for barge making).[108]

Nevertheless, it is clear that by 1729 some good tobacco was arriving in France from Louisiana. The invoices of receipt of some of this at the company's manufactory at Tonneins were sent back to Louisiana in 1729 to be shown to the planters as an incentive to greater efforts.[109]

In retrospect, between 1723 when the Indies Company was restored and 1729 when the entire condition of the company was again reviewed, the policy of the company towards the Louisiana tobacco trade had passed through several phases. The new syndics and directors found in 1723 that the earlier efforts of Law had come to nothing and that no tobacco was arriving from Louisiana. Committed to a policy of developing there a supply of tobacco for France, they at first seemed to assume that if they offered high enough prices, supplies would be forthcoming. This policy, embodied in their *ordonnances* of November 1724 and June 1725 setting prices at 30 and 40 *l.t.* per quintal did not in fact bring forth the desired supplies because of a labor shortage within the colony (and the relative attractiveness of other labor uses). The company had therefore to make more serious efforts to send slaves there which began to show results in 1727-28. The quality of the new production did not, however, give satisfaction. Starting in 1727, the company made efforts to solve this problem by obtaining Chesapeake seed and sending an "expert" to the colony to demonstrate the correct method of growing, harvesting, drying, bunching in hands and packing tobacco. They also resolved to use price incentives to get the quality they wanted, ordering that from 1729 lower prices would be paid for tobacco not of the first quality. By the end of that year, the problem of quality had not been completely solved: although much good tobacco was arriving in France, other was still being unladen in an unusable condition. Quantitative progress was noticeable but still modest. Perhaps 150,000 lb. had been delivered in France from the crop of 1728, not all of it usable; 300,000 lb. were promised from the crop of 1729. (France was then importing over six million pounds annually from England alone.)

It is obvious that by 1728–29 well-informed persons in France had reason to be rather disenchanted about Louisiana's tobacco prospects. Some might well have wondered whether anything would ever come of all that talk and promise except stinking, rotting, worm-eaten leaves. Jean-Daniel Kolly, managing partner of the St. Catherine's concession at Natchez, was sufficiently concerned to go out to Louisiana with his son in 1728 to see for himself. He, it will be remembered, had made a fortune during the "System" and had purchased that concession in 1721 from the former *ordonnateur*, Marc-Antoine Hubert. He subsequently acquired a plantation at Choupetoulas from the local merchants Massy and Guénot.[110] In addition, he came out armed with a power of attorney to manage the concession of "Madame de Chaumont."[111] She was the notorious speculator reputed to have made an enormous fortune in Law's time. (She had compounded for three millions at the time of the Chamber of Justice of 1716, but was taxed eight millions by the Visa of 1722—the largest single assessment!) [112] She had early acquired a concession at the Pascagoula River.[113] It would thus appear that "smart money" had become disturbed.

Not only private proprietors began to worry. The company's whole position in Louisiana came under question. As exploiter of the tobacco monopoly, the Indies Company had a political obligation to do all in its power to try to develop a national source of tobacco in Louisiana. As a firm trading on a limited capital, the Indies Company had a more pressing obligation to avoid activities that resulted in continuing large-scale losses. Louisiana was a losing trade for the company. Its expenses there were high and its returns negligible. One calculation showed the company's losses in its trade to that colony between 1721 and 1731 as 8.7 million *l.t.* gross or seven million net after budgeted allowance for bad debts and post-1731 recoveries were deducted.[114] A substantial part of these losses resulted from bad debts. To help develop the colony, the company sold the settlers European goods, provisions, and slaves on long credits. Much of the sums so advanced proved difficult or impossible to collect. This was reflected in the rising figures in the company's accounts for debts owing in Louisiana:

31 January 1725	2,601,217 *l.t.*
31 January 1726	3,147,713 *l.t.*
22 April 1727	3,917,119 *l.t.*
30 April 1728	4,432,892 *l.t.*

In drawing up the effective balance of the company as of 30 April 1728, 50 percent was deducted from overseas debts generally, but 80 percent was written off for Louisiana.[115]

With expenses remaining high[116] and losses increasing rapidly, the question obviously was how long could the company continue to "encourage" Louisiana. Some were prepared to argue that the company had already lost so much in Louisiana that a little more wouldn't make too much difference. One memoir writer insisted that if only the company would persevere with its existing arrangements and be prepared to invest about 300,000 l.t. annually for the next six or so years, Louisiana would be brought to the point where it could start making major returns to France. The author was well informed and cited the losses suffered during the first generation of Virginia's settlement as proof of what could come from even the most discouraging beginnings.[117] The orthodox government attitude was suggested in an earlier memoir of 1728 by Louis Fagon, *intendant des finances* and formerly one of the commissioners of council in charge of the company during the receivership of 1721–23. For him, it was self evident that France had to develop a colonial supply of tobacco to free itself from paying three million annually to the English and Dutch for imported leaf. Louisiana was the only colony available for such production. Hence, "of all the activities of the government, there is none so essential to the State as sending to that colony ample and continuous aid."[118] There was nothing in this formulation about continuing the existing position of the Indies Company in Louisiana; thus by omission it was implied that if the company could not continue, other means would have to be found to support that colony.

The Indies Company's own straitened circumstances made some decision necessary. In the latter months of 1729 and the early months of 1730, as we observed in the last chapter, there ensued an extended debate within the company and government about the firm's condition. Its earnings, although considerable, were insufficient to cover the high dividends to which it had become pledged in 1723. Its trading capital was shrinking and proving inadequate for the many branches of trade for which it was responsible. It logically occurred to some that if the company farmed out the tobacco monopoly for a higher rent than it was then receiving from its own management and gave up its unprofitable or capital-expensive branches of trade, it could devote its liberated capital resources to the highly profitable East India trade, to the obvious advantage of its annual trading balance.

Such a suggestion had actually been discussed in the annual report of the syndics and directors of the company in 1727, but rejected then as inconsistent with important state objectives, including the development of an autarkic supply of tobacco in Louisiana.[119] Such suggestions were, however, to sprout on every side during 1729–30. Some came from avowed enemies of the company. The farmer-general Desvieux suggested abolishing the company, transferring the tobacco farm to the united farms and all its trading activities to a new company.[120] Another memoir from a merchant discussed the possibility of setting up a new company to take over the Louisiana trade. The author was no friend of the Indies Company, but admitted that no new company could do any better faced with shipping costs, the tendency of

Louisiana tobacco to spoil in transit, and a tobacco monopoly in France. He recommended waiting until the Indies Company voluntarily offered to surrender Louisiana and then throwing open the trade thither.[121]

Much more important was the debate which took place within the camp of the friends of the company. One such memoir written in 1729 for the controller-general asserted that the company would then have been in a flourishing condition if it had concentrated on the East India trade since 1721, giving up its trade to Africa and Canada and ceding Louisiana to the king. It would pay the king to take over Louisiana, even if it would cost his treasury more at first, because that colony was on the verge of becoming a major producer of tobacco which ultimately would save the kingdom the millions annually it then spent on English tobacco. Upon the retrocession of Louisiana to the king, the trade thither should be thrown open to all French merchants, though the company should still be obliged to bring 500–600 slaves there yearly and to buy all the tobacco produced in the colony. Private merchants could not be counted on to bring slaves in quantity at first, and the company (which still had the tobacco monopoly) could use the slave ships to bring tobacco back to France.[122] A simliar but more complicated "mixed" scheme was advanced in another memoir. Its author would also throw open the import trade in Louisiana to all French merchants who would be free to carry away all goods except tobacco. The company would retain the tobacco and Spanish trades and would share responsibility with the Senegal Company and private merchants for bringing slaves to the colony; it would be obliged to buy all tobacco grown in the colony at a price to be fixed by the king. The king would also take over some of the administrative and transportation expenses then born by the company.[123]

Such "mixed" schemes were answered by another memoir writer, also strongly in favor of getting the Indies Company out of Louisiana and every other commitment so that it could concentrate on the trades to the East Indies and China. He therefore rejected the suggestion that, after handing over Louisiana to the crown, the company should still be obliged to bring slaves there and to buy all the tobacco grown there. He was one of those who wanted the company to farm out its tobacco monopoly in France and so free more of its capital for the East Indies trade. Since one ship with European goods could buy enough tobacco in Louisiana to freight four ships back with tobacco, he argued that transport costs would always make the Louisiana tobacco trade a losing proposition and the Indies Company was best out of it. If the government wanted tobacco from Louisiana, they could issue an order that nothing else might be exported from thence. They could similarly always create a market for Louisiana tobacco in France by excluding foreign tobaccos.[124]

Plissay, probably a naval official, a conservative friend of Louisiana, attacked the rather offhand suggestions in the previous memoir that tobacco cultivation might be made compulsory in Louisiana. The colony must be left free to develop according to its natural advantages and disadvantages. He insisted, however, that the Indies Company or whoever succeeded it as tobacco monopolist in France must be obliged in law to buy all the tobacco brought back from Louisiana at a previously announced schedule of prices. This would encourage private ships to carry tobacco back to France and would result in the most economical freight rates possible. For the rest, he accepted the necessity of the company shedding most of its ancillary activities.[125] He may well have been very influential for his ideas were closest to those ultimately adopted.

Such was the rather indecisive state of the discussion in March 1730 when, as described in the last chapter, the affairs of the company were so rudely shaken by the arrival in Paris (ca. 14 March) of word of the massacre at Natchez, followed a few days later (19 March) by the financial scandal within the company which led to the dismissal of the controller-general Le Peletier Des Forts, commonly regarded as a friend of the company.[126] From the time Montplaisir and "the Clairacs" settled at Natchez in 1720, that area had been the principal center of tobacco growing in the colony. The various farms, plantations, and concessions of the French there were scattered in and among the villages of the Natchez Indians, a settled, agricultural but very warlike tribe. This had been a disadvantage from the beginning. During the Second Natchez War of 1723, Kolly's St. Catherine's concession had been raided and horses and cattle killed.[127] This was of course nothing compared to the events of 28 November 1729. Alarmed by the land-grabbing proclivities of the new commander, the Natchez formed a successful conspiracy and in the course of one night stealthily killed the greater part of the French population thereabouts: 145 men, 36 women, and 56 children. (Other women and children were taken prisoners and subsequently ransomed. Most of the slaves were also taken prisoners by the Indians.) The Le Blanc and St. Catherine's concessions were totally lost with all their staff. Among those slaughtered by the banks of the great river were the "Mississippi" millionaire Jean Daniel Kolly and his son, who had arrived the day before to inspect their St. Catherine's concession.[128]

Although the fort was eventually reestablished, the work of that night effectively extinguished for many years the agricultural activity about Natchez. The Negro slaves were killed, abducted, or dispersed. It was at once recognized in Paris that since Natchez was the principal center of tobacco production in Louisiana, its destruction ended any immediate prospects of the Indies Company being able to supply much leaf from that colony. A "free trade" memoir writer immediately argued that, should the company thereafter retrocede Louisiana to the crown, there was no longer any point in requiring it or its successor in the tobacco monopoly to buy all the tobacco produced in Louisiana, for there was unlikely to be much grown there for many years.[129]

All the same, the ultimate details were to be very much along the lines suggested earlier by Plissay. In July 1730, as we have seen, the Indies Company came to an agreement with the United General Farms on the terms under which the former would lease the tobacco monopoly to the latter. The terms were ultimately embodied in a contract between the two of 5 September 1730 confirmed by a *résultat du conseil* of the same date. By article iii of the *résultat,* the united farms, as the new lessees of the tobacco monopoly, were obliged to purchase all tobacco delivered from Louisiana—at the price they paid for Virginia tobacco![130] (This was a reversion to the provisions of the 1721 lease.) Having thus farmed out the tobacco monopoly on terms not disadvantageous to itself, the Indies Company had only to rid itself of the incubus of Louisiana to be most comfortably rid of both halves of Law's unhappy alliance.

On 22 January 1731, the full court of the company offered to retrocede Louisiana to the crown. The *délibération* recited the company's great hopes for and devotion to the colony, and all they had done for it, including the twenty millions they had spent there—but the massacre by the Natchez, in wiping out the most flourishing and promising part of the colony, had rendered all those hopes and efforts futile and forced the company, however reluctantly, to offer to surrender the colony.[131] Privately the company had indicated that it would be willing to surrender to the crown its political position and administrative responsibilities in Louisiana while retaining the trading monopoly, including the obligation to supply the colony with victuals and 500 slaves a year—or, alternatively, to be rid of the colony and pay the crown compensation for the obligations it was surrendering.[132] The Council of State, by the *arrêt* of 23 January 1731, accepted the latter alternative.[133] The controller-general Orry wrote the same day to the company that the secretary of state Maurepas estimated that they should pay the king 3.5 million for the various obligations they were throwing off in Louisiana; the king, however, to help the company had reduced the figure to 1.45 millions payable over ten years. These terms were accepted by the company's *délibération* of 24 January.[134] Thus were the Natchez tomahawks made to cut the Gordian knot.

For the moment, the Louisiana tobacco trade seemed extinguished indeed. By the *résultat* of 5 September 1730, the united farms were obliged to buy Louisiana tobacco delivered in France only at the price they paid for Virginia tobacco there. In practice such terms would have meant the total extinction of tobacco cultivation for export along the Mississippi: transportation costs were so much higher from Louisiana than from Virginia that little would have been left for the planters. Louisiana tobacco had recently seemed to need a European price twice that for Virginia. Maurepas, however, as we shall see in the next chapter, was too orthodox a colonial minister to permit anything as unorthodox as a free market to last very long.

CHAPTER 13

Louisiana Tobacco under "Free Trade," 1731–63

The Age of Maurepas, 1731–49

Jean-Frédéric Phélypeaux, count of Maurepas, followed his grandfather and father as secretary of state for the navy. When his father, Jérôme Pontchartrain, was forced, after the death of Louis XIV, to give up his secretaryship of state, he had arranged to surrender it to his fourteen-year-old son. The young Maurepas assumed the title and functions of a secretary of state in 1718 when he was seventeen but was not assigned the navy department until 1723 (on the death of Dubois) when he was twenty-two. He retained the office until a witty offense to Madame de Pompadour led to his dismissal and banishment in 1749. Though his father and grandfather were still alive when he took up his departmental duties in 1723 and could have given him much valued advice, he was very slow in asserting himself as a policy-maker during either the prime ministership of the duke of Bourbon (1723–26) or the controller-generalship of Le Peletier Des Forts (1726–30). He early showed a flare for paperwork, but was never to be a very creative policy formulator. However, with the replacement of Des Forts in 1730 by the much less significant Orry, Maurepas, now approaching thirty, began to show a bit more administrative initiative.

In November 1727, Maurepas exhibited his emerging bureaucratic personality by drawing up a memoir delimiting the respective authority of the secretary of state for the navy and the controller-general in the affairs of the Indies Company. The secretary was to be responsible for all the overseas affairs of the company, including the encouragement of tobacco cultivation in Louisiana in the interests of national self-sufficiency. Yet, though the agricultural and other internal affairs of Louisiana were to be under the secretary, the foreign trade of that colony was to be under the supervision of the controller-general—including the slave trade thought so necessary for realizing the agricultural potential of the colony. Then too, the entire management of the tobacco monopoly in France, from its purchasing policy down to the hiring of guards and manufacturing employees, was left under the supervision of the controller-general.[1] It was an awkward division unless the two officials worked unusually well together. That it worked at all must have been due to the self-effacement of the young secretary of state. Even after the fall of Des Forts, in a report of September 1730 to the *conseil royal de commerce,* Maurepas pointedly refrained from saying anything about Louisiana or the activities of the Indies Company inasmuch as such topics belonged entirely to the jurisdiction of the controller-general.[2]

Only after the changes of 1730–31 could Maurepas assert himself in the then much less controversial affairs of Louisiana. Once the Indies Company had farmed out the tobacco monopoly and had given up Louisiana, the affairs of that colony became much less important as political questions and were allowed to pass in fact under the almost exclusive attention of the secretary of state for the navy. No one else really cared. Although matters concerning the tobacco monopoly under the united farms still remained within the cognizance of the controller-general, even there Maurepas was able to take a certain amount of initiative.

The immediate problem facing Maurepas as the Indies Company surrendered their privileges in Louisiana (as of 1 July 1731) and ceased trading thither was to persuade private traders to venture their ships there. Such ships would have to be sent immediately to supply the colony and take away its produce or the entire experiment there would collapse. Maurepas thus wrote hurriedly to the officers of his ministry in the western ports, instructing them to urge local merchants to send ships to Louisiana; as compensation for unfamiliar risks, the king promised an unspecified subsidy on all victuals and other European goods sent to the colony. When Belamy, the *commissaire de la marine* at La Rochelle, conveyed this information to the Chamber of Commerce there, they not unexpectedly inquired how much the subsidy would be. Characteristically, Maurepas had no idea and had to write back to Belamy asking how much would be necessary.[3] Privately, Maurepas wrote to Jacques Rasteau (Râteau), a leading merchant at La Rochelle, offering him a subsidy of 40 *l.t.* per ton on all goods sent to Louisiana plus an attractive contract to carry government flour there for the garrison.[4] Rasteau thus became the first private French merchant to send a vessel, the *St. Paul,* to Louisiana after the retrocession. These favorable terms were soon extended to other merchants such as Jean Jung of Bordeaux and Fro(s)tin of St. Malo,[5] though later the subsidy was changed to only 20 *l.t.* on goods sent out, with a further 20 *l.t.* per ton on goods returned.[6] In addition, an *ordonnance* of 4 August 1731 exempted all merchant vessels bound for Louisiana from the general obligation to carry indentured servants or muskets there free.[7] The next year, an *arrêt* of the council of state exempted goods bound to or from Louisiana from export or import duties in France or from river tolls on the Seine or Loire.[8] (Even most foreign goods bound thither were exempted.) It is thus clear that from the very start of the "free trade" period of Louisiana's commercial history, the government recognized: (a) that high freight rates (caused by exceptional distance and unbalanced trade) could strangle the trade of the colony in its infancy unless brought down by state subsidies; and (b) that high costs of labor in Louisiana could further restrict the marketability of its produce in Europe unless partially modified by exemptions in France from import and even export duties (to reduce the cost of living in Louisiana).

These measures were all designed to encourage the trade to Louisiana generally. From the first, however, merchants and bureaucrats realized that tobacco, though monopolized in France, would be one of the principal "free trade" returns from capital-poor Louisiana, despite the destruction of Natchez. Thus, when informed early in 1731 of the government's desire that they trade to Louisiana, the La Rochelle Chamber of Commerce understandably asked Belamy whether the united farms would buy the tobacco they might bring back from Louisiana and, if so, at what price. Maurepas replied that he would try to get the farmers-general to agree in advance to take Louisiana tobacco at a set price.[9] He was not at first successful: on 22 May 1731, he wrote to the governor and *ordonnateur* of Louisiana that the united farms refused to give any such guarantee until they knew more about the quality of tobacco from Louisiana; he expected, however, that as soon as the new monopolists had seen one good crop, they would agree to a price advantageous to the colony.[10] Such vague assurances were hardly likely to settle the doubts of the merchants of La Rochelle: a few weeks later, their Chamber of Commerce asked for a guaranteed price of 50 *l.t.* per quintal on all tobacco returned from Louisiana.[11] However one calculates freight, this was well above the prices paid by the Indies Company in the 1720's and 150 percent above the prices then being paid by the monopoly for Virginia tobacco delivered. Maurepas did not have the power to concede such demands but he assured the La Rochelle chamber collectively[12]—and Rasteau privately[13]—that if the tobacco their ships brought back from Louisiana was of acceptable quality, the united farms would take it at a price well above what they paid for Virginia tobacco. The gap between the Virginia price (20 *l.t.*) and their asking price (50 *l.t.*) was so wide that this promise was not as reassuring as it might seem.

Maurepas was warned that without a guaranteed price for tobacco, the merchants and supercargoes in Louisiana would not pay more for the leaf than 15 *l.t.* per quintal: this was hardly a price to encourage the planters.[14] Maurepas preferred to wait and see. In March 1732, the king's flute the *Gironde* returned to La Rochelle from New Orleans, the first vessel to arrive from the colony since 1 July 1731, the effective date of the retrocession. She had on board three light hogsheads of tobacco (weight, 1,019 lb.) belonging to de Latre, a merchant of that port, and 16,039 lb. in light hogsheads and barrels which Nicolas Chauvin de la Fresnière, a planter and trader in Louisiana, had consigned on his own account to Vivier, a merchant at La Rochelle. The tobacco was placed in a sealed warehouse at La Rochelle where, at Maurepas' urging, it was inspected by de la Porte, the senior farmer-general and head of the company's tobacco purchasing and manufacturing committee. All but two barrels were accepted experimentally, but the price remained to be settled.[15] In June, when Rasteau's ship the *St. Paul* arrived in La

Rochelle from Louisiana with 103,000 lb. of tobacco on his own account, Maurepas assured him that the united farms would take his leaf tobacco as it had taken that on the *Gironde*. The secretary was fearful, though, that they would not take the manufactured tobacco (*en rolles et en carottes*) which had also been brought back.[16] Maurepas was bringing pressure on the controller-general Orry to get the prices settled as soon as possible, so that two vessels about to leave for Louisiana, one from La Rochelle and one from Bordeaux, should know before departing what they could expect to get for tobacco on their return.[17]

In the event, the price decision was postponed until August, by which time the monopoly would have had some reports from their manufactory at Tonneins on the results obtained from working up the first Louisiana leaf. Maurepas was urging a price of about 30 or 35 *l.t.* per quintal; Orry, to avoid having to make a decision, suggested to the united farms that they negotiate privately with each merchant for the sale price. On or about 1 August, the farmers-general submitted a long memoir to the council stating their position. They could not negotiate privately with the merchants because the latter, knowing the government's great interest in Louisiana, would hold out for an excessive price. Although it was highly desirable to establish tobacco production in a French colony, Louisiana tobacco was still unknown to French consumers; to force it on them might create great hostility. Earlier experiments in manufacturing it at the Indies Company's manufactory at Le Havre had produced an unsatisfactory product tasting of yellow wax and anise. Nevertheless, out of consideration for the state objectives involved, the united farms were prepared to buy the tobacco now coming from Louisiana, manufacture it carefully, mixing it with other tobaccos, and thus gradually introduce it to the French consumer and hopefully develop a taste for it. They only hoped that if consumers refused absolutely to take it, the council would relieve them of the commitment.

The united farms felt that they had to be very careful about the price: although the quantities then involved were very small, if an excessively generous price were promised, production might rise very rapidly in Louisiana and bankrupt the farm. In an average year they manufactured eight million pounds of leaf to produce six million pounds of consumable tobacco products. Of this, only about one-third was sold at the full monopoly price of 50 *sols* per lb.; the rest was sold at much lower prices in the army, in frontier areas exposed to smuggling, and in impoverished districts. The *résultat* of 5 September 1730 obliged them to buy Louisiana tobacco only at the price they paid for Virginia leaf: the latter then cost them only 19 *l.t.* 1 *s.* per quintal delivered in France, all expenses included. Even this price was a favor to Louisiana for its tobacco was not as good as that of Virginia. Under the circumstances, the farmers-general, during their existing lease of 1730–38, could not offer to pay more than their Virginia price (19 *l.t.* 1 *s.*). If that was enough for Virginia growers whose tobacco had to pass through the

British entrepôt, it should be enough for Louisianans who shipped directly to France.[18]

It is unlikely that the farmers-general in fact imagined that a price of 19 *l.t.* 1 *s.* delivered in France would be sufficient to encourage tobacco cultivation in Louisiana. In all probability, they made that offer for the record, to establish a claim to compensation in the event that the council decided on a higher price. At this impasse, the entire matter was referred to some high official in the office of the controller-general (perhaps Fagon) who early in August worked out the accepted solution. He reported that the merchants wanted a price of 40 *l.t.* per quintal claiming that their tobacco cost them 30 *l.t.* in Louisiana. However, they obtained their tobacco there with European goods which they marked up 100 percent over cost price. Thus, the prime cost of the tobacco to them was nearer 15 *l.t.*, excluding freight. Even so, the price offered by the united farms of only 19 *l.t.* 1 *s.* was totally inadequate. As a compromise, he suggested that the price be fixed at 35 *l.t.* per quintal for 1732 and 1733, declining by stages to 25 *l.t.* after 1738, and that, of this price, only 25 *l.t.* per quintal be paid by the united farms, anything over to be charged against the annual rent which the united farms paid the Indies Company. That company could well afford the modest sums involved (unlikely to go above 30,000 *l.t.* annually) because they had been permitted to throw off their losses in Louisiana and yet received a rent of 7.5–8 millions annually from the united farms for the tobacco monopoly.[19]

This scheme was accepted by the council in its general outlines though with a slightly accelerated decline in prices. On 6 August 1732, the controller-general Orry wrote formally to Maurepas that the united farms had agreed to pay 25 *l.t.* and that the king had decided to establish a declining schedule of prices for Louisiana tobacco: 35 *l.t.* per quintal during 1732 and 1733; 30 during 1734 and 1735; 27:10 during 1736 and 1737 and 25 in 1738 (the last year of the monopoly's existing lease). Anything over 25 *l.t.* per quintal paid by the united farms was to be recovered from the Indies Company in a manner to be worked out between the two companies.[20] On 12 August, Maurepas sent a circular letter to the naval officials in the principal ports informing them of the newly fixed prices and instructing them to notify the merchants in their respective ports.[21] Word was of course also sent to Louisiana for the encouragement of planters there.[22]

The main lines of Maurepas' policy had been worked out (and the most active phase of his interest terminated) with these new arrangements of 1732 for the Louisiana tobacco trade. He had obtained a seemingly adequate price for Louisiana tobacco in France, at least for the short run. He had also obtained a significant subsidy for shipping to and from that colony. Only the future would reveal whether those prices and subsidies were enough.

Shipping did not at first seem a crucial problem. From scarcely two ships a year during 1731–34, shipping to the colony rose by the end of the decade to around six vessels annually from France, four from La Rochelle alone.[23] How much tobacco these vessels brought back to France would depend upon the spread between Louisiana and French prices and upon freight rates. Since tobacco weighed less per cubic foot than did rice or indigo, the alternative productions of Louisiana, it took up more space in a ship's hold in proportion to its weight than they did and consequently had to pay a higher freight per pound. (Even on the king's ships, whose freight rates were kept artifically low, tobacco was charged twice as much by weight as were rice or cotton in seed.) [24] Whether the supercargoes of French merchants would choose to buy tobacco in Louisiana rather than some other commodity would depend upon their estimate of the probable gross profit per pound in France multiplied by the ship's capacity by weight in each commodity. The supercargo probably had excess credits in Louisiana for his purchases,[25] but he might be hindered in profitable loading by insufficient supplies of certain local products, traceable ultimately to the colony's small labor force. A census of January 1732 showed that the total population of Louisiana proper (New Orleans and the lower Mississippi) was only 5,199, including 3,695 slaves.[26] Insofar as no arrangements had been made by Maurepas for major additions to the labor supply during the early years, 1732–35, when tobacco prices were to be relatively high, it was inherently unlikely that those prices by themselves would lead to a "breakthrough" in Louisiana tobacco production. By itself, that colony was still too dubious a proposition to attract the attention of private slave traders, particularly when markets in the Antilles were so much greater, so much more affluent and so much nearer.

Once he had achieved the price settlement of August–September 1732, Maurepas devoted himself thereafter to relative trivia in his efforts to encourage the Louisiana tobacco trade: he was in frequent correspondence with merchants, particularly at La Rochelle, and in their interest used the influence of his office to prod the united farms (through the controller-general) to be prompt and generous in their dealings with merchants importing tobacco from Louisiana. For example, he was successful in persuading the farmers-general to buy the *manufactured* tobacco which Rasteau had imported from New Orleans even though the company was not formally obliged to do so; at the same time, he tried but failed to get them to pay a premium price for it.[27] Through Michel Begon, *intendant de la marine* at Le Havre, he encouraged merchants there to join those of La Rochelle, Bordeaux, and St. Malo in the Louisiana and tobacco trades.[28] At the same time, he successfully fended off suggestions of the farms that all merchants trading to Louisiana be obliged to deliver their tobacco only to Bordeaux, Le Havre, Dieppe, or Morlaix—a suggestion which would have been most prejudicial to those of La Rochelle, the principal traders to Louisiana.[29]

As might be expected, the principal immediate difficulty was quality. Although the bulk of the leaf tobacco delivered was satisfactory, individual parcels caused trouble. The united farms also objected because the tobacco received in 1732 contained too high a proportion of the smaller, inferior leaf of the second and third growths from the same roots. Though Maurepas was able to get these objections brushed aside for that year,[30] he realized that a solution to these problems would have to be found in Louisiana. Thus, both in the memoir of instructions sent from the king to Bienville and Salmon on 2 September 1732 and in a less formal letter of the same date, the government, after notifying the governor and *ordonnateur* of the new prices fixed for Louisiana tobacco during the next six years, reminded them of the importance of seeing that none but good tobacco was sent home from their colony.[31] At the request of the united farms, Maurepas subsequently instructed the same two officials that henceforth all tobacco was to be shipped from Louisiana in dried leaf, that no manufactured tobacco would be received and that each hogshead must contain at least one-third leaf of the first growth and not more than one-sixth leaf of the third growth. Forty *sols* per quintal would be deducted for shortages in the "first sort" and thirty *sols* per quintal for excesses of the "third sort."[32]

When these new instructions reached Louisiana, the governor and the *ordonnateur* issued an *ordonnance et règlement* on 18 March 1733 announcing the new metropolitan prices and establishing the new packing rules; no tobacco was to be embarked until passed by a public inspector.[33] A subsequent *ordonnance* of Salmon (6 November 1734) reinforced the inspection provisions and named the old "Clairac" Descairac as inspector, but the latter died shortly afterward.[34]

In the field, tobacco production was recovering only very slowly from the terrible blow of the Natchez massacre of 1729 and the confusion attendant upon the retrocession of 1731. Maurepas realized immediately in 1730 that the "affaire des Natchez" would interrupt the hoped for rapid increase in the colony's tobacco production.[35] Governor Périer thought some good might be extracted from this disaster. Although from Hubert's time, local expert opinion had for agricultural promise looked to Natchez and areas farther up the river, where there was much open land, Périer had long felt that areas lower down the river might be better for most crops despite the extra labor needed to clear the very thick forests.[36] In the event, circumstances directed developments along the lines preferred by Périer, even though he was not long to remain the colony's governor. Although Fort Rosalie was reestablished at Natchez, no significant agricultural activity was attempted there, even after the feared Natchez were exterminated. Travelers in later years reported that the soldiers of the garrison there grew a little tobacco for use and sale, but this was not commercially significant.[37] Instead the principal area of resumed tobacco cultivation ultimately became that about Pointe Coupée on the west bank of the river about forty leagues above New Orleans, roughly half way between that city and Natchez.[38]

The most obvious reason why tobacco cultivation survived in Louisiana after the destruction of Natchez was simply that there was still in the colony a significant number of small planters who either could not grow anything else or who did not find any other crop more remunerative. This, rather than any specific policy pushed by Maurepas or Orry, guaranteed continuity in the short run. Even while offering the freight subsidies and the other measures of 1731 to encourage merchants to send ships to the Mississippi, Maurepas was rather pessimistic about the future of tobacco there. On the one hand, he fixed freight for tobacco on the king's ship at a modest 50 l.t. per ton (less than one-half the Chesapeake rate) and urged the planters to grow good tobacco; on the other hand he hesitated to push the united farms on the price.[39] The formal instructions about the retrocession sent to Périer and Salmon did not even mention tobacco![40] The king's particular instructions to the *commissaire-ordonnateur* Salmon, while recommending indigo, were pessimistic about tobacco: after the destruction of Natchez, it was feared that little could be done with tobacco in Louisiana until such time as the colony was sufficiently well populated to support a shipbuilding industry to construct the ships to carry the tobacco to Europe.[41]

When they received these pessimistic words, Périer and Salmon replied immediately that, even so, tobacco must remain the principal product of the colony. They agreed that the general agricultural development was impeded by insufficient labor. At the same time, the planters were wary of indigo after disappointments in price during the company's days; rice they grew primarily for domestic consumption. Everyone, though, could grow tobacco and thus it still was the principal cash crop, which, for the colony's sake, must sell well in France.[42] Other letters from the colony in the next few months reiterated the same theme.[43] These urgings, as well as the importunities of the west coast merchants, drove the initially skeptical Maurepas to fight for the 1732 price arrangements.

Once Maurepas had been persuaded that tobacco must remain the principal product of Louisiana, he was prepared to stick to that policy. For the next few years, he sent out annual appeals to the governor and *ordonnateur* to urge the settlers to grow more and better tobacco.[44] The institutional arrangements he had established for that trade were only moderately successful. We need not be too concerned about the complaints of a merchant like Rasteau who insisted that, despite the high prices established for tobacco, he lost money on his early ventures to Louisiana; he had his subsidies to justify.[45] The fact that the number of ships sent annually to the colony tended to increase during the 1730's would suggest that, with the subsidies included, the trade must have been profitable for the merchants.[46]

The planters on the other hand were soon disenchanted with the new arrangements, and for better reason: they had assumed that because the merchants sold their European goods in Louisiana at advances of from 100 to 300 percent, they would buy the planters' tobacco at the full price offered in France by the united farms and reimburse themselves for the costs of freight home out of their selling profits in the colony. The merchants in fact had no such eleemosynary intentions. The price of tobacco was determined by the local market: when two or more ships were in the colony at once and competing for trade, it might approach the theoretical maximum (7 *sols* per lb. or 35 *l.t.* per quintal in 1732–33); when one ship had the colony to itself for any protracted period, as was usually the case at first, the planters and local traders had difficulty getting more than five *sols* per lb., the prevailing price in 1732–33. It was to go much lower later. When the gap between local and French prices became too glaring, some local people consigned to France on the king's ships rather than sell in the colony. However, the delays were so great in getting the tobacco to France and in getting returns from thence that both the local officials and Maurepas considered consignment a drag on the economic development of the colony. They agreed that the only solution was to encourage more trading vessels to visit the colony each year.[47]

The new quality controls proclaimed in the colony in 1733 were slow in having the desired effect. The numerous disputes during 1733 and 1734 between the merchants in France and the monopoly over deliveries could be blamed on bad habits developed under the Indies Company and on understandable delays in the diffusion of the new regulations.[48] Maurepas warned however that the monopoly had only so much complaisance and would soon refuse to take manufactured tobacco under any conditions.[49] By 1734, Bienville and Salmon, eager to please, could report that the quality problem had been solved in Louisiana.[50] Yet planters continued to work their tobacco up into small pressed *carottes* for local consumption and possible export to the Antilles. When ship captains or supercargoes could not otherwise obtain a full cargo homeward—as in 1734–35—they bought some of these *carottes* to help fill their ships, even though contrary to the *ordonnance* and the declared policy of the united farms. Maurepas initially urged the farms to be indulgent about buying such manufactured tobacco, but, from March 1735 onward, supported them in their refusal to buy anything but dried leaf tobacco.[51] More seriously, in 1735[52] and again in 1739,[53] the inspectors of the farm rejected a hundred and more hogsheads at a time because of bad odor. In both cases, the tobacco having been delayed in the colony because of inadequate shipping,[54] Maurepas used his influence to get the greater part of it accepted, if at lower prices.[55] He seems to have done this primarily as a special favor to Rasteau, owner of the tobacco and the greatest trader to Louisiana. It is doubtful if he would have done as much for any other merchant. The quality problem had not been solved to the degree that tobacco could wait a year or more at New Orleans for shipping without danger of deterioration.

Yet the chief problem faced by the planters in Louisiana at first was not government regulation nor even prices—but nature. (Even in years of short crops, tobacco prices might be kept from rising if the ships from France came singly and months enough apart.) The weather of the Gulf of Mexico, rarely benign, was particularly unkind to tobacco growers in the age of Maurepas. 1728 and 1729 had been years of ruinous rains; 1730 was abnormally dry.[56] After the political turbulences of 1730 and 1731, the year 1732 witnessed a hurricane on 29 August[57] and 1733 a drought in April and May followed by torrential rains in June and a windstorm in July,[58] destroying in each year the greater part of the crop in field or shed. So small was the 1731 crop that a single La Rochelle vessel (Rasteau's *St. Paul*), taking on 100,000 lb. in March 1732, exhausted the crop. When the first Bordeaux vessel arrived in April, there was no tobacco left. It was hoped that the 1732 crop would be about 300,000–400,000 lb.[59] but, after the hurricane, only 150 hogsheads (75,000–100,000 lb.) could be sent home. In 1733, a crop of 300,000–400,000 lb. was again expected;[60] but expectations were radically reduced after the storms of June and July.[61] In 1734, the crop succeeded only at Pointe Coupée where it still fell short of 100,000 lb.[62]

The merchants meanwhile had found tobacco such a dubious proposition that vessels arriving in the summer of 1733 from Bordeaux and St. Malo were under instructions to take no tobacco (!), forcing what little there was to wait for the next king's ship.[63] So little had in fact been made that, when the next king's ship, *La Somme,* arrived in February, Bienville and Salmon doubted that there was enough tobacco to fill her. She actually carried home only 116 hogsheads and 11 chests, perhaps 60,000–100,000 lb., the greater part of the crop of 1733. Another 105 hogsheads of the same crop had been purchased for Rasteau but were left behind for the king's ship by his captain who instead took on a cargo of timber, pitch, and tar for the Antilles where he could easily get a more remunerative homeward cargo of sugar, and other goods.[64] (This was to become a common shipping pattern in the Louisiana trade.) In the event, the commander of the next king's ship, the *Charente,* refused to take Rasteau's tobacco because, after loading that of the planters, he felt he needed ballast rather than more light tobacco;[65] he arrived back in France in 1735 with only 65 hogsheads on board (35,000–52,000 lb.), virtually the whole crop of 1734.[66] Maurepas regretted the loss this delay had caused Rasteau (though the risk had been taken knowingly)[67] but he censured other merchants like Jung whose ships had brought back little tobacco.[68]

To meet the double discouragements[69] of bad weather and low prices, various expedients were tried or recommended. To help the planters after the hurricane of August 1732, Bienville and Salmon reduced the freight on tobacco shipped homeward on the king's ships in 1733 from 50 to 25 *l.t.* per ton.[70] At the same time, they recommended that the sliding scale recently adopted be abandoned and that prices be kept at the high level of 1732–33. They also suggested that the united farms take tobacco in *carottes* to save freight space and maintain an agent at New Orleans who would buy the tobacco directly from the planters for bills of exchange and ship it back to France at the company's expense.[71] The *ordonnateur* Salmon was so depressed that in a private letter to Pontchartrain, the father of Maurepas, he suggested restoring Louisiana to the care of a monopoly company.[72]

The discouragement of the early 1730's became even more acute in the latter part of the decade as the downward-sliding scale of prices adopted in 1732 went about its discouraging business. In 1735, no one in the colony raised any tobacco except for a little at Pointe Coupée which the planters made up into *carotte* for sale in the colony and to the sailors and inferior officers on board the king's ships. The growers were discouraged not so much by prices or policy as by the terrible succession of too dry or too wet weather that had ruined so many crops. By this time, the smaller planters had turned to victuals, the larger to indigo again. Maurepas found this "annoying" (*fâcheux*), a favorite adjective.[73] His continued exhortations to stay with that "promising" crop did not in fact induce many settlers along the Mississippi to plant tobacco.[74]

In 1737, Bienville and Salmon reported their fears that the last tobacco planters at Pointe Coupée might give it up completely. Though crops were small, the prices paid by the merchant ships had dropped from 5 *sols* per lb. a few years before to 3*s*. 6*d*., in part reflecting the downward sliding scale. The government and united farms had meanwhile, starting in 1735, tried to encourage experiments with tobacco in Canada. Instructions were sent out on planting and the monopoly promised to take all grown at a uniform price. What with worms and low prices, nothing came of the Canadian experiment but exaggerated tales of it reached Louisiana: wild rumors that the farmers-general were paying 10 *sols* per lb. in Canada fed the anger of the men of Pointe Coupée at their wretched prices. Bienville and Salmon again urged that the price of tobacco in Louisiana be set at 7 *sols* per lb., or double the price of that year. Maurepas said he would look into the matter, but nothing came of it.[75] As a measure of temporary relief, the freight charges for tobacco homeward on the king's ships were again temporarily reduced, this time from 50 *l.t.* to 30 *l.t.* per ton.[76]

Equally futile were the rather extended efforts during these same years to increase the labor supply in the colony. Since the white population was little disposed to work in the fields, this could only mean increasing the slave population. With the end of the Indies Company's monopoly in 1731, there was no one legally charged with bringing slaves to Louisiana. In April 1734, Bienville and Salmon wrote to the secretary of state suggesting that the colony could pay for one frigate's load of slaves annually at 900 *l.t.* per head. Even if the whole tobacco crop were lost one year because of poor weather, the slaves could be paid for in furs, pitch, and tar. It would of course be necessary to send a second ship over from France to help bring back all the pitch and tar.[77] Maurepas was quite interested and entered into negotiations with Orry de Fulvy, the brother of the controller-general, who had charge of the Indies Company, to see whether that company would agree to supply Louisiana with several hundred slaves annually. The company was prepared to make a contract for 200–300 slaves a year for as little as 600 *l.t.* per head (compared with 1,000 *l.t.* in the free market in the Antilles) provided that payment could be guaranteed without advance of credit. On this rock, the negotiations of 1734 foundered.[78]

In 1736–37, the matter was reopened at the initiative of Jacques Rasteau of La Rochelle, the leading Louisiana trader of the 1730's. He proposed to supply slaves at the rate of 850 *l.t.* for males of ages sixteen to thirty years, 750 *l.t.* for females of the same ages, 650 *l.t.* for males of ten to fifteen, 550 for females of those ages and children "in proportion." These rates, he claimed, compared very favorably with St. Domingue prices of 1,200–1,300 *l.t.* for adults, particularly considering that Louisiana was farther away. The slaves were to be paid for in such goods as tobacco, indigo, and furs, one-half the price from the current crop, the other half in one year's time. Tobacco would be taken at only 3*s.* 6*d.* per lb., the current price. Rasteau wanted the planters to agree collectively to take *all* the slaves delivered at these prices and to indicate informally in advance how many each wanted.[79] Early in February 1737, the principal planters called together at New Orleans by the *ordonnateur* Salmon agreed to the general lines of the Rasteau proposal. They asked only that the price allowed for tobacco be raised to 4*s.* per lb. and that payment be made not in two but in three installments, one-third from the current crop, one-third one year later, and one-third two years later. Twenty planters and officials present at the meeting signed for 208 slaves, but indicated that there were other planters at Mobile, Pointe Coupée, Natchitoches, and even Illinois who would also want slaves.[80] On 10 February 1737, twelve planters submitted a further memorial to Salmon supporting both Rasteau's proposals and their counterproposals, neither of which, they argued, were inimical to the unused slave trading privileges of the Indies Company.[81]

Maurepas worked on these schemes,[82] but was unable to develop a formula that would satisfy Rasteau or any other metropolitan venturers. Disgusted, some merchants and large planters of Louisiana (including six who had subscribed the previous year to take slaves under Rasteau's scheme) formed a company of their own in 1738 and offered to supply the colony with slaves, provided that: (1) they be given a monopoly for a number of years; (2) the government remit 150,000 *l.t.* from Louisiana to France for them at par; (3) the government either allow them the use of a royal vessel on favorable terms, or alternatively grant them a subsidy of so much per slave imported; (4) royal conscription be used to man their vessels for the Guinea coast; and (5) exemption be granted them from the duties paid by private slave traders to the Indies Company. Although these proposals were forwarded by Bienville and Salmon, and one of the company went over to negotiate, nothing came of them either.[83] The concessions demanded probably seemed excessive.

The initiative had for the time passed to the colonists themselves. In 1741, the *ordonnateur* Salmon reported to the minister that no slaves had been imported into the colony for fourteen years. Rasteau and all other merchants who had promised any had failed to deliver. To replace the old slaves who were dying off, they had perforce to rely on kind treatment and natural reproduction. Thus, two-thirds of the 4,000 slaves then in the colony were native born in contrast to the Antilles where almost all were imported. Since they were relatively so successful in "breeding," even a small importation of slaves might result in a large ultimate increase in the slave population. Two local residents were prepared to undertake the trade: Claude Joseph Villars Dubreuil, the contractor for public works, and Etienne Dalcourt, an old settler. With the support of the government, the two would undertake to supply the colony with one ship of 300 slaves yearly. Salmon endorsed the project and the projectors and recommended Dalcourt who was going to France to obtain the support of the minister.[84]

The two adventurers persisted despite the most awkward difficulties. Dalcourt could not persuade the Indies Company to supply him with a cargo of slaves, though they did agree to waive their duty of 10 *l.t.* per head. Therefore, he decided that he and Dubreuil should send their own ship from France to Africa. To do this it was necessary to remit a large amount of their wealth in Louisiana to France to fit out the ship. To encourage them and to facilitate this transfer, Maurepas authorized Salmon to supply them with 30,000 *l.t.* in bills of exchange on France, to give them 100 tons free freight in the first king's ship for France in 1742 and to reserve for them two-thirds of the freight capacity in all the king's ships visiting the colony in 1742 and 1743. Dalcourt was to go back to Louisiana in the autumn of 1741 to arrange for the transfer of his funds and then return to France in early 1742 to supervise the fitting out of the ship for Africa.[85] When Dalcourt returned to Louisiana, he found that insufficient warning had been given to accumulate the goods necessary to transfer the large sums needed to France. Tobacco crops had improved somewhat since the mid-1730's but 1741 had not been a good year, and the leaf was poor in color. Nevertheless, in order to buy a mere 50,000 lb., Dalcourt and Dubreuil caused the price to rise from 4s. 3d. to 6s. per lb. Yet the two persevered: they were prepared to borrow if they could not remit enough funds to France or persuade some La Rochelle merchant to join them. They boldly made agreements with tobacco growers at Pointe Coupée for large deliveries from future crops.[86]

Dalcourt on his return to France in the spring of 1742 was in fact unable to persuade his La Rochelle friends to join the venture, yet pushed on nevertheless. The Indies Company agreed to sell him 200 slaves at Senegal, to be paid for half in cash on the spot, half in Paris in July 1743. The crown gave every encouragement to the venture, even guaranteeing the debt to the Indies Company. The vessel was ready late in 1742[87] and Dalcourt sailed with it from La Rochelle to Senegal and arrived at Louisiana with 190 surviving slaves in August 1743.[88] Various other proposals by Dubreuil, Dalcourt and others were considered, but this modest shipment of 1743 proved to be the only importation of slaves into Louisiana from Africa between the retrocession of 1731 and the start of the British-French hostilities in 1744.

The war, of course, led to the suspension of all such schemes until its termination in 1748.

One reason why the government was prepared to give stronger support to the Dalcourt-Dubreuil scheme of 1741–43 than it had to earlier schemes was the changed international situation after 1739. Maurepas' interest in the Louisiana tobacco trade showed signs of weakening in the later 1730's but was to revive as the approaching prospect of war with Great Britain exposed the weaknesses of having a major branch of the French state revenue dependent upon a source of supply from a potential enemy. Voices of criticism had not been entirely absent, even during the British-French *rapprochement* of the 1730's. In December 1736, October 1738 and again in October 1740, the estates of Brittany instructed their deputies at court to ask the king to order the united farms to buy more tobacco from the French colonies.[89] The most effective statement of the problem, however, came from the young Etienne de Silhouette, the future controller-general.

The young Silhouette lived for a number of years during the 1730's in Great Britain, originally as a student. It was during these years that he translated Pope into French and began those literary correspondences that established much of his salon reputation. During these same years, he advanced his economic education and from 1735 helped support himself— as we shall see in a subsequent chapter—by helping purchase British tobacco for the united farms.[90] We do not know the details, but it seems that Silhouette either resigned or was relieved of his tobacco employment in Britain in 1739. He thus found himself at that time with a good knowledge of the British tobacco market and of the farms' practices and with a possible private grievance against that organization. This knowledge and apparent grievance both found expression in a long memoir on tobacco which he distributed just before the British declaration of war on Spain in October 1739. So many copies of this memoir have survived that we can at the very least assume that it had a wide circulation. One copy found its way into the hands of British intelligence where it was taken very seriously.[91] In addition, Silhouette seems to have prepared a second more general memoir on the British and French colonies in which he repeated many of the points made in the special memoir on tobacco.[92]

In the first or tobacco memoir, Silhouette described the importance of that trade in the power struggles of Britain and France, whom he likened to Rome and Carthage. Silhouette had used his time in Britain to good advantage, acquiring a fairly accurate knowledge of the volume of tobacco imports and exports there, the principal reexport markets, the organization of the trade to Virginia and Maryland. Through the forty million pounds of her tobacco reexported to various European countries, Britain, he explained, extracted a tribute with which she sustained her two great colonies in the Chesapeake and a navigation employing 200 ships yearly. Shamefully among these tributary countries was France which paid 3.4 million *l.t.* for 14,000–

15,000 hogsheads annually (11–12 million lb.), quite apart from what was smuggled in or imported legally through Dunkirk for the use of the eastern frontier provinces. It was dangerous for the king of France to depend for fifteen (sic) millions of his revenues on a commodity whose supply could in time of war be cut off by his enemies or rendered costly by British punitive export duties or indirect shipment via Holland.

Hence, it appeared self-evident to Silhouette that the French government must do all in its power to stimulate the cultivation of tobacco in Louisiana to the point where all France's needs could be satisfied from thence. He realized that one key to the problem lay in the price offered by the tobacco farm, but was rather facilely optimistic about its solution. It was not necessary to go back to the high prices of Colbert's time, because tobacco was no longer grown by white settlers but by slaves who required much less. He thought that if the united farms guaranteed to take Louisiana tobacco at the price they paid for Virginia tobacco delivered to France—tobacco bought in London for 2d.¼ sterling per lb. cost them about 25 $l.t.$ per quintal delivered in France—they would be offering enough for the planters on the Mississippi. He argued that since Louisiana tobacco did not have to go through the British entrepôt, as did that from the Chesapeake, the French planter in saving those extra freight and entrepôt charges would net 88 percent more than would the British from the same price. He was aware that a round trip to Louisiana took three months longer than a trip to the Chesapeake and hitherto had required higher freight charges, but thought that rates from Louisiana could be brought down to the Chesapeake levels by elimination of the three months "sojourn in the country," so costly to Chesapeake traders. If really big merchants were encouraged to trade to Louisiana, they could have agents buying tobacco in advance of their ships and thus eliminate totally turn-around delays and bring freight from Louisiana down to Chesapeake rates. (Only a very brash and inexperienced young man could have made such an argument, considering that Louisiana was more than twice as far from Europe as Virginia. Nor did he consider whether French ships customarily carried as much freight as British ships of the same theoretical capacity.)

Finally, Silhouette realized that even if the metropolitan price and the freight rates were satisfactory, any marked expansion of tobacco production in Louisiana would require a great increase in the slave labor supply. He believed that if one could eliminate unreasonable profits and unnecessary costs, such as bad debts and tolls to the Indies Company, slaves from Africa could be economically supplied to Louisiana for as little as 500 $l.t.$ per adult head. At that price, slaves would pay for themselves growing tobacco in Louisiana even if they lived only four years on an average. (Slaves were calculated to survive on an average only seven years in the Antilles but much longer in Louisiana where there was a significant native born slave population.)

Having established the "economics" of the problem, Silhouette proceeded to make a concrete proposal to the government. He would himself undertake to carry the scheme into operation provided that: (1) the government gave him a large land grant on the Mississippi near New Orleans; (2) that the united farms guaranteed to take all tobacco delivered to France at 25 *l.t.* per quintal, they paying all harbor, landing, and warehouse charges; and (3) that the government advanced to him free of interest no less than 600,000 *l.t.* for fourteen years, of which 500,000 *l.t.* would be used for a thousand slaves and the rest for miscellaneous expenses.[93]

Although the British received word that Silhouette's proposal was to be accepted, nothing in fact ever came of it. Silhouette himself explained to Cardinal Fleury that it had been read with approval by Maurepas, by the *intendants des finances* Fagon and Trudaine, and by the senior farmers-general de la Porte and Lallemant de Betz; only the opposition of Orry and the outbreak of the British-Spanish war prevented its execution.[94] The controller-general's lack of enthusiasm is understandable, considering the very large advances required by the scheme. (If the government had wanted to spend more money on this sort of development, they could have accomplished more for less by simply offering a small subsidy on slaves imported.) Then too, there is nothing in his memoir that indicates that Silhouette had any great knowledge about Louisiana. His calculations, while always reasonable, are usually stretched a bit too far for prudence: in practice, something would have to be allowed on all his prices and freight rates. Yet, his memoir was a well thought out effort by a person of considerable ability. Its analysis highlights the three crucial impediments to the development of a Louisiana tobacco industry: French monopsony prices, high freight rates, and inadequate labor supply.

Though he may have read and approved Silhouette's memoir, Maurepas was in general little inclined to integrated analysis or planning; he was much more addicted, as his father and grandfather had been before him, to improvisation and detail. His characteristic response to the dangers posed by the deteriorating international situation was to do nothing about prices or freight rates, but to worry once more about quality. Annoyed by the difficulties caused by the refusal of the farmers-general to accept part of a large shipment received by Rasteau in 1739, Maurepas decided that efforts must be renewed in the colony to improve the quality, packing, and stowing of tobacco, to reduce deterioration at sea.[95] Bienville and Salmon were not sure whether the defective quality reported from France was the result of deceit on the part of the planters or careless stowage by the ship captains. To make sure that it was not the former, Salmon issued an *ordonnance* on 12 July 1740 ordering each planter to have a distinctive mark to be placed on each hogshead of tobacco produced by him. If any tobacco was found defective upon arrival in France, the original producer was to refund the purchase price.[96] A further comprehensive *ordonnance* on quality controls was issued by Bienville and Salmon on 22 May 1741.[97] In addition, to take the place of Descairac, the tobacco inspector who had died, they appointed Ricard of Pointe Coupée, another old Clairac hand going back to the original settlement in Law's time.[98] Such an "inside" appointment was unlikely to raise quality much.

In August 1741, Maurepas, as requested by Bienville and Salmon, asked Lallemant de Betz whether the united farms could not be a little more indulgent about packing requirements.[99] The farmers general, however, adamantly refused concessions facilitating the fraudulent intermixing of first, second, and third growth. If a small planter had to put these in the same hogshead, then he must observe the *ordonnances* and pack them in separate layers within the hogshead so that they could be readily separated when the hogshead was opened. This position of the farms was duly forwarded to Bienville and Salmon in Louisiana by Maurepas, with instructions to devote less time to excuses and more to persuading the planters to grow better tobacco.[100]

A year later, when de Vaudreuil was sent out to succeed Bienville as governor of Louisiana, the various instructions to him and Salmon repeated all the familiar injunctions about the necessity of controlling the quality of tobacco, the economic backbone of the colony; considerable dissatisfaction was expressed at the failure of Bienville to follow similar instructions.[101] For some years, too, people had been writing Maurepas that tobacco took up too much space in ships for its weight. For every ton of rated capacity, a French ship (in contrast to a British) could allegedly carry only half a ton of tobacco. If sand or stone had to be used as ballast, then the tobacco carried would have to bear the full freight homeward and most of the freight outward (when the vessels went substantially in ballast); this burden tobacco could not bear at current prices. It was argued that, until such time as Louisiana produced enough lead or copper to be used as ballast homeward in place of sand, tobaccos could not be carried at an economic freight.[102] Maurepas recognized these arguments to the point of reviving for Vaudreuil the old but impractical instruction to encourage the building of ships in Louisiana (as was done in Virginia and Maryland) to eliminate the uneconomic outward voyage.[103]

Though Maurepas seemed incapable of devising any practical scheme to stimulate a large-scale expansion of the Louisiana tobacco trade, both he and the farmers-general themselves were sufficiently disturbed by the deteriorating international situation to look about for other sources of supply. We have already mentioned the experiments in Canada. In 1739, de la Croix, intendant at Martinique, had raised the question of supplying tobacco once more from the Antilles; Maurepas had referred the matter to the united farms who were discouraging. In late 1740, after the start of hostilities in Europe, the governor of Guadeloupe sent home some local tobacco, which Maurepas asked to have manufactured with Virginia. The results were successful. Maurepas, excited, wrote in February 1741, both to the united farms and to the governors in the Antilles, suggesting that more might be done along these lines. From the farmer-general Lallemant de Betz he received in reply a fatherly lecture: the contracted price of the united farms was calculated upon an estimated yield of the tobacco monopoly based on a stable price of British tobacco at about 22–23 *l.t.* per quintal. The farms were prepared to pay 25–26 *l.t.* for Louisiana tobacco only because not more than 100,000 lb. annually came from there. If the densely populated Antilles turned to tobacco, they might produce much more. This would throw off the cost calculations upon which the price of the farm had been set. Any such change was clearly improper within the life of a contract. Tobacco had best be left to Louisiana; the Antilles were better occupied in sugar. Under no circumstances would the farm pay more than 25 *l.t.* for any tobacco.[104] From the Windward Islands, Maurepas received an equally disenchanting reply: no price that the farmers-general were likely to offer would be enough to make it economic to grow tobacco on those islands where land and labor were dear. Hence, the officers there also thought that tobacco had best be left to Louisiana.[105] Once more, Maurepas had flapped his wings but had not gotten off the ground.

Despite the complete futility of almost everything then attempted, tobacco cultivation struggled on at Pointe Coupée. The later 1730's and early 1740's were not as catastrophic as the weather troubled years of the early 1730's. The crop of 1737 marketed in 1738 may have reached 350,000 lb.[106] That of 1738, however, was reduced by drought to 130,000 lb.;[107] that of 1739 was "fairly good,"[108] while that of 1740 was expected to reach 400,000 lb.[109] A well-informed memoir of 1747 suggested that 250,000–300,000 was a normal year's export from Louisiana to France.[110] As late as 1739, there had only been 50 *habitations* with a total of only 180 slaves at Pointe Coupée.[111] In 1741, five or six substantial planters from the New Orleans area moved to Pointe Coupée with their slaves, finding tobacco more attractive than indigo.[112] By 1746, it was reported that there were nearly 200 households there with about 400 slaves.[113] Except for a trifling amount (perhaps 5,000–6,000 lb.) grown at Natchitoches on the Red River, this single settlement continued to supply the total commercial tobacco production of the colony.[114]

With the advent of the war between Britain and France in 1744, the tobacco trade of Louisiana languished once more. The united farms, as we shall see in Chapter 15, obtained special permission from both governments to continue importing tobacco from Great Britain in wartime. They thus had no occasion to improve the prices they were offering for Louisiana tobacco. With the trade only marginally profitable in peacetime, the higher freight rates, risks and insurance charges of wartime were sure to render it a "losing trade" for most merchants. Fewer vessels came safely to Louisiana and those that came looked for commodities more profitable than tobacco.

In the 1740's, the indigo revival was proceeding apace. Thus, during the mixed war and peace years of 1743–46, total tobacco exports from the colony averaged 170,000 lb., worth only 29,750 *l.t.*, as is shown in Table I.

TABLE I

Exports from Louisiana, 1743–46[115]
(annual averages)

To Metropolitan France:

50,000 lb. furs, skins, etc.	at 30*s.* per lb.	82,500 *l.t.*
20,000 lb. indigo	at 60*s.* per lb.	60,000 *l.t.*
170,000 lb. tobacco	at 3*s.* 6*d* per lb.	29,750 *l.t.*
Total		172,250 *l.t.*

To Caribbean:

timber, etc.	18,750 *l.t.*
pitch, tar, etc.	20,000 *l.t.*
goods traded to Spaniards (reexports)	29,000 *l.t.*
Total	67,750 *l.t.*
Grand total	240,000 *l.t.*

In the last years of the war, tobacco's situation grew worse. In the spring of 1747, Governor Vaudreuil reported that Pointe Coupée was growing in numbers but that the tobacco trade there was under great discouragements. The merchant ships were loading up with sugar and logwood (from Yucatan) and leaving the tobacco behind. Over the preceding two years, about 400 hogsheads (up to 320,000 lb.) had accumulated but the king's flute would at most be able to take 100 of them. The backlog, of course, depressed prices still further. Though many of the settlers wanted to give up the crop, Vaudreuil allegedly persuaded them to continue with it. He only wished the government would find means to raise the price, for the commodity was still important for settlers with few or no slaves.[116] The next year, the situation was even worse. The 1747 crops had been good and tobacco was piling up in the colony. Because of the loss of the *Chameau* the previous year, no planter would consign his tobacco on the king's flute, the *Parham*, which had to return to France in ballast. With stocks of tobacco and furs accumulating, prices were wretched but many merchant vessels still refused to buy a cargo at New Orleans but followed the increasingly common practice of selling their European goods for bills of exchange on France and taking on such cargo as timber for St. Domingue where they could get a more profitable homeward freighting of sugar.[117]

Such was the unhappy situation of the Louisiana tobacco trade in 1747–48, as the war and the long administration of Maurepas were alike drawing to a close. There were by 1746 about 3,200 whites and 4,730 Negroes in the colony,[118] but less than 10 percent of the latter were engaged in tobacco cultivation. Even had Maurepas been much more successful than he was in persuading private merchants to send slaves to Louisiana, it is unlikely that the proportion working on tobacco would have been raised much if at all. Under the sliding scale adopted in 1732, the price paid by the United General Farms for Louisiana tobacco delivered in France had declined from 35 *l.t.* per quintal in 1732–33 to 25 *l.t.* in 1738 at which price the farms left it for the next two leases or twelve years, 1738–50. A price of 25 *l.t.* per quintal or five *sols* per lb. in France could not support a price much above three *sols* per lb. in Louisiana. This was equivalent to 1*d.* ½ sterling, a low but not unusual price in the Chesapeake. For distant Louisiana with its much higher living costs, this was empirically an inadequate price. As the years went by, Maurepas showed less and less inclination to fight with the ever more influential farmers-general over this price. He preferred to fritter away his time writing letters about quality control. His successor strove mightily but was in the end hardly more successful.

The Last Years of French Louisiana, 1748–63

The "peace" interlude of 1748–56 was a period of remarkable activity in French colonial history: the system of Dupleix reached its apogee in India, while in North America the French military position in the valleys of the St. Lawrence and Ohio was greatly strengthened and expanded. In the history of the Louisiana tobacco trade, these were also years of great activity, though much of it took the form of projecting and proposing and commencing, rather than of executing and accomplishing. The period is in part marked from that which preceded it by the dismissal in April 1749—through the influence of the insulted Madame de Pompadour—of the perennial minister of the navy, the count of Maurepas, the third and last of his family to hold that high office. His successor as minister was Antoine Louis Rouillé, scion of a new but rapidly rising family.[119] For what it is worth to the reputation of the rather ineffectual Maurepas, it should be noted that much of the "activity" that followed his disgrace had its origin during his term of office.

During the pause caused by the war of 1744–48, the government had a chance to review its whole policy toward Louisiana and the tobacco trade there. Numerous memoirs were submitted from every side.[120] One of these came from Jacques Rasteau *fils,* son of the merchant of La Rochelle who had sent the first and greatest number of vessels to Louisiana in the 1730's. The son had himself resided in the colony and had as good a knowledge of affairs there as any man in France. His proposal is remarkable for the clarity and perception with which it analyzed the problem and for the impracticality of the solution it recommended.

France, Rasteau *fils* asserted, consumed sixteen million pounds of British tobacco (rather too high an estimate). Calculating that each rated ton of British shipping carried not more than 1,600 lb. of tobacco, French purchases thus gave employment to 10,000 tons of shipping in the British-Chesapeake trade and approximately 1,000 seamen; other work was created for thousands both in Britain and in the Chesapeake. If France wished to cease benefiting Britain in this manner and to create instead work for her own mariners, manufacturers, and planters, she would have to multiply the 200,000 lb. of tobacco she then obtained from Louisiana; this meant making the Louisiana tobacco trade profitable. To do this Rasteau *fils* first suggested that the government should pay a subsidy of 400 *l.t.* per couple (male and female) for 1,000 slaves to be brought to Louisiana over three or four years and sold to the planters for 1,800 *l.t.* per couple payable in tobacco at the market price. He felt sure that once this thousand slaves had been delivered, the productive capacity of the colony would have been sufficiently enhanced so that thereafter the colony would be able to support a private slave trade without subsidy. Rasteau recognized that these slaves might in fact be put to work raising not tobacco but indigo which grew more readily in the lower parts of the colony and which competed with the production of the French Antilles. To prevent this, he recommended that the slaves be sold preferably for tobacco and that the state award a subsidy for ten years of nine *deniers* per pound on all tobacco grown in the colony. Since tobacco was then selling for about three *sols* per pound in the colony, this would mean a subsidy of 25 percent to the producers, about the same as that to the slave traders. Finally, to make it worth while for merchant ships to carry back tobacco rather than denser commodities, he recommended a shipping subsidy on tobacco returned to France of 30 *l.t.* per ton of 1,600 lb. of tobacco. All this was to be executed by private persons without special privileges or monopolies. He admitted that these various subsidies would come to 697,500 *l.t.* annually even after the slave subsidy had expired (and perhaps 764,000 *l.t.* during the first three years when the slaves were coming).[121] His scheme was impractical only in imagining that the government would spend 700,000 *l.t.* annually on subsidies for ten years; in its analysis of where the wheels had to be greased, it was one of the most "practical" documents ever submitted on Louisiana.

Few others attempted such frank or comprehensive analyses or recommendations. In a memoir submitted in November 1747, André Fabry de la Bruyère, a minor naval official formerly resident in Louisiana, admitted in passing that more slaves were needed but placed his chief emphasis upon freight costs. The higher costs of operating French ships made it uneconomic to bring back tobacco from Louisiana at current prices. There were two solutions: the first was to raise the price paid for tobacco in France from 25 to 30 *l.t.* per quintal. Hardé, a merchant of La Rochelle, had told him that this would be enough to make the trade profitable. Alternatively, he thought the farmers-general might well send out an agent to buy tobacco in the colony for 15 *l.t.* per quintal or three *sols* per lb., payable in bills of exchange on

France. The company could charter whole ships to bring it back to France at *two* sols per lb., thus keeping their total costs within the existing five *sols* per lb. or 25 *l.t.* per quintal. Fabry envisioned no difficulty in chartering vessels at two *sols* per lb. since vessels could then be had to bring sugar from St. Domingue to France for one *sol* per lb. (Tobacco could at that time be shipped from Virginia to Britain for around ½d. sterling per lb. or 12d. in French money, just half the figure suggested by Fabry for Louisiana.) Thus a vessel which would earn 15,000 *l.t.* carrying 300,000 lb. of sugar from St. Domingue homeward would earn 20,000 *l.t.* carrying 200,000 lb. of the less dense tobacco from Louisiana: the extra 5,000 *l.t.* would be adequate compensation for the extra distance and risks to and from New Orleans. If none of these alternatives worked, Fabry recommended granting tobacco free freight home on the king's ships for a few years as a special encouragement.[122]

These same points were gone over in a significant memoir of about 1748 by Beletrus, a senior clerk *(commis)* in the navy ministry at Versailles. Beletrus was very well informed about everything that had happened in the Louisiana tobacco trade during the preceding thirty years; he had obviously read everyone else's memoirs and his views may be taken to represent the departmental synthesis. He was less optimistic than Fabry—or at least his calculations were more cautious. He also thought that a price in the country of three *sols* per lb. was enough for the planters, but he thought that 1s. 2d. per lb. should be allowed for the costs of the inspection at New Orleans, the costs of loading and unloading as well as insurance. As might be expected in one who had read all the correspondence, he placed great emphasis upon inspection to guarantee quality control in Louisiana. For the freight homeward, he reckoned that one would have to allow not two *sols* but 2s. 6d. per lb. at first, though he hoped that this might ultimately be reduced. Putting these all together, he recommended a price in France of 6s. 6d. per lb. or 32 *l.t.* 10s. per quintal in place of the price of 25 *l.t.* paid by the united farms since 1738; he conceded, though, that a price of 30 *l.t.* per quintal or six *sols* per lb. might be barely sufficient. Though this was a higher price than the farms paid for English tobacco, it could be justified by reasons of state.[123] As we might expect, the recommendations of Beletrus were to be most influential.

These and many other similar contemporary memoirs were not composed in a void. All during the last year of the war, Maurepas had been writing to Louisiana about the importance of continuing and expanding the tobacco plantations there and of improving their quality. For his part, he had had a great scheme to help that trade ready when the war intervened; as soon as the war was over, he would bring that scheme forward again; in the meantime, he would see if it were at all possible to get the farmers-general to raise their price.[124] With the war over, new instructions had to be drafted for Michel de la Rouvillière, the newly appointed *commissaire-ordonnateur*.

The formal instructions to Governor Vaudreuil and Michel jointly repeated the now traditional items about quality and shipbuilding.[125] The private instructions to Michel were, however, more informative. The king was represented as recognizing that the 25 *l.t.* per quintal price prevailing since 1738 was inadequate and as determined to rectify this as soon as possible.[126] The advice of Beletrus had been taken.

Nothing was in fact done about the price of tobacco, though, until 1750. This delay can be in part ascribed to the confusion following upon the dismissal of Maurepas in April 1749; it can also be explained by the existing six-year contract of the united farms which was not to expire until 30 September 1750. Shortly before the expiry of the old contract, Rouillé, the new navy minister, brought pressure to bear to improve the price of Louisiana tobacco.[127] The relevant *arrêt* was finally issued on 13 October 1750. The price of 25 *l.t.* per quintal paid by the farms for Louisiana tobacco since 1738 was raised to 30 *l.t.* for the next lease of the farms (Jean Girardin, 1750–56). Of this sum, 2 *l.t.* 10s. per quintal would be reimbursed to the farms by the king. Louisiana tobacco was to be imported only as dried leaf tied in bunches or hands (*en manoque*); manufactured tobacco was prohibited. The ports of importation, the rights of entrepôt, and other terms were restated as in previous legislation.[128]

This modest rise in price was to be the only concrete result that came out of the flood of memoirs that filled the years from 1747 to 1751. Many other sweeping measures were, however, seriously considered. The most important of these were measures designed to increase the importation of slaves into Louisiana. This was a matter attracting considerable state attention at the end of the war in 1748, when two substantial new slave-trading companies were formed. The two younger Paris brothers, whom we last encountered going into exile in 1726, had returned to court and influence in the later 1730's; in the 1740's they were active again as army suppliers and sponsored both the rise of Madame de Pompadour and the downfall of the controller-general Orry.[129] Throughout they retained their concessions in Louisiana and their interest in that colony.[130] In September 1748, the youngest of the brothers, Jean Paris de Montmartel, helped organize an Angola Company to engage in the slave trade on a large scale. The "expert" member of the company was the great Irish slave trader of Nantes, Antoine-Vincent Wailsh; its financial affairs were in the hands of the Paris bankers, Tourton & Baur. Two months later, in answer to this challenge from "outsiders," a large number of farmers-general and persons with Indies Company connections formed a rival Guinea Company under the leadership of Charles-Claude-Ange Dupleix de Bacquencourt (brother of the Indian governor and son of the old tobacco farmer); its "technical" partners were the equally great Nantes slave trading firm of Grou & Michel; its Paris banker was Jean Cottin. After a short period of intense competition, the two companies cooperated in 1750 in taking over jointly from the Indies Company the Senegal slave export trade. The Angola Company was not successful and was wound up in 1753, but the new Guinea Company continued active for a generation.[131]

With the creation of these big slave trading companies in 1748, powerful centers of influence were created in whose interest it might well be for the government to "encourage" the importation of slaves into Louisiana. Even before the formation of the Angola and Guinea companies, David Gradis & Son, the great Bordeaux West India merchants, had suggested a scheme whereby the government would contract with private slave traders to buy 10,000 slaves delivered to Louisiana—2,000 annually for five years. The price —at least 1,000 *l.t.* per head for men, women, and children mixed—would be paid by the king, one-third in advance, two-thirds on delivery; the king's officers would then sell the slaves to the planters, with the crown not the merchants assuming all risk of the buyers' debts.[132]

This proposal was immediately answered by a memoir from the prolific Fabry de la Bruyère, the former resident of Louisiana, whose not ineffective memoir of the preceding year had recommended raising the price of tobacco from 25 to 30 *l.t.* In a new memoir or memoirs written in the summer or fall of 1748, Fabry calculated that 10,625 field hands making 1,600 lb. of tobacco each annually would be needed to make the seventeen million pounds of tobacco he thought France needed. However, if too many slaves were imported at once—as under the Gradis scheme—the planters would lack the means of paying for them. If the crown sold the slaves on credit, it would lose vast sums through bad debts, just as the Indies Company had done earlier. Instead of the heavy initial importation suggested by Gradis, Fabry proposed a graduated importation starting with 200 the first year and rising with the ability of the planters to pay. If word were sent out at once to Louisiana that the king was sending out 200 slaves in 1750 to be sold for tobacco, the planters could be counted on to increase the number of slaves working on tobacco from about 250 to 500 who, at 1,600 lb. each, would produce 800,000 lb. tobacco in the first year (1749 or 1750, depending on when word was sent out) or enough to buy the 200 slaves at 4,000 lb. of tobacco each. The next year, with their added labor force, the planters could grow more tobacco and thus buy a larger number of slaves. In each succeeding year, a larger labor force would enable the planters to grow more tobacco and thus to purchase an even larger number of slaves than the year before. By 1759, there would be 10,325 slaves in the colony working on tobacco (the 500 original ones plus 9,825 newly imported) who would produce 16,520,000 lb. of tobacco.

Fabry did not think that his scheme would cost the crown anything in the end. The slaves would be sold for tobacco only, thus eliminating all losses on credit. He thought that the government could contract with big French slave dealers to deliver slaves to Louisiana for an average price of 600 *l.t.* per head payable in Paris (compared to Gradis's suggested price of

1,000 *l.t.*). Each of the slaves thus costing the government 600 *l.t.* would be sold in turn to planters for 4,000 lb. of tobacco, which would be returned to France at the government's expense and sold to the farmers-general for 25 *l.t.* per quintal, realizing 1,000 *l.t.* on each slave. From the resulting margin of 400 *l.t.* per slave, 240 *l.t.* would have to be deducted for the freight back to France of the 4,000 lb.; this would still leave a profit of 160 *l.t.* per slave. Fabry admitted that his freight rate of only 60 *l.t.* per 1,000 lb. was low. (This rate was of course equivalent to only six *l.t.* per quintal compared to the ten *l.t.* per quintal which Fabry had allowed in his 1747 memoir and the 12 *l.t.* 10 *s.* rate which Beletrus had thought necessary in his memoir.) He thought that a six *l.t.* rate homeward would pay if the ships carried out a remunerative cargo to St. Domingue and if the wait for tobacco in Louisiana was significantly shorter than the usual wait for sugar at St. Domingue. As in his earlier and later memoirs, Fabry recognized that one of the chief competitive disadvantages of Louisiana was that French vessels were more expensive to operate than their British rivals. But he did not feel that these cost differentials were irreducible. If French merchants refused either to supply slaves at 600 *l.t.* each or to carry tobacco back to France for six *l.t.* per quintal, the government should deal with British or Dutch merchants who would do business at those prices; he felt sure that once their bluff was called, the French *traitants* and shipowners would meet the foreign price.[133]

The Fabry scheme seems to have passed in many versions through many hands. In its original version, its key idea was that the king himself should be entrepreneur for the supply of slaves to Louisiana and the return of tobacco; others were prepared to turn his scheme on its head and use his ideas and data as arguments for a private monopoly company. The count of Magnières, a contemporary Franco-Irish writer, published a scheme proposed by a company of substantial merchants which in fact incorporated the ideas, data, and ten-year tables of Fabry. The scheme was, however, less advantageous both to the united farms and to the planter than that of Fabry, though presumably more advantageous to the merchant-undertakers. They asked that the tobacco price paid by the united farm be raised from 25 *l.t.* to 30 *l.t.* per quintal (as was subsequently done in 1750). For their part, they would agree to deliver slaves to Louisiana at the accelerating rate suggested by Fabry's tables, there to be sold to the planters for 900 *l.t.* per head. In exchange for the slaves, they would accept only tobacco, at a rate of 17 *l.t.* 10*s.* per quintal or 3*s.* 6*d.* per lb., the ordinary price in Louisiana.[134] In practice, however, this would mean that the planter would have to deliver 5,143 lb. of tobacco for one slave instead of Fabry's 4,000 lb.

The company which proposed this scheme can almost certainly be identified with the Angola Company of Paris de Montmartel.[135] There is other writing emanating from that circle which calls for a monopoly company to supply slaves to Louisiana.[136] According to Magnières, the company's scheme came into the hands of Anne-Simon Piarron de Chamousset, *maître des requêtes* (brother of the philanthropist), who submitted it to the minister of the navy (probably Maurepas, just before his fall). The minister forwarded it to S. F. A. Le Normant, *commissaire-ordonnateur* in Louisiana, 1744–48, who had just returned to France to become *intendant de la marine* at Rochefort. On the basis of Le Normant's observations, the company amended its scheme, though not enough to get it accepted.[137]

Various versions have survived of the Fabry scheme as amended by the new company. The most general is a report from a seemingly neutral expert (probably Beletrus), quite familiar with the affairs of the colony, to whom the matter had been referred. The author reviewed the history of the slave supply in Louisiana from the days of the Indies Company. He was fully aware of all the difficulties, pointing out that although the old company had sold slaves for as little as 660 *l.t.* each and bought tobacco for as much as 5s. per lb. (25 *l.t.* per quintal), it had been unable to obtain the tobacco it had hoped for. He recommended proceeding more slowly along the lines suggested by Fabry. Unlike Fabry, he insisted upon the necessity for a monopoly company to supply the slaves. Unlike Fabry too, he would let the settlers pay for these slaves in money or any commodity, but he would give every preference to tobacco: e.g., the price for a slave would be 1,000 *l.t.* in cash, but 900 *l.t.* in tobacco at 3s. 6d. per lb. (17 *l.t.* 10s. per quintal); the price of tobacco in France was to be raised from 25 *l.t.* to 30 *l.t.* per quintal—precisely the terms of the company.[138]

Another memoir, annotated "M. de Lad.," sketched the working details for a company with a twenty-year monopoly. The sale price was reduced slightly to 900 *l.t.* for male adults and 820 *l.t.* for women, to be paid for in tobacco still at 17 *l.t.* 10s. per quintal.[139] A detailed scheme very much along these lines was in fact drawn up by Le Normant, intendant at Rochefort, and sent by the minister to Nantes for the opinion of the slave traders there. To their *observations,* Le Normant submitted his own further *réponses*.[140] The authors of the Nantes *observations* objected to the principle of monopoly, but Le Normant argued that free trade had been given its chance since 1731 and had failed to supply the colony. Le Normant also had little patience with the Nantes objections to the clause that would have forbidden private merchants to export tobacco. He insisted that none of them had actually been doing so; all the tobacco carried back to France went instead in the king's vessels. Eighteen out of twenty private vessels preferred the triangle trade carrying European goods to Louisiana, timber thence to the Antilles, and a cargo of sugar home to France. He also defended as justified the proposed price of slaves (900 *l.t.* for men and 820 for women), which Nantes thought too low, and the price offered for tobacco which Nantes held too high. (The Nantais preferred 15 *l.t.* instead of 17 *l.t.* 10s. per quintal.) There was less dispute about the technical clauses obliging the company to take tobacco first in preference to other goods, obliging it to deal directly with the planters and not with middlemen and protecting it as creditor. The Nantais suggested, though, that more radical changes in prices would be necessary in time of war to cover higher freight and insurance charges.

One further version of the monopoly company scheme has survived, probably drawn up late in 1749 or early 1750, which seems an attempt to answer some of the practical objections of Nantes. Most of the old clauses are repeated, but with significant changes: the monopoly was reduced from twenty years to ten; the price at which the slaves were to be sold was raised from 900 (for men) and 820 (for women) to 1,000 and 900 respectively, but as compensation the price of tobacco was to be raised to 20 *l.t.* per quintal. (This would reduce the price of an adult male slave from 5,143 to 5,000 lb. of tobacco.) As compensation, the new scheme asked that the price of tobacco in France be raised from 30 to 32 *l.t.* 10*s*. All promised schedules of delivery were abandoned and, in event of war, the company could surrender its contract.[141]

We do not know precisely who was supporting and who was opposing the company scheme. Fabry, one of the busiest and most knowledgeable memoir writers of these years, had always been opposed to monopoly companies. In 1749 he rethought his arguments and became more cautious. On 1 April 1749, he submitted an amazingly detailed plan for a model plantation near New Orleans, filled with physiographic data on the country and precise calculations on how much each slave and hired laborer would cost. Here, as in his earlier memoirs, he despaired of getting freight cheaply enough from French shipowners and recommended chartering or buying a flute on the king's account in Holland.[142] Later that year, he submitted a new version of his earlier scheme for a ten-year program of planned accelerating slave importations. He wanted the slaves sold to the planters for his old price of 4,000 lb. of tobacco, now expressed as 800 *l.t.* per head payable in tobacco at 20 *l.t.* per quintal. The tobacco would be sold to the united farms in France for only 25 *l.t.* per quintal, requiring a very low freight home. He repeated his attacks on schemes for a private company, insisting that prices could be kept in line and the scheme made to work only if the latter were carried out on the king's account. The king should contract with private traders to bring slaves to Louisiana for only 600 *l.t.* per head and guarantee them a tobacco freight back to France at the remarkably low figure of 40 *l.t.* per hogshead (compared to 60 in his earlier scheme). He admitted that no French slave traders would deal on these terms and therefore suggested that until such times as French merchants became more reasonable, the king should contract with Englishmen who would accept these terms.[143]

Thus both Le Normant, the advocate of a monopoly company, and Fabry, the advocate of royal trading, became involved in ever more intricate and self-defeating cost calculations. Neither side could prove satisfactorily that they could make a large-scale slave importing scheme work without the heavy state subsidies which Rasteau *fils* had earlier claimed were necessary. We do not know the grounds, but eventually the negotiations were broken off. On 5 April 1750, after about a year of negotiation, Rouillé wrote to Wailsh of the Angola Company that the conditions his company proposed were "too onerous."[144] The next day, the minister wrote to Dupleix of the Guinea Company inviting that company to submit propositions of its own.[145] We do not know what resulted from this invitation, except that nothing concrete developed.[146] In the end, as earlier noted, the government the following October contented itself with raising the price paid by the farm for Louisiana tobacco from 25 to 30 *l.t.* per quintal.

The idea of some special arrangement to encourage the importation of slaves into Louisiana, though seemingly "shelved" in 1750, stayed in circulation during the remaining years of peace. In 1752, we find traces of Silhouette (now an influential figure in government circles) intervening on behalf of a sieur Brignon who proposed to import "foreign slaves" into Louisiana. Rouillé was at first interested but denied permission when informed that two private vessels were about to be sent out by French merchants to carry slaves to Louisiana: one by (Pierre?) Salles of Paris, the other by a merchant of Morlaix.[147] There is no evidence of any such vessels ever getting to Louisiana.

More schemes came forth in 1754. Of one from a sieur Laugeois, we know no details.[148] Another, emanating from a sieur Colom was similar to the Le Normant schemes of 1749–50; it called for a company with a capital of 1.5 million *l.t.* to bring slaves to Louisiana with some monopoly privileges. Unlike the earlier projects, it did not emphasize tobacco but envisioned the company's ships carrying timber to the Antilles (as suggested in some of Fabry's memoirs).[149] The plan was opposed as an undesirable monopoly by the new governor, de Kerlérec, and nothing ever came of it.[150] With the advent of hostilities in 1755, interest in such schemes evaporated.

In Louisiana, meanwhile, the tobacco trade slumbered through the peace interlude of 1748–56 much as it had during the prewar years. Crops at Pointe Coupée were reported poor some years and better other years, but the quantities never seem to have been large.[151] In 1754, the annual crop was estimated at 160,000 lb. (or at most 200,000 lb.), below the levels reached in the 1730's and 1740's.[152] When Louis de Kerlérec was sent out as governor in 1752, the instructions to him and the *ordonnateur* Michel repeated the old platitudes about encouraging tobacco and shipbuilding and controlling quality that had appeared in the instructions to Vaudreuil and Salmon and went back to 1731.[153] Much the same instructions accompanied de Rochemore when he was sent out as *ordonnateur* in 1758.[154] Little in fact was done. A memoir describing the colony prepared shortly after 1755 reported some sixty to eighty settlers at Pointe Coupée growing tobacco successfully; the 30–40 settlers at Natchitoches on the Red River made "a little tobacco"; at Natchez, where "excellent tobacco" had been grown in the 1720's, "some soldiers of the garrison diverted themselves by making some once more."[155] Memoirs written about 1740 had said much the same thing.[156] Kerlérec wished he had some hard-working Germans or Lorrainers to send to Natchez to restart tobacco growing there,[157] but none were forthcoming.

With the advent of the Seven Years' War, the affairs of the feeble Louisiana tobacco trade naturally went from bad to worse. With the market for dried leaf tobacco becoming very uncertain, the settlers at Pointe Coupée turned increasingly to maize and subsistence agriculture; what little tobacco they did grow they manufactured into *carottes* for its better preservation and sale in America. In 1758 all their crops failed.[158] In 1759, there was a sudden spurt of schemes for companies to develop Louisiana, emphasizing its timber trade with the French Antilles. One "under the name of Bertrand Duvernet" wanted a great territorial concession near New Orleans;[159] another was to be based on Mobile Bay.[160] Both wanted temporary permission to buy slaves from the British and Dutch and import supplies from the English colonies. Both requested, however, that, once they were established, the French colonies be obliged to buy all forest products from them and not the British. Such schemes were obviously designed to meet wartime shortages in the West Indies. In the event, nothing came of them.

In 1763, as in 1731, the tobacco "industry" in Louisiana produced only enough tobacco to fill one ship a year. The failure of French governmental efforts to develop that trade was based upon a persistent misunderstanding about costs. Labor was expensive in Louisiana and freight was dear. Yet Louisiana tobacco was expected to compete in price in the French market with Virginia tobacco grown in an established colony with a much more adequate labor force (free and slave) and much closer to Europe, hence with much cheaper freight rates. The farmers-general quite understandably were not prepared to pay a premium for Louisiana tobacco and, except for the *arrêt* of 1750 raising the French price from 25 to 30 *l.t.* per quintal, the government was not prepared to require them to do so. A price of 30 *l.t.* per quintal, one-quarter to one-third above what the united farms paid in peacetime for Virginia tobacco delivered, was not enough to solve the Louisiana problems. The French government had been prepared to pay limited subsidies on shipping to the Mississippi; it was also prepared to spend millions on the military and civil establishments there. These expenditures created a money supply in the colony which made it worth while for French merchants to send ships to Louisiana with European produce. Such merchants did not however find it in their interest to have their ships return to France with much Louisiana produce except a little indigo and furs. For the most part, they took on cargoes of forest products (timber, pitch, tar) for the Antilles where they could easily get a remunerative cargo of sugar homeward. Thus there was little demand among the merchant ships—fairly numerous by the 1750's—for tobacco. Many saw this problem; only the merchant Rasteau *fils* dared make recommendations sweeping enough to break the cycle of frustration. His recommendation for a frank policy of subsidies for slave importations and for tobacco shipments from Louisiana to France went unheeded. The government had no compunctions about subsidizing the slave trade elsewhere but in Louisiana it would spend millions on the garrison and next to nothing on "economic development." War ultimately solved the problem.

After the Loss of Louisiana, 1763–75

The cession of the right bank of the Mississippi and New Orleans to Spain in 1762 and the left bank to Great Britain in 1763 altered fundamentally the prospects of the tobacco trade in that valley. On the British side we can find memoirs of 1763 debating whether or not Britain should encourage tobacco planting about its new acquisition at Natchez to compete with its older plantations in the Chesapeake.[161] On the French side, there was great confusion. The treaty of cession of October 1762 was at first kept secret and its implementation was long delayed. Thus, with the approach of peace, steps were recommended and even taken to revivify the colony and its tobacco trade. The war years had been marked by significant published writing defending Louisiana against the hostile interests of the united farms.[162] In 1762, with peace imminent, but before the treaty of cession to Spain had been decided upon, the navy minister urged the controller-general to renew and extend the various privileges and exemptions previously granted to the trade of the colony.[163] With the terms of the British treaty known but those of the Spanish treaty still a secret, a memoir writer hastened to urge that the loss of the left bank should not discourage France from developing the right bank of the Mississippi where much good tobacco could be grown—if the price were sufficiently attractive.[164]

The residents of Louisiana were not themselves informed of the cession of New Orleans and the west bank to Spain until the middle of 1764. They could thus nurture illusions. On 17 October 1763, a number of merchants and planters signed a memorial urging French government support for the renewed development of the Louisiana tobacco trade. Their representation included an eleven year plan for the gradual introduction of slaves and expansion of production along the lines of earlier schemes by Fabry *et al*. The scheme was presented to d'Abbadie, director-general in Louisiana, who forwarded it to the duke of Choiseul, navy minister, in April 1764.[165] With the public announcement of the decision to cede the remainder of Louisiana to Spain, nothing could of course be done about such representations.

The actual situation in Louisiana was unattractive, but not absolutely bleak. In 1764, Rivoire, a merchant newly returned to New Orleans from France, wrote to the marquis of Grimaldi, Spanish foreign minister, about the prospects of the colony. Tobacco cultivation there, he reported, had declined by three-fourths during the war. Nevertheless, he felt it could and should be revived: there were promising market potentialities both in France itself and in Denmark![166] (Thus did the "pipe-dreams" waft from French history into Spanish.) In the years between the peace of 1763 and the establishment of effective Spanish administration in 1769, there actually was a modest revival of tobacco production for regional trade. One of the last French estimates of the economy of Louisiana placed tobacco production in the mid-1760's at 300,000 lb., or about at the level of the late 1720's.[167] During the period of confusion, merchants of all nations established at New Orleans were able to supply manufactured tobacco from Pointe Coupée and Natchitoches, to the French and Spanish colonies and to the British in the Floridas. When effective Spanish control was established at New Orleans in 1769, a rival British trading station was established up the river on the east bank at Manchac, where tobacco could be obtained from Pointe Coupée on the other side to send to the now British ports of Mobile and Pensacola. There was of course also a legitimate trade in Pointe Coupée and Natchitoches tobacco to Vera Cruz and elsewhere in the Spanish empire.[168]

With Louisiana going or gone, there was naturally some discussion in France during the years following the Seven Years War of the possibility of reviving tobacco cultivation in Martinique or Guadeloupe, but it was soon enough seen once more that this would be impractical.[169] Far more serious was the related grand project taken up by Choiseul late in 1762 to develop French Guiana (Cayenne) as a replacement for Louisiana and as a source of French tobacco supplies. Settlers for the new colony on the Kourou west of Cayenne, were recruited particularly from Alsace and Lorraine where experienced tobacco growers could be found and where there were serious signs of overpopulation, thousands emigrating from those provinces in the 1760's to Germany, Hungary, and Russia. The farmers-general agreed to take the first 10,000 lb. of tobacco grown in the colony for an experimental purchase. In the event, the Kourou settlements of 1763–64 were inadequately planned and grossly mismanaged by those in charge: the chevalier Turgot, the principal projector and brother of the famous controller-general, and Chanvalon, a professional colonial administrator. Of the 12,000–17,000 poor emigrants sent out, only a little over a hundred (35 families) settled and stayed, some 3,000 returning to France while the remainder died in the jungle of one disease or another. Despite this gruesome fiasco, a few years later (1768), Choiseul's cousin and successor as navy minister, the duke of Choiseul-Praslin, took up the idea once more and chartered a new company to establish a colony at Approuague, to the east of Cayenne. (Both cousins had received very large land grants between the Kourou and the Dutch frontier.) Although the scale and death toll of this experiment were lower, the failure was as complete, both company and government losing their entire investments.[170] There the scheme and schemers rested until hopes stirred once more with the start of the American Revolution. (The quite different conditions prevailing after 1775 will be discussed in Part III.)

Surveying the three-quarters of a century from the abandonment of the St. Domingue tobacco cultivation and the foundation of Louisiana, about

1700, to the start of the American Revolution in 1775, we cannot help being still a little surprised at the utter failure of the French to develop a national source of tobacco supply. The commodity was after all relatively easy to grow.[171] The French government had, it would seem, to take one of two difficult decisions. Either it had to force the farmers-general to buy French colonial tobacco at a sufficiently high price to make its cultivation and transportion worthwhile (probably twice the price of Virginia tobacco) or it had to subsidize the trade for as long as might be necessary to get it started. The first would have had to be paid for indirectly by the French state in the price of the farm; the latter would have been paid for directly. In the end, fiscal stringency and fiscal conservatism made either decision impossible. The dozens of other schemes (mentioned in this chapter) which were considered at the time were all merely commentaries on that inability to act decisively.

CHAPTER 14

The Tobacco Monopoly under the United Farms: The Leases of 1730–86

By the lease, *résultat,* and *arrêts* of September 1730, the farm of the tobacco monopoly, it will be remembered, was sublet by the Indies Company to the United General Farms for eight years (1 October 1730–30 September 1738). This period corresponded to the last two years of the lease of the united farms under the name of Pierre Carlier (1726–32) plus the full six years of their upcoming lease under the name of Nicolas Desboves (1732–38). For this sublease, the united farms were to pay the Indies Company 7.5 million *l.t.* p.a. during the first four years, 1730–34, and eight million during the last four, 1734–38.[1] Since the gross receipts of the monopoly in the early 1730's were about thirteen million *l.t.* and sales tended upward,[2] the contract price seemed well covered and there was ample opportunity for profit through careful management.

The tobacco monopoly thus acquired by the united farms turned out to be a very good thing for the farmers-general. From papers relating to a subsequent lawsuit between the farmer-general Le Riche de la Popelinière and his brother Le Riche de Cheveigné, we learn that each of the forty farmers-general was asked to put up only 100,000 *l.t.* extra capital for the tobacco monopoly; it proved so immediately profitable that no further calls of capital were made. Over and above the 10 percent interest paid on the capital thus advanced, each farmer-general received as dividends from the profits of the tobacco monopoly alone 125,000 *l.t.* for the two Carlier years (1730–32) and 302,500 *l.t.* for the six Desboves years (1732–38). (The slight drop in the annual rate can be explained by the rise in the yearly price of their farm from 7.5 to eight million in 1734.) Over the eight years, the forty farmers-general together received 17,100,000 *l.t.* from tobacco alone, or 2,137,500 *l.t.* p.a.[3]

The profits made by the farmers-general at this time from tobacco were characteristic of their enviable position under Fleury. Aside from interest and salaries, total profits of each farmer-general during the Forceville lease of 1738–44 were reported by Le Riche de Cheveigné to have exceeded one million *l.t.*[4] From 1726 to 1750, the united farms were leased by the company at a price that rose very little and which was commonly and understandably considered to be well below the true value of those revenues. All sorts of rumors, sound and wild, circulated about the great profits which the farmers were supposedly making both on the united farms and on tobacco.

When these leases came up for renewal in 1737–38, there were suggestions that the entire arrangement made for the tobacco monopoly in 1730 should be reconsidered. Some attacked the Indies Company and asserted that it had no right to a revenue of eight million a year from that privilege, particularly after it had given up any pretense of developing Louisiana. Several answering memoirs have survived from these years defending the Indies Company and its rights to its eight millions p.a.[5] Other critics attacked the United General Farms. One account estimated that they sold six million pounds of tobacco yearly at an average price of 50 *sols* per lb., thus grossing fifteen millions; since the author of the account estimated that the farm's operating expenses were only three millions p.a., he put its profits at twelve million *l.t.* gross, or four million net, after payment of the annual rent to the Indies Company.[6] This shrewd estimate was probably a bit high in estimating the average price at which tobacco was sold by the farm, but probably a bit too conservative in estimating the farm's total sales. All in all, though, it was not far from the mark, as was shown in the event.

While the entire question of the renewal of the farms was under consideration in the fall of 1737, a company of unknown composition came forward and offered to farm the tobacco monopoly separately for ten or eleven million *l.t.* annually. Cardinal Fleury, ultimately responsible for the reestablishment of the general farms in 1726 and for their disappointing yield since then, seems to have been annoyed that anyone should disturb the tidy arrangements he had made for the tobacco monopoly. He decided to leave it in the hands of the united farms, but to raise its annual value in his private calculations from eight to ten and eventually eleven million *l.t.* The extra three million were added on to the price of the united farms but not acknowledged as coming from tobacco. The Indies Company thus continued to receive only eight millions a year from its tobacco monopoly and was defrauded by the crown of the growing value of the monopoly, which technically should have gone to it.[7] In this roundabout and unacknowledged way, tobacco was responsible for the three million rise in the yield of the united farms by the Jacques Forceville lease (1738–44), the only significant rise in the farms' yields between 1730 and 1750. (See Table III.)

When the general lease came to be renegotiated in 1743–44, France was engaged in a land war in Germany and the Low Countries and was drawing closer to a sea war with Britain. Such circumstances were not psychologically propitious for raising the price of the farms. The farms were in the event relet for the Thibault La Rue lease of 1744–50 at virtually the same rent as had prevailed during the previous six years. There is nothing to suggest that, in calculating the price of the whole, the valuation of the tobacco farm at eleven million was changed.

During the war years, the entire question of the relationship of the tobacco farm to the Indies Company came under consideration. Only the eight millions which that company received from the united farms for the tobacco monopoly enabled it to pay dividends; its trading activities resulted in no net profits. As already mentioned, the matter had previously been considered in 1737-39. A scheme had been put forward then suggesting that the king redeem the eight million p.a. pledged to the Indies Company by repaying to them the ninety million *l.t.* capital which he owed them. This could be done by having the king surrender his 10,000 shares in the company for thirty million; by having the king borrow thirty million from the united farms to be paid to the Indies Company and employed by them as working capital; and by granting the company thirty million (capital value) worth of 3 percent *rentes* to produce 900,000 *l.t.* annually. With ten millions in such *rentes* which the Company already possessed producing another 300,000 *l.t.*, they would have an assured income of only 1.2 million *l.t.* annually. Castanier, for the company, pointed out that even if the crown decided to reduce the dividend on their shares to 50 *l.t.* per share (from the 150 pledged in the 1720's), this 1.2 million would be enough for dividends on only 24,000 shares. The king would therefore have to be at enormous expense to call in the excess 22,000 shares. Castanier tried to prove that when the costs of all the capital needed for such transactions and dividends forgone were computed, the king would save very little by the proposed changes.[8] Whether or not his arguments were persuasive, nothing was in fact done at the time to disturb the income of the Indies Company from the tobacco monopoly.

When the matter was next taken under consideration, it was in a manner not hostile to but rather solicitous of the interests of the Indies Company. Cardinal Fleury, for so long the principal minister, had died in 1743 and Orry, controller-general since 1730, was dismissed in 1745, the first vengeance of Madame de Pompadour (acting in behalf of the restored Paris brothers): both departed ministers had been notoriously more responsive to the interests of the united farms than to those of the Indies Company. The heroic achievements of the young Dupleix in India during the war with Britain now made the government much more sympathetic to the needs of the company. At the same time, the growing productivity of the tobacco monopoly made it particularly inconvenient to have such a valuable branch of the revenue granted in perpetuity to the Indies Company and sublet to the united farms with the excess value of the monopoly, which should have gone to the company, hidden in the total price of the farms. All this indirection and camouflage was ended by an edict of June 1747. The title to the tobacco monopoly was once and for all taken away from the Indies Company and resumed by the crown from 1 July 1747. As compensation for the eight million annual income thus lost, the company received 180 millions (nominal value) in royal perpetual annuities (*rentes*) at 5 percent to produce nine millions annually. (The nine millions were secured as a first charge on the income from the tobacco farm.) The other privileges of the company were confirmed.[9] Thus was the connection between the tobacco monopoly and the Indies Company forged by Law finally severed. Henceforth, the united farms would have to deal only with the government in fixing the price and terms of the tobacco monopoly.

With the death of Fleury in 1743, the dismissal of Orry in 1745, and the return of peace in 1748, public affairs had at last reached that conjuncture at which a major increase in the yield from the united farms was possible. The new and very able controller-general Machault reputedly learned from his close friend, the farmer-general Bouret, that the united farms had been making nine millions in profits during the La Rue lease—despite the war—and on entering into negotiations in 1749 determined to raise the rent to the crown by that amount. Thus during the Jean Girardin–Jean-Baptiste Bocquillon lease of 1750–56 the united farms paid 102,765,000 *l.t.* annually, compared to 92 million under the previous lease.[10] Tobacco accounted for only a proportionate part of this 10.8 million *l.t.* increase. Instead of about eleven millions, the tobacco monopoly was now valued at twelve millions[11] plus 600,000 *l.t.* for the new tobacco import duty established in the eastern provinces outside the monopoly.[12]

Thus ended the stagnant period in the yields of the farms other than tobacco. The farmers-general were not happy about this abrupt rise in their obligations for the farms generally or for tobacco in particular. Their yields failed to rise as much as was hoped from the peace, and they were forced to look at themselves and their company with newly critical eyes. On 13 March 1753, the marquis of Argenson, former secretary of state for foreign affairs, noted in his journal:

> One of the farmers general said to me yesterday that the operation of the general farms could not long be maintained as it now is, because of the bad management of that great machine; that the tobacco yield was beginning to diminish each week. That company of forty associates doesn't contain six persons who do any work, and the others understand exactly nothing about it and are good for nothing except collecting their dividends. They are reversioners and court favourites who pay a lot for their places. The employees are insolent fellows and rogues whom they catch stealing from the company or neglecting it totally; there is a prodigious number of them to whom positions are given as sinecures *(en pensions sèches)* to get rid of them. The company, not controlling these jobs, cannot dismiss the poor workers nor promote the good ones. With all this, the wretchedness of the times diminishes consumption; so that, says this man, one would be amazed if one knew what the company really earned; they hid these shortcomings so as not to weaken the company's credit.

The farmer-general also complained to Argenson of the host of petty subfarmers who survived in many of the excises, though long since eliminated in tobacco. Changed with every new lease at the whim of the controller-general, such subfarmers tried to squeeze all they could from the public in each six years. The pessimistic informant also feared that the great advances from the farmers-general to the crown, then 27 millions, would ruin their credit and them. He claimed that several of those "money-bags" (*richards*) had asked the controller-general for permission to retire but had been refused for fear of discrediting the company.[13]

Argenson's informant was, perhaps calculatingly, overly pessimistic. It seemed clear, however, that if the government wished to push the yields of the united farms any higher, certain "reforms" would have to be made. During his brief tenure as controller-general, Machault's successor, Jean Moreau de Séchelles (1754–56), effected a number of such changes. The remaining subfarms (27 companies containing 215 farmers) were abolished and promises were made that the government would thereafter allow the national company complete autonomy in engaging and dismissing its employees. In return, the number of farmers-general was raised from forty to sixty to bring in new talent and to make an unprecedentedly large new advance to the king.[14] Séchelles decided to finance the coming war by borrowing and obliged each farmer-general to advance one million for a sixty million loan from the company to the crown. In the previous lease, the farmers-general had had enough of their own funds free to supply working capital; now with all their own resources advanced to the crown, they had to borrow another sixty million for working capital, with the most serious results.[15]

At the same time (1755), the price for the coming Pierre Henriet lease of 1756–62 was set at 110 millions, over seven million more than in the preceding lease. Tobacco contributed more than two-fifths of this increase, the valuation of the monopoly being increased from 12.6 to 15.6 million (i.e., fifteen million for the monopoly and 600,000 for the duty in the eastern frontier provinces).[16] Thus, by 1756, the monopoly had reached a contract price double the 7.5 million which the united farms had first paid for it in 1730–34, and ten times its contract price at the beginning of the century.

The Seven Years' War marks a turning point in the fiscal history of eighteenth-century France. The quiet, crisis-free years of slowly mounting revenues that had followed the collapse of Law's System in 1720 now came to an end. The war initiated a new period of heavy borrowing that lasted with only brief respites down to the Revolution. From this time onward, the revenues of the French state were never equal to its commitments. Although the tobacco farm was quite prosperous in the early years of the war, it inevitably became involved in many ways in the economic difficulty of the French state at this time. By 1758, a year of heavy borrowing and heavier public expenditure, the desperate stratagems of the latest of the controllers-general, Jean-Baptiste de Boullongne (1757–59), reached the tobacco farm.

All responsible employees of the united farms, particularly those who handled money, were understandably required to give bonds for the due performance of their offices and trusts. By an *arrêt* of 30 April 1758, all such officials, including those of tobacco, were discharged of their bonds but required instead to deposit as a pledge with the company at 5 percent interest a sum of money varying in amount with their salaries or earnings. The company in turn was obliged to lend all sums so received to the crown at the same 5 percent. This hurt the monopoly by reducing the trading capital of those distributors (*entreposeurs*) who worked on commission.[17] In short, the crown having extracted a sixty million loan from the farmers-general themselves in 1756, now extracted millions more from the farmers' employees and agents.

This forced loan of 1758 was a half-way house back to the evil old system of 1694 (abolished in 1717) under which offices in the united farms and the tobacco monopoly had been sold for the profit of the crown. Under the new system, as under the old, the farmers could not dismiss an incompetent employee without refunding to him the capital he had advanced. When such half-way measures were being adopted, it was only natural that imaginative projectors should come forward with schemes to sell these offices outright as in 1694. One variant, presented during Silhouette's brief controller-generalship (1759), called for selling the offices of hereditary retailers of salt and tobacco for an annual fee; if 40,000 such retailers paid only 30 *l.t.* annually, their offices would produce 1.2 million p.a.; life annuities to this amount could be sold at 10 percent to produce 12 million capital for the government immediately.[18] Another scheme, calling for the more orthodox sale of these same offices for a capital sum was referred to a farmer-general for his comment. He pointed out the failures of the 1694–1717 experiment: many of the offices created were never sold and those sold often had been acquired by incompetents or worse who had had to be bought out. It was always to be feared that anyone who bought such an office intended to make more than normal profits out of it by fraud.[19]

Far more serious than these raids on the pockets of the employees of the farms were the direct attacks on the tobacco farm itself and on its customers. Up to 1758, tobacco had been exempted from a 20 percent surtax levied on other components of the united farms. In that year, tobacco was at last swept up in Boullongne's desperate improvisations. A royal *déclaration* of 24 August 1758 established a 20 percent surcharge (four *sols* in the *l.t.*) on the retail price of tobacco, to be collected by the united farms on a special account for the king's benefit. This meant that tobacco hitherto sold to the consumer for fifty *sols* per pound would thereafter cost sixty, and so in proportion for other grades. The new duty was to start 1 October 1758 and last ten years.[20] It was, however, subsequently extended by a *déclaration* of 17 March 1767[21] for six more years and from 1774 incorporated into the regular leases of the monopoly.[22]

The new surcharge of 1758 caused considerable trouble. Barbier noted in his diary at the time that such a substantial jump in price was a heavy tax indeed on an item by then in almost universal use.[23] Well-to-do customers who bought a pound or more at a time at the *entrepôts* had to pay the full 20 percent extra, their price for the most popular variety, superior roll tobacco *en carottes,* going up from about 50 to about 60 *sols* per lb. Smaller buyers who purchased snuff by the ounce from retailers were, however, spared the rise in price. Since the retailers were already authorized to charge 5*d.* per oz. or 80*s.* per lb. for their snuff, the company made them absorb the price rise in their grinder's margin. These pricing changes made it henceforth less worth while for the larger purchasers to buy from the *entrepôts* and gave the disgruntled retailers added inducement to mix into their snuff either contraband tobacco or foreign matter.[24] The *cour des aides* also made trouble about the farm's *entrepôt* prices[25] and in 1758 and again at the renewal of the surcharge in 1767 remonstrated to the king about the encouragement to fraud implicit in these higher prices for tobacco.[26]

The year 1759 was one of crisis for the United General Farms, really unprecedented since their restoration in 1726. With their entire capital advanced as a loan to the crown, the company had to finance their current operations by borrowing, primarily through the issue of interest bearing *billets des fermes.* With confidence weak and the company overextended, a drop in revenues that year forced the farms to suspend payment temporarily on their *billets* (the suspension being authorized by an *arrêt* of 21 October 1759).[27] One of the more obvious causes of this crisis was the fall in the revenues of the farms during the fiscal year 1 October 1758–30 September 1759, following the adoption of the measures of 1758. This was true of the farms generally but was particularly true of the tobacco farm as is shown in Table I.

TABLE I

Gross and Net Receipts of the United Farms and of the Tobacco Farm
1756–60[28]

Receipts:	United Farms		Tobacco Farm	
	Gross	Net	Gross	Net
	(in millions of livres tournois)			
1756–57	156.7	124.4	32.4	21.9
1757–58	162.0	126.5	33.4	19.8
1758–59	147.0	110.8	26.1	12.7
1759–60	154.6	118.5	28.7	16.1

When we remember that the price of all the united farms together during the Henriet lease was 110 million *l.t.,* we can see that even during the worst year the company remained nominally in the black, even if it could not meet its obligations. When we remember too that in calculating that 110 millions, the tobacco farm had been estimated at fifteen millions, we realize exactly how profitable this branch of the company's revenues was during the first two years of that lease, 1756–58, and just how disastrous the slump of 1759 was. British spies at the time reported that the drop in consumption had been so marked (1.8 million lb. in six months) that the new surtax was going to be dropped.[29] In later years, the farmers-general were to allege that their gross tobacco receipts never fully recovered from the slump of 1759 brought on by the new surtax.[30] This allegation was undoubtedly exaggerated, but it does suggest something of the shock of that year.

Before the end of the terrible 1759, Silhouette had fallen, to be replaced by the old government hand, Bertin, a sometime physiocrat, but a rather traditional controller-general. It was his unenviable task to drag French finances through the last disheartening phase of the Seven Years' War (1759–63).[31] The Henriet lease of the united farms was scheduled to expire on 30 September 1762. The negotiations for its renewal thus had to be carried on in wartime, with the precise date of the peace quite indefinite. The farmers-general spread stories in 1761, as the bargaining started, that the tobacco farm could only be restored by a removal of the 20 percent surtax of 1758 and a substantial reduction in the price to the consumer.[32] Bertin, however, bargained with remarkable skill considering the difficulties of the time. The data cited above in Table I were undoubtedly prepared for him at this time to enable him to proceed more knowingly.

The total annual rent of the united farms (somewhat redefined but for our purposes still excluding Lorraine) during the lease in the name of Jean-Jacques Prévost (1762–68) was set at 115.4 millions in war and 121.4 millions in peace—compared to 110 millions in the previous lease.[33] In making the arrangements for tobacco, Bertin ceded to the united farms the proceeds of the supplementary 20 percent duty of 1758 which had been collected for the king's account during 1758–62. We know that even during the depressed year 1758–59, this supplementary duty produced 4,180,575 *l.t.* 14*s.* 4*d.* for the king.[34] In succeeding years it must have produced something closer to five millions. The surrender of this nearly five millions to the company enabled Bertin to raise the estimated value of the tobacco farm from 15.6 million in the previous lease to 21,850,000 *l.t.* in wartime and 22,208,000 *l.t.* in peacetime for the Prévost lease.[35] The yield of the tobacco farm had now reached about three times its 1730 price. Succeeding events made the terms obtained by Bertin in the very difficult times of 1761–62 seem very good indeed. Not until the 1780's was the government able to extract substantially higher figures for either the united farms generally or the tobacco farm in particular.

In 1763, Bertin got into a prolonged and bitter fight with the *parlements* over direct taxation and was hounded out of office before the year was over. In what appeared a conspicuous surrender to the courts, he was replaced as controller-general by the inexperienced L'Averdy, a *conseiller au parlement*. At the end of 1763 Paris was swept by rumors of great changes impending in finance: the United General Farms were to be abolished; the entire tax structure was to be overhauled; the cultivation of tobacco was to be permitted again in France as an encouragement to agriculture. Even after the rumors so dangerous to the credit of the united farms were officially denied, other rumors of change persisted through 1764, including stories that the salt and tobacco monopolies would be replaced by simple duties.[36]

Far from effecting any basic reforms in the revenue structure of the French state, the inexperienced and ineffectual L'Averdy was unable even to preserve the status quo. In negotiating the Prévost lease for 1762-68, the advance from the farmers-general to the crown had been increased from 60 to 75 millions. Although provision was made for repaying most of this during that and the next lease, in fact, nothing was repaid.[37] This, combined with his own lack of talent and the dubious "success" of most of the fiscal strategems he had adopted since 1763,[38] makes it not at all surprising that L'Averdy in renegotiating the lease of the united farms in 1767 failed to obtain terms very much better than those of the existing Prévost lease of 1762-68. Although France was at peace and privately quite prosperous in 1767 (while it had been engaged in a disastrous and fiscally ruinous war in 1761-62 when Bertin negotiated the last lease), L'Averdy was able to raise the annual rent of the united farms by only eight millions (6.5 percent), from 124 to 132 millions—or without Lorraine, from 121.4 to 128.9 millions. The tobacco farm (the monopoly plus the continuing 20 percent surtax) contributed very little to this increment, rising from 22,208,000 to only 23,125,208 *l.t.*[39]

The new Julien Alaterre lease of 1768-74 also provided for increasing the advance from the company to the crown to 92 millions. Of this sum, twenty millions were supposed to be repaid in the course of the lease by quarterly deductions from the rent paid by the company to the crown, but in fact were not. As had been the case since 1756, the working capital of the company continued to be largely borrowed. The twenty millions hopefully to be refunded during the Alaterre lease were intended by the company to strengthen its working capital and provide greater backing for its *billets*. This relief did not materialize and under the combined pressures of the increased advances to the crown, economic distress from bad harvests and disappointing revenue yields, the company again found itself strained beyond its resources. An *arrêt* of 18 February 1770 once more permitted it to suspend payment on its *billets;* another *arrêt* of 13 November 1770, provided for the resumption of payments in March 1771 but spread over many years.[40] Under such circumstances, it need cause no surprise that the lease Alaterre (1768-74) was the only one between 1726 and the Revolution during which we know definitely that the farmers-general lost money in several years.[41]

Just as the new lease was starting (October 1768), the inept L'Averdy was replaced by the apparently more apt Maynon d'Invau, grandson of the farmer-general and tobacco farmer of 1697-1718. He was, however, tied too closely to the declining fortunes of the duke of Choiseul and, before the year 1769 was over, was in return replaced by the abbé Terray, an obscure *parle-*

mentaire protected by the chancellor Maupeou and the newly triumphant madame du Barry. Terray was tough, unscrupulous, and effective, very much in the style that characterized the last years of Louis XV in contrast to the ineffective moderation of the 1760's.[42]

When it came time to renegotiate the lease of the united farms in 1773–74, Terray demanded to see full accounts. The farmers-general produced the relatively unsatisfactory figures for the first four years (1768–72) of the Alaterre lease. Terray saw no virtue in consistency. For each branch of the farms, he preferred to make his own calculations upon the best three or four years he could find in the two leases since 1762. Thus, for tobacco, he used not the first four years of Alaterre, in which gross receipts averaged only 35,805,659 *l.t.* but rather the first three years of Prévost (1762–65) in which they had averaged 36,306,901.[43] The farmers-general argued that this base was unjustified since a new convention with Spain signed in 1768, making many concessions on freedom of navigation, etc., had allegedly encouraged smuggling and increased their patrolling expenses by 400,000 *l.t.* annually.[44] In the end, the abbé Terray succeeded in continuing the 92 million advance and in raising the annual contract price of the united farms excluding Lorraine from 128,853,912 under Alaterre to 157,764,752 *l.t.*[45] for the Laurent David lease (1774–1780) —in great part by adding new revenues not formerly included. He projected the gross receipts of tobacco at 37,808,305 *l.t.* and set its net value at 24,083,567 *l.t.*, an increase of only 958,359 *l.t.* over the Alaterre valuation.[46] It will be observed that the various figures suggested at this time (1773) for the gross receipts of the tobacco farm, i.e., 35–38 millions, are somewhat above the equivalent data for 1756–58 (33.4 millions) given in Table I. It should be remembered, however, that since 1762 the gross receipts had included the 20 percent surtax of 1758, yielding 4–5 millions. With due allowance made for this last component, all these figures suggest both continuation of the slump in tobacco sales that set in upon the adoption of that surtax and the end of the great expansion in French tobacco consumption that had continued from 1713 to 1758. Thus, Terray had had to squeeze very hard indeed to get any further revenue from tobacco.

Although the Laurent David lease of January 1774 was negotiated by one of the toughest-minded, most ruthless and best informed of the controllers-general of the eighteenth century, it yet proved a very advantageous contract for the company, so great was the prosperity of France in the ensuing years.[47] With the advent of Louis XVI (10 May 1774), Terray was replaced by the more radically reforming Turgot (August 1774) —but the many other enemies the latter made brought him down (May 1776) before he could seriously touch the united farms. After an interlude, he was succeeded by that exotic outsider, the Swiss banker Necker, who undertook to finance the American war by borrowing, to spare the monarchy the unpopularity of increasing taxes. In negotiating the Nicolas Salzard lease for 1780–86, Necker took *aides* (primarily excises on wines), and *domaines* from the united farms and entrusted them to commissioners to administer on crown account. He reduced the number of farmers-general from sixty back to forty and in general brought the company under even greater government supervision.[48]

The "reforms" of Necker completed a process which had gradually whittled away the financial independence and secrecy of the united farms. Machault had been able to get accounts from the company only by collusion. Bertin and his successors obtained them both by right and by the necessity of accounting. The process was, ironically, formalized under the ineffective L'Averdy. An edict of December 1764 creating a new Sinking Fund (*caisse d'amortissement*) established for the benefit of that fund a tax of 10 percent on all interest payments from the crown, as well as on salaries and profits received by revenue farmers, receivers-general, and *trésoriers-généraux*. At the height of the financial crisis of 1770, the abbé Terray, newly installed as controller-general, obtained an *arrêt du conseil* of 4 February raising this tax on the incomes of farmers-general to 30 percent, retroactive to the beginning of the current (Alaterre) lease in 1768. After negotiating the David lease in January 1774, he issued another arbitrary *arrêt* replacing this tax on the farmers-general with a higher but declining scale of rates: 50 percent of the first four million *l.t.* profits in the next lease, 40 percent on the next four million, 30 percent on the next four, and 20 percent on anything over 12 million. These arrangements were in 1780 continued and formalized as "royal participation" by Necker, with the added proviso that the first four million of profits should go entirely to the crown, after which Terray's sliding scale would operate.[49] Whether called taxes before 1780 or "royal participation" thereafter, profit sharing required accounting and was hardly consistent with older ideas of revenue farming. In effect, the Royal General Farms were becoming something like a management contract on commission (*régie intéressée*).

In computing the price for the truncated united farms during the Salzard lease (October 1780–December 1786), Necker imposed a valuation of 26 millions on tobacco; this was based upon annual gross profits of 26.4 million in the previous lease when the price was only 24.1 millions. Despite the prosperity of the united farms during the outgoing David lease, this higher price for tobacco was impressive, considering that the American war had so disrupted the world tobacco market that leaf was costing the united farms about treble what it had before the war.[50] After the fall of Necker in June 1781, his successor Joly de Fleury (1781–83) abandoned the no new taxation policy and by an edict of August 1781 levied a further ten percent (two *sols* in the *livre*) surtax on most existing taxes. For tobacco, however, the surtax was only four *sols* per pound weight, or about 5–7 percent. This new four *sols* was temporarily to be collected and accounted for to the crown separately; in fact, the company absorbed it itself or took it from the profit margins of its retailers, leaving the price to the consumer unchanged. (They wished to avoid the difficulties of 1758 when a sudden rise in retail prices on *carottes* hurt sales badly.) [51]

Although the conservative Joly de Fleury (1781–83) for the moment shielded the farmers-general, Necker's reforms of 1779–80 had destroyed the legend of the inviolability of that company and left their future open to much speculation. When the "prime minister" Maurepas died in 1781, his empty dignity as president of the Finance Council was transferred to the foreign secretary Vergennes, an inveterate enemy of the united farms, who soon made it known that he intended to take advantage of his new position to interfere in financial administration. As expected, this forced the resignation of Joly de Fleury; he was replaced as controller-general by Le Fèvre d'Ormesson, as ardent as Vergennes in his hostility to the farms. In his few months in office in 1783, Ormesson continued Necker's work by taking the customs duties (*traites*) out of farm, though leaving them with the farmers-general to be managed as a *régie* on government account. This reduced the farming business of the "United General Farms" to only three significant revenues: the royal monopolies of salt and tobacco and the *entrées de Paris* (tolls on goods entering the capital). When the determined Ormesson next ordered the conversion of the truncated remainder of the united farms into a *régie*, he provoked a panic in the unprepared Paris financial community and a rush to cash or sell the farms' notes (*billets des fermes*). At this juncture, Vergennes lost his nerve, ordered the withdrawal of the order (*arrêt*) against the united farms and let Ormesson go.[52]

The new controller-general, Calonne (1783–87), proved much less hostile toward the united farms. In negotiating the Jean-Baptiste Mager lease for 1786–92, he did continue *traites* as a *régie* on government account, avowedly to facilitate a planned reform and unification of customs. That same lease established a complex pricing arrangement for the tobacco monopoly: although the four *sols* per pound surtax of 1781 was now incorporated into the lease, the nominal price of the monopoly was only raised from 26 million to 27 million *l.t.*: however, should the yield go above 27 millions, the first two millions of the excess were to go entirely to the crown, while any further surplus was to be divided half to the crown and half to the company. (This was similar to Necker's arrangement of 1780, but with the sliding scale dropped.) For the "budget" of 1788, a government expert estimated that the net yield of the monopoly was about 32 million *l.t.*, with 30.5 million going to the crown. Final figures for the same year actually showed a net of about 33.5 million, with 31.25 presumably going to the state.[53]

The ability of the government to drive ever harder bargains made the united farms more and more a public utility and less and less a private speculation. (Public utilities can, of course, be excellent investments.) For the tobacco monopoly, this meant that "profits" realized by the farmers-general tended to stagnate or even decline, though sales and receipts grew steadily. This is clearly shown in Table II.

TABLE II

Receipts and Profits of the Tobacco Farm, 1728–88[54]

Years	Gross Receipts	Operating Profit	Price of Lease	Apparent Book Profit
	(in millions of livres tournois)			
1728–29	12.5	6.8–7.5		
1730–31	13.0		7.5	
1730–38 (av.)			7.5–8.0	2.14 (net distributed)
1756–60 (av.)	30.2	17.6	15.6	2.0
1762–65 (av.)	36.3		22.2	
1768–72 (av.)	35.8		23.1	
1774–80 (av.)	37.8 (est.)	26.4	24.1	2.3
1774–83 (best yr.)	43.0 48–49			
1788 (est.)		32.0	30.5	1.5
1788 (actual)	51.1	33.5	31.25	2.25

However stagnant or disappointing the ultimate profits of the tobacco monopoly might have been to the farmers-general, quite different were the results for the state. The 30.5 or 31.25 million *l.t.* realized in 1788 was more than four times the price agreed upon for 1730–34 when the united farms first took over the monopoly and about sixty times the price obtained by Colbert in 1674. Table III summarizes the progress since 1730.

The increasing importance of tobacco in French public revenues cannot be understood simply in terms of rising absolute figures. When the tobacco farm was first included in the price of the united farms during the 1680's and 1690's, it accounted for a little over one percent of that price. When the much more important tobacco monopoly was restored to the administration of the united farms in 1730, it accounted for 8.6 percent of the total price paid by the farms to the state and the Indies Company. This proportion rose gradually to 14.2 percent in the contract price for the Henriet lease of 1756–62. The imposition of the 20 percent surtax in 1758 raised the monetary yield of the tobacco farm, to be sure, but by discouraging legitimate consumption and by encouraging fraud ended the period of the most prosperous natural growth of the monopoly. Tobacco's share of the total yield of the united farms shot up to 18.9 percent in the first year of the Prévost lease of 1762–63 but declined gradually thereafter to 15.2 percent in the David lease of 1774–80. One should not be confused by the higher per-

Table III

Tobacco Monopoly under the United Farms, 1730–91[55]

Lease Name	Years	—A— Un. Farms Total Rent Paid to State & Ind. Co.	—B— Tob. Farm Price Paid to Ind. Co.	—C— Tob. Farm Total Price Paid to State & Ind. Co.	—D— C as Percentage of A
		(in millions of livres tournois)			
Pierre Carlier (1730–32) Nicolas Desboves (1732–38)	1730–34 1734–38	87.5 88.0	7.5 8.0	7.5 8.0	8.6% 9.1
Jacques Forceville	1738–44	91.1	8.0	10–11	11–12.1
Thibault La Rue	1744–50	91.2 *w* 92.0 *p*	8.0 8.0	[c. 11] [c. 11]	12.1 12.0
Jean Girardin & Jean-Baptiste Bocquillon	1750–56	102.8	–	12.6	12.3
Pierre Henriet	1756–62	110.0	–	15.6[a]	14.2
Jean-Jacques Prévost	1762–68	115.4 *w* 121.4 *p*	– –	21.85 *w* 22.21 *p*	18.9 18.3
Julien Alaterre	1768–74	128.9	–	23.13	17.9
Laurent David	1774–80	157.8	–	24.08	15.2
Nicolas Salzard	1780–86	[122.0]*	–	26.0[b]	–
Jean-Baptiste Mager	1786– [92] 1788[e]	[144.0+]* [150.1]* 250.3†	– – –	27.0+ 30.5 30.5	– [20.3] 12.2

w = war.   *p* = peace.
* = noncomparable totals of reduced farms (minus *aides, domaines,* etc., but including Lorraine and *traites*).
† = artificial total (for comparison) of reduced united farms plus *aides, domaines,* etc., as had existed before 1780.
a = does not include product of 20% surtax of 1758.
b = does not include product of surtax of 1781.
e = contemporary estimate.

---

centages which could be shown for the 1780's. The united farms were then only a truncated fraction of their former self. If, for purposes of comparison, we add, as we do in the last line of the table, to the 150.1 million yield of the united farms in 1788 the yield of the *aides* (50.2 million) and *domaines* (50 million) which had been under the united farms before 1780, the share of tobacco in the reconstituted whole drops from 20.3 percent to 12.2 percent, indicating a continuation of the declining proportion manifest since 1762.

The United General Farms between their restoration in 1726 and the Revolution accounted for something under one-half of the total revenues of the French crown. As difficult as it is to ascertain the yields of the united farms and its components, it is even more difficult merely to estimate the total revenues of the French crown. Nevertheless, a rough attempt has been made in Table IV in order to show the relative importance of the tobacco revenue.

TABLE IV

Tobacco Revenue in the Total Revenues of the French Crown

Year	Total Revenues[56]	Tobacco Revenues	Percentage
	(in millions of livres tournois)		
1715	166	2.0	1.2%
1756	253	12.6	5.0%
1763	320	21.85	7.0%
1768–69	317	23.1	7.3%
1776	377	24.1	6.4%
1788–89	475 (est.)	30.5 (est.)	6.4%

Again we find something of a peak in the 1760's and a modest decline in relative importance thereafter.

Many readers will at this point wonder whether a revenue which at its peak only accounted for 7.3 percent of total state revenue was all that important. One might answer that few states in any period have treated lightly the source of seven or even five percent of their income—but that is to miss the point. The interrelationship of the tobacco revenues and the total revenues of the French crown lies not in the relative importance which someone today would ascribe to the former, but rather in the condition of the latter felt at the time: so precarious were the finances of the French crown all through the eighteenth century that a monopoly which produced seven or even five percent of those revenues ranked as an unassailable interest. The exigencies of French finance were such that a long succession of French statesmen, highly varied in talents, opinions and importance, all accepted as axiomatic the proposition that the tobacco monopoly must be run on principles that would maximize its yield—regardless of whether those principles were consistent with the colonial and highest state objectives of that same French monarchy.

Only if one can conceive of the unassailable importance of that five to seven percent of French crown revenues will one understand the tobacco purchasing policy pursued by successive tobacco monopolists between the restoration of peace in 1713 and the outbreak of the American Revolution in 1775.

CHAPTER 15

Purchasing Policy and Its Critics, 1721–75

The Purchasing Policy of the Monopoly, 1721–75

The great increases in the yield of the tobacco monopoly in the eighteenth century—fifteenfold between 1715 and 1788—could not, even in the least corrupt of regimes, have taken place without a most far-reaching increase in consumption. Unfortunately, we can only perceive the general contours of this increase, not its details. Few year-by-year or district-by-district accounts of sales of the monopoly have survived. One interesting report surviving does, however, give us the geographical breakdown of sales during the first three years of the Laurent David lease, 1774–77. Total sales at this time were about fourteen million pounds (including 500,000 lb. *tabac de cantine* for the troops), almost ten times the sales of a century before (1,471,114 lb. in 1676).[1]

The most interesting aspect of this account is what it shows of the geographic distribution of tobacco consumption. In Louis XIV's time, it will be remembered, tobacco consumption was heavily concentrated in maritime districts, particularly in Normandy and Brittany. Consumption then was radically lower in all inland districts, even those like the *généralités* of Paris and Lyons containing great urban populations.[2] By Louis XVI's time, tobacco-taking was noticeably more evenly diffused throughout the whole country, though significantly heavier in *généralités* with large urban populations than in those with primarily rural populations. This tends to confirm what the *chevalier* d'Eon, among others, wrote at the time about tobacco-taking being an urban habit that had not yet reached significant sections of the rural population.[3] Thus, a ranking of the farms' 40 *directions* by consumption per household in 1774–77 shows Paris in the lead, followed by areas either noticeably urban (Lyons) or urban-maritime (the *directions* of St. Malo, L'Orient, and Nantes in Brittany, Marseilles and Toulon in Provence, and Amiens and Rouen along the Channel). Eastern frontier districts highly exposed to smuggling by land (Lorraine, Langres in Champagne, Belley in Burgundy, and Valence in Dauphiné) were all in the bottom quarter of the list. There too we find the *directions* serving the more rural parts of Normandy (Caen, Alençon) and the very rural west between La Rochelle and Tours, both areas also exposed in part to maritime smuggling.

The new pattern was the result of marked differentials in the growth of consumption over the preceding century. While Paris and the country as a whole had increased estimated consumption per capita by about tenfold, the northern maritime districts (Brittany, Normandy, and Picardy), whose consumption had been precocious in 1676, had increased theirs by only two to fourfold. At the other extreme, in the *généralités* of Bordeaux, Montauban and Auch, where, because of planting, legitimate consumption had been almost nil in the seventeenth century, the increase in per capita legal consumption was over one hundred fold. Most inland districts, where tobacco taking penetrated later, had increases well above the national average. Although France as a whole, with a per capita consumption of about 0.65 lb. per annum in 1774–77, had still not caught up with England and Wales (between 1.0 and 1.5 lb.),[4] the difference in consumption patterns between France and northern Europe had considerably narrowed since the seventeenth century.

Our consumption data for the years 1774–77 are summarized in Table I. Since the *directions* of the farms for which we have sales data do not correspond to the royal *généralités* for which population estimates are available, we have used hearth or household counts instead.

To supply any volume of sales, the monopoly had to buy leaf weighing approximately 50 percent more, inasmuch as about one-third of the pur-

TABLE I
Tobacco Sales and Consumption in the Monopolized Provinces, 1774–77[5]

Direction	Hearths or Households	Sales p.a. lb.	Sales per Household lb.
Paris	289,731	1,751,568	6.05
St. Malo	133,441	771,863	5.78
L'Orient	112,981	635,744	5.63
Marseilles	88,867	387,934	4.37
Amiens	101,255	418,331	4.13
Lyons	149,990	559,221	3.73
Bayonne (excl. free port)	86,572	300,698	3.47
Rouen	191,988	618,378	3.22
Nantes	52,217	166,002	3.18
Toulon	49,529	148,853	3.01
Toulouse	167,420	501,821	3.00
Laval	103,600	309,540	2.99
Bordeaux	266,910	770,738	2.89
Chalon/s/Saône	60,730	170,159	2.80
Limoges	173,021	484,915	2.80
Le Mans	56,291	150,226	2.67
Auch	97,985	260,133	2.65
Metz	58,761	151,144	2.57
Dijon	58,170	149,571	2.57
Bourges	81,469	205,909	2.53

TABLE I (Continued)

Direction	Hearths or Households	Sales p.a. lb.	Sales per Household lb.
Soissons	81,355	194,449	2.39
Moulins	136,667	318,816	2.33
Orléans	138,081	317,912	2.30
Grenoble	74,459	166,966	2.24
Châlons/s/Marne	82,804	180,833	2.18
Charleville	33,939	74,131	2.18
Montpellier	148,304	321,086	2.17
St. Quentin	69,856	150,606	2.16
Villefranche-de-Rouergue	162,495	349,896	2.15
Angers	127,248	266,124	2.09
Lorraine	167,537	348,874	2.08
Tours	99,497	205,206	2.06
Caen	251,229	512,577	2.04
Poitiers	54,971	107,100	1.95
Valence	60,189	117,353	1.95
Belley	36,867	69,482	1.89
Langres	71,707	133,977	1.87
Alençon	97,616	175,657	1.80
Narbonne	35,600	63,796	1.79
La Rochelle	130,211	221,158	1.70
Total	4,441,906	13,208,747	2.97

	Estimated Population[6]	Sales p.a. lb.	Sales per Head lb.
Same Forty Directions	21,688,700	13,208,747	0.609

		Estimated Total Legal Consumption[7]	
Same Forty Directions		14,000,000	.645

chase weight of the leaf was lost in manufacture and transport through spoilage, dessication, and the cutting out of the midrib.[8] Thus, about 21 million lb. of leaf would have to be bought to obtain 14 million lb. of processed tobacco for sale (Table II). After the abolition of the domestic plantations in 1720, these millions of pounds had all to be imported; because the monopoly preferred not to buy the leaf grown in the exempted provinces (particularly Alsace and Flanders), and, with the crops in Louisiana remaining disappointingly small, these imports had to be purchased from foreigners. At a moderate peacetime price of 25 *l.t.* per quintal delivered, 21 million lb. would cost about 5.25 million *l.t.* (or £210,000 sterling). War and rising consumption could send the figure much higher.

TABLE II

Purchases and Sales by the Monopoly, 1730–86[9]

	Purchases (Leaf)	Sales (Manufactured)
Ca. 1730	8–9,000,000 lb. p.a.	6,000,000 lb. p.a.
Oct. 1762–Sept. 1768	–	12,565,502
Oct. 1768–Sept. 1774	–	13,223,290
Oct. 1774–1781 (?)	–	14,557,793
Oct. 1776–Sept. 1780	24,988,553	15,194,411
Oct. 1780–Dec. 1786	25,895,254	14,526,880
1788		15,224,464
1789		15,049,377

The reader will remember from colonial Chapters 12 and 13 that in all the discussions concerning Louisiana and the tobacco monopoly in the 1720's and 1730's—culminating in Silhouette's long memoir of 1739—Great Britain was always referred to as the country from which the French monopolists then obtained their tobacco. This antinational purchasing policy was of course based upon the availability in Great Britain of large quantities of inexpensive Chesapeake tobacco in qualities suitable for France. Price was the most immediately relevant factor. With the return of peace in 1713, the relative price attractiveness of Chesapeake tobacco gradually returned, helped by deflationary conditions prevailing after 1720 and by Walpole's concession of full drawback of import duties in 1723.[10] One British memoir writer of the early 1730's boasted that the resulting "low price of Tobacco in all the Countries of Europe prevented the French (our great rivals in the Plantation Trade) from going forward with their Plantations of Tobacco in their new Settlem.ts up the Mississippi &c."[11]

With the passage of years, quality, price, and convenience joined to make the French monopoly almost totally dependent upon British supplies. In his calculations for the lease of 1774, Lavoisier estimated that the company would need about twenty million pounds of leaf a year, of which about nineteen (95 percent) would come from Britain and about one million pounds (5 percent) from Amersfort in the United Provinces.[12] On the eve of the dissolution of the monopoly, a farmer-general (probably Lavoisier again) prepared a memoir (May 1790) estimating the needs of the monopoly by then at 24 million lb. annually of which perhaps 10 percent would be bought from Holland, the rest from North America.[13] Thus, from its restoration in 1721 until its abolition in 1791, dependence upon Chesapeake supplies was to be one of the most striking features of the French tobacco monopoly.

For the earlier decades, the age of Fleury, we do not have any systematic data on French tobacco imports, but we have accounts of British exports. Those specifying shipments to France, reproduced in the Appendix and summarized in Table III, are for England only, but there is reason to believe that until about 1740, French tobacco purchases in Scotland were relatively minor. The table has been constructed to show how the upward tendency of French purchases from Britain persisted through all the major changes in the status of the monopoly, including Law's company in 1719, the return to the Indies Company in 1723, the transfer to the united farms in 1730, and the renewal of their lease in 1737.

TABLE III
English Tobacco Exports to France and Flanders (in Pounds), 1711–43
Annual Average by Periods[14]

	Flanders	France	Flanders and France
1711–18	986,176	2,328,846	3,315,022
1719–20	671,263	6,150,442	6,822,065
1721–23	1,865,526	2,984,002	4,849,528
1724–29	725,547	6,057,334	6,782,881
1730–36	1,783,761	8,897,423	10,681,184
1737–43	4,426,443	11,606,914	16,033,357

One of the great problems presented by these figures is the inexplicable fluctuations in the English exports to Flanders. This English customs designation included both the French free port of Dunkirk and the ports of Austrian maritime Flanders, particularly Ostend. Before 1744, however, literary evidence suggests that in practice tobacco sent to "Flanders" went primarily to Dunkirk. We shall discuss the affairs of this port in Chapter 18.[15] Suffice it to remark here that tobacco sent from England to Dunkirk, a great tobacco manufacturing center, might be consumed in that port or in the eastern provinces of France outside the monopoly (Flanders, Artois, Hainault, Cambrésis); it might also be shipped legally into the Austrian Netherlands, Liège, or the Rhineland, or sold for shipboard use to the many craft visiting the port. Less legitimately, it might be smuggled by sea into Britain or France or even Spain, or by land into France, the Austrian territories, or Lorraine. Then too the tobacco farm itself maintained a manufactory first at Charleville, later at Valenciennes,[16] to supply separate farms in the frontier districts and *tabac de cantine* for the troops.[17] Charleville alone took 545 hogsheads of English tobacco annually in 1728–30.[18] It would be hard to say in what proportions increased fraud or increased *tabac de cantine* for the troops caused the steady increases of English tobacco shipments to Flanders in the 1730's and 1740's. (We can only speculate idly about what acts or omissions of the short-lived du Verdier company may have caused the freakish jump in shipments there in 1722–23.)

Corroboration of a sort for these English export figures comes from certain French data which passed into the hands of Sir Robert Walpole, the British prime minister. Walpole received from an unknown source detailed accounts of French tobacco imports from England during the last two years that the tobacco farm was in the hands of the Indies Company[19] and the first two years that it was managed by the united farms.[20] Combining these two reports, we obtain the following picture of French tobacco imports from England.

			French Pounds Weight	English Pounds Weight (approx.)
1 Oct. 1728–30 Sept. 1729	7,841	hhd.	4,904,650	5,370,592
1 Oct. 1729–30 Sept. 1730	11,010	hhd.	7,857,570	8,604,039
1 Oct. 1730–30 Sept. 1731	14,000	hhd.	[9,478,000]	[10,378,410]
1 Oct. 1731–30 Sept. 1732	15,000+	hhd.	[10,155,000]	[11,119,725]
Total			32,395,220	35,472,766

If we add up the English figures shown in the Appendix for exports to France in 1729, 1730, 1731, and 1732 (not quite the same period), we obtain for the latter four years the total of 33,182,440 English pounds. That this is less than the French estimates of imports from England can be explained if the 350,000 French lb. (or 383,250 English lb.) sent annually to Charleville were in fact imported, as is likely, via Dunkirk or from Holland and not through France proper.[21] Correcting for Charleville, the French and English data are remarkably close—perhaps meaninglessly close considering that the periods are not identical and the French figures for the last two years are only estimates. But the French accounts seem to suggest that whatever inaccuracies may lie in the English data, the margin of error is unlikely to be statistically significant.

During the generation between the fall of Law and the start of the British-French war (1720–44), the only country, other than Great Britain, from which the French monopoly bought tobacco was the United Provinces. There was a long established tobacco cultivation in the provinces of Utrecht, Gelderland, and Overyssel. This cultivation had expanded in the 1690's and had been particularly extensive and prosperous in the generation 1700–1720 when the war and other factors made British Chesapeake tobacco particularly expensive on the continent. After 1723, when Walpole removed the last retained duty on Chesapeake tobacco passing through the British entrepôt, the Dutch cultivation languished under lower prices until the time of the American Revolution. The most famous Dutch tobacco was that grown about Amersfort in the bishopric of Utrecht.[22] Although the early French tobacco monopolies had bought Dutch manufactured tobacco in the seventeenth century and in wartime, it was not the policy of the restored monopoly to do so after 1721 for the same reason the monopoly refrained from buying Rhenish or Flemish tobaccos—it did not want the French consumer to acquire a taste for tobaccos which could be easily procured by overland smuggling.

To this ban on the importation of continental tobaccos, exception was made solely for the output of the Amsterdam manufacturing firm of Scholt (or Scolthen). The elder Scholt, who had started out as a messenger boy in a wholesale warehouse, developed a secret sauce applied to spun Amersfort tobacco after the spinning. With substantial purchases by the monopoly as early as 1691, a taste for this particular tobacco was speedily developed in France. By the 1720's, his son was master of a great manufacturing house in Amsterdam turning out annually hundreds of thousands of pounds weight of a unique spun tobacco. Most of his output went to the Indies Company of France for 11 Dutch *sols* per lb. When the united farms took over the monopoly in 1730, the farmer-general Lallemant de Betz forced down the price to nine Dutch *sols* per lb. and obliged the younger Scholt to agree to sell the entire output of his house to the French farm. This was done deliberately to prevent any of the output falling into the hands of smugglers. Other Dutch manufacturers had attempted to imitate Scholt's sauce but the French consumer could tell the difference. In France, in making pressed *carottes,* strands of Scholt's *tabac de Hollande* were mixed with Chesapeake tobacco spun in France in the ratio of one part in three or four.[23]

One account estimates French imports from Holland during 1728–30 at 1,000 "chests" of about 400 lb. each or 400,000 lb. annually.[24] Another account of 1733 places the output of Scholt's manufacture, all of which went to France, at 1,000 rolls packed in chests *(caisses)* containing about 380 lb. each —or 380,000 lb. annually.[25] The two accounts are comfortingly consistent. They also indicate, though, that French imports of this specialized product from Holland were only about 6 percent of imports from Britain in 1728–30 and 4½ percent in 1732–33.

In the 1730's, the farmers-general also imported significant quantities of Amersfort leaf from the United Provinces. They used this to make a superior roll tobacco which eventually permitted them to dispense with Scholt's product. Instead of mixing pieces *(bouts)* of spun Holland and spun Virginia in their *carottes,* the Amersfort and Chesapeake leaf were mixed in the spinning stage, with the large Amersfort being used for the wrapper and Virginia for the filler. Some Lille tobacco was also used for wrappers, though it was less suitable. In the 1740's, for reasons unknown, the farmers-general decided to eliminate the use of Amersfort and to make *supérieure* entirely from Virginia leaf.[26]

With the advent of the British-French war in 1744, the monopoly's established practice of supplying most of its needs in Britain approached its greatest crisis until the American Revolution. So important, however, was this revenue to the French state, so specifically had French consumer taste been molded and so settled had the monopoly's buying practices become that the united farms could conceive of no alternative to continued purchases from Britain. They apparently had very little difficulty obtaining permission and licenses from the French government, but had, as we shall see in another chapter, greater but not insuperable difficulty in getting passes from the British government.[27] The alternation of war and peace is reflected in the records of English exports (Table IV).

TABLE IV
Selected English Tobacco Exports (in Pounds), 1743-48[28]

Year Ending Christmas	Flanders	France	Flanders & France	Holland
1737-43 (av.)	4,426,443	11,606,914	16,033,357	11,409,280
1743	6,622,949	9,334,461	15,957,410	13,611,531
1744	3,649,146	6,812,779	10,461,925	16,105,474
1745	2,027,100	2,732,123	4,759,223	13,021,148
1746	304,371	7,248,909	7,553,280	12,727,459
1747	–	8,334,781	8,334,781	16,151,067
1748	3,203,826	13,822,211	17,026,037	13,383,355

This table, if read carefully, reflects rather sensitively the changing political-military situation in northwest Europe. War was declared between Britain and France in March 1744; though some special passes were soon procured, it was not until September of 1745 that regular arrangements were completed for the general resumption of the British-French tobacco trade under routine licenses. This policy hesitation is reflected in declining English tobacco exports to France in 1744 and 1745 and the marked recovery of 1746. The almost fourteen million pounds shipped in 1748 more than announces the return of peace. Similarly, the independent tobacco dealers and manufacturers of the free port of Dunkirk seem to have foreseen the coming of the war by abnormally high importations (to "Flanders" in the table above) in 1743. The advent of war is marked by much lower exports to Flanders in 1744 and 1745, nearly all of which after March 1744 must have gone to Austrian Flanders, particularly Ostend. After the capture of Ostend by the French in the summer of 1745, exports to Flanders virtually disappear in 1746 and 1747. Exports to Holland also seem to reflect happenings elsewhere. In 1744, when the normal Anglo-French tobacco trade was temporarily interrupted, English exports to Holland jump. Some of these we know were transshipped to France in neutral or licensed Dutch vessels as in previous wars.[29] Similarly, when all English exports to Flanders, French and Austrian, ceased in 1747, exports to Holland once again surged. It is highly likely that some of these were carried from Holland into the French occupied territories under some kind of license.[30] Conversely, when the return of peace saw leaps in exports to Flanders and France, those to Holland slumped in what was otherwise an exceptionally active year.

The great limitation to these figures taken from the English inspector-general's accounts is that they do not include Scotland—and by the 1740's France was importing a significant proportion of her British tobacco from Scotland. A clearer picture of the whole can be obtained by adding up the licenses granted by the British government for the export of tobacco to France during the last three years of the war.

TABLE V
British Licenses under the Great Seal for Tobacco Exports to France during the War of the Austrian Succession [31]

Year	From England	From Scotland
1745 (from 18 Sept.)	4,685 hogsheads	400 hogsheads
1746	8,269 hogsheads	9,433 hogsheads
1747	9,990 hogsheads	9,920 hogsheads
1748 (to 17 May)	8,344 hogsheads	4,760 hogsheads
Total	31,288 hogsheads	24,513 hogsheads

The above table indicates clearly how important Scotland had become as a source of French tobacco by 1746 and how fatal it would be at this stage to use only English data. The total figure for hogsheads licensed from England and Scotland during 1745–48 are in the ratio of 100 to 78.35. If actual exports from England and Scotland were in the same proportion, one could calculate that to the 32,138,024 lb. of tobacco exported from England to France during 1745–48 shown in Table IV, there should be added something like 25,180,142 lb. for Scotland—making a total for British shipments to France during these years of 57,318,166 lb. or 14,329,541 lb. annually. There does not seem in this light to have been any decline in French tobacco imports from Britain caused by the war.

As a check upon the figures shown by the licenses, I have searched the port books for Port Glasgow[32] and Greenock[33] for the four quarters ending Christmas 1747. (These two ports accounted for 79 percent of Scottish tobacco imports during 1737–47.) *All* the ships licensed for France from these two ports can be found actually sailing—although the aggregate number of hogsheads shipped was something less than the total shown on the licenses. While 7,600 hogsheads were licensed for those two ports in 1747, we find only 6,889 shipped totalling 6,659,810 lb. Adding to this Clyde figure, the data for the lesser Scottish ports which also exported to France then (Ayr, Kirkcudbright, and Dumfries), we can reconstruct total shipments in 1747 to France (minus Dunkirk) from Scotland and Britain:

	Hogsheads Licensed	Pounds Shipped
England	9,990	8,334,781
Scotland	9,920	8,318,616
Britain	19,910	16,653,397

This compares with 14,948,528 lb. for 1743 (similarly calculated).[34] Thus, once the difficulties of obtaining passes had been settled, British tobacco exports to France in wartime resumed at levels fully comparable with peacetime.

In addition to the tobacco purchased by the French in the normal way during the war of 1744–48, the monopoly had available tobacco captured by French privateers from British vessels returning from the Chesapeake. During the war of the 1690's, when French consumption was only a small fraction of what it had become by the 1740's, such captures were enough to supply the monopoly's customers in northern France.[35] French privateers were quite successful against British vessels in the Chesapeake trade during 1744–48, much more so than they had been in the latter years of the Spanish Succession or were to be in the Seven Years' War.[36] However, even if they had been generally as successful as they had been during the war of the 1690's —they were not—they could not have hoped to supply the same proportion of French demand, for consumption had multiplied many times since the 1690's. A contemporary list of 769 British vessels known to have been captured by the enemy, French or Spanish, during the first two years of the French war (1744–46) gives the names of 63 vessels taken when bound from Virginia or Maryland to Britain. Of these, however, only 39 are shown as definitely having been condemned in a French port: 28 in ports of the monopoly, 11 in Bayonne or St. Jean de Luz, where normally the farm did not buy; the rest were carried to Spanish or unknown ports, lost at sea, or recaptured by the British.[37] Assuming these 28 vessels brought into the controlled ports had carried an average of 250,000 lb. of tobacco each, their capture brought the monopoly 7,000,000 lb. or 3,500,000 lb. each year.

From the point where the preceding account breaks off—11 March 1745/6—to the end of the war in 1748, rough data on British vessels lost to the French can be patched together from the periodical press.[38] From such sources it would appear that the British-Chesapeake trade lost in these months:

	Vessels
Taken eastbound by the French or into French ports	49
Taken eastbound by the Spanish or into Spanish ports	16
Taken, but retaken or ransomed	20
Taken outward bound to the Chesapeake	17
Taken by the French and lost or burned	4
Total mercantile loss	106

Of the 49 vessels taken by the French homeward bound from the Chesapeake with tobacco, only 11 are known to have been taken into ports within the monopoly; the remainder went to Bayonne and St. Jean de Luz (18), Bergen in Norway (3) or unknown ports (17). If those taken into unknown ports were redistributed proportionately among the known ports, then instead of 11 we should have 17 tobacco vessels brought into French ports by privateers during the last two and one-quarter years of the war or roughly eight p.a.: at 250,000 lb. of leaf each, these eight would have provided a supply of two million pounds annually, considerably less than the 3.5 million lb. p.a. produced by captures in the first two years of the war. Combining both periods, we get for the whole war (1744–48) tobacco supplies from such privateering averaging 2.7 million lb. p.a., or 18 percent of prewar imports from Britain of about 15 million lb. in 1743. If a significant proportion of the tobacco were of grades (e.g., superior York River sweet-scented) or varieties (Maryland bright leaf) not normally bought for France, it would be unlikely that Chesapeake prizes in the war of 1744–48 could have supplied more than 10 or 15 percent of French needs.

During the peace interlude of 1748–56, French tobacco imports from England resumed at a high but erratic level, as is shown in Table VI.

TABLE VI
English Tobacco Exports (in Pounds) to France and Flanders, 1748–56[39]

Year Ending Christmas	Flanders	France	Flanders & France
1737–43 (av.)	4,426,443	11,606,914	16,033,357
1744–47 (av.)	1,495,154	6,282,148	7,777,302
1748	3,203,826	13,822,211	17,026,037
1749	6,811,983	7,377,211	14,189,194
1750	5,093,646	5,118,588	10,212,234
1751	6,252,339	6,759,985	13,012,324
1752	10,005,363	11,040,859	21,046,222
1753	7,448,201	14,692,254	22,140,455
1754	8,116,325	13,888,647	22,004,972
1755	7,764,004	1,335,707	9,099,711
1756	5,603,551	390,362	5,993,913

In this table, something of a pattern is discernible. The lease of the united farms was renewed in 1750 and 1756. In both cases, there seems to have been a slowing down in purchases toward the end of the lease, perhaps to reduce the stocks that would need to be carried over from one lease to another. However, the second drop in shipments from England in 1755–56 must also be associated with the deterioration of relations between Britain and France at that time, culminating in the declaration of war by Britain on France in May 1756, and a not unrelated rise in prices.

English tobacco exports to Flanders became a major problem for the united farms in the 1740's. The company, as we shall see in Chapter 18, had become seriously alarmed by the sudden spurt in these shipments during 1737–43. (Cf. Table III.) After the wartime check, shipments resumed at an even higher level with the restoration of peace in 1748. These danger signals coinciding with the negotiations for the renewal of the lease of the united farms in 1749, the company—as partial compensation for the much higher price exacted from them then—induced the government to adopt a very high duty (30 *sols* per lb.) on all foreign tobacco entering the eastern provinces outside the monopoly. Even though Dunkirk was exempt as a free port, the new toll cut off the manufacturers in that port from their legitimate marketing area in French Flanders, Hainault, and Artois. The duty also sent part of Dunkirk's normal business to Ostend.[40] Thus the very high figures for English exports to Flanders in the 1750's represent for the first time substantial shipments to Austrian Ostend rather than to French Dunkirk.

Such data on purely English shipments are by this time particularly unsatisfactory, inasmuch as Scotland continued in the peace, as in the war just ended, to account for a major proportion of British exports to France. As a corrective, we have extracted data from the Scottish port books for 1751 to reconstruct the totals exported that year to France from that part of Britain and from the whole kingdom.[41]

	lb.
Scottish exports to Dunkirk	417,775
Scottish exports to France (minus Dunkirk)	10,084,220
English exports to France (minus Dunkirk)	6,759,985
British exports to France (minus Dunkirk)	16,844,205

From 1755 onward, Scottish export data similar to the English data used above become available. We can therefore state with some precision the volume of British exports to France between that year and the American Revolution. We must, however, correct for Dunkirk, for that port was considered part of France in Scottish calculations and part of Flanders in English.

British shipments to France, Table VII indicates, were acutely depressed during the coming of the war in 1755 and 1756. Late in 1756, however, passes were again made available for a tobacco trade between the belligerents[42] and the trade slowly returned to "normal" by 1759. Available evidence does not explain very much of the year-by-year fluctuations in purchases. Prices, in particular, which will be discussed in Chapter 25, leave much unexplained. (The reduction of purchases in 1761 was a conscious effort to reduce prices after the heavy buying of the previous year: it also characteristically came towards the end of the Henriet lease. On the other hand, shipments were again reduced in 1765 although prices were abnormally low that year.) We also have little information about the supplementary supplies which the French might have got from prizes during the Seven Years' War. Some evidence suggests that in the earlier years of the war, tobacco prizes brought into French ports may have been about the level

TABLE VII

British Tobacco Exports (in Pounds) to France, minus Dunkirk, 1755-75[43]

	FROM SCOTLAND			ENGLAND	BRITAIN
	Official Total	− Dunkirk	= France Proper		
1755	1,034,875	?		1,335,707	
1756	1,879,407	?		390,362	
1757	5,365,165	0	5,365,165	4,288,578	9,653,743
1758	5,486,917	0	5,486,917	4,964,319	10,451,236
1759	6,970,744	0	6,970,744	9,254,448	16,225,192
1760	16,409,840	0	16,409,840	11,186,479	27,596,319
1761	4,941,682	0	4,941,682	3,905,855	8,847,537
1762	7,716,212	o?	7,716,212	8,851,081	16,567,293
1763	8,806,011	?		6,882,723	
1764	14,658,701	?		6,487,779	
1765	6,197,608	3,420,520	2,777,088	3,207,933	5,985,021
1766	10,985,746	1,193,589	9,792,157	5,878,654	15,670,811
1767	9,268,919	1,012,457	8,256,462	5,871,604	14,128,066
1768	16,121,886	2,096,047	14,025,839	8,170,291	22,196,130
1769	14,335,064	2,197,477	12,137,587	223,383	12,360,970
1770	16,501,175	3,099,301	13,401,874	2,192,045	15,593,919
1771	16,955,232	4,891,752	12,063,480	1,865,796	13,929,276
1772	22,514,188	2,148,969	20,365,219	9,899,955	30,265,174
1773	24,406,240	2,539,794	21,866,446	7,343,883	29,210,329
1774	10,721,409	5,158,973	5,562,436	3,850,519	9,412,955
1775	11,218,515	2,357,888	8,860,627	4,136,131	12,996,758

of the last years of the previous war (i.e., about eight ships a year).[44] On the other hand, the *Annual Register* printed some detailed accounts indicating that about 55 vessels homeward bound from the Chesapeake were captured by the French in 1761. Assuming that twelve of these were ransomed (the general proportion indicated) and that only four-elevenths of the remaining 43 were carried to ports of the monopoly (as in 1756–58), we find the farm left with at most 16 tobacco vessels carrying approximately four million pounds, a not insignificant supply. (For this date, we know definitely that the monopoly got none of Bayonne's large take.)[45]

Taken together, British figures suggest something approaching an eightfold growth in tobacco shipments to France between 1711–18 and 1766–75. Are there no French data by which such figures could be checked? The French government had in 1713–16 established a *bureau de la balance du commerce* to collect accounts of French imports and exports and to calculate France's commodity balance of trade. The agency was established in imitation of the office of the English Inspector-General of Imports and Exports, though its reports were neither as full nor as esteemed as those of its English prototype.[46] The question of reliability is of particular relevance to tobacco data. In Britain, tobacco paid a heavy duty at importation and (after

1723) drew back the full duty at exportation. British customs therefore kept the most detailed records of tobacco transactions, specific to the last pound. In France, however, tobacco was imported on the account of the farmers-general themselves and thus paid nothing in customs (*traites*). The farmers-general themselves had to supply such data as the clerks of the *bureau de la balance* received on the monopoly's tobacco imports. It is not impossible that the farmers-general misrepresented the extent of their own importations.

Most of the annual reports of the *bureau de la balance du commerce* have disappeared. The earliest located is for 1752. Though it gives only values, it indicates clearly the preponderance of Britain as a source for French tobacco imports. Out of 3,630,208 *l.t.* worth of tobacco imported, 3,582,458 *l.t.* 15 *s.* worth (over 98 percent) came from Britain. From Holland came 140,091 *l.t.* worth of leaf tobacco, 1,001 *l.t.* worth of snuff and 873 *l.t.* worth of manufactured tobacco. (Scholt's production seems to have disappeared.) From Spain came 5,390 *l.t.* worth of snuff. From no other country did there come as much as 1,000 *l.t.* worth.[47]

From other sources, M. Morineau reports similar value data for French tobacco imports from the United Provinces and Britain only for the three preceding years, 1749–51. These are quite consistent with our 1752 figures, showing about 94 percent of the combined total coming from "Angleterre," the remaining 6 percent from "Hollande."[48] Such values can be converted into physical quantities without too much difficulty, assuming that the British tobacco was valued at 25 *l.t.* per quintal or five *sols* per lb. (the value commonly used by the *bureau*, ca. 1749–75). However, when we attempt to compare the physical quantities thus obtained with British data on exports to France, difficulties appear.

TABLE VIII
British Tobacco Shipments to France (excluding Dunkirk), 1749–52
French and British Data Compared[49]

Year	Reported French Leaf Tob. Imports from Britain (values) l.t.	Equivalent Quantities at 25 l.t. per Quintal French lb. (millions)	English lb. (millions)	British Reported Tob. Exports to France English lb. (millions)
1749	2,745,000	10.98	12.08	[18.45]
1750	2,056,000	8.22	9.05	[12.8]
1751	2,209,000	8.84	9.72	16.84
1752	3,582,459	14.33	15.76	[27.6]
Total	10,592,459	42.37	46.61	[75.74]
p.a.	2,648,115	10.59	11.65	[18.94]

The French and British statistical services used different fiscal years, that for France ending on 30 September, that for Britain ending at Christmas. Most of this discrepancy can be eliminated, however, by considering only the average of the four years in the last line. When we compare our computed data on British exports to France (18.94 in last column) with our French data on imports from Britain converted into English pounds weight (11.65 in third column), we find that it would appear that the farmers-general were under-reporting their tobacco imports from Britain by almost 40 percent.

In subsequent years, our better Scottish data make it possible to substitute reported for computed figures on British exports, but the gaps do not disappear. Some surviving French accounts for these years give only the total value of tobacco imported from all sources. This is usually the same as imports from Britain, for 95–99 percent of French imports are known to have come from there. We can convert these values into quantities at the same price of 25 *l.t.* per quintal. When we do, however, we obtain quantities after 1763 that again bear little resemblance to British data on exports to France. (The reverse discrepancy of 1758 may be explained by prizes and temporarily large imports from Holland and Russia in wartime. Neither were continued with the peace.)

TABLE IX
British Tobacco Shipments to France (excluding Dunkirk), 1758–74
French and British Data Compared

Year	Reported Total French Leaf Tob. Imports (values) [50] l.t.	Equivalent Quantities at 25 l.t. per Quintal French lb. (millions)	English lb. (millions)	British Reported Tob. Exports to France[51] English lb. (millions)
1758	3,016,193	12.1	13.3	10.5
1766	2,143,196	8.6	9.4	16.9
1770	2,439,895	9.8	10.7	18.7
1771	5,074,718	20.3	22.3	18.8
1773	2,406,004	9.6	10.6	31.8
1774	1,080,975	4.3	4.8	14.6

For 1772 and 1775, we have other more detailed accounts from the *bureau de la balance du commerce*. Out of total French tobacco imports in 1772 worth 3,298,736 *l.t.*, no less than 3,145,983 *l.t.* worth or 95 percent still came in leaf from Britain: 12,451,212 lb. out of 13,017,178 lb. total imported. The British preponderance is still clear. (From Holland, the next most important supplier there came only 493,184 lb. of leaf, worth 129,091 *l.t.*) [52] The only difficulty again is that British data for the same year (Table VII) show exports to France (minus Dunkirk) of 30,265,174 lb.! Similarly in 1775, while more than 90 percent of imports are shown coming from Britain, the quantities and values are suspiciously small:[53]

Leaf from Britain	4,449,542 lb. worth	1,148,365 *l.t.*
Leaf from Holland	466,687 lb. worth	116,671 *l.t.*
Manufactured from W.I.	500 lb. worth	1,500 *l.t.*
Total	4,916,629 lb. worth	1,266,536 *l.t.*

During this same year—1775—British accounts (Table VII) show exports to France (minus Dunkirk) of 12,996,758 English lb., just under twelve million French pounds. A later French account, drawn from the records of the farmers-general themselves, shows foreign tobacco purchases in 1775 worth four to five million *l.t.* or three to four times the value shown by the *bureau de la balance*.[54]

The only conclusion that can be drawn is that in the years between the War of the Austrian Succession and the American Revolution, the farmers-general were sufficiently alarmed at hostile criticisms to falsify the tobacco data they supplied to the *bureau de la balance*. (This could have been done easily by giving the correct number of hogsheads imported—easily checked—but suggesting an artificially low average weight per hogshead.) The farmers were, of course, particularly subject to criticism on two grounds: (1) they bought so much tobacco from Britain, a country with which France had a chronically adverse balance of trade;[55] and (2) taken as a whole, so much more was spent on imports of raw tobacco than was received from exports of the manufactured product. The grounds for criticism on both these points could be reduced if accounts were "doctored" to minimize the value of tobacco imported from Britain and to exaggerate the value of manufactured tobacco exported to Italy, Switzerland, and other countries.

This suggestion of "doctoring" is not pure speculation. There is much persuasive evidence that the accounts of the *bureau de la balance* give less than an accurate or even fair picture of France's tobacco trade. Even a cursory glance at some of its national summaries will show that, while tobacco imported was commonly valued at about five *sols* per lb., manufactured exports carried the unrealistically high full French monopoly retail price of 60–80 *sols* per lb.[56] A much closer view of the practices of the *bureau* can be obtained from their accounts for the Breton ports available from 1749.[57] Imports and exports are always given in physical quantities—either pounds or hogsheads—and then valued. In 1749, 1757–60, 1763–69, and 1775, British leaf tobacco imports were given by the pound and valued at five *sols* per lb., while in 1761–62 and 1770–74, they were similarly entered but valued at six *sols* per lb. However, in 1753–56, tobacco imports from Britain were given in hogheads only and valued at 120 *l.t.* per hogshead. (In 1759, such imports were given partly in pounds at five *sols* and partly in hogsheads at 180 *l.t.*) The choice between the conventional five or six *sols* per lb. for valuing imports seems arbitrary and bears no relationship to the fluctuations of world prices.[58] Five *sols* per lb. since 1726 had been the equivalent of 2d.½ sterling. Since the French pound was almost 10 percent heavier than the English, it really corresponded to an English price of 2d.¼, or roughly twopence per pound for the tobacco bought in Britain and farthing per pound for commission and transportation to France. Now, there were times in every decade between 1725 and 1775 when the French did buy tobacco in Britain for twopence per lb. or less. More often than not, however, they went over twopence and during the Seven Years' War even bought in London at over fourpence per pound.[59] This means that the bureau's practice of valuing tobacco imports from Britain at five or even six *sols* per lb., seriously underestimated the cost of that tobacco to France.

Much more serious were the discrepancies in the years when the tobacco was recorded in hogsheads only. As noted above, these hogsheads were usually valued at 120 *l.t.* At the low price of five *sols* per lb., this conversion implied that the average hogshead weighed only 480 lb. (Any higher price per pound would have implied an even lighter hogshead.) This was a good weight for a hogshead when the *bureau de la balance* was established in 1716. However, by the late 1740's and early 1750's, the average Chesapeake hogshead had come to weigh about 900 French pounds or 985 English pounds.[60] The error on the hogsheads' weight compounded the error on the price, in extreme cases reducing the amounts actually spent in Britain by almost three-fourths. For these reasons, we shall make only very limited use of the data in the accounts of the *bureau de la balance du commerce,* preferring to use—for all their gaps and problems—the relatively less challengeable ledgers of the English Inspector-General of Imports and Exports and his Scottish deputy.

We do not know whether the errors in the tobacco data of the *bureau de la balance* were due more to its own spirit of routine or rather more to the misrepresentations of the united farms. The mood of defensiveness in the united farms which might have led to such misrepresentation will be more understandable after we look at some of the pressures the company was subject to during and after the Seven Years' War.

Russia, the Seven Years' War, and Purchasing Policy[61]

For the tobacco monopoly, the Seven Years' War was an unprecedented crisis. The annual rent of the tobacco farm had by 1756 grown to ten times its price during the War of the Spanish Succession. This meant, roughly speaking, that in this war ten times more tobacco had to be purchased than in the war of a half century before—and without help from domestic supplies. This war, unlike its predecessors, was much more clearly a war against Britain; court and "public" opinion were therefore less likely to accept with good grace the monopoly's allegedly unchallengeable need to continue importing leaf tobacco from Britain in wartime.

The Seven Years' War was also different in that Russia, long hostile to or suspicious of France, was now by the accidents of history an ally of France. Between 1748 and 1755 there had been no French diplomatic representation of any sort at St. Petersburg. Political reconciliation led to the despatch there in 1757 of an ambassador, the marquis of L'Hôpital, and a consul-general, Jean Baptiste de Cury de Saint Sauveur, who had previously served in the same capacity at St. Petersburg in the 1740's. Both were experienced public servants, anxious to do all in their power to promote better relations between Russia and France, political and commercial.[62]

Russia by this time had a considerable tobacco cultivation, particularly in the Ukraine (the districts of "Godinski" and "Rominski")[63] and along the lower Don near the Sea of Azov. The seed used was indifferent and the preparation of the tobacco left much to be desired. Yet it sufficed for the bulk of the rather limited Russian consumption. The use of tobacco was far from universal among the mass of the population while fashionable circles preferred imported foreign tobaccos no matter how expensive. Little or none of the Russian tobacco had up to then ever been exported commercially but the idea had interesting possibilities. Although there was a considerable demand in Russia for French wines, brandies and articles of luxury, Russian-French trade since Colbert's time had been impeded by a relative lack of good return cargoes. If France could transfer its extensive tobacco purchases from Britain to Russia, the millions of *livres* so spent would go far towards the creation of a major Franco-Russian commerce. This was a matter meriting the most careful attention from a consul-general, an ambassador and the highest officers of state.[64]

The tobacco supply problem of the French monopoly was particularly difficult during the opening months of the Seven Years' War. After very heavy imports from Great Britain during 1752–54, the company had virtually ceased purchases there during 1755 and 1756.[65] The reasons for this stoppage are unknown, though it may have been associated with both the diplomatic situation and the sexennial renewal of the lease of the united farms in 1756. This was the moment when the controller-general Moreau de Séchelles raised the number of farmers-general from forty to sixty. The transition from the old lease to the new was therefore likely to have been particularly complex in 1756. Although licenses to export tobacco from Britain to France were authorized almost immediately after the declarations of war in May 1756, it was well into 1757 before any substantial quantities of tobacco arrived in France from Britain.[66] Even at that, the shipments of 1757 and 1758 at about 9–10 million lb. annually were well below "normal" shipments of about 15 million lb. Not until 1759 and 1760 was the last figure reached.[67] Thus, the evidence would seem to suggest that, despite prizes, the monopoly probably had a serious supply problem during 1756–58 and a particularly acute one during the last months of 1756 and early 1757.

Among the senior farmers-general in 1756 was the Paris merchant-financier, Jean-François de la Borde, originally from Bayonne, since 1725 a deputy in the Council, now "Bureau," of Commerce (first representing Bayonne, then the farmers-general). Through his wife, he was connected to Mme de Pompadour and had risen through that influence.[68] Allied commercially to La Borde was the Paris mercantile house of Beaujon & Goossens, specializing in the northern trade and supplying the French navy. Nicolas Beaujon, formerly a merchant of Bordeaux, now a Paris financier and receiver-general of La Rochelle, was later famous as the banker of Madame du Barry; Pierre-François Goossens was an important merchant and banker of Dutch origin, resident in Paris. In 1759, when the royal treasury was in desperate straits, Beaujon and Goossens were part of a syndicate of five which undertook to raise 44 millions for the treasury, engineers, and navy. They were also closely tied to the great Amsterdam financial and mercantile house, Hope & Co., also important suppliers to the French navy.[69] Both La Borde and Beaujon & Goossens were thus houses of considerable political as well as financial-commercial importance.

In Russia, by contrast, there were few French mercantile houses and these were of little financial importance. So weak in fact was the credit of the few French houses in St. Petersburg that the French court banker after 1759 (Jean-Joseph de la Borde) chose to make remittances to the French diplomats in St. Petersburg through a British house there, even when France and Britain were at war.[70] The most important French houses in St. Petersburg, about 1756, were those of Michel, Raimbert, Godin, and Baudouin. Nicolas Baudouin, of Rouen, was apparently the least important, being primarily a factor or commission agent for Beaujon & Goossens of Paris. Godins of St. Petersburg were affiliated with Godin & Co. of Rouen and Vidal & Co. of Montpellier. Joseph Raimbert, who had come to St. Petersburg in 1749, was associated with Lousmeau du Pont of Lyons (silks being one of the French products sought by the Russians). He (or a younger brother whom he brought out to Russia) was vice-consul at St. Petersburg from 1764 to 1794.[71] Jean Michel, also of a Rouen family, was the son of a Frenchman who accompanied Peter the Great back to Russia after the czar's visit to France in 1717. Brought up in Russia, the young Michel became from the early 1740's an importer of French fashions, much favored by the ladies of the court. He also became a protégé of the vice-chancellor Vorontsov, leader of the pro-French element in the Russian court. Michel's business required him to make an annual trip to France, during which he frequently carried messages and performed errands valued by the French and Russian courts.[72]

Various schemes were brought forward in 1756–57 to establish one or more great French houses in St. Petersburg which would be able to expand Franco-Russian commerce and recapture the bulk of the existing trade between the two countries controlled by English and Dutch intermediaries.[73] In one such scheme, of February 1757, Beaujon & Goossens proposed to do it all themselves, working through factors they would set up in St. Petersburg and through Hope & Co. of Amsterdam—provided the French government gave them all its financial and naval stores business in Russia. Goossens had earlier made such proposals individually in 1749 and 1751. The latest version was referred to St. Sauveur, consul-elect at St. Petersburg, before he left Paris for his new post. That old Russia hand advised against it on the grounds that any firm that worked through Hope & Co. would be regarded by the Russians as a Dutch and not as a French house.[74] Thus, even before St. Sauveur arrived in Russia at the end of 1757, his high patriotic line and opposition to the cosmopolitan schemes of Beaujon & Goossens were clear.

Goossens had since 1753 been actively interested in the possibility of supplying France with tobacco from Russia. Sometime during 1753–55, he obtained samples of Ukrainian tobacco and had them examined by experts in Holland and England. The reports being highly satisfactory, Beaujon & Goossens entered into negotiations with count Peter Ivanovich Shuvalov, proprietor of vast territories in the Ukraine, and persuaded him to obtain the tobacco export monopoly, to expand production on his own lands in the Ukraine and to sell them tobacco on mutually agreeable terms. Shuvalov was the cousin of Elizabeth's favorite, Ivan Ivanovich Shuvalov, and in his own right an important figure in the Russian army and court.[75] It is unclear exactly when Peter Shuvalov received his monopoly, though it can hardly have been later than 1755. Two memoirs of the latter part of 1756 refer to the monopoly as already in operation. According to one by Raimbert, the monopoly had already established processing centers at Moscow and St. Petersburg, although there was still some question of quality.[76]

With terms agreed upon with Shuvalov, Goossens approached the farmers-general in the latter part of 1756, that is, immediately upon the start of the new lease. He offered to supply them with 100,000 quintals or ten million pounds of Ukrainian tobacco delivered in France at a fixed price. (This would have been analagous to the fixed price contracts which the London purchasing agent, George FitzGerald, made with the farmers-general for 1744–50 and 1756–57.) Jean-François de la Borde, who was authorized by the company to negotiate with Goossens, told him that the company would prefer to take delivery directly from Shuvalov in Russia. Goossens then prepared an alternative scheme along those lines, with his firm acting only as factors on commission for the united farms. When this second scheme was shown to Perrinet de Jars, head of the tobacco purchasing committee, he replied that in those dangerous times it would be more prudent for the farmers-general to take delivery in France. Goossens then prepared a third memoir offering to supply the same ten million pounds for a set price of 26 *l.t.* per quintal delivered in France. (The monopolist had allegedly been getting the equivalent of 20 *l.t.* for his tobacco at St. Petersburg recently; the margin would cover transportation, insurance, risks, and profit.)

If the farmers-general agreed, Goossens was prepared to contract after he had received approval from his "associate" in St. Petersburg.[77] In other words, Beaujon & Goossens were not acting on their own at this stage, but rather in collaboration with a merchant house in St. Petersburg. This we know from later evidence to have been the house of William Gomm, a leading British merchant and banker deeply involved with the Russian government in financial transactions, shipbuilding and monopoly export trades.[78]

Early in 1757, Goossens appears to have reached some sort of informal understanding with La Borde, acting for the farmers-general, along the lines of the third proposal above. As soon as word of this was conveyed to Gomm, the latter entered into serious negotiations with the Russian monopolist, count Peter Shuvalov. On 14 May 1757, Gomm signed a twenty-year contract with Shuvalov, allegedly for exports to France of 300,000 *poods* annually (equivalent to 12 million Russian, 10.8 million English, or 9.6 million French lb.).[79] It was too late, however, to do anything about planting such enormous quantities that year. Thus, the implementation of the contract had to wait until the next year. In the interval, however, there were to be great changes in St. Petersburg.

The new French ambassador, L'Hôpital, arrived in St. Petersburg in July 1757; the new consul, St. Sauveur, in November. Neither was pleased with the news that it was an English merchant who had contracted to buy Shuvalov's tobacco for export to France. The consul wrote to the minister of the navy in January 1758 explaining how damaging the ambassador and he felt this would be to French national and commercial prestige in Russia.[80] The opportunity came in February when the pro-British chancellor Bestuzhev was dismissed and his place at the head of the government and in the conduct of foreign affairs taken by the strongly pro-French vice-chancellor Vorontsov. Then, L'Hôpital could intervene via Vorontsov to persuade Peter Shuvalov that it would be in the interests of Franco-Russian amity for him to transfer his business from the Englishman Gomm to the Frenchman, Joseph Raimbert.

In the summer of 1757, Raimbert had prepared a memoir in answer to some queries that had been sent to him on Russian trade. At that time, he thought that the tobacco matter had been entirely sewn up by Goossens acting through Gomm.[81] By January 1758, however, he put his scruples aside and was prepared to step forward under the powerful protection of L'Hôpital and St. Sauveur as the "chosen instrument" of French national interest as seen in St. Petersburg. He of course knew that he was sailing dangerously close to a lee shore since he had no authorization from the farmers-general nor any friends in that company. Nevertheless, the opportunity to "break into the big time" was too tempting. After a protracted struggle in February–March 1758 with Gomm[82] (allegedly supported by the English minister, Robert Keith), Shuvalov was finally induced to break his contract with the Englishman and to give a similar contract to Raimbert on 11/22 March. At the last moment, Jean Michel, another French merchant in St. Petersburg, was, at the behest of the ambassador and consul, added to the contract as Raimbert's partner.[83] Michel added much political, if little financial, strength to the new arrangement. He had long been a confidant of Vorontsov and had, it will be remembered, been employed by him and by the French government in many quasi-diplomatic errands.

By the terms of the imperial grant of the export monopoly to Shuvalov, he was to pay the government ten kopeks (less than a shilling) per *pood* (40 Russian, 36 English or 32.75 French lb.) on all tobacco exported, in lieu of all other duties and tolls.[84] This quite moderate duty Shuvalov could easily recover from the prices he charged to those who bought his tobacco for export. His contract with Gomm (acting with Goossens) was for 300,000 *pood* (12 million Russian lb.) annually for twenty years at an unknown price. There is mention of Gomm's contracting to pay Shuvalov 16,000 rubles annually: this may have been a supplementary payment or a guaranteed minimum.[85] The new contract with Raimbert and Michel signed in March 1758 was for up to 300,000 *pood* annually for six years only. The price appears to have been 115 kopeks per *pood*.[86] As tobacco normally cost 40–50 kopeks per *pood* in the Ukraine and with transport to St. Petersburg at 30–35 kopeks per *pood*[87] and the duty at 10 kopeks, Shuvalov should have made a gross profit of 5–25 kopeks per *pood*. Other clauses in the contract provided that, although the buyers (Raimbert and Michel) were to pay freight and insurance, both the shipping invoices and insurance were to be made out in the name of Shuvalov. Since Britain and Russia were not at war, this should have protected Russian and neutral vessels carrying the tobacco from British privateers. If any troubles ensued on that account, Shuvalov was to use his influence with the Russian court to obtain official protection for the vessels and their cargoes.

Although persuaded by L'Hôpital to break the Gomm-Goossens contract and transfer the concession to Raimbert and Michel, Shuvalov (probably well informed by Gomm) retained a certain obvious skepticism about the French merchants' ability to fulfill the contract and sell the tobacco to the farmers-general. He had therefore insisted on inserting a clause stipulating that the new contract would be void unless confirmed within four months, i.e., by 11/22 July 1758, well before the harvest in the Ukraine.[88] Before Raimbert and Michel could confirm it, they would have to make a sales contract with the united farms. This time limit put Raimbert and Michel under very great pressure for they had no known friends among the farmers-general and do not appear to have been able to make any preliminary soundings. That great company had every reason to be most incensed that two outsiders like Raimbert and Michel, commercial adventurers and financial nonentities, should upset the carefully made arrangements between La Borde and Goossens and try to force themselves upon the united farms as the company's recognized agents and/or suppliers.

A month after the contract was signed, Michel in some anxiety set out from St. Petersburg for Paris to solicit the concurrence of the farmers-general. He went equipped with samples and letters from St. Sauveur, as well as one from Vorontsov to the abbé de Bernis, minister of foreign affairs.[89] St. Sauveur also sent a long memoir which tried to answer the criticisms of the Raimbert-Michel contract already being made by Goossens by showing how closely the new plan paralleled Goossens' own proposals of 1757; he claimed the support of Trudaine, *intendant des finances,* Vincent de Gournay, member of the Bureau of Commerce, and of the merchant deputies in that council. Nevertheless, the memoir requested various evidences of public support for the project, including a royal loan to Raimbert and Michel of 1.2 million *l.t.* They allegedly could borrow this money elsewhere, but a crown loan would be a sign of favor which would attract business their way from firms in France which up to then had been placing their Russian orders through British houses in St. Petersburg.[90] The implication remains, however, that Raimbert and Michel lacked more than the approval of the farmers-general.

Even while Michel was on his way, disturbing letters from Paris to St. Petersburg passed him on the road, bearing tidings that boded ill for his mission. Earlier, when it still appeared that the Goossens-Gomm arrangements were secure, the farmer-general Roslin, new head of the tobacco purchasing committee, had on 18 January written to the ambassador L'Hôpital (whose wife was his first cousin) stating that the monopoly was having difficulty getting tobacco from Great Britain and needed two million pounds of Russian tobacco quickly. On 28 March (after Paris would have heard of the ambassador's démarche in behalf of Raimbert, but before they knew its results), Roslin wrote back to L'Hôpital that the farmers-general had recently received large shipments from Britain and no longer needed Russian tobacco urgently. If, however, Michel should get the contract with Shuvalov and bring samples with him to France, the farmers-general would have the most careful experiments made at their manufactories with such leaf; when they had learned the results of those experiments, the farmers-general would be able to decide how much Ukrainian tobacco they needed. St. Sauveur and Raimbert saw immediately that such tests would serve as an excuse for the farmers-general to refrain from supporting the contract of 11/22 March. Briefed by Raimbert, St. Sauveur sent off another memoir pointing out that the farmers-general had received samples in 1756 and asking why the farmers-general now needed more samples from Raimbert and Michel when they had a few months before been prepared to go ahead with the La Borde–Goossens–Gomm arrangements without further experimentation. (Raimbert blamed the farmers' coolness on Goossens' intrigues.) The consul pleaded that the contract (countersigned by himself and the ambassador) must be honored, even if the deliveries (ca. 10 million lb. annually) had to be spread over twelve rather than six years.[91]

Actually, there was little point in inveighing against the "hypocrisy" of the farmers-general in refusing to deal with Raimbert and Michel upon terms which they had accepted from Goossens and Gomm. The whole point was that a great company like the farmers-general could not let outsiders of no financial standing force themselves upon the company by political intrigue. If Raimbert and Michel had had the financial standing of Goossens or Gomm, the situation might have been slightly different. Nor was there any more point in inveighing against the equal hypocrisy of tests and experiments. Trudaine, *intendant des finances,* who attempted to mediate the matter for the controller-general, wrote to St. Sauveur that in fact the samples of Ukrainian tobacco brought by Michel had proved far from satisfactory, and that he suspected the profits of Raimbert and Michel would be excessive.[92]

Following his arrival at the end of May, Michel attempted to treat with both the farmers-general and the government. In this, he continued the negotiations begun before his arrival by his Paris correspondents and backers, the merchant-bankers Gilly and Bouffé. Despite the good offices of Trudaine,[93] the farmers-general were adamant and the deadline of 22 July passed without the contract being ratified in Paris. St. Sauveur and Raimbert sent anguished memoirs from St. Petersburg urging that the contract be confirmed even though the deadline had passed; Shuvalov could be mollified if the contract were ratified no more than two months late. Otherwise, all would be ruined, the French ambassador and consul rendered ridiculous, and the worst Russian suspicions about France confirmed; neither the Russians in general nor Shuvalov in particular would ever consent to have commercial dealings with the French again.[94] Despite such dire warnings, there were in fact grounds for compromise: it still remained in the French interest to experiment with Russian tobaccos, if not necessarily to contract blindly for ten million pounds yearly; similarly, it was still in Shuvalov's interest to attempt to open a market for his tobaccos in France. Moreover, the controller-general de Boullongne had a personal interest in working out a compromise since he was the father-in-law of the ambassador L'Hôpital, and the uncle of the key farmer-general Roslin, as well as being officially the protector of the united farms.

In his negotiations with the farmers-general (led by Roslin) in June, Michel found that the company professed to find his proffered contract impracticable because (a) his price of 25 *l.t.* 5 *s.* per quintal delivered in France was too high; (b) the transport problems in wartime were too great and they were not impressed with his plan to ship by Dutch ships as far as Holland and then transship to French vessels which would carry the leaf to France in winter when few British privateers were out; (c) they were not sure about quality; (d) nor were they sure French consumers would accept Ukrainian tobacco alone or in mixture. Michel even offered to surrender the primary Shuvalov contract to them provided that he and Raimbert were employed as their commission agents in Russia, but the farmers were still not interested. Michel hard-headedly realized by then that it would take two years to make extensive tests with Ukrainian tobacco in France: tobacco ordered then (June 1758) would be shipped from the Ukraine to St. Petersburg in the winter months, December-February, when the ground was frozen, and could not arrive in France before June 1759; by the time it was sent to the manufactories, processed and distributed to consumers and the results collected and analyzed, another year would have passed. Under the circumstances, in a memoir of June 1758, Michel suggested that the Shuvalov contract of March 1758 be postponed for two years and that during the experimental interval, interim contracts be arranged for from 500,000 to one million pounds annually. Raimbert and he could execute these at their own risk or as factors for the farmers-general, and would need only a small advance. In fact, a fixed price contract along these lines between

Michel and the farmers-general was signed in late July (a few days after the four months' grace on the original Shuvalov contract had expired). Michel was afraid that Shuvalov would not cooperate in such a piddling contract and induced Bernis to write to L'Hôpital to persuade that grandee to participate.[95] Even though St. Sauveur and Raimbert, infuriated at this scaling down, predicted that the count would not agree,[96] in fact Shuvalov did.

The corresponding new contract between count Peter Shuvalov and Raimbert and Michel, signed in September, provided for the sale by the monopolist to the French merchants of 30,000 *pood* (1.2 million Russian lb. or about one million French lb.) annually in 1759 and 1760. The price (115 kopeks per *pood*) and terms were to be the same as in the abandoned March contract. Of the 69,000 rubles due Shuvalov for the two years' sale of 60,000 *pood*, 45,532½ were to be paid immediately, the remainder in September and October 1759. The substantial advance (a much more rapid payment than provided for in the March contract) was the price Raimbert had to pay for Shuvalov's approval. Gilly and Bouffé were not expecting this and he was in some trepidation lest his bills on Amsterdam not be honored. If the tobacco proved satisfactory, Raimbert and Michel had the option of continuing the contract for four more years up to the maximum quantities specified in the March contract. They were to have the preference over other equal bidders, but Shuvalov could sell to others offering more.[97]

The farmers-general still made some difficulties about the interposition of Gilly and Bouffé, but this was eventually settled satisfactorily. As St. Sauveur now admitted, Raimbert and Michel "are not capitalists and have never been presented as such"; they were simply the best French merchants available in St. Petersburg. They needed Paris backers of means and Gilly and Bouffé were well suited for the role, analagous to that Goossens would have played if Gomm's contract had stood.[98] Both Gilly and Bouffé were leading figures in the Protestant banking community of Paris, the Gilly coming originally from Montpellier, the Bouffé from La Rochelle. Simon Gilly was then a director of the Indies Company of which Gabriel Julien Bouffé was an important shareholder and customer.[99] The Indies Company connection suggests participation in a milieu with a long history of rivalry vis-à-vis the farmers-general.

Despite these personal troubles, and despite the availability of technical reports questioning the suitability of Ukrainian tobacco,[100] the contract got off to a good start in 1759. In March, London was alarmed by rumors that the full ten million lb. were intended, rather than the one million of the second contract.[101] In fact, the quota was over-shipped. Instead of the 30,000 *pood* (1.2 million Russian lb.) called for by the contract, over 38,000 *pood* were shipped on five vessels.[102] Trouble, however, followed quickly enough.

Even before the tobacco reached France, difficulties were encountered at Elsinore, where the Danes demanded a Sound Toll payment equivalent to 9 percent of the reported cost of the tobacco on board at St. Petersburg. This came as something of a shock to Raimbert and Michel and to Gilly and Bouffé, for the Sound Toll on other merchandise normally came to only ½ to 2 percent. Gilly and Bouffé claimed that the Danes were using an old valuation for tobacco suitable perhaps for expensive manufactured tobaccos shipped from west to east, but hardly reasonable for the cheap Ukrainian leaf tobacco. The French and Russian governments intervened diplomatically at Copenhagen, but the Danes were adamant. Several years of memoir writing and negotiation left the situation unchanged.[103] This was a serious blow to Raimbert, Michel and associates: they had contracted with Shuvalov for their supply at a fixed price and had also contracted for their sales to the farmers-general at a fixed price. Thus, the "nine percent" duty had to come out of their profit margin.

If this were not enough, when the 1759 tobacco arrived in France, it was found to be inferior in quality to that of the Chesapeake and badly deteriorated through fraud and carelessness in packing and transport. Little attention had been paid to the instructions sent by the farmers-general for drying and packing in the Chesapeake manner. Green and inadequately dried leaves had been included. In tying the tobacco leaves into bunches or "hands" (*manoques*), instead of using another dried tobacco leaf for binding, the Ukrainians used green leaves or vines that rotted and damaged the tobacco. Instead of hogsheads, canvas wrapped bales were used in shipment, which gave inadequate protection to the tobacco and were too bulky (30 *pood* or 1,200 Russian lb.) for easy handling. Stowage became an expensive problem when the tobacco came to be loaded on board ship at St. Petersburg, particularly when ships were chartered at a flat rate and not by cargo carried. The bales too made it easy to add water or snow to the tobacco to increase its weight before sale. The employees of Raimbert and Michel sent to inspect the tobacco at purchase were insulted and assaulted by Shuvalov's men when they tried to stop some of these frauds and reject tobacco as defective.[104]

Despite all these disappointments in the shipments of the first year, the farmers-general kept to the letter of their contract and accepted the deliveries provided for the second year, 1760. This "good will" can perhaps be explained by the fact that the prices of Chesapeake tobacco in 1759 were at their highest levels in more than thirty years (about double prewar prices) while the stocks of the united farms were so low that the company had been forced to make very large purchases in Britain at these exceptionally high prices.[105] Thus, in 1760 the company accepted contractual shipments of about 900,000 Russian or 720,000 French lb.[106] These too proved disappointing in quality.[107]

In August 1760, Raimbert and Michel submitted to count Peter Shuvalov a report on all the defects found in the tobacco sent to France in 1759.[108] The two years of their existing contract having effectively expired, they were prepared to contract only for another million pounds for the next year, 1761, provided that certain conditions were met: (1) they would take only well-conditioned tobacco two years old: (2) no green leaf or foreign matter was to be used in securing the "hands"; (3) no snow, etc., was to be used to increase the weight of the tobacco; (4) their agents were to have unimpeded rights to inspect and reject tobacco at delivery; (5) the tobacco was to be packed in oak hogsheads, provided either by Shuvalov or by themselves, deducting cost from their price.[109] When Shuvalov rejected these terms, Raimbert and Michel in October announced their intention of retiring from the trade.[110]

A complete breakdown at this stage was, however, averted by diplomatic intervention. With Shuvalov prepared by January 1761 to make some concessions, an initiative by the French minister Breteuil led to an agreement continuing the count's contract with Raimbert and Michel for a third year. Shuvalov promised improvements in quality, but nothing firm was agreed upon concerning packing.[111] In the event something over a million pounds was shipped to France in 1761, making a grand total for the three years 1759–61 of about 3.5 million Russian or 2.9 million French lb.[112] The farmers-general were in a much more independent position by 1761, having taken advantage of the lower prices in Britain in 1760 to make exceptionally large purchases.[113] Nevertheless, they let themselves be persuaded by Gilly and Bouffé to accept the third year's "trial" on the same terms. However, the contract with Shuvalov not being concluded till January, the tobacco was very late in coming to St. Petersburg and the contractors had to pay heavy demurrage to the chartered Dutch ships. Being paid this year by weight, the Dutch masters broke open the bales to cram more into their holds and much of the tobacco was damaged by exposure or by lack of ventilation. The deliveries of 1761 proving not significantly better than those of the two preceding years, the farmers-general declined to contract further with Raimbert and Michel who perforce had to let their own arrangements with Shuvalov lapse.[114]

Quite early in the story, Raimbert, Michel and the consul St. Sauveur had realized that Shuvalov's monopoly (Goossens' brainchild) was not a help but a major obstacle in the development of the Franco-Russian tobacco trade. In 1758, at their own expense, Raimbert and Michel had sent an "expert," one Nottbek, to the Ukraine, to instruct in the preparation and packing of the tobacco, to distribute the printed translations of the directions sent by the farmers-general and to supervise the receipt of the tobacco destined for France. He had received nothing but harassment from Shuvalov's agents and had had to be recalled after a few months.[115]

At the same time, however, Raimbert and Michel entered into a friendly correspondence with the councillor, courtier, and dilettante, G. N. Teplov. In 1759, on his own lands in the Ukraine near Glukhov, Teplov began experiments in growing tobacco from Virginia seed. Part of the cultivation was managed by Nottbek, the remainder by himself. That winter,

Teplov sent large samples of the tobacco thus grown to Raimbert and Michel who reported that the quality was excellent. The merchants realized, however, that there was no point in sending commercial quantities to St. Petersburg as long as the Shuvalov monopoly persisted. St. Sauveur wrote as admiringly of the broad vision of Teplov as he did despairingly of the narrow self-interest of Shuvalov.[116]

In 1760, the baron of Breteuil was sent to St. Petersburg as French minister, at first to assist the ambassador L'Hôpital, later to act for him after his return on leave to France. (In fact, L'Hôpital's star had been in the descendent ever since the downfall of his father-in-law, the controller-general de Boullongne, and Paris de Montmartel, in 1759.) Part of Breteuil's ostensible mission was to investigate the possibilities of making a commercial treaty with the Russians as favorable as that long enjoyed by the British.

On 28 October 1760, St. Sauveur presented to Breteuil—and to L'Hôpital—a memoir which he had drawn up in the names of Raimbert and Michel. It reviewed the history of the tobacco contract from the beginning down to Shuvalov's rejection of their August proposals for a third year. They declared to the ambassador and minister their determination to withdraw from the affair and their conviction that the question would have to be taken up with the Russian ministers at a diplomatic rather than consular or private level if anything was to be saved of the French-Russian tobacco trade. They also suggested that prospects for that trade would be more encouraging if Shuvalov's monopoly were abolished and a free trade substituted.[117] When both French ministers in St. Petersburg suggested that it would create a very bad impression if Raimbert and Michel broke off negotiations with Shuvalov, those merchants submitted a further memorial to Breteuil in November repeating their argument and emphasizing more strongly the need for a free trade.[118]

Although Raimbert and Michel took Breteuil's advice and contracted with Shuvalov in January 1761 for a third year's shipment, their libertarian effort had not been in vain. On both a copy of the Russian-British treaty and a draft of a proposed French-Russian treaty which Breteuil sent home early in 1761, he added notes suggesting the advisability of abolishing the Shuvalov monopoly.[119] Although Breteuil's suggestions had no immediate results, the next year, mid the great political upheavals that then shook Russia, the tobacco export monopoly of count Peter Shuvalov was in fact abolished on 31 July 1762, shortly after Catherine's "accession."[120]

In the new regime, a prominent and important place was to be played by Teplov, who eventually became a "secretary of state" and a senator. In his new role, he retained his former agrarian interests. In February 1763, a *ukase* was issued providing for the abolition of the export duty on tobacco, for the payment of premiums for its cultivation in the Ukraine, and for the free distribution of superior Virginia and Amersfort (Dutch) seed. As "director-general of tobacco plantations in the Ukraine," Teplov was in charge of carrying out these new policies. He also composed and had distributed in the tobacco growing areas a manual on the cultivation and preparation of tobacco in the approved American manner.[121] (Raimbert and Michel had earlier had similar instructions sent them from France printed and distributed, though with less success.)

By 1765, Teplov's work had made sufficient progress for him to suggest to the marquis of Bausset, then French minister in St. Petersburg, that a new French experiment might be made. He offered to supply the farmers-general with 40,000 *pood* annually, that is, 1.6 million Russian or 1.3 million French lb. This was a small enough amount to leave the normal business of the tobacco monopoly in France undisturbed but large enough for the farmers-general to make the most extensive experiments in the properties and marketability of Ukrainian tobacco. The scheme was endorsed by Rossignol, the new French consul-general in St. Petersburg. It also was pushed by Raimbert who made a trip home in 1765[122] and revived the interest of Gilly who in turn submitted a memoir in February 1766 suggesting that the farmers-general contract to take three to four million pounds yearly for nine or ten years.[123] These proposals seem to have been based upon the grant to Teplov of some sort of control over exports, either a bureaucratic or personal monopoly. The growers in the Ukraine were by 1766 for the first time sufficiently interested in the export market to protest against this to the empress and to request the restoration of full freedom of export.[124]

Nothing came of the 1765 proposals, but Teplov raised the matter with Raimbert again in 1768. Since quality rather than price seemed to be the stumbling block, he suggested that the farmers-general send their own agent to the Ukraine both to instruct and inspect. Although such an agent would be paid and directed by the farmers-general, he would receive an official title and authority from the Russian government to facilitate his work. He would also be authorized to make purchases in Teplov's name, circumventing the Russian anti-alien laws. Teplov would also make warehouses and other facilities available to him for handling and forwarding purchases made for the farmers-general. His headquarters would be at Romny in the heart of the growing region. The plan was strongly endorsed by Raimbert but it proved impossible to arouse the interest of the farmers-general.[125]

The Russian purchases of 1759–61 were thus the only significant effort by the united farms to develop a new source of tobacco supply between their assumption of the monopoly in 1730 and the advent of the American Revolution. It is hard to imagine even this limited effort being undertaken were it not for the extraordinary atmosphere and supply problems of the Seven Years' War. The farmers-general first became interested in Ukrainian leaf in 1756 when their reserves were low and when it was quite uncertain how much tobacco they would be able to get from Britain during the war. The high prices and financial crisis of 1759 kept their interest aflicker even after the intrusion of Raimbert et al. made the affair riskier and politically distasteful to them. With the very large shipments from Britain in 1760 at moderate prices, the objective needs of the farmers-general disappeared and their never more than tepid interest in Ukrainian tobacco conspicuously cooled.

This cooling was facilitated by the political changes in France of 1758–59. The duke of Choiseul was much less interested in cultivating Russia than his predecessor Bernis had been. Choiseul's protégé, Jean-Joseph de la Borde, the new court banker, was also a farmer-general, while his predecessor, Paris de Montmartel, had represented a different and hostile interest. (Raimbert, Michel, Gilly, and Bouffé all seem to have had some connection with Montmartel but none with the farmers-general.) Finally, the controller-general de Boullongne (1757–59) had some interest in supporting his son-in-law the ambassador L'Hôpital, while his successors Silhouette and Bertin, under circumstances of the most acute financial strain, could be counted on to give the normal support of their office to the farmers-general. (Bertin's negotiations for the renewal of the farms' lease in 1761–62 at a markedly higher price would have made him particularly careful about protecting the interests of that company.)

None of these attendant circumstances would, in and of itself, have been decisive if Ukrainian tobacco had been of a quality more readily acceptable in France. It was offered at prices that were competitive with those paid for British tobacco in normal years and which appeared markedly cheap when Chesapeake prices rose in 1758 and 1759. However, the monopolists dared not force Ukrainian leaf on the French consumers. The marked fall in sales in 1759 that followed the price rise of 1758 had shown that consumer resistance could be very real in France. Ultimately, then, it was the French consumer and not the monopolists who rejected the opportunity to substitute Ukrainian tobacco for Virginian.

During and after the Seven Years' War, active minds were also to suggest countries other than Russia as possible sources of tobacco imports that would free France from its disgraceful dependence on Britain. There were in particular those ancient centers of the tobacco trade, Spain and Portugal. From time to time through the century, the esteemed tobaccos of Cuba were brought home by French West Indian traders, but only for entrepôt and transshipment to other European markets.[126] As French and Spanish policy grew closer together in the war, a Spanish memoir writer of about 1760 suggested closer commercial cooperation. In particular, he thought that Cuba could supply all the tobacco which France then purchased from Britain. Transport costs might be something of a problem, but he thought these could be reduced.[127] Nothing came of such schemes probably because total Cuban shipments to Europe were much less than French needs alone and the price of "Havana" leaf was three or four times that of Chesapeake in Europe.[128]

Much more serious were the suggestions that France might buy more Brazilian tobacco. The monopoly had after all bought considerable quantities from Portugal in Louis XIV's time before French taste abandoned chewing tobacco for snuff. About 1740, when the farmers-general and government were actively investigating West Indian and other possible tobacco supplies that would free them from dependence on Britain, samples were sent from Portugal for trial. The farmers-general reported, however, and Orry agreed that the Portuguese prices were too high and the quality not suited to current French tastes. As in the previous century, this tobacco was grown principally about Bahia and to the northward. In the ensuing decades, much further south about Sacramento on the Plate, the Brazilians developed a new cultivation of tobacco in the Virginia style, suitable for snuff. In August 1763, some of this was sent to the French government and farms by the Lisbon merchant, Jacome Ratton. A memoir from the French minister in Portugal, the *chevalier* de Saint Priest, of 13 March 1764 urged the most serious consideration of this possibility.[129] Nothing was in fact done, though a surviving draft memoir from the controller-general's office of about 1766–70 indicates that someone there was quite sympathetic to the Portuguese supply scheme.[130] Assuming that the quality of Sacramento tobacco was satisfactory, price and quantity still posed serious problems. Production could not have been very large, for the territory attached to the *Colonia do Sacramento* (really only a fortified trading station) was minute and Spanish guards saw to it that it was not enlarged. (In the end, under constant Spanish harassment, the colony on the Plate was abandoned in 1777.)

Thus, the Spanish and Portuguese projects of the 1760's were in the end to prove but another chapter in the literary rather than the commercial history of the French tobacco monopoly.

The Monopoly's Purchasing Policy and the Critics of 1758–63

The military defeats of the Seven Years' War and the state financial crisis of 1759 brought forth a flurry of published criticism remarkable for the reign of Louis XV. The censor had eventually to stop this outpouring at the return of peace. In this brief hour of free discussion, every aspect of French public finance was criticized.[131] It was inevitable that the tobacco monopoly should attract its share of criticism. Though much of this writing was ill informed, and none of it exceptionally well informed, a few of the works at least deserve a brief mention. All of them gave critical attention to the monopoly's purchasing policy.

One of the better informed works was Forbonnais' *Recherches et considérations sur les finances de France* (1758).[132] Forbonnais was a confidante and advisor of Silhouette, briefly controller-general in 1759. His work shows a marked sympathy toward Louisiana that is quite consistent with Silhouette's position in his 1739 memoir on tobacco discussed above.[133] Forbonnais estimated that only four million people in France took tobacco but that they consumed five pounds per annum each, making a total national consumption of twenty million pounds. Of this, he thought two-thirds or 13.3 million lb. were provided by the monopoly, the rest smuggled in. These were very shrewd guesses, particularly if we include in the smuggled total all the tobacco consumed in the provinces outside the monopoly.[134] To Forbonnais (who shows the influence here of John Law) it seemed that the costs of the monopoly were so high that an import duty of only half the nominal rate would produce as much net revenue; that is, that there were severe economies in administrative costs to be made through an import duty, even though the needed expenditures on guards would have to be at least those of a monopoly. The varieties smuggled from the Rhineland and elsewhere were of such vile quality that Forbonnais felt smuggling would cease once a free trade had been established under a moderate duty. By contrast, the tobaccos of the French colonies were of such excellent quality that they would in an open market drive out all European leaf. With a little customs preference, they would also drive out the other American tobaccos. Only such a free trade could save the economy of Louisiana for whose tobaccos Forbonnais had the highest praise. They were much better than those of Virginia and it was a scandal that France spent four million *l.t.* annually on British leaf.[135]

Forbonnais' rosy view of Louisiana as the solution to France's tobacco supply problems reflects not only his close intellectual connection with Silhouette (who had been arguing in this fashion in 1739) but also the considerable volume of Louisiana publicity that had appeared in the preceding five years. In 1753, the abbé Jean-Baptiste Le Mascrier published his *Mémoires historiques sur la Louisiane,* based upon notes left by the engineer Dumont de Montigny who had served in Louisiana for twenty-five years starting about 1720. The author(s) gave considerable space to Louisiana tobacco, praising in particular those of Pointe Coupée and Natchez, the latter of which he (they) reported to be superior to that of St. Domingue or Virginia.[136] Similar praise can be found in the 1758 work on Louisiana by Le Page du Pratz, another old settler from Law's time (1718-34).[137] Even more to the point was the 1754 work on international trade, previously discussed, by the Franco-Irish publicist, the count of Magnières. He emphasized the unique opportunities provided by Louisiana for France to free herself from dependence on British tobacco supplies and publicized the projects of the mercantile groups vying to get a government contract to supply that colony with slaves.[138] Even a contemporary commentator on Sir Josiah Child, when he came to the chapters on the "Balance of Trade" and "Colonies" felt obliged to note how much more advantageous it would be for France to get its tobacco from Louisiana rather than from Britain, even if it cost the monopoly three or four times as much.[139]

Forbonnais (like these contemporary writers and like John Law) accepted the basic tenets of a traditional Colbertian policy: France's primary objective should be to develop its own colonial tobacco trade; to this end it was justified in continuing the suppression of the domestic cultivation of tobacco. By contrast, there were contemporary writers of a more physiocratic orientation who were prepared to argue that, since France could grow tobacco, she should in fact do so, thereby employing thousands of poor laborers and saving millions in foreign exchange.[140] A similar polarization had appeared sixty years before in the time of the first deliberations of the Council of Commerce.[141]

Much the most famous work to appear at this time was the *Théorie de l'impôt* (1761) of Mirabeau the father. He was primarily concerned to show that the farmers-general in all their revenues were making exorbitant profits. He placed French tobacco consumption at 48 million lb. annually, of which half was supplied by contraband, the other half by the monopoly, (about twice actual sales). He assumed that they sold all their tobacco at the full legal price of 64 *sols* per lb. (allowing nothing for *cantine* or frontier zones) from which he deduced they had gross receipts of 76.8 million *l.t.* from tobacco. (His original exaggeration of sales had been compounded by the enhancement of the sales price.) From this he deducted only 12 million for the price of the lease (actually 15.6 million excluding Lorraine) but he allowed an excessively high purchase price for tobaccos of 14 *s*. per lb. In the end he "calculated" that the monopoly made profits of 31.15 million annually on tobacco.[142] His figures can be compared with those for 1759–60 submitted to the controller-general.[143]

	Mirabeau	*Official*
Gross Receipts	76.8 million *l.t.*	28.7 million *l.t.*
Net Receipts	43.15 million *l.t.*	16.1 million *l.t.*
Farm Price	12.0 million *l.t.*	15.6 million *l.t.*
Net Profit	31.15 million *l.t.*	.5 million *l.t.*

There is little wonder that Mirabeau's work made such a great stir at the time.

With very detailed and sometimes confusing and self-defeating calculations, Mirabeau tried to prove that, if France permitted a free trade and a domestic plantation under a low duty on the cultivation of only 3 *sols* per lb., legitimate consumption would rise from his estimated 24 million to 40 million lb.[144] (Even here, his argument is incomplete for a three *sol* tax on 40 million lb. would only produce six million *l.t.*)

A well-informed discussion of some of this literature on French public finance was published in the *Journal de Commerce* of Brussels in 1761 by the merchant-physiocrat of Nantes, Jean-Gabriel Montaudouin de la Touche. In general, Montaudouin had a high regard for the argument of Forbonnais whose calculations and judgments he cited with great respect. Nevertheless, he felt that the dominant position which Chesapeake tobacco then held in the world market was due to its intrinsic quality. No good snuff was then manufactured anywhere in Europe which did not mix some Virginia and Maryland tobacco in with the local (particularly Dutch and German) leaf. He thought Mirabeau knew very little about the tobacco trade and consequently exaggerated the ease of underselling Virginia with "superior" French leaf. Tobacco grown in France might be better than other European growths but not than that of the Chesapeake. Montaudouin pointed out that Mirabeau failed to allow for the depressing effect upon Chesapeake prices of a French production of forty or more million pounds annually. The planters in Virginia would suffer a little from such a decline but a cheaper Chesapeake product could compete all the more effectively in Europe. European prices could fall far below the six *sols* (3*d*. sterling) used by Mirabeau. Similarly, Montaudouin, an experienced merchant, considered that Mirabeau had grossly exaggerated the opportunities for France to develop a great export trade in tobacco manufactured from its own leaf. French manufactures were not really that good. In addition to the very famous private manufactures of Scolthen (Scholt) in Amsterdam, Boulongaro in Frankfort, and Brouwer in Brussels, there were elsewhere in Europe an "infinity of others all superior to the French manufactures."

Finally, the merchant critic doubted Mirabeau's calculation that France spent twenty million *l.t.* annually for foreign tobacco. He followed Forbonnais in estimating that the farmers-general imported thirteen million pounds annually at 5 *sols* per lb. (3.25 million *l.t.*) while the smugglers probably brought in seven million pounds at 20 *sols* (7 million *l.t.*), making a total foreign expenditure of only about ten million *l.t.* (He failed to allow for the loss of weight between purchase and manufacture which would have added 50 percent or 1.625 million to the monopoly's purchases.)

Despite his physiocratic interests, Montaudouin thought it ridiculous to argue for the restoration of tobacco cultivation in France on general philosophical grounds. The tobacco monopoly produced a great revenue for the state almost painlessly: no one had to take tobacco if he did not want to. Yet, while arguing thus and deflating the exaggerated calculations of Mirabeau, the merchant *philosophe* was no blind defender of the farmers-general or of the status quo. From Forbonnais, he had picked up a very high opinion of the quality of Louisiana tobacco. If France could get even a moderate quantity of these good Mississippi tobaccos, she could free herself from dependence on Britain by mixing them with the cheaper if inferior tobaccos of Holland, the Rhineland and Swabia. He thought that the farmers-general had refrained from using European tobacco in the past because it required extra years of aging, tying up more capital. He had also heard very good things about Ukrainian tobacco and wondered why the French had not experimented more with that. He understood that Brouwer in Brussels was then conducting some very successful trials with samples sent him from Russia.[145]

A few months later, a parallel critique of purchasing policy came from the *parlement* of Provence. They recommended that the monopoly be required to buy only Levant tobacco, to the obvious benefit of Marseilles.[146] (In fact, the monopoly had been making smoking tobacco at Marseilles from Levantine leaf, but the demand for such in France proved limited.)

And so the circle was completed. The less people knew about the tobacco trade the easier they found it to criticize the heavy dependence of the French monopoly on supplies from Britain. Those who knew something about the trade and accepted a justification of monopoly for fiscal reasons could only suggest experiments with Louisiana or Ukrainian tobaccos. In fact, the farmers-general had tried both and found them either unsuitable in quality (Ukrainian) or else unprocurable in large enough quantities at competitive prices (Louisiana).

But Mirabeau was to have the last laugh. Although all his arguments could be proved ridiculous by the knowing, it was in fact his advice that was followed by the revolutionary National Assembly in 1791. France then decided once and for all that she was no longer going to be totally dependent upon an imported supply of an agricultural commodity that she could grow herself. That decision involved costs for the French fisc and consumer but it was a permanent decision.

CHAPTER 16

The Internal Structure and Operation of the Tobacco Monopoly, 1721–91

The Manufacturing Establishments

In the days of the Bernard-Crozat-Maynon tobacco monopoly (1697–1718), it will be remembered, the farm conducted most of its own manufacture in two large establishments at Dieppe in Normandy and Morlaix in Brittany. The company also had a small workshop at Paris for snuff and outside their own territories maintained a further *manufacture* at Charleville near the frontier of the Southern Netherlands to supply the local tobacco monopoly, which they also farmed, as well as *tabac de cantine* for the troops. Manufacture by supervised private workshops was still permitted at Tonneins in the Agenais and elsewhere in the parishes where tobacco cultivation was still tolerated. In addition, throughout the south, the private syndicates which subfarmed the tobacco monopoly in individual provinces maintained several minor tobacco workshops in their respective jurisdictions.[1]

When the tobacco monopoly was temporarily abolished by John Law in 1720, the various manufactories of the monopolist (then the Indies Company) and the subfarmers were sold at auction, many of them passing into the hands of one company, Jean Maurice de Montigny & Co. When the monopoly was reestablished in 1721, most of these premises were reacquired by the new monopoly (the Edouard du Verdier company) or by the single subfarming company for the south.[2] Some of the old *manufactures* in the south—such as those at Mondragon, St. Esprit, and Montpellier[3]—appear, however, not to have been reestablished at this time and disappear from the record.

Starting with the du Verdier company of 1721–23 (and its southern subfarmer) and continuing under the Indies Company (1723–30) and the United General Farms (1730–91), the successive administrators of the tobacco monopoly found it necessary to establish new manufactories to meet growing consumer demand in France. The farmer-general Dupin listed eight *manufactures* in 1732: Dieppe, Le Havre, Toulouse and Charleville for twist (*corde*) only; Morlaix and Tonneins for twist and snuff; Arles and Clermont-en-Auvergne for snuff only.[4] These same sites minus Charleville but plus Paris and Cette occur in a subsequent list compiled some time after 1750.[5] In later lists of 1768–74, Clermont has disappeared, Marseilles has been acknowledged, and Valenciennes has taken the place of Charleville.[6] The united farms were also responsible for the works at Nancy in Lorraine whose monopoly they leased separately. A final authoritative list of 1790 dropped Marseilles and showed ten establishments: seven general (Paris, Dieppe, Le Havre, Morlaix, Tonneins, Cette, Valenciennes), two for smoking tobacco only (Toulouse, Nancy), and one for snuff only (Arles).

Each of these *manufactures* was in charge of an *inspecteur* or works manager assisted by one or two *contrôleurs*. At Morlaix in 1729, the *inspecteur* received 2,000 *l.t.* p.a. and the *contrôleurs* 1,200. These salaries were relatively modest, but, as a perquisite, the officers in charge received the proceeds of the ashes of burnt tobacco stems, midribs, and refuse sold to launderers and others. Though the ashes from 100 pounds of stems brought only 50 *sols,* on six million pounds annually this could come to 150,000 *l.t.* to be divided among the two or three top officers of the seven general manufactories. There appears to have been considerable stability in the higher managerial ranks of the works, and, in at least one case, Desmarest of Dieppe, a veteran manager (*inspecteur*) of a manufactory was rewarded by promotion to a farmer-generalship.[7]

The workers in the manufactories had less cause for satisfaction. The women, children, and unskilled laborers employed were poorly paid but caused relatively little trouble. Far more truculent were the better paid, skilled adult male workers. In quiet times, they seem to have been constantly if almost imperceptibly usurping various perquisites in pay, working conditions, and "samples." Periodically, the company would find itself forced to tighten discipline and retract some of these concessions, sometimes provoking strikes, always provoking labor unrest among these skilled workmen. It was they, not the less skilled, who in 1790 petitioned the National Assembly against the rules, discipline, and pay of the monopoly.[8]

Probably the oldest of the manufactories was that at Dieppe. We have already noted how a significant manufacturing trade had been started there by private merchants in the 1660's. After the establishment of the monopoly in 1674, the private manufacturers at Dieppe were probably permitted to continue for a year or two under license but were soon replaced by the monopoly's own works in 1676. New premises were built in 1684 but destroyed by the Anglo-Dutch bombardment of 1694. The works were then rebuilt in a more spacious location. In a memoir of the 1690's, Vauban put Dieppe's output at one million *l.t.* yearly.[9] By 1715, that establishment was employing 1,000–1,100 workers and was having the serious labor trouble described in Chapter 7.

Because of these labor troubles or the inconveniences arising out of the location and character of the port or other difficulties, the restored monopoly of the 1720's seemed disenchanted with Dieppe. The du Verdier company (1721–23) wanted to continue the lease of a part of their premises at Dieppe owned by a sieur de Varneville at the old rent of 750 *l.t.* p.a. and became involved in extensive litigation with him when he obtained an order from the *bailliage* of the city raising the figure to 1,100 *l.t.*[10] When the Indies Company took over the monopoly in 1723, they wanted to move the entire manufactory to the more convenient port of Le Havre. The local magistrates fought this proposal vigorously, pointing out that the works by then employed 1,500 persons in the town and that its removal would create grave social problems. They were successful in preventing the move, though a separate manufactory was soon thereafter established at Le Havre.[11] The decision to stay in Dieppe was confirmed by the decision in 1732-33 to build a great new works there, costing more than 140,000 *l.t.* for the building alone. The new premises were opened in 1737.[12]

The decision taken in 1733 to build the new Dieppe manufactory may have been motivated by a desire to tighten industrial discipline and increase efficiency. As the oldest manufacturing establishment of the monopoly, Dieppe suffered from generations of accumulated laxities and perquisites. In December 1729, there were serious riots and a sit-in strike, when the Indies Company removed a *gratification* which the workers had formerly enjoyed. The whole affair was rather similar to the disturbances of 1715, though much more successful from the workers' standpoint. In 1729, no one was punished and the *gratifications* were restored. When the united farms took over in 1730, a new spirit of even more efficiency led to a steady rise in work norms. Worker grumbling became so pronounced that troops were summoned in 1733 to check a threatened riot before it started. Several of the ringleaders were dismissed and the new work norms confirmed. It was thereafter possible to maintain output at Dieppe with a reduced work force.[13] A detailed report of survey in 1738 showed only 615 workers in place of the 1,000-1,500 a generation earlier.[14]

We know rather less about the other old manufactory at Morlaix, the decaying linen center in north Brittany. In Chapter 7, we suggested that the works had possibly been established during 1681-87, when the monopoly in Brittany was subfarmed to a separate company, and subsequently taken over by the united farms in 1687 when the subfarm was discontinued. The workshop there was also damaged by enemy bombardment during the 1690's and was replaced by larger premises on a hill outside the town.[15] This site proving inconvenient, new premises conveniently placed for water traffic were built in the 1730's on the new quay de Léon south of the town.[16] In 1733, the *intendant* of Brittany, des Gallois de la Tour, reported that from 1,000 to 1,200 persons were employed in the tobacco manufactory in and near Morlaix.[17] Of these, only about 250 could have been adult males rated for local taxes—the rest being either women or children.[18] When the farmer-general Brissat visited Morlaix in 1741, he reported that at least 700 persons of both sexes and all ages were employed there.[19] On the eve of the French Revolution, employment was relatively unchanged at 700-900. Working conditions were not ideal and there was some discontent among the workers, though this was *not* expressed in their *cahier*.[20]

We get a rather precise if not necessarily exact idea of the volume of activity at Morlaix from surviving data on tobacco imports in the Rennes customs district (*direction*) which included all of Brittany except Nantes and the Loire estuary. As Morlaix was the only tobacco manufacturing center in the district, these figures can be substantially equated with imports at Morlaix. (It will be observed that the dominance of British imports, observed in Chapter 15 for the country as a whole, was also characteristic of Morlaix.)

TABLE I

Tobacco Imports in the Rennes Customs District, 1749–75[21]

Year	From: Britain	Holland	Other	Total
		(in French lb. weight)		
1749	2,098,989	9,000	—	2,107,989
1750	—	115,418	2	115,420
1751	—	—	—	—
1752	4,776,300	71,250	—	4,847,550
1753	243,900	86,100	—	330,000
1754	5,970,300	136,875	—	6,107,175
1755	885,600	87,775	—	973,375
1756	1,011,420	251,817	—	1,263,237
1757	2,597,385	285,551	12	2,882,948
1758	3,170,600	539,593	20	3,710,213
1759	1,909,544	290,339	—	2,199,883
1760	4,762,606	255,697	—	5,018,303
1761	387,683	159,368	313,800	860,851
1762	2,248,212	—	—	2,248,212
1763	2,504,123	168,648	1,609	2,674,380
1764	2,556,504	147,235	2	2,703,741
1765	3,502,655	—	6	3,502,661
1766	992,918	260,588	—	1,253,506
1767	3,383,846	138,317	—	3,522,163
1768	2,041,670	283,715	—	2,325,385
1769	2,627,647	120,548	—	2,748,231
1770	3,278,975	290,050	—	3,569,025
1771	3,599,390	61,499	—	3,660,889
1772	5,294,262	115,916	—	5,410,178
1773	3,797,314	163,331	—	3,960,645
1774	1,823,240	256,350	—	2,079,590
1775	2,199,472	376,650	—	2,576,122

The last of the old tobacco manufactories in northern France going back to before Law's time was that at Charleville in the sovereign territory on the eastern frontier whose tobacco monopoly was still leased in the 1730's from the Condé family. From 1703, the monopoly had had a general *manufacture* there, supplying cheap tobaccos for the local monopoly, the French army and those exposed frontier areas within France proper where the full prices of the monopoly could not be charged. The works used the whole production of Charleville leaf (about 34,000 lb. annually) plus some from Alsace and considerable quantities of Virginia leaf to turn out 621,700 lb. of its distinctive tobaccos in an average year of the 1730's.[22]

These older works were to be supplemented by new in the generation following the reestablishment of the monopoly in 1721. Some of these new foundations, of course, also had links with the past, particularly the great works at Tonneins on the Garonne. The town was in the middle of the jurisdictions in the Agenais where tobacco growing had been permitted until 1720, and had served as the manufacturing center of that region. When tobacco cultivation was prohibited, not only were numerous peasant families left without a valued cash crop, but hundreds and perhaps thousands of laborers in the private workshops of Tonneins were left without employment. When the monopoly was reestablished in 1721, the new monopolists almost immediately established a large manufactory at Tonneins. It has been suggested that this move was designed to exploit the persisting reputation of the tobacco formerly grown in the district.[23] This seems improbable; more likely the new establishment was designed simply to create work in an area distressed by the change in government policy and to utilize the considerable pool of skilled labor in the vicinity.[24]

The manufactory at Tonneins proved to be one of the most successful in the country. Although a survey of 1730–32 reported only 400–500 workers were employed there (at wages of from three to twenty *sols* daily),[25] a comparable survey of 1762 reported 600 employees.[26] A generation later, Latapie's surveys of 1778 and 1782 and his report of 1785 mention 1,200 workers,[27] while, by 1789, the number employed had reportedly risen to 1,400–1,500.[28] The manufactory at Tonneins was supposed to supply only Lower Guienne, Gascony, and Béarn, but its product (distinctively marked) was so popular that it was in fact in heavy demand in many other parts of the country. A map in Lavoisier's papers shows Tonneins directly supplying La Rochelle, Poitiers, and Limoges, and indirectly (via Toulouse) serving Perpignan, Lyons, and Grenoble. The farmers-general themselves were curious about this popularity and ordered a comparative test and chemical analysis made in 1758. The report concluded that Tonneins tobacco was identifiably superior to those of other works of the company, but that this superiority could only be ascribed to the local water; a later writer suggested the superior skill of the workmen.[29] When the government inspector of manufactures Latapie visited Tonneins in 1778 and subsequent years, he was less pleased with the quality of the goods produced there. He had heard that the tobacco works were putting cantharides ("Spanish fly") into their snuff. He, however, was strongly opposed to tobacco in any form and his report perhaps ought not to be taken literally.[30]

The manufactory at Toulouse was established in 1722 by the syndicate which subfarmed all the southern provinces from the du Verdier company. When subfarming ceased after 1723, the works were taken over by the Indies Company and later the united farms. However, under both the Indies

Company and the united farms, Toulouse continued to supply the provinces it had supplied under the subfarm: Languedoc, Roussillon, Provence, Dauphiné, the Lyonnais (and later Avignon). Some of the surplus production was sent to Paris.[31] Although formally "founded" in 1722 to supply this larger region, the Toulouse works probably represented some sort of continuation of an older smaller establishment of the subfarmers of Languedoc. In 1737, for an annuity of 1,500 l.t. annually, the united farms purchased from one Pierre Jacob the building on the Rue de la Pomme in which the manufactory at Toulouse was located. Now, one Jacques Jacob de St. Elie had been the dominant figure in the Languedoc subfarm from 1690 to 1718.[32] Even earlier, we noted a snuff works at Toulouse in the 1680's and 1690's. Toulouse thus appears not so much a new foundation in 1722 as the solitary survival of the days of the small subfarms in the south. In the last years of the monopoly, however, it was reduced to a manufactory of smoking tobacco only, chopping up stemmed leaf received from Tonneins and Cette.[33]

The foundation or refoundation of the manufactories at Tonneins and Toulouse in 1721 and 1722 had immediate repercussions upon tobacco traffic in the port of Bordeaux. The works in those towns before 1720 had depended primarily upon locally grown tobaccos. Tobacco planting having been abolished in the Garonne valley in 1719–20, the reestablished manufactories had to depend upon foreign tobaccos imported via Bordeaux. Though insignificant before 1720, tobacco imports became a major activity of that port in the succeeding decades. The data on tobacco imports at Bordeaux furnish us with a valuable index of the combined activity of the establishments at Tonneins and Toulouse.

TABLE II

Tobacco Imports at Bordeaux, 1717–76[34]

Year	From: Britain leaf	Holland leaf	mfd.	snuff	French America mfd.	leaf
			(in French lb. weight)			
1717	—	—	—	2,895	100	—
1718	—	—	200	13,820	—	—
1719	—	45,000	—	30,130	—	9,625
1720	60,000	2,325*	3,025	26	—	215
1721	—	—	6	9,055	—	—
1723	144,000	—	—	—	—	1,000
1724	320,900	—	59,925	—	—	—
1725	40,000	4,500	—	—	—	—
1726	788,250	—	—	—	—	—
1728	409,500	—	—	2,635	—	—
1729	100,000	—	—	4,935	—	—
1730	583,450	6,160	—	51,860	—	—
1731	1,431,825	42,325	14,813	33,560	—	—
1732	3,604,300	—	—	—	—	—
1733	799,865	—	2,870	49,485	—	—

Table II (Continued)

Year	From: Britain leaf	Holland leaf	mfd. (in French lb. weight)	snuff	French America mfd.	leaf
1734	1,604,550	—	—	355	—	—
1735	239,800	—	—	—	—	—
1736	800,200	—	—	—	—	—
1737	1,576,400	181,380	—	—	—	—
1738	1,042,875	—	—	—	—	—
1740	—	40,000	—	680	—	—
1741	2,347,950	—	—	93	550	1,110
1742	5,164,750	—	—	360	—	287,925
1743	3,352,460	3,075	—	—	—	7,800
1744	1,602,050	2,135,375*	—	1,103	—	—
1745	2,701,150	—	—	—	—	140
1746	4,917,493	50,075	20	—	—	—
1747	4,371,578	—	—	—	—	575
1748	3,633,908	—	—	—	—	—
1749	4,346,565	—	—	—	—	99
1750	4,747,161	—	—	—	9,811	—
1751	4,637,168	—	—	—	1,131	183
1752	6,878,031	—	—	—	16,165	—
1753	6,723,685	—	—	—	—	—
1754	5,548,615	—	—	—	—	6,725
1755	3,845,287	—	—	—	—	12,295
1756	939,940	—	—	—	—	—
1757	2,703,222	—	—	—	—	—
1758	5,036,395	—	—	—	—	—
1759	6,479,050	—	—	—	—	—
1760	7,854,680	—	—	—	—	—
1761	7,061,336	—	30	—	—	—
1762	1,495,271	—	—	—	20	—
1763	1,527,850	—	—	—	57	—
1764	5,822,644	—	—	—	—	—
1765	861,640	—	—	—	—	48
1766	2,355,550	—	—	—	—	35
1767	1,937,578	—	—	—	—	20
1768	2,202,075	—	—	—	—	—
1769	3,523,510	—	—	—	—	—
1770	3,367,080	—	—	—	—	—
1771	3,127,205	—	—	—	—	55
1772	4,630,640	—	—	—	50	—
1773	4,885,686	—	—	—	136	—
1774	1,334,600	—	—	—	77	—
1775	1,400,480	—	—	—	—	—
1776	3,442,750	117,782	—	—	134	—

*Virginia tobacco from Holland.

These figures would seem to suggest that although the Tonneins and Toulouse manufactories were organized in 1721-22, imports for them at Bordeaux did not become aggregatively important until after the united farms took over the tobacco monopoly in 1730. Though we cannot be absolutely sure, this may be something of a statistical illusion: the united farms may have reported their imports more fully to the Chamber of Commerce than did the privileged Indies Company. There is other evidence to suggest that considerably more tobacco than is shown in Table II was actually imported at Bordeaux from Britain for the monopoly about 1728-30.[35]

If Tonneins and Toulouse were in reality revivals, much more clearly a new foundation was the manufactory at Le Havre founded by the Indies Company about 1724-26. The existing establishment at Dieppe apparently could no longer itself supply the growing demand in north central France, while the smaller works in Paris made only snuff. Expansion at Dieppe seems to have been out of the question, probably owing to the position of the port, labor troubles there, and frequent quarrels between the monopoly and the municipality over such matters as quay duties and the burning of refuse stalks.[36] Le Havre by contrast was more conveniently situated for traffic up the Seine and its corporation, in order to attract the manufactory, offered to waive all municipal tolls.[37] The new tobacco manufacturing works at Le Havre began operation in an old tennis court until their new buildings were ready for occupation in 1728.[38] Perhaps because labor was relatively expensive (12-60s. per day in 1738), the work force was kept relatively stable, being 503 in 1738 and only 400-500 in 1785-88.[39]

A memoir drawn up by a local antiquary in the early 1740's (before the declaration of war) tells us that from 30 to 35 vessels came annually to Le Havre from London with tobacco for the royal manufactory there. Some smaller amounts came also from Holland.[40] A book published subsequently by the same authority reports that in the immediate postwar years—1749-52—about 6,000 hogsheads were imported there from Great Britain annually in 30 to 40 vessels—besides some 400 basketfuls from Holland.[41] Both these estimates suggest imports at Le Havre from Britain alone of well over five million pounds annually—not impossible, but as estimates probably a bit high. Dardel, the modern authority on the ports of the lower Seine, reports rather lower figures for the whole customs district (*direction*) of Rouen—including both Dieppe and Le Havre (Table III).

In the generation after the united farms took over the monopoly in 1730, there were no further foundations of major new manufactories—though there were significant administrative changes. Following the establishment of King Stanislas in Lorraine in 1737—by French diplomacy and French arms—the united farms of France contracted to lease the tobacco monopoly in Lorraine and its works at Nancy. By the 1780's, this too had been reduced to the manufacture of smoking tobacco, processing stemmed leaf received from Paris.[42] On the other hand, about 1744, the united farms gave up their lease

TABLE III

Tobacco Imports in the Customs District of Rouen[43]

Year	From:	Britain	Holland	Portugal
		(in thousands of French lb. weight)		
1730		2,969	578	—
1732		6,570	379	4
1738		3,446	376	6
1767		3,179	568	—
1769		3,513	866	—
1771		4,068	496	—
1774		301	447	—
1776		[ca. 1,800]	544	—

of the tobacco monopoly and *manufacture* in the principality of Charleville; this seems to have followed upon their taking over in 1738 of the management of the tobacco monopoly in Hainault and its manufactory at Valenciennes from which they could as easily supply French troops in the eastern frontier provinces with *tabac de cantine*.[44] In the 1740's too, the old Paris snuff works was moved to more spacious quarters in the Hôtel de Longueville near the Tuilleries where part of the tobacco administration was also centered. That manufactory came to specialize in a type of snuff called *tabac d'Hollande*.[45]

The area least well served with manufactories at this time was the south, most of which from the Lyonnais to Roussillon was supplied from Toulouse. The small establishments at Arles and Clermont-Ferrand made only snuff and the latter disappears from the record some time after 1750.[46] The old works at Marseilles had a very limited output, primarily of smoking tobaccos. To correct this apparent shortage of manufacturing facilities in the south, the united farms chose in 1751 to establish a new manufactory at Cette (Sète) on the coast of Languedoc.

Although Cette had been a legal port for the exportation of domestic tobacco, 1676-1719, and after the abolition of planting (1719) became one approved for imports, there was very little tobacco traffic of any sort at that port in the first half of the eighteenth century. Accounts of the town's imports during 1717 and during 1732-39 show no tobacco. However, with the establishment of the manufactory there by the monopoly in 1751, Cette became a fixture in the international tobacco trade, receiving ten or more British tobacco ships a year with two million and more pounds of Chesapeake tobacco.[47]

At Marseilles, there was a very ancient tobacco trade going back to the beginning of the seventeenth century. During the earlier part of the eighteenth century, under successive monopolies, this trade languished, being confined to occasional importations of Levant and Spanish tobaccos, largely in entrepôt for reexport.[48] In 1724, for example, total tobacco imports at the port consisted of 1,280 lb. of Spanish snuff and 28,970 lb. of "Levant" tobacco, probably from Salonika.[49] There was a small local manufactory in the port, similar to the snuff works at Arles, which seems to have continued from the days of the subfarms before 1718 through into the days of the United General Farms. It seems to have been most active in the 1740's when perhaps two ships a year were sent from Britain to Marseilles on the monopoly's account. After the opening of the manufactory at Cette, such shipments to Marseilles became rare once again.[50] In the succeeding generation—the zenith of the age of snufftaking—the Marseilles establishment was used only to make a special mixture of Virginia and Levant tobacco for smokers![51] It appears to have ceased processing operations about 1774, with the manufacture of smoking tobacco transferred to Toulouse.

It is rather difficult from the above French data to get any clear idea of the relative importance over time of the various manufacturing establishments of the united farms or of their changing scale of operations. We have found figures for the number of workers employed in some of the works, but not all—and then only for isolated years. Except for Bordeaux and Morlaix, the French port traffic data are also for isolated years only. From accounts of the destinations of British exports, we can, however, get a rough idea of the ranking and activity of the several French manufactories at certain periods.

TABLE IV

Shipments of Tobacco from England to Various French Manufactories
1 October 1728–30 September 1730[52]

	1728–29		1729–30	
	hhds.	*lb.*	*hhds.*	*lb.*
Dieppe	1,436	860,273	2,137	1,498,331
Morlaix	1,468	914,272	3,420	2,465,317
Le Havre	2,031	1,288,438	2,697	1,880,062
Tonneins	2,419	1,547,639	2,153	1,602,170
Charleville	487	294,028	603	403,690
Total	7,841	4,904,650	11,010	7,857,570

The Le Havre figure undoubtedly included material intended for Paris while that for Tonneins included leaf for Toulouse (shipped up the Garonne from Bordeaux by way of Tonneins). If we assume that one-third of the tobacco shipped to Tonneins ultimately went to Toulouse, then we can see that as of 1728–30 the new manufactories of the south had not yet surpassed the older established works of the north.

When we come to the wars of the midcentury, we get a reasonably clear idea of the relative ranking of the French manufactories by the destinations specified in the passes issued by the British government. A crude measurement can be obtained by counting the number of passes or ships

TABLE V

Destinations of Vessels Licensed by the British Government
(Under the Great Seal) to Carry Tobacco to France in Wartime

A. *War of the Austrian Succession, 18 September 1745 to 12 May 1748*[53]

Year	Bordeaux	Morlaix	Dieppe	Le Havre	Marseilles	Dunkirk	Total
1745	0	2	5	5	1	0	13
1746	18	3	12	13	0	0	46
1747	3	10	27	19	2	2	63
1748	15	5	5	12	4	0	41
1745–48	36	20	49	49	7	2	163

B. *The Seven Years' War, 1 June 1756 to 12 November 1762*[54]

Year	Bordeaux	Morlaix	Dieppe	Le Havre	Marseilles & Dunkirk	Cette	Total
1756–57	14	13	15	11 (12)	0	0	54
1758	14	17	10	18	0	1	60
1759	21	6	25	10	0	5	67
1760	29	23	49	0	0	5	106
1761	5	0	25	0	0	6	36
1762	0	10	32	0	0	9	51
1756–62	83	69	156	39 (40)	0	26	374

(Table V). A clearer picture of the relative manufacturing activity in different parts of France can be obtained by ignoring annual fluctuations and calculating not ships but the total number of hogsheads licensed for export in each war (Table VI). Shipments for Bordeaux, it should be remembered, were intended primarily for the manufactory at Tonneins, secondarily for that at Toulouse.

Tables V and VI would suggest that although absolute activity was rising at Bordeaux (for Tonneins and Toulouse) and at Cette, the relative

TABLE VI

Number of Hogsheads of Tobacco Licensed for Shipment by British
Government to Various French Ports in Wartime[55]

	1745–48	*1756–62*
Bordeaux	12,130	26,285
Morlaix	7,110	19,145
Dieppe	16,299	44,605
Le Havre	17,118	11,855
Marseilles	2,044	—
Cette	—	9,430
Dunkirk	700	—
Total	55,401	111,320

TABLE VII

Ports of Destination of Tobacco Shipped from Glasgow
(Port Glasgow and Greenock) in 1743 and 1771

	1743[56]	*1771*[57]
	(in English lb. weight)	
Dieppe	912,261	1,180,023
Le Havre	2,446,590	4,918,784
Seine ports total	3,358,851 (72%)	6,098,807 (39%)
Morlaix	1,310,993	4,629,569
Bordeaux	—	3,150,875
Cette	—	1,683,007
Marseilles	—	198,469
French total	4,669,844	15,760,727
(Dunkirk)	*84,476*	*5,014,116*
(France plus Dunkirk)	*4,754,320*	*20,774,843*

preeminence of the northern centers was still unchallenged. In both wars, more than half the passes issued and hogsheads licensed were for the Norman ports of Dieppe and Le Havre. (Because of the British blockade of Le Havre, shipments for both ports in the last years of the war had to be sent to Dieppe.[58]) This pattern suggests that Paris and the Seine valley still dominated French consumption.[59] The concentration, however, was gradually breaking down as southern consumption and manufacture developed. This dispersal can be detected by examining the destinations of Glasgow exports to France, 1771, and of French purchases from all sources, 1778–79 (Tables VII, VIII).

The principal manufacturing procedures can be briefly described. They were common to all the larger establishments of the monopoly. The

TABLE VIII

Manufactories of Destination of Tobacco Purchased by the
Farmers-General, October 1778–September 1779[60]

	(in French lb. weight)
Paris	3,407,597
Le Havre	4,705,258
Dieppe	4,558,166
Seine area total	12,671,021 (41%)
Morlaix	5,854,106
Tonneins (via Bordeaux)	5,146,905
Toulouse (via Bordeaux)	3,442,423
Cette	3,624,834
Valenciennes	264,880
French total	31,004,169

tobacco arrived at the manufactory in hogsheads weighing, by 1770, up to 1,050 French lb. or 1,150 English lb.—though 1,000 English lb. was about average. After the hogshead was opened, a master workman went through the contents tossing the "hands"—bunches of leaves tied together—into three heaps according to quality: the best for *andouille supérieure;* the middling for *andouille ordinaire, Virginie pressé,* and *demi-andouille;* and the "third sort" for *tabac de cantine* for the troops. The tobacco was then delivered to the manufactory proper where each master spinner had his own table with a crew of about seven: one or two women sorters (*plieuses, robeuses*) who sorted the leaves, picking out the best for wrappers (*robes*) when special Dutch leaf was not purchased for this purpose; one or two boy stemmers (*écoteurs*) who cut out the midribs on the ordinary leaf given to them by the *robeuses;* a rover or slubber (*boudinier, bougieur*) who twisted the stemmed leaf fragments into rough rovings (*boudins, bougies*); a boy *donneur de feuilles* who smoothed out the individual wrapper leaves and passed them to the spinner; the master spinner himself (*fileur*) who wrapped the outside leaf over the rovings and fed the continuous cord into the machine; a laborer (*tourneur, torqueur*) who turned the wheel (*tour de fer*) which spun the tobacco. The master spinner was paid a flat sum for the daily quota of his table (100 to 150 lb.) plus so much per pound extra for any excess production; his assistants were paid by the day only. (The subsequent processes of manufacture employed primarily unskilled labor on day wages for rolling and unrolling the spun tobacco, cutting it up, and operating the great presses.)

The first operation at spinning was to untie the hands and brush off the dirt. Then after sorting, the midribs were cut out by the stemmer. The tobacco was then wetted and left to sit on racks for two or three days to absorb the moisture and become suppler. It was then spun and wound onto rolls of 20 to 70 lb. each. The cheap variety known as *Virginie pressé* (used for smoking) was passed under rollers after spinning and wound onto smaller rolls; it was then ready for sale off the roll. The other varieties were usually described as spun *à l'andouille,* i.e., "stuffed rolls," probably because of the relationships of the bigger outer wrapper leaves to the scrappier materials inside. They required further manufacture. When ready, the entire roll might be dumped into a vat containing an appropriate "sauce" and then allowed to ferment for about four or five days. The roll was then unwound and cut into pieces, or strands, twenty inches (*pouces*) long. A number of these strands (as few as two or three in cheap *cantine* or *demi-andouille,* but from five to eight in *supérieure*) were then placed in sets of molds which were placed under presses for from 24 to 48 hours depending on thickness. (These great presses took from eight to fifteen men to operate.) The product which came out of the press was known as a *carotte*. At the beginning of the century it was sold in that form. From the 1720's onward, however, to make the *carotte* firmer for rasping into snuff, it was next wound round with a string

Table IX

Input and Output of the Manufactories at Tonneins and Le Havre, 1786 and 1789[61]

A. The Spinning Works (Fabrique en Rolles)

	Tonneins (1786)	Le Havre (1789)
(1) Input	lb.	lb.
Virginia leaf	2,873,080	3,655,495
Maryland leaf	86,135	366,088
Amersfort leaf	325,432	157,498
Other Dutch leaf	77,298	372,432
Miscellaneous	—	9,439
Weight added by moistening	155,726	150,720
Sticks, paper, string, etc.	—	12,885
Total	3,517,671	4,724,557
(2) Output		
Rolls: *andouille supérieure*	898,360	1,138,661
Rolls: *andouille ordinaire*	2,695	247,843
Rolls: *demi-andouille*	—	64,171
Rolls: *tabac menufilé*	5,998	—
Rolls: *tabac de cantine*	57,530	95,020
Scaferlati (smoking tobacco)	42,210	—
Stemmed leaves	1,634,698	2,018,880
Midribs	805,565	1,026,806
Spoilage	66,345	115,276
Sweepings	4,270	17,900
Total	3,517,671	4,724,557

B. The Carotte-making Works (Fabrique du Ficelage)

	lb.	lb.
(1) Input		
Rolls: *andouille supérieure*	827,081	897,035
Rolls: *andouille ordinaire*	—	22,767
Rolls: *demi-andouille*	—	62,835
String for wrapping *carottes*	13,528	16,750
Weight gained in manufacture	1,001	—
Total	841,610	999,387
(2) Output		
Pieces bound in string *(tabac ficelé)*	841,610	995,126
Sweepings	—	1,594
Loss in manufacture	—	2,667
Total	841,610	999,387

along its full length. The *carotte* wound in string was known as *tabac ficelé:* in an age when almost everyone took snuff, it was for decades the principal product of the monopoly.

The entire manufacturing process was characterized by elaborate controls and account-keeping to see that work norms were met and that no pilfering took place. Even the midribs cut out by the stemmers were carefully weighed and inventoried and periodically burned with all the precautions one might associate with the destruction of old paper money[62] (the ashes being sold for the profit of the local inspectors). The farmers-general, fearful of their reputation, refused to use the midribs in manufacture, although in both Britain and Holland, these cuttings (called "stems" in America and "stalks" in Britain) were widely used to make snuff and cheap smoking tobacco. About 1774, a company offered to buy from the united farms for export all the midribs then being burned.[63] During the American War, when tobacco became scarce and expensive, the united farms in fact ordered burning stopped and the midribs saved—ostensibly for export, but conceivably for domestic use.[64]

The only surviving detailed accounts of physical input and output for the manufactories of the monopoly are from the 1780's. For comparative purposes, we have extracted the data for Tonneins in 1786 and Le Havre in 1789. Separate accounts were kept for each stage of the manufacture (Table IX).

In the last generation before the French Revolution, the united farms, as a measure to check fraud, began to make increasing quantities of their own snuff—rather than let the consumer rasp his own from a *carotte* or the re-

TABLE X

Input and Output of the Snuff-Grinding Works at
Tonneins, 1780–81, 1785–86, and 1789[65]

	Oct. 1780–Sept. 1781	Oct. 1785–Sept. 1786	1789
		(1) Input	
	lb.	lb.	lb.
Spun tobacco (*Andouille supérieure*)	1,387,398	—	—
Defective *carottes*	—	3,754	—
Leaf chopped up	285,695	1,177,336	1,488,235
Scraps	1,553	—	—
Contraband seized	10,949	8,009	—
Total	1,685,595	1,189,099	1,488,235
		(2) Output	
Snuff (*rapé*)	1,597,777	1,137,920	1,424,816
Tobacco dust	2,744	5,810	6,658
Loss in manufacture	85,074	45,369	56,761
Total	1,685,595	1,189,099	1,488,235

tailer rasp it for him. (We shall discuss the administrative considerations involved in Chapter 17.) To supply the great quantities of snuff needed, snuff works were started or revived at some of the principal manufactories. At first they made snuff from roll tobacco much as a small retailer might do. In the 1780's, they began making the snuff directly from leaf in the British fashion. The results can be seen in the large output of "stemmed leaves" in Table IX (page 424) not made into roll. The changeover can be seen more closely by comparing the input data at Tonneins (the only snuff works for which we have exact data) for 1781 and 1786. Notice the disappearance of spun tobacco as an input (Table X, page 425).

Despite this impressive volume, the snuff-grinding operations of the monopoly remained essentially manual in technique and power until the end of the farmers-general. (At Morlaix in 1752, huge stone mortars were used which took four men to operate.) By contrast, contemporary snuff-grinders in Dunkirk used equipment driven by windmills while those in England and Scotland had banks of mortars and pestles driven by watermills. In the 1770's and 1780's, the farmers-general (and Lavoisier in particular) were experimenting with large, more efficient snuff-grinding machines, though the designs still called for man or horse power.[66]

From the above accounts we get a fairly clear idea of the activity of some of the larger manufactories of the monopoly on the eve of the French Revolution. The place of their individual output in the total operations of the monopoly is more difficult to establish. We do know that about 1788–89, the monopoly was buying about 24–25 million lb. of leaf annually from which it sold about 15–16 million lb. of manufactured tobacco. The balance was accounted for by spoilage and loss of weight in transport and storage, and wastage in manufacture. For 1789, the following sales figures are reported:[67]

snuff (company ground)	8,514,829 lb.
tabac ficelé (to be rasped into snuff by consumer)	4,320,591 lb.
smoking tobacco (roll)	2,213,957 lb.
Total	15,049,377 lb.

What such figures meant for the earnings of the monopoly is hard to say for we have virtually no detailed accounts of costs. The nearest we can get are some summary data for 1756–60 (Table XI).

It will be seen at once that, of the purely commercial expenses of the tobacco monopoly, by far the most important was the prime cost of the raw material. Direct expenditures on manufacturing (primarily for labor) were relatively secondary. Transport alone in the said account came to almost as much as all direct manufacturing costs. Overland transport was very slow and five times more expensive than water carriage: for example, it took 16 days and cost the monopoly 6 *l.t.* 10 *s.* per quintal to send tobacco overland

Table XI
Summary Accounts of the Tobacco Monopoly, 1756–60[68]

	1756–57	1757–58	1758–59	1759–60
		(in *livres tournois*)		
Receipts (gross)	32,412,907	33,422,316	26,059,080	28,749,021
Expenses:				
a. Administration, distribution & guards	4,085,722	4,067,734	3,849,891	3,824,177
b. Purchases	4,182,708	7,136,260	7,404,266	5,809,215
Transport	788,602	1,076,524	918,848	1,422,402
Manufacturing	1,064,229	1,010,470	906,180	990,054
Total (b)	*6,035,538*	*9,223,254*	*9,229,294*	*8,221,672*
c. Lease of farms in frontier territories	252,759	252,750	252,382	252,854
d. Bad debts, etc.	145,429	51,399	—	358,348
Total expenses (a–d)	10,519,449	13,595,137	13,331,567	12,657,052
Gross Profit	21,893,458	19,827,179	12,727,513	16,091,969
Total expenses and profit	32,412,907	33,422,316	26,059,080	28,749,021

from Paris to Moulins; but cost them only 12 *l.t.* 12 *s.* per *1,000* lb. to send the same by river from Orléans to Nantes—approximately the same distance.[69] Nevertheless, in time of war, when coastal shipments were excessively risky, overland transport would have to be used more. In the table above, transport costs jumped markedly in 1760 when Le Havre was blockaded by the British fleet. However, a perennial and much greater expense was the cost of the elaborate establishment of guards, inspectors, auditors, and the like required by a monopoly. The above account would suggest rather graphically that the two overwhelming concerns of the monopoly should have been: (1) its raw material supply; and (2) its great administrative effort to suppress smuggling and maximize legitimate consumption.

The Organization of the Monopoly, 1730–91

The United General Farms of France was one of the most elaborate and efficient bureaucratic organizations in the *ancien régime*. (Whenever we stumble upon one of their letters in the records of some government department, we are struck by its modern appearance—the letter numbered in four figures, the department and subdepartment carefully noted in the heading, etc.) A book on the tobacco monopoly is not the place for a full description of the many cells of that complex organism.[70] Suffice it to say that the regime

GENERALITIES AND
INTENDANCIES
1789

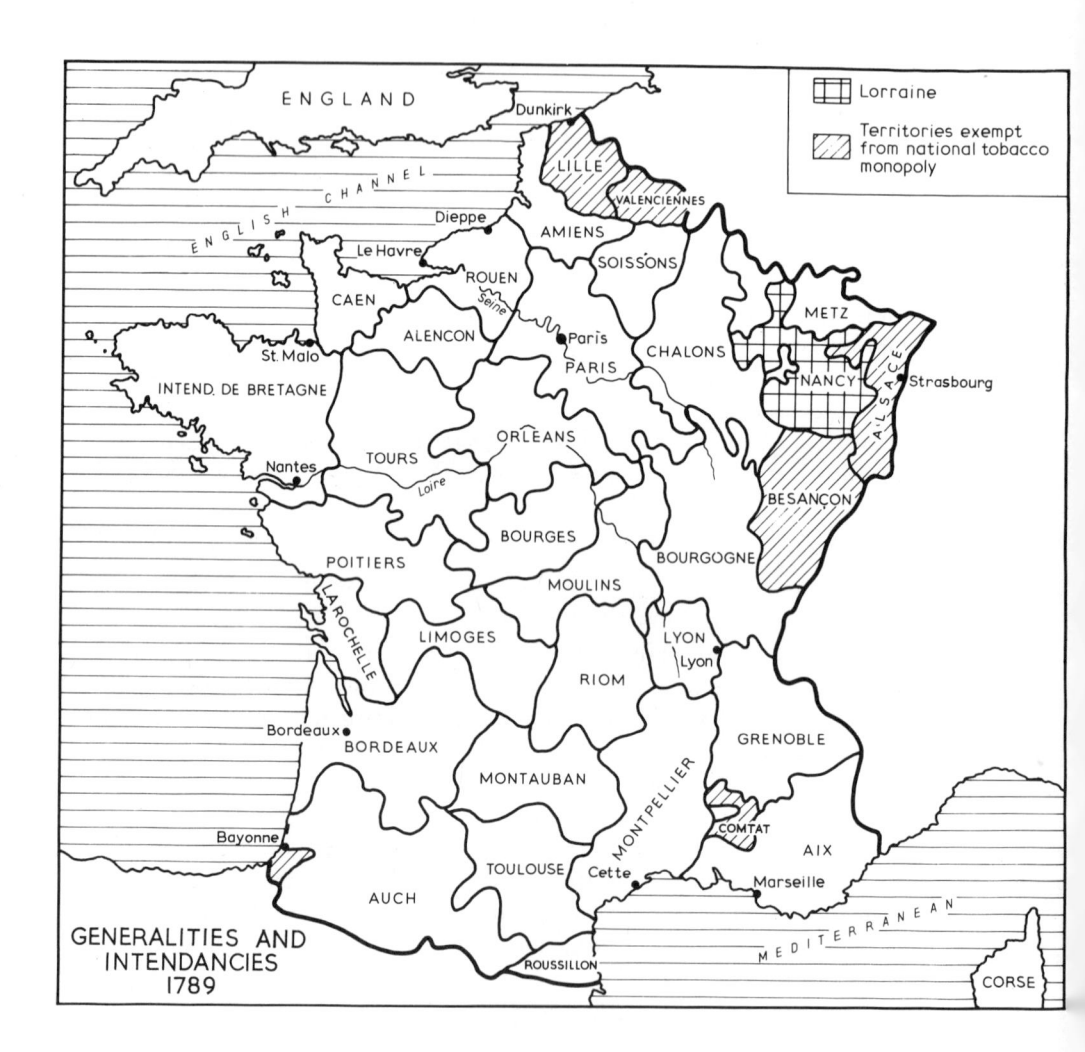

of departmental organization, correspondence and tours of inspection to which the tobacco monopoly was subject was characteristic of that prevailing through the other sections of the united farms as well.

Very little business of the united farms was handled in the full assemblies of the forty or (after 1756) sixty farmers-general. Instead, the work of the farms was quite naturally divided into *départements,* each under the supervision of an *assemblée* or committee of the company. The membership on these committees was decided by the controller-general and legally established by an *arrêt du conseil.* In most cases, it is to be presumed, the controller-general merely accepted the departmental assignments suggested by the leaders of the company—but this did not always have to be. Boullongne advanced his nephew, the younger Roslin, and the abbé Terray did as much for his niece's husband, Jacques Paulze.[71] Nevertheless, despite frequent changes in the controller-generalship, there was remarkable continuity in the membership of the committees of the united farms. Although some lesser figures were transferred about after two to four years on a given committee, the important members—the ones who made the decisions and did the work—remained on the same committees for decades. For example, Lallemant de Betz served on the tobacco committees continuously from the time the monopoly was taken over by the united farms in 1730 until 1758; Dangé from 1756 to 1777; the younger Roslin from 1756 to 1787; and de Saint Amand, the last head of the company and of tobacco, from 1769 to 1791. Many other such examples could be given.[72]

The number and responsibility of the committees of the company were frequently changed. Throughout, however, there was always one committee charged with general supervision of all the affairs of the company and its dealings with the government. It was technically a general auditing committee, but can be readily identified, despite changing titles, as the first committee on all printed lists. Informally it was commonly styled the *caisses* before 1780 and the *comité d'administration* thereafter. From 1721 onward, under *régie* as well as *ferme,* this committee was headed by Jean François de la Porte, the son of a farmer-general, a farmer-general himself since 1695 and head of the united farms, *circa* 1726–43. In the 1730's and 1740's, there was also a Fifth Committee charged with dealing with provincial estates and *chambres des comptes,* whose membership was identical with that of the First Committee.

When the tobacco monopoly was taken over by the united farms, in 1730, its supervision was divided among three committees. First and foremost, a committee was set up to supervise the purchasing of tobacco, the manufacturing establishments and the shipment of processed tobacco from the works to the distribution centers all over the country. (We shall henceforth refer to this as the Purchasing Committee.) Significantly, its membership was identical with that of the First (and Fifth) Committees, i.e., the most important people in the company. Like the First Committee, it was headed by de la Porte, the leading farmer-general. Thus, from the very first, responsibility for buying millions of *livres* worth of tobacco abroad and employing thousands of persons to manufacture it in France was placed at the very center of the company. Although the identical First, Fifth and Purchasing Committees were filled with farmers-general of great seniority (de la Porte, Le Normant, Chevalier, Desvieux, de Lalive, Lallemant de Betz, in particular), it was necessary to add to them two newcomers, Bonnevie and de la Gombaude, who had been active in the previous tobacco monopolies of 1721–30 and who could furnish both experience and continuity.

In addition to the Purchasing Committee, an even larger committee (19 members) was set up to supervise the *régie* or administration of the tobacco monopoly. Its duties included supervision of the numerous regional and local distribution centers, the retailers, the inspectorate and guards of the company, and the collection of receipts. This committee, hereafter referred to as the (Tobacco) Administrative Committee, was headed by Lallemant de Betz. Finally there was a smaller committee (eleven members), headed by Bonnevie, charged with the "examination of the general and particular accounts of the tobacco monopoly." Most but not all of the members of this Tobacco Auditing Committee were also members of the Administrative Committee. Five farmers-general (Lallemant de Betz, Bonnevie, Mazade, Darlus, and de la Gombaude) were members of all three tobacco committees (Purchasing, Administration, Auditing). Of them, Lallemant de Betz seems to have been the dominant spirit in the management of the tobacco monopoly from 1730 till some time before his death in the late 1750's. (He had earlier been interested in the du Verdier tobacco monopoly company of 1721–23.) All surviving letters of these decades from the united farms to the government concerning tobacco are signed by Lallemant de Betz. (He succeeded de la Porte as head of the united farms, ca. 1743, but was removed by the controller-general Machault, ca. 1749, in favor of the more compliant Bouret.)[73]

These arrangements of 1730 for the tobacco monopoly survived substantially unchanged until 1756. In 1744, however, to the three existing committees responsible for the tobacco monopoly, a fourth was added for the supervision of all activities in Paris, including manufacture and distribution. As all the members of this new, small Paris Committee were also members of the Administrative Committee, this reorganization probably amounted to little more than adding an extra meeting weekly to give special attention to the metropolis.[74] During these same years, there were of course subtler changes in the committees arising from changes in personnel. Of the five key members on all tobacco committees in 1730–32, de la Gombaude died in 1732 and Bonnevie in 1733, and Mazade retired from the committees in 1743 (and died in 1750) with Darlus following him in 1748. As those above them died or retired, more junior farmers-general, who had hitherto only been on the big tobacco Administrative Committee, by seniority acquired further positions on the more important Purchasing Committee (identical with the key First Committee): Le Riche, Perrinet, Grimod de la Reynière, Le Monnier, Hocquart, and others. Perrinet did not reach the Purchasing Committee till 1743, but in 1749–50 replaced Lallemant de Betz as head of that as well as of the Administrative, Auditing and Paris Committees. Etienne Perrinet retained this preeminent position in tobacco until 1762, though he did not head Purchasing after 1756.

The stability which characterized the administration of the tobacco monopoly within the united farms from 1730 to 1756 came to an end during the Seven Years' War. We have already noticed how the war disrupted French finances and through the supplementary levy of 1758 interrupted the steady, prosperous growth of the yields of the tobacco monopoly. The new age of financial stress had also to be an age of experimentation and financial improvisation. The changing character of administration was marked by the sudden elevation by the controller-general Boullongne of his nephew, the younger Roslin (who had just succeeded his father as farmer-general), to the headship of the Tobacco Purchasing Committee in 1758. Under de la Porte, Lallemant de Betz, and Perrinet, prosperity had paid great deference to seniority; now, crisis shook the ladder, letting agile newcomers scramble much more quickly to the top.[75]

From 1756 onward, we also find much more frequent changes in the distribution of functions among committees of the united farms. Only two committees concerned with the tobacco monopoly—the Administrative and Auditing Committees—remained substantially unchanged in function from 1756 down to 1791. The special Paris Committee was abolished in 1758 and then reestablished in 1768 as a special committee for tobacco and *aides* (excise duties) in the city and *plat-pays* of Paris; this joint Paris committee was in turn abolished in 1772, only to be resurrected in another Paris Tobacco Committee for the lease of 1774–80. Similarly, the severe crisis which the united farms experienced in 1770 led to the appointment of a small special committee "for the improvement of the tobacco administration throughout the kingdom." In personnel, it was really a subcommittee of the Administrative Committee and lasted only two years.

The most strategic committee was of course the Purchasing (and Manufacturing) Committee and it had the most erratic career of all. In 1756, when the company of the United General Farms was expanded from forty to sixty members, it was apparently felt that some sort of stronger central direction was needed to coordinate the varied activities of the now more diffusely composed company. The Tobacco Purchasing Committee, among others, was abolished and its functions transferred to the First Committee charged with responsibility for "all the most important business." This committee of twenty, nominally headed by the aged Lallemant de Betz, had to meet four times a week to carry out its varied functions. This arrangement apparently proved unsatisfactory for the next year a separate Tobacco Purchasing Committee was reestablished, at first under Jean-François de la Borde, but from 1758 under the younger Roslin. Throughout, substantially the same people remained responsible for the same areas of decision.

In 1759, the remaining functions of the First or supervisory Committee were divided between two committees with identical membership. During the lease of 1762–68, the separate Tobacco Purchasing Committee was once more abolished and its purchasing functions transferred to the new First or Audit Committee while the supervision of the tobacco manufactures and personnel was relegated to the identical Second or Operations Committee. During the first four years of the Alaterre lease of 1768–74, a separate tobacco purchasing committee was once more reestablished, though the supervision of the manufacture was left with the General Operations Committee: during the last two years of the lease, 1772–74, the separate tobacco purchasing committee was abolished and the responsibilities reunited with those of the manufactures in the Second or General Operations Committee. During the Laurent David lease of 1774–80, a return was made to the practice of 1762–68, with the First or Audit Committee of the company in charge of tobacco purchases and the Second or Operations Committee in charge of the tobacco manufactures. As before, both committees had the same members. During the Salzard (1780–86) and Mager (1786–) leases, these same arrangements persisted, except that Operations now became the First Committee and the other supervisory functions (including tobacco buying and relations with the ministry) placed second.

Throughout all these changes, one fact remained constant: though the routine administration of the tobacco monopoly might be relegated to some of the younger and less important members of the company, the decisions about purchases and personnel were made by the inner circle of senior farmers-general who were the political powers in the society. Of these, the most important for our purposes after the departure of Lallemant de Betz in 1758 and Perrinet in 1762 were the younger Roslin (1758–87), Paulze more briefly in the 1770's, and Saint-Amand in the 1780's.

Below the levels of the farmers-general, active or *fainéants,* who served on the supervisory committees were the senior employees of the company or *directeurs* who headed the various departments. Of them we know even less. One Sonnois who had been General Cashier of the Tobacco Administration under the Indies Company continued to appear in the *Almanach Royal* from 1730 to 1759 as *chef de bureau* or *directeur* for tobacco accounts. Not until 1750–51 was he joined there by Mahieu as *directeur* for tobacco generally and by Fournier as *directeur* for tobacco manufacture and supply. Jean-Baptiste-Louis Fournier, an employee from the Indies Company's time, who under cover of tobacco purchases had managed diplomatic communications with Great Britain during the war of 1744–48, became a farmer-general in 1756. (He and Desmarest were the only employees of the tobacco monopoly so to rise after the death of de la Gombaude in 1732, though several had risen to the rank of *fermier-général* earlier.)

From 1757, we find *directeurs* for four separate offices within the tobacco monopoly: (1) the tobacco monopoly generally; (2) accounts;[76] (3) foreign correspondence and purchases; (4) manufacture and supply of regional distribution centers. Some of these offices were headed by a single *directeur*, others by two or three *directeurs* acting jointly. In 1761, the general office (1, above) disappeared, only to reappear in 1764 as a general administrative office, along with a new office for Paris and vicinity. With minor changes, these five offices persisted until the end of the monopoly. After 1746, the headquarters of those departments concerned with the manufacture and transport of tobacco were consolidated at the Hôtel de Longueville (where the Paris manufactory was also moved) acquired for that purpose, but other departments seem (from the *Almanach Royal*) to have remained at the Hôtel des Fermes, where their operation could be coordinated with those of other branches of the farms.[77]

Below the level of the central administration, the entire country was divided by the united farms into districts called *directions*. These often but not always coincided with the *généralités* or intendancies into which France was divided for purposes of royal administration. Thus, though there were only 31 or 32 *généralités*, there were 41 to 45 *directions*. In each, there were usually two *directeurs*, one in charge of *traites, gabelles et tabacs* (import duties, salt and tobacco monopolies), the other in charge of the remaining revenues farmed (excises, stamp duties, etc.). Immediately below the *directeur* for tobacco and associated revenues in each *direction* were usually one or two (but sometimes three or four) general auditors and inspectors styled *contrôleurs-généraux*, each in charge of an area or *contrôle-général*. For tobacco, each *direction* within the monopoly's jurisdiction was also divided into two or more districts or *recettes générales*, each centered upon a *bureau-général* or regional distribution center. (A *recette générale* of the tobacco monopoly was normally coterminous with a single *contrôle-général* of the united farms, but sometimes included two *contrôles-généraux*.)[78] To the *bureaux-généraux*, tobacco was carried directly from the manufactories by private carriers under contract to the monopoly.[79] In classic fashion, the principal officers at each such *bureau* were a receiver-general in immediate charge (at ca. 1,200–1,500 *l.t.* p.a. in the 1780's), and a controller (at ca. 800–1,200 *l.t.* p.a.) who kept a parallel set of books and acted as a check upon the activities of the receiver-general. (The controller's functions were not strenuous and the position seems to have been used partly for the semi-retirement of old, valued employees.) Each *bureau-général* in turn supplied tobacco to a half dozen or more local distribution offices or *entrepôts*, each in charge of an officer called an *entreposeur*. Unlike the higher officials, the *entreposeurs* received not a salary but a commission to cover both their remuneration and their expenses (rent, transport, etc.).[80]

Virtually every market town had an *entrepôt* of the tobacco monopoly. Members of the public who wanted to buy their tobacco in quantities of a pound or more at a time could buy directly from these *entrepôts*. Most, however, preferred to buy in smaller quantities from the licensed retailers scattered through town and country. These last were not employees of the monopoly, but private shopkeepers authorized to sell tobacco under conditions prescribed by the monopoly. The company was anxious to see that there were enough retailers in the villages so that country people would not deal with smugglers as a matter of convenience.[81] They were also concerned to see that there were not too many retailers in any given town lest some of them, earning too little, be driven by want to buy from smugglers. Elaborate surveys of retailers were made. Among the few documents of the farm that have survived is a map of the town of Rethel in the 1780's showing the location of each current and suppressed licensed retailer.[82] For the much greater city of Nantes, we have a detailed report of 1778 giving the name, address, and character of each of sixty licensed retailers in that great port. Some sold only tobacco; others were grocers and the like. A few were former employees of the monopoly. The list also noted neighborhoods where there were too many or too few retailers.[83] In the country as a whole, there were in 1774 40 *directions*, 55 *bureaux-généraux* for tobacco, and 553 *entrepôts*; by 1782, the last had grown to 556 serving 43,000 retailers.[84]

The entire system was intensively regulated and supervised. Licensed retailers received printed instructions, which included what records they were to keep and the manner in which they were to display and store their tobacco.[85] It was the duty of the *entreposeur* or officer-in-charge of each local distribution office to visit periodically each licensed retailer in his jurisdiction. The same retailers might be visited at other times by lesser officials and guards of the monopoly.[86] In Paris, there was a special *controlleur-ambulant* assisted by a squad of town agents (*commis-parville*) who went about in pairs visiting licensed retailers. The *controlleur-ambulant* had to make written weekly reports to the *directeur* in charge of Paris.[87] In the provinces, the controllers-general in each *direction* had similarly to visit periodically each *entrepôt* in their jurisdiction and to examine books there. The books themselves were sent up annually to Paris for audit. At the next higher level, the *directeur* in charge of tobacco in each *direction* was not only expected to visit and inspect at least four times yearly every *bureau-général*, *entrepôt* and retail establishment in his *direction*, but also was responsible for the mobile guards who scoured the countryside looking for smugglers, searching vehicles along the roads and visiting rural retailers. The guards too had to keep detailed records of all seizures and the *directeur* was responsible for seeing that these seizures were duly prosecuted.[88]

Despite the elaborate system of controls which thus existed on paper, administration was always difficult. If the retailers were constantly tempted by fraud, the employees of the monopoly seem more afflicted by incompetence and indifference. The better-paid officials were chosen through the patronage of individual farmers-general or courtiers and were not easily removed.[89] After 1758, the company did not have a free hand in selecting staff, for each higher employee was required to make a large cash deposit (lent by the company to the crown) in place of the bond formerly given as security. This new system restricted employment in the more responsible positions in the monopoly to those who could raise these large sums.[90] To keep them zealous, the company had to resort to a number of stratagems.

At the lowest level, to make sure that all the 20,000 guards and officers were diligent in making seizures and in reporting and prosecuting them once made (rather than arranging private compositions with the smugglers), the monopoly had long agreed that the value of the tobacco, wagons, or horses seized and condemned be divided among the guards and officers making the seizures, with a share also going to the local director, controller, and receiver. To the sums realized from the seizures, the monopoly itself added cash awards for each smuggler captured, ranging from 3 *l.t.* for a woman or child to 30–50 *l.t.* for an adult male member of an armed band. Starting with the temporary tobacco monopoly of 1721–23, we find frequent elaborate published announcements of the manner in which the proceeds from these seizures and awards were to be distributed.[91]

These arrangements seemed to have caused some grumbling among the guards, who saw no reason why the local director, receiver-general, controller-general, and entreposeur in whose jurisdiction a seizure had been made should share in the rewards when they had incurred none of the risks of the seizure. Therefore, about 1738, the company ordered that henceforth only the guards making a seizure should share in the rewards. A new and subtler system of incentives was adopted for higher officials. By a *délibération* or minute of 1 August 1738, the company ordered that a quota be set for each *entrepôt*, slightly below the average sales of the preceding few years. Thereafter, each manager (*entreposeur*) was to receive a bonus of a certain percentage on all sales exceeding that quota, in addition to his regular commission. A subsequent *délibération* of 18 December 1739 threatened with dismissal all managers who fell short of their quotas, while a still further *délibération* of 5 April 1740 extended the system to higher officials. If the total sales by all the *entrepôts* in a *contrôle-général* exceeded the total quotas for that district, then the controller-general also received a bonus. If the total sales by all the *contrôles-généraux* in a *direction* exceeded the sum of the quotas for that *direction,* then the *directeur* too received a bonus. Such incentives were proportionately higher in the *directions* near the exposed eastern frontier than elsewhere in the kingdom.[92] At the beginning of the La Rue lease in 1744, the system was continued at more generous levels, the highest rates still going to the eastern provinces, followed by rates slightly lower in the maritime provinces, and lower still in the safe inland areas.[93] All these bonuses were in addition to salaries and normal commissions.

When the 20 percent surcharge was imposed on tobacco in 1758, the commissions regularly paid to *entreposeurs* and others for each pound sold automatically went up an equivalent amount. At the same time, as explained in Chapter 14, sales tended to languish in many areas and the monopoly entered a much less profitable era. In recognition of the higher regular commissions, and as a measure of economy, at the start of the Prévost lease in 1762 the bonuses for sales over quotas were abolished. In compensation, annual supplementary payments were made to *directeurs* and controllers-general but not to *entreposeurs* whose regular commissions had benefited from the twenty percent surcharge. At the start of the Alaterre lease in 1768, the regular commissions paid to *entreposeurs* were reduced by one-sixth (i.e., back to what they had been before 1758) but the bonuses for excess sales were reestablished. There was great dissatisfaction over the levels at which the quotas had been set, which allegedly did not reflect changed local conditions: thus, at the beginning of the David lease in 1774, it was again suggested that the bonuses be abolished and higher normal commissions given to the *entreposeurs*.[94] Though we do not have details of later arrangements, one thing is clear in all this: higher prices and relatively stagnant sales after 1758 led also in this matter to a period of constant administrative experimentation, in contrast to the much stabler arrangements that prevailed before 1758.

The central and local administrations of the tobacco monopoly and of the united farms generally were coordinated through two institutions, correspondence and inspection. A single farmer-general was given the responsibility for corresponding with the senior officials of the farms responsible for various branches of the farmed revenues in several *directions*.

Thus, since import duties (*traites*) and the salt and tobacco monopolies were usually linked together, a farmer-general who sat on the administrative (*régie*) committees for those three revenues would usually be charged with corresponding with the *directeurs* responsible for those three revenues in each of several *directions*. An energetic farmer-general might bring under his personal control all details of those revenues in his *directions,* even though his function formally was merely to transmit to the local people the decisions of the respective administrative committees. A less energetic farmer-general must merely have signed documents drafted for him by the *directeurs* of the appropriate *bureaux* in Paris.[95]

The ultimate control was attempted by the tours of inspection which six or eight farmers-general made every year in the provinces. A fair number of the reports from these *tournées* have survived.[96] Some are fatuous in the extreme, filled with such trivia as physical descriptions of the buildings in which the tobacco manufactures were located.[97] Others were very businesslike.[98] What a tour could mean in the tobacco monopoly is very clearly conveyed by a memoir written about 1770 by the farmer-general Jacques Paulze when his son, a future farmer-general, was about to set out on his first tour with the farmer-general Tronchin.

The father began by describing the operation of a manufactory. The inspecting farmer-general must first establish the exact quantities of the input and output of the works. He must ascertain precisely how much weight was lost in transit between the time the tobacco was purchased in Britain and the time it arrived at the factory; how much weight was lost after arrival by dessication through improper storage, by spoilage or by manufacturing operations, and how much added through the moistening. (All this was designed to prevent pilfering being disguised as natural losses.) He was also to check into the number of workers employed in each grade, their wages, and the competence of the supervisors.

At the regional distribution centers (*bureaux généraux*) the visiting farmer-general was to make sure that the tobacco was carefully stored in well-ventilated warehouses; he was to see that all records were properly kept, and that losses of weight in transit or in storage were not unreasonable. He was to determine how much tobacco was supplied monthly to each of the dependent *entrepôts,* and was in particular to make sure that the accounts kept by the receiver agreed with those of the controller. When the farmer-general visited an *entrepôt,* he was to look into much the same details. He was to find out how many retail outlets there were in each town or village, how much each sold annually, and whether sales seemed reasonable in proportion to the size of the place. He was in particular to establish the population of the district served by each *entrepôt,* compare sales within the district year by year, and, by computation per capita, with that in nearby districts. On his travels, the son was finally recommended to converse courteously and attentively with the guards of the farms he met, listen to their complaints and suggestions and make note of them, for, to Paulze, they were the key to the successful administration of the whole.[99]

Paulze's advice to his son to collect detailed statistical information on the population and sales in each area served by a tobacco *entrepôt* was hardly a new idea; such had in fact been the policy and practice of the monopoly for two generations. Ever since the united farms took over tobacco in 1730, the more modern farmers-general on tour had been trying to work out quantitative methods to judge the efficiency of their local administrations.[100] In the early 1730's, in reports like that of Dedelay de la Garde on Poitou, we find data comparing sales in various *entrepôts* during 1731–32 with sales the previous year.[101] The most "scientific" results came, not unexpectedly, from the more learned farmers-general like Dupin and Helvetius.

In the report of the farmer-general Claude Dupin on his tour of the *département* of Châlons-sur-Marne in 1732, we can find pages of material which he subsequently published in his *Oeconomiques*,[102] as well as a most interesting method. He collected population data and tried to calculate probable consumption. Since the use of tobacco was not yet fully established in this interior district, he assumed that none of the women and only half the men took tobacco. Those that did he assumed consumed six pounds annually, a low estimate in his opinion. At that, he had to conclude that fully a third of the consumption in his frontier district was met by smuggling. He made a similar calculation for each *entrepôt* district within the department.[103]

Similar but more extensive data were collected in succeeding years by the farmers-general Fontaine, Helvetius, and Villemur, the first in his 1734 survey of the interior departments or *directions* of Moulins, Clermont, Limoges, Bourges, and Orléans, the latter two in their 1737-39 and 1743-44 surveys of the three *directions* in or attached to Champagne (Châlons-sur-Marne, Charleville, Langres) and the two in Burgundy (Chalon-sur-Saône and Dijon). None of the three attempted to estimate or calculate population, but for the district served by each *entrepôt* recorded simply the number of parishes and hearths or households therein. The number of parishes served usually ranged from 25 to 75, though it could be fewer, particularly in the Massif Central, or much more numerous, when the *entrepôt* was in a large town like Dijon or Orléans. The number of households served by an *entrepôt* ranged from 29,000 for Orléans and 21,000 for Langres down to barely 1,000 in the east, or even less in some rural districts near Orléans. Fontaine, Helvetius, and Villemur also recorded current sales at each *entrepôt*, as well as the figures for the preceding year. They did not attempt, as had Dupin, to calculate what sales ought to have been, but the data in their reports would have made it possible to pinpoint problem areas.[104]

After the sales quota and bonus system was established in 1738, farmers-general on inspection naturally also reported how sales compared to quotas at the various *bureaux généraux* and *entrepôts*.[105] The elaborate forms of data collecting developed in the 1730's by Dupin, Helvetius, and others remained typical of the general farms, if not of all farmers-general, to the end of the *ancien régime*.[106] For the lease of 1774-80, printed forms have survived specifying the number of households served by each of the 553 *entrepôts* and providing blanks for reporting annual sales.[107]

Farmers-general on tour did not of course just collect statistics. Among all the things mentioned in Paulze's memoir to his son, the itinerants seem to have devoted particular attention to the number and distribution of retail shops[108] and to the character and efficiency of the *directeurs* and controllers-general.[109] Some carried their investigations much further—few further than the farmer-general and chemist, Lavoisier. Antoine-Laurent Lavoisier became a farmer-general in 1768 and in 1769 went on an extended tour of inspection in Champagne. For this tour, we have his almost daily letters to the farmer-general Paulze in Paris, his future father-in-law, then charged with the correspondence relating to the tobacco and salt monopolies in that province. Lavoisier sent in the usual reports about personnel and the organization and distribution of the guards along the frontiers. As a more individual touch, he devised a simple chemical test to detect the presence of ash, the most common impurity found mixed in snuff. In each town he visited, he would have an agent posing as a customer buy an ounce or less of each variety of snuff sold by each retailer in the place. These would then be brought to Lavoisier for a test with sulfuric acid (*vitriol*). The ash, if any were mixed in, would immediately identify itself by its burning or sparking. Through these tests, about 20 or 25 percent of the retailers in some town were shown to be deceiving the company and public; many of them were dismissed. More interestingly, such tests suggest the extreme sophistication of the inspection apparatus of the company and of the lengths to which that organization went to protect both its interests and those of the public.[110]

CHAPTER 17

Administrative Problems of the Tobacco Monopoly, 1721–91

Laws and Authorities

The few months in 1720 when, at John Law's advice, the tobacco monopoly had been abolished and the trade thrown open to all constituted something of a break in the legal history of the monopoly. When the "exclusive privilege" was restored in 1720–21, it was found necessary or convenient to provide it with new legal "codes," freshly compiled, if not innovating in content, codifications in fact of all the numerous laws and orders adopted for the tobacco monopoly between the great *ordonnance* of 1681 and the advent of Law.

The *déclaration* of 17 October 1720 reestablished only the import monopoly. Its various clauses reenacted the former regulations designed to prevent tobacco smuggling in ports, along seacoasts and on the land frontiers. The local fiscal courts (*élections*) were reestablished as courts of first instance in all cases concerning the monopoly, with appeal to the regional *cours des aides*.[1] Much more important was the legislation of 1721. Following the refoundation of the full monopoly by the *arrêt* of 29 July, a royal *déclaration* was issued on 1 August establishing general regulations for the entire operation of the tobacco farm: in fact, it was a codification of the legislation of the previous two generations, with minor alterations.[2] For the next seventy years, this *déclaration* of 1721 was the principal piece of legislation cited in all cases concerning the tobacco privilege—just as the *ordonnance* of 1681 had been during the preceding forty years.

The only other general measures for the regulation of the tobacco monopoly were the leases themselves. These spelled out in great detail the rights of the farmers against both the government and their own successors and the terms on which the farm was to operate. They were very important in guaranteeing the property rights of the farm in civil law, but were infrequently cited in criminal cases. Like all good, proven legal documents, the leases of the united farms and of tobacco tended to be quite conservative, repeating the same tested clauses generation after generation.[3]

Although the foundations were thus securely laid, some further pieces of legislation were required to explain or clarify the measures of 1720–21. Some judges, for example, had been remiss or lenient in their interpretations of the criminal code reestablished by the *déclaration* of 1 August 1721. A further *déclaration* had therefore to be issued on 1 March 1723 specifically restoring the full fines and other punishments prescribed by Maynon's *déclaration* of 6 December 1707, even where such conflicted with milder penalties established during the Law interlude.[4]

The *déclaration* of 17 October 1720 had made one important innovation in the criminal code: tobacco smuggling in bands of three or more armed civilians was made punishable by death.[5] Tobacco smuggling in armed bands of soldiers had already been made liable to the death penalty in 1709.[6] Confusingly, a subsequent *déclaration* of 12 July 1723 ordered the death penalty for the smuggling of all commodities into Paris in armed bands of *five* or more;[7] these latter provisions were confirmed and extended to all France in a more general *déclaration* of 2 August 1729. Henceforth, smugglers who used force were to be condemned to death even though they were carrying no contraband at the time of the offense. Employees of the farms who cooperated with smugglers were also to be punished by death. (This clause was enforced in several known cases relating to tobacco.) Lesser crimes against the tobacco monopoly were to be punished at the first offense by three years on the galleys and a 500 *l.t.* fine, and, for a second offense, by the galleys for life and a 1,000 *l.t.* fine. Persons harboring smugglers were to be punished by a 1,000 *l.t.* fine. Since poor peasants likely to be caught under this clause could not pay such a fine, it would normally have been automatically commuted to three or more years on the galleys.[8] Some ambiguity persisting in tobacco offenses, a further *déclaration* of 27 January 1733 was needed to explain that in tobacco cases, either armed participation in an armed band of three, or unarmed participation in an armed band of five, alike incurred the death penalty.[9]

Further criminal legislation was later thought necessary to explain under what conditions persons sentenced to the galleys for offenses against the tobacco and salt monopolies were to be branded,[10] and how persons so condemned for nonpayment of their fines could escape such punishments by late payments;[11] or to provide for the speedier condemnation of animals and vehicles seized in tobacco smuggling cases,[12] and to prohibit the raising of large dogs (*chiens matins*) useful in tobacco or salt smuggling.[13]

In its early days, it will be remembered, the monopoly had had great trouble with corporations and courts of law whose privileges seemed to conflict with those of the farm.[14] After 1721, we find very few traces of such conflicts with municipalities and other corporations.[15] By contrast, conflicts with courts of law continued to be quite numerous, particularly in the 1720's and 1730's. In some cases, the noncooperation of the lower courts went as far as the arrest and prosecution of officers of the monopoly for actions connected with the lawful exercise of their offices. More common were cases in which fiscal courts failed in tobacco cases to levy the fines called for by the law. Orders of council were issued in great number in the 1720's calling upon the crown prosecutors in local courts to explain certain actions of their courts against the employees of the monopoly.[16] Decisions in local courts without fiscal jurisdiction were voided and their officers fined 1,000 *l.t.* for interfering in the affairs of the monopoly.[17] Officers of local fiscal courts were similarly punished for levying fines in tobacco cases far below the high levels established by law (e.g., 30 *l.t.* instead of 1,000 *l.t.*).[18] Other orders merely raised fines to the legal levels.[19] The intervention of still other orders from the Council of State was required to disallow technicalities on which local fiscal courts had discharged or weakened cases brought by the employees of the monopoly,[20] as well as to check the tendency of the same courts to allow the accused illegal delays. (Some courts, for example, were humanely reluctant to convert unpaid fines into galley sentences after the prescribed time had elapsed.)[21] The monopoly's right to the expeditious written legal procedures long granted it had still to be guarded against court encroachments.[22] So did the monopoly's right to keep accused smugglers in prison while it appealed their acquittal.[23]

By the 1740's, decisions on appeal seem to suggest that the law was being quite rigorously enforced: the *cour des aides* of Paris regularly set aside orders of lesser fiscal courts which had been lenient in cases involving only a few pounds of tobacco—a full thousand *livre* fine or the galleys were to be demanded even in cases involving as little as ten ounces of tobacco.[24] Similar orders came from the council[25] and the *parlement* of Brittany.[26] In one extreme case, the full fine was levied for a case involving one ounce of illicit tobacco.[27]

In the years 1750–80, improper decisions by lower fiscal courts in tobacco cases continued to be successfully appealed by the united farms, though the number of printed decisions does not seem to have been as large as during 1721–50. The lower courts seem to have been most difficult in the years after 1763 when the whole judicial order was obstreperous. In these decades, the lower courts caused trouble for the same reasons as before: they refused on technicalities to convict tobacco smugglers or illicit traders,[28] they levied fines below the levels prescribed by law;[29] they harassed the monopoly by trying to force retailers to register their commissions and thus enhance the revenues of their courts.[30]

Although the monopoly's principal troubles were with the local fiscal courts (*élections*), the higher courts were not always fully cooperative either. There was a small flurry of cases in the 1730's in which the monopoly had to appeal from the *cour des aides* of Paris[31] to the Council of State—but these were atypical. More numerous were the cases involving the *cour des aides* of Rouen (Normandy)[32] and Bordeaux (Guienne).[33] These, particularly the Bordeaux cases, frequently involved larger sums of money. The arguments of lawyers were important here, rather than the mere pity for the poor accused shown in many local cases.

The controlling idea in fiscal litigation under the *ancien régime* seemed to be to place cases in courts where they would be most speedily and "sympathetically" handled. Thus, ordinary courts were normally forbidden to hear cases involving the royal revenues which were reserved to the local fiscal courts (*élections*) and on appeal to the higher fiscal courts (*cours des comptes, cours des aides*). When one or more local *élections* seemed inadequate to handle the cases connected with a given branch of the revenue, special procedures might have to be devised to have those cases decided quickly and "correctly." In one bizarre case in 1739, the failure of the officers of the *élection* of Langres (in Champagne) to observe the tobacco regulations induced the Council of State to remove tobacco cases from their cognizance to that of the local salt monopoly magistrates.[34] More frequently, the tobacco monopoly preferred to have its cases heard at higher levels when local benches proved inadequate.

In the years following the reestablishment of the tobacco monopoly in 1721, particularly after the resumption of control by the Indies Company in 1723, we find numerous orders of the Council of State removing specific tobacco cases from *élections* and *cours des aides* and evoking them to the council itself or referring them to the local intendant. The latter usually acted as a special commissioner of the council for that case which he heard assisted by some local magistrates or officials named by himself. (Paris cases were similarly referred to the *lieutenant-général de police*.) Such procedures were most likely to have been used in cases involving riots, physical attacks upon the employees of the monopoly, particularly bold displays of force by smugglers, or egregious disregard of the law by local courts.[35]

It was understandably inconvenient for the Indies Company, every time a difficult tobacco case developed, to have to go to the Council of State for an extraordinary order evoking the case from an inferior court and/or referring it to an intendant. To obviate this awkward necessity, two general orders were obtained in September 1728. One permanently charged the intendants in the northeastern provinces of Ile de France, Picardy, and Champagne with responsibility for trying all cases within their *généralités* involving the smuggling of tobacco and other contraband in armed bands.[36] The other established an extraordinary tribunal consisting of the *lieutenant-général de police* and the magistrates at the Châtelet, Paris, with jurisdiction over certain cases involving the illicit armed traffic in tobacco—primarily in the capital but also in other towns.[37] This authority was extended the following March to include unlimited competence to try as a court of last resort all cases involving contraband (particularly tobacco, salt, and Indian textiles).[38] From time to time, intendants in other provinces received equivalent powers.[39] Other extraordinary commissions (modeled on that of Paris) were set up at Valence on the Rhone in 1733 and at Reims in 1740. The former had jurisdiction over all smuggling cases in the provinces of the southeastern frontier from Burgundy to the Mediterranean; the latter was responsible for the same in the provinces of the eastern frontier: Champagne, Picardy, Soissonnais, and the Three Bishoprics. Both were very successful and highly resented emanations of the *conseil d'état,* independent of the highest regional courts.[40]

These extraordinary tribunals developed during 1728–40 appear to have been adequate for the next generation. Though they heard most serious cases, ordinary petty cases of tobacco fraud continued in most known instances to be tried in the local fiscal courts. From time to time, particularly in the 1730's, orders had to be obtained from the Council of State evoking tobacco cases from such courts and referring them to the intendants.[41] A more difficult period ensued, however, after the 20 percent surcharge was placed on tobacco in 1758. This considerably encouraged fraud just at a time when the finances of the united farms were severely strained. Established procedures again seemed no longer adequate, circumstances calling as before for extraordinary facilities for trial. However, under the milder regime of L'Averdy, such facilities were given more "constitutional" forms.

On 23 August 1764, letters-patent were issued establishing a new special commission to sit at Saumur and, as a court of last resort, try all cases involving contraband traffic in the *généralités* of Bourges, Moulins, and Poitiers (and in Brittany for salt only). In those particular provinces, such a tribunal was probably concerned much more with salt than with tobacco cases. Unlike the independently constituted Valence and Reims commissions, that at Saumur was composed of three members of the *cour des aides* of Paris and local magistrates added as needed.[42] Saumur was to serve as a model in the coming years. By letters-patent of 21 November 1765, the tribunal at Reims was reconstituted to consist of two members of the *cour des aides* of Paris and one member of that of Metz.[43] When this new commission at Reims came into conflict with the *chambre des comptes* of Nancy (for Lorraine), the Council of State by an *arrêt* of 7 March 1773 supported it fully and added Lorraine and the Barrois to its jurisdiction.[44]

The extraordinary tribunal at Reims was well situated to act against the overland smuggling of tobacco along the northeastern frontiers of France. Its jurisdiction was less well defined to check smuggling by sea. As this form of contraband became particularly important in the 1760's, letters-patent of 8 January 1767 provisionally added the three Norman *généralités* (Rouen, Caen, Alençon) to Reims's jurisdiction for two years.[45] This experiment proving only partly successful, further letters-patent of 9 October 1768 established yet another special commission at Caen with equivalent jurisdiction over the three Norman *généralités*. Its members were drawn from the *cour des comptes, aides et finances* of Rouen.[46] Although the continuation of this commission caused great controversies with the *cour des aides* of Rouen, in fact it lasted with unimpaired powers down to the Revolution.[47]

These provincial tribunals had jurisdiction over every form of contraband. Under the rigorous controller-generalship of the abbé Terray, a new special commission was created in 1771 for tobacco cases in Paris and vicinity consisting only of the *lieutenant-général de police,* with the king's attorney (*procureur*) at the Châtelet acting as prosecutor.[48] Under the more constitutional controller-generalship of Turgot, this one-man tribunal was replaced in 1775 by a more usual special commission for tobacco consisting of the *lieutenant-général de police* plus five members of the Paris *cour des aides*.[49]

The united farms seem to have hoped that these extraordinary tribunals would not only facilitate their prosecutions and litigation but would stand as threats of the direst punishment to those contemplating fraud. Many judgments of these special courts, sentencing contrabanders to heavy fines, the galleys, and branding (but none to death), were printed for general distribution. A fair number of these surviving cases involve tobacco, the Paris[50] punishments appearing milder than those at Caen[51] or Reims.[52] Perhaps the most notorious was that at Valence. Surviving records show 765 convictions for contraband between 1733 and 1771: 631 of the condemned were sent to the galleys, 77 to the gallows and 57 ordered broken on the wheel. This averages out as sixteen galley sentences and three and one-half death sentences annually, with perhaps one-half or two-thirds ascribable to tobacco. Even heavier volumes of punishment can be found at the less noted commission at Reims where at least 65 percent of the cases involved tobacco. Out of 140 decisions in the two very busy years, 1741–42, 92 involved tobacco, sending 119 persons (in 68 cases) to the galleys and 17 (15 cases) to death. Activity in the next decade was less than half as heavy but still above the Valence average. Negative evidence would suggest that after the accession of Louis XVI in 1774, both galley and death sentences for smuggling became markedly rarer, the latter almost disappearing by 1789. Even so, the special commissions (sometimes dubbed "chambres ardentes") were regarded as instruments of tyranny and were all abolished on 23 September 1789.[53]

There was nothing extraordinary in the reluctance of the *chambres ardentes* to decree the death penalty in tobacco cases after 1774. By the end of the *ancien régime,* there was a wide gap between the gruesome letter of the "tobacco code" and its enforcement. In the 1780's, Mahy de Cormeré could report that, in an average year, 466 men, 155 women, and 31 children were arrested for tobacco fraud; some 2,903 seizures of tobacco were made, coming to perhaps 200,000 pounds.[54] Yet the results of all this police and legal activity were not what one would assume from reading the texts of edicts and *déclarations*. In a normal year, there were no death sentences and very few commitments to the galleys. Only rarely too was the full fine of 1,000 *l.t.* levied. In the average case, the arrested person proving to be without means, a local philanthropist would come forward and offer to pay a composition of 200–300 *l.t.* (£8–12 sterling) to save the arrested from the galleys; the offer was usually accepted by the courts. These local humanitarians were in fact the "protectors" of the smugglers, i.e., the persons (often respectable local businessmen) who hired them to do the smuggling and who profited by their fraud. The reformers of the 1780's were unwilling to advocate more frequent use of the galleys, though one suggested higher fines in the more serious cases.[55]

Smuggling by Sea, 1718–91

Whatever initial difficulties the tobacco monopoly, after its restoration in 1721, may have had with the fiscal courts of the country, it is clear that, after 1728, in the intendants and special commissions, it had access to sympathetic courts of effective jurisdiction. The heart of its administrative problems between 1721 and at least 1782 lay thus not in laws or public institutions, but in the economics of monopoly and poverty. The successive tobacco farms were trying to extract monopoly prices from a population in which there were an embarrassing number of wretched, idle, and desperate persons prepared to run tobacco despite the pains and penalties of the law and the sometime rigor of its judges.

A country facing outward both to sea and land, France knew much of smuggling both on its coasts and across its frontiers. We have already discussed in Chapter 5 the various forms of illicit traffic with which the tobacco monopoly had had to contend in its early decades, 1674–1718.[56] With the abolition of domestic cultivation in the 1720's, one source of illicit tobacco had since been eliminated. For the rest, the restored monopoly faced substantially the same sorts of fraud as had its predecessors—though on a much larger scale. The growth of French tobacco consumption after 1713 increased both smuggling and the war against it many, many fold. We shall deal first with smuggling by sea, as the easiest to understand, if not necessarily the most serious danger to the revenue.

Most of the forms of smuggling by sea discussed in Chapter 5 continued after 1721. With the elimination of the domestic plantations, however, the problem of the surreptitious relanding of exported Guienne tobacco disappeared. The controls adopted in the 1680's and later also made many of the simpler forms of smuggling more difficult. The smuggling after 1721 along the Mediterranean coast of France was almost never the work of a French merchant or shipowner. Most cases seem to involve a vessel with Spanish or Italian papers taking on tobacco at Genoa for Spain or perhaps at Amsterdam for Italy and putting into a bay or harbor on the French coast on some pretext; anchored off-shore for a week or more at a time, "waiting for the wind to change," such a vessel was in a position to supply small craft that might come out from the French shore to buy its tobacco. These sales seem to have been both arranged in advance and improvised on the spot.[57]

On the west coast of France, tobacco smuggling after 1721 as before seemed to be a less serious problem than in the Mediterranean. The establishment of offices of the tobacco monopoly on all the major western islands except Yeu (that on Belle-Ile in 1715) precluded their use as bases for very extensive tobacco smuggling.[58] Nevertheless, there are traces in the English records of a contraband trade at Bristol and Bideford shipping tobacco to St. Martins on the Isle of Ré and occasionally to Bordeaux and Nantes. Even though this disappears after the united farms took over the farm in 1730, the monopoly's sales in Poitou remained conspicuously low.[59] The tobacco smuggling via the Isles of Ré, Yeu, or Bouin was probably the work of professional smugglers carrying little else; that run in the major ports, by contrast, was usually concealed on larger vessels carrying other cargo. At Bordeaux, there were some interesting cases involving fairly large scale smuggling of this sort by merchants of the port.[60] On vessels returning from the West Indies, there was of course always the chance that some of the crew would bring along a little Macouba or Havana snuff or St. Domingue or Louisiana roll tobacco.[61] Nevertheless, the west seems to have been the least active area in tobacco smuggling.

By far the busiest area was the north coast. It was all too easy for a foreign vessel to take on a cargo of tobacco in Holland or at the free port of Dunkirk (a great tobacco manufacturing center) and with papers purporting a voyage to Spain or the Mediterranean hover off the Norman coast and deliver the tobacco to small craft that ran it ashore. Off the Brittany coast, it was not even necessary to have a "mother ship" to supply tobacco to the small craft, for the Channel Islands sat like great smuggling vessels a few miles off shore, within easy reach of many kinds of small craft from the French coast. Jersey, Guernsey, and Alderney were all outside British customs jurisdiction and as virtual free ports made excellent bases for every kind of illicit trade.

In Chapter 5 (Table I), we already noted how as early as the 1690's, English tobacco exports to the Channel Islands reached levels ten times the estimated consumption (50,000 lb.) of those places.[62] Exports at these suspiciously high levels resumed with the peace in 1713 and remained high down to the American Revolution, except for wartime (Table I). These figures cover England only. Only rarely after the 1740's, however, did Scotland send a vessel to the Channel Islands. Were we to convert the last column (for which we have data) to include shipments from Scotland as well, we should have to change only two years, raising the totals for 1766 to 1,480,854 lb. and for 1767 to 643,125 lb.

It can be seen at a glance that, except for war years, there were, conservatively speaking, supplies on the Channel Islands for at least 500,000 lb. of tobacco smuggling annually. There were manufactories there to turn this leaf into roll or snuff.[63] We noted in Chapter 5 that even in the 1690's, English officials wondered whether all this was actually run into France rather than into England. Informed opinion, including that of clergymen on the islands, assured the government that it went to France.[64] In 1764, the British Treasury under the reforming George Grenville made a comprehensive survey of the smuggling problem on the Channel coast. None of the

TABLE I

English Exports of Tobacco to the Channel Islands, 1711–76[65]

(*in thousands of English lb. weight*)

Year		Year		Year	
1711	79*	1733	1,204	1755	230*
1712	289	1734	291	1756	395*
1713	494	1735	506	1757	421*
1714	505	1736	772	1758	73*
1715	181	1737	344	1759	159*
1716	851	1738	1,067	1760	532*
1717	1,039	1739	1,559	1761	31*
1718	1,111	1740	887	1762	21*
1719	222	1741	625	1763	484
1720	452	1742	753	1764	659
1721	336	1743	767	1765	615
1722	308	1744	86*	1766	990
1723	387	1745	360*	1767	483
1724	171	1746	175*	1768	429
1725	441	1747	85*	1769	681
1726	443	1748	479*	1770	455
1727	848	1749	311	1771	342
1728	587	1750	933	1772	746
1729	688	1751	899	1773	825
1730	368	1752	1,341	1774	685
1731	787	1753	1,385	1775	415
1732	782	1754	969	1776	32

* = war years.

reports from the collectors and comptrollers of the various southern ports mentioned tobacco as a commodity smuggled into England from the Channel Islands.[66] The officers at Weymouth did mention it, though, as being smuggled from the Channel Islands into France.[67] The captain of a revenue cutter thought it was smuggled from the islands both into France and England.[68] The English customs "register" on Guernsey (who had no official cognizance of the exports of the island) thought that the tobacco "is for the most part carried into France."[69]

It is very likely that tobacco from the Channel Islands was smuggled both into France and into England, but that far more of it was smuggled into France than into England, not simply because the islands were much closer to France, but because that country was a much more profitable market. On the one hand, legitimate tobacco cost more in France than in England (perhaps 60 percent more after prices were raised in 1758). On the other hand, there were other commodities which were far more remunerative than tobacco for running into Britain. There was little reason for a professional smuggler on the English south coast to run tobacco, on which the duty was only six or eight pence per pound through most of the eighteenth century, when he could instead run tea on which the duty was four shillings per pound and more.[70]

On the French side, there is evidence enough of tobacco smuggling from Guernsey and Jersey after 1721 as before.[71] The area most affected was understandably northern Brittany where the very independent and impoverished local nobility more than tolerated the fraud. When Dupleix, for many years in charge of the tobacco farm in Brittany, became administrative head of the national tobacco monopoly under Law in 1718, he used his new position of authority to obtain *lettres de cachet* for the arrest of many poor Breton gentlemen and obstreperous noblemen who had been engaged in this traffic during the preceding ten years. The most important of these were the marquesses of Pontcallec and Salarum, the former powerful enough to overawe the guards of the monopoly, the latter the brother-in-law of the *procureur général* of the *parlement* of Rennes. Although these two grandees were never actually imprisoned, Dupleix's attack helped provoke them into joining the abortive Breton revolt of 1719.[72]

Dupleix's severity did not end the problem. In 1723, a smuggling "company" was active in the *pays de Lamballe,* led by the cadet of a very ancient noble Breton family and including both gentlemen and peasants. Being warned by a fisherman on 23 August 1723 that an English ship had come with their tobacco, and would go into the bay of La Fresnay that night, the "company" immediately assembled near Pléhérel. One of them went on board the English vessel and purchased 6000 lb. of tobacco which they ran ashore in small craft and carried in carts to the forest of La Hunaudaye for hiding. The peasants then were sent away with the carts and, while some of the gentlemen stayed on guard, another of them went into Lamballe to sell the tobacco. However, someone informed the agents of the monopoly who sent nineteen guards the next day into the forest. The gentlemen there were, however, too heavily armed and drove off the guards with gunfire and a bayonet charge, killing five and wounding two. The case caused a great stir and the intendant himself presided at the trial, sentencing twelve to hanging and eight others to the galleys, and levying heavy fines. The galley sentences were actually carried out against the peasant culprits, but the gentlemen who had incurred the gallows escaped by fleeing the country. Some years later, their friends obtained pardons permitting their return. The ensuing years saw other cases involving *nobles* and the public opposition of the Estates to the monopoly's authority to search residences of clerics and gentlemen.[73] There could have been few in Brittany during those years who had not heard of tobacco smuggling.

It was no accident that the intendant personally heard that case.[74] The government had little confidence in the regular courts of Brittany in such matters. When the united farms took over the tobacco monopoly in 1730, they complained to the controller-general Orry that extraordinary measures would be needed, for the tobacco smugglers in Brittany went about in armed bands greater in strength than the brigades of their guards. It was impossible under those circumstances to arrest the greatest smugglers caught in the act. Orry instructed the intendant that, if normal procedures could not cope with tobacco smuggling in Brittany, he should inform Paris of flagrant cases, so that *lettres de cachet* could once more be issued for the arrest, imprisonment and even banishment to the colonies of those implicated.[75]

Though rarely so lurid, the problem did not diminish with the passage of time. A memoir of the 1760's describes the tobacco smuggling problem as it then existed in Brittany. The tobacco run came originally either from Jersey and Guernsey or from Holland. That from the Channel Islands was made up there into little rolls, *carottes* or snuff and run in French vessels which went thither specially to get it. That manufactured in Holland, both snuff and *carottes,* was packaged in small boxes of a pound or so bearing the names of the Dutch manufacturers. It was carried in foreign ships—frequently those of the Channel Islands—to the Breton coast. Spanish vessels sometimes landed theirs on the islands of Bouin and Noirmoutier, near the mouth of the Loire, not yet under effective royal control. Armed bands, still including some gentlemen, came to escort the tobacco from the coast to some inland wood where it was hidden. It was next sold to professionals who hawked it about the countryside on horseback. Even the clergy were implicated. By the 1770's, the south Breton coast from Lorient eastward seems to have replaced the north as the chief smuggling zone.[76]

The basic French policy against tobacco smuggling by sea was to prohibit what the English called "hovering," i.e., small vessels anchoring or sailing suspiciously close to the coast. In November 1718, Dupleix, through John Law, obtained an unprecedentedly severe order from the Council of State, permitting the cutters of the Occident Company (the then tobacco monopolists) to stop and search any foreign vessel found in a French harbor or within two leagues of the French coast. The preamble declared that this was necessary because of the great amount of tobacco run ashore into Normandy and Brittany from small foreign vessels purporting to be going to Spain or Portugal. If such searches disclosed any tobacco, the vessel was to be confiscated and the master fined 1,000 *l.t.*[77] Another order the next month extended the control zone to all waters within two leagues of any French offshore islands.[78] Full jurisdiction in all such cases was given to the intendants.[79]

When, after Law's brief experiment in open trade, the tobacco import monopoly was restored, the *déclaration* of 17 October 1720 reenacted both the 1718 prohibitions against foreign vessels hovering and the controls on French vessels going back to the *ordonnance* of 1681.[80] The measures seem to have been moderately successful. In the very first days of November 1718, several Jersey vessels were seized and confiscated under the new law. Despite much litigation, the confiscations stood.[81] Thereafter, British and Channel

Islands craft seem normally to have left this risky business to others. When the farmer-general de Nantouillet visited Normandy in 1738–39, he found receipts from tobacco rising thanks to increased patrols along the coast and the lower reaches of the Seine.[82]

One difficulty, of course, in enforcing this rigorous policy against hovering was that foreign governments might view with extreme displeasure the seizure of vessels under their flags on the open seas, even if close to the French coast. To avoid unnecessary friction, the government issued new regulations in 1733 explaining the old rules going back to 1681 about tobacco on foreign ships carried for the use of the crew. Such tobacco still had to be declared immediately on entering a French port, sealed and deposited in the warehouse of the monopoly until the ships' departure. However, a ship's master was permitted to draw out twelve ounces per week for each member of his crew while in the French port.[83]

Nevertheless, there remained ample grounds for friction, since foreign vessels were much better suited to tobacco smuggling than French. Although the British government usually ignored complaints[84] from its subjects so implicated, other courts were less cautious. In 1729, the Austrian minister at Genoa complained to the French consul there about the seizure by the French tobacco monopoly of a vessel with Neapolitan papers. The master-owner was a Catalan naturalized Neapolitan for convenience, although he had not visited Naples since 1721. His trade was buying tobacco in Genoa and selling it off the Provençal coast. He would anchor in a protected harbor for a week or two "waiting for the wind to change" and then move on to another haven further down the coast, always claiming to be bound for Spain. Although the litigation went on for three years, the French government enforced the letter of the law.[85] In explanation, the controller-general wrote to the secretary of state for the navy that many small vessels with Spanish or imperial flags frequented the French coast smuggling tobacco or salt. They tried to cover their operations by reference to treaties between their crowns and France, even when those treaties were not applicable. The French, he felt, treated such craft with more leniency than they deserved.[86]

The Spanish were the most troublesome of all, for it was French policy from the 1730's onward to stay on as good terms with Spain as possible. Thus, the Council of State in 1733, while confirming the condemnation of 18 Catalan barques for running tobacco or salt along the coast of Provence and Languedoc, ordered that, as an act of grace, the prisoners be released, the fines remitted and the vessels restored to their owners, leaving only the contraband confiscated.[87] Nevertheless, this mixture of leniency and rigor toward the Spaniards seemed to work well enough for the united farms until 1762.

In July 1762, as part of the price for enticing Spain into the war against Britain, Louis XV granted letters-patent conferring special privileges on subjects of that crown resident in and visiting France.[88] On the one hand,

Spaniards in France were treated as Frenchmen (exempt from the *aubaine*, for example); on the other hand, Spanish consuls could claim special consideration for their vessels when the rights of Frenchmen were not enough. In practice, this new pro-Spanish policy (closely associated with Choiseul, minister for both the navy and foreign affairs) made it very difficult for the united farms to check tobacco smuggling by Spanish craft during the Prévost lease (1762–68): receipts in all coastal areas suffered visibly. A maritime convention of 1768 between France and Spain was supposed to clarify the question and check smuggling by Spanish vessels—but did not at first. To make matters still worse, the *cour des aides* ruled in 1769 that Spanish vessels could not be seized simply for hovering, that running or the intent to run tobacco had to be proved.[89]

With the decline of Choiseul's influence between 1768 and his ultimate disgrace in 1770, and with the arrival of the tough-minded abbé Terray at the controller-generalship in 1769, there came an end to the period of leniency for Spanish vessels. Significant judgments were once again printed in which Spanish vessels with large cargoes of tobacco were condemned.[90] In one interesting case, a vessel with 77,000 lb. of tobacco was condemned by the special commission at Caen, over the objections of the Spanish ambassador, on the grounds that the owner and crew of the vessel were really French and that the Spanish papers had been obtained under false pretenses.[91] The results of this new tougher policy and increased patrols were immediately perceived in higher yields from the tobacco monopoly in the maritime districts of Normandy and Brittany. (The Spaniards reciprocated in kind by sending in troops to crush the smuggling of French snuff into Catalonia along the borders of Roussillon.)[92]

Nevertheless, the united farms were not happy. The convention with Spain made in 1768 was quite unsatisfactory for them: to make it work at all, they had had to spend an extra 500,000 *l.t.* on guards in coastal regions. In negotiating for the new David lease in 1774, the farmers-general asked for and got a considerable tightening up of the agreement of 1768.[93] The new convention of 27 December 1774[94] was technically an explicatory addition to that of 2 January 1768, designed to prevent the running of tobacco and salt into both countries. No vessel of either country could by the new terms enter a port of the other country with either salt or tobacco, on pain of confiscation of the cargo. French and Spanish vessels were to carry papers giving full details of their crews and of all salt and tobacco on board; vessels exporting such cargo were to return certificates of delivery at their avowed destinations. Passports for vessels carrying those commodities were to specify the routes to be followed. The French and Spanish consuls at Dunkirk and Ostend were to exchange complete lists, which included all their national vessels clearing, cargoes, and destinations. The revenue-cutters of either country were permitted to search vessels of the other country under 100 tons burthen found within two leagues of either coast. If any tobacco or salt were found during such a search, or on any vessel in port, the contraband was to be confiscated and the vessel itself and the rest of its cargo placed at the disposal of the consul of the vessel's homeland, to be disposed of as directed by his government. These terms were not as rigorous as those originally adopted in 1718-19, but seem to have been reasonably effective. We hear no more of the question.

Special, but more limited, difficulties in enforcing the antismuggling regulations for tobacco in the Mediterranean were created by local institutions there. The tobacco monopoly was particularly upset by the quarantine regulations controlled by health commissioners (*intendants du bureau de la santé*) at Marseilles and Toulon. The farmers felt that during the weeks in which ships were undergoing quarantine or their passengers and cargo segregated in the lazarettos, there were far too many opportunities for tobacco smuggling. Thus again, during Law's brief but ruthless ascendency, the tobacco farm obtained an order from the Council of State (22 May 1719) permitting their agents to breach the quarantine walls: (1) agents of the monopoly were permitted in the special offices (*consignes*) in which arriving ship captains were interrogated by the health officials; (2) at that time, the captains were to declare under penalty how much tobacco they had on board; and, most seriously, (3) the agents of the monopoly were to be permitted to search the lazarettos and ships in quarantine as they pleased, taking only such health precautions as they themselves thought necessary.[95] These new regulations caused the most violent protests from the health officers at both Marseilles and Toulon to the Regent and the count of Toulouse (head of the navy council). The officers felt that these new rules, quite apart from insulting their staffs, were a violation of the whole spirit of quarantine.[96] Nevertheless, despite the great Provençal plague of 1720-22, the new rules were not revoked, though we cannot know to what extent the monopoly took advantage of its dangerous powers. Years later, in the 1760's, the monopoly had further trouble with the health commissioners who insisted that tobacco ships from Britain for the manufactory at Cette do quarantine at Marseilles and refused to establish a lazaretto at Cette where tobacco from leaky ships might be landed for safety.[97]

Equally difficult were the free port transit privileges of Marseilles. Tobacco might be brought there from Holland, Dunkirk and Italy in transit for reexport. Smuggling was self-evidently involved, for tobacco was monopolized not only in France but in Iberia and Italy as well. However, the monopoly did not in fact seem to mind as long as it felt that the tobacco reexported was going to foreign parts. However, a report of the early 1770's suggested that much of that exported from Marseilles might be returning to France.[98] The Marseilles merchants at that time were importing 450,000–600,000 lb. of tobacco in 60–80 large vessels annually from Dunkirk. They insisted upon the right to transship it in the harbor to smaller vessels without going formally through the *entrepôt*. This was an obvious invitation to fraud and the monopoly wanted them to enter and clear the tobacco formally so that supervision might be easier. The monopoly won its point by 1785, only at the expense to Marseilles of having much of this "transit" trade redirected to Genoa and Leghorn.[99]

In concluding, one point must be kept in mind: whether it was run ashore on the south, west, or north coasts of France, whether it was manufactured into roll or snuff in Holland, Dunkirk, or the Channel Islands, the tobacco smuggled by sea into France after 1721 seems to have been preponderantly Virginia in origin. For this, there was a ready market in France created by monopolistic policy since the 1690's. On the land frontiers, the problem was more complex.

Smuggling by Land, 1721–91

At least as serious as the running along the seacoasts was the contraband activity along France's land frontiers. This problem, as already explained in Chapter 5, was particularly acute along France's long exposed eastern frontier.[100] In the Rhineland and the United Provinces, millions of pounds of tobacco were raised and manufactured annually; in France's own privileged eastern provinces outside the tobacco monopoly—Flanders, Artois, Alsace, Franche-Comté—more millions were grown and worked up each year. The French monopoly normally bought little or none of this frontier, Rhenish or Netherlandish tobacco, nurturing instead a consumer preference in France for Virginia tobacco, less easily procured by the eastern frontier smugglers. Nevertheless, the manufacturers of Dunkirk, St. Omer, and Strasbourg could and did obtain large quantities of Virginia leaf which they mixed with local tobaccos to make products both good enough and cheap enough for smuggling purposes.

The activities of the smuggling bands were by no means confined to the immediate neighborhood of the frontiers. Tobacco smuggled from Artois into Picardy in the 1740's was carried into the lower Seine valley in Normandy.[101] To the southward, the smugglers reached the forest of Orléans where they established great stores, from which they supplied the country roundabout as far as Paris.[102] Tobacco from the Franche-Comté naturally plagued all sections of Burgundy within the monopoly.[103] Others carried it southward through Burgundy and the Lyonnais into the northern parts of Languedoc (the Vivarais, Velay and Gevaudan) and thence into Rouergue and Auvergne.[104] The celebrated smuggler Mandrin, operating out of Savoy in 1754–55, carried his tobacco via Dauphiné into Rouergue, Auvergne, the Lyonnais and Burgundy.[105]

From the earliest days of the monopoly, increasing attention had been paid to guards along the frontiers. One of the reasons for transferring the monopoly to the united farms in 1730 had been to increase the efficiency of its patrols and reduce their cost by combining them with those of the salt monopoly (*gabelles*) and customs (*traites*). Nevertheless, from the very beginning, it had been realized that a thin line of guards could never cover the whole frontier if smugglers were permitted to bring their goods up to the very frontier itself. Thus, as explained in Chapter 5, a series of regulations had been evolved in the 1670's and 1680's under which it was prohibited to grow, manufacture or store tobacco in that part of Artois (outside the monopoly) lying within three leagues of the frontier of Picardy (within the monopoly). The only exception was the small amount of tobacco each household was permitted to keep for home use. By 1686, these rules had been extended to those parts of Hainault and the Cambrésis also lying within three leagues of the monopoly's territories.[106]

When the privilege was reestablished after Law's experiments, the *déclaration* of 1 August 1721 confirmed the ban on planting and full right of search in the three league zone in Artois, Hainault and the Cambrésis.[107] After much litigation and some violence, the zone itself was gradually restored in the 1720's.[108] This was the most intensively patrolled "frontier" of France. During the 1730's, there was further controversy before the Council of State concerning certain parishes or groups of parishes in Artois and Hainault which claimed to be outside the three league zone but which were at the test ruled to be within it.[109] The most complex and difficult cases involved Artesian villages enclaved in Picardy and Picard villages enclaved in Artois. The law in such cases was interpreted leniently within the limits of revenue security.[110] Enforcement remained difficult, however, and by the early 1740's, the united farms had become dissatisfied with the general operation of the laws restricting traffic in tobacco—and salt—in the whole three league zone of Artois, Hainault, and the Cambrésis. In 1741, they submitted a long memoir to the government complaining about that frontier. Their expenditures on three lines of foot and horse patrols along that boundary had increased from 817,838 *l.t.* in 1736 to 926,569 *l.t.* and yet tobacco sales in those *entrepôts* nearest the frontier remained trivial. St. Pol in Artois was an open center of the smuggling trade, but neither the local nor the provincial authorities would cooperate in any way with the united farms. That company challenged the legal basis of Artois' claims to exemptions from the tobacco monopoly.[111]

In answer to such complaints, the government conceded only the *déclaration* of 9 April 1743, codifying and stiffening the regulations relating to the three league zone.[112] This limited innovation led to protests from the estates of Artois and the Cambrésis and had to be explained by further *déclarations* of 13 May[113] and 8 September 1746.[114] The rights of search in houses and vehicles in transit in the zone were carefully limited and defined. As a control, registers of all inhabitants above the age of six (presumably the smoking age) were to be prepared annually by village officials throughout the three league zone and forwarded to the agents of the monopoly. These same village officials were to issue passes to those of their residents who wished to bring tobacco for family use from the free parts of Artois, Hainault, or the Cambrésis into the three league zone. In the Cambrésis, the same results were sought by having licensed retailers in each village alone authorized to bring tobacco into the three league zone and to supply each family with its monthly quota. A special *ordonnance* was also required covering the needs of troops stationed in the zone.[115]

The three league zone, having proved itself on the northern frontiers of the monopoly, came inevitably to be extended elsewhere. Such had in fact been authorized by the *déclaration* of 1721, but not at first enforced. By an order of the Council of State of 12 September 1724, the three league principle was applied to the frontiers of Franche-Comté (outside the monopoly) contiguous to Burgundy, Bresse, and Champagne (inside the monopoly). Although the tobacco trade and cultivation were free elsewhere in the county, in that newly defined zone, containing more than 500 named towns and villages as well as the lands best suited for tobacco, it was prohibited to plant, manufacture, or even store any tobacco over the two pounds allowed each household for its monthly use. Full rights of search were given to the monopoly.[116] By a subsequent order of 29 December 1725, eight shopkeepers (*marchands*) in Dôle, four in Gray, and two in Lons-le-Saunier within the three league zone were alone licensed to deal in tobacco for the use of the inhabitants of the zone. At the same time, a special commission was set up consisting of the intendant and four members of the *parlement* of Besançon to try all tobacco cases arising in Franche-Comté.[117]

The three league ban seems to have stirred resentment in Franche-Comté at least as great as that earlier aroused in Artois.[118] The government and the monopoly had to be adamant here, for the Jura was one of the most notorious smuggling districts. The intendant found it necessary to issue an *ordonnance* on 6 August 1729 repeating and codifying the various measures taken since 1721. Beyond that, he provided that in an additional one league zone beyond the three leagues from the frontier, no one could sell tobacco unless he lived in a walled town. This was an effort to cut off smugglers from their rural suppliers. For the same reason, no wholesale tobacco dealer could have a warehouse west of the river Saône whose crossings were to be check points for tobacco traffic.[119] The comprehensiveness of this *ordonnance* suggests that a large part of the rural population was helping the smugglers.

Further restrictions followed apace. After the united farms took over the tobacco monopoly, the intendant in 1732 was given exclusive power to try as a court of last resort all tobacco cases in Franche-Comté.[120] A month later, he issued an *ordonnance* repeating in more draconian terms his 1729 regulations. The entire province outside the three league zone was now also brought under control. All tobacco dealers had to register with the intendant; it was forbidden to sell more than sixty pounds of tobacco to anyone not a registered dealer. Retailers were forbidden to sell tobacco to anyone not a resident of their localities. Tobacco entering the province from

Alsace or elsewhere had to be declared at the frontier and be accompanied by transit papers. Yet, the agents of the monopoly were forbidden to make searches outside the three league zone and a new survey of that zone was promised to avoid disputes about where planting was permitted.[121] Two years later, the intendant (Charles de la Neuville) issued still another *ordonnance* prescribing such details as records to be kept by licensed dealers and certificates to be returned by exporters.[122] The various measures of the intendant de la Neuville and his successor were given more lasting authority by a comprehensive order of the Council of State in 1736. Through the province, a tight system of declarations, passes and receipts was now established for all plantings and movements of tobacco and for all sales over two pounds.[123] An extraordinarily close regime of control had now been established in whose operation local authorities up to the *parlement* of Besançon were forbidden to interfere.[124]

In 1745, the new intendant of Besançon, Jean-Nicolas Megret de Serilly, proposed to tighten controls even further while winning over the most important of the local corporations, the municipality of Besançon: after conferences with its officials, he produced a scheme for a provincial monopoly, with its own manufacture at Besançon, the whole to be dominated by the magistrates of that town. With the concurrence of the corporation, letters patent for the new arrangements were obtained on 14 September 1745, but the *parlement* of Besançon refused to register them on the grounds that the new arrangements were detrimental to the populace who wanted cheaper tobacco, particularly that of Alsace. The new controller-general Machault was forced to intervene and suppressed both the *remonstrance* of the *parlement* to the king and the Besançon monopoly scheme itself.[125]

The status quo persisting from the 1730's did not indefinitely satisfy the farmers-general: the higher rents they had to pay for the tobacco monopoly from 1750 onward made them, as we shall see, much more attentive to all the administrative arrangements in the frontier provinces. In return for the much higher rent to be paid from 1750, they extracted from the government the valuable *déclaration* of 4 May 1749 (to be discussed in the next chapter) establishing a very high entry duty of 30 *sols* per lb. on all foreign tobacco entering the French frontier provinces exempt from the monopoly. By article ii of that *déclaration,* tobacco legally grown within the frontier provinces, exported and then reimported had to pay the full 30s. duty. This meant that the popular Alsatian tobacco would have to pay the duty on importation into the Franche-Comté since the main road from Belfort to Besançon passed through the foreign (Württemberger) county of Montbéliard. Given the available roads and the points legally prescribed for entering tobacco into the Franche-Comté, there was no legal way for tobacco from Alsace to evade this duty.[126]

Up to this time, the tobacco problem in the Franche-Comté had involved merchants and retailers almost exclusively, planting and manufacturing being relatively unimportant. However, the new duty, increasing the price of both foreign and Alsatian tobacco several hundred percent, created overnight in the province the sharpest incentives for planting. Some of the peasantry were not slow to respond. To check this tendency, the monopoly obtained an *arrêt du conseil* (17 February 1750) confirming all the existing paper controls on planting. To make cultivation as difficult as possible, the intendant, Jean-Louis Moreau de Beaumont, issued an *ordonnance* on 1 June 1752 providing that planting permits had to be applied for by 1 December of the previous year and would be granted for plots of from one to four *journaux* only. This was used administratively to confine cultivation in the province to 600 *journaux*. Not satisfied, the monopoly obtained a further *arrêt du conseil* (9 April 1754) reducing the planting quota to 500 *journaux* for 1754, 450 for 1755, and 400 for 1756 and subsequent years. On top of this, the new intendant Bourgeois de Boynes established a tax of 100 *l.t.* on all planting permits (*ordonnance* of 4 December 1754). In vain did the *parlement* of Besançon protest in its own *arrêt* of 14 December 1754 which attempted to reaffirm the right of free cultivation in all parts of the province outside the three league zone: they were overruled and their competence denied by an *arrêt du conseil* of 6 January 1755.

Thereafter, for all practical purposes the Franche-Comté came within the effective control of the tobacco monopoly, even though its residents did not pay full monopoly prices. This was soon recognized in form as well as in fact. Although the Franche-Comté was regularly and explicitly listed as one of the exempted provinces in leases of the tobacco monopoly, at least through 1738,[127] it was no longer so listed in the lease of 1755.[128] The 400 *journaux* or *arpents* of cultivation thereafter permitted (about 500 English acres) could produce about 500,000 lb. of tobacco, or almost the entire consumption of the province. It is unlikely, though, that the full quota was grown, considering the poor quality of the local leaf and the limit of one *journal* to each registered cultivator. According to a report on the farms in 1774, the tobacco of the monopoly was sold in competition with local growth throughout the province.[129] Just before the Revolution, a well-informed official estimated the consumption of the province at 600,000 lb. of which 250,000 were supplied by the monopoly.[130] The restrictive policy of the farms was, all in all, successful in that very little of the permitted production of the Franche-Comté could have been available for smuggling into France proper.

Eventually, something like the three league zone ban was extended to the inner frontiers of almost all the provinces outside the jurisdiction of the tobacco monopoly. Only in the case of Franche-Comté, however, were analagous if more limited controls applied to all tobacco movements in the rest of the province as well. The very exceptionalness of these measures indicates not merely the vigor with which the united farms moved when it took over the monopoly in the 1730's but also the extreme seriousness with which they regarded the problem in Franche-Comté, the land where smuggling seemed a part of the normal way of life.

There were, of course, other frontiers unsuited to the application of the principle of the three league zone. Because Spain had its own very severe tobacco monopoly, smuggling along the Pyrenees was not a serious problem for the French monopoly except near the privileged territory about Bayonne. (That problem will be discussed in the next chapter on the French territories outside the jurisdiction of the monopoly.) Another frontier of great complexity lay in the Ardennes where the northernmost stretches of Champagne beyond the Aisne reached the frontier of the Austrian Netherlands. Immediately to the east, also along the frontier of Austrian Luxembourg, lay an area of confused boundaries where territories of the Three Bishoprics (in France proper and within the tobacco monopoly), Lorraine and independent "sovereignties" lay intermixed. This jumble of jurisdictions so close to a hostile frontier created ideal conditions for illicit activity in a poor and backward area whose inhabitants also regarded smuggling as a normal village activity.[131]

The jurisdictions administered by the intendant of the Three Bishoprics (Metz, Toul, and Verdun) were frequently separated from each other and from France proper by the territories of Lorraine. Districts not originally part of the Three Bishoprics when acquired in 1559 had been added to them for administrative purposes: their rights and privileges were governed by many separate treaties and there was no uniformity of status throughout the intendancy. Thus, when the very intelligent farmer-general Dupin made a tour of the Three Bishoprics in 1732, he found matters in great confusion. "International" trade of great complexity regularly crisscrossed French territory from one enclave to another, all guaranteed by treaty rights. Moreover, without any treaty justification that he could find, the four towns and territories of Longwy, Sarrelouis, Sarrebourg, and Phalsbourg, acquired from Lorraine in 1661, had usurped the right to plant and trade in tobacco. Longwy, in particular, on the border of Luxembourg, used this liberty to import 120,000 lb. of tobacco annually from Alsace and the Austrian Netherlands for smuggling into France, the local inhabitants not consuming more than 6,000 lb. annually.[132] From the 1720's onwards, elaborate regulations had been adopted prescribing routes, passes, and bonds for tobacco passing from Alsace across Lorraine and the Three Bishoprics to the Austrian Netherlands or other foreign destinations. Nevertheless, as late as the 1740's, it was possible to discover a foreign village of thirty households enclaved in the Three Bishoprics importing 63,662 lb. of tobacco from Alsace in two years and ruining the legitimate sales of the monopoly in surrounding territories.[133]

When Dupin in 1732 moved further west into the Ardennes to the area about Sedan and Charleville, very close to the imperial frontier, he found that tiny foreign jurisdictions lying immediately outside French territory, like the duchy of Bouillon, and others too small to appear on any map, were perfectly situated to act as *entrepôts* for vast smuggling operations into France. Bouillon was the most important, importing tobacco from Alsace, the Palatinate and Cologne and manufacturing it locally for smuggling purposes; the tobacco trade had become the principal source of new local wealth. But Dupin concluded rather skeptically that, if the trade were stopped at Bouillon, it would only go somewhere else along the frontier.[134]

The attitude of the tobacco monopoly toward these annoying petty frontier sovereignties and appanages was simple: buy up their tobacco monopolies. In 1686, it will be remembered from Chapter 5, the then united farms had contracted to lease the tobacco monopolies in Charleville, Rethel, and the Clermontois (including Clermont, Stenay, Dun, and Jamets).[135] When, however, Law's company took over the French tobacco monopoly in 1718, it failed to obtain the transfer of the Clermontois farm which its predecessors had leased from the prince of Condé.[136] The control of tobacco in these awkwardly placed territories was reacquired by the French monopoly by the 1730's,[137] but the new lease was not continued after 1744.[138] Similarly, Charleville, which also belonged to the princes of Condé after 1708, and where the monopoly had had an important manufacture from 1703,[139] was no longer leased after 1744. By the 1760's, the tobacco monopoly in both Charleville and the Clermontois was in the hands of a Dunkirk tobacco manufacturer who used them as depots for fraud. The united farms were forced to come to terms with the then prince of Condé, resuming the lease of the tobacco monopoly in both Charleville and the Clermontois from 1 January 1771.[140] The crown finally purchased all the fiscal rights of the prince of Condé in the Clermontois in 1784.[141]

There were of course other sovereignties and appanages which the monopoly also strove to control. Although the *déclaration* of 1 August 1721, like the leases going back to 1687, provided that the monopoly included the western islands of Ré, Belle-Ile, Bouin, Noirmoutier, and Oléron, in fact the monopoly was unable to establish itself effectively on the prince of Conde's Noirmoutier until the prince sold his rights to the crown in the last ruthless days of Louis XV.[142] The crown had arbitrarily suppressed the tobacco plantation in the viscounty of Turenne in the 1720's[143] but only settled its pretensions definitively when it purchased the appanage from the duke of Bouillon in 1738. About the same time, the united farms induced the duke of Maine to suppress tobacco planting in his principality of Dombes (north of Lyons) though that appanage retained its own distinct tobacco monopoly until reunited to the crown in 1762. Only in 1768 was the local monopoly fully absorbed into that of France with the elimination of the last local price differentials.[144]

In the south, the principality of Orange, acquired by the treaty of Utrecht, was merged in the tobacco monopoly by the lease of 1714. The nearby Comtat Venaissin, belonging to the pope, remained outside the farm's control. In the seventeenth century, tobacco cultivation had spread into that territory from nearby French Mondragon; concentrated on the rich low lands near the Rhone and in the Haut-Comtat, a papal enclave in Dauphiné, tobacco culture had reached economically significant levels by the turn of the century. The yields were remunerative enough to pay for heavy manuring and thus enable tobacco cultivation to be alternated with wheat without a fallow. The crop was bought and manufactured by dealers in Avignon and the principal towns of the Comtat, primarily for sale to French smugglers. This troublesome trade seems to have grown greatly after tobacco cultivation was prohibited in France in 1719. By the early 1730's, production was thought to be near or above 800,000 lb. annually.

Both the Provençal tobacco subfarmers in 1708 and the Indies Company in 1728 had tried to reach some sort of understanding with the papal government for the suppression of cultivation, but in both cases local interests were able to block agreement in Rome. Matters became much more serious after the united farms took over the tobacco monopoly in 1730. The patience of the French government was worn thin by the role of the Comtat in smuggling tobacco, in the manufacture of printed silks ("indiennes") prohibited in France, and in irregular monetary operations. A war of trade prohibitions and boycotts started in 1730 as each side tried to gain a stronger negotiating position at the expense of the other; in it, the population of the Comtat suffered considerably by the cutting off of food supplies from France. By 1733 (with the start of the War of the Polish Succession), both sides were ready for compromise. Despite the objections of many in the Comtat, the papal nuncio in Paris was instructed to get the best terms he could. By an agreement of 4 December 1733, confirmed by a concordat signed at Paris on 11 March 1734, the manufacture of *indiennes* and the cultivation and trade in tobacco were prohibited in Avignon and the Comtat. The tobacco trade in those territories was made a papal monopoly which, by a contract signed at Avignon on 31 March 1734, was leased for eight and one-half years to François Cornelli, citizen of Avignon, straw man for the united farms of France. The rent (really an indemnity) was 230,000 *l.t.* annually, suggesting that the French monopoly valued rather highly the illicit possibilities of this territory.[145]

If the Comtat Venaissin was ten or twenty times as important as the petty jurisdictions along the Ardennes frontier, the great duchy or kingdom of Lorraine was at least ten times as important as the Comtat. The Bernard-Crozat-Maynon tobacco monopoly, it will be remembered, had succeeded in farming the tobacco monopoly of Lorraine from 1708 onward.[146] When the tobacco monopoly in France passed from them to Law's Occident Company in 1718, the Lorraine lease passed with it.[147] When Law decided to abolish the tobacco monopoly in France, he had no further interest in keeping the Lothringian monopoly. The court of Lorraine therefore (by a lease of 3 November 1719) farmed its tobacco monopoly for 130,000 *livres* (Lorraine) annually for eleven years to the company farming its other revenues. Although the principals in this company (in the name of Jean Baptiste Bonnedame) were French, they are not known to have had any connection with either the Indies Company or the united farms of France.

The new tobacco farm in Lorraine could expect to pay its 130,000 *livres* (Lor.) annually, compared to the 55,000 contracted in 1714, only because tobacco consumption was rapidly growing in these years in Lorraine as in France. (In 1725, it reportedly earned 226,000 *livres*.) Taxes on tobacco lands were reduced and other concessions made to encourage tobacco planting in the duchies. That grown near Neufchâteau had a relatively good reputation, though none was superior. Manufactures were established at Nancy, Neufchâteau, and elsewhere. Other measures were taken to discourage tobacco smuggling *into* Lorraine. These steps were moderately successful; when the united farms of Lorraine were renewed in 1730, the tobacco sector was valued at 150,000 *livres* (Lor.). The new farmers-general of Lorraine (under the name of Pierre Gillet) chose not to manage tobacco themselves but to sublease it and some other revenues to a separate company under the name of Jean-Baptiste Christophe.

The prosperity of these successive tobacco farms in Lorraine could only have had adverse effects upon that of the tobacco monopoly in France. Hardly had the treaty of Vienna been signed in 1737, ceding Lorraine to the French protégé, King Stanislas, late of Poland, father-in-law of Louis XV, when an order of the new king (6 September 1737) abrogated the leases of the various farms of Lorraine and Bar and transferred them all to the farmers-general of France under the name of Philippe Le Mire. (Tobacco was valued at 270,000 *livres* in fixing the farms' rent at 3.3 million.) The unesteemed tobacco plantations in the two duchies (around 1,800 arpents or 2,250 English acres on the eve of the union) were progressively suppressed and the manufacture confined to Nancy.[148] Thanks therefore to a major war and a European-wide territorial settlement, the united farms of France regained control over the tobacco monopoly of Lorraine which Law had so improvidently let slip from French control.

Even though the united farms of Lorraine remained legally separate from those of France until 1762 and administratively distinct until 1780,[149] from the very first they were operationally one. Farmers-general were sent out from Paris to inspect Lorraine much as they might the most ancient province of France.[150] Legally, the guards of the French farms were given permission to pursue and arrest smugglers on the soil of Lorraine, while the employees of the farms of Lorraine could make similar pursuits and arrests across the French frontier.[151] Yet, in other ways, the united farms of France indulged Lorraine, their lease there being profitable, particularly in tobacco.[152] Not till 1771, therefore, were tobacco prices in the duchies raised to the levels prevailing in comparable French provinces.[153]

The Struggle against Illicit Trade within the Frontiers of the Monopoly, 1721–91

By close patrolling of its own frontiers and the three leagues in French territories beyond, as well as by acquiring control of tobacco monopolies in sovereignties and appanages outside its jurisdiction, the successive tobacco monopolists of France sought to secure those frontiers against the activities of smugglers who constantly threatened to inundate France with fraudulent tobacco. Yet the battle could not be fought only at the frontiers. Just as the activity of the smugglers reached to almost every corner of the kingdom, so had the monopoly to be on guard everywhere against the frauds that could destroy it. No form of influence or privilege could be permitted to stand unchallenged before the unanswerable logic of its administrative necessity.

During the long wars of Louis XIV, it will be remembered, *ordonnances* had rolled regularly from the press forbidding soldiers to smuggle tobacco under the heaviest of penalties: death was ordered for those smuggling in armed bands; lesser offenders were promised the galleys.[154] The tobacco monopoly changed hands many times, but the harsh punishments for the troops subsisted. The opportunities for military smuggling created by the Catalonian campaign in the brief war with Spain, 1718–20, obliged Law in December 1719 to obtain yet one more *ordonnance* tightening the control on the movements of individual soldiers and making officers responsible for the fines of their men.[155] Shortly after the united farms took over the monopoly in 1730, they found it necessary to obtain yet a further *ordonnance* codifying once more the regulations against the smuggling by soldiers of tobacco, salt and other goods.[156] During the wars of 1740–48 and 1756–63, further *ordonnances* had to be published prohibiting smuggling[157] and regulating with increasing tightness the supply of *tabac de cantine* to the troops. To prevent soldiers from selling their cantine tobacco to civilians, the monopoly was given the right to dole out their allowance of one pound per month in rations of as little as one ounce at a time.[158] Finally, during the War of the American Revolution (when tobacco became very expensive), the soldier's allowance itself was cut to one-half pound per month, allegedly to check sales to civilians.[159]

We hear less of the military problem after 1721 than under Louis XIV, but it was never eliminated. It might not seem very serious that some sailors and marines in Brittany sold part of their *tabac de cantine* to civilians in 1729.[160] Yet, after the start of the war in 1740, it was reported that legitimate sales of tobacco had declined 30,000–60,000 lb. annually in the Rouen area alone because of the troops in winter quarters thereabouts.[161] The same was reported from Burgundy in the same years.[162]

Equally traditional, equally a continuation of the administrative struggles under Louis XIV, was the unending campaign of the monopoly against every form of privilege which could act as a cover to fraud. Exemptions of course were normal rather than exceptional under the *ancien régime*. There has survived a manuscript guide of the early eighteenth century, which under the name of each *direction* of the united farms lists the exemptions which local noblemen, ecclesiastical bodies, and municipalities had to specific duties.[163] Tobacco, in contrast to older branches of the revenue, was relatively untouched by such privileges. The *déclaration* of 1 August 1721, repeating older provisions, permitted the employees of the tobacco monopoly to search anywhere, even in privileged places and convents.[164] The enforcement of this right was to be a more difficult matter.

As soon as the Indies Company resumed control of the tobacco monopoly in 1723, it found it expedient to get an order from the Council of State stating unequivocally that officers of the tobacco monopoly, like those of the *gabelles*, could, accompanied by two witnesses, search any ecclesiastical, noble, or bourgeois domicile. No magistrate or officer of a local court need be present.[165] Efforts of local fiscal and other courts to restrict this unequivocal right of search were overruled by the *cour des aides* and Council of State.[166] Although the new regulations were literally enforced against houses of monks and friars,[167] some concessions had to be made for convents of nuns. Except in emergencies, searches were to be made only with the permission of the diocesan bishop and had always to be in the presence of a local magistrate and a chaplain of the convent.[168]

Of all privileged orders, government officials were sometimes the most insistent on their rights. The navy ministry was quite upset in 1715 when the home of a naval ensign was searched in Le Havre and contraband tobacco seized.[169] Particularly troublesome were the rules governing the searching of coaches. An *ordonnance* of 9 April 1729 provided that every coach entering Paris, even those belonging to the king, was to be stopped and searched.[170] Tobacco was found being smuggled even in the courier wagons of the ministry of foreign affairs in 1747. Although the ministry then waived any exemptions for its vehicles,[171] it had to bestir itself when the same eager employees of the united farms at Péronne in Picardy seized tobacco on coaches belonging to the Prussian and Genoese ministers in Paris. They had to instruct the farms to seize the tobacco but to let the coachmen and coaches go.[172]

Tobacco fraud embraced not only the king's coaches, but his residences as well. So scandalous did the selling of contraband tobacco in and about Versailles become that the king was obliged to issue an *ordonnance* on 10 April 1762 permitting employees of the monopoly accompanied by a court official to search anywhere in the palaces and their related buildings. The rule applied equally to all other residences of the king, the royal family, and the princes of the blood. Palace residents or functionaries found harboring or selling fraudulent tobacco were to be deprived of their lodgings and/or dismissed from their employments and subjected to the full penalties of the law.[173] Other royal *ordonnances* extended these rules to all privileged places in Paris[174] and prohibited functionaries or domestics in royal or other privileged residences from even selling tobacco without written permission from the monopoly.[175]

But ambassadors' coaches and royal palaces were but the exotica of tobacco smuggling. Infinitely more important were the tens of thousands of ordinary coaches and wagons that might convey fraudulent tobacco and the tens of thousands of country inns and simple barns that might be used to hide the same. It wasn't enough to decree that everyone must keep his barns and sheds locked or be responsible for any salt or tobacco found therein,[176] or to punish innkeepers on whose premises contraband tobacco in transit had been found.[177] To enforce such rules in rural areas and small towns required expensive patrols. Thus, the net yield of the monopoly in rural France was characteristically low. It was estimated in 1738 that 33 percent of the net yield of the tobacco farm came from the city of Paris alone—or 42 percent if the *plat pays* thereabouts was included.[178] To protect this disproportionate yield, the tobacco monopoly helped persuade the united farms to build the hated new wall around Paris in the 1780's.[179] But rural France could not be immured. Ultimately, the monopoly was forced to think through its position, to go beyond a regime of walls and punishments, even terror, and to attack the very economics of fraud itself.

From the very first days of the monopoly, the crown had regulated the maximum prices at which tobacco could be sold. In this tradition, the *déclaration* of 1 August 1721 had provided the following maximum prices per pound:

	Wholesale	*Retail*
superior twist (mostly foreign leaf)	50 *sols*	60 *sols*
inferior twist (all domestic leaf)	25 *sols*	32 *sols*
Brazil tobacco	70 *sols*	80 *sols*

Snuff maxima continued according to the complex but largely irrelevant scale established in 1681.[180] These same prices were confirmed when the monopoly was transferred to the united farms in 1730.[181] (Twenty percent was added in 1758 and four *sols* per lb. weight in 1781.) [182] Since tobacco growing was now prohibited within the monopoly's territories and since interest in Brazil tobacco was waning, the important prices were the 50 and 60 *sols* established for superior twist (*corde*). These were undeniably high prices by contemporary standards. (Devaluation reduced the value of 60 *sols tournois* after 1726 to 2*s.* 6*d.* sterling, but equivalent twist in England then sold retail for about 1*s.* 6*d.* per lb. or 40 percent less.) From the very first, however, the monopolists of the 1720's and the united farms after 1730 realized that it was inexpedient to try to extract these prices everywhere. In areas between the frontier and the first major river or other effective barrier, twist was sold retail at the reduced prices of 33s. for superior and 16s. for inferior. This system proved hard to control for many persons carried tobacco from the low price zones near the frontiers of the monopoly into the full priced zones of the interior. (This was as understandable as people in the United States today buying cigarettes "across the state line" when it is cheaper.) The united farms found it necessary to obtain an order from the Council of State in 1733 recognizing this variable pricing policy, but declaring it a misdemeanor subject to serious fines for anyone to carry tobacco from the low price zone into the areas where full prices were charged.[183]

To make this multi-price system work, the monopoly seems to have worked out a system of selling slightly different varieties of twist in the different price zones so that the inspectors could tell easily and quickly whether any cheap tobacco had been carried into a more expensive district. By 1735, there were three zones: (1) the full price zone where "superior Virginia" was sold; (2) a middle priced zone where ordinary *andouille, demi-andouille,* and *gros-rouge* were sold; and (3) a cheap price zone where common twist (*menu filé*) was sold.[184] The actual practice was rather more complex. When the farmer-general Helvetius reported on his inspection of Champagne in 1737–38, he described a great variety of pricing practices near the frontier. The most expensive style, called "Hollande," everywhere sold wholesale for 50s. per lb., while the *cantine* for the troops uniformly sold for only 12s. per lb. However, the style called *vignettes bleues* (Blue Label) sold for 26s., 29s. and 32s. There was also a considerable variety of cheaper tobaccos from 16s. to 22s. per lb.[185] Yet everywhere he went, Helvetius reported irregular traffic from low priced districts to higher priced ones, distorting sales data everywhere. These operations seem to have become more pronounced when prices in some districts near the frontier were raised in 1738.[186]

There seems to have been some controversy within the company as to the utility of this variable price policy. In his *Oeconomiques* (published in 1745), the farmer-general Dupin reported quite favorably on the administration of the tobacco monopoly. Yet he felt that to check smuggling, the farms should either reduce tobacco prices generally or alternatively introduce a new cheaper grade of tobacco. He alone of contemporary writers seems aware of the consumer, insisting that large sectors of the rural population had not yet, because of expense, acquired the tobacco habit.[187] On the other hand, the maverick farmer-general Bouret, in his advice to the controller-general Machault in 1749–50, argued that the gradual elimination of all price discrepancies would raise yields by five million *l.t.* annually.[188]

Yet the existing system persisted in a somewhat simplified fashion. In the lease of 24 August 1755 for the farm of 1756–62, prices were prescribed on a geographical basis. The old "inferior twist" made from domestic leaf had disappeared. Only two basic styles were recognized: twist suitable for smoking at 48 *sols* per lb. wholesale; and string-bound twists (*tabac en corde et ficelé*) for use in making snuff on a rasp, at 52 *sols* per lb. (The two *sols* over the legal maximum of 50 *sols* was chargeable to the cost of the string.) These full prices were established throughout the greater part of the kingdom. Lower prices of 40 *sols* for *ficelé* and 36 *sols* for smoker's twist were fixed for partially exposed frontier districts: the Calésis, the Boulonnais, the frontier *élections* of Picardy and Champagne, Lorraine and Bar west of the Moselle, Lower Dauphiné. Still lower prices of 36 for *ficelé* and 32 for smoker's twist were ordered for yet more exposed districts: the Three Bishoprics, Lorraine east of the Moselle, Franche Comté, and Upper Dauphiné.[189] This geography makes quite clear the extent to which the monopoly was worried about the land frontier and not the sea frontier in 1755.

In 1762, most price differentials appear to have been eliminated. The schedules announced that year for the next lease established a uniform set of prices, for all *entrepôts*.[190] Faced with declining sales after the adoption of the 20 percent surtax in 1758, the monopoly appears to have taken the easy way out and raised prices in most of the exposed zones. The same policy and prices seem to have been in effect at least until 1774.[191] Although this price rise allegedly did not lead to any decline in consumption, there is evidence of some price variation reappearing in 1774 and later.[192]

In the last years of the monopoly, with less interest being shown in lower price zones, the administrators of the farm became increasingly convinced that the greatest weakness in their defenses against fraud lay in the unreliability of their own staff and agents. Even though most employees were appointed and promoted through personal patronage, some effort seems to have been made from time to time to check such disloyalty. Court decisions were occasionally printed in which employees of the farms were sentenced to death or to the galleys for smuggling tobacco.[193] Yet the problem of the dishonest guard was trivial compared to the problem of the dishonest retailer. We have already mentioned how Lavoisier tried to devise tests which would detect the presence of foreign matter in the retailers' snuff. Even more serious was their ability to mix contraband with what they purchased from the monopoly. Few of them made more than a meagre living from their licenses: the temptation to fraud was obvious. With 43,000 of them to watch by 1782,[194] the supervisory problem might well have seemed impossible. If only one in ten were dishonest, the farm could still easily have lost millions.

In the seventeenth century, tobacco was most commonly smoked or chewed; snuff taking was quite exotic. In the eighteenth century, by contrast, smoking and chewing were largely confined to rustics and boors; only snuff taking was acceptable in the fashionable world and everyone aped the world of fashion: respectable bourgeois, domestic servants as sophisticated as their masters, even common soldiers, all made snuff taking part of their daily lives. Although this new fad multiplied the business of the monopoly after 1713, it also created new problems of administration. It was fairly easy to mark with a seal the twists, weighing about a pound, sold to smokers and chewers. Since the seal at one end was not normally discarded until the twist was totally consumed, it was quite easy to ascertain who was carrying legitimate tobacco and who illicit. (To keep his tobacco fresh, a smoker would normally only cut up a pipeful or so at a time.) Snuff, however, whether ground or grated, could not readily carry a seal or mark. Its growing popularity posed therefore a most serious challenge to the controls of the monopoly.

If retailers were permitted to make snuff on their own premises, they could easily mix illicit tobacco in with that which they purchased from the monopoly. If on the other hand, retailers were forced to buy their snuff ready-made from the monopoly and forbidden to own snuff-grinding equipment, their opportunities for fraud would be seriously curtailed. If the retailer were forbidden even to sell snuff, his opportunities for this kind of fraud would disappear. Any inspector could tell in a few minutes whether all the roll tobacco in a shop was legitimate. Not even a Lavoisier could say as much about the snuff.

When the united farms had first taken over the tobacco monopoly in 1680, they had issued prohibitions against snuff making anywhere except in the workshops of the farm.[195] Save for the imported, all snuff then sold in France was supposed to be made in the monopoly's own workshops in Paris and Mondragon, though its distribution was largely left to subfarmers.[196] In the 1690's, however, a new fad developed embarrassing the yield of the snuff subfarms. Rather than pay the higher prices demanded, snuff takers purchased pieces (*bouts*) of cheaper spun tobacco and grated it themselves. An active little trade sprang up in those years supplying elegantly decorated snuff rasps or grates to be carried in the pocket and used as needed. This practice may well have started among soldiers during the war of the 1690's and gradually spread up the social scale. The snuff takers readily discovered that, although it saved them money, grating their own was an awkward business as the twists sold by the monopoly for smoking and chewing were not thick or solid enough to hold firm at the rasp. To meet the new demand, retailers soon began to take several strands of spun tobacco and press them into a *carotte,* thick and sturdy enough to hold together during grating. The best form of *carotte* for snuff making was *tabac ficelé* around which string had been wrapped to keep it extra firm. Unfortunately, in pressing *carottes,* the seals attached to the pieces (*bouts*) of spun were necessarily broken and had to be removed, making it all too easy for a retailer to mix illicit with legal spun in making his *carottes.*[197] Thus, the monopoly during the years of the Bernard-Crozat-Maynon company, 1697–1718, had been forced to go into the business of making its own *carottes.*

All these problems were attacked forthrightly in the *déclaration* of 1 August 1721. Retailers were forbidden to have any equipment for chopping up, grinding, or rasping tobacco; they were also forbidden to have presses for making *carottes* or *tabac ficelé*. Tobacco for snuff takers (the principal demand by then) was to be supplied by the monopoly only in string-wrapped *carottes* and these were not to be undone by the retailer except with the written permission of the monopoly.[198] By 1726, the Indies Company had ceased delivering pieces (*bouts*) of spun, insisting that the retailers take only the company's *ficelé*. Since the latter product was readily identifiable by its mark and by its distinctive string wrapping, the new system seemed fraud-proof. In fact it was not.

When snuff taking was still a novelty, as it had been in the 1690's, grating one's own was an exciting participation in the mysteries of a select cult. When, by the 1730's, almost everyone seemed to be taking snuff, making it yourself became for many a bit of a bore. (The fashion or rage of the elaborately decorated snuff-box hit Paris, ca. 1719–20.) Demand developed for ready-ground snuff at or near prevailing tobacco prices, far below the levels charged in the *entrepôts* of the monopoly for exotic Spanish and other imported foreign snuffs. If the licensed retailers of the monopoly would not sell moderately priced ready-made snuff, then others would. Keepers of places of public resort (*cabaretiers, limonadiers*) began to keep a little made-up snuff on hand for the use of their customers. Porters in privileged buildings added a small sideline. Faced with this new illicit competition, many licensed retailers, in an effort to keep their customers, also made up some snuff for ready sale. The whole control system seems to have broken down about 1738.[199] In December 1739 alone, we hear of six *limonadiers* and one *faiencier* (crockery dealer) in Paris heavily fined for making and selling snuff.[200]

Enforcement became very difficult without totally alienating both the tens of thousands of retailers of the monopoly and the general public which wanted to purchase ready-made snuff. An order and letters-patent were ultimately obtained from the Council of State on 28 May 1743[201] forbidding licensed retailers and all others from selling snuff under any pretext without the written permission of the monopoly. In the 1740's, there are isolated examples of retailers being prosecuted and heavily fined under this law.[202] However, after the more compliant Bouret replaced Lallemant de Betz at the head of the united farms in 1749, a more tolerant policy seems to have been followed. Permits to make and sell snuff were freely given to all licensed retailers who applied for them.[203] By 1758, the director of the farms at Marseilles could issue a public announcement saying that it was the policy of the monopoly to encourage retailers to sell snuff provided they made it on their own premises and did not sell it for more than five *sols* per ounce.[204] Comparable instructions for Paris issued in 1773 provided that the retailers must make their snuff only on their own premises and only during specified daytime hours.[205]

This tolerant, complacent policy seemed to work reasonably well till the war and the financial crisis of 1759. The 20 percent surcharge on tobacco exacted by the state in 1758 came out of the retailer's profit margin on snuff, and led, as previously noted, to a sharp drop in legal sales in 1759.

Many suspected that retailers were compensating for their smaller margins by mixing in contraband. Although there was some recovery in 1760 and succeeding years, the foundations of complacency had been shaken. Some of the "young Turks" in the company, led by the farmer-general to be, Jacques Delahante, thought that the monopoly should stop manufacture by the retailers and make all the snuff in its own workshops. Delahante's scheme was ignored until he succeeded the aged Fournier as president of the Tobacco Administration Committee in 1768. In the next few years, Lavoisier's chemical tests, in exposing many of the frauds of the retailers, gave added support to the advocates of reform.[206] (Simultaneously, Lavoisier was investigating new machinery for the more efficient large scale manufacture of snuff.) [207] In 1772, Delahante formally presented his snuff-manufacturing scheme to the company, but it was blocked again by the farmer-general Paulze, head of the Tobacco Purchasing and Manufacturing Committee and nephew by marriage to the controller-general, the abbé Terray. Delahante was nevertheless permitted to continue his experiments with snuff manufacture at the old works at Paris and Morlaix and in the frontier provinces managed by the farm, Lorraine, the Three Bishoprics, the Clermontois (taken over in 1771), and Hainault. Though defeated at the time, Delahante managed, by persuading individual colleagues, to get his scheme applied to the southern provinces of Guyenne, Languedoc, and Dauphiné (with snuff coming from the manufactories at Tonneins, Toulouse, and Arles) and the manufacture at Morlaix expanded to serve all Brittany.

The year 1774 saw the death of Louis XV, the dismissal of the abbé Terray and the reconstruction of the farms for the new David lease of 1774–80. Delahante joined the *caisses* or First Committee and was able to extend his experiments to further areas. In 1777–78, he proposed once more that the new snuff manufacture policy be extended to the whole country, but was again blocked by Paulze. The farmers-general in charge of the provinces where the new system was in force supported it, while those responsible for the provinces where retailers were still permitted to do their own snuff grinding preferred the old ways. The decision to continue with the status quo and not extend company grinding was made by the controller-general Necker. In 1781–82, during the controller-generalship of Joly de Fleury, Delahante's new system was finally adopted over the solitary objection of the by then ultraconservative but demoted Paulze and despite the misgivings of the controller-general. It was claimed for the farms that where grinding by retailers had been eliminated, total tobacco sales improved, with 80 percent of sales accounted for by company ground snuff and only 20 percent by unground *corde* for home rasping, chewing or smoking. Nevertheless, the new system never became totally effective everywhere, for Joly de Fleury instructed the farm (July 1782) to introduce their own snuff but to let those retailers who still had the right to grind continue grinding. In fact, the monopoly deprived the retailers of this right wherever they dared but the *parlements* protected some of the grinding retailers (who were connected to local influence via their landlords and those who lent them money) and the new controller-general Calonne did not want to have to fight the courts everywhere over this issue.[208]

Under the new system formally adopted in 1782 (though on trial for more than a decade by then) retailers wherever possible were forbidden to grind any tobacco into snuff—even at the request of a customer—and were obliged to sell only the snuff furnished them ground by the company. Consumers, however, were not obliged to take their snuff prepacked or sight unseen but could examine the various varieties displayed in earthenware pots and make their own selection. By these arrangements, the retailers lost all chance to profit legally or illegally from the manufacture of snuff. Hurt in their pockets, many of the 43,000 retailers sought revenge by spreading stories: everything imaginably wrong with the snuff was blamed on the company's new practice of manufacturing in its own workshops and forbidding retailers to do any grinding or rasping. Empirical evidence lent credence to these stories. When Chesapeake tobacco became scarce during the War of the American Revolution, the farmers-general for mixing had purchased much cheaper Netherlands and Rhenish tobacco and even some Russian tobacco which tended to spoil more quickly than other varieties. Even in normal times, there was a danger of spoilage. To keep the snuff reasonably moist, some water was added at the manufactory after grinding. Should a careless worker add a trifle too much water at this stage, an undesired further fermentation of the tobacco could take place. The public, however, aroused by the retailers, was all too ready to believe that this excessive moistening was a plot against its health caused by the monopoly's desire to make its snuff weigh more at sale.[209]

The story of the revolt of the great law courts against the tobacco monopoly in the 1780's has been told in detail by several authors.[210] It is an important phase of the prehistory of the French Revolution. The barest outline will suffice here. In those hectic events, we see very clearly the breakdown of that privileged legal position which the monopoly had so carefully built up for itself from its earliest days. From the beginning of the century, various *cours des aides* had tried to interfere in the affairs of the tobacco monopoly on behalf of the consuming public by sending court agents to inspect the facilities of the company and the salubrity of its tobacco. Again and again, the monopoly had obtained orders from the Council of State rebuffing these investigations and ordering the courts not to interfere in the internal affairs of the company except in connection with an authentic civil suit. Such orders went to the *cours des aides* of Clermont-Ferrand in 1717[211] and Aix in 1722,[212] and to the *élections* (local fiscal courts) of Lyons in 1738,[213] and Grenoble in 1752.[214] This long established position was now to be successfully challenged.

When the *cour des aides* of Aix complained to Necker of excessive moisture in the snuff sold in Provence, the controller-general sent a farmer-general to investigate. The latter was able to blame it all on the retailers and ordered all their grinding equipment removed.²¹⁵ However, the more this policy of snuff manufacture by the company was extended, the less defense the monopoly was to have against succeeding attacks. In 1782, shortly after the new system was introduced into Dauphiné, there were complaints about the quality of 63 hogsheads of snuff sent into the province: this particular shipment had been made from wartime substitutes of non-Virginia leaf and had been an exceptionally long time in transit (going from Tonneins to Toulouse to Grenoble to Briançon). The *parlement-cour des aides* of Dauphiné ordered an investigation and subsequently directed that eleven hogsheads be destroyed. Instead of complaining about the invasion of its privileges, the monopoly apologized for the admitted deterioration of the snuff and ordered the rest of the 63 hogsheads also destroyed. In return, the court let it resume the sale of premanufactured snuff.²¹⁶ With the door thus opened, numerous other high courts started their own investigations: Aix, Nancy, Metz, Montpellier, Pau, Bordeaux, Montauban, Clermont-Ferrand, Rouen, and Rennes.²¹⁷ Most of these attacks were to prove harmless or at worst merely embarrassing; that at Rennes was to be more serious.

With its long tradition of particularism and independent institutions, Brittany was to be one of the most truculent of provinces on the eve of the Revolution of 1789: on no question was its belligerency more striking than on that of snuff. From about 1772, the monopoly had noticed declining sales, particularly in the area of Lorient. This decline became much more noticeable in 1775 (perhaps associated with the influx of American tobacco ships to Nantes and Lorient). The company, ascribing the decline to the ease with which snuff-making retailers could obtain fraudulent tobacco to mix with legitimate, tightened controls in late 1775 and early 1776 and extended to the St. Malo and Lorient *directions* the new system, hitherto in operation only near Morlaix, which forbade retailers to grind their own snuff and required them to sell only that made at the monopoly's Morlaix works. At this time, roughly the years of Turgot's incumbency, 1774–76, Brittany was swept with tax resistance and antifiscal disturbances fed by rumors that the united farms were to be abolished. Both the *parlement* at Rennes and the intendant in particular found it all too easy to blame part of the trouble on the poor quality of the new snuff and lack of choice so irksome to the consumer. Delahante prepared many able memoirs refuting this argument. Though few may have been convinced, the crisis passed for the moment with the dismissal of Turgot.²¹⁸

Far more serious was the postwar attack on the monopoly's snuff emanating not from the administration but from the *parlement* at Rennes and its subordinate courts. Despite its ultimate very broad political implications, the origins of this phase of the Breton tobacco controversy were probably commercial. The American Revolution, while causing a temporary tobacco shortage in Europe, opened dazzling vistas of a great direct trade between France and the United States. With its convenient location, Lorient in particular attracted a fair share of the American trade during the war; to encourage such trade after the peace, it was in 1784 declared a free port for all goods from the United States. With its new status it became immediately the principal port of resort for American vessels and the chief tobacco trading center in France. Its commission merchants hoped that by capturing most of the monopoly's business, Lorient would replace London and Glasgow as the great European market for American tobacco. In these expectations they were to be disappointed. The farmers-general were unhappy about the high prices for Chesapeake tobacco prevailing in Europe in 1783 and 1784 and kept their American purchases to a minimum, substituting Dutch, Flemish, and Alsatian tobacco, as in wartime. Trying but failing to reach some understanding with the monopoly, the Breton merchants, led by the very influential Bérard brothers, exerted pressure on the government to get the monopoly to buy more from them. In this, they were ultimately successful in 1786–87. Although we do not have any direct evidence connecting Lorient with events at Rennes, we do know that the protests on quality made by the Breton *parlement* in 1784 and succeeding years forced the farmers-general back into the market for Chesapeake tobacco and ultimately worked to the advantage of Lorient.[219]

On 11 September 1784, at precisely the time when the farmers-general were rejecting Lorient's most serious offer to contract for all the needs of the monopoly, the police court at Rennes ordered the suspension of snuff sales by the monopoly and the seizure and examination of all stored tobacco in its jurisdiction. When the local agent of the monopoly refused to obey, the matter was evoked to the *chambre des vacations* of the *parlement* of Rennes which confirmed the police court's orders and named four local "experts" (two physicians and two apothecaries) to examine the tobacco. These highly irregular incursions into the privileges of the monopoly were not unexpectedly referred to Paris and voided by an *arrêt du conseil* of 1 October. Before the last could be registered, however, the local experts' report was rushed to the *parlement* which on 12 October issued a further *arrêt* ordering the burning of all the seized snuff and requiring the monopoly to cease distributing its own snuff and to return grinding equipment to all retailers within the Rennes police jurisdiction. (A further *arrêt* of 15 October extended these procedures to the entire province.) By this time, the matter was attracting national attention and a very sharp *arrêt du conseil* was issued on the nineteenth (passed extraordinarily in the king's presence) to overrule the *parlement's* action of the twelfth. (A further *arrêt du conseil* of 21 November voided the *parlement's* related action of 15 October.)[220]

Despite this ostensible firmness, the new controller-general Calonne decided that it would be expedient to make a partial retreat. He was advised by the intendant Bertrand de Moleville that many consumers did not like the excessive moisture in the monopoly's snuff and that it might be better to let retailers resume grinding and give the consumer more choice.[221] Instead, the farmers-general were secretly authorized to make emergency purchases of superior Virginia tobacco in London and Amsterdam and new regulations for the tobacco monopoly were publicly adopted by an order of the Council of State of 16 October 1784. Blaming all on the false rumors circulated by retailers deprived of the opportunity for fraud, the new regulations confirmed to the monopoly the exclusive right to manufacture snuff commercially in its own workshops. At the same time, the company was ordered to set up additional shops (*ateliers*) for the manufacture of snuff so that no *entrepôt* would be further than thirty leagues from a grinding works; to take great care in the said manufacture; and to provide all *entrepôts* with an adequate supply of *carottes* so that *consumers* who wished to grate their own snuff could do so. All snuff arriving from the manufactory at a *bureau-général* was to be inspected by the intendant or one of his subdelegates before being sent on to the local *entrepôts*. While the old prohibitions against interference were nominally confirmed, the local fiscal courts were empowered, on receipt of complaints about snuff, to investigate such complaints and send reports thereon to the controller-general in Paris.[222]

Despite these concessions, the *parlement* of Brittany remained intransigent. Their answer to the royal *arrêts* of 1 and 19 October and 21 November was further *arrêts* of their own on 27 November, 17 December 1784 and 4 March 1785 ordering a continuation of searches, inspections, and burning of defective tobacco. This evoked another *arrêt du conseil* on 19 March 1785, again in the king's presence, voiding the new batch of orders from Rennes.[223]

By letters-patent of the same day (19 March), however, Calonne made additional concessions to public opinion. The *arrêt* of 21 November had provided for the despatch to Brittany of two well-known Paris chemists (both academicians) to inspect the controversial tobacco. They reported that all was in order except for the excessive moistening of the snuff after grinding; this they recommended should be markedly reduced.[224] The new letters-patent for the regulation of the tobacco monopoly accepted this advice and provided that thenceforth no moisture was to be added to the snuff after grinding in the workshops or warehouses of the monopoly or in the retailers' shops. Not only fiscal but police and other local judges were given fuller powers to receive and investigate complaints about the quality of the monopoly's snuff, and to make provisional seizures where defective products were found. Reports of such investigations and seizures were thenceforth to be sent not to the fiscally minded controller-general but to the more judicious chancellor (or Keeper of the Seals).[225] Although these new regulations were ultimately accepted and enrolled by most high courts,[226] they were not so received in Brittany. The *parlement* of Rennes drew up remonstrances (that of 9 July 1785 being printed and widely disseminated) justifying its conduct and attacking Calonne as a pawn of the united farms.[227] The government, i.e. Calonne, replied strongly, forcing the registration of the letters-patent of 19 March by *lettres de jussion* and *lit de justice* on 18 August 1785.[228] The *parlement* retaliated by a series of *arrêts* between August and November ordering all local fiscal and police judges to report on defective tobacco to it and not to Paris and authorizing interference in other internal affairs of the monopoly. These gestures were met by another *lit de justice* by the governor of the province which forced the registration of new letters-patent of 4 December 1785 cancelling the intervening offending acts of the *parlement*.[229]

At the same time, Calonne kept seeking some measure of accommodation. He considered a scheme whereby two sets of retail stores would be set up in Brittany, one selling snuff made in the company's workshops, the others selling snuff made by the shopkeeper himself. No mixing would be possible, but the customer could choose between shops. On 22 January 1786, the court permitted a delegation from the *parlement* of Rennes to appear before the king and present their case with supporting written evidence; notwithstanding, on 5 February, the king told the delegates that he had considered their complaints in council but approved and took full responsibility for all the actions of the council against which they complained. The *parlement* of Brittany was not in the future to impede the execution of orders of the Council of State. The language was awesome, but the intent was less imperious. If, on the next day (6 February 1786), letters-patent were issued merely confirming and explaining those of 19 March 1785, Calonne also spoke obligingly to the delegates and seems to have promised more.[230] A few months later, he communicated to their *parlement* a letter he had written on 26 April to the united farms informing them of the king's intention to appoint a royal inspector of tobacco manufacture and, in the next lease, to permit retailers to make snuff once more.

No such clauses, however, had been included in the next or Jean-Baptiste Mager lease of the united farms made on 19 March 1786. (Calonne reportedly asked the farmers-general to give up their own snuff grinding, but was persuaded to change his mind.) When the lease was sent out for registration under letters-patent in August, the *parlement* of Rennes saw that it had been misled and retaliated in rage. On 19 September 1786, it registered the lease but ordered the united farms to provide *carottes* to its retailers who were to be permitted to have grinding equipment and make their own snuff. By this and a subsequent order of 14 November 1786, the local fiscal courts in Brittany were also instructed to resume a close inspection of the affairs of the monopoly. When this challenge to the monopoly and crown went unanswered, the *parlement* of Rennes went one great step further on 29 March 1787; it forbad the sale by retailers in Brittany of any snuff made in the works of the monopoly, though permitting the company to continue such sales in its own *entrepôts*.[231]

We do not know how effective was this last eruption of the *parlement* of Rennes against the tobacco monopoly. The royal snuff manufactories kept working at Morlaix as elsewhere. The product must have been sold. At the political level, of course, this was a much more profound challenge to royal authority.

From the very beginning of its existence in 1674, the tobacco farm had found its monopoly difficult to enforce. The necessity for enforcement led it to pursue two main lines of policy. On the one hand in its early days it sought ever sterner punishments against those who violated its privileges. The enforcement of these laws was resisted in many local courts and from the first created friction between the farm and the magistrates. Insofar as the monopoly sought escape from these entanglements by extraordinary procedures and extraordinary tribunals, they drew upon themselves the perpetual suspicion of the magistrates as a class. On the other hand, the monopoly sought to make its privileges more effective by various rational, businesslike devices: giving the customer the qualities he preferred, lower prices near frontiers, bonuses and commissions for its agents and employees, and—finally—the centralized manufacture of snuff in its own factories. Only the last caused trouble, in part because of the distaste of consumers, more because of the hostility of the retailers whose illicit profits were thus circumscribed—but, most of all, because the great law courts saw in the *râpage* an issue on which they could assume a popular stance and challenge at once an unpopular monopoly, an unpopular minister and their ancient enemy, bureaucratic centralization. Thus, in the end as in the beginning, the resistance of the courts emerges as a great thread of continuity in the administrative history of the tobacco monopoly.

CHAPTER 18

French Territories outside the Monopoly and the 1749 Import Duty

From its inception in 1674–81, the tobacco monopoly did not extend to France's newly acquired eastern provinces: Alsace, Franche-Comté, Artois, Flanders, Hainault, and the Cambrésis. Nor did it automatically apply to the eighteenth-century French territorial acquisitions, the principality of Orange, Lorraine, and Corsica. In practice, the "rights and privileges" of these territories were rather differently regarded. Lorraine and Orange were almost immediately brought under the control of the monopoly, as we have seen in earlier chapters. Corsica was geographically and politically so separate a case that we can ignore it in this work.[1] Of the seventeenth-century acquisitions, Franche-Comté, as we have just seen, lost most of its tobacco privileges in the decades after 1721, while most of the privileges of Hainault and the Cambrésis were in effect bought out by the monopoly.[2] In contrast, Alsace, Flanders, and Artois retained their exemptions from the tobacco monopoly almost intact: almost, but not entirely.

The common element in the history of all these territories—and the exotic territory of Labourd—was the threat they posed to the security of the frontiers of the monopoly. To guard against their use as bases for smuggling, we have seen how the monopoly obtained the three league "tobacco-free" zone just beyond most of its eastern frontiers.[3] The monopolists were not primarily concerned that tobacco *grown* in these exempted territories would be smuggled into France. None had any great reputation; and the farmers had taken effective care to keep the consumers of France ignorant of and hence uninterested in Rhenish and Flemish tobaccos. Rather were the monopolists concerned that these frontier territories would become great depots for the supply to smugglers of Virginia and other foreign tobaccos known and liked in France. Since these exempted territories all had their tobacco manufacturing trades, such foreign tobaccos could be prepared in any form demanded by French smugglers and consumers. In fact, within these territories, at Dunkirk and Strasbourg, lay two of the greatest tobacco manufacturing industries in Europe.

The monopoly could never persuade the French government to abolish the privileges of the exempted provinces. The furthest the government would go was the import duty of 30 *sols* per lb. established by Machault in 1749 on all foreign tobacco coming into those frontier provinces. (The surcharges of 1758, 1771 and 1781 carried this ultimately to 45*s*.) This tax was designed to make foreign tobaccos so expensive in the exempted provinces that it would be uneconomic to smuggle them into the territories of the monopoly.[4] The farmer-general Bouret hoped that success in this would also permit the company to eliminate lower prices in those parts of the monopoly near the eastern frontiers. Insofar as the lower price system seems to have been abandoned in part after about 1758, there seems to be some objective evidence of the success of the thirty *sols* duty. Against this success must be weighed the bitter resentment of all the tobacco interests—except the growers—in the exempted provinces, supported by their local estates and corporations. The universal if not uniformly successful resistance to this and related encroachments in all the frontier territories will be the unifying theme of this chapter.

Bayonne and the *Pays de Labourd*

The tiny *pays de Labourd* lay at the southwesternmost extremity of the realm bordered by Guienne, Navarre, Spain, and the sea. Separated from France proper by the desert wastes of the Landes, it was commonly treated by French administration as an island or overseas territory. Under English kings and French (from 1451), its capital Bayonne retained many of the privileges of a Basque town. Culturally and commercially, it looked toward its neighbor Basque ports, San Sebastian and Bilbao. Neither the port nor the surrounding territory had ever been administratively or fiscally integrated into France. Bayonne was particularly favored in the seventeenth century as the center of a great Spanish trade—licit and illicit—through which France earned much silver.

When the tobacco monopoly was established in 1674, nothing was said about Bayonne and Labourd. They were not specifically exempted from the monopoly as were the eastern provinces. Nevertheless, they did not receive the monopoly. In 1686, the intendant of Béarn raised the possibility of extending the monopoly to Bayonne, but nothing was done about it at the time.[5] In 1688 and 1691, the farmers-general proposed annexing Labourd to the monopoly with the understanding that they would continue to sell tobacco there only at the low price then prevailing. They insisted that tobacco was being smuggled from Bayonne into French Navarre and Béarn and carried ultimately into Languedoc, Auvergne, and Limousin. Again, nothing came of the proposals, probably because of the opposition of the intendant of Bordeaux, Louis Bazin de Bezons. In 1695, he also prevented the united farms from moving their checkpoints several leagues closer to Bayonne.[6]

The tobacco traffic at Bayonne about 1688–1713 appears to have been only modestly active. In the year ending September 1698, some 33,925 lb. of tobacco were imported into the port and 46,980 lb. exported—all to Spain. The excess of exports may have come from old stocks, local growth, or prizes. Since tobacco was also a monopoly in Spain, these exports meant either direct smuggling into that kingdom or, more likely, shipments to the privileged ports of Bilbao and San Sebastian, much greater smuggling centers.[7] The only question was whether the king of France gained more by Bayonne tobacco smuggled into Spain than he lost by the same smuggled into France.

The king of France shared with the duke of Gramont the proceeds from the local customary tolls (*droits de la coutume*) at Bayonne. These were collected by the united farms of France which maintained an office at Bayonne for that limited purpose. This office would also seal packages of tobacco being carried from Bayonne overland toward Spain. Such seals exempted the carriers from searches along the roads of Labourd and Béarn and were thought to prevent running the tobacco into Béarn. However, when the tobacco monopoly was separated from the united farms in 1697, even this elementary check disappeared.[8] The tobacco farmers of the Bernard-Crozat-Maynon company seem to have become increasingly dissatisfied with this anomaly. They tried to push their own patrols ever closer to Bayonne, during 1715–17, and to inspect river traffic. When they made their proposals of 12 July 1714 for the renewal of their lease at a higher rent, they asked for the addition to the monopoly of the territories of Orange and Labourd, the latter to be administered as an ordinary part of the *généralité* of Bordeaux.[9] The crown, however, surrendered Orange but not Labourd.

In March 1717, letters-patent were issued by the new regime confirming the privileges of Bayonne. During John Law's experiments with the tobacco monopoly, 1719–21, the local agent of the Indies Company, Larrard, tried unsuccessfully to establish a tobacco *bureau* in the town and then to surround the place with patrols but was stopped by the town authorities aided by their governor, the duke of Gramont, and by the marshal duke of Berwick, governor of Guienne. The latter wrote to the magistrates (22 April 1720) that the Regent still intended to preserve the tobacco privileges of Bayonne.[10] The documents of 1720–21 restoring the tobacco monopoly in France again said nothing about the *pays de Labourd*. In practice, this meant that its long standing, if never defined, exemption from the monopoly would continue.

With the passage of years, the restored tobacco monopolists became less and less happy about the privileges of Labourd. Because tobacco was tightly monopolized in Spain, tobacco smuggling into France was not ordinarily a serious problem along the Pyrenees frontier—except in Navarre and Béarn adjacent to Labourd.[11] The magistrates of Bayonne and Labourd in the 1720's, perceiving the return of the spirit of an orthodox and rigorous fiscality, were rather cautious and conciliatory. At the full restoration of the united farms in 1726, they permitted the farmers to move their guards four leagues closer to the very outskirts of Bayonne and to establish patrol boats behind Bayonne where the Nive runs into the Adour.[12] None of this benefited the tobacco monopoly which was then in the hands of the Indies Company. In 1729, that company pressingly requested a royal *déclaration* requiring tobacco leaving Bayonne by land to give a bond to be discharged by the return of a certificate of actual export.

To this suggested reform Bayonne was violently opposed. Its tobacco trade had greatly expanded since 1714, especially when the king of Spain temporarily deprived his privileged ports of Bilbao and San Sebastian of their right to traffic in tobacco (ca. 1717–22). This of necessity sent all the Spanish tobacco smugglers to Bayonne. Her merchants through their correspondents in the West Indies established direct contact with Cuban traders who agreed to supply "Havana" tobacco surreptitiously via the French islands, particularly St. Domingue. This leaf was manufactured at Bayonne and St. Jean de Luz for sale to Spanish smugglers. The trade was at its height about 1729 when the Indies Company asked for security on export. The town's deputy on the Council of Commerce in Paris, Jean-François de la Borde, prepared a memoir arguing ably that such controls would ruin the port's tobacco trade and much of its prosperity. Their struggling West Indian trade could not be entirely dependent on sugar. It also needed the freedom to bring back Havana tobacco and snuff which in turn was sold at Bayonne to smugglers from Spain for silver. The main smuggling route was up the Nive valley through French Navarre into Spanish Navarre, Castile, and Aragon. It was impossible to return certificates from Spain. If certificates of export were issued at the last customs checkpoint in France, the exporters would be exposed to detection by the Spanish guards. Even if the Indies Company lost 20,000–50,000 *écus* (60,000–150,000 *l.t.*) annually from tobacco smuggling into France, Bayonne would lose far more if this trade were prohibited. Its best sailors by the thousands would leave for the Spanish Basque ports and, by some logic, take the fishing trade with them.[13]

With the aid of the count of Maurepas, secretary of state for the navy, and the united farms, who did not yet have the monopoly, La Borde was able to stop the weakening Indies Company in 1729. He was, however, sadly deceived when he reported that the transfer of the tobacco monopoly to the united farms the next year would confirm the liberties of Bayonne's trade.[14] Almost at once, the guards of the united farms, already stationed in Labourd, began to interfere with the tobacco trade—notwithstanding an order from the *cour des aides* of Bordeaux restoring some tobacco seized in Labourd[15] and assurances to de la Borde from the farmer-general Mazade that such seizures were all a mistake.[16] Spanish "merchants" and ship captains, feeling that the French customs guards were in collusion with the Spaniards, became very cautious in their activities at Bayonne.[17] When the farmer-general Grimod du Fort issued a formal order requiring all tobacco exported from Bayonne to give bond and return certificate, the matter was appealed to de Pomereu, intendant of Auch (in which jurisdiction Bayonne lay after 1716);[18] he, adhering to the policy of his predecessor Leclerc de Lesseville, ordered (6 September 1731) that tobacco exports be permitted from Labourd without bonds or certificates until such time as the matter was decided by the Council of State in Paris.[19] Detailed memoirs were sent there in 1731–32 by the united farms and the town, the former insisting the trade was really rather unimportant, the latter claiming it had a million pounds of Havana tobacco then in store.[20] Nothing was decided at the time, though Maurepas, ever sympathetic to the West Indian trade, wrote to the magistrates of Bayonne that he personally considered their claims vindicated.[21]

Matters remained tense through the 1730's. The farmers-general considered Bayonne the source of all the contraband tobacco in Guienne, Gascony, Armagnac, Rouergue, and western Languedoc.[22] In the single month of August 1734, the intendant Pomereu sentenced eleven persons to be hanged and others sent to the galleys for tobacco smuggling in armed bands about Cambo, inland from Bayonne.[23] Bit by bit, the monopoly seemed to be whittling away the privileges of the port. The Spanish smugglers continued to complain that the employees of the French monopoly were cooperating with the Spanish frontier guards.[24] In 1735, the farmer-general Bergeret, on tour in those parts, issued new orders governing the export of tobacco from Bayonne. These further alarmed the Spanish "traders" and the magistrates of Bayonne had once more to appeal to the king in council through their protector, the secretary of state Maurepas.[25] As a result of these representations, Balosre, the new intendant of Auch, issued a new *ordonnance* (19 October 1735) confirming that issued in 1731 by Pomereu and forbidding the united farms from making any regulations that impinged on the freedom of the tobacco trade at Bayonne.[26] The farmers-general could only issue passes to accompany the tobacco from Bayonne to the Spanish frontier.[27]

This uneasy truce continued until the late 1740's. In 1748, there were riots against the united farms at St. Jean de Luz.[28] More seriously, on 4 May 1749, came the king's *déclaration* establishing the duty of 30 *sols* per lb. on all foreign tobacco imported into French territories outside the tobacco monopoly.[29] At first the merchants of Bayonne did not think that the *déclaration* applied to them. (It did not apply to Dunkirk, but Dunkirk was a more influential place than Bayonne, with more carefully chartered freedoms.) When the merchants of Bayonne discovered that the united farms intended to collect the new duty in Labourd, they complained bitterly,[30] as did their neighbors in St. Jean de Luz and nearby Ciboure. The latter complained to Rouillé that, because of the post-1730 influx of guards of the united farms, the cutomary tolls on the trade of St. Jean de Luz had declined from 30,000 to 7,000 *l.t.* per annum.[31]

Rouillé, successor to Maurepas as navy minister, actively attempted to help Bayonne. When the employees of the united farms tried to collect the new 30 *sols* per lb. from Sallenave, the first Bayonne merchant to import tobacco from Louisiana after the new duty went into effect, Rouillé interceded on his behalf with the controller-general but to no avail. Machault decided against Sallenave and the pretensions of Bayonne. During 1750–52, Rouillé kept encouraging Sallenave to appeal and brought pressure on the *intendants des finances,* Orry de Fulvy and Trudaine, to reopen the case and recommend a change of policy to Machault.[32]

The extent as well as the limits of Rouillé's influence were made quite explicit in 1750. In a letter of 29 July 1750 to Machault on the Sallenave affair, the navy minister complained that the prices offered by the united farms to the merchants for their Louisiana tobacco were insufficient.[33] In answer to this and like pleas, an order of the Council of State was issued the following October raising that price from 25 to 30 *l.t.* per quintal. This order included Dunkirk and Bayonne among the ports to which Louisiana tobacco could be brought but provided that at those two ports outside the monopoly, the 30 *sols* per lb. duty was to be paid immediately unless the tobacco was sold to the united farms or placed in sealed customs warehouses.[34] This was no concession at all to Bayonne for two reasons. First, even though it had been sending an occasional ship to Louisiana since 1741, its tobacco trade was not primarily in Louisiana or other French colonial leaf but rather in Havana and other Spanish tobaccos brought back by its West Indian traders. Although Governor de Kerlérec of Louisiana asked that the Bayonne free *entrepôt* facilities be extended to Spanish American tobaccos obtained by the French in West Indian trade,[35] nothing seems to have been done about it. Second, while Dunkirk reexported much of its *entrepôt* tobacco by sea, that from Bayonne commonly went overland to Spain. Such shipments on leaving the customs warehouse at Bayonne would therefore either have to pay the 30 *sols* per lb. duty or be sealed and give export bond. Neither was compatible with the smuggling trade to Spain.

It thus transpired that the merchants of Bayonne and St. Jean de Luz had complained with good reason in 1750. Their comfortable trade of selling Havana tobacco (illegally procured in the Antilles) to Spanish "traders" for illegal transmission into Spain was thenceforth rendered impossibly difficult and went into a marked decline. Some of the local people sought an alternate supply of untaxed tobacco by turning to planting in the early 1750's. Within two or three years, production in the *pays de Labourd* is reported to have exceeded 500,000 lb. annually. The monopoly responded brutally in September 1753 by sending in armed men to destroy the tobacco in the fields without warning.[36] This bitterly resented action was regularized after the event by an order of the Council of State of 1 January 1754 prohibiting planting in the district. These measures left the condition of Labourd quite ambiguous: by collecting the 30 *sols* per lb. duty on foreign tobaccos, the united farms treated it as a territory outside the monopoly, while the planting ban of 1754 seemed to imply (without saying so) that it was within the monopoly. When the Chamber of Commerce of Bayonne complained of this inconsistency, the court settled the matter in the last harsh days of Louis XV and the abbé Terray by an order of the Council of State of 4 May 1773 which incorporated Bayonne and all of Labourd into the territories of the monopoly and prohibited any private trade in tobacco. News of the new arrangements evoked riots in Bayonne and strenuous protests to Paris from the local authorities.[37]

Before the new rigorous regime could be put into operation, however, Louis XV died (10 May 1774) and the harsh and unpopular controller-general, the abbé Terray, was soon after dismissed by the young, complaisant king, Louis XVI. The new reforming controller-general, Turgot, from his experiences as an intendant, was keenly aware of the manner in which fiscal policy could impoverish a district. By a simple letter, he suspended the order of the Council of State of 4 May 1773 which never became operative.[38] Nevertheless, although Labourd escaped formal annexation to the territories of the tobacco monopoly, the united farms continued to collect the 30 *sols* per lb. duty on tobacco, to enforce the 1754 ban on planting, and to distribute their own tobacco through the district, in competition with that of the private trade.[39] The tobacco trade to Spain remained ruined—much to the chagrin of the local traders.

Appreciating the new air of concessions and greater "constitutionality," however, the inhabitants of the *pays de Labourd* immediately began to agitate for the repeal of the hated measures of 1749 and 1754 and the restoration of the remainder of their lost liberties. One rather old-fashioned faction in Bayonne simply called for the return of their traditional "freedoms" without any clarification of what they were. A more enlightened party, controlling the town council and chamber of commerce of Bayonne, proposed instead that the customs frontier of France be established at the river Adour, leaving Bayonne, St. Jean de Luz, and the greater part of Labourd outside the united farms' customs boundaries, hence once again free ports. (The old-fashioned faction, probably owners of warehouses, didn't like this compromise because it meant that goods arriving in the port destined for France would not be landed in the free port of Bayonne but would go instead to St. Esprit across the river in the territories to be conceded to the farms.) Memoirs containing arguments on both sides were printed in 1774.[40] Neither, however, found much sympathy from Turgot. In 1776, the memoirs were sent to Dupré de St. Maur, the new intendant of Bordeaux (to which jurisdiction Bayonne was attached after 1775). St. Maur took a great interest in the plight of Bayonne and brought the whole matter to the attention of Necker after he took charge of finance.

Despite an extensive correspondence during 1777–79 between Necker, Dupré de St. Maur, and spokesmen for Bayonne,[41] little was accomplished. Tobacco from the new United States was brought to Bayonne during the war, but the port and district remained subject to the authority of the united farms in tobacco and all else. At one stage, the matter was referred by Necker to the deputies of commerce in Paris who suggested that, should the other liberties of Labourd be restored, tobacco ought still to stay under tight control.[42] The entire matter was ultimately referred by Necker to the inspector-general of commerce, P. S. Dupont, who did extensive research and accumulated a library of documents on Bayonne going back to the previous century. (He even went so far as to purchase from the heirs of Trudaine memoirs which that defunct *intendant des finances* had written when the matter was under consideration in the early 1750's.)[43] These studies made Dupont an ardent advocate of the pretensions of Bayonne, St. Jean de Luz, and the *pays de Labourd*. In his first report of 1 September 1779, he advocated creating a free trade zone (*réputé étranger*) out of that portion of Labourd lying beyond the Nive, including Bayonne and St. Jean de Luz. (The merchants and magistrates of Bayonne in 1774 had asked for the free trade in the larger area lying up to the Adour.) He disagreed with the suggestion of the deputies of commerce that such concessions should not include tobacco.[44]

Despite all these reports, nothing was in fact done about Bayonne when Necker arranged the new leases of the united farms in 1779–80. After his fall, Dupré de St. Maur raised the question anew with the principal minister, Vergennes. He reviewed all the arguments made for the district since 1774. Under the oppression of the united farms, the population of Bayonne had declined from 22,000 in 1713 to 11,242 in 1764 and 9,452 in 1778, while that of St. Jean de Luz had fallen from 14,000 in 1713 to 4,000. St. Maur, like Dupont, wanted the reestablishment of a free port and a formal withdrawal of the unenforced 1773 order incorporating Labourd within the tobacco monopoly.[45] Similar demands were made in a printed memoir from the town and chamber of commerce of Bayonne in 1783.[46] The farmers-general remained able to fight off such requests until the accession of Calonne to the controller-generalship in November 1783.

One of the first actions of Calonne was to make Dupont a councillor of state and give him the title of *commissaire-général du commerce*. With his new power, Dupont immediately revived in 1784 his unsuccessful proposals of 1779 for a free port at Bayonne. In the changed political situation, he now found himself able to argue away the expected protests of the united farms.[47] Letters-patent of 4 July 1784 confirmed and restored to Labourd its position outside the French customs frontiers (*à l'instar de l'étranger effectif*) going back to 1483. Its position outside the tobacco monopoly was also confirmed and, as a special favor, it was exempted from the 1749 import duty of 30 *sols* per lb. on foreign tobacco which most other French territories outside the monopoly had to pay. However, that portion of Labourd lying between the Adour and the Nive was declared a frontier zone (analogous to the three league zones in other exempted provinces) in which no one could plant or store tobacco or keep more than two pounds per household at a time. The parish priest and jurats in each village were to be responsible for distributing tobacco to the inhabitants of this frontier zone. Beyond the

Nive, Bayonne and St. Jean de Luz were left free to resume their free trade in tobacco interrupted in 1749.[48]

Bayonne never became a major center of the international tobacco trade. Its smuggling activity was always a much greater menace to the revenues of Spain than to those of France. Nevertheless, the history of its relations with the tobacco monopoly is very interesting for the extremely clear measurement it provides of degrees of rigor over time in the French administrative temperament: the strong position of the port vis-à-vis the relatively weak monopolists under Louis XIV, based in great part on the state's need for Spanish silver; the continued weakness of the monopoly under the Indies Company in the 1720's; the progressively stronger line taken by the united farms after 1730, first in sending patrols throughout the territory, then in suppressing the tobacco import trade in 1749 and the planting in 1754, and finally in attempting to absorb the district into the monopoly in 1773; thereafter, the rectifications by Turgot and the major concession—the reestablishment of the free import trade at Bayonne—under Calonne. Thus we have a rather complete curve of the rise and fall of administrative rigor in eighteenth-century France. Much the same curve will be discernible in the more complex case of Alsace.

The Alsatian Tobacco Trade and the Monopoly

Although the administrative and fiscal history of tobacco in Alsace bore some resemblance to that in the *pays de Labourd,* the situations were economically of quite different magnitudes. Bayonne was a smuggling *entrepôt* through which a few hundred thousand pounds of West Indian tobacco annually passed into Spain and France. Lower Alsace, by contrast, was a major producer of tobacco, part of the great tobacco producing zone stretching down the Rhine to Utrecht (including the Palatinate, the Hanau district on the Main, Cleves and Gelderland and Overyssel in the United Provinces), together the greatest tobacco producing area in the world after the Chesapeake. In addition, Strasbourg was with Amsterdam and Dunkirk one of three great tobacco manufacturing centers on the continent. Thus, Alsace was for the tobacco monopolists of France a problem of infinitely greater complexity than Labourd.

Alsace of all French provinces has not lacked for historians, and all historians of eighteenth-century Alsace have touched upon tobacco. (A definitive monograph on the history of tobacco in Alsace, however, remains to be written.) Most modern scholarship accepts the traditional account that the commercial cultivation of tobacco was introduced into Lower Alsace, about 1620, by a Strasbourg merchant named Robert Koenigsmann who had lived for some time in London. Because of this association, his property near Hönheim outside Strasbourg on which the first experiments were made was called the *Engelländische Hof* or *Cour d'Angleterre.* The cultivation spread through the district in the mid-1620's.[49] Another more Gallophil story has the tobacco seed first brought into Lower Alsace by one Benjamin Maucler, one of the French colonists introduced by the duke of Deux-Ponts (Zweibrücken). His experiments near Bischwiller with monopoly privilege led both to illegal competition and to unrest among the peasantry who believed that tobacco polluted the air and caused fogs and storms. To calm them, the cultivation was forbidden at Bischwiller in 1631, but not before it had spread into other jurisdictions in the vicinity.[50]

This hostility of the local peasantry was characteristic of the resistance of conservative inland provinces to the introduction of this new product. We have already noted this in Burgundy. In Upper Alsace, numerous municipalities adopted regulations against the use of tobacco about 1649–62.[51] Even in Strasbourg, municipal regulations, about 1651–68, forbad smoking in public houses. Despite these islands of hostility, both the use and cultivation of tobacco seem to have become reasonably well established in Alsace by the mid-seventeenth century.

By that time, Strasbourg had become an active manufacturing center. From the 1650's onward, the municipal records contain numerous references to tobacco-makers and tobacco-spinners and their problems. At first, they were not a recognized craft and so could not obtain protection against hawkers and peddlers on the one hand, or against engrossers of the trade on the other. As early as 1669, some "protected strangers" in the town were employing twelve to fifteen hired hands each in tobacco manufacture in addition to their own families. A municipal regulation of 1672 tried to protect the smaller tobacco-makers from the competition of the bigger firms by limiting the number of employees the latter could have; it was not, however, observed. By 1691, one manufacturer with thirty tables (employing therefore at least 150 hands) had twenty agents buying tobacco for him in the countryside.[52]

That busy manufacturer of 1691 claimed he needed his twenty buying agents because his trade had become very brisk since the start of the war in 1688. The Strasbourg tobacco manufacturers ascribed their success to a secret sauce developed about 1700,[53] but the hostilities were probably more important. All our evidence suggests that the wars of 1688–1715 gave a great stimulus not just to the Alsatian but to all the Rhenish tobacco plantations from Strasbourg to the bishopric of Utrecht. The long and unprecedented naval wars between the maritime powers and France interrupted the normal operation of the English-Chesapeake tobacco trade. Thanks to the heavy activity of French privateers, risks and insurance rates between the Capes of Virginia and England rose more than freights, discouraging vessels from venturing in this trade. This tended to drive down prices in the Chesapeake (causing production to stagnate between the 1690's and 1720's) while forcing up prices for Chesapeake tobacco in Europe. These high prices for overseas leaf in an age of expanding consumption made the tobacco business in Europe very profitable for more than a generation. Cultivation was greatly expanded up and down the Rhine, not the least in Lower Alsace.[54]

The tobacco monopolists in France normally preferred to ignore all this Rhenish production because they were not satisfied with its quality and because they did not want to familiarize French consumers with varieties of tobacco readily procured by smuggling. Partly for this reason, we have very few good accounts or estimates of Alsatian production. In 1696, one Jules de Pflügk wrote to the controller-general suggesting that 48 million pounds of tobacco were raised annually in Alsace (80,000 arpents producing 600 lb. each)! He suggested a tax of one *l.t.* per quintal to produce 480,000 *l.t.* annually.[55] At the other extreme, another fiscal projector wrote to the government in 1702 suggesting a tax of one *sol* per lb. on all tobacco manufactured in Alsace which he would farm for 60,000 *l.t.* annually. This suggests a production of only a little more than 1.2 million lb. annually.[56] The truth lay somewhere between these extremes of 1.2 and 48 million lb.

In 1697, the intendant Jacques de la Grange reported that there were then 1,500 persons employed in the Strasbourg manufacture, with an output worth 400,000–500,000 *l.t.* annually. He thought that two-thirds of the export went to Germany and Switzerland, the remainder towards Lorraine and the Saar (and hence, by implication, available for smuggling into France). He did not estimate total production but noted that the sale had reached 1,200 quintals weekly.[57] A later intendant, Le Pelletier de la Houssaye, prepared a similar memoir in March 1701 in which he put tobacco manufacture, Strasbourg's principal trade, at 50,000 quintals annually.[58] With the continuation of the wars and high prices, the trade understandably continued to grow. By 1718, according to a later account, 78 Strasbourg tobacco manufacturers employed 8,000 workers (up from 1,500 in 1697) while their output had risen to 80,000 quintals or eight million pounds. The production figure is reasonable, though that for the labor force seems unduly high since the total population of Strasbourg was then only 35,000.[59]

The golden age of the Rhenish tobacco industries came to an end around 1720. After the crashes of that year and the ensuing deflation, commodity prices throughout Europe were generally lower.[60] Tobacco was noticeably affected. To make matters worse, in 1723, Sir Robert Walpole had Parliament refund the last halfpenny per pound of the import duty which had since 1660 been retained when tobacco was reexported from Britain.[61] This had the effect of reducing the price of British tobacco in continental markets by close to ½d. sterling per lb., equivalent after 1726 to one *sol* per lb. or five *l.t.* per quintal. The loss of this price margin was obviously depressing to continental growers; in 1785, for example, the price paid to producers in Alsace was only 12 *l.t.* per quintal.[62]

The resulting stagnation of the Alsatian tobacco industry is made quite apparent from the data on tobacco entries into Strasbourg. A municipal toll had been collected there since 1689, but its records survive only from

Table I
Leaf Tobacco Consumed in Strasbourg Manufacture, 1726–85[63]
(in quintals of 100 lb.)

Year		Year		Year	
1726	54,138	1746	48,804	1766	47,592
1727	60,300	1747	42,858	1767	43,524
1728	49,770	1748	45,660	1768	42,174
1729	33,480	1749	62,400	1769	37,704
1730	42,396	1750	45,258	1770	36,744
1731	18,234	1751	33,240	1771	41,742
1732	70,314	1752	50,838	1772	59,874
1733	84,738	1753	51,048	1773	39,704
1734	65,442	1754	58,530	1774	41,188
1735	45,042	1755	53,538	1775	39,756
1736	70,704	1756	50,364	1776	45,410
1737	21,900	1757	45,378	1777	40,956
1738	62,358	1758	63,426	1778	42,126
1739	85,206	1759	30,414	1779	57,904
1740	44,544	1760	86,844	1780	65,410
1741	46,212	1761	59,190	1781	31,169
1742	44,550	1762	59,754	1782	47,533
1743	62,886	1763	48,948	1783	44,685
1744	54,906	1764	39,414	1784	53,724
1745	34,470	1765	41,184	1785	39,967
Total	1,051,590		1,017,090		898,887
Average	52,579		50,854		44,943

1726. The above raw material input figures can be roughly equated with manufactured output at Strasbourg. Correctly, from one-quarter to one-third should be deducted for weight lost in manufacture. However, that was compensated for in advance by a fictitious tare of 30 percent, deliberately granted from 1689 as compensation to the manufacture for the aforesaid losses in weight.

The stagnation pattern is clear. Against a reported output of 80,000 quintals in 1718, we have annual averages here declining from 52,579 quintals (1726–45) to 50,854 (1746–65) and to 44,943 quintals (1766–85). The average for the last two decades would have been even lower if the American Revolution had not given an artificial stimulus to all the branches of the old Rhenish tobacco trade. At that, there were (in a generous estimate) only 1,500–1,600 persons employed in the Strasbourg manufacture in 1787, no more than had been reported for 1697.[64]

It was commonly estimated that Strasbourg accounted for at least three-fourths of the tobacco manufactured in Alsace. An authoritative account of 1791 gives the following distribution of manufactories:

Strasbourg district (modern *arrondissement*):
    Strasbourg   42
    Hittenheim (Ittlenheim)   2
    Haguenau   2
    Bischwiller   2

Sélestat (Schelestat) district (modern *arrondissement*):
    Schelestat   1
    Benfeld   3
    Erstein   1

Other:
    Wissembourg   1
    Ingwiller   1

Most of these manufactories specialized in snuff, but a few at Strasbourg, Bischwiller, Benfeld, and Erstein made pipe tobacco. In addition, many of the growers made pipe tobacco at home and exported it by wagon to Switzerland or Germany.[65]

Before 1749, as we shall see, the Strasbourg manufacturers were so busy that the Alsatian growers could not keep them fully supplied and tobacco had to be imported from the Palatinate and Holland. Though legal importation was rendered prohibitively expensive in 1749, the Strasbourg and nearby manufacturers were still busy enough about 1760 to consume almost all the leaf grown in the province.[66] By the 1780's, however, there is evidence that the declining manufacture had left a large margin of leaf available for export unworked. Some rather extreme calculations put the total crop of the province then at 12.2 million lb. However, an official report from Strasbourg's merchants in 1787 estimated production at only 5–6 million lb.[67] A subsequent more political statement to the National Assembly from the deputies of Strasbourg put production slightly above 7.5 million lb., grown in no less than 97 "principal places" of cultivation. The chief were:

Strasbourg district (arrondissement):
    Strasbourg   5,000 quintals
    Hittenheim (Ittlenheim)   2,000
    Schiltigheim   1,500
    Weyersheim   1,500
    Bischwiller   1,500

Schelestat district (modern Sélestat *arrond.*):
    Nordhausen   1,800 quintals
    Erstein   5,000

Matzenheim	2,000 quintals
Sand	1,500
Benfeld	4,000
Kogenheim	2,000
Kertzfeld	2,000
Westhausen	2,000
Hilsenheim	2,000

Upper Alsace (in present Altkirch *arrond.*):

Habsheim	1,800 quintals
Zimmersheim	1,500

The cultivation then seems to have been concentrated in the valley of the Ill between Sélestat and its confluence with the Rhine below Strasbourg, with a northern continuation around Bischwiller and Haguenau; in addition a more scattered cultivation could be found all along the Rhine from New Brisach in Upper Alsace down to the border of the Palatinate. About two-thirds of this crop was consumed by workshops within the province, the remainder going to manufacturers in Cologne, Augsburg, and Switzerland.[68]

Strasbourg's manufactured tobacco and snuff were widely known and well thought of.[69] (Even in contemporary England and America, any moist rasped or grated snuff was commonly styled "Strasbourg rappee," in contradistinction to the drier ground "Scotch snuff.")[70] To handle this important local product, there were in the 1780's no fewer than forty-two manufacturers and thirteen firms of wholesale tobacco traders and factors at Strasbourg.[71] Most of their business was external, for only a small part of production was consumed in Alsace—not more than 500,000 lb.[72] The rest was exported, most going to Germany.[73] At the time of the Revolution, the deputies of the town boasted that their markets included Saxony, Prussia, Poland, Russia, Switzerland, and Italy.[74] Although the Swiss and Italian markets were important, the greater bulk of the tobacco products shipped from Strasbourg went down the Rhine.[75]

In all of this, one thing is clear: although Alsace had a major tobacco industry, producing over five million pounds annually throughout the century, little or none[76] of this was ever purchased by the French monopolists—except in extraordinary periods such as the Spanish Succession or the American Revolutionary War. To the succeeding French monopolists, Alsatian tobacco was normally simply another troublesome product of the exempted zones that could too easily be smuggled into France. Their own interest and its alleged inferiority justified them in keeping this product outside the experience of the French consumer. The monopolists themselves, of course, could not ignore it as an object of smuggling.

Alsace was in great measure a free-trade zone, with a large transit trade between Switzerland and the lower Rhine valley. In the interests of the tobacco monopoly, the province's transit privileges were first modified by an order of the Council of State of 11 December 1736 which required exporters to declare the contents as well as the weight of all packages leaving Alsace. When passing from Alsace into France, the said goods were to be inspected by the guards of the united farms and any, including tobacco, not declared would be subject to confiscation plus a 300 *l.t.* fine.[77] A more restrictive order of 14 August 1745 required tobacco carried on the highways of Alsace to be bonded against smuggling and to be accompanied by a pass.[78]

These were trivial measures compared to the sweeping *déclaration* of 4 May 1749 which established the 30 *sols* per lb. tax on all tobacco entering Alsace and the other provinces outside the monopoly.[79] As explained before, this was the major concession extracted by the united farms from Machault in return for a much higher annual rent to the crown for the tobacco and other farms. A subsequent order of 17 June 1749 named five places in Alsace—Landau, Beinheim, and Fort-Louis-du-Rhin in the north; Strasbourg itself; and St. Louis near Basel on the Swiss frontier—as the places where tobacco imported into Alsace must pay the new duty and get passes.[80] As Landau was an enclave in the Palatinate and as Beinheim and Fort-Louis were on an exposed frontier difficult to patrol, a subsequent order of 20 January 1750 moved the "tobacco frontier" in northern Alsace back to the river Moutre or Moder and established new entry points at Haguenau and Drusenheim in place of those abandoned at Landau, Beinheim, and Fort-Louis. That part of Lower Alsace north of the Moder was left free to import foreign tobacco free of duty but could not send any into the rest of the province.[81]

Needless to say, these new regulations provoked bitter protests in Alsace, particularly from Strasbourg. The authorities there denied that their tobacco was sold for smuggling into France. Since the Franche-Comté market had recently been closed to them, their entire vent had become foreign—Italy, Germany, Switzerland, and the Baltic. They would have no objection, they alleged, if the new duty of 30 *sols* per lb. on foreign tobacco were applied only to Dutch and overseas tobacco—they could do without them—but they could not do without the leaf from the Palatinate and Hanau on the Main which they needed for mixing. If they had to pay the duty on these cheap German tobaccos, they could no longer compete in foreign markets with their German competitors whose supplies were not so taxed. Almost immediately, they claimed, manufacturers and workers had started leaving Strasbourg for Freistadt and Lichtenau across the Rhine or for Seltz just north of the Moder (which belonged to the duke of Zweibrücken). They were particularly unhappy about fixing the "tobacco frontier" on the Moder lest this give an advantage to their fellow-Alsatian manufacturers north of that line and compromise, they averred, the king's pretensions to sovereignty in that area.

Finally, the magistrates of Strasbourg claimed that the new duty not only compromised the tobacco trade but all the traffic that passed through the city. The freedoms of the city had attracted a great number of foreign merchants and business and made the place the great *entrepôt* for trade between the Low Countries and the upper Rhine and Italy. English, Dutch, and other foreign merchants routed their trade through Strasbourg because they knew that the privileges of the town exempted goods in transit from search and from all tolls except a small one in Upper Alsace calculated by weight without opening packages. Now that anything might be opened in search for tobacco, much of this trade would be driven to the other side of the Rhine where attractive concessions were even then being offered.[82] Only on this last point did the then ministers attempt to mollify Alsace. By an order of 9 July 1754, goods in transit through Alsace could be sealed and pass through without being opened.[83]

Hardly was Louis XV dead (May 1774) and the relentless Terray replaced as controller-general by the reforming Turgot (August) when Strasbourg, like every other aggrieved corporation in the realm, made its complaints heard against the "unconstitutional" incursions of the late monarch.[84] Turgot was even more generous to Alsace than he had been to Bayonne. By an order of the Council of State of 23 October 1774, the collection of the 1749 duty of 30 *sols* per lb. on imports of foreign tobacco was suspended in Alsace. In return, for the security of the tobacco monopoly in France, the three league zone system was extended to Alsace. No tobacco could be planted, manufactured, or stored in Alsace within three leagues of its frontiers with Lorraine, the Three Bishoprics, Franche-Comté or even independent Montbéliard (belonging to Württemberg).[85] A subsequent *arrêt* of 9 November 1775 named the towns in the three league zone in which a limited number of dealers would be licensed to supply local consumer needs.[86] Thus the manufacturers and merchants of Strasbourg were freed from the shackles of the 1749 duty only at the cost of placing the townsmen and peasantry of inland Alsace under the much tighter scrutiny of the three league system. In practice, this meant that at Belfort, for example, forty retailers were replaced by three licensees and the big smuggling trade from that town through alien Montbéliard into Franche-Comté was ended.[87]

The effects which the 1749 duty on foreign leaf tobacco imports had on the tobacco manufacturing industry in Lower Alsace have probably been much exaggerated by contemporary complainants[88] and later historians. From Table I, it can be calculated that average entries of tobacco into Strasbourg during 1726-48 were 51,692 quintals. There were exceptionally heavy shipments in during 1749, undoubtedly anticipating the new duty, and compensatingly lighter shipments during the next two years. However, during 1752-63, thanks in part to the Seven Years' War, the inflow at Strasbourg remained at or above the pre-1749 level. Only after the conclusion of the war in 1763, did activity there drop consistently below the 1726-48 level. It stayed below even after the 30 *sols* per lb. duty was removed in 1774—except for 1779–80 when exceptional demand during the American War[89] gave Strasbourg a belated breath of prosperity. The beginning of Strasbourg's real distress in 1763 and the absence of recovery after 1774 suggest that the 30 *sols* per lb. duty on foreign tobacco really had very little to do with the city's difficulties. We also hear of difficult days in the Amsterdam tobacco trade about 1763. Together, they suggest that the troubles of Strasbourg were probably due to basic changes in the tobacco market in Europe—particularly to the development of local manufactures in Italy, Germany, and the Baltic, changing the composition of the international trade in tobacco from the finished product to the raw material. Thus, the Alsace cultivation suffered less than the Strasbourg manufacturing trade. Alsace may also have been affected by changes in taste that created a preference for the cheap and abundant Chesapeake leaf. One cannot expect British tobacco exports to the continent to have quadrupled between the early 1720's and the early 1770's (to ca. 85 million lb. annually) without some adverse effects upon continental producers.[90]

The Northern Provinces and Dunkirk

The last areas outside the tobacco monopoly remaining to be investigated are the northern provinces of Artois, Flanders, Hainault, and the Cambrésis, acquired by Louis XIV between 1659 and 1678. By the acts of capitulation of the various major towns and by the treaties transferring sovereignty, all the ancient rights, privileges, and freedoms of the towns and provinces were recognized by their new sovereign. In practice, the exemption from new royal taxation was taken to include exemption from the tobacco monopoly.

For our purposes, the four provinces vary greatly in importance. The Cambrésis, of course, was the smallest and least important. After the three league zone was extended to it and the tobacco monopoly in the town of Cateau taken over by the united farms of France—both in the 1680's—we hear no more of its problems.[91] Similarly, we hear relatively little of French Hainault after the three league zone was extended to it at the same time. In 1725, the estates of Hainault and the crown converted an existing excise on snuff into a provincial tobacco monopoly which they leased to the tobacco farm of France (the Indies Company) with the understanding that tobacco would be sold in their province at prices much lower than those prevailing in most of France. Cultivation was closely regulated but not prohibited. At first, the French monopoly subleased the farm in Hainault to others, but from 1738 the farmers-general managed it themselves, though continuing the customary lower prices. At Valenciennes in Hainault, the united farms from 1738 had a major tobacco manufactory for the supply of that province, the troops along the frontier and those adjacent parts of France where cheaper tobaccos were sold by the monopoly. (In these latter functions, it replaced the older frontier manufactory at Charleville which was given up, ca. 1744. Valenciennes on the Scheldt was better situated than Charleville for obtaining supplies.) [92]

Much more important—though for different reasons—were the two larger northern provinces of Artois and French Flanders. In Artois, a significant tobacco cultivation about St. Omer dated from the 1630's and 1640's: by 1660, there was an important trade at St. Omer manufacturing snuff, chewing and smoking tobacco, with a smaller center at nearby Aire. When both were finally annexed to France in 1678, these manufactures survived outside the monopoly and prospered considerably after 1720. They mixed local leaf with American and other foreign tobaccos imported via Dunkirk. (In 1739–40, almost 1.5 million lb. of Virginia tobacco were shipped annually from Dunkirk to St. Omer alone.) By 1750, there were 17 tobacco workshops in St. Omer, and 28 by 1789, at which time some 450 hands were employed at that trade. The output of St. Omer was consumed locally and exported to Germany, the Low Countries and further afield, but, from the earliest days of the monopoly, much of it was smuggled into the territories of the farm.[93]

Artois, with these indigenous resources and its long, exposed frontier with Picardy and the Boulonnais, had long attracted the attention of the French monopoly as a supply base for overland smuggling. As such, it had been the first frontier province subjected to the three league frontier control system: in close to a thousand square miles of Artois, no tobacco could be planted, manufactured, or stored.[94] This rigor at first greatly reduced the dimensions of the Artesian problem. By contrast, Flanders, which did not have a common frontier with the territories of the monopoly, was to prove a less immediate but more intractable problem in that it contained about Lille a more important major tobacco growing area and at Dunkirk one of the greatest centers of the European tobacco trade.

Tobacco may have been grown in Flanders in the sixteenth century.[95] It was sufficiently well established by 1635 to be made the subject of a temporary toll (*octroi*) at Lille granted by Philip IV of Spain for the support of a local church. The toll eventually became permanent at Lille and was followed by similar taxes at other towns in Flanders, Artois and Hainault and rural districts or chatellanies. When Louis XIV occupied Lille in 1667 (his sovereignty there being established by the treaties of 1668 and 1678), he confirmed both the fiscal privileges of the towns and chatellanies and their taxes voluntarily raised for local purposes.[96]

Yet, despite this long history, there is evidence that the cultivation of tobacco in French Flanders may have been a very small thing in the seventeenth century. Except in tariffs of tolls, mentions of tobacco at the time are quite few and late. According to a memoir of 1697–98, leaf tobacco grown at Werwick (Werwicq) and about Warneton (both near Lille) were among the exports of the province,[97] but shipments from Flanders into Artois were only 3,000 lb. annually.[98] In 1706, the intendant at Lille reported that Wervick tobacco had difficulties finding markets and ought to be helped.[99] (Both Wervick and Warneton had complex statuses, part of the latter being an imperial enclave in French Flanders and half of the former lying across the Lys in imperial territory.) The cultivation thus seems to have been confined to a very few places near Lille, about 1700, in contrast to the scores of places at which it was to be reported about 1760. This impression of a relatively modest production until well into the eighteenth century is confirmed by the earliest accounts we have of cultivation in Flanders. In order to protect the yield of their local taxes, including a tax on tobacco land, the bailiffs of the chatellany of Lille required growers to register the amount of land on

TABLE II
Land Registered for Tobacco Cultivation in the Chatellany
(*châtellenie*) of Lille, 1712–39,[100] and Estimated Production[101]

Year	Land verges	Est. Prod. lb.	Year	Land verges	Est. Prod. lb.
1712	48,104	171,240	1726	185,000	658,600
1713	46,829	166,680	1727	154,000	548,240
1714	76,231	271,360	1728	160,000	569,600
1715	99,287	353,440	1729	148,000	526,880
1716	110,163	382,160	1730	196,000	697,760
1717	97,614	347,480	1731	215,000	765,400
1718	89,100	317,160	1732	206,000	733,360
1719	66,956	238,360	1733	192,000	683,520
1720	157,212	559,640	1734	174,000	619,440
1721	126,761	451,240	1735	148,000	526,880
1722	106,250	378,240	1736	160,000	569,600
1723	106,430	378,880	1737	172,000	612,320
1724	162,000	576,720	1738	183,000	651,480
1725	174,000	619,440	1739	208,000	740,480

which they intended to plant tobacco. From Table II, we get a clear picture of a steadily growing but relatively modest production. Even if we were to double these figures to allow for production elsewhere in French Flanders (probably too generous an allowance), the impression would not be radically changed. Although Flemish production about 1712–39 was economically important for the poor peasants whom it supported on very small holdings, it was still modest—compared both to what it would become after 1750 and to the five million pounds then being grown annually in Lower Alsace.

If the beginnings of tobacco culture in French Flanders—centered on Lille—were modest and hesitant, the same cannot be said of the tobacco manufacture centered on Dunkirk. When that town was purchased by Louis XIV from Charles II of England in 1662, its new sovereign conferred upon it the most generously defined privileges of a free port. So valuable to the French crown was Dunkirk, as a major center of wartime privateering against Britain and of peacetime smuggling of French textiles, brandies, and tea into southern England, that its privileges were never compromised or trimmed under the *ancien régime*.[102] We do not know when tobacco manufacture started at Dunkirk, but it was well established there by the end of the 1660's. According to one theory, Dunkirk was at first just a transfer point for the importation and transshipment of English and other seaborn tobaccos destined for St. Omer, a few miles inland, where an established manufacture was in existence by 1660. After Dunkirk became French in 1662, some of the St. Omer manufacturers decided to reduce their transport costs and moved thither.[103] The characteristic tobacco manufactured at St. Omer, Valenciennes, Dunkirk, and elsewhere in the northern provinces was styled "Saint Vincent," a trade jargon term having little or nothing to do with the French West Indian island of that name. Actually, only modest amounts of tobacco were ever grown on St. Vincent. Its name was borrowed by the trade to refer to a spun tobacco or snuff normally consisting exclusively of Virginia, though sometimes perhaps mixed with northern (Flemish, Artesian, Hainault) leaf.[104]

Dunkirk was also much better situated than St. Omer to supply the seaborn smuggling trade. We have already noted how the Marseilles free port imported tobacco from Dunkirk for resale to Italian smugglers and how small craft pretending to be bound from Dunkirk to Spain were common smugglers along the coasts of Normandy and Brittany.[105] England was a closer and greater market for the Dunkirk smuggling trade. As early as April 1671, a report to the English government described Dunkirk as the chief center for the English "relanding" trade. Chesapeake tobacco was legally reexported from England to Dunkirk and most of the import duties drawn back. At Dunkirk, the tobacco was manufactured into "cut tobacco" for smoking—an English specialty; it was prepared in the English fashion, with tools and machines specially sent out from London, and then sold to smugglers to be "relanded" in England.[106] Much the same picture, though with much greater detail, came to light at the time of Walpole's "Excise Crisis" of 1733 when Parliament considered the general state of the tobacco trade. Dunkirk was described as a great tobacco smuggling center. Eight or nine Irish sloops were permanently employed carrying leaf tobacco from thence for illegal landing in England and Ireland. Since English smugglers preferred the manufactured product for easy disposal after running into England, Dunkirk tobacco was not only manufactured in the English style but was packaged in the forged printed wrappings of well-known London tobacconists. One witness described much the same activity at Ostend, though apparently on a much smaller scale there. Many of the dealers and manufacturers at both Dunkirk and Ostend seem to have acted on commission for principals in London who financed and controlled the entire operation.[107]

Although Dunkirk was importing tobacco from Portugal about 1700[108] and seems to have drawn some "Clairac" tobacco from Bordeaux until the Guienne plantations were destroyed in 1720,[109] it was heavily dependent upon Chesapeake tobacco imported from Britain to supplement and improve the local tobaccos. We do not have to depend upon purely verbal testimony to establish this close relationship between London and Dunkirk, for we have some data on British tobacco exports thither. The problem is one of interpretation. Under the English navigation act of 1660 (passed when Dunkirk belonged to England) and subsequent legislative and administrative rulings, Dunkirk was considered part of Flanders and not part of France, even after it passed into French possession. Thus, when the English foreign trade statistics were started in 1696, the clerks calculated shipments to Dunkirk, like those to Ostend, as shipments to "Flanders."[110] Since we cannot "disaggregate" this total, we are forced to postulate, on the basis of literary evidence, that down to at least 1749, three-fourths or more of all tobacco shipments from England to "Flanders" were in fact shipments to Dunkirk.[111] The Dunkirk-English tobacco trade was obviously a substantial affair even at the turn of the century, though its real importance dates only from the late 1730's and 1740's, despite a wartime interruption.

TABLE III
English Tobacco Exports to Flanders, 1699–1749[112]

1699–1701	946,377 lb. p.a.
1711–1718	986,176 lb. p.a.
1719–1720	671,623 lb. p.a.
1721–1723	1,865,526 lb. p.a.
1724–1729	725,547 lb. p.a.
1730–1736	1,783,761 lb. p.a.
1737–1743	4,426,443 lb. p.a.
1744	3,649,146 lb.
1745	2,027,100 lb.
1746	304,371 lb.
1747	— lb.
1748	3,203,826 lb.
1749	6,811,983 lb.

The possible tobacco trade between Scotland and Dunkirk is more difficult to establish. To complicate matters, under Scottish administrative practice, Dunkirk was considered part of France, hence exports to "Flanders" meant only Austrian Flanders. However, we can with some safety ignore the Scottish-Flemish tobacco trade before 1749 as yet unimportant, either at Dunkirk or Ostend.[113]

At first both the French government and the tobacco monopoly ignored the growing tobacco trade of Dunkirk and French Flanders. A memoir from the intendant in 1699 fails to include tobacco in its discussion of the manufactures of Maritime Flanders.[114] As late as the 1720's, the chief concern about tobacco smuggling in Flanders seemed to come from the local authorities who were concerned about the yields of their *octrois*. In 1723, the bailiffs and justiciars of the chatellany of Lille, to increase the yield of their tobacco tax, gave its farmer the right to name exclusive distributors of tobacco in each village, thus inhibiting the distribution of untaxed tobacco.[115] At their behest, the secretary of state issued printed instructions to the local mounted constabulary (*maréchaussée*) ordering them to cooperate in the suppression of tobacco smuggling.[116]

After the united farms took over the national tobacco monopoly in 1730, much more attention was given to the tobacco problem in the northern provinces. (The 1730's, it will be remembered, saw the extension of the tobacco monopoly's effective control over Lorraine, Franche-Comté, and the Comtat Venaissin.) The new rigor reached the north at the end of the decade. In 1739, a Dunkirk merchant applied for a routine ship pass to bring tobacco stems, midribs and scraps from Holland to Dunkirk on a British vessel. Such "refuse" was to be used for the "filler" in making spun tobacco, wrapped in Flemish or Virginia leaf. Against the advice of the chamber of commerce of Lille (who apparently foresaw the dangers of inviting governmental interference), the bailiffs of the chatellany of Lille, on behalf of the tobacco growers of French Flanders, appealed to the intendant to forbid such importations; the use of such "trash," they claimed, would give Flemish tobacco a bad name in the markets of the Austrian Netherlands and Germany. Earlier intendants had banned such imports in 1685 and 1709. Hardly had this request been made when the united farms of France appeared on behalf of the bailiffs of Lille and the growers of Flanders. The company recommended not only banning the importation of all stems and midribs, but also levying an import duty of 10 *sols* per lb. on all Virginia and other foreign tobacco (including that from Austrian Flanders) imported into the northern provinces. This would have been equivalent to an *ad valorem* duty of 200 percent for Virginia leaf could then be bought in London for delivery at Dunkirk for five *sols* per lb. (2*d*.½ sterling). Such a duty, of course, would have well protected the growers of Flanders from foreign competition. It would also have made prohibitively expensive in Flanders and the other northern provinces the Virginia leaf so much in demand for use in mixtures designed for smuggling into France. Needless to say, this suggested duty was violently opposed on behalf of the tobacco merchants and manufacturers by the estates of Lille, Maritime Flanders, Artois, Hainault, and the Cambrésis, as well as by the municipalities of Dunkirk and St. Omer. Numerous memoirs on each side were presented to the government during 1739-40. The proposal was stillborn at the time; it is, however, an important indication of the thought of the united farms in 1739. (The decision to do nothing may have been influenced by the very harsh winter of 1740 which left the laboring population of Flanders in great want.) [117]

Although defeated on the issue of the import duty, the united farms of France continued their war of memoirs against the northern provinces—particularly Artois with its long, exposed frontier with the territories of the monopoly. Seizures along this frontier by the guards of the monopoly were mounting steadily:

October 1734–September 1735	56,041 lb.
October 1735–September 1736	69,178 lb.
October 1736–September 1737	82,232 lb.
October 1737–September 1738	125,969 lb.
October 1738–September 1739	139,637 lb.

Since the united farms estimated that the guards seized only about one-tenth of the contraband smuggled, they became understandably alarmed at this upward progression of seizures. They investigated and found to their consternation that the situation was indeed deteriorating. From the records of the checkpoint where goods left the free port of Dunkirk, they established that during 1732–38, 875,000 lb. of Virginia tobacco had been shipped annually from the free port to Flanders and Artois; in 1738–39 this had risen to 1,662,777 lb., and in 1739–40 to 2,275,661 lb.! Of this, 1,500,812 lb. went to Artois, mostly to the great manufacturing center at St. Omer (1,472,465 lb.). (The much more populous Flanders took only the 774,849 lb. remaining.) In addition to these imports from Dunkirk, Artois received 483,521 lb. from the Austrian Netherlands, making total imports of 1,984,333 lb. To this must be added another one or two million pounds of leaf grown in Artois or imported without record from the chatellany of Lille. (This last estimate of the united farms is undoubtedly high.) What could Artois do with two to four million pounds of tobacco? In Hainault, where the tobacco monopoly was separately leased by the united farms of France, and where tobacco was deliberately sold cheaply, a population of 97,200 persons consumed 293,688 lb. of tobacco in 1739. By the same proportions the 196,778 inhabitants of Artois should have consumed about 600,000 lb. and not two to four million. The united farms were sure that the balance was smuggled into the territories of the monopoly. Four villages in Artois near the edge of the three league zone were observed for several months by agents of the monopoly: tobacco arrivals were noted equivalent to fifteen times the possible consumption of the villages. St. Pol was the center of the smuggling trade as St. Omer was of the manufacturing.

Various excuses were advanced by the estates of Artois. It was even argued that dealers had been stocking up since 1732, in anticipation of a war with Britain. It was also claimed that much of this Virginia tobacco was subsequently reexported to the Austrian Netherlands or to the bishopric of Liège. The united farms insisted, however, that Liège was supplied from the Austrian Netherlands, which in turn got all its Virginia tobacco from Dunkirk or directly from England via Ostend and Nieuport. Thus, all the tobacco shipped from St. Omer in wagons for Philippeville, Givet, and Mariembourg, though ostensibly bound for Liège, was actually carried into Hainault and thence run into Champagne and the Soissonnais.[118] All that seems to have come of this memoir writing were the measures of 1743 and 1746 strengthening the three league zone system in Artois, and the Cambrésis. That of 13 May 1746 extended to the Cambrésis the Flemish system of restricting the sale of tobacco to one licensed retailer in each rural parish.[119]

The entire tobacco question in the frontier provinces was of course infinitely complicated by the French-Austrian war of 1740–48. As a war measure, Maria Theresa had prohibited the importation of French Flemish tobacco into her Belgian dominions. When the French armies occupied most of those territories in 1745, the French authorities reciprocated by permitting the importation of French tobaccos into the Austrian territories free of any duty. At the same time, the controller-general saw to it that the conquered provinces did not become a base for smuggling Virginia tobacco into France: by an *ordonnance* of 1 June 1746 and an order of the Council of State of 1 June 1747, the import duty on Virginia leaf tobacco in the Austrian Netherlands was raised from two florins, ten *sols* (or *patars*) per quintal to 4 *fl.*: 10*s*. and 6 *fl.* 15*s*.[120] These were still modest duties by French standards. (Four Flemish florins equalled five *livres tournois*.)

With the return of peace, matters soon came to a crisis. Strong measures were needed to assuage France's war-strained finances. In return for additional millions from the farmers-general, the controller-general Machault conceded, inter alia, the now familiar *déclaration* of 4 May 1749.[121] By this draconian measure, an import duty of thirty *sols* per pound was established on all foreign tobacco entering the French provinces outside the jurisdiction of the tobacco monopoly—including Flanders, Artois, Hainault, and the Cambrésis. It amounted to a toll approaching 600 percent and was quite frankly designed to prevent those provinces accumulating any Virginia tobacco for smuggling into France proper. It seems to have burst upon the world unexpectedly[122] and caught unprepared the various northern estates and corporations which had successfully resisted the much more modest duty of 10 *sols* per lb. proposed in 1739.[123] These bodies now protested to little avail. Times had changed.

If Paris had no ears for the plaints of French Flanders, the newly restored government of the Austrian Netherlands was all attention. Those who governed for Maria Theresa openly welcomed tobacco manufacturers and artisans who contemplated emigrating after 1749 from the French to the Austrian territories. Between 1731 and 1763, 64 permits were granted by the government in Brussels for the establishment of privileged tobacco manufactures, almost all between 1750 and 1757:

1731–38	0	or	0	p.a.
1739–42	3		0.75	
1743–49	0		0	
1750–51	18		9	
1752–57	42		7	
1758–63	1		0.17	

This striking concentration of foundations between 1750 and 1757 can be explained fiscally. In contrast to the new French duty of near 600 percent, the new tariff on English and Dutch goods adopted in the Austrian Netherlands on 27 January 1749, while raising the duty on Virginia leaf above its 1680 level (from 2 *fl.* 10s. to 4 *fl.* 12s. 6d. per quintal), left it at the modest rate of about 30 percent. Ostend and Nieuport, like Dunkirk, were free ports —but they were also placed in a much better position to capture some of Dunkirk's transit trade. In 1751, the toll on foreign goods passing in transit across the territories of the Austrian Netherlands was reduced from 2½ percent to 1 percent, and in 1755 reduced again to ½ percent. Of necessity, tobacco bound for Liège, Aachen and the nearby parts of Germany would henceforth pass preferably through Austrian territory; these rates were probably low enough to take some transit trade away from Holland as well. These attractive conditions were modified after 1757 by the higher taxes necessitated by the war and perhaps the new French alliance.[124]

With the Austrian (and other) territories so invitingly open, it is not surprising that one reaction to the new duty of 1749—in French Flanders as in Alsace—was emigration. Paris soon heard stories of mass movements. The marquis of Argenson, for example, noted in his journal on 17 March 1750 that the new duty had driven 1,500 families out of Flanders and 4,000 out of Alsace.[125] From Lille came stories of exports vanishing, workshops empty, thousands of laborers destitute, and an employer of eighty moving his establishment to Ypres.[126] In Dunkirk, where the tobacco industry was much larger, the situation was much more acute. Manufacturers at Lille and St. Omer used a large proportion of local leaf but at Dunkirk, five-sixths of the annual input of six million pounds was in Virginia leaf. The manufacturers in the free port of Dunkirk could still get their Virginia leaf free, but they were cut off from their licit and illicit markets in northern France and places adjacent by the new duty, collected as their goods moved from the free port area to the *basse-ville* of Dunkirk. Thus, hardly had the new duty been proclaimed when workshops at Dunkirk were reported letting off laborers and even closing. Employment in the Dunkirk tobacco manufacture, which had by early 1749 recovered from its wartime low of 1,500 back to its

1744 figure of 4,000 declined again apace. Workers dismissed or fearful of dismissal were reported emigrating. In January 1750 alone, according to one seemingly exaggerated account, 600 families of tobacco workers, containing 2,000 persons, left Dunkirk. Masters emigrated as well as men. A more sober account has seventeen manufacturers and 1,572 workers leaving for the Austrian territories on the adoption of the new duty. By March 1750, we are told elsewhere that the migrants from Dunkirk had set up many new workshops in the Austrian dominions: twenty alone at Nieuport, just a few miles from Dunkirk, two at Poperinghe, two at Warneton, two in the Austrian part of Wervick, two at Furnes, one at Ostend, four at Bruges, one at Alost, three at Malines, four at Charleroi, two at Fleurus, two at Louvain—plus two at Maestricht in the territories of the United Provinces and many in the lands of the bishop of Liège. By about 1753, there were only 60 tobacco workshops left in Dunkirk employing 1,400 to 1,500 workers, compared to the 200 shops and 4,000 workers of 1749.[127]

There is considerable external verification for the tale of woe which came from the spokesmen of Lille and Dunkirk. We have already seen that the extraordinary number of 61 tobacco manufactories were licensed with privileges in the Austrian Netherlands between 1750 and 1758.[128] On the British side, we see evidence of enhanced activity in tobacco shipments to

TABLE IV
British Tobacco Exports to "Flanders," 1748–75[129]

	English Exports to French and Austrian Flanders	*Scottish Exports to Austrian Flanders Only*
	(in thousands of lb. per annum)	
1730–36	1,784	probably under 100
1737–43	4,426	probably under 100
1748	3,204	probably under 100
1749	6,812	probably under 100
1750	5,094	probably under 100
1751	6,252	probably under 100
1752	10,005	probably under 100
1753	7,448	probably under 100
1754	8,116	?
1755–62	4,410	336
1763	4,344	?
1764–70	4,135	1,904
1771–75	5,612	1,026

both Flanders. English exports to the two Flanders were very buoyant in the years following the conclusion of peace in 1748. Any decline in shipments to Dunkirk after the duty of 1749 went into effect was more than made up for by increased shipments to Ostend. The extraordinarily high shipments of 1752–54, the highest of the century, probably reflected increased shipments through Ostend after the transit duties in the Austrian Netherlands were reduced in 1751. When 1756 brought war with both France and Austria, British shipments to both Ostend and Dunkirk were demonstrably inhibited.[130]

Unfortunately, we do not have any data which would let us measure exactly what proportion of English exports to "Flanders" went to the French and Austrian parts respectively. It is likely that the pre-1749 situation in which at least 75 percent had gone to Dunkirk had given way to a situation in which between 45 percent and 65 percent was going to Ostend. As much was implied in consular reports received by the British government in 1765 stating that tobacco had then become the principal article in trade between London and Ostend (and a major item from Liverpool, as well).[131] Scottish data also show a marked though not as pronounced rise in the proportion of tobacco exports to Flanders going to Ostend rather than Dunkirk. We

TABLE V
Scottish Tobacco Exports to Dunkirk and Ostend[132]

Year	Dunkirk	Ostend
	lb.	lb.
1742–44 (Mich.)	42,238 p.a.	0
1747	354,104	0
1751	367,763	0
1755	?	124,827
1756	?	965,680
1757	?	1,446,273
1758–61	?	0
1762	?	149,803
1764	?	808,832
1765	3,420,520	2,158,363
1766	1,193,589	1,292,816
1767	1,012,457	812,457
1768	2,096,047	2,263,617
1769	2,197,477	2,953,477
1770	3,099,301	3,030,355
1771	4,891,752	4,418,239
1772	2,148,969	710,937
1773	2,539,794	0
1774	5,158,973	0
1775	2,357,888	0

can only speculate as to what might have "killed" the Ostend market for Scotland in 1772.[133] The diversion of the English market from Dunkirk to Ostend was more permanent.[134]

Despite the loss of much of its tobacco trade to Ostend after 1750, Dunkirk was far from finished as a tobacco manufacturing center. Some strength came from consolidation. Instead of 200 houses in 1749 and 60 in 1753, we are told that there were only 30 manufacturing establishments in the port in 1768 and 37 just before the American Revolution, but they were turning out from 2.5 to 5.5 million lb. annually. By 1789, there were again 60 manufactories reported, employing 800 presses and 4,000–5,000 workers and consuming about six million pounds of leaf. New and old markets were developed in Germany, the Baltic, the kingdom of Naples and particularly in northern Italy (via Marseilles, Genoa, Leghorn, and Cività Vecchia).[135] Much of this Italian market was a smuggling market, though we do know that the Neapolitan monopoly also obtained tobacco from Dunkirk.[136] There remained the ship's stores market and the substantial sales to sea smugglers for running into northern France, Ireland, Scotland and England. Only one market was lost by the new 30 *sols* duty—that of supplying the French smugglers for overland carriage into France. As intended, the new duty had indeed driven this trade out of Dunkirk and French Flanders—but not very far. In the 1760's, it is reported that the principal market for the tobacco manufactured in the Austrian Netherlands was the smuggling trade into France.[137] The area about Wervick, where there was tobacco growing on both sides of the border (the river Lys) seems to have been the center of this contraband activity.[138]

If tobacco manufacturing at Dunkirk, St. Omer, and Lille was in varying degrees seriously hurt by the 30 *sols* duty of 1749, the same cannot be said of tobacco growing. With Virginia and other imported leaf subject to a duty approaching 600 percent, the local tobacco cultivators were well protected indeed. There was even less need of foreign leaf for mixing now that snuff taking was the dominant form of consumption.[139] We have already noted that tobacco cultivation in Alsace did not follow the Strasbourg manufacture into decline after 1749. About Lille, the story was much more dramatic. In the 1730's (Table II) tobacco produced in the chatellany of Lille had fluctuated around a mere 600,000–700,000 lb. annually. With the adoption of the new duty, the cultivation burgeoned, spreading from Wervick and Warneton to no less than 121 places all over the chatellany. The

TABLE VI
Land Registered for Tobacco Production in the Chatellany of Lille and Estimated Production, 1758–61[140]

Year	Land	Estimated Production
1758	500 hectares	2,000,000 lb.
1759	591 hectares	2,364,000 lb.
1760	650 hectares	2,600,000 lb.
1761	505 hectares	2,020,000 lb.

TABLE VII

Tobacco Production in the Chatellany of Lille, 1773–90[141]

Year	lb.	Year	lb.
1773	4,325,000	1782	9,621,000
1774	5,110,000	1783	7,069,000
1775	4,808,000	1784	7,580,000
1776	5,450,000	1785	7,045,000
1777	9,774,000	1786	5,916,000
1778	19,144,000	1787	3,090,000
1779	12,985,000	1788	4,747,000
1780	11,148,000	1789	5,493,000
1781	11,594,000	1790	8,312,000

Average   7,956,166 lb. p.a.

trade flourished during the Seven Years' War and reached heroic heights during the American Revolution when tobacco became very expensive in Europe. It remained throughout a crop of the very smallest peasants.[142]

When the farmer-general Bouret persuaded the controller-general Machault to levy the import duty of 30 *sols* per lb. on foreign tobacco entering the frontier provinces outside the monopoly, he and his company undoubtedly hoped that they would destroy in the northern provinces the manufacture of Virginia and mixed tobaccos so much in demand for smuggling. What they really succeeded in doing was both confining the manufacture of foreign tobaccos to the free port of Dunkirk and encouraging its establishment in the nearby Austrian territories. Although the limits of Dunkirk were easy to watch, the long frontier between French and Austrian Flanders was much more difficult to patrol, in great part because there was a legitimate private tobacco culture and trade on the French side of the frontier. Even more discouraging for the company, the high duty gave an obvious encouragement to the plantation of tobacco in Walloon Flanders (Lille). When we consider the millions of pounds of increased growth after 1750—in both French and Austrian Flanders[143]—we must conclude that the high duty of 1749 was in great measure self-defeating in the northeastern provinces.

The united farms tried to bring all the frontier territories outside the tobacco monopoly under the effective police of that monopoly. Where this was not possible, the extraordinary duty of 4 May 1749, it was hoped, would prevent those provinces from becoming bases for smuggling foreign tobacco into France. The monopoly was much less concerned with native tobacco little demanded by the French consumer. In the case of Franche-Comté, the police had been so effectively established by the 1730's that the 1749 duty was anticlimactic. Its incidence has been ignored in this chapter.[144] Elsewhere the 1749 duty hurt and was complained against bitterly. Alsace escaped from it in 1774, Bayonne in 1784. Flanders and Artois never did. This is some measure of the seriousness with which even the ministers of Louis XVI took the smuggling problem on the northeast frontier. Ironically, though, the close proximity of the new tobacco industry in Austrian Flanders probably made the 1749 duty less truly effective on the northern frontier where it was retained than elsewhere where it was abandoned.

Part II
Britain and the Chesapeake: Monopsonistic Elements in an Open Market

CHAPTER 19

Britain and the French Market up to the Treaty of Utrecht

The Beginnings (to 1711)

THE HISTORY of the British-Chesapeake tobacco trade, for our present purposes, can be divided into three roughly defined periods. The first, extending from the start of tobacco cultivation in Virginia down to 1689, was characterized by expanding production, declining prices, and burgeoning markets in the British Isles and in Europe as the tobacco habit spread. In the ensuing period, the wars of 1689–1713 led to relative stagnation. High wartime freight and insurance rates discouraged the sending of ships to Chesapeake, at once depressing prices in the colonies and raising them in Europe. The former phenomenon tended to discourage further expansion of tobacco cultivation in Virginia and Maryland, while the latter gave a great stimulus to production in Europe. This period of relative stagnation persisted after the war into the 1720's.[1] Recognizing the export market problem, Sir Robert Walpole in 1723 had Parliament remove the last halfpenny per pound of the import duty retained (since 1660) at export.[2] This considerably narrowed the price advantage of continental tobaccos and facilitated rising reexports from the late 1720's. This and related phenomena stimulated renewed growth in the Chesapeake where production trebled between the early 1720's and early 1770's.[3]

British interest in or even consciousness of the French tobacco market varied with the general condition of the trade. In the decades before 1689 when other continental markets seemed able to take all the Chesapeake leaf available for reexport, there was hardly a mention of the possibilities of a French vent. In the difficult decades after 1689, however, English merchants and officials became slowly but increasingly aware of the desirable possibility of selling more tobacco to the French monopoly. This awareness was of course greatly stimulated by the monopoly's increasing purchases of tobacco in England after 1697; it reached its peak during the War of the Spanish Succession in the debates over trading with the enemy and over the contents of the Commercial Treaty of Utrecht. In the third period, 1724 to 1775, there was much less public talk about the French market. With the development of a great vent for British tobacco in France after 1713, particularly after 1723, it seems to have been tacitly understood that France was best left to merchants lest government intervention spoil everything.

In Chapter 7, we have already examined the English-French tobacco trade before and immediately after the establishment of the monopoly in 1674. What little we know of this subject is summarized in Table I. When

TABLE I
English Tobacco Exports to France, 1660–87[4]

Year	London	Outports (in English lb.)	Total
1660	33,084	[c. 16,542]	[c. 49,726]
Mich. 1668– Mich. 1669	160,818	[c. 80,409]	[c. 241,227]
Mich. 1685– Mich. 1686	131,783	59,769	191,552
Mich. 1686– Mich. 1687	169,778	325,903	496,281

we consider that total English tobacco *exports* had already reached the level of eight million pounds in 1668–69[5] and more than doubled in the next thirty years,[6] we can readily perceive that the quantities sent to France before 1689 were relatively trivial.

A treaty of commerce was under negotiation between England and France between 1669 and 1677. In a 1669 proposed draft sent to Paris by the French ambassador in London, there is no mention of tobacco.[7] When discussions were resumed, some English merchants trading to France explained what they wanted in a memorial of 29 November 1674 printed for presentation to the English commissioners negotiating the treaty. Although the tobacco monopoly had just been established in France (September 1674), they referred neither to it, nor to the French market for tobacco. They were much more concerned about the Dutch market, England having just made peace with the United Provinces while the French-Dutch war continued. The only mention of tobacco came in a discussion of contraband of war. The English merchants asked,

> That the English may freely trade to all Ports and Places, tho' in Enmity with the *French,* and carry any Corn, Fish, or other Provisions, as also Lead in Pigs and Bars, Tobacco, Sugar, and all other Commodities, those only excepted which shall be particularly enumerated in this Treaty, and declared *Contrabanda.*[8]

When the treaty came ultimately to be concluded in February 1677, tobacco was in fact included among the goods that were *not* to be considered contraband of war.[9] Neither the government nor the merchants of England had anything more to ask of France in respect to tobacco.

At the conclusion of the War of the League of Augsburg in 1697, Secretary Trumbull's office wrote to the new Board of Trade asking for advice should there be any commercial negotiations at Ryswick. The board returned a list of points for negotiation: again there was no mention of tobacco.[10] By contrast, the Dutch, in their commercial negotiations with France at Ryswick, demanded the abolition of the tobacco, saltpeter, and other French monopolies as contrary to their treaties of 1662 and 1678. Up to then, of course, they had been selling more tobacco to France than did England. The French replied that, as Dutch merchants were treated on the same basis as were French merchants, there was no infraction of the older treaties. Dutch merchants sending tobacco to France could either sell to the monopoly or reexport without paying duty. No one was treated better.[11] In the end, nothing was said about tobacco in the Ryswick treaties.

Though nothing was done about tobacco then, 1697 was nonetheless to mark an important turning-point in the history of the English-French tobacco trade. In Chapter 7, we have already seen how France came to be supplied with Virginia tobacco during the war of 1689–97, thanks to the brilliant successes of the French privateers. French consumers liked what they had to take.[12] We have also seen in Chapter 3 how, in September 1697, the controller-general, the elder Pontchartrain, decided to take the tobacco monopoly away from the united farms and grant it to the Bernard-Crozat-Maynon company. The new tobacco monopoly company decided by 1700 that it would be in their interest to buy tobacco in increased quantities in the English market.

TABLE II
English Tobacco Exports to France, 1697–1707[13]

Year	(in English lb.)
Mich. 1696–Mich. 1697	0
Mich. 1697–Christmas 1698 (15 months)	110,926
Christmas 1698–1699	296,990
Christmas 1699–1700	1,756,244
Christmas 1700–1701	2,241,041
Christmas 1701–1702	191,550
Christmas 1702–1707	0

With the advent of the war in 1702, a period of extraordinary difficulty ensued for Chesapeake planters, English merchants, and French buyers alike. Privateers did not bring as many Virginia ships into French ports in this war as they had in the last, and, faced with increasing consumption, the monopoly was hard pressed to obtain needed supplies. Its difficulties were rendered all the more acute by the comparatively strict economic warfare measures adopted by the principal belligerents during the early years of the war, 1702–5. The monopoly could get special passes from the French government, but they could at first do nothing about the very strict English and Dutch bans against trading with the enemy. It was during this difficult period that the company had recourse to such dangerous and expensive devices as having their agents in London ship Virginia tobacco to correspondents in Gothenburg, Sweden, who in turn transshipped the same in Swedish vessels to France.[14]

In England, official sentiment was unusually adamant on the question of trading with the enemy under the Tory-dominated government of 1702–4, and for some time afterward. Considerable pressure was brought to bear on the Dutch to break off postal communication with France. The declaration of war of 4 May 1702 brought into operation a body of existing legislation against exporting contraband to or having any other dealings with the enemy. This was at first interpreted to mean that British merchants could not *export* to France, while a subsequent act prohibited the *importation* of any French or French colonial goods into England after 25 March 1705.[15] The Dutch, however, were not so rigorous. By 1704, they were thoroughly tired of the trade bans and allowed most of them to lapse. The French government on its side was by 1705 prepared to permit trade with the Dutch to resume along traditional lines. Starting that year, a long series of orders were issued by the Council of State, defining the conditions under which Dutch vessels might visit French ports and the commodities they could bring in and carry away.[16] This general policy, of course, made it easier for the French monopoly to obtain tobacco from Holland and affected tobacco markets throughout northern Europe. Even as the English Parliament was passing the 1705 ban on imports from France, a Liverpool M.P. and tobacco merchant could write to his partner at home that tobacco prices were staying up at London because of the Dutch: "it's said the Dutch carry it [tobacco] for France and no doubt a way will be found [by them] to carry it to Spain [which] will help that Trade very much."[17]

With the London mercantile community so clearly aware of what the Dutch were doing, it must naturally have occurred to many that, if English merchants could obtain permission to trade with the French as the Dutch did, many branches of English trade would benefit. There seems, however, to have been such hostility in Parliament to traffic of this sort that the tobacco merchants of London were slow to request permission. Instead, during 1705 and the early months of 1706, they devoted their collective energies to complaining to the government about the two groups of English merchants competing for the monopoly of tobacco exports to Russia.[18] Some, however, had their eyes elsewhere.

Early in 1706, Colonel Robert Quary, surveyor-general of customs in North America, was preparing to return to his station after a visit of some months in England. Quary had had an extended quarrel with the Assembly of Virginia[19] and seems to have thought it advisable to mend his home fences before crossing the Atlantic. On the eve of his departure he flooded the government with memorials suggesting ways of helping the distressed tobacco trade. On 2 February 1705/6, he sent to Lord Treasurer Godolphin a memorial on the tobacco trade which was in due course referred through Secretary Hedges to the Board of Trade (22 February). Quary blamed the chaos and depression in the trade on the irregularity of the convoy system. Recently three great convoys had arrived from the Chesapeake within fourteen months, disorganizing and depressing the tobacco market in Europe. Prices had fallen so low that the tobacco sent could not realize enough to cover the bills of exchange drawn by planters which had to be returned protested. It would be worse if ships sailed without convoy, for their capture by the French would supply the normal continental market. Although he referred to the prewar French, Spanish, and Flemish markets now being supplied by the Dutch, he did not suggest any remedies except a reform in the convoy system.[20]

The board and the merchants spent the next few weeks discussing the convoy question until their attention was redirected by a most informative memorial presented on 15 March by John Linton, a London tobacco manufacturer. He concentrated upon the great expansion of the Dutch cultivation and manufacture since 1688 and on the many markets they had taken away from the English. One of these was the French, where the Dutch but not the English could then trade: "The French Trade for tobacco they [the Dutch] have by our Prohibition intirely ingrost, Send thither (as I am informed) : 3: or: 4 Sorts of their owne Growth made into Roll . . . Their Tobacco being brought into vse there, deprives vs of the vend of: 8 or 10,000 h'h'ds of Leafe, wee Sold them yearly before this warr. . . ." To strengthen the English export potential, Linton's recommendations (aside from those concerned with Russia and the Baltic) included permitting exports to France in neutral vessels as well as exports to Spain for the ostensible use of English and allied troops there. He also asked for the remission of the last halfpenny of the import duty not then refunded on exportation—a concession not granted until 1723.[21] In a slightly later revised version of his suggestions, Linton dropped the duty drawback suggestion but added a request that English merchants be permitted to export tobacco to all parts of Spain subject to the Archduke Charles without having to deal with the local monopoly.[22]

The Board of Trade was very much impressed by Linton's memorial which they considered at length on 18 and 19 March, at which times they seem to have been waited on by some tobacco merchants who supported Linton's suggestion for exporting tobacco to enemy France in neutral vessels. The commissioners immediately instructed their secretary to write to the advocate general, Sir John Cooke, asking "by what Law, Order or Instruction" such export was forbidden.[23] Cooke replied on 9 April that such trade was prohibited generally by the "Laws of war and of nations" as well as by the words in the queen's declaration of war of 4 May 1702 prohibiting her "subjects to hold any correspondence or communication with France or Spain, or their subjects." Nevertheless, the queen might "by contrary declarations and instructions, allow such trade," but it would be necessary to obtain the concurrence of the States General of the United Provinces lest Dutch ships seize neutral vessels carrying from Britain to France. (English vessels earlier were seizing Dutch vessels legally trading to France, until the queen gave contrary orders.)[24]

Meanwhile Linton had been in correspondence with Quary who was becalmed at Plymouth on his way to America. From Plymouth on 2 April 1706, Quary sent two versions of a new memorial to the Board of Trade and to Lord Treasurer Godolphin. In it, he repeated Linton's information about the growth of tobacco cultivation in the United Provinces as well as Linton's specific recommendations for the relief of the English tobacco trade—including permitting exports to France in neutral vessels. To this he added the recommendation that experts be sent over to inspect the Dutch operations, including John Linton who had "manufactured more than any man in England."[25] When Quary's latest memorial came before the Board of Trade on 11 April, they asked him immediately for further information on France and convoys, and inquired of the great tobacco merchant, Micajah Perry, how much tobacco was then being exported to Spain and Portugal (not very much).[26] They also wrote Secretary Hedges of their progress but suggested that, rather than send a special agent to the United Provinces, the English envoy at the Hague could engage someone to make inquiries.[27] Either Hedges or Godolphin expected more, for, on the sixteenth, the secretary of state wrote back to the board referring to them the Treasurer's version of Quary's last memorial and asking them for their "further thoughts" on the matter.[28]

At their meeting of 18 April, the Board of Trade had in hand Secretary Hedges' prod, Micajah Perry's authoritative confirmation of the possibilities of the French, Spanish, and Portuguese markets, and Sir John Cooke's opinion that there were no statutory impediments to an export trade to France in wartime.[29] They summoned for the next day some prominent tobacco merchants of London headed by Micajah Perry, leader of the Virginia trade, and John Hyde, leader of the Maryland trade. These merchants in person and in writing a few days later supported Quary's proposal to permit tobacco export to France in neutral vessels—provided that assurances could be given that they would not be seized by either British or Dutch warships.[30] In their formal report to the queen on 26 April 1706, the board recommended *inter alia* that the export of tobacco be permitted to France in neutral vessels and that the English ambassadors in Spain and Portugal be instructed to assist the sale of English tobacco in those countries.[31]

What this record means is far from clear. The proposal to permit tobacco exports to France came originally from Quary, a minor official, and John Linton, an unsuccessful manufacturer who wanted the government to send him to Holland. When the Board of Trade wrote to Sir John Cooke on

19 March for his opinion on the legality of exports to France, they referred to an application for such permission from "several merchants of tobacco."[32] There is no other trace of such application in the records of the Board. The tobacco merchants of London took no part in the solicitation until specifically questioned by the board. One gains the impression that interested parties working behind the scenes were reaching Godolphin and Hedges. Who they were, or whether they had anything to do with the French monopoly, we can only guess.

There were of course other more important things going on behind the scenes, including the efforts of Marlborough and Godolphin to reconstruct the ministry to increase the role of their Junto Whig supporters. This involved replacing Hedges with the earl of Sunderland as secretary of state for the southern department. While this great dispute was raging at court, the Board of Trade's representation on the tobacco trade was forgotten. Nothing came of a petition to the queen from the Virginia merchants asking for action on the board's representation.[33]

With the reconvening of Parliament and the final replacement of Hedges by Sunderland (3 December), the air rather cleared. If the tobacco merchants held back, others were less reluctant. On 17 December 1706, a motion was made in the House of Commons "That Leave be given to bring in a Bill for the taking off the Prohibition of importing *French* Wines." It failed[34] for rather obvious reasons of state: as one tobacco merchant pointed out to another; "it was not thought convenient at this time for that it might be prejudicial to our alliance with Portugall."[35] Although there was no obvious connection between the proposed bill and the tobacco trade, Virginia merchants were rightly interested in it, for imports of wine would pay for and facilitate exports of tobacco to France—as at least one draft pamphlet among Harley's papers argued.[36]

On 19 May 1707, the reconstituted Board of Trade (packed with Whig hacks) seemingly on its own initiative took up its dormant representation of 26 April 1706 on the tobacco trade. During the next six weeks, they held frequent conferences with Perry, Hyde, Linton, and others representing the tobacco trade. Further petitions and memorials were presented,[37] as well as reports on the growing Dutch competition: one house in Amsterdam allegedly manufactured one million pounds of roll tobacco annually for the French monopoly; before the war they had used all Virginia, but were then mixing half Dutch ("inlands") tobacco with their Virginia leaf.[38] Finally, at a meeting of the board on 27 June, the draft of a new representation was read to the merchants, "with which they were well satisfied."[39] The new representation of 1 July 1707 from the board to the queen summarized the various evidence presented by the merchants on the continental markets and Dutch competition; it repeated most of the specific recommendations of the previous April, including that of permitting the export of tobacco to

France in neutral ships.[40] The contents of this representation were repeated the following November in a long report made by the Board of Trade to the House of Lords on the state of the trade of the kingdom.[41]

After further unexplained delays, the Board of Trade's representation of 1 July 1707 was finally taken up at the Privy Council on 18 January 1707/8. By an order in council of that date, the secretaries of state were ordered to instruct the envoys in Spain, Portugal, Sweden, and Russia to do all possible to encourage British tobacco exports to those parts. (Nothing ever came of this.) At the same time, the proposal for permitting tobacco exports to France in neutral vessels was referred to Lord Treasurer Godolphin, and for legal opinions to the attorney-, solicitor-, and advocate-general.[42] On further referral the customs commissioners reported to the Lord Treasurer on 28 January 1707/8 that they found no law prohibiting such exportation in wartime, but feared that permitting a direct trade then might provide an opportunity for British subjects to send goods to France under assumed names and use the proceeds to buy wines and other French goods. Such permission might be inexpedient "during the session." Godolphin, who was then distracted by his great fight with Harley, merely sent the customs' report to the queen on 28 January without comment. A few weeks later, after his victory and the dismissal of Harley, Godolphin called in the customs commissioners on 17 February, reconsidered the matter, and decided that "all proper encouragement be given to trade; and what is desired being not against any law his Lordship will propose it at the Privy Council."[43]

On 20 February 1707/8, on a report from the Lord Treasurer, the queen in council finally ordered that tobacco might be exported to France in neutral vessels. Appropriate notice was to be sent to customs, to commanders of ships of war and privateers and to the Dutch government.[44] It is clear that the final decision was Godolphin's. It is also clear that both Hedges and Harley had to go before this decision could be made. We may surmise that those two Tory ministers, realizing well that trading with the enemy was intensely unpopular with back bench, country gentry members of Parliament— whether Tory, country party, or independent—had been reluctant to take any initiative in this matter.

The new British policy of permitting tobacco exports to France was slow to have any effect: no tobacco was in fact exported to France in 1708. (The French monopoly's affairs were distracted that year by the great financial crisis and by the renewal of their lease; they also were reported to have had ample stocks on hand or contracted for, and may have hoped by holding back to drive down the London price.) In 1709, the French did take over one million pounds but in 1710 again bought nothing, as their government tightened up commercial controls after the failure of the peace negotiations of the previous year (Table IV).

Needless to say, the tobacco merchants of London and the outports were not at all happy in 1708 about the failure of the order-in-council of 20

February to result in immediate exports to France. Providentially, Colonel Edmund Jennings, president of the council and acting governor of Virginia, was to write a long report on 24 June 1708 on the economic state of his colony: so desperate had the tobacco trade become that the impoverished planters were forced to turn to linen and woolen manufactures. No remark could be better calculated to catch the attention of the Board of Trade. When this paragraph was read at the board on 8 November, the Virginia merchants were immediately summoned. Micajah Perry, Isaac Millner, and others duly appeared on 11 November and explained that the planters had been reduced to such straits in part because the outbound Virginia fleet with £200,000 worth of manufactures which was supposed to have left England in August 1707 did not in fact depart until March 1708. When asked by the board whether they had not received any relief from the order-in-council of 20 February 1707/8, they replied that they had not because the Dutch had made long term advance contracts to supply many markets.[45] They were obviously referring to France, for only a monopoly can contract for a country's needs a year or more in advance.

Two weeks later, the tobacco merchants were back at the Board of Trade with their solution: if freedom to export tobacco to France had so far had no effect, it was necessary to go further. In a memorial of 26 November 1708, they proposed that anyone not an enemy alien should not only be free to export tobacco or any other British goods to France in neutral ships, "but as an encouragement thereto, may be permitted to import into this Kingdom, (in the same ships that Transported the Tob:º or other goods before mention'd) a Loading of French Wines paying their Majesties Customs charg'd thereon, before the Prohibition."[46] This memorial was read at the board on 29 November without any decision being reached. On 16 December, Richard Perry (son and partner of Micajah), John Linton, and other tobacco merchants again attended the board without any further success. They informed the board that they intended to print up their "Reasons" for presentation to the House of Commons.[47]

Simultaneously, the tobacco merchants of London had been conducting a somewhat more successful solicitation at the Treasury. Their "Reasons" for the tobacco-wine trade had on 26 November been referred to the customs commissioners who reported *the next day:*

> Wee have no objection to the Merchants applying to Parliament to obtain such a Law, and are humbly of Opinion That the Importation of Wine from France by Law in exchange for British Commodities will not only very much advance the Customs, but may in great measure prevent the present practice of Running Wines, and carrying out the Coin of the Kingdom.

The report was on 1 December read by Godolphin, who had "no objection."[48]

To understand the great furor this proposition caused, we must consider the interests involved. France had been the preponderant supplier of English wine imports before the parliamentary ban of 1678 and again between the resumption of trade in 1685 and the outbreak of hostilities in 1689. The very high discriminatory duties placed on French wines from 1689 had diverted this trade from France to Spain, Portugal, and Italy. The Anglo-Portuguese (Methuen) commercial treaty of 1703 (granting Portuguese wine duties at least one-third under those on French wines, in return for the preferred admission of English woolens into Portugal) and the parliamentary ban on French wine imports in 1705 merely confirmed what was already taking place.

TABLE III

English Wine Imports, 1688, 1701, and 1708[49]

	1688 (London only)	1701 (London)	1701 (Outports)	1708 (London)	1708 (Outports)
French	14,219 tons	1,733 t.	319 t.	120 t.	216 t.
Portuguese	541 tons	6,373	1,036	7,516	2,118
Spanish	3,252 tons	8,478	1,296	1,415	825
Italian	282 tons	1,289	124	1,671	22
Rhenish	885 tons	669	129	524	46

This reorientation of the wine trade had created a considerable vested interest among British merchants trading to Portugal and Italy and among the woolen manufacturers and dealers from whom they bought. (The merchants trading to Spain for the most part supported those trading to Portugal because they expected to resume their great wine importations from Spain once the duke of Anjou was driven out.)

Why did the tobacco merchants raise the wine question and thus attack this strong vested interest? Part of the answer may lie in their close political association with some of the wine merchants. Since about 1700, the wine and tobacco trades had been acting jointly in approaches to the government over customs bonds, a very serious problem common to both trades as importers of heavily taxed commodities.[50] The spokesman for the wine trade in these negotiations was Samuel Shepheard, M.P. for London, 1705–8, one of the principal promoters and directors of the new East India Company of 1698, a great merchant described in 1710 as "an excellent merchant for shipping and foreign trade by far the first in England."[51] Shepheard seems to have been more influential with Lord Treasurer Godolphin than anyone in the tobacco trade[52] and it would have been only natural for the Chesapeake merchants to have followed his leadership and advice in dealings with the British government.

There was of course also the French government to deal with. The tobacco trade was all the more ready to support the wine scheme because they saw that there was no reason for the French to buy tobacco directly from England for cash, when they could buy the same thing from Holland in exchange for wine. (It was the oft avowed French policy in permitting such dealings in wartime to have no unbalanced trades.) The only difficulty in talking about a balanced trade in wartime was that tobacco was a monopoly in France. Thus those who controlled French tobacco purchases in England might also control French wine exports thither. This immediately raised the spectre of who in London was really "on the inside" with the French tobacco monopoly.

The agents of the French tobacco monopoly in London at this time were the Huguenot firm of Tourton & Guiguer (whom we shall discuss in the next chapter).[53] Behind them loomed the much more important figure of John Lambert, the London agent of Antoine Crozat and probably of Samuel Bernard.[54] Lambert was also a Huguenot, though of English descent, born on the Isle of Ré, but educated in London where he returned and commenced business after the revocation of the Edict of Nantes. He became a great merchant and shipowner, interested over his career in eighty vessels, a man who later claimed to have exported over £500,000 worth of British manufactures in eight years.[55] He was particularly active in the wine trade, in which he sometimes shared ventures with Samuel Shepheard.[56] Like Shepheard, he was a big shareholder in such "Whiggish" ventures as the Bank of England and the new East India Company.[57] In addition to his other business for Bernard, there is reason to suspect that he may have been the paymaster for the tobacco monopoly in London, paying for the purchases nominally made by others.[58] Even at the time, most of his activities must have appeared mysterious; it would have been all too easy, however, to imagine that should a bill pass for exchanging tobacco for wine, that trade would in fact fall into the hands of a few like Tourton & Guiguer, Shepheard, and Lambert. This may not have been the entire "in-group"; that there was an "in-group" was certain.

Word was out very soon that Godolphin had "no objection" to the Virginia trade soliciting the House of Commons, and counteractivity followed. The merchants of London trading to Portugal, Spain, and Italy got up a counter petition to the Treasurer with 85 signatures. It was referred by Godolphin to customs on 22 December 1708, but not reported on by them till 20 January 1708/9. The petitioners of course argued that permission to import wine from France would ruin the wine trade from the more southerly countries and with it the export of British woolens and Newfoundland fish thither. Since the French were already buying British tobacco, this permission would not expand total tobacco exports at all. No one would benefit except those few men who had contracted with the monopolists in France for the export of tobacco and who would thus have a monopoly of the return trade in wine. The customs commissioners replied that even if the act passed, Portuguese wine would be well protected in the British market by duties only half those of French wines. They doubted if exports of British woolens would be adversely affected. They knew nothing of schemes to engross such a trade—but pointed out that the Portuguese merchants would have an opportunity to raise the question when the bill was before Parliament.[59] The sympathy of customs to the scheme, in contrast to the coolness of the Board of Trade, is perhaps to be explained by the duties which wine imports from France would have to pay.

As the season for parliamentary action approached, both sides took to the printing press, publishing broadsides and pamphlets for distribution to members of the House of Commons. Those issued in behalf of the scheme stressed the distress of the tobacco trade,[60] and the amount of French wine already entering the country through smuggling,[61] while denying that any real monopoly would result.[62] The publications on the other side repeated the arguments made in the Portuguese merchants' petition to the Lord Treasurer, stressing that the only beneficiaries would be "such as can make a private agreement with the farmers of Tobacco in *France*, or their Agents here," particularly since the French would not buy anything from Britain except tobacco.[63] These arguments were by no means confined to merchants in the Portuguese trade. A well-informed, well-argued manuscript pamphlet from that time, written by Arthur Bayley, a prominent tobacco merchant, analyzed the situation of the tobacco trade and attacked the French wine scheme as tending toward monopoly.[64]

On 5 February 1708/9, a petition was presented to the House of Commons from "the merchants, trading to Virginia and Maryland, on behalf of themselves, and the planters of tobacco in those colonies" describing that trade's distress owing to the loss of export markets in Sweden, Russia, Poland and, particularly since the start of the war, in France and Spain, all of which had so lowered the price of tobacco that the inhabitants of those colonies were being forced to turn to woolen, linen and cotton manufacture. The petitioners asked only "that the present state of the tobacco plantations in America may be taken into consideration, and such encouragement given for the exporting tobacco, as to the House shall seem meet"—but everyone knew what was meant.[65]

When the petition came up for consideration by the house on 10 February, a motion to reject it was defeated, 114 for, 173 against. (This was a large house, implying some effort on both sides to get members in.) It was then "ordered, that leave be given to bring in a bill, for the encouraging the exportation of tobacco, and other commodities, and manufactures, of the growth and product of Great Britain, and dominions thereunto belonging; and that Mr. Bridges, Sir Henry Bunbury, Mr. Poulteney, Mr. Steward and Mr. Lowndes, do prepare, and bring in, the bill."[66] As James Brydges was paymaster-general, John Pulteney a member of the Board of Trade and William Lowndes secretary to the Lord Treasurer, this was clearly a government bill. The bill was read a first time on 18 February and a second time on

24 February. On the latter occasion, a petition was presented against the bill from "divers merchants, and others, trading to Portugal, Spain and Italy" claiming the bill would ruin woolen exports to those countries. Opposition to the bill was mounting, for the motion to read the bill a second time passed only 155 to 147, while that to commit it to a committee of the whole passed only 159 to 154.[67] In the next two weeks, further petitions against the bill were received from the "traders in the woollen manufacture, inhabitants of the town and vicarage of Hallifax," the merchants, weavers and traders of Norwich, and the "Governors of the Dutch Bay Hall in Colchester, and . . . the Bay-makers, Say-makers, Perpetuana-makers, and the Makers of the other Woollen Manufactures in and near the said Town." With pressures mounting, motions to go into a committee on the bill were defeated on 9 March (144 to 117, 152 to 122). The bill was not heard of again.[68]

A contemporary account ascribes the defeat of the bill in part to lobbying among the members by the minister from Portugal, in part to the consideration that it would be "to the Advantage of *France,* and to the Benefit of Five or Six Persons in *Great Britain* only." [69] Part of its failure may also have been due to the unpopularity of Lambert and Shepheard. The latter had once been expelled from the house because of election frauds. In 1713, another bill to help the tobacco trade was thrown out by the House of Lords because it contained extraneous clauses ("tacks") which were too obviously a "job" to help Lambert and Shepheard.[70]

The final chapter in this wine and tobacco controversy was something of an anticlimax. In 1710, of course, there occurred the great political upheaval in which Queen Anne dismissed Godolphin and the Whig ministers. As the new ministers were determined on peace, they were much less solicitous of the sensibilities of Portugal. These ministerial changes almost immediately split that dominant group of new "Whiggish" financiers who had emerged in the 1690's and scored their greatest successes in the foundation of the Bank of England in 1694 and the new East India Company in 1698. Some of them—particularly those at the head of the Bank—remained loyal to Godolphin; among these were Sir Gilbert Heathcote, Sir William Scawen, Francis Eyles, and Nathaniel Gould who waited upon the queen in June 1710 and asked her not to dismiss the Lord Treasurer lest it "tend to lessen the credit of the public funds." After that minister's dismissal, these "loyalists" withheld their support and greatly embarrassed Harley (soon to be earl of Oxford) in his early financial measures.[71] On the other hand, there were those who deserted the inner circles of financial Whiggery and offered Harley their services, much appreciated in the circumstances: the best known names in this group were Sir Theodore Janssen, (Sir) Joseph Martin, (Sir) John Lambert, and Samuel Shepheard. Lambert was part of a syndicate that arranged to remit £450,000 to the army in Flanders a few days after Godolphin's dismissal in 1710 and received a baronetcy as a reward.[72] Samuel Shepheard became deputy- and subgovernor of Oxford's new South Sea Company in which the others were directors.[73] (When the treaty of Utrecht took the Asiento away from Samuel Bernard's French company, it placed it in the hands of an English company whose directors were by no means unfamiliar to him.)

Early in 1711, the new government brought in a bill to repeal the act of 1705 prohibiting the importation of French wines. The bill was brought in on 17 February 1710/1 and, despite a petition from Bristol and Exeter, passed its third reading on 10 March, slipping through the Lords by the 16th (despite more petitions) and receiving the royal assent the next day.[74] There was much less publicity connected with this successful bill of 1711 than with the unsuccessful one of 1709. In the government sponsored *Review*, edited by Daniel Defoe, an article did mention the distressed condition of the tobacco colonies as one reason for supporting the bill.[75]

The act of 1711 permitted wine imports from France only in vessels carrying British produce thither and limited such imports to the value of British goods exported.[76] As French regulations did not permit the import of most British produce or the export of wine in most foreign vessels,[77] the French-British wine trade failed to revive to the degree anticipated. Nevertheless, the French tobacco monopoly was able to take advantage of the act to ship wine from Bordeaux to its agents in London to pay for the tobacco it needed. This exchange helps explain the great surge of English tobacco exports to France in 1711. The failure in 1712 of Tourton & Guiguer, the London agents,[78] probably explains much of the subsequent decline of 1712–13.

TABLE IV
English Tobacco Exports
to France, 1703–13[79]

Years	(in English lb.)
1703–8	0
1709	1,121,382
1710	0
1711	3,505,807
1712	864,376
1713	790,800

The great fight over opening the wine and tobacco trades with France during the war was to be but a "practice run" for the fight over the commercial treaty of Utrecht.

The Commercial Treaty of Utrecht, 1709–14

In the year 1709, abortive peace negotiations were undertaken between the allies and France. Since it was likely that a commercial treaty would be part of any general peace settlement, various agencies of the British government began collecting data that would be needed in such a negotiation. On 16 May 1709, the secretary of state, the earl of Sunderland, wrote to the Board of Trade asking them to review all commercial treaties since about 1660. The board wrote to the mayors of Bristol and Exeter for advice and asked groups of merchants for their opinions. On 23 May, a group of tobacco importers, including Micajah Perry, Arthur Bayley, and John Hyde, attended the board with a memorial discussing the tobacco monopoly in France. Because of the monopoly, they argued: (a) tobacco consumption was held down in France by excessively high prices, and (b) Britain and Holland could sell only leaf tobacco to the farm, whereas formerly they had sold manufactured. Both the plantations and employment in Britain were thus hurt. They asked "that in a Treaty, it may be provided that a free Importations of Tobacco both Leafe and Manufactured may be allowed to the Subjects of both Nations [Britain and Holland] under as easie a duty as Can be Obtained, not Subject to aney Farme or Monopoly Whatsoever."[80]

Others consulted by the Board of Trade that year repeated the arguments of the London merchants. The mayor of Bristol, after consultation with the merchants of that port, recommended that a free trade in tobacco in France, under a moderate duty "would encrease the consumption there and very much improve our Plantations, and . . . Navigation."[81] Much the same came from the mayor of Exeter,[82] and from Samuel Locke[83] and Henry Gaultier,[84] merchants of London. All these communications were taken into account when the board considered the matter in September, and in their report to Sunderland on 18 October 1709, the commissioners indicated that "the merchants desire (if it can be obtained) that a free Importation of Tobacco, in Leaf & Manufactured, may be allowed, under a Duty not exceeding what shall be paid for Tobacco of European Growth, and that it be not subject to any Farm or monopoly."[85] However, the commissioners could not have considered this too promising a point, for they omitted any mention of it in their draft treaty sent to Sunderland that same day.[86]

With the failure of the peace negotiations of 1709, the projects for a commercial treaty were stillborn. Matters of trade had to be left on the shelf until the political-military situation was such that negotiations could be renewed in 1712. Work was then resumed where interrupted in 1709 without further solicitation of opinions.[87] On 18 December 1711, Secretary St. John wrote to the Board of Trade for information on a commercial treaty with France. They replied immediately by sending him a copy of their draft treaty of 1709.[88] During the next three months, the draft treaty was worked on in St. John's office, by whom and in consultation with whom we do not know. It was only at this stage that an article was added ending the tobacco monopoly in France, the clause requested in vain by the merchants in 1709.[89] In all probability, St. John was trying to make his treaty more attractive politically to draw more mercantile support both to it and to the ministry.

On 18 March 1711/2, Secretary St. John sent to the Board of Trade the Latin draft of the commercial treaty prepared in his office. Article xiii contained the provisions for an open trade in tobacco in France.[90] When the board came to consider the draft on 26 March, they immediately gave orders "that letters be writ to Sir John Lambert, Mr. Stephen Seignoret, Mr. Samuel Shepheard, Mr. Samuel Locke, Mr. Laurence Galdie, Sir Patrick Johnson, Sir William Johnson, and Mr. Thomas Smith, to desire them to consult with such gentlemen as they should think proper, and to let their lordships have, as soon as they could conveniently, what they may have to offer in relation to the said Treaty."[91] The first five were London merchants trading to France, close to the government; the last three were Scots: Sir Patrick Johnstone, M.P. for Edinburgh, Thomas Smith, Dean of Gild of Glasgow and M.P. for the Glasgow burghs, Sir William Johnstone of Westerhall, Bart., member of a prominent Dumfrieshire family and shortly to be M.P. for the Dumfries burghs. This was a very limited group and foretold by its exclusiveness much of the later troubles of the treaty.

Those consulted had many suggestions to make about the draft treaty, but none affecting article xiii on tobacco. Only the memorial presented by the three Scotsmen contained a paragraph calling for the end of the tobacco monopoly in France.[92] (Scotland had not been consulted in 1709.) Nevertheless, when the Board of Trade returned the draft treaty to Secretary St. John on 15 April 1712, they suggested that the tobacco clause be strengthened. The proposed clause said only:

> Likewise the Duties upon Tobacco in the leaf or wrought to be brought into France shall from henceforward be reduced to the same moderate Rate which the Tobacco of the Growth of any Country in Europe brought into France does or shall enjoy, neither shall the British Merchants be prohibited for the time to come to Sell the said Tobacco to any Buyer they shall think fit.

The Board of Trade wanted this clause extended to include commodities other than tobacco, with a general prohibition of all monopolies added: "Nor shall there be for the future in either Kingdom any Farm or Monopoly of any Goods, Commodities or Merchandizes whatsoever."[93] St. John, probably foreseeing difficulties, did not accept the change.

The congress of Utrecht began its long and arduous negotiations in January 1712, the British and French having already agreed on the general outlines of a peace. In May-June 1712—about the time that the British suspended military operations against the French—St. John and Torcy, the French foreign minister, agreed that commercial difficulties should not hold up the general treaty: any details about trade that could not be settled at Utrecht would be left to special commissioners.[94] In August 1712, St. John, now viscount Bolingbroke, went to Paris with Matthew Prior to conclude the formal suspension of hostilities.[95] On his return, he left Prior there. In November 1712, Bolingbroke wrote to Torcy that since the North American and commercial articles seemed to be the principal affairs holding up negotiations at Utrecht, he had instructed Prior to try to settle these matters by direct negotiations at Paris.[96]

Among the commercial clauses causing most trouble at Utrecht was article xiii in the British draft. As finally drawn in Bolingbroke's office, it provided that the English Levant and East Indies companies could carry their wares to France on the same terms as the French companies and that British tobacco could be imported into France, paying the same duties as European tobacco, and sold to anyone without restriction.[97] To this the French plenipotentiaries at Utrecht replied that no foreign nation had such freedoms, nor could they be claimed under "most favored nation" status.[98]

In the course of the fall, the British plenipotentiaries at Utrecht made a major concession on this point. In a revised version of the draft treaty (the second British propositions), they gave up the demand for the abolition of the monopoly and in the tobacco section (now article xi) asked only: that duties on British tobacco, manufactured or unmanufactured, imported into France should be reduced to the level enjoyed by other European and American tobaccos; and that British merchants importing tobacco into France should pay the same duties and have an "equal liberty to sell" subject to the same laws as French merchants importing tobacco.[99] This was hardly any liberty at all. The French negotiators at Utrecht, seeming not to realize that the British had conceded almost everything in article xi, continued to make difficulties about tobacco. On 12/23 December 1712, the English negotiators wrote from Utrecht, "Art: 11th concerns Tobacco, in which the ffrench Ministers are very positive their Court canot grant what we would have."[100] On 22 December/1 January 1712/3, the British plenipotentiaries wrote again that, although the French were prepared to concede the tariff of 1664 on most goods, they could not reach any agreement on the four excepted categories (woolens, fish, sugar, and tobacco) which the French thought should be left to the special commissioners.[101]

By that time, however, both sides began to have second thoughts about article xi, recognizing it for what it was—a brave verbal display to disguise a complete retreat by the British in their tobacco demands. A memoir (probably from the Council of Commerce) explained to the French foreign minister that although this clause seemed contrary to French laws in that it spoke of "liberty of selling," closer examination showed that such was to be only "according to the laws of France"; thus, the imagined difficulties disappeared and "this article can be left as is."[102] In London, about the same time, there began to be some realization that too much perhaps had been conceded in the wording of article xi. In a rather ambiguous letter of 24 December (o.s.) to the plenipotentiaries at Utrecht, Bolingbroke tried to strengthen the article by interpretation:

> As to the 11th Article . . . , I am to add further that her Ma:^ty intends hereby only that her Subjects carrying Tobacco into ffrance may freely sell the same there to whom they judge proper. . . . If however the ffrench are so very positive and unwarrantable in respect to ye Tobacco ffarmers her Ma:^ty will be very sorry to find a matter so prejudicial to both Nations, so much encouraged, for the consequence will infalliby be, that as there is a Monopoly of Tobacco in ffrance so there will be one of the same Commodity created by Merchants here in concert with the ffarmers of ffrance to the disadvantage of open Traders whereby great mischiefs will accrue on both sides.[103]

Bolingbroke may have written this only for the record, for in it he did not instruct the plenipotentiaries to do anything specific about the weak wording of article xi.

A week earlier in Paris, Matthew Prior had in much the same way tried to strengthen the import of article xi. In the third clause of his memoir of 21 (24) December (n.s.) presented to the controller-general Desmaretz, he raised the tobacco question most delicately: "As Tobacco is farmed in France, and as the English Merchants can only sell it to the employees of the farmers of tobacco, which is a great prejudice to the English, entirely obstructing the freedom of commerce in that respect, it was hoped that the French would find suitable means to mitigate this inequality in commerce." Desmaretz referred the memoir to the Council of Commerce who interpreted it as a return to the demands of article xiii of the first British project: "It was changed in article xi of the second project and agreed [sic] that the English should be treated in France in respect to tobacco in the same manner as were the subjects of the [French] king; thus this was a settled matter reopened by this memoir."[104] The same sentiments in somewhat politer form were conveyed by Desmaretz to Prior.[105]

The French were not to be budged. On 8/19 January 1712/3, Prior wrote Bolingbroke from Paris that Desmaretz had told him and Torcy had told the duke of Shrewsbury the same thing: "the Farm of Tobacco they insist is an Annual fund appropriate to the Kings use, and more certain as to its Produce than any other in France and that our Merchants in this Case have no other reason to Complain than their own, being Both upon an equal Foot."[106] The next day at Utrecht, the French representatives replied more formally, "The English shall be permitted to sell their Tobacco as the French do. We cannot deviate from the established Usage on this article in France."[107] Bolingbroke not surprisingly decided that the tobacco farm was not to stand in the way of his great arrangements. On 19/30 January 1712/3, he wrote to Prior not to delay signing the commercial treaty because of minor points such as the tobacco farm, but to leave all such matters for later negotiation with the special commercial commissioners then being sent to London.[108]

Word soon got about in London that Bolingbroke was making important concessions in the commercial treaty with France. On 16/27 January 1712/3, l'Hermitage, Dutch representative in London, wrote to the States General, "On the rumor which has spread that the two commissioners who have come here to negotiate trade for France will not agree to let [the British] ship refined sugar and tobacco [to France], the principal merchants who trade to America have presented a memorial explaining that a very great number of the English colonies on that continent will be ruined if they can't sell those commodities as they did formerly but can't do now to France. . . ."[109] The memorial in question was a long document with several pages devoted to an attack on the French tobacco farm and customs system.[110] Others were similarly astir in January: Cornelius Denne, a tobacco merchant of London, wrote to Treasurer Oxford on the distress of the tobacco trade and the need for an open monopoly-free trade into France;[111] Sansome, British-consul elect at Bordeaux, before setting out for that post, submitted memorials both to the Board of Trade[112] and to Secretary of State Dartmouth calling for the abolition of the tobacco monopoly in France.[113] His claim that the French king would increase his revenues by an open trade under a moderate duty is reminiscent of the arguments advanced from French mercantile circles about 1701.

Despite these murmurings, Bolingbroke pushed on: the definitive treaty of navigation and commerce between Great Britain and France was signed at Utrecht on 31 March o.s. or 11 April n.s. 1713. Tobacco was dealt with in article x, which was *verbatim* the same as article xi in the second project of 1712. It provided:

> The Duties on Tobacco imported into France, either in the Leaf, or prepared, shall be reduced hereafter to the same moderate Rate, as the said Tobacco, of the growth of any Country in *Europe* or *America*, being brought into *France*, does or shall pay. The Subjects on both sides shall also pay the same Duties in *France* for the said Tobacco; There shall be likewise an equal liberty of Selling it; and the *British* Subjects shall have the same Laws as the Merchants of *France* themselves have and enjoy.[114]

The ninth article of the treaty provided that matters which had not yet been concluded at the time of signing should be referred to commissioners from both sides for settlement. By a convention signed the same day as the treaty, the plenipotentiaries on both sides specified the issues and claims that were to be referred to the commissioners. Item three kept alive the British pretensions on tobacco: reserved for future discussion was the demand that "the British Merchants shall not hereafter be forbidden to Sell the Said Tobacco to any Buyer whom they please for which purpose the letting out the Dutys on the said Tobacco to Farmers which has been hitherto practised shall cease neither shall such farming be used again hereafter."[115] However, long before the special commissioners could be appointed and their discussions begin, the promise of the treaty was hopelessly compromised in June 1713 by the failure of the House of Commons to enact legislation removing the prohibitions and reducing the duties on French goods, as called for in articles viii and ix of the treaty.

The story of Bolingbroke's failure is well known: the bill introduced with every prospect of success in May was defeated in June 1713 when scores of independent and Tory M.P.'s deserted the government under pressure from the silk, linen, and woolen trades in their constituencies. The Spanish, Portuguese, and Italian merchants who had been defeated in 1711 had their revenge in 1713. Convincing the woolen interest that their existing market in Portugal was worth more than a hypothetical market in France was the master stroke of the opposition. For our present purposes, it should be noted that the failure to include in the treaty clauses really solicitous of the interests of the tobacco and sugar trades gave to those great interests no really strong reason either to support or oppose the bill. In fact, there really were no interests who thought they would benefit very much from the bill[116] except would-be wine importers from France—and, however effective Sir John Lambert and Samuel Shepheard were in the closet, there were limits to their effectiveness in Parliament or "out of doors."

While the bill was before Parliament and for about a year afterwards, a considerable propaganda battle was waged. Many tried to argue that the treaty would, for example,[117] bring great benefits to the tobacco trade. In May 1713, the Board of Trade delivered to the House of Lords copies of all the documents it had received since 1697 on the trade with France, including the memorials of 1709 from the Virginia merchants asking for an open tobacco trade to France.[118] In October 1713, Daniel Defoe in the government sponsored *Mercator: or, Commerce Retrieved* suddenly discovered the tobacco interest which he had neglected all summer in his arguments for the treaty. In issue after issue during the next few months, he tried to use that trade in defense of the treaty. Sometimes he argued that too little tobacco was being exported to France because the bill had failed; in other issues, he used the great amount of tobacco being exported to France as evidence of the soundness of the treaty's objectives. In general, the *Mercator* of these months seems piqued at the Virginia trade for failing to support the treaty as their interest should have dictated.[119] Much the same arguments were made in Defoe's pamphlets defending the treaty.[120]

The argument on the other side was much stronger. In a private communication to the Lord Treasurer, John Crookshanks of Twickenham (a frequent informant on commercial matters to Oxford and later Walpole) explained that in article x on tobacco, "the words are smooth but . . . don't inferr any positive engagement on the french King's part, in favour of England." He agreed that it would be a good thing for the tobacco trade if article iii in the supplementary convention were ever enacted. However, he explained very carefully why it was not in the French king's fiscal interest to do any such thing.[121] The same points were made in stronger language by the Italian merchant, Nathaniel Torriano, in a memorial which he presented to the House of Lords on 8 June against the treaty[122] and in a pamphlet.[123] Another pamphleteer argued rather illogically that since the French would buy tobacco in England only when prices were low, their purchases would never raise prices for the planters.[124]

Whatever the strength of the arguments, most M.P.'s from places with any tobacco trade voted against the bill and treaty: the M.P. from the Glasgow burghs (and most other Scottish burgh members), all the members for Cumberland, both members from Lancashire and both from Liverpool (the last two being tobacco merchants), one member from Bristol (the other not voting) and three of the four members from the City of London.[125] Most of these may have voted as they did not out of economic interest but out of partisan hostility to the government. Nevertheless, it is rather clear that Bolingbroke's treaty did not succeed in appealing to or mobilizing a wide enough spectrum of commercial or industrial interests. It left the tobacco trade hostile or disinterested.

After the defeat of their bill, the government faced the difficult problem of what to do about the rest of the commercial treaty. Even if articles viii and ix had not been given effect by Parliament, could they persuade the French that the remainder of the treaty was legally in force? Should they appoint the special "commissaries" for further negotiation provided for in article ix? Early in September 1713, a fortnight after he moved from the northern to the southern department, Bolingbroke took the matter in hand and instructed the Board of Trade to look into these questions and report.[126] They considered the matter with more than due deliberation and did not report until after the English "commissaries" were appointed in December. On the 18th, the board attended a meeting of the "cabinet council" in Bolingbroke's office and reported, not unexpectedly, that, even though the conditional articles viii and ix had not been made operative, the unconditional remainder of the commercial treaty was binding. Among other points, they demonstrated at length that the rather meaningless article x on tobacco was absolute and not conditional.[127]

The English "commissaries" appointed on 13 December 1713 to negotiate with the French included several persons who knew a great deal about the tobacco trade.[128] In January 1714, the convention of the royal burghs of Scotland petitioned the queen that they be instructed to ask of the French the abolition of the tobacco monopoly.[129] Although such a point had been included in the supplementary agenda appended to the commercial treaty of Utrecht, it was not in fact raised in the Board of Trade's report of 18 December or in the instructions to the commissioners of 14 February 1713/4.[130] It would have been futile, for the ministry's defeat in Commons in June 1713 had changed the objectives of the "commissaries." Originally, they had been intended to extend as well to clarify the commercial treaty; by February 1714, their goal had shrunk to the salvaging of some parts of the treaty from the wreck of the whole.

The negotiations for the commercial treaty of Utrecht were the only effort of the London government in the century 1674–1775 to use diplomacy to expand the French market for British colonial tobacco. That solitary essay failed. Ironically, though, in the following decades, without the assistance of Whitehall, British tobacco exports to France expanded beyond the wildest dreams of the men of 1713. French convenience effected what British purpose could not accomplish.

CHAPTER 20

The French Agency in London: The Early Agents, 1697–1739

When in the years following 1697, the French monopoly decided to buy tobacco in England, they created a new force in the English tobacco market, a single large buyer. When French buying in Britain reached consistently high levels after 1723, a monopsonistic factor of some weight was introduced into that market. All correspondence relating to the trade becomes filled with references to "the French" and "the French price." For their part, the French monopolists had the difficult choice of deciding whether to employ one single agent in Britain or dividing their business between several. A single agent would have the maximum monopsonistic power in the market but might be difficult to supervise or control. By employing several agents, they could use one as a check upon another—but there would always be the danger that the competition of their own agents in a tight market would drive up prices. For a merchant, the French tobacco buying agency was a great plum, not only for the commissions it earned but because of the large sums handled in cash and bills of exchange and the great credit they conveyed. The rivalry for the agency was intense and the highest political pressures were used to obtain it. The history of that agency is thus at once a history of commercial practice and of commercial politics—and a history of the highest interest.

We know very little about the agents in England of the Bernard-Crozat-Maynon tobacco monopoly company of 1697–1718. The first absolutely sure datum we have is that about 1707–11 the agency was held by the London Huguenot house of Tourton & Guiguer, an affiliate of the great Parisian house of the same name. It is quite possible that this same firm had been the London agents since 1697; we cannot be absolutely sure.[1]

The families of Tourton and Guiguer were closely connected.[2] Sprung from a long line of notaries at Annonay-en-Vivarais, Claude Tourton became a banker at Lyons in the decades preceding the revocation of the edict of Nantes and married Jeanne Guiguer, by whom he had seventeen children. These included Louis of Lyons; Jean Claude, founder of the great Paris bank; Jean, banker at Amsterdam from the 1670's; and Jean André and (Jean) Nicholas, both merchants of London. Nicholas Tourton appears to have been settled in London as a merchant and banker from about the time of the revocation. He received letters of denization in 1687 and was naturalized in 1691.[3] He was an original subscriber to the Bank of England in 1694[4] and a director of the *old* East India Company, about 1706–8.[5] During the wars of 1689–1713, he was actively interested in remitting government money abroad.[6] His brother Jean Claude of Paris was even more active in such undertakings for the French government, was very close to Torcy and was employed by that minister in secret negotiations with the Grand Pensionary Heinsius in the last years of the War of the Spanish Succession.[7]

The Guiguer (originally Geiger) were a Swiss protestant family established at Lyons. Leonard Guiguer (1632–1710), of Swiss birth, married Elizabeth Tourton, by whom he had eleven children, including George Tobie (1672–1752) and Isaac (1664–1715), merchants in London; Jeanne (1662–1712), wife of Théophile Thellusson, a Genevan citizen established in trade at Lyons, and mother of Isaac Thellusson, the great banker and diplomat; and Louis (1675–1747), partner of Jean Claude Tourton in the Paris bank of Tourton & Guiguer, subsequently baron de Prangins. Among his other interests, Louis Guiguer was very much concerned in revenue farming (particularly the *domaine d'Occident*) in the years following 1697.[8] George Tobie (later Tobias) Guiguer was naturalized in England in 1696, his brother Isaac in 1708.[9] Though originally less prominent than his cousin and partner Nicholas Tourton, George Tobie Guiguer lived to play a prominent and variegated part in the life of the City of London. He was an original subscriber to the Bank of England[10] and to the *new* East India Company of 1698, a shareholder in the South Sea Company, about 1714–17,[11] and for many years a director of the Royal Exchange Assurance Company (founded in 1720).[12]

We first hear of the London firm of Tourton & Guiguer in 1690 when it consisted of Nicholas Tourton and Samuel Guiguer;[13] in 1701, the firm consisted of (Jean) Nicholas Tourton, Jean André Tourton and George Tobie Guiguer. About 1704, Jean André Tourton moved to Lyons where he headed the family's mercantile house, his place in the London firm taken by Isaac Guiguer.[14] During both great wars, in addition to the private ventures of Nicholas Tourton, the London firm of Tourton & Guiguer was actively involved in remitting government money abroad, particularly to Switzerland and Italy.[15] We do not know when they first began to buy tobacco in London for the French monopoly, but they were heavily involved in this at their end. When the act of Parliament of 1711 opened the wine trade from France, the French tobacco monopoly (the Bernard-Crozat-Maynon company) sent large shipments of wine on their own account from Bordeaux to London to pay for the more than three million pounds of tobacco they bought there in 1711. To pay the heavy British import duties on this wine, they authorized Tourton & Guiguer to draw £10,000 on their correspondents in Amsterdam. Although Tourton & Guiguer of London do not appear to have been affected by the great "stoppages" in France in 1708–9 which affected such great firms as Bernard & Nicolas, Hogguer, and the Lyons Tourton & Lefort,[16] their own affairs were in disorder by the early months of 1712. They were probably affected by a very heavy fine in 1712 for customs irregularities[17] and by the wave of bankruptcies in London about 1711 (which particularly affected the tobacco trade).[18] Whatever the cause, the tobacco monopolists in Paris notified the controller-general Desmaretz in April 1712 that Tourton & Guiguer in London were insolvent and were heavily in debt to them for the money advanced to pay the wine duties. The wine itself they had dishonestly used as security for loans to themselves. The monopolists wanted Desmaretz to request the foreign secretary Torcy to ask the British government that the wine in question be seized and turned over to them as their property. Desmaretz wisely refused to take any action lest the wine be seized in London as the property of French subjects illegally imported into England.[19]

A commission of insolvency was taken out against Tourton & Guiguer in the Court of Bankruptcy, London, in August 1712 on the petition of James Bradley, a tobacco merchant of London.[20] However, George Tobie Guiguer must have been able to reach some sort of settlement with his creditors very quickly because in December 1712, he opened a new Drawing Office account at the Bank of England in his own name.[21] It is apparent that he kept the French tobacco buying contract, for the "debit" column in his new account is from the start filled with payments to well-known names in the tobacco trade: Bradley, Taylor, Falconar, Corbin, Nelthorpe, Milner, Dawkins, Scarth, Cary, Hyde, Bowles, Lloyd, Perry. Not everyone was pleased that the late bankrupt George Tobie Guiguer should keep the French buying contract. Jean Anisson, deputy from Lyons in the Council of Commerce, in London during 1713–14 on government business relating to the commercial treaty of Utrecht, wrote to Desmaretz on 13 June 1713 describing the Whig opposition to the treaty, abetted by the canards of émigré Huguenot merchants in London:

> Among these French merchants who have raised the excitement the most, there is one among others who has a commission from France which is worth a rather considerable sum to him each year; he well deserves the punishment of being deprived of that commission from France, since there is no sort of filth which he has not vomitted up against our government. If Your Lordship judges that this would be an example to make, I should be honored to give him notice after all our business is done, since [otherwise] we should not be safe from the resentment of such a scoundrel.[22]

Those sentiments immediately suggest the hostility of a member of the official French business community against Huguenot outsiders like Guiguer who knew how to make a good thing out of the exigencies of France. In the longer run, it hints at the passionate competition which that agency was to evoke.

The Virginia trade names continue to fill the accounts of George Tobie Guiguer through 1718; they become progressively less frequent in 1719–20 and disappear completely thereafter. We may probably conclude that he retained the tobacco buying commission until the end of the Bernard-Crozat-Maynon company in 1718. Thereafter he was probably "winding up" his tobacco business, though he may also have handled speculative purchases and shipments of tobacco for private persons during the free trade months of 1720. Lüthy reports that he failed again in 1720. If so, the matter was settled privately with his creditors, for his name does not appear on the records of the Court of Bankruptcy at that time.[23]

As of 1 October 1718, the French tobacco monopoly passed from the Bernard-Crozat-Maynon syndicate to Law's company. We know a little bit about the history of the London agency at this time because the Indies Company, as well as John and William Law personally, employed George Middleton, the Strand goldsmith, as their banker in London.[24] Middleton's firm has survived to the present as Coutts & Co., still in the Strand. Some of the firm's records of this time have also survived.[25] From them, we can reconstruct much of the history of the London agency during 1718–20.[26] At some time prior to 2 February 1718/9, Law must have decided to transfer all or part of the London tobacco purchasing agency from George Tobie Guiguer to his own brother, William Law. Between that date and July, William Law received almost £15,000 from Guiguer, whose financial services were still used. More important, the debit side of his account shows payments to most of the leading names in the London tobacco trade: Perry, Hyde, Lee, Bradley, Falconar, Geo. Hatley & Co., Jonathan Forward, Jonathan Scarth, and noticeably Tobias Bowles, the Virginia and Maryland merchant and shipowner.[27] These payments stop abruptly in August when William Law went over to Paris, except for some large payments in September and October to Tobias Bowles. In certain cases, the ledger clearly shows William Law's account being credited with receipts from the French Indies Company and debited simultaneously with payments to Bowles. On 17 August, an account was also opened in the name of John Law in which during the next two months, receipts from the Indies Company are balanced by payments to Claude Bettifort (Bettefort). From this and later evidence, it is clear that, after William Law stopped handling tobacco purchases directly, they were managed by Bettefort and perhaps Bowles and paid out of the personal accounts of the two Laws. (William shared in the commissions.)[28] On 12 October 1719, six weeks after William went over to Paris, the matter was somewhat regularized: an account was opened in Middleton's ledgers in the name of the "Directors of the French India Company." In it frequent large payments are recorded to Bettefort, Bowles, and others. From the letters of January-March 1720, it is clear that Bettefort was doing most of the tobacco buying for the company,[29] with Bowles, Middleton, and others handling ships and other supplies for the company. We know little about Claude Bettefort, or about the James Douglas[30] and "Mr. Harrold"[31] who made private tobacco purchases for William Law for speculative shipment to France in the open trade months of 1720. Bettefort appears to have been a well-connected young man from Dunkirk (a great tobacco port, of course) sent over to London just for this business.[32] Douglas was a much more important West India merchant of London who acted as London agent for several Scottish receivers-general.[33] "Mr. Harrold" was presumably Martin Harrold of London, related to Stephen Harrold, a minor merchant of Bristol. It is possible but unlikely that Douglas's purchases for William Law were actually made in Scotland and Harrold's in Bristol. Middleton also handled payments from the company to Stephen Peloquin of Bristol, but these were probably not for tobacco.[34]

Middleton received a "brokerage" and commission for the sums he paid out for the company's tobacco purchases in London. He reimbursed himself by drawing on André Pels & Son of Amsterdam, the company's correspondents there. When the Pels became difficult about the volume of the bills being drawn on them, the company in April 1720 transferred its Amsterdam agency to Abraham Mouchard, but his credit was not as good as that of Pels. George Tobie Guiguer to whom the company still owed £9,000 complained that he could not get bills on Mouchard discounted.[35]

When, after the crash, the Indies Company's accounts come to be drawn up in 1722, its creditors included Middleton (32,500 l.t.), Peloquin (74,000), Pels (80,000) and Mouchard (650,000). Claude Bettefort, who had overdrawn up to £10,000 at Middleton's to buy tobacco for the company, managed to end up owing it 127,553 l.t.[36] Middleton suspended payments (but did not fail) on 12/23 December as Law was fleeing France. George Tobie Guiguer's troubles were similarly timed.

In the confusions following the collapse of the "System," we lose track completely of the London tobacco agency for a few months. In August 1721, the full monopoly was reestablished as of 1 September by the triumphant Paris brothers and conferred upon a separate company under the name of Edouard du Verdier. The Paris brothers were not avowedly members of that company but, we are told, reserved for themselves the contract for making tobacco purchases in England for a substantial commission and ½ percent per month for any funds advanced.[37] That the brothers Paris, at the height of their power, should want the tobacco buying contract shows that it was beginning to become something substantial, well worth having. We have no inkling of what English firms collaborated with the brothers in making these purchases during the 25 months that the du Verdier concession lasted. Whoever was doing the business, however, was not without observant critics and competitors. In January 1723, the dramatist Philippe Néricault Destouches, unofficial agent of Cardinal Dubois in London, wrote to that minister recommending a memorial from a London merchant in the tobacco trade. The last named claimed that the persons then doing the tobacco purchasing were defrauding the monopoly in price and quality; he himself had great stocks of tobacco on hand intended for Holland which he offered to sell the farm on advantageous terms. The merchant claimed to be close to Lord Carteret who, Destouches thought, would also recommend the business to the cardinal.[38] Nothing more is known of the scheme or its fate.

The picture becomes somewhat clearer after the monopoly returned to the Indies Company (as of 1 October 1723). As already explained, this transfer was followed by increased imports of tobacco from Great Britain. This new buying program ran into trouble in 1725 when tobacco shipments from the Chesapeake to Britain dropped to the lowest level in ten years and European tobacco prices soared.[39] We do not know who had been buying in London for the monopoly during 1723–25, but the crisis prices of 1725 obviously induced change. To manage tobacco purchases in London, no less a person was sent over than Pierre Cavalier, one of the syndics of the company. Cavalier was a Paris banker (in partnership with his brother Jean), who had been interested in the Indies Company and its predecessors since 1717, and had been chosen a syndic by the shareholders in 1721 and again in 1723.[40]

An account in the name of "Peter Cavalier" was opened at the Bank of England on 3 November 1725 and closed on 13 July 1733.[41] In it, we can find frequent large payments to such well-known names in the London tobacco trade as Hyde, Bradley, Forward, Scarth, Dawkins, Bowles, and Randolph, the first two being by far the most important. (He also made large payments to Lord Bolingbroke.) As we shall see in a later chapter, Cavalier, the first really large French buyer in the London market, acquired a legendary reputation among merchants and planters for his ability to drive prices down.[42] There is also evidence in the ledgers of the Bank of England to suggest that he was doing some buying in the provinces and in Scotland.[43]

Some monthly cash accounts for the Indies Company have survived which show that it was remitting money to two persons in London during 1729–30:[44]

		"M. Cavalier"	"M. Hays"
November	1729	1,801,962 l.t.	174,562 l.t.
December	1729	235,897	434,324
January	1730	204,452	66,864
February	1730	566,400	—
April	1730	652,348	51,719

The Hays were a prosperous Huguenot family of London, originally of Calais, connected by marriage to other even more prominent émigré families.[45] The member here referred to is almost surely Daniel Hays (1659–1732), substantial London merchant, big shareholder in the Bank of England and new East India Company, sometime "assistant" of the Africa Company and director of the South Sea Company (1715–18). He had left Calais for Ireland as a boy in 1670, but had been active in London since 1688 and was naturalized there in 1695.[46] Since we know that Cavalier was the only tobacco buyer in London,[47] the money sent by the company to Hays—if it was for tobacco—must have been for purchases elsewhere, in the outports or in Scotland. That Hays had some connection with the company's tobacco purchases is the more likely because of his family connections.[48]

Following the transfer of the tobacco farm in 1730 from the Indies Company to the united farms, the new monopolists decided in 1731 to take their principal London tobacco agency away from Pierre Cavalier and entrust it instead to one Louis Guillemau. They adhered to this decision even though the chevalier de Chavigny, French minister in London, tried to persuade Chauvelin, the minister of foreign affairs, to have Cavalier kept in London as a useful source of information on British financial and commercial matters.[49] Louis or Lewis Guillemau appears to have been a native of Lées in Béarn. He must have been at least a nominal Protestant, for he became a naturalized British subject in 1727. His wife, Catharina Maria Radburne, was English. He was a merchant with close connections in Spain, particularly at Cadiz and Valencia.[50] After he acquired the tobacco contract, we find him buying Breton linens at Morlaix, seat of one of the monopoly's tobacco manufactories, for shipment to Cadiz.[51] Perhaps some of the ships that carried tobacco from London to Morlaix continued on to Cadiz and returned to England with Spanish wine. Guillemau's account at the Bank of England shows considerably fewer payments to "tobacco names" than did the account of Cavalier, but, as an active merchant, Guillemau would have had many other ways of settling with those from whom he bought tobacco.[52] Then also, unlike Cavalier, Guillemau did not have the London commission exclusively to himself.

Lewis Guillemau died in December 1735. Even before that time, others were buying tobacco for the French in England. One such buyer was the important merchant John Bance (c. 1694–1755), former director of the United East India Company (1722–31), director of the Bank of England (1731–55, with interruptions), and M.P. for Westbury (Wilts) 1734–41 and Wallingford (Berks) 1741–47.[53] More interestingly, he was the London correspondent of Samuel Bernard in the 1720's.[54] He was a public spokesman for the dissenters[55] and a trustee in 1737 for the £320,000 "Copper Loan" to the Emperor Charles VI, that is, the loan secured upon the coppermines of Hungary.[56] He was involved in speculative wheat shipments to France, about 1739–42, both on his own account[57] and for Isaac Thellusson and François Tronchin, of Paris,[58] as well as in tobacco exports in the 1730's to Holland and Spain.[59]

His account at the Bank of England seems to suggest that Bance first became active in tobacco about the year 1732. If we are correct in assuming that Daniel Hays had been buying tobacco outside of London for the French monopoly, then Bance may have succeeded him in this business when Hays died in 1732. Under the multiple agency policy adopted by the united farms early in the 1730's, he was probably also employed in London buying in competition with Guillemau. The debits on his account contain London tobacco names as well as those from Liverpool, Bristol, and Scotland.[60]

One tobacco port which the French buyers seem to have neglected in the 1730's was Whitehaven. In 1734, the tobacco merchants there wrote to their landlord and county member, Sir James Lowther, Bart., asking him, as patron of their port, to speak to John Bance about buying their tobacco. He replied:

> I saw Mr Bance yesterday, he does not know whether he shal have the Whiteh[ave]n Tobacco, w[hi]ch is offer'd him at 2^{d}¾ a pound but as they [the Whitehaven merchants] are in Treaty with another [French buyer], they [the French buyers] dont care to bid ag[ain]st each other, if the other dont agree, he thinks of sending to view it.[61]

In the event, the French buyers left Whitehaven alone for the time being.

Tobacco names become very rare in John Bance's bank account after 1739. It was most probably at this time, following upon the death in 1738 of his Paris correspondent, Samuel Bernard, that the tobacco buying commission was taken away from Bance and given to others. (There were several major changes at this juncture.) Bance was furious and in retaliation tried to corner the British tobacco market and force the French monopoly to reinstate him; his allies among the London tobacco merchants could not hold out, however, and the scheme miscarried.[62]

During Bance's ascendancy, 1732–39, the tobacco trade name which his bank account shows receiving the largest sums is "Buchanan." They were a numerous tribe whose achievements and failures fill the history of the Glasgow tobacco trade between 1707 and 1775. Though they provided the most sensational bankruptcies in that town's celebrated trade, their name is still remembered there in Buchanan Street. About 1728–31, the largest firm in the young Glasgow tobacco trade was Andrew Buchanan & Co.,[63] whose partners were the brothers Andrew, Archibald and Neil.[64] The last was M.P. for Glasgow burghs from 1741 until his death in 1744. The brothers' London agent was a kinsman, James Buchanan, a Virginia merchant handling business in the capital for several Glasgow firms, from about 1727 until his death in 1758.[65] In 1741, fearful of Spanish privateers, both James and Neil Buchanan petitioned the government separately for convoy to and from Morlaix for three Glasgow vessels carrying tobacco to France.[66]

In the early 1730's, purchases for the French appear to have been handled separately in Scotland by Andrew Buchanan & Co., the Glasgow merchants, and by William Alexander, an Edinburgh merchant and director of the Royal Bank of Scotland, with close family and commercial connections in Glasgow.[67] From November 1730, William Alexander had been selling the Royal Bank large drafts on London which he most probably acquired from his French tobacco business.[68] Buchanans of course could furnish the same, as the Court of Directors minutes at the Royal Bank of 6 February 1734/5 show:

> Andrew Buchanan Merchant in Glasgow having Propos'd In his own Name, and in Name of his Brothers Merchants in Glasgow To give the Bank Bills upon London to the Extent of Six thousand pounds sterling drawn by Monsr Silowette payable to and Indors'd by the said Andrew Buchannan and Brothers at Sixty days date, upon receiving value thereof at Glasgow, And having likewise laid before the Court, Copies of a Letter of Credit by Mr Simon and Company Merchants in London, in favour of the said Monsr Silowette.
>
> Order'd That the Cashier write to Mr Buchanan, advising him That the Directors Agree to his having Two or Three thousand pounds Sterling immediatly upon their Bills drawn and Indors'd as above, And That he shall have the remainder of the said Six thousand pounds, upon the Directors receiving information from London of the Character and Sufficiency of the said Mr Simon and Company.[69]

The "Monsieur Silowette" here referred to is none other than the young Etienne de Silhouette, future controller-general of France. Silhouette's father was *homme des affaires* to the family of the duke of Noailles (president of the Finance Council, 1715–18, inter alia); in such and related work he prospered sufficiently to purchase the honorary ennobling title of *secrétaire du roi* (1712) and the office of receiver of the *tailles* at Limoges and to be taxed 350,000 *l.t.* by the Chamber of Justice of 1716.[70] The son is known to have traveled extensively as a young man, acquiring a literary reputation for his travel accounts and translations. From his years in England came well-received translations of Pope, Bolingbroke, and Warburton.[71] Shortly after reaching his majority, he is reported to have visited London in 1731–32, staying with the Huguenot "banker" James Benezet—but there is nothing explicit to connect this visit with commerce.[72] In 1734, he was again in England, staying, while in London, at the house of the merchant, Peter Simond, who handled his finances. (Simond, we shall see, was a former partner of Benezet.) Silhouette's circle of acquaintances in England included George Tobie Guiguer. While on a visit to Oxford during February–June 1734, he ordered many books from dealers in London, including a large proportion on British government and trade.[73] From Oxford, he sent Chauvelin, the foreign minister, a report on the parliamentary session of 1734.[74]

None of Silhouette's biographers has explained his relationship with tobacco buying. It would appear that at some time in late 1734 or early 1735 an unknown family crisis (probably a quarrel with his father) deprived him of his income and forced him to earn his own living. In these straits, he found himself "obliged to devote myself to commerce which up till then I had studied only from curiosity and not from necessity." The friendship of de la Porte, head of the united farms, obtained for him a commission to buy tobacco in Great Britain for that company.[75] In 1735, he made the buying trip to Scotland mentioned above—his first dated connection with the tobacco agency. Fragments of other evidence hint at his tobacco buying activity in the next few years, none of it seemingly on a very large scale. In the ledgers of the Bank of England, we see that the Royal Bank of Scotland was credited with £860 from Silhouette in 1736 (presumably bills given to merchants in Scotland) while Benezet was debited with £1,300 paid him in October 1737 and Simond with £2,200 paid him between September 1737 and January 1737/8; the last payment to Silhouette noted in the ledgers of the Bank was £2,400 on 25 June 1741.[76]

By 1739, the ambitious Silhouette seems either to have tired of or to have become dissatisfied with the tobacco buying commission and began looking about for ways to improve himself. In the middle of that year, he wrote a long and widely circulated memoir[77] on tobacco which we have already discussed in the chapter on Louisiana.[78] In it, he recommended that France cease buying tobacco from Britain and develop Louisiana instead. Maurepas, de la Porte, Lallemant de Betz, and everyone else important liked his memoir—everyone except the controller-general Orry. Silhouette himself recognized that the outbreak of the British-Spanish war that October made the inauguration of his ambitious scheme impractical.[79]

Silhouette had, however, succeeded in calling himself to the attention of those in power. Before the year 1739 was up, the marquis of Argenson noted in his journal:

> They have just given the official cyphers to the sieur Silhouette, a very learned fellow who lives in London buying tobacco for the farmers-general. Each post, he writes M. Amelot [the minister of foreign affairs] everything he hears, all of which discredits M. de Cambis [the ambassador] more and more and renders him useless.[80]

Silhouette was neither a spy nor a diplomat but an authorized if unofficial agent and observer. In the diplomatic archives, we can read the reports and analyses which he sent from London between November 1739 and his return to France early in 1742.[81] Other evidence shows him busy in London during 1738-40, writing letters to various other important people in France, including Maurepas, and being of help—interestingly enough—to the visiting DuTot, the former clerk turned literary defender of John Law.[82] Silhouette most probably gave up his tobacco agency about the time his diplomatic reporting began late in 1739; there is no mention of it in his 1741 correspondence requesting permission to return home.

When we turn to Silhouette's host and banker, Peter (né Pierre) Simond, we return to the mainstream of London's commercial life and to the mainstream of Huguenot émigré experience between the revocation of the edict of Nantes and the French Revolution. His father, Pierre, was a pastor at Embrun in Dauphiné who fled to Zeeland in 1686. Following his marriage there to a refugee from Normandy, the elder Pierre went out to the Cape of Good Hope as minister to a group of Huguenots being sent thither by the Dutch East India Company. There his two sons, Pierre and Jacques Cléopas, were born, the former in 1690. In 1703, the Reverend Pierre Simond and his young family returned to Holland.[83] His son, Pierre, who was trained as an apprentice and clerk in the counting house of the well-connected Amsterdam Huguenot firm of Fizeaux,[84] emigrated to England, about 1715, and as Peter Simond was naturalized in 1717. (His brother "James Cleopas" followed him but was not naturalized until 1730.)[85] On 16 June 1720 (at the height of the South Sea Bubble) an account was opened at the Bank of England in the name of Simond, Benezet & Simond, the partners being Peter and James Cleopas Simond and James (Jacques) Benezet. In 1728, Benezet (with whom Silhouette stayed in 1731) withdrew and formed his own firm, for a time in partnership with his brother John Stephen (Jean-Etienne) until the latter, a Quaker, went out to Philadelphia in 1732 (where he is remembered as the father of Anthony Benezet, the early Quaker antislavery agitator).[86] By the 1730's, the Simonds of London were an important firm of West India merchants, with additional trading interests in South Carolina and Georgia, Peter Simond in fact being the London commercial agent for the trustees of Georgia at its first settlement.[87] Peter Simond married one daughter to the eleventh baron St. John of Bletsoe and another to the fourth Trevelyan baronet of Nettlecombe, Somerset, from whom descend an eminent progeny. He died in 1785 at the age of 95, living long enough to have an estate in South Carolina confiscated during the American Revolution.[88] The firm he founded in 1720 survives to this day as a London West India house.[89]

The degree of Peter Simond's involvement in the French tobacco buying agency in the 1730's is unknown. He may have been only the banker for Silhouette. It seems unlikely, though, that Silhouette would freely *choose* a banker unknown in Scotland for the payment of purchases there. It seems more likely that by 1735, Simond was an agent of the French united farms forced to share his commission with the needy, young Silhouette.

Some years later, in 1756, the London firm of Sir Joshua Van Neck, Baronet, & Co., in petitioning the government for permission to export tobacco to France in wartime, stated "that for upwards of twenty five Years past . . . [they had] been employed in exporting Tobacco's to France."[90] This would suggest that the Van Necks had been so employed ever since the united farms took over the tobacco monopoly in 1730. Their connection with the French tobacco purchasing contract was to be longer and more important than that of any other British mercantile house.

The brothers Gerard and Joshua Van Neck came from a distinguished family of the Dutch office-holding patriciate. They were born in The Hague, sons of Cornelis Van Neck, Paymaster General of the Land Forces of the United Provinces. Four of their brothers remained in Holland: Abraham, attorney-general of Holland, Jacobus, magistrate of The Hague, Lambert, Pensionary of Rotterdam, and Willem, professor at Maestricht.[91] Gerard came over to London in 1718 and set up immediately as a merchant on his own account; he was naturalized in 1720. His younger brother Joshua joined him in 1722 and was naturalized in 1733.[92] Although Dutch by birth, the brothers were intimately connected with the Huguenot community in London. In 1734, Gerard Van Neck married the widow of Sir Dennis Dutrey, Bart., a lady allegedly worth £100,000; she was the daughter of Hillary Reneu, a merchant originally from Bordeaux.[93] Joshua Van Neck two years before had married Marianne, daughter of Stephen Daubuz, also a Huguenot merchant of London. Huguenot churches as well as Dutch churches, and Huguenot friends even more than Dutch friends were mentioned in the will of Gerard Van Neck when he died in 1750.[94]

The firm of Gerard & Joshua Van Neck remained active in the City for 163 years;[95] its first like its last years are, however, rather obscure. Although there are early references to them as merchants and shipowners trading to Holland,[96] they became famous principally as financiers. Gerard was briefly a director of the East India Company from 1729 to 1732. In 1737, he appeared in the more characteristic role of trustee—along with John Bance and John Gore—for the £320,000 "Copper Loan" to the emperor.[97] In 1744, he was a trustee for taking the subscriptions for a £200,000 loan to the king of Sardinia[98] and in 1749, he and John Gore were trustees for a 100,00 ducats loan to the United Provinces.[99] Loans going the other way were, however, much more common and these became a specialty of the Van Necks: through their hands from at least 1720 passed much of the Dutch capital seeking investment in the British public funds and great monied companies.[100] For a government loan of £1.8 million early in 1744, Gerard Van Neck subscribed £150,000, the third largest subscription.[101] In the next war, his brother Joshua was always first: £500,000 in the loan of 1757;[102] £1.2 million out of £8 million in 1759—a larger subscription than that of the Bank of England![103] It is therefore not surprising that when Gerard Van Neck died in 1750, he was reputedly worth £240,000 (and had his will published in the press) ;[104] nor that his brother and principal heir Joshua should be made a baronet in 1751.

Although much evidence has survived of the Van Necks' buying tobacco for the French in the 1740's and 1750's, we know nothing of the character or scope of their activity in that role in the 1730's. In their account at the Bank in the later 1730's, we find a few large payments to Silhouette and Simond and Buchanan and some tobacco names (too few to be meaningful) .[105] Whatever their role in the French tobacco purchases, we need not assume automatically that it was in competition with that of Bance and Simond; the contrary is as possible. Gerard Van Neck had served with Bance on the directorate of the East India Company and the "Copper Loan." His relations with Simond were even closer. Both had come over from Holland to London about the same time. Peter Simond was the executor of Gerard's will in 1750 (along with Joshua Van Neck).[106] When Simond's own daughters married in the 1750's, Sir Joshua Van Neck, Bart., was a trustee of the marriage settlements in both cases.[107]

Putting together the bits and pieces of our meager evidence for the 1730's, we can detect the probable outline of a coherent evolution. When the united farms took over the monopoly in 1730, they found Peter Cavalier alone buying in London and Daniel Hays buying in Scotland. The farmers-general abandoned the exclusive agency principle and immediately added the Van Necks as a competing London buyer. The next year, 1731, they replaced Cavalier with Lewis Guillemau. In 1732, upon the death of Daniel Hays (who had been working with William Alexander in Scotland) his Scottish and other business was transferred to John Bance (working with the Buchanans in Scotland). About the time of Guillemau's death in 1735, a small share was transferred to young Silhouette, working with Peter Simond. The triple division of the agency between Van Necks, Bance-Buchanan, and Simond-Silhouette persisted through 1735–39.

From its origins around the turn of the century down to the mid-1730's, the history of the London agency of the French tobacco monopoly has been hazy and conjectural. The surviving evidence is very thin and often anonymous. (We shall leave to Chapter 25 the discussion of the economic-institutional implications of the work of these agents.) Some of those discussed may as merchants seem mildly bizarre. When we come to the late 1730's, our evidence becomes fuller. This will enable us to examine much more closely the infinitely more bizarre operations of those more professional eighteenth-century adventurers—the abbé Huber, Daniel MacKercher, and the FitzGerald clan.

CHAPTER 21

The French Agency in London: The Rise of the Abbé Huber and the FitzGeralds

The MacKercher-Huber Mission of 1737–38[1]

At their meeting on 27 April 1737, the lieutenant governor and council of Virginia were disturbed by the news that "two Gentlemen going by the names of M! Hubert & M! Mackircher [have] lately arrived here under pretence of traveling through his Maj!s Plantations on the Continent, but have produced no Letters or other Credentials to Manifest what their business is." To the board it seemed that "at a time when his Maj!s plantations on the Continent are threatned with an Invasion by the Spaniards it may prove of dangerous Consequences to Admit Strangers to too easy an Access whereby they may have oppertunity to Discover the Strength and Scituation of our ports & Harbours." They therefore delegated two of their more accomplished members, William Byrd II and John Robinson, "to discourse with the said Two Strangers and Endeavour to find out their Quality their Business here and to what place they are bound."[2] On being interrogated, the travelers produced letters of introduction from Lord Baltimore to various persons of prominence in Maryland. They described themselves as agents of the French United General Farms intending to purchase tobacco in Virginia and Maryland for shipment to France via Great Britain. Their interrogators satisfied, the strange voyagers were allowed to proceed on their way.[3]

Well might Governor Gooch and his advisers have sniffed espionage, for Williamsburg was confronted by two of the more bizarre examples of that eighteenth-century type—the international adventurer. Their project was intrinsically alarming: tobacco was the most valuable British import from North America and France the most important reexport market. The scheme, even if technically legal, would have subverted the entire spirit and intent of the Acts of Trade and Navigation.[4] Who then were these "Gentlemen going by the names of M! Hubert & M! Mackircher" and how came they to be meddling in the all too well managed affairs of the French tobacco monopoly?

The more forward of the two we know to have been a Scot, Daniel MacKercher, whose part in this affair has been preserved in chapter 98 of *Peregrine Pickle*.[5] The novelist, Smollett, a friend and protégé of MacKercher, probably received the account from his patron:[6] MacKercher became quite famous in the eighteenth century as the champion of James Annesley, claimant to the earldom of Anglesea.[7] To this sensational case, with its "stolen" peerage, Smollett devoted the bulk of a long chapter. As its preamble, he went at some length into the earlier career of MacKercher in Europe and America. For all its irrelevance, this lengthly *MacKercherei* detracted nothing from the contemporary success of the novel.[8] Smollett, the journalist, well knew the public appetite for the morsels, choice and coarse, of the Annesley case. Smollett the Glaswegian was also aware of a public interest in "that valuable branch of our trade . . . which gives employment to two great provinces, and above two hundred sail of ships"[9] and from which the wealth of so many of his Clydeside friends was drawn.[10] And so into chapter 98, to MacKercher's evident embarrassment,[11] went details mercantile as well as amorous of that adventurer's earlier career in Europe and America.

Daniel MacKercher, the reader of *Peregrine Pickle* is told, was born, in classic Scots fashion, into a noble but impoverished house, his father a minister in the national kirk. Orphaned at an early age, he was soundly educated for the church by an uncle, but ran off during "the '15" to join the victorious army. Filling his early years with modest adventures, military and civil, he came in course to move in politer circles and traveled extensively on the continent where he formed many valuable friendships. During the War of the Polish Succession, he visited the French army in the field; and, in the officers' mess, Smollett tells us, made those useful connections that ultimately were to lead him to Virginia.[12] (We know, in fact, that among the officers present at the siege of Philippsbourg—visited by MacKercher—was Lieutenant James FitzGerald of Dillon's Regiment in the Irish Brigade of the French army. He was the nephew of George FitzGerald of London, a merchant with, as we shall see below, the most extensive and valuable connections in French mercantile and financial circles.) [13]

In his wanderings, MacKercher, according to Smollett, became quite knowledgeable in the trade, manufactures, and finances of Britain, France, and Holland. He was particularly impressed by the British tobacco trade to France, "the most considerable branch of our commerce with that people" and by its importance to the French revenue and to the Chesapeake planter. He was shocked to learn of the very low prices paid by the united farms for the tobacco they bought in Britain and of their power to depress the British price in time of glut. He concocted a scheme for retaining part of the duty at export, by which the British treasury would have gained over £100,000 sterling and the French obliged to pay more. The Treasury lords, we are told, engrossed in the excise scheme of 1733, at first disregarded MacKercher's proposal, then accepted it "but discovered a surprising backwardness to carry it into execution."[14]

Rejected at home, MacKercher turned his wits abroad. "By the interposition of his friends," he was enabled to present a memorial to the French farmers-general setting forth the possible advantages their company might realize by buying in America at a price fixed by themselves the tobacco which they needed and "which best suited the taste of the public and their manufacture." He would himself undertake to obtain for them in America any quantity of sound tobacco "at the price which they paid in the port of London" for the worst of the market. "After some dispute, they agreed to his proposal, and contracted with him for fifteen thousand hogsheads a-year, for which they obliged themselves to pay ready money, on its arrival in . . . Great Britain." On signing the contract, MacKercher immediately set out in high spirits for America, taking with him "by way of companion, . . . a little French Abbé, a man of humour, wit, and learning, with whom he had been long acquainted, and for whom he had done many good offices."[15]

Thus far, Smollett's narrative, though impossible to corroborate in details, seems reasonable and consistent with what is otherwise known. When, however, the novelist introduces his "little French Abbé," we are forced to recognize that Smollett received his information only from Mac-Kercher and thus can tell us only his friend's side of the story. Smollett's picture of MacKercher as paragon[16] may well have been true; it was hardly the whole truth. For the "little French Abbé," far from being a mere traveling companion, was a major participant in the inception and execution of Daniel MacKercher's grand design.

The person styling himself John James Huber in America and the abbé Hubert in France was born Jean-Jacques Huber in Geneva in 1699, scion of a distinguished family of the mercantile patriciate of that very Protestant city. His father was a prosperous member of the privileged Swiss Protestant merchant community at Lyons; his older brother Jacob was to become a prominent banker in Paris. (Jacob's marriage to Catherine Vasserot in 1719 was a great social event of the Bubble, attended by everyone from John Law downward.) But not everyone in the family was a merchant or pastor. Jean-Jacques' nephew was Jean Huber, portraitist of Voltaire; his sister was Marie Huber, one of the more celebrated bluestockings of that age, a lady theologian, a mystical deist. She is chiefly remembered now as Lamartine's "sybil of the Alps," a probable source of many of the theological ideas of that other Genevan, Jean-Jacques Rousseau. If Marie Huber sought refuge from her family's rather perfervid and incontinent Protestant pietism in an austerer deism, her brother's flight from Geneva took rather a Roman and sybaritic course.[17]

A difficult juvenile who had at the age of seventeen been detained by his family for more than a year in the Geneva House of Correction, the young Jean-Jacques at twenty fled from his father's counting house in Lyons to Turin where he lived for three years, becoming a Roman Catholic, taking minor orders and acquiring the degree of licentiate in theology. From thence he turned to Paris and a career of wits. By 1725, he reintrudes upon the record in the brilliant if disreputable circle surrounding the cardinal de Rohan, whom he served in some secretarial capacity.[18] He next comes to light in London in 1731–32, ostensibly an intellectual tourist, visiting savants. He talked of becoming a historian and attempting a life of Peter the Great.[19] At the same time, from this trip he acquired something of a reputation as an expert on British politics.[20]

On his return to Paris in 1732, the abbé Huber established himself in the home of a new protector, Alexandre-Jean-Joseph Le Riche de la Popelinière (or Pouplinière), financier, farmer-general, and patron of arts and artists[21] (including Rameau[22] the composer and La Tour,[23] the pastellist). By this time, it would seem, the abbé's reputation as a "man of parts" and a wit was beginning to attract to him that European-wide acquaintance that was to include a prince of Brunswick,[24] a Rousseau[25] and even a Daniel MacKercher.

Le Riche, of course, was in a position to find employment for the abbé Huber in the united farms, though few posts in that employment would have been exactly to his taste. A much more promising prospect opened up in the fall of 1733 when the abbé de Cosnac (soon to be bishop of Die), a protégé of the cardinal de Rohan, introduced Huber to the foreign secretary Chauvelin. That minister and his wife proved at first the abbé's most effective patrons. Shortly thereafter, Huber was sent to Switzerland in 1734 on a secret mission (behind the back of the French ambassador there) for both Chauvelin and the united farms, on business involving the sale of French salt to the canton of Berne.[26] The abbé Huber's success in this opened up for him prospects of further employment in a quasi-diplomatic capacity.

In 1735, Huber was once more traveling toward London, ostensibly to obtain subscriptions for the publication of a learned tome. In June, the British ambassador in Paris wrote home in some alarm of "a french Abbé called Hubert . . . gone for England upon some secret Errand from the Garde des Sceaux [Keeper of the Seals, i.e., Chauvelin], . . . his figure is remarkable for it is very crooked, Brownish Complexion with a sprightly Look; He is reckoned a very good for nothing Fellow, but has parts and will undertake any thing for money."[27] The secretary of the embassy added that the abbé was "always willing to procure Intelligence for me, and to furnish me with lights in some branches of the French Commerce in which I employ'd him more than once; . . . If he be thought an Object worth notice in England, I dare say 'twill be no difficult matter to gain him."[28]

Unable, though, to obtain from Cardinal Fleury any adequate explanation of the abbé's business in London, and fearing him to be a tool of Chauvelin's hostility and duplicity, the British ministers looked for ways to turn the abbé to their own account. Knowing Chauvelin (the principal enemy of Britain in the French court) to be peculiarly susceptible to money, the duke of Newcastle, secretary of state, toyed with the idea of using the abbé ("a Creature of Madame Chauvelin's") and Madame herself as "Instruments" in bribing the Garde des Sceaux, but dropped the scheme when it became apparent that that great man's power was slipping.[29] With no further use for Huber, the British ambassador the next year used his credit with Fleury to block the fading Chauvelin's plans for sending the abbé back yet again to London, this time as secretary to the new French ambassador.[30] In these exchanges, it is apparent that the British ministry particularly disliked the abbé because of the "Company, that He frequents" in London, persons "in the most avowed Opposition to His Majestys Measures."[31] Huber, it will be seen, had entree into Jacobite circles through his friendship with the FitzGeralds,[32] as well as into Tory circles through a family connection with Lord Bolingbroke.[33] He must also have cultivated the antiministerial opposition centered about the Prince of Wales; a prime adornment of this last circle was Charles, 5th lord Baltimore, gentleman of the bedchamber to the prince, proprietor of Maryland and author of the letters of introduction which Huber brought with him to America.[34]

Thus, at the very moment when the impending fall of Chauvelin and the opposition of the British government blocked his diplomatic career, the abbé Huber was able to use his other connections with La Popelinière, Chauvelin, and Lord Baltimore (and presumably MacKercher) to launch an American career. We know only that on 30 November 1736, the abbé wrote to the Garde des Sceaux for help in the tobacco buying project. Ministerial support was apparently vital, for La Popelinière was not yet a member of the responsible tobacco purchasing committee of the united farms. In the letter, Huber said nothing of MacKercher but took full credit for the project whose details were already familiar to Chauvelin. The farmers-general, particularly the aged de la Porte, head of the company and of the tobacco buying committee, were, he reported, convinced of the practicability, utility, and profitability of the scheme, and were to meet that week to make their final decision. The abbé wanted only to be sent to Maryland to set the project going there: a word from Chauvelin would do the trick. He assured the keeper that he thought himself in all humility best qualified for this task because of his "liaisons avec Myl[ord] Baltimor Gouverneur perpetuel du Pays." If granted this slight favor, he would not only be able to serve the company and obtain some slight advantage for himself, but would also undertake to investigate in detail the English colonies and their competitive strength against the French.

If, however, for some unforeseen reason, the Maryland project should fall through, the prescient Huber begged the Keeper for some little means of subsistence, such as *all or part* of the contract to make the French tobacco purchases in London. M. de la Porte knew how well acquainted he was with that business and the Keeper knew equally well what other sorts of services his useful *protégé* could render in London, while ostensibly busying himself with tobacco.[35] With the death of Guillemau in December 1735, there must have been a great scramble for the London agency in 1736 which brought out many schemes and schemers. The projects of Huber and MacKercher should undoubtedly be viewed in that context.

We know nothing of the subsequent fate of the Huber and MacKercher proposals to buy tobacco directly in America—except that, despite opposition by Silhouette and the other London agents, they were in some form accepted by the united farms.[36] The two adventurers probably sailed from London at the very end of March 1737. They are first heard of in America when they attracted the frightened attention of the Virginia council on 27 April.[37] On producing their letters of introduction and explaining their mission and their desire to keep it secret till announced publicly in Maryland, the adventurers were allowed to proceed on their way. After some months north of the Potomac, MacKercher returned alone to Williamsburg early in August 1737, from which time the adventurers' paths separated.[38] The abbé was presumably to manage the Maryland end of the affair, where his *liaisons* with Lord Baltimore would prove most useful, while MacKercher assumed direction in Virginia where his Scots and Fairfax connections might be of greater help:[39] it should be remembered that Huber spoke only of Maryland in his letter to Chauvelin, while Smollett mentioned only Virginia in his representation of MacKercher's version of the affair.

Thus, in June 1737 there was published in Maryland under the signature of John-James Huber a pamphlet entitled, *A Memorial Relating to the Tobacco-Trade,* setting forth the terms of purchase proposed on behalf of the farmers-general.[40] Daniel MacKercher, for his part, on his return to Williamsburg on 3 August 1737, presented the very same proposals to the planters of Virginia, first orally, then in the *Virginia Gazette* of 5 August and, a few days later, in a pamphlet dated Williamsburg, 8 August 1737. MacKercher's Virginia proposals, in both printed versions, bore the same title and were virtually *word for word* the same as Huber's earlier Maryland offering. MacKercher's version differed from Huber's only in the computations, which the Scot concocted more imaginatively, making his scheme seem more attractive to the prospective seller. Later that year, MacKercher's pamphlet was reissued with quite substantial textual changes, though still bearing the old title and date "Williamsburg, August 8, 1737."[41] Earlier and later versions of both authors followed the same general argument: the strength of the French as monopsonistic buyers in the British tobacco market was stressed, the inadequacy of the price received by the planters of Virginia and Maryland conceded; the obvious solution was for the planters to deal directly with the united farms and thus save themselves much of the service charges in British ports and effect economies of scale in freight; the French would agree to take 15,000 hogsheads (about 13,500,000 lb.) a year delivered in London or any other British port at a fixed price of 2d. per pound. Although this was less than the 2d.1/4 they had been paying in London during the two preceding years, it would net the planters more because of economies in by-passing the London commission merchants and London business charges. Detailed sample accounts were included to show (in MacKercher's versions) that on a typical hogshead weighing 790 lb. in

Virginia, the planter's net receipt would rise by 22s. from £2:17:5 to £3:19:5, or 38 percent. (Huber's less dazzling figures promised a gain of only 5s. on a hogshead of 933 lb.) [42]

In the year following the announcement of the scheme in August 1737, the Williamsburg and Philadelphia papers were filled with news accounts and controversial correspondence relating to it.[43] Yet the planters held aloof. There were doubts about the legality of the scheme, about the credit of the persons involved and about the wisdom of the planter assuming all the risks of shipment in a fixed price sale. Nonetheless, Governor Gooch was strongly impressed by the scheme and in his first report to the Board of Trade ventured a striking prediction:

> But if, . . . instead of the Planters running the Risque of the Tobacco home, and receiving their Price as it weighs upon its delivery at the King's Scales, as the Gentlemen at first proposed, these Farmers will consent to Purchase & pay the Price Here, in Money or Bills of Exchange, and run the hazard themselves of the Voyage, the Planters I'l answer for them will come into it; for it would turn not only to their Advantage, but to the Benefit of the Trade in General, being disburthened of that load of mean Tobacco, which now lyes heavy on the M^rchants hands, ...[44]

In short, MacKercher had great difficulty in converting a courteous interest in his scheme into a firm commitment by the great shipping planters. Under the circumstances, it is quite understandable that, as in Smollett's version, he should decide to return to Europe "to consult his Principals," leaving the abbé Huber behind in Maryland. MacKercher most probably left America in the fall of 1737, Huber following him in August 1738 or shortly thereafter. Before leaving, each promised Governor Gooch that he would present the plan to the Board of Trade in London and bring back some definite written assurance or "license" of its legality.[45]

Before Huber left, he was able to push the plan to the brink of success. Agents were appointed in each colony: in Maryland, Philip Thomas of Ann Arundel county; in Virginia, Edward Barradall, a prominent Williamsburg lawyer.[46] These were public figures of the first rank. Thomas had just become a farmer of the Lord Proprietor's quitrents in Maryland and was a few years later to sit on the council of state there.[47] Barradall was to become attorney-general of Virginia by royal warrant in the course of that very year (1738).[48]

In January and February 1737/8, a formal offer to buy 15,000 hogsheads of tobacco on stated terms was made in the Williamsburg and Philadelphia press in the name of Philip Thomas.[49] Public and private negotiations with the planters continued during the following months. Finally, on 1 May 1738 at a meeting held in Williamsburg, an agreement was reached by Thomas and Barradall with a large group of Virginia planters. Thirteen persons signed the formula of May 1, including several councillors and others prominent in the colony; further subscriptions were invited.[50] No such agreement was ever reached in Maryland, though it seems to have been understood that if the Virginia arrangement worked out satisfactorily, Maryland might follow in course.[51]

Huber's "Proposals" of 1 May 1738 retreated far from the original offer of 1737, ending with terms that met all Governor Gooch's initial doubts. Originally, Huber and MacKercher had proposed to buy tobacco for the account of the united farms at a fixed price of 2d. per lb., netting the consigning planter more than the 2d.1/4 which the farms paid for the same tobacco in London in 1736 because the farmers would accept delivery of the tobacco at the King's Beam (customs weighing scales) upon landing, thus saving the consigner most of the London charges and any subsequent loss of weight. The planter still had to employ a London "factor" (commission merchant) to attend the unloading and weighing and receive the proceeds from the agents of the united farms, but the commission should have been much less than that hitherto paid. (The French buyer assuming all responsibility for paying and drawing back the large duty, the factor ought not any longer include the value of the duty in calculating his commission.) Of the original schemes, MacKercher's more flamboyant version had promised the planter some 22s. more per hogshead through savings of 9s. in commission, 8s. in weight not lost and some 10 or 11s. in minor expenses avoided. (Huber promised less.) In addition to these direct gains, both MacKercher and Huber held out prospects of additional savings by chartering whole vessels and thus reducing freight costs to the planter up to 30 percent.[52]

The gains promised by MacKercher's tables in particular were somewhat deceptive. For one thing, he assumed that most of the weight lost in a hogshead between first shipping and final sale took place in the London merchant's cellars and not on shipboard. This was contrary to commonsense, to planters' complaints, and to government observations.[53] This misapprehension was compounded by further confusions in accounting.[54] Second, MacKercher's calculation was based upon a hogshead weighing only 772 lb. at the King's Beam, somewhat below the Virginia average.[55] Charges per hogshead would weigh relatively more heavily upon the lighter unit. (Huber, by contrast, who based his calculation upon a hogshead of 933 lb. and who avoided MacKercher's confused accounting could only promise a gain of about 5s. per hogshead in his initial announcement.) [56] Third, many of the economies promised by both MacKercher and Huber were uncertain at the very least. What if handling costs could not be reduced to the extent suggested? What if merchants could not be found to venture ships at lower freights or to perform their reduced factorial duties for a reduced commission? The projectors foresaw some of these questions and promised to get all the ships themselves for the first year's business and to find pushing, new factors if the old merchants would not cooperate.[57] Last, there was the question of risk. Not only would the planter have to stand the hazard of the ocean crossing, but he was asked to chance his all in the hands of persons unknown to himself and of whose good credit he knew nothing. This was the one question the adventurers had not attempted to answer in their *Memorials*.

Thus, Huber was not able to negotiate along the lines originally suggested and had to change his terms. In the proposal made by Philip Thomas in Maryland in January 1737/8, all the risks, except that of the sea, were now assumed by the buyer: the tobacco was to be delivered in Maryland and the price, though not paid till the arrival of the tobacco in London, was to be calculated on the Maryland weight. With the purchaser paying all freight and incidental charges and sustaining all losses by wastage, the gross price offered was reduced from 16s. 8d. per 100 lb. to about 11s. The final net price to be realized by the planter was admittedly a shade lower than in the August 1737 schemes (£4 instead of £4:1s.:1d. per 800 lb. hogshead) but supposedly much more secure.[58] Still, reasonable critics of the project could argue that the price was not good enough and that the planter, although ostensibly selling his tobacco "in the country" at a country price, had actually to run the risk of the sea and to wait a considerable time for his money.[59] Thus, in the final agreement with the Virginia planters at Williamsburg on 1 May 1738, Huber was forced to raise the price slightly and to agree to take delivery unconditionally in Virginia and to pay in cash or bills of exchange at par (25 percent premium for sterling). No hogsheads under 800 lb. would be accepted: those weighing 800 lb. or more would be paid for at the rate of £4:4s. per 800 lb. (1.26d. sterling per lb.); those weighing 850, £4:12s. (1.3d. per lb.) and 11s. per 100 lb. for anything over; hogsheads weighing 900 lb. or more at the rate of £5 per 900 lb. (1.33d. per lb.).[60]

During the first half of 1738, the abbé Huber became involved in an extensive newspaper debate involving the *Virginia Gazette,* Franklin's rather friendly *Pennsylvania Gazette,* and the very hostile *American Weekly Mercury,* published by Franklin's chief Philadelphia rival, Bradford. The details of this rather arid debate need not detain us here.[61] It did, however, suggest that Maryland, much of whose tobacco was unsuited to the French market, was much less sympathetic to Huber's scheme than was Virginia. Some Marylanders pointed out that the abbé was offering them less (by the January terms) than he conceded to the Virginians by the May terms. There may have been good reason for this. Not only were the French uninterested in the Maryland bright tobaccos, but the Virginia inspection law guaranteed buyers a minimum quality and thus justified better terms in Virginia than could be risked in Maryland.[62]

"John James Huber" left the Chesapeake late in the summer of 1738. Were it not for the taunts by his foes in the press that only "328 Hogsheads" had been subscribed in Virginia,[63] one might imagine that he sailed in a blaze of glory. The terms reached with the Virginia planters on 1 May were so attractive and so practicable, the list of planters subscribing so distinguished. There was talk of building a Virginia merchant marine to take the tobacco to Europe. The subscribing grandees offered to act as subscription agents;[64] and the press was filled with friendly warnings from Thomas and Barradall urging all planters to sign up before it was too late.[65] A Rappahannock planter wrote the *Pennsylvania Gazette* that "the Subscriptions daily Increase, tho' the dry Season we have had, has been some Obstruction."[66] An enthusiastic account appeared in the Bristol and London press concluding with the news that Barradall and Thomas "have not only contracted for the Year 39 and 40; and expect in a short Time to have a sufficient Power to contract for Four Years more. *And perhaps, in four Years more, the French will contract for the whole Main.*"[67]

When Huber left Virginia, everything seemed so promising that the cautious Gooch made the abbé promise to send no ships till he had explained the project to the Board of Trade and obtained some sort of clearance from them. After his return to Europe, the abbé wrote the governor "that he has gott the better of all Opposition and intends shortly to return to" Virginia. In mid-1739, the governor was still a faithful believer in the scheme.[68] But the abbé did not return to Virginia, and in London the Board of Trade waited in vain for a MacKercher or a Huber to appear to defend the project. No one even appeared to attack it.[69] Finally, early in 1740, Governor Gooch was forced to close the government's dossier on the "French Scheme":

> [The abbé] not returning to this Colony, according to his Agreement with me, and the subscribers, and no Body on the Spott for him to produce the Power [from the Board of Trade], or to pay the money at the time prefixed, the project is sunk. A ship came hither last Fall [1739], as it was said, in that Interest, but the Contract being determined [i.e., terminated] by a failure on his Part, she had her Loading to seek; and as the Gentleman, who came hither in her, lives in London, and is concerned with one M.r Fitzgerald an eminent Merchant there, was obliged to put himself upon the foot of a common purchaser, I judged he had a Right to Trade.[70]

Why then did this brilliant project fail? Was it, as in the novel, the abbé's "unparalleled piece of treachery" that led the adventurers to fall out? Reading Smollett alongside our other evidence, a pattern emerges. During 1737, while MacKercher was in America, the Genevan moved in the shadow of the Scot. Once MacKercher left, however, the abbé's peculiar talents showed themselves. Not only did he burst into print as the leading publicist of three colonies; more significantly, he abandoned his and MacKercher's early impractical plan and pushed those private negotiations with the leading planters in MacKercher's Virginia which resulted in the agreement of 1 May 1738. This is what we can read between Smollett's lines:

> He secretly wrote a memorial to the company, importing that he found by experience M——— could afford to furnish them at a much lower price than that which they had agreed to give; ... and that, if they thought him worthy of such a trust, he would undertake to furnish them at an easier rate, in conjunction with some of the leading men in Virginia and Maryland, with whom he said, he had already concerted measures for that purpose.[71]

Even if the abbé did not actually betray his colleague to their employers, reasons for jealousy and quarrel were ready enough at hand. Though Huber at his return wrote Gooch that he had conquered all opposition,[72] the project itself died. Smollett insists MacKercher killed it by withdrawing in anger at the abbé's perfidy. This may have been the anger of pride or defeat or indignation at sharing Virginia with a bungler whose own Maryland expectations had gone awry. Smollett suggests as much and more when he writes that the farmers "afterwards used all their endeavours to persuade him [MacKercher] to be concerned with that little traitor in his [the abbé's] undertaking (by which he might still have been a considerable gainer)." The virtuous and belatedly patriotic MacKercher, we are told, "resisted all their solicitations, and plainly told them, in the Abbé's presence, that he would never prostitute his own principles so far, as to enter into engagements of any kind with a person of his character, much less in a scheme that had a manifest tendency to lower the market-price of tobacco in England."[73]

At the test, the farmers-general may themselves have killed the project.[74] With the experts at each other's throat, their own doubts must have been reinforced. There were of course also the hostile voices of the Bance and Simond-Silhouette interests.[75] Moreover, the approaching war between Great Britain and Spain, midst other hazardous prospects, promised a rise in freight and insurance rates. This had become critically relevant since one of Huber's concessions of May 1738 was to have the buyer assume the cost and risk of the ocean crossing. Revenue farming was a business intrinsically incompatible with avoidable risks.

There remains one minor thread yet to unravel. In their *Memorials,* MacKercher and Huber were anxious to establish the ability of the farmers-general, who bought so far ahead, to depress the London market at will, if necessary by stopping all purchases for a while. To prove that their employers could that very year force the price down from $2d.1/4$ to $2d.$, the projectors revealed that "Two very topping Merchants of *London* have offer'd to oblige themselves by Contract to supply them always at this Price [$2d.$] in the present Course of the Trade, and to give Security for the Performance of the Contract . . . provided the *Farmers* would grant them the Commission, and defer the buying of the Tobacco for some Months."[76] This information immediately set tongues going in the two colonies. Experience had convinced many in Virginia and Maryland that there were tobacco merchants in London, factors though they might be, who were prepared to act against the interest of their principals for their private gain. Such suspicions, when particularized, could be disastrous in a trade where reputation still counted for everything. To prevent rumor hurting specific individuals, the abbé Huber was forced to write his first letter to the press:

> ... I never meant, nor insinuated to mean any Merchant in the Tobacco-Trade, but Two Merchants well known at *London;* each of them offer'd a Bail of 100,000 Crowns [£12,000], if not complying with his Promise. Their Names (tho' it was useless to set them in Print) I never refused to tell, even when not enquired for, as having it under their Hands, and being obliged to no Secrecy.[77]

The revealing phrase "having it under their Hands" immediately suggests that Huber (and perhaps MacKercher) was in communication with two great London merchants (not in the tobacco trade) who had been trying for some time to obtain the London tobacco purchasing contract from the French farmers-general. The identity of these "Two very topping Merchants" is suggested by Gooch's last letter. The governor reported that the supercargo of the vessel that came to Virginia in the fall of 1739 in the Huber "Interest" lived "in London, and [was] ... concerned with one Mr Fitzgerald an eminent Merchant there."[78] The two merchants are thus almost surely George FitzGerald, uncle and nephew, merchants of London and partners (from 1739) of Jean-Jacques Huber.[79] If we may believe Smollett, it was an encounter with their kinsman, James FitzGerald, at the siege of Philippsbourg, that first brought MacKercher into touch with the whole world of Paris high finance.

In the end, things turned out much as the abbé had foreseen, if not exactly as Daniel MacKercher liked. It will be remembered that when Huber had in 1736 applied to Chauvelin for that minister's support, he had suggested that, if the Chesapeake buying experiment proved unsuccessful, he be compensated by all or part of the London agency of the united farms.[80] That is exactly what happened on the abbé's return to France late in 1738. Sometime not too long thereafter, the united farms decided or were persuaded to give a substantial part of their British buying business to the abbé Huber for five years starting 1 September 1739, in effect for the remainder of the Forceville lease (1738–44). If we are correct in inferring in the last chapter that both Bance and Silhouette gave up or lost their tobacco commissions in 1739, then these new arrangements were simply the transfer of part of the British agency from Bance, Silhouette, and Simond to Huber and associates. On 10 May 1739, a partnership contract was in fact signed between Jean-Jacques Huber and the two George FitzGeralds of London to undertake the tobacco commission.[81] According to a later gossipy memoir, this transfer of the agency from Bance to the FitzGeralds in 1739 was effected through Huber's connection with the controller-general Orry; the FitzGeralds were required to pay a *pot de vin* of 52,000 *l.t.* annually, of which Huber kept 12,000 *l.t.*, the remaining 40,000 *l.t.* going presumably somewhere indicated by Orry.[82] When the war started in 1744, the younger FitzGerald petitioned the British government for licenses to carry to France tobacco purchased "by order of John James Huber Esq! of Paris & for account of the Farmers Generall of France." The quantities so purchased were large and scattered among Glasgow, Ayr, Kirkcudbright, Aberdeen, and Whitehaven.[83] It would seem, therefore, as if the contract given by the united farms to Huber and the FitzGeralds in 1739 was for tobacco purchases outside of London, specifically in the north of England and Scotland. The London contract remained in the hands of others, the Van Necks first of all.

Thus, in his later years, the abbé Huber found that solid mercantile prosperity which had eluded him ever since he fled his father's counting house in Lyons twenty years before. In 1739, he could move out of the residence of La Popelinière into a town house of his own. When he died in 1744, his will included coaches, horses, servants, and *objets d'art*. (In 1743, he had also established near Paris, under a monopoly patent, a calendry for finishing cloth.) He left small bequests to most of his brothers and sisters and to friends, including two pictures to the controller-general Orry, the enemy of Silhouette. His executor was the important Paris banker, Isaac Vernet (also of a Genevan family), his residuary legatee the pastellist, Maurice-Quentin de la Tour, who did several well-known portraits of him. Himself to the end, the abbé Huber cut off his own mother and grandmother with twelve *sols* or fifty pounds of chocolate each and left not a sou to repay the considerable sums "advanced for him by M[acKercher], in order to prevent his rotting in jail."[84] MacKercher, however, sued and the estate, thus embarrassed, was a long time being settled. Most of the small bequests were eventually paid but with the tobacco accounts not yet settled and the MacKercher suit still pending, La Tour in 1748 surrendered all claims as residuary legatee to Vernet for 10,000 *l.t.*[85]

The MacKercher-Huber expedition of 1737–38 can be viewed in two lights. Under one, it was simply another phase in the long, behind-the-scenes struggle for the united farms' tobacco buying commission—a struggle which, as we shall see, grew more intense as that commission became more valuable. Seen thus, the chapter ends simply with MacKercher worsted and Huber and the FitzGeralds carrying away part of the commission. In a more "serious" light, the incident can be viewed as a conscious effort by the French monopoly and government to subvert the entire spirit if not the letter of the British Acts of Trade and Navigation and deal directly with the tobacco planters in Virginia and Maryland. Conscious it certainly was—but how serious was it? We have seen again and again that, at the test, the united farms were governed by bookkeeping considerations. Buying directly in Virginia and Maryland would be attractive to the united farms only if it could be done more cheaply than buying in London. But could it?

Huber, MacKercher, the farmers-general, and the articulate planters of Virginia and Maryland all seemed to regard the London market and London costs as unnecessary burdens on the trade which could be cut away to the profit of all concerned. In practice, however, these obvious economies proved very difficult to realize. It was expensive to do business in London, but the London market and the London factors, for all that was said against them, did perform services not easily dispensed with, as their critics discovered at the test. Silhouette pointed all this out at the time in his criticism of the Huber-MacKercher project.[86] There were, however, inefficiencies in the tobacco trade as conducted in the 1730's: the consignment system under which hogsheads were sold individually at considerable cost was ill suited to the needs of small planters growing ordinary grades of tobacco, as well as to the needs of the great French buyer who wanted to contract for thousands of hogsheads. Much more suitable for both, we shall see, was the system used in the outports where costs were lower and whose merchants bought tobacco on their own account in the Chesapeake. Huber and the FitzGeralds must have realized this when they took over the outport buying commission in 1739.[87]

Who Were the FitzGeralds?

Thus far we have spoken of the FitzGeralds of London only as allies of the abbé Huber. They were much more than that. They were important merchants on their own account in London with most valuable connections in the highest Paris financial circles. If the career of Peter Simond, with its South African, Dutch, French, and English chapters, seems to epitomize many of the most striking features of the history of the Huguenot exile in the century following the revocation, so does the history of the FitzGerald (properly fitz Gerald) family embody many of the most dramatic features of the history of the Irish Diaspora in the decades following the Catholic defeat at the Boyne.

The FitzGeralds of Waterford were a very cadet branch of the family of the Geraldine earls of Kildare.[88] They remained true to the old faith, prospered with it and suffered with it. When Catholics ruled Ireland, Richard FitzGerald, a merchant with a most numerous progeny, was sheriff of Waterford in 1650. He or his merchant son of the same name was probably the Richard FitzGerald who was mayor of the same city in 1687, in James II's time.[89] The FitzGeralds were closely intermarried with other leading Catholic families of the city, as well as with county families and mercantile families in other Irish ports. With the Williamite conquest, this vast cousinhood was dispersed over the face of Europe. No fewer than twenty-one FitzGeralds were attainted in County Waterford, including several sons of the sheriff.[90]

Their flight and resettlement overseas was to a considerable degree directed and assisted by cousins settled at St. Malo and elsewhere since Cromwell's time.[91]

By his first wife, Maria Browne, sheriff Richard FitzGerald had a son John (born ca. 1637), who eventually settled in London and prospered there as a merchant, and a daughter, Margaret, who married Luke Hore, a merchant of Dublin. In 1685–86, Luke Hore was national treasurer of the association for Catholic emancipation;[92] after the Boyne, he was proscribed and fled to St. Malo where his wife, Margaret, died in 1698.[93] By his second wife, Frances Xaveria, daughter of Nicholas Wyse of Kingsmeadow and of St. John's Priory, County Waterford, Richard FitzGerald had ten sons and three daughters. The eldest of these daughters, Maria, married Nicholas Porter, merchant of Waterford, while the youngest married James Butler. Both Porters[94] and Butlers,[95] proscribed at home, established themselves in France after 1690 where over three generations they kept in touch with their Fitz-Gerald relations, even when marrying into good French families.

Of the ten sons of Richard FitzGerald of Waterford by his second wife, the sixth, Richard, was a regimental commander in King James's army and was killed at the Boyne. Thomas, the eighth, had died in St. Domingue before 1716. (He may be the sieur Geraldin who was director there for the Company of St. Domingue, ca. 1708–9.)[96] The other brothers scattered over Ireland, England and France.[97] The youngest, Edward, remained in Waterford as a merchant. Yet, his grandson James FitzGerald joined the Irish Brigade of the French army in 1730, won a colonel's brevet in the field at Fontenoy (1745), rose to the rank of brigadier (1758) and *maréchal de camp* (1762) and commanded Clare's regiment during the minority of the earl of Thomond.[98] (Young James was close to the London FitzGeralds and was also remembered in the will of the abbé Huber.)[99]

The eldest of the ten sons of Waterford, Nicholas, was pardoned by William III and remained in Ireland where he appears to have reacquired his grandfather Wyse's small property, for he is described in later records as "of King's Meadow, Waterford, Esq." His eldest son Richard was admitted to Gray's Inn in 1731[100] and became a barrister in London. Nicholas's older half-brother, John, the wealthy merchant of London, left his entire estate to this Richard when he died (aged 97) in 1734.[101] Nicholas is probably the "Mr. FitzGerald, a Papist of the county of Waterford" who applied to Lord Perceval in 1733 for his aid in getting a private act of Parliament in Great Britain to permit him, contrary to statute, to purchase land in Ireland worth £1,000 yearly for his children. "He said his brother, who is a reputable merchant of London, having no children, had promised to settle 20,000 *l.* on his nephews and nieces, the children of this FitzGerald, in case he would lay it out in land in Ireland, but not otherwise, and therefore as it was a compassionate case, and as his family had been very serviceable to the Protestants of Ireland in King James' reign in protecting their persons, houses, and goods,

... he hoped he should succeed." Perceval, though sympathetic, thought it improper that the British Parliament should intercede in an Irish affair and refused to act.[102] Richard FitzGerald of Gray's Inn nevertheless acquired a considerable landed estate in Staffordshire, Lancashire, and Flintshire by his marriage to an English Catholic heiress, Rebecca Grove, daughter of Thomas Grove of Worcester. Richard FitzGerald protected his wife's land against suits brought by her Protestant relations by becoming a nominal Protestant himself.[103] On his death in 1763, Richard FitzGerald, by then quite wealthy, left all his and his late wife's real estate to the eldest surviving son of John FitzGerald of Williamstown, County Waterford, son of Edward FitzGerald, tenth son of Sheriff Richard. Unlike his first cousin, that other grandson of Edward, the *maréchal de camp* James FitzGerald, the heir of Richard of Gray's Inn was brought up a Protestant and lived to be sheriff of both Waterford and Flintshire.[104]

The mercantile members of the family had less reason to become Protestant than the landed. Gregory, the second of the ten sons of Sheriff Richard FitzGerald by his second marriage, is probably the Gregory FitzGerald whom we find as a merchant and Jacobite consul at Nantes from 1689 to 1692.[105] Subsequently, he settled in Santa Cruz de Tenerife in the Canaries, where he died sometime after 1718, leaving a daughter Frances Xaveria married to Bernard Walsh, a merchant on the island.

George, the ninth son, with whom we are principally concerned, also settled on Tenerife where he was in business at La Oratava for some years in partnership with his niece's husband, Bernard Walsh. (The wine trade from the Canaries to England prospered after 1689 and John FitzGerald, his older half-brother, the merchant in London, was also in the wine trade.) [106] In 1711, George FitzGerald visited St. Malo, that great center of Irish emigration, where he married Servanne-Marie Browne, of another expatriate family. Through his wife, George FitzGerald became connected by marriage with the Cranisbourg (Cranisborough), a Waterford family established in commerce at Morlaix, and more importantly, with the Wailsh (Walsh), the great Irish merchants and slave traders of Nantes.[107] In 1718, George FitzGerald dissolved his partnership with his nephew Bernard Walsh and moved from Tenerife to London.[108] In January 1734/5, he took in as partner his nephew, George FitzGerald the younger, son of his oldest brother, Nicholas of King's Meadow, and younger brother of Richard of Gray's Inn.[109] George FitzGerald the elder died in 1744 leaving a will filled with familial and charitable bequests. His business he left to his nephew, namesake, and partner.[110]

We have gone into this much detail because it is important to see the FitzGeralds of London not simply as two merchants looking for business, but as part of a vast family network stretching over Ireland, England, France, and Spain, with its own system of communications and its own system of loyalties, able to exert influence in its own way in strange places. Long before cousin James FitzGerald became a colonel in the Irish Brigade, another cousin, Sir Thomas FitzGerald (Don Tomás Geraldino), was Spanish governmental representative on the directorate of the South Sea Company, 1732–37, and minister in London, 1737–39.[111] The London FitzGeralds were drawn almost inevitably to politics, which could be good or bad for business. The elder George FitzGerald found it difficult to get favors from the British government because of his "imprudently declared attachment for the Pretender."[112] George the younger was known to the papal representatives in London as a "zelante Cattolico" (even though his brother Richard became a Protestant) and was consulted about plans for Catholic schools in Ireland.[113] His family and business connection, Antoine Wailsh of Nantes, was deep in the plots for "the '45," even supplying the ship which carried the Young Pretender to Scotland.[114] Dr. Florence Hensey, a physician acting as French spy in London and apprehended by the British government, revealed in 1758 that George FitzGerald was the Jacobite banker in London (performing services analogous to those performed by Lawrence Woulfe, George and John Waters, and Charles Selwyn in Paris).

> He is very closely connected with Marshal Thomond [Charles O'Brien, earl of Clare and of Thomond, marshal of France] with whom he corresponds regularly. His house is a Rendezvous of Jacobites. All those that come from abroad upon errands are addressed to him. He has placed many of his Relations in the Irish Brigade and supports them genteely. Among the rest is one James FitzGerald a Colonel Who was aide de camp to the late Marshal Saxe. I have seen him often in London. Many come over here incog [sic] from the Irish Brigade and else where. Some he accomodates at his own house, but most of them are sett down at the Bull Inn gate in Holbourn which he took some years ago for his servant James Hutton.... This Inn is seldom without some persons of this sort.

Hensey implied that some of this FitzGerald did "in order to ingratiate himself at the french Court" and keep his tobacco contract.[115]

The London FitzGeralds had even better commercial than political connections. In 1748, Antoine-Vincent Wailsh and Paris de Montmartel put together a syndicate that obtained a royal charter for the slave trading Angola Company. The company operated from Nantes, its Paris affairs being handled by its partners, the bank of Tourton & Baur (a successor to Tourton & Guiguer). Its London agent was George FitzGerald.[116] Thus we see the younger Fitzgerald as part of one of the most powerful financial-commercial networks in France. Banished in 1726, Duverney and Montmartel, the surviving Paris brothers were, in part through the influence of Samuel Bernard, permitted to return to the capital in the later 1730's. They regained their preeminent influence at court during the 1740's when they were once more important army contractors; Montmartel became principal court banker. George FitzGerald, according to Dr. Hensey, worked closely with Montmartel, helping to discount and circulate his bills via Amsterdam.[117] FitzGerald's relations were probably even closer with Tourton & Baur who were for many years his Paris correspondents.[118] Another link with this last connection is suggested by the fact that about 1736–38, George FitzGerald the younger was a director of the Royal Exchange Assurance Company, the very company on whose board George Tobie Guiguer also sat as a director![119] In a not too literal sense, the FitzGeralds may perhaps be thought to have "inherited" the old Tourton & Guiguer interest in the tobacco buying contract.

As merchants, the FitzGeralds of course had interests in Ireland.[120] They also had connections with privateering.[121] On the continent, their correspondence was most diverse.[122] Their greatest activity seems to have been directed toward Spain and its possessions.[123] (In 1736, we find George FitzGerald & Co. chartering a ship for Colabeau of Paris to carry wheat from Calais to the Spanish Mediterranean coast. Charles Colabeau, syndic of the French Indies Company, was subsequently actively interested in Wailsh's Angola Company of 1748.) [124] As a house, the FitzGeralds seem to have been peculiarly adept at trade that violated the navigation acts of many nations. As early as 1709, we find a Mr. FitzGerald, one of the owners of the ship *St. Francis Xavier* of La Palma in the Canaries, applying to the British Board of Trade for a license for that vessel to carry British goods to the Canaries, thence proceed to Caracas and elsewhere in the Spanish West Indies for trade and thence return to Britain.[125] From his base on Tenerife before 1718, George FitzGerald the elder had sent ships to Havana.[126] He was later suspected of shipping wheat to hostile Spain in the famine year 1740 through collusive captures by Spanish privateers.[127]

The full complexity of the dealings in and out of the Spanish empire in which the FitzGeralds specialized can rather interestingly be seen in the history of their ship *King's Meadow* (named after the family property in County Waterford). The ship's captain, Thomas Mansfield, had citizenship in the Austrian Netherlands to facilitate its operations. In 1737–38, the ship was employed on a voyage from Amsterdam to Ireland to Jamaica to Santiago de Cuba and thence back to England and Hamburg. This venture was made in collaboration with the South Sea Company and presumably did not violate any British law. The next year (1738–39), the ship took on pipe staves, wheat, and barley at Hamburg; some of the pipe staves were unloaded at Cadiz (Strange & Mullone being the consignee) and 1,800 silver dollars taken on; the remainder of the pipe staves and the grain were then discharged at Malaga (Mathew & Thomas Quilty & Co.); then the ship proceeded to Madeira where the dollars were consigned to Holloran & Gordon and 38 pipes of wine taken on; the wine was delivered to Taylor & Verdon at Jamaica from whence the ship proceeded to the Bay of Honduras for logwood and thence back to Jamaica and London: all on account of George FitzGerald & Co. of London. In 1740, the vessel was innocently employed to Le Havre, probably with tobacco for the monopoly, and thence less innocently to the Channel Islands. In 1741, the firm chartered the ship to the Victualling Commissioners to carry wine, which the commissioners had purchased from another London merchant, from the Canaries to the British forces in the West Indies; in order to get that wine from the enemy's islands, the *King's Meadow* went to Holland where it acquired a Dutch crew and false Dutch papers; with these it proceeded to the Canaries and took on a lading of wine; on its way to the West Indies it met a Spanish man-of-war and in panic the master threw overboard his British papers. Thus, when the vessel reached Jamaica, it was seized and condemned for violating the British navigation acts. Although the decision was reversed on appeal, ten years of litigation ensued in Jamaica, England, and Scotland.[128]

George FitzGerald, uncle and nephew, were thus not obscure hangers-on of the abbé Huber but were themselves affluent merchants with exceptional financial, commercial, and political connections in France. As specialists in the most devious of international operations, they were peculiarly suited to dabble in the French tobacco buying contract.

CHAPTER 22

The Purchasing Commission during the War Years, 1739–63

From 1739 to 1744, commissions to purchase tobacco in England and Scotland for the French were, we have seen, held by the FitzGeralds via the abbé Huber and by the Van Necks; the older agencies of Silhouette, working with Peter Simond, and of Bance probably ended about 1739. The business papers of none of these persons have survived, nor are most of their records at the Bank of England very revealing. By this time, most active merchants in London had accounts with a private banker in "the City" as well as with "the Bank." Frequently, they used their facilities with the latter only to handle large discounting operations; their Drawing Office records therefore reveal little of their everyday trade. An exception, however, was the bank account of the FitzGeralds between June 1741 and early 1743.

During the 1730's, the FitzGeralds banked with Ironside & Belchier; their account at the Bank of England was relatively inactive. In 1741, for reasons unknown, the FitzGeralds decided to make greater use of the Bank Drawing Office; their account there became very active in June 1741 and remained so until January 1742/3, more than a year before the death of the elder George FitzGerald. Among the payments from the account during this year and a half to persons with names associated with the tobacco trade, we find:[1]

Alexander	(Edinburgh)	£13,400: 0: 0
How	(Whitehaven)	4,017:18: 0
Gildart	(Liverpool)	1,968: 1: 4
Buchanan	(Glasgow)	1,550: 8: 0
Buck	(Bideford)	700: 4: 7
Peloquin	(Bristol)	350: 0: 0

In addition, £2,400 was paid to Silhouette, but this probably was no longer for tobacco. The figures themselves are probably fragmentary and thus not too meaningful (except in suggesting a preponderant place for Alexander). They do show something of the geographic range of the FitzGeralds' activity and some of the houses with whom they dealt. It was an outport business, heavily oriented toward the north and Scotland.

Up to the time the FitzGeralds and Huber obtained their commission in 1739, most of the French tobacco had been bought in London. Although, as we shall see in the next chapter, the outport and Scottish share rose dramatically under the FitzGeralds, the London agency still remained important. It is therefore unfortunate that we know little about it at this time except that Bance and the Van Necks, and Simond and Silhouette until at least 1739, were vaguely involved in it. Only in the early 1740's, do we begin to find concrete evidence of the Van Necks' activity. For the 1730's, all is dark, except for a single payment from their bank account to Silhouette in 1736.[2] There is nothing to connect them then to Huber or FitzGerald, although they were not entirely strangers to the milieu from which Huber came. In subsequent years, we find them in close correspondence with Isaac Vernet, the banker and executor of the abbé Huber, and with Vernet's successors, Thellusson, Necker & Co. (a firm also less immediately descended from the Paris Tourton & Guiguer).[3] However, with the return of Silhouette to Paris in 1742, Van Necks' activity in the French tobacco agency noticeably increases. Their account at the Bank of England shows that suddenly, early in 1743, they started paying large sums (£22,253 in six months) to FitzGeralds with whom of late they had had no business at all.[4] A letter of 1743 acknowledges them and the FitzGeralds to be the only agents of the French monopoly in London.[5] By the start of the French-British war, whole shiploads of tobacco were being cleared from London to France in the names of Gerard and Joshua Van Neck of London.[6] These scraps of evidence may be misleading, but they do tend to suggest that Van Necks were taking an increasingly important part in French tobacco purchases even before the war pushed them into a leading position.

The start of the British-Spanish war in 1739 and the War of the Austrian Succession in 1740 did not seem to make very much difference at first in the conduct of the tobacco export trade from Britain to France; those two powers were still at peace with each other. The Spaniards, however, did seize at least one neutral vessel carrying British tobacco to the French monopoly. In 1741, Neil Buchanan of Glasgow had to obtain a convoy for three

TABLE I
English Tobacco Exports to France: Nationality of Shipping, 1737–44[7]

Year	In British Vessels	In Foreign Vessels	Total
	(in English lb.)		
1737	17,364,899	—	17,364,899
1738	7,539,724	56,000	7,595,724
1739	9,370,842	2,431,095	11,801,937
1740	4,851,519	888,256	5,739,775
1741	5,940,619	9,029,597	14,970,216
1742	7,684,005	7,057,385	14,741,390
1743	4,916,807	4,453,654	9,370,461
1744	3,249,110	3,563,669	6,812,779

of his Glasgow tobacco ships from the Cornish coast to Morlaix. A month later, James Buchanan of London applied for a convoy for the same three vessels out of Morlaix till clear at sea on their way to Virginia.[8] The other suppliers seem to have taken their chances, or to have employed foreign vessels (Table I). Thus, in 1737–38, virtually no non-British vessels had been used to carry tobacco to France (presumably for economic reasons); by 1741–44, with the threat of Spanish privateers, fully half the tobacco sent to France was being carried in foreign ships. No comparable data are available for Scotland during all these years. However, after the Scottish port books start at Michaelmas 1742, we find evidence of an even more striking use of foreign craft, French primarily, but a few from Hamburg, in the eighteen months ending with the French declaration of war on Britain on 20/31 March 1744 (Table II).

TABLE II
Scottish Tobacco Exports to France: Nationality of Shipping
29 September 1742–20 March 1743/4 o.s.[9]

	In British Vessels	In Foreign Vessels (in English lb.)	Total
Port Glasgow	913,385	3,783,413	4,696,798
Greenock	67,669	2,737,026	2,804,695
Ayr	124,993	936,917	1,061,910
Kirkcudbright	108,279	–	108,279
Total	1,214,326	7,457,356	8,671,682

All these arrangements, whether improvised or of longer standing, were rudely shaken by the events of 1744. Regardless of the international situation, the Forceville lease of the United General Farms was due to expire on 30 September; all commissions and appointments under it would expire at the same time, though most could expect to be renewed for the next six-year lease of the farms. The five-year partnership contract between Huber and the FitzGeralds was due to expire on 1 September, but would undoubtedly have been continued if their commission from the farms had itself been renewed. However, within a few weeks all these expectations were smashed. On 20/31 March, France declared war on Britain; the same day, George FitzGerald the elder dropped dead;[10] on 31 March/11 April Britain declared war on France; a few days later (5/16 April) the abbé Huber was dead. In the resulting confusion, George FitzGerald the younger seems to have made a serious bid to take over the entire tobacco buying contract.

At first, it seemed obvious that war would mean the end of the French market and a sharp contraction in the trade. Sir James Lowther, Bart., M.P.

for Cumberland, heard from his well-informed agent at Whitehaven, a few days before the outbreak of hostilities, "The uncertain Scituation of Publick Affairs makes Trade of all kinds very precarious. . . . If there is a French War that Market will be lost, & . . . it will make a great change amongst them [the tobacco merchants]. People of sense are lessening their Trade & Winding up as fast as they can. Mr. How sends fewer ships [to Virginia] than formerly."[11] But within a few weeks, Lowther in London was picking up rumors of another sort. "I suppose," he wrote back to Whitehaven on 31 March, "our Merch[an]ts will now be thinking of some round about way of getting their Tobacco sold to the French."[12] At first, Sir James suspected it would be by way of Holland and feared that the Dutch rather than the English merchants would benefit by such a routing.[13]

The most pressing problem was that of ships loading or on their way to France when the war broke out. On 24 March 1743/4, four days after the French declared war, and before Britain reciprocated, an order-in-council was issued placing an embargo on all French ships in British ports.[14] An eager customs officer at Gravesend stopped an English and a Danzig vessel carrying tobacco for the Van Necks to France, but was ordered by the Treasury on 30 March to permit them to proceed on their way.[15] Other cases had to be referred to the Privy Council.[16] A particularly zealous officer at Falmouth held up the *Rose* of Appledore with tobacco from Barnstaple for Morlaix, shipped by David and John Peloquin of Bristol; the officer insisted that the tobacco was not the Peloquins' property but had been shipped, as the ship's papers showed, on the account of the farmers-general. The Privy Council ordered her released.[17] At least one admittedly French ship had been caught in an English port (Whitehaven) at the outbreak of the war, but Sir James Lowther, principal landlord and patron of the port, was able to get an order-in-council in June releasing her. (Peter How, FitzGerald's collaborator at Whitehaven, was very close to Lowther.) In July, George FitzGerald even wangled a pass from Lord Carteret's office, permitting the vessel to carry tobacco on its return voyage to France.[18]

Meanwhile, a more formal effort was being undertaken to reopen the tobacco trade to France. By May 1744, it must have been clear that the French government would give the necessary passes for neutral or British vessels to import the tobacco needed by the monopoly. Knowing this, "several Merchants of the City of Glasgow"—no doubt after consultation with FitzGerald and/or the Van Necks—petitioned the Treasury "praying leave to Export Tobacco . . . to France in Neutrall Vessells, or in British Ships, under such Restrictions as My Lords shall think fitt." On 23 May, the petition was referred for report to the customs commissioners of Scotland and England.[19] When favorable reports were received from those boards in July, the Treasury consulted the attorney- and solicitor-general who advised them that the granting of such passes was not properly a Treasury function. However, the Treasury minute on 19 July ends ambiguously, "And as to the other part of the Merch[an]ts Mem[oria]l, My Lords would have the Comm[issione]rs of the Customes proceed in their usual Method."[20] What this meant in unveiled language was that customs could continue to turn a blind eye to the export of tobacco to France in neutral vessels.

As early as 9 June 1744, Sir James Lowther wrote his agent at Whitehaven that he had been talking to Henry Pelham, First Lord of the Treasury, about the possible ill effects of the war on the port's tobacco trade, and reported that Pelham replied "the Tobacco Trade to France w[ou]ld be carried on in Neutral Ships from Wh[itehave]n as before, w[hi]ch shows he knows more of that Trade than I imagin'd."[21] In fact, a week or so later, a Dutch and a Danish vessel arrived at Whitehaven with French passes. There was another Dutch ship at Whitehaven in July and seven more in August, all sent by George FitzGerald to carry tobacco to France.[22] In Scotland, during the same months, two Dutch vessels came to Greenock and one to Port Glasgow to take on tobacco for Bordeaux.[23]

From the very first it was evident that this use of neutral vessels would be expensive since it was most likely that the Dutch or Danish vessels would have to go in ballast to Whitehaven or Scotland where FitzGerald was doing most of his buying for the French; the farmers-general would of course have to pay these higher freights. It would thus be in the fiscal interest of the united farms to get licenses for British vessels to bring tobacco despite the war. British vessels could do this very cheaply while outward bound for Virginia. If Pelham would not go beyond neutral vessels, there were other ministers—particularly Carteret—to whom FitzGerald could apply. FitzGerald's collaborator at Whitehaven, the great local Virginia merchant, Peter How, confided regularly to Sir James Lowther's local agent, John Spedding, to whom he was connected by marriage. Through this channel, Lowther heard as early as 1 July:

> [The tobacco] trade is likely to go on with France as well now as in time of peace by means of passes obtain'd from some of our Ministers of State, & M[r] How thinks those passes will be granted as well to our own ships as to those of Neutrall Nations. . . . He is Applying for a pass for the ship Hope of this Town to go to France with another Loading of Tob[o], & says they will have a protection if France is to secure them from being taken for 12 days after they depart from any port of that Kingdom in their way to Virginia or any where Else, so that he Expects most of our ships that go to Virg[a] will take a Loading of Tob[o] to France when they go out, w[ch] will be a great help to their Freights.[24]

FitzGerald indeed got the pass for How's *Hope* which sailed with some Dutch ships for France early in August.[25] How also received other royal passes in July and August 1744 to send the ships *Charity* and *Nelson* to

France on the grounds that neutral vessels were not available at Whitehaven; the tobacco they carried had all allegedly been purchased for the late "John James Huber of Paris" before the start of the war.[26] In August, Lowther also heard from young Anthony Bacon, Spedding's cousin, then a Whitehaven ship captain about to settle as a merchant in London, that tobacco was also being sent from London to France with French passes.[27]

By early September, FitzGerald felt confident enough to flood Secretary Carteret's office with petitions. Peter How, his Whitehaven agent, and William Alexander, his Scottish agent, wanted permission to import French produce to the value of the freight and commissions owing them in France from the estate of the late "John James Huber."[28] Even John Bance, dismissed since about 1739, applied for permission to export 200 hogsheads of tobacco to France on board a French ship that had come to London with a special pass. Most of the surviving petitions, dating from 7 to 13 September, were, however, from George FitzGerald himself. In them, he asked permission to export to France certain specified quantities of tobacco purchased before the war "by order of John James Huber Esqr of Paris & for account of the Farmers Generall of France." The ports in France to which the tobacco was intended were specified as well as the ports in Britain where the tobacco was lying: Glasgow (900 hogsheads), Ayr (250 in one petition, 210 in another), Aberdeen (140), Kirkcudbright (337) and Whitehaven (375).[29] From the Scottish port books (with only Ayr defective), we can ascertain that all these applications were granted as were some later ones which have not survived. All in all, during the first eighteen months of the war (Lady Day 1744–Michaelmas 1745), at least 24 vessels (16 British, 7 Dutch and 1 French) sailed from Scotland with tobacco for France; they all received sign manual passes from the office of Lord Carteret:

Lady Day–Midsummer	1744	nil			
Midsummer–Michaelmas	1744	4 ships	1,055 hhd.	961,459 lb.
Michaelmas–Christmas	1744	8 ships	1,644 hhd.	1,481,089 lb.
Christmas–Lady Day	1745	6 ships	2,408 hhd.	2,134,108 lb.
Lady Day–Midsummer	1745	4 ships	1,078 hhd.	958,022 lb.
Midsummer–Michaelmas	1745	2 ships	578 hhd.	509,543 lb.
Total		24 ships	6,763 hhd.	6,044,221 lb.[30]

Secretary Carteret's pass register (not necessarily complete) shows 43 such tobacco passes, 25 for Scotland (6,505 hogsheads) and 18 for England (5,125 hogsheads), all issued between June and September 1744. (Only two can be found in Secretary Newcastle's books.) Except for the one to Bance, all in Carteret's register were outside London and were to FitzGerald, save one to David Peloquin of Bristol for a shipment from Bideford. The passes used in Scotland in the winter of 1744–45 were thus all issued in September

1744 or earlier. This chronology probably reflects the departure of Granville (Carteret) from office in November 1744,[31] and fears in Whitehall that this trade could be used as a cover for Jacobite plotting (as was very likely in the case of FitzGerald).[32]

Inasmuch as the supply of passes surreptitiously available from a secretary of state's office was at best quite limited, other and more open approaches had to be used if normal levels of tobacco exports to France were to continue in wartime. The tobacco merchants of Glasgow, it was noted above, had openly petitioned the Treasury in May for regular permission to export to France in wartime, but the matter had been put aside in July when the attorney-general questioned the competence of the Treasury. The matter was at this juncture carried to the Privy Council, not by FitzGerald or the Glasgow merchants, but by Gerard and Joshua Van Neck. For the first time, the brothers stepped from the shadows and openly took the lead in matters relating to the French tobacco contract. Whatever useful connections FitzGerald may have had in Paris, in Whitehall he was known as a Jacobite. Someone with a stronger position in London was needed to take charge of the French business. As major lenders to the British government and as individuals with personal access to the Pelham brothers, the Van Necks were particularly well suited for such a role. In fact, the age of the Pelhams in politics, 1743–62, was to be the age of the Van Necks in finance.

On 18 September 1744, a petition from Gerard & Joshua Van Neck was read at the Privy Council and referred to the committee on colonial affairs. The petitioners stated that France had in recent years been buying £160,000 sterling (roughly 4 million *l.t.*) worth of tobacco in Britain, employing sixty ships and taking off varieties of tobacco not suited to other continental markets. If the French could not continue to obtain their tobacco from Britain during the war, they would be forced to develop their own colonial supplies, to the permanent prejudice of the British tobacco trade. ". . . The French Court has given liberty to the Farmers General to import into France in English or Neutral Bottoms all such Quantitys of Tobacco as they shall think proper since which the Farmers General have applyed to the Petitioners to Obtain His Majestys Royal License for the Exporting such Tobacco's from Great Britain into the Ports of France free of Capture which Licence must be a Common Benefit to His Majestys Trading Subjects especially as the French Court neither Asks or expects any French or other Effects to be taken by His Majestys Subjects in lieu of the Tobacco or any other Equivalent whatsoever." The petitioners needed only British passes.[33]

On 20 September, the committee of the Privy Council referred the matter to the Treasury and to the attorney- and solicitor-general—not to report on the propriety of granting such passes, but merely to advise on their form and detail.[34] After consulting the customs board, the Treasury recommended on 12 October that the trade be confined to British vessels of at least 200 tons (to hinder smuggling in Britain), that no French goods be brought back and that full details of the ship, including port of despatch and destination, be given in the pass.[35] The attorney- and solicitor-general recommended on 29 October "that the Passes . . . be under the Great Seal and Inrolled in the Court of Chancery."[36] The question was then allowed to slumber in the committee of Privy Council for five months. Part of this delay may have been due to the ministerial crisis of November 1744 that led to the dismissal of Granville (Carteret); part must also have been due to the reluctance of those extremely cautious brothers, Henry Pelham and the duke of Newcastle, to undertake something as politically explosive as "trading with the enemy."

On 18 October 1744, Sir James Lowther, ever solicitous of Whitehaven's tobacco trade, wrote again from London to his agent, "There has bein some bustle about a new contract or Licence to carry Tobacco to France, hearing of I call'd yesterday on Mr. FzGerald at the Exch:[ange] but he could not tell me how it was lik to go, it is to be manag'd by Messrs Van Eck if it is allow'd of by the ministry."[37] However, by 6 November, Lowther reported, "It is thought the consideration of allowing the sending Tobacco to France will be putt of til the Parl[iamen]t sitts & be brought before the two Houses to determine about it, if so shal speak to as many as I can in the mean time."[38] A fortnight later, he learned that basic strategic considerations were holding up the licenses.

> . . . I have enquir'd a good deal of the Com.rs & other Officers of the Customs ab[ou]t carrying on the Tobacco Trade to France & I hear both the Great folks [the ministry] & the Merch[an]ts are hugely divided ab[ou]t it for tho' 'tis allowed that it will help the Kingdom to a great deal of ready money yet the ffrench make such prodigious advan[ta]ge of the Tobacco by selling it again that it is tho[ugh]t the ffrench wo[ul]d be a vast deal more distrest in their Revenue than we can be by our prohibitting that Trade . . . .[39]

Little was heard about the question in the next few months, though tobacco continued to be sent to France in neutral vessels or via Holland. Funds were reasonably plentiful in the tobacco ports patronized by the French.[40] Nevertheless, with the government taking no action on the Van Necks' September petition and doing nothing about bringing the matter before Parliament, George FitzGerald decided to take the initiative once more. On a signal from him, early in March 1745, the Whitehaven tobacco merchants wrote all the M.P.'s from Cumberland about the necessity of exporting tobacco to France. (They were stirred in part by a passing fear of the Dutch getting into the war and thus blocking that channel to France.) Sir James Lowther agreed to present a petition to the House of Commons from Whitehaven but advised FitzGerald to have petitions presented first from Liverpool and Bristol, since the Londoners were particularly suspicious of Whitehaven's sudden preeminence in the tobacco trade.[41] The petitions from the outports for a tobacco trade to France were supposed to have been presented on 22 March but had to be postponed when the House adjourned early for the weekend. Before they could be presented the next week, they were withdrawn on some sort of understanding being received from the ministry that the matter would be handled administratively without recourse to Parliament. (Lowther, for example, was in touch both with John Hill, an important member of the customs board, and with the duke of Argyle, a member of the cabinet.) [42]

On 29 March 1745, after five months pause, the committee of the Privy Council resumed consideration of the tobacco trade to France and asked the attorney- and solicitor-general to revise the draft pass they had prepared the previous October in order to include the points recommended by the customs board.[43] The attorney- and solicitor-general returned the amended pass on 8 April, but nothing was done thereon for the next six weeks.[44] By this time, it was evident that the tobacco merchants of London, angry at the recent transfer of much of the French buying to Whitehaven and Scotland, had been using their influence against the proposals.[45] Lowther and other friends of the outports exerted themselves and the corner was turned. By 8 May, FitzGerald was so confident of carrying the point that he had written to Peter How in Whitehaven to resume purchases and to start loading a British vessel for Marseilles.[46] Yet the matter dragged on.

When the committee of the Privy Council next took up the tobacco question on 23 May, the Van Necks pleaded that, although they were prepared to give bond not to bring back any French goods on ships taking tobacco to France, they did not want such a restriction written into the pass lest it provoke the French and hurt the trade. The secretary of the committee wrote directly to customs asking whether it would be safe to change the passes as requested.[47] Though no concession was made on this point, an altered form of the pass was ultimately approved by the committee on 2 July and authorized by an order-in-council of 4 July. In the final form, the minimum tonnage for vessels exporting tobacco to France was reduced from 200 to 150 tons.[48] On 23 July, the order-in-council was transmitted by the Treasury to the customs boards for England and Scotland charged with its enforcement.[49] The first passes were issued in September.

In general, the pass system worked well during the war, there being only isolated and minor complaints about violations by French privateers.[50] On the British side, the arrangements had to be altered only once: on 15 March 1745/6, the Privy Council ordered the passes amended to forbid the carrying on tobacco ships of passengers from or to France[51]—a precaution suggested by the Scottish uprising and the Jacobite reputation of FitzGerald. There appear to have been no difficulties about arranging payments through bill operations via Amsterdam.

In one important respect, however, the pass system disappointed the early expectations of the merchants. They had hoped to be able to send their ships to France and thence directly to America. In that way, the French passes good for ten or twelve days after the vessel left a French port would carry the Chesapeake-bound ships beyond the normal range of French privateers. The passes specified, however, that the tobacco ships must return directly to a British port; this was the only way the British government could make sure that the passes were used as intended and that the vessels did not take on any French goods for export to the colonies. This understandable rigor made it less attractive for a merchant to try to combine a tobacco shipment to France with an outward bound sailing to the Chesapeake.

In summary, it would seem that George FitzGerald, despite his strong position in Paris, was unable to obtain the needed passes from the British government and was forced in September 1744 to surrender to the Van Necks an enlarged share in the French tobacco buying contract and the handling of all relations with the British government. To appreciate the quality of the Van Necks' relations with the duke of Newcastle, we must make a brief excursion from economic into diplomatic history.

The marshal count (later duke) of Belleisle was arrested in Germany in 1744 and kept prisoner at Windsor Castle for most of the year 1745. During that time, he maintained a correspondence with the British secretary of state, the duke of Newcastle, through the intermediary of Gerard Van Neck, who handled the prisoner's finances and at whose home the marshal was entertained and met British ministers.[52] After the marshal returned to France, he continued to correspond with Van Neck and, through him, with the duke of Newcastle. Sometimes Belleisle used the channel to explore the possibility of peace, sometimes he only asked that, as special favors, the British government permit the export of thirty or forty horses for Louis XV, or of some other goods desired by French courtiers.[53]

By the end of the year 1744, there was distinct if unavowed feeling in both the British and French governments that perhaps the declaration of war of the previous March had been a mistake. The fall of Granville in November gave the Pelhams more freedom to maneuver. Persons like Gerard Van Neck, whose business required correspondence even in wartime at well-informed levels on both sides, were in a position to pick up and transmit such sentiments. Interest was greatest on the French side and by the end of the year a proposal was made (perhaps by the controller-general Orry) to send an agent to London, ostensibly on tobacco buying business, who would in fact be in a position to receive proposals from the British government. The person suggested was Jean-Baptiste-Louis Fournier, *directeur* of the farms at Paris in charge of tobacco purchasing and manufacturing. (He had served in the monopoly since the 1720's and subsequently became a farmer-general, ca. 1759–68.) From his position at the head of the

Purchasing Office, Fournier was naturally quite familiar with the Van Necks and with the general situation in London; he also seems to have known Lord Chesterfield, then a member of the government. Bussy, the former French minister in London, thought the scheme too cumbersome and too difficult to keep secret since merchants were such gossips and everyone in London knew that such an emissary wasn't needed to get tobacco. Nevertheless, Argenson, the foreign minister, perhaps under pressure from Orry, to whom Fournier was to report, finally authorized the trip. Fournier went to London in mid-April 1745.[54]

Gerard Van Neck immediately sent to Newcastle the draft of a letter for "a friend" in Paris concerning chances for peace and ways of opening negotiations.[55] The Pelhams, however, were afraid to offend the king and their continental allies or to give an opening to their domestic political opponents, particularly Granville. Fournier therefore waited for months without hearing anything definite from the British government. He saw Van Neck weekly, who kept assuring him that the Pelhams, Harrington, Hardwicke, and Chesterfield were all for peace but were prevented from moving by political and diplomatic impediments. By June, Van Neck had introduced Fournier to Newcastle and other ministers but the *directeur* received nothing more than Van Neck's own general ideas. The French victories in the summer of 1745 made the British ministers even more reluctant to take the initiative lest they seem to be begging for peace.[56] In July, Fournier was permitted to see Belleisle before the marshal's return to France: this and newspaper reports about Fournier's mission unnecessarily alarmed an Austrian representative in London who feared that the "sous-fermier" would be instructed to continue the peace negotiations he imagined the marshal to have begun.[57]

When Fournier returned to Paris in November, he explained with strained correctness to Argenson that he had been extremely reluctant to enter into political discussions in London. However, a "person highly trusted by those [British] ministers and strongly bound by friendship to sieur Fournier [i.e., G. Van Neck] often talked to him about the disposition of the British ministers for peace." Only after the most pressing solicitation, Fournier now reported, did he agree to speak to Newcastle and Harrington, the two secretaries of state, but had insisted that they treat him only as a courier and not as a negotiator.[58]

In fact, Fournier's departure from London in November coincided with the Young Pretender's invasion of England. The British ministers who had held aloof all summer felt obliged to send some message back with him. Newcastle explained the situation candidly to Chesterfield in Dublin:

> There is also another incident which might (if we were masters to do what was really right for the publick) turn to our advantage, but otherwise, I am afraid, may embarrass us. My Lord Harrington and

> I and M^r [Gerard] Van Neck had a meeting with your friend, Mr Fournier, the night before he went to France, wherein we gave him strong assurances of our disposition to peace. This has produced an answer from him which M. Vanneck brought me this morning, proposing the sending of persons of confidence on each side immediately to Roterdam to treat upon conditions of peace.[59]

Chesterfield thought that every opportunity for negotiation should be seized, noting that "Monsieur Fournier's is to go through [Lambert] Vanneck of Rotterdam, who is Pensionary Vanderheim's right hand, ..." On 30 November, Newcastle informed Chesterfield that the ministry had "taken the resolution to enter into your friend Fournier's proposal," and were looking for someone to send to Rotterdam.[60] Chesterfield beseeched him, "for God's sake cherish my friend Fournier."[61] In the end, nothing came of the overtures because the French refused to negotiate while the fate of the rebellion in Scotland was still unknown. Newcastle informed Chesterfield of the failure on 6 January 1745/6, adding that "your friend, Fournier, probably since Orry's removal, is quite dumb."[62] (The controller-general Orry had been dismissed in 1745.)

Although nothing concrete came out of his negotiations with marshal Belleisle or Fournier, this diplomatic interlude of 1745–46 suggests to us clearly the position of confidence which Gerard Van Neck held vis-à-vis the duke of Newcastle, a position which explains much of his success in the tobacco business.

Because of opposition within the administration, eighteen months were required to establish a regular system for the issuance of passes under the Great Seal for the shipment of British tobaccos to France in wartime: hostilities between France and Britain began in March 1744; the Van Necks commenced their ultimately successful petitioning in September 1744; their petition was accepted and the procedures established by the Lord Justices' order-in-council of 4 July 1745; the first passes under the new procedure were issued in September 1745. Between that month and May 1748, a total of 163 tobacco passes passed under the Great Seal; of these two were for Dunkirk (to Samuel Bosanquet of London and William Alexander of Edinburgh), the remaining 161 for France proper, i.e. the provinces of the tobacco monopoly. The distribution of those 161 is indicated by Table III. Each pass represents one ship carrying an average of 340 hogsheads or 300,000 lb.

The reader will see at a glance the degree to which French buying had by this time left London and the south of England and become concentrated in the north (Whitehaven and Scotland). This shift will be explored at length in the next chapter. The reader will be equally struck by the preponderant position of the Van Necks. Peter How was George Fitz-

TABLE III

Passes under the Great Seal for Tobacco Export to France, 1745-48[63]

Port of Shipment	Van Necks	P. How	W. Alexander	LeMaistres	Total
London	19	—	—	—	19
Bideford	6	—	—	—	6
Liverpool	10	—	—	—	10
Whitehaven	42	5	—	—	47
Pt. Glasgow	32	—	1	9	42
Greenock	8	—	—	10	18
Ayr	9	—	—	1	10
Dumfries	3	—	—	3	6
Kirkcudbright	2	—	—	1	3
Total	131	5	1	24	161

Gerald's correspondent and collaborator at Whitehaven; William Alexander was the same at Edinburgh. Their passes were all issued in the first few months, after which their names disappear from the record. But what about George FitzGerald himself? There can be no question of his having been excluded from the buying contract. In a remarkably well-informed memoir, written in 1786, the aged farmer-general Paulze reviewed the history of the tobacco buying agency over the preceding fifty years. He devoted great attention to the years 1744-50, for during that lease the united farms did not employ an agent or agents on commission in London but, in order to protect themselves against price rises in wartime, contracted with George Fitz-Gerald of London for their needs at a flat price, all the risks of the market falling on FitzGerald.[64] What seems to have happened then is that Fitz-Gerald contracted to supply the French for six years starting 1 October 1744. Realizing that he could not handle the British government on his own, he took the Van Necks in as partners in this contract, they acting for him in all subsequent negotiations with the London government. This interpretation is corroborated by the fact that the ships mentioned in the Port Glasgow, Greenock, Ayr, and Dumfries passes issued to Gerard and Joshua Van Neck were all entered outward (in the Port Books) for the account of William Alexander of Edinburgh,[65] the Scottish agent of George FitzGerald; and, all during the war, Alexander in Edinburgh, to reimburse himself for his tobacco purchases for France, drew on George FitzGerald of London.[66] In other words, though we do not know the particulars, during 1744-50 the Van Necks, George FitzGerald, Peter How, and William Alexander were all one interest and not competitors.

Who, though, were the LeMaistres? The recipients of the tobacco passes in 1745-48 were described therein as Peter and Caesar LeMaistre, merchants of London. We know for sure only that they were Huguenots, naturalized in the 1730's, natives of Paris, and brothers, sons of Pierre and Louisa

LeMaistre of Paris.[67] It is conceivable that they were connected in some way to the family of the farmer-general, Jacques LeMaistre (d. 1706) ; much more immediately relevant, they were almost certainly the brothers-in-law of the important current farmer-general, Etienne Perrinet de Jars.[68] Caesar died in 1758, Peter predeceasing him, about 1750.[69] We do not know when their connection with the French tobacco purchasing began. Peter LeMaistre's account at the Bank of England was opened in June 1735, shortly after he was naturalized. During 1736–37 (i.e., immediately following the death of Guillemau), tobacco names are relatively common in this account, including one large (£3,293:16:2) payment to Silhouette in January 1736/7; such names become much less frequent thereafter and disappear in the 1740's.[70] During the late 1740's, the passes show that the LeMaistres' purchases were all in Scotland; the Scottish port books[71] indicate that they were made for them there by Alexander Grant, merchant of Edinburgh. Such purchases would not require any special competence on the part of the LeMaistres beyond the ability to forward the money to Scotland. They do not seem to have had any special connection with the British government. As an encouragement to trade (and perhaps as compensation for the costs of having all their passes issued under the Great Seal), Newcastle gave the French tobacco agents free postal franking privileges for the duration of the war. The Post Office refused to extend this to the LeMaistres and the Van Necks had to write on their behalf to Newcastle, explaining that the LeMaistres stood "immediately and equally" with themselves, vis-à-vis the farmers-general.[72] It seems likely that the LeMaistres were persons with good connections within the united farms company who, through some jobbery, were given a small share of the Scottish commission to be executed by the presumably competent Alexander Grant.

With the return of peace in 1748, the French tobacco agency in Britain returned to "normal." With the start of the new lease of the United General Farms on 1 October 1750, the six-year fixed-price contract with FitzGerald expired and the French purchases in Britain were once more made on commission. FitzGerald and the Van Necks also seem to have ceased their collaboration and to have reverted to the older arrangement under which they divided the commission between them, each acting separately. The LeMaistre firm continued its minor participation in the agency for a while. In 1751, the Van Necks' account at the Bank shows payments to them for the last time.[73] That same year, the Scottish port books show Alexander Grant, the LeMaistres' agent, shipping tobacco from Scotland to France, along with William Alexander, who bought for George FitzGerald.[74] At some time between 1751 and 1756, the LeMaistres' connection with the French agency ended.

While keeping its old style for foreign business, the firm of Gerard & Joshua Van Neck was reorganized in 1750, shortly before Gerard's death, as Van Neck, Walpole & Olivier; Gerard retired and Joshua took in as partners Thomas Walpole and Daniel Josias Olivier, both of whom had previously been apprentices and clerks in the firm.[75] The Hon. Thomas Walpole was a younger son of Horatio, lord Walpole of Wolterton, younger brother of the prime minister, Sir Robert Walpole. "Old Horatio" had significantly married Marie Magdalene Lombard, daughter of Peter (Pierre) Lombard, merchant of London, a wealthy Huguenot émigré from Nîmes. Their youngest son, the Hon. Richard Walpole, went to sea but in 1758 gave up the life of a captain of an East Indiaman to become a partner in the bank of Cliffe, Walpole, & Clarke. Thomas and his older brother Horatio became members of Parliament in 1754; Richard, in 1768. Similarly, Thomas in 1750 married Elizabeth, daughter of Joshua Van Neck, while Richard followed in 1757, marrying Van Neck's younger daughter Margaret. From the very first, young Thomas Walpole had wide interests transcending the Van Neck firm. In 1753–54, he was a director of the East India Company; from 1752 to 1762, he was a contractor for supplying the garrison at Gibraltar, in partnership with Merrick Burrell (governor of the Bank of England) and Zacharias Fonnereau. They appear in the London directories for 1763 as Fonnereau, Walpole, & Burrell, merchants, Warnford Court, Throgmorton Street—but Thomas Walpole broke off about that time as the partners split both commercially and politically.[76]

By contrast, the other junior partner, Daniel Josias Olivier, confined his activities to the premises of Van Neck & Co. on New Broad Street. His grandfather, Jourdain Olivier, a Huguenot minister at Pau in Béarn, fled to Holland in 1685 where he became minister of émigré churches at Breda and The Hague. Daniel's father, Jerome Olivier, was minister at the French church of the Savoy in London and married Julie de la Motte, herself the daughter of a Huguenot minister. Through the influence of Alderman John Porter (originally La Roche) and his mother, née Daubuz, related both to the Oliviers and to Sir Joshua Van Neck's wife, Marianne Daubuz, young Daniel Josias Olivier, though originally intended for the ministry, was placed an apprentice in the Van Neck house in 1738. Through the patronage of the childless Gerard Van Neck, he was advanced to a very junior partnership in the firm and enabled to marry Susanne Massé, daughter of James Massé, a London merchant, and niece of J. B. Massé, the miniaturist of Louis XV, and also connected to the Loubier and Boissier and other prominent Huguenot mercantile families of London. Daniel Josias Olivier appears to have been the technical manager of Van Neck & Co., supervising the numerous foreign investment accounts the firm handled. Writing in 1756, Daniel Josias Olivier referred to that house as "perhaps the greatest Merchants in London." He was not inclined to exaggerate.[77]

With the formal start of the new war in 1756, arrangements were made much more quickly for passes to continue the tobacco trade to France despite hostilities. Sir Joshua Van Neck was still very close to those in power. In 1755, he had been used as a channel by which the French ambassador in London and ministers in Paris sent messages to Newcastle of their peaceful intentions. (Van Neck also employed his young partner, Thomas Walpole, and the latter's father, "Old Horatio," to impress upon Newcastle the seriousness of these French offers.) In the early months of 1756, in an effort to avert the war, both Silhouette, one of the commissioners for settling the boundaries in North America, and Carpentier, a French agent in London ostensibly concerned with prisoners, also entered into serious correspondence with Sir Joshua. During both years, the regular correspondence of Van Neck with his Paris banking correspondent, Isaac Vernet (the executor of the abbé Huber), became increasingly political, with Vernet at his end showing many of the letters to the minister of foreign affairs, Rouillé.[78] Sir Joshua's good offices were much appreciated by the French government and, at the declaration of war, he was specifically designated by the king's council as French agent in London for the issuance of certificates needed by British investors to collect their annuities in Paris.[79] (Van Neck took advantage of this position, however, to have his Paris correspondents. Thellusson, Necker & Co., the new style of the Vernet firm, purchase more French public debt for himself and his son-in-law Thomas Walpole—as was revealed in correspondence intercepted by the secretary of state Pitt.) [80] Early in 1761, the farmer-general and court banker, Jean-Joseph de la Borde, as a confidant of Choiseul wrote to Van Neck offering to come to London to talk about peace.[81] A year later, we find a comparable letter from Isaac Vernet.[82] Not until after the resignation of Newcastle in May 1762 is there any hint that the political influence of Sir Joshua Van Neck had in any way been diminished.

In the Seven Years' War, as in the preceding war, therefore, all negotiations with the British government concerning tobacco shipments to France were handled by a Van Neck, although George FitzGerald's interest was at least as important. Early in 1756, after the beginning of hostilities in North America and on the seas and after the suspension of trade with France, but well before the French attack on Minorca and the formal British declaration of war in May, Sir Joshua Van Neck, Bart., petitioned the crown for permission to export tobacco to France during the suspension of trade. On 2 March, the petition was referred to a committee. Unlike 1744–45, when it took the government eighteen months to make up its mind, this time all was promptness and despatch. Ten days later, on 12 March, the committee reported that it had examined the precedent of the 1740's and had been shown passes signed by the French king on 22 February indicating that the tobacco would be received in France without unacceptable restrictions. They recommended that passes be issued similar to those of the previous war.[83] By an order-in-council of 18 March, the king declared his intention of issuing passes as before and specified their wording. On 26 March, the Treasury sent the appropriate instructions to the customs boards for England and Scotland.[84]

On the technical side, the pass system worked much as in the previous war.[85] There were, however, difficulties arising from the greater seriousness with which the Seven Years' War was fought. The tobacco ships were closely guarded in French ports, the crews confined on board, and the masters permitted off only on pressing business and when accompanied by an authorized interpreter. Nevertheless, for security reasons, four tobacco vessels at Morlaix were refused permission to leave for several months in the spring of 1758. This subjected them to great danger as their three month British passes expired while they were detained and their French six-month passes were on the verge of expiring.[86] In August 1759, the British government for its part amended the passes to specify that they did not apply to French ports being blockaded by the Royal Navy.[87] On 17 March 1760, Van Neck complained to Newcastle "that the Exportation of Tobacco to France is greatly inconvenienced by the Fleet under Admiral Rodney preventing any ships from going into Havre de Grace where the principal manufactory of Tobacco is established, & the Farmers General suffer very heavy Charges & great Damage of the Tobacco by the Land Carriage from other ports to Havre de Grace." Although Van Neck asserted that the Admiralty had no objections to letting the tobacco ships through, there is no record of anything having been done about his complaint.[88]

The Paulze memoir of 1786 tells us that during the Seven Years' War, George FitzGerald contracted to supply the united farms with tobacco once more at a flat price—rather than on commission. However, Paulze adds, without explanation, that after one year this arrangement was terminated and a return made to the commission system.[89] This report is substantially confirmed by the passes issued. The first model pass was issued on 1 June 1756 to Sir Joshua Van Neck. After that, no further passes were issued in 1756, except two in August and two in December, all four to George FitzGerald. This delay may have been caused by the transition to the new lease of the united farms on 1 October 1756. During January-March 1757, the trade resumed at normal proportions, 21 passes being issued, all to FitzGerald. Only in April 1757 does the name of Sir Joshua Van Neck reappear, sharing the passes in the next three years with FitzGerald. We can only speculate about what might have been going on behind the scenes to explain this disappearance and reappearance of Sir Joshua Van Neck. One thing, however, is certain: during the Seven Years' War, unlike the previous war, FitzGerald and Van Neck acted competitively, rather than cooperatively, in the French interest.

The history of the French tobacco agency during the war may be conveniently divided at December 1759. From June 1756 through December 1759, 179 effective passes were issued under the Great Seal for the export of tobacco to France. (In this war, the passes averaged 299 hogsheads each and, allowance made for underutilization, each probably represented an actual export of about 270,000 lb.) Of these 179 passes, 123 were in the name of

George FitzGerald, the remaining 56 in the name of Sir Joshua Van Neck, Bart. They were divided among all the usual ports of England and Scotland. If, however, we subdivide the years 1756–59 at May 1758, an interesting pattern emerges, as shown in Table IV.

TABLE IV
British Passes for Tobacco Export to France, 1756–59[90]

Port of Shipment	1 June 1756– 24 May 1758 Van Neck	FitzGerald	29 May 1758– 31 Dec. 1759 Van Neck	FitzGerald	Total
Glasgow	7	36	12	23	78
Ayr	4	8	0	4	16
Leith	1	0	0	1	2
Whitehaven	11	11	0	8	30
Liverpool	3	0	1	4	8
Bristol	3	0	1	2	6
Bideford	2	2	0	1	5
London	5	0	6	23	34
Total	36	57	20	66	179

When compared with the data on the previous war in Table III, the above totals reveal the increasing importance of Glasgow (Port Glasgow and Greenock) in French purchases, the disappearance of the lesser Scots ports of Dumfries and Kirkcudbright, the declining importance of Whitehaven, the reappearance of Bristol, and the renewed importance of London. When subdivided into the two periods before and after May 1758, interesting differences appear. Most obviously, the lead of FitzGerald over Van Neck in the French business increases from 1.6:1 in the initial period to 3.3:1 in the later period. More interestingly, in the earlier period, FitzGerald's shipments were all from Scotland, Whitehaven, and Bideford, places where his purchasing activity had been concentrated since he first started buying for the French in 1739.[91] By contrast, in the later period, he began shipping from Liverpool (from May 1758), Bristol (only from September 1759), and most noticeably London (from April 1759). In fact, the declining importance of Whitehaven and the rising importance of London, previously noted, is attributable entirely to a shift in FitzGerald's buying pattern between March 1759, when he last obtained passes for Whitehaven, and the start of his London passes in April. Taken as a whole, the bare data of the passes seem to suggest that during 1756–59, FitzGerald was competing aggressively and successfully with Van Neck and by 1758–59 had obtained commissions from the farmers-general to make purchases in London and other English ports hitherto reserved to Van Neck. Since FitzGerald did not have the financial resources of the Van Necks and since 1759 was the year of the highest tobacco prices since 1725,⁹² we can well imagine that his financial position may have been strained by his strenuous competition during 1758–59.

This inference that George FitzGerald was extending himself in 1758–59 in order to get more of the French business from Van Neck is born out by the information which Dr. Hensey, the convicted Jacobite spy, gave the government in July 1758.

> George FitzGerald Merchant supplies the french farmer Generals with Tobacco from England by virtue of a Contract. . . I was in paris eight years ago when he went over to renew it. Several attempts have been made by others to supplant him in this beneficial Commission which produces between three or four thousand pounds yearly. He has had interest enough to baffle all their efforts. However he is obliged to do many things and he does many with pleasure in order to ingratiate himself at the french Court. He has been endeavouring some time to get as much of the french business as he could out of the hands of Mess.ʳˢ Vanneck and has aimed at shewing that he was as able and willing to serve them [as Van Neck]. I remember his having offered . . . to lend M. [the marshal duke of] Mirepoix . . . between ten and fifteen thousand pounds at a low interest in order to pay off a Mortgage . . . and I heard . . . that he has assisted in negociating or discounting Paris de Monmartels bills which are made at six and twelve months usances and are generally discounted upon the Change of Amsterdam I think at 7½ or 8 p cent loss and this is . . . the method the french Government has to raise money upon an emergency, the credit of MonMartel being especially in Holland superior to that of the french Government.⁹³

Thus it would appear that, in competing with Van Neck about 1758, George FitzGerald had not only extended himself in buying more tobacco but had also undertaken other financial favors that could prove embarrassing to him in a crisis.

The ambitions of George FitzGerald need not have proved too dangerous if the situation in France had been more stable. On 13 October 1758, a British spy in Paris reported to Pitt that Paris de Montmartel had been dismissed as court banker and replaced by La Borde, the famous Bayonne merchant recently come to Paris. On 16 March following, he corrected this by reporting that Montmartel was reinstated and was sharing the office with La Borde.⁹⁴ Since FitzGerald was close to Montmartel, these rumors were upsetting, quite apart from La Borde's closeness to Van Neck. More profoundly serious for all concerned were the general finances of France which Pitt and everyone else knew were desperate by the end of 1758.⁹⁵ The surtax levied in 1758 on the tobacco farm and most other branches of French revenue had proved a great disappointment, leading in many cases to a diminution of receipts.

In this critical situation, Etienne de Silhouette became controller-general in March 1759. (We last met him buying tobacco in Britain, ca. 1735–39.) Though a master of requests and a former chancellor to the duke of Orléans, he was a complete outsider to the world of the court and the higher administration. He achieved his high office largely because of his reputation as a financial expert and a man of ingenuity, qualities desperately needed in the exigencies of the hour. (He got many of his ideas from the financial writer, Véron de Forbonnais, whom he consulted regularly.) Silhouette was pushed forward by the marshal duke of Belleisle and madame de Pompadour (who earlier had been close to the Paris brothers) and was opposed from the start by Paris de Montmartel. At first he achieved great popularity by striking measures such as the partial reduction of pensions and the abolition of *croupes* or hidden "cuts" or pensions on the places of the farmers-general. Half the enhanced profits of the farmers-general were recovered by the crown and used to finance the sale to the public of 72 million *l.t.* in so-called "shares" in the united farms, really just another five percent state loan with a speculative extra. Silhouette's popularity and reputation for painless financial wizardry disappeared in September 1759 when he introduced a great body of new taxes, involving him in a serious struggle with the *parlements*. So desperate had the state's financial position become that, on 26 October 1759, orders were issued by the Council of State (dated the 21st) delaying the payment of all public short-term debt, including the *billets* of the united farms and the *rescriptions* of the receivers-general. Such *billets* and *rescriptions* had hitherto enjoyed a very high reputation and were in general circulation. A crisis of credit ensued, violently shaking the financial and business communities and destroying what was left of the reputation of Silhouette. He was dismissed on 21 November 1759, less than nine months after he had taken office.[96]

Early in 1759, before Silhouette's elevation, with French royal finances approaching a crisis, Jean Paris de Montmartel had given up his governmental financial business, his functions being divided between Jean-Joseph de la Borde, the new court banker, and a syndicate of five headed by Nicolas Beaujon, receiver of La Rochelle, then close to Mme. de Pompadour and later banker to Mme. du Barry; Beaujon's collaborators were his mercantile partner, Pierre-François Goossens, a Dutch banker in Paris, Joseph Micault d'Harvelay, grand nephew of Paris de Montmartel and his successor as *garde du trésor royal*, Gabriel Michel, director of the Indies Company and *trésorier-général de l'artillerie*, and Jean Le Maître de la Martinière, *trésorier-général des fortifications*, and close to Paris de Montmartel. While La Borde kept responsibility for most army and diplomatic expenses, the syndicate of five (styled Beaujon, Goossens & Co.) agreed to provide the king in 1759 with thirty-six million *l.t.* for the navy, six million for fortifications and military engineering, and two millions for the general use of the Treasury. In return, they were reimbursed by *rescriptions* on the receivers-general which were negotiable. The five raised much of the funds advanced by circulating bills of exchange. These arrangements were, however, compromised by the *arrêt* of 21/26 October 1759 which suspended payment of the *rescriptions*. To protect the syndicate and enable them to fulfill their obligations towards the crown, a further order (*arrêt*) was made by the Council on 14 November 1759 (not published until the 30th) suspending or delaying the payment of the obligations of the five great financiers toward their own creditors. This wrought further havoc upon private credit in France and throughout Europe.[97]

George FitzGerald's business in Paris in the past had normally been handled by the bankers Tourton & Baur;[98] in addition, he was, as late as 1758, extensively engaged with Paris de Montmartel. In 1759, he also became heavily involved with "Beaujon, Goossens & Co." of Paris. This designation has confused historians.[99] It was the style used by the syndicate of five financiers (just referred to) and must be distinguished from that of "Beaujon & Goossens," a mercantile firm active in the northern trade from about 1756 whose two partners were the same Nicolas Beaujon and Pierre-François Goossens.[100] FitzGerald was continuing to perform for the syndicate of five the services which he had previously rendered to Paris de Montmartel in aiding a bill circulation to support short term loans to the French state.

The *dénouement* is recorded in the court minutes of the Royal Bank of Scotland, William Alexander, FitzGerald's agent for Scotland, being a director of that bank.

> 15 December 1759: Messrs William Alexander and Sons merchants in Edinburgh Represented to the Court in writing that they had advice of the 8th Instant [December] from Mr George Fitzgerald of London Merchant one of their Correspondents there signifying "That the Post of the day before [7th] brought him a Letter from Mess.rs Beaujon Goossens and Company of Paris with whome he was involved wherein they say, That they would neither accept or pay his Bills, and that [refusal was authorized] by the French Kings Edict of the 30th Ultimo, That he was less prepared for this as by a Letter received about Two Posts before, they assured him, in the Strongest manner that all their foreign Engagements shou'd be punctually comply'd with, That he thought it necessary to give them this early Advice, for Unless some sudden and almost unexpected supplys reached him he fear'd the worst ... tho' the world must allow his situation to have been one of the Best upon the Exchange of London."[101]

In other words, Beaujon, Goossens & Co. at first wrote FitzGerald that despite the *arrêt de surséance* of 14/30 November, they would honor their foreign obligations—and then wrote him two posts later that they could not do so. This ruthlessness also brought down simultaneously the Amsterdam bank of John Testas & Son, on whom FitzGerald had drawn heavily.[102]

George FitzGerald's failure in December 1759 revealed an extensive correspondence stretching from Saxony to Ireland to Cadiz.[103] Among his British collaborators in the French tobacco business, Peter How of Whitehaven (as we shall see in the next chapter) was ultimately brought down in 1763;[104] William Alexander & Sons of Edinburgh, who had more than £20,000 in bills on FitzGerald outstanding at the time of his failure, were fortunate enough to receive extraordinary help from the Royal Bank of Scotland and survived.[105] Robert Alexander, son of Provost William, was in fact one of the assignees in FitzGerald's bankruptcy. George FitzGerald himself died in 1762.[106] The important point for purposes of this study is that the failure of George FitzGerald was due to his financial operations and not to his tobacco business. The farmers-general honored all their obligations for tobacco purchases. Thus, Van Necks were totally unaffected. There was a great flurry of alarm in tobacco circles in Britain and America—some fearing that the farmers-general had failed and the French market lost—until it was made clear that the credit of the united farms as a tobacco purchaser was unimpaired.[107] Individual merchants and planters whose tobacco had been sold to George FitzGerald on credit of course suffered. They stood as ordinary creditors and it seems unlikely that they ever recovered much more than five shillings in the pound.[108] Among them it was rumored that FitzGerald's debts would reach one million sterling.[109]

The failure of George FitzGerald in December 1759 left Van Neck & Co. in solitary possession of the French agency for England and Scotland. They were in a strong negotiating position inasmuch as their own credit was so firm and that of the French so weak. The farmers-general seem to have made no immediate move to redivide the agency.[110] After several months of inactivity, in February 1760, Van Necks resumed buying tobacco for the French and applying for shipping passes. The trade actually continued at a somewhat higher level than during the first years of the war. Between 20 February 1760 and 12 November 1762 (hostilities ceasing on the 26th), some 193 passes were issued, compared to only 179 for the slightly longer period between June 1756 and December 1759. All were now issued in the name of Sir Joshua Van Neck. The tendency to concentrate more and more of the French purchases in Glasgow continued in this last period, with 107 passes of the 193 total for the Clyde ports. This was done primarily at the expense of Whitehaven which received only six passes; the renewed interest of "the French" in London, manifest in 1759, continued during the next three years (40 passes).[111]

With the return of peace in 1763, Van Neck & Co. retained the primary French purchasing commission until that great firm was itself disrupted in 1765. In 1760, Elizabeth, daughter of Sir Joshua Van Neck and wife of the Hon. Thomas Walpole, died, dissolving one bond that united those two men.[112] In May 1765, the firm was apparently fighting to keep the agency, for Horace Walpole wrote then to the earl of Hertford, "If Mr. Walpole loses this vast branch of trade [tobacco], he and Sir Joshua Vanneck must shut up shop."[113] Nevertheless, before that year was out, the Hon. Thomas Walpole, his partner Olivier wrote, "having acquired a very handsome Fortune chose to retire from our Business." The old firm, still using the style "Gerard and Joshua Van Neck," was reorganized from 1 January 1766 as a partnership between Sir Joshua Van Neck, Bart., his youngest son Joshua, and Daniel Josias Olivier.[114] They maintained Paris connections and in 1771 were referred to as the "agent of the French court," buying up shares in the British East India Company on French account.[115] Walpole, for his part soon organized his own merchant house, Walpole & Ellison. In the shuffle, Walpole ran off with the French buying contract. His very success, however, was to encourage emulation and to introduce a period of bitter struggles for the French contract that were to fill the years 1766–75 and will be the subject of Chapter 24.

The war years 1744–62 are perhaps the most revealing in the century or more covered by this work. The entire pass system indicates most graphically the moral surrender of French statecraft to the narrowest fiscal considerations. Trading with the enemy in wartime was an accepted practice in the seventeenth and eighteenth centuries; governments regularly condoned it and attempted to control it by issuing passports and licenses. When Louis XIV permitted his tobacco farm to import tobacco from Holland and England during the War of the Spanish Succession, he did attach some conditions; the enemy vessels had to take away wine and other surplus French goods and not money. The English thus could share very little in this trade until Parliament permitted the import of French wine in 1711. By contrast, during the wars of 1744–48 and 1756–62, so unquestioned a consideration had the yield of the tobacco farm become that the raw material supply of the monopoly became a major state objective. Despite efforts to obtain tobacco from Russia in the Seven Years' War, there was never any serious thought of doing without British supplies. Thus, France had to obtain those supplies on exclusively British terms: the tobacco was to be paid for in cash (i.e., bills of exchange on Amsterdam) and carried to France in British ships which were to return in ballast. That these terms were refused in Louis XIV's time and accepted in Louis XV's is a measure of the growing importance of tobacco consumption and the tobacco revenue in France—and of much else besides.

Postscript to Chapter 22

There are certain other London firms which may have had some sort of share in the French tobacco business between 1740 and 1765. The surviving evidence is inadequate. They should at least be mentioned.

(*I.*) Daniel Frederick Colb appears in the London directories about 1740 as a merchant of Lime Street. The discount book of Martin's Bank shows that, about 1734, the executors of the late John Hyde and James Buchanan, tobacco merchants, were discounting large bills (ca. £800–£1,000) drawn on Colb.[116] Colb also appears in 1738 as an agent of the French government purchasing wheat in London.[117] When we examine his very active account at the Bank of England (opened 1733, closed at his death in 1743), we are struck by the frequency with which the names of the French tobacco circle in London appear, particularly on the debit, but also on the credit side of his account: Van Neck, FitzGerald, Simond, Benezet, Guillemau, LeMaistre. In addition, for a limited period between December 1733 and August 1735, we find a significantly numerous sprinkling of the names of London tobacco merchants in his debit column (i.e., receiving payments from him): Perry, Hyde, Hanbury, Forward, Cary, Buchanan, Bradley.[118]

When D. F. Colb died in 1743, the balance of his account at the Bank of England was paid to one *Michael* Rouge, his attorney.[119] Michael Rouge was one of the Friday night convivial circle that met at the home of Gerard Van Neck and were each remembered in his will by a bequest of £100.[120] From 1747 to 1760, there was an account at the Bank of England in the name of *Samuel* Rouge, who appears in the directories of the time as a merchant of Copthall Court, Throgmorton Street. In it, Van Neck appears frequently in the debit column for large round sums (e.g., £5,000) that suggest bill operations rather than commercial transactions.[121] The Rouge connection is probably unimportant, but it would be useful to know more about Daniel Frederick Colb.

(*II.*) The commission merchants of London who received tobacco on consignment from the planters of Virginia and Maryland regularly sent to their correspondents in the Chesapeake "accounts of sale" indicating the sales history of each hogshead consigned. When examining the scattered accounts of sale that have survived in various archives in Virginia and Maryland, one is struck by the frequency with which the names "Fonblanque," "Thellusson," or "Fonblanque & Thellusson" appear. John Fonblanque, son of Abel de Grenier de Fonblanque, a Protestant nobleman of Languedoc, came over to England in the mid-1740's and was naturalized in 1748. He was joined in the early 1750's by his brother, Anthony Fonblanque (naturalized 1758).[122] For a time, about 1755, they were in business together, then about 1758–60, had separate houses, only to join together again as partners shortly before the death of John in November 1760. In the 1763 directories, their firm appears as "John & Anthony Fonblanque & Thellusson, Flemish merchants, Great Tower Street."[123] Their new partner was Peter Thellusson (1737–97), son of Isaac Thellusson, the continuator of the old Tourton & Guiguer bank in Paris, subsequently Genevan minister to the French court. Another son of Isaac, George-Tobie Thellusson was a partner in the Paris bank of Thellusson & Necker, itself a continuation from 1756 of the house of Isaac Vernet, the banker and executor of the abbé Huber.[124] Peter Thellusson appears to have come over to London about the time of FitzGerald's failure in 1759; he was naturalized in 1760.[125] By 1770, he had left the Fonblanques to establish his own house; in 1775, Thellusson & Co. was importing tobacco in a small way directly from Virginia.[126] By the 1790's, Peter Thellusson Sons & Co. was famous as the most important London merchants handling French *émigré* funds.[127] Since the Paris house of Vernet/Thellusson & Necker was the close correspondent of Van Neck & Co., it is possible that Van Necks gave their London affiliate some of the English buying business on subcontract. It is known that there were such subordinate *commisionaires* in London as well as in the outports. We cannot be certain, however. Sometimes the price data seem to suggest that Fonblanque & Thellusson were buying at the "French price"; sometimes they seem to be paying more. As Flemish merchants it is of course possible that they were really buying for export to Dunkirk and Ostend. On this firm, therefore, our data are at best only suggestive.

CHAPTER 23

The French Agency in the English Outports and in Scotland, 1725–65

The General Situation

During the first quarter of the eighteenth century, British tobacco imports stagnated at little over thirty million pounds annually. Growth resumed in the late 1720's (just as French purchases began to become a major factor in the market); by 1771–73 or 1771–75, the import trade reached a level more than three times that of 1721–25. This growth, however, was not distributed evenly throughout the trade, as is suggested by Table I. The tripling was effected by a growth rate through that half century of 2.29 percent per annum. Growth was, however, not uniform over that time, being most rapid (2.82) from the late 1720's to the early 1740's, slightly lower (2.42) during the war and postwar years of the later 1740's and early 1750's, and significantly lower (1.76) from the start of the Seven Years' War to the American Revolution. When we break down the growth rates by geographical areas, we find more striking variations. Over the half century, the growth rate was radically higher in Scotland (4.59) than in London or the English outports. This was, however, largely a post-1740 phenomenon, for, in the first period (1721–25 to 1738–43), the Scottish rate was only average and was markedly exceeded by that of the English outports (4.0). In the middle period, when Scottish growth was most hectic (8.36), that of the English outports dropped back to 2.24 while London stagnated again. More remarkably, in the last period, when Scottish growth dropped back to its secular level, London's rate picked up modestly, while the English outports went into absolute decline. These variant growth rates meant that, in an advancing trade, London's share was to drop from about 57–58 percent in the 1720's to under 40 percent after 1748; the English outports maintained a share of 27.6–35.6 percent down to 1756–62, but thereafter dropped to 16.4 percent in 1771–73. Acting reciprocally, the Scottish share, after stagnating at about 13–15 percent from 1721–25 to 1738–43 rose precipitously to levels exceeding 40 percent after 1762.

When we speak of "the English outports" and "Scotland" we are referring to deceptive aggregates. From 80 percent (in the 1740's) to 98 percent (in the 1770's) of Scotland's tobacco trade was accounted for by the two Clyde harbors of Port Glasgow and Greenock, both satellite shipping points for the commercial center at Glasgow city (too far up the unimproved Clyde

TABLE I

Tobacco Imports at London, the English Outports and Scotland,
1685–1775: Annual Averages and Growth Rates[1]

	London	Outports	England	Scotland	Britain

A. *Annual Averages* (in thousands of lb.) *and Percentages*

	London	Outports	England	Scotland	Britain
1685m–88m	14,501 (51.8)	13,495 (48.2)	27,996 (100)		
1696m–1702x	21,186 (64.4)	11,720 (35.6)	32,905 (100)		
1703–7			23,690 (100)		
1708–11			28,785 (95.2)	1,449 (4.8)	30,235
1712–14			27,128		
1715–17			25,242 (91.2)	2,449 (8.8)	27,691
1718–20			33,350		
1721–25	19,271 (57.2)	9,291 (27.6)	28,562 (84.8)	5,100 (15.1)	33,662
1726–31	26,099 (58.1)	13,035 (29.0)	39,133 (87.1)	5,813 (12.9)	44,946
1732–37	25,722	13,398	39,120		
1738–43	28,641 (52.3)	18,447 (33.7)	47,088 (86.0)	7,637 (14.0)	54,726
1744–48	24,259 (41.8)	20,638 (35.6)	44,896 (77.4)	13,149 (22.6)	58,045
1749–55	29,030 (40.3)	23,806 (33.1)	52,836 (73.4)	19,187 (26.6)	72,024
1756–62	22,885 (35.3)	19,659 (30.3)	42,544 (65.6)	22,258 (34.3)	64,802
1763–69	(39.4)	(19.8)	45,680 (59.2)	31,453 (40.8)	77,132
1770–75			52,791 (54.6)	43,832 (45.4)	96,623
1771–73	39,415 (38.6)	16,777 (16.4)	56,192 (55.1)	45,849 (44.9)	102,041

B. *Growth Rates* (per centum per annum)

	London	Outports	England	Scotland	Britain
1721–25 to 1771–73	1.48	1.22	1.39	4.59	2.29
1721–25 to 1738–43	2.3	4.0	2.9	2.34	2.82
1738–43 to 1749–55	0.12	2.24	1.01	8.36	2.42
1749–55 to 1771–73	1.54	−1.73	0.31	4.45	1.76

to be reached then by ocean-going craft). The English outports were a more heterogeneous lot. At least two dozen of them received more than accidental or trivial tobacco shipments in the eighteenth century. Only four, however, need concern us here: Bideford (including Barnstaple), Bristol, Liverpool, and Whitehaven. They did not share equally in the growth of the outports during the 1740's, as is suggested by Table II. The gap in Table II between 1750 and 1771 can be filled in partially by data on exports from Virginia—though the omission of Maryland tends to exaggerate the importance of Glasgow and Bristol and to underrepresent the relative importance of London (Table III).

Many interesting patterns can be detected, from the study of the three tables. The trade of all the ports did not move parallelly. It is not surprising that the Clyde ports, after the military uprising of 1745–46, should

Table II

Tobacco Imports at the Six Principal Centers, 1721–73[2]

Year Ending Christmas	London	Bideford & Barnstaple	Bristol	Liverpool	Whitehaven	Port Glasgow & Greenock
	(in thousands of lb. weight)					
1722	19,457*	808	4,109	1,728	1,119	6,533m**
1723	20,581*	875	3,900	1,569	859	4,166m**
1724	18,400*	868	3,076	2,008	1,410	5,311m**
1725	14,272*	685	3,182	1,203	756	4,162m**
1726	20,114*	1,418	3,809**	2,250	1,955	3,616m
1727	27,671*	1,760	6,870**	2,962	1,877	6,537m
1728	28,563*	1,359	4,851	4,051	1,442	6,696m**
1729	27,296*	1,601	3,945	3,276	1,896	6,383m**
1730	23,981*	2,172	3,410	2,491	2,011	4,495m**
1731	28,860*	1,950	4,508**	2,431	1,472	3,266m
1738	24,889*	2,638	3,816	4,351**	3,168	3,745
1739	30,516*	2,801	3,799	4,310	3,942	4,713**
1740	17,437*	1,967	4,748	5,358**	4,457	4,255
1741	40,025*	2,125	2,927	5,468	5,413	6,434**
1742	23,360*	2,221	4,311	5,312	6,970	8,569**
1743	36,254*	3,541	3,840	6,129	9,443**	9,148
1744	22,805*	673	3,791	4,248	9,359**	8,832
1745	24,373*	1,624	3,243	5,770	7,073	11,173**
1746	18,407*	365	3,979	7,195	9,145**	8,194
1747	28,189*	1,341	3,256	9,380	9,266	10,021**
1748	27,782*	1,149	2,861	8,161	10,622	13,537**
1749	21,438*	639	4,690	6,004	10,556	17,783**
1750	25,668*	1,663	4,806	5,563	9,013	14,361**
1771	43,542**	—	4,433	7,020	2,940	48,148*
1772	38,789**	—	4,713	6,537	3,576	43,427*
1773	34,913**	—	4,668	7,593	7,212	44,471*

* = 1st place
** = 2d place
m = year ending Michaelmas (only where indicated)

Table III

Tobacco Exports from Virginia to the Six Principal British Centers, 1750–62[3]

Year	London	Bideford & Barnstaple	Bristol	Liverpool	Whitehaven	Port Glasgow & Greenock
	(in hogsheads of about 1,000 lb. each)					
1750	14,948	187	4,865	2,233	7,981	15,940
1758	13,241	158	6,436	3,081	6,569	16,311
1761	16,315	202	5,486	5,062	5,213	16,489
1762	17,274	0	3,755	5,315	6,672	22,496

suffer a setback in 1746 not experienced elsewhere. More difficult to explain are the sharp setbacks in London's trade in 1742, 1744, and 1746 while many other ports (particularly Whitehaven) were increasing their trade. It would appear that London (whose trade was mostly on consignment) received what was left after the agents of the outport merchants (who traded on their own account) purchased what they needed in the colonies to fill their ships. Thus, shipments to London reflect, in exaggerated form, the fortunes of the crops in the Chesapeake. Privateering during the war of 1744–48 affected the southern ports much more severely than the northern. Much traffic was in fact diverted by the war to the safer north-about-Ireland route. Thus Bristol's trade languished during the war but recovered with the peace, while Liverpool's boomed during the war and fell off somewhat with the peace. More difficult to explain are the fortunes of Whitehaven and the Clyde ports. Their trade also boomed during the war, but showed no signs of decline with the peace. In other respects, the fate of Whitehaven and the Clyde ports did not run parallelly. The Clyde had been the leader of the outports during 1715–30, yielding first place only to London, at a time when Whitehaven's share in the tobacco trade had been relatively minor.[4] Port Glasgow and Greenock lost this preeminent position during the 1730's and, to regain it from 1747 onward, had to fight against the considerably expanded trades of both Liverpool and Whitehaven. To understand some of these vagaries in the growth of the import trade, it will be useful to examine some data on the export trade.

From 1721 to 1775, at least 70 percent of the tobacco imported into England was reexported. For Scotland, where the data are less complete, the reexport proportion was generally near or above 90 percent. For Great Britain as a whole, even under the discouraging conditions of the war years 1755–62, the share exported did not fall below 79.9 percent and was considerably higher in peacetime. At London, reexports were close to the English average.[5] At only one significant tobacco port—Bristol—was more than 50 percent of the import retained for domestic consumption. At the other extreme, Whitehaven and the Clyde ports reexported more than 90 percent of their imports.[6] They were significantly the most dynamic sections of the trade, particularly in the exuberant 1740's.

Although all the ports with above average growth rates in the tobacco trade also had exceptionally high reexport ratios, not all ports with exceptionally high reexport ratios were equally able to sustain their early growth rates of the 1740's throughout the forty years preceding the American Revolution. There were, it would seem, instabilities in the reexport market. It is unlikely that any conditions prevailing in the chief "open" markets (Holland, Germany, Ireland) could abruptly give and as abruptly take away any advantage which one British port might hold over another. However, the individuals who decided buying policy for the monopsonistic French market had just such discretionary power. Table 3 in the Appendix indicates what we know about where the French bought their tobacco in Britain. The reader should observe the very sudden changes in quantity and location of shipments under monopsonistic conditions.

When the French monopoly started buying tobacco in significant quantities from England during 1699–1701, they made their purchases almost exclusively in London. Table 3a in the Appendix suggests that the French preference for London over the English outports continued in the 1720's and 1730's. However, shortly after Huber and FitzGeralds acquired their purchasing contract in 1739[7]—a commission which did not include London—the absolute and relative importance of the English outports increased markedly. These ports were most important as French suppliers from about 1742 to 1754, after which the monopoly lost interest in them noticeably (except for an isolated spree in 1773). Though the French neglected the English outports after 1754, London was able to attract back the custom it had enjoyed before 1743 only in part during the brief interludes, 1753–54, 1759–60 and 1772. Instead, the French business went increasingly to Scotland. Although the regular annual Scottish trade accounts start only with 1755, the Scottish port books have survived from Michaelmas 1742, recording individual ship clearances and cargoes. From these we have computed the Scottish totals for 1743, 1747, and 1751 shown, with later data for comparison, in Table IV.

TABLE IV

Origin of British Tobacco Exports to France (excluding Dunkirk), 1743–75[8]

Year	London	Outports	England	Scotland	Great Britain
		(in thousands of lb.)			
1743	2,659	6,675	9,334	5,614	14,949
1747	1,368	6,966	8,335	8,319	16,653
1751	1,547	5,213	6,760	10,084	16,844
1757–62 (av.)	3,555	3,521	7,075	7,815	14,890
1766–75 (av.)	—	—	4,943	12,633	17,576

It will be seen at once that in 1743, the first year for which we have data on Scottish shipments to France, Scotland was already a major supplier of tobacco to France, well ahead of London and close to the total of the English outports. By 1747, Scotland had not only surpassed the latter but was sending more tobacco to France than all of England. From that time onward, Scotland attracted an ever increasing share of the relatively stable French business, 72 percent by 1766–75.

The only surviving data indicating how the French tobacco purchases were distributed among the English and Scottish outports are the passes for wartime shipments to France discussed in the previous chapter. These are summarized in Table V. (Each period is approximately three years.)

TABLE V

British Passes (under the Great Seal) for
Tobacco Exports to France in Wartime[9]

Port of Shipment	1745–48	1756–59	1760–62
Glasgow (incl. Greenock)	60	78	107
Ayr	10	16	12
Leith	0	2	3
Other Scottish ports	9	0	0
Whitehaven	47	30	6
Liverpool	10	8	14
Bristol	0	6	8
Bideford	6	5	3
London	19	34	40
Total	161	179	193

In the 1740's, the French were buying just under half their tobacco in Scotland, with almost another 30 percent accounted for by Whitehaven; the share of London and the southern English ports was trivial. By 1760–62 (after the failure of George FitzGerald), the Scottish share had risen to almost two-thirds, largely at the expense of the now neglected Whitehaven; there was also a revived interest in London and the south English ports which in this last period accounted for over 25 percent of shipments to France.

In 1766, someone in London prepared a memoir for the Piedmontese tobacco farmers on the structure of the British tobacco market. The author described with knowledge the buying practices of the French. Tobacco, explained the memoir, could be purchased more cheaply and with better selection in the English and Scottish outports than in London. Nevertheless, London was the communications and commercial center of the country. Provincial merchants had regular agents or correspondents there whom they kept informed about commercial conditions in their ports, including the supplies and prices of tobacco. Therefore, the French saw fit to maintain their primary agent in London where he could survey market conditions in all the lesser ports and decide where and under what conditions purchases might most advantageously be made.[10] With the persistence of the conditions described in the memoir, French tobacco buying in Britain continued to be managed from London right down to the American Revolution—even though as early as the 1740's most of the tobacco bought was being shipped from ports in the north of England and Scotland.

Of French buying at Bristol, Bideford and Liverpool, we know very little. The Bideford tobacco trade was dominated by the Buck and Strange families and went into decline after the deaths of John and George Buck around 1745. When it was at its height, around 1730–45, it was almost entirely a reexport trade, with the French taking almost half the port's imports. Purchases there then appear to have been made by David and John Peloquin of Bristol, though the Bucks and George Strange may also have dealt directly with the French agents in London.[11]

At Bristol itself, the attention of overseas merchants in the eighteenth century became increasingly concentrated upon the West Indies sugar trade, the tobacco trade showing no long-term signs of growth between 1720 and the American Revolution. The tobacco reexport trade at Bristol was proportionately less important than at Bideford, though here too we can trace regular sales to the French of two or three shiploads annually from the 1730's to the 1760's. The monopoly's Bristol purchases were handled primarily by David and John Peloquin (1730–53), by David Peloquin alone (1755–63) and by James Daltera (around 1764–72). The Peloquin were a Huguenot family established at Bristol since the Revocation. (Stephen Peloquin had bought ships there for the Indies Company in 1720.) [12] The Daltera were an Irish Huguenot family who established mercantile branches at Bristol and Liverpool in the mid-eighteenth century.

At Liverpool, it is likely, at least in the 1730's and 1740's, that one of the Gildarts was buying for the French; by the 1770's the minor agency there had been transferred to Joseph Daltera. French purchases on the Mersey never became too important, in part because the Liverpool merchants (increasingly specialists in the more speculative slave trade) were reluctant to cut their tobacco prices to the level prevailing in Whitehaven and Glasgow. They seem to have preferred waiting for a rise in the market, even if this meant letting a lot of their capital sit idle in the king's warehouse.[13] While Liverpool waited, its competitors to the north, preferring rapid turnover to short-term maximization of profits, forged ahead in the tobacco trade.

Thus, both the nature of our documentation and the nature of the trade force us, in our investigation of French buying activity outside London, to concentrate upon Whitehaven and Scotland, the ports which supplied from two-thirds to three-fourths of French purchases in Britain from the 1740's onward.

French Buying at Whitehaven, 1742–75

The port of Whitehaven, situated near the westernmost extension of Cumberland, was the most northerly port of any significance on the west coast of England in the eighteenth century. The port was developed in the later seventeenth century and extended in the eighteenth in great part by the Whitehaven branch of the Lowther family as an outlet for the coals mined on their nearby property.[14] Coal shipments to Ireland throughout the eighteenth century provided the sure "bread-and-butter" trade for the considerable merchant fleets of Whitehaven and nearby Workington. The larger coal carriers could also cross the Atlantic, and in the late seventeenth century, because of, rather than despite, its isolated position, Whitehaven developed an extensive Chesapeake trade. By the Act of Navigation of 1660, as amended in 1671, tobacco could not be shipped from the English colonies directly to either Scotland or Ireland, but had first to be landed in England. Whitehaven, the first English port reached by vessels coming from the Chesapeake on the short "great circle" route north about Ireland, was ideally situated to be an entrepôt for the transshipment of English colonial tobacco to Ireland and Scotland. With shipping available—thanks to the coal trade —and costs relatively low, a modestly prosperous trade developed there by the end of the seventeenth century, importing tobacco from Virginia and reexporting to the two nearby kingdoms.

Whitehaven could compete in its limited reexport markets because its tobacco was cheap. About 1700, it was recognized that tobacco generally sold there for halfpenny per pound less than at London. This was enough of a margin to encourage Scottish merchants to buy tobacco there for speculative shipments to Sweden and the Baltic. Whitehaven's own merchants were less venturesome, for they lacked commercial connections at most continental ports.[15]

Whitehaven's modest prosperity as an entrepôt for the importation and reexportation of tobacco to Ireland and Scotland was seriously undermined by the Act of Union of 1707. Scotland could now import its own tobacco directly from America and no longer had need of the Cumberland way-station; worse still, the Scots were soon competing in the reexport trade to Ireland. Tradition has it that the merchants of Glasgow, lacking oceangoing vessels at the time of the Union, chartered those of Whitehaven for their first ventures to the Chesapeake.[16] Such arrangements persisted for some time. Lists prepared in the 1720's show that half the Whitehaven vessels engaged in the Virginia trade sailed to and from Scotland (25 in 1722; 14 in 1725). Comparable conditions prevailed among the smaller number of Workington ships in the same trade.[17] If such chartering meant employment for the mariners and earnings for the shipowners of Cumberland, it did not mean much bustle along the quays of Whitehaven or profits for its merchants. Under such circumstances, we are not surprised to find quite specific evidence of stagnation in the port's Virginia trade after 1707. Tobacco imports at Whitehaven in the five years 1698–1702 averaged 1.4 million lb. annually;[18] during the ten years 1722–31, they averaged only 1.5 million lb.[19] This standstill was quite obviously associated with limited markets. Whitehaven was situated in a remote corner of the kingdom far from the chief centers of English population and consumption; it could thus have only a limited domestic market for its tobacco. When we examine the Whitehaven port books for 1719, we find the markets for tobacco narrowly limited: except for a few small shipments to Norway and the Isle of Man, all the tobacco exported from Whitehaven went to Dublin and Belfast.[20]

Whitehaven's stagnation in the first quarter of the century paralleled a general stagnation of the English tobacco trade. Like the trade as a whole, activity at Whitehaven began to pick up in the later 1720's: imports rose from an average of 1.2 million during 1722–26 to 1.7 million during 1727–31.[21] Rapid growth continued in the 1730's, imports reaching 3.9 million annual average during 1738–1740,[22] representing a growth rate well above the national average. (English imports went up about 50 percent while those at Whitehaven had increased more than 300 percent since the early 1720's.)[23] An important factor contributing to the growth of Whitehaven's tobacco trade in the 1730's was the development of a new market in Holland. While the port books for 1719 show a trade overwhelmingly oriented toward the traditional market in Ireland,[24] those for 1739–41 show an equally marked export orientation toward Holland:[25]

	1739	*1740*	*1741*
to Holland	3,441,372 lb.	4,020,693 lb.	4,783,838 lb.
to Ireland	1,102,245	1,198,309	929,521
to Norway	25,641	—	35,388
to unspecified	15,779	—	260,000

Many individuals and circumstances contributed to the boom in the tobacco import trade at Whitehaven in the 1730's and in the reexport trade there to Holland. The town produced in this generation a very enterprising breed of merchants, well represented by the Lutwidges, who aggressively pushed the development of the harbor, the trade to the Chesapeake and the reexport trade to Holland. (The Lutwidges specialized in the Maryland trade which produced the varieties of tobacco preferred in Holland.)[26] Specialized houses appeared in Holland closely connected to the rising tobacco ports of the north of England and Scotland. The most interesting of these was the house of the Herries brothers, originally from Dumfries, established at Rotterdam about 1730, just as the Dutch tobacco transit trade was moving there from Amsterdam.[27] By far the most important group, however, was that centering about Sir James Lowther, Bart., of Whitehaven (1673–1755), principal landowner in and about the town, M.P. for the county of Cumberland (1708–22, 1727–55) and most active member of a family that dominated or attempted to dominate the public life of the counties of Cumberland and Westmorland for more than a century. In 1756, the property of Lowther of Whitehaven, following that of two other branches of his family, passed to his kinsman, the young Sir James Lowther of Lowther, Bart., subsequently earl of Lonsdale, the famous "borough-monger" and "king" of Cumberland and Westmorland, the "richest commoner in England" before he became a peer. Very close to the older Sir James Lowther was his Whitehaven estate manager and political agent, John Spedding.[28] The latter's son, Lowther Spedding, married (1739) Jane Walker, stepdaughter of Peter How, an important tobacco merchant in Whitehaven. How himself subsequently married (1755) Christian, widowed second wife of Lowther Spedding. John Spedding's cousin was Anthony Bacon whom Spedding trained in Lowther's estate office as his successor but who preferred to go to sea as a captain in the

Maryland trade. Bacon subsequently settled as a merchant in London where he was not too successful until in 1752 his cousin Spedding induced How and other Whitehaven tobacco merchants to make him their agent. From that happy turn dates the prosperity which made Bacon an important government contractor in the Seven Years' War, an M.P., and subsequently a major figure in the coal and iron industries of Cumberland and particularly South Wales.[29]

Sir James Lowther the elder contributed in many ways to the remarkable rise of the Whitehaven tobacco trade in the 1730's and 1740's. As M.P. for the county, a large amount of his time in London was devoted to the management of bills for road and harbor improvements, and for the solicitation of petty administrative favors for the port. In his private capacity, he was even closer to the tobacco merchants of Whitehaven. He was supposed to be worth about one million pounds when he died in 1755. Like his father before him, he had continuously reinvested his income in his mines and other property and in acquiring more land. Some of this wealth went into shipping, both for the Virginia and coal trades. As early as 1693–94, we find his father Sir John Lowther taking one-eighth shares in vessels built for the Virginia trade.[30] By the late 1730's and 1740's, we find Sir James Lowther investing in a score and more vessels, in some cases owning five-eighths, three-fourths, and even seven-eighths of individual ships. He seems to have deliberately expanded his investment in local shipping in the late 1730's to facilitate the export of his coal to Ireland. He was quite satisfied if a vessel were used on a six-month or so trip to Virginia in the earlier part of the year but was available to carry coal in the late summer and fall. When the tobacco trade boomed in the 1740's, some local merchants tried to squeeze in two trips to Virginia in one year and abandoned the coal trade entirely, much to Lowther's vexation.[31] In addition, Sir James Lowther made short and medium term loans of several thousand pounds each to local merchants, including Peter How and even the politically hostile Walter and Thomas Lutwidge.[32] Such short term credit was particularly important at Whitehaven where there was a total absence of banking facilities. When the tobacco ships returned from the Chesapeake, the shippers were extremely pressed for cash to pay the freight (or sailors' wages if they were ship owners too) as well as that part of the tobacco duties (the "old subsidy") which had to be paid in cash, rather than bonded. If a merchant had a second ship come in from Virginia before he had sold or reexported the tobacco from his first ship, his shortage of cash could become acutely embarrassing. Under such circumstances, the wealth of the Lowthers, whether invested in shipping or lent to the merchants on short-term loans, must be seen as a most significant addition to the capital stock and credit facilities of the Whitehaven tobacco trade in its most remarkable hour.

A different but just as successful approach to the capital and credit shortage at Whitehaven can be observed in the career of Peter How, another member of the Lowther-Spedding group, and the most important for the purposes of our study. The 1719 Whitehaven port books show Peter How & Co. as a small tobacco importer, just starting in the Virginia trade.[33] By 1740, the firm, now How & Kelsick, was importing about 1.3 million lb. in a year and stood head and shoulders above the rest of the trade in the port.[34] Part of Peter How's preeminence had a political base. In 1739, through his own politicking (and without the knowledge of Sir James Lowther) he obtained for himself the commission to receive and remit to London the excise receipts for Cumberland. This meant that he would always have on hand a ready supply of hard cash so useful when ships came home. While ordinary receivers of revenue had to buy bills of exchange on London in the open market, Peter How could count on having balances in London through his trading operations which could be used by him to settle his excise accounts: the large sums earned by the tobacco which he and other Whitehaven merchants sold in Holland were normally remitted to London by bills of exchange; provincial merchants normally kept a good part of their cash balances in London, for London bills were as good as cash for most mercantile purposes.

Sir James Lowther was not happy about Peter How's obtaining the excise receivership. Lowther was a great receiver of rents in Cumberland, a good part of which Spedding remitted to London for him by buying bills of exchange. (Lowther lived in London about eight months in the year and managed his investments from there.) In buying bills on London, Spedding had to bid against the government revenue receivers for the limited supply offered by traders. Sir James Lowther often complained about the great paucity of London bills in Cumberland (which exported so little) and instructed Spedding to take from good merchants longer term bills than revenue collectors could handle. Most of the short term loans of Lowther money which Spedding made to the Whitehaven merchants when their ships came in were actually repaid by 60-120 day bills on London. Lowther was accordingly very much pleased by the development of tobacco sales to Holland from about 1735 onward for this increased the supply of London bills in Whitehaven. He was less pleased with How's getting the excise remittance contract, for How had up to then been one of the chief suppliers to Spedding of London bills, for which he would now have other uses. (Lowther only hoped that the 1 percent discount which How charged the other merchants when he gave them cash in return for 60-day London bills would send them to Spedding for cash on easier terms.) Sir James wrote Spedding in 1739 that when his, Lowther's cousin, Walter Fletcher, died, his position as receiver-general of the land tax in Cumberland and Westmorland should not be allowed to fall into the hands of anyone in Whitehaven but should be given to someone in Carlisle who would buy London bills from the cattle drovers there, whose bills Lowther did not like, and thus not compete for the Whitehaven supply.[35] In the event, however, when Walter Fletcher died in 1743, Peter How also acquired his position as land tax receiver for the two counties, this time with the help of Lowther.[36] The reason Lowther by 1743 no longer feared How's role in the bill market was that in the intervening years, the French had started making large scale tobacco purchases in Whitehaven, ending overnight the bill scarcity there.

There is no record of the French buying any tobacco at Whitehaven before 1742. The surviving port books for the 'teens show no shipments to France; when the port books resume after a hiatus, they show no shipments to France in 1739, 1740 or 1741.[37] Nor do the accounts at the Bank of England of the French buyers Peter Cavalier, Lewis Guillemau and John Bance show any Whitehaven names.[38] The French trade bursts suddenly upon the record on 17–18 February 1741/2 when the *St. Stephen* of Bordeaux entered outward at Whitehaven for Bordeaux with 165,000 lb. of tobacco shipped by Peter How on account of the farmers-general of France. The tobacco had been imported from Virginia on the *Cumberland* a month before by How & Kelsick and by young James Spedding, John's merchant son.[39] About the same time, old John Spedding wrote Sir James Lowther that there were five French ships in the harbor and more expected;[40] How was busy buying tobacco for the French which he paid for by bills drawn on George FitzGerald of London. The first payment to "How" in FitzGerald's account at the Bank of England is dated 15 March 1741/2.[41] From that moment Peter How was in the enviable trading position of having, as a revenue receiver, a regular supply of local cash, and, as buyer for the French, an unrivaled facility for drawing bills on London. These two roles both balanced and strengthened each other. How at once became the principal, indeed almost the only, source of London bills for the Lowther account (tens of thousands of pounds sterling annually) and was much cherished by Sir James for it. At the same time, he could in buying tobacco offer the local merchants their choice of cash or London bills of early maturity.[42] In return for such courtesies, he could force the merchant sellers to accept a relatively low price for their tobacco. A few years later, Thomas Lutwidge, who remained loyal to the Dutch market, explained to Robert Herries of Rotterdam that many Whitehaven merchants preferred selling to How for the French at an execrable price rather than shipping to Holland because How as a revenue receiver could always give them the quick and hard cash they needed for the "old subsidy" and other pressing expenses.[43] It would be difficult to imagine anyone better situated than Peter How to do the French business at Whitehaven.

From the start, the French buying at Whitehaven was a very big thing. The surviving Whitehaven port books end in 1743. However, those for 1742 and 1743 show the following distribution of tobacco exports:[44]

	1742	1743
France	3,024,322 lb.	5,434,719 lb.
Holland	3,170,728	3,403,096
Ireland	793,707	1,132,612
Other	30,391	650

Thus, from nothing in 1741, the French market jumped to 55 percent of the tobacco export trade at Whitehaven in 1743.

At the same time, of course, the import trade at Whitehaven had to grow rapidly to meet this suddenly opened large new market. Though the Whitehaven tobacco trade, stimulated by the Dutch market, had been growing very rapidly in the late 1730's, it was to grow even more rapidly in the 1740's under the whip of French demand.[45] The very substantial shipments to France could not have begun suddenly in February 1742 unless some sort of preliminary arrangements had been made the previous year. In all probability George FitzGerald had reached some sort of agreement or understanding with Peter How early in 1741, encouraging some of the Whitehaven tobacco merchants to send more ships to the Chesapeake that year than they normally would have done. Thus, the rise in Whitehaven imports in 1741, the year of the transition, probably represents some French influence, while that in 1742 and succeeding years shows the full force of French demand: Whitehaven imports in 1742 were 81 percent above the 1738–40 level; and 144 percent above in 1743–44. It was at this juncture that there occurred those "wonder-years"—1743, 1744, and 1746—in which Whitehaven passed Bristol, Liverpool and even the combined Clyde ports to be for a moment the leading tobacco port in the kingdom after London.[46]

It would appear that in the 1740's, all the tobacco at Whitehaven suitable for the French market was actually bought for France. The superior grades of James and York River tobacco which merited premium prices were sorted out and sent to Ireland; the bright "Oronoko" leaf from the Patuxent and other northerly districts of Maryland had still to be sent to Holland, for the French would not take it. Everything else from Virginia and even the leaf from the Potomac and eastern shore districts of Maryland were sold to the French. Most of this was delivered to Peter How for the French immediately upon importation. There is evidence that How had contracted for purchase with the importers well before the tobacco had arrived at Whitehaven.[47]

Despite this great boom of 1742–46, Whitehaven was apparently not able to satisfy the French fully in price and quantity. Early in 1746, the last year in which Whitehaven led in the provincial tobacco trade, Sir James Lowther heard that more of the French business was going to Glasgow and was suitably alarmed for his port.[48] The French in fact were sending more of their business to the Clyde, but continued to make major purchases at Whitehaven. Between September 1745 and the end of the war in 1748, 60 vessels were licensed to carry tobacco from the Clyde to France and 47 from Whitehaven, more than all the other English ports put together. The French seemed, however, to have grown less enthusiastic about Whitehaven in the 1750's. After the start of the Seven Years' War, of the 179 vessels licensed to carry tobacco to France during 1756–59, only 30 sailed from Whitehaven, compared to 78 from the Clyde and 34 from the Thames. After the failure in December 1759 of George FitzGerald, through whom most French orders came to Peter How, the French business almost disappeared at Whitehaven: of 193 vessels licensed to carry tobacco to France during 1760–62, only six cleared from Whitehaven.[49]

From its beginnings in 1742, the French purchases in Whitehaven were made exclusively by Peter How. He in turn worked solely with George FitzGerald of London. At first all the bills of exchange on London which How furnished Spedding were drawn on George FitzGerald. During the pass period, 1745–48, when FitzGerald and the Van Necks were forced to combine their activities in the French interest, How drew a few bills on the Van Necks. However, with the return of peace, he seems to have reverted to his primary connection with George FitzGerald.[50] Thus, when FitzGerald failed in December 1759, How was peculiarly exposed. He survived the immediate blow and struggled on until the end of 1763 before finally failing himself for £40,000–50,000.[51] His collapse was a serious blow to the whole town of Whitehaven, for he was not only indebted to many there, but was the proprietor of a large tobacco manufacturing works. Were his assets to be sold in the normal way, it was likely that the manufacture would be destroyed, to the detriment of the town.

The failure of Peter How brought into play the whole power structure of Cumberland and Westmorland, then dominated by the struggle for preeminence between the younger Sir James Lowther (the future earl of Lonsdale) and the duke of Portland. The assignees under the bankruptcy looked to the duke of Portland for protection. A dissident group of creditors, led by Spedding's cousin Anthony Bacon, now a great merchant of London, and those interested in preserving the tobacco manufacture looked to Sir James Lowther for protection. In 1758, John Spedding died; his successor as chief steward and political manager for the Lowther interest in Cumberland and Westmorland was John Robinson, a local lawyer and landowner (subsequently secretary to the Treasury under Lord North). Robinson early established a very close political friendship with Charles Jenkinson, secretary to the Treasury under George Grenville (1763–65), who sat in Parliament for the Lowther borough of Cockermouth.[52]

Immediately upon How's failure in December 1763, the future (Portlandite) assignees complained to the government that How had just before the bankruptcy transferred some of his assets to the London firm of Bacon, Franklyn & Co. (Anthony Bacon, Gilbert Franklyn, and Anthony Richardson). (Ultimately, ca. 1769, Bacon & Co. surrendered some of the real estate involved.) Immediately thereafter, in January 1764, Bacon and other dissident creditors complained to the Treasury that the assignees were dilatory in selling some semi-manufactured tobacco which would soon spoil. They asked that the government transfer the crown's attachment or "extent" upon the estate of Peter How to Sir James Lowther who would sell what needed to be sold immediately and guarantee the full debt to the crown. (As a receiver of the land tax, How owed the government £10,129.) The real negotiation was conducted between Robinson and Jenkinson. George Grenville coolly brushed aside the objections of the duke of Portland and had the Treasury agree to the proposition. The assignees, however, appealed to the Court of the Exchequer which found in their favor in May-June 1764. Whereupon, Lowther, Anthony Bacon and three other dissident creditors offered to pay by installments all of How's debts and asked that the Court of Bankruptcy discharge the existing assignees and name Bacon, James Spedding, and three others as new assignees. Lowther's motivation in this seems to have been to keep How's tobacco manufacture going and to protect the other local interests at Whitehaven involved in How's fall. The move was unsuccessful and the liquidation of How's estate commenced. Nevertheless, the entire question was still under litigation in 1792, long after most of the principals had died.[53] When How himself died in 1772, he was described in the London press as "Receiver-General of the Land-Tax, Window-Tax, and Excise, for the Counties of Cumberland and Westmoreland upwards of 20 Years, and for 40 Years one of the most principal Merchants in the North of England."[54]

The failures of George FitzGerald in 1759 and Peter How in 1763 struck a grievous blow at the prosperity of the Whitehaven tobacco trade. In 1757, old John Spedding had instructed the young Sir James Lowther that "the Merchants in this Town . . . could not carry on the Tobacco Trade without Selling a great part of what they import to the French for ready Money."[55] In 1758, on the eve of the first disaster, Spedding reported to Lowther that the Whitehaven merchants were pushing the tobacco trade lustily and were sending over fifty ships to the Chesapeake that year.[56] All this ended suddenly. We have already noted how French purchases at Whitehaven fell off markedly in the latter part of 1758 and 1759 and almost ceased during 1760–62, after FitzGerald's failure.[57] This must have forced the still substantial Whitehaven tobacco trade back onto a dangerously heavy dependence upon the Dutch export market; the failure of Peter How, already weakened by FitzGerald's stop, at the end of 1763 was probably not unconnected with the great Amsterdam financial crisis of July-November of that same year. As early as 1763, signs of a serious and sudden contraction in the Whitehaven tobacco trade were evident.[58] In May 1764, Robinson wrote to Jenkinson of Sir James Lowther's disappointment in the failure of the Treasury to prevent the "distress [of] the tobacco trade of the town of Whitehaven, and no inconsiderable branch it was, though too much depressed at present."[59] The slump continued through the 1760's. When Pennant visited Whitehaven in June 1772, he learned that "The tobacco trade is much declined: formerly about twenty thousand hogsheads were annually imported from *Virginia;* now scarce a fourth of that number; *Glasgow* having stolen that branch: but to make amends, another is carried on to the *West-Indies.*

. . ."[60] Pennant's figures are exaggerated, but other data show tobacco imports at Whitehaven in 1771–72 at about one-third the level of 1743–49.[61]

Thus, the French market proved the undoing of the Whitehaven tobacco trade in the 1760's as it had proved its making in the 1740's. Yet, for all its disappointments and sorrows, the glittering French prize still appeared worth striving for in Whitehaven. It went ultimately to Samuel Martin of a Quaker Anglo-Irish family with Virginia and other valuable connections. His father, Col. John Martin, had lived for some time in Virginia where he had acquired a considerable landed estate. In the 1750's, Col. John Martin, having returned to Ireland, was interested in a Dublin merchant house in partnership with his sons George and Samuel. Among other business, this firm received consignments of Virginia tobacco via England. The colonel's daughters married into leading Anglo-Irish landed families, including that of the earl of Shannon. His son Samuel married a daughter of Peter Gale of Whitehaven, merchant, member of a prominent anti-Lowther family. Shortly after his father's death in 1760, Samuel withdrew from the Dublin firm and moved to Whitehaven (1761), where he established a successful house in the Irish trade. In 1762, he wrote to his cousin, Samuel Martin (Sr.) of Antigua:

> I brought some very strong recommendations also in hopes of succeeding to the present Fr[en]ch Agent Peter How Esq[r] (who is old and infirm) in case of surviving him who is the sole purchaser of Tobacco at this port for the Farmers Gen[l] of France, which is in the Gift of Sir Joshua Vanneck & Co. of London who since M[r] FitzGeralds failure; has succeed'd to the whole Business of the Farmer's Gen[l], and as I am perfectly acquainted with the quality of Tobacco & have so good a stake in Virginia from whence I can constantly have the surest & earliest intelligence, I think if I can get it I shall make as much of it as the present Gent[n] does, wh[ic]h may be between three and four hundred a year.

To get this contract, Samuel Martin had brought into play some of the most significant lines of influence in British-Irish society. Among the letters of recommendation which he had brought over with him from Dublin was one from George Stone, archbishop of Armagh and primate of Ireland, to his brother Andrew Stone, former undersecretary and confidant of the duke of Newcastle, subsequently secretary to the Prince of Wales, 1756–60, and at this time treasurer to Queen Charlotte (1761–73), one of the most influential men behind the scenes of British politics. Another letter was from John Ponsonby, speaker of the Irish House of Commons, to his brother-in-law, Lord Walpole of Wolterton. Ponsonby, Archbishop Stone, and the earl of Shannon were probably the three most powerful men in Ireland in the age of the "Undertakers." Lord Walpole was, of course, the brother of the

Hon. Thomas Walpole, son-in-law and partner of Sir Joshua Van Neck. Lord and Lady Walpole assured Martin "of their Friendship" to which he added the recommendations of the influential merchant-M.P.'s Sir Samuel Fludyer, Arnold Nesbitt, Robert Jones, Samuel Touchet, and Sir William Baker as well as those of other influential merchants. On his next trip to London, he planned to speak to his cousin Samuel Martin, secretary to the Treasury (son of Samuel Martin of Antigua).[62] It is therefore not entirely surprising that shortly after the failure of Peter How in December 1763, Samuel Martin received the French agency at Whitehaven, which he seems to have retained intermittently until 1775. The commission, however, under his administration was never to be that dominant force in the life of the port which it had been in Peter How's heyday in the 1740's and 1750's.

In summary, then, the Whitehaven tobacco trade reached its greatest heights in the 1740's and 1750's when that port furnished a significant part of the French tobacco purchases. During those same decades the whole economic life of the port seems to have received a considerable quickening from the easing of credit and payments problems arising from French cash purchases.

The French Agents in Scotland

The story of French tobacco buying in Scotland was the Whitehaven tale writ large. Scotland generally and Glasgow in particular had entered the Chesapeake tobacco trade very vigorously immediately following the Union in 1707. By 1714–17, Glasgow had pushed ahead of all the English outports to become the leading tobacco trading center in the realm after London. However, the combination of the business depression that followed the collapse of the South Sea Bubble in 1720 and the customs reforms of 1723–24 led to a stagnation in the Glasgow tobacco trade and a loss of relative rank.[63] During the 1730's and early 1740's, we find Bristol, Liverpool, and Whitehaven each successively pushing ahead of the Clyde ports (Port Glasgow and Greenock) for a few years each. However, about 1740, Glasgow's tobacco trade began to grow again and by the late 1740's the Clyde ports had regained that important position in the tobacco trade which they were to retain until the American Revolution.[64] There is a marked coincidence in time between Glasgow's resumption of growth about 1740 and the expansion of French purchases there that very year.

We do not know when the French monopoly began tobacco purchases in Scotland. The Scottish Inspector-General's reports, giving aggregate data on exports and destinations, only begin in 1755; the Scottish port books, with ship-by-ship entries from which similar information can be calculated, only resume in 1742. At both these dates, shipments to France were already a significant proportion of Scottish tobacco exports. By contrast, there is almost nothing to indicate any French purchases in Scotland in the twenty or so years after the Union of 1707. Scottish names are rare in the bank accounts of the monopoly's agent, George Tobie Guiguer, during 1711–19. The James Douglas who bought for William Law during the open trade interlude of 1720 may have bought in Scotland,[65] but there is nothing to indicate that John Law sent any of the monopoly's business there in 1718–19. Neither, except for a few suggestive references to "Buchanan" is there anything in the bank account of Peter Cavalier, agent of the restored Indies Company, to indicate that he was making any tobacco purchases in Scotland during 1725–30.[66] It is possible, perhaps likely, that such outlying purchases were by 1728 being handled by the other French agent, Daniel Hays.[67] Nevertheless, it is certain that the French *were* buying in Scotland during the very last years of the Indies Company's management.

On 27 November 1730, the Bogles of Glasgow wrote to their Rotterdam correspondent:

> . . . the French Company have given Orders for buying above one Thousand Hhds in this place, and as the Crop in Virginia was Worse Last year, and only about four Thousand Hhds Imported to Glasgow this year [,] the Gentlemen who buy here for the French are Oblidged to take More Indifferent Tobaco than they used to Do, tho' they buy none but the very best they Can get & pay 2½ for the lb' Ready Money which is a tollerable Good Price. . . .[68]

This important letter is the only concrete evidence we have of the beginnings of French tobacco purchases at Glasgow. It reveals that certain "Gentlemen" at Glasgow (probably the Buchanans) had been buying for the French there for several years and already were a major force in the market, buying 1,000 hogsheads at a time when annual imports were only 4,000. However, the 600,000–700,000 lb. contained in those 1,000 hogsheads were only a small fraction of total French purchases in Britain at this time; during 1730–31, shipments from England alone to the French monopoly averaged over eight million pounds annually.[69] What little we know suggests that the French continued to make only a relatively small proportion of their total purchases in Scotland through the 1730's.

For about twenty-five years after the United General Farms took over the tobacco monopoly in 1730, it appears that they usually employed two competing agents in Scotland, just as they did at London. From about 1730 to about 1744, the French purchasing in Scotland appears to have been divided (or perhaps alternated) between Andrew Buchanan & Co. of Glasgow and William Alexander & Co. of Edinburgh; from about 1744 to about 1755, the contract similarly appears to have been divided between the same Alexanders, who had the major share, and Alexander Grant & Co. of Edinburgh, who had a minor share; from 1756 until 1771, however, the contract appears to have been held exclusively by the Alexander firm. Thus, the history of French buying in Scotland between 1730 and 1771 is in great part that of the Alexanders of Edinburgh, through whom we can most usefully follow the French activity north of the Tweed.

Like many Scottish merchants of the eighteenth century, the Alexanders of Edinburgh were cadets of an ancient and noble house, theirs being that headed by the earls of Stirling. Robert Alexander (1604–87), a solicitor in Paisley, purchased the properties of Boghall and Blackhouse in Ayrshire, which passed through his son, James, "of Boghall," a Presbyterian minister, to his grandson John (ca. 1660–1712), a wealthy merchant and burgess of Glasgow. This John married Janet, daughter of Alexander Cuninghame of Craigends, Renfrewshire, by whom he had two sons and a daughter. The daughter Anna married Peter Murdoch, Lord Provost of Glasgow in 1731, and by an earlier marriage father and father-in-law of other provosts of that town. (Through this marriage the Alexanders were connected to the leading "tobacco lords" of Glasgow.) The elder son of John Alexander, Robert, "of Blackhouse" became principal Clerk of Session (the highest court in Scotland) at Edinburgh. The younger son William became a merchant and banker of Edinburgh.[70]

The early career of William Alexander (born ca. 1690) is rather mysterious. Someone by that name appears as a small shareholder of the South Sea Company in 1714.[71] There is evidence that our particular William Alexander was in Paris during the excitement of "the System" in 1719–20.[72] While in France, he married (February 1720) Mariamne Louisa de la Croix of La Rochelle. She came of a prominent Huguenot family of Dutch origin (their name being originally Crucius), active in many great drainage schemes of the seventeenth century. Although Alexander family histories would have it that her family had left La Rochelle at the time of the Revocation,[73] in fact they were active there throughout the eighteenth century. She was a first cousin of Theodore de la Croix, a leading La Rochelle merchant of mid-century, who was connected by marriage to the Girardot, Cottin and other great Protestant banking families of Paris.[74] William Alexander and wife were in London in January 1722 where their newborn son John was baptized at the French Church, Threadneedle Street.[75] Although this son appears to have died as an infant, they subsequently had three other sons who lived to maturity—Robert, William (II), and Alexander John.[76]

William Alexander's Paris residence, about 1720, is quite interesting because it was precisely at this moment that the important Scottish banker, Alexander Alexander, began his Paris career.[77] Although it is not possible to connect the last named (apparently a friend of John Law) with any particular branch of the Alexander family in Scotland, he did have commercial dealings with our William Alexander as well as with a wide range of exiled and traveling Britons, including Lord Bolingbroke[78] and Robert Knight, fugitive cashier of the South Sea Company.[79] His house acted as Paris correspondent for important London banks (e.g., Middleton's, Martin's) [80] and was much favored by British tourists in Paris, including the young Horace Walpole.[81] Just before Alexander Alexander failed in 1740, his banking premises, Rue St. Appolline, were sold to Charles Selwyn, an English merchant, who continued a bank there for the English community in Paris until about 1763.[82]

In 1722 or shortly thereafter, William Alexander returned to Scotland and established himself as a merchant and banker at Edinburgh. He was eventually to have a distinguished public as well as commercial career there. Although he did not become a burgess of the town until 1733, he ultimately was to play a prominent part in its public life, serving as a member of its town council during 1746-51 and as Lord Provost in 1752-54, and ultimately representing it in the House of Commons during the Parliament of 1754-61. The central government recognized his importance by naming him one of the twenty-one trustees for fisheries and manufactures in Scotland (1738) and one of the commissioners for forfeited estates (1755-60).[83]

The foundation for William Alexander's public career in Edinburgh was of course his success as a merchant and banker. At the beginning of the next century, old men in Edinburgh remembered Provost Alexander as "the only banker in Edinburgh" in their youth, the man to whom was addressed the only letter that arrived in some mails from London.[84] He had extensive commercial connections throughout Scotland and England, extending to Spain, France and the West Indies. The importation of wine was one of his regular activities.[85] At the time of his death, in 1761, the foreign correspondents of his house included such great names as Thellusson, Necker & Co. of Paris, Delalande Magon frères & Co. of St. Malo, as well as Pierre de Bacque of Dunkirk, Ménager of Le Havre, John Black & Co. of Bordeaux, not to mention the St. Domingue houses of Shea & Sheridan at Léogane and John Stewart at "the Cape."[86] Earlier correspondents had included Butler, Powers & Co. of Cadiz[87] and of course, George FitzGerald of London.[88]

Rather more is known of William Alexander's activities as a banker and director of the Royal Bank of Scotland. At the time of the Union in 1707, former shareholders of the ill-fated Darien (Scottish Indies) Company and other debtors and claimants were issued government obligations or "debentures"—the so-called "equivalent." As the payment of interest on these debentures was slow, they sold at a discount and most passed into the hands of English speculators. In 1724, the debenture holders were by act of Parliament chartered as the "Equivalent Company," with headquarters in London. Prevented from engaging in banking in London by the charter of the Bank of England, the leaders of the Equivalent Company (including Daniel Hays, one of the French tobacco agents in London) obtained a charter in 1727 under the Great Seal of Scotland for a company to conduct banking in Scotland only. In contrast to the old Toryish Bank of Scotland (founded 1696), the new Royal Bank of Scotland had a pronounced Whig, even official, character and soon was handling virtually all of the government business in Scotland. It also dealt regularly in English and foreign bills of exchange which the old bank then would not touch.[89]

Reflecting its close alliance with ruling Whig circles and public finance, the directorate of the Royal Bank of Scotland during its first half century was dominated by politicians, judges, and handlers of public money (such as receivers-general and paymasters). The initial board of directors of 1727 did not contain a single merchant. A slight change occurred in 1728 when William Alexander and Patrick Crawfurd, Jr., both merchants of Edinburgh, were elected "extraordinary directors." In 1730, Alexander became one of the ordinary directors, which position he continued to fill for the next thirty years. For much of that time, he was the only person styled "merchant" on the board, though later he was joined by one or two others, particularly, from 1743, Provost John Coutts, founder of another equally important mercantile and banking house in Edinburgh. From the first, the new Royal Bank of Scotland attracted considerable business from Glasgow, whose tobacco merchants needed short term credits. With his origins and close family connections in the highest Glasgow mercantile circles, William Alexander frequently acted as the channel through which Glasgow merchants were introduced to the Royal Bank and their requests presented to its board. By its pioneering experiments with "overdrafts," the Royal Bank was comparatively well equipped to provide the services the Glasgow merchants desired. (The old Bank of Scotland was forced to follow its example to attract Glasgow business.)

Shortly after the United General Farms took over the French tobacco monopoly on 1 October 1730, William Alexander was named one of their buying agents in Scotland. It is possible that he owed both this appointment and his seat on the directorate of the Royal Bank to a family connection with Daniel Hays of London. In any event, these two positions supported each other usefully. At Edinburgh, just as at Whitehaven at this time, exchange on London was chronically short and usually sold at a premium (instead of at the discount that would have naturally reflected the 30 or 60 days during which the bill seller had use of the buyer's money). As tobacco buyer for the French in Scotland, William Alexander would have to draw large bills on London and thus was a man well worth having on the bank's directorate.[90] On 17 November 1730, just a few weeks after the changes in Paris, William Alexander informed the Royal Bank for the first time that he had occasion to draw £4,000 on London for which bills he could get 1¼ percent premium in the town; instead, he agreed to give them at par to the Bank (whose policy it then was not to pay premia for exchange) for immediate cash. By April 1732, he had supplied the Bank with over £7,000 in London bills, but something of a lull followed.[91] (This pause may have been associated with Daniel Hays' death in 1732.)

What little evidence we have suggests that Alexander's French commissions in the 1730's were rather a small affair. Total French purchases in Scotland were most likely modest, and such buying business as there was had to be split between him and the Buchanan brothers of Glasgow—Andrew, Archibald, and Neil. Their share may have been as big or bigger than his. When Silhouette visited Scotland in 1735, he dealt with Buchanans and it was Andrew Buchanan, not William Alexander, who sold £6,000 of Silhouette's bills on Simond in London to the Royal Bank.[92] In the account of Louis Guillemau at the Bank of England, 1732-35, we find payments to "Buchanan" but not to Alexander; in the same accounts of John Bance, 1732-41, we find payments both to Buchanans and Alexander, but rather more to the former.[93]

All this was to change in the 1740's. Just as we can pinpoint the entrance of the French into the Whitehaven market at 1741-42, so we can with some assurance place the turning point in Scotland a year or so earlier. As we have already explained, in the latter part of 1739, the united farms gave a substantial part of their British purchasing business to the abbé Huber and the FitzGeralds acting as partners. The FitzGeralds either were obliged or chose to make most of their purchases outside of London. Just as they chose to deal exclusively with Peter How at Whitehaven, so they decided to handle all their soon-to-be substantial Scottish business through William Alexander. The first indication we have of the new changes came on 24 October 1740 when the Royal Bank's directors agreed to buy at par a £1,200 bill drawn by Alexander on George FitzGerald in London. On the thirty-first, he agreed to give the Royal Bank all his tobacco bills on London drawn at 90 days and they in turn agreed to discount all the good Edinburgh bills remitted him from London if not more than 40 days from maturity. This is the first mention of such a transaction between Alexander and the bank since 1732. Thereafter, throughout the 1740's, the Royal Bank's directors' minutes are filled with such references: as Alexander's supply of bills grew, the other directors were able to force down the duration of par bills from 90 to 60 days.[94] At the London end, we can also find payments to "Alexander" becoming very frequent in the Bank of England account of George FitzGerald & Co.[95]

The intimation given by the banking records of a vast upsurge in French tobacco purchases in Scotland in the 1740's is more than born out by the Scottish port books which start at Michaelmas 1742 (Table VI A, B). These figures reveal rather clearly the revolutionary impact of French buying upon the Scottish tobacco trade in the 1740's and the importance of the year 1740 as a turning point. As late as 1739, Scotland provided only 11 percent of total British tobacco exports; by 1751, this had reached 35 percent of a considerably expanded total. While total British tobacco exports in these twelve years increased less than 50 percent, those from Scotland increased

TABLE VI (A)

Scottish and British Tobacco Exports, 1743, 1747, and 1751[96]

Year	Scottish Exp. to France (minus Dunkirk)	Scottish Exp. to World	British Exp. to France (minus Dunkirk)	British Exp. to World
		(in thousands of lb.)		
(1739)	?	4,834	?	43,054
1743	5,614	10,853	14,949	57,555
1747	8,319	12,907	16,653	51,991
1751	10,084	21,929	16,844	61,226

TABLE VI (B)

Scottish and British Tobacco Exports (Percentages), 1743, 1747, and 1751

Year	Scot. Exp. to Fr. as % of Br. Exp. to Fr.	Scot. Exp. to Fr. as % of Scot. Total Exp.	Br. Exp. to Fr. as % of Br. Total Exp.
1743	38%	52%	26%
1747	50%	64%	32%
1751	60%	46%	28%

more than 350 percent. Almost all of this increase down to 1747 was accounted for by the growth of the French market. Scotland, we have seen above,[97] was supplying hardly 10 percent of British tobacco exports to France, about 1730–31; there is nothing to indicate that the percentage was any higher as late as 1739. But the French policy change, which we detected in the banking records at about 1740, was felt in Scotland sharply and suddenly. By 1743 (the first complete year in the port books), Scotland was providing 38 percent of total British tobacco exports to France; this was to become 50 percent by 1747 and 60 percent by 1751.

This increased French buying was to have the most far-reaching effect upon the Scottish tobacco trade as a whole. While the French monopoly in these years took only 26–32 percent of total British tobacco exports (and rarely took more in the century), they were taking from 46 to 64 percent of Scottish exports (compared to 10 or 15 percent at the most in 1730–31). Thus the "golden age" of the Scottish tobacco trade, 1740–75, is the age of the French market. To meet this suddenly enhanced demand from France, Scottish merchants had to increase their purchases in the Chesapeake. Scottish tobacco imports rose precipitously from an average of 5.5 million lb. annually during 1738–40 to an average of ten million pounds annually during 1741–44 and, with the return of peace, reached twenty million pounds annually during 1749–53! In relative terms, the Scottish share rose from about 10 percent of British imports in 1738 to 20 percent in 1744 (and was ultimately to reach 30 percent in 1757 and 40 percent in 1765). The French market not only provided an outlet for these increased imports, but the prompt and assured French payments provided the underpinning for the whole credit structure that made this expansion possible.

The new directions taken by the tobacco trade in the revolutionary decade of the 1740's continued in the succeeding years down to the American Revolution. After a marked slump during 1754–57 (contemporary to an almost complete suspension of exports to France during 1755 and 1756), the Scottish sector led the British trade as a whole into a new generation of growth; by 1771–75, Scottish imports averaged 45 million lb. annually (more than double the high level of 1749–53)—and constituted 45 percent of total British imports. Almost all the tobacco imported into Scotland was reexported, with France continuing the preeminent destination (Table VII A, B).

TABLE VII (A)

Scottish and British Tobacco Exports, 1757–75[98]

Year	Scottish Exp. to France (minus Dunkirk)	Scottish Exp. to World	British Exp. to France (minus Dunkirk)	British Exp. to World
	(in thousands of lb. annual averages)			
1757–62	7,815	22,129	14,890	55,213
1766–75	12,633	36,712	17,576	75,509

TABLE VII (B)

Scottish and British Tobacco Exports (Percentages), 1757–75

Year	Scot. Exp. to Fr. as % of Br. Exp. to Fr.	Scot. Exp. to Fr. as % of Scot. Total Exp.	Br. Exp. to Fr. as % of Br. Total Exp.
1757–62	52%	35%	27%
1766–75	72%	34%	23%

After the difficult earlier phase of the Seven Years' War when the French made their only serious effort to find alternate sources of tobacco supplies, British tobacco exports to France resumed their upward course quantitatively and regained the relative share of total British tobacco exports they had held in 1751. The Scottish share of British exports to France became even more predominant than before the war, though the French market was not quite as important to the much expanded Scottish trade as it had been during the "take-off" of the 1740's.

The Scottish tobacco trade was always overwhelmingly the trade of the Clyde ports—Port Glasgow and Greenock, service ports for Glasgow city. Their share of total Scottish imports had been 91 percent in the three years Michaelmas 1714–Michaelmas 1717 and again in the ten years Michaelmas

1721–Michaelmas 1731 but declined to 79 percent for the ten years Christmas 1737–Christmas 1747, only to rebound to 98 percent during the final decade Michaelmas 1766–Michaelmas 1776.[99] All the significant centers of the Scottish import trade were heavily oriented toward the reexport trade which took 90 percent or more of their imports. Understandably, the French purchasing business was heavily concentrated in the Clyde ports; however, at times the French gave a slightly disproportionate share of their business to the lesser Scottish ports: 25 percent, for example, in 1747.[100] However, their interest in the lesser ports declined over time, as is suggested by the division of the export passes in wartime (Table VIII).

TABLE VIII

Great Seal Passes for Scottish Tobacco
Exports to France in Wartime[101]

Year	Port Glasgow & Greenock	Lesser Scottish Ports
1745–1748	60 (76%)	19 (24%)
1756–1759	78 (81%)	18 (19%)
1760–1762	107 (88%)	15 (12%)

The lesser ports patronized by the French were those in the southwest, along the coast between Glasgow and Whitehaven, the most important being Ayr, followed by Dumfries and Kirkcudbright. At all three, about 1743–51, just as at the Clyde ports, more than half the tobacco export trade was directed toward France. (Only at Aberdeen on the east coast was there a significant tobacco export business independent of France.) Indeed it would seem that the only thing that permitted the lesser ports of southwest Scotland to play as large a role in the tobacco business as they did in the 1740's and 1750's was the French market. When this business faded away after 1760, so did their tobacco trades.

At the Clyde ports, the French market remained the most important single export market. However there, as in Scotland generally, the French market was most important during the crucial explosive decade of the 1740's and relatively less important later on as other markets were expanded or developed (Table IX).

TABLE IX

Tobacco Exports at Port Glasgow and Greenock, 1743–73[102]

Year	To France	To Dunkirk	To World
1743	4,698,301 lb. (54%)	84,476 lb.	8,721,842 lb.
1747	6,305,706 (66%)	354,104	9,546,960
1751	8,470,243 (49%)	372,263	17,118,749
1770	15,706 hhd. (41%)	2,907 hhd.	37,938 hhd.
1771	16,098 (36%)	5,309	44,799
1771	15,760,727 lb. (36%)	5,014,116 lb.	43,881,611 lb.
1773–74 (av.)	13,313 hhd. (34%)	4,256 hhd.	39,643 hhd.

In addition to this useful import-export data, the port books available after Michaelmas 1742 give us precise information on who was buying tobacco for the French in Scotland.[103] The books for 1742–45 unfortunately tell us nothing because it was then local custom to list the importer as exporter *pro forma*. Only once at Port Glasgow was this not done; then the clerk wrote "William Gordon for William Alexander," Gordon being the local broker who handled the physical shipment for Alexander of Edinburgh. (At Greenock the same services were then performed by one Robert Gilmor.) By 1747, the procedure at the customs houses had been changed and the actual exporters were generally listed. For that year, we can also compare the entries in the port books with the passes issued by the privy council for tobacco shipments to France in wartime.

At Greenock in 1747, all the tobacco ships to France carrying passes in the name of George FitzGerald or the Van Necks were shown in the port books as cleared out by "William Watson for Alexander Brown and William Alexander" or some abbreviation thereof. Watson had taken Gilmor's place as the local shipping agent; Alexander Brown was another Edinburgh merchant with whom William Alexander was then seemingly sharing part of the French business.[104] At Port Glasgow that same year, ships with FitzGerald or Van Neck passes were cleared by William Gordon for the same or for "William Alexander & Son." At both ports, all ships with passes issued to Peter & Caesar Le Maistre were cleared by Samuel Taylor and/or Allan Gibb, local brokers acting for Alexander Grant, merchant of Edinburgh.[105] At Ayr all the entries outward were made for William Alexander. At Dumfries, ships with Van Neck passes were cleared outward by a local broker, George McMurdo for Alexander Brown or William Alexander, while vessels with Le Maistre passes were cleared by the importers acting for Alexander Grant. (At Kirkcudbright and Leith, exports were still entered outward in the name of the importers.)

With the return of peace in 1748, the passes to France cease, but we can still trace in the port books the division of French purchases between the Alexander (FitzGerald-Van Neck) and the Grant (Le Maistre) interests (Table X).

TABLE X

Scottish Shipments to France and Their Purchasers, 1747–51[106]

	1747 W. Alexander/ A. Brown	1747 A. Grant	1751 W. Alexander	1751 A. Grant
Pt. Glasgow & Greenock	5,001 hhd.	1,988 hhd.	6,331 hhd.	2,532 hhd.
Dumfries	811	281	64	462
Ayr	347	—	216	—
Total	6,159 (73%)	2,269 (27%)	6,611 (69%)	2,994 (31%)

Thus, the inference, suggested by the banking evidence, that William Alexander played the leading role in making French purchases in Scotland after 1740 is confirmed by the port books. The bulk of the business was securely in his hands by 1747 and probably much earlier. The fraction retained by the Le Maistre-Grant interest was to disappear by the time the war passes started again in 1756.

With purchases of this magnitude to make, William Alexander probably had to draw on London for nearly £100,000 annually in 1747 or 1751 and more in other years. As such, he probably had a greater supply of London bills than any other merchant or banker in Scotland, and with it had the wherewithal to oblige the Royal Bank and others worth cultivating. Thus, we find Alexander at the height of his influence in the 1750's, Lord Provost, M.P. and bank director. The last position caused him some difficulty after the Glasgow merchants set up banks of their own about 1750—the "Ship Bank" (Dunlop, Houstoun & Co.) and the "Glasgow Arms Bank" (Cochrane, Murdoch & Co.), the leading principals in the latter, Provosts Andrew Cochrane and John Murdoch of Glasgow being connected to him by marriage. Alexander had always been something of a "consul" of Glasgow at Edinburgh and his position probably became very difficult during the ensuing "bill-cashing" wars between the Edinburgh and the Glasgow banks. Yet, at the height of the bitterness, Alexander was regularly reelected to the directorate of the Royal Bank. The bank could hardly dispense with a director who could furnish that much exchange upon London.[107]

The only close picture we get of Provost William Alexander at work for the French comes from an extended lawsuit he had with John Miller, a tobacco dealer at Greenock, who acted as agent there for many great Chesapeake merchants of Glasgow. The agent swore to imports and exports as a partner in the firm of his principals, but his only real share therein was his commission. It was the practice of tobacco importers to sort out their tobacco, reserving the best for the domestic, Irish and Norwegian markets, holding the common for the French and sending anything else the French wouldn't take to Holland (both varieties unappreciated in France and qualities unacceptable there). In order to get a certain proportion of superior tobaccos for the French without paying extra for it, Alexander frequently contracted with Glasgow houses to take the entire contents of a ship from a suitable river, the Glaswegians reserving only ten hogsheads out of 100. The farmers-general were thus assured of getting some superior mixed in with their common. To make sure that the French got the shiploads they bought, all hogsheads so purchased were immediately marked with the letters "FFG." Alexander and the Glasgow merchants agreed only on the price and number of hogsheads. Everything else was left to the agents of the two sides at Port Glasgow or Greenock. At Greenock, William Watson acted for Alexander for many years, while Miller represented a number of Glasgow houses. On the side, he was a petty tobacco wholesaler, buying from importers, sailors, and customs sales, and selling a hogshead at a time to inland manufacturing tobacconists. Having in his custody at one time hundreds of hogsheads belonging to Glasgow merchants or the farmers-general, Miller had many opportunities for fraud. He apparently removed the better grades of tobacco from whole shiploads sold but not yet delivered to the French and substituted inferior tobacco which he had bought from sailors or at customs sales. In one two-year period, the farmers-general complained that among Alexander's purchases delivered to Le Havre, Morlaix, and Tonneins were nearly 200,000 lb. of defective tobacco. Alexander sued Miller for damages and was successful, though the case was appealed all the way to the House of Lords.[108] The case is most interesting in revealing a fully developed marketing mechanism in which whole shiploads were sold unseen by seller or buyer, who knew only the river of origin. (Of course, a certain minimum quality was assured by the Virginia inspection law of 1730.)

Twenty years and more of profitable "French business" for Provost William Alexander almost came to an end in December 1759 when George FitzGerald of London failed. Following the Beaujon, Goossens & Co. suspension, FitzGerald broke owing £4,000 to the farmers-general and near £25,000 to Provost Alexander. (The provost's oldest son Robert was one of the assignees in the bankruptcy.) £20,200 in unpaid bills of exchange which Alexander & Sons had drawn on FitzGerald and sold to the Royal Bank came home to Edinburgh for settlement. The provost's health broke under the strain; although reelected to the directorate of the Royal Bank in 1760 and 1761, he was no longer active and did not stand for reelection to Parliament in 1761. He died in July of that year very much under a cloud.[109]

Yet the firm of William Alexander & Sons survived and was to prosper again. With extraordinary help from the Royal and the old Banks of Scotland, the firm met the immediate crisis. In the longer run, their retention of the exclusive French commission in Scotland gave them both the earnings and the credit (now based on Van Neck & Co.) that loomed large in the Edinburgh of the 1760's.[110]

Of the provost's three sons, the youngest, Alexander John Alexander, had gone out to the Chesapeake in 1756 from whence he moved on to the Caribbean in the last year of the war. The older two, Robert and William (II) remained in Edinburgh where they had effective control of the family firm from the time of their father's election to Parliament in 1754.[111] They were characteristic figures of the new metropolis then aborning, the Edinburgh of the "Scottish Renaissance" and the "New Town." Robert Alexander moved with the *literati* in the Select Society; he introduced into Edinburgh the Paris literary "supper"; according to Henry Mackenzie, "the Northern Addison," these suppers "were frequented by all the literary and most of the fashionable persons of the time." His younger brother, William, threw himself, more traditionally, into the politics of the General Assembly of the Church of Scotland where he was active in the "popular call" faction opposed to the "patronage" party of Principal Robertson, the moderator. He was remembered in later years as a "strange adventurer, . . . who of all the men I have known had the strongest propensity to plotting, with the finest talents for such a business."[112] The brothers never became directors of the Royal Bank, nor did they achieve the municipal or parliamentary positions of their father; yet they obviously cut a figure in the greater world. When Benjamin Franklin visited Edinburgh in the 1760's, he was drawn inevitably into their society. Favors were exchanged and lifelong friendships formed. It was in fact Robert Alexander who commissioned the famous Martin portrait of Franklin which now hangs in the White House.[113]

When not entertaining the *literati* or stirring up the General Assembly, the brothers continued their father's mercantile and banking house with apparent success. They financed the first cudbear (a dyestuff) manufacture, set up at Leith. They made one other relevant extension of activity. To their father's business as tobacco buying agent for the French, they added a direct involvement in the tobacco trade to America. As early as 1754, William Alexander the younger was interested in Alexander Brown's ventures to the Chesapeake. Such activity was expanded in 1756 at the start of the war when George FitzGerald once more contracted with the farmers-general to supply them at a flat price during the war—rather than on commission. Although this arrangement was abrogated after only one year, the Alexanders apparently made a very good thing of it while it lasted.[114] After the French purchasing returned to the normal commission arrangement in 1757, the Alexander firm continued to interest itself in ventures to the Chesapeake, with or without the cognizance of the united farms we do not know. Such activity seems to have continued through the 1760's.[115]

In the decade or so preceding the American Revolution, when the British-Chesapeake tobacco trade was at its height, France (minus Dunkirk) took only 23 percent of the total British tobacco exports and 34 percent of Scottish exports. Those figures, however, do not measure the ultimate importance of the French market in the growth of the trade. In this chapter, we have examined in some detail the special cases of Whitehaven and the Clyde ports. In both places, the French market accounted for something over 50 percent of the whole during the crucial decade of the 1740's when the trade in those places experienced its most rapid growth. At first the growth at Whitehaven was even more sensational than that at Glasgow; but the Clyde won out in the end. There are many reasons for this. In the 1740's, Whitehaven merchants could borrow larger sums from Sir James Lowther than Glasgow merchants could get on overdrafts from the Edinburgh banks (£1,000 being the normal maximum at the Royal Bank). The shoe was however on the other foot after the foundation of the tobacco merchants' own two banks at Glasgow, about 1750. The death of the elder Sir James Lowther of Whitehaven in 1755 and of his agent John Spedding in 1758 were also serious blows to the Cumberland port for there is no indication that their successors—Sir James Lowther of Lowther and John Robinson—ever equally understood the Whitehaven tobacco trade and its financial needs. Thus, Glasgow not only retained the French business and saw it increase, but also saw its general tobacco trade increase even more rapidly so that the French market was relatively less important to it in 1766–75 than it had been in 1747–51. By contrast, when Whitehaven lost most of its French market after the double failures of George FitzGerald (1759) and Peter How (1763), its tobacco trade received a blow from which it never fully recovered. If the full effects of French demand were geographically limited, they were nonetheless of extreme importance in the areas of maximum impact.

CHAPTER 24

The Last Great Struggle for the French Agency in Great Britain, 1766–75

For the greater part of its existence, the history of the French tobacco agency in Britain is a rather shadowy affair. No business records have survived of Guiguer, Cavalier, Guillemau, Bance, the Van Necks, or the FitzGeralds. When, however, we come to the last decade, 1766–75, our documentation suddenly becomes remarkably full. From the surviving correspondence of many of the principals involved, we are not only able to reconstruct in some detail the fight for the agency in this hectic decade, but are able to place those happenings in the broader context of French court history. For, ultimately, the struggle for the London tobacco agency was but a reverberation at the periphery of struggles for power and influence at Versailles and Paris.

The most important person in the French government in the 1760's was the duke of Choiseul, minister of foreign affairs, 1758–61, 1766–70, minister of war, 1761–70, minister of the navy, 1761–66. Married to the fabulously wealthy granddaughter of Antoine Crozat, closely supported by Madame de Pompadour, he dominated court, society, and government alike. The great drama at the French court in the years following the death of Pompadour in 1764 was the rise and triumph of an anti-Choiseul faction centered around the dukes of Richelieu and Aiguillon and the chancellor Maupeou. Choiseul played into the hands of his enemies by refusing to accept the rise of Madame du Barry and by advocating a strong pro-Spanish, anti-British war policy in 1770 which French finances could not support. Events moved rapidly once the king's relationship with du Barry was established in 1768: Maupeou became chancellor in September 1768; du Barry was formally presented at court in April 1769; in December of that year, the abbé Terray, a creature of Maupeou, and close to du Barry, was made controller-general; one year later, in December 1770, the duke of Choiseul was dismissed and exiled from court.[1]

Tremors from these upheavals in the great world were of course felt in the world of Paris finance. When Terray arrived at the controller-generalship, the functions of court banker were divided between Magon de la Balue, of the great St. Malo financial family,[2] and the newly recalled Jean-Joseph de la Borde,[3] an obscure trader from Bayonne who had risen to the top of the Paris financial community through the patronage of the duke of Choiseul. Both had been farmers-general, though La Borde retired permanently from the company in 1768. French government finances were in desperate straits at the beginning of the Terray's administration; the disorder of heavy short-term indebtedness left behind by the Seven Years' War had not been cleaned up.[4] To keep the government going, the royal bankers, La Borde and Magon, used Samuel Bernard's old desperate technique of borrowing by selling foreign bills of exchange. The job of keeping such bills in circulation fell upon the French financial agents abroad, Horneca, Hogguer & Co. at Amsterdam and the Hon. Thomas Walpole in London. Similar work, it will be remembered, had been done in the 1750's, when Paris de Montmartel was royal banker, by Jean Testas & Co. at Amsterdam and George Fitz-Gerald at London. When both were ruined in December 1759 by the Beaujon, Goossens & Co. suspension, the whole Testas business was taken over immediately by Horneca (Horneca, Hogguer & Co. after 1762), while Walpole succeeded to FitzGerald's role either then or after his split with Van Neck in 1765.[5]

Early in 1770, the duke of Choiseul, irked by the independent line being taken by the abbé Terray, decided to use his protégé La Borde to get rid of the controller-general. As minister of war, he reported that there would be no cash to pay the troops in March 1770 unless further advances were forthcoming from La Borde. At his suggestion, we are told, La Borde refused to make such advances except on the most onerous terms. Realizing where the trouble originated, Terray fought back: unknown to anyone except the chancellor Maupeou, he persuaded the king to consent to two emergency *arrêts* on 18 February 1770 suspending the payment of the *billets* of the united farms and the *rescriptions* of the receivers-general. Choiseul, realizing that he had miscalculated, had La Borde come forward and announce that he had found the needed sums and that it would not be necessary to issue the orders of suspension. The controller-general, however, told La Borde that his terms were too dear and dismissed him as royal banker. When the *arrêts* were published, there was great fear that it might be 1759 again. There were serious doubts abroad about the credit of Magon de la Balue, now the sole remaining court banker, whose failure would have brought down Horneca in Amsterdam and Walpole in London—just as in 1759. Those gentlemen rushed to Paris to point out the urgency of the situation. Though Terray suspected that Magon, like La Borde before, was feigning financial difficulties only to embarrass him, the king's council was sufficiently impressed to agree to an emergency transfer of four million *l.t.* from the Indies Company, in order to support Magon, Horneca and Walpole, and French state credit abroad. Nevertheless, within a few months, Magon de la Balue had yielded his post as court banker to Nicolas Beaujon, now banker to Madame du Barry.[6]

All this was, as we shall see below, obviously relevant to Thomas Walpole's career as French tobacco agent in London. Equally relevant were changes of power within the company of the United General Farms. Its principal figures were hostile to the abbé Terray during his first few months at the controller-generalship, 1769-70. The disgrace of the duke of Choiseul at the end of 1770 meant therefore that the company had miscalculated and would have to adjust its policies and leadership to the new locus of power within the state. This readjustment took the form of the advancement to the front of the company of the hitherto obscure Jacques Paulze, husband of a niece of the abbé Terray. Paulze is remembered today only as the father-in-law of Lavoisier (who became an adjunct farmer-general in 1768); they were to die together on the same scaffold in 1794. Paulze became a full farmer-general only in 1768.[7] As a junior member of the company, he was assigned only to the more routine committees. In April 1771, however, shortly after the disgrace of Choiseul, he was moved to the head of the most important committees—including the tobacco purchasing committee. At the same time, to make room for Paulze, Magon de la Balue, the disgraced court banker, was dropped from the tobacco purchasing committee (of which he had been the formal "head" during 1763-68). A very apparent transfer of power had taken place within the United General Farms.[8] (La Borde had already withdrawn from the company in 1768.)

These profound changes in the structure of power and influence in France inevitably had their impact upon the French tobacco agency in London. Firms hitherto far outside the charmed circle now saw their opportunity to strike for that coveted prize. The most successful of the new contenders were the Herries, a Scottish family with ramifications in London, Rotterdam, Ostend, throughout the Mediterranean, and—not the least—in Paris.

Robert Herries (I) of Halldykes, Dumfriesshire, a petty Scottish laird (d. 1728) had four sons: the eldest of these, William (ca. 1697-1777) inherited Halldykes and other property, but dissipated his inheritance.[9] The younger brothers, Robert (ca. 1700-1791), John (1721-59), and Charles became merchants. The most important of these was Robert: "He was a handsome young man, of a good family in Annandale, who had not succeeded in business at Dumfries, and had been sent over [to Rotterdam] by ... Provost Bell, of that town, as their agent and factor—as at that time they dealt pretty deep in the tobacco trade. He had immediately assimilated to the manners of the Dutch and was much respected among them."[10] Robert Herries (II) prospered in the 1730's and 1740's as a factor for Whitehaven and Scottish merchants at Rotterdam where most of the Netherlands tobacco transit trade was becoming centered. In 1751, when the lands of his extravagant older brother William were sold at auction to pay his debts, Robert of Rotterdam purchased Halldykes and retired there, though he continued to take an interest in some commercial ventures.[11]

The extravagant oldest brother, William, late of Halldykes, had three sons, Robert (III), Charles, and William. Deprived by their father's mismanagement of any expectation of inheritance, all three became merchants. Robert, the eldest (with whom we are principally concerned), was trained in his uncle Robert's house in Rotterdam. When the elder Robert retired to

Halldykes in 1751, young Robert continued the business there in partnership with his uncle John. This did not prove mutually satisfactory and in 1754 young Robert withdrew to set up his own business at Barcelona, upon the advice and with the assistance of Hope & Co., the great Scottish mercantile and banking house at Amsterdam. He prospered at Barcelona and acquired interests in houses at Montpellier and Valencia—Honorius Dalliot & Co.—and elsewhere.[12] (At one time he was contractor for farming the papal forests!) [13] A good part of the business of his Barcelona firm consisted in shipping spirits to the Channel Islands and the Isle of Man where they were ultimately resold to the smugglers who ran them into England, Scotland, and Ireland.[14] His Barcelona and Valencia houses, in years of shortages, also did a big business importing wheat. This brought them into correspondence with wheat exporting firms in the middle colonies of North America and the Chesapeake—including the very important house of Willing & Morris of Philadelphia.[15]

In the 1760's, the history of the Herries was to become closely intertwined with that of another Scottish family, the Coutts. John Coutts, originally from Montrose, had established a mercantile and banking business at Edinburgh about 1730. It prospered and he became provost of Edinburgh, 1742-44, and joined William Alexander on the directorate of the Royal Bank of Scotland. When he died in 1750, his firm was carried on by his four sons, Patrick, John, James, and Thomas. In 1752, Patrick (the eldest) and Thomas (the youngest) established a branch house at Jeffreys Square, St. Mary Axe, London, leaving John and James to manage the Edinburgh end. However, in 1755, James Coutts married the niece and heiress of George Campbell, proprietor of the long established Campbell or Middleton bank in the Strand, which we have met earlier as the London correspondents of John Law and Alexander Alexander of Paris. At the time of his marriage James Coutts left his family's Edinburgh bank and became a partner in George Campbell's "West End" bank. When Campbell died in 1760, James Coutts took his brother Thomas out of the family's Jeffreys Square branch and made him a partner in the Strand bank (which has survived to this day as Coutts & Co.). This left the brother John Coutts alone in charge of the family's old Edinburgh firm and Patrick in charge of the City branch. A crisis ensued in 1761 when John Coutts died and Patrick went insane. Neither James nor Thomas Coutts was prepared to leave the prosperous Strand bank, but wanted to continue their old family houses in Edinburgh and London (Jeffreys Square) as provision for some needy relatives. New partners were required. These were found for the Edinburgh end in Sir William Forbes, a landless baronet, son of an Edinburgh barrister, and James Hunter (later Sir James Hunter Blair, Bart.), son of a merchant of Ayr, then both clerks in the Edinburgh counting-house. At the same time— 1762—a senior managing partner at London was added in the person of Robert Herries of Barcelona; he was known to the brothers from his Rotterdam days when the late John Coutts had been operating a smuggling business from there. The remaining partners were the Coutts uncles William Cochrane and John Stephens, who were pensioned off in 1766 and 1771 respectively. Though the partners were the same, the London house (Jeffreys Square) used the style Herries, Cochrane & Co. (Herries & Co. after 1766), while the Edinburgh house was known as John Coutts & Co., later (1773) Sir William Forbes, James Hunter & Co. Separate books were kept. The Edinburgh firm was primarily a bank, while the London sister was more of a mercantile house.

When he took over the management of the former Coutts firm in Jeffreys Square in 1762, Robert Herries agreed to give up his interest in his houses at Montpellier and Valencia while retaining his interest in that at Barcelona.[16] About 1768, the partners in the Barcelona firm of Robert Herries & Co. were the brothers, Robert, Charles and William Herries, plus Thomas Cleghorn (originally a clerk in the house) and David Steuart (trained at Coutts's in Edinburgh).[17] At the same time, the partners in the Valencia house styled Honorius Dalliot & Co. were Dalliot, Charles Herries and David Boswell, son of Lord Auchinleck and brother of James Boswell.[18] To this spectrum of interests,[19] Robert Herries (III) added a "West End" bank in 1772. Utilizing his friendship with Hope & Co. of Amsterdam and their European-wide circle of correspondence, Herries in 1769 devised a "circular exchange note" or traveler's check which could be cashed at any one of 78 commercial centers on the continent from Moscow to Lisbon. Since this facility was designed for the wealthier sort of English traveler on the continent, the Jeffreys Square location was inconvenient. As the Coutts brothers were not interested in the idea, Herries felt no compunctions about opening his own West End house in St. James's Street, the London Exchange Banking Company. The new bank, opened on 1 January 1772, was headed and managed by his old, retired uncle, Robert Herries of Halldykes, who came up to London for this purpose. The partners were Robert Herries the nephew (Sir Robert Herries from 1774), his brothers Charles and William Herries (who returned from Barcelona about this time), his aforementioned uncle Robert Herries of Halldykes, his partners Forbes and Hunter, his wife's brother, George Henderson, her cousin Sir William Maxwell of Springkell, Bart. and his own Dumfriesshire friend, the very wealthy William Johnstone Pulteney. In October 1770, he had also arranged to have a quarter interest in the City or Jeffreys Square house made over to his brothers Charles and William and his brother-in-law George Henderson. The last links with the Coutts were broken as of 1 January 1773.

Herries' City and West End houses were always quite distinct. After Cochrane withdrew, the Jeffreys Square firm appears in the directories as Herries & Co., merchants, subsequently Sir Robert Herries & Co. (from 1774) and Charles Herries & Co. (from 1784); it disappeared from the directories about 1801. The St. James's Street house dropped the style London Exchange Banking Co. after a few years and appeared in the directories as Robert Herries [Senior] & Co., bankers, subsequently Sir Robert Herries & Co. (from ca. 1780), and, from about 1799, as Herries Farquhar & Co. (In 1893, it was absorbed into Lloyds Bank, Ltd., but still does business in St. James's Street as the "Herries, Farquhar branch" of that great company.)[20]

With all his manifold interests, it is not surprising that Robert Herries, the nephew, should sooner or later dream of taking over the French tobacco agency in Britain. He himself had started out in life in his uncle's tobacco house in Rotterdam; his partner James Hunter was the son of a tobacco merchant at Ayr who sold to the French; the Coutts firm in Edinburgh and Jeffreys Square, London, had a long association with the tobacco trade.[21] Between 1754 and 1770, Herries had occasion to make numerous coach trips across France as business took him to and from his Barcelona house. On these long trips, he made the acquaintance of a number of useful Frenchmen, including in 1754 the Swiss banker at Lyons, Jean-Robert Tronchin, Voltaire's financier, whom the controller-general Bertin was in 1762 to make the first foreign or Protestant farmer-general of the century. Through Tronchin, Herries became friendly with many other farmers-general.[22] By the late 1760's, circumstances were more than propitious for a siege of the agency.

Upon the failure of George FitzGerald in 1759, it will be remembered, the primary French tobacco commission in Britain had passed exclusively into the hands of the London firm of Sir Joshua Van Neck, the Hon. Thomas Walpole and Daniel Josias Olivier. This was a reversal of a thirty years' policy of the farmers-general of dividing the primary commission among at least two competing London houses. Once the war was over, it was bound to occur to many that the exclusive contract might be too much of a good thing for Van Neck & Co. The Grenville ministry was reported anxious that they lose it because of their traditional attachment to the Newcastle Whigs. In the spring of 1765, it was rumored in well-informed quarters that Van Necks had in fact lost the contract. That they did not seems due both to the fall of Grenville that year and to Thomas Walpole's cousinhood with Horace Walpole and his older brothers, who were in turn cousins of the Conway brothers.[23] Under the Grenville ministry (1763–65), Francis Seymour Conway, earl of Hertford, was British ambassador in Paris; under the succeeding Rockingham and Chatham ministries (1765–68), his younger brother Henry Seymour Conway was secretary of state.

The Van Necks' "victory" of 1765 was to prove only a reprieve. At the end of that year, Thomas Walpole withdrew from the firm which continued without him. Shortly afterwards, he set up a new firm of his own in partnership with Robert Ellison.[24] An obscure scuffle then ensued, but when the dust cleared, Thomas Walpole had walked off with the French contract. In May 1767, his brother Robert wrote him from Spain (where he was secretary to the embassy) congratulating him on his victory over Sir Joshua.[25] Thomas Walpole at this point was at the height of his career. As a politician, he had successfully translated himself from the Rockingham to the Chatham camp and was very close to that great man at the beginning of his ministry (1766–68). (Through his cousins, the sons of the great Robert Walpole, he was, we have seen, also connected to General Henry Seymour Conway, secretary of state, in 1765–68.) In 1769, Walpole, in collaboration with Samuel Wharton, Benjamin Franklin and many leading Philadelphia merchants, promoted the Grand Ohio or Vandalia Company (also called the "Walpole Company") which obtained a large land grant on the Ohio from the government. Its London shareholders included Lord Camden, George Grenville and his brother Lord Temple, General Conway and his brother Lord Hertford, as well as the influential secretary to the Treasury, Thomas Bradshaw, and his successor John Robinson.[26] In Paris, which Thomas Walpole visited frequently from 1765 onward, he, like his cousin Horace, moved easily in the circle about Madame du Deffand and made a good impression upon the duke and duchess of Choiseul.[27] As early as 1764, he was on friendly terms with the important farmer-general Roslin, a member of the tobacco purchasing committee. When in Paris, he sometimes stayed with La Borde with whom he had the most extensive business dealings.[28]

Yet, Thomas Walpole had his enemies. One of these was a London "Spanish" merchant named George Bryan. Bryan had for many years been employed as a subagent in London to buy tobacco for the French. George FitzGerald's account at the Bank of England in the 1740's is filled with payments to Bryan.[29] This arrangement persisted during the years 1760–66, when Van Neck & Co. had the exclusive primary buying commission. However, when Thomas Walpole took over the contract (probably ca. January 1767), he dropped Bryan. That gentleman, however, had his own connections in Paris and immediately set to work to see if he could not supplant Walpole. In July 1767, he approached James Hunter, who was managing the Jeffreys Square counting house of Herries & Co. while Robert Herries was on a trip to Scotland, and inquired whether "John Coutts & Co." (the Edinburgh sister house of Herries & Co.) would be interested in handling tobacco purchases in Scotland if he, Bryan, got the French contract. Hunter, Forbes, and Herries were all most interested but Bryan could do nothing at the time.[30] By the next January, however, Bryan had supplied the French monopoly with detailed accounts of the Alexanders' purchases for them in Scotland showing that Walpole had charged the monopoly £12,000–13,000 sterling more than the prices actually paid by the Alexanders. This information had been obtained for Bryan by Herries, Forbes, and Hunter through their Glasgow correspondents, Colin Dunlop & Sons. (Besides being a great tobacco merchant, Provost Colin Dunlop was a founding partner in the "Ship Bank," Dunlop, Houstoun & Co., a Glasgow rival of the Cochrane, Murdoch bank run by the Alexanders' Glasgow connections.) The farmers-general were suitably incensed and a party of them wanted to take the contract away from Thomas Walpole.

Between January and March 1768, there was a great flurry of activity as opposing forces scrambled for the loose contract. Thomas Walpole rushed to Paris and offered to cease buying on commission and contract instead to supply the French at a fixed price. George Bryan wanted to bid for such a contract too, but Herries warned him that Walpole and the Alexanders would drive the contract price too low in a competition, in order to keep the business, counting on their ability to force the market down once they had a long term contract in hand and ready cash.[31] Bryan suspected that Walpole "notwithstanding all that has happen'd, will still get in again by means of the Kings Banker [La Borde] with whom he is engaged in vast sc[h]emes of circulation for national purposes—But whenever the present Minister [Choiseul] goes out the Banker must follow and then his [Bryan's] friends will be watchful for him."[32] But the farmers-general deceived even the perceptive Bryan. Unable to make up their minds between him and Walpole, they secretly decided to employ Hope & Co., the great Amsterdam Scots house, as their principal agents for the year 1768. The London end was handled by Gurnell, Hoare & Harman, correspondents of the court banker La Borde and a most prestigious Quaker house. Late in January, unusual people acting for Hopes started buying tobacco "for the French" in Bristol, Glasgow, Hamburg, and Holland. Speculators in league with the Alexanders were unjustifiably suspected. When the deception was revealed in March, the contenders Bryan and Walpole felt rather silly, but, realizing that the employment of the Hopes was just a stop-gap, both decided to continue their efforts.[33]

Other strange things happened in the summer of 1768. At Glasgow, Simson, Baird & Co. were buying tobacco as the acknowledged local representatives of Hope & Co., the monopoly's primary agent. In July, however, George Oswald & Co., big tobacco merchants, received instructions via Alexanders in Edinburgh, allegedly from John Pott, a wealthy Rotterdam merchant with whom they had not hitherto dealt, instructing them to buy about a thousand hogsheads of tobacco for him. Simultaneously, John Liotard and Giles Godin, Italian and Spanish merchants of London, wrote authorizing Oswalds to draw on them for the tobacco purchased on Pott's account; Alexanders would help dispose of the London bills in Edinburgh (but without endorsing them) if Oswalds had any difficulties selling them in Glasgow. Oswalds wondered whether this was just a scheme to supply Alexanders (whose credit was shaky) with needed London exchange or whether Sir Joshua Van Neck stood behind the "front man" Pott and was trying to force his way back into the French contract. In any event, Oswalds thought themselves adequately covered and purchased and shipped 850 hogsheads of tobacco to "Pott" before the unknown London speculators tired of the affair in September, cancelled the commission, and instructed them to dispose of the remaining purchased but unshipped tobacco as best they could.[34] In France, this activity was interpreted as an attempt by someone to corner the market and dictate terms to the monopoly; Herries heard that the farmers-general were determined to buy none of the Oswald purchase under any circumstances.[35]

Meanwhile, Robert Herries had from March onward become increasingly interested in the possibility of doing something himself in the French tobacco business. As Bryan would not take him in as an equal, he would have to proceed on his own. If the dropping of Walpole meant the dropping of Alexanders, he wondered if his own Edinburgh house ("John Coutts & Co.") might not get the "inspectorship" or chief agency in Scotland under Hopes. His own affairs required him to be in Barcelona in August 1768. It would be very easy to travel out via Amsterdam and Paris.[36] At Amsterdam, he learned that Hopes' position was tenuous and that they did not expect to be continued in the tobacco contract beyond that year 1768; Herries had overestimated their services to and influence upon the French ministry; they were totally dependent on La Borde's good will. Herries decided nevertheless to persevere in his own behalf without their assistance.[37] At Paris, his old friend, the farmer-general Tronchin, was mildly encouraging but explained that nothing would be decided till after the first of October when the new lease of the united farms started. In the meanwhile, Herries arranged for Tronchin "to pave the way" till his return, devising "a method to interest him heartily in our Success without offending his delicacy." He also planned to use the Dutch and Danish ministers at Paris—he was Danish consul in Barcelona—and asked his Edinburgh partners to "get me any letters to Lord Rochford [ambassador at Paris, 1766–68], As well as from David Hume [secretary to the embassy, 1765–66] to some of his female Acquaintances."[38] At Barcelona, Herries discovered that Juan de Larra(r)d, his partner in a business at Reus (near Tarragona), knew La Borde well: they both came from the same district, near Bayonne. He thus left Barcelona in October 1768 with letters from Larrard to La Borde, to a "lady of quality" at court related to Larrard, and to other important people in Paris.[39]

After business stops at Montpellier and Lyons, Herries returned to Paris on 1 November 1768 to find himself none too early. Not only was Thomas Walpole busy there before him, but the letters to La Borde had become useless inasmuch as that great financier had in October given up his places as farmer-general and (temporarily) as royal banker. This meant that Hopes of Amsterdam, La Borde's great friends, would not be continued and that there was no point in Herries' trying to work through them.[40] Herries decided to strike out on his own, ignoring Bryan who was also in Paris, but working through Tronchin (who unfortunately was not on the tobacco purchasing committee) and other friends in Paris. If he could not get the whole British contract, he hoped to be able to get the Scottish part separate from the rest; he thought that this would be more valuable than the English because it would not involve his company in performing miscellaneous credit services in London for the French government and company. He was guardedly optimistic, but had to concede failure within a few weeks. The reorganization of the united farms at the start of the new lease in October had strengthened the hands of those in the company friendly to Walpole. Even so, this was not enough and Walpole had to use court influence. However, Herries learned that some of the farmers-general were "much piqued at Mr Walpole for endeavoring to force himself on them by Court Interest—I am persuaded this was his last Resource—I think it very probable it may succeed with him, yet my friends are desirous that I should go on as if I knew nothing of the matter and by this means lay the foundation at least of Success another time, for he will not they think remain long their Agent."[41] The contract was in fact restored to Thomas Walpole (and his allies the Alexanders) in November. On 28 November, his brother, Lord Walpole, wrote from Wolterton welcoming Thomas back to London, hoping that his Paris tobacco mission was successful.[42] Walpole in fact regained the contract, but only, as Herries explained to his partners, by undertaking to perform financial services for the French (circulating the royal banker's international bills) which Herries would not have his own house touch. Herries was optimistic; he was also prescient.[43]

During the ensuing year 1769 and the first half of 1770, all mention of tobacco disappears from the correspondence of Robert Herries with his partners—but their eyes were open. (James Hunter, one of the partners, made a trip to Paris in June 1769.)[44] Essentially, they were waiting for Thomas Walpole's overcommitments to bring him down. For these same months, a private letterbook of Thomas Walpole has survived. His principal confidential correspondent in Paris at the time was the court banker and farmer-general, Magon de la Balue, with whom he discussed both financial transactions and the management of his tobacco agency. The confusions of 1768 made tobacco buying in 1769 very difficult. During the former year, Hope & Co. had been authorized to go as high as 3d. per lb. in their British purchases, a high price for peace time. Realizing that their tobacco contract would not be renewed, Hope & Co. made no effort to lower prices but rather sought to buy as much as they could at the upper price limit, maximizing their own commission. Their Glasgow representatives, Simson, Baird & Co., not only bought all they could at 3d. but even made contracts at that price for whole shiploads not yet arrived. Thus when Walpole and the Alexanders resumed buying in January 1769, they found very little tobacco on hand and much of that arriving already sold to Simson, Baird, or so it was pretended. To make matters even more difficult, Walpole was committed to pay no more than 2d.3/4 per lb. Thus, it was May before he could ship his first 208 hogsheads to France—one shipload. He wrote frequently to Magon, explaining the character of the tobacco trade, and assuring him that he would be able to make great purchases in the fall, and even force the price down to

$2d.½$ per lb., once he had brought to heel the by then oversupplied tobacco merchants. The great difficulty to efficient buying, he explained, was the nervousness of some farmers-general who wanted to see all the purchases scheduled for a given year made in the first few months for complete security. As it was, they bought more than a year ahead. Walpole must have been able to give the farmers-general some satisfaction, for he mentions tobacco much less in his letters of the latter part of 1769.[45]

From July 1769 onwards, Walpole's correspondence with Magon de la Balue was concerned almost entirely with their growing financial imbroglio. To purchase Portuguese gold or to raise short term funds, Magon de la Balue, as court banker, had worked out an arrangement with Walpole & Ellison whereby he, Magon, drew bills on them at 60 or 90 or 120 days. These bills were sent to Magon's other correspondent in London, Jonas (Josias?) Cottin & Son; upon acceptance by Walpole & Ellison, Cottins would have the bills discounted at the Bank of England, preferably, and remit the proceeds to Magon. When the bills became due, Walpole & Ellison obtained funds to meet them by drawing bills on Magon and selling them in London.[46] This was an expensive way of borrowing but Magon had no choice. During the spring and summer of 1769, the affairs of the French Indies Company were also in great disorder, with some shareholders, inspired in part by the Swiss banker Jacques Necker, wanting to continue the company, even though this meant further heavy borrowing, while others, led by another Swiss banker, Isaac Panchaud (recently moved from London to Paris) wanting to wind up the company's Asian trade and convert it into a discount bank. The controller-general Maynon d'Invau turned some accounts of the company over to the abbé Morellet who prepared a memoir, read to the shareholders on 20 July, calling for the suppression of the company; despite the flag-waving reply of Necker, the *arrêt* suspending the trading privileges of the Indies Company was signed on 13 August 1769. The winding up of the company took another generation.[47] Although Maynon d'Invau had decided by July 1769 to get the Indies Company out of the Indian trade, he was faced with the immediate problem of meeting its pressing obligations of the next few months until the funds were in hand from its autumn sales. This short term advance he asked Magon de la Balue to provide; Magon could only meet it by drawing on Walpole & Ellison in London, to whom he wrote asking for an additional £167,000 credit for funds needed by the Indies Company by early September. Walpole & Ellison were at first doubtful that they could provide the full sum, but Cottin persuaded the Bank of England to discount up to £250,000 of Walpole & Ellison's paper for this operation, in bills with not more than 90 days to run. Walpole & Ellison were covered both by a letter of authorization from the controller-general to Magon de la Balue and by *billets* of the Indies Company, deposited with Magon, payable from the first receipts of the company's fall sales.[48] Nevertheless, Thomas Walpole would have preferred also being able to draw upon a strong Amsterdam house. By drawing on Amsterdam as well as on Paris, he could avoid depressing the London rate on Paris (and thereby calling attention to the operations of his house). He tried unsuccessfully to induce the important Amsterdam firm of George Clifford & Co. to come in, but they held back, fearful of another 1720.[49]

All went well until 21 December 1769 when Maynon d'Invau, under attack from Maupeou and in despair at the bankruptcy of the state, resigned as controller-general and was replaced the next day by the more ruthless abbé Terray. For a short time, the Paris money market in panic lost all confidence in the government's ability or determination to satisfy its obligations. With a complete suspension of trading in state paper, Magon de la Balue found inconvertible all the *billets* of the Indies Company and other government "effects" in his vaults and had to write Walpole & Ellison that he no longer knew whether he would be able to meet their bills on him about to fall due:

```
3,276,927  l.t.  2s.  1d.   for species purchases
2,592,599  l.t.  9s.  8d.   for Indies Company
  297,544  l.t.  9s.  2d.   for other operations

6,167,071  l.t.       11d.  total (ca. £246,683 stg.)
```

Almost the entire capital of Walpole & Ellison was involved in this outstanding paper. Bills drawn by them on Magon and not paid would of course come back to them in London for settlement.[50] There was no hope of looking to Amsterdam for help for Magon's correspondents there, Horneca, Hogguer & Co., were more heavily compromised than Walpole & Ellison. In fact, Magon wanted the latter to send £75,000 sterling worth of gold to Hornecas in Amsterdam for their relief and for reimbursement to draw long bills on five houses in Italy; Walpole refused.[51] Instead, he sent Ellison over to Paris post haste with a large amount of Portuguese gold consigned for sale to Nogué, La Borde's brother-in-law. With the proceeds of this sale, Ellison had enough cash to meet all of his firm's bills on Magon through January if the royal banker could not meet them himself. At the same time, Walpole appealed for support to the temporarily retired La Borde and, through the count du Châtelet-Lomont, the French ambassador in London, to the duke of Choiseul. Also at this time, Magon was instructed that, if he could not meet the bills drawn on him, he should turn over to Ellison the 2.6 million in *billets* of the Indies Company which had been deposited with him as security for the bill operation undertaken by Walpole & Ellison for that company. Lest Magon balk at this, Walpole warned him that there were still over £60,000 sterling (about 1.5 million *l.t.*) outstanding in bills of exchange drawn by him on Walpole & Ellison. If he did not cooperate with Ellison in meeting their bills on him, they would of course be obliged to refuse his bills on them.[52] We do not know the precise details of what next ensued but by 12 January 1770, the crisis had passed. Confidence had apparently been temporarily restored on the Paris money market and Ellison had, one way or another, seen to it that all his firm's bills on Magon were met.

Although the credit of Walpole & Ellison had survived the crisis of December 1769 intact, that of Magon de la Balue and Horneca had not. On 12 January 1770, Walpole wrote to Magon forbidding him or Horneca, Hogguer & Co. in Amsterdam to draw any more bills on Walpole & Ellison.[53] It would appear that it was at this point that there occurred the events described by Coquereau. With French revenues committed a year in advance and with Magon de la Balue unable to make any further substantial advances, La Borde, who had retired in 1768, was asked to return and share the responsibilities of court banker. He agreed only on condition that he could withdraw at any time. (La Borde, it appears, raised money at this juncture by the usual foreign bill operations with Hopes of Amsterdam and Gurnell, Hoare & Harmans of London; the last named extended the "chain" by selling bills on Marseilles and other Mediterranean centers; they also bought Portuguese gold in London for La Borde: these were all commissions just refused by Walpole.) In February, allegedly at the suggestion of his patron Choiseul, La Borde refused further advances except on the most onerous terms. Terray responded swiftly, secretly and brusquely by the *arrêts* of 18 February 1770 suspending payment of the *billets* of the united farms and the *rescriptions* of the receivers-general. La Borde was dismissed and a new crisis of confidence ensued. It was rumored in foreign money markets that other forms of government paper would also be dishonored and the failure of Magon was believed imminent. Walpole rushed from London and Horneca from Amsterdam to plead with the French government the necessity of sustaining Magon. Magon actually closed one afternoon but that same evening, Choiseul carried the council against Terray and four million of the Indies Company's funds were transferred to Magon, the proceeds of a lottery-loan authorized on 9 February. (This was probably reimbursement for advances previously made by Magon to the Indies Company.) This enabled Magon to reopen and the crisis passed.[54]

Coquereau's story is in part supported by a letter from Madame du Deffand to Horace Walpole on 3 March 1770. The *arrêts* of 18 February were not published until the twenty-first, on the afternoon of which day, midst great confusion, Magon closed his doors. Choiseul, according to Madame du Deffand, was informed at dinner and went immediately to the controller-general and made him aware of the danger to the state. They immediately had three million *l.t.* sent to Magon who reopened the next morning and the crisis passed. According to Madame du Deffand, "Half the public believe that the Controller made a great mess of things and showed his ignorance and bad faith; others say that he was forced to it by the intrigues of M. de Choiseul, who, in communication with La Borde and La Balue, made them refuse to make the loan for the year, at least not without an exorbitant increase in interest." Madame du Deffand admitted that she did not know all the details, but—except for her omission of the council meeting—her account is in substantial agreement with that of Coquereau.

During the crisis, Madame du Deffand reported, Robert Walpole, the British minister in Paris, "went about distracted because his brother [Thomas] was concerned for sixteen million" *l.t.* By 3 March, however, he assured the good lady that all was well, as the Paris papers also claimed.[55] The private letter book of Thomas Walpole is blank for the month of February 1770, in all probability because he was in Paris himself during the height of the crisis. When the confidential letters resume in March, all is serene but the alienated Magon has disappeared as correspondent. While maintaining a correct correspondence between his firm and Magon, acting for the tobacco committee, Walpole had begun a new private correspondence with the farmer-general Douet concerning those same tobacco purchases. There are no further letters on financial matters, Walpole having ceased his great bill-circulating operations for the French court.[56]

In March 1770, Madame du Deffand reported that the duke of Choiseul was "extrêmement content de votre cousin et de son frère," i.e. Robert and Thomas Walpole.[57] That might have been some satisfaction to Walpole & Ellison were it not obvious to all that their firm was, along with La Borde and Magon, hopelessly implicated in the party of the duke of Choiseul whose star was in decline. It was evident to many that once Choiseul fell, Walpole could not long thereafter hold onto the tobacco buying contract; the sharks began to gather. Walpole's correspondence with Douet during 1770 reveals a business that is not going well.

Thomas Walpole subsequently admitted that he had entered into the great bill operations with Magon de la Balue in 1769 principally "because Monsieur de la Balue was the master of the business of the farm and would control it entirely in my favor."[58] Once Magon's influence began to slip in 1770, it became evident that there were within the company of the united farms individual farmers-general who were not sympathetic to Walpole. (One of these was Tronchin, the old and close friend of Herries.) To embarrass Walpole, such individuals leaked to Herries, and presumably to others, details of Walpole's dealing with the company. False rumors circulated with true. Thus, when Walpole in 1770 promised the farmers-general that he would buy tobacco for them in London for 2*d*.3/4 per lb., word was "leaked" in London that he had *contracted* to supply a large quantity at that price. Believing him to be desperate to buy, the London tobacco merchants held out for a higher price. To break the ring, Thomas Walpole in March had to go to 2*d*.7/8 to get 6,000 hogsheads, embarrassing him with the company. Rumors were then circulated that he was once more charging the company more than he paid in Britain, and he felt obliged to prove his innocence. It was also reported in Glasgow that Hope & Co. of Amsterdam were to be given a new commission to buy for the farmers-general in Scotland. When George Oswald & Co. bought a thousand hogsheads for an unknown account, as they had in 1768, it was assumed that they were acting for Hopes or someone else buying for the French. Walpole in turn demanded proofs of innocence from the monopoly. Yet, by persuading the company not to rush its purchases and by out-bluffing the London merchants who thought (correctly) that the company's stocks were low, Walpole eventually regained control of the market. By May 1770, he was able to purchase another 9,000 hogsheads at 2d.3/4 (compared to the 2d.7/8 paid in March).[59] Over the summer, he finally forced the price down to 2d.5/8 as he purchased 6,000 hogsheads more. He was quite satisfied with his own performance and had hopes of pushing the price down further in 1771 provided that the difficulties between Britain and Spain did not develop into war.[60] Yet, even while he seemed to be succeeding, the foundations of his "interest" in Paris were crumbling.

After his failure to get the French commission in 1768, Robert Herries remained very quiet. There are no references at all to the agency in his correspondence with his Edinburgh partners Sir William Forbes and James Hunter in 1769 and early 1770. His hopes began to revive only toward the end of the latter year. "I have been thinking," he wrote Hunter in August, "That as it is in the month of Oct: that the Farmers Gen! renew their annual Tobacco orders, it might not perhaps be amiss if I would make a Short trip to Paris for a week or two about that time to see what fruit we may really expect from the hopes M: T[ronchin] has from time to time given us."[61] When Herries arrived in Paris towards the end of October, on his way again to Barcelona, he found matters so encouraging that he immediately wrote in great secrecy to Forbes and Hunter for detailed information, including the size of the current tobacco crop in relation to that of the previous seven years, tobacco on hand in Glasgow, prices, and credit terms.[62] When Herries got back to Paris from Barcelona in January 1771, the great and long expected revolution had taken place: in December the duke of Choiseul had been dismissed as minister and banished from court. Anything was now possible and Herries' friends encouraged him to expect "one of the best Commissions that any Trade can afford." He no longer had to worry about George Bryan who, he learned, had been bought off by Walpole a year or two before for a pension of 20,000 l.t. annually.[63]

Yet affairs moved rather more slowly than Herries had been led to expect. On the advice of his friends, he returned to London, leaving events in Paris to take their own inevitable course. As he explained to Forbes,

> ... what I had in view at Paris must soon or late come round, and that too in the most agreeable way that could be wished, I mean without solicitation on my part and for no other cause than that the present managers find that they have been ill served and the majority of them resolved to change at once all their Agents in a certain branch of trade not only in great Britain but in Holland—They may

perhaps declare this resolution in less than a month or perhaps not in less than 6 or even in twelve months but whenever they do I am pretty certain my friend [Tronchin] will be empower'd by his co-interested to make proposals to new Agents and I am as certain that he will make them to me, because independent of late assurances I have had seventeen years experience of his unbounded confidence & friendship—He foretold to me what was to happen four months ago, But forbad me strictly to mention it . . . to any person breathing, Because he was not sure of the strong reasons that since [have] been discover'd to make a total change necessary and it was only on that discovery he putt materials into my hand for forming a new Plan, which I had the good luck to do so much to his satisfaction that tho my name was not mention'd to the rest he assured me the majority greatly approved it, . . .

In other words, the farmers-general were highly irked at having their London agent chosen for them by court intrigue and were sympathetic toward Herries precisely because he had hitherto refrained from using any court or other outside connections.[64]

Thomas Walpole, however, still had effective friends in the united farms. Through some financial operations, they saw to it that large sums belonging to the company were in March 1771 lodged with Walpole & Ellison and then used this as an excuse to give that firm a buying order for 6,000 more hogsheads at 2d.3/8 and 2 1/4 to liquidate the credit.[65] That same month, Magon de la Balue wrote Walpole informing him of the charges against him (referred to by Herries above). Essentially, Walpole was accused of being irregular, incomplete and inaccurate in reporting his purchases as he made them. His defense was simply that the selling merchants were not exact in their deliveries and he had to deal with them gently and fill in as best he could. How important after all, he asked, were inaccuracies of a few hundred hogsheads out of the 36,000 he had purchased in the preceding two years.[66]

This was the last help Thomas Walpole was to receive from Magon de la Balue. In April 1771, Magon was removed from the presidency of the tobacco buying committee and replaced by the hitherto obscure farmer-general Jacques Paulze, husband of the niece of the controller-general, the abbé Terray. This meant that there was no longer a merchant member of the committee familiar with British conditions; hence much more respect would be paid to the advice of the outside farmer-general Tronchin, Herries' friend, who had such knowledge. Shortly before, Magon had also been replaced as court banker by Nicolas Beaujon, the financier of Madame du Barry. Although Thomas Walpole had handled payments to the count du Châtelet-Lomont, French ambassador in London, 1768–70, Beaujon soon let it be known that payments to the new French ambassador, the count of Guines, would be made through Van Necks. This was a public and particularly mortifying rebuff to Walpole.[67]

Walpole's only remaining effective friend in the inner circles of the united farms was the farmer-general Roslin, who defended him when Walpole's accounts were challenged in the tobacco buying committee in March-April 1771. To him Walpole explained that "M. [Magon] de la Balue was my particular friend and I have not had the good fortune to be known at all to M. Paulze who perhaps has connections hostile to me."[68] Walpole by correspondence attempted to cultivate Paulze, emphasizing his recent great services to the monopoly in reducing the price from 2d.3/4 or 7/8 to 2d.3/8 per lb. and his expectations of reducing it further in the summer. Paulze, who seems to have been leading him on, wrote in return of his plans of expanding French tobacco purchases in Britain, obtaining there not only the common grades of tobacco, as in the past, but even the smaller quantities of the more expensive grades which the united farms had hitherto purchased in Holland. Even while hearing this heartening news from Paris, Walpole was disturbed by reports from Scotland that persons acting for would-be competitors were approaching the leading tobacco merchants, inquiring about terms for the purchase of 10,000 hogsheads (ten million pounds) for France.[69] Feeling himself sinking, Walpole grasped at every straw. In May, Jacques Necker (the great Swiss banker in Paris) proposed, on behalf of the French government, that Walpole facilitate a large six month credit (probably to buy grain) via drawing and redrawing operations between Paris and London. Walpole, whose relations with Necker had not been close since he left Van Necks in 1766, said that he would be interested only on condition that his tobacco contract be continued. He also wanted the status of a preferred creditor of the French state, inasmuch as he still had six million *l.t.* (£240,000–250,000) nominal value of French government debt as a souvenir of his earlier similar dealings with Magon de la Balue.[70]

Meanwhile, throughout the spring of 1771, Robert Herries kept quiet but attentive watch on the whole tobacco world. From Scotland, his partners Forbes and Hunter kept him informed of the condition of the Glasgow market, of purchases and rumored purchases, current and future, by the Walpole-Alexander interest. His Paris informants assured him that, as soon as the advance of the united farms' funds in Walpole's hands had been worked down, a transfer would be made.[71] From March through May, Herries was in correspondence with Paris over the detailed terms on which he would take the contract. Finding that the Glasgow sellers would never agree to the inspection (and possible rejection) of their tobacco in France—instead of at delivery in Scotland, as was then customary—he proposed to the farmers-general, in return for a 4 percent commission, to assume all the risks of spoilage during shipment between Britain and France. By 21 May, he had received specific "Proposals" from Paris; fearing that Walpole might try to frighten him off by privately "cornering" the market, Herries authorized his partner Hunter to let the Glasgow tobacco merchants know that a change was imminent. By 27 May, the "word" was obviously out, for both Alexander brothers and James Simson (of Simson, Baird, & Co., the Glasgow buyers for Hopes in 1768) hurriedly left Scotland about then for Paris.[72]

By 4 June, perturbed by the unaccountable delay and by Tronchin's absence on an inspection tour, Herries resolved upon a secret trip to Paris, letting it be thought "that I am gone down to Margate to Bath in the Sea."[73] When he got to Paris, he found the place thick with competitors for the agency. When the matter came up for decision in the tobacco committee, six of the ten members were for an immediate contract transferring the agency to Herries, two were neutral or absent, while two were for postponing the entire matter. Majority rule prevailed and the final orders were being prepared when unexpectedly a command came from Controller-General Terray to postpone any decision. One of the new suppliants for the agency had developed an interest at court (probably by bribing the baroness de la Garde, mistress to Terray). The majority six, headed by Terray's own nephew, the president Paulze, made remonstrance after remonstrance to the controller-general and threatened to resign. Herries felt that if the matter came before the whole company, they would be 57 to 3 for him; nevertheless, he recognized those three as dangerous. The new candidate, who had obtained the delay order, became alarmed at the fervor of the farmers-general. He offered to withdraw in Herries' favor in return for a "consideration" of £3,000 sterling, admitting that "he finds the farmers General themselves firm in . . . [Herries'] favors, and that tho he may be forced upon them they would soon or late force him out again." Herries, however, refused to buy court favor because he wanted to come in as the candidate of the farmers-general themselves, the symbol of their independence and their victory. He was only worried lest this impasse work to the advantage of the agent in place, Thomas Walpole.[74]

Herries, standing now openly as the official candidate of the farmers-general battling court intrigue, worked feverishly to attract countervailing and respectable support. Although the Dutch ambassador and Danish envoy in Paris were "particularly active" in his behalf, the British ambassador, Lord Harcourt, held aloof. Herries tried unsuccessfully through his brother Charles in London to get letters from various influential people to Harcourt. It was generally recognized that the most Herries could hope for was Harcourt's neutrality "as there was little doubt but Lord H—— would use his Interest for his Secretary's Brother or for some other Candidate through his means."[75] This was not a reference to Thomas Walpole and his brother Robert, secretary (1768–69) and minister (1769–71) at the embassy in Paris, but rather to a brother of Lt. Col. John Blaquière, Harcourt's secretary who became secretary to the legation in July. The Blaquière were a Huguenot mercantile family of London connected to the Van Necks.[76] Though nowhere visible, Sir Joshua Van Neck must have been a presence disturbing alike to Walpole and Herries.

By early July, Herries saw that it was not enough to be supported by 57 farmers-general to three when "these three or two of them . . . are back'd by all the power of the ministry and the Underlings & kept Mistresses's in pay of the present Agent." It was not simply the "pensions" paid by Walpole to the baroness de la Garde, her brother and others; the extensive financial services which Walpole was performing for the French state in his bill operations with Necker formed a consideration which no controller-general could overlook; Herries had categorically refused to become involved in such transactions.[77] In May, about the same time that "Proposals" had been sent to Herries by the united farms, a document was sent to Walpole listing charges against him and queries about future conduct. The farmers-general were not satisfied with the quality of tobacco received, the charges, or the commissions; in addition, they suspected that Walpole was actually paying the tobacco sellers lower prices than he charged the united farms, under the guise of a deduction for prompt payment—with the farms' money. Walpole answered these charges as best he could; for the future, he made various proposals but insisted on a 5 percent commission to cover all miscellaneous expenses, compared to the 4 percent offered by Herries.[78] Neither his proposals nor his answers to charges were satisfactory to the majority of the farmers-general. During May and June, Walpole had been frequently asked to come over to Paris; on 2 July all ten members of the tobacco purchasing committee signed a letter urging an immediate visit. Walpole refused to come, insisting that his negotiations with the British government for the Ohio lands required his presence in London.[79] In his absence his friends among the farmers-general (notably Roslin) proposed a compromise: Walpole would "repay all past overcharges & serve them in future for less than [he] had aggreed to act." This seemed reasonable to Controller-General Terray who "therefore without using his authority beg'd that they [the farmers-general] would favour all in their power one who had been so deeply engaged for the Court." The six pro-Herries men on the tobacco committee "therefore aggreed to give Mr W[alpole] all manner of fair play & full time to justify himself on condition that if he could not do this, the other two [pro-Walpole members] should join them in ratifying their propositions to" Herries.

In this inconclusive way, the matter was allowed to rest during July and August 1771. Herries had returned to London by 9 July. His friends among the farmers-general were still confident of ultimate victory though they warned him that it might be necessary to bribe one person.[80] Towards the end of August, Walpole finally went over to Paris to justify himself. He was still trying to block Herries & Co. by vast purchases of tobacco unauthorized by the farmers-general, a tactic destined to be futile in a year of exceptionally heavy imports. Although Walpole's friends in Scotland spread stories of his carrying all before him in Paris, in fact, he met a "mortifying rebuff." Although he offered in writing to refund £3,000 in overcharges to the company, the farmers-general told him that they liked neither his excuses nor his proposals. Even his three friends were silent. The farmers warned him too that if he succeeded in using the court against them, they would "leak" the entire story to the public press.[81]

The affair reached its crisis in September. Through channels unknown, the matter was brought to the attention of the king; the amount of money which the baroness de la Garde and her brother were accepting from applicants for the tobacco and other contracts had become a public scandal offensive even to that tolerant monarch. The baroness was exiled from court. Herries hoped that "her disgrace may perhaps be a means to reconcile our friend P[aulze] with his Uncle [Terray]."[82]

With that troublesome lady out of the way, the tobacco matter was speedily settled. Early in September, even before her exit, Herries & Co. had been given a secret experimental commission to purchase several thousand hogsheads in Scotland—the farmers-general hoping to make the experiment permanent.[83] Thomas Walpole stayed on in Paris until 10 October to fight this, but without success. Madame du Deffand could tell by his external appearance that he had suffered a great defeat.[84] The eventual "compromise" was that Herries & Co. would be the buying agents for Scotland where the French made at least 75 percent of their purchases. Thomas Walpole would remain the London agent and would also be paymaster for the agents in Scotland and the English outports. Herries did not want to be paid through Walpole whom he suspected of "some dark intention of leaving us in the lurch." Nevertheless he had to accept this arrangement, if only for the time being. He explained to his partners,

> T[hellusson] N[ecker] & C? are deeply engaged with the Court B——k—r [banker, Nicolas Beaujon] and of course have great influence with the Ministry—They are at the same time deeply engaged for A[lexander] & W[alpole] in a course of circulation and would be hurt imensely by a fall of either—The last [Walpole] is I believe not only jointly With them [Thellusson & Necker] but singly engaged in great engagements for the Court And must still have had further Motives than those that appear visible for wishing & getting his Protectors to insist on his being our paymaster.[85]

It had been agreed with his partners that Robert Herries would bear all the costs of solicitation in Paris, successful or not. In return he personally would have one-half of all the profits arising from the French contract. The rest would be thrown into the general profits of the Edinburgh and London firms.[86] The actual purchases were to be made or supervised in Scotland by

James Hunter, who as the son of a tobacco merchant in Ayr had been raised in that trade. The great Glasgow house of Colin Dunlop & Sons, from whom Herries had got most of his information during the years he was soliciting for the contract, were rewarded by being made the local agents or brokers. They handled much of the negotiation with the other merchants and did some of the purchasing themselves. At a lower level, William Hamilton at Greenock and Robert Douglas at Port Glasgow were employed to supervise the physical receipt and shipment of the tobacco. Most important of all, the partners expected to have the money of the farmers-general in their hands for about thirty days between receipt and expenditure for tobacco. Precise rules were worked out so that both the Edinburgh house ("John Coutts & Co.") and the London house (Herries & Co.) shared the use of this money for 15 days each. These arrangements must have left considerable sums in the hands of each firm since the practice was to draw thousands of pounds weekly on Paris during the buying operations. Little wonder that Herries could refer to this as "the most important Commission business of any in Europe."[87]

At the end of 1771, everything looked rosy for Herries & Co. Robert Herries could inform his Edinburgh partners "that my friends in the [tobacco] Committee now carry all before them—Two of the three in opposition seem to submitt chearfully to reason & power and the other is obliged to be silent—M.r P[aulze] is quite reconciled with his Uncle the M[iniste]r [Terray] & is consulted by him on all occasions, But for reasons of State he [Paulze] proposes to keep up appearances with M.r W[alpole] til march or april next when the whole [agency] will enter with us."[88]

Walpole, however, had his own sources of information and was not inclined to yield any more without a fight. It had been understood that while Herries and partners were buying in Scotland for 2d.1/8 per lb., Walpole was to buy in London at 2d.1/4, maintaining at 1/8d. per lb. the constant difference between the Glasgow and London prices which had once been as much as 1/2d. Walpole, however, perhaps to embarrass Herries, raised the London price to 2d.3/8 enabling him to buy more than his provisional quota and making Herries' purchases in Scotland more difficult when he tried to preserve the 2d.1/8 price. There were also difficulties over quality: Hamilton, Herries' agent at Greenock, rejected part of a shipment sold by John Glassford, greatly irritating the latter, but even what he passed did not please the farmers-general. Herries suspected that Glassford had deliberately delivered damaged tobacco to embarrass him. Actually, many of the greatest "tobacco lords"—Glassford, William Cuninghame, James Ritchie—had long standing friendships with the Alexander brothers whose firm had done them many favors in the forty years it bought for the French.[89] They not only tried unsuccessfully to force Herries to yield the full London price but went so far as to organize a syndicate of eight Glasgow and two London merchants who offered to supply the farmers-general with 20,000 hogsheads (or 20 million lb.) of tobacco annually at a flat price for as many years as the farmers-general chose to contract.[90] Herries had to go over to Paris in March-April 1772 to head off these machinations and to persuade the farmers-general to let him raise his Glasgow price slightly. He was authorized to delay purchases as long as necessary and Walpole in London was forbidden to make any further purchases till October and then at only 1/8d. above the Glasgow base price. With this new weapon, Herries was able to mollify Glasgow, disintegrate the opposition against him there and make large purchases.[91] But, by that time, the business situation had changed and Glasgow needed Herries desperately.

Thomas Walpole, in these early months of 1772, was unable to profit from Herries' difficulties. The farmers-general wanted him to refund the several thousands pounds sterling he had promised the previous August. He insisted that that offer had been conditional on his retaining the whole tobacco agency, three-quarters of which had in fact been taken away from him. He seems to have appeased the company only by agreeing to make £150,000 available to them for six months by a bilateral bill drawing and redrawing operation between Paris and London. They were to start their drawing on him in June 1772, the worst possible month that could have been chosen since the peace.[92]

The panic of June 1772 has yet to be studied in its widest ramifications.[93] In many ways, it is the first modern financial panic, developed endogenously within the private sector of the economy, unrelated to the advent of war or peace or to public debt management (à la 1720). The preceding two or three years had been characterized by a rising volume of business activity associated with a great expansion of credit. In Scotland, this expansion of credit was facilitated by the foundation in 1769 of a great new bank, Douglas, Heron & Co.—"the Ayr bank"—with branches all over the country. The Scottish bankers, particularly the Ayr bank, were so generous in extending credits to businessmen and landowners that they compromised their liquidity. To compensate for this, they raised cash by "chains of bills," large scale bill drawing and redrawing operations, between Scotland and certain Scottish houses in London. Among the firms most heavily involved in these operations was William Alexander & Sons of Edinburgh. Among those least involved were Herries & Co. of London and its Edinburgh alter ego, "John Coutts & Co.," Herries being particularly suspicious of Scottish banking. In April 1772, he wrote to his Edinburgh partners that he did not like the looks of things and wanted them to retrench by calling in some of their Edinburgh debts and building up a cash reserve in London: they were not to touch the paper of the Ayr bank.[94]

The precarious state of affairs, of which the Royal Bank of Scotland[95] and the Bank of England were fully aware, was rendered shakier still by extensive speculation, including deep (over £100,000) operations in East Indies Company stock by Sir George Colebrooke, chairman of that company, and the London Scottish banker, Alexander Fordyce, a partner in the house of Neale, James, Fordyce & Downe.[96] Fordyce's stopping on 10 June 1772 brought down the whole house of cards, ruining twenty major firms in London and Edinburgh in the process. A Scottish merchant in London, who unsuccessfully attempted suicide at the height of the crisis, later in a more collected mood described the events of June to his brother in India:

> You must know then, that on the 10th of June last /a day remarkable in Scotland/ Alexander Fordyce stopt Payment, he had met with great Losses in his Stock Speculations & stopt for about £200,000—his House in the Banking Business [Neale, James, Fordyce & Downe] stopt also that Day for a large Sum—Fordyce Grant & Co were connected with him to the amount of £56,000 & Charles Fargusson [Ferguson] was engaged with Fordyce Grant & Co. to the amount of £30,000—so that both these Houses stopt the 10th of June with the Banker—At this Turn Money Matters were very easy & Credit & a general Confidence was established beyond anything you ever knew, but all of a sudden the very Reverse took place & the most rigid Diffidence & Suspicion . . . was established everywhere—In this Situation Things remained from the 10th till the 20th of June when there was a total overthrow of us all together . . . it was impossible to command a single shilling of Cash on any Security . . . On that Day Messrs Glyn & Halifax the Bankers—Messrs Adams—Edie & Laird, . . . & many others were Bankrupt— . . . In Scotland it was as Bad or rather worse than it was here—Fordyce Malcolm & Co [the Edinburgh affiliate of Fordyce of London] you may be sure were knocked up as were the Alexanders, Gibson & Balfour—Andrew Sinclair & Co—Francis Garbott & Co, Arbuthnot & Guthrie & many others—at Glasgow they held it out surprizingly well only Simson Baird & Co of Note . . . & some few others of little Consequence—Tho at this Time Coutts [of London] were protesting the Bills of both their [Glasgow] Banks, & in Holland Davison-Manson, Jas Crawfurd & others were protesting the Bills of Glassford, Colin Dunlop, Speirs, Cochrane [the greatest Glasgow tobacco firms] & many others.
>
> In short the South Sea affair was a Trifle to what has now happened—The great Douglas Heron & Co Bank in Scotland who had £700,000 of Bank Notes circulating in that Country also stopt. . . .
>
> What contributed greatly to our affairs having a different aspect was that the Bank of England saw it necessary to support Messrs Glyn & Hallifax & Mesrs Alexanders, by which a great Many will be relieved such as the Adams, Edie & Laird & others.[97]

One of the reasons why Glasgow suffered so little from the panic compared to Edinburgh was that such a large proportion of its principal export

—tobacco—was sold to the French for cash, instead of being exported to Holland or Hamburg from whence the proceeds could be realized only slowly by multiple bill drawings through London. Thus, Glasgow merchants who sold to the French did not have extensive bills of exchange outstanding which in the crisis might have been returned unpaid from Holland or London. Herries & Co. and its Edinburgh affiliate had come through the panic unscathed.[98] A few days after the worst Edinburgh failures, Herries and Forbes arrived in Glasgow with authorization from the French to make extensive purchases at a price slightly above the 2*d*.1/8 the merchants had been refusing all spring. They "were received with open arms."[99] And, to secure their triumph, down in the crash had gone Simson, Baird, & Co., the Glasgow correspondents of the Hopes and a major local rival for the French agency.

Other rivals were also eliminated, though less absolutely. The failure of Glyn & Halifax in London had forced the Edinburgh house of William Alexander & Sons (i.e., Robert and William Alexander II) to close their doors, seriously imperiling Thomas Walpole of London. As these were major houses, the Bank of England came to the rescue and made a £160,000 advance to Glyn & Halifax and Alexanders, guaranteed by Thomas Walpole. This permitted Glyn & Halifax and Alexanders to reopen in July: Glyns survive to the present day as Glyn, Mills & Co. but Alexanders lasted only till 1775 when they failed, all but ruining Thomas Walpole in the process. The subsequent complicated history of Thomas Walpole and the Alexanders will be discussed in Chapter 26.[100] For our immediate purposes, the important thing is that, although Walpole and the Alexanders survived the panic of 1772, they did so with an enormous debt to the Bank of England and with severely compromised reputations. (Walpole, in the backlash of the June panic, had also lost by the failure of the foreign houses of Romayne & Dumoulin and Verduc & Co. of Cadiz.)[101]

Herries' expanding tobacco operations were supported by a £30,000 running credit from the farmers-general. To realize that credit, he had of course to draw on his "paymasters," Walpole & Ellison in London. By early September 1772 he was experiencing difficulty in having his accepted bills on Walpole & Ellison discounted in London, and informed the farmers-general thereof.[102] On 11 September Herries wrote confidently to his partners that he thought it likely that the farmers-general would change their London "paymaster" or "cashier"; if they were reluctant to combine that function with the Scottish agency which his firm already held, he would suggest that it be given to his other house, "the London Exchange Banking Company" in St. James's Street which had a few extra affluent partners.[103] By the eighteenth, he could be "glad that we are now to have no more to do with a certain House here, . . . That house [Walpole's] is so engaged with Messrs A[lexanders] that the one must rise or the other fall in time."[104] Although Walpole still kept his small London agency for the French, Herries was authorized to draw thenceforth directly on Paris and not through Walpole & Ellison.[105] These drafts at the rate of 75,000 *l.t.* weekly on Colin de St. Marc, the farmers-general's cashier, started in October.[106] Walpole at first hoped that these new arrangements were temporary and wrote to the farmer-general Roslin as well as to "old friends" such as Magon, La Borde and Necker about the united farms' shabby treatment of himself and of Herries' scandalous profiteering from the large sums left in his hands. He also accused Herries of buying several thousand hogsheads which had not yet arrived—a normal practice but one of which Walpole strongly disapproved. By the end of the year, however, Walpole at last realized that, owing to Paulze's domination of the company and implacable hostility towards himself, he had nothing more to expect from the United General Farms of France. His current account with them was closed.[107]

Although Herries & Co. and affiliated firms had emerged untouched from the debacles of 1772, the general reputation of Scottish credit had not. Herries was very sensitive on this point, for he knew that he had enemies in Paris who might try to attack him by casting doubts on the credit of all Scots houses. After the final closing of the Ayr bank in August 1773, there were efforts at Ayr itself to start new banks—the so-called "second" and "third Ayr banks"—to fill the void and pick up some of the debris left by the collapse of the "first Ayr Bank," Douglas, Heron & Co. One of these new foundations was Hunters & Co., in which several of James Hunter's kinsmen were partners. James Hunter himself took a share in it, though he had full responsibility for all the tobacco purchases in Scotland. Herries objected violently, noting the unfortunate effect in Paris of his having a partner involved in anything called an "Ayr bank." A thick and bitter correspondence ensued before Hunter yielded.[108] It was at this point—February 1774—that Herries thought it necessary to procure a knighthood for himself to refurbish for his French critics both his reputation and that of the Scots nation. The farmers-general were sufficiently impressed or otherwise mollified to add to his responsibilities that of London buying agent and paymaster to the lesser agents in the English outports.[109] (The London agency was up till then nominally held by Walpole, but no tobacco had been bought there for export to France in 1773.) [110]

Thus, by the beginning of 1774, Herries & Co. had become the French "cashiers" for all purchases in Great Britain as well as the buying agents for Scotland and London.[111] Three small agencies remained outside their total control, including that of Daltera in Liverpool and Samuel Martin in Whitehaven. Herries in 1774 thought it would be possible for him to take over "the three little agencies" too, but considered it imprudent to push for so exclusive a position. As Herries suspected, the farmers-general did not want to become entirely dependent on one agent and in 1773-74 increased their orders to Daltera in Liverpool and Samuel Martin in Whitehaven. An order was sent to the latter for three million pounds in 1773, which, as Herries pointed out, was almost equal to total imports at the port. Martin could not fulfill his contract at Whitehaven and so made some purchases at Glasgow. Daltera was suspected of the same practice. Herries complained sharply and strict orders were sent from Paris for Daltera and Martin to remain within their own bailiwicks,[112] French purchases in the English outports becoming much lower in 1774–75 than they had been in 1773.[113]

Robert Herries had taken over the French business at a propitious time. The late 1760's had been years of poor crops and relatively high prices. Starting in 1771, however, just when he took over the agency, came five years of exceptionally heavy imports and declining prices. Total British imports rose from an annual average of 74 million lb. in 1764–70 to 100 million in 1771–75. The French took advantage of this to make their heaviest purchases of the century in Britain in 1772 and 1773.[114] Most of these purchases were made in Scotland where Herries & Co. were the agents (Table I). (Even a 4 percent commission on 20 million lb. at only 2d.¼ per lb. average price would have come to £7,500 exclusive of the commission on the shipping and insurance and the value of the funds of the farm constantly in hand.) [115]

TABLE I

British Tobacco Exports to France (Exclusive of Dunkirk), 1771–75[116]

Year	London	Outports	England	Scotland	Britain
		(in thousands of lb.)			
1771	0	1,866	1,866	12,063	13,929
1772	7,020	2,880	9,900	20,365	30,265
1773	0	7,344	7,344	21,866	29,210
1774	305	3,545	3,851	5,562	9,413
1775	1,943	2,193	4,136	8,861	12,997

Herries took advantage of the substantially expanded supplies of tobacco available in Britain after 1771 to exact better terms from the tobacco merchants of Glasgow. Clyde practice differed from that of London in several significant details. At Glasgow it was the practice for a merchant whose tobacco had lost weight in storage to add enough loose leaf to a hogshead to bring it up to its import weight so that he could draw back the full duty at exportation. This altering of hogsheads was contrary to British law, involved false swearing at exportation and was no longer practiced at London. From the standpoint of the French buyer, it gave the sellers or their agents fraudulent opportunity for removing superior tobacco and replacing it with inferior. Herries announced in 1773 that henceforth the London rules would apply at Glasgow and no repacking would be permitted. The Glasgow merchants fought collectively and vigorously against this "innovation," and for several months refused to sell Herries any tobacco. He tried unsuccessfully at first to break their resistance by offering them one-half farthing per pound less for their tobacco with the old Glasgow rules than with the proposed

London rules. By September 1773, however, he had broken down their resistance and was able to make the most extensive purchases on his own terms. During these same months, he fought an attempt by the Scottish banks to offer only par for his firm's thirty-day bills on London while they were taking other people's sixty-day London bills at par. Since this was an insult to the credit of the farmers-general, he instructed his Edinburgh partners to refuse to sell London bills or give them in payment for tobacco at less than sixty days par. As the firm's bills were a major part of the Scottish supply of London exchange, he was able to starve the Edinburgh and Glasgow bankers into compliance by April.

Midst his other triumphs of 1773, Herries had reduced the "French price" at Glasgow to the very low level of 1*d*.7/8 per lb. (His offer of 1*d*.3/4 if the Glaswegians wanted to keep their old rules had been declined.) [117] Convinced that there were enormous stocks of tobacco still on hand in Britain, he advised and was instructed by the farmers-general in March 1774 to offer only 1*d*.3/4 per lb. for common at Glasgow in 1774. (This amounted to a cumulative reduction of almost 42 percent from the 3*d*. per lb. paid in 1768.) When the merchants refused to go below 1*d*.7/8, preferring to take their chances on speculative reexports to Holland and Germany, Herries advised the monopoly to stick to their offer and content themselves with reduced deliveries in 1774. He felt sure that once the merchants found the Dutch and German markets fully stocked and the 1774 crop in America as large as ever, they would have to accept the French price. The monopoly could safely hold out because they had great stocks on hand from their very large purchases in 1772 and 1773. In any event, there would most likely have been some modest reduction in purchases in 1774 because of stocks on hand and because that was the year of transition from one sexennial lease of the farms to another when forward commitments were always reduced. But the farmers-general, acutely embarrassed at the time by Terray's financial exactions, cut back much further. They seized upon Herries' advice and in July 1774 decided to make no further substantial purchases till spring 1775 and to stick to their offered price at least until they learned the size of the current Chesapeake crop. Although this meant a sharp reduction in the commissions earned by his own firm, Herries felt that he would triumph in the end, establish the 1*d*.3/4 price and fix himself permanently in the farmers' favor.[118] In actuality, he almost undid himself.

By the winter of 1774–75, of course, the coming American Revolution was already casting its shadow before it, and prices of North American produce were beginning to rise. Moreover, great changes had taken place in Paris which undermined much of the solidity of Herries' position vis-à-vis the farmers-general. Louis *le bien aimé* died on 10 May 1774. With his death, the entire court power structure based on Madame du Barry and her allies dissolved. For a few months, there was some uncertainty as to the direction the new king, his grandson, would take, but on 24 August, the chancellor Maupeou was banished from the court, and the abbé Terray, model of the ruthless harshness of the last years of Louis XV, was replaced as controller-general by the reformer Turgot. This change automatically undermined the position of Paulze, Terray's nephew by marriage, as guiding spirit of the united farms and president, inter alia, of its tobacco buying committee. Although Paulze wrote Herries that the dismissal of his uncle would not affect the company or his position in it, Herries had his doubts. In October, Herries went over to Paris to mend his fences, equipped with a letter of introduction to Turgot from David Hume. The new controller-general was delighted to hear from the philosopher, but for Herries things were not the same.[119]

Yet, Herries went on, ever venturing onto thinner and thinner ice. In 1773, when the French bought absolutely no tobacco at London and probably none at Bristol, Herries became aware that quantities of the common grades of tobacco, normally sold to the French, could be picked up at those two ports at or below the French price: at a time when his representatives were paying 1d.7/8 in Scotland for the French, parcels were offered to him in London at 1d.1/2 and 1d.5/8. Since the farmers-general were resolved to do no buying in the south at that time, he decided to speculate on his own account. Operating in the name of a distant kinsman, Michael Herries, a merchant of London, and through a broker, Tindal, who seems to have been a former employee of his, Robert Herries made substantial speculative purchases in London and Bristol for shipment to Dunkirk, Rotterdam, and Hamburg.[120] Merchants who got wind of this thought that the purchases were really for the French, but the matter was kept a total secret from the farmers-general.[121] Herries made these purchases in ports where the French were not buying, but did not long limit himself thus. In 1774, when French purchases in Scotland were radically reduced by insistence on the 1d.3/4 price, Herries instructed Colin Dunlop & Sons (who bought for the French at Glasgow under Hunter's supervision) to buy for his own firm's account at 1d.7/8; these purchases were also shipped off speculatively to Dunkirk, Rotterdam, and Hamburg. On one occasion, Herries even instructed Dunlop to stop his desultory efforts for the French until Herries' own purchases were made.[122]

In August 1773, when the Glasgow merchants were still arguing with Herries about the London conditions of sale and threatening to boycott him, Herries wrote his partners, "But if none of them were ever to sell us another hh^d, We shall gett orders to buy in the Colonies & land at Glasgow until another sett of importers take up the trade & you may tell them so."[123] This was the old Huber-MacKercher scheme seemingly revived only to frighten the Glasgow merchants. Although the Clyde resistance quickly crumbled, Herries actually persisted with the scheme. (He probably knew that the Alexanders had profitably experimented along these lines in 1756–57.)[124] Working again through Michael Herries and through Willing &

Morris of Philadelphia, his "old friends" in the Mediterranean grain trade, Herries had whole shiploads of tobacco purchased in Virginia.[125] Local firms, such as Jenifer & Hooe, the correspondents of Willing & Morris at Alexandria, Virginia, were also employed to make these purchases.[126] In the course of 1774, Herries perceived that the extremely reduced purchases the French were then making would necessitate correctively heavy purchases early in 1775, which might be difficult to make. In order to avoid having to raise the price markedly when purchases resumed then, Herries suggested to Paulze and the farmers-general that they authorize him to make prior purchases on their account in America.[127] Although no such authorization was given, no less than 1824 hogsheads entering the port of London in 1775 were addressed to Herries & Co.[128]

Herries' own Edinburgh partners, Sir William Forbes and James Hunter, did not approve of all these speculations—piled onto others in hops and brandies; their disapproval was one of the principal reasons for the dissolution of the partnership when the existing contract expired at the end of 1775. Thereafter, the Edinburgh house of Sir William Forbes, James Hunter & Co. went about its circumspect way as a model bank, while the London (Jeffreys Square) house of Sir Robert Herries & Co. pursued its more adventurous mercantile course.[129]

When the French refused to pay above 1*d*.3/4 in 1774, most Glasgow and other merchants preferred speculative shipments to Holland, Flanders and Germany where they found they could net more no matter how much they sent. With little tobacco remaining on hand in Glasgow, Herries saw little point in raising the price. In October 1774, it was reported that there were only 2,000 hogsheads at Port Glasgow and 500 of those were being loaded for Dunkirk.[130] This left both the farmers-general and Herries in the most exposed of positions. At the beginning of November, the resentful and ever watchful Thomas Walpole rushed to the French chargé d'affaires in London, Charles-Jean Garnier, with the news he had just received from America that Virginia and Maryland had agreed to suspend the export of tobacco after August 1775. This, as Walpole had warned, was bound to raise British prices precipitously, and was made all the worse for the farmers-general by Herries' own substantial exports that year to Dunkirk and Holland. Garnier sent this information to the minister of foreign affairs, the count of Vergennes, from whom it was passed to the controller-general Turgot and thence to the farmers-general. Early in December, word got back to Herries who rushed to explain to Garnier (and through him to Vergennes) that the shipments he had made to Dunkirk and Holland in the summer were with the knowledge of the farmers-general and designed to bring down prices in those places and to bluff the sellers in Scotland into thinking that the farmers-general were fully supplied. The plan worked for a while in August but was soon disrupted by news from America which prevented purchases at the monopoly's price since that time. Herries suspected that false reports of his subsequent buying at high prices to send to Holland were spread by speculative purchasers who were trying to force the market ever higher.[131]

Herries was not content with a merely literary defense. The news from America finally persuaded the farmers-general to drop their unrealistic 1774 price of 1d.3/4. With his new freedom, and alarmed by growing criticism of him in Paris, Herries moved vigorously, offering 2d.1/2 in Scotland in January 1775. The Glasgow merchants, however, hearing that he was buying in London and the English outports "Virginia & ordinary Maryland from 2 3/4^d to 3 1/4^d & Upper Marylands at 3 1/2 & 3 3/4^d," demanded 3d. for common.[132] Herries' partner, Hunter, wouldn't give the 3d. demanded, even though prices were continuing to rise in Holland and elsewhere.[133] Then, suddenly at the end of February, the great Glasgow house of Speirs, Bowman & Co. announced that they were prepared to buy 6,000 hogsheads of common tobacco at 3d. per lb.; 6,600 hogsheads were immediately subscribed by the trade. It was then announced that this purchase had been made for the farmers-general of France acting through their Whitehaven agent, Samuel Martin.[134]

Herries had been suspicious of Speirs, Bowman & Co. as early as December 1774.[135] During January and February, he had heard rumors about Samuel Martin and had specifically written to Paris asking bluntly what truth there might be to these stories. He had been assured that Martin would be given no contract in Scotland. Paulze even arranged to have Herries see "by accident" the contents of a spurious letter to Martin refusing him a buying commission. This led Herries to deny publicly that Martin was buying for the French, only to appear ridiculous a few days later when the truth got out. The company's stratagem was defended by reference to Herries' private speculations.[136] There seems in fact to have been a struggle within the farmers-general between the friends and foes of Herries, provoked by the dangerous state of the company's tobacco supplies. A vote to take the commission away from Herries & Co. lost by only one vote in the tobacco buying committee. The secret commission to Martin was a compromise to gain time and test the market, and was supposed to be a once-only arrangement.[137] In April, Herries personally bought 2,000–3,000 hogsheads at Glasgow by conceding 3d.1/4.[138] His purchases did not however satisfy the French in quantity and in August Martin was back in the Scottish market but could not get anything at his 3d. limit.[139] In October, Herries had to go over to Paris for a climactic fight against his foes within and without the company.[140] He triumphed and was confirmed in his London and Scottish agency for the remainder of the existing lease, 1774–80.[141] It was, however, a hollow victory, for within a few months tobacco had ceased arriving in Britain from the Chesapeake.

It would be a mistake to see the farmers-general's London tobacco agency during 1768–75 as simply the plaything of court intrigue. Its award was the product of a complicated interplay of interests within and without the united farms. The great mistake that Thomas Walpole made was to imagine that if his influence at court was great enough, he could overcome the hostility of even 57 out of 60 farmers-general. Had Choiseul lasted, he might very well have, but buying Madame de la Garde's favors was no substitute for the loss of that great friend in power. Herries was favored precisely because he chose to stand as the candidate not of court intrigue but of the company itself: he would compete in merchant fashion by underbidding. Yet even he had his personal connections with Tronchin and worked hard to cultivate Terray and Turgot in turn. The collective interest of the farmers-general as a business company and the influence of individuals could never be entirely separated.

CHAPTER 25

The French Monopoly as a Monopsonistic Buyer in the British Tobacco Market, 1700–1775: Some Economic Implications

The French tobacco buying commission was a very attractive piece of business for those who shared it. The principal agents received commissions of from two to five percent (varying with the services rendered). Lesser commissions were paid to the subagents (*commissionaires*) in London, the English outports, and Scotland who made the actual purchases and whose credit was involved in drawing bills for payment. Petty commissions had also to be paid to great merchants (such as Colin Dunlop at Glasgow) who acted as brokers and to the less important men in Port Glasgow and Greenock who supervised the receipt and shipment of the tobacco.[1] As valued as the commissions earned were the profits on exchange and the large sums of the united farms' money which lingered for a while in the hands of the principal agents. Even Sir William Forbes in his circumspect memoirs remembered these sums as one of the most attractive features of the commission.[2] In May 1771, the Hon. Thomas Walpole confided to Necker that he had £40,000–50,000 of the farms' funds in his hands, equivalent to a six or seven weeks' supply once the buying started.[3] To get the commission, Herries had to give the farmers-general better terms, but he counted on having their funds in his hands for thirty days. These, he admitted, were in the vicinity of £30,000 at a time, though Walpole accused him of holding onto £50,000.[4] These retardations of funds in transit were managed by the timing of the payments for tobacco purchased. In Scotland, for example, under Herries & Co., tobacco was paid for by thirty- or sixty-day "tobacco notes." When due, these notes could be redeemed either in cash (Scottish bank notes) or in bills of exchange on London (usually at sixty days date). The Scottish bank notes could of course be readily obtained from any of the banks for the same sixty-day London bills.[5] For bankers and great dealers in exchange, the funds and credit of the farmers-general were a most attractive adjunct to the buying commission.

The funds so obtained could be put to good use by the agents in their mercantile and banking businesses. They could even use the farms' funds to discount (for their own profit) bills drawn on themselves for tobacco bought for the farms.[6] The funds could also be used to make advances to the tobacco importers (particularly at the necessitous moment when their ships came in from the Chesapeake) placing them in a position of dependence in which they would be readier to sell to the French on "reasonable" terms.[7] Funds in hand gave bargaining power. The farmers-general put large sums in the hands of their principal London agents because they felt that their purchases would in the final accounting be made more cheaply that way.

From the standpoint of the tobacco importers in England and Scotland, the French agents with their great commissions, vast funds, and seemingly unlimited ability to delay purchases were a diabolic force in the market to whom could be traced all disconcerting ups and downs and starts and stops. As early as the War of the Spanish Succession, astute observers of the London market had pointed out the baleful consequences of a single large French buyer.[8] This awareness became general in the years following 1723[9] when the Indies Company greatly expanded its purchases in Britain and placed its London agency in the hands of a single person, its own syndic Pierre Cavalier. The situation was explained to Sir Robert Walpole, about 1729–30, in a memoir from a London tobacco merchant:

> The whole Trade for Tobacco in France is in a Farm, at present in the possession of their East India Comp: . . . the far greatest part of what they consume, they ever had, & still must have from us, in former years we have had good prices from them, but of late years they have done what they pleased.
>
> For as that Company have the Sole vending of Tobacco in France, So they have been so cunning, to employ but one Agent at one time, to buy all the Tobacco they want from England, whose Gentlemen have ever been our Masters, but the Gentleman [Cavalier] that at present has that Commission, has exceeded all his Predecessors in Politicks, he had laid a Scheme that must for ever have kept down the price of Tobacco, & would have been the ruin of the Plantations, it is true we have of late by means taken among ourselves, given that Gentleman a Check in his Career but as he has the Power of the Purse, I am afraid he will still be too hard for us, he being but One, & we so many. . . .
>
> And yet were that oppression only for Tobacco for the consumption of France I should not be so much concerned, But what that one Gentleman does, Affects all the Tobacco imported into Great Britain, for all other Buyers govern themselves by what that one man does, . . . So that in effect, the Wellfare of all the people in Virginia & Maryland . . . has depended upon the good will & pleasure of that one single Gentleman. . . .[10]

In this document, the entire eighteenth-century bill of complaints against the French agent was set forth: as the great single buyer, his monopsonistic "power of the purse" enabled him to lower the price not just of the tobacco he bought, but of the market generally. There is only one effective response to the weight of a monopsonistic buyer in a market of many sellers and that is a "countervailing" union among the sellers giving them equivalent bargaining powers. That such united action was attempted in the 1720's we can infer from the claim in the above document that "we have of late by means taken among ourselves, given that Gentleman a Check." What those "means" were we know in part by the fortuitous presence in London during 1727–28 of Henry Darnall of Maryland who reported on them in print to his fellow provincials upon his return to the Chesapeake.[11]

In the 1720's, Maryland had not yet come to specialize in the strong, bright-leaf tobaccos whose market lay almost exclusively in Holland and the north of Europe. For the milder, brown Oronokos, then also grown extensively in Maryland, the French market was as important as it was for equivalent leaf produced in Virginia. When Pierre or Peter Cavalier began his activities in London in 1725, thanks to short crops the year before in the Chesapeake, prices were higher than they were ever to be again until the American Revolution. In the course of 1726–27, however, with more normal crops, he was able to effect a reduction in price of about one-third. This serious decline (which proved to be secular) to a level of prices lower than those known for thirty years[12] provoked the trade into an attempt at concerted action. They already had a very loose organization, primarily for political lobbying; to it, all tobacco merchants were supposed to contribute 3d. per hogshead imported, but many were in arrears. This dormant organization was revivified at a general meeting of the Virginia and Maryland trade of London on 7 March 1727/8: it was agreed then to meet thereafter regularly once a month, to continue the 3d. per hogshead levy and collect arrears and to appoint a committee of six Virginia and six Maryland merchants to consider further steps. The committee appointed was headed by Alderman Micajah Perry, M.P. for London, leader of the Virginia trade, and Samuel Hyde, partner with his father John Hyde in the largest Maryland house in London; other members included the Maryland merchant John Falconar and the Virginia merchant, Edward Randolph, a native of the colony.[13]

Within a week of its establishment, the committee received a memorial from John Falconar, one of its less important but most zealous members. "It is well known to us all," Falconar insisted, "that the chief Cause of the Depression of the Trade is from the great Ascendant the *French* Agent has got over us," an inevitable condition since "he being but One, and so very considerable a Buyer, must have a great Advantage over so many Sellers, acting without any manner of Consultation or Agreement." With his great funds, the French agent—Peter Cavalier—bought up whole shiploads from needy merchants; these he sorted out himself, sending what was proper to France and the remainder to Holland where it was deliberately dumped on the market to lower the "world" price and thus facilitate cheaper purchases by the French in London. Acknowledging his power, all the other buyers in

London governed their prices by those offered by the French agent. To Falconar it seemed that such conditions could be remedied only by the united action of the trade, bargaining collectively and enforcing minimum prices.[14]

After considering Falconar's analysis and his detailed proposals, the committee recommended to the trade that their organization be formalized: that the general trade meet monthly, with intervening monthly meetings by the committee (elected annually) a fortnight later; that a two-thirds vote be required for action; that fines be levied for nonattendance; and that a paid secretary be appointed. All these proposals were accepted by a special general meeting of the trade at the Black Swan Tavern on 21 March 1727/8 and confirmed at the first regular meeting on 4 April. Alderman Micajah Perry was continued as "Treasurer" or head of the trade. The only proposal of the committee turned down by the general meeting was one authorizing the sending to Virginia and Maryland of the names of those failing to subscribe to the agreement or to observe its terms. This single defeat deprived the scheme at its inception of effective discipline, for only the threat of informed planters withholding consignments could be counted on to bring into line every last importer.

With its organization seemingly taken care of, the trade had to concert concrete measures. At the April meeting, they had only agreed provisionally that no tobacco even of the poorest quality be sold to anyone for less than 2d.½ per lb.[15] Falconar had recommended an arrangement pointed more directly at the French buyer. Virginia tobacco might be divided into three grades: (a) best, not bought by the French; (b) superior "for the French"; and (c) "good" or common, "for the French." The committee should reach an agreement with the French buyer fixing a price of 3d. per lb. for large purchases of James River, most suitable for France, containing equal parts of b and c grades. Other rivers and grades, whether bought by the French or not, would be priced by the committee according to their normal price relationship to James River.[16]

Falconar's plans were not acceptable to Samuel Hyde, son of John Hyde, first in the Maryland trade and major supplier to the French. Rather than oppose Falconar's scheme, the Hydes apparently decided to bring forward a scheme of their own so ambitious that it would drive every other out, and so top-heavy that it would collapse of its own weight. At the meeting of 2 May, Samuel Hyde suggested that the committee arrange to examine and grade every hogshead of tobacco at arrival from America. Separate minimum prices would then be set for each variety and grade. Reports would be sent to the "naval officer" (shipping inspector) of each river in the Chesapeake, announcing the minimum prices adopted and listing the grading given to each hogshead sent from his river. Each consigning planter could ascertain from these lists exactly how each hogshead of his own tobacco was classified; by checking these gradings against the accounts of sale he received from his factor in London, he could see whether that merchant had adhered to the minimum prices set by the trade. No denunciatory letters would be needed to inform the planters. Hyde's overly ambitious plan was referred by the trade to the committee where it was forgotten.[17] Nothing was settled beyond the 2d.½ absolute minimum earlier agreed upon. Yet in April, tobacco was being sold to the French monopoly for 2d.¼ and before May was up Cavalier was boasting that he would smash all their combinations. Falconar turned most pessimistic.[18]

By August 1728, the planters in the Chesapeake had received word of developments in London that spring, together with a plea from Falconar that pressure be brought to bear on the merchant-factors. A letter signed by 83 principal planters of Maryland was sent to the London trade, collectively supporting the principle of combination and threatening to boycott any noncooperative merchant.[19] When this letter was read at the October meeting of the trade, the zealots (Falconar, Randolph, etc.) moved that the chairman, Alderman Micajah Perry, M.P., query each merchant present about his sales conduct since the 2d.½ minimum was adopted in the spring. Minor derelictions were charged against or admitted by Jonathan Scarth, James Bradley, Philip Smith, and John Hanbury and more serious ones against the Hydes. At the end, the chairman himself admitted that of the 1,000 hogsheads he had sold since the spring, 400 had been below the 2d.½ minimum; he had been forced to do this, he explained, when he found out that the Hydes and others had broken the price line on a wide front.

It soon became evident that the Hydes were the principal villains in everyone's eyes. Randolph claimed that in a vain effort to keep up prices, he had offered to take a "parcel" of hogsheads from Hyde at a price higher than that offered by "the French Man," but had been refused.[20] (Peter Cavalier's account at the Bank of England shows that between 31 July and 31 October, he paid from that source alone almost £10,000 to "Hyde.")[21] An extensive and bitter exchange of letters ensued in the *Maryland Gazette* during January–June 1729 between the attackers and defenders of the Hydes.[22] It was alleged that the great indebtedness of many Maryland planters to this house, the largest in the Maryland trade, prevented collective countermeasures in the colony and made the firm insensitive to colonial opinion.[23] A letter in defense of the house, written by a master of one of its ships, was quite earnest but had few hard facts to cite. The attackers placed great emphasis upon the Hydes' French sales: not only did the break in the 2d.½ minimum price come through their sales to the French agent, but it was even rumored that Samuel Hyde had "been concern'd with a Person in *Holland,* and Mr. Cavallier, in a Contract with the Farmers in *France* to supply that Kingdom with Tobacco." The last charge was so serious that a resolution of denial absolving the Hydes had formally been entered in the minutes of the June 1728 meeting of the trade and signed by all present.[24]

Individual planters were, however, sufficiently aroused to write strong letters to the Hydes about their alleged practice of selling whole shipments to Cavalier, the French agent. To one of them, the firm replied:

> Observe you are apprehensive it is not for the interest of our Principalls [the consigning planters] to sell all sorts of Tobacco to the French Buyer [;] this we agree would be the Case if the same Person that bought for France did not likewise buy for other Marketts & the Prizes [prices] he gives for what he sends to Holland is regulated by what other Buyers give for the Same Sorts: & we Can assure you we have allwayes had as good a price from him as we Could have had from any other Buyer & have never sold to him but when we have thought it most for the interest of our Principalls so to do, ...

Their ship captains would satisfy verbally "the Charge of Breaking agreements."[25] In other words, John Hyde & Co. felt they had little on their record that needed explanation or apology. As the firm extending the greatest credit in Maryland, they were probably peculiarly dependent upon the assured quick cash from the French buyer and could not have changed their selling practices if they had wanted to.

The Hydes aside, little was at first argued in defense of the general failure to enforce the price agreements except that combinations to fix prices were illegal by common law and statute.[26] A fuller defense was prepared in a letter of 7 November 1728, signed by 37 tobacco consignment merchants of London and published in Maryland the following April. It was frankly admitted that the agreement for a $2d.1/2$ minimum as well as a later one to fix a $2d.3/4$ minimum for better grades had both failed and that tobacco was then selling at and under $2d.$ per lb. Falconar had earlier argued that unless the London merchants found ways to keep prices up, planters would no longer find it worth their while to consign to commission merchants there, but would sell their tobacco "in the country" to outport traders; the London merchants now pleaded that they no longer controlled enough of the trade for them to do anything about fixing prices.

> *London* used formerly to have a much great Share of the Trade from *Maryland* and *Virginia*, than of late Years it has had, and consequently, it was then much more in the Power of the Merchants of *London* to govern the Markets, than now they can pretend to; for very near one half of all the Tobacco that comes to *Great-Britain*, goes to the Out-Ports. *Glasgow* alone, imported last Year above 10,000 Hogsheads that give them a Weight in Trade, that is not at all for your Interest; for they being Traders chiefly on their own Account [rather than commission merchants like the Londoners], and living at a great distance from us, it cannot be expected that they will come into Measures with us to raise the Price, which we know by Experience they have not been very careful about.[27]

In the latter half of 1729, the planters lost interest in the question which disappeared from the *Maryland Gazette* abruptly. This sudden change was probably due to "great rains" in the summer of 1729 which "Destroy'd great part of this Crop [and] . . . makes the Comodity rather look up."[28] For the future, however, the planters preserved no illusion that the monopsonistic power of the French buyer could be curbed by any united action of the London merchants. As the greatest planter-merchant in Maryland wrote to a friend visiting London a few years later:

> What you was so kind to hint of the Merch[an]ts mismanagem[en]t in the Tobacco trade, find has proved too true. And understand the French have gaind the Point, As am afraid they always will while the Trade so disperst, and into some needy hands.[29]

After the farmers-general took over the tobacco monopoly in 1730, it will be remembered that they divided Cavalier's sole commission among two or more houses. The planters were rather confused as to exactly what this meant for the bargaining power of the French buyers, as one of them wrote to the press:

> Sometimes we have been told, that the Agents of the *French* Commission at *London,* act as one Man, and by that Unanimity, have been able to reduce the Price of Tobacco as they pleased. At other times, that these very Agents, vying with one another, who should purchase the largest Quantity of Tobacco, thereby to inhance the Commissions arising upon their Purchase, have been the Means of raising the Price of it.[30]

And yet, despite all this, despite the failure of the 1728 London pricing ring, despite the dispersal of the trade among many "needy hands," and despite the division of the French agency among several houses, some sort of collective bargaining procedure seems to have been worked out in the ensuing decades. This usually took the form of the French buyers at London, Whitehaven, or Glasgow meeting informally with the local "trade" and thrashing out a generally agreed upon price. This usually left no trace in surviving correspondence except an occasional phrase like *"we* agreed." Sometimes a merchant wrote more, as did Silvanus Grove in 1759 about the competition between the two French agents:

> . . . last Saturday the Trade were Summon'd to meet in the Evening when we were acquainted Mr Fitzgerald thought the Trade had not used him well in selling Tob.^{o} to Sr Joshua Van Neck at 3^{d}7/8 as he was the first that offered that price but however if we could let him have a quantity worth his while he would advance the price[;] he had accordingly bought Two thousand seven hundred H'h'ds at 4^d . . . .[31]

In this case, when prices were exceptionally high, collective bargaining was in the interest of the French buyer. George FitzGerald did not want to raise his offer to 4d. unless he could be guaranteed "a quantity worth his while" at that price. In the 1770's, we find references to similar bargaining at the initiative of the French agents.[32] This negotiation was largely the work of the big sellers; the small men could come in or not as they pleased. At Glasgow, for example, in the 1760's, James Lawson, a smaller merchant, did not take part in the discussions with the French representatives. Instead, he corresponded with William Alexander & Sons in Edinburgh, French agents in Scotland from 1730 until 1771, offering his tobacco—sometimes whole shiploads not yet arrived—at a certain price. Lawson's offers were most likely to be accepted when they followed the price already agreed upon between Alexanders and the bigger Glasgow importers.[33]

At other times, the interest in collective bargaining might come rather from the sellers. In 1759, the London merchants by collective action forced their French price up to 4d., even though the less cooperative Glaswegians were not able to get theirs up to an equivalent price of 3d.3/4.[34] At other times, joint action was less successful. In 1769–70, according to a London merchant, expecting higher prices because of exaggerated rumors of poor crops in the Chesapeake:

> the Glasgow people stood out for 3ᵈ with the *French* from December till May & it was well known they [the French] wanted Tobacco, little doubt was made but they must have given the price demanded; We [the Londoners] therefore made a stand here in full expectation of geting 3ᵈ 1/4 from them for all the ordinary & bad Tobacco; but some houses at Glasgow having large Quantities on hand, (and suppose heavy Bills drawn thereon) & finding much more Tobacco was likely to be imported this year than had been expected, induced them to sell to the French . . . at 2ᵈ 3/4 & since at 2ᵈ 5/8.[35]

Shortly after this, Thomas Walpole wrote to Paulze explaining that the French agent had to deal "with a numerous body of merchants united in the desire to keep up the price of their commodity, constantly on the alert against all the measures of the agent, and at the same time extremely jealous of each other." The agent had to exploit these jealousies and the need of some sellers for cash "to prevent their combinations."[36]

When conditions were sufficiently threatening, the trade might be induced, as in 1728, to take extraordinary measures. Such in fact happened in 1773, when Herries was engaged in his successful double offensive to lower the "French price" and to force the Glasgow merchants to accept the London sales terms. In June 1773, the Glasgow importers entered into bonds of £2,000 each not to accept the "London allowance."[37] When Herries' Edinburgh house secretly approached the leading Glasgow house of William

Cuninghame & Co., offering to buy 700 hogsheads, the Cuninghame partners replied that they could not consider such an offer without consulting with the trade as a whole.[38] All the same, the Glasgow merchants yielded to Herries on price and terms by September.

In short, there was a tradition of joint action in dealing with the French in both the London and Glasgow tobacco trades from the 1720's to the 1770's. This mechanism was often encouraged by the French agents to guarantee themselves the quantities they needed. Collective action was less frequently used successfully as a bargaining weapon by the trade against the French agents.

Countervailing force against a monopsonistic buyer could develop in forms other than collective action by many small sellers; it could manifest itself in the emergence of a relatively few large sellers able to deal with the "monopsonist" on more equal terms. The French agents probably preferred and encouraged the larger sellers:[39] it was easier and surer buying from firms that could sell hundreds and thousands of hogsheads, that could contract in advance of arrival and be counted on to deliver. We have already noted the very heavy purchases of Peter Cavalier in the 1720's from John Hyde & Co. Among the dozen or so tobacco names found at any given time on the debit side of the Bank of England drawing accounts of the French agents from the 1710's to the 1730's, Hydes and a very few others account for the lion's share.[40] In later years, the pattern was even more pronounced. In 1759, for example, James Russell of London sold 900 hogsheads (three shiploads) to the French at one time.[41] At Whitehaven in 1743, although eighteen importing firms supplied the 5.4 million lb. of tobacco which Peter How exported to France for the farmers-general, the two largest firms supplied almost half, the top four over two-thirds and the first seven together accounted for 82 percent:[42]

How & Kelsick	1,831,543 lb.	
William Hicks	830,500	
William Gale	496,000	
Thomas Lutwidge	494,300	
total 1st four	3,652,343	(67%)
Edwd. Tubman & Co.	300,000	
James Spedding & Co.	296,792	
John Lewthwaite	219,054	
total 1st seven	4,468,189	(82%)
8 firms (87–134,000 ea.)	869,330	(16%)
3 firms (9–51,000)	97,100	(2%)
Total	5,434,619 lb.	

At Glasgow, a comparable situation can be found at the same time. Of the 8.4 million lb. shipped to the farmers-general from Port Glasgow and Greenock between Michaelmas 1742 and Michaelmas 1744, almost half was supplied by three groups of firms (Bogles, Dunlops, and McCalls), while the top seven (adding Berries, Ritchies, Oswalds, and Donalds) accounted for more than three-fourths of French supplies.[43]

The emergence of a few large firms supplying the bulk of French purchases in London, Whitehaven and Glasgow both reflected and influenced a parallel pattern of concentration in the trade as a whole. From a relatively dispersed condition, about 1700, the London trade had reached a degree of concentration in 1733 in which six merchants accounted for four-sevenths of the tobacco bonds outstanding.[44] In 1775, in a doubled trade, the top six merchants in London (all importing more than 2,000 hogsheads each) accounted for 51 percent of the trade while the top eleven (all importing more than 1,000 hogsheads) accounted for 68 percent.[45] In Glasgow at the same time, the eight firms making up the three Glassford, Speirs, and Cuninghame groups accounted for 55 percent of the trade.[46] The French market can probably be considered a significant factor contributing to the general concentration of the trade, not simply in that concentration in supplying the French seems to have appeared earlier in a more extreme form than in the trade generally, but also because France was the only important market, foreign or domestic, in which the large dealer had a pronounced advantage.

Intimately associated with this concentration among French suppliers was the development of buying in advance. Sometimes this might imply nothing more than a single merchant selling at the current price the cargo of a ship expected in a few days or weeks.[47] Sometimes the transactions were more impressive. An anonymous memoirist in London in May 1766 claimed that the French agents there had contracted at 2d.¼ per lb. for virtually all the tobacco expected to arrive before the first of August.[48] The Hon. Thomas Walpole, in his memoirs to the united farms of 1769–1773, bitterly attacked this practice of advance contracting as practiced by Simson, Baird in 1768 and by Herries after 1771. In effect, he argued, it was *forestalling,* and deprived the French buyers of the depressing effects on prices which large imports should have had.[49] Whether these contracts were ever for more than three or four months in advance, we do not know.[50]

The necessary preference of the French buyers for the big sellers with whom they could best deal had significant effects on both the institutional and geographical structure of the trade in Great Britain. Institutionally, French buying favored merchants trading on their own account over those who acted as commission agents or factors for planters or (less frequently) merchants in the Chesapeake. The commission system seems to have been at its height in the generation of high European prices between about 1690 and about 1720.[51] From the late 1720's, with the advent of lower prices, it was reported to be in decline and by 1733 to account for no more than one-third of the tobacco arriving in Britain. The relative decline of consignment was not unrelated to the French market. A merchant trading on his own account could in absolute propriety sell whole warehousefuls to the French, including shiploads not yet unloaded and examined, or even arrived. He knew that what he was selling unseen was mixed in quality and tried to sell at a price that adequately reflected the probable distribution of qualities within a shipload. By contrast, a commission merchant received tobacco from scores of planters, each of whom expected each of his hogsheads to be sold individually according to its quality. This was easy enough if the tobacco were in the top tenth by quality and suitable for the domestic market. For the common grades, suitable only for export to France, Holland or Germany, such careful selling was impractical. Yet, the planters never could be convinced of this. The greatest London commission merchants of the 1720's and 1730's, the Perrys and the Hydes, sold hundreds of hogsheads at a time to the French and appeased the planters as best they could. However, the intrinsic inconsistency of such activity proved too much for those once great houses: they both failed in the 1740's. Although right down to the American Revolution, we can still trace sales to the French in "accounts of Sale" received by planters from London and Liverpool factors, the overwhelming bulk of French purchases after 1740—in London as well as the outports— were made from merchants trading on their own account.

For merchants trading on their own, the French market was particularly strategic. The great book profit of such businesses normally came not from the sales of tobacco sent home but rather from the mark-ups on European goods sold in America. These could vary from 40 to 50 percent on wholesale transactions to 150 percent and more on retail sales. The latter were commonly made on credit to planters, to be repaid with tobacco from the next crop. With such profits "assured" from the sale of its European goods, the firm was generally satisfied if it "broke even" on paper in its tobacco returns. Book losses were common when the price of tobacco was too high in the Chesapeake. (Even the indebted planter was commonly entitled to the prevailing price in his county.) In such years, the company's agents in the Chesapeake were authorized to sell "in the country" all tobacco not absolutely needed to fill the company's ships and to remit the proceeds in bills of exchange. Tobacco and bills of exchange were thus alternative forms of remittance, each to be used in appropriate circumstances. More often, of course, the remittance was made in tobacco.

The European manufactures sold to the planters at these great advances were themselves usually purchased on credit in Britain, particularly the fabrics supplied by the London linendrapers and the Scottish linenmanufacturers. Somewhere in the vast chain of credit stretching from the cottage crafts of Silesia and Scotland to the debt-ridden planters of the Chesapeake, there had to be a source of hard and quick cash. Such cash was acutely needed when a ship came in from the Chesapeake for, all at once, a host of payments had to be made in coin or bank notes: the ship's freight or the crew's wages; part of the customs duties (the "Old Subsidy") even if it was later to be drawn back; customs fees; the charges of unloading (lighterage, porterage, and carting). Hardly any of the available markets for tobacco provided quick cash. The smaller domestic manufacturers paid good prices but expected to receive long credits. Only at London were there bigger manufacturers and jobbers who could pay relatively quickly for larger purchases. Exports to Holland, Hamburg, and Ireland were commonly on consignment and the tobacco might lie months at its destination before sale. Some German buyers bought through correspondents in London and presumably paid quickly, but such practices were limited and brought no relief to Whitehaven or Glasgow. For the great importers there and at London, the only regular vent for quick cash was the French market.[52] The French buyers, as noted at the beginning of this chapter, paid for their tobacco in cash at exportation or in 30- or 60-day notes which could readily be discounted for cash; in addition, they often lent the importers money to meet the expenses of vessels arriving. (The French buyers also chartered the tobacco importers' vessels to carry their purchases to France—an easy source of cash earnings for vessels otherwise outward bound to the Chesapeake in ballast.) Thus, even if a merchant sold only 30 or 40 percent of his importation to the French, it was such sales alone which provided the assured cash which enabled him to support his slower if more profitable sales elsewhere. Cheap cash sales to the French were thus the *liquidity* grease which kept in motion the entire sluggish mechanism of the British-Chesapeake trade.

In helping to explain the transition from the consignment system to direct trading, the French market of course simultaneously helps explain the geographic shift in the trade from south to north. London was the classic center of the consignment trade. (Experienced planters consigned a small proportion of their output to Liverpool or Bristol to purchase goods which might be cheaper at those outports than at London.) By contrast, the trades at Whitehaven and Glasgow were conducted primarily on the merchants' own account. At the beginning of the century, some stray consignments came their way, but by mid-century, the Glaswegians were turning down consignment business as more trouble than it was worth.[53] As early as 1728–29, we have seen the London commission merchants justify their failure to act together vis-à-vis the French by asserting that they no longer could control the market inasmuch as half the trade had passed into the hands of merchants dealing on their own account in the English outports and Scotland. Despite the added expenses for commissions, monetary transfers, postage and perhaps freight, it was inevitable that the French would experiment with northern purchases. Yet, as we have seen in Chapter 23, their purchases in Whitehaven and Glasgow remained on a relatively modest scale until the 1740's. In all probability, they had been restricted at first by the paucity of firms in those ports that could deal on the French scale. Not only had such firms emerged by about 1740, but the outbreak of the Spanish War in 1739 gave an added advantage to the safer and cheaper north-about-Ireland route used by the traffic from the Chesapeake to Whitehaven and the Clyde. The wartime exaggeration of the normal price advantage of the northern ports, coinciding with the appearance of the necessary institutional preconditions, goes far to explain the sudden shift of French buying to the north; this shift in turn is the principal explanation for the meteoric rise of both Whitehaven and the Clyde ports in the 1740's. By 1750, a Glasgow merchant could write that "the French agents take all [our] Virginia Tobacco after we withdraw whats fitt for other merkats."[54]

In the Chesapeake, at one step further removed, we can detect effects of French demand upon the institutions, geography and rate of growth of the tobacco economy.

Trade in the Chesapeake had long been carried on in three distinct forms: the independent merchant, the planter-consigner and the supercargo-store systems. Of great antiquity but of least importance for the tobacco trade were the independent merchants resident in the Chesapeake. Though long established in the country, most independent merchants found it difficult with their meagre capital to compete in the direct trade to Great Britain and found more profitable use for their limited resources in the trade to the West Indies and (later) southern Europe. Their prosperity in these southerly trades and their numbers (swelled by immigrants from Scotland) made Baltimore and Norfolk the two great commercial centers of the Chesapeake in the generation before the American Revolution. Though specializing in the West Indian trade, all independent merchants in the Chesapeake had correspondents in London and sometimes elsewhere in Great Britain who bought European and Asian goods for them and who handled their bill business. The independent merchants in the Chesapeake naturally received some tobacco in payment for the European, Asian and West Indian goods which they sold locally; this tobacco they might "sell in the Country" for cash or consign to a merchant correspondent in Britain for sale on their own account; in years of unusual price fluctuations, they might even receive orders to buy tobacco speculatively for the account of their British correspondents. Tobacco was, however, incidental and not central to their main southward-looking business.

Even in the seventeenth century, some larger planters had tried to circumvent middlemen and obtain for their tobacco the full metropolitan price, including all trading profits. They took over the consignment system normally practiced between relatively equal merchant correspondents and found merchant houses in London, Bristol, and Liverpool who agreed to act as their factors on commission, to sell their consigned tobacco, and to purchase European goods. The more socially sophisticated planters looked for factors who could be trusted to purchase ladies' and gentlemen's clothing, house furnishings, and carriages in the latest and most correct style; such correspondents were also expected to supervise the education of children sent to England for schooling and to act as political agents, particularly in the solicitation of offices.[55] Most important of all, the factor was used as a source of short-term credit whenever possible. The planter-consignment system received a great stimulus from the disparity between Chesapeake and English prices in the war years of the 1690's, and was at its height in the period of relatively high prices from the 1690's until about 1725. In the period of much lower prices that followed, metropolitan factors appear to have become much more conservative in granting credits. (Disaster struck the great houses of Hyde and Perry in the 1740's with great advances outstanding to planters.) With credit harder to get and prices in Britain discouraging, more and more planters cut back on their consignments and instead sold their tobacco "in the country." Complaints of the decline of the planter-consignment system, we already noted, were noticeable from the late 1720's and 1730's. By the 1760's and 1770's, a few big London factors found their capital underemployed in the volume of planter business they were receiving. Some of them tried to generate new business by extending big credits to independent merchants in the Chesapeake (hitherto confined to a minor role in the direct Chesapeake-British trade by the limitations of available capital and credit): in this new "cargo trade," substantial shipments of European goods were supplied by London commission merchants on credit to independent merchants in the Chesapeake, to be paid for by the return shipment of tobacco on consignment. The development of the new "cargo trade" was cut short by the American Revolution. It does nevertheless suggest the availability of substantial underutilized capital and credit in the hands of London commission merchants; and if it illuminates retrospectively the decline in the planter consignment system in the preceding half-century, it also foreshadows the superior credit facilities and institutions that were to draw American trade back to Britain after the war.

The third and most important mode of dealing in Chesapeake tobacco was direct trade. From the earliest days of settlement in the seventeenth century, supercargoes from English ships had bartered their wares for the tobacco of local planters and petty shopkeepers. To facilitate such trade, supercargoes were ultimately instructed by their metropolitan employers to establish first temporary and then permanent "stores" on shore. With the stores permanent, barter was replaced by credit sales to the smaller planters (the characteristic customers of these stores) to be repaid by tobacco (or sometimes wheat) deliveries from the next crop. From these modest foundations, there developed, particularly from the 1740's, great chains of stores belonging to a single firm usually seated in Glasgow, but sometimes to the southward. By the American Revolution, the largest of these firms had more than £100,000 in credit outstanding to thousands of customers in the Chesapeake. Together, the direct-trading "stores" probably controlled two-thirds of the annual crop of the Chesapeake.[56]

The ultimate lead of the direct-trade stores over both the independent local merchants and the planter-consigner system cannot be understood without reference to the French market. We have already noted more than once the coincidence of the shift, about 1740, of French buying to Glasgow and Whitehaven, and the very rapid development at those ports in the 1740's of tobacco imports acquired through the direct-trading "store" system. In this expansion, the availability of capital and credit must have played a crucial limiting role. In neither did Glasgow or Whitehaven have any significant advantage over London: the Scottish merchants tried to make up for their lack of capital by large partnerships utilizing the resources of sleeping partners, by borrowing on bond, and by the formation of their own small banks after 1750. Even so, they seem to have operated on a narrow capital base. To compensate for this, the great Glasgow (and Whitehaven) houses seem to have decided upon a policy of the quickest possible tobacco sales at home with minimal regard to book profits. (Since the greatest and most dependable profits were made by the sale of European goods in America, it was necessary to tie up capital in the stocks of stores in the Chesapeake and in advances to planters; there was much less need to tie up capital in tobacco stocks held in Britain or on the continent.) However, the full option for the quick sale of tobacco and rapid turnover of capital did not really exist for the merchants of Glasgow and Whitehaven until the French started buying in quantity from them in the 1740's. Before that time, the trade at those ports had been inhibited by a limited domestic market and by the long delays before proceeds could be realized on speculative reexports to Amsterdam or Hamburg. (A ship might make a round-trip to the Chesapeake before a shipment to a sluggish Dutch market produced any cash.)

In short, the French after 1740 were attracted to Glasgow and Whitehaven because tobacco was slightly cheaper there (particularly in wartime) and because there were in those ports firms trading on their own account large enough to make big sales but not strong enough to be extortionate at the bargaining table. The great expansion of French cash purchases at the northern ports in the 1740's gave the merchants there, already trading on their own account through the "store" system in the Chesapeake, the opportunity to turn over their capital much more rapidly and thereby to expand greatly their operations in the tobacco colonies. (Even if the French took only 25 percent of British tobacco exports, they took over 50 percent of Glasgow and Whitehaven exports in the crucial 1740's and thus gave to local merchants a very real option of turning over their capital more rapidly.) Thus, the northward shift of French purchases in the 1740's was a logical precondition for the exceptional expansion in that decade both of the Glasgow-Whitehaven tobacco trades and of the store system, at the expense of competing ports and of competing modes of trade in the Chesapeake.

French demand and the associated institutional changes in the trade must also be taken into consideration when we consider the rate of growth of the Chesapeake tobacco trade. We have frequently noted that tobacco imports at Whitehaven and in southwestern Scotland experienced their years of most rapid growth in the 1740's, just after substantial French buying was transferred thither. Taking the British trade as a whole, we can detect a rather clear secular pattern of growth. After a period of very rapid growth in the mid-seventeenth century during which exports from the Chesapeake to England increased about tenfold from the 1630's to 1660's, expansion slowed, shipments merely doubling between 1668–69 and the end of the century; this slowing down was succeeded by complete stagnation during the first quarter of the eighteenth century. Growth resumed after 1725, and by 1771–75 shipments had reached a level treble that of a half century before.[57] The slowing down of 1669–1725 can readily be explained on the supply side by labor shortage and rising costs, and on the demand side by the saturation of the European market, declining prices (particularly ca. 1660–90), and growing continental competition during the wars of 1688–1713.[58] The abrupt resumption of growth after 1725 is harder to explain. Consumption per capita and population were relatively static in Great Britain; even if consumption were rising on the continent, the effect would hardly have been so abrupt. Walpole, of course, removed the last halfpenny (actually 3/8 of a penny) of retained duty in 1723, permitting tobacco to move thereafter through the British entrepôt without fiscal burdens.[59] This made British tobacco much better able to compete on the continent with Dutch and German tobaccos. Yet exports to Holland, Germany and the Baltic increased only moderately at first. Only the French monopoly responded by really massive increases in British purchases. In the generation following the changes of 1723, well over half of the increased imports into England was to be absorbed by increased exports to France alone, while the increased exports to France and Flanders together took over 70 percent of the growth.[60] (Had we equivalent figures for Scotland before and after 1739, the pattern would undoubtedly have been equally if not even more marked.)

TABLE I

English Tobacco Imports and Exports Compared, 1721–23, 1737–43[61]

Year	Imports Total	To France	Exports To Fr. & Flanders
	(annual averages)		
1721–23	31,709,386 lb.	2,984,002 lb.	4,849,528 lb.
1737–43	47,533,994	11,606,914	16,033,357
Increase	15,824,608 lb.	8,622,912 lb. (54.5%)	11,183,829 lb. (70.7%)

The mechanism through which increased French demand after 1723 transmitted itself to the Chesapeake and elicited increased production there is not at first glance clear. We lack good price series for the Chesapeake at this time. In Europe, however, tobacco prices during the generation after

1725 were markedly lower than those prevailing during 1695–1725. It seems unlikely that the simple price mechanism by itself (i.e., conscious planter response to market price changes) can account for the full spurt in production after 1725. Institutional-financial circumstances probably need also to be brought in. The generation of stagnation in the trade can be accounted for in part by a relative shortage of capital. During the war years, 1689–1713, delays in the sending and return of convoys tied up large amounts of trading capital; when a year's crop came home in a single convoy, maximum prices would only be realized by slow sales, tying up more capital in unrecovered freight charges and customs deposits. Peace facilitated the more rapid turnover of trading capital, as did the customs reforms of 1714 and 1723. To balance these, the great wave of linked bankruptcies which hit the London trade in 1711 markedly reduced for a time the total effective capital employed in the trade.[62]

Capital turnover was slow in all tobacco resale markets except the French. In the domestic market, sales were slow to the small manufacturers—a hogshead at a time—and frequently on extended credit. Only at London were there merchants who regularly bought for export (either on their own account or more likely on foreign order); elsewhere, the importing merchants at Glasgow, Whitehaven, and Liverpool normally reexported the tobacco on their own account; when the tobacco reached Rotterdam or Hamburg, it might sit for months before sale and then be sold on credit; further delays might be involved in the remittance of the proceeds. The French agents, however, bought for cash or immediately discountable notes and helped the importers with short term loans. Thus the French market uniquely facilitated the more rapid turnover of capital in the tobacco trade. By selling a substantial proportion of his imports to the French, the merchant accelerated the turnover of his capital and thus the total volume of his transactions. He could turn his ships around and send them back to the Chesapeake more rapidly and with more goods. By maintaining larger stocks of goods in his stores in the tobacco colonies, he enabled his storekeepers ("factors") there to have more tobacco purchased in anticipation of the arrival of the ships and thus to turn the ships around more quickly in the Chesapeake too. The result might be that phenomenon much boasted of at Glasgow and Whitehaven, if seldom realized—a ship making two voyages to the Chesapeake in one year.

Within the tobacco colonies, the more rapid turnover of mercantile capital facilitated by the French market meant an increase in the number of Scottish and Whitehaven stores, an increase in the total volume of merchandise available therein and an increase in the total volume of credit available to the planters. Credit was the magnet which drew the subsistence settler into the market economy. The availability of such credit diminished the need for savings for disaster, permitted the expenditure of scarce cash for the purchase of slaves as well as the diversion of labor from subsistence to market activities. Store credits were supposed to be cleared by deliveries from the current or following crop. A small planter assuming a larger than normal burden of debt was assuming an obligation to grow more tobacco than usual in the next crop year. An intelligent storekeeper might encourage a planter to increase his debt, but only within the limits of his ability to grow tobacco and repay. Tobacco merchants generally recognized that, with prudence, the surest ways of "pushing the trade" were opening more stores and extending more credit. If credit expansion by any one store might simply draw business from its competitors, credit expansion by the whole system had to elicit a greater production of tobacco or collapse of its own weight. Thus, at several stages removed, did increased French demand for British tobacco after 1723 create its own supply: large French cash purchases permitted merchants to turn over their capital more rapidly and thereby to expand their gross annual operations; expanded credit facilities at their local stores encouraged and enabled planters to grow more tobacco. (All these sharp influences emanating from increased French demand were ultimately reinforced by the weaker influences emanating from the more slowly expanding demand from other continental countries.)

French demand was not uniformly felt throughout the Chesapeake. We must first distinguish between the older productive areas in Tidewater and the new areas of settlement and tobacco production in the Piedmont, or more loosely "above the fall line." The half-century, 1725 to 1775, that saw a trebling of tobacco exports from the Chesapeake also saw a reduction of production on the eastern shore and expansion inland of that on the western shore. After overcoming initial difficulties in clearing the land and opening roads to navigable water, the tobacco planters of the Piedmont found themselves with compensating advantages. With lands generally suitable for both tobacco and wheat, they more frequently had a real market choice in choosing a crop. With fresh lands, they not only got good tobacco crops but produced leaf of a recognized superior quality that obtained a higher price than tobacco grown lower down the same river. This helps account for the great tobacco boom, about 1750–75, on the south side of James River, in the areas behind Richmond and Petersburg. By the 1770's, the customs Upper District of James River (everything above Williamsburg) accounted for about half the tobacco being exported from Virginia.[63] To these frontier areas with their superior leaf, the Scottish stores came willingly. The bigger firms like William Cuninghame & Co. established headquarters stores near the heads of navigation at Petersburg and Richmond, and at Fredericksburg and Falmouth on the Rappahannock, with dependent stores supplied from thence further inland. They would have gone into these new areas with their many small planters and good tobaccos even if there had been no French market. However, since the French market was important to the financing and growth of the Scottish store firms, its existence accelerated their expansion on the Piedmont and thus stimulated the economic development of that region.

Even while pushing their stores upriver and onto the Piedmont, the Scottish firms did not abandon older trading areas in Tidewater. Cuninghames had major stores at Cabin Point on the lower James River and at Dumfries on the Potomac. The opposite Maryland shore of the latter river was thick with Scottish stores. For these declining areas of Tidewater, producing in most cases an inferior, lower priced grade of tobacco, the French market may have been even more strategic. Thence came the cheap tobaccos, "common for France," which Glasgow merchants sold sight-unseen by the shipload to the French agents. One of the several firms managed by John Glassford of Glasgow had in its articles a rule that no store was to be established on the James River above Flowerdew Hundred (on the south shore below the confluence of the Appomattox). When Neil Jamieson, the partner managing the American end from Norfolk, complained of this restriction, Glassford insisted that doing business further up the James River involved too much capital (higher prices and longer credits to the planters): "It was all along his plan to carry on a Business from which a pretty large Importation of ordinary Tobacco can be made with the least Sinking of large Sums and the French Sales was what was in View for said Tobacco excepting any little good Tobacco that might be in it. . . ." If Jamieson couldn't get enough tobacco on the lower James, he could establish a branch on the Rappahannock.[64] In this light, it may well have been the French market that was holding up the decaying tobacco cultivation of Tidewater Virginia; and thus it would later have been the disappearance of a French market after 1791 that accounted for the ultimate collapse of Tidewater cultivation.

In addition to the very general distinction between Piedmont and Tidewater, we must distinguish between the tobacco produced in the various river-valleys of Virginia and Maryland. Not all were equally acceptable or equally suitable for the French market. Right through the century, it was recognized that the strong, bright leaf of Maryland (produced principally along the Patuxent and to the northward) was not liked in either Britain or France but was popular in Holland and Germany. The Maryland trade thus was much more heavily dependent upon the Dutch reexport market than was the Virginia. Of the brown, milder leaf grown in Maryland, Thomas Walpole explained in a memoir of 1769 that both that grown along the Potomac and that grown on the declining eastern shore (Sassafras, Chester and Choptank Rivers) were suitable for the French. That grown on Chester River was particularly acceptable to the French, but relatively little was available. The greatest quantities sent them from Maryland came from the much ampler production of the Potomac. Among the Virginia products, according to Walpole, the French took none of the famous and expensive York River "sweet-scented," in demand in Britain and for reexport to Ireland, Spain and Germany. Nor did they get any of the Rappahannock then in demand for domestic consumption within Britain. The bulk of their

Virginia purchases came from James River, with a smaller share from the Potomac.[65] Other accounts are in substantial agreement with that of Walpole, although they include Rappahannock among the varieties commonly taken by the French.[66] No tobacco was exported from the Virginia eastern shore or Accomack District after about 1730.[67]

There is a rough correlation between the location of the Scottish stores and activity and the geographic varieties of tobacco preferred by the French. In Maryland, the preference of the French for the cheap and milder tobaccos of the Potomac was reflected in the concentration of Scottish stores along that shore.[68] From the port of Annapolis, by contrast, there were hardly any shipments to Glasgow or Whitehaven in the 1750's and 1760's.[69] In the very busy quarter, 5 July–10 October 1775, of total Glasgow (Port Glasgow and Greenock) imports of 5,453 hogsheads from Maryland, 58.8 percent came from the North [shore of] Potomac District, 26.6 percent from Annapolis, and only one shipload each from the eastern shore (7.9 percent) and the important Patuxent district (6.7 percent).[70] The French coolness toward Maryland tobaccos generally was paralleled by a relative lack of attention to this province by the Scots. Whereas, during 1768–72, 32.5 percent of North American tobacco shipments to Great Britain came from Maryland,[71] only 24.5 percent of Scottish imports in the same years came from Maryland[72] (or only 22.7 percent for 1769–74).[73] This relative neglect of Maryland by French and Scots may help explain the slower growth of the Maryland tobacco trade, compared to that of Virginia. There is evidence that, about 1701–4, Maryland accounted for over 40 percent of British North American output.[74] This had declined to 36.4–37.5 percent by 1758–66 (according to a contemporary estimate),[75] to 32.5 percent by 1768–72,[76] and to only 22 percent by 1773.[77]

In Virginia, of much greater importance to French and Scots, there was also a rough correlation between areas producing tobacco sought by the French, areas having the greatest number of Scots stores and areas of the most rapid increases in output. The French, it will be remembered, bought no York River, little Rappahannock, and a fair amount of Potomac, but their great purchases were from the sleepy Lower and burgeoning Upper Districts of the James River. (The Upper James District it will be remembered, included both the James above Williamsburg and its major tributary, the Appomattox.)[78] This pattern of preference is reflected to a significant degree in the distribution of Scottish stores: none on the eastern shore or along the lower York River; very few along the lower Rappahannock; a sprinkling along the Potomac and in the upper Rappahannock valley behind Fredericksburg (where they drew as much Potomac tobacco as Rappahannock); and a heavy concentration along the James River and its southern tributaries.[79] In the busy quarter, 5 July 1775–10 October 1775, more than half of the tobacco imports from Virginia at Port Glasgow and Greenock came from the Upper District of James River:[80]

District	Hogsheads
Upper James River	9,403
Lower James River	2,697
York River	337
Rappahannock River	3,146
South Potomac	3,208
Total	18,791

When we reflect that nearly half the tobacco coming out of the Rappahannock may have been classed "Potomac" by the trade, we see how clearly Glasgow's imports reflected French demand.

Evidence for the measurement of the regional growth of tobacco cultivation in Virginia is hard to come by. What there is, however, seems to suggest that the areas attracting the most French and Scottish business also had the fastest rates of growth. In 1713–14, the York and Rappahannock customs districts accounted for 59 percent of the receipts from the Virginia tobacco export duty; these were the districts relatively unaffected by French demand and their share of total shipments was to fall to 31 percent sixty years later (1773–74). The Potomac district about held its own, while the shares of the Upper and Lower Districts of James River, most affected by French demand via the Scots, rose from 22 percent to 52 percent of the total.[81] From the "naval officers' accounts" (registers of shipping entered and cleared), we get a comparable picture (Table II).

TABLE II

Virginia Tobacco Exports to Britain by Districts, 1737–73[82]

	Upper James	Lower James	James Unspec.	York	Rappahannock	South Potomac	Unspec. (York & Northern)
			(in hogsheads)				
1737 E	6,969	828	0	12,720	6,235	2,538	0
S	1,720	71	0	0	3,443	1,463	0
B	8,689	899	0	12,720	9,678	4,001	0
1738 E	5,400	936	0	9,884	4,558	1,073	0
S	1,408	0	0	195	2,515	724	0
B	6,808	936	0	10,079	7,073	1,797	0
1739 E	4,676	939	0	11,910	7,763	2,909	0
S	1,384	193	0	0	2,998	1,925	0
B	6,060	1,132	0	11,910	10,761	4,834	0
1740 E	5,332	965	0	8,085	7,044	3,040	0
S	1,788	112	0	158	3,097	1,557	0
B	7,120	1,077	0	8,243	10,141	4,597	0

TABLE II (continued)

	Upper James	Lower James	James Unspec.	York	Rappahannock	South Potomac	Unspec. (York & Northern)
			(in hogsheads)				
1741 E	5,574	1,062	0	15,107	7,571	3,131	0
S	2,313	86	0	362	2,506	2,110	0
B	7,887	1,148	0	15,469	10,077	5,241	0
1742 E	6,023	941	0	9,148	9,502	2,241	0
S	3,134	553	0	524	2,901	2,920	0
B	9,154	1,494	0	9,672	12,403	5,161	0
1743 E	5,342	807	0	11,654	9,800	2,805	0
S	1,837	622	0	779	3,434	2,930	0
B	7,179	1,429	0	12,433	13,234	5,735	0
1744 E	4,448	659	0	7,801	7,248	2,416	0
S	4,673	123	0	549	3,638	2,273	0
B	9,121	782	0	8,350	10,886	4,689	0
1745 E	6,264	1,356	0	11,625	9,446	2,781	0
S	3,917	536	0	814	3,724	5,539	0
B	10,181	1,892	0	12,439	13,170	8,320	0
1750 E	6,881	1,500	0	11,957	8,934	1,697	0
S	6,516	648	0	1,278	7,003	4,768	0
B	13,397	2,148	0	13,235	15,937	6,465	0
1758 E	6,323	762	0	10,466	8,224	4,227	0
S	6,896	1,347	0	1,514	5,382	3,788	0
B	13,219	2,109	0	11,980	13,606	8,015	0
1761 E	9,144	827	0	10,199	9,785	3,078	0
S	7,775	774	0	1,191	5,571	2,216	0
B	16,919	1,601	0	11,389	15,356	5,294	0
1762 E	8,816	966	0	9,809	10,883	3,059	0
S	13,177	712	0	1,695	4,844	4,702	0
B	21,993	1,678	0	11,504	15,727	7,761	0
1768 B	16,838	2,640	0	6,258	9,132	6,817	0
1770–71 B	25,010	2,303	5,221	9,075	12,020	11,549	1,779
1771–72 B	21,733	3,167	4,632	8,634	14,549	10,716	1,777
1772–73 B	30,890	4,797	0	8,248	13,244	10,541	1,857

E = to England; S = to Scotland; B = to Great Britain

From the above table, it can be seen rather clearly that the York District had reached its peak by 1737 and was not growing thereafter, while Rappahannock reached its full development about 1750 and stagnated for the next generation. By contrast, the districts affected by French demand and the heaviest Scots attention, maintained impressive growth right down to the American Revolution. The table also suggests that it was precisely in the mid-1740's, when French demand became a major factor at Glasgow, that the Scots pushed ahead of the English on the Potomac and began the shift of the main center of their activity from northern Virginia southward to the James River.

It is not our intention to claim that either the pattern of the aggregate growth of the tobacco economy in the Chesapeake or the fate of particular regions can be explained entirely in terms of the French market. Obviously, for a total explanation, other factors have to be taken into consideration, including the relative price attractiveness of other crops, transport costs, soil suitability and exhaustion, clearance and other development costs, and labor supply. Even the last three, however, were not independent variables, for general market and credit conditions affected the demand for slaves as well as the decision to abandon old lands and open new. (We hope to explore these and other aspects of the Chesapeake economy in another book.) All that we have attempted to argue here is that the growth of the tobacco economy cannot be understood without reference to quantitative and qualitative demand. Uniquely important among markets was the French—because of its monopsonistic character. The administration of French demand is the best single explanation we have for the timing of the resumed growth of the English tobacco trade about 1724–43 and for the great multiplication of the Scottish trade in the 1740's. To keep a proper perspective, we must always remember that by 1771–75, while exports to France accounted for 26.3 percent of total British exports and 22.5 percent of total British imports, they accounted for 42.8 percent of Scottish exports and 38.3 percent of Scottish imports.[83] In those areas of the Chesapeake particularly affected by French demand via the Scots—the Upper and Lower Districts of James River, the Virginia and Maryland sides of the Potomac—tobacco for the farmers-general must have accounted for from 40 percent to 50 percent of production.

Appendix to Chapter 25: The French in the British Tobacco Market, 1748–75: A Price Chronicle

Thus far in this chapter, we have been concerned with the most general of institutional and statistical trends. Before concluding, it will be interesting to attempt to describe how the British tobacco market actually responded to French demand. Before 1748, we have only isolated reports of market conditions and the "French price." Therefore, we shall have to confine this chronicle to the years 1748–75.

In 1739, the French united farms were paying about 2d.¼ per lb. for their tobacco in London and about 2d. per lb. elsewhere (Bristol, Liverpool, Scotland).[84] Because of the very rapid rise in British imports, prices remained low throughout the wars of 1739–48 at both London and Amsterdam.[85] By 1748, tobacco had become relatively scarce in Britain and prices were tending slightly upward.[86] Even so, the French did not pay more than 2d.5/16 for their Whitehaven spring purchase and 2d.3/8 at London in the fall.[87] With the end of the war, the French, with adequate stocks on hand, ceased purchases from November 1748 until about April 1749; prices sagged as tobacco flowed in from America.[88] In April, 1749, the French resumed purchases at Glasgow and Whitehaven at 2d.1/8, but were able to get the price still lower by the start of the next year. All during 1750, 1751, and 1752, they gave only 2d. for the large quantities they bought in the outports and Scotland and no more than 2d.1/4 for the lots they picked up in London;[89] these were the same prices they had paid in 1739 and something approximating the "normal peacetime price." All the same, by the third year, 1752, there were strong complaints of glut developing in the market,[90] and, under the weight of exceptionally heavy imports during 1752–54, the French price was by 1754 driven down to 1d.7/8 in London,[91] suggesting approximately 1d.5/8 or 3/4 for the outports and Scotland.

The French appear to have taken advantage of these low prices and to have bought heavily during 1752–54, accumulating stocks that enabled them to reduce purchases markedly during the troubles attending the coming of the war in 1755–56. The approach of war and short crops in the Chesapeake in 1755, causing abnormally low imports in 1756, evoked a rise in prices despite large stocks and little French buying. In Scotland, the market rose from 1d.5/8–3/4 in July 1755 to 2d.1/2–3/4 in March 1756, even before the formal declaration of war.[92] When the French resumed large scale purchases under license in 1757, they were of course obliged to pay more, but their shrewd managers (FitzGerald and Van Neck) kept the Scottish price from rising more than from 2d.5/16 in early 1757 to 2d.5/8 in early 1758.[93] The London price in the early fall of 1758 was only 2d.3/4.[94]

Then the market exploded. In 1758, the crop was exceptionally poor in the Chesapeake, leading to a very short importation in 1759. As an excessive number of ships arriving in the Chesapeake in the spring and summer of 1758 had cleaned out the great crop of 1757, there was no carryover to mitigate the effects of the short crop of 1758: prices almost trebled in the Chesapeake, reaching 45s. local currency per hundred pounds, or 5.4d. per lb., equivalent to about 3d.1/2 sterling at the then distorted rate of exchange.[95] Tobacco bought at these prices would be a losing proposition in Britain unless the metropolitan price could be forced up radically. In November 1758, when the London merchants learned of the true dimensions of the situation, they agreed together to hold out for a French price of 4d. per lb., which they expected would enable them to get 5d. from other buyers. The Londoners wrote to the outports and Scotland, urging the importers there to hold out for 3d.3/4. Liverpool followed the London lead, but Glasgow early in November 1758 had been thinking of only a 3d. price from the French. While the disgusted Londoners and Liverpudlians held out, the merchants of Glasgow and Whitehaven sold 2,000 hogsheads to the French between November and January at prices rising from 3d. to 3d.1/2 and much larger quantities at the latter price between January and March 1759. Nevertheless, the Londoners had the last laugh for Whitehaven and Glasgow were not able to satisfy the very great French needs: in April 1759, FitzGerald and Van Neck, offering 3d.7/8 to the Londoners and getting less than 2,000 hogsheads, were forced finally to concede the 4d. demanded since the previous November. News of this raised the Glasgow price to 3d.5/8 by June; before the peak was reached in July-September 1759, the London French price reached 4d.1/4 and that at Glasgow hit 3d.11/16.[96] The French had to pay through the nose in 1759 because their stocks had been depleted by below normal purchases during the preceding four years. Planters (unless their crops had been exceptionally reduced) should have benefited greatly from these higher prices, whether they consigned or sold in the country. Merchants, however, had to pay such high prices for their tobacco in Chesapeake that many, particularly at Glasgow, were not able to recover costs fully on all sales and suffered some book losses.[97] Had the Glasgow merchants been less dependent on the French for their working capital, they might have held out more effectively and extracted higher prices from the French during the panic winter of 1758–59. The Londoners, being less dependent on the French, got more from them.

The panic bubble of 1758–59 was bound to burst; at the beginning, there had actually been larger carry-over stocks of the 1757 crop in Britain and Holland than buyers suspected; by the autumn of 1759 word began to get around that the crop of that year in the Chesapeake would be larger than normal. With stocks at last deemed adequate by the farmers-general, the French agents abruptly ceased buying in October in an effort to force down the price.[98] When Van Neck resumed purchases in February 1760 (FitzGerald having failed in December), he offered 3d.3/4 in London and 3d.1/4 in Glasgow. He easily got 5,000 hogsheads in London and much more in Glasgow: although the price spread between Scotland and London was greater than normal, the great Glasgow houses were frightened and quickly sold the French virtually all they had on hand or expected. (Tobacco exports to France set a new record in 1760, to be exceeded only twice thereafter.) So great were the quantities offered that the French agents were able to conclude their record 1760 purchases in May at 3d.1/8 and withdraw from the market. They returned tentatively during the summer to force the price down to 2d.3/4 both at Glasgow in July and at London by September (a full penny per pound below what they had been paying in the spring) and then withdrew again for the rest of the year.[99]

The very high prices in the Chesapeake during the winter of 1758–59 encouraged heavy planting that spring and helped make the 1759 bumper crop. Imports into Britain were therefore at record levels in 1760. By November and December of that year, there was a warehouse shortage at Glasgow.[100] Except for trial purchases, the French let the glut and pressure build up by staying out of the market from September 1760 until June 1761. (Their restraint was facilitated by exceptionally numerous captures of Virginia prizes early in 1761.) This inactivity forced prices down throughout Europe, for, as John Glassford explained, "the price given for Tob° by the french regulates the prices in great measure in all the markets & when they bear off long from buying at all, it is fully worse as the [other European] Markets are glutted by the Qualities [sic, i.e., quantities] that poured in upon them from the want of a french sale." The long withdrawal of the French also meant a money shortage at Glasgow, causing general retrenchment there.[101] The French agents sampled the market by buying limitedly at Glasgow in December 1760 at $2d.1/4$–$3/8$, at Liverpool in March 1761 at $2d.1/4$ and at London at $2d.1/2$, but refused offers in the spring of $2d.3/16$ and $2d.1/8$ at Glasgow. They finally returned to the market generally in June, offering $2d.1/4$ at London, $2d.1/16$ at Liverpool and $2d$. at Glasgow. An attempt to raise these prices in August failed and they persisted until September 1762 by which time the French had stopped all but intermittent buying at Glasgow and Liverpool.[102]

With the advent of peace, the French agents were able early in 1763 to force prices down to $2d$. at London and $1d.15/16$ and $7/8$ in Scotland. With the seas now open, a new record for importation was established that year, enabling the French to force the Glasgow price down from $1d.7/8$ in May-July to $1d.3/4$ in October-November. By April 1764, the price was down to $1d.5/8$ at both Glasgow and Whitehaven, and reached $1d.9/16$ there in February-July of 1765.[103] Three things must be noted about these three years of very low prices—1763, 1764, and 1765. French purchasing in Britain since 1760 was under the direction of a single agent (Van Neck & Co.), whereas from 1730 to 1759 it had been divided among two or more competing firms. Second, the Amsterdam financial crisis of 1763 had had repercussions in Scotland and had left credit very tight there in 1763-64, making it more difficult for sellers to hold out. Third, imports during these three years averaged 86.8 million lb. yearly, the highest on record thus far and about 7.5 million lb. higher than the annual average of the previous three years of record imports, 1752, 1753, 1754, when prices were also very low.

By contrast, British tobacco imports in the next four years, 1766–69, were abnormally low, averaging only 69.9 million lb. annually, or almost 17 million lb. below the average of the preceding three years. This can be blamed in part upon climatic conditions in the Chesapeake. It is also worth noting that wheat prices everywhere in Europe in 1766–68 were exceptionally high and that Britain in 1767–68 became temporarily a substantial net importer of cereals.[104] The sequence of very low tobacco prices during 1763–65 with rising cereal prices culminating in the peak of 1766–67 may have led planters consciously to turn from tobacco to wheat in the mid-1760's.[105]

Whatever the reasons, the abnormally low British tobacco imports of 1766-69 were bound to affect the "French price." The first short crop in the Chesapeake was that of 1765, shipped in 1766. By October 1765, word of the changed conditions reached Britain and a London merchant was glad to report that "Tobacco hath got well up, upon the first Accounts of a short Crop in Virg.ᵃ we rise all the Smoak we could [i.e., we spread the report about] and the price is now d½ p' li' higher than last winter all over Europe."[106] This is confirmed at Glasgow where at the beginning of October the base price was already 2d.1/16, a full halfpenny per pound above the French price of July.[107] The French stayed out of the market to their later distress, for in January, it was reported, "Tob° is on the Rise, as the French are in Want & cannot get themselves supplied at Glasgow."[108] It was at this point of vexing miscalculation that the French agency in London was transferred in 1766 or early 1767 from Van Neck & Co. to the Hon. Thomas Walpole. (High prices also help to explain its transfer within the next few years to Hopes of Amsterdam in 1768, back to Walpole in 1769 and to Herries in 1771.) In January 1766, the French agents reentered the market and offered to take at 2d.¼ almost all suitable tobacco the merchants had on hand or expected to receive by August.[109] The offer was accepted at Glasgow in March and a price at or just below this level seems to have persisted through 1766 and, with some sagging, into the summer of 1767: at London, their price had declined to 2d.1/8 by May-August 1767, at Liverpool from 2d.1/16 in February to 2d. in April and at Glasgow from 2d. in January to 1d.15/16 in April; in June, some foolish Glaswegians sold them 1,000 hogsheads at 1d.7/8 because unsold stocks were accumulating in Rotterdam.[110]

In the fall of 1767, however, when word came of the third successive bad crop in America (caused this time by frosts), prices jumped suddenly 3/8 of a penny per lb. (or to 2d.1/4 "French price" at Glasgow).[111] At this juncture, the farmers-general transferred their purchasing commission for 1768 from Walpole to Hope & Co. of Amsterdam, working principally through Simson, Baird & Co. of Glasgow. The new managers did not perform well for their employers. They began their Glasgow purchases in January 1768 at 2d.3/8 (compared to Walpole's last price of 2d.1/4) but were forced up to 2d.1/2 by May. When their London agents incautiously offered 3d., they were forced to raise the Glasgow price to 2d.3/4; by July, they were giving 3d. at Glasgow and 3d.1/4 in London.[112] At these prices, they made very heavy purchases. When Thomas Walpole regained the buying commission in January 1769, he was at first hindered by the large volume of advance contracts at 3d. which Simson, Baird had made at Glasgow at the end of 1768 for later deliveries. These absorbed much of the tobacco available in January and February. From March onward, he was able to make the more modest purchases of 1769 at 2d.3/4.

In the fall of 1769, characteristically exaggerated reports reached Britain of the crop damage caused by a hurricane on 8 September. Taking this information at face value, the principal importers agreed among themselves to hold out for a French price of 3$d.$ per lb. in Glasgow and 3$d.$1/4 in London. However, as ships arrived in early 1770, it was realized that damage reports had been much inflated: in the end, 1770 imports were higher than any since 1765. By March 1770, some houses were prepared to sell 6,000 hogsheads to the French for 2$d.$7/8, but some Glasgow and all London great houses held out. In May, however, the Glasgow resistance collapsed and 6,000 more hogsheads went for 2$d.$3/4; in the summer, more was sold at 2$d.$5/8, redeeming the position of Thomas Walpole.[113]

The crop of 1770 in America was the first of five enormous crops that resulted in average British imports of 100 million lb. annually during 1771–75. (The previous extended peak had been the 86.8 million lb. average during 1763–65.) These greater outputs would seem to have been evoked by the higher metropolitan prices of 1768–70 and by a great expansion of credit throughout the trade which prosperity encouraged. The depressing effect on price which these great crops should have had was at first limited by the general credit inflation in Britain in the two years or so preceding the crisis of June 1772. Thus, despite the great crop of 1770, Thomas Walpole was only able to lower Scottish prices further from the 2$d.$5/8 of the summer of 1770 to 2$d.$3/8 in the first half of 1771.[114] When, in September 1771, the agency was divided between Walpole for London and Herries for Scotland, it was agreed that the former should offer 2$d.$1/4 in London, while the latter would give 2$d.$1/8 in Glasgow. The latter price (or something very close to it) was in fact given at Glasgow and Whitehaven in the latter part of 1771 and all through 1772; at London, however, Walpole, to increase his purchases, was permitted to raise his price to 2$d.$3/8 early in 1772 but dropped back to 2$d.$1/4 in the latter part of the year.[115] The crisis of 1772 effectively eliminated Walpole and greatly strengthened Herries' hand against the sellers. Purchases were suspended at London but 22 million lb. were purchased in Scotland in 1773 at 1$d.$7/8. (Total British shipments to France minus Dunkirk approached or exceeded 30 million lb. in both 1772 and 1773, the high point of the century.) In 1774, Herries attempted to drive prices down further by offering only 1$d.$7/8 in London, 1$d.$13/16 in Liverpool and 1$d.$3/4 in Glasgow. In this, he and his French employers miscalculated, as explained in the last chapter: the great Glasgow houses preferred speculative shipments to Holland and Germany, and French purchases in 1774 fell off by two-thirds. With the arrival of disturbing news from America in January 1775, tobacco prices rose abruptly all over Europe. The French agents (Martin and Herries) were forced that year to concede 3$d.$ and 3$d.$1/4 in Glasgow and up to 3$d.$3/4 in London.[116]

Throughout, the "French price" remained not a market price at which countless small transactions took place, but rather a special price negotiated between monopsonistic buyers and partially united sellers for very large sales of mixed lots of passable "mean," "common" and "middling" grades. (When tobacco was plentiful, the French in later years took almost all Virginia; when it was scarcer, they took increasing proportions of Maryland too.) The "French price," in short, was not so much a classic market price as a more or less administered base price upon which the market prices for the several grades were built.

Lavoisier's Map of Distribution Network
of French Tobacco Monopoly, ca. 1780
Courtesy Cornell University Library.